TEACHER'S EDITION

L. Carey Bolster

H. Douglas Woodburn

Scott, Foresman and Company
Editorial Offices: Glenview, Illinois

Regional Offices: Sunnyvale, California •
Tucker, Georgia • Glenview, Illinois •
Oakland, New Jersey • Dallas, Texas

PROGRAM Two-Year Program

Mathematics in Life, Second Edition, followed by *Consumer and Career Mathematics, Second Edition,* provides a two-year general mathematics program. However, either book may be used independently at any grade level.

Mathematics in Life

Recommended for a first course in general mathematics. Emphasis in each chapter on basic mathematical skills and problem solving in consumer and career applications.

Unit 1 Whole Numbers

Unit 2 Decimals and the Metric System

Unit 3 Fractions, Mixed Numbers, and Probability

Unit 4 Ratio, Percent, and Statistics

Unit 5 Algebra

Unit 6 Geometry and Right-Triangle Relations

Consumer and Career Mathematics

Recommended for a final course in general mathematics, or for a course in consumer mathematics. Emphasis on mathematics needed in consumer and career situations with review of basic computational skills in Unit 1.

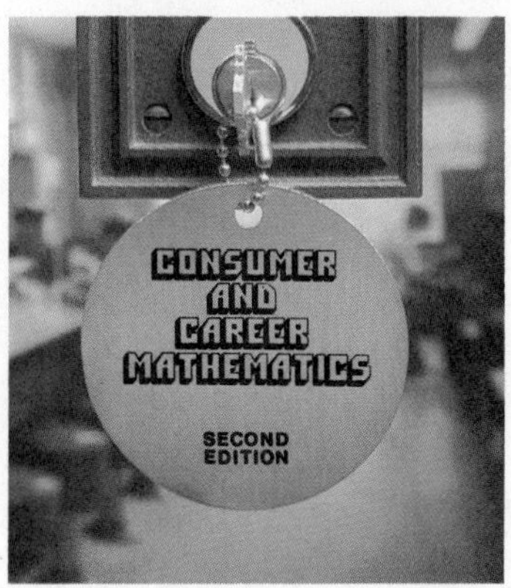

Unit 1 Mathematics Skills

Unit 2 Income, Banking, and Credit

Unit 3 Transportation

Unit 4 Housing

Unit 5 Taxes, Insurance, and Investments

Unit 6 Purchasing and Budgeting

ISBN: 0-673-23431-2

12345678910-KPH-9392919089888786

CONTENTS Table of Contents

Teacher's Edition

Student's Text

Unit and chapter titles are listed below. For a complete table of contents including lesson titles, tests, and features, see pages iii–viii in the student's text which follows after page T80.

MATERIALS Program Materials

Student's Text

480 pages including answers to odd-numbered exercises

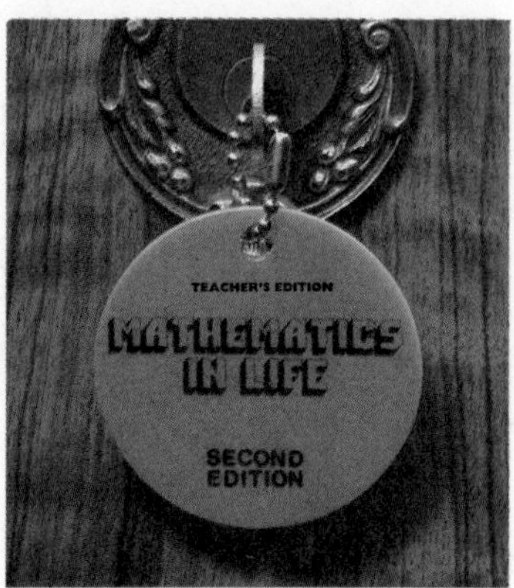

Teacher's Edition

560 pages including reproduced student's pages with answers and notes overprinted plus 80 teacher pages at the front of the book.

Supplementary Materials

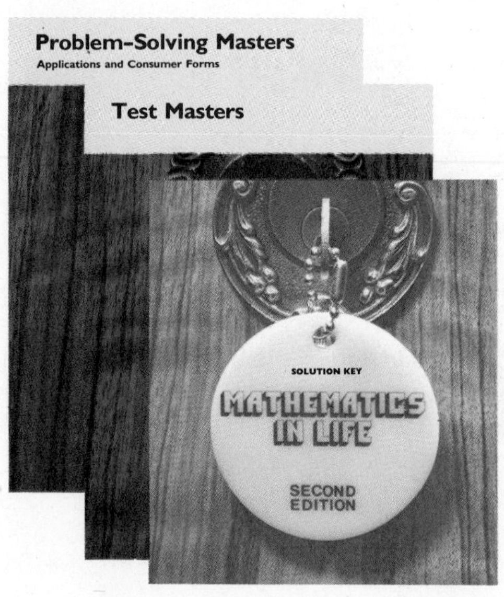

Problem-Solving Masters
Applications and Consumer Forms

64 duplicating masters. Provides applications that reinforce and extend problem-solving lessons in the student's text. Also includes consumer forms, such as checks and deposit slips, that can be used with lessons in the student's text.

Test Masters

60 duplicating masters. Provides an alternate form for each chapter, unit, end-of-book, and competency test.

Solution Key

Contains answers for all exercises in the student's text. Steps needed to obtain answers are shown for selected exercises.

Mathematics in Life, Second Edition

Skills	**Skills Pretest** with items keyed to examples in **Skills Lessons** emphasizing estimation skills• in examples keyed to exercise sets keyed to a **Skills Posttest** to build mastery of all basic skills	*pages 47–58*
Problem Solving	**Consumer Applications** in each chapter followed by **Career Applications** followed by a special lesson on **Developing Problem-Solving Strategies•** to teach problem-solving skills needed for survival in everyday life	*pages 59–69*
Built-in Testing	Skills Pretest, Skills Posttest, and Chapter Test in student's text; and Unit Test, End-of-Book Test, and Competency Test• in the teacher's edition to help teachers assess students' needs on a regular basis	*page 70*
Enrichment Maintenance	Skills Tune-up, Calculator Applications, and Computer Literacy• at the end of each unit, with Break Times interspersed among the skills lessons, and a Skills File• in the back of the student's text to allow ample flexibility in meeting individual differences	*pages 71–73*
Complete Teacher's Edition	Overprinted notes with helpful teaching suggestions, a suggested time schedule, and reference charts listing objectives including those designated as minimum computational skills objectives• to make the book extremely easy to manage	*pages T14–T45*
Supplementary Materials	*Problem-Solving Masters: Applications and Consumer Forms,*• *Test Masters,* and *Solution Key* to provide even greater flexibility in using the program	*page T4*

•Indicates a new feature in *Mathematics in Life, Second Edition*

AUTHORS Authors and Readers/Consultants

Authors

L. Carey Bolster

Mr. Bolster is a Supervisor of Mathematics for the Baltimore County Public Schools. He works with elementary and secondary teachers in curriculum development and instruction, and often conducts in-service workshops. He is coauthor of mathematics programs for the elementary and secondary levels.

H. Douglas Woodburn

Mr. Woodburn is Chairman of the Mathematics Department of Perry Hall Middle School in Baltimore County, Maryland. He has taught at the junior high, senior high, and college levels. He has reviewed articles submitted for publication in *The Mathematics Teacher* and *Arithmetic Teacher*.

Authors of Supplementary Materials

Glenn Prigge
Problem-Solving Masters

Dr. Prigge is a Professor of Mathematics at the University of North Dakota. He has conducted workshops at national and regional mathematics meetings. He has written articles published in various mathematical journals.

Dora A. Serna Cantu
Test Masters

Ms. Cantu is an Instructor of Mathematics at Laredo Junior College in Laredo, Texas. She has also taught mathematics at the secondary level. She has conducted workshops for elementary and secondary teachers.

Readers/Consultants

Thelma Thomas Daley

Ms. Daley is a Supervisor of Guidance for the Baltimore County Public Schools. She is a former Chairman of the National Council on Career Education and has written articles related to career education.

Marita H. Eng

Ms. Eng is Chairman of the Mathematics Department of Sandalwood Junior-Senior High School in Jacksonville, Florida. She is coauthor of a series of computational skills workbooks.

Robert Y. Hamada

Mr. Hamada is an Instructional Specialist, Mathematics, in the Office of Instruction of the Los Angeles Unified School District. He is coauthor of an elementary-school mathematics program.

Linda Borry Hausmann

Ms. Hausmann is an Instructional Coordinator at the Minnesota Educational Computing Consortium in St. Paul, Minnesota. She is author of a computerized music theory package.

Sidney Sharron

Mr. Sharron is a Supervisor in the Instructional Media and Resources Branch of the Los Angeles Unified School District. He has taught mathematics at the high school and college levels.

FEATURES Organization

Units The text is divided into six units.

Chapters Each unit contains three chapters. There are 18 chapters in all.

Within chapters See the sample table of contents given below. Each chapter focuses first on skills and then on problem solving in consumer and career applications with a special lesson that develops problem-solving strategies. See pages T8–T13 for samples of lessons, tests, and special features.

		Chapter 3 Dividing Whole Numbers
Skills	**Skills Pretest**	Pretest *47*
	Skills Lessons	Dividing with One-Digit Divisors *48* Dividing with Two-Digit Divisors *50* Dividing with Zeros in the Quotient *52* Dividing with Three-Digit Divisors *53* Using Order of Operations *54* BREAK TIME *55* Solving Multiplication and Division Equations *56* BREAK TIME *57*
	Skills Posttest	Posttest *58*
Problem Solving	**Consumer**	CONSUMER Computing Monthly and Weekly Salaries *59* CONSUMER Finding the Price per Item *60* CONSUMER Painting a House *62*
	Career	CAREER Bottling-Plant Supervisor *64* CAREER Appliance-Store Buyer *66*
	Developing Problem-Solving Strategies	DEVELOPING STRATEGIES Tactics: Reading a Table, Interpreting Remainders *68*
Chapter Test		Chapter 3 Test *70*
End-of-Unit Materials		Skills Tune-up *71* Calculator Applications *72* Computer Literacy *73*

FEATURES Skills

Pretest on skills Each chapter begins with a pretest on the skills that are taught in the chapter. For each skill on the pretest, there is a page reference to a skills lesson. Each skill is then broken down into types of exercises. Each type appears as a lettered item on the pretest and each item corresponds to a lettered example and exercise set in the skills lesson.

Skills lesson Skills lessons follow the pretest and each lesson is on either one page or on two facing pages. The lesson title indicates the skill that is being taught.

Examples Each example in a skills lesson is the same type of exercise as the pretest item with the same letter. Examples are lettered consecutively throughout a chapter.

page 47

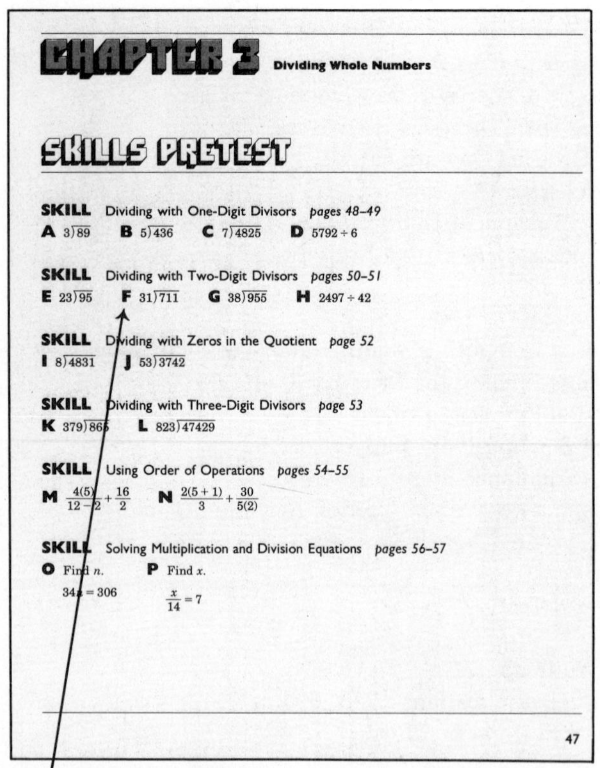

CHAPTER 3 Dividing Whole Numbers

SKILLS PRETEST

SKILL Dividing with One-Digit Divisors *pages 48–49*

A 3)89 **B** 5)436 **C** 7)4825 **D** 5792 ÷ 6

SKILL Dividing with Two-Digit Divisors *pages 50–51*

E 23)95 **F** 31)711 **G** 38)955 **H** 2497 ÷ 42

SKILL Dividing with Zeros in the Quotient *page 52*

I 8)4831 **J** 53)3742

SKILL Dividing with Three-Digit Divisors *page 53*

K 379)865 **L** 823)47429

SKILL Using Order of Operations *pages 54–55*

M $\frac{4(5)}{12-2} + \frac{16}{2}$ **N** $\frac{2(5+1)}{3} + \frac{30}{5(2)}$

SKILL Solving Multiplication and Division Equations *pages 56–57*

O Find n. $34n = 306$ **P** Find x. $\frac{x}{14} = 7$

47

Item F on a pretest is the same exercise type as . . .

page 50

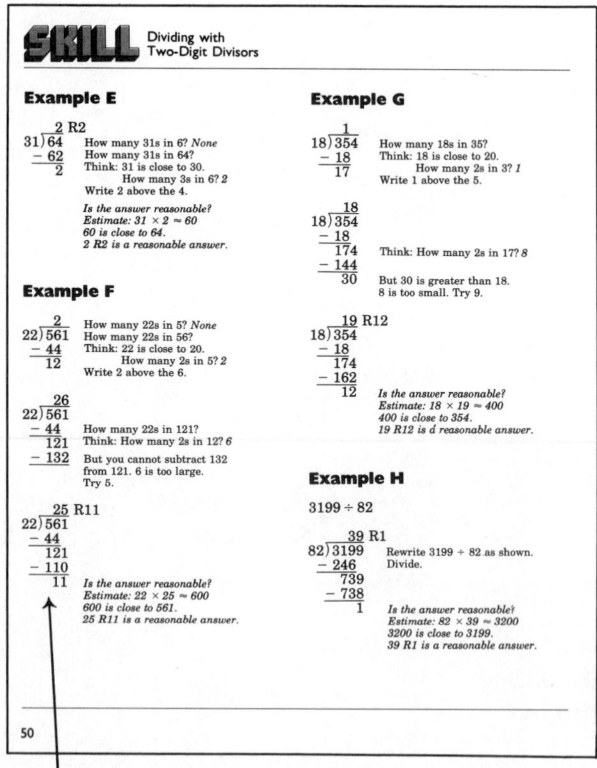

SKILL Dividing with Two-Digit Divisors

Example E

```
   2 R2
31)64
 - 62
    2
```

How many 31s in 6? *None*
How many 31s in 64?
Think: 31 is close to 30.
How many 3s in 6? *2*
Write 2 above the 4.

Is the answer reasonable?
Estimate: 31 × 2 ≈ 60
60 is close to 64.
2 R2 is a reasonable answer.

Example F

```
    2
22)561
 - 44
   12
```

How many 22s in 5? *None*
How many 22s in 56?
Think: 22 is close to 20.
How many 2s in 5? *2*
Write 2 above the 6.

```
   26
22)561
 - 44
   121
 - 132
```

How many 22s in 121?
Think: How many 2s in 12? *6*
But you cannot subtract 132 from 121. 6 is too large.
Try 5.

```
   25 R11
22)561
 - 44
   121
 - 110
    11
```

Is the answer reasonable?
Estimate: 22 × 25 ≈ 600
600 is close to 561.
25 R11 is a reasonable answer.

Example G

```
    1
18)354
 - 18
   17
```

How many 18s in 35?
Think: 18 is close to 20.
How many 2s in 3? *1*
Write 1 above the 5.

```
   18
18)354
 - 18
   174
 - 144
    30
```

Think: How many 2s in 17? *8*

But 30 is greater than 18.
8 is too small. Try 9.

```
   19 R12
18)354
 - 18
   174
 - 162
    12
```

Is the answer reasonable?
Estimate: 18 × 19 ≈ 400
400 is close to 354.
19 R12 is d reasonable answer.

Example H

3199 ÷ 82

```
    39 R1
82)3199
 - 246
   739
 - 738
     1
```

Rewrite 3199 ÷ 82 as shown.
Divide.

Is the answer reasonable?
Estimate: 82 × 39 ≈ 3200
3200 is close to 3199.
39 R1 is a reasonable answer.

50

Example F in a skills lesson and as . . .

Exercise sets Each exercise set contains exercises that are the same type as the example with the same letter.

Mixed practice A special set of exercises contains additional mixed practice on the types of exercises introduced in the lesson.

Posttest on skills A posttest on skills follows the skills lessons in a chapter. The posttest is an alternate form of the pretest with the same page references to skills lessons and with similar lettered test items.

page 51

Exercises

Set E

1. 34)68
2. 24)96
3. 53)60
4. 81)92
5. 32)74
6. 76)96
7. 29)81
8. 52)77
9. 21)64
10. 41)88
11. 80)95
12. 33)87

Set F

1. 83)412
2. 74)281
3. 53)301
4. 31)243
5. 24)819
6. 23)829
7. 54)701
8. 22)568
9. 52)673
10. 24)286
11. 33)514
12. 43)676
13. 62)927
14. 21)794
15. 34)620
16. 14)463
17. 34)928
18. 42)829
19. 12)817
20. 13)604

Set G

1. 25)114
2. 57)286
3. 65)344
4. 79)317
5. 28)226
6. 37)199
7. 26)842
8. 19)790
9. 17)879
10. 18)385
11. 15)927
12. 16)978
13. 39)743
14. 48)773
15. 35)994
16. 36)831
17. 28)732
18. 26)995
19. 15)898
20. 25)896

Set H

1. 3157 ÷ 42
2. 7796 ÷ 24
3. 9980 ÷ 63
4. 17,562 ÷ 51
5. 82,621 ÷ 23
6. 82,197 ÷ 36
7. 73,329 ÷ 46
8. 147,177 ÷ 32
9. 448,127 ÷ 77
10. 4,194,347 ÷ 56

Mixed Practice

1. 35)846
2. 42)78932
3. 76)9992
4. 55)4509989
5. 94 ÷ 23
6. 929 ÷ 33
7. 602 ÷ 24
8. 719 ÷ 18
9. 19)546873
10. 31)86
11. 22)99556
12. 14)723604
13. 811 ÷ 41
14. 1379 ÷ 53
15. 76 ÷ 54
16. 739 ÷ 27

51

the exercises in Set F and as . . .

page 58

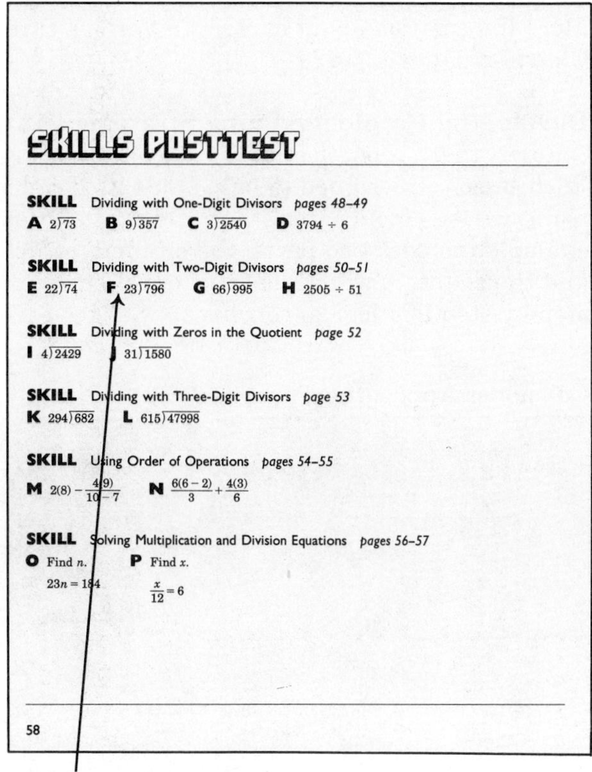

SKILLS POSTTEST

SKILL Dividing with One-Digit Divisors *pages 48–49*

A 2)73 **B** 9)357 **C** 3)2540 **D** 3794 ÷ 6

SKILL Dividing with Two-Digit Divisors *pages 50–51*

E 22)74 **F** 23)796 **G** 66)995 **H** 2505 ÷ 51

SKILL Dividing with Zeros in the Quotient *page 52*

I 4)2429 **J** 31)1580

SKILL Dividing with Three-Digit Divisors *page 53*

K 294)682 **L** 615)47998

SKILL Using Order of Operations *pages 54–55*

M $2(8) - \frac{4(9)}{10 - 7}$ **N** $\frac{6(6-2)}{3} + \frac{4(3)}{6}$

SKILL Solving Multiplication and Division Equations *pages 56–57*

O Find n. $23n = 184$

P Find x. $\frac{x}{12} = 6$

58

item F on the posttest.

Problem Solving

Problem-solving lessons following the skills lessons in each chapter utilize skills taught previously in the book and emphasize the use of skills taught in the chapter itself. Each problem-solving lesson is clearly identified in the title. The title also alerts students to one of the three types of problem-solving lessons in each chapter:

Consumer Applications After the posttest on skills in each chapter, there are one or more consumer lessons. These lessons show how the skills previously taught in the book are used in everyday life. Each lesson is on either one page or two facing pages.

Career Applications Following the consumer lessons in each chapter, there are one or more career lessons. These lessons show how the skills taught previously are used in various careers. The lesson title gives the name of the career. More information about careers in various career clusters is given in the Careers Chart on pages 426-429.

Developing Problem-Solving Strategies After the career lessons in each chapter, there is one lesson that focuses on developing problem-solving strategies. Each lesson is designed to help students develop a problem-solving strategy by using various tactics (tools) for solving the problem. A carefully worked-out example includes two parts: the problem, which poses a question to be answered, and the solution, which contains questions with answers that lead the student step-by-step to a logical conclusion. See pages T24-T25 for additional information.

Consumer Applications pages 248-249

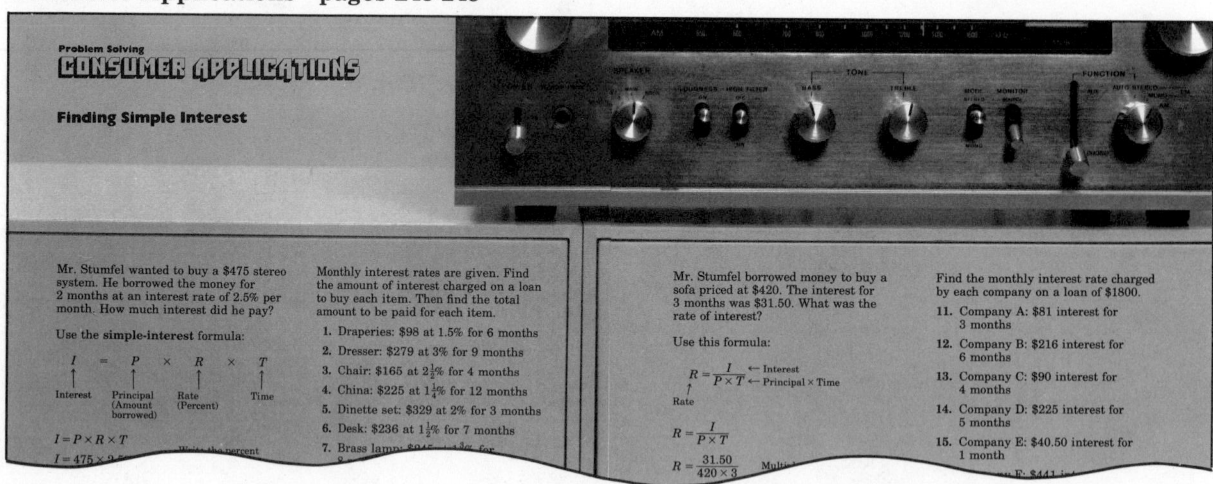
Problem Solving

CONSUMER APPLICATIONS

Finding Simple Interest

Mr. Stumfel wanted to buy a $475 stereo system. He borrowed the money for 2 months at an interest rate of 2.5% per month. How much interest did he pay?

Use the **simple-interest** formula:

$I = P \times R \times T$

Interest — Principal (Amount borrowed) — Rate (Percent) — Time

$I = P \times R \times T$

Monthly interest rates are given. Find the amount of interest charged on a loan to buy each item. Then find the total amount to be paid for each item.

1. Draperies: $98 at 1.5% for 6 months
2. Dresser: $279 at 3% for 9 months
3. Chair: $165 at $2\frac{1}{2}$% for 4 months
4. China: $225 at $1\frac{1}{4}$% for 12 months
5. Dinette set: $329 at 2% for 3 months
6. Desk: $236 at $1\frac{1}{2}$% for 7 months

Mr. Stumfel borrowed money to buy a sofa priced at $420. The interest for 3 months was $31.50. What was the rate of interest?

Use this formula:

$R = \frac{I}{P \times T}$ ← Interest / ← Principal × Time; R: Rate

$R = \frac{I}{P \times T}$

$R = \frac{31.50}{420 \times 3}$

Find the monthly interest rate charged by each company on a loan of $1800.

11. Company A: $81 interest for 3 months
12. Company B: $216 interest for 6 months
13. Company C: $90 interest for 4 months
14. Company D: $225 interest for 5 months
15. Company E: $40.50 interest for 1 month

Career Applications pages 90-91

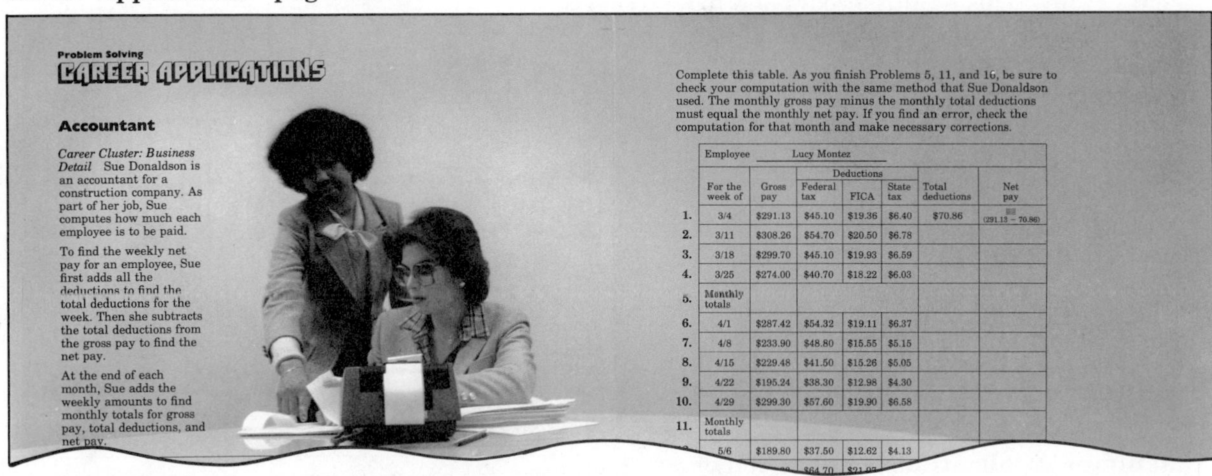

Problem Solving

CAREER APPLICATIONS

Accountant

Career Cluster: Business Detail Sue Donaldson is an accountant for a construction company. As part of her job, Sue computes how much each employee is to be paid.

To find the weekly net pay for an employee, Sue first adds all the deductions to find the total deductions for the week. Then she subtracts the total deductions from the gross pay to find the net pay.

At the end of each month, Sue adds the weekly amounts to find monthly totals for gross pay, total deductions, and net pay.

Complete this table. As you finish Problems 5, 11, and 16, be sure to check your computation with the same method that Sue Donaldson used. The monthly gross pay minus the monthly total deductions must equal the monthly net pay. If you find an error, check the computation for that month and make necessary corrections.

Employee Lucy Montez

	For the week of	Gross pay	Deductions: Federal tax	Deductions: FICA	Deductions: State tax	Total deductions	Net pay
1.	3/4	$291.13	$45.10	$19.36	$6.40	$70.86	▒ (291.13 − 70.86)
2.	3/11	$308.26	$54.70	$20.50	$6.78		
3.	3/18	$299.70	$45.10	$19.93	$6.59		
4.	3/25	$274.00	$40.70	$18.22	$6.03		
5.	Monthly totals						
6.	4/1	$287.42	$54.32	$19.11	$6.37		
7.	4/8	$233.90	$48.80	$15.55	$5.15		
8.	4/15	$229.48	$41.50	$15.26	$5.05		
9.	4/22	$195.24	$38.30	$12.98	$4.30		
10.	4/29	$299.30	$57.60	$19.90	$6.58		
11.	Monthly totals						
	5/6	$189.80	$37.50	$12.62	$4.13		

Developing Strategies pages 118-119

Problem Solving

DEVELOPING STRATEGIES

Tactic: Selecting Necessary Data

Sheila Braniff, an architect, must consider town ordinances when designing a building complex.

Building Type	Phase I	Phase II	Phase III
A 28—1 B.R. apartments 10—2 B.R. apartments Building area—21,106 sq. ft.		1 Bldg. 38 units	
B 18—1 B.R. apartments 6—2 B.R. apartments Building area—12,205 sq. ft.	7 Bldg. 168 units	5 Bldg. 120 units	1 Bldg. 24 units
C 8—2 B.R. apartments Building area—5,640 sq. ft.			2 Bldg. 16 units
D 12—3 B.R. apartments Building area—9,247 sq. ft.	5 Bldg. 60 units		3 Bldg. 36 units

Total land area—1,935,983 sq. ft.

TOWN OF WHEATFIELD

BUILDING ORDINANCES

- Minimum distance between buildings—50 feet.
- 1.5 parking spaces per living unit.
- Minimum of 1 parking space per 400 sq. ft. of commercial building.
- All streets to be posted "NO PARKING."
- 1 waste station (64 sq. ft.) per building.
- Minimum distance between street lights—500 feet.
- Maximum building area permitted is 0.25 of total land area.

Problem

According to town ordinances, how many parking spaces must be included in phase III of the building complex?

Solution

The following questions show Sheila's strategy for solving the problem. The tactics she used included selecting necessary data from available information.

a. How many units of each building type are in phase III? Select necessary data.

Type A	Type B	Type C	Type D
0	24	16	36

b. What is the total number of units in phase III? Add. $24 + 16 + 36 = 76$

c. How many parking spaces must be allowed per unit? Read ordinances. 1.5 per unit

d. How many parking spaces are needed? Multiply. $1.5 \times 76 = 114$

Conclusion: The design for phase III of the building complex must include 114 parking spaces.

118

Related Problems

1. According to the town ordinances, how many parking spaces must be included in phase I of the building complex?
2. Find the number of parking spaces necessary for phase II.
3. Sheila's original design included a total of 628 parking spaces for the three phases. Had she planned for enough parking spaces according to the town ordinances?
4. The complex has 16,800 square feet set aside for commercial use. What is the minimum number of parking spaces required by town ordinance?
5. The complex has two swimming pools. Each pool area needs 20 parking spaces. Find the total number of spaces required for the complex.

Extensions

6. Parking lot X contains 36 parking spaces as required by ordinance. How many units are in building X?
7. The design for building Z allows for 2.5 parking spaces per unit. If the parking lot contains 30 spaces, how many units are in building Z?
8. Buildings E and F share a parking lot. As required by ordinance, the lot contains 57 parking spaces. Building E has two more units than building F. How many units are in building E? How many units are in building F?

119

FEATURES Enrichment

Break Time This feature occurs one to four times within the skills lessons of each chapter. It can be either a recreational puzzle or a problem.

page 219

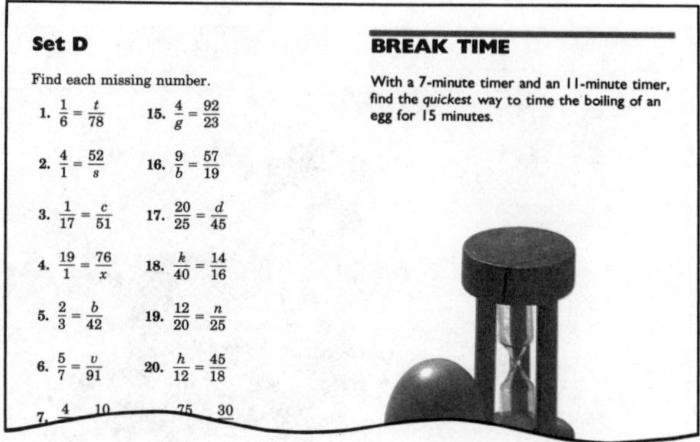

Set D

Find each missing number.

1. $\frac{1}{6} = \frac{t}{78}$
2. $\frac{4}{1} = \frac{52}{s}$
3. $\frac{1}{17} = \frac{c}{51}$
4. $\frac{19}{1} = \frac{76}{x}$
5. $\frac{2}{3} = \frac{b}{42}$
6. $\frac{5}{7} = \frac{v}{91}$

15. $\frac{4}{g} = \frac{92}{23}$
16. $\frac{9}{b} = \frac{57}{19}$
17. $\frac{20}{25} = \frac{d}{45}$
18. $\frac{k}{40} = \frac{14}{16}$
19. $\frac{12}{20} = \frac{n}{25}$
20. $\frac{h}{12} = \frac{45}{18}$

BREAK TIME

With a 7-minute timer and an 11-minute timer, find the *quickest* way to time the boiling of an egg for 15 minutes.

Calculator Applications At the end of each unit is a page of consumer problems to be solved by using a four-function calculator. Key sequences are suggested.

page 72

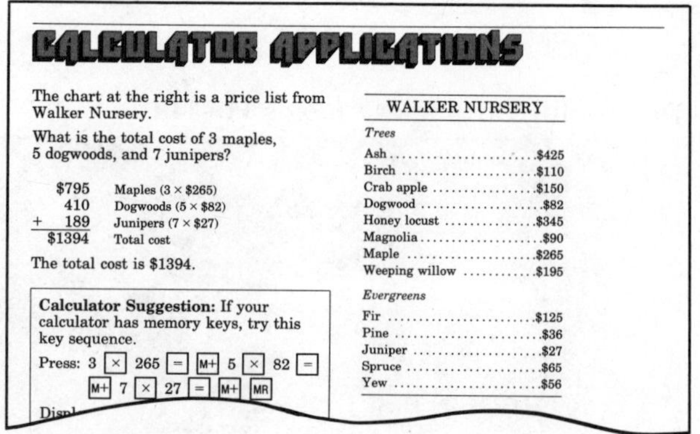

CALCULATOR APPLICATIONS

The chart at the right is a price list from Walker Nursery.

What is the total cost of 3 maples, 5 dogwoods, and 7 junipers?

\$795	Maples (3 × \$265)
410	Dogwoods (5 × \$82)
+ 189	Junipers (7 × \$27)
\$1394	Total cost

The total cost is \$1394.

Calculator Suggestion: If your calculator has memory keys, try this key sequence.

Press: 3 [×] 265 [=] [M+] 5 [×] 82 [=] [M+] 7 [×] 27 [=] [M+] [MR]

WALKER NURSERY	
Trees	
Ash	\$425
Birch	\$110
Crab apple	\$150
Dogwood	\$82
Honey locust	\$345
Magnolia	\$90
Maple	\$265
Weeping willow	\$195
Evergreens	
Fir	\$125
Pine	\$36
Juniper	\$27
Spruce	\$65
Yew	\$56

Computer Literacy At the end of each unit is a page focusing on BASIC programming. All of the programs and exercises have been written so that they can either be run on a computer or be used as paper-and-pencil activities.

page 73

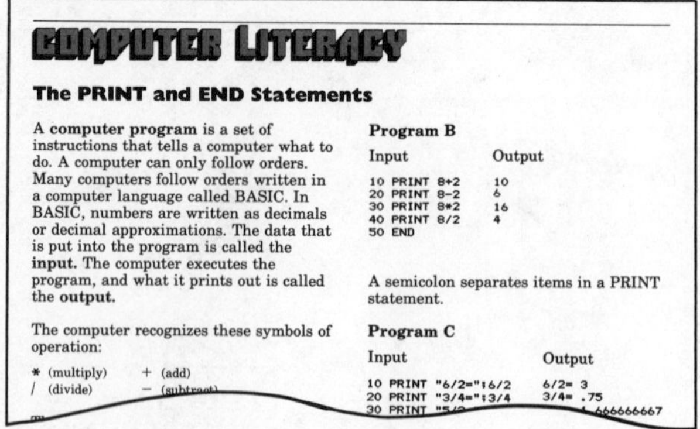

COMPUTER LITERACY

The PRINT and END Statements

A **computer program** is a set of instructions that tells a computer what to do. A computer can only follow orders. Many computers follow orders written in a computer language called BASIC. In BASIC, numbers are written as decimals or decimal approximations. The data that is put into the program is called the **input.** The computer executes the program, and what it prints out is called the **output.**

The computer recognizes these symbols of operation:

* (multiply) + (add)
/ (divide)

Program B

Input	Output
10 PRINT 8+2	10
20 PRINT 8-2	6
30 PRINT 8*2	16
40 PRINT 8/2	4
50 END	

A semicolon separates items in a PRINT statement.

Program C

Input	Output
10 PRINT "6/2=";6/2	6/2= 3
20 PRINT "3/4=";3/4	3/4= .75

Maintenance and Testing

page 347

SKILLS TUNE-UP

Multiplying and Dividing Fractions and Mixed Numbers, pages 149–160

1. $\frac{3}{4} \times \frac{7}{10}$
2. $\frac{7}{15} \times \frac{5}{28}$
3. $\frac{7}{8} \times \frac{1}{2}$
4. $\frac{4}{5} \times \frac{1}{2} \times \frac{5}{8}$
5. $9 \times \frac{4}{7}$
6. $\frac{3}{7} \times 49$
7. $\frac{5}{11} \times 2\frac{4}{9}$
8. $1\frac{19}{20} \times 12$

Percent, pages 235–246

Write each percent as a decimal.

1. 9%
2. 35%
3. 92.1%
4. 0.35%
5. 6.24%
6. 0.1%
7. 27%
8. $5\frac{1}{4}$%

Write each decimal as a percent.

9. 0.04
10. 0.923
11. $0.37\frac{1}{2}$
12. 2.36
13. 0.79
14. 0.243
15. 0.8
16. 0.03

Percent, pages 235–246

1. Find 4% of 65.
2. Find 54% of 60.
3. Find 8% of 85.
4. Find $33\frac{1}{3}$% of 63.
5. Find 25% of 32.
6. Find 125% of 40.
7. 27 is what percent of 45?
8. 23 is what percent of 115?
9. 7 is what percent of 35?
10. 86 is what percent

Skills Tune-up At the end of each unit is a page containing sets of exercises that maintain skills taught previously in the book. References at the beginning of each set indicate pages on which the skill was taught.

page 419

SKILLS FILE

Use after page 51.

1. 5)97
2. 3)83
3. 6)879
4. 8)345
5. 4)8932
6. 7)2144
7. 5)32693
8. 8)15718
9. 24)98

Use after page 52.

1. 6)185
2. 4)362
3. 8)3442
4. 2)6015
5. 9)4776
6. 7)2802
7. 6)18157
8. 5)37604
9. 8)48643

Use after page 79.

1. 17.4 + 6.7
2. 48.5 + 72.8
3. 3.76 + 5.92
4. 4.68 + 12.25
5. 0.096 + 0.243
6. 7.427 + 8.395
15. 20.98 + 0.53 + 18.46
16. 15.67 + 2.35 + 7.23
17. 8.956 + 3.409 + 6.738
18. 5.215 + 0.779 + 2.241
19. 0.036 + 0.42 + 0.98

Skills File The skills file at the back of the student book contains sets of exercises that provide additional skills practice. Each set is keyed to an appropriate skills lesson.

page 256

CHAPTER 11 TEST

1. Write 7% as a decimal.
2. Write 0.594 as a percent.
3. Write 35% as a fraction in lowest terms.
4. Write $\frac{3}{4}$ as a percent.
5. Find 58% of 72.
6. Find $4\frac{3}{4}$% of 900.
7. Find $66\frac{2}{3}$% of 51.
8. 13 is what percent of 20?
9. 22 is what percent of 24?

13. Linda Lauer wanted to buy tires priced at $275. She borrowed the money for 6 months at an interest rate of 1.5% per month. How much interest did she pay? Use this formula: $I = P \times R \times T$
14. Mr. Doughty borrowed $1400 to buy a dining room set. The interest for 12 months was $420. What was the monthly interest rate? Use this formula: $R = \frac{I}{P \times T}$
15. The balance on Mr. Stillman's charge account was $192. He made a $25 monthly payment. Then he was charged 2% for a finance charge. What was the new balance on his account?

Chapter Test The test at the end of each chapter contains items from each skills lesson and each problem-solving lesson in the chapter. Skills pretest and posttest are described on pages T8 and T9.

Additional testing available in the Teacher's Edition includes six unit tests, an end-of-book test, and a suggested competency test. Alternate forms of the chapter tests, unit tests, end-of-book test, and suggested competency test can be found in the *Test Masters*.

FEATURES Teacher's Edition

Teaching Aids

Management The management guide suggests ways of planning, testing, and individualizing while using *Mathematics in Life, Second Edition.* See page T16.

Time Schedule The suggested time schedule is a general guide to allocating periods of time to chapters within each unit. See page T17.

Reference Charts A reference chart for each unit keys objectives to text pages, to pretest and posttest items, and to chapter test items. See pages T18-T23.

Teaching Notes Notes and activities for each chapter include additional information and teaching suggestions. Also included are specific suggestions for teaching problem-solving lessons as well as calculator and computer pages. See pages T24-T45.

Reproducible Tests Six unit tests, an end-of-book test, and a competency test are provided. See pages T55-T79.

Answers and Lesson Notes

① **Objective** A brief statement of the objective for the lesson. The same objective appears in the reference charts.

② **Type of Exercise** An indication of the specific type of exercise that is taught in the example.

③ **Mixed Practice Reference** Keys each exercise in the set of mixed practice to the type of exercise shown in the corresponding example.

④ **Skills File Reference** Keys skills lessons to additional practice exercises in the back of the student's text.

page 52

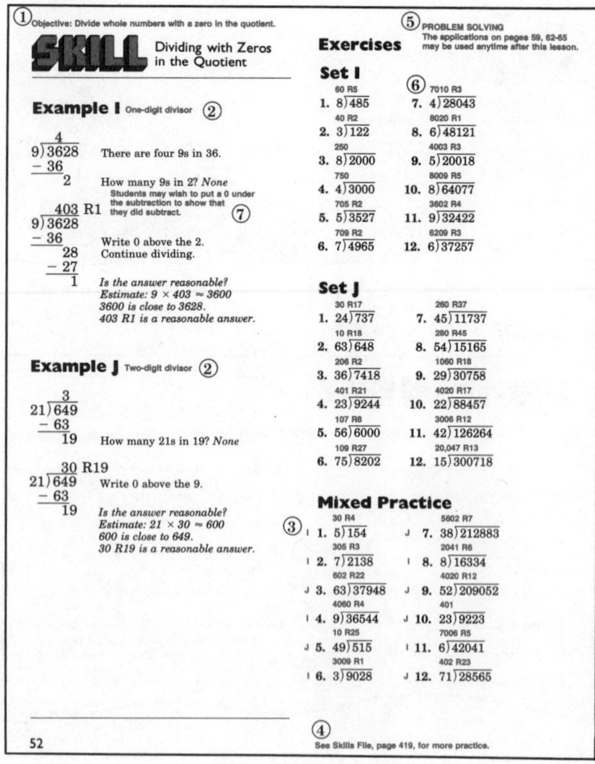

① Objective: Divide whole numbers with a zero in the quotient.

SKILL Dividing with Zeros in the Quotient

Example I One-digit divisor ②

9)3628 → 4; − 36; 2 — There are four 9s in 36.

How many 9s in 2? *None*

Students may wish to put a 0 under the subtraction to show that they did subtract. ⑦

9)3628 → 403 R1; − 36; 28; − 27; 1 — Write 0 above the 2. Continue dividing.

Is the answer reasonable?
Estimate: 9 × 403 ≈ 3600
3600 is close to 3628.
403 R1 is a reasonable answer.

Example J Two-digit divisor ②

21)649 → 3; − 63; 19 — How many 21s in 19? *None*

21)649 → 30 R19; − 63; 19 — Write 0 above the 9.

Is the answer reasonable?
Estimate: 21 × 30 ≈ 600
600 is close to 649.
30 R19 is a reasonable answer.

Exercises

⑤ PROBLEM SOLVING
The applications on pages 59, 62-65 may be used anytime after this lesson.

Set I ⑥

Exercise	Answer	Exercise	Answer
1. 8)485	60 R5	7. 4)28043	7010 R3
2. 3)122	40 R2	8. 6)48121	8020 R1
3. 8)2000	250	9. 5)20018	4003 R3
4. 4)3000	750	10. 8)64077	8009 R5
5. 5)3527	705 R2	11. 9)32422	3602 R4
6. 7)4965	709 R2	12. 6)37257	6209 R3

Set J

Exercise	Answer	Exercise	Answer
1. 24)737	30 R17	7. 45)11737	260 R37
2. 63)648	10 R18	8. 54)15165	280 R45
3. 36)7418	206 R2	9. 29)30758	1060 R18
4. 23)9244	401 R21	10. 22)88457	4020 R17
5. 56)6000	107 R8	11. 42)126264	3006 R12
6. 75)8202	109 R27	12. 15)300718	20,047 R13

Mixed Practice ③

Ref.	Exercise	Answer	Ref.	Exercise	Answer
I	1. 5)154	30 R4	J	7. 38)212883	5602 R7
I	2. 7)2138	305 R3	I	8. 8)16334	2041 R6
J	3. 63)37948	602 R22	J	9. 52)209052	4020 R12
I	4. 9)36544	4060 R4	J	10. 23)9223	401
J	5. 49)515	10 R25	I	11. 6)42041	7006 R5
I	6. 3)9028	3009 R1	J	12. 71)28565	402 R23

52

④ See Skills File, page 419, for more practice.

(5) **References to Problem-Solving Lessons** References on some skills lessons indicate when the student has had the skills needed to do certain applications in the chapter.

(6) **Answers** Answers printed on a full-size replica of the student's page.

(7) **Notes** Helpful information and teaching suggestions.

(8) **Materials** A list of materials other than paper and pencil that are needed by the student to do the lesson.

(9) **Scoring Table** A table to convert raw test scores to percentage scores on each pretest, posttest, and chapter test.

(10) **References to Types of Exercises** A letter next to a chapter test item indicating the exercise type being tested.

(11) **References to Duplicating Masters** References to *Test Masters* and to *Problem-Solving Masters* where appropriate.

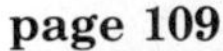

page 109

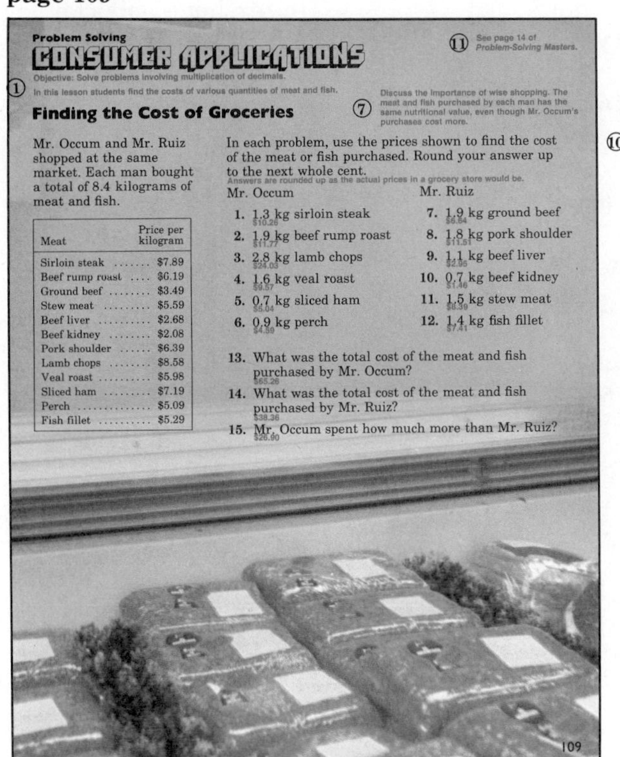

Problem Solving

CONSUMER APPLICATIONS

(11) See page 14 of *Problem-Solving Masters.*

(1) Objective: Solve problems involving multiplication of decimals.

In this lesson students find the costs of various quantities of meat and fish.

(7) Discuss the importance of wise shopping. The meat and fish purchased by each man has the same nutritional value, even though Mr. Occum's purchases cost more.

Finding the Cost of Groceries

Mr. Occum and Mr. Ruiz shopped at the same market. Each man bought a total of 8.4 kilograms of meat and fish.

Meat	Price per kilogram
Sirloin steak	$7.89
Beef rump roast	$6.19
Ground beef	$3.49
Stew meat	$5.59
Beef liver	$2.68
Beef kidney	$2.08
Pork shoulder	$6.39
Lamb chops	$8.58
Veal roast	$5.98
Sliced ham	$7.19
Perch	$5.09
Fish fillet	$5.29

(10) In each problem, use the prices shown to find the cost of the meat or fish purchased. Round your answer up to the next whole cent.

Answers are rounded up as the actual prices in a grocery store would be.

Mr. Occum

1. 1.3 kg sirloin steak $10.26
2. 1.9 kg beef rump roast $11.77
3. 2.8 kg lamb chops $24.03
4. 1.6 kg veal roast $9.57
5. 0.7 kg sliced ham $5.04
6. 0.9 kg perch $4.59

Mr. Ruiz

7. 1.9 kg ground beef $6.64
8. 1.8 kg pork shoulder $11.51
9. 1.1 kg beef liver $2.95
10. 0.7 kg beef kidney $1.46
11. 1.5 kg stew meat $8.39
12. 1.4 kg fish fillet $7.41

13. What was the total cost of the meat and fish purchased by Mr. Occum? $65.26
14. What was the total cost of the meat and fish purchased by Mr. Ruiz? $38.36
15. Mr. Occum spent how much more than Mr. Ruiz? $26.90

109

page 326

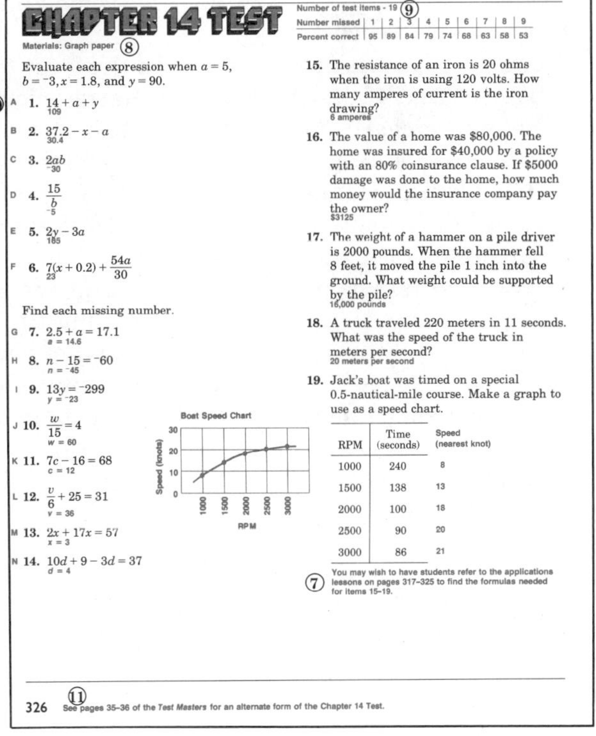

CHAPTER 14 TEST

Materials: Graph paper (8)

Number of test items - 19 (9)

Number missed	1	2	3	4	5	6	7	8	9
Percent correct	95	89	84	79	74	68	63	58	53

Evaluate each expression when $a = 5$, $b = {}^{-}3, x = 1.8$, and $y = 90$.

(10) A 1. $14 + a + y$ 109

B 2. $37.2 - x - a$ 30.4

C 3. $2ab$ ⁻30

D 4. $\frac{15}{b}$ ⁻5

E 5. $2y - 3a$ 165

F 6. $7(x + 0.2) + \frac{54a}{30}$ 23

Find each missing number.

G 7. $2.5 + a = 17.1$ $a = 14.6$

H 8. $n - 15 = {}^{-}60$ $n = {}^{-}45$

I 9. $13y = {}^{-}299$ $y = {}^{-}23$

J 10. $\frac{w}{15} = 4$ $w = 60$

K 11. $7c - 16 = 68$ $c = 12$

L 12. $\frac{v}{6} + 25 = 31$ $v = 36$

M 13. $2x + 17x = 57$ $x = 3$

N 14. $10d + 9 - 3d = 37$ $d = 4$

15. The resistance of an iron is 20 ohms when the iron is using 120 volts. How many amperes of current is the iron drawing? 6 amperes

16. The value of a home was $80,000. The home was insured for $40,000 by a policy with an 80% coinsurance clause. If $5000 damage was done to the home, how much money would the insurance company pay the owner? $3125

17. The weight of a hammer on a pile driver is 2000 pounds. When the hammer fell 8 feet, it moved the pile 1 inch into the ground. What weight could be supported by the pile? 16,000 pounds

18. A truck traveled 220 meters in 11 seconds. What was the speed of the truck in meters per second? 20 meters per second

19. Jack's boat was timed on a special 0.5-nautical-mile course. Make a graph to use as a speed chart.

RPM	Time (seconds)	Speed (nearest knot)
1000	240	8
1500	138	13
2000	100	18
2500	90	20
3000	86	21

(7) You may wish to have students refer to the applications lessons on pages 317–325 to find the formulas needed for items 15–19.

326 (11) See pages 35–36 of the *Test Masters* for an alternate form of the Chapter 14 Test.

MANAGEMENT

Plan/Teach

Long range
- Table of contents
- Suggested time schedule on page T17
- Problem-solving notes on pages T24–T25
- Calculator and computer notes on pages T26–T27
- Objectives (including minimum computational skills objectives) listed on pages T18–T23
- Competency test keyed to skills objectives and consumer topics

Intermediate
- Overview of each chapter in notes on pages T28–T45
- Reference charts that key skills pretest items, skills posttest items, and chapter test items to objectives and text pages

Short term
- Teaching suggestions overprinted on page
- Overprinted notes identifying exercise type for each teaching example
- ABC system of keying test items to exercises in the student's text
- Additional notes found on pages T28–T45

Test

In the student's text
- 18 skills pretests
- 18 skills posttests
- 18 chapter tests on skills and problem solving
- Teacher-constructed skills tests made by choosing one exercise from each lettered set

In the teacher's edition
- 6 multiple-choice unit tests
- 1 multiple-choice end-of-book test
- 1 multiple-choice competency test

In the Test Masters
(alternate forms of tests in the student's text and the teacher's edition)
- 18 chapter tests
- 6 multiple-choice unit tests
- 1 multiple-choice end-of-book test
- 1 multiple-choice competency test

Maintain/Enrich

In the student's text

Maintain
- Skills Tune-up
- Skills File
- Skills exercises not previously assigned

Enrich
- Break Time
- Calculator Applications
- Computer Literacy

In the teacher's edition
- Activities to *maintain* and *enrich* both computational and problem-solving skills suggested in teacher's notes on pages T28–T45
- Overprinted notes on lesson page

In supplementary items
- *Problem-Solving Masters: Applications and Consumer Forms* that *maintain* and *enrich* problem-solving skills taught in the student's text

Suggested Time Schedule

The suggested schedule given below is a general guide to allocating periods of time to chapters within each unit. The schedule is based on a school year of 170 days.

	Chapter	Pages	Title	Days
Unit 1	1	3–24	Adding and Subtracting Whole Numbers	8
	2	25–46	Multiplying Whole Numbers	9
	3	47–70	Dividing Whole Numbers	12
Unit 2	4	75–94	Adding and Subtracting Decimals	7
	5	95–120	Multiplying and Dividing Decimals	12
	6	121–144	The Metric System	10
Unit 3	7	149–170	Multiplying and Dividing Fractions and Mixed Numbers	11
	8	171–192	Adding and Subtracting Fractions and Mixed Numbers	11
	9	193–210	Probability	9
Unit 4	10	215–234	Ratio, Proportion, and Similarity	8
	11	235–256	Percent	11
	12	257–278	Statistics	9
Unit 5	13	283–302	Positive and Negative Numbers	8
	14	303–326	Expressions and Equations	10
	15	327–346	Graphing	8
Unit 6	16	351–370	Perimeter and Area	8
	17	371–392	Surface Area and Volume	10
	18	393–414	The Pythagorean Rule and Trigonometry	9

REFERENCE CHART

Unit I
Whole Numbers

Objectives	*Text pages*	*Pretest, Posttest items*	*Chapter Test items*
Chapter 1 Adding and Subtracting Whole Numbers, Pages 3–24			
1. Round whole numbers.	4	A, B, C	1–3
2. Estimate sums and differences using rounded numbers.	5	D, E, F	4–6
*3. Add whole numbers.	6–7	G, H, I, J	7–10
*4. Subtract whole numbers.	8–9	K, L, M	11–13
5. Compute following order of operations involving addition and subtraction.	10–11	N, O	14–15
6. Solve addition and subtraction equations.	12–13	P, Q	16–17
7. Solve problems involving addition and subtraction of whole numbers.	15–21		18–21
8. Solve problems by reading a scale.	22–23		22
Chapter 2 Multiplying Whole Numbers, Pages 25–46			
9. Multiply multiples of powers of 10.	26	A, B	1–2
10. Estimate products using rounded numbers.	27	C, D	3–4
11. Multiply whole numbers by a one-digit multiplier.	28–29	E, F, G, H	5–8
*12. Multiply whole numbers by a two-digit multiplier.	30–31	I, J, K, L	9–12
13. Multiply whole numbers by a three-digit multiplier.	32–33	M, N, O	13–15
14. Compute following order of operations involving addition, subtraction, and multiplication.	34–35	P, Q	16–17
15. Solve problems involving multiplication of whole numbers.	37–43		18–21
16. Solve problems by reading a table and using a formula.	44–45		22
Chapter 3 Dividing Whole Numbers, Pages 47–70			
17. Divide whole numbers by a one-digit divisor.	48–49	A, B, C, D	1–4
*18. Divide whole numbers by a two-digit divisor.	50–51	E, F, G, H	5–8
19. Divide whole numbers with a zero in the quotient.	52	I, J	9–10
20. Divide whole numbers by a three-digit divisor.	53	K, L	11–12
21. Compute following order of operations involving addition, subtraction, multiplication, and division.	54–55	M, N	13–14
22. Solve multiplication and division equations.	56–57	O, P	15–16
23. Solve problems involving division of whole numbers.	59–67		17–21
24. Solve problems by reading a table and interpreting remainders.	68–69		22

*Minimum computational skill See page T72.

REFERENCE CHART

Unit 2
Decimals and the Metric System

Objectives	*Text pages*	*Pretest, Posttest items*	*Chapter Test items*
Chapter 4 Adding and Subtracting Decimals, Pages 75–94			
25. Write and compare decimals.	76–77	A, B, C	1–3
*26. Add decimals.	78–79	D, E, F, G	4–7
*27. Subtract decimals.	80–81	H, I, J, K	8–11
28. Round decimals.	82	L, M	12–13
29. Estimate sums and differences using rounded numbers.	83	N, O, P	14–16
30. Solve problems involving addition and subtraction of decimals.	85–91		17–20
31. Solve problems by obtaining information from a picture.	92–93		21
Chapter 5 Multiplying and Dividing Decimals, Pages 95–120			
*32. Multiply decimals.	96–97	A, B, C	1–3
33. Estimate products using rounded numbers.	98–99	D, E	4–5
*34. Divide a decimal by a whole number.	100–101	F, G, H	6–8
35. Multiply or divide a decimal by 10, 100, or 1000.	102–103	I, J, K, L	9–12
36. Divide decimals.	104–105	M, N, O	13–15
37. Round quotients.	106–107	P, Q, R	16–18
38. Solve problems involving multiplication and division of decimals.	109–117		19–23
39. Solve problems by selecting necessary data from given information.	118–119		24
Chapter 6 The Metric System, Pages 121–144			
40. Estimate and measure the length of a segment to the nearest centimeter or millimeter.	123	A, B	1–2
41. Choose sensible measures and do conversions involving metric units of length.	124–125	C, D	3–4
42. Find areas of figures and do conversions involving metric units of area.	126	E, F	5–6
43. Find volumes of figures and do conversions involving metric units of volume.	127	G, H	7–8
44. Choose sensible measures and do conversions involving metric units of capacity.	128	I, J	9–10
45. Choose sensible measures and do conversions involving metric units of mass.	129	K, L	11–12
46. Write measures for given amounts of water using related units of volume, capacity, and mass.	130	M, N	13–14
47. Choose sensible measures involving metric units of temperature.	131	O, P	15–16
48. Solve problems involving metric units of measure.	134–141		17–20
49. Solve problems by measuring.	142–143		21

*Minimum computational skill See page T72.

REFERENCE CHART

Unit 3 Fractions, Mixed Numbers, and Probability

Objectives	*Text pages*	*Pretest, Posttest items*	*Chapter Test items*
Chapter 7 Multiplying and Dividing Fractions and Mixed Numbers, Pages 149–170			
50. Write fractions and mixed numbers.	150–151	A, B	1–2
51. Rename fractions and mixed numbers.	152	C, D, E	3–5
52. Write a fraction as a decimal.	153	F, G	6–7
*53. Multiply fractions.	154–155	H, I, J, K	8–11
54. Multiply mixed numbers.	156–157	L, M, N, O	12–15
*55. Divide fractions and mixed numbers.	158–159	P, Q, R, S	16–19
56. Solve problems involving multiplication and division of fractions and mixed numbers.	161–167		20–23
57. Solve problems by using estimated information.	168–169		24
Chapter 8 Adding and Subtracting Fractions and Mixed Numbers, Pages 171–192			
58. Find common denominators.	172	A, B	1–2
59. Compare fractions and mixed numbers.	173	C, D, E	3–5
*60. Add and subtract fractions.	174–175	F, G, H, I, J, K	6–11
*61. Add mixed numbers.	176–177	L, M, N, O	12–15
62. Subtract mixed numbers with the same denominator.	178–179	P, Q, R	16–18
*63. Subtract mixed numbers with different denominators.	180–181	S, T, U	19–21
64. Solve problems involving addition and subtraction of fractions and mixed numbers.	183–189		22–25
65. Solve problems by drawing a picture.	190–191		26
Chapter 9 Probability, Pages 193–210			
66. Find probabilities and make predictions.	194–195	A, B, C	1–3
67. Find probabilities using tree diagrams.	196–197	D, E	4–5
68. Find probabilities involving independent events using multiplication.	198–199	F, G	6–7
69. Find probabilities involving dependent events using multiplication.	200–201	H	8
70. Solve problems involving probability.	203–207		9–11
71. Solve problems by using a simpler case.	208–209		12

*Minimum computational skill See page T72.

REFERENCE CHART

Unit 4
Ratio, Percent, and Statistics

Objectives	*Text pages*	*Pretest, Posttest items*	*Chapter Test items*
Chapter 10 Ratio, Proportion, and Similarity, Pages 215–234			
72. Write ratios and lists of equal ratios.	216–217	A, B	1–2
*73. Find a missing number in a proportion by using cross-products.	218–219	C, D	3–4
74. Identify similar figures and name corresponding angles and sides.	220–221	E, F	5–6
75. Find missing dimensions in similar triangles by using proportions.	222–223	G, H	7–8
76. Solve problems involving ratio, proportion, and similarity.	225–231		9–12
77. Solve problems by using proportions and interpreting remainders.	232–233		13
Chapter 11 Percent, Pages 235–256			
78. Write percents as decimals and decimals as percents.	236–237	A, B	1–2
79. Write percents as fractions and fractions as percents.	238–239	C, D	3–4
*80. Find a percent of a number.	240–241	E, F, G	5–7
*81. Find what percent one number is of another.	242–243	H, I	8–9
82. Find a number when a percent of it is known.	244–245	J, K	10–11
83. Solve problems involving percent.	247–253		12–16
84. Solve problems by reading a table, reading a scale, and working backward.	254–255		17
Chapter 12 Statistics, Pages 257–278			
85. Find the mean for a set of data.	259	A	1
86. Find the median and the mode for a set of data.	260–261	B, C	2–3
87. Read and make a bar graph.	262–263	D, E	4–5
88. Read and make a line graph.	264–265	F, G	6–7
89. Read and make a circle graph.	266–267	H, I, J	8–10
90. Solve problems involving statistics.	270–275		11–13
91. Solve problems by making a table and interpreting data.	276–277		14

*Minimum computational skill See page T72.

REFERENCE CHART Unit 5 Algebra

Objectives	*Text pages*	*Pretest, Posttest items*	*Chapter Test items*
Chapter 13 Positive and Negative Numbers, Pages 283–302			
92. Write, compare, and order positive and negative numbers.	284–285	A, B, C	1–3
93. Add positive and negative numbers.	286–287	D, E, F, G	4–7
94. Subtract positive and negative numbers.	288–289	H, I, J, K, L, M	8–13
95. Multiply positive and negative numbers.	290–291	N, O, P, Q	14–17
96. Divide positive and negative numbers.	292–293	R, S, T, U	18–21
97. Solve problems involving positive and negative numbers.	295–299		22–24
98. Balance a check register by using positive and negative numbers.	300–301		25
Chapter 14 Expressions and Equations, Pages 303–326			
99. Evaluate expressions.	304–305	A, B, C, D	1–4
100. Evaluate expressions involving order of operations.	306–307	E, F	5–6
101. Solve addition and subtraction equations involving integers and decimals.	308–309	G, H	7–8
102. Solve multiplication and division equations involving integers and decimals.	310–311	I, J	9–10
103. Solve two-step equations.	312–313	K, L	11–12
104. Combine like terms to solve equations.	314–315	M, N	13–14
105. Solve problems involving equations.	317–323		15–18
106. Solve problems by using a formula and making a graph.	324–325		19
Chapter 15 Graphing, Pages 327–346			
107. Give ordered pairs for points, and locate points for ordered pairs.	329	A, B	1–2
108. Read a graph on a grid, and draw the graph of an equation.	330–331	C, D	3–4
109. Give ordered pairs of integers for points in four quadrants, and locate points for ordered pairs of integers.	332–333	E, F	5–6
110. Read a graph on a four-quadrant grid, and draw the graph of an equation on a four-quadrant grid.	334–335	G, H	7–8
111. Solve problems involving coordinate graphing.	338–343		9–11
112. Solve problems by reading and interpreting graphs.	344–345		12

REFERENCE CHART Unit 6 Geometry and Right-Triangle Relations

Objectives	*Text pages*	*Pretest, Posttest items*	*Chapter Test items*
Chapter 16 Perimeter and Area, Pages 351–370			
113. Find the perimeter of a geometric figure.	352–353	A, B	1–2
114. Find the circumference of a circle.	354–355	C, D	3–4
115. Find the area of a rectangle, a square, and a parallelogram.	356–357	E, F, G	5–7
116. Find the area of a triangle and a trapezoid.	358–359	H, I	8–9
117. Find the area of a circle.	360–361	J, K	10–11
118. Solve problems involving perimeter and area.	363–367		12–14
119. Solve problems by obtaining information from a picture, using a formula, and selecting necessary data.	368–369		15
Chapter 17 Surface Area and Volume, Pages 371–392			
120. Find the surface area of a rectangular prism.	373	A	1
121. Find the surface area of a cube.	374	B	2
122. Find the surface area of a cylinder.	375	C	3
123. Find the volume of a rectangular prism and a cube.	376–377	D, E	4–5
124. Find the volume of a cylinder.	378–379	F, G	6–7
125. Find the volume of a pyramid and a cone.	380–381	H, I	8–9
126. Find the volume of a sphere.	382	J, K	10–11
127. Solve problems involving surface area and volume.	385–389		12–14
128. Solve problems by obtaining information from a picture, using a formula, and reading a table.	390–391		15
Chapter 18 The Pythagorean Rule and Trigonometry, Pages 393–414			
129. Find powers of numbers by using positive exponents, and find square roots of numbers by trial and error.	395	A, B	1–2
130. Find squares and square roots of numbers by reading a table.	396–397	C, D, E	3–5
131. Find the length of a side of a right triangle by using the Pythagorean Rule.	398–399	F, G	6–7
132. Write the tangent, the sine, and the cosine of a given angle as a ratio and as a decimal.	400–401	H, I, J	8–10
133. Give the tangent, the sine, and the cosine of a given angle by reading a table.	402–403	K, L, M	11–13
134. Find the length of a side of a right triangle by using a trigonometric ratio.	404–405	N, O, P	14–16
135. Solve problems involving the Pythagorean Rule and Trigonometry.	408–411		17–18
136. Solve problems by drawing a picture and using trigonometric ratios.	412–413		19

The ability to solve problems is a very important goal of mathematics education. In *Mathematics in Life, Second Edition,* each chapter is divided into a skills section and a problem-solving section. The section featuring problem solving is divided into three types of lessons.

Consumer Applications In these lessons, students can use the skills taught previously by applying them to real-world situations featuring consumer topics.

Career Applications In these lessons, students can use skills previously taught to solve problems related to specific career situations. Additional information about careers can be found in the Careers Chart, pages 426–429.

Developing Problem-Solving Strategies In these lessons, students first focus on developing a strategy (overall plan) to solve a problem. Then they use varied problem-solving tactics (tools) to execute the plan. The chart below shows a complete listing of all the problem-solving tactics taught in *Mathematics in Life, Second Edition.* Each tactic is keyed to the chapters and text pages where it is taught and used.

Tactic	Chapter	Page
Reading a Scale	1 11	22 254
Reading a Table	2 3 11 17	44 68 254 390
Using a Formula	2 14 16 17	44 324 368 390
Interpreting Remainders	3 10	68 232
Obtaining Information from a Picture	4 16 17	92 368 390
Selecting Necessary Data	5 16	118 368
Measuring	6	142

Tactic	Chapter	Page
Using Estimated Information	7	168
Drawing a Picture	8 18	190 412
Using a Simpler Case	9	208
Using Proportions	10	232
Working Backward	11	254
Making a Table	12	276
Interpreting Data	12	276
Using Positive and Negative Numbers	13	300
Making a Graph	14	324
Reading and Interpreting Graphs	15	344
Using Trigonometric Ratios	18	412

Each lesson devoted to developing strategies guides students step-by-step through the solution of a problem. However, if students can solve the problem by using another strategy, they should not be penalized for this kind of creative thinking. Listed are some of the highlights of the lesson below.

① **Tactic** is a tool used in implementing a strategy (overall plan).

② **Problem** includes some given information plus a question to be answered.

③ **Solution** shows how one person used various tactics and specific questions as part of his/her strategy.

④ **Conclusion** is the answer to the problem.

⑤ **Related problems** provide additional problems that give students more practice in using the strategy developed in the example.

⑥ **Extensions** expand the topic and give students the opportunity to develop strategies for slightly harder problems. Extensions are intended for the more able student.

pages 232-233

Problem Solving

DEVELOPING STRATEGIES

① **Tactics: Using Proportions, Interpreting Remainders**

Lauri Stephen works for a stable that boards horses. One of her responsibilities is to buy food for the horses. Each horse eats a combination of hay and sweet feed every day.

Hay: 25-kg bales
$2 per bale

Sweet feed: 25-kg bags
$5.25 per bag

② **Problem**

Buster eats 113 kilograms of hay in 4 weeks. At this rate, how much would it cost to feed Buster hay for one year? (1 year = 52 weeks)

③ **Solution**

The following questions show Lauri's strategy for solving the problem. The tactics she used included using proportions and interpreting remainders.

a. How many kilograms of hay will Buster eat in one year? Write a proportion and solve.

$$\frac{113}{4} = \frac{x}{52} \begin{matrix} \longleftarrow \text{Kilograms of hay} \\ \longleftarrow \text{Number of weeks} \end{matrix}$$

$$x = 1469$$

b. How many bales are needed? Divide and interpret remainder.

$$25\overline{)1469} = 58 \text{ R}19 \longrightarrow 59$$

c. How much will the hay cost for one year? Multiply.

$$\begin{array}{r} 59 \longleftarrow \text{Number of bales} \\ \times\ 2 \longleftarrow \text{Dollars per bale} \\ \hline 118 \end{array}$$

④ *Conclusion:* If Buster continues to eat hay at a rate of 113 kilograms in 4 weeks, the cost of the hay for one year will be $118.

232

⑤ **Related Problems**

1. Buster eats 70 kilograms of sweet feed in 4 weeks. At this rate, how much will it cost to feed Buster sweet feed for one year?
2. What is the total cost of feeding Buster for one year?
3. Lucky Kate eats 90 kilograms of sweet feed in 4 weeks. At this rate, how much will it cost to feed her sweet feed for one year?
4. Lucky Kate eats twice as much hay as sweet feed. At this rate, how much will hay for one year cost?
5. What is the total cost of hay and sweet feed for feeding Buster and Lucky Kate for one year?
6. Thunderbolt eats 15 kilograms of hay in 5 days. Bongo eats twice as much hay as Thunderbolt. At this rate, how many bales of hay are needed to feed Bongo for one year? Round your answer to the nearest whole number. (1 year = 365 days)
7. How much will hay for Thunderbolt and Bongo cost for one year?

⑥ **Extensions**

8. Lauri needs 100 bales of hay to feed Beulah for one year. To the nearest kilogram, how much hay does Beulah eat in 5 days?
9. Wild Walker eats 3 bags of sweet feed in 4 weeks. How many kilograms of sweet feed does she eat in one year?

233

 **Calculator**

Ways to Use the Calculator with
Mathematics in Life, Second Edition

1. **Not at all**
   You may choose to omit the optional feature called "Calculator Applications" at the end of each unit and not use calculators at all during the year.

2. **With Calculator Applications**
   You may choose to use calculators with only the special feature called "Calculator Applications" at the end of each unit. This feature focuses on ways of using a calculator with selected consumer topics.

3. **With problem-solving lessons**
   Since the focus of these lessons is on solving problems and developing strategies, calculators could be used so that students can concentrate solely on problem solving and not be concerned with paper-and-pencil computation.

4. **With skills lessons in Chapters 9–12, 14, 16–18**
   These chapters, e.g., Chapter 16 on perimeter and area, present mathematical concepts that use but don't teach computation. Using calculators with these chapters will help students learn the math skills without being slowed down by paper-and-pencil computation.

5. **Any combination of items 2–4**
   You may choose any combination that you prefer.

The use of the calculator with *Mathematics in Life, Second Edition,* is strictly optional. If you do plan to use the calculator in your classroom, however, a simple, four-function calculator that adds, subtracts, multiplies, and divides is sufficient. You might want to be aware of the following variations in calculators and **have students consult the manual for their specific calculator to determine the correct operating procedure.**

Variations

Most calculators have algebraic logic: 2 [×] 3 [=] . Some have reverse logic: 2 [ENTER] 3 [×] . The logic greatly affects how key sequences are performed.

Most calculators will do operations in the order they are entered. However, some (not many) are internally programmed to do multiplication before addition.

Many calculators have a feature that is referred to as "automatic constant." Try pressing 2 [×] 3 [=] [=] [=] . Some calculators "remember" the first number that is pressed; others "remember" the second. Some calculators have the automatic constant feature for all four operations, while others have it for only multiplication and division. Still others do not have this feature at all.

Many calculators have memory keys. [M+] and [M−] keys are common. They work somewhat differently from [MS] or [STO] keys.

Many simple calculators have a percent key. The use of the percent key varies a great deal from calculator to calculator. On some calculators, pressing the [=] key immediately after the [%] key may produce unwanted results.

Ways to Use Computer Literacy Pages with *Mathematics in Life, Second Edition*

1. **Not at all**
   These pages are optional and can be omitted if you wish.

2. **As paper-and-pencil activities**
   All of the exercises have been written so that students can complete them as paper-and-pencil activities without running them on a computer. Using this plan, all students can gain exposure to the BASIC programming language.

3. **With a computer**
   The programs have been written so that students can run them on a computer. But you may choose to assign the exercises first as paper-and-pencil activities to provide exposure to BASIC programming concepts before having students run the exercises on the computer to verify the answers. Because there are variations in computers, it is recommended that you run these programs before assigning them to your students.

The use of the computer with *Mathematics in Life, Second Edition,* is strictly optional. A feature on computer literacy is included at the end of each unit. These pages provide exposure to the BASIC programming language and are not intended to represent a complete course in BASIC programming. See the box at the left for ways to use these pages as a part of your complete course of instruction.

Liberties have been taken in explaining some concepts to make them easier for students to understand; e.g., the computer does not return to the FOR statement as explained. This explanation was given to make the concept of the loop easier for students to understand.

Features vary from computer to computer. You might want to be aware of the following variations and **have students consult the manual to determine correct operating procedure for the specific computer being used.**

Variations

With most computers, a statement does not have to fit on one line; and the computer will automatically go to the next line to continue the same statement.

When a comma is used to separate items in a PRINT statement, it causes each item to be printed in a different zone. The number of characters in a zone and the number of zones vary among computers.

Try pressing 2/3. Some computers round the answer (.66666667); others truncate (.66666666). You may notice the number of significant digits can also vary.

You should be aware that it is not important that all students' programs be identical in appearance to be correct.

 **Chapter 1**

Adding and Subtracting Whole Numbers, pages 3–24

Overview

The main focus of Chapter 1 is a review of adding and subtracting whole numbers. Estimation is taught as a skill and is shown with each example in the addition and subtraction skills lessons. The first lesson in the chapter reviews rounding whole numbers, a skill necessary for estimation. The five problem-solving lessons use addition and subtraction skills in practical situations involving diet, travel costs, buying power, fuel delivery, and use of electricity.

Lesson Notes and Activities

page 4 A review of numeration and place value may be necessary before beginning this lesson.

The general rule for rounding is introduced here and will be used when estimating answers to computation throughout the text.

page 5 Discuss with your students the importance of estimation both in the classroom and in everyday life. In some cases an estimated answer is all that is needed. In other cases, an estimate may be used to determine if an actual answer is reasonable.

pages 6-7 For remedial students, you may want to review addition and subtraction basic facts before beginning whole-number computation.

pages 8-9 You might want to review some subtraction examples with consecutive zeros in the minuend. Exercises of this type appear in Set L and in Mixed Practice.

pages 10-11 In this lesson, the operations of addition and subtraction are used together. Therefore, the order or grouping of the numbers used might change the answer. You may want to discuss the commutative and associative properties for addition. You could give students some more difficult exercises such as these: $(55 - 17) - (3 + 29)$ [6]
$28 - [(4 + 17) - 3]$ [10]

pages 12-13 Discuss with students the idea of "undoing" an operation. Use physical ideas such as opening and closing a door.

pages 16-17 If possible, obtain current schedules and fare information, and have students plan a trip.

pages 18-19 After students have completed the table on page 19, you might use the information to discuss varying situations. For example, compare the increase in buying power with the increase in net income after a $1000 raise.

pages 20-21 Remind students that the temperatures are given in degrees Celsius and be sure they are familiar with this scale.

Some Sunday newspapers publish the number of degree-days for the week in the weather section.

pages 22-23 As an extension of this lesson, you might have students compare amounts of electricity used in their homes during various months. They could find this information on the stubs of past electric bills. Discuss possible reasons for more electricity being used during certain months. You might also have students discuss ways to reduce their use of electricity and thus conserve energy.

 Chapter 2

Multiplying Whole Numbers, pages 25–46

Overview

In Chapter 2, students learn to multiply whole numbers by one-, two-, and three-digit multipliers. They estimate products by rounding the factors and multiplying with multiples of 10, 100, and 1000. They use the standard order of operations to evaluate expressions involving addition, subtraction, and multiplication. In the problem-solving lessons, students use multiplication skills in a variety of situations including apartment costs, gasoline costs, corn production, catering, and fire fighting.

Lesson Notes and Activities

page 26 Have students write as many pairs of factors as they can for a product like 36,000. Restrict the factors so that each has only one nonzero digit. [6 × 6000, 60 × 600, 9 × 4000, 90 × 400, 4 × 9000, 40 × 900]

page 27 You may wish to mention settings where estimated products might be used. For example, gate receipts at a sports event, seats in a stadium, names in a phone book, books in a library.

You could have students check their estimates by using a calculator to find the actual products.

pages 28–29 To provide more practice, write the digits 6, 4, 7, 9, and 3 on the chalkboard. Ask the students to put the digits in these boxes to form the greatest possible product and the least possible product.

```
  ■■■■      [9 × 7643 = 68,787]
×    ■      [3 × 4679 = 14,037]
―――――
```

pages 30–31 In Example J, you might use these two exercises to explain why the final step is to add.

```
  36       36       36
×  8     × 20     × 28
 288      720      288 ⟵ 8 × 36
                   720 ⟵ 20 × 36
                  1008
```

pages 32–33 To provide more practice, have students complete self-checking puzzles like this. Answers are shown in brackets.

(× across; × down)

14	8	[112]
27	6	[162]
[378]	[48]	[18,144]

page 37 Newspaper want ads contain information that can be used to generate additional problems similar to those in the lesson.

pages 38–39 Point out that 7 kilometers per liter is about the same as 16 miles per gallon; and 16 kilometers per liter is about the same as 37 miles per gallon.

pages 40–41 One thousand square meters is about one-tenth of the area of a football field. You might also mention that a metric ton, which is 1000 kilograms, is about the weight of a subcompact car.

pages 44–45 You might ask students to investigate the reasons for the variations in flow and nozzle pressure.

NOTES Chapter 3

Dividing Whole Numbers, pages 47–70

Overview

In Chapter 3, students learn to divide whole numbers by one-, two-, and three-digit divisors. Included in these lessons is division with zeros in the quotient. Also, students use the standard order of operations in evaluating expressions and they solve multiplication and division equations. The problem-solving lessons focus on the use of division in settings involving salaries, price per item, painting, assembly lines, inventories, and egg packing.

Lesson Notes and Activities

pages 48–49 Review the terms *dividend, divisor, quotient,* and *remainder*.

In discussing Example A, you might point out that sometimes it is better to express an answer as a quotient with a remainder rather than as a mixed number or decimal. If the problem were how many $7 books can be bought for $88, an answer of 12 books with $4 left over would make more sense than an answer in mixed-number or decimal form.

Remind students that they can multiply and add to check an answer. For example, here are two ways to show a check for Example B.

$$\begin{array}{r} 73 \\ \times\ \ 6 \\ \hline 438 \\ +\ \ \ 1 \\ \hline 439 \end{array} \qquad (6 \times 73) + 1 = 439$$

Students who have trouble with the exercises in Set A may need a review of division basic facts.

You might demonstrate short division with a problem like the one below. In each step, students multiply and subtract mentally and then write the remainder in front of the next digit in the dividend.

$$\begin{array}{r} 4\ \ 2\ \ 6\ \text{R}1 \\ 7\overline{)2\ \ 9\,^{1}8\,^{4}3} \end{array}$$

page 59 Students could divide the weekly salary by 40 to find the hourly salary, ignoring all remainders.

If students are interested in salaries for jobs in various parts of the country, they can find information in the *Occupational Outlook Handbook* in the library or in the guidance office.

pages 60–61 To add realism to the lesson, have students do similar problems from local newspaper ads.

For problems involving just basic facts, such as 3 for 22¢, an alternate method is to round the price up to the next multiple of 3 and then divide. $24 \div 3 = 8$.

pages 66–67 Inventory turnover rate is an indication of how fast goods are being sold. However, it does not indicate the store's profit. Profit depends on other factors as well, such as overhead costs and mark-up on items.

pages 68–69 Discuss the difference between retail and institutional use. Ask students to give examples of each. [Retail: grocery store; Institutional: school, hospital]

You might ask students to find out how eggs are graded.

Calculator Applications

page 72 If students do not have calculators with memory keys, they can write intermediate answers on paper instead of storing them in the calculator's memory.

 **Chapter 4**

Adding and Subtracting Decimals, pages 75–94

Overview

Students begin this chapter by writing and comparing decimals. The next two lessons deal with addition and subtraction, with exercises given in both horizontal and vertical form. Students also use rounded decimals to estimate sums and differences involving decimals. Addition and subtraction of decimals are used to solve problems involving catalog purchases, maintaining a checking account, payroll computations, and reading blueprints.

Lesson Notes and Activities

pages 78–79 You may wish to have less-able students write zeros when adding decimals with different numbers of decimal places.

8.625 + 0.3 $\qquad \begin{array}{r} 8.625 \\ +\ 0.300 \\ \hline \end{array}$

pages 80–81 You can use this device to reinforce addition and subtraction computation with decimals. Answers are shown in brackets.

(+ across, + down)

[0.09]	1.3	1.39
0.28	[2.6]	[2.88]
0.37	3.9	[4.27]

page 85 Since discount stores are basically warehouses, they have a low overhead and usually charge lower prices than retail outlets. However, point out that discount catalog stores are not always cheaper because special sales at retail outlets sometimes feature lower prices.

You may wish to have students use a discount catalog and newspaper ads to compare prices of similar items.

pages 88–89 The check register shown uses the double-line method for recording checks. This provides students with a place to do the computation. The new balance always appears in the gray area of the balance column. You may wish to discuss the single-line method. In this method, the purpose of the check is not written, the amount of the check or deposit is written once, and only the new balance is listed in the balance column.

You might want to discuss the use of the other two columns in the check register. The column marked T can be used when reconciling the statement to check off checks that have cleared. Or, T may be written in the column to indicate items that may be used later for income tax deductions. The fee column is used to record service charges or fees for each check.

You may wish to take a field trip to a bank for further information on banking services. If possible, obtain some sample checks. These could be used to generate several problems such as those in the lesson.

pages 90–91 Point out that the amount of federal and state tax withheld varies according to the number of dependents claimed by the wage earner.

You may want to discuss the types of deductions that may be made: federal income tax, state income tax, FICA, insurance, contributions, retirement fund, etc.

pages 92–93 The industrial arts department may have blueprints to show to your class. Point out that machinists must often calculate dimensions from blueprints.

 Chapter 5

Multiplying and Dividing Decimals, pages 95–120

Overview

In Chapter 5, students learn to multiply decimals. Some products need extra zeros before placing the decimal point. They estimate products by rounding one or both factors. Division is developed in a sequence of lessons: dividing a decimal by a whole number, dividing by a decimal, and rounding quotients. Some exercises require annexing zeros in the dividend. Shortcuts are given for multiplying and dividing by powers of 10. Multiplication and division are used in the problem-solving lessons to plan parking lots, and find the cost of electricity, postage, groceries, and monthly car payments.

Lesson Notes and Activities

pages 96-97 In Example A, some students may profit by using the "looping method" to count the number of decimal places in the product.
3 7.2 8 1 ⟵3 decimal places

Throughout this chapter, and in several other chapters, you may wish to have students check their work by using calculators. Ample practice has been provided, so you might choose to assign some of the exercises to be done on the calculator.

pages 98-99 Point out that we frequently use estimation in finding the product of decimals. Examples include price of gasoline times number of gallons, or unit price times number of units purchased.

pages 100-101 Show students how to check division problems by multiplying or by using a calculator.

pages 106-107 Discuss with students the fact that quotients are often rounded to a particular decimal place. In dealing with money, to give an answer to the nearest cent, the quotient is rounded to the nearest hundredth. In baseball statistics, batting averages are given to the nearest thousandth.

page 109 Use the grocery advertisements in the newspaper to discuss differences in prices of various cuts of meat, as well as differences in prices from store to store.

pages 110-111 This lesson shows that even families with low or moderate incomes can eat well-balanced meals. Information on nutrition is available from such sources as: American Dietetic Association, 620 North Michigan Avenue, Chicago, Illinois 60611, and The United States Department of Agriculture, Office of Information, Washington, D.C. 20250.

pages 112-113 Remind students that when buying a car it pays to shop around to find the best financing. Interest rates and loan payments will be dealt with in further detail in Chapter 11.

pages 114-115 Have students use their families' electric bill to find the rate charged for electricity in your area. Then have them work problems 1-15 using that rate.

pages 116-117 You might have students investigate the cost of sending packages by means other than the mail (bus, truck, train, and air freight).

The Metric System, pages 121–144

Overview

In this chapter, students study the commonly used metric units of length, area, volume, capacity, mass, and temperature. They measure to the nearest centimeter and millimeter. They choose sensible measures for familiar objects, and convert measures within the metric system. They also study the relationship among metric units used to describe an amount of water. The problem-solving lessons use metric measures in cooking, sewing, and medicine dosages. Other lessons involve measuring X rays of teeth and metal fasteners to the nearest millimeter.

Lesson Notes and Activities

page 123 You may wish to have students bring to class food labels and newspaper advertisements in which metric units are used. Students could use these to make a bulletin board display.

pages 124–125 Relating metric prefixes to a place value chart might help some students remember what each prefix means.

thousands	hundreds	tens	ones	tenths	hundredths	thousandths
kilo-	hecto-	deka-		deci-	centi-	milli-

To convert from one unit to another, count how many places the second unit is from the first on the chart and in which direction and then move the decimal point accordingly.

page 126 You might have students estimate and measure the area of the chalkboard in square meters and the area of tracings of their hands in square centimeters.

page 127 For students who have trouble visualizing the figures shown, you might use one-centimeter cubes to construct the figures.

page 129 The force of gravity on an object as measured on a bathroom scale is different on the earth than on the moon. This force is referred to as "weight." The amount of substance in an object as measured on a balance scale is the same everywhere. This is referred to as "mass" but is also called "weight" in common usage. The United States Bureau of Standards has stated that for everyday purposes, *weight* and *mass* can be used interchangeably.

page 130 You might use the ideas on the page in the following experiment to find the volume of a rock. Measure the level of water in a graduated cylinder, say 27 mL. Submerge the rock. Record the new height of the water, 38 mL. Subtract. The rock displaced 11 mL of water, so it has a volume of 11 cm^3.

pages 136–137 The International Standard Organization (ISO) is developing a system for standardizing clothing sizes throughout the world. Tags with pictures will be attached to all garments and will show dimensions of garments in centimeters.

Computer Literacy

page 147 LET statements are often used as counters within a program. Starting with LET X = 0 and then using LET X = X + 1, keeps track of the number of times X is used in the program. This use of the LET statement would be with a GO TO statement or loops which are explained in later lessons.

Chapter 7

Multiplying and Dividing Fractions and Mixed Numbers, pages 149–170

Overview

In Chapter 7, students write fractions and mixed numbers for pictured situations. They reduce fractions to lowest terms, change improper fractions to whole or mixed numbers and mixed numbers to improper fractions. They write terminating and repeating decimals for fractions. Students multiply and divide fractions, whole numbers, and mixed numbers. Rules are given for estimating so that the student can check if the answer is reasonable. The problem-solving lessons use these skills in situations involving exercise times and distances, a "C" clamp, scale drawings, duck decoys, and lawn work.

Lesson Notes and Activities

pages 150-151 If reinforcement is needed, students may be asked to draw figures similar to those shown.

As an alternative to Example B, you could relate mixed numbers to the markings on a ruler.

page 152 Point out that the process of reducing does not actually reduce the *fraction;* it only reduces the *terms* of the fraction.

pages 154–155 Other methods of estimating could be used to check if an answer is reasonable. One method involves rounding the factors to the nearest whole number. Since common denominators are not introduced until Chapter 8, a number line could be used to see which whole number a fraction or mixed number is closer to.

pages 156–157 Another aid for estimating is to find a range for the answer. For example, the product of $7\frac{2}{3} \times 3\frac{1}{5}$ is between 21 (7×3) and 32 (8×4).

page 161 This lesson may be extended by giving various lengths of the track, such as 400 meters. Students could then compute distances when given numbers of laps, or find the number of laps for a run of a certain distance.

pages 162–163 You can find the distance from the top of one thread to the top of another by counting the number of grooves in 1 inch of the bolt. If there are 20 grooves in 1 inch, then the distance between threads is $\frac{1}{20}$ inch.

The "C" clamp is similar to the more precise micrometer. Bring a micrometer to class, and have students compare the two measuring devices.

pages 164–165 Build on this lesson by having the students construct the scale drawings on grid paper. Also, provide the students with copies of other simple scale drawings, and have them draw the objects in actual size.

pages 166–167 The craft of decoy carving began as a functional part of the sport of duck and goose hunting. Many decoys were placed in the water around the hiding place of the hunter to lure ducks to that location. These were called "working decoys" and were actual size. The decorative decoys, mostly in demand by collectors, are more brilliantly and accurately painted.

pages 168–169 Have students estimate the size of different areas; for example, how much larger the gym is than the classroom.

 Chapter 8

Adding and Subtracting Fractions and Mixed Numbers, pages 171–192

Overview

Students begin by finding equal fractions with a common denominator and comparing fractions and mixed numbers. They add and subtract fractions with the same and different denominators. They add mixed numbers with sums that may need renaming. They subtract mixed numbers in two lessons. The denominators are the same in one lesson and different in the other. Both lessons have minuends that may need renaming. Examples show estimation by rounding to the nearest whole number. The problem-solving lessons use addition and subtraction in settings involving wages, the stock market, toy manufacturing, efficiency reports, and ceiling tiles.

Lesson Notes and Activities

page 173 You might show students how to use cross-products to compare fractions.

$\frac{3}{8} > \frac{2}{7}$ $\quad\quad$ $\frac{3}{4} < \frac{7}{9}$

$3 \times 7 > 8 \times 2$ $\quad\quad$ $3 \times 9 < 4 \times 7$

pages 174-175 Have more-able students group addends to help them find answers more quickly in problems such as these.

$\frac{2}{8} + \frac{3}{8} + \frac{6}{8} = \left(\frac{2}{8} + \frac{6}{8}\right) + \frac{3}{8} = 1\frac{3}{8}$

$\frac{1}{7} + \frac{4}{7} + \frac{6}{7} = \left(\frac{1}{7} + \frac{6}{7}\right) + \frac{4}{7} = 1\frac{4}{7}$

pages 178-179 Have students work several exercises like Example P under your supervision before assigning Set P.

You may wish to use this method with less-able students. Have them add the same fraction to both the minuend and the subtrahend so that the subtrahend is a whole number as in this example.

$$\begin{array}{r} 8\frac{1}{4} + \frac{1}{4} = 8\frac{2}{4} \\ -\ 5\frac{3}{4} + \frac{1}{4} = 6 \\ \hline 2\frac{2}{4} = 2\frac{1}{2} \end{array}$$

page 183 You might have students answer questions that are extensions of the problems on the page, such as these.

1. How many hours did the carpenter work during this six-week period? [203 hours]
2. How much did the carpenter earn in this six-week period? [$3045]
3. Did he work more hours in the third or fourth week? [Third]
   How many more? [3 hours]
4. Did he earn more money in the first or second week? [Second]
   How much more? [$45]

pages 184-185 Be sure students are aware that a net change such as $-2\frac{3}{8}$ indicates that the last price paid per share was $2\frac{3}{8}$ dollars lower than the last price paid the day before.

Mention that money not only can be earned in the stock market but can be lost as well. You may wish to have students choose a stock and follow it for a period of several weeks to see if the final result is a gain or loss.

In addition, you could use the newspaper to generate problems such as those shown in the lesson.

pages 186-187 Point out that a fraction of a cent can make a tremendous difference in profit on an item that is mass produced. $\frac{7}{8}$ cent per item on one million items is $8750.

Be sure students understand that all expenses, such as salaries, overhead, and so on, must be deducted from gross profit to determine net profit.

 Chapter 9

Probability, pages 193–210

Overview

In Chapter 9, students learn to find probabilities of independent and dependent events and make predictions. They also learn to use tree diagrams and multiplication in counting the number of possible outcomes. The problem-solving lessons use the skills of finding probabilities and predicting outcomes in working with license plates, concession supplies, mortality tables, and game development.

Lesson Notes and Activities

pages 194–195 For further practice in giving probabilities, have students look at the month of September on a calendar. Then ask them questions similar to the following. What is the probability that a date picked at random will

1. be on a Monday?
2. be on a weekend?
3. be an even number?
4. be greater than 50?
5. be less than 35?

Discuss situations where the probability of an outcome is 0 and others where it is 1.

Explain to the students that probability is a way of predicting the number of times an event will occur. Emphasize that mathematical probabilities do not tell us what future events *will* be, only what they are *likely* to be.

pages 196–197 Tree diagrams not only assist in counting choices; they provide a complete list of the choices.

To give students further practice in making tree diagrams, ask them to make one to show all the three-digit numbers that can be written using each of the digits 4, 7, and 9 exactly once.

pages 198–199 Be sure students are convinced that multiplication and tree diagrams give the same results in counting possible outcomes. If necessary, take the time to do several examples both ways.

In Exercise 6, the nine favorable outcomes are 10, 20, 30, 40, 50, 60, 70, 80, and 90.

In Exercise 10, the list of nine favorable outcomes begins with 100 and ends with 900.

In Exercise 13, the list of ninety-nine favorable outcomes begins with 100 and ends with 9900.

In Exercise 16, the list of ninety-nine favorable outcomes begins with 1000 and ends with 99,000.

pages 200–201 Emphasize to the students that in Example H the outcome of the first event influences the outcome of the second event.

In the Break Time, each figure is a traversable network because it has 0 or 2 odd vertices. A vertex is odd if an odd number of paths meet at that point.

page 203 You may wish to extend this lesson by including questions based on the format of the license plates used by your state.

pages 204–205 Point out to the students that sometimes outcomes are not equally likely and that actual data can be used to estimate probabilities. The more conclusive the data, the more accurate the estimation is likely to be.

 Chapter 10

Ratio, Proportion, and Similarity, pages 215–234

Overview

In Chapter 10, students learn to write ratios, list equal ratios, and find a missing number in a proportion by using cross-products. Students also learn to identify similar figures and name corresponding angles and sides of similar triangles. In addition, they find missing dimensions in similar triangles by using proportions. The problem-solving lessons focus on the uses of proportions and similarity in filling prescriptions, feeding horses, and in determining tree heights, ground distances, and travel times.

Lesson Notes and Activities

pages 216–217 Explain that a ratio expresses a comparison between two quantities. Point out that ratios can be applied to a variety of situations. For example, the exercises in Set A deal with gasoline consumption, measurement conversion, mixtures, rates, prices, maps, scale models, and so on.

pages 220–221 To describe similarity, you might say that if a figure is enlarged or reduced and then rotated and/or flipped, the resulting figure has the same shape of the original figure and is therefore similar. You might move the overhead projector to demonstrate this. Point out that figures that have the same size and shape, congruent figures, are also similar.

You might have students draw a figure on a grid with small squares and then draw an enlargement of the figure on a grid with larger squares.

In Set F, students can check for corresponding parts by placing a tracing of one triangle over the other triangle.

pages 222–223 You can demonstrate that the measures of corresponding angles in similar triangles are equal by drawing similar triangles on separate acetates and then sliding an angle of one triangle over the corresponding angle in the other triangle.

page 225 Remind students that the order in which quantities are compared must be the same in both ratios of the proportion.

You might have students use road maps to plan other trips. Students can use the rates given in the lesson to find driving time, liters of gasoline used, and food and motel expenses for their own trips.

pages 226–227 Other problems of this type can be found in scouting manuals and in other camping books.

pages 230–231 Mention that the problems in this lesson apply only to photographs taken in a vertical line to the ground.

pages 232–233 There are other expenses when caring for a horse such as blacksmith fees, veterinary fees, and so on. Ask students to investigate some of these costs in your area.

Percent, pages 235–256

Overview

Students begin this chapter by writing percents as decimals and fractions and writing decimals and fractions as percents. Then they find a percent of a number, what percent one number is of another number, and a number when a percent of it is known. In working with the three cases of percent, they write equations in which only the position of the variable differs from case to case. In the problem-solving lessons, students apply their knowledge of percent to discount buying, simple interest, finance charges, tolerance ranges for resistors, and cleaning solutions.

Lesson Notes and Activities

pages 236-237 Point out to students that 100% of something is *all* of it. Likewise, 0% of something is *none* of it. Mention situations in which percents greater than 100% do occur, such as price increases. Also mention situations in which percents greater than 100% are not appropriate, such as votes, surveys, and so on.

pages 240-241 For Set G, if students cannot remember the fraction equivalent for a percent, they could multiply the number in the percent by $\frac{1}{100}$. For example, to find $33\frac{1}{3}\%$ of 60, follow these steps:

$$33\tfrac{1}{3} \times \tfrac{1}{100} \times 60 = \frac{\overset{1}{\cancel{100}}}{\underset{1}{\cancel{3}}} \times \frac{1}{\underset{1}{\cancel{100}}} \times \frac{\overset{20}{\cancel{60}}}{1} = 20$$

The three types of percent problems can also be solved using proportions. For example: to find 7% of 4.1, follow these steps:

$$\frac{7}{100} = \frac{n}{4.1}$$
$$7 \times 4.1 = 100 \times n$$
$$28.7 = 100n$$
$$0.287 = n$$

pages 242-243 For students having difficulty with the equation method, proportions can be used. For example: 7 is what percent of 35?

$$\frac{n}{100} = \frac{7}{35}$$
$$n \times 35 = 100 \times 7$$
$$35n = 700$$
$$n = 20$$

pages 244-245 Proportions can be used for these problems also. For example: 22 is 40% of what number?

$$\frac{40}{100} = \frac{22}{n}$$
$$40 \times n = 100 \times 22$$
$$40n = 2200$$
$$n = 55$$

page 247 Point out the advantages of buying items on sale. Use local newspapers to generate problems involving amount of discount and sale price.

pages 248-249 Discuss the importance of investigating various sources before borrowing money. Ask students to contact banks and savings and loan companies to gather information.

pages 252-253 Point out that an ohm is a measure of resistance the same as a degree is a measure of temperature.

 Chapter 12

Statistics, pages 257–278

Overview

In Chapter 12, students learn to apply the statistical measures of mean, median, and mode to a set of data. They also learn to obtain information from bar, line, and circle graphs. In addition, they translate data into bar, line, and circle graphs. The problem-solving lessons use various types of graphs and tables, and stress the interpretation of data presented by those media. The lessons deal with electric bills, temperature, precipitation, air pollution, and sales reports.

Lesson Notes and Activities

pages 260–261 Have students find the mean, the median, and the mode for sets of real data, such as points scored by professional sports teams, Olympic medals won by countries, etc. The students could be assigned the task of gathering data interesting to them.

pages 262–263 Discuss with your class how choices of different values for the vertical scale can affect the appearance of a graph and vary its impact. To emphasize this point, you may wish to have students construct the graph in Example D using a vertical scale numbered by 1s or 4s.

In discussing the exercises in Set D, you may wish to point out that the Olympic Games were canceled in 1916, 1940, and 1944 because of World Wars I and II.

pages 266–267 Point out that a circle graph is used to highlight a division of a whole rather than to show trends.

Students could use a compass or the edge of a protractor to draw circles.

pages 270–271 The graph shows a great increase in expenses during the winter months because the home was heated electrically.

You may wish to have students make a bar graph to show the same information and then generate such questions as: "What type of graph best shows trends and comparisons?" [Line graph]

pages 272–273 A world almanac contains information that can be used to generate problems similar to those in the lesson.

pages 274–275 Hydrocarbons are gaseous residue, a result of unburned fuel. By themselves they are not toxic; but they help to form ozone. Carbon monoxide is a colorless, odorless, and poisonous gas also produced by incomplete burning of fuel. Ozone is one of the major ingredients in smog. It is a toxic form of oxygen, formed when hydrocarbons combine with nitrogen oxides.

You may wish to explore with the class various pollutants in air and water and the effect they have on animal and plant life.

pages 276–277 Sales information for the Style 98 shoes could be used for additional problems similar to the Extensions.

Calculator Applications

page 280 If the students do not have calculators with an automatic constant feature, they can simply continue to reenter the desired operation and number.

NOTES Chapter 13

Positive and Negative Numbers, pages 283–302

Overview

Students begin this chapter by writing, comparing, and ordering positive and negative numbers. Then they learn to add, subtract, multiply, and divide positive and negative numbers. The problem-solving lessons involve using positive and negative numbers to chart football plays, to find the times and heights of morning and evening high tides, to read a wind-chill table, and to balance a check register.

Lesson Notes and Activities

pages 284-285 Discuss with the students the uses of integers in real-life situations. Discussions may include the following examples: temperatures, golf scores, profits and losses, stock market changes, and countdowns for launching space vehicles.

pages 286-287 In an addition magic square, the sum for each row, each column, and each diagonal is the same. Have students tell which of these are magic squares and give the magic sum.

-2	2	3
6	1	-4
-1	0	4

Yes. [3]

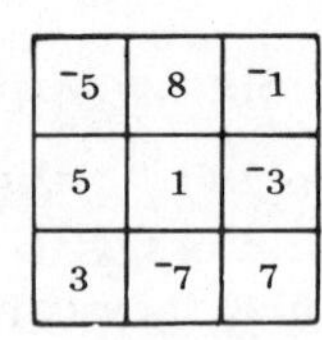

-7	0	-8
-6	-5	-4
-2	-10	-3

Yes. [-15]

-5	8	-1
5	1	-3
3	-7	7

No.

pages 288-289 Use a device such as this to reinforce addition and subtraction of integers. Each answer is shown in brackets.

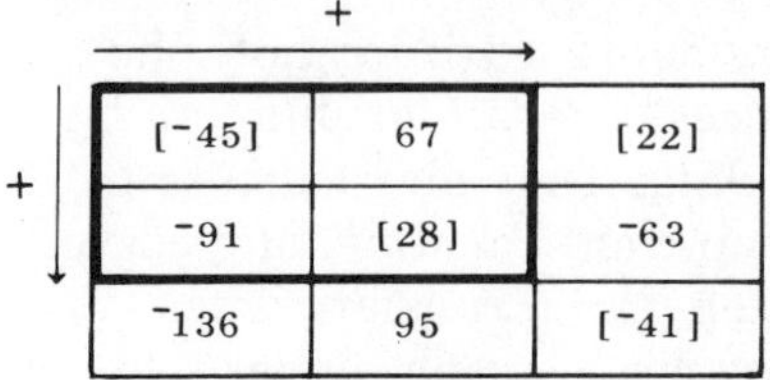

[-45]	67	[22]
-91	[28]	-63
-136	95	[-41]

pages 290-291 Have students make a multiplication table for the integers -3 through 3. The patterns that will occur in this table should help convince students of the rules for multiplication of integers.

Have students tell which of these are multiplication magic squares and give the magic product.

-3	36	2
4	-6	9
18	1	-12

Yes. [-216]

24	18	-4
2	-12	72
-36	8	3

No.

pages 292-293 Use a device such as this to reinforce multiplication and division of integers.

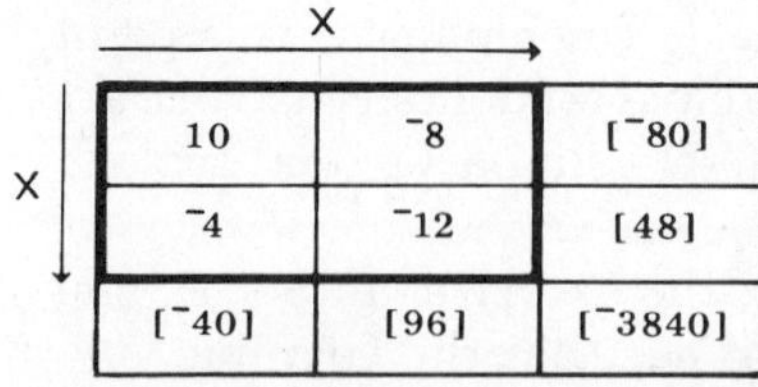

10	-8	[-80]
-4	-12	[48]
[-40]	[96]	[-3840]

pages 298-299 For extra practice, you may give the students the thermometer reading and the wind-chill index and ask for the wind speed; or you may give the wind speed and the wind-chill index and ask for the thermometer reading.

NOTES Chapter 14

Expressions and Equations, pages 303–326

Overview

In Chapter 14, students evaluate expressions involving integers, decimals, and order of operations. Then they solve equations which contain those types of expressions. Students solve single-step equations with missing addends, missing minuends, missing factors, and missing dividends by "doing the same thing" to both sides of the equation. They also solve two-step equations and equations in which they need to combine like terms. The problem-solving lessons use formulas in settings dealing with electricity, insurance, construction, police work, and boating.

Lesson Notes and Activities

pages 304-305 In Examples A–D, have students evaluate each expression using other values for the variables.

As an additional activity, have students find all values of n for which the value of the expression $\frac{240}{n}$ is a whole number. Remind students that zero is not a possible replacement for n. [1, 2, 3, 4, 5, 6, 8, 10, 12, 15, 16, 20, 24, 30, 40, 48, 60, 80, 120, 240]

page 309 In the Break Time, have the students withdraw $1 at a time to show that the sum of the balances is not related to the sum of the withdrawals.

pages 312–313 For students having trouble with these problems, you might try this procedure for finding n.

$4n + 12 = 32$	
n is multiplied by 4.	M 4
12 is added to $4n$.	A 12
To solve, do the opposite.	
Subtract 12.	S 12
Then divide by 4.	D 4

page 317 Fuses or circuit breakers are used to protect electrical equipment. You could extend the lesson to solve problems such as this: "How many watts can be used in a 110-volt circuit with a 20-amp fuse?"
$W = EI$
$W = 110(20)$
$W = 2200$
(2200 watts can be used.)

pages 320–321 The practice of sinking piles is common in building homes in resort areas near beaches where the ground is sandy and there is flooding. Students may be most familiar with the piles that are used to support boat docks. Also mention that other supporting structures, such as steel beams imbedded in concrete, are often used for very tall buildings.

pages 322–323 The electronic equipment contains a timer, an odometer, and a calculator. The operator must qualify to use the equipment, and must demonstrate the ability to determine speeds within a very small range for error.

pages 324–325 A knot is a unit of speed and equals one nautical mile per hour. The term "mile" commonly refers to statute mile which is 5280 feet. A nautical mile is approximately 6076 feet. So, one nautical mile is approximately equal to 1.15 statute miles. Therefore, one knot is approximately equal to 1.15 miles per hour.

The abbreviation for both knot and knots is Kn.

Graphing, pages 327–346

Overview

In Chapter 15, students learn to give ordered pairs for points on both first-quadrant and four-quadrant grids. They also learn to locate points on both grids when given ordered pairs. A subsequent skill is the reading of graphs on first-quadrant and four-quadrant grids. The students then draw graphs of linear equations on both grids. In the problem-solving lessons, students read, make, and interpret various types of graphs and use four-quadrant grids to locate points. The lessons involve antifreeze, a drill press, layers of rock, and sales graphs.

Lesson Notes and Activities

page 329 Use a city or state map and ask students to locate specific points. The map should have letters and numbers along the borders so that a point can be located by a letter and a number, such as (C, 7).

pages 330–331 To extend Set C, have students take an informal look at equations in the general form $y = \blacksquare x + \blacksquare$. Ask what is true about the graph when the first number is positive. [The line slopes upward from left to right.] Negative? [It slopes downward from left to right.] What happens as the second number increases? [The line moves up.] Decreases? [The line moves down.]

pages 332–333 Point out that by convention the four quadrants are labeled I, II, III, and IV, counterclockwise starting with the upper right quadrant.

You might have students write four ordered pairs, plot the four points, and connect them. Then ask what happens to the figure when the sign on the first number in each pair is changed. [The figure is flipped over, or reflected about, the y-axis.] What happens if the sign of the second number in each pair is changed? [The figure is reflected about the x-axis.]

pages 342–343 A geophone is a small microphone. Either many geophones are placed in the ground at one time, each at a different depth, or one geophone is placed at different depths at different times. When a charge of dynamite is set off, compression waves travel through the rock. The faster the waves travel, the more dense is the rock. Different rates of travel (different slopes on the graph) indicate different layers of rock. The information from the geophones is displayed above the ground on a seismograph.

pages 344–345 Discuss with students the main reason for increases in sales dollars: inflation. You might also point out that the steep increase at the end of each year corresponds with the holiday season. The earlier peak in 1981 corresponds with Thanksgiving week.

You might want to have students determine average sales per quarter or per week. You may also wish to point out that even though total sales were greater in 1981, the amount of increase actually decreased as the year progressed.

Computer Literacy

page 349 Although the majority of computers presently being sold can perform this function, check your computer before assigning the exercises.

NOTES Chapter 16

Perimeter and Area, pages 351–370

Overview

In Chapter 16, students learn to find the perimeter of rectangles and other polygons and the circumference of circles using either the diameter or the radius. They also learn to find the area of rectangles, squares, parallelograms, triangles, trapezoids, and circles. The problem-solving lessons present situations in which these skills are used to compute amounts of fertilizer needed, lengths of pipes, the cost of carpeting, and areas of swimming pools.

Lesson Notes and Activities

pages 352-353 You might ask students to suggest some uses of calculating perimeters. Examples could include fencing a yard, making picture frames, bordering a quilt, putting molding around a room, caulking around a window, and edging a garden.

pages 354-355 To develop the concept of pi, use a circle that has a 21-cm diameter. Then use a 21-cm string, marked in seven equal segments, to show that it takes $3\frac{1}{7}$, or 3.14, diameters to "wrap around the circle," or measure the circumference.

$$\pi = \frac{C}{d}$$

pages 356-357 Have students draw a parallelogram on grid paper, cut the figure in two pieces—making the cut perpendicular to the bases, and rearrange the pieces to form a rectangle.

$A = bh$

pages 358-359 Have students draw a triangle on grid paper, cut the figure in two pieces—making the cut parallel to the base at the midpoint of the height, and rearrange the pieces to form a parallelogram. Multiply its base (base of triangle) times its height (one-half the height of the triangle).

$A = b(\frac{1}{2}h)$

Have students draw a trapezoid on grid paper, cut the figure in two pieces—making the cut parallel to the bases at the midpoint of the height, and rearrange the pieces to form a parallelogram. Multiply its base (top base plus bottom base of the trapezoid) times its height (one-half the height of the trapezoid).

$A = (a + b)\frac{1}{2}h$

pages 360-361 Have students cut a circle into 16 equal pie-shaped pieces. Then arrange the pieces side-by-side to form a figure that looks like a parallelogram. Multiply its base (one-half the circumference) times its height (radius).

$A = \frac{1}{2}C(r)$

Since $C = 2\pi r$, $\frac{1}{2}C = \pi r$. So $A = \pi r^2$.

page 363 Have students find the cost of carpeting a room in their homes, choosing carpeting from catalogs or newspaper advertisements.

pages 364-365 Be certain students understand that they must always round answers *up* to the next whole number, or they would not buy enough fertilizer.

pages 368-369 This lesson might stimulate a discussion on safety standards, the use of smoke and fire detectors, and so on.

NOTES Chapter 17

Surface Area and Volume, pages 371–392

Overview

In Chapter 17, students use formulas to find the surface area and volume of a rectangular prism, a cube, and a cylinder. They also compute the volume of a pyramid, a cone, and a sphere by using formulas. The problem-solving lessons make use of surface area and volume in finding engine displacement and in computing costs of materials to make candles, build a garage, and pave certain surfaces.

Lesson Notes and Activities

page 373 Some students may have difficulty visualizing surface area. Have students take a box and paint the faces so that faces with the same dimensions are the same color. Through discussion, show how the formula is derived. If necessary, some students can find the area of each face and then find the sum.

page 375 Students might have trouble seeing that the length of the rectangle is the circumference of the base. Cut apart a salt box or other cylindrical container, and demonstrate how the rectangle "wraps around" the circular base. For some students, provide exercises in which the diameter, rather than the radius, is given.

pages 376–377 For a review of cubic units, refer to the lesson on page 127.

page 378 To extend the first five Skill lessons, have available models of rectangular prisms, cubes, and cylinders, such as cereal boxes and canned foods. For each, have students measure the dimensions and then compute the surface area and/or volume.

page 379 You might give students the following hint to solve the Break Time. To find the volume of the space in the middle of the four elevators, first find the volume of the square formed by the centers of the elevators.

pages 380–381 Classroom models of prisms and pyramids are helpful. Try to use a prism and a pyramid with congruent bases and equal heights. Fill the pyramid with water or sand and show that its volume is $\frac{1}{3}$ the volume of the prism. Use a similar approach to show the cone-cylinder relationship.

page 385 Hobby stores often have price lists that include candle molds, dies, wicks, and scents. Have students obtain such lists and then compute the cost of making various candles.

pages 386–387 In Problem 13, the conversion given is $1 \text{ m}^2 = 1{,}000{,}000 \text{ mm}^2$. The metric unit commonly used for measuring concrete blocks is the millimeter. However, if this conversion is too difficult for your students, have them use the centimeter. $1 \text{ m}^2 = 10{,}000 \text{ cm}^2$.

pages 388–389 This lesson might stimulate a discussion on automobile repair and maintenance. More information concerning the piston engine should be available from the Driver Education Department in your school.

 Chapter 18

The Pythagorean Rule and Trigonometry, pages 393–414

Overview

Students begin this chapter by finding powers of numbers and square roots of numbers. They use the Pythagorean Rule to find the hypotenuse or a missing leg. The tangent, sine, and cosine ratios are introduced, and students use these trigonometric ratios to find the length of a side of a right triangle. The problem-solving lessons apply the Pythagorean Rule and trigonometric ratios to situations involving baseball diamonds, pipelines, and antenna towers.

Lesson Notes and Activities

page 395 Emphasize to the students that the definition given is true if and only if the exponent is a natural number.

You may wish to show that any number to the 0 power equals 1. Show this by putting several examples on the board like the one given here, and ask students to find the pattern.

$3^4 = 81$	
$3^3 = 27$	$81 \div 3 = 27$
$3^2 = 9$	$27 \div 3 = 9$
$3^1 = 3$	$9 \div 3 = 3$
$3^0 = 1$	$3 \div 3 = 1$

page 396 The square root symbol used here denotes the principal or nonnegative square root of the number.

pages 398-399 To develop the Pythagorean Rule, have students use grid paper to draw right triangles with legs of lengths 5 and 12, 7 and 24, 3 and 4, 8 and 15. Students can use a strip of the grid paper as a ruler to measure the length of each hypotenuse. They can square the lengths of the sides in each triangle to discover that the sum of the squares of the legs equals the square of the hypotenuse. You might also have students actually draw squares on the sides of the triangles. The sum of the areas of the squares on the legs equals the area of the square on the hypotenuse.

pages 400-401 You might have students use a grid to draw three similar right triangles with sides of 3, 4, and 5; 6, 8, and 10; and 9, 12, and 15. A strip of the grid paper can be used to check the length of each hypotenuse. Then choose an acute angle in one triangle and identify the corresponding angle in each of the other triangles. These corresponding angles have the same measure. Have students write the tangent, the sine, and the cosine of each of the three angles as ratios and as decimals. Conclude that any angle of that same size will have the same tangent, sine, and cosine, regardless of the size of the right triangle that contains the angle.

pages 402–403 Emphasize that most of the numbers in the table are approximations.

pages 410–411 Demonstrate why the run is half the diagonal in a 30°- 60°- 90° triangle by showing the triangle as half of a 60°- 60°- 60° triangle.

ANSWERS Additional Answers

Page 41

1. a. 3720 L	2. a. 279,000 kg	3. a. 279 metric tons
b. 1320 L	b. 99,000 kg	b. 99 metric tons
c. 5760 L	c. 432,000 kg	c. 432 metric tons
d. 6960 L	d. 522,000 kg	d. 522 metric tons
e. 1560 L	e. 117,000 kg	e. 117 metric tons
f. 3000 L	f. 225,000 kg	f. 225 metric tons
g. 1440 L	g. 108,000 kg	g. 108 metric tons
h. 3960 L	h. 297,000 kg	h. 297 metric tons
i. 3240 L	i. 243,000 kg	i. 243 metric tons
j. 11,400 L	j. 855,000 kg	j. 855 metric tons
k. 4200 L	k. 315,000 kg	k. 315 metric tons
l. 11,520 L	l. 864,000 kg	l. 864 metric tons
m. 6720 L	m. 504,000 kg	m. 504 metric tons
n. 2520 L	n. 189,000 kg	n. 189 metric tons

Page 143

10. 25-mm reamer; 5-mm adjustment
11. 20-mm reamer; 5-mm adjustment
12. 25-mm reamer; 2-mm adjustment
13. 20-mm reamer; 2-mm adjustment
14. 30-mm reamer; 5-mm adjustment
15. 20-mm reamer; 4-mm adjustment
16. 20-mm reamer; 1-mm adjustment
17. 15-mm reamer; 1-mm adjustment
18. 25-mm reamer; 1-mm adjustment

Page 191

10. $1\frac{3}{8}$ feet by $1\frac{1}{4}$ feet
11. $1\frac{11}{16}$ feet by $1\frac{7}{8}$ feet
12. $1\frac{1}{8}$ feet by $\frac{15}{16}$ feet
13. $2\frac{1}{2}$ feet by $1\frac{1}{2}$ feet

Page 203

2. $\frac{1}{6,760,000}$
3. $\frac{2}{6,760,000}$ or $\frac{1}{3,380,000}$
4. $\frac{10,000}{6,760,000}$ or $\frac{1}{676}$
5. $\frac{676}{6,760,000}$ or $\frac{1}{10,000}$
6. $\frac{260}{6,760,000}$ or $\frac{1}{26,000}$
7. $\frac{676,000}{6,760,000}$ or $\frac{1}{10}$
8. $\frac{130,000}{6,760,000}$ or $\frac{1}{52}$
9. $\frac{7000}{6,760,000}$ or $\frac{7}{6760}$
10. $\frac{10}{6,760,000}$ or $\frac{1}{676,000}$

Page 206

1. $\frac{15}{9912}$ or $\frac{5}{3304}$
2. $\frac{12}{9794}$ or $\frac{6}{4897}$
3. $\frac{17}{9665}$
4. $\frac{23}{9373}$
5. $\frac{38}{9173}$
6. $\frac{216}{6801}$ or $\frac{72}{2267}$
7. $\frac{303}{4130}$
8. $\frac{288}{2626}$ or $\frac{144}{1313}$
9. $\frac{107}{468}$

14. $\frac{9480}{9665} \approx 0.98$
15. $\frac{2626}{7699} \approx 0.34$
16. $\frac{8762}{9982} \approx 0.88$
17. $\frac{9480}{9743} \approx 0.97$
18. $\frac{9173}{9241} \approx 0.99$
19. $\frac{1311}{2626} \approx 0.50$
20. $\frac{4130}{9806} \approx 0.42$

Additional Answers

Page 213

4. Answers may vary.

```
10 INPUT X
20 IF X=0 THEN 50
30 PRINT (2*X)+(3*X)
40 GO TO 10
50 END
```

5. Answers may vary.

```
10 INPUT A
20 INPUT B
30 IF A=0 THEN 120
40 IF A=B THEN 100
50 IF A>B THEN 80
60 PRINT A;"<";B
70 GO TO 10
80 PRINT A;">";B
90 GO TO 10
100 PRINT A;"=";B
110 GO TO 10
120 END
```

Page 261

1. 4.9	6. 75.4	11. 357	16. 205.9	21. 19.9
2. 5	7. 175.8	12. 985	17. 3163.8	22. 62.9
3. 5.5	8. 777.9	13. 10.9	18. 8764.9	23. 33.4
4. 6.3	9. 27.8	14. 19.1	19. 19.1	24. 371.8
5. 14.6	10. 36.4	15. 77.4	20. 70	25. 8549.2

Page 263 Set E

1. U.S. Olympic Gold Medals, 1956–1976

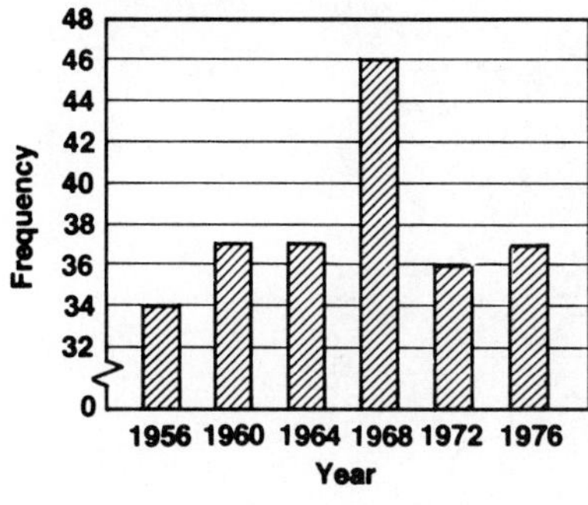

2. U.S.S.R. Olympic Gold Medals, 1956–1976

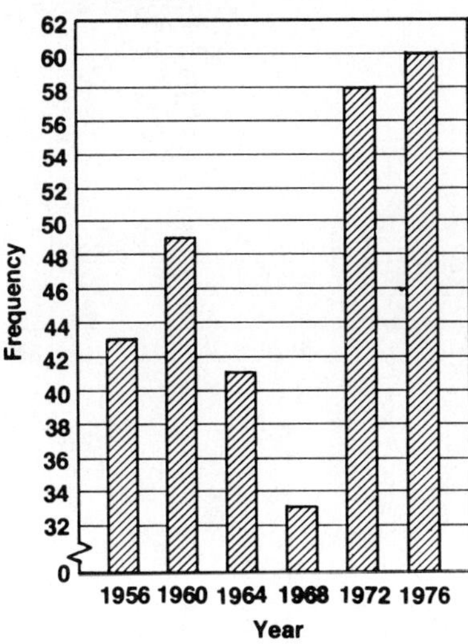

3. Winter Olympic Medals, 1980

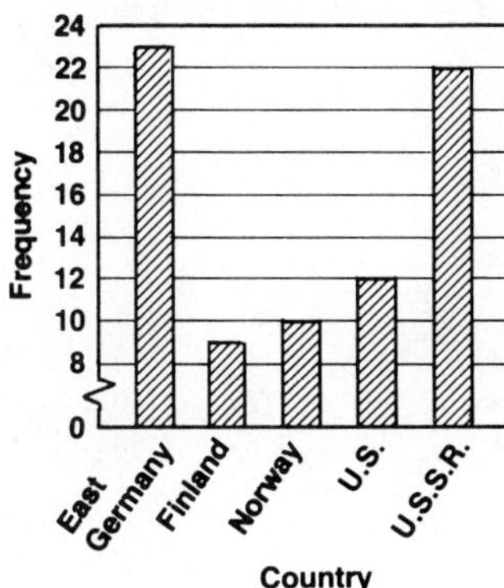

ANSWERS Additional Answers

Page 267 Set J

1. **Elements of Earth's Crust**

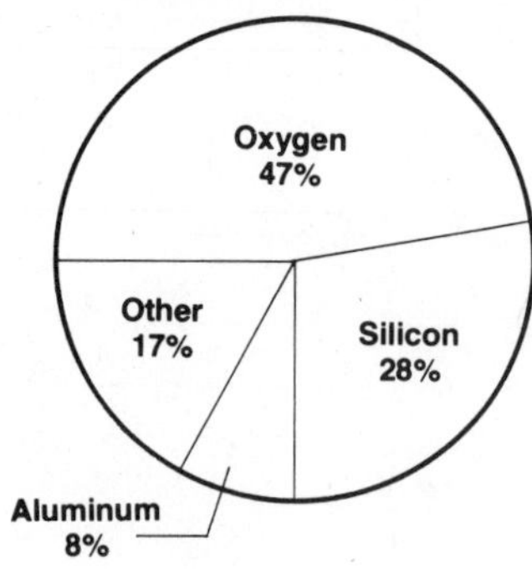

2. **Sources of Water Pollution**

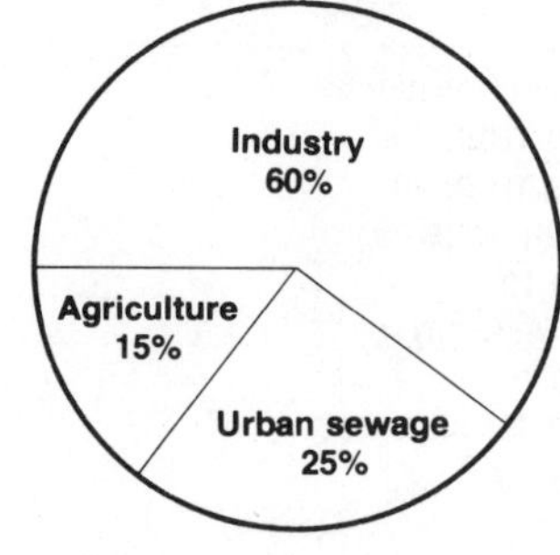

3. **Sources of Air Pollution**

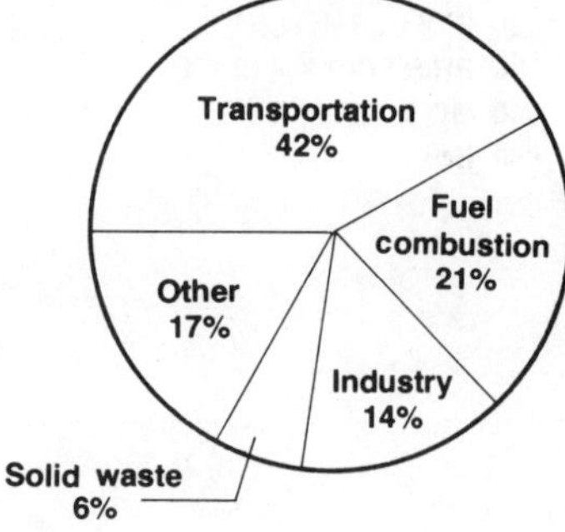

4. **Earth's Water**

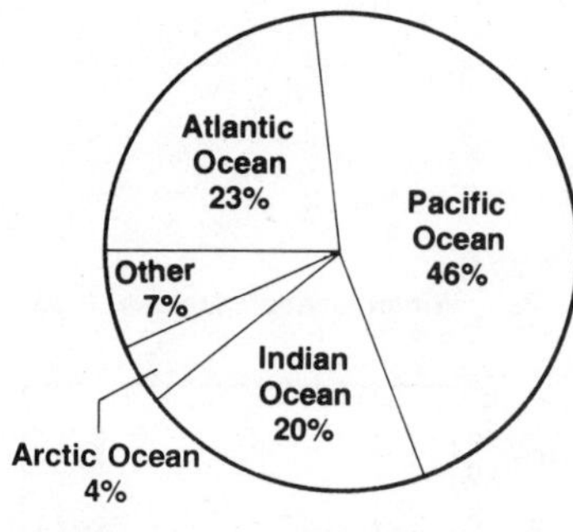

5. **Earth's Land**

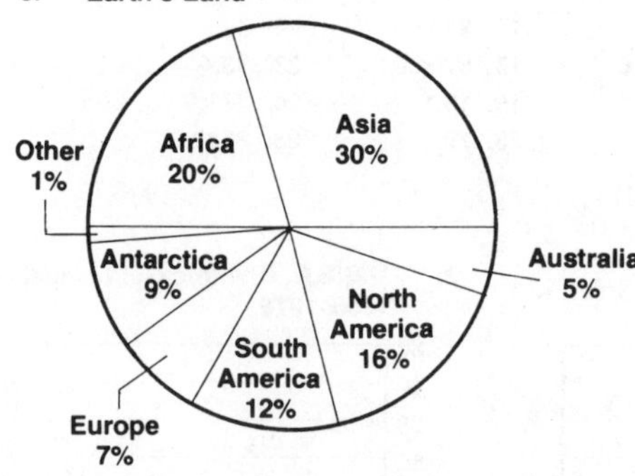

Page 271

		Jan.	Feb.	Mar.	Apr.	May	June	July	Aug.	Sept.	Oct.	Nov.	Dec.
13.	1978	$110	$105	$ 80	$ 60	$ 40	$ 45	$ 55	$ 50	$ 60	$ 65	$ 65	$ 85
14.	1979	$175	$130	$ 90	$ 75	$ 45	$ 65	$ 65	$ 60	$ 70	$ 55	$ 70	$105
15.	1980	$140	$160	$120	$ 85	$ 60	$ 70	$ 90	$ 70	$ 75	$ 75	$100	$115

	Highest bill		Lowest bill		Difference
	Year	Amount	Year	Amount	
19.	1979	$175	1978	$110	$65
20.	1980	$160	1978	$105	$55
21.	1980	$ 85	1978	$ 60	$25
22.	1980	$ 90	1978	$ 55	$35
23.	1980	$ 75	1979	$ 55	$20
24.	1980	$115	1978	$ 85	$30

Additional Answers

Page 272

2.

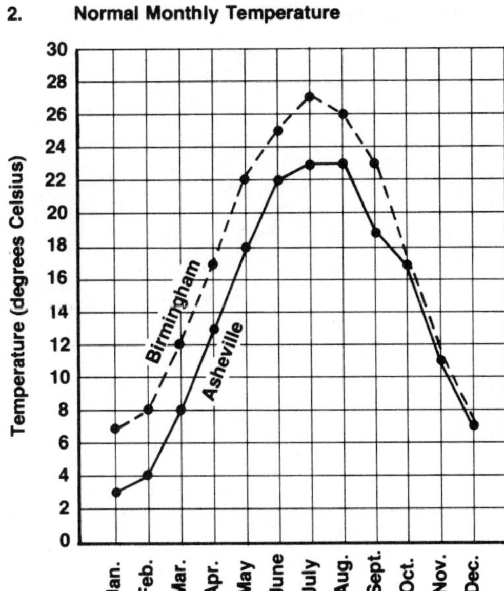

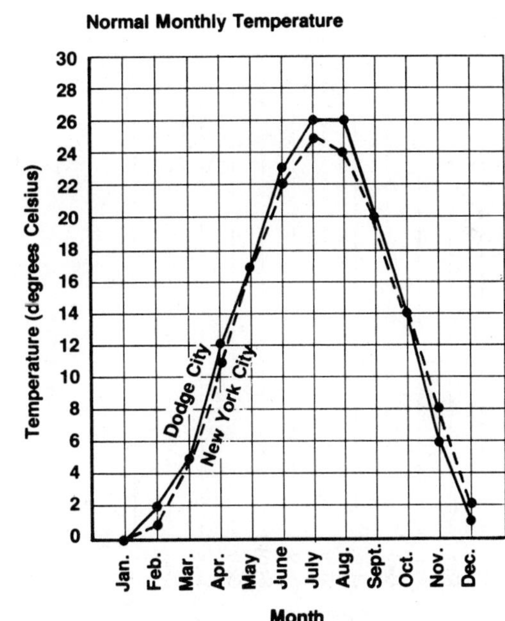

Page 273

4.

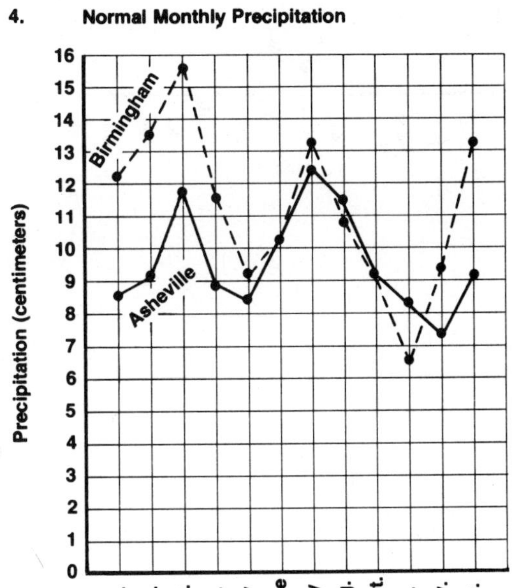

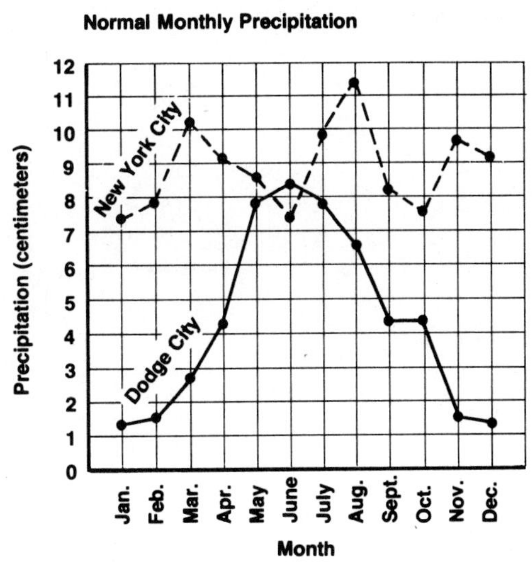

Additional Answers

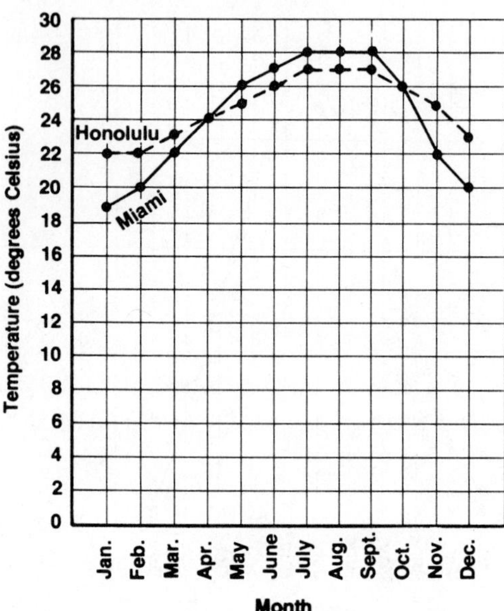

Page 273

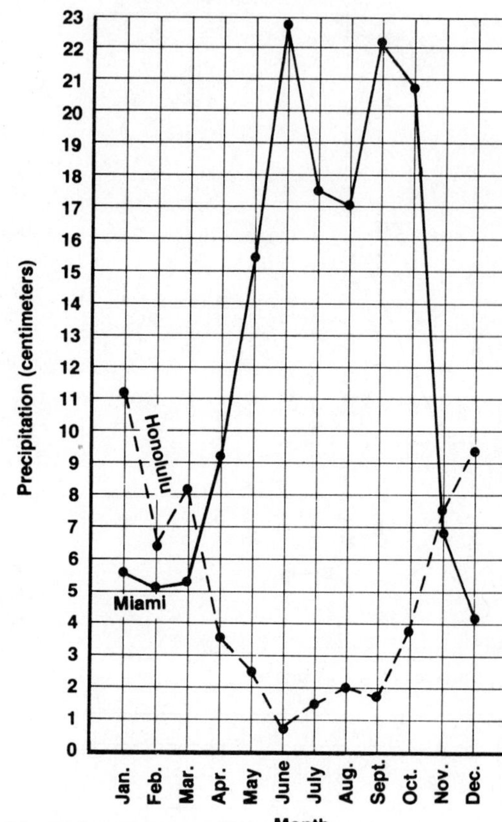

Additional Answers

Page 277

10. *Shoe Sales – Style 98, July*

983-8 // ②	986-8 ⓪	987-8 // ②
983-9 // ②	986-9 // ②	987-9 ⓪
983-10 ~~////~~ / ⑥	986-10 ~~////~~ /// ⑧	987-10 //// ④
983-11 // ②	986-11 ~~////~~ / ⑥	987-11 // ②
983-12 ⓪	986-12 // ②	987-12 // ②

11.

Blue	**Gray**	**Green**
Size 8: 2 pairs	Size 9: 2 pairs	Size 8: 2 pairs
Size 9: 2 pairs	Size 10: 8 pairs	Size 10: 4 pairs
Size 10: 6 pairs	Size 11: 6 pairs	Size 11: 2 pairs
Size 11: 2 pairs	Size 12: 2 pairs	Size 12: 2 pairs

12. Size 8: 4 pairs; Size 9: 4 pairs; Size 10: 18 pairs; Size 11: 10 pairs; Size 12: 4 pairs

18.

Tan	**Black**	**Navy**
Size 5: 3 pairs	Size 6: 3 pairs	Size 6: 3 pairs
Size 7: 6 pairs	Size 7: 15 pairs	Size 7: 9 pairs
Size 8: 21 pairs	Size 8: 6 pairs	Size 8: 12 pairs
Size 9: 6 pairs		Size 9: 6 pairs

Page 278

5. Summer Birthdays

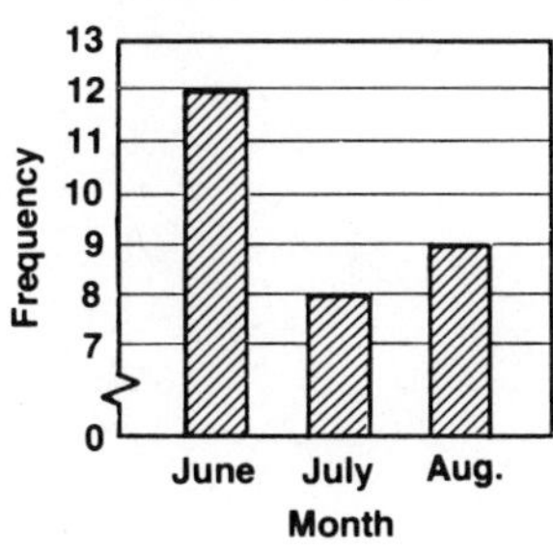

7. Egg Use per Person

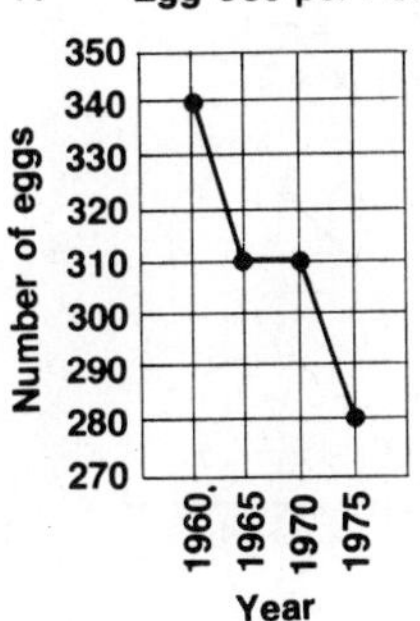

10. Fabric Blend Fibers

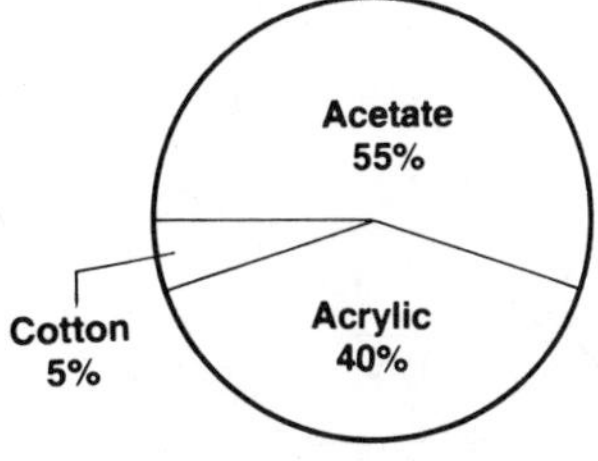

Page 325

1. Speed Chart for the *Morning Star*

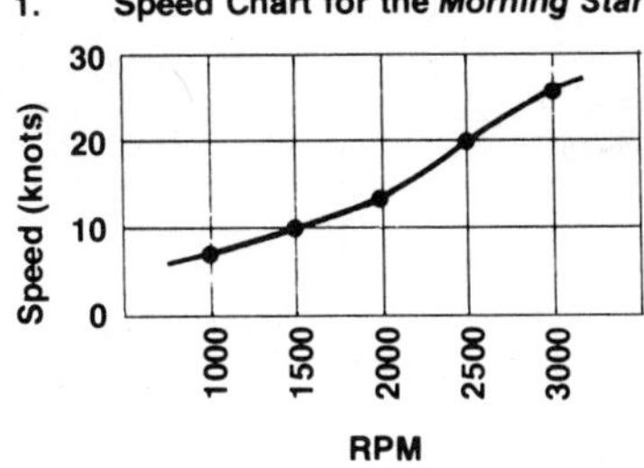

2. Speed Chart for the *Friendship*

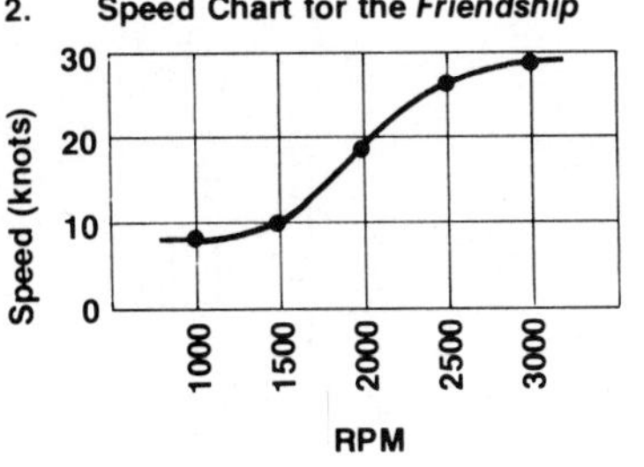

3. Speed Chart for the *Felicidad*

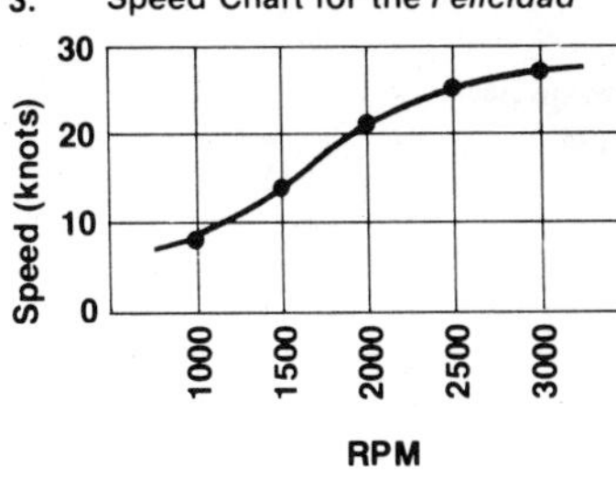

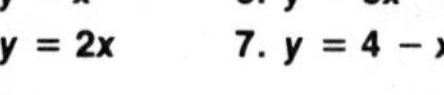

Additional Answers

Page 331 Set D

1. $y = x$
2. $y = x + 3$
3. $y = 2x$
4. $y = 2x - 1$
5. $y = 3x - 5$
6. $y = x - 4$
7. $y = 4 - x$
8. $y = 8 - 2x$

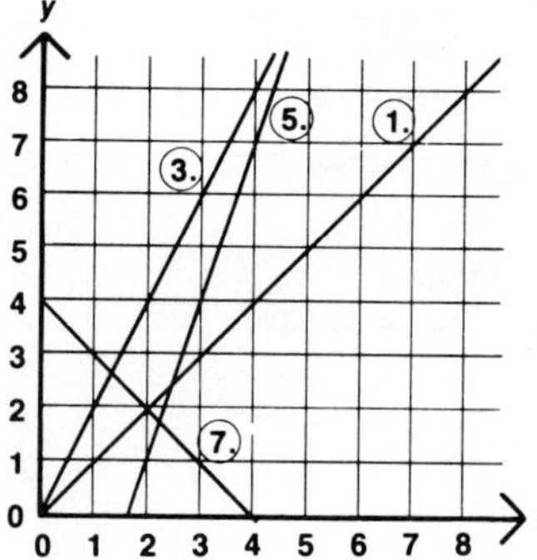

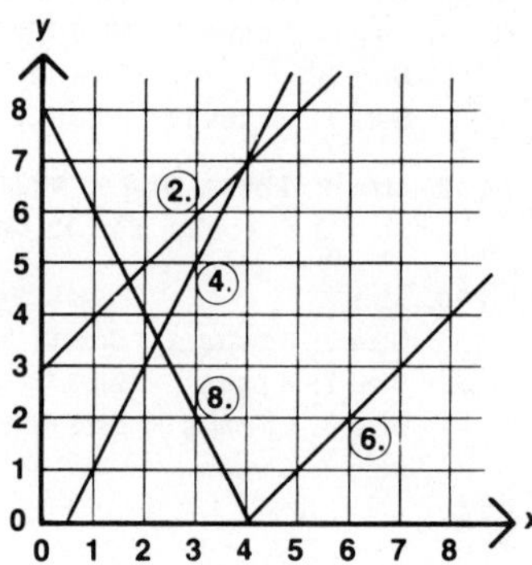

Page 333 Set F

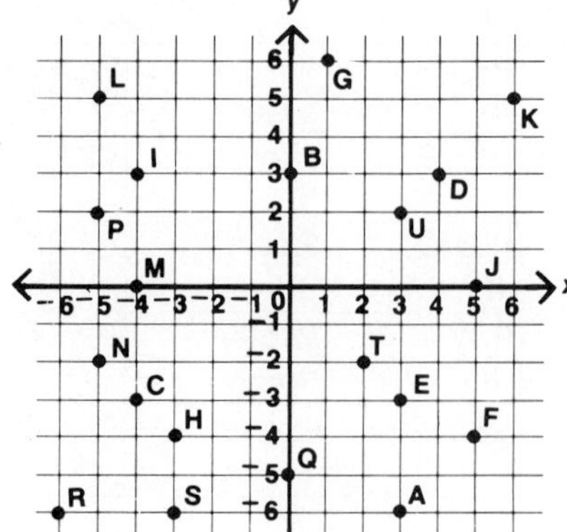

Page 335 Set H

1. $y = x + 1$
2. $y = {}^{-}2x$
3. $y = x - 3$
4. $y = x$
5. $y = 2x - 1$
6. $y = {}^{-}2 - x$
7. $y = 3 - x$
8. $y = x + 3$

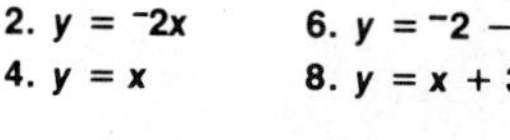

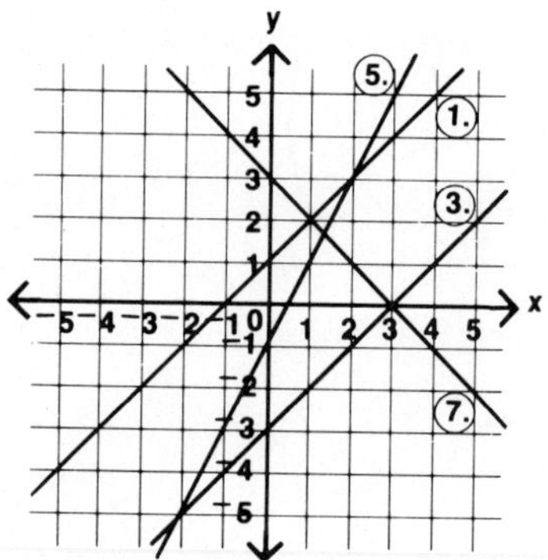

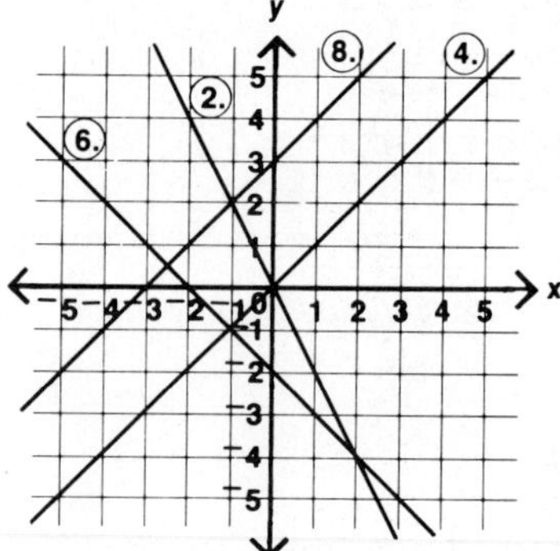

Page 341

1–4

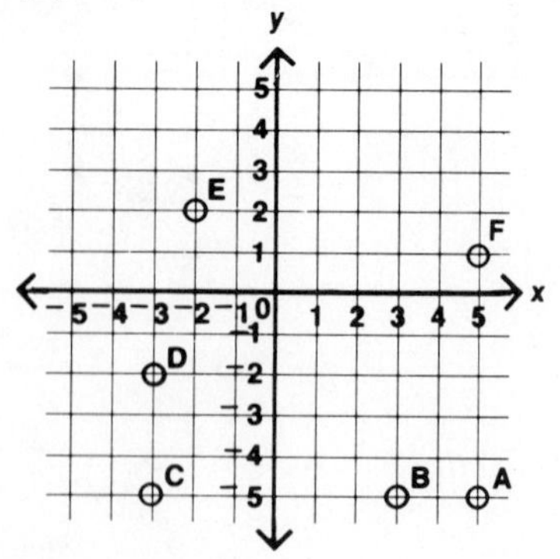

5–10

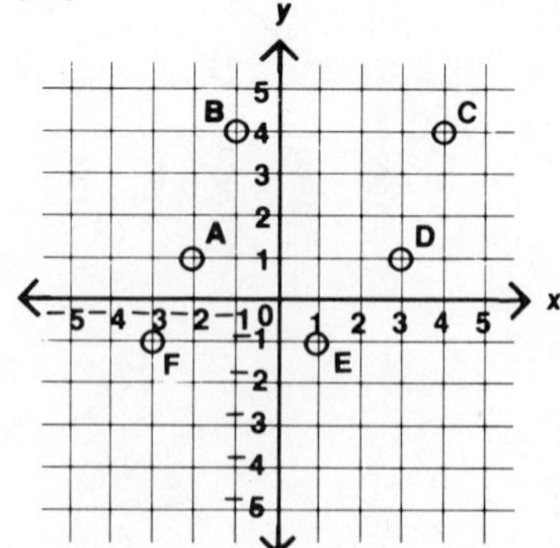

11–18

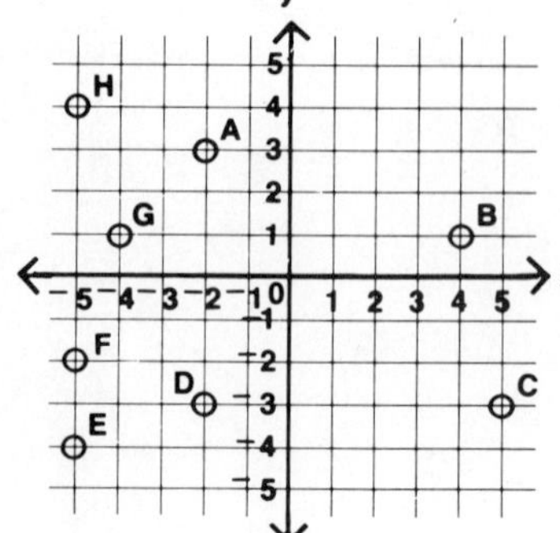

Additional Answers

Page 343 1. and 3.

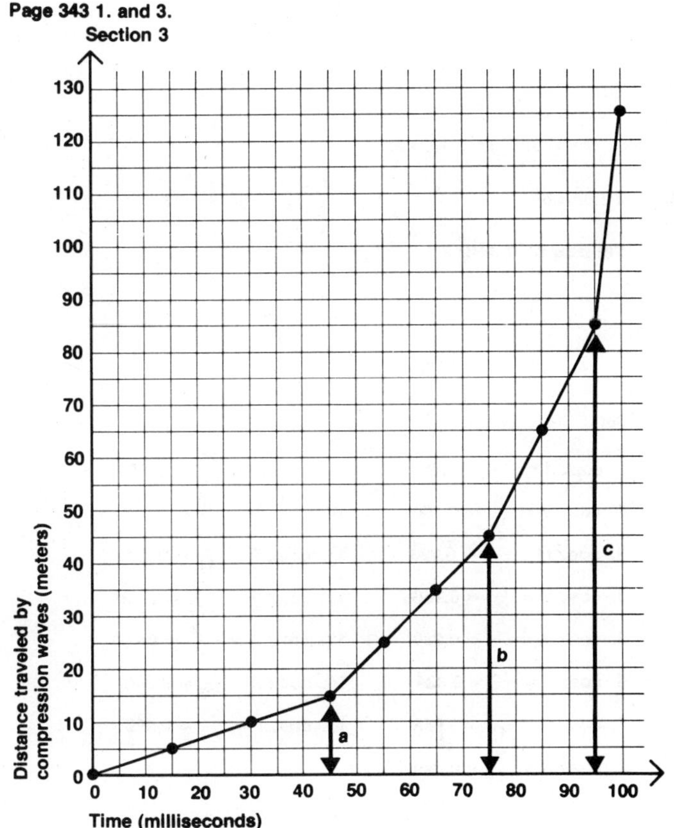

Page 349

1. ? 3
   3 IS AN ODD NUMBER.
   ? 6
   6 IS AN EVEN NUMBER.
   ? 10
   10 IS AN EVEN NUMBER.
   ? 15
   15 IS AN ODD NUMBER.
   ? 24
   24 IS AN EVEN NUMBER.
   ? 25
   25 IS AN ODD NUMBER.
   ? 0

Page 349

2. ? 24
   DIVISORS OF 24 ARE:
   1
   2
   3
   4
   6
   8
   12
   24
   ? 36
   DIVISORS OF 36 ARE:
   1

2. *continued*
   2
   3
   4
   6
   9
   12
   18
   36
   ? 41
   DIVISORS OF 41 ARE:
   1
   41
   ? 64

2. *continued*
   DIVISORS OF 64 ARE:
   1
   2
   4
   8
   16
   32
   64
   ? 120
   DIVISORS OF 120 ARE:
   1
   2
   3

2. *continued*
   4
   5
   6
   8
   10
   12
   15
   20
   24
   30
   40
   60
   120
   ? 0

ANSWERS Additional Answers

Page 349

3.
```
? 12
? 3
 12 IS A MULTIPLE OF 3
? 15
? 6
 15 IS NOT A MULTIPLE OF 6
? 51
? 3
 51 IS A MULTIPLE OF 3
? 63
? 12
 63 IS NOT A MULTIPLE OF 12
? 0
```

5. Answers may vary.
```
10 INPUT N
20 IF N=0 THEN 100
30 IF INT(N/2)=N/2 THEN 60
40 PRINT N;"IS NOT DIVISIBLE BY 2 AND 3."
50 GO TO 10
60 IF INT(N/3)=N/3 THEN 80
70 GO TO 40
80 PRINT N;"IS DIVISIBLE BY 2 AND 3."
90 GO TO 10
100 END
```

Page 401 **Set I**

1. $\sin\angle J = \frac{20}{29} \approx 0.690$
2. $\sin\angle V = \frac{8}{10} \approx 0.800$
3. $\sin\angle M = \frac{5}{13} \approx 0.385$
4. $\sin\angle Y = \frac{7}{25} \approx 0.280$
5. $\sin\angle K = \frac{24}{25} \approx 0.960$
6. $\sin\angle T = \frac{35}{37} \approx 0.946$
7. $\sin\angle X = \frac{12}{37} \approx 0.324$
8. $\sin\angle S = \frac{28}{53} \approx 0.528$
9. $\sin\angle D = \frac{45}{53} \approx 0.849$
10. $\sin\angle B = \frac{9}{41} \approx 0.220$
11. $\sin\angle P = \frac{40}{41} \approx 0.976$
12. $\sin\angle R = \frac{154}{170} \approx 0.906$
13. $\sin\angle G = \frac{72}{170} \approx 0.424$
14. $\sin\angle Z = \frac{63}{65} \approx 0.969$
15. $\sin\angle F = \frac{16}{65} \approx 0.246$

Set J

1. $\cos\angle J = \frac{21}{29} \approx 0.724$
2. $\cos\angle V = \frac{6}{10} \approx 0.600$
3. $\cos\angle M = \frac{12}{13} \approx 0.923$
4. $\cos\angle Y = \frac{24}{25} \approx 0.960$
5. $\cos\angle K = \frac{7}{25} \approx 0.280$
6. $\cos\angle T = \frac{12}{37} \approx 0.324$
7. $\cos\angle X = \frac{35}{37} \approx 0.946$
8. $\cos\angle S = \frac{45}{53} \approx 0.849$
9. $\cos\angle D = \frac{28}{53} \approx 0.528$
10. $\cos\angle B = \frac{40}{41} \approx 0.976$
11. $\cos\angle P = \frac{9}{41} \approx 0.220$
12. $\cos\angle R = \frac{72}{170} \approx 0.424$
13. $\cos\angle G = \frac{154}{170} \approx 0.906$
14. $\cos\angle Z = \frac{16}{65} \approx 0.246$
15. $\cos\angle F = \frac{63}{65} \approx 0.969$

Page 417

4.
```
BOWLING AVERAGE
 134
 127
OUT OF DATA AT LINE 20
```

5.
```
 4
 9
 7
OUT OF DATA AT LINE 10
```

6. Answers will vary.
```
10 READ B,H
20 LET A=B*H/2
30 PRINT "AREA OF TRIANGLE:";A
40 GO TO 10
50 DATA 4,5,8,12,3,19
60 END
```

TESTS Information and Answers

Information about the tests

On the following pages, you will find a test for each unit, an end-of-book test, and a suggested competency test. Each of these tests may be copied and reproduced for classroom use. Blackline masters have been provided with this Teacher's Edition.

Answers for the unit and end-of-book tests are given below and are circled on the following pages. Answers for the suggested competency test are circled on the test pages in this Teacher's Edition.

Each unit test consists of 20 to 25 items. Each skill objective in a unit is related to one item on the test corresponding to that unit. Notice that the items relating to applications have been placed at the end of each test.

There are 50 items on the end-of-book test. The first 40 items relate to skills and the remaining 10 items relate to applications.

An alternate form of each of these tests is included in the *Test Masters*.

Answers for the tests

Unit 1	Unit 2	Unit 3	Unit 4	Unit 5	Unit 6	End-of-book	
1. C	**1.** D	**1.** A	**1.** C	**1.** C	**1.** B	**1.** B	**26.** B
2. B	**2.** B	**2.** C	**2.** B	**2.** C	**2.** C	**2.** B	**27.** B
3. C	**3.** B	**3.** A	**3.** A	**3.** D	**3.** D	**3.** D	**28.** A
4. A	**4.** C	**4.** B	**4.** C	**4.** A	**4.** C	**4.** D	**29.** C
5. A	**5.** B	**5.** C	**5.** B	**5.** D	**5.** D	**5.** D	**30.** D
6. C	**6.** D	**6.** D	**6.** D	**6.** D	**6.** C	**6.** A	**31.** A
7. D	**7.** C	**7.** C	**7.** B	**7.** D	**7.** B	**7.** C	**32.** D
8. C	**8.** C	**8.** A	**8.** D	**8.** D	**8.** D	**8.** A	**33.** D
9. B	**9.** A	**9.** D	**9.** C	**9.** A	**9.** D	**9.** B	**34.** A
10. A	**10.** C	**10.** C	**10.** B	**10.** C	**10.** B	**10.** A	**35.** D
11. D	**11.** B	**11.** B	**11.** B	**11.** C	**11.** B	**11.** A	**36.** C
12. A	**12.** C	**12.** B	**12.** D	**12.** B	**12.** C	**12.** A	**37.** C
13. B	**13.** B	**13.** A	**13.** C	**13.** B	**13.** D	**13.** D	**38.** C
14. D	**14.** A	**14.** C	**14.** A	**14.** B	**14.** B	**14.** C	**39.** C
15. B	**15.** D	**15.** B	**15.** A	**15.** C	**15.** A	**15.** C	**40.** B
16. D	**16.** D	**16.** A	**16.** D	**16.** A	**16.** A	**16.** D	**41.** A
17. A	**17.** A	**17.** D	**17.** C	**17.** B	**17.** A	**17.** A	**42.** B
18. A	**18.** A	**18.** B	**18.** A	**18.** C	**18.** A	**18.** D	**43.** B
19. C	**19.** A	**19.** C	**19.** A	**19.** D	**19.** B	**19.** D	**44.** D
20. D	**20.** C	**20.** D	**20.** C	**20.** A	**20.** C	**20.** B	**45.** B
21. B	**21.** C					**21.** A	**46.** B
22. A	**22.** B					**22.** D	**47.** C
23. D						**23.** B	**48.** A
24. B						**24.** C	**49.** B
25. C						**25.** A	**50.** A

TEST Unit I
Whole Numbers pages 3–70

Choose the correct answer.

1. Round 3782 to the nearest hundred.
   - A 3700
   - B 3780
   - (C) 3800
   - D 4000

2. Estimate. 259 + 531
   - A 700
   - (B) 800
   - C 900
   - D 950

3. $\begin{array}{r} 795 \\ 63 \\ +1058 \\ \hline \end{array}$
   - A 1716
   - B 1906
   - (C) 1916
   - D 2483

4. $\begin{array}{r} 6057 \\ -\ 865 \\ \hline \end{array}$
   - (A) 5192
   - B 5282
   - C 6192
   - D 6812

5. 901 − (763 + 49)
   - (A) 89
   - B 187
   - C 191
   - D 1713

6. Find *x*. $x - 17 = 27$
   - A 10
   - B 34
   - (C) 44
   - D 459

7. 6000 × 300
   - A 18,000
   - B 90,000
   - C 900,000
   - (D) 1,800,000

8. Estimate. 632 × 49
   - A 24,000
   - B 25,000
   - (C) 30,000
   - D 35,000

9. $\begin{array}{r} 8064 \\ \times\ \ 9 \\ \hline \end{array}$
   - A 72,556
   - (B) 72,576
   - C 74,594
   - D 81,567

10. $\begin{array}{r} 5417 \\ \times\ 38 \\ \hline \end{array}$
    - (A) 205,846
    - B 205,966
    - C 206,526
    - D 215,606

11. $\begin{array}{r} 273 \\ \times 169 \\ \hline \end{array}$
    - A 41,682
    - B 45,037
    - C 46,047
    - (D) 46,137

12. 64 − 3(18 − 9)
    - (A) 37
    - B 40
    - C 488
    - D 549

13. $7\overline{)2645}$
    - A 377
    - (B) 377 R6
    - C 379 R6
    - D 380 R5

14. $33\overline{)784}$
    - A 22 R25
    - B 22 R35
    - C 23
    - (D) 23 R25

15. 2957 ÷ 58
    - A 50
    - (B) 50 R57
    - C 500 R5
    - D 599 R8

16. $197\overline{)34602}$

A 165 R107   C 175 R97

B 170 R112   (D) 175 R127

17. $\frac{30}{2(3)} - \frac{2(3 + 1)}{2}$

(A) 1   C 3

B 2   D 4

18. Find x. $14x = 672$

(A) 48   C 686

B 658   D 9408

19. Find the total number of calories.

Food	Calories
1 glass of milk	160
3 strips of bacon	240
2 boiled eggs	154
1 slice of bread	63

A 507 calories   (C) 617 calories

B 607 calories   D 711 calories

20. The meter on an oil truck read 2738 liters before an oil delivery and 1854 liters after the delivery. How many liters of oil were delivered?

A 134 liters   C 874 liters

B 834 liters   (D) 884 liters

21. How much rent would you pay over a 6–month period if the rent is $375 a month?

A $2150   C $22,500

(B) $2250   D $22,530

Use this formula for item 22.

NP + FL = EP

Nozzle pressure (NP) plus friction loss (FL) equals engine pressure (EP).

22. The friction loss is 18 pounds for each 100 feet of rubber-lined hose. What is the engine pressure needed for 400 feet of hose when the nozzle pressure is 85 pounds?

(A) 157 pounds   C 800 pounds

B 1570 pounds   D 7285 pounds

23. Annual salary: $22,152

Find the monthly salary.

A $1736   C $1845

B $1836   (D) $1846

24. 3 cans for 79¢

Find the price if you buy just 1 can.

A 26¢   C 28¢

(B) 27¢   D $2.27

25. How many cartons will be needed to pack 857 eggs if each carton holds 12 eggs?

A 70 cartons   (C) 72 cartons

B 71 cartons   D 73 cartons

TEST Unit 2
Decimals and the Metric System pages 75–144

Choose the correct answer.

1. An equivalent decimal for 0.4 is:
   A 0.0004 C 0.040
   B 0.004 (D) 0.40

2. $\begin{array}{r} 13.6 \\ 0.24 \\ +\ 5.083 \\ \hline \end{array}$
   A 18.823 C 19.67
   (B) 18.923 D 21.083

3. $\begin{array}{r} 14.63 \\ -\ 8.91 \\ \hline \end{array}$
   A 4.32 C 6.72
   (B) 5.72 D 23.74

4. $\begin{array}{r} 2.53 \\ \times\ 1.4 \\ \hline \end{array}$
   A 1.265 (C) 3.542
   B 3.532 D 35.42

5. $7\overline{)0.252}$
   A 0.0036 C 0.36
   (B) 0.036 D 3.6

6. 100 × 12.3
   A 1.23 C 123
   B 12.300 (D) 1230

7. 16.8 ÷ 0.012
   A 14 (C) 1400
   B 140 D 14,000

8. Round 16.38 to the nearest tenth.
   A 10 (C) 16.4
   B 16.3 D 20

9. Round the quotient to the nearest hundredth.
   $6\overline{)2.293}$
   (A) 0.38 C 0.39
   B 0.385 D 10.39

10. Estimate. 7.82 − 3.18
   A 3 (C) 5
   B 4 D 6

11. Estimate. 4.78 × 0.325
   A 0.15 C 12
   (B) 1.5 D 15

12. Choose the most sensible measure for the height of a house.
   A 10 mm (C) 10 m
   B 10 cm D 10 km

13. Count the squares to find the area of this figure in square centimeters.

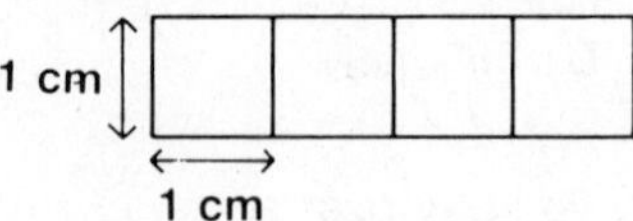

   A 3 cm^2 C 10 cm^2
   (B) 4 cm^2 D 12 cm^2

14. Count the cubes to find the volume of this figure in cubic centimeters.

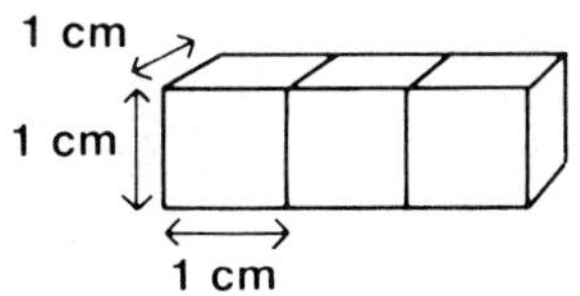

(A) 3 cm^3 C 9 cm^3
B 6 cm^3 D 12 cm^3

15. Choose the most sensible measure for the amount of milk a pitcher holds.

A 2 mL   C 200 mL
B 20 mL   (D) 2 L

16. Choose the most sensible measure for the mass of a man.

A 80 mg   C 80 g
B 800 mg   (D) 80 kg

17. Complete this statement.

6 cm^3 of water is ☐ mL of water and has a mass of ☐ g.

(A) 6, 6   C 60, 6
B 6, 60   D 60, 60

18. Choose the most sensible temperature for a glass of cold water.

(A) 6°C   C 87°C
B 48°C   D 100°C

19. Find the net pay.

Gross pay	Deductions			Net pay
$250.84	$40.13	$16.55	$5.02	

(A) $189.14   C $234.29
B $194.16   D $245.82

20. Ed Cohoe is borrowing money to buy a new car. The balance due after his down payment is $3204. Interest on the loan is $453.96 per year for three years. If Ed pays back the loan in 36 equal payments, what will be the amount of each payment?

A $1.27   (C) $126.83
B $12.68   D $1268.30

21. A recipe calls for 160 mL of milk. How much milk is needed for a triple recipe?

A 48 mL   (C) 480 mL
B 80 mL   D 4800 mL

22. Find the distance *d* between the centers of the holes. The measures are given in centimeters.

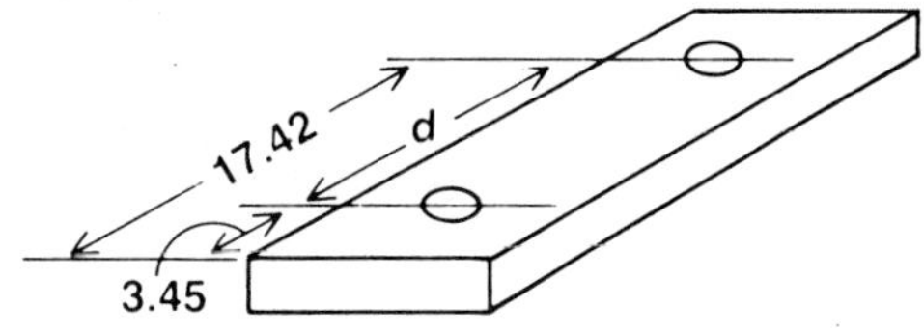

A 10.52 cm   C 14.07 cm
(B) 13.97 cm   D 20.87 cm

TEST Unit 3
Fractions, Mixed Numbers, and Probability pages 149–210

Choose the correct answer.

1. Write a mixed number for point S.

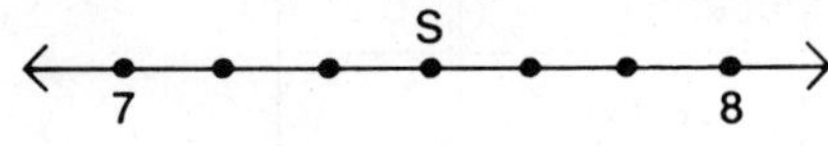

Ⓐ $7\frac{1}{2}$ C $7\frac{2}{3}$

B $7\frac{3}{5}$ D $8\frac{1}{2}$

2. Reduce $\frac{18}{24}$ to lowest terms.

A $\frac{1}{2}$ Ⓒ $\frac{3}{4}$

B $\frac{2}{3}$ D $\frac{6}{8}$

3. Write $\frac{3}{5}$ as a decimal.

Ⓐ 0.6 C 2.3

B 1.5 D 6

4. $\frac{3}{8} \times \frac{8}{9}$

A $\frac{11}{72}$ C $\frac{11}{17}$

Ⓑ $\frac{1}{3}$ D $\frac{24}{17}$

5. $2\frac{1}{2} \times 1\frac{1}{4}$

A $1\frac{3}{8}$ Ⓒ $3\frac{1}{8}$

B $2\frac{1}{8}$ D $3\frac{1}{4}$

6. $2\frac{1}{2} \div \frac{3}{8}$

A $\frac{15}{16}$ C $5\frac{4}{5}$

B $2\frac{5}{8}$ Ⓓ $6\frac{2}{3}$

7. Write $\frac{2}{3}$ and $\frac{4}{5}$ as fractions with a common denominator.

A $\frac{2}{15}, \frac{4}{15}$ Ⓒ $\frac{10}{15}, \frac{12}{15}$

B $\frac{7}{15}, \frac{7}{15}$ D $\frac{10}{8}, \frac{12}{8}$

8. Compare the numbers $4\frac{2}{3}$ and $4\frac{5}{6}$.

Ⓐ $4\frac{2}{3} < 4\frac{5}{6}$ C $4\frac{2}{3} = 4\frac{5}{6}$

B $4\frac{2}{3} > 4\frac{5}{6}$ D $4\frac{5}{6} < 4\frac{2}{3}$

9. $\frac{1}{2} + \frac{2}{3}$

A $\frac{2}{5}$ C $\frac{5}{6}$

B $\frac{3}{5}$ Ⓓ $1\frac{1}{6}$

10. $4\frac{2}{3} + 3\frac{5}{6}$

A $7\frac{2}{3}$ Ⓒ $8\frac{1}{2}$

B $7\frac{7}{9}$ D $8\frac{2}{3}$

11. $8\frac{1}{3} - 5\frac{2}{3}$

A $2\frac{1}{3}$ C 3

Ⓑ $2\frac{2}{3}$ D $3\frac{1}{3}$

12. $6\frac{1}{6}$
$-2\frac{1}{4}$

A $3\frac{1}{12}$
C $4\frac{1}{12}$
(B) $3\frac{11}{12}$
D $4\frac{11}{12}$

13. Give the probability that the roll of a number cube will show three.

(A) $\frac{1}{6}$
C $\frac{1}{2}$
B $\frac{1}{4}$
D $\frac{2}{3}$

14. Multiply to find the number of possible outcomes for tossing three coins.

A 4
(C) 8
B 6
D 16

15. Give the probability of drawing two of these cards at random that show *D* if the first card is *not* replaced before the second draw.

O	D	D	S

A $\frac{2}{24}$
C $\frac{3}{4}$
(B) $\frac{2}{12}$
D $\frac{2}{2}$

16. Jill jogs around a track at a speed of one lap every $4\frac{2}{3}$ minutes. How many laps can she complete in 14 minutes?

(A) 3 laps
C 6 laps
B 4 laps
D 10 laps

17. Bill cut a lawn in $2\frac{1}{4}$ hours. At that rate, how long should he estimate that it would take him to cut a lawn 2 times as large?

A $1\frac{1}{2}$ hours
C 4 hours
B $3\frac{1}{2}$ hours
(D) $4\frac{1}{2}$ hours

18. How many seconds did Luis use to drill all three braces?
1st brace, $15\frac{7}{10}$ seconds
2nd brace, $16\frac{1}{2}$ seconds
3d brace, $15\frac{3}{5}$ seconds

A $46\frac{4}{5}$ seconds
C $47\frac{9}{10}$ seconds
(B) $47\frac{4}{5}$ seconds
D $48\frac{9}{10}$ seconds

19. If the probability that a cup of lobster chowder will be sold is $\frac{26}{135}$ and a total of 600 cups of chowder will be sold, about how many cups of the total sold will be lobster chowder?

A 46 cups
(C) 116 cups
B 78 cups
D 200 cups

20. The game **OK** uses cards similar to the one shown. If the numbers 1–8 are used for the **O**-column and 9–16 are used for the **K**-column, how many different cards are possible? (Remember, a number cannot appear more than once on a card.)

O	K
4	10
7	13

A 56 cards
C 128 cards
B 64 cards
(D) 3136 cards

TEST **Unit 4**
Ratio, Percent, and Statistics pages 215–278

Choose the correct answer.

1. Write the ratio for sit-ups to seconds.

   6 sit-ups in 9 seconds

   A $\frac{1}{9}$ (C) $\frac{6}{9}$

   B $\frac{1}{6}$ D $\frac{9}{6}$

2. Find the missing number in this proportion.

   $\frac{10}{8} = \frac{t}{12}$

   A 6 C 40

   (B) 15 D 120

3. The triangles are similar. Which side corresponds to side ST?

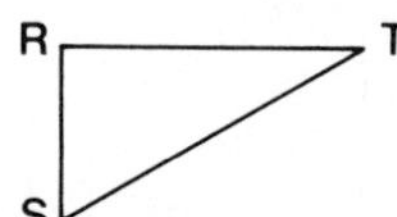

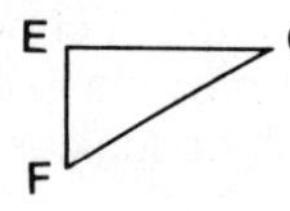

   (A) side FG C side RS

   B side EG D side EF

4. The triangles are similar. Use a proportion to find n. All lengths are in meters.

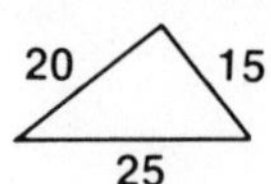

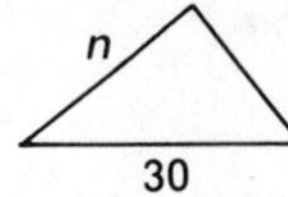

   A 4 meters (C) 24 meters

   B 18 meters D 36 meters

5. Write 4% as a decimal.

   A 0.004 C 0.4

   (B) 0.04 D 4

6. Write 45% as a fraction in lowest terms.

   A $\frac{1}{25}$ C $\frac{3}{10}$

   B $\frac{3}{20}$ (D) $\frac{9}{20}$

7. Find 12% of 60.

   A 5 C 50

   (B) 7.2 D 72

8. 17 is what percent of 25?

   A 1.47% C 17.25%

   B 17% (D) 68%

9. 10 is 25% of what number?

   A 25 (C) 40

   B 30 D 250

10. Find the mean of 72, 83, 76, 81, and 93.

    A 72 C 83

    (B) 81 D 93

11. Find the median of 11, 9, 2, 4, 7, 6, and 4.

    A 2 C 9

    (B) 6 D 10

12. In which month does Buffalo receive less than 40 centimeters of snow?

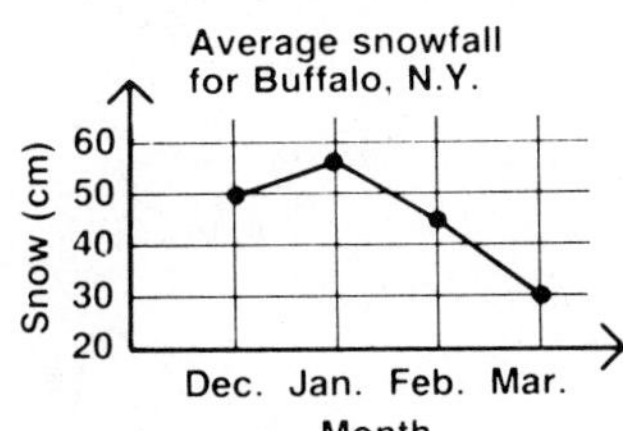

A December　　**C** February

B January　　(**D**) March

13. In which year was the volume of mail more than 80 billion?

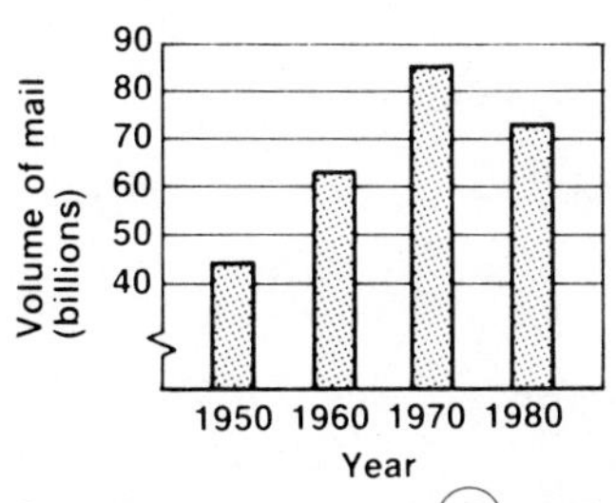

A 1950　　(**C**) 1970

B 1960　　**D** 1980

14. Which material makes up 30% of this concrete mix?

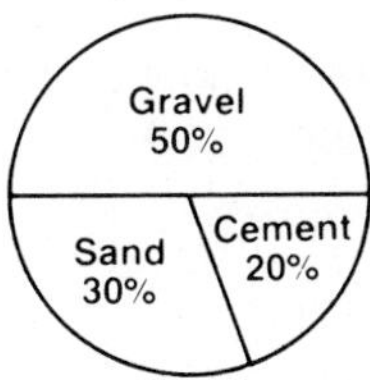

(**A**) sand　　**C** gravel

B cement　　**D** concrete

15. If it takes 6 hours to drive 435 kilometers, how long does it take to drive 580 kilometers?

(**A**) 8 hours　　**C** 12 hours

B 10 hours　　**D** 16 hours

16. A certain horse eats 140 kilograms of hay in 4 weeks. At this rate, how many kilograms of hay does this horse eat in one year? (1 year = 52 weeks)

A 324 kg　　**C** 1680 kg

B 972 kg　　(**D**) 1820 kg

17. The regular price of a sweater was $28. How much did Dean save if he bought it at a 25% discount?

A $3.50　　(**C**) $7

B $4　　**D** $21

18. The recommended concentration of a solution of Scour cleaner is 12%. A tank containing 400 liters of solution has a 9% concentration of Scour. How many liters of Scour need to be added to the solution to raise the concentration close to the recommended level?

(**A**) 12 L　　**C** 120 L

B 86 L　　**D** 3600 L

19. High ozone readings for two consecutive days were 29 and 45. Find the increase.

(**A**) 16　　**C** 30

B 24　　**D** 74

20. Shoe Sales—Style 87

872-6	875-6	877-6
|||	~~||||~~ ||	||

How many pairs of Style 87 shoes in size 6 were sold? (Last digit is size.)

A 3 pairs　　(**C**) 12 pairs

B 7 pairs　　**D** 14 pairs

TEST Unit 5 Algebra pages 283–346

Choose the correct answer.

1. Arrange these numbers in order from the least to the greatest.
   4 $^{-}3$ $^{-}7$ 6

   A $^{-}3, 4, 6, ^{-}7$ — C $^{-}7, ^{-}3, 4, 6$
   B $^{-}3, ^{-}7, 4, 6$ — D $4, 6, ^{-}3, ^{-}7$

2. $7 + ^{-}3$

   A $^{-}10$ — C 4
   B $^{-}4$ — D 10

3. $14 - ^{-}8$

   A $^{-}22$ — C 6
   B $^{-}6$ — D 22

4. $^{-}9 \times 3$

   A $^{-}27$ — C 12
   B $^{-}6$ — D 27

5. $^{-}35 \div ^{-}5$

   A $^{-}7$ — C 0.7
   B $^{-}0.7$ — D 7

6. Evaluate $15 - x + y$ when $x = 2$ and $y = 3$.

   A 9 — C 11
   B 10 — D 16

7. Evaluate $5a + 3b$ when $a = 3$ and $b = 4$.

   A $^{-}3$ — C 11
   B 3 — D 27

8. Find d. $d - 2.5 = 6.4$

   A 2.9 — C 4.1
   B 3.9 — D 8.9

9. Find w. $9w = ^{-}207$

   A $^{-}23$ — C 198
   B 23 — D 216

10. Find n. $7n + 15 = 113$

    A $^{-}14$ — C 14
    B 5.1 — D 91

11. Find t. $18t + 6 - 5t = 45$

    A $^{-}22$ — C 3
    B $^{-}3$ — D 22

12. Give the ordered pair for point A.

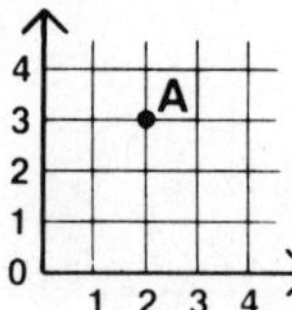

    A (2, 2) — C (3, 2)
    B (2, 3) — D (3, 3)

13. Read the graph below to find the value of y when $x = 4$.

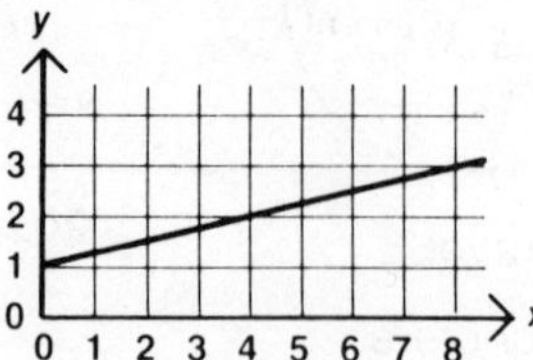

    A 1 — C 4
    B 2 — D 8

14. Give the ordered pair for point P.

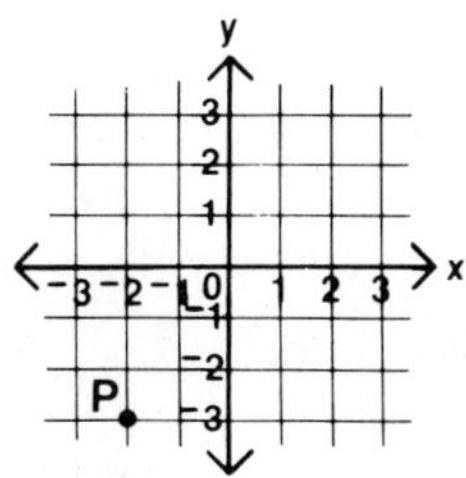

A (⁻3, ⁻2) **C** (2, ⁻3)

B (⁻2, ⁻3) **D** (2, 3)

15. Read the graph below to find the value of y when $x = 3$.

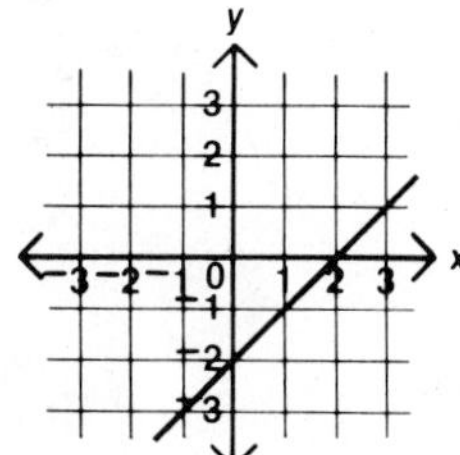

A ⁻2 **C** 1

B 0 **D** 5

16. Find the balance in the checking account after the deposit listed in the check register.

PAYMENT/DEBIT (−)	√ T	FEE (IF ANY) (−)	DEPOSIT/CREDIT (+)	BALANCE
				$ 67 20
$ 86 90		$	$	
			60 00	

A $40.30 **C** $109.70

B $96.40 **D** $152.50

17. A morning tide height for Boston was 2.71 m. The height difference of the tide in Kodiak was ⁻0.52 m. What was the height of the morning tide in Kodiak?

A 0.52 m **C** 2.9 m

B 2.19 m **D** 3.23 m

18. A car traveled 360 meters in 12 seconds. What was the speed of the car in meters per second? (Use the formula $D = RT$.)

A 12 m/s **C** 30 m/s

B 23 m/s **D** 36 m/s

19. What is the freezing point for solution that is 10% antifreeze?

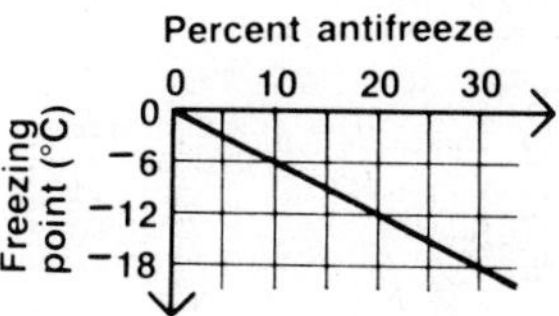

A ⁻24°C **C** ⁻12°C

B ⁻18°C **D** ⁻6°C

20. What were total sales for the first six weeks for the Bargain Mart?

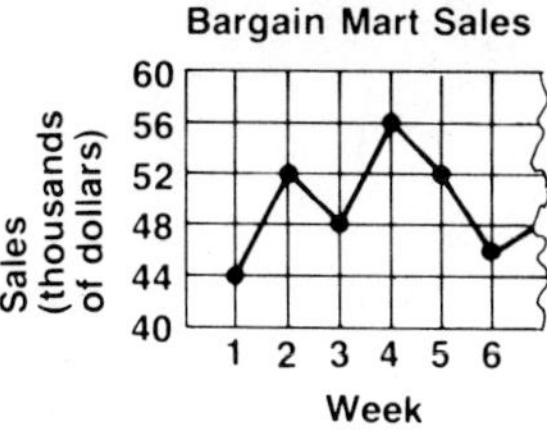

A $298,000 **C** $304,000

B $300,000 **D** $308,000

TEST Unit 6
Geometry and Right Triangle Relations pages 351–414

Choose the correct answer.

1. Find the perimeter.

   $P = 2l + 2w$

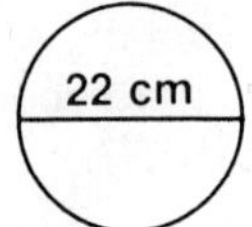

   A 42 cm
   (B) 84 cm
   C 112 cm
   D 168 cm

2. Find the circumference.

   $C = \pi d$

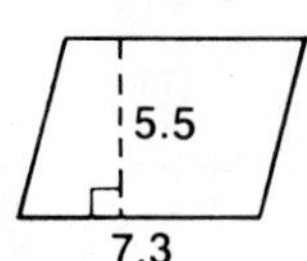

   A 34.54 cm
   B 66 cm
   (C) 69.08 cm
   D 138.16 cm

Find the area. Each dimension is in centimeters.

3. $A = bh$

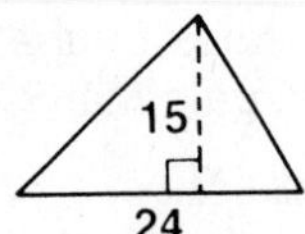

   A 12.8 cm^2
   B 25.6 cm^2
   C 30.03 cm^2
   (D) 40.15 cm^2

4. $A = \frac{1}{2}bh$

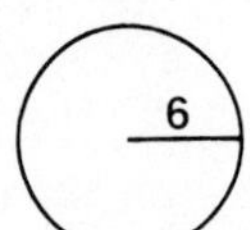

   A 19.5 cm^2
   B 90 cm^2
   (C) 180 cm^2
   D 360 cm^2

5. $A = \pi r^2$

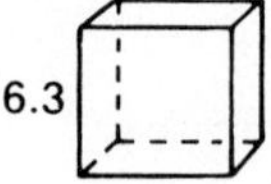

   A 15.14 cm^2
   B 27.68 cm^2
   C 36 cm^2
   (D) 113.04 cm^2

Find the surface area. Each dimension is in centimeters.

6. $A = 6s^2$

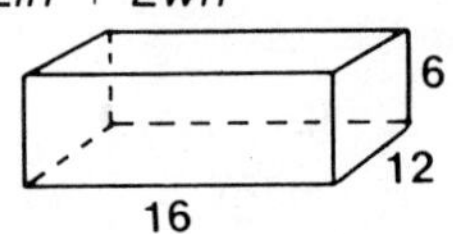

   A 39.69 cm^2
   B 75.6 cm^2
   (C) 238.14 cm^2
   D 1428.84 cm^2

7. $A = 2lw + 2lh + 2wh$

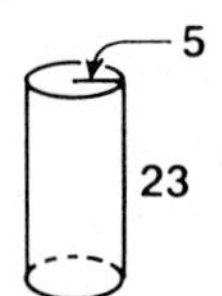

   A. 68 cm^2
   (B) 720 cm^2
   C 1152 cm^2
   D 2304 cm^2

8. $A = 2\pi rh + 2\pi r^2$

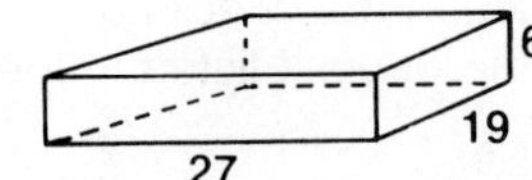

   A 332.84 cm^2
   B 722.2 cm^2
   C 785 cm^2
   (D) 879.2 cm^2

Find the volume. Each dimension is in meters.

9. $V = lwh$

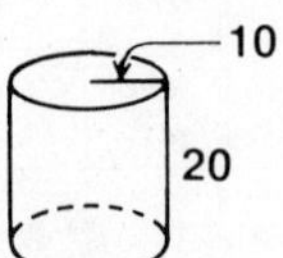

   A 37 m^3
   B 1368 m^3
   C 1468 m^3
   (D) 3078 m^3

10. $V = \pi r^2 h$

   A 942 m^3
   (B) 6280 m^3
   C 9420 m^3
   D 12,560 m^3

11. $V = \frac{1}{3}\pi r^2 h$

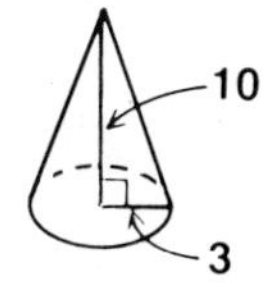

A 62.8 m²   C 282.6 m²

(B) 94.2 m²   D 942 m²

12. $V = \frac{4}{3}\pi r^3$

A 376.8 m^3 (C) 113.04 m^3

B 84.78 m^3 D 339.12 m^3

13. Compute 5^3.

A 8   C 75

B 15   (D) 125

14. Use $a^2 + b^2 = c^2$. Find the length of side FG.

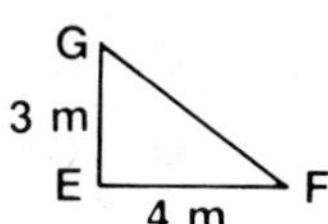

A 4 m   C 5.5 m

(B) 5 m   D 6 m

15. Use the triangle in item 14. Give the tangent of ∠F as a ratio.

(A) $\frac{3}{4}$ C $\frac{7}{4}$

B $\frac{4}{3}$ D $\frac{7}{3}$

16. Carpeting costs $16 per square meter. Find the cost of carpeting a living room with these dimensions.

Length: 7 m   Width: 5 m

(A) $560   C $1920

B $580   D $2020

17. Find the total length of this pipe.

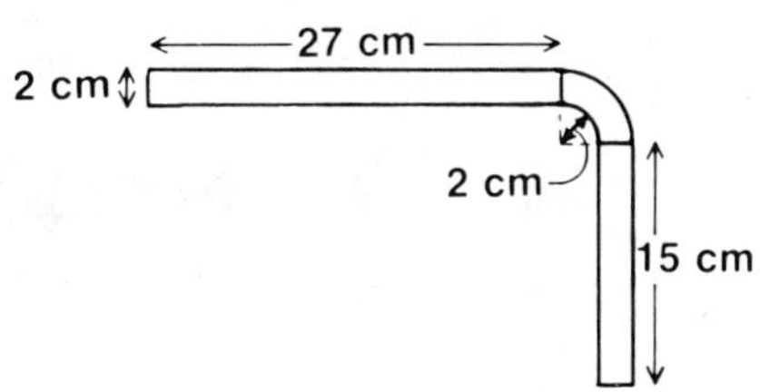

(A) 47 cm   C 67 cm

B 55 cm   D 92 cm

18. Pool specifications state that there must be one lifeguard stand per 2000 square feet of water surface. How many lifeguard stands must there be for the Albion Pool?

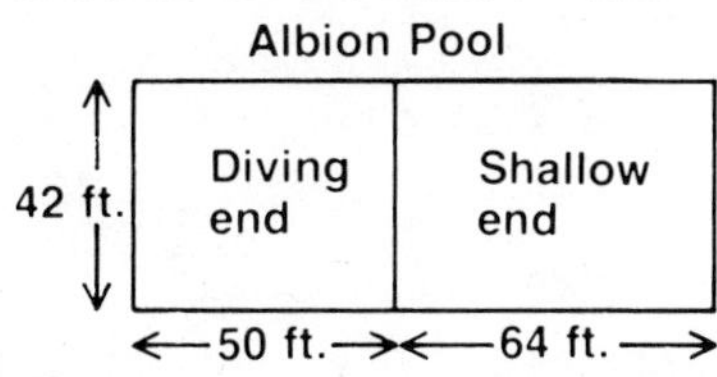

(A) 3 stands   C 6 stands

B 4 stands   D 8 stands

19. How many cubic meters of concrete are needed for a footing that is 5.7 m by 0.3 m by 0.9 m?

A 0.625 m^3 C 6.25 m^3

(B) 1.539 m^3 D 15.39 m^3

20. These sides form a right angle. What is the length of side ST?

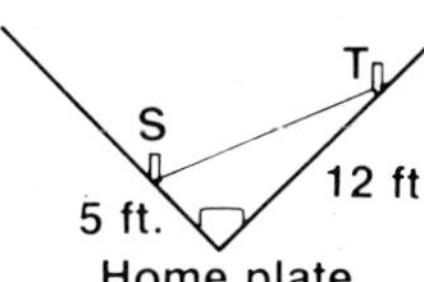

A 10 feet   (C) 13 feet

B 12 feet   D 15 feet

TEST End-of-Book

Choose the correct answer.

1. $\begin{array}{r} 672 \\ +344 \\ \hline \end{array}$

   A 916   (B) 1016   C 1026   D 1126

2. $\begin{array}{r} 7046 \\ -\ \ 865 \\ \hline \end{array}$

   A 6081   (B) 6181   C 7081   D 7181

3. Find *n*. $n - 26 = 15$

   A 11   B 21   C 31   (D) 41

4. $\begin{array}{r} 7093 \\ \times \quad 8 \\ \hline \end{array}$

   A 6344   B 6584   C 56,724   (D) 56,744

5. $\begin{array}{r} 2168 \\ \times \quad 37 \\ \hline \end{array}$

   A 22,050   B 79,816   C 80,208   (D) 80,216

6. $16 - 5(6 - 4)$

   (A) 6   B 9   C 26   D 66

7. $6\overline{)3442}$

   A 507   B 577   (C) 573 R4   D 5713 R4

8. $34\overline{)2287}$

   (A) 67 R9   B 67 R11   C 72 R32   D 610 R18

9. $\begin{array}{r} 15.8 \\ +\ \ 0.37 \\ \hline \end{array}$

   A 15.53   (B) 16.17   C 19.5   D 42.8

10. $\begin{array}{r} 26.43 \\ -\ \ 9.81 \\ \hline \end{array}$

    (A) 16.62   B 17.62   C 124.51   D 166.2

11. $\begin{array}{r} 35.4 \\ \times 0.12 \\ \hline \end{array}$

    (A) 4.248   B 35.52   C 42.48   D 424.8

12. $7\overline{)1.141}$

    (A) 0.163   B 1.63   C 16.3   D 163

13. 100×14.3

    A 1.43   B 14.3   C 143   (D) 1430

14. $0.12\overline{)4.2}$

    A 0.35   B 3.5   (C) 35   D 350

15. Choose the most sensible measure for the width of a hallway.

    A 3 mm   B 3 cm   (C) 3 m   D 3 km

16. 6.2 kg = ☐ g

    A 0.0062   B 6.2   C 62   (D) 6200

17. $\frac{2}{5} \times \frac{3}{4}$

A $\frac{3}{10}$ C $\frac{3}{5}$

B $\frac{1}{2}$ D $\frac{6}{7}$

18. $2\frac{1}{3} \div \frac{2}{3}$

A $1\frac{5}{9}$ C 3

B 2 D $3\frac{1}{2}$

19. $\begin{array}{r} 3\frac{1}{2} \\ +5\frac{5}{8} \\ \hline \end{array}$

A $2\frac{1}{8}$ C $8\frac{3}{4}$

B $8\frac{1}{8}$ D $9\frac{1}{8}$

20. $\begin{array}{r} 7\frac{1}{2} \\ -1\frac{2}{3} \\ \hline \end{array}$

A $5\frac{1}{3}$ C $6\frac{1}{6}$

B $5\frac{5}{6}$ D $6\frac{1}{2}$

21. Give the probability that a roll of a number cube will show a three.

A $\frac{1}{6}$ C $\frac{1}{2}$

B $\frac{1}{4}$ D $\frac{4}{3}$

22. Multiply to find the number of possible outcomes for tossing four coins.

A 4 C 8

B 6 D 16

23. Find the missing number. $\frac{6}{9} = \frac{n}{24}$

A 8 C 21

B 16 D 36

24. The triangles are similar. Use a proportion to find *n*.

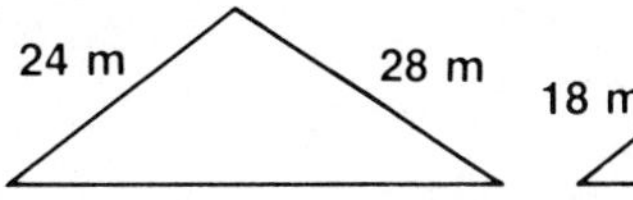

A 16 m C 21 m

B 20 m D 24 m

25. Write 9% as a decimal.

A 0.09 C 9

B 0.9 D 90

26. Find 16% of 40.

A 0.64 C 64

B 6.4 D 640

27. Find the mean of 87, 95, 78, and 92.

A 86 C 86.5

B 88 D 89.5

28. How many cans of apricots were produced in 1979?

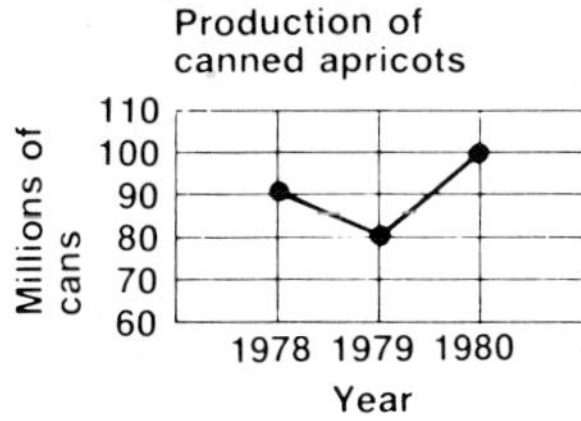

A 80 million C 100 million

B 90 million D 110 million

29. $8 + {}^{-}6$

A $^{-}14$ | C 2 (circled)
B $^{-}2$ | D 14

30. $16 - {}^{-}9$

A $^{-}25$ | C 7
B $^{-}7$ | D 25 (circled)

31. $^{-}7 \times 6$

A $^{-}42$ (circled) | C 13
B $^{-}1$ | D 42

32. Evaluate $3a - 2b$ when $a = 5$ and $b = {}^{-}4$.

A $^{-}22$ | C 7
B 2 | D 23 (circled)

33. Find h. $h - 3.7 = 4.8$

A 1.1 | C 7.5
B 3.5 | D 8.5 (circled)

34. Find x. $^{-}5x + 14 = 119$

A $^{-}21$ (circled) | C 15
B $^{-}15$ | D 21

35. Read the graph below to find the value of y when $x = 2$.

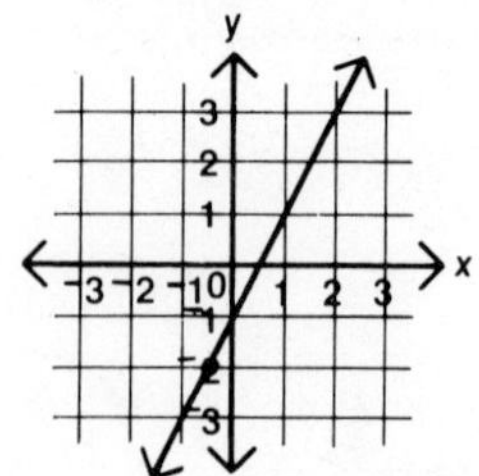

A $^{-}3$ | C 1
B 0 | D 3 (circled)

36. Find the perimeter.

$P = 2l + 2w$

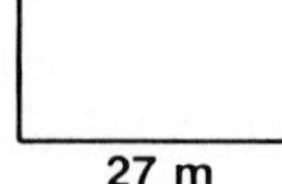

A 43 m | C 86 m (circled)
B 66 m | D 432 m

37. Find the circumference.

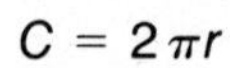
$C = 2\pi r$

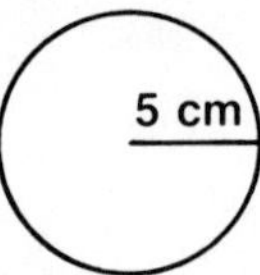

A 3.14 cm | C 31.4 cm (circled)
B 6.28 cm | D 62.8 cm

38. Find the surface area.

8 m
12 m

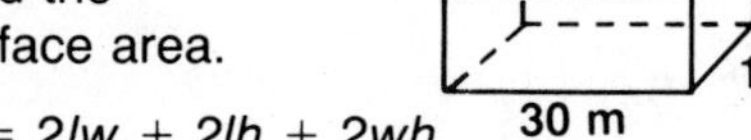
$A = 2lw + 2lh + 2wh$

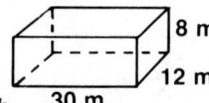

A 792 m^2 | C 1392 m^2 (circled)
B 1180 m^2 | D 5760 m^2

39. Find the volume.

$V = \pi r^2 h$

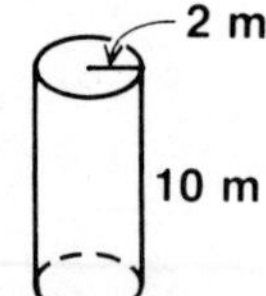

A 12.56 m^3 | C 125.6 m^3 (circled)
B 314 m^3 | D 3140 m^3

40. Use $a^2 + b^2 = c^2$ to find the missing length.

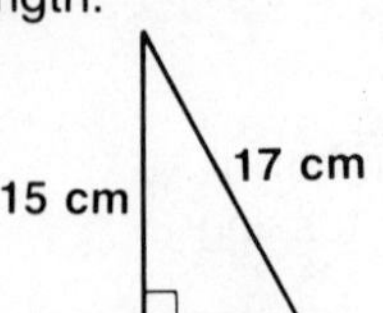

A 6 cm | C 10 cm
B 8 cm (circled) | D 12 cm

41. How much rent would you pay over a 6-month period if the rent is $358 a month?

(A) $2148 C $2310

B $2748 D $4296

42. How many cartons will be needed to pack 642 eggs if each carton holds 12 eggs?

A 53 cartons C 55 cartons

(B) 54 cartons D 62 cartons

43. Find the distance d between the centers of the holes. The measures are given in centimeters.

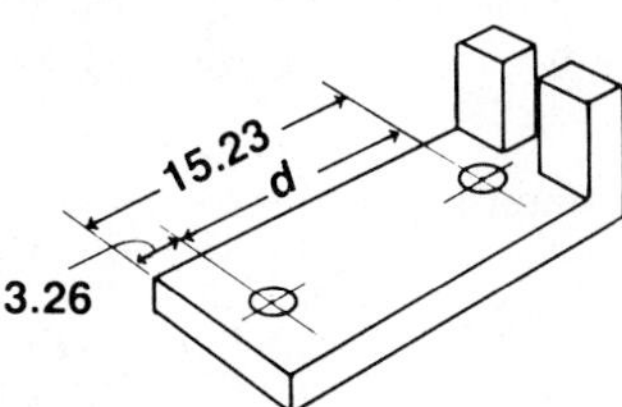

A 8.71 cm C 18.49 cm

(B) 11.97 cm D 21.75 cm

44. What is the cost of 2.5 meters of material at $4.80 per meter?

A $4.80 C $11

B $9.60 (D) $12

45. Randy rides his bicycle at a speed of one lap every $1\frac{1}{2}$ minutes. How long will it take him to complete 10 laps?

A 10 minutes C 20 minutes

(B) 15 minutes D 24 minutes

46. If it takes 6 hours to drive 459 kilometers, how long does it take to drive 765 kilometers?

A 8 hours C 12 hours

(B) 10 hours D 16 hours

47. The balance on Ms. Greico's charge account was $238. She made a $20 payment. Then she was charged 2% for a finance charge. What was the new balance on her account?

A $218 (C) $222.36

B $220 D $222.76

48. Find the balance in the checking account after the deposit listed in the check register.

PAYMENT/DEBIT (−)		√ T	FEE (IF ANY) (−)	DEPOSIT/CREDIT (+)		BALANCE	
						$ 33	40
$ 65	20		$	$			
				40	00		

(A) $8.20 C $31.80

B $25.20 D $138.60

49. A truck traveled 240 meters in 12 seconds. What was the speed of the truck in meters per second?

A 12 m/s C 21 m/s

(B) 20 m/s D 24 m/s

50. How many cubic meters of cement are used for a rectangular patio that is 7 m by 8 m and is 0.3 m deep?

(A) 16.8 m^3 C 56 m^3

B 45 m^3 D 168 m^3

Suggested Competency Test

This test is designed to evaluate students' performance with computational skills and measure how well they can use these skills in everyday life. It is an example of the type of competency test that many schools require for graduation. Thirty-two items, keyed to book objectives, test computational skills. Thirty items, keyed to consumer topics, test problem solving in consumer and career applications. Answers to the competency test are circled on the test pages.

Interpretation of test scores is left up to the individual teacher. However, to demonstrate overall competence in the content, a student should answer correctly at least one item keyed to each objective or consumer topic.

Computational skills

Book objective	Test items	Pages
3. Add whole numbers.	1–2	6–7
4. Subtract whole numbers.	3–4	8–9
12. Multiply whole numbers with a two-digit multiplier.	5–6	30–31
18. Divide whole numbers with a two-digit divisor.	7–8	50–51
26. Add decimals.	9–10	78–79
27. Subtract decimals.	11–12	80–81
32. Multiply decimals.	13–14	96–97
34. Divide a decimal by a whole number.	15–16	100–101
53. Multiply fractions.	17–18	154–155
55. Divide fractions and mixed numbers.	19–20	158–159
60. Add and subtract fractions.	21–22	174–175
61. Add mixed numbers.	23–24	176–177
63. Subtract mixed numbers with different denominators.	25–26	180–181
73. Find a missing number in a proportion by using cross-products.	27–28	218–219
80. Find a percent of a number.	29–30	240–241
81. Find what percent one number is of another.	31–32	242–243

Consumer topics

Topics	Test items	Pages
Income (salaries)	33–34	59, 183
Net income	35–36	18–19, 90–91
Deposit slips	37–38	86–87
Check register	39–40	88–89, 300–301
Interest	41–42	248–249
Monthly payments	43–44	112–113
Unit price	45–46	60–61
Sale discount	47–48	247
Sale price	49–50	247
Living expenses	51–52	37, 109, 110–111
Utilities	53–54	114–115, 270–271
Automobile expenses	55–56	38–39
Travel expenses	57–58	16–17
Travel distances	59–60	225
Floor plans	61–62	363

Competency Test

Choose the correct answer.

1. $\begin{array}{r} 357 \\ +285 \\ \hline \end{array}$

A 532 C 632
B 542 (D) 642

2. $\begin{array}{r} 8712 \\ 435 \\ +\quad 36 \\ \hline \end{array}$

A 8173 (C) 9183
B 8183 D 9273

3. $\begin{array}{r} 403 \\ -127 \\ \hline \end{array}$

A 226 C 326
(B) 276 D 376

4. $\begin{array}{r} 6174 \\ -\quad 926 \\ \hline \end{array}$

(A) 5248 C 6258
B 5858 D 6848

5. $\begin{array}{r} 512 \\ \times\quad 95 \\ \hline \end{array}$

A 7168 (C) 48,640
B 47,430 D 71,590

6. $\begin{array}{r} 836 \\ \times\quad 43 \\ \hline \end{array}$

A 5852 C 36,638
(B) 35,948 D 37,158

7. $21\overline{)987}$

A 39 (C) 47
B 42 D 407

8. $34\overline{)884}$

A 20 (C) 26
B 22 D 206

9. $\begin{array}{r} 3.4 \\ +4.75 \\ \hline \end{array}$

A 7.15 C 9.25
(B) 8.15 D 50.9

10. $\begin{array}{r} 0.07 \\ 4.26 \\ +6.93 \\ \hline \end{array}$

A 10.16 C 12.13
(B) 11.26 D 18.19

11. $\begin{array}{r} 3.794 \\ -1.286 \\ \hline \end{array}$

A 1.492 C 2.418
B 1.512 (D) 2.508

Go on to the next page.

12. $\begin{array}{r} 51.45 \\ -\ 9.7 \\ \hline \end{array}$

(A) 41.75 C 50.48

B 42.38 D 58.35

13. $\begin{array}{r} 2.12 \\ \times\ 3.8 \\ \hline \end{array}$

A 2.322 C 7.976

B 7.946 (D) 8.056

14. $\begin{array}{r} 4.67 \\ \times 0.05 \\ \hline \end{array}$

A 0.2005 C 0.2305

B 0.2035 (D) 0.2335

15. $7\overline{)4.13}$

A 0.059 (C) 0.59

B 0.509 D 5.09

16. $6\overline{)0.426}$

(A) 0.071 C 7.01

B 0.701 D 7.1

17. $\frac{2}{3} \times \frac{4}{5} =$

A $\frac{2}{15}$ C $\frac{3}{4}$

(B) $\frac{8}{15}$ D $\frac{6}{8}$

18. $5 \times \frac{2}{3} =$

(A) $3\frac{1}{3}$ C $5\frac{2}{3}$

B $4\frac{1}{3}$ D $7\frac{1}{2}$

19. $\frac{1}{6} \div \frac{2}{5} =$

A $\frac{1}{15}$ C $\frac{1}{3}$

B $2\frac{2}{5}$ (D) $\frac{5}{12}$

20. $\frac{3}{4} \div 2 =$

(A) $\frac{3}{8}$ C $2\frac{2}{3}$

B $\frac{2}{3}$ D $2\frac{3}{4}$

21. $\begin{array}{r} \frac{4}{6} \\ +\frac{1}{6} \\ \hline \end{array}$

A $\frac{1}{9}$ C $\frac{5}{12}$

B $\frac{1}{4}$ (D) $\frac{5}{6}$

22. $\begin{array}{r} \frac{11}{12} \\ -\frac{4}{12} \\ \hline \end{array}$

A $\frac{4}{11}$ C $\frac{3}{4}$

(B) $\frac{7}{12}$ D 7

Go on to the next page.

23. $3\frac{1}{2}$ $+2\frac{3}{8}$

A $1\frac{1}{16}$
C $5\frac{2}{5}$
B $1\frac{1}{3}$
(D) $5\frac{7}{8}$

24. $4\frac{2}{5}$ $+5\frac{1}{3}$

A $9\frac{1}{5}$
C $9\frac{1}{2}$
B $9\frac{3}{8}$
(D) $9\frac{11}{15}$

25. $7\frac{8}{9}$ $-4\frac{2}{3}$

A $1\frac{1}{3}$
C $4\frac{16}{27}$
(B) $3\frac{2}{9}$
D $12\frac{5}{9}$

26. $8\frac{3}{4}$ $-3\frac{2}{5}$

A $4\frac{3}{10}$
C $6\frac{8}{15}$
(B) $5\frac{7}{20}$
D $12\frac{3}{20}$

27. Find the missing number.
$\frac{4}{6} = \frac{x}{9}$

A 4
(C) 6
B 5
D 7

28. Find the missing number.
$\frac{12}{t} = \frac{3}{8}$

(A) 32
C 34
B 33
D 35

29. Find 5% of 60.

A 1
(C) 3
B 2
D 4

30. Find 40% of 85.

A 28
C 45
(B) 34
D 57

31. 9 is what percent of 25?

A 16%
(C) 36%
B 29%
D 44%

32. 12 is what percent of 20?

A 8%
C 24%
B 16%
(D) 60%

Go on to the next page.

Competency Test continued

33. Larry Smith earned $19,084 last year. There are 52 weeks in a year. On the average, how much did Larry earn per week?

A $191 C $498

(B) $367 D $992

34. Lena Arnholt makes $12 per hour. Tuesday she worked 7.5 hours. How much did she earn on Tuesday?

A $80 (C) $90

B $85 D $95

35. Mary Ching's gross income from her part-time job was $5607. Her total taxes (federal and social security) were $738. What was her net income?

(A) $4869 C $5979

B $5131 D $6345

36. Juan Perez's gross income for the year was $18,194. His federal tax was $3258. His social security tax was $1210. What was his net income?

A $12,736 C $14,334

(B) $13,726 D $22,662

37. What is the net deposit?

CASH	CURRENCY	36	00
	COIN		52
LIST CHECKS SINGLY		125	06
TOTAL FROM OTHER SIDE			
TOTAL			
LESS CASH RECEIVED		25	00
NET DEPOSIT			

(A) $136.58 C $161.58

B $146.06 D $186.58

38. What is the net deposit?

CASH	CURRENCY	137	00
	COIN	5	48
LIST CHECKS SINGLY			
		286	04
		550	00
TOTAL FROM OTHER SIDE			
TOTAL			
LESS CASH RECEIVED		0	00
NET DEPOSIT			

A $741.52 C $868.42

B $863.04 (D) $978.52

39. Find the new balance.

PAYMENT/DEBIT (−)		√ T	FEE (IF ANY) (−)	DEPOSIT/CREDIT (+)		BALANCE	
						$692	34
$57	88		$	$			

(A) $634.46 C $650.71

B $645.54 D $750.22

Go on to the next page.

40. Find the new balance.

PAYMENT/DEBIT (−)		√ T	FEE (IF ANY) (−)	DEPOSIT/CREDIT (+)		BALANCE	
						$342	07
$			$	$35	88		
123	63						

A $182.56 **C** $429.82

(B) $254.32 **D** $501.58

41. Gina wanted to buy a television set priced at $520.00. She borrowed the money for 3 months at an interest rate of 2% per month. How much interest did she pay? Use the formula $I = P \times R \times T$.

A $10.40 **C** $26.00

B $15.60 **(D)** $31.20

42. Martin wanted to buy a camera. He borrowed $275 for 2 months at an interest rate of 2.5% per month. How much interest did he pay? Use the formula $I = P \times R \times T$.

A $5.50 **(C)** $13.75

B $6.85 **D** $14.00

43. James borrowed $1000. The amount of interest is $140. If he pays back the loan in 12 equal payments, what will be the amount of each payment?

(A) $95 **C** $140

B $120 **D** $168

44. Mr. and Mrs. Hardwick borrowed $5000 from the bank. The amount of interest for each year is $716. They want to pay back the loan in 2 years. If the loan is paid back in 24 equal payments, what will be the amount of each payment?

A $238 **C** $348

(B) $268 **D** $358

45. How much does one can of soup cost?

Soup Sale
3 cans for 99¢

A 32¢ **C** 34¢

(B) 33¢ **D** 35¢

46. How much does one tire cost?

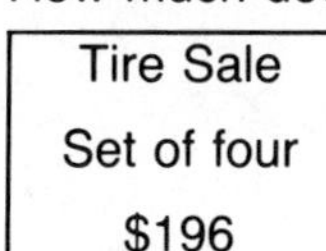

A $46 **C** $48

B $47 **(D)** $49

47. Find the amount saved (discount).

Canoe Sale	
Regular price	$456.95
Now 20% off	

(A) $91.39 **C** $314.24

B $114.24 **D** $365.56

Go on to the next page.

48. Find the amount saved (discount).

Sewing Machine Sale	
Regular price	$345.00
30% Discount	

A $69.50 (C) $103.50

B $92.50 D $241.50

49. What is the sale price?

Lawn Mower Sale	
Regular price	$408.00
Now 25% off	

A $102.00 C $224.40

B $122.40 (D) $306.00

50. What is the sale price?

Freezer Sale	
Regular price	$448.00
Now 15% off	

A $358.40 C $403.20

(B) $380.80 D $425.60

51. How much rent would you pay in one year if the rent is $308 a month?

A $3080 (C) $3696

B $3524 D $3706

52. Lean ground beef costs $4.26 per kilogram. Find the cost of 2.5 kilograms.

A $1.67 C $8.52

B $6.76 (D) $10.65

53. The rate charged for electricity in a certain city is $0.06 per kilowatt-hour. What is the cost for using 1600 kilowatt-hours?

(A) $96 C $108

B $102 D $114

54. Find the average of the four electric bills.

Month	Electric Bill
January	$86
February	$72
March	$63
April	$75

A $72 (C) $74

B $73 D $75

55. Gasoline costs 40¢ per liter. How much would 42 liters cost?

A $9.45 C $12.60

B $10.50 (D) $16.80

Go on to the next page.

56. Carla's station wagon goes 4.8 kilometers per liter of gasoline. If gasoline costs 36¢ per liter, find the cost of gasoline to drive the station wagon 2100 kilometers.

A $108.36 **C** $200.00

(B) $157.50 **D** $278.40

57. Find the total cost of the trip.

Gasoline and maintenance	$356
Meals	$117
Lodging	$168

A $512 **(C)** $641

B $532 **D** $711

58. How much could John save by traveling round trip by bus rather than by airplane?

Airplane

Coach fare	$716
Meals	No charge

Bus

Fare	$236
Meals	$83

(A) $397 **C** $480

B $407 **D** $633

59. Ann's car goes 15 kilometers per liter of gasoline. The gasoline tank holds 40 liters. How far should the car go on a full tank of gasoline?

A 55 kilometers **C** 550 kilometers

B 400 kilometers **(D)** 600 kilometers

60. The Dudley family drove 1947 kilometers in 3 days. What was the average distance driven each day?

A 600 kilometers **(C)** 649 kilometers

B 612 kilometers **D** 673 kilometers

61. Find the area of the living room. The length is 6 meters and the width is 5 meters. Use the formula $A = l \times w$.

A 11 square meters **C** 61 square meters

(B) 30 square meters **D** 70 square meters

62. Find the area of this room.

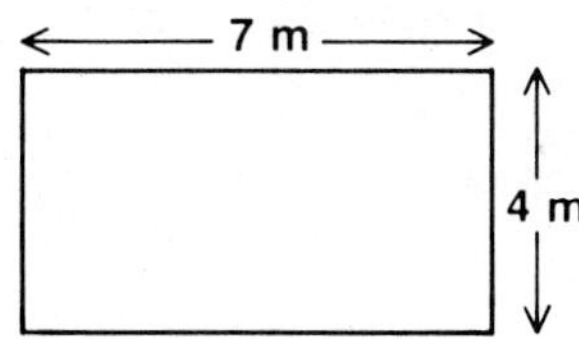

(A) 28 square meters **C** 48 square meters

B 32 square meters **D** 64 square meters

Stop. End of test.

L. Carey Bolster

H. Douglas Woodburn

Scott, Foresman and Company
Editorial Offices: Glenview, Illinois

Regional Offices: Sunnyvale, California •
Tucker, Georgia • Glenview, Illinois •
Oakland, New Jersey • Dallas, Texas

Authors

L. Carey Bolster
Supervisor of Mathematics
Baltimore County Public Schools
Towson, Maryland

H. Douglas Woodburn
Chairman of the Mathematics Department
Perry Hall Middle School
Baltimore County, Maryland

Reader/Consultants

Thelma Thomas Daley
Supervisor of Guidance
Baltimore County Public Schools
Towson, Maryland

Marita H. Eng
Mathematics Department Chairman
Sandalwood Junior-Senior High School
Jacksonville, Florida

Robert Y. Hamada
Instructional Specialist, Mathematics
Los Angeles Unified School District
Los Angeles, California

Linda Borry Hausmann
Instructional Coordinator
Minnesota Educational Computing Consortium
St. Paul, Minnesota

Sidney Sharron
Supervisor, Instructional Media and Resources Branch
Los Angeles Unified School District
Los Angeles, California

ISBN: 0-673-23430-4

12345678910-KPH-939291908988786

Acknowledgments

For permission to reproduce indicated information on the following pages, acknowledgment is made to:

Deposit slip, checks, and check registers on 86 and 88–89 reprinted by permission of Glenview State Bank. Break Time on 377 from TOPS DECK AA, Problem 37. Reprinted by permission of Dale Seymour Publications, P. O. Box 10888, Palo Alto, CA 94303.

Unless otherwise credited, all photographs are the property of Scott, Foresman and Company. For permission to reproduce photographs on the following pages, acknowledgment is made to:

Photo on 40–41, J. C. Allen and Son. Photo on 184–185, Edward Pieratt/Black Star. Photo on 230–231, U. S. Navy. Photo on 272–273, David Baumhefner, NCAR. Seismograph in photo on 342–343 courtesy of Soiltest, Inc., Evanston, Illinois.

UNIT ONE Whole Numbers

Chapter 1
Adding and Subtracting Whole Numbers

Chapter 2
Multiplying Whole Numbers

Chapter 3
Dividing Whole Numbers

End-of-Unit Materials

UNIT TWO Decimals and the Metric System

Chapter 4
Adding and Subtracting Decimals

Skills

Problem Solving

Chapter 5
Multiplying and Dividing Decimals

Skills

Problem Solving

Chapter 6
The Metric System

Skills

Problem Solving

End-of-Unit Materials

UNIT THREE Fractions, Mixed Numbers, and Probability

Chapter 7
Multiplying and Dividing Fractions and Mixed Numbers

Skills

Problem Solving

Chapter 8
Adding and Subtracting Fractions and Mixed Numbers

Skills

Problem Solving

Chapter 9
Probability

Skills

Problem Solving

End-of-Unit Materials

UNIT FOUR Ratio, Percent, and Statistics

Chapter 10
Ratio, Proportion, and Similarity

Chapter 11
Percent

Chapter 12
Statistics

End-of-Unit Materials

UNIT FIVE Algebra

Chapter 13
Positive and Negative Numbers

Skills

Problem Solving

Chapter 14
Expressions and Equations

Skills

Problem Solving

Chapter 15
Graphing

Skills

Problem Solving

End-of-Unit Materials

UNIT SIX Geometry and Right-Triangle Relations

Chapter 16
Perimeter and Area

Chapter 17
Surface Area and Volume

Chapter 18
The Pythagorean Rule and Trigonometry

End-of-Unit Materials

End-of-Book Materials

MATHEMATICS
IN LIFE
SECOND
EDITION

UNIT ONE Whole Numbers

CHAPTER 1

Adding and Subtracting Whole Numbers

On each Pretest, Posttest, and Chapter Test a table such as this is given to help score the test. For scores of 50% correct or better, the percent correct is listed below the number of test items missed.
You may prefer to record particular items missed by each student, rather than using percent scores.

Number of test items - 17

Number missed	1	2	3	4	5	6	7	8
Percent correct	94	88	82	76	71	65	59	53

SKILLS PRETEST

SKILL Rounding Whole Numbers *page 4*

A Round 342 to the nearest ten.
340

B Round 8671 to the nearest hundred.
8700

C Round 17,522 to the nearest thousand.
18,000

SKILL Estimating Sums and Differences *page 5*

D Estimate. 547 + 386
900

E Estimate. 4817 − 2154
3000

F Estimate. 315 + 24 + 8
350
Answers may vary.

SKILL Adding Whole Numbers *pages 6–7*

G $432 + 57$
489

H $678 + 374$
1052

I $218 + 47 + 62$
327

J 38 + 247 + 8563 + 12
8860

SKILL Subtracting Whole Numbers *pages 8–9*

K $3875 - 1263$
2612

L $2043 - 485$
1558

M 12,841 − 1857
10,984

The Pretest for each chapter assesses student understanding of the skills developed in that chapter. Each skill is broken into exercise types. These exercise types appear on the Pretest, in the skills lessons, and on the Posttest. They are lettered A, B, C, and so on, consecutively throughout the chapter.
Item A on the Pretest is the same exercise type as Example A in the skills lesson (page 4), and as the exercises in Set A (page 4), and as item A on the Posttest (page 14). Notice that the skills for a chapter are tested again on the Chapter Test (page 24) along with applications.

SKILL Using Order of Operations *pages 10–11*

N 34 − 9 + 7
32

O 18 − (8 + 4)
6

SKILL Solving Addition and Subtraction Equations *pages 12–13*

P Find x.

$x + 26 = 94$
$x = 68$

Q Find a.

$a - 87 = 114$
$a = 201$

You may choose to individualize assignments for your students according to the items missed on the Pretest. On the other hand, you may choose to use the Pretest simply as a preview of the skills to be taught in the chapter. If all students do well on the Pretest, you may choose to go directly to the applications (pages 15–23).

See pages T18–T23 for a listing of all the objectives in each chapter.

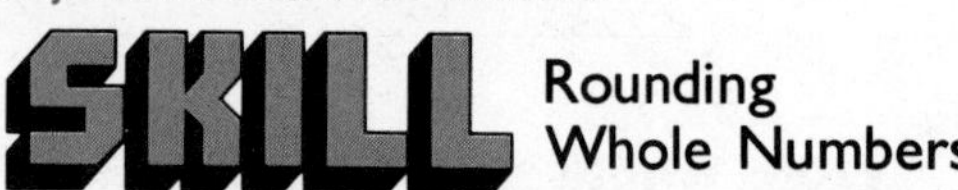

Rounding Whole Numbers

The lesson title names the mathematical skill taught in the lesson.

Example A To the nearest ten

Each skill is broken into exercise types. The exercise type is given here.

Round each number to the nearest ten.

82 — Find the tens place. Look at the digit to the right. It is less than 5.

80 — Do not change the digit in the tens place. Write a zero for the digit to the right.

$82 \approx 80$ $\approx$ means *is approximately equal to.*

378 — Find the tens place. Look at the digit to the right. It is 5 or greater.

380 — Add 1 to the digit in the tens place. Write a zero for the digit to the right.

$378 \approx 380$

Example B To the nearest hundred

Round 4793 to the nearest hundred.

hundreds place ↓

$4793 \approx 4800$ The digit to the right of the hundreds place is greater than 5. Round up.

Example C To the nearest thousand

Round 16,583 to the nearest thousand.

thousands place ↓

$16{,}583 \approx 17{,}000$ The digit to the right of the thousands place is 5. Round up.

The exercises in Set A correspond to Example A, those in Set B correspond to Example B, and so on, throughout the chapter.

Exercises

Answers to odd-numbered exercises are given at the end of the student's text on pages 434–467.

Set A

Round to the nearest ten.

1. 62 (60)	8. 471 (470)	15. 1002 (1000)
2. 17 (20)	9. 263 (260)	16. 2468 (2470)
3. 86 (90)	10. 575 (580)	17. 4325 (4330)
4. 24 (20)	11. 142 (140)	18. 5001 (5000)
5. 93 (90)	12. 829 (830)	19. 8 (10)
6. 38 (40)	13. 287 (290)	20. 95 (100)
7. 45 (50)	14. 975 (980)	21. 4397 (4400)

Set B

Round to the nearest hundred.

1. 645 (600)	8. 6248 (6200)	15. 11,843 (11,800)
2. 371 (400)	9. 5351 (5400)	16. 25,578 (25,600)
3. 750 (800)	10. 8234 (8200)	17. 1008 (1000)
4. 839 (800)	11. 3180 (3200)	18. 4906 (4900)
5. 124 (100)	12. 7096 (7100)	19. 85 (100)
6. 452 (500)	13. 2308 (2300)	20. 976 (1000)
7. 285 (300)	14. 2555 (2600)	21. 7981 (8000)

Set C

Round to the nearest thousand.

1. 7456 (7000)	8. 5132 (5000)	15. 73,028 (73,000)
2. 2347 (2000)	9. 7506 (8000)	16. 18,541 (19,000)
3. 1834 (2000)	10. 1890 (2000)	17. 17,009 (17,000)
4. 6058 (6000)	11. 9087 (9000)	18. 20,199 (20,000)
5. 4509 (5000)	12. 1099 (1000)	19. 788 (1000)
6. 8666 (9000)	13. 36,253 (36,000)	20. 9643 (10,000)
7. 3750 (4000)	14. 93,521 (94,000)	21. 29,541 (30,000)

Objective: Estimate sums and differences using rounded numbers.

SKILL Estimating Sums and Differences

Example D
Estimating sums, addends have same number of digits

Estimate. 329 + 456

$329 + 456$

$300 + 500 = 800$

Round each number. Add the rounded numbers to get an estimate.

$329 + 456 \approx 800$

Example E
Estimating differences, minuend and subtrahend have same number of digits

Estimate. 5124 − 1729

$5124 - 1729$

$5000 - 2000 = 3000$

Round each number. Subtract the rounded numbers to get an estimate.

$5124 - 1729 \approx 3000$

Example F
Estimating sums and differences, different numbers of digits are involved

Estimate. 2342 + 486 + 78

$2342 + 486 + 78$

$2300 + 500 + 100 = 2900$

Round the numbers to the same place. Add.

$2342 + 486 + 78 \approx 2900$

Explain to students that estimation can be done in many ways. One way is to round both numbers so that the addition or subtraction becomes a basic fact, as shown in Examples D and E. When the numbers involved have different numbers of digits, one way is to round them to the same place, as in Example F. Choose a place that will allow simple computation without destroying the purpose of the estimate.

Exercises

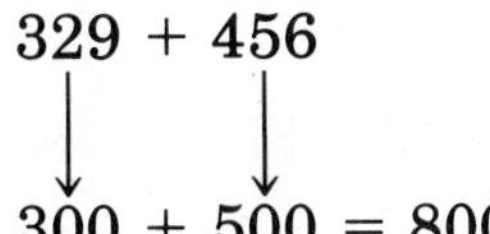

Set D

Estimate each sum.

1. 49 + 23
70
2. 17 + 64
80
3. 365 + 249
600
4. 657 + 198
900
5. 186 + 308
500
6. 915 + 308
1200
7. 378 + 876
1300
8. 623 + 187
800
9. 3099 + 1387
4000
10. 8479 + 2974
11,000
11. 5628 + 4382
10,000
12. 6290 + 1873
8000

Set E

Estimate each difference.

1. 91 − 27
60
2. 53 − 19
30
3. 847 − 228
600
4. 362 − 157
200
5. 812 − 474
300
6. 784 − 427
400
7. 9003 − 1931
7000
8. 4814 − 2187
3000
9. 4295 − 1821
2000
10. 9386 − 4432
5000
11. 78,261 − 32,895
50,000
12. 67,827 − 11,889
60,000

Set F

Estimate each answer.
Answers may vary.

1. 3526 + 193
3700
2. 1276 + 128 + 293
1700
3. 1517 + 423 + 58
2000
4. 6829 + 91 + 423 + 6
7300
5. 12,346 + 2927 + 1156 + 896
17,000
6. 7283 − 916
6400
7. 6490 − 873
5600
8. 4573 − 87
4500
9. 34,861 − 2175
33,000

Objective: Add whole numbers.

SKILL Adding Whole Numbers

Example G Without renaming

Estimate: 250 + 30 = 280

```
  247
+  31
  278
```

Add ones.
Add tens.
Add hundreds.

Example H With renaming

Estimate: 400 + 900 = 1300

```
   11
  395
+ 897
 1292
```

Add ones.
Carry 1 into tens column. Add.
Carry 1 into hundreds column. Add.

Example I Three or more addends

Estimate: 900 + 0 + 100 = 1000

```
   12
  865
   39
+ 128
 1032
```

Add numbers in each column.
Carry when necessary.

The estimates given in Examples I and J are based on rounding each addend to the nearest hundred.

Example J Horizontal form

370 + 284 + 5458 + 43

Estimate:
400 + 300 + 5500 + 0 = 6200

```
  121
  370
  284
 5458
+  43
 6155
```

Rewrite as shown, lining up columns correctly.
Add. Carry when necessary.

Exercises

Set G

1. 34 + 55 — 89
2. 45 + 23 — 68
3. 371 + 28 — 399
4. 247 + 52 — 299
5. 423 + 502 — 925
6. 206 + 721 — 927
7. 8743 + 152 — 8895
8. 7485 + 113 — 7598
9. 3425 + 2561 — 5986
10. 4081 + 5417 — 9498
11. 14326 + 3051 — 17,377
12. 83458 + 2501 — 85,959

Set H

1. 37 + 29 — 66
2. 57 + 35 — 92
3. 847 + 58 — 905
4. 528 + 73 — 601
5. 65 + 435 — 500
6. 999 + 99 — 1098
7. 429 + 573 — 1002
8. 762 + 819 — 1581
9. 675 + 1345 — 2020
10. 258 + 5978 — 6236
11. 5647 + 6081 — 11,728
12. 9138 + 6927 — 16,065
13. 86457 + 5843 — 92,300
14. 98384 + 9528 — 107,912

Each exercise in Mixed Practice is the same type of exercise as in one of the other sets in the same lesson. The type is referenced next to the exercise.

Set I

1. $\begin{array}{r} 35 \\ 48 \\ +\ 79 \\ \hline 162 \end{array}$

2. $\begin{array}{r} 301 \\ 572 \\ +\ 648 \\ \hline 1521 \end{array}$

3. $\begin{array}{r} 55 \\ 62 \\ 39 \\ +\ 78 \\ \hline 234 \end{array}$

4. $\begin{array}{r} 567 \\ 42 \\ +\ 2311 \\ \hline 2920 \end{array}$

5. $\begin{array}{r} 2035 \\ 767 \\ 8 \\ +\ 25 \\ \hline 2835 \end{array}$

6. $\begin{array}{r} 3684 \\ 15 \\ 278 \\ +\ 54110 \\ \hline 58{,}087 \end{array}$

7. $\begin{array}{r} 78091 \\ 823 \\ 65 \\ +\ 4602 \\ \hline 83{,}581 \end{array}$

8. $\begin{array}{r} 249 \\ 71 \\ 1006 \\ 5 \\ +\ 987 \\ \hline 2318 \end{array}$

9. $\begin{array}{r} 8175 \\ 24 \\ 63 \\ 807 \\ +\ 248 \\ \hline 9317 \end{array}$

Set J

1. 510 + 6758
7268
2. 1007 + 573
1580
3. 34,795 + 6832
41,627
4. 18 + 234 + 5420
5672
5. 195 + 34 + 5764
5993
6. 21 + 63 + 95 + 72
251
7. 84 + 25 + 71 + 76
256
8. 16 + 4721 + 8 + 754
5499
9. 589 + 2309 + 9 + 876
3783
10. 389 + 4054 + 2003 + 18
6464
11. 7 + 68 + 112 + 4 + 199
390
12. 3 + 17 + 498 + 5 + 256
779

Mixed Practice

H 1. $\begin{array}{r} 149 \\ +\ 307 \\ \hline 456 \end{array}$

I 2. $\begin{array}{r} 82 \\ 67 \\ 425 \\ 13 \\ +\ 1482 \\ \hline 2069 \end{array}$

G 3. $\begin{array}{r} 64 \\ +\ 23 \\ \hline 87 \end{array}$

H 4. $\begin{array}{r} 465 \\ +\ 2439 \\ \hline 2904 \end{array}$

I 5. $\begin{array}{r} 37 \\ 55 \\ 84 \\ +\ 97 \\ \hline 273 \end{array}$

G 6. $\begin{array}{r} 521 \\ +\ 347 \\ \hline 868 \end{array}$

H 7. $\begin{array}{r} 2635 \\ +\ 794 \\ \hline 3429 \end{array}$

I 8. $\begin{array}{r} 147 \\ 2497 \\ 38 \\ +\ 355 \\ \hline 3037 \end{array}$

G 9. $\begin{array}{r} 235 \\ +\ 41 \\ \hline 276 \end{array}$

H 10. $\begin{array}{r} 8997 \\ +\ 3546 \\ \hline 12{,}543 \end{array}$

I 11. $\begin{array}{r} 57409 \\ 71 \\ 898 \\ 14 \\ +\ 5226 \\ \hline 63{,}618 \end{array}$

G 12. $\begin{array}{r} 3258 \\ +\ 6531 \\ \hline 9789 \end{array}$

H 13. $\begin{array}{r} 643 \\ +\ 1987 \\ \hline 2630 \end{array}$

I 14. $\begin{array}{r} 352 \\ 276 \\ 35 \\ 6 \\ +\ 9108 \\ \hline 9777 \end{array}$

H 15. $\begin{array}{r} 37408 \\ +\ 9653 \\ \hline 47{,}061 \end{array}$

I 16. $\begin{array}{r} 72 \\ 9 \\ 18 \\ 45 \\ 3 \\ +\ 12 \\ \hline 159 \end{array}$

J 17. 381 + 642
1023
J 18. 16 + 5 + 284
305
J 19. 932 + 57
989
J 20. 7460 + 865
8325
J 21. 47 + 38 + 29
114
J 22. 459 + 5530
5989
J 23. 28,007 + 6449
34,456
J 24. 12 + 345 + 6 + 7890
8253
J 25. 6537 + 2351
8888
J 26. 5689 + 7883
13,572
J 27. 8175 + 24 + 63 + 807 + 33
9102
J 28. 8 + 76 + 345 + 99
528
J 29. 624 + 5078 + 8855 + 25
14,582
J 30. 237 + 86 + 1414 + 7 + 88
1832

See Skills File, page 418, for more practice.

Objective: Subtract whole numbers.

Subtracting Whole Numbers

Example K Without renaming

Estimate: 5000 − 2000 = 3000

```
  4897
− 1625
  3272
```

Subtract ones, tens, hundreds, and thousands.

Remind students that they can check their answers by adding.

Example L With renaming

Estimate: 4000 − 800 = 3200

```
      1 12
  4 0 2 2
−   8 3 7
        5
```

Rename to get 10 more ones. Subtract ones.

```
 3 10 1 12
  4 0 2 2
−   8 3 7
        5
```

You need more tens. First rename to get 10 more hundreds.

```
    9 11
 3 10 1 12
  4 0 2 2
−   8 3 7
  3 1 8 5
```

Then rename to get 10 more tens. Subtract tens, hundreds, and thousands.

Example M Horizontal form

73,541 − 1867

Point out that the first number is the minuend and goes on top when the subtraction is written vertically.

Estimate: 74,000 − 2000 = 72,000

```
     14 13
   2  4  3 11
 7 3  5  4  1
−  1  8  6  7
 7 1  6  7  4
```

Rewrite 73,541 − 1867 as shown, lining up columns correctly. Subtract. Rename as necessary.

Exercises

Set K

1. 48 − 37 = 11
2. 56 − 24 = 32
3. 847 − 235 = 612
4. 655 − 241 = 414
5. 189 − 52 = 137
6. 296 − 65 = 231
7. 9427 − 8304 = 1123
8. 3974 − 1652 = 2322
9. 2864 − 743 = 2121
10. 4783 − 251 = 4532
11. 58206 − 17104 = 41,102
12. 28947 − 8006 = 20,941

Set L

1. 82 − 26 = 56
2. 94 − 75 = 19
3. 745 − 326 = 419
4. 481 − 157 = 324
5. 260 − 172 = 88
6. 836 − 798 = 38
7. 924 − 38 = 886
8. 871 − 85 = 786
9. 2613 − 893 = 1720
10. 5192 − 304 = 4888
11. 6235 − 470 = 5765
12. 1263 − 375 = 888
13. 7381 − 96 = 7285
14. 1903 − 56 = 1847

PROBLEM SOLVING
The applications on page 15–23 may be used anytime after this lesson.

15. 3105 − 921 = 2184

16. 1200 − 248 = 952

17. 4824 − 957 = 3867

18. 3204 − 579 = 2625

19. 8010 − 5478 = 2532

20. 4000 − 2181 = 1819

21. 25712 − 6333 = 19,379

22. 47821 − 8939 = 38,882

23. 43657 − 25489 = 18,168

24. 85163 − 37274 = 47,889

Set M

1. 72 − 58 (14)
2. 96 − 37 (59)
3. 325 − 64 (261)
4. 531 − 46 (485)
5. 127 − 35 (92)
6. 250 − 19 (231)
7. 648 − 59 (589)
8. 401 − 83 (318)
9. 170 − 156 (14)
10. 574 − 231 (343)
11. 4215 − 77 (4138)
12. 5421 − 85 (5336)
13. 8324 − 572 (7752)
14. 4209 − 695 (3514)
15. 8654 − 1333 (7321)
16. 7543 − 1928 (5615)
17. 36,104 − 5237 (30,867)
18. 47,312 − 4859 (42,453)

Mixed Practice

K 1. 368 − 142 = 226

L 2. 7025 − 1819 = 5206

L 3. 4608 − 345 = 4263

K 4. 8426 − 104 = 8322

L 5. 75490 − 682 = 74,808

L 6. 18406 − 9520 = 8886

L 7. 7123 − 4658 = 2465

L 8. 53400 − 38642 = 14,758

L 9. 9111 − 482 = 8629

M 10. 6471 − 583 (5888)

M 11. 65 − 38 (27)

M 12. 922 − 474 (448)

M 13. 5300 − 61 (5239)

M 14. 847 − 96 (751)

M 15. 3508 − 752 (2756)

M 16. 789 − 37 (752)

M 17. 462 − 85 (377)

M 18. 92 − 53 (39)

M 19. 4916 − 258 (4658)

L 20. 6152 − 394 = 5758

K 21. 597 − 243 = 354

L 22. 5746 − 4089 = 1657

L 23. 39721 − 539 = 39,182

L 24. 60000 − 9387 = 50,613

L 25. 403 − 86 = 317

L 26. 39584 − 768 = 38,816

L 27. 60241 − 59946 = 295

L 28. 60035 − 56174 = 3861

M 29. 9261 − 6875 (2386)

M 30. 46,031 − 999 (45,032)

M 31. 86,054 − 54,681 (31,373)

M 32. 3712 − 872 (2840)

M 33. 34,123 − 7777 (26,346)

M 34. 8007 − 79 (7928)

M 35. 45,149 − 26,873 (18,276)

M 36. 273 − 195 (78)

M 37. 80,005 − 4376 (75,629)

M 38. 73,020 − 24,561 (48,459)

See Skills File, page 418, for more practice.

Objective: Compute following order of operations involving addition and subtraction.

Using Order of Operations

Example N Without parentheses

55 − 12 + 3 — Add or subtract in order from left to right.

43 + 3

46

Point out the importance of working from left to right. In this case, if the addition were done first, the answer would be 40.

Example O With parentheses

15 − (8 + 3) — First do operations within parentheses. Then add or subtract.

15 − 11

4

Emphasize that operations inside parentheses must be performed first. You might give students exercises such as these:

Insert parentheses, if necessary, to make each statement true.

1. 25 − 16 − 8 = 17 [25 − (16 − 8)]
2. 31 − 10 − 9 = 12 [not necessary]
3. 42 + 6 − 3 = 45 [not necessary]
4. 17 − 12 + 3 = 2 [17 − (12 + 3)]
5. 70 − 30 + 5 = 35 [70 − (30 + 5)]
6. 61 − 57 − 18 = 22 [61 − (57 − 18)]
7. 84 + 16 + 3 = 103 [not necessary]
8. 52 + 20 − 17 = 55 [not necessary]

Exercises

Set N

1. 32 − 7 − 18
   7
2. 2 + 25 − 11
   16
3. 13 − 10 + 22
   25
4. 45 + 6 + 19
   70
5. 60 − 3 − 17
   40
6. 4 + 26 − 15
   15
7. 37 − 10 + 5
   32
8. 41 + 17 − 2
   56
9. 75 − 35 − 16
   24
10. 12 + 3 + 29
    44
11. 63 − 27 + 4
    40
12. 7 + 52 − 36
    23
13. 81 + 13 − 9
    85
14. 23 − 19 + 38
    42
15. 64 − 35 − 12
    17
16. 11 + 43 − 26
    28
17. 6 + 55 − 9
    52
18. 59 − 10 + 8
    57
19. 16 + 53 − 60
    9
20. 3 + 71 − 48
    26
21. 85 − 23 − 51
    11
22. 94 − 64 + 70
    100
23. 19 + 380 − 84
    315
24. 264 − 21 − 97
    146
25. 79 + 126 − 35
    170
26. 427 − 92 − 16
    319
27. 57 + 95 − 121 + 4
    35
28. 350 − 45 − 6 + 1
    300

Set O

1. 25 − (17 − 4)
12
2. (28 − 16) + 5
17
3. (36 − 9) − 20
7
4. 24 − (7 + 6)
11
5. 51 + (10 − 8)
53
6. (35 − 20) − 9
6
7. (6 + 41) + 75
122
8. 48 − (27 + 12)
9
9. (83 − 64) + 5
24
10. (52 − 18) − 4
30
11. 9 + (18 + 140)
167
12. 39 − (51 − 48)
36
13. 66 − (23 + 15)
28
14. (12 + 71) − 46
37
15. (73 − 68) − 5
0
16. 54 + (9 + 27)
90
17. (35 + 14) + 62
111
18. 53 + (91 − 89)
55
19. 50 − (97 − 68)
21
20. (15 + 8) + 16
39
21. (131 + 25) + 6
162
22. 75 − (44 − 19)
50
23. 125 − (66 + 47)
12
24. (230 − 85) + 152
297
25. 99 + (780 − 371)
508
26. (602 − 98) + 75
579
27. 30 − (964 − 959)
25
28. 340 − (56 + 82)
202

Mixed Practice

N 1. 15 − 8 + 6
13
N 2. 49 + 8 − 21
36
O 3. (49 + 8) − 21
36
O 4. 79 − (23 + 12)
44
N 5. 61 + 83 − 14
130
O 6. (81 − 65) − 8
8
N 7. 16 + 14 − 30
0
O 8. 4 + (4 − 4)
4
O 9. (35 − 8) − 17
10
N 10. 12 − 8 + 12
16
O 11. (56 − 29) + 9
36
O 12. 15 − (8 − 2)
9
O 13. 68 − (13 − 9)
64
N 14. 12 + 12 + 12
36
N 15. 15 − 9 + 16
22
O 16. 43 − (12 + 18)
13
O 17. (27 + 8) − 35
0
N 18. 34 + 16 + 8
58
N 19. 25 − 20 − 3
2
O 20. 25 − (20 − 3)
8
O 21. (25 − 20) − 3
2
N 22. 62 + 18 + 7
87
N 23. 82 + 31 − 61
52
O 24. (140 + 8) − 29
119
O 25. 61 − (37 + 2)
22
O 26. 118 − (29 + 41)
48
N 27. 46 + 8 − 12
42
O 28. 100 − (80 + 19)
1

BREAK TIME

Arrange these four dominoes in the square pattern shown below so that the total number of dots on each side of the square is the same.
12 dots on each side.

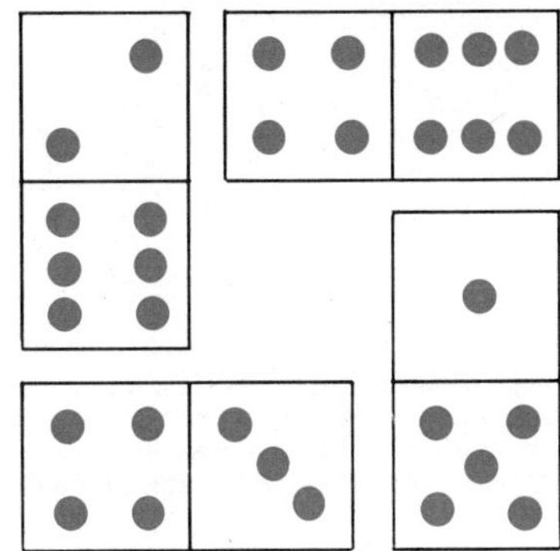

Break Times are recreational puzzles that occur in the skills lessons of each chapter. You can use them in a variety of ways—assign them to students who complete their regular work early; use them for class discussion; create a puzzle corner in your classroom; have problem-solving contests. Encourage students of all ability levels to try the Break Times.

Objective: Solve addition and subtraction equations.

Solving Addition and Subtraction Equations

Example P Missing addend

Find n.

Point out that the variable represents a number. Any letter could be used for the variable.

$$n + 47 = 83$$

$$n + 47 - 47 = 83 - 47$$

$$n = 36$$

47 is added to n. To undo the addition and get n by itself on one side of the equation, subtract 47 from $n + 47$. To keep the equation in balance, also subtract 47 from 83.

Check:
Does 36 + 47 = 83? *Yes*

Check by substituting 36 for n in the original equation.

Example Q Missing minuend

Find x.

Encourage students to examine the equation before solving for x. Point out that the value of x must be greater than 137.

$$x - 86 = 137$$

$$x - 86 + 86 = 137 + 86$$

$$x = 223$$

86 is subtracted from x. To undo the subtraction, add 86 to $x - 86$. Also add 86 to 137.

Check:
Does 223 − 86 = 137? *Yes*

Check by substituting 223 for x in the original equation.

Solving simple equations is introduced in this lesson and on pages 56–57 so that students will be able to work with variables when needed. Formulas, tables with variables, and equations are used in various chapters throughout the book. A more complete study of solving equations is given in Chapter 14.

Exercises

Set P

Find each missing number.

1. $x + 18 = 53$ $x = 35$
2. $q + 35 = 96$ $q = 61$
3. $a + 26 = 51$ $a = 25$
4. $c + 19 = 43$ $c = 24$
5. $71 + t = 83$ $t = 12$
6. $23 + n = 45$ $n = 22$
7. $54 = d + 29$ $d = 25$
8. $104 = 82 + b$ $b = 22$
9. $79 = z + 22$ $z = 57$
10. $93 = r + 58$ $r = 35$
11. $753 + g = 817$ $g = 64$
12. $k + 247 = 1258$ $k = 1011$

Set Q

Find each missing number.

1. $k - 8 = 25$ $k = 33$
2. $b - 25 = 13$ $b = 38$
3. $a - 9 = 14$ $a = 23$
4. $d - 19 = 8$ $d = 27$
5. $n - 52 = 87$ $n = 139$
6. $v - 37 = 7$ $v = 44$
7. $94 = g - 35$ $g = 129$
8. $68 = c - 15$ $c = 83$
9. $31 = y - 59$ $y = 90$
10. $14 = f - 71$ $f = 85$
11. $x - 864 = 21$ $x = 885$
12. $t - 347 = 899$ $t = 1246$

Mixed Practice

Find each missing number.

P **1.** $c + 29 = 50$ c = 21

P **2.** $21 + p = 49$ p = 28

Q **3.** $d - 42 = 44$ d = 86

Q **4.** $r - 36 = 22$ r = 58

P **5.** $73 = h + 46$ h = 27

Q **6.** $98 = a - 5$ a = 103

Q **7.** $h - 71 = 52$ h = 123

P **8.** $g + 15 = 80$ g = 65

Q **9.** $86 = j - 71$ j = 157

P **10.** $25 + x = 91$ x = 66

P **11.** $45 = 32 + v$ v = 13

P **12.** $29 + y = 83$ y = 54

Q **13.** $b - 52 = 0$ b = 52

Q **14.** $d - 56 = 34$ d = 90

P **15.** $k + 59 = 94$ k = 35

Q **16.** $38 = w - 20$ w = 58

P **17.** $a + 41 = 59$ a = 18

Q **18.** $p - 73 = 46$ p = 119

P **19.** $w + 42 = 55$ w = 13

P **20.** $63 + f = 110$ f = 47

Q **21.** $n - 8 = 106$ n = 114

Q **22.** $28 = s - 33$ s = 61

P **23.** $205 + a = 525$ a = 320

P **24.** $449 = b + 287$ b = 162

Q **25.** $w - 63 = 282$ w = 345

P **26.** $52 + h = 267$ h = 215

P **27.** $c + 89 = 132$ c = 43

Q **28.** $x - 147 = 53$ x = 200

BREAK TIME

How many cubes will balance with the sphere on the third scale?
3 cubes

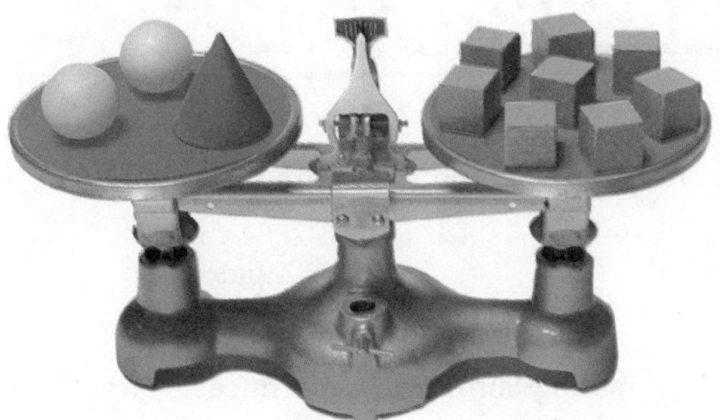

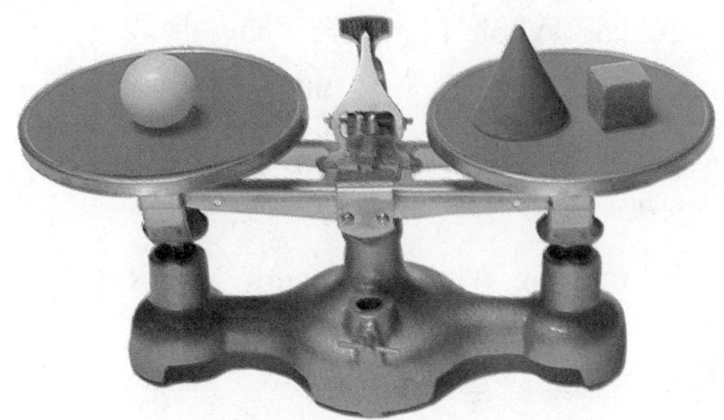

SKILLS POSTTEST

Number of test items - 17

Number missed	1	2	3	4	5	6	7	8
Percent correct	94	88	82	76	71	65	59	53

SKILL Rounding Whole Numbers *page 4*

A Round 762 to the nearest ten.
760

B Round 2584 to the nearest hundred.
2600

C Round 37,560 to the nearest thousand.
38,000

SKILL Estimating Sums and Differences *page 5*

D Estimate. $745 + 198$
900

E Estimate. $6128 - 2855$
3000

F Estimate. $214 + 18 + 5$
240
Answer may vary.

SKILL Adding Whole Numbers *pages 6–7*

G $125 + 34$
159

H $596 + 217$
813

I $193 + 54 + 86$
333

J $1237 + 82 + 569 + 98$
1986

SKILL Subtracting Whole Numbers *pages 8–9*

K $5368 - 4147$
1221

L $3605 - 927$
2678

M $14{,}312 - 2523$
11,789

SKILL Using Order of Operations *pages 10–11*

N $53 - 8 + 6$
51

O $27 - (9 + 5)$
13

SKILL Solving Addition and Subtraction Equations *pages 12–13*

P Find x.

$x + 19 = 75$
$x = 56$

Q Find y.

$y - 23 = 62$
$y = 85$

The Posttest parallels the Pretest, item for item. Students who miss items on the Posttest can refer to the pages listed to find a worked-out example and a set of practice exercises.

Problem Solving

CONSUMER APPLICATIONS

Objective: Solve problems involving addition and subtraction of whole numbers.

In this lesson students compute the total number of calories and grams of carbohydrates for a given menu.

See page 1 of *Problem-Solving Masters.*

Three types of Problem-Solving lessons occur after the Skills lessons in each chapter: Consumer Applications, Career Applications, and Developing Strategies. The problems in these lessons use the skills from that chapter and from previous chapters.

Counting Calories and Carbohydrates

Bob wants to maintain his weight. His doctor told him that his daily food intake should provide about 2800 calories and about 100 grams of carbohydrate.

1. Find the totals in each column for Monday and Tuesday.

Monday		
Food	Calories	Grams of carbohydrate
2 fried eggs	200	0
3 strips of bacon	240	0
1 glass of milk	160	12
1 buttered toast	110	11
1 beef patty	250	0
2 slices of cheese	220	2
2 glasses of milk	320	24
2 pork chops	600	0
1 salad	150	3
1 serving of corn	80	18
2 apples	160	40
Totals	2490	110

Tuesday		
Food	Calories	Grams of carbohydrate
1 bowl of cereal	230	36
1 muffin	145	28
1 orange	77	19
1 meat sandwich	292	24
1 glass of milk	160	12
1 bowl of soup	150	20
1 banana	80	21
1 macaroni dinner	201	34
1 lemonade	60	15
1 fruit salad	70	18
1 granola bar	120	15
Totals	1585	242

2. On Monday, Bob was under his recommended food intake by how many calories?
310 calories

3. On Tuesday, he was over his limit by how many grams of carbohydrate?
142 grams

4. On Wednesday, Bob started to find the totals for his breakfast and lunch. For each day below, find how many calories and grams of carbohydrate Bob can have for supper.

	Totals for breakfast and lunch				
	Wednesday	Thursday	Friday	Saturday	Sunday
Calories	1785	1965	1450	2130	1535
Grams of carbohydrate	62	53	48	59	73
Supper Calories	1015	835	1350	670	1265
Supper Grams	38	47	52	41	27

Problem Solving

CONSUMER APPLICATIONS

See page 2 of *Problem-Solving Masters*.

Objective: Solve problems involving addition and subtraction of whole numbers.

In this lesson students find the difference in travel costs using various forms of transportation.

Comparing Costs of Traveling

Mr. and Mrs. Irwin are planning a trip from New York to Miami to visit friends. They want to find the most economical way to travel.

Approximate round-trip costs for two adults are listed below. Add to find the total cost for each form of transportation.

NEW YORK TO MIAMI

1. *Airplane*

Coach fare	$768
Meals	No charge

$768

2. *Train*

Coach fare	$342
Meals	$63

$405

3. *Bus*

Fare	$392
Meals	$59

$451

Gasoline and maintenance costs listed for the automobile trips are based on an average cost of 28¢ per mile. Remind students that this includes more than just gasoline and immediate repairs.

4. *Automobile*

Gasoline and maintenance	$732
Tolls	$20
Meals	$116
Lodging	$136

$1004

5. Which form of travel is most economical?
Train

How much money would the Irwins save traveling

6. by bus instead of by automobile?
$553

7. by bus instead of by airplane?
$317

8. by train instead of by airplane?
$363

9. by train instead of by automobile?
$599

10. The trip from New York to Miami takes about 3 hours by airplane and about 48 hours by automobile. How much time would the Irwins save traveling round trip by airplane rather than by automobile?
90 hours

The method of travel chosen determines other expenses. These factors must be taken into consideration when finding the total cost of a trip.

Approximate round-trip costs for two adults are listed below. Find the total cost for each form of transportation.

WASHINGTON TO DENVER

11. *Airplane* (4 hours one way)
Coach fare $944
Meals No charge
$944

12. *Train* (42 hours one way)
Coach fare $492
Meals $98
$590

13. *Bus* (44 hours one way)
Fare $614
Meals $68
$682

14. *Automobile* (72 hours one way)

Gasoline and maintenance	$905
Tolls	$6
Meals	$174
Lodging	$136

$1221

15. How much money could a couple save traveling round trip by bus rather than by automobile?
$539

16. How much time could a couple save traveling round trip by bus rather than by automobile?
56 hours

Approximate round-trip costs for two adults are listed below. Find the total cost for each form of transportation.

CHICAGO TO SAN FRANCISCO

17. *Airplane* (5 hours one way)
Coach fare $1392
Meals No charge
$1392

18. *Train* (50 hours one way)
Coach fare $502
Meals $109
$611

19. *Bus* (53 hours one way)
Fare $700
Meals $123
$823

20. *Automobile* (120 hours one way)

Gasoline and maintenance	$1199
Tolls	$1
Meals	$290
Lodging	$272

$1762

21. How much money could a couple save traveling round trip by airplane rather than by automobile?
$370

22. How much time could a couple save traveling round trip by airplane rather than by automobile?
230 hours

Problem Solving

CONSUMER APPLICATIONS

Objective: Solve problems involving subtraction of whole numbers.

In this lesson students find the amount of real buying power for a certain income, when given the amounts of taxes and the decrease in buying power for one year.

Finding Real Buying Power

Each year, your annual net income will buy about 10% less than it did the year before.

You may wish to discuss such terms as inflation and recession. Point out that during inflationary periods, the value of the dollar decreases. When the inflation rate is high, the decrease in buying power is greater than 10%.

Ann Chong is a student with a part-time job. Her gross income last year was $6000. If her salary and taxes remain the same this year, you can find her real buying power for this year by following these steps.

Gross income	$6000
Subtract federal tax.	− 427
Income less federal tax	$5573
Subtract social security tax.	− 399
Net income	$5174
Subtract 10% of net income for decrease in buying power.	− 517
Real buying power	$4657

The federal income tax figures used in this lesson are based on 1980 tax tables for a single person, not head of household.

The social security tax is figured at the rate of 6.65% and rounded to the nearest dollar.

This year Ann's net income will be $5174. But $5174 this year will buy goods and services worth only $4657 last year.

Complete the table to find the real buying power for these incomes.

	Gross income	Federal tax	Income less federal tax	Social security tax	Net income	Decrease in buying power	Real buying power
	$6000	$427	$5573	$399	$5174	$517	$4657
1.	$7000	$607	$6393	$466	$5927	$593	$5334
2.	$8000	$792	$7208	$532	$6676	$668	$6008
3.	$9000	$982	$8018	$599	$7419	$742	$6677
4.	$10,000	$1182	$8818	$665	$8153	$815	$7338
5.	$11,000	$1392	$9608	$732	$8876	$888	$7988
6.	$12,000	$1609	$10,391	$798	$9593	$959	$8634
7.	$13,000	$1849	$11,151	$865	$10,286	$1029	$9257
8.	$14,000	$2092	$11,908	$931	$10,977	$1098	$9879
9.	$15,000	$2352	$12,648	$998	$11,650	$1165	$10,485
10.	$16,000	$2613	$13,387	$1064	$12,323	$1232	$11,091
11.	$17,000	$2913	$14,087	$1131	$12,956	$1296	$11,660
12.	$18,000	$3213	$14,787	$1197	$13,590	$1359	$12,231
13.	$19,000	$3513	$15,487	$1264	$14,223	$1422	$12,801
14.	$20,000	$3829	$16,171	$1330	$14,841	$1484	$13,357

Problem Solving

CAREER APPLICATIONS

Objective: Solve problems involving addition and subtraction of whole numbers.

In this lesson students solve problems involving degree-days and deliveries of heating oil.

Dispatcher

See the Careers Chart beginning on page 426 for more information about the careers in this cluster.

Career Cluster: Business Detail

Ms. Liester is a dispatcher for a fuel company. In order to determine when heating oil should be delivered, she uses a unit called a **degree-day.**

If the average daily temperature is less than 18 degrees Celsius (18°C), the number of degree-days is found by using this formula.

$$18 - \text{Average temperature} = \text{Number of degree-days}$$

On October 5 the average temperature was 12°C.

$18 - 12 = 6$

Six degree-days were counted for October 5.

Find the number of degree-days for each date.

	Date	Average temperature	
1.	October 7	13°C	5 degree-days
2.	October 8	17°C	1 degree-days
3.	October 9	16°C	2 degree-days
4.	October 10	11°C	7 degree-days
5.	October 11	4°C	14 degree-days
6.	October 12	9°C	9 degree-days
7.	October 13	0°C	18 degree-days

8. Find the total number of degree-days for October 7–13.
56 degree-days

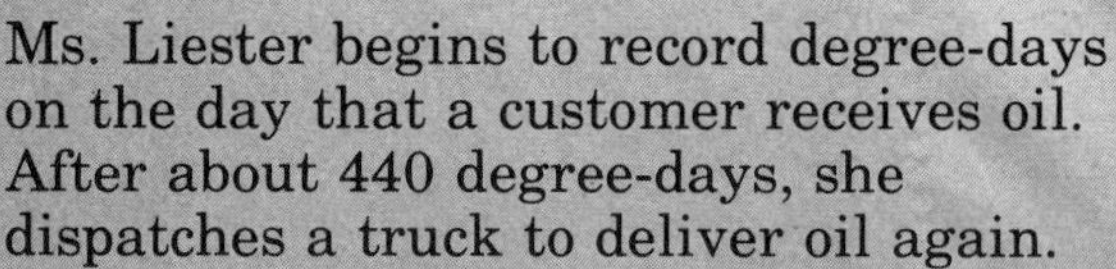

Ms. Liester begins to record degree-days on the day that a customer receives oil. After about 440 degree-days, she dispatches a truck to deliver oil again.

9. The list below shows the number of degree-days recorded for each week of January. Find the total.
428 degree-days

Week of	Number of degree-days
January 4–10	75
January 11–17	120
January 18–24	109
January 25–31	124

10. The Kaylor home received heating oil on January 4. After January 31, how many more degree-days will be recorded before oil is delivered again?
12 degree-days

11. The Steins received oil January 18. After January 31, how many more degree-days will be recorded before oil is delivered again?
207 degree-days

See pages 57–58 of *Problem-Solving Masters.*

Ms. Liester uses truck drivers' tickets to find the amount of heating oil that has been delivered.

Each truck has a meter that tells the number of liters of oil left in the truck. The driver reads the meter after each delivery.

Find the amount of oil delivered to each address and the total amount delivered by each truck.

The amounts of oil delivered are given in liters.

	Truck 31			
	Address	Meter before	Meter after	Amount delivered
12.	514 Locust St.	9475	8417	1058
13.	268 Locust St.	8417	7605	812
14.	301 Holly Ave.	7605	6671	934
15.	915 Maple Ave.	6671	5968	703
16.	362 Spruce Dr.	5968	4833	1135
17.	890 Pine St.	4833	3481	1352
18.			Total	5994

	Truck 56			
	Address	Meter before	Meter after	Amount delivered
19.	3910 Ellis	8320	7348	972
20.	1415 Frolic	7348	6050	1298
21.	1508 Baldwin	6050	5067	983
22.	2802 Ellis	5067	3972	1095
23.	500 Grand	3972	3263	709
24.	652 Lewis	3263	2276	987
25.			Total	6044

The meter referred to here is called a Preset Quantrol meter. It works like an odometer on a car, but it counts backward from maximum quantity to minimum quantity.

Problem Solving

DEVELOPING STRATEGIES

The last lesson in each chapter deals with developing strategies for solving problems.

Objective: Solve problems by reading a scale.

In this lesson students compare the number of kilowatt-hours used during each of the first six months of successive years.

Tactic: Reading a Scale

Daniel Cruz is concerned about conserving energy. He has decided to compare the amount of electricity used this year with the amount used last year. The electric meter on the Cruz family's house measures the number of kilowatt-hours used. The meters below show the readings for January first and February first of this year. When reading the meter, Daniel records the locations of the pointers from left to right. If a pointer is between two numbers, he uses the smaller number. If a pointer is between 9 and 0, he thinks of the 0 as 10, and then uses the smaller number, 9.

January 1

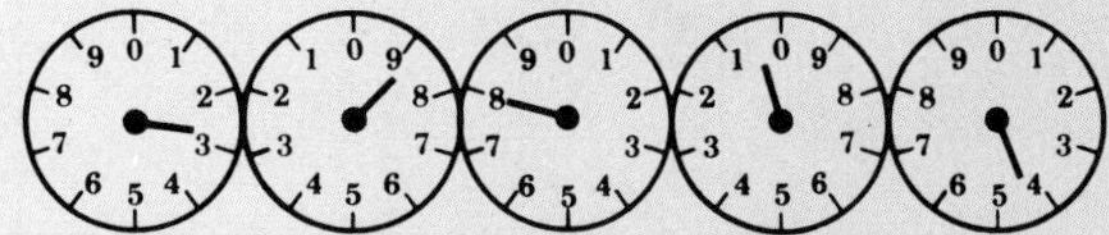

February 1

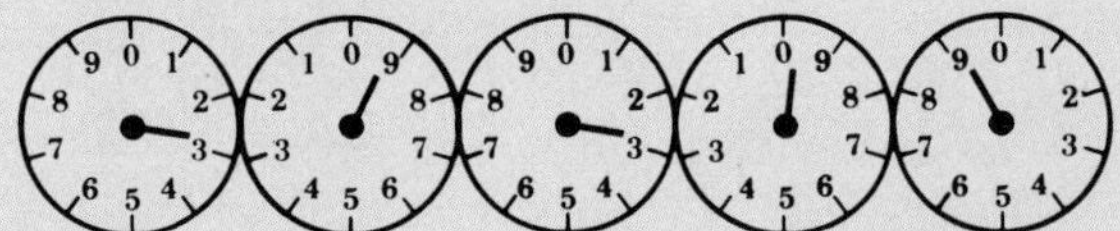

Problem

Daniel's records show that the family used 534 kilowatt-hours during January last year. How much less electricity did they use during January this year?

Solution

In his strategy for solving this problem, Daniel used the tactic of reading scales. He asked himself these questions.

a. How much electricity did the family use in January last year? This information is given in the problem. — 534 kilowatt-hours

b. How much electricity did the family use in January this year? Read the meters and subtract.

$$\begin{array}{r} 29299 \leftarrow \text{Feb. 1} \\ -\ 28804 \leftarrow \text{Jan. 1} \\ \hline 495 \end{array}$$

c. How much less electricity did the family use in January this year than in January last year? Subtract.

$$\begin{array}{r} 534 \leftarrow \text{last year} \\ -\ 495 \leftarrow \text{this year} \\ \hline 39 \end{array}$$

Conclusion: The family used 39 kilowatt-hours less in January this year than in January last year.

The number of dials on electric meters varies, but the method of reading the meter is consistent. Point out to the student that the dials have alternating faces. That is, the numbers are in a clockwise position on the first dial, counterclockwise on the second, and so on.

See page 3 of *Problem-Solving Masters.*

Related Problems

Read the meter for each month shown for this year.

1. March 1 29748

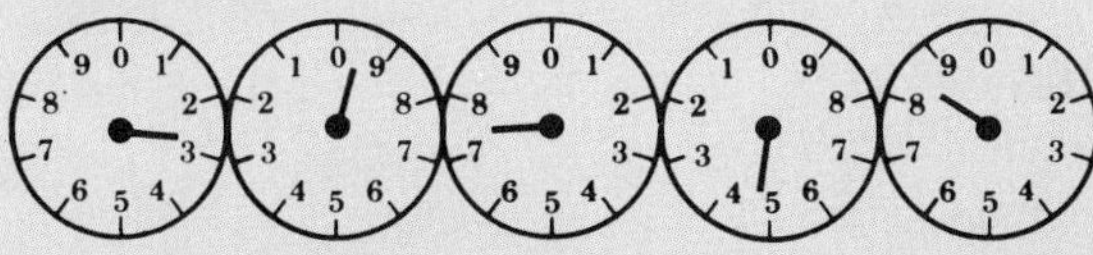

2. April 1 30170

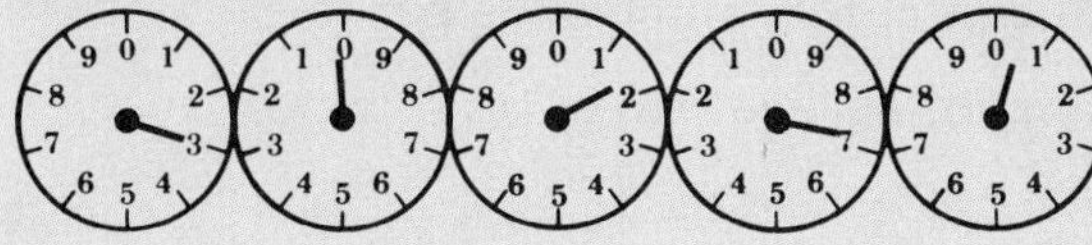

3. May 1 30602

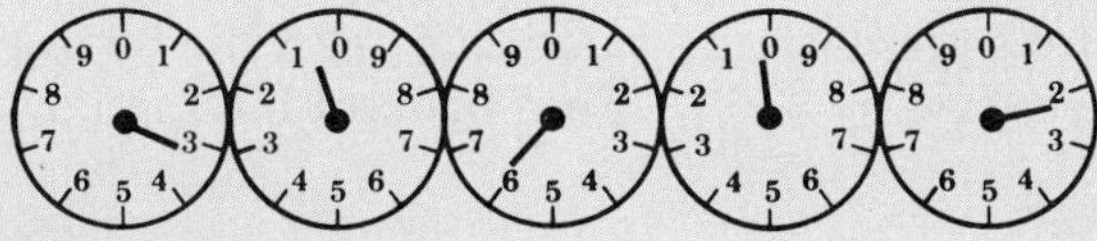

4. June 1 31084

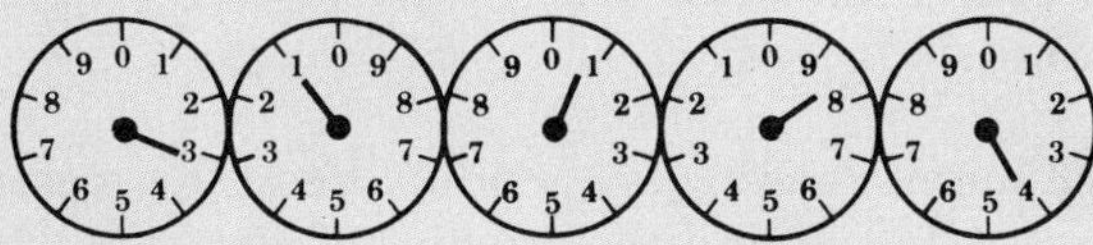

5. July 1 31653

This list shows the number of kilowatt-hours used during each of the first six months of last year.

January	534	April	458
February	483	May	517
March	446	June	603

For each month, find how much less electricity the Cruz family used this year than last year. Use the list above and the meter readings for this year.

6. February 34 kilowatt-hours
7. March 24 kilowatt-hours
8. April 26 kilowatt-hours
9. May 35 kilowatt-hours
10. June 34 kilowatt-hours

Extension

11. How much less electricity did the Cruz family use during the first six months of this year than during the first six months of last year?
192 kilowatt-hours

CHAPTER 1 TEST

Number of test items - 22

Number missed	1	2	3	4	5	6	7	8	9	10	11
Percent correct	95	91	86	82	77	73	68	64	59	55	50

The letter in color next to a test item indicates the skills exercise type that is being tested.

A **1.** Round 643 to the nearest ten.
640

B **2.** Round 9781 to the nearest hundred.
9800

C **3.** Round 28,561 to the nearest thousand.
29,000

D **4.** Estimate. $629 + 857$
1500

E **5.** Estimate. $5621 - 2529$
3000

F **6.** Estimate. $826 + 15 + 4$
850 Answers may vary.

G **7.**
$$\begin{array}{r} 173 \\ +\ 24 \\ \hline \end{array}$$
197

H **8.**
$$\begin{array}{r} 596 \\ +348 \\ \hline \end{array}$$
944

I **9.**
$$\begin{array}{r} 12 \\ 998 \\ +\ 47 \\ \hline \end{array}$$
1057

J **10.** $3651 + 7 + 92 + 458$
4208

K **11.**
$$\begin{array}{r} 5983 \\ -3842 \\ \hline \end{array}$$
2141

L **12.**
$$\begin{array}{r} 3017 \\ -\ 428 \\ \hline \end{array}$$
2589

M **13.** $35{,}162 - 6704$
28,458

N **14.** $74 - 6 + 3$
71

O **15.** $27 - (15 + 8)$
4

P **16.** Find d. $37 + d = 72$
$d = 35$

Q **17.** Find t. $t - 21 = 17$
$t = 38$

18. Find the total number of calories.
614 calories

Food	Calories
1 glass of milk	160
1 ham sandwich	216
1 serving of corn	88
1 salad	150

19. Find the total cost of this automobile trip.
$321

Gasoline and maintenance	$195
Meals	$58
Lodging	$68

20. Bill's net income for last year was $16,368. If his gross income and taxes remain the same this year, his buying power will decrease by $1637. Find his real buying power for this year.
$14,731

21. The meter on an oil truck read 2645 liters before an oil delivery and 1798 liters after the oil delivery. How many liters of oil were delivered?
847 liters

22. On July 1 the meter reading was 84627. Read the meter below for August 1, and find the amount of electricity used in July.
854 kilowatt-hours

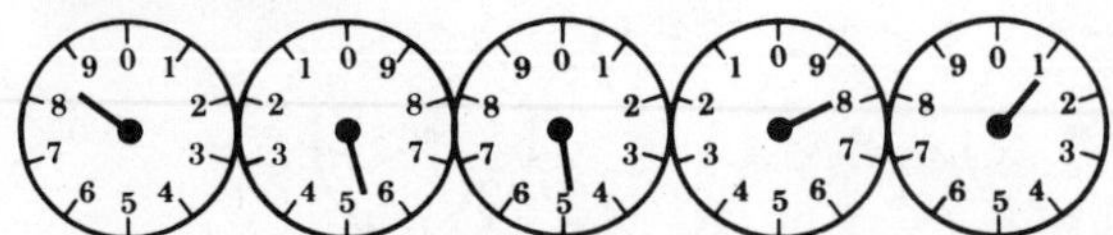

The Chapter Test covers both the skills lessons and the applications in a chapter. On this test, items 1-17 correspond to exercise types A–Q in Chapter 1. Test items 18–22 correspond to the applications found on pages 15–23.

For each Chapter Test in the student's text, there is an alternate form of the test in the *Test Masters*. The alternate form matches the Chapter Test, item for item. The alternate form of the Chapter 1 Test can be found on pages 1-2 of the *Test Masters*.

CHAPTER 2 Multiplying Whole Numbers

SKILLS PRETEST

Number of test items - 17

Number missed	1	2	3	4	5	6	7	8
Percent correct	94	88	82	76	71	65	59	53

SKILL Multiplying with Multiples of 10, 100, and 1000 *page 26*

A 30×1000
30,000

B 6000×700
4,200,000

SKILL Estimating Products *page 27*

C Estimate. 9×495
4500

D Estimate. 834×3786
3,200,000

SKILL Multiplying with One-Digit Multipliers *pages 28–29*

E 82×4
328

F 59×7
413

G 9084×6
54,504

H 8×342
2736

SKILL Multiplying with Two-Digit Multipliers *pages 30–31*

I 67×50
3350

J 79×24
1896

K 8126×36
292,536

L 45×649
29,205

SKILL Multiplying with Three-Digit Multipliers *pages 32–33*

M 843×600
505,800

N 279×704
196,416

O 531×495
262,845

SKILL Using Order of Operations *pages 34–35*

P $8(7) - 3(6)$
38

Q $3(9) - 6(1 + 3) + 7$
10

Objective: Multiply multiples of powers of 10.

Multiplying with Multiples of 10, 100, and 1000

Example A
Multiplying with a power of 10

70×1000

$70 \times 1000 = 70{,}000$

1 zero — 3 zeros — 4 zeros

The number of zeros in the product equals the total number of zeros in the factors.

Example B
Multiplying with multiples of powers of 10

6000×400

$6000 \times 400 = 2{,}400{,}000$

3 zeros — 2 zeros — 5 zeros

Multiply the nonzero digits. Then write as many zeros in the product as there are in all the factors.

Point out a case like 40 × 500 in which the product of the nonzero digits ends in zero. This zero is not included in the total number of zeros in all the factors.

$40 \times 500 = 20{,}000$

1 zero — 2 zeros — 3 zeros

Exercises

Encourage students to do the exercises mentally without rewriting them in vertical form.

Set A

1. 100×80 8000
2. 6×1000 6000
3. 10×10 100
4. 70×100 7000
5. 1000×5 5000
6. 100×100 10,000
7. 200×1000 200,000
8. 1000×1000 1,000,000
9. 46×100 4600
10. 1000×72 72,000
11. 5000×1000 5,000,000
12. 1000×300 300,000
13. $10{,}000 \times 1000$ 10,000,000
14. 4000×1000 4,000,000
15. $100 \times 80{,}000$ 8,000,000
16. $10{,}000 \times 900$ 9,000,000

Set B

1. 30×40 1200
2. 70×20 1400
3. 600×6 3600
4. 4000×70 280,000
5. 60×3000 180,000
6. 8×800 6400
7. 200×50 10,000
8. 500×700 350,000
9. 50×600 30,000
10. $30 \times 70{,}000$ 2,100,000
11. $90{,}000 \times 60$ 5,400,000
12. 600×800 480,000
13. 400×5000 2,000,000
14. $90{,}000 \times 300$ 27,000,000
15. $700 \times 80{,}000$ 56,000,000
16. 8000×500 4,000,000

Mixed Practice

B 1. 90×200 18,000
A 2. $50{,}000 \times 10$ 500,000
A 3. 100×400 40,000
B 4. 600×9000 5,400,000
B 5. 7000×6000 42,000,000
A 6. 100×100 10,000
A 7. 68×1000 68,000
B 8. 5000×2000 10,000,000
A 9. 1000×1000 1,000,000
B 10. 800×30 24,000
B 11. 600×5000 3,000,000
A 12. 1000×35 35,000
A 13. $60 \times 10{,}000$ 600,000
B 14. $70{,}000 \times 900$ 63,000,000
B 15. $400 \times 80{,}000$ 32,000,000
A 16. 100×300 30,000

Objective: Estimate products using rounded numbers.

Estimating Products

Example C Rounding one factor

Estimate. 4×59

4×59

$\downarrow \quad \downarrow$

$4 \times 60 = 240$

Round to get factors that have one nonzero digit.

Then multiply.

$4 \times 59 \approx 240$

Example D Rounding both factors

Estimate. 308×2915

308×2915

$\downarrow \quad \downarrow$

$300 \times 3000 = 900{,}000$

Round each factor to get a number with one nonzero digit.

Then multiply.

$308 \times 2915 \approx 900{,}000$

Exercises

Set C

Estimate each product.

1. 4×39 160
2. 3×91 270
3. 78×5 400
4. 51×4 200
5. 696×6 4200
6. 9×805 7200
7. 8×606 4800
8. 7×893 6300
9. 616×3 1800
10. 4×789 3200
11. 6×5938 36,000
12. 7092×5 35,000
13. 9045×8 72,000
14. 7×6953 49,000

Set D

Estimate each product.

1. 37×22 800
2. 91×59 5400
3. 569×73 42,000
4. 304×41 12,000
5. 68×7156 490,000
6. 52×4893 250,000
7. 93×285 27,000
8. 42×856 36,000
9. 596×497 300,000
10. 294×718 210,000
11. 818×386 320,000
12. 792×608 480,000
13. 5032×904 4,500,000
14. 795×6983 5,600,000

Mixed Practice

Estimate each product.

D 1. 52×28 1500
D 2. 378×64 24,000
C 3. 7×794 5600
D 4. 89×3989 360,000
C 5. 9057×8 72,000
D 6. 468×6435 3,000,000
D 7. 379×421 160,000
C 8. 4×6892 28,000
D 9. 504×4038 2,000,000
D 10. 77×83 6400
D 11. 32×5687 180,000
C 12. 592×6 3600
D 13. 82×287 24,000
D 14. 723×874 630,000

Objective: Multiply whole numbers by a one-digit multiplier.

Multiplying with One-Digit Multipliers

Example E
Two-digit multiplicand, without renaming

Estimate: 2 × 60 = 120

$$\begin{array}{r} 62 \\ \times\ 2 \\ \hline 124 \end{array}$$

2 × 2 = 4
2 × 6 = 12

Example F
Two-digit multiplicand, with renaming

Estimate: 5 × 50 = 250

$$\begin{array}{r} 49 \\ \times\ 5 \\ \hline 245 \end{array}$$

5 × 9 = 45 Carry 4.
5 × 4 = 20 20 + 4 = 24

Writing the carry numbers might be helpful for some students.

Example G
Three or more digits in the multiplcand

Estimate: 9 × 5000 = 45,000

$$\begin{array}{r} 5038 \\ \times\ \ \ 9 \\ \hline 45342 \end{array}$$

9 × 8 = 72 Carry 7.
9 × 3 = 27 27 + 7 = 34 Carry 3.
9 × 0 = 0 0 + 3 = 3
9 × 5 = 45

You might demonstrate additional examples involving zeros before students do Sets G and H.

Example H
Horizontal form

7 × 9512

Estimate: 7 × 10,000 = 70,000

$$\begin{array}{r} 9512 \\ \times\ \ \ 7 \\ \hline 66584 \end{array}$$

Rewrite 7 × 9512 as shown.
Multiply.

Students who make many errors or work very slowly might benefit from additional oral or written work on multiplication basic facts.

Exercises

Set E

1. 24 × 2 = 48
2. 13 × 3 = 39
3. 81 × 4 = 324
4. 92 × 4 = 368
5. 64 × 2 = 128
6. 31 × 5 = 155
7. 72 × 2 = 144
8. 41 × 3 = 123
9. 83 × 2 = 166
10. 73 × 3 = 219

Set F

1. 25 × 7 = 175
2. 68 × 4 = 272
3. 55 × 6 = 330
4. 29 × 2 = 58
5. 47 × 7 = 329
6. 38 × 6 = 228
7. 99 × 4 = 396
8. 35 × 3 = 105
9. 64 × 9 = 576
10. 94 × 6 = 564
11. 38 × 4 = 152
12. 85 × 7 = 595
13. 29 × 5 = 145
14. 34 × 9 = 306
15. 76 × 6 = 456
16. 84 × 8 = 672

PROBLEM SOLVING
The applications on pages 38–39 and 44–45 may be used anytime after this lesson.

Set G

1. 836×4 — 3344
2. 985×3 — 2955
3. 805×2 — 1610
4. 409×6 — 2454
5. 677×3 — 2031
6. 376×4 — 1504
7. 5714×9 — 51,426
8. 7519×7 — 52,633
9. 8056×5 — 40,280
10. 6024×5 — 30,120
11. 9703×7 — 67,921
12. 6804×4 — 27,216
13. 73524×8 — 588,192
14. 87714×9 — 789,426
15. 45807×6 — 274,842
16. 35609×8 — 284,872

Set H

1. 7×51 — 357
2. 67×9 — 603
3. 4×72 — 288
4. 39×8 — 312
5. 6×926 — 5556
6. 4×603 — 2412
7. 589×3 — 1767
8. 6×804 — 4824
9. 5864×4 — 23,456
10. 7562×6 — 45,372
11. 5×3175 — 15,875
12. 3×8247 — 24,741
13. 9507×6 — 57,042
14. 7×6043 — 42,301
15. $6 \times 34{,}572$ — 207,432
16. $57{,}683 \times 4$ — 230,732
17. $40{,}079 \times 8$ — 320,632
18. $9 \times 60{,}028$ — 540,252
19. $7 \times 61{,}354$ — 429,478
20. $71{,}566 \times 5$ — 357,830

Mixed Practice

F 1. 29×7 — 203
G 2. 784×6 — 4704
G 3. 2078×5 — 10,390
F 4. 38×8 — 304
G 5. 73906×4 — 295,624
E 6. 32×3 — 96
G 7. 687×7 — 4809
G 8. 8477×6 — 50,862
F 9. 46×4 — 184
H 10. 9×409 — 3681
H 11. 93×2 — 186
H 12. 7368×7 — 51,576
H 13. 5×96 — 480
H 14. $87{,}496 \times 2$ — 174,992
H 15. 6×81 — 486
H 16. 379×4 — 1516
H 17. 9×63 — 567
H 18. 5602×8 — 44,816
H 19. $23{,}080 \times 9$ — 207,720
G 20. 97807×3 — 293,421
E 21. 43×3 — 129
G 22. 935×5 — 4675
G 23. 37236×8 — 297,888
G 24. 4094×5 — 20,470
G 25. 897×3 — 2691
F 26. 54×3 — 162
G 27. 6951×6 — 41,706
G 28. 53657×7 — 375,599
H 29. 229×8 — 1832
H 30. 5×71 — 355
H 31. 3207×9 — 28,863
H 32. 8×84 — 672
H 33. 9578×4 — 38,312
H 34. 2×64 — 128
H 35. $67{,}943 \times 5$ — 339,715
H 36. 6×75 — 450
H 37. 508×7 — 3556
H 38. $9 \times 45{,}060$ — 405,540

Objective: Multiply whole numbers by a two-digit multiplier.

Multiplying with Two-Digit Multipliers

Example I Two-digit multiplicand, zero in the multiplier

Estimate: 30 × 60 = 1800

$$\begin{array}{r} 59 \\ \times\ 30 \\ \hline 1770 \end{array}$$

Write 0 in the ones place.
Then multiply 3 and 59.

Example J Two-digit multiplicand

Estimate: 30 × 40 = 1200

$$\begin{array}{r} 42 \\ \times\ 28 \\ \hline 336 \\ 840 \\ \hline 1176 \end{array}$$

[8 × 42

[20 × 42 Write 0 in the ones place.
Then multiply 2 and 42.

[Add 336 and 840. Students need not write a zero in the ones place if they are not used to doing so.

Example K Three or more digits in the multiplicand

Estimate: 50 × 600 = 30,000

$$\begin{array}{r} 629 \\ \times\ \ 45 \\ \hline 3145 \\ 25160 \\ \hline 28305 \end{array}$$

[5 × 629

[40 × 629 Write 0 in the ones place.
Then multiply 4 and 629.

[Add 3145 and 25160.

Example L Horizontal form

97 × 4705

Estimate: 100 × 5000 = 500,000

Rewrite 97 × 4705 as shown.
Multiply.

$$\begin{array}{r} 4705 \\ \times\ \ \ 97 \\ \hline 32935 \\ 423450 \\ \hline 456385 \end{array}$$

Exercises

Set I

		Answer			Answer
1.	64 × 30	1920	6.	65 × 70	4550
2.	85 × 20	1700	7.	51 × 80	4080
3.	47 × 60	2820	8.	95 × 90	8550
4.	68 × 40	2720	9.	76 × 90	6840
5.	57 × 50	2850	10.	52 × 40	2080

Set J

		Answer			Answer
1.	46 × 18	828	9.	84 × 29	2436
2.	38 × 24	912	10.	95 × 37	3515
3.	64 × 53	3392	11.	54 × 39	2106
4.	45 × 63	2835	12.	32 × 47	1504
5.	36 × 83	2988	13.	25 × 88	2200
6.	77 × 42	3234	14.	75 × 44	3300
7.	65 × 17	1105	15.	98 × 76	7448
8.	56 × 19	1064	16.	79 × 86	6794

PROBLEM SOLVING
The applications on pages 37 and 42–43 may be used anytime after this lesson.

Set K

1. 594 × 78
46,332
2. 657 × 49
32,193
3. 803 × 67
53,801
4. 709 × 56
39,704
5. 4681 × 83
388,523
6. 9458 × 37
349,946
7. 6507 × 34
221,238
8. 3508 × 78
273,624
9. 8060 × 46
370,760
10. 9070 × 64
580,480
11. 42763 × 75
3,207,225
12. 89752 × 36
3,231,072
13. 91508 × 97
8,876,276
14. 72604 × 68
4,937,072
15. 30024 × 49
1,471,176
16. 50039 × 95
4,753,705

Set L

1. 53 × 90
4770
2. 70 × 84
5880
3. 42 × 67
2814
4. 39 × 74
2886
5. 87 × 58
5046
6. 65 × 97
6305
7. 527 × 37
19,499
8. 29 × 643
18,647
9. 936 × 73
68,328
10. 64 × 877
56,128
11. 8512 × 83
706,496
12. 58 × 6415
372,070
13. 7684 × 60
461,040
14. 90 × 8345
751,050
15. 79 × 40,708
3,215,932
16. 60,903 × 86
5,237,658
17. 36 × 95,324
3,431,664
18. 86,543 × 45
3,894,435
19. 32,067 × 28
897,876
20. 46 × 41,086
1,889,956

Mixed Practice

K 1. 827 × 73
60,371
I 2. 25 × 90
2250
K 3. 9032 × 37
334,184
K 4. 78623 × 65
5,110,495
K 5. 645 × 44
28,380
J 6. 53 × 16
848
K 7. 3465 × 82
284,130
K 8. 35070 × 57
1,998,990
K 9. 509 × 75
38,175
L 10. 17 × 935
15,895
L 11. 7008 × 63
441,504
L 12. 47 × 80
3760
L 13. 5433 × 76
412,908
L 14. 45 × 480
21,600
L 15. 806 × 33
26,598
L 16. 29 × 58
1682
L 17. 54,003 × 84
4,536,252
L 18. 92 × 26,431
2,431,652
L 19. 30 × 70,586
2,117,580
K 20. 8023 × 64
513,472
K 21. 47060 × 93
4,376,580
K 22. 875 × 26
22,750
J 23. 42 × 18
756
K 24. 744 × 68
50,592
K 25. 45312 × 83
3,760,896
K 26. 4735 × 28
132,580
I 27. 39 × 60
2340
K 28. 603 × 87
52,461
L 29. 70 × 56
3920
L 30. 87,009 × 43
3,741,387
L 31. 842 × 19
15,998
L 32. 704 × 66
46,464
L 33. 38 × 79
3002
L 34. 67 × 9006
603,402
L 35. 21,542 × 94
2,024,948
L 36. 48 × 6372
305,856
L 37. 650 × 74
48,100
L 38. 30,467 × 50
1,523,350

Objective: Multiply whole numbers by a three-digit multiplier.

Multiplying with Three-Digit Multipliers

Example M
Three-digit multiplicand, two zeros in the multiplier

Estimate: 400 × 600 = 240,000

```
   612
 × 400
244800
```

Write 0 in the ones place and tens place.
Multiply 4 and 612.

Example N
Three-digit multiplicand, one zero in the multiplier

Estimate: 700 × 900 = 630,000

```
   892
 × 706
  5352     [6 × 892
624400     [700 × 892  Write 0 in the ones place and tens place. Then multiply 7 and 892.
629752     [Add.
```

Example O
Three or more digits in multiplicand, no zeros in the multiplier

Estimate: 700 × 400 = 280,000

```
   421
 × 675
  2105     [5 × 421
 29470     [70 × 421  Write 0 in the ones place. Then multiply 7 and 421.
252600     [600 × 421  Write 0 in the ones place and tens place. Then multiply 6 and 421.
284175     [Add.
```

Exercises

Set M

1. 578 × 300 — 173,400
2. 663 × 400 — 265,200
3. 826 × 600 — 495,600
4. 542 × 700 — 379,400
5. 706 × 900 — 635,400
6. 807 × 800 — 645,600
7. 643 × 700 — 450,100
8. 534 × 600 — 320,400
9. 398 × 400 — 159,200
10. 489 × 500 — 244,500

Set N

1. 629 × 106 — 66,674
2. 328 × 207 — 67,896
3. 253 × 409 — 103,477
4. 673 × 304 — 204,592
5. 734 × 505 — 370,670
6. 735 × 804 — 590,940
7. 647 × 908 — 587,476
8. 278 × 603 — 167,634
9. 523 × 704 — 368,192
10. 875 × 507 — 443,625
11. 683 × 730 — 498,590
12. 892 × 940 — 838,480
13. 409 × 270 — 110,430
14. 508 × 790 — 401,320
15. 804 × 604 — 485,616
16. 903 × 509 — 459,627

PROBLEM SOLVING
The applications on pages 40–41 may be used anytime after this lesson.

Set O

1. 253 × 376 = 95,128
2. 432 × 689 = 297,648
3. 529 × 467 = 247,043
4. 738 × 348 = 256,824
5. 1824 × 742 = 1,353,408
6. 2156 × 634 = 1,366,904
7. 62194 × 328 = 20,399,632
8. 19243 × 549 = 10,564,407
9. 6507 × 957 = 6,227,199
10. 8307 × 742 = 6,163,794
11. 50708 × 836 = 42,391,888
12. 90805 × 459 = 41,679,495

Mixed Practice

N 1. 723 × 507 = 366,561
O 2. 4972 × 678 = 3,371,016
N 3. 480 × 208 = 99,840
O 4. 947 × 825 = 781,275
O 5. 19746 × 429 = 8,471,034
M 6. 739 × 800 = 591,200
N 7. 649 × 760 = 493,240
N 8. 190 × 309 = 58,710
M 9. 938 × 600 = 562,800
N 10. 563 × 904 = 508,952
O 11. 654 × 837 = 547,398
N 12. 846 × 790 = 668,340
O 13. 3856 × 962 = 3,709,472
O 14. 21483 × 438 = 9,409,554

See Skills File, page 418, for more practice. Exercises include practice with 1-, 2-, and 3-digit multipliers.

BREAK TIME

Here are 17 straws.

Move 3 straws to make 5 squares that are the same size.
Answers may vary.

Start over again.
This time remove 5 straws so that exactly 3 squares remain.
Answers may vary.

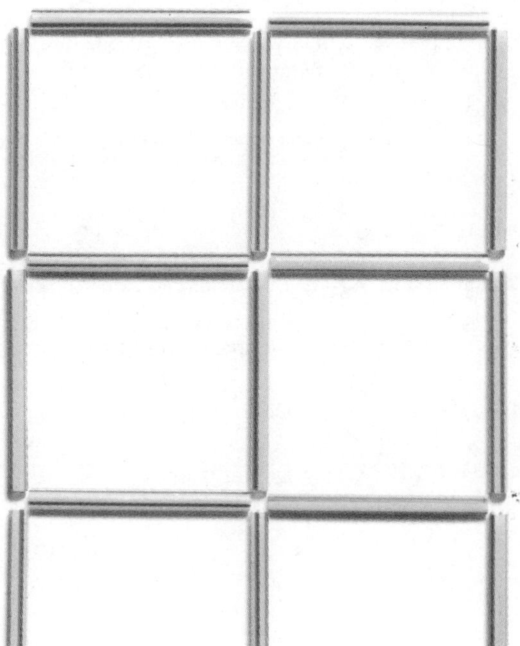

Objective: Compute following order of operations involving addition, subtraction, and multiplication.

Using Order of Operations

Example P Without operations inside parentheses

$32 + 7(3) - 4$

Follow these general rules.

First do all operations inside parentheses.

Then do remaining multiplications.

Then do remaining additions and subtractions from left to right.

$32 + 7(3) - 4$	Do multiplication.
$32 + 21 - 4$	Do remaining operations from left to right.
$53 - 4$	
49	Point out that if the addition had been done first, the answer would be 113.

Example Q With operations inside parentheses

$6(5) + 4(9 - 2)$	Follow rules in Example P. Do operations inside parentheses.
$6(5) + 4(7)$	Do multiplications.
$30 + 28$	Do addition.
58	

Order of operations involving addition and subtraction was introduced in Chapter 1, pages 10-11. Here, multiplication is included. In Chapter 3, pages 54-55, division is included. Additional work on order of operations is provided in Chapters 13 and 14.

Exercises

Set P

1. $5 + 3(6)$ 23
2. $8(7) - 9$ 47
3. $32 - 8(3)$ 8
4. $14 + 2(30)$ 74
5. $9 + 4 + 6(5)$ 43
6. $8 + 9(2) + 4$ 30
7. $2 + 4(6) - 7$ 19
8. $12 + 7 - 3(2)$ 13
9. $6(7) + 5(4)$ 62
10. $8(5) + 6(3)$ 58
11. $2 + 3(5) + 1$ 18
12. $28 + 15 - 3(7)$ 22
13. $6(9) - 2(9)$ 36
14. $9(7) - 8(3)$ 39
15. $10(4) - 13 + 6$ 33
16. $15 + 6(7) - 1$ 56
17. $21 + 4(9) - 7$ 50
18. $11(3) - 14 + 5$ 24
19. $6(2) - 5(2) + 6$ 8
20. $4(8) + 3(5) - 9$ 38
21. $50 - 2(3)(4)$ 26
22. $14 + 7(6)(3)$ 140
23. $9(2)(4) + 22$ 94
24. $8(4)(2) - 9$ 55
25. $20(4) - 3(2)(3)$ 62
26. $5(4)(3) + 6(6)$ 96
27. $9 + 3(2)(4) + 6(2)$ 45
28. $5(2)(7) + 4(3) - 6$ 76

Set Q

1. $5(14 - 8)$
30
2. $7(12 - 4)$
56
3. $(6 + 8)3$
42
4. $(7 + 9)4$
64
5. $3(8 + 4) - 20$
16
6. $5(18 - 9) - 41$
4
7. $25 + (5 + 3)$
33
8. $6(15 - 8) + 17$
59
9. $55 - (16 - 8)$
47
10. $24 + 3(2 + 4)$
42
11. $4(14 - 6) + 12$
44
12. $65 - 4(16 - 9)$
37
13. $7(19 + 22 - 11)$
210
14. $8(32 - 18 + 6)$
160
15. $5(7 + 6 + 8)$
105
16. $6(42 - 9 - 8)$
150
17. $3(2) + 8(4 + 1)$
46
18. $5(4) + 2(1 + 6)$
34
19. $12 + 7(8 - 3) - 20$
27
20. $18 + 9(7 - 4) - 15$
30
21. $(24 - 9)3 + 4(6) - 17$
52
22. $(21 - 7)4 + 3(7) - 13$
64
23. $2(6 + 3) - (7 + 1) + 5$
15
24. $6(5 + 2) - (3 + 9) + 7$
37
25. $(4 + 3)2 + (9 - 1)5$
54
26. $(3 + 2)7 + (12 - 9)8$
59
27. $7(5)(2) - 5(6 + 1) + 9$
44
28. $5(3)(4) - 6(4 + 2) + 8$
32

Mixed Practice

P 1. $6(4) - 8$
16
Q 2. $17 - (3 + 2)$
12
Q 3. $2(48 - 19 - 4)$
50
P 4. $4(3) + 5(2)$
22
P 5. $12 - 2(3)$
6
Q 6. $5(7 + 8) - (9 - 6)6$
57
Q 7. $4(3 + 9 + 12)$
96
Q 8. $7 + 3(4 + 8)$
43
Q 9. $4 + 6(3 + 2) - 1$
33
P 10. $6(2) + 37$
49
Q 11. $(8 + 9)3 - 2(5 + 8)$
25
P 12. $24 - 4(2)$
16
P 13. $4(3)(8) - 16$
80
Q 14. $(34 - 17 - 6)5$
55
Q 15. $(5 + 6)3 + (7 - 2)5$
58
P 16. $4 + 3(8)(2) - 6$
46
Q 17. $(7 + 12)20$
380
Q 18. $17 - (4 + 2 - 3)5$
2
Q 19. $75 - 3(4 + 1)$
60
Q 20. $7(2) + 4(2 + 8)$
54
P 21. $16(2) + 4(9)$
68
Q 22. $7(8 + 3 + 4)$
105
Q 23. $57 - (6 + 9 - 5)3$
27
Q 24. $16 - (4 + 3)2 + 27$
29
P 25. $7 + 3(5)(6) - 21$
76
P 26. $129 - 6(8)(2)$
33
Q 27. $4(4) + 4(4 + 4)$
48
Q 28. $(6 + 5)2 + 7(6 + 2)$
78

BREAK TIME

Draw 16 dots on your paper as shown below.

Connect all 16 dots with only 6 strokes. Do not lift your pencil from the paper.
Answers may vary.

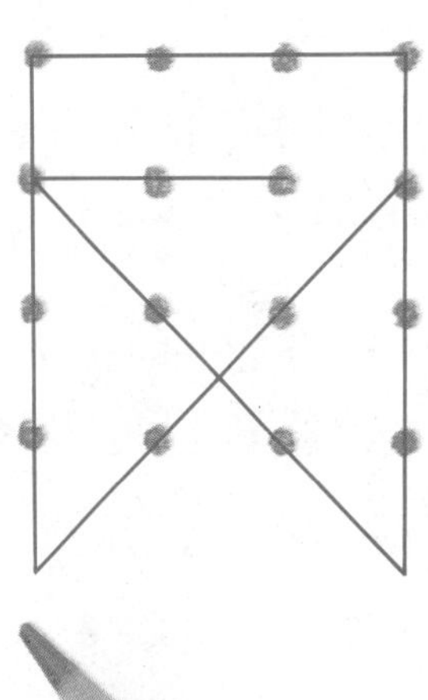

SKILLS POSTTEST

Number of test items - 17

Number missed	1	2	3	4	5	6	7	8
Percent correct	94	88	82	76	71	65	59	53

SKILL Multiplying with Multiples of 10, 100, and 1000 *page 26*

A 80×1000 80,000 **B** 4000×900 3,600,000

SKILL Estimating Products *page 27*

C Estimate. 7×693 4900 **D** Estimate. 574×3215 1,800,000

SKILL Multiplying with One-Digit Multipliers *pages 28–29*

E 92×3 276 **F** 48×9 432 **G** 7026×8 56,208 **H** 6×472 2832

SKILL Multiplying with Two-Digit Multipliers *pages 30–31*

I 39×40 1560 **J** 68×29 1972 **K** 4317×54 233,118 **L** 35×867 30,345

SKILL Multiplying with Three-Digit Multipliers *pages 32–33*

M 584×700 408,800 **N** 637×903 575,211 **O** 452×386 174,472

SKILL Using Order of Operations *pages 34–35*

P $9(7) - 2(8)$ 47 **Q** $8(5) - 4(9 - 3) + 9$ 25

Problem Solving

CONSUMER APPLICATIONS

See page 4 of *Problem-Solving Masters.*

Objective: Solve problems involving multiplication of whole numbers.

In this lesson students compute the costs involved in renting an apartment.

Computing Apartment Costs

The cost of living in an apartment includes more than the rent. Often a security deposit is required before a person can move into an apartment. The amount of the deposit is usually the same as one month's rent. The cost of gas and electricity may also add to the cost of apartment living.

NOW RENTING

ENCHANTED FOREST TOWERS

Acorn (1 bedroom)	$265 per month
Mapleway (2 bedroom)	$317 per month
Woodview (2 bedroom)	$345 per month
Oak Trail (3 bedroom)	$378 per month
Evergreen (3 bedroom)	$395 per month

Gas and Electricity Extra
Security Deposit Required

Penguin Realty Development

1. Curt Wolf lives at the Enchanted Forest Towers in a one-bedroom apartment. How much does he spend for rent in 6 months?
   $1590
2. Carl and Janet Howard rent a Mapleway apartment. How much rent do they pay in 7 months?
   $2219
3. The Kugel family rents an Evergreen apartment. The Millers rent an Oak Trail apartment. In one year, how much more will the Kugels pay for rent than the Millers?
   $204
4. The Taylors live in a Woodview apartment. What is the cost (deposit plus rent) of the apartment for 5 months?
   $2070
5. Ed Colfax rented an Acorn apartment for 5 months. Then he moved to a Mapleway apartment for 7 months. How much did he pay for that one year? (Remember to add the increase in the security deposit.)
   $3861
6. Naomi Madlem's gas and electricity bills averaged $52 each month. How much money does Naomi pay for gas and electricity in one year?
   $624
7. Irene Reilly rents a Woodview apartment. Each month she pays about $20 for gas and $30 for electricity. Find the total cost (deposit + rent + gas + electricity) for 6 months.
   $2715
8. The Cohen family rented an Oak Trail apartment for one year. The gas and electricity bills averaged $46 each month. Find the total cost of the apartment for one year.
   $5466
9. Mr. and Mrs. William Rehm rented an Evergreen apartment for 9 months. Their gas and electricity bills averaged $59 each month. When they moved, $350 of their security deposit was refunded to them. Find the total cost of the apartment for the 9 months.
   $4131

In Problem 5, the security deposit for the Acorn apartment is $265. Upon moving into the Mapleway apartment, Ed would pay $52 to increase his security deposit to $317.

Problem Solving

CONSUMER APPLICATIONS

Objective: Solve problems involving multiplication of whole numbers.

In this lesson students find the cost of automobile fuel by reading a table.

Finding the Annual Cost of Automobile Fuel

You can use this chart to find the approximate annual cost of gasoline if the price of gasoline is 40¢ per liter.

Annual Cost of Gasoline										
Kilometers traveled per year	Kilometers per liter 7	8	9	10	11	12	13	14	15	16
8000	$457	$400	$356	$320	$291	$267	$246	$229	$213	$200
10,000	571	500	444	400	364	333	308	286	267	250
12,000	686	600	533	480	436	400	369	343	320	300
14,000	800	700	622	560	509	467	431	400	373	350
16,000	914	800	711	640	582	533	492	457	427	400
18,000	1029	900	800	720	655	600	554	514	480	450
20,000	1143	1000	889	800	727	667	615	571	533	500
22,000	1257	1100	978	880	800	733	677	629	587	550
24,000	1371	1200	1067	960	873	800	738	686	640	600
26,000	1486	1300	1156	1040	945	867	800	743	693	650
28,000	1600	1400	1244	1120	1018	933	862	800	747	700
30,000	1714	1500	1333	1200	1091	1000	923	857	800	750
32,000	1829	1600	1422	1280	1164	1067	985	914	853	800

Find the annual cost of gasoline for each of these situations.

	Kilometers traveled per year	Kilometers per liter
1.	12,000 $686	7
2.	12,000 $343	14
3.	22,000 $1257	7
4.	30,000 $1500	8
5.	18,000 $554	13

See page 5 of *Problem-Solving Masters.*

Here are some data for eight cars.

Car	Description and number of cylinders	Kilometers per liter	
A	Minicompact, 4 cyl.	15	6. $533
B	Subcompact, 4 cyl.	16	$500
C	Compact, 4 cyl.	12	$667
D	Intermediate, 4 cyl.	11	$727
E	Intermediate, 6 cyl.	9	$889
F	Full-sized, 6 cyl.	8	$1000
G	Station wagon, 4 cyl.	10	$800
H	Station wagon, 8 cyl.	7	$1143

6. The average car is driven about 20,000 kilometers per year. At this rate, what is the annual cost of gasoline for *each* of cars A–H?
See above.

At 20,000 kilometers per year, how much would a driver spend on gasoline

7. for car C in 2 years?
$1334

8. for car C in 5 years?
$3335

9. for cars B and G in 1 year?
$1300

10. for cars B and G in 5 years?
$6500

11. for cars D and H in 3 years?
$5610

At 26,000 kilometers per year, how much money would a driver save on gasoline by driving

12. car C instead of car D?
$78

13. car B instead of car E?
$506

14. car D instead of car G?
$95

15. car A instead of car H?
$793

For each driver below, find the total cost of the car plus gasoline *for 5 years*. Each driver travels about 24,000 kilometers per year.

	Driver	Price of car	Kilometers per liter
16.	Mr. Diaz $11,470	$6135	9
17.	Ms. Todd $10,229	$7029	15
18.	Ms. Chin $8925	$5495	14

19. Which driver's total cost for 5 years was greatest?
Mr. Diaz

Problem Solving

CAREER APPLICATIONS

Objective: Solve problems involving multiplication of whole numbers.

In this lesson students solve problems involving production and packaging of canned corn.

Farm Manager

See the Careers Chart beginning on page 426 for more information about the careers in this cluster.

Career Cluster: Technology Wilbur Pearce is the farm manager at the Mitchell Parker Corn Packing Company. The corn is grown in fields that the company either owns or leases.

Field	Field location	Size in thousands of square meters
a	North Miller Pond	310
b	South Miller Pond	110
c	Curley Avenue	480
d	Tassel Street	580
e	Husk Hollow	130
f	Johnson property	250
g	Santos property	120
h	Old Homeplace	330
i	River Road	270
j	North Perryman	950
k	South Perryman	350
l	Little Care's Stable	960
m	Glenville South	560
n	Lower Chesapeake	210

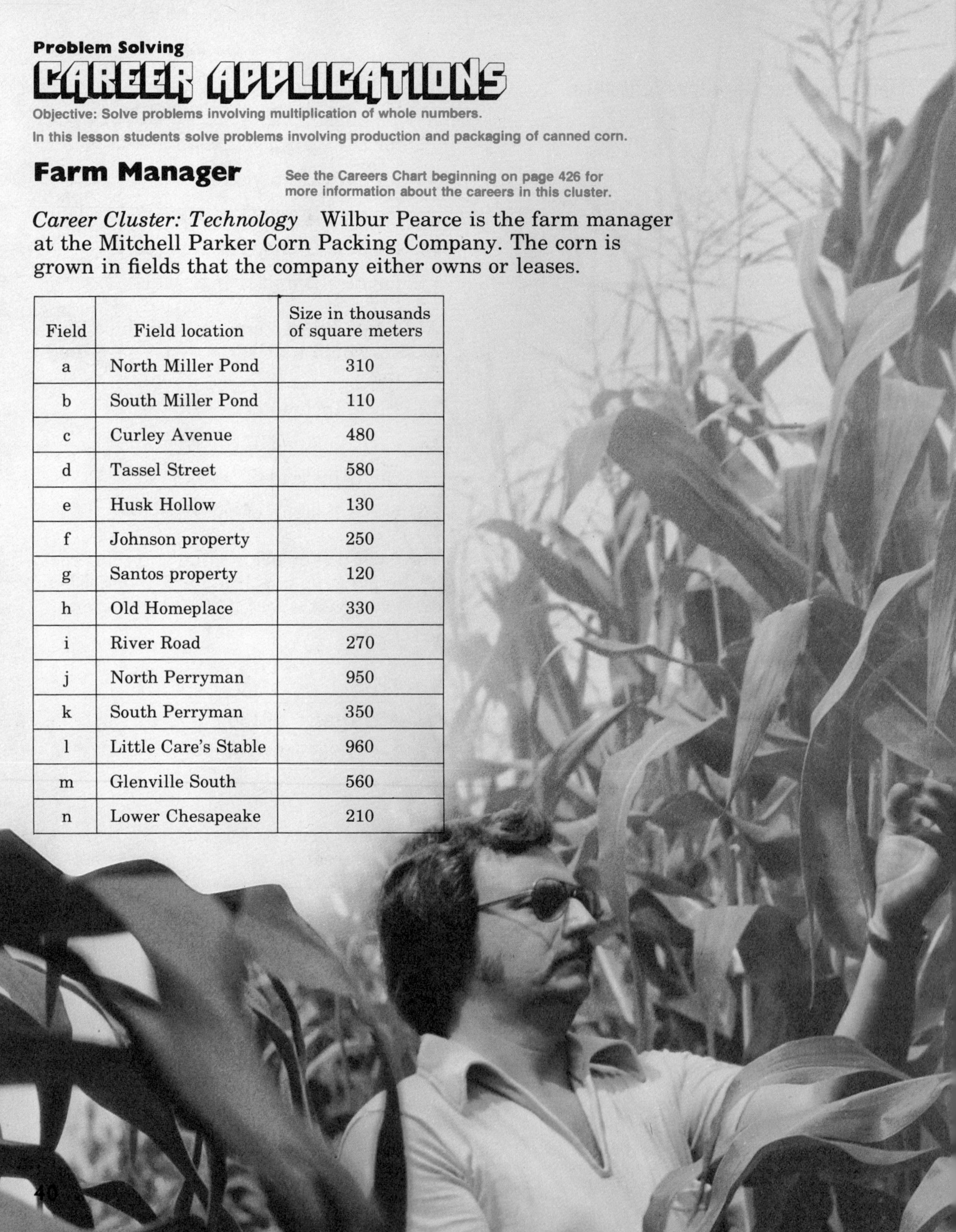

See pages 6–7 of *Problem-Solving Masters.*

Here are the steps involved in producing and packing the corn. Wilbur oversees each step until the corn reaches the packing house.

Plow, fertilize, and plant fields.

1. 12 liters of fertilizer were used per thousand square meters.

How many liters of fertilizer were used on *each* field?
See Additional Answers on page T46.

Harvest crop.

2. 900 kilograms of corn were produced per thousand square meters.

How many kilograms of corn were produced by *each* field?
See Additional Answers on page T46.

3. 1000 kilograms is 1 metric ton.
156,000 kilograms is 156 metric tons.
250,000 kilograms is 250 metric tons.

How many metric tons of corn were produced by *each* field?
See Additional Answers on page T46.

4. How many metric tons of corn were produced in all?
5049 metric tons

Transport corn to packing house.

Transport trucks are weighed on large scales. Subtract the EVW from the LVW to find the weight of each load of corn.

	Empty vehicle weight (EVW) in kilograms	Loaded vehicle weight (LVW) in kilograms	
5.	5044	10,470	5426 kilograms
6.	5552	12,778	7226 kilograms
7.	6498	14,596	8098 kilograms
8.	7340	15,988	8648 kilograms
9.	6210	13,876	7666 kilograms
10.	5487	11,862	6375 kilograms

Husk corn, separate from cob, pack and seal in cans, cook in cans, label cans, pack in cases, ship cases.

11. 28 cases of corn were processed from each metric ton of corn.

How many cases of corn were processed in all? (Use answer from Problem 4.)
141,372 cases

12. 24 cans were packed per case.

How many cans were needed in all?
3,392,928 cans

13. Each case sold for $8. What were the total sales of the Mitchell Parker Company that season?
$1,130,976

Problem Solving

CAREER APPLICATIONS

Objective: Solve problems involving multiplication of whole numbers.

In this lesson students solve problems involving preparation of food and ordering supplies for a catering service.

Caterer

See the Careers Chart beginning on page 426 for more information about the careers in this cluster.

Career Cluster: Business Contact Mr. and Mrs. Perez are caterers. They use special stacking ovens to prepare large amounts of food.

Complete the chart below. $S \times P \times C = T$

Notice that the number of pan changes per hour (C) depends on the cooking time.

	Dish	Cooking time in minutes	Servings on 1 pan (S)	Number of pans (P)	Pan changes per hour (C)	Total servings per hour			
						1 oven (T)	2 ovens ($2 \times T$)	3 ovens ($3 \times T$)	4 ovens ($4 \times T$)
1.	Beef patties	15	8	6	4	192	384	576	768
2.	Steaks	8	6	6	7	252	504	756	1008
3.	Cutlets	12	6	6	5	180	360	540	720
4.	Sausages	9	6	6	6	216	432	648	864
5.	Liver	6	6	6	10	360	720	1080	1440
6.	Rolls	17	13	3	3	117	234	351	468
7.	Pastries	10	10	6	6	360	720	1080	1440

Mr. and Mrs. Perez order supplies every two weeks. Complete this table to find what needs to be ordered.

	Item	Number used per day	Number needed for 2 weeks (14 days)	Reserve needed	Total needed for 2 weeks	Number on hand	Number to be ordered
8.	Napkins	500	7000 (14 × 500)	500	7500 (7000 + 500)	1000	6500 (7500 − 1000)
9.	Hot cups	150	2100	100	2200	300	1900
10.	Cold cups	100	1400	100	1500	200	1300
11.	Plates	300	4200	200	4400	600	3800
12.	Bowls	180	2520	150	2670	210	2460
13.	Forks	600	8400	400	8800	500	8300
14.	Coasters	280	3920	180	4100	240	3860
15.	Placemats	200	2800	80	2880	110	2770

Problem Solving

DEVELOPING STRATEGIES

Objective: Solve problems by reading a table and using a formula.

In this lesson students find the engine pressure needed to maintain the flow of water necessary to fight fires.

Tactics: Reading a Table, Using a Formula

Ann Sorenson is a pump operator on a fire engine. She calculates the engine pressure necessary to provide enough water to extinguish a fire. To find the necessary pressure, Ann uses this formula.

$$NP + FL = EP$$

Nozzle pressure (NP) plus friction loss (FL) equals engine pressure (EP).

NOZZLE PRESSURE: pressure loss due to resistance of water moving through nozzle

FRICTION LOSS: pressure loss due to resistance of water moving through hose

ENGINE PRESSURE: pressure provided by the engine to maintain the flow of water and to overcome pressure losses due to the nozzle and friction

FLOW: rate at which water is used measured in gallons per minute (GPM)

Friction loss per 100 feet of rubber-lined hose

Flow (GPM)	Diameter of hose		
	$2\frac{1}{2}$-inch	3-inch	4-inch
260	16	6	2
280	19	7	2
300	21	8	2
320	24	9	2
340	27	11	3
360	30	12	3
380	33	13	3
400	36	14	3
425	41	16	4
450	45	18	4
475	50	20	5
500	55	22	5

Problem

Find the engine pressure necessary to maintain a flow of 280 GPM through 400 feet of $2\frac{1}{2}$-inch hose with a nozzle pressure of 50 pounds.

Solution

The following questions show Ann's strategy for solving the problem. She used the tactics of reading a table and working with a formula.

a. How many pounds of pressure are lost due to the nozzle? This information is given in the problem.

50 pounds

b. How many pounds of pressure are lost due to friction? Read the table, and then multiply.

19 pounds lost per 100 feet
× 4 hundreds of feet of hose
76 pounds of pressure lost

c. What is the necessary engine pressure? Use the formula, and then solve the equation.

$NP + FL = EP$
$50 + 76 = EP$
$126 = EP$

Conclusion: The engine pressure must be 126 pounds to overcome the pressure losses due to friction and the nozzle while maintaining a flow of 280 GPM.

Related Problems

1. Find the engine pressure necessary to maintain a flow of 260 GPM through 600 feet of $2\frac{1}{2}$-inch hose with a nozzle pressure of 92 pounds.
   188 pounds
2. Find the engine pressure necessary to maintain a flow of 425 GPM through 300 feet of 4-inch hose with a nozzle pressure of 78 pounds.
   90 pounds
3. Find the engine pressure necessary to overcome a nozzle pressure of 54 pounds and maintain a 340 GPM flow through 400 feet of $2\frac{1}{2}$-inch hose.
   162 pounds
4. If 800 feet of 3-inch hose is used to fight a fire, find the engine pressure necessary to maintain a flow of 450 GPM with a nozzle pressure of 85 pounds.
   229 pounds
5. A 1000-foot hose was made from 600 feet of $2\frac{1}{2}$-inch hose and 400 feet of 3-inch hose. Find the engine pressure necessary to maintain a flow of 380 GPM with a nozzle pressure of 62 pounds.
   312 pounds
6. Find the engine pressure necessary for a 900-foot hose made from 300 feet of $2\frac{1}{2}$-inch hose and 600 feet of 4-inch hose. The flow is 500 GPM and the nozzle pressure is 59 pounds.
   254 pounds

Extensions

7. The flow through a 700-foot, 3-inch hose was 425 GPM. If the engine pressure was 191 pounds, what was the nozzle pressure? (NP = EP − FL)
   79 pounds
8. Find the nozzle pressure used if the engine pressure was 247 pounds and the flow was 400 GPM through a 500-foot, $2\frac{1}{2}$-inch hose. (NP = EP − FL)
   67 pounds

CHAPTER 2 TEST

Number of test items - 22

Number missed	1	2	3	4	5	6	7	8	9	10	11
Percent correct	95	91	86	82	77	73	68	64	59	55	50

A **1.** 60×1000
60,000

B **2.** 5000×700
3,500,000

C **3.** Estimate. 9×596
5400

D **4.** Estimate. 283×8415
2,400,000

E **5.** $\begin{array}{r} 74 \\ \times\ 2 \\ \hline \end{array}$
148

F **6.** $\begin{array}{r} 39 \\ \times\ 6 \\ \hline \end{array}$
234

G **7.** $\begin{array}{r} 8043 \\ \times\ \ \ 7 \\ \hline \end{array}$
56,301

H **8.** 4×649
2596

I **9.** $\begin{array}{r} 58 \\ \times 30 \\ \hline \end{array}$
1740

J **10.** $\begin{array}{r} 89 \\ \times 17 \\ \hline \end{array}$
1513

K **11.** $\begin{array}{r} 3156 \\ \times\ \ 46 \\ \hline \end{array}$
145,176

L **12.** 28×493
13,804

M **13.** $\begin{array}{r} 752 \\ \times 800 \\ \hline \end{array}$
601,600

N **14.** $\begin{array}{r} 287 \\ \times 609 \\ \hline \end{array}$
174,783

O **15.** $\begin{array}{r} 913 \\ \times 542 \\ \hline \end{array}$
494,846

P **16.** $9(6) - 4(7)$
26

Q **17.** $7(5) - 2(6 + 3) + 8$
25

18. How much rent would you pay over an 8-month period if the rent is $317 a month?
$2536

19. What is the total cost of gasoline for both cars in 3 years?
$3846

Gasoline cost	
Car 1	$467 per year
Car 2	$815 per year

20. One metric ton of corn yields 28 cases of processed corn. How many cases of processed corn will 180 metric tons of corn yield?
5040 cases

Use this information for item 21.

Servings on 1 pan (S): 8
Number of pans (P): 6
Pan changes per hour (C): 7

21. Multiply $S \times P \times C$ to find the total servings per hour for the oven.
336 servings per hour

Use this formula for item 22.

$$NP + FL = EP$$

Nozzle pressure (NP) plus friction loss (FL) equals engine pressure (EP).

22. The friction loss is 19 pounds for each 100 feet of rubber-lined hose. What is the engine pressure needed for 700 feet of hose when the nozzle pressure is 52 pounds?
185 pounds

 See pages 3–4 of the *Test Masters* for an alternate form of the Chapter 2 Test.

CHAPTER 3 Dividing Whole Numbers

SKILLS PRETEST

Number of test items - 16

Number missed	1	2	3	4	5	6	7	8
Percent correct	94	88	81	75	69	63	56	50

SKILL Dividing with One-Digit Divisors *pages 48–49*

A $3\overline{)89}$ 29 R2 **B** $5\overline{)436}$ 87 R1 **C** $7\overline{)4825}$ 689 R2 **D** $5792 \div 6$ 965 R2

SKILL Dividing with Two-Digit Divisors *pages 50–51*

E $23\overline{)95}$ 4 R3 **F** $31\overline{)711}$ 22 R29 **G** $38\overline{)955}$ 25 R5 **H** $2497 \div 42$ 59 R19

SKILL Dividing with Zeros in the Quotient *page 52*

I $8\overline{)4831}$ 603 R7 **J** $53\overline{)3742}$ 70 R32

SKILL Dividing with Three-Digit Divisors *page 53*

K $379\overline{)865}$ 2 R107 **L** $823\overline{)47429}$ 57 R518

SKILL Using Order of Operations *pages 54–55*

M $\frac{4(5)}{12-2}+\frac{16}{2}$ 10 **N** $\frac{2(5+1)}{3}+\frac{30}{5(2)}$ 7

SKILL Solving Multiplication and Division Equations *pages 56–57*

O Find n.

$34n = 306$

$n = 9$

P Find x.

$\frac{x}{14} = 7$

$x = 98$

For items A-L and Exercise Sets A-L, have students give answers as quotients with remainders. Remind them that the answers could also be written as mixed numbers.

Objective: Divide whole numbers by a one-digit divisor.

SKILL Dividing with One-Digit Divisors

Each division example will show how estimation can be used to check if an answer is reasonable.

Example A Two-digit dividend

```
   1
4)78
 - 4
   3
```

How many 4s in 7? *1*
Write 1 above the 7.
Multiply 1 × 4. Subtract.

```
  19 R2
4)78
 - 4
  38
- 36
   2
```

Bring down the 8.
How many 4s in 38? *9*
Multiply 9 × 4. Subtract.
The remainder is 2.

Is the answer reasonable?
Estimate: 4 × 19 ≈ 80 4 × 19 ≈ 4 × 20
80 is close to 78.
19 R2 is a reasonable answer.

Review the rules for estimating products taught in Chapter 2. The rules are used here to determine if an answer is reasonable.

Example B Three-digit dividend

```
    7
6)439
 - 42
    1
```

How many 6s in 4? *None*
How many 6s in 43? *7*
Write 7 above the 3.
Multiply. Subtract.

```
   73 R1
6)439
 - 42
   19
 - 18
    1
```

Bring down the 9.
How many 6s in 19? *3*

Is the answer reasonable?
Estimate: 6 × 73 ≈ 420
420 is close to 439.
73 R1 is a reasonable answer.

Example C Four or more digits in dividend

```
     3
8)3180
 - 24
    7
```

How many 8s in 3? *None*
How many 8s in 31? *3*

```
    39
8)3180
 - 24
    78
  - 72
     6
```

Bring down the 8.
How many 8s in 78? *9*

```
   397 R4
8)3180
 - 24
    78
  - 72
     60
   - 56
      4
```

Bring down the 0.
How many 8s in 60? *7*

Is the answer reasonable?
Estimate: 8 × 397 ≈ 3200
3200 is close to 3180.
397 R4 is a reasonable answer.

Example D Horizontal form

8962 ÷ 3

```
  2987 R1
3)8962
 - 6
   29
 - 27
    26
  - 24
     22
   - 21
      1
```

Rewrite 8962 ÷ 3 as shown.
Divide.

Is the answer reasonable?
Estimate: 3 × 2987 ≈ 9000
9000 is close to 8962.
2987 R1 is a reasonable answer.

Exercises

Set A

1. $3\overline{)57}$ 19
2. $6\overline{)90}$ 15
3. $3\overline{)84}$ 28
4. $4\overline{)56}$ 14
5. $4\overline{)87}$ 21 R3
6. $6\overline{)95}$ 15 R5
7. $2\overline{)93}$ 46 R1
8. $7\overline{)94}$ 13 R3
9. $5\overline{)88}$ 17 R3
10. $8\overline{)97}$ 12 R1

Set B

1. $7\overline{)581}$ 83
2. $6\overline{)348}$ 58
3. $9\overline{)263}$ 29 R2
4. $6\overline{)520}$ 86 R4
5. $7\overline{)508}$ 72 R4
6. $8\overline{)679}$ 84 R7
7. $3\overline{)173}$ 57 R2
8. $5\overline{)481}$ 96 R1
9. $2\overline{)570}$ 285
10. $3\overline{)555}$ 185
11. $4\overline{)729}$ 182 R1
12. $5\overline{)909}$ 181 R4
13. $3\overline{)814}$ 271 R1
14. $5\overline{)807}$ 161 R2
15. $4\overline{)758}$ 189 R2
16. $4\overline{)953}$ 238 R1

Set C

1. $8\overline{)4600}$ 575
2. $4\overline{)2528}$ 632
3. $7\overline{)9303}$ 1329
4. $2\overline{)5316}$ 2658
5. $9\overline{)2652}$ 294 R6
6. $3\overline{)2917}$ 972 R1
7. $6\overline{)7535}$ 1255 R5
8. $5\overline{)6711}$ 1342 R1
9. $2\overline{)15326}$ 7663
10. $3\overline{)28096}$ 9365 R1

PROBLEM SOLVING
The applications on pages 60-61 may be used anytime after this lesson.

11. $7\overline{)26543}$ 3791 R6
12. $4\overline{)33367}$ 8341 R3
13. $6\overline{)91422}$ 15, 237
14. $5\overline{)83355}$ 16,671
15. $3\overline{)172630}$ 57,543 R1
16. $4\overline{)186275}$ 46, 568 R3
17. $8\overline{)924135}$ 115,516 R7
18. $6\overline{)1342761}$ 223,793 R3

Set D

1. $47 \div 2$ 23 R1
2. $73 \div 5$ 14 R3
3. $156 \div 2$ 78
4. $228 \div 3$ 76
5. $975 \div 3$ 325
6. $770 \div 5$ 154
7. $781 \div 4$ 195 R1
8. $829 \div 6$ 138 R1
9. $8092 \div 7$ 1156
10. $7404 \div 4$ 1851
11. $6843 \div 5$ 1368 R3
12. $9587 \div 2$ 4793 R1
13. $95{,}114 \div 4$ 23,778 R2
14. $91{,}357 \div 8$ 11,419 R5
15. $389{,}952 \div 4$ 97,488
16. $764{,}317 \div 9$ 84,924 R1
17. $856{,}754 \div 2$ 428,377
18. $860{,}498 \div 7$ 122,928 R2

Mixed Practice

C 1. $6\overline{)3376}$ 562 R4
B 2. $9\overline{)684}$ 76
C 3. $3\overline{)261719}$ 87,239 R2
A 4. $5\overline{)83}$ 16 R3
B 5. $4\overline{)671}$ 167 R3
C 10. $7\overline{)49952}$ 7136
B 11. $5\overline{)476}$ 95 R1
C 12. $4\overline{)9253}$ 2313 R1
C 13. $2\overline{)15125}$ 7562 R1
C 14. $5\overline{)3426781}$ 685,356 R1

D 6. $289 \div 3$ 96 R1
D 7. $2151 \div 9$ 239
D 8. $66{,}598 \div 8$ 8324 R6
D 9. $623 \div 7$ 89
D 15. $817 \div 7$ 116 R5
D 16. $5213 \div 8$ 651 R5
D 17. $79 \div 6$ 13 R1
D 18. $716{,}347 \div 5$ 143,269 R2

Objective: Divide whole numbers by a two-digit divisor.

Dividing with Two-Digit Divisors

Example E
Two-digit dividend, first estimate works

```
   2 R2
31)64
 - 62
    2
```

How many 31s in 6? *None*
How many 31s in 64?
Think: 31 is close to 30.
How many 3s in 6? *2*
Write 2 above the 4.

Is the answer reasonable?
Estimate: 31 × 2 ≈ 60
60 is close to 64.
2 R2 is a reasonable answer.

Example F
Three-digit dividend, some estimates too large

```
    2
22)561
 - 44
   12
```

How many 22s in 5? *None*
How many 22s in 56?
Think: 22 is close to 20.
How many 2s in 5? *2*
Write 2 above the 6.

```
   26
22)561
 - 44
  121
- 132
```

How many 22s in 121?
Think: How many 2s in 12? *6*
But you cannot subtract 132 from 121. 6 is too large.
Try 5.

```
   25 R11
22)561
 - 44
  121
- 110
   11
```

Is the answer reasonable?
Estimate: 22 × 25 ≈ 600
600 is close to 561.
25 R11 is a reasonable answer.

Remind students that only one digit at a time can be written in the quotient.
For example:

```
     9
32)3167
 - 288
   287
```

How many 3s in 31? ***10***
Try 9.
Continue dividing.

Example G
Three-digit dividend, round divisor up, some estimates too small

```
    1
18)354
 - 18
   17
```

How many 18s in 35?
Think: 18 is close to 20.
How many 2s in 3? *1*
Write 1 above the 5.

```
   18
18)354
 - 18
  174
- 144
   30
```

Think: How many 2s in 17? *8*

But 30 is greater than 18.
8 is too small. Try 9.

```
   19 R12
18)354
 - 18
  174
- 162
   12
```

Is the answer reasonable?
Estimate: 18 × 19 ≈ 400
400 is close to 354.
19 R12 is a reasonable answer.

Example H
Four or more digits in dividend, horizontal form

3199 ÷ 82

```
    39 R1
82)3199
 - 246
   739
 - 738
     1
```

Rewrite 3199 ÷ 82 as shown.
Divide.

Is the answer reasonable?
Estimate: 82 × 39 ≈ 3200
3200 is close to 3199.
39 R1 is a reasonable answer.

Exercises

Set E

1. $34\overline{)68}$ (2)
2. $24\overline{)96}$ (4)
3. $53\overline{)60}$ (1 R7)
4. $81\overline{)92}$ (1 R11)
5. $32\overline{)74}$ (2 R10)
6. $76\overline{)96}$ (1 R20)
7. $29\overline{)81}$ (2 R23)
8. $52\overline{)77}$ (1 R25)
9. $21\overline{)64}$ (3 R1)
10. $41\overline{)88}$ (2 R6)
11. $80\overline{)95}$ (1 R15)
12. $33\overline{)87}$ (2 R21)

Set F

1. $83\overline{)412}$ (4 R80)
2. $74\overline{)281}$ (3 R59)
3. $53\overline{)301}$ (5 R36)
4. $31\overline{)243}$ (7 R26)
5. $24\overline{)819}$ (34 R3)
6. $23\overline{)829}$ (36 R1)
7. $54\overline{)701}$ (12 R53)
8. $22\overline{)568}$ (25 R18)
9. $52\overline{)673}$ (12 R49)
10. $24\overline{)286}$ (11 R22)
11. $33\overline{)514}$ (15 R19)
12. $43\overline{)676}$ (15 R31)
13. $62\overline{)927}$ (14 R59)
14. $21\overline{)794}$ (37 R17)
15. $34\overline{)620}$ (18 R8)
16. $14\overline{)463}$ (33 R1)
17. $34\overline{)928}$ (27 R10)
18. $42\overline{)829}$ (19 R31)
19. $12\overline{)817}$ (68 R1)
20. $13\overline{)604}$ (46 R6)

Set G

1. $25\overline{)114}$ (4 R14)
2. $57\overline{)286}$ (5 R1)
3. $65\overline{)344}$ (5 R19)
4. $79\overline{)317}$ (4 R1)
5. $28\overline{)226}$ (8 R2)
6. $37\overline{)199}$ (5 R14)
7. $26\overline{)842}$ (32 R10)
8. $19\overline{)790}$ (41 R11)
9. $17\overline{)879}$ (51 R12)
10. $18\overline{)385}$ (21 R7)
11. $15\overline{)927}$ (61 R12)
12. $16\overline{)978}$ (61 R2)
13. $39\overline{)743}$ (19 R2)
14. $48\overline{)773}$ (16 R5)
15. $35\overline{)994}$ (28 R14)
16. $36\overline{)831}$ (23 R3)
17. $28\overline{)732}$ (26 R4)
18. $26\overline{)995}$ (38 R7)
19. $15\overline{)898}$ (59 R13)
20. $25\overline{)896}$ (35 R21)

Set H

1. $3157 \div 42$ (75 R7)
2. $7796 \div 24$ (324 R20)
3. $9980 \div 63$ (158 R26)
4. $17{,}562 \div 51$ (344 R18)
5. $82{,}621 \div 23$ (3592 R5)
6. $82{,}197 \div 36$ (2283 R9)
7. $73{,}329 \div 46$ (1594 R5)
8. $147{,}177 \div 32$ (4599 R9)
9. $448{,}127 \div 77$ (5819 R64)
10. $4{,}194{,}347 \div 56$ (74,899 R3)

Mixed Practice

G 1. $35\overline{)846}$ (24 R6)
F 2. $42\overline{)78932}$ (1879 R14)
G 3. $76\overline{)9992}$ (131 R36)
G 4. $55\overline{)4509989}$ (81,999 R44)
H 5. $94 \div 23$ (4 R2)
H 6. $929 \div 33$ (28 R5)
H 7. $602 \div 24$ (25 R2)
H 8. $719 \div 18$ (39 R17)
G 9. $19\overline{)546873}$ (28,782 R15)
E 10. $31\overline{)86}$ (2 R24)
F 11. $22\overline{)99556}$ (4525 R6)
F 12. $14\overline{)723604}$ (51,686)
H 13. $811 \div 41$ (19 R32)
H 14. $1379 \div 53$ (26 R1)
H 15. $76 \div 54$ (1 R22)
H 16. $739 \div 27$ (27 R10)

See Skills File, page 419, for more practice.

Objective: Divide whole numbers with a zero in the quotient.

Dividing with Zeros in the Quotient

Example I One-digit divisor

$$\begin{array}{r} 4 \\ 9\overline{)3628} \\ -36 \\ \hline 2 \end{array}$$

There are four 9s in 36.

How many 9s in 2? *None*

Students may wish to put a 0 under the subtraction to show that they did subtract.

$$\begin{array}{r} 403 \text{ R1} \\ 9\overline{)3628} \\ -36 \\ \hline 28 \\ -27 \\ \hline 1 \end{array}$$

Write 0 above the 2.
Continue dividing.

Is the answer reasonable?
Estimate: 9 × 403 ≈ 3600
3600 is close to 3628.
403 R1 is a reasonable answer.

Example J Two-digit divisor

$$\begin{array}{r} 3 \\ 21\overline{)649} \\ -63 \\ \hline 19 \end{array}$$

How many 21s in 19? *None*

$$\begin{array}{r} 30 \text{ R19} \\ 21\overline{)649} \\ -63 \\ \hline 19 \end{array}$$

Write 0 above the 9.

Is the answer reasonable?
Estimate: 21 × 30 ≈ 600
600 is close to 649.
30 R19 is a reasonable answer.

PROBLEM SOLVING
The applications on pages 59, 62-65 may be used anytime after this lesson.

Exercises

Set I

1. 8)485 — 60 R5
2. 3)122 — 40 R2
3. 8)2000 — 250
4. 4)3000 — 750
5. 5)3527 — 705 R2
6. 7)4965 — 709 R2
7. 4)28043 — 7010 R3
8. 6)48121 — 8020 R1
9. 5)20018 — 4003 R3
10. 8)64077 — 8009 R5
11. 9)32422 — 3602 R4
12. 6)37257 — 6209 R3

Set J

1. 24)737 — 30 R17
2. 63)648 — 10 R18
3. 36)7418 — 206 R2
4. 23)9244 — 401 R21
5. 56)6000 — 107 R8
6. 75)8202 — 109 R27
7. 45)11737 — 260 R37
8. 54)15165 — 280 R45
9. 29)30758 — 1060 R18
10. 22)88457 — 4020 R17
11. 42)126264 — 3006 R12
12. 15)300718 — 20,047 R13

Mixed Practice

I 1. 5)154 — 30 R4
I 2. 7)2138 — 305 R3
J 3. 63)37948 — 602 R22
I 4. 9)36544 — 4060 R4
J 5. 49)515 — 10 R25
I 6. 3)9028 — 3009 R1
J 7. 38)212883 — 5602 R7
I 8. 8)16334 — 2041 R6
J 9. 52)209052 — 4020 R12
J 10. 23)9223 — 401
I 11. 6)42041 — 7006 R5
J 12. 71)28565 — 402 R23

See Skills File, page 419, for more practice.

Objective: Divide whole numbers by a three-digit divisor.

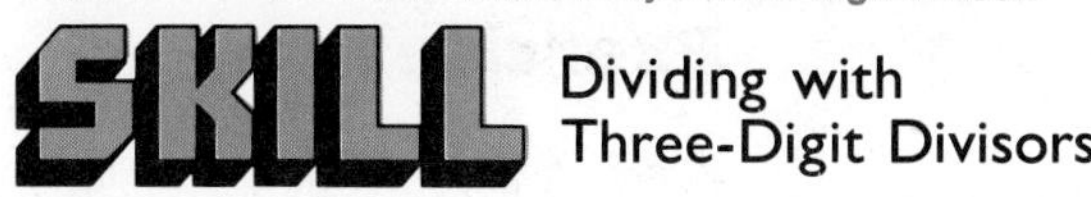

Dividing with Three-Digit Divisors

Example K Three-digit dividend

```
       2 R51
287)625
   -574
     51
```

How many 287s in 625?
Think: 287 is close to 300.
How many 3s in 6? *2*

Is the answer reasonable?
Estimate: 287 × 2 ≈ 600
600 is close to 625.
2 R51 is a reasonable answer.

Example L Four or more digits in dividend

```
        5
714)37218
   - 3570
      151
```

How many 714s in 3? *None*
In 37? *None* In 372? *None*
In 3721?
Think: 714 is close to 700.
How many 7s in 37? *5*

```
       52 R90
714)37218
   - 3570
     1518
   - 1428
       90
```

Think: How many 7s in 15? *2*

Is the answer reasonable?
Estimate: 714 × 52 ≈ 35,000
35,000 is close to 37,218.
52 R90 is a reasonable answer.

Exercises

PROBLEM SOLVING
The applications on pages 66–69 may be used anytime after this lesson.

Set K

1. 107)875 — 8 R19
2. 920)976 — 1 R56
3. 278)820 — 2 R264
4. 576)682 — 1 R106
5. 315)927 — 2 R297
6. 190)985 — 5 R35
7. 186)950 — 5 R20
8. 116)575 — 4 R111
9. 275)879 — 3 R54
10. 433)823 — 1 R390
11. 342)904 — 2 R220
12. 261)796 — 3 R13

Set L

1. 903)5005 — 5 R490
2. 688)9215 — 13 R271
3. 317)9240 — 29 R47
4. 197)7984 — 40 R104
5. 735)61394 — 83 R389
6. 611)24713 — 40 R273
7. 412)12255 — 29 R307
8. 331)60917 — 184 R13
9. 692)34976 — 50 R376
10. 261)53538 — 205 R33
11. 921)802114 — 870 R844
12. 352)635947 — 1806 R235

Mixed Practice

L 1. 912)611783 — 670 R743
K 2. 186)825 — 4 R81
L 3. 304)56432 — 185 R192
L 4. 437)2507 — 5 R322
K 5. 231)653 — 2 R191
L 6. 173)52917 — 305 R152
K 7. 260)784 — 3 R4
L 8. 181)7249 — 40 R9
L 9. 412)160680 — 390
L 10. 394)26589 — 67 R191
K 11. 118)846 — 7 R20
L 12. 579)7528 — 13 R1

Objective: Compute following order of operations involving addition, subtraction, multiplication, and division.

Using Order of Operations

Example M Without operations inside parentheses

$$\frac{8(5)}{10} - \frac{6+8}{9-2}$$

Follow these general rules.

First do all operations inside parentheses; also do any operations above and below division bars.

Then do all remaining multiplications and divisions.

Then do all remaining additions and subtractions from left to right.

$\frac{8(5)}{10} - \frac{6+8}{9-2}$	Do all operations above and below division bars.
$\frac{40}{10} - \frac{14}{7}$	Do remaining divisions.
$4 - 2$	Do remaining subtraction.
2	

Example N With operations inside parentheses

$\frac{6(8-5)}{2} - \frac{25}{9-4} + 2(2)$	Follow rules from Example M. Do operation inside parentheses.
$\frac{6(3)}{2} - \frac{25}{9-4} + 2(2)$	Do operations above and below division bars.
$\frac{18}{2} - \frac{25}{5} + 2(2)$	Do remaining multiplication and divisions.
$9 - 5 + 4$	Do remaining addition and subtraction from left to right.
8	**Emphasize that the remaining addition and subtraction must be done in order from left to right to obtain the correct answer.**

Exercises

Set M

1. $\frac{2(8)-4}{3}$ **4**
2. $\frac{27+9}{8+4}$ **3**
3. $\frac{12+48}{5(4)}$ **3**
4. $\frac{28+5}{3(2)+5}$ **3**
5. $35 - \frac{5+3}{7-5}$ **31**
6. $\frac{40}{2(4)} - 3$ **2**
7. $\frac{72}{9} - \frac{21+3}{4}$ **2**
8. $\frac{8(2)}{4} + \frac{7(4)}{2}$ **18**
9. $3(7) + \frac{15-3}{2}$ **27**
10. $\frac{16-4}{3(2)} + 4(2)$ **10**
11. $\frac{9(4)}{3(2)} - \frac{8(6)}{4(2)}$ **0**
12. $\frac{10-4}{17-15} + \frac{18+42}{6(2)}$ **8**
13. $\frac{20}{4} + \frac{6(3)}{2} + \frac{21}{5+2}$ **17**
14. $4(5) - 7(2) + \frac{100}{25}$ **10**

Set N

1. $\dfrac{36}{3(7-3)}$
3

2. $\dfrac{80}{4(5-3)}$
10

3. $\dfrac{2(8+4)}{3(9-7)}$
4

4. $\dfrac{32}{8} - (11-9)$
2

5. $\dfrac{6(5)}{3} - (5+2)$
3

6. $\dfrac{6(9+1)}{3} - 11$
9

7. $17 - \dfrac{2(5+3)}{4}$
13

8. $\dfrac{2(1+4)}{5} + \dfrac{20}{4}$
7

9. $\dfrac{30}{5} + \dfrac{3(7-5)}{2}$
9

10. $\dfrac{4(7+3)}{5} - \dfrac{24}{12}$
6

11. $\dfrac{25}{5} - \dfrac{2(3+7)}{4}$
0

12. $3(6) + \dfrac{5(7-5)}{5-3}$
23

13. $\dfrac{8(2)}{4} - \dfrac{6(3+2)}{10}$
1

14. $\dfrac{45}{9} - \dfrac{4(7+2)}{3+9} + \dfrac{3(8)}{12(2)}$
3

Mixed Practice

N 1. $\dfrac{42}{2(9-6)}$
7

M 2. $\dfrac{5(6)}{4+1} - \dfrac{16+2}{1+8}$
4

M 3. $\dfrac{24-8}{12-8} + \dfrac{54-9}{5}$
13

N 4. $\dfrac{7(8+4)}{4} + \dfrac{24}{12}$
23

M 5. $\dfrac{6(8)}{4} - \dfrac{7+8}{5}$
9

N 6. $\dfrac{56}{8} - (13-6)$
0

M 7. $\dfrac{3(9)}{7-4} - \dfrac{8+8}{2+2}$
5

M 8. $29 + \dfrac{9(4)+14}{36-11}$
31

N 9. $\dfrac{49}{4+3} + \dfrac{2(11-3)}{4}$
11

N 10. $\dfrac{32}{8} - \dfrac{22}{6+5} + \dfrac{6(4+5)}{3(2)}$
11

N 11. $\dfrac{7(5+4)}{3} - \dfrac{4(10-2)}{16}$
19

M 12. $\dfrac{81}{9} + \dfrac{37+13}{5}$
19

N 13. $9(8) - \dfrac{(6+2)4}{16} + \dfrac{21}{7}$
73

N 14. $\dfrac{64}{2(12-8)}$
8

BREAK TIME

Copy this figure. Show how to divide it into 2 equal parts. Each part must have the same size and shape.

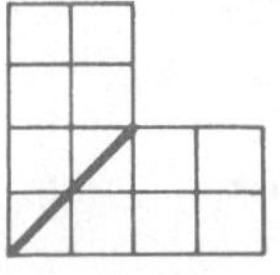

Copy the figure again. Show how to divide it into 3 equal parts.

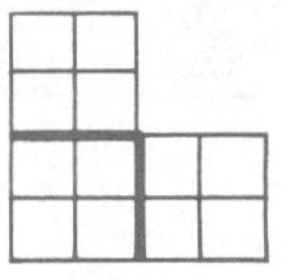

Copy the figure again. Show how to divide it into 4 equal parts.

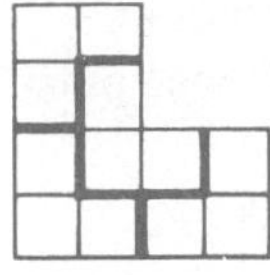

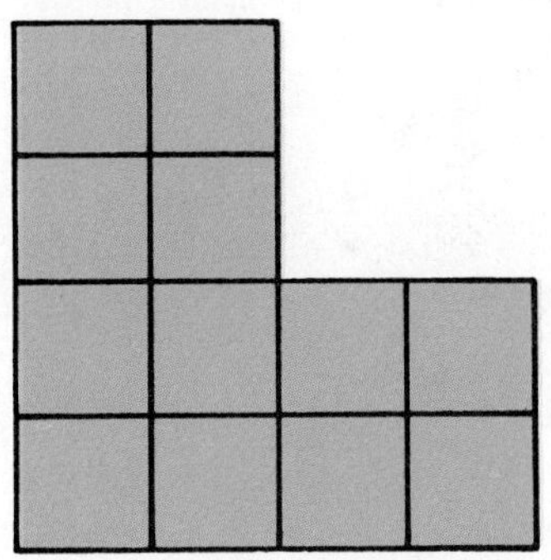

Objective: Solve multiplication and division equations.

Solving Multiplication and Division Equations

Example O Missing factor

Find n.

$25n = 375$ — n is multiplied by 25. To undo the multiplication and get n by itself on one side of the equation, divide both sides of the equation by 25.

$$\frac{25n}{25} = \frac{375}{25}$$

$$n = 15$$

Check:
Does $25(15) = 375$? *Yes* — Check by substituting 15 for n in the original equation.

Example P Missing dividend

Find x.

$\frac{x}{35} = 20$ — x is divided by 35. To undo the division, multiply both sides of the equation by 35.

$$(35)\frac{x}{35} = (35)20$$

$$x = 700$$

Check:
Does $\frac{700}{35} = 20$? *Yes* — Check by substituting 700 for x in the original equation.

Addition and subtraction equations are found in Chapter 1 on pages 12–13. A more complete study of equations is given in Chapter 14.

Exercises

Set O

Find each missing number.

1. $3c = 78$ c = 26
2. $6w = 102$ w = 17
3. $126 = 3q$ q = 42
4. $108 = 4b$ b = 27
5. $6z = 150$ z = 25
6. $8a = 112$ a = 14
7. $126 = 7t$ t = 18
8. $752 = 8w$ w = 94
9. $9y = 126$ y = 14
10. $4x = 340$ x = 85
11. $35n = 140$ n = 4
12. $12n = 132$ n = 11
13. $891 = 33r$ r = 27
14. $385 = 11y$ y = 35
15. $12v = 192$ v = 16
16. $25f = 25$ f = 1
17. $207 = 23d$ d = 9
18. $0 = 71y$ y = 0
19. $57c = 342$ c = 6
20. $24t = 120$ t = 5
21. $51 = 17u$ u = 3
22. $160 = 32g$ g = 5
23. $15d = 120$ d = 8
24. $18x = 270$ x = 15
25. $98 = 14h$ h = 7
26. $352 = 32m$ m = 11

Set P

Find each missing number.

1. $\frac{e}{4} = 13$
e = 52

2. $\frac{v}{3} = 25$
v = 75

3. $95 = \frac{s}{5}$
s = 475

4. $42 = \frac{k}{7}$
k = 294

5. $\frac{a}{7} = 61$
a = 427

6. $\frac{n}{6} = 91$
n = 546

7. $20 = \frac{s}{4}$
s = 80

8. $23 = \frac{m}{6}$
m = 138

9. $\frac{k}{12} = 9$
k = 108

10. $\frac{n}{15} = 5$
n = 75

11. $3 = \frac{n}{45}$
n = 135

12. $6 = \frac{n}{32}$
n = 192

13. $\frac{x}{35} = 9$
x = 315

14. $\frac{w}{26} = 5$
w = 130

15. $8 = \frac{t}{14}$
t = 112

16. $7 = \frac{b}{31}$
b = 217

17. $\frac{w}{13} = 13$
w = 169

18. $\frac{c}{15} = 55$
c = 825

19. $62 = \frac{s}{24}$
s = 1488

20. $53 = \frac{t}{39}$
t = 2067

21. $\frac{x}{21} = 14$
x = 294

22. $\frac{g}{36} = 12$
g = 432

23. $8 = \frac{n}{100}$
n = 800

24. $9 = \frac{y}{200}$
y = 1800

25. $\frac{m}{8} = 160$
m = 1280

26. $\frac{b}{6} = 270$
b = 1620

27. $15 = \frac{t}{300}$
t = 4500

28. $21 = \frac{s}{400}$
s = 8400

Mixed Practice

Find each missing number.

P 1. $12 = \frac{g}{500}$
g = 6000

O 2. $37t = 777$
t = 21

P 3. $29 = \frac{t}{29}$
t = 841

O 4. $5x = 95$
x = 19

P 5. $\frac{a}{9} = 26$
a = 234

O 6. $0 = 56z$
z = 0

P 7. $\frac{c}{15} = 17$
c = 255

O 8. $908 = 4w$
w = 227

P 9. $57 = \frac{y}{11}$
y = 627

O 10. $713 = 23m$
m = 31

P 11. $\frac{b}{2} = 127$
b = 254

O 12. $14s = 882$
s = 63

P 13. $\frac{d}{35} = 45$
d = 1575

O 14. $6n = 78$
n = 13

P 15. $\frac{x}{600} = 9$
x = 5400

O 16. $980 = 7z$
z = 140

BREAK TIME

If it takes 12 minutes to cut a log into 3 pieces, how long would it take to cut the log into 4 pieces?
18 minutes

SKILLS POSTTEST

Number of test items - 16								
Number missed	1	2	3	4	5	6	7	8
Percent correct	94	88	81	75	69	63	56	50

SKILL Dividing with One-Digit Divisors *pages 48–49*

A $2\overline{)73}$ 36 R1 **B** $9\overline{)357}$ 39 R6 **C** $3\overline{)2540}$ 846 R2 **D** $3794 \div 6$ 632 R2

SKILL Dividing with Two-Digit Divisors *pages 50–51*

E $22\overline{)74}$ 3 R8 **F** $23\overline{)796}$ 34 R14 **G** $66\overline{)995}$ 15 R5 **H** $2505 \div 51$ 49 R6

SKILL Dividing with Zeros in the Quotient *page 52*

I $4\overline{)2429}$ 607 R1 **J** $31\overline{)1580}$ 50 R30

SKILL Dividing with Three-Digit Divisors *page 53*

K $294\overline{)682}$ 2 R94 **L** $615\overline{)47998}$ 78 R28

SKILL Using Order of Operations *pages 54–55*

M $2(8) - \frac{4(9)}{10 - 7}$ 4 **N** $\frac{6(6 - 2)}{3} + \frac{4(3)}{6}$ 10

SKILL Solving Multiplication and Division Equations *pages 56–57*

O Find n.

$23n = 184$

$n = 8$

P Find x.

$\frac{x}{12} = 6$

$x = 72$

Problem Solving

CONSUMER APPLICATIONS

See page 8 of *Problem-Solving Masters.*

Objective: Solve problems involving division of whole numbers.

In this lesson students use annual salaries to compute monthly and weekly salaries.

Computing Monthly and Weekly Salaries

Shanu Ahmed was deciding on a career. To help plan his future, he looked up average annual salaries for various occupations.

Complete his chart below.

	Occupation	Salary		
		Annual	Monthly	Weekly
	Apprentice barber	$9360	$780 (9360 ÷ 12)	$180 (9360 ÷ 52)
1.	Automobile mechanic	$15,912	$1326	$306
2.	Bricklayer (journeyman)*	$14,976	$1248	$288
3.	Bulldozer operator*	$14,040	$1170	$270
4.	Carpenter*	$15,288	$1274	$294
5.	Cook	$9516	$793	$183
6.	Custodian	$11,232	$936	$216
7.	Electrician	$19,656	$1638	$378
8.	Fabric worker	$10,296	$858	$198
9.	Nurse	$14,664	$1222	$282
10.	Painter	$14,508	$1209	$279
11.	Photoengraver	$19,812	$1651	$381
12.	Police officer	$19,188	$1599	$369
13.	Sheet-metal worker	$19,500	$1625	$375
14.	Social worker	$11,544	$962	$222
15.	Tilesetter	$17,940	$1495	$345

*Seasonal outside work. Salary affected by weather conditions.

Problem Solving

CONSUMER APPLICATIONS

Objective: Solve problems involving division of whole numbers.

In this lesson students find the price for one item, when given the price for more than one item.

Finding the Price per Item

When Mr. and Mrs. Housum shop for groceries, they keep a running total of their purchases.

Applesauce: 3 jars for 97¢

They bought 1 jar of applesauce.
How much will they pay for 1 jar?

$$\begin{array}{r} 32 \rightarrow 33 \\ 3\overline{)97} \\ -9 \\ \hline 7 \\ -6 \\ \hline 1 \end{array}$$

There is a remainder.
Round up to the next cent.

One jar of applesauce will cost 33¢.

For each problem, find the price if just 1 item is purchased.

	Item	Marked price
1.	Bean soup 42¢	2 cans for 84¢
2.	Cat food 30¢	3 cans for 89¢
3.	Tomato sauce 20¢	5 cans for 98¢
4.	Cucumbers 25¢	4 for 99¢
5.	Peas 44¢	2 cans for 87¢
6.	Vegetable soup 32¢	3 cans for 94¢
7.	Salt 37¢	2 boxes for 74¢
8.	Corn 24¢	4 cans for 96¢
9.	Fruit cocktail 46¢	2 cans for 92¢
10.	Beans 25¢	4 cans for 97¢
11.	Tomatoes 33¢	3 cans for 98¢
12.	Mustard 35¢	2 jars for 69¢
13.	Bread 45¢	2 loaves for 89¢
14.	Hand soap 28¢	3 bars for 84¢
15.	Facial tissues 50¢	2 boxes for 99¢

In each problem, the prices are for the same size can. Tell which brand is a better buy if just 1 can is purchased.

	Brand X	Brand Y	
16.	4 for 78¢	5 for 94¢	Brand Y
17.	3 for 51¢	4 for 73¢	Brand X
18.	4 for 97¢	2 for 53¢	Brand X
19.	3 for 56¢	5 for 98¢	Brand X
20.	3 for 67¢	4 for 86¢	Brand Y
21.	4 for 93¢	2 for 46¢	Brand Y
22.	5 for 72¢	6 for 79¢	Brand Y
23.	2 for 31¢	5 for 84¢	Brand X
24.	4 for 89¢	3 for 72¢	Brand X
25.	3 for 39¢	5 for 58¢	Brand Y
26.	6 for 99¢	4 for 63¢	Brand Y
27.	2 for 59¢	3 for 82¢	Brand Y
28.	3 for 40¢	6 for 87¢	Brand X
29.	5 for 56¢	8 for 99¢	Brand X
30.	2 for 47¢	3 for 75¢	Brand X

Problem Solving

CONSUMER APPLICATIONS

Objective: Solve problems involving division of whole numbers.

In this lesson students find the amount of paint or stain needed to cover a given area.

Painting a House

Dora and Jim Willoya need to paint their storage shed and part of their house. They used a chart like the one below to decide how much paint to buy.

Surface	Type of paint or stain	Square meters covered with 1 liter of paint	
		First or primer coat	Second coat
Frame siding	Exterior house paint	12	13
	Aluminum paint	13	15
Shingle siding	Exterior house paint	8	10
	Shingle stain	4	6
Shingle roofs	Exterior oil paint	4	6
	Shingle stain	3	5
Cement and cinderblock walls	Cement water paint	3	4
	Exterior oil paint	5	6
Walls and ceilings (smooth finish)	Flat oil paint	13	15
	Latex base	13	17
Cement floors and steps	Porch and deck paint	11	15
	Stain and finish	12	12

Dora will paint the bedroom ceilings. She will use two coats of latex-base paint to cover 78 square meters. How many liters of paint will she need?

First coat: 6 liters

$$13\overline{)78}$$

↑ Square meters covered with 1 liter of paint (Read from chart.)

↑ Square meters

Second coat: 4 → 5 liters

$$\begin{array}{r} 4 \\ 17\overline{)78} \\ -\,68 \\ \hline 10 \end{array}$$

There is a remainder. Round up to 5 liters.

Total number of liters: 6 + 5, or 11

See page 9 of
Problem-Solving Masters.

Complete the table below. Remind students to find both the correct surface and the correct type of paint or stain in the chart on page 62.

	Surface	Type of paint or stain	Square meters	First coat (liters)	Second coat (liters)	Total (liters)
1.	Downstairs ceilings	Latex base	130	10	8	18
2.	Living room	Latex base	52	4	4	8
3.	Bedrooms	Latex base	117	9	7	16
4.	Kitchen	Flat oil paint	39	3	3	6
5.	Cement basement walls	Exterior oil paint	130	26	22	48
6.	Cement basement floor	Stain and finish	96	8	8	16
7.	Cement patio floor	Porch and deck paint	22	2	2	4
8.	Shingle siding on shed	Shingle stain	72	18	12	30
9.	Shingle roof on shed	Exterior oil paint	32	8	6	14
10.	Frame siding on house	Exterior house paint	216	18	17	35

Problem Solving

CAREER APPLICATIONS

Objective: Solve problems involving division of whole numbers.

In this lesson students solve problems involving production and deliveries in a bottling plant.

Bottling-Plant Supervisor

See the Careers Chart beginning on page 426 for more information about the careers in this cluster.

Career Cluster: Trades Carla Johnson supervises assembly lines in a bottling plant.

Assembly line 1 fills returnable liter bottles.
Assembly line 2 fills returnable half-liter bottles.
Assembly line 3 fills nonreturnable, two-liter bottles.

Complete the table.

		Line 1	Line 2	Line 3
	Bottles per minute	156	336	72
	Bottles per case	12	24	6
1.	Cases per minute	13 (156 ÷ 12)	14 (336 ÷ 24)	12
2.	Cases per hour (60 min.)	780 (60 × 13)	840 (60 × 14)	720
3.	Cases per day (8 hours)	6240 (8 × 780)	6720	5760
4.	Cases per week (5 days)	31,200 (5 × 6240)	33,600	28,800

How many cases can be filled

5. on line 1 in 3 minutes? (3 × 13)
   39 cases
6. on line 1 in 5 minutes? (5 × 13)
   65 cases
7. on line 1 in 2 hours? (2 × 780)
   1560 cases
8. on line 2 in 10 minutes?
   140 cases
9. on line 2 in 4 weeks?
   134,400 cases
10. on line 3 in 5 hours?
    3600 cases
11. on line 3 in 52 weeks?
    1,497,600 cases

Carla received these orders. Divide by the number of cases per minute to find how many minutes it would take to fill each order.

12. 78 cases of returnable liter bottles (Line 1; 78 ÷ 13)
6 minutes

13. 360 cases of nonreturnable, two-liter bottles (Line 3; 360 ÷ 12)
30 minutes

14. 252 cases of returnable half-liter bottles
18 minutes

15. 650 cases of returnable liter bottles
50 minutes

16. 84 cases of nonreturnable, two-liter bottles
7 minutes

17. 1170 cases of returnable liter bottles
90 minutes

18. 630 cases of returnable half-liter bottles
45 minutes

Bottled water is delivered these two ways.

Bulk delivery vans:
1200 cases per van

Conventional delivery trucks:
250 cases per truck

How many cases can be delivered by

19. 3 bulk delivery vans?
3600 cases

20. 20 bulk delivery vans?
24,000 cases

21. 8 conventional delivery trucks?
2000 cases

22. 5 bulk delivery vans and 12 conventional delivery trucks?
9000 cases

23. 40 bulk delivery vans and 100 conventional delivery trucks?
73,000 cases

Vans deliver to large supermarkets. Trucks deliver to small grocery stores and to coin-operated machines.

Problem Solving

CAREER APPLICATIONS

Objective: Solve problems involving division of whole numbers.

In this lesson students compute inventory turnover rates for appliance stores.

Appliance-Store Buyer

Career Cluster: Business Detail
John Blake is a buyer for Daley's Appliance Store.

He needs to know how fast merchandise is being sold.

First he finds the **total cost of goods sold** during the last six months.

Cost of goods sold	
January	$2470
February	1675
March	2572
April	2863
May	3347
June	4521
Total	**$17448**

The total cost of goods sold is the total amount that the store, *not* the customers, paid for the goods.

Then he finds the **average cost of inventory** for the store. Inventory was taken 3 times during the six months.

Cost of inventory (goods in stock)	
On February 28	$4127
On April 30	4698
On June 30	4261

To find the average, add and divide the total by 3.

$$\begin{array}{r} 4127 \\ 4698 \\ +\,4261 \\ \hline 13086 \end{array} \qquad 3\overline{)13086}\ \ 4362$$

The average cost of inventory was **$4362.**

Then John computes the **inventory turnover rate** for six months.

$$\frac{\text{Total cost of goods sold}}{\text{Average cost of inventory}} = \text{Inventory turnover rate}$$

$$\frac{17448}{4362} = 4$$

The inventory turnover rate for six months was 4. This means that the store turned over (sold) its inventory about 4 times during six months.

Here are some data for three other appliance stores.

Cost of goods sold

Month	Happ's Store	Greco's Store	Lee's Store
January	$3145	$2530	$2945
February	2976	1819	2383
March	4042	2240	3104
April	3416	2701	3062
May	2759	3142	3406
June	3617	4221	2312

Cost of inventory

Date	Happ's Store	Greco's Store	Lee's Store
February 28	$3519	$2379	$3972
April 30	4766	2087	4530
June 30	3688	2671	4407

1. For *each* of the three stores, find
   a. the total cost of goods sold.
   Happ's: $19,955 Greco's: $16,653 Lee's: $17,212
   b. the average cost of inventory.
   Happ's: $3991 Greco's: $2379 Lee's: $4303
   c. the inventory turnover rate.
   Happ's: 5 Greco's: 7 Lee's: 4
2. Which of the three stores had the greatest total cost of goods sold?
   Happ's
3. Which store had the greatest inventory turnover rate?
   Greco's

Happ's store sold more dollars worth of goods, but Greco's store sold its goods faster.

DEVELOPING STRATEGIES

Objective: Solve problems by reading a table and interpreting remainders.

In this lesson students solve problems involving the packaging of eggs for retail and institutional sales.

Tactics: Reading a Table, Interpreting Remainders

The chart shows the number of eggs shipped to Doug Morgan by six farmers. Doug sells eggs for retail and institutional use.

RETAIL—12 eggs per carton
Empty cartons are purchased in cases that each hold 250 cartons.

INSTITUTIONAL—30 eggs per flat
Empty flats are purchased in cases that each hold 500 flats.

Morgan Farms, Inc.			
	Number of eggs		
Farmer	Shipped	Broken	Unbroken
Niatum	4294	23	
Bowen	8649	50	
Gorski	5816	20	
Reynolds	2296	12	
Sanchez	3614	15	
Wilcox	3149	22	
		Total	

Problem

How many cartons will Doug need if all the unbroken eggs that he received from Gorski, Reynolds, and Sanchez will be sold retail?

Solution

The following questions show Doug's strategy for solving the problem. He used the tactics of reading a table and interpreting remainders.

a. How many unbroken eggs were received from Gorski, Reynolds, and Sanchez? Read the table, and then subtract.

$5816 - 20 = 5796$
$2296 - 12 = 2284$
$3614 - 15 = 3599$

b. What is the total number of unbroken eggs received? Add. $5796 + 2284 + 3599 = 11{,}679$

c. How many cartons that hold 12 eggs will be needed? Divide. $11{,}679 \div 12 = 973 \text{ R}3$

Conclusion: Doug will need 973 cartons that will hold 12 eggs each and one carton to hold the remaining 3 eggs. Therefore, he will need a total of 974 cartons.

Related Problems

The unbroken eggs received from Wilcox will be sold for retail use.

1. How many cartons will be needed to pack the eggs?
   261 cartons
2. How many cases of cartons will be needed to pack the eggs?
   2 cases

The unbroken eggs received from Niatum and Bowen will be sold for institutional use.

3. How many full flats can be filled with the eggs from Niatum?
   142 flats
4. How many eggs from Niatum will be in the unfilled flat?
   11 eggs
5. How many full flats can be filled with the eggs from Bowen?
   286 flats
6. How many eggs from Bowen will be in the unfilled flat?
   19 eggs
7. If the eggs from Niatum and Bowen are sold together, how many flats are needed to pack the eggs?
   429 flats
8. How many cases of flats will be needed if the eggs are sold together?
   1 case

Extension

9. A grocery store orders eggs by the pallet. A pallet holds 30 boxes of eggs. There are 30 cartons of eggs in a box. If a grocery store sells 6265 cartons in one month, how many pallets will be needed for 2 months?
   14 pallets

CHAPTER 3 TEST

Number of test items - 22

Number missed	1	2	3	4	5	6	7	8	9	10	11
Percent correct	95	91	86	82	77	73	68	64	59	55	50

A **1.** $3\overline{)77}$ 25 R2

B **2.** $6\overline{)295}$ 49 R1

C **3.** $8\overline{)3914}$ 489 R2

D **4.** $4938 \div 5$ 987 R3

E **5.** $31\overline{)75}$ 2 R13

F **6.** $43\overline{)981}$ 22 R35

G **7.** $38\overline{)994}$ 26 R6

H **8.** $4577 \div 52$ 88 R1

I **9.** $7\overline{)4251}$ 607 R2

J **10.** $43\overline{)2942}$ 68 R18

K **11.** $281\overline{)807}$ 2 R245

L **12.** $725\overline{)24730}$ 34 R80

M **13.** $\frac{6(6)}{9} + \frac{24}{15 - 7}$ 7

N **14.** $\frac{2(8)}{4} - \frac{5(7 - 4)}{5}$ 1

O **15.** Find n. $24n = 144$ $n = 6$

P **16.** Find x. $\frac{x}{17} = 5$ $x = 85$

17. Annual salary: $12,324

Find the monthly salary.
$1027

18. 3 cans for 82¢

Find the price if you buy just 1 can.
28¢

19.

Type of paint	Square meters covered with 1 liter of paint	
	First coat	Second coat
Latex base	13	17

Find how many liters of paint should be bought to cover 65 square meters with two coats of latex-base paint.
9 liters

20. An assembly line fills 14 cases of bottles per minute. How many minutes does it take to fill 588 cases?
42 minutes

21. Find the average cost of inventory below.
$1200

Date	Cost of inventory
February 28	$1250
April 30	1000
June 30	1350

22. How many cartons will be needed to pack 789 eggs if each carton holds 12 eggs?
66 cartons

See pages 5–6 of the *Test Masters* for an alternate form of the Chapter 3 Test.
For a test on Unit 1, see pages T56–T57 of this book and pages 7–8 of the *Test Masters*.

SKILLS TUNE-UP

A Skills Tune-up page occurs at the end of each unit. It contains sets of maintenance exercises that can be used at any time. The exercise sets are referenced to pages where the particular skills are taught.

Adding and Subtracting Whole Numbers, pages 3–14

1. 24 + 65
   89
2. 73 + 25
   98
3. 404 + 356
   760
4. 57 + 62 + 131
   250
5. 55 + 29 + 17
   101
6. 264 + 559 + 36
   859
7. 30 + 34 + 56
   120
8. 58 + 73 + 89
   220
9. 5327 + 674 + 39 + 12
   6052
10. 56 + 15 + 2
    73
11. 2423 + 1727
    4150
12. 32,572 + 5633
    38,205
13. 4 + 59 + 145 + 47
    255
14. 971 + 713 + 44 + 7
    1735
15. 78 − 16
    62
16. 2572 − 33
    2539
17. 807 − 188
    619
18. 8350 − 689
    7661
19. 7003 − 458
    6545
20. 5493 − 836
    4657
21. 5386 − 3338
    2048
22. 65,413 − 47,087
    18,326
23. 4062 − 293
    3769
24. 8452 − 7694
    758
25. 30,104 − 9947
    20,157
26. 74,283 − 17,347
    56,936

Multiplying Whole Numbers, pages 25–36

1. 29 × 3
   87
2. 48 × 37
   1776
3. 20 × 775
   15,500
4. 9 × 420
   3780
5. 63 × 191
   12,033
6. 814 × 9
   7326
7. 163 × 500
   81,500
8. 600 × 90
   54,000
9. 34 × 58
   1972
10. 55 × 378
    20,790
11. 25 × 1200
    30,000
12. 26 × 7053
    183,378
13. 74 × 453
    33,522
14. 22 × 2104
    46,288
15. 42 × 329
    13,818
16. 5 × 1960
    9800
17. 4000 × 300
    1,200,000
18. 409 × 638
    260,942
19. 3 × 3650
    10,950
20. 14 × 326,099
    4,565,386
21. 46 × 2313
    106,398
22. 70,000 × 800
    56,000,000
23. 110 × 4687
    515,570
24. 54 × 5083
    274,482
25. 266 × 15,486
    4,119,276
26. 700 × 40,000
    28,000,000
27. 728 × 737
    536,536

Dividing Whole Numbers, pages 47–58

1. 724 ÷ 4
   181
2. 4500 ÷ 9
   500
3. 7250 ÷ 4
   1812 R2
4. 3974 ÷ 13
   305 R9
5. 1429 ÷ 41
   34 R35
6. 507 ÷ 56
   9 R3
7. 48,000 ÷ 80
   600
8. 773 ÷ 37
   20 R33
9. 80,304 ÷ 4
   20,076
10. 855 ÷ 19
    45
11. 5840 ÷ 730
    8
12. 7582 ÷ 800
    9 R382
13. 2905 ÷ 83
    35
14. 8846 ÷ 385
    22 R376
15. 3293 ÷ 67
    49 R10
16. 7496 ÷ 7
    1070 R6
17. 27,000 ÷ 300
    90
18. 2377 ÷ 59
    40 R17
19. 9600 ÷ 16
    600
20. 3159 ÷ 63
    50 R9
21. 58,248 ÷ 72
    809
22. 16,884 ÷ 28
    603
23. 10,358 ÷ 287
    35 R313
24. 6001 ÷ 94
    63 R79
25. 98,847 ÷ 523
    189
26. 60,273 ÷ 27
    2232 R9
27. 90,067 ÷ 345
    261 R22

CALCULATOR APPLICATIONS

Calculator Applications occur at the end of each unit. They are optional, but all students are encouraged to do them if calculators are available. The applications use the skills from previous chapters.

The chart at the right is a price list from Walker Nursery.

What is the total cost of 3 maples, 5 dogwoods, and 7 junipers?

	$795	Maples (3 × $265)
	410	Dogwoods (5 × $82)
+	189	Junipers (7 × $27)
	$1394	Total cost

The total cost is $1394.

Calculator Suggestion: If your calculator has memory keys, try this key sequence.

Press: 3 [×] 265 [=] [M+] 5 [×] 82 [=] [M+] 7 [×] 27 [=] [M+] [MR]

Display: 1394

Answer: $1394

If your display does not show 1394, consult the instruction book for your calculator to find out how the memory keys work. Be sure to clear the memory before starting each problem.

WALKER NURSERY

Trees	
Ash	$425
Birch	$110
Crab apple	$150
Dogwood	$82
Honey locust	$345
Magnolia	$90
Maple	$265
Weeping willow	$195
Evergreens	
Fir	$125
Pine	$36
Juniper	$27
Spruce	$65
Yew	$56

For each problem, find the total cost of the items.

1. 2 weeping willows, 3 crab apples
$840
2. 8 pines, 6 firs, 2 honey locusts
$1728
3. 4 dogwoods, 5 yews, 1 spruce
$673
4. 25 firs, 9 yews, 1 ash
$4054
5. 1 honey locust, 6 maples, 1 birch
$2045
6. 10 magnolias, 15 dogwoods, 5 pines
$2310
7. 8 yews, 12 junipers, 1 spruce, 1 maple
$1102

Find each answer.

8. The Clarks purchased 2 maple trees, 7 dogwood trees, 4 junipers, and 8 yews. The delivery charge for these items was $75. What was the total cost of these items delivered?
$1735
9. Mrs. Ortez bought 2 crab apple trees, 10 junipers, and 6 yews. The delivery charge was $45, and the labor charge for planting them was $545. What was the total cost including delivery and labor?
$1496
10. Mr. Federico bought 2 yews and 4 junipers. He paid the nursery $250. How much change did he receive?
$30
11. The Olsons bought 2 birch trees, 3 spruces, and 2 firs and had them delivered. The delivery charge was $33. They paid the nursery $700. How much change did they receive?
$2

The calculator suggestion is intended to show students how to solve the problem with one key sequence. Since simple calculators vary somewhat, students should be aware of how their particular calculator works.

COMPUTER LITERACY

Computer Literacy lessons occur at the end of each unit.

The programs and exercises have been written so that they can be used either with a computer or as a pencil and paper activity.

The PRINT and END Statements

A **computer program** is a set of instructions that tells a computer what to do. A computer can only follow orders. Many computers follow orders written in a computer language called BASIC. In BASIC, numbers are written as decimals or decimal approximations. The data that is put into the program is called the **input.** The computer executes the program, and what it prints out is called the **output.**

The computer recognizes these symbols of operation:

*	(multiply)	+	(add)
/	(divide)	−	(subtract)

The instructions to a computer are called statements. The PRINT statement causes the computer to print what is between quotation marks, or answers to calculations.

The END statement stops the program. It should be the last statement in a program.

Program A

Input

```
10 PRINT "JOHN"
20 PRINT "TAUGHT"
30 PRINT "THE COMPUTER"
40 PRINT "TO COMPUTE."
50 END
```

Output

```
JOHN
TAUGHT
THE COMPUTER
TO COMPUTE.
```

Every statement of a program is numbered. Although the statements do not have to be typed in order, the computer always executes them in numerical order.

Program B

Input

```
10 PRINT 8+2
20 PRINT 8-2
30 PRINT 8*2
40 PRINT 8/2
50 END
```

Output

```
10
6
16
4
```

3. 9+4= 13
8−5= 3
4*7= 28
3/2= 1.5

A semicolon separates items in a PRINT statement.

A semicolon used at the end of a PRINT statement causes the computer to print the next PRINT statement on the same line.

Program C

Input

```
10 PRINT "6/2=";6/2
20 PRINT "3/4=";3/4
30 PRINT "5/3=";5/3
40 END
```

Output

```
6/2= 3
3/4= .75
5/3= 1.666666667
```

Give the output for each program.

1.
```
10 PRINT "KATHY LIKES"
20 PRINT "TO WRITE"
30 PRINT "PROGRAMS."
40 END
```
KATHY LIKES
TO WRITE
PROGRAMS.

2.
```
10 PRINT 5+2
20 PRINT 7-4
30 PRINT 6*8
40 PRINT 9/3
50 END
```
7
3
48
3

3.
```
10 PRINT "9+4=";9+4
20 PRINT "8-5=";8-5
30 PRINT "4*7=";4*7
40 PRINT "3/2=";3/2
50 END
```
See above.

4. Write a program that will print your name, address, city, state or province.
Answers will vary. A sample answer is given below.

5. Write a program to compute $6 + 3$, $6 - 3$, 6×3, and $6 \div 3$.
Answers may vary. A sample answer is given below.

4.
```
10 PRINT "MARY FRASER"
20 PRINT "831 COLLEGE"
30 PRINT "BELOIT"
40 PRINT "WISCONSIN"
50 END
```

5.
```
10 PRINT 6+3
20 PRINT 6-3
30 PRINT 6*3
40 PRINT 6/3
50 END
```

Statement numbers can be any integer from 1 to 99,999. Some computers have an automatic numbering feature.

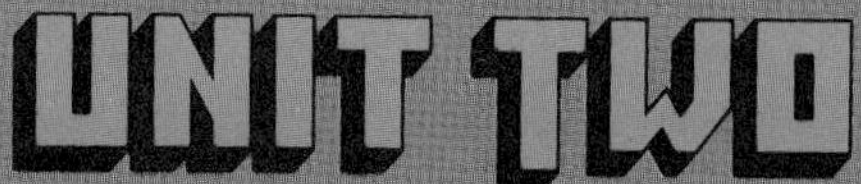

UNIT TWO Decimals and the Metric System

CHAPTER 4 Adding and Subtracting Decimals

SKILLS PRETEST

Number of test items - 16

Number missed	1	2	3	4	5	6	7	8
Percent correct	94	88	81	75	69	63	56	50

SKILL Writing and Comparing Decimals *pages 76–77*

A Give the place value of the 4 in 336.0524.
ten-thousandths

B Write an equal decimal for 0.6 in thousandths.
0.600

C Compare these decimals. Replace ● with <, >, or =.
0.7 ● 0.701
<

SKILL Adding Decimals *pages 78–79*

D
5.4
24.7
+ 3.5
33.6

E
3.002
45.73
+ 12.8
61.532

F 27.25 + 0.37 + 6.04
33.66

G 6.1 + 8.53 + 7
21.63

SKILL Subtracting Decimals *pages 80–81*

H
9.63
− 0.42
9.21

I
15.6
− 9.37
6.23

J 12.5 − 4.8
7.7

K 8.26 − 4.3
3.96

SKILL Rounding Decimals *page 82*

L Round 5.862 to the nearest one.
6

M Round 0.6358 to the nearest hundredth.
0.64

SKILL Estimating Sums and Differences *page 83*

N Estimate.
38.4 + 243.8
280

O Estimate.
7.34 − 4.91
2

P Estimate.
0.27 + 0.64
0.9

See page T31 for additional notes on Chapter 4.

Objective: Write and compare decimals.

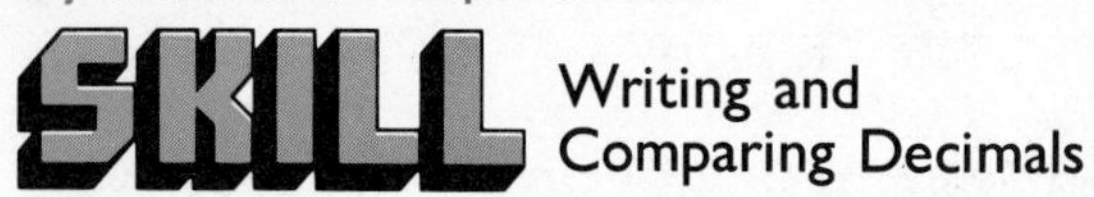

Writing and Comparing Decimals

In this text, zero will be placed to the left of the decimal point when a number is less than one.

Example A Place value

Give the place value of the 6 in each of these numbers.

435.6892
2.136
50.317926

thousands	hundreds	tens	ones	tenths	hundredths	thousandths	ten-thousandths	hundred-thousandths	millionths
	4	3	5	6	8	9	2		
			2	1	3	6			
		5	0	3	1	7	9	2	6

435.6892 — 6 tenths
2.136 — 6 thousandths
50.317926 — 6 millionths

Example B Equal decimals

Write an equal decimal for 0.8 in hundredths and in thousandths.

0.8 = 0.8**0**
0.8 = 0.8**00**

You can write zeros to show equal decimals.

Write an equal decimal for 0.4700 in hundredths and in thousandths.

0.4700 = 0.47
0.4700 = 0.470

You can drop zeros to show equal decimals.

Example C Comparing decimals

Compare these decimals.
Replace ● with <, >, or =.

0.374 ● 0.422
0.374 < 0.422

374 thousandths is less than 422 thousandths.

0.042 ● 0.02
0.042 ● 0.020

Write an equal decimal for 0.02 in thousandths.

0.042 > 0.020
0.042 > 0.02

42 thousandths is greater than 20 thousandths.

0.34 ● 0.3400
0.34 ● 0.34

Write an equal decimal for 0.3400 in hundredths.

0.34 = 0.34
0.34 = 0.3400

34 hundredths is equal to 34 hundredths.

You might want to give the students these whole numbers to compare for a short review of the symbols < and >.

68 ● 75 [<]	896 ● 895 [>]
32 ● 34 [<]	597 ● 579 [>]
98 ● 45 [>]	1079 ● 1709 [<]
757 ● 759 [<]	3845 ● 3485 [>]

You could use number lines to show students that 0.8 = 0.80 = 0.800. Notice that the number lines are calibrated in tenths, hundredths, and thousandths.

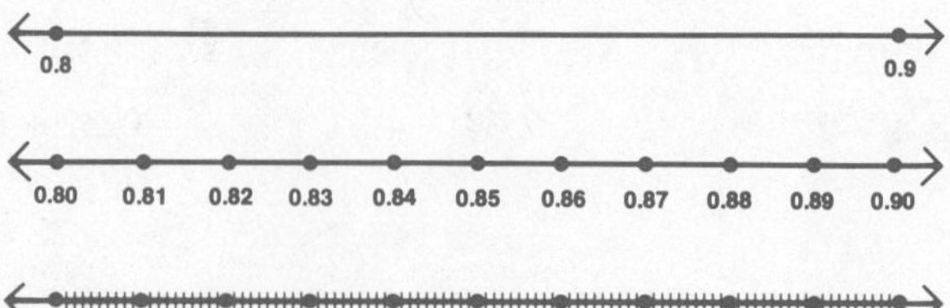

Exercises

Set A

Give the place value of the 3 in each number.

1. 7.138
   hundredths
2. 6.309
   tenths
3. 1.2873
   ten-thousandths
4. 13.67
   ones
5. 218.003
   thousandths
6. 136.51
   tens
7. 8.01673
   hundred-thousandths
8. 719.3
   tenths
9. 310.6
   hundreds
10. 0.019653
    millionths
11. 216.03
    hundredths
12. 75.013
    thousandths
13. 21.38
    tenths
14. 3016.2
    thousands
15. 0.874093
    millionths
16. 0.92315
    thousandths
17. 0.71683
    hundred-thousandths
18. 6.0153
    ten-thousandths
19. 13,675.1
    thousands
20. 0.01763
    hundred-thousandths
21. 5384.6
    hundreds
22. 6.0653
    ten-thousandths

Set B

Write an equal decimal for each number in hundredths and in thousandths.

1. 0.6
   0.60, 0.600
2. 0.4200
   0.42, 0.420
3. 0.3800
   0.38, 0.380
4. 0.2600
   0.26, 0.260
5. 0.1
   0.10, 0.100
6. 0.2
   0.20, 0.200
7. 0.9100
   0.91, 0.910
8. 0.7
   0.70, 0.700
9. 0.6300
   0.63, 0.630
10. 0.5800
    0.58, 0.580
11. 0.9
    0.90, 0.900
12. 0.3
    0.30, 0.300
13. 1.6
    1.60, 1.600
14. 0.8200
    0.82, 0.820
15. 0.3700
    0.37, 0.370
16. 7.6100
    7.61, 7.610
17. 0.5
    0.50, 0.500
18. 2.9
    2.90, 2.900
19. 3.2500
    3.25, 3.250
20. 0.4
    0.40, 0.400

Set C

Compare these decimals.
Replace ● with <, >, or =.

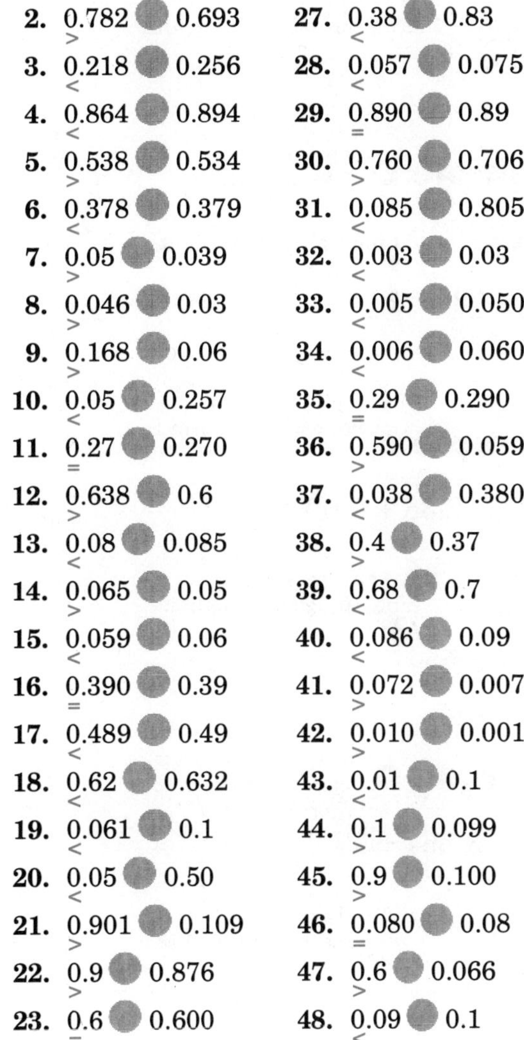

1. 0.29 ● 0.31
   <
2. 0.782 ● 0.693
   >
3. 0.218 ● 0.256
   <
4. 0.864 ● 0.894
   <
5. 0.538 ● 0.534
   >
6. 0.378 ● 0.379
   <
7. 0.05 ● 0.039
   >
8. 0.046 ● 0.03
   >
9. 0.168 ● 0.06
   >
10. 0.05 ● 0.257
    <
11. 0.27 ● 0.270
    =
12. 0.638 ● 0.6
    >
13. 0.08 ● 0.085
    <
14. 0.065 ● 0.05
    >
15. 0.059 ● 0.06
    <
16. 0.390 ● 0.39
    =
17. 0.489 ● 0.49
    <
18. 0.62 ● 0.632
    <
19. 0.061 ● 0.1
    <
20. 0.05 ● 0.50
    <
21. 0.901 ● 0.109
    >
22. 0.9 ● 0.876
    >
23. 0.6 ● 0.600
    =
24. 0.01 ● 0.005
    >
25. 0.009 ● 0.01
    <
26. 0.652 ● 0.7
    <
27. 0.38 ● 0.83
    <
28. 0.057 ● 0.075
    <
29. 0.890 ● 0.89
    =
30. 0.760 ● 0.706
    >
31. 0.085 ● 0.805
    <
32. 0.003 ● 0.03
    <
33. 0.005 ● 0.050
    <
34. 0.006 ● 0.060
    <
35. 0.29 ● 0.290
    =
36. 0.590 ● 0.059
    >
37. 0.038 ● 0.380
    <
38. 0.4 ● 0.37
    >
39. 0.68 ● 0.7
    <
40. 0.086 ● 0.09
    <
41. 0.072 ● 0.007
    >
42. 0.010 ● 0.001
    >
43. 0.01 ● 0.1
    <
44. 0.1 ● 0.099
    >
45. 0.9 ● 0.100
    >
46. 0.080 ● 0.08
    =
47. 0.6 ● 0.066
    >
48. 0.09 ● 0.1
    <
49. 0.056 ● 0.560
    <
50. 0.06 ● 0.060
    =

Objective: Add decimals.

Adding Decimals

Example D Same number of decimal places

```
   7.6    Line up decimal points.
  12.8    Add tenths, ones, and tens.
+  9.2    Place decimal point in sum.
  29.6
```

Example E Different number of decimal places

```
   4.3      Line up decimal points.
  12.75     Add.
+  0.093
  17.143
```

Example F Horizontal form, same number of decimal places

36.47 + 2.38 + 0.09

```
  36.47   Rewrite as shown.
   2.38   Line up decimal points.
+  0.09   Add.
  38.94
```

Example G Horizontal form, different number of decimal places

0.07 + 3.864 + 17.2

```
   0.07    Rewrite as shown.
   3.864   Line up decimal points.
+ 17.2     Add.
  21.134
```

You might want to give students these additional exercises before assigning Set G.

7.2 + 59.5 + 0.491 [67.191]
3.2 + 0.84 + 7.605 [11.645]
0.09 + 0.8 + 7 + 0.46 [8.35]
0.25 + 4.7 + 6 + 0.387 [11.337]

Exercises

Set D

1. 10.8 + 7.9 — 18.7
2. 67.3 + 89.4 — 156.7
3. 9.72 + 5.46 — 15.18
4. 8.59 + 14.32 — 22.91
5. 0.072 + 0.135 — 0.207
6. 25.38 + 9.27 — 34.65
7. 2.934 + 5.708 — 8.642
8. 9.362 + 8.487 — 17.849
9. 219.6 + 0.4 + 58.3 — 278.3
10. 10.34 + 0.96 + 25.41 — 36.71
11. 16.842 + 0.061 + 2.954 — 19.857

Set E

1. 0.5 + 0.204 + 0.16 — 0.864
2. 0.386 + 0.01 + 0.5 — 0.896
3. 0.675 + 0.9 + 0.38 — 1.955
4. 6.943 + 0.2 + 3.57 — 10.713
5. 4.251 + 7.9 + 0.38 — 12.531
6. 31.6 + 1.892 + 7.05 — 40.542
7. 12.48 + 0.673 + 9.1 — 22.253
8. 25.6 + 3.841 + 9.02 — 38.461
9. 50.001 + 3.96 + 27.8 — 81.761
10. 29.387 + 0.8 + 1.62 — 31.807

Set F

1. 4.2 + 3.7
   7.9
2. 6.4 + 3.5
   9.9
3. 0.81 + 0.57
   1.38
4. 2.06 + 7.29
   9.35
5. 1.96 + 3.75
   5.71
6. 0.062 + 0.814
   0.876
7. 1.039 + 3.684
   4.723
8. 8.013 + 1.789
   9.802
9. 0.2 + 0.6 + 0.4
   1.2
10. 0.75 + 0.83 + 0.47
    2.05
11. 0.684 + 0.703 + 0.541
    1.928
12. 1.098 + 8.635 + 2.174
    11.907
13. 3.2 + 6.8 + 7.4 + 9.1
    26.5

Set G

1. 0.09 + 3.6
   3.69
2. 2.8 + 0.139
   2.939
3. 0.437 + 2.59
   3.027
4. 78.1 + 5
   83.1
5. 8.45 + 0.652 + 1.5
   10.602
6. 0.91 + 0.2 + 0.078
   1.188
7. 0.942 + 0.7 + 0.48
   2.122
8. 1.2 + 2.86 + 0.093
   4.153
9. 8.725 + 0.23 + 2.46
   11.415
10. 5.37 + 2.938 + 0.05
    8.358
11. 0.72 + 3.921 + 7.5
    12.141
12. 4.9 + 0.72 + 3.6 + 0.01
    9.23
13. 1.8 + 2.63 + 0.012 + 6
    10.442

Mixed Practice

D 1. $\begin{array}{r} 6.75 \\ +\ 8.96 \\ \hline \end{array}$
   15.71

E 2. $\begin{array}{r} 5.74 \\ 1.8 \\ +\ 0.071 \\ \hline \end{array}$
   7.611

E 3. $\begin{array}{r} 17.48 \\ 9.074 \\ +\ \ 0.36 \\ \hline \end{array}$
   26.914

D 4. $\begin{array}{r} 5.829 \\ +\ 6.743 \\ \hline \end{array}$
   12.572

F 5. 5.9 + 2.4
   8.3

G 6. 0.16 + 0.014
   0.174

G 7. 17.5 + 2.46 + 8.3
   28.26

F 8. 1.35 + 2.76
   4.11

F 9. 5.348 + 9.215
   14.563

G 10. 32.5 + 0.43
    32.93

G 11. 7 + 0.096 + 1.8
    8.896

F 12. 0.395 + 0.627
    1.022

G 13. 0.62 + 2.5 + 0.3
    3.42

F 14. 16.89 + 3.21 + 12.05
    32.15

F 15. 5.487 + 4.396
    9.883

G 16. 4.9 + 6 + 3.25
    14.15

G 17. 96.3 + 0.68 + 1.7 + 1.5
    100.18

G 18. 0.675 + 2 + 5.432
    8.107

G 19. 65.39 + 7.064
    72.454

G 20. 13.04 + 8 + 2.1 + 0.79
    23.93

F 21. 1.8 + 13.6 + 2.9
    18.3

F 22. 0.013 + 0.208 + 0.009
    0.23

G 23. 0.098 + 1.7 + 0.6
    2.398

See Skills File, page 419, for more practice.

BREAK TIME

Move *only one* glass so that the empty glasses alternate with the full glasses.

Move only the second glass. Pick it up and pour the liquid into the fifth glass. Return the glass to its position.

Objective: Subtract decimals.

Subtracting Decimals

Example H

Same number of decimal places

```
  4.72
- 2.65
  2.07
```

Line up decimal points.
Subtract hundredths, tenths, and ones.
Place decimal point in difference.

Example I

Different number of decimal places

```
  7.6
- 4.362
```

Line up decimal points.

```
  7.600
- 4.362
  3.238
```

Write zeros to show thousandths.
Subtract.

Review the fact that annexing zeros does not change the value of the decimal. See Example B.

Example J

Horizontal form, same number of decimal places

14.25 − 8.59

```
  14.25
-  8.59
   5.66
```

Rewrite 14.25 − 8.59 as shown.
Line up decimal points.
Subtract.

Example K

Horizontal form, different number of decimal places

18.76 − 5.9

```
  18.76
-  5.9
  12.86
```

Rewrite 18.76 − 5.9 as shown.
Line up decimal points.
Subtract.

You might want to give students these additional exercises before assigning Set K.

8.296 − 4.32 [3.976]
6.2 − 3.18 [3.02]
9 − 1.6 [7.4]
7.1 − 5.076 [2.024]

Exercises

Set H

1. 5.6 − 3.2 — 2.4
2. 7.8 − 0.9 — 6.9
3. 0.67 − 0.28 — 0.39
4. 9.75 − 4.67 — 5.08
5. 5.81 − 3.96 — 1.85
6. 12.03 − 8.15 — 3.88
7. 0.892 − 0.371 — 0.521
8. 0.943 − 0.217 — 0.726
9. 0.769 − 0.085 — 0.684
10. 9.138 − 2.079 — 7.059
11. 8.602 − 5.314 — 3.288
12. 7.001 − 6.358 — 0.643

Set I

1. 5.9 − 1.86 — 4.04
2. 4.7 − 2.63 — 2.07
3. 7.1 − 3.45 — 3.65
4. 3.67 − 1.8 — 1.87
5. 4.3 − 2.68 — 1.62
6. 7.2 − 4.91 — 2.29
7. 0.59 − 0.372 — 0.218
8. 0.64 − 0.258 — 0.382
9. 0.581 − 0.39 — 0.191
10. 4.35 − 1.762 — 2.588
11. 7.251 − 2.37 — 4.881
12. 7.6 − 3.789 — 3.811

PROBLEM SOLVING
The applications on pages 85–93 may be used anytime after this lesson.

Set J

1. $4.6 - 3.2$
   1.4
2. $9.4 - 5.8$
   3.6
3. $6.83 - 4.27$
   2.56
4. $7.41 - 5.63$
   1.78
5. $5.362 - 1.491$
   3.871
6. $0.312 - 0.045$
   0.267
7. $15.37 - 9.48$
   5.89
8. $35.21 - 26.35$
   8.86
9. $8.215 - 7.326$
   0.889
10. $5.106 - 3.724$
    1.382
11. $7.284 - 2.395$
    4.889
12. $38.154 - 17.237$
    20.917
13. $0.7684 - 0.0369$
    0.7315

Set K

1. $8.75 - 2.6$
   6.15
2. $7.2 - 3$
   4.2
3. $9.4 - 7.25$
   2.15
4. $8.256 - 4.13$
   4.126
5. $4.28 - 2.195$
   2.085
6. $7.18 - 5.091$
   2.089
7. $8.164 - 3.89$
   4.274
8. $7.639 - 4.1$
   3.539
9. $6.8 - 4.521$
   2.279
10. $7.5 - 3.276$
    4.224
11. $17.365 - 12.19$
    5.175
12. $39.32 - 24.732$
    14.588
13. $28 - 15.36$
    12.64

Mixed Practice

H 1. $\begin{array}{r} 5.73 \\ -\ 4.28 \\ \hline \end{array}$
1.45

I 2. $\begin{array}{r} 15.4 \\ -\ 8.673 \\ \hline \end{array}$
6.727

I 3. $\begin{array}{r} 281.4 \\ -\ 4.828 \\ \hline \end{array}$
276.572

H 4. $\begin{array}{r} 13.462 \\ -\ 8.521 \\ \hline \end{array}$
4.941

J 5. $8.1 - 6.7$
1.4

K 6. $8.37 - 6.4$
1.97

J 7. $8.03 - 2.16$
5.87

K 8. $9.13 - 5.062$
4.068

K 9. $18.21 - 18.096$
0.114

J 10. $0.81 - 0.64$
0.17

K 11. $9 - 6.7$
2.3

J 12. $4.362 - 1.475$
2.887

K 13. $8.104 - 5$
3.104

J 14. $9.35 - 7.48$
1.87

K 15. $8.1 - 5.23$
2.87

J 16. $27.58 - 16.79$
10.79

K 17. $49.2 - 36.895$
12.305

J 18. $1.826 - 0.739$
1.087

K 19. $6.35 - 3.182$
3.168

K 20. $18.1 - 3.105$
14.995

J 21. $9.001 - 5.382$
3.619

K 22. $0.01 - 0.009$
0.001

K 23. $37.389 - 26$
11.389

J 24. $65.003 - 58.351$
6.652

J 25. $12.013 - 8.136$
3.877

BREAK TIME

During the restoration of an old clock, it was discovered that the clock face had been cracked into four pieces. The interesting fact was that the sum of the individual symbols on each piece was 20.

Copy the clock face below and draw the cracks.

Note: IIII was often used in place of IV.

See Skills File, page 420, for more practice.

Objective: Round decimals.

Rounding Decimals

Example L To the nearest one

Round each decimal to the nearest one.

3.876 — Find the ones place. The digit to the right is 5 or greater.
↓
4 — Round up. Drop all digits to the right of the ones place.

$3.876 \approx 4$

26.32 — Find the ones place. The digit to the right is less than 5.
↓
26 — Do not change the digit in the ones place. Drop all digits to the right of the ones place.

$26.32 \approx 26$

Example M To the nearest tenth, nearest hundredth, or nearest thousandth

Round each decimal.

Round 3.075 to the nearest tenth.

$3.075 \approx 3.1$

tenths place
3.075
↓
3.1

Round 0.4852 to the nearest hundredth.

$0.4852 \approx 0.49$

hundredths place
0.4852
↓
0.49

Round 2.9872 to the nearest thousandth.

$2.9872 \approx 2.987$

thousandths place
2.9872
↓
2.987

Exercises

You may want to have students refer to the place-value chart on page 76.

Set L

Round to the nearest one.

1. 7.8 — 8
2. 3.4 — 3
3. 16.21 — 16
4. 42.708 — 43
5. 58.069 — 58
6. 49.91 — 50
7. 94.51 — 95
8. 20.81 — 21
9. 104.26 — 104
10. 2.684 — 3
11. 201.10 — 201
12. 371.80 — 372
13. 598.60 — 599
14. 423.5 — 424
15. 0.3218 — 0

Set M

Round to the nearest tenth.

1. 2.3094 — 2.3
2. 1.56 — 1.6
3. 0.072 — 0.1
4. 47.193 — 47.2
5. 0.35 — 0.4
6. 0.3892 — 0.4
7. 101.29 — 101.3
8. 6.53 — 6.5
9. 72.448 — 72.4
10. 0.802 — 0.8
11. 27.19 — 27.2
12. 9.3365 — 9.3
13. 0.8801 — 0.9
14. 2.451 — 2.5
15. 11.98 — 12.0

Round to the nearest hundredth.

16. 5.327 — 5.33
17. 0.6194 — 0.62
18. 12.053 — 12.05
19. 6.11749 — 6.12
20. 95.1302 — 95.13
21. 0.3851 — 0.39
22. 24.054 — 24.05
23. 3.1657 — 3.17
24. 41.977 — 41.98
25. 0.0082 — 0.01
26. 4.932 — 4.93
27. 1.441 — 1.44
28. 28.668 — 28.67
29. 7.5023 — 7.50
30. 0.3967 — 0.40

Round to the nearest thousandth.

31. 0.00367 — 0.004
32. 5.1922 — 5.192
33. 0.2847 — 0.285
34. 6.1008 — 6.101
35. 0.42831 — 0.428
36. 9.0161 — 9.016
37. 0.20453 — 0.205
38. 1.9801 — 1.980
39. 8.3384 — 8.338
40. 7.2531 — 7.253
41. 0.62588 — 0.626
42. 0.0079 — 0.008
43. 71.1135 — 71.114
44. 2.4364 — 2.436
45. 0.3796 — 0.380

Objective: Estimate sums and differences using rounded numbers.

Estimating Sums and Differences

Example N
Sums or differences with numbers greater than 10

Estimate. 54.8 + 286.3

$$54.8 + 286.3$$
$$\downarrow \quad \downarrow$$
$$50 + 290 = 340$$

When the numbers are greater than 10, round as with whole numbers.

Then add or subtract.

$$54.8 + 286.3 \approx 340$$

Example O
Sums or differences with numbers between 1 and 10

Estimate. 8.93 − 4.17

$$8.93 - 4.17$$
$$\downarrow \quad \downarrow$$
$$9 - 4 = 5$$

When the numbers are between 1 and 10, round to the nearest one.

Then add or subtract.

$$8.93 - 4.17 \approx 5$$

Example P
Sums or differences with numbers less than 1

Estimate. 0.38 + 0.54

$$0.38 + 0.54$$
$$\downarrow \quad \downarrow$$
$$0.4 + 0.5 = 0.9$$

When the numbers are less than 1, round to the same place.

Then add or subtract.

$$0.38 + 0.54 \approx 0.9$$

In Set P, the numbers in Exercise 5 could be rounded to the nearest hundredth to give 0.14. The numbers in Exercise 6 could be rounded to the nearest tenth to give 0.6.

In Mixed Practice, the numbers in Exercise 9 could be rounded to the nearest hundredth to give 0.55. The numbers in Exercise 12 could be rounded to the nearest tenth to give 0.7.

Exercises

Set N

Estimate each answer.

1. 42.6 + 89.7
130
2. 378.4 + 67.9
450
3. 51.96 − 39.8
10
4. 872.93 − 89.3
780
5. 38.12 + 942.8
980
6. 616.2 − 21.68
600

Set O

Estimate each answer.

1. 7.16 − 1.72
5
2. 8.3 − 5.88
2
3. 3.463 + 5.81
9
4. 5.32 + 7.681
13
5. 9.37 − 2.986
6
6. 7.777 + 5.89
14

Set P

Estimate each answer.

1. 0.58 + 0.62
1.2
2. 0.92 − 0.38
0.5
3. 0.617 − 0.473
0.1
4. 0.793 + 0.361
1.2
5. 0.82 − 0.675
0.1
6. 0.62 + 0.035
0.66

Mixed Practice

Estimate each answer. Then find the actual sum or difference.

O 1. 9.27 − 5.8
3; 3.47
N 2. 305.4 + 621.7
900; 927.1
O 3. 2.3 + 7.95
10; 10.25
P 4. 0.88 − 0.65
0.2; 0.23
N 5. 239.65 − 83.7
160; 155.95
O 6. 6.47 + 2.83
9; 9.3
P 7. 0.57 + 0.28
0.9; 0.85
N 8. 878.2 − 358.7
500; 519.5
P 9. 0.93 − 0.382
0.5; 0.548
O 10. 7.2 − 3.84
3; 3.36
N 11. 347.8 + 51.72
400; 399.52
P 12. 0.085 + 0.57
0.66; 0.655

SKILLS POSTTEST

Number of test items - 16

Number missed	1	2	3	4	5	6	7	8
Percent correct	94	88	81	75	69	63	56	50

SKILL Writing and Comparing Decimals *pages 76–77*

A Give the place value of the 5 in 782.0459.
thousandths

B Write an equal decimal for 0.2 in thousandths.
0.200

C Compare these decimals. Replace ● with <, >, or =.
0.9 ● 0.091
>

SKILL Adding Decimals *pages 78–79*

D 12.7 + 3.5 + 9.1
25.3

E 21.9 + 3.067 + 16.39
41.357

F 16.72 + 0.38 + 5.09
22.19

G 8.3 + 1.65 + 9
18.95

SKILL Subtracting Decimals *pages 80–81*

H 7.25 − 0.14
7.11

I 12.9 − 6.35
6.55

J 16.3 − 10.7
5.6

K 9.35 − 7.4
1.95

SKILL Rounding Decimals *page 82*

L Round 7.54 to the nearest one.
8

M Round 0.849 to the nearest hundredth.
0.85

SKILL Estimating Sums and Differences *page 83*

N Estimate.
47.2 + 323.5
370

O Estimate.
6.27 − 3.85
2

P Estimate.
0.47 + 0.38
0.9

Problem Solving

CONSUMER APPLICATIONS

Objective: Solve problems involving subtraction of decimals.

In this lesson students read the code for a discount catalog and compute the savings between the list price and discount price.

Buying from a Discount Catalog

Mario plans to buy this blender from a discount catalog.

14-SPEED BLENDER
Features easy access and positive push-button control. Hi-Lo switch doubles blending speed instantly. Large 44 oz. shatterproof container. Cord storage. Almond.

226 24E 2397 .... $34.95

Stock number (226 24E) · Discount price (2397) · List price ($34.95)

He subtracted to find how much money he would save if he purchased this blender at the discount price rather than the list price.

\$34.95	List price
− 23.97	Discount price
\$10.98	Savings

How much money would be saved by purchasing each appliance at the discount price rather than the list price?

1. BLENDER A
   Harvest Gold.
   242 23E 2175 .... $29.95
   $8.20
2. BLENDER B
   Avocado.
   261 09E 2894 .... $37.95
   $9.01
3. BLENDER C
   Black and Chrome.
   242 22E 3787 .... $51.95
   $14.08
4. BLENDER D
   Almond and Chrome.
   261 08E 3247 .... $43.95
   $11.48
5. FOOD PROCESSOR A
   Harvest Gold.
   6570 H 10984 .... $145.95
   $36.11
6. FOOD PROCESSOR B
   White and Chrome.
   6867 H 13789 .... $219.95
   $82.06
7. FOOD PROCESSOR C
   Almond.
   6284 H 19987 .... $279.95
   $80.08
8. FOOD PROCESSOR D
   Almond.
   4735 H 12177 .... $199.99
   $78.22

You might discuss reasons for the differences in prices of blenders and food processors, such as number of speeds, size, quality, number of attachments, and brand names.

Problem Solving

CONSUMER APPLICATIONS

Objective: Solve problems involving addition and subtraction of decimals.

In this lesson students compute the total and the net deposit that are recorded on a deposit slip.

Writing a Deposit Slip

When James opened a checking account at a bank, he made out a deposit slip for $61.74. He kept the receipt the bank gave him as proof that the deposit had been made.

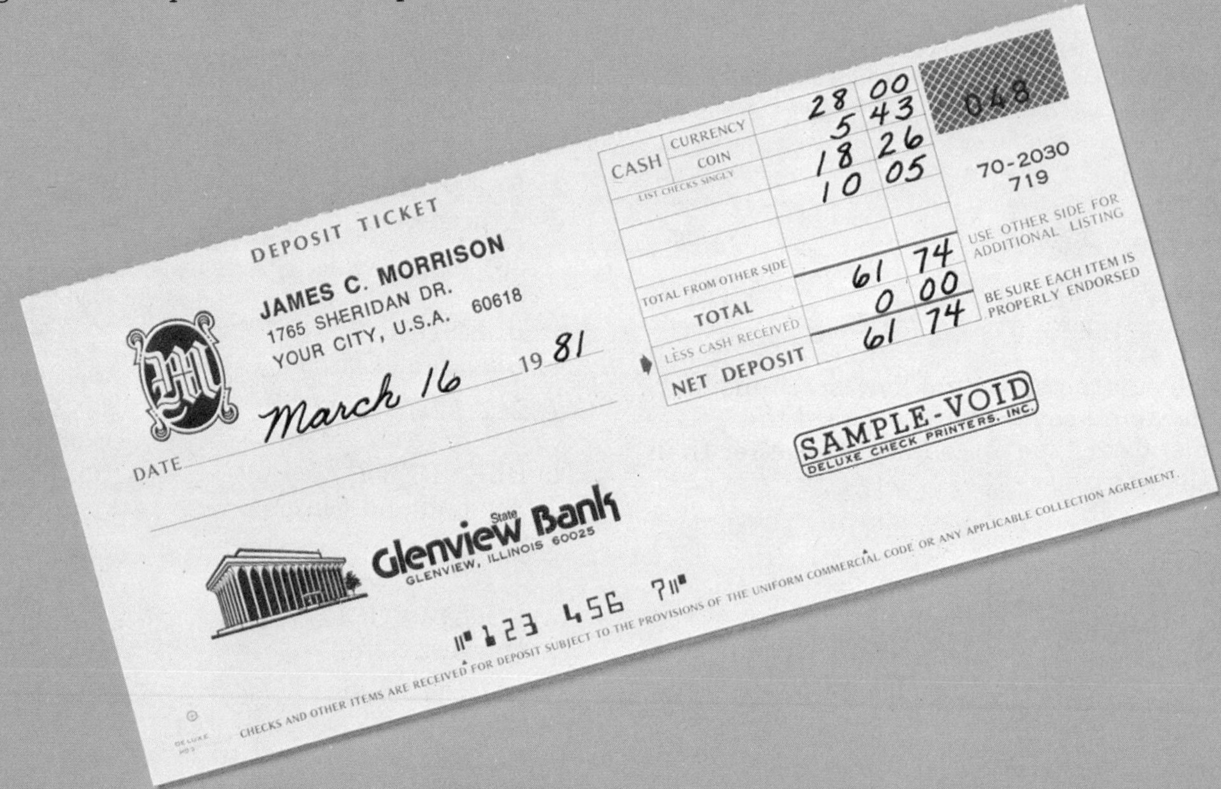

DEPOSIT TICKET

JAMES C. MORRISON
1765 SHERIDAN DR.
YOUR CITY, U.S.A. 60618

DATE March 16 19 81

CASH	CURRENCY	28	00
	COIN	5	43
LIST CHECKS SINGLY		18	26
		10	05
TOTAL FROM OTHER SIDE			
TOTAL		61	74
LESS CASH RECEIVED		0	00
NET DEPOSIT		61	74

048

70-2030
719

USE OTHER SIDE FOR ADDITIONAL LISTING

BE SURE EACH ITEM IS PROPERLY ENDORSED

SAMPLE-VOID
DELUXE CHECK PRINTERS, INC.

Glenview State Bank
GLENVIEW, ILLINOIS 60025

⑆123 456 7⑆

CHECKS AND OTHER ITEMS ARE RECEIVED FOR DEPOSIT SUBJECT TO THE PROVISIONS OF THE UNIFORM COMMERCIAL CODE OR ANY APPLICABLE COLLECTION AGREEMENT.

Find the total and the net deposit for each deposit slip.

1.

CASH	CURRENCY	37	00
	COIN	6	38
LIST CHECKS SINGLY		25	71
		16	89
TOTAL FROM OTHER SIDE			
TOTAL		85	98
LESS CASH RECEIVED		0	00
NET DEPOSIT		85	98

2.

CASH	CURRENCY	25	00
	COIN	2	61
LIST CHECKS SINGLY		19	18
		67	34
TOTAL FROM OTHER SIDE			
TOTAL		114	13
LESS CASH RECEIVED		0	00
NET DEPOSIT		114	13

The vertical line on the deposit slip serves in place of the decimal point to separate dollars and cents. The dollar sign is not used here, but it is understood that these are amounts of money.

See pages 10 and 60 of *Problem-Solving Masters.*

Problems 1–4 are like the example on page 86.
Problems 5–8 involve receiving cash while making a deposit.
Problems 9–10 involve larger deposits (especially coins), such as for a business.

3.

CASH	CURRENCY	175	00
	COIN		
LIST CHECKS SINGLY		82	51
		125	00
		396	28
TOTAL FROM OTHER SIDE			
TOTAL		778	79
LESS CASH RECEIVED		0	00
NET DEPOSIT		778	79

7.

CASH	CURRENCY		
	COIN		
LIST CHECKS SINGLY		509	62
		142	38
		12	73
TOTAL FROM OTHER SIDE			
TOTAL		664	73
LESS CASH RECEIVED		75	00
NET DEPOSIT		589	73

4.

CASH	CURRENCY	92	00
	COIN	5	15
LIST CHECKS SINGLY		276	37
		65	42
		114	87
TOTAL FROM OTHER SIDE			
TOTAL		553	81
LESS CASH RECEIVED		0	00
NET DEPOSIT		553	81

8.

CASH	CURRENCY		
	COIN		
LIST CHECKS SINGLY		106	91
		250	64
		718	12
TOTAL FROM OTHER SIDE			
TOTAL		1075	67
LESS CASH RECEIVED		280	90
NET DEPOSIT		794	77

5.

CASH	CURRENCY		
	COIN		
LIST CHECKS SINGLY		487	25
		109	82
TOTAL FROM OTHER SIDE			
TOTAL		597	07
LESS CASH RECEIVED		98	00
NET DEPOSIT		499	07

9.

CASH	CURRENCY	1025	00
	COIN	138	16
LIST CHECKS SINGLY		927	53
		4096	75
		6130	92
TOTAL FROM OTHER SIDE		343	52
TOTAL		12,661	88
LESS CASH RECEIVED		0	00
NET DEPOSIT		12,661	88

6.

CASH	CURRENCY		
	COIN		
LIST CHECKS SINGLY		275	49
		386	53
		92	18
TOTAL FROM OTHER SIDE			
TOTAL		754	20
LESS CASH RECEIVED		150	00
NET DEPOSIT		604	20

10.

CASH	CURRENCY	1725	00
	COIN	258	12
LIST CHECKS SINGLY		1014	98
		8536	51
		7102	49
TOTAL FROM OTHER SIDE		827	19
TOTAL		19,464	29
LESS CASH RECEIVED		0	00
NET DEPOSIT		19,464	29

Discuss receiving cash while making a deposit, recording it on the deposit slip, and signing for it.
When receiving cash while making a deposit, the signature of the depositor is required on the line below the date.

Problem Solving

CONSUMER APPLICATIONS

Objective: Solve problems involving addition and subtraction of decimals.

In this lesson students write a check and complete a check register.

Using a Checkbook

James pays each of his bills with a check. He completes the check register before he writes the check. Then he knows how much money will be left in his account. He keeps each canceled check as proof that payment has been made.

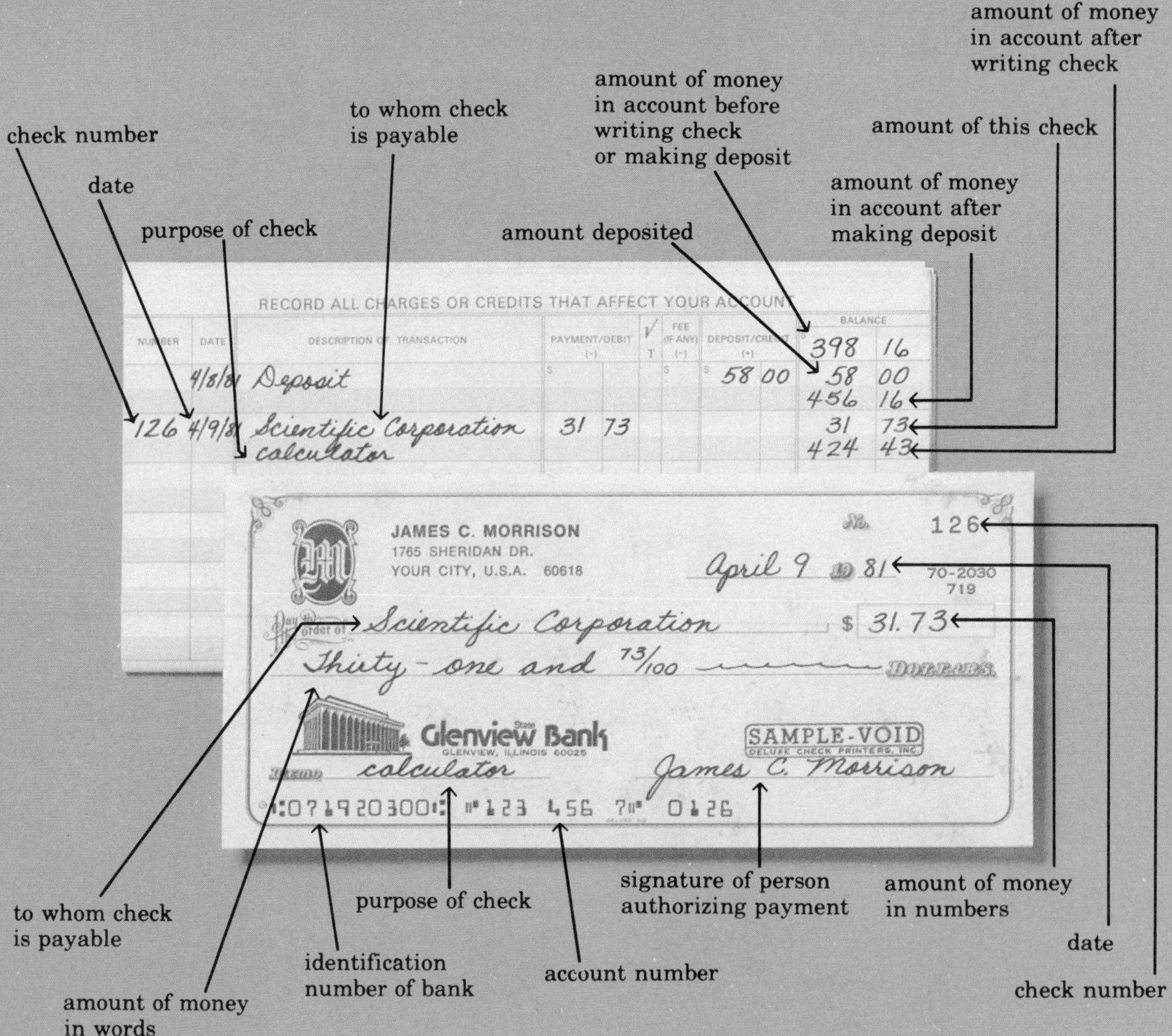

See pages 11-13 and 59, 61-62 of *Problem-Solving Masters.*

Use the data on the check register to complete the data missing on the check.

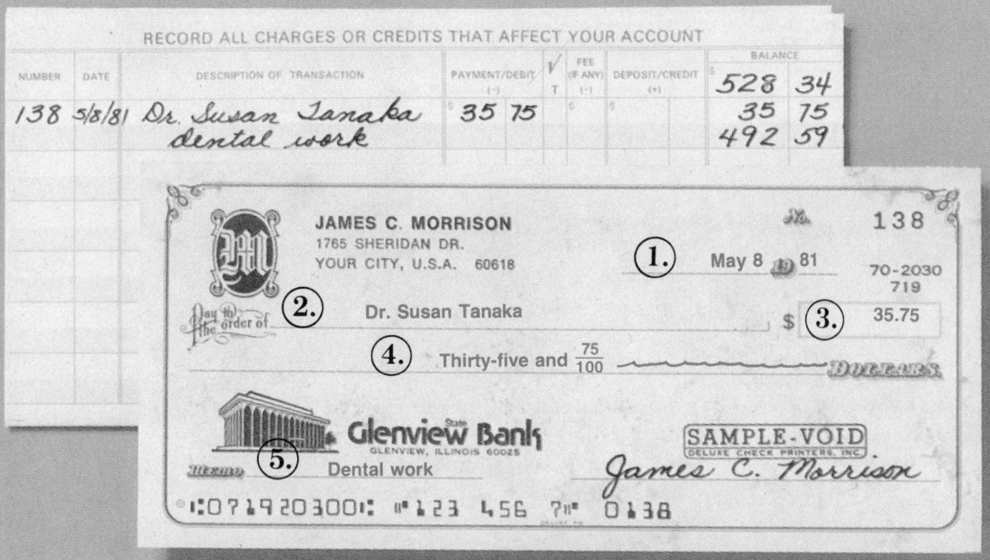

Find each new balance. The last balance on each page of the check register becomes the beginning balance for the next page of the check register.

	PAYMENT/DEBIT (−)	√ T	FEE (IF ANY) (−)	DEPOSIT/CREDIT (+)	BALANCE
					$ 358 23
	$ 15 74		$	$	15 74
6.					342 49
	48 50				48 50
7.					293 99
				85 00	85 00
8.					378 99
	19 95				19 95
9.					359 04
	32 28				32 28
10.					326 76
				115 39	115 39
11.					442 15
	225 50				225 50
12.					216 65
	21 97				21 97
13.					194 68

	PAYMENT/DEBIT (−)	√ T	FEE (IF ANY) (−)	DEPOSIT/CREDIT (+)	BALANCE
14.					$ 194 68
	$ 15 92		$	$	15 92
15.					178 76
	37 89				37 89
16.					140 87
				352 18	352 18
17.					493 05
	243 98				243 98
18.					249 07
	114 68				114 68
19.					134 39
				164 38	164 38
20.					298 77
	16 73				16 73
21.					282 04
	13 98				13 98
22.					268 06

As you discuss the items on page 88, point out that the check register is a record kept by the consumer.

Although some banks do so only on request, canceled checks are often routinely returned to the consumer.

Problem Solving

CAREER APPLICATIONS

Objective: Solve problems involving addition and subtraction of decimals.

In this lesson students find the total deductions and net pay for an employee.

Accountant

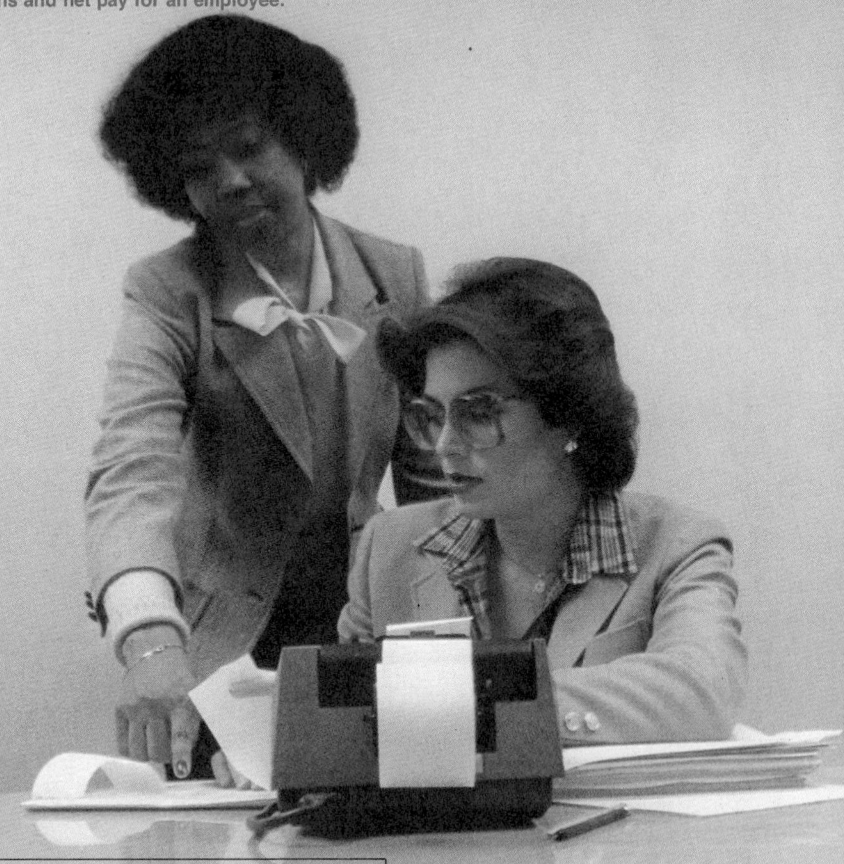

Career Cluster: Business Detail Sue Donaldson is an accountant for a construction company. As part of her job, Sue computes how much each employee is to be paid.

To find the weekly net pay for an employee, Sue first adds all the deductions to find the total deductions for the week. Then she subtracts the total deductions from the gross pay to find the net pay.

At the end of each month, Sue adds the weekly amounts to find monthly totals for gross pay, total deductions, and net pay.

Employee: Mike Merrill

For the week of	Gross pay	Deductions: Federal tax	Deductions: FICA	Deductions: State tax	Total deductions	Net pay
3/4	\$244.55	\$47.50	\$16.26	\$5.38	\$69.14	\$175.41
3/11	\$164.25	\$35.70	\$10.92	\$3.61	\$50.23	\$114.02
3/18	\$313.90	\$62.15	\$20.87	\$6.91	\$89.93	\$223.97
3/25	\$232.90	\$48.00	\$15.49	\$5.12	\$68.61	\$164.29
Monthly totals	\$955.60				\$277.91	\$677.69

Sue uses the monthly totals to check her computation. The monthly gross pay minus the monthly total deductions must equal the monthly net pay. (\$955.60 − 277.91 = \$677.69)

Complete this table. As you finish Problems 5, 11, and 16, be sure to check your computation with the same method that Sue Donaldson used. The monthly gross pay minus the monthly total deductions must equal the monthly net pay. If you find an error, check the computation for that month and make necessary corrections.

Employee Lucy Montez

	For the week of	Gross pay	Deductions: Federal tax	Deductions: FICA	Deductions: State tax	Total deductions	Net pay
1.	3/4	$291.13	$45.10	$19.36	$6.40	$70.86	$220.27 (291.13 − 70.86)
2.	3/11	$308.26	$54.70	$20.50	$6.78	$81.98	$226.28
3.	3/18	$299.70	$45.10	$19.93	$6.59	$71.62	$228.08
4.	3/25	$274.00	$40.70	$18.22	$6.03	$64.95	$209.05
5.	Monthly totals	$1173.09				$289.41	$883.68
6.	4/1	$287.42	$54.32	$19.11	$6.37	$79.80	$207.62
7.	4/8	$233.90	$48.80	$15.55	$5.15	$69.50	$164.40
8.	4/15	$229.48	$41.50	$15.26	$5.05	$61.81	$167.67
9.	4/22	$195.24	$38.30	$12.98	$4.30	$55.58	$139.66
10.	4/29	$299.30	$57.60	$19.90	$6.58	$84.08	$215.22
11.	Monthly totals	$1245.34				$350.77	$894.57
12.	5/6	$189.80	$37.50	$12.62	$4.13	$54.25	$135.55
13.	5/13	$330.33	$64.70	$21.97	$7.27	$93.94	$236.39
14.	5/20	$248.20	$49.20	$16.51	$5.46	$71.17	$177.03
15.	5/27	$292.00	$54.70	$19.42	$6.42	$80.54	$211.46
16.	Monthly totals	$1060.33				$299.90	$760.43

Gross pay is total earnings without deductions.
FICA (Federal Insurance Contributions Act) is social security.
Net pay is "take-home" pay.

In each exercise, the weekly gross pay varies due to the number of hours worked. Also, the percent deducted for federal tax was increased after March.

Problem Solving

DEVELOPING STRATEGIES

Objective: Solve problems by obtaining information from a picture.

In this lesson students find dimensions on drawings of machine parts.

Tactic: Obtaining Information from a Picture

In his job as a machinist, John Carr makes metal parts for machines. He works from drawings or blueprints that specify the exact dimensions of the finished part. He plans the sequence of machine operations that is needed to make the part, prepares the machine tools to do the job, and sets the speed at which the work will be fed into the machine.

John is working from this drawing of a machine part to set up a drill press to drill the holes in the correct positions. All measures are given in centimeters.

Problem

What is the distance a between the centers of the holes?

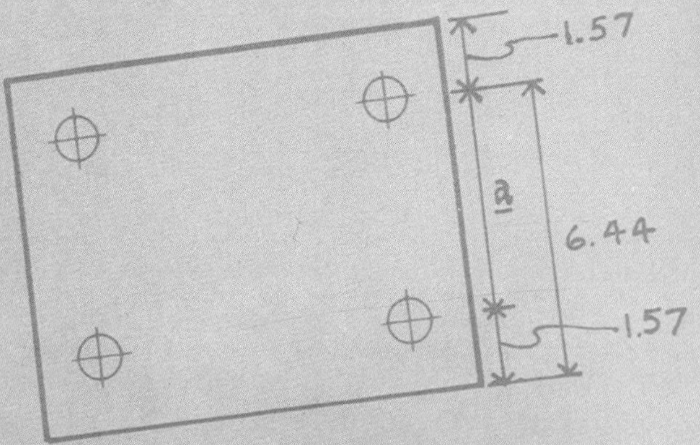

Solution

In his strategy for solving this problem, John used the tactic of obtaining information from a picture.

a. What is the distance from the center of the top hole to the bottom edge of the part? Obtain information from the picture. 6.44 cm

b. What is the distance from the center of the bottom hole to the bottom edge of the part? Obtain information from the picture. 1.57 cm

c. What is the distance a between the centers of the holes? Subtract.

$$\begin{array}{r} 6.44 \\ -\,1.57 \\ \hline 4.87 \end{array}$$

Conclusion: The distance a between the centers of the holes is 4.87 centimeters.

Related Problems

All measures are given in centimeters.

John used these drawings to set up other drill presses.

1. Find the distance d between the centers of the holes.
   23.24 cm

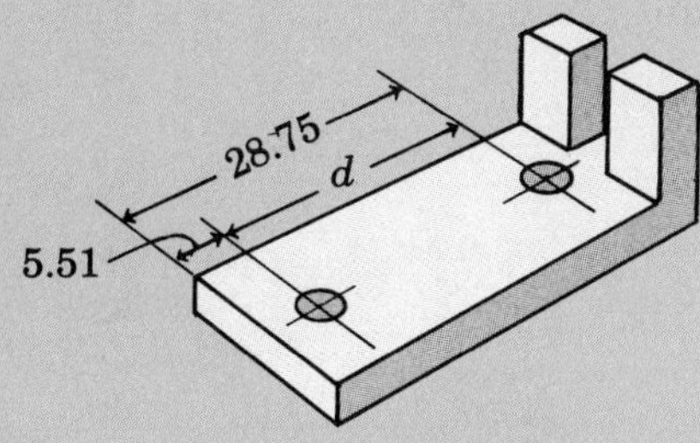

2. Find the distance f between the centers of the holes.
   18.2 cm

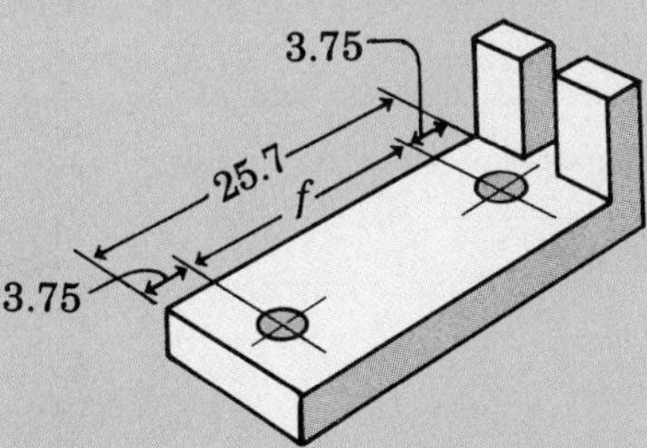

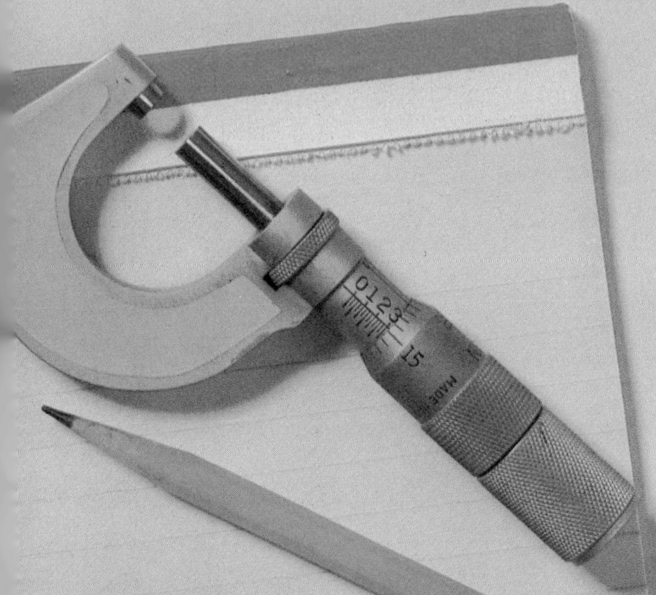

John needed to determine the total dimensions for this machine part.

3. Find the total length g.
   6.426 cm
4. Find the total width h.
   2.01 cm

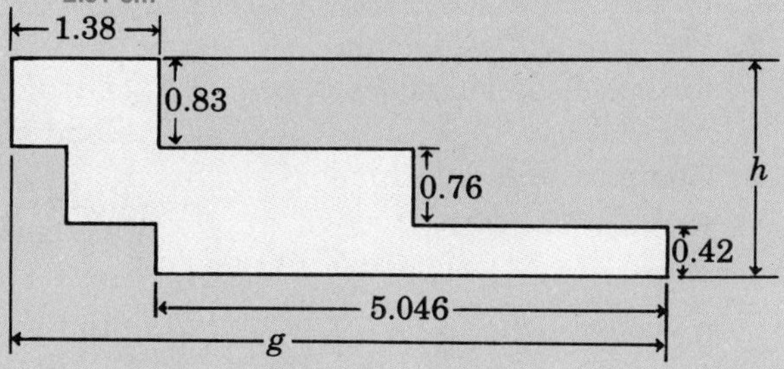

5. Find the total length l.
   3.25 cm
6. Find the total height m.
   1.7 cm

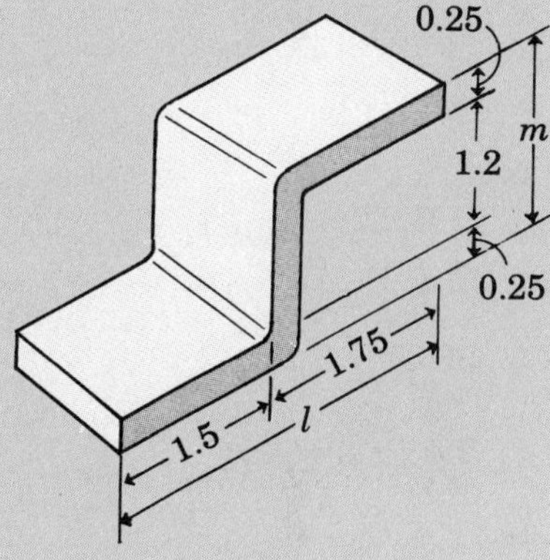

Extensions

7. Find the inside diameter n.
   3.342 cm

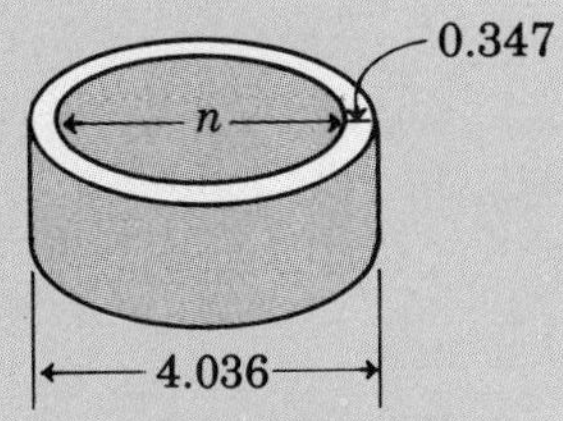

8. Find the outside diameter.
   3.472 cm

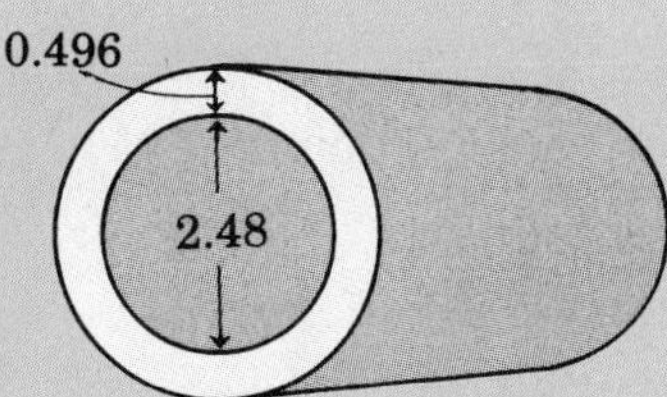

CHAPTER 4 TEST

Number of test items - 21

Number missed	1	2	3	4	5	6	7	8	9	10
Percent correct	95	90	86	81	76	71	67	62	57	52

A **1.** Give the place value of the 9 in 457.0009.
ten-thousandths

B **2.** Write an equal decimal for 0.9 in thousandths.
0.900

C **3.** Compare these decimals. Replace ● with <, >, or =.

0.89 ● 0.8
>

D **4.**
$$\begin{array}{r} 3.5 \\ 16.8 \\ +\ 4.3 \\ \hline \end{array}$$
24.6

E **5.**
$$\begin{array}{r} 0.5 \\ 6.078 \\ +\ 3.54 \\ \hline \end{array}$$
10.118

F **6.** 36.47 + 0.35 + 2.71
39.53

G **7.** 7.43 + 6 + 2.8
16.23

H **8.**
$$\begin{array}{r} 14.76 \\ -\ 3.62 \\ \hline \end{array}$$
11.14

I **9.**
$$\begin{array}{r} 4.12 \\ -\ 1.865 \\ \hline \end{array}$$
2.255

J **10.** 12.48 − 5.39
7.09

K **11.** 25.72 − 6.8
18.92

L **12.** Round 9.385 to the nearest one.
9

M **13.** Round 0.437 to the nearest hundredth.
0.44

N **14.** Estimate.

83.4 + 421.7
500

O **15.** Estimate. 8.26 − 5.84
2

P **16.** Estimate. 0.29 + 0.62
0.9

17. How much money would be saved by purchasing this blender at the discount price rather than at the list price?
$8.16

BLENDER Harvest Gold.
286 43E 2879 ....$36.95

18. Find the total and the net deposit.

CASH	CURRENCY	21	00
	COIN	6	34
LIST CHECKS SINGLY		548	25
		101	36
TOTAL FROM OTHER SIDE			
TOTAL		676	95
LESS CASH RECEIVED		0	00
NET DEPOSIT		676	95

19. Find the new balance.

PAYMENT/DEBIT (−)		√ T	FEE (IF ANY) (−)	DEPOSIT/CREDIT (+)		BALANCE	
						$ 298	15
$ 19	34		$	$		19	34
						278	81

20. Find the total deductions and net pay.

Gross pay	Deductions			Total deductions	Net pay
$218.74	$35.16	$14.55	$4.81	$54.52	$164.22

21. Find the distance d between the centers of the holes. The measures are given in centimeters.
10.92 cm

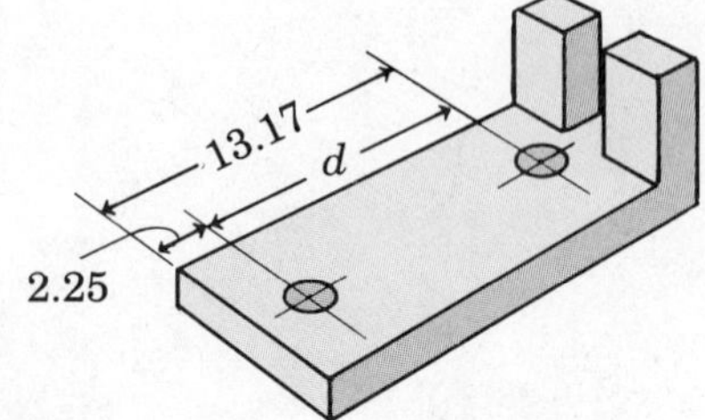

 See pages 9–10 of the *Test Masters* for an alternate form of the Chapter 4 Test.

CHAPTER 5 Multiplying and Dividing Decimals

SKILLS PRETEST

Number of test items - 18

Number missed	1	2	3	4	5	6	7	8	9
Percent correct	94	89	83	78	72	67	61	56	50

SKILL Multiplying Decimals *pages 96–97*

A $\begin{array}{r} 3.28 \\ \times\ \ 6.7 \\ \hline \end{array}$
21.976

B $\begin{array}{r} 0.453 \\ \times\ \ 0.08 \\ \hline \end{array}$
0.03624

C 3.9×6.4
24.96

SKILL Estimating Products *pages 98–99*

D Estimate. 0.05×6.8
0.35

E Estimate. 4.8×0.5189
2.5

SKILL Dividing a Decimal by a Whole Number *pages 100–101*

F $6\overline{)14.82}$
2.47

G $4\overline{)0.268}$
0.067

H $18.72 \div 39$
0.48

SKILL Multiplying and Dividing a Decimal by 10, 100, or 1000 *pages 102–103*

I 100×3.615
361.5

J 1000×7.4
7400

K $896.4 \div 10$
89.64

L $9.2 \div 100$
0.092

SKILL Dividing Decimals *pages 104–105*

M $0.9\overline{)47.88}$
53.2

N $0.007\overline{)6.02}$
860

O $394.8 \div 0.056$
7050

SKILL Rounding Quotients *pages 106–107*

P Round the quotient to the nearest tenth.

$3\overline{)1.78}$
0.6

Q Round the quotient to the nearest hundredth.

$6.1\overline{)0.324}$
0.05

R Round the quotient to the nearest thousandth.

$8\overline{)0.774}$
0.097

Objective: Multiply decimals.

Multiplying Decimals

Example A
Without writing zeros in the product

```
   8.67 ←— 2 decimal places
 ×  4.3 ←— 1 decimal place
  2 601
 34 680
 37.281 ←— 3 decimal places
```

To multiply decimals, multiply as with whole numbers. The number of decimal places in the product is the total number of decimal places in the factors.

Example B
With writing zeros in the product

```
    0.32 ←— 2 decimal places
 × 0.004 ←— 3 decimal places
 0.00128 ←— 5 decimal places
```

When you multiply decimals, sometimes you need to write one or more zeros in the product.

Example C
Horizontal form

5.9×2.7

```
   2.7
 × 5.9
  2 43
 13 50
 15.93
```

Rewrite 5.9×2.7 as shown. Multiply.

Exercises

Set A

1. 43.7×0.6 — 26.22
2. 40.5×9 — 364.5
3. 5362×0.08 — 428.96
4. 1.08×7 — 7.56
5. 5.8×6.3 — 36.54
6. 0.42×1.9 — 0.798
7. 1.17×3.4 — 3.978
8. 1.75×2.6 — 4.55
9. 3000×1.2 — 3600
10. 900×0.28 — 252
11. 21.6×3.8 — 82.08
12. 9.56×1.7 — 16.252
13. 56.7×3.2 — 181.44
14. 2.08×7.5 — 15.6
15. 1.407×8 — 11.256
16. 14.28×9.3 — 132.804
17. 6700×0.193 — 1293.1
18. 12.8×9.05 — 115.84
19. 56.3×129 — 7262.7
20. 8.33×2.56 — 21.3248

Set B

1. 2.31×0.002 — 0.00462
2. 7.8×0.003 — 0.0234
3. 4.27×0.015 — 0.06405
4. 6.7×0.009 — 0.0603
5. 0.316×0.07 — 0.02212
6. 0.53×0.008 — 0.00424

7. 0.095×0.02
0.0019

8. 0.0055×0.08
0.00044

9. 0.9312×0.06
0.055872

10. 3.05×0.009
0.02745

11. 0.17561×0.03
0.0052683

12. 9.2175×0.007
0.0645225

13. 0.42×0.12
0.0504

14. 0.0082×0.29
0.002378

15. 0.634×0.0017
0.0010778

16. 0.468×0.13
0.06084

17. 1.09×0.062
0.06758

18. 0.2056×0.071
0.0145976

19. 0.0598×0.032
0.0019136

20. 0.972×0.048
0.046656

21. 0.0951×0.174
0.0165474

22. 0.0507×0.638
0.0323466

Set C

1. 35.7 × 0.5
17.85
2. 0.09 × 2.36
0.2124
3. 1.36 × 0.8
1.088
4. 0.043 × 0.7
0.0301
5. 0.004 × 9.6
0.0384
6. 4.9 × 0.006
0.0294
7. 0.3 × 102.9
30.87
8. 7.15 × 0.004
0.0286
9. 0.6 × 0.1051
0.06306
10. 0.507 × 0.02
0.01014
11. 42.1 × 4
168.4
12. 0.08 × 0.307
0.02456
13. 0.23 × 0.082
0.01886
14. 3.8 × 2.6
9.88
15. 0.58 × 25
14.5
16. 72 × 9.3
669.6
17. 0.613 × 0.15
0.09195
18. 3.6 × 0.0219
0.07884
19. 7.38 × 2.1
15.498
20. 62.1 × 3.7
229.77
21. 0.19 × 5.367
1.01973
22. 4.573 × 2.8
12.8044

Mixed Practice

B 1. 0.3081×0.15
0.046215

A 2. 108.2×0.03
3.246

A 3. 93.06×0.06
5.5836

B 4. 0.526×0.035
0.01841

A 5. 0.166×4.7
0.7802

B 6. 4.4517×0.0152
0.06766584

A 7. 1569×0.16
251.04

B 8. 0.08×0.46
0.0368

B 9. 0.1285×0.024
0.003084

C 10. 9.58 × 16.3
156.154
C 11. 0.45 × 6.3
2.835
C 12. 1.781 × 0.018
0.032058
C 13. 6.9 × 0.2
1.38
C 14. 35.16 × 1.2
42.192
C 15. 0.74 × 0.035
0.0259
C 16. 38 × 0.12
4.56
C 17. 125 × 7.68
960
C 18. 0.124 × 0.4
0.0496
C 19. 14 × 21.3
298.2

B 20. 21.4×0.0018
0.03852

B 21. 3.5099×0.0052
0.01825148

A 22. 11.9×8
95.2

B 23. 0.062×0.455
0.02821

A 24. 1.48×860
1272.8

B 25. 0.0654×0.004
0.0002616

B 26. 2.754×0.011
0.030294

B 27. 0.1897×0.009
0.0017073

A 28. 276×0.005
1.38

C 29. 0.04 × 1.064
0.04256
C 30. 3.0355 × 0.026
0.078923
C 31. 47.8 × 2.4
114.72
C 32. 0.028 × 3.6
0.1008
C 33. 2.5 × 21
52.5
C 34. 317 × 0.012
3.804
C 35. 196.6 × 1.27
249.682
C 36. 0.098 × 0.25
0.0245
C 37. 19.2 × 2.7
51.84
C 38. 0.0367 × 0.25
0.009175

See Skills File, page 420, for more practice.

Objective: Estimate products using rounded numbers.

Estimating Products

Example D Rounding one factor

Estimate. 0.03×7.9

$$\begin{array}{l} 0.03 \times 7.9 \\ \downarrow \quad\quad \downarrow \\ 0.03 \times 8 = 0.24 \end{array}$$

Round to get factors that have one nonzero digit.

Then multiply.

$0.03 \times 7.9 \approx 0.24$

Example E Rounding both factors

Estimate. 3.87×0.2156

$$\begin{array}{l} 3.87 \times 0.2156 \\ \downarrow \quad\quad \downarrow \\ 4 \times 0.2 = 0.8 \end{array}$$

Round each factor to get a number with one nonzero digit.

Then multiply.

$3.87 \times 0.2156 \approx 0.8$

Exercises

Set D

Estimate each product.

1. 0.5×4.9 2.5
2. 6.15×0.3 1.8
3. 0.312×0.4 0.12
4. 0.6×59.45 36
5. 2×7.18 14
6. 0.29×5 1.5
7. 29.56×8 240
8. 7×3.94 28
9. 0.06×9.08 0.54
10. 6.93×0.07 0.49
11. 0.89×0.05 0.045
12. 0.09×0.395 0.036

Set E

Estimate each product.

1. 2.87×0.5134 1.5
2. 4.17×0.68 2.8
3. 5.9×3.99 24
4. 0.92×0.2897 0.27
5. 0.75×0.21 0.16
6. 4.02×0.41 1.6
7. 58.46×0.82 48
8. 0.506×0.7015 0.35
9. 9.23×0.487 4.5
10. 0.079×0.81 0.064
11. 8.35×0.067 0.56
12. 0.0059×49.87 0.3

PROBLEM SOLVING
The applications on pages 109–111 may be used anytime after this lesson.

Mixed Practice

Estimate. Then find the actual product.

E **1.** 0.678×0.52
0.35; 0.35256

D **2.** 4×38.79
160; 155.16

E **3.** 5.03×5.06
25; 25.4518

E **4.** 0.296×0.6985
0.21; 0.206756

D **5.** 0.6×0.392
0.24; 0.2352

E **6.** 78.6×9.1
720; 715.26

D **7.** 0.49×0.03
0.015; 0.0147

E **8.** 7.34×0.0057
0.042; 0.041838

E **9.** 0.8017×0.405
0.32; 0.3246885

E **10.** 0.55×3.24
1.8; 1.782

D **11.** 0.9068×5
4.5; 4.534

D **12.** 0.4×7.1
2.8; 2.84

D **13.** 5.95×0.08
0.48; 0.476

E **14.** 0.028×0.32
0.009; 0.00896

E **15.** 0.42×0.48
0.2; 0.2016

E **16.** 67.98×0.093
6.3; 6.32214

D **17.** 8×80.62
640; 644.96

E **18.** 0.058×0.624
0.036; 0.036192

D **19.** 0.7×0.7016
0.49; 0.49112

E **20.** 2.8×41.7
120; 116.76

D **21.** 0.596×9
5.4; 5.364

E **22.** 0.049×79.86
4; 3.91314

D **23.** 8.1×0.3
2.4; 2.43

D **24.** 0.82×0.02
0.016; 0.0164

E **25.** 0.0061×2.04
0.012; 0.012444

E **26.** 3.98×89.27
360; 355.2946

E **27.** 0.074×7.56
0.56; 0.55944

BREAK TIME

Match each figure with its top view.

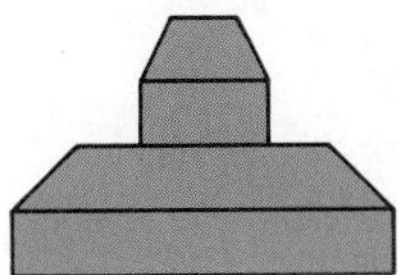
Figure 1
F

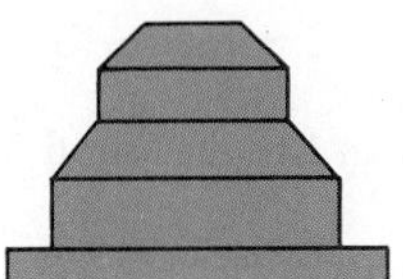
Figure 2
B

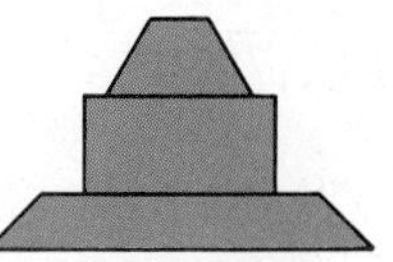
Figure 3
G

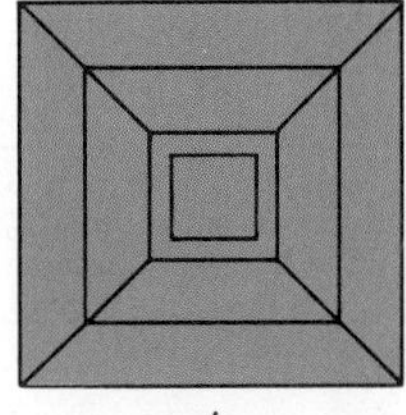
A

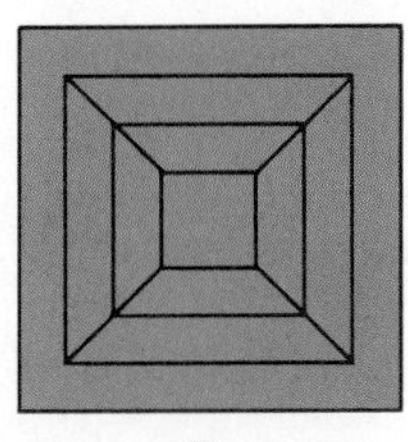
B

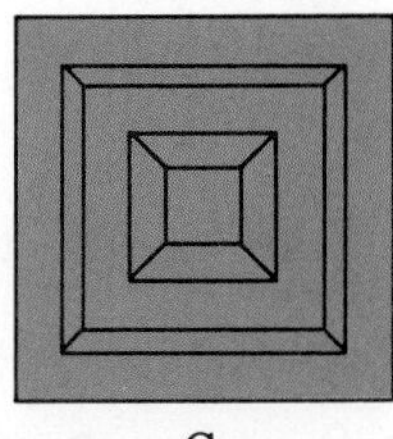
C

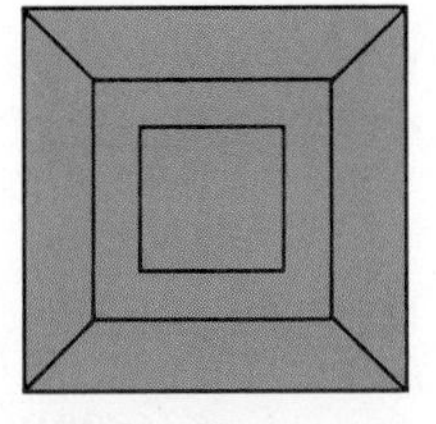
D

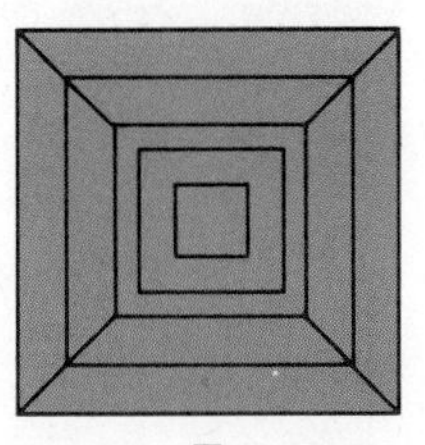
E

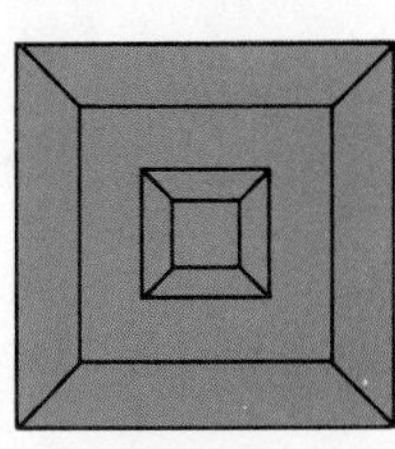
F

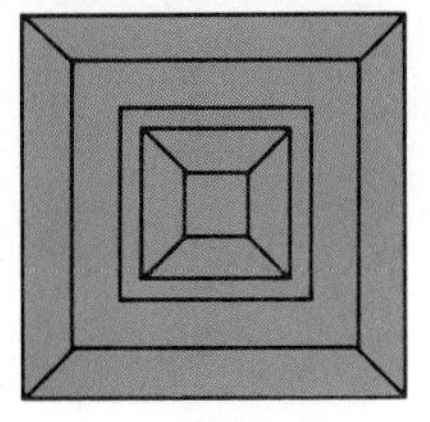
G

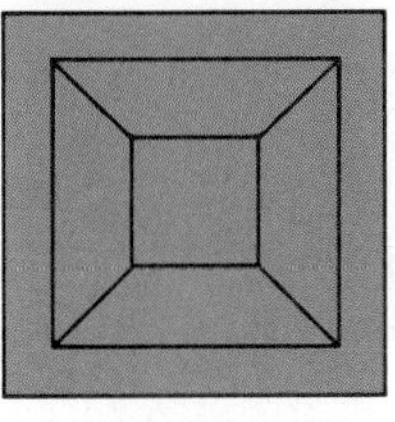
H

I

Dividing a Decimal by a Whole Number

Example F
Without writing zeros in the quotient

$$\begin{array}{r} . \\ 4\overline{)3.72} \end{array}$$

Place the decimal point in the quotient directly above the decimal point in the dividend.

$$\begin{array}{r} 0.93 \\ 4\overline{)3.72} \\ -\,3\,6 \\ \hline 12 \\ -\,12 \\ \hline 0 \end{array}$$

Divide as with whole numbers.

Is the answer reasonable?
Estimate: 4 × 0.93 ≈ 3.6
3.6 is close to 3.72.
0.93 is a reasonable answer.

The estimation method used in this lesson was taught in Examples D and E.

Example G
With writing zeros in the quotient

$$\begin{array}{r} 0.0 \\ 5\overline{)0.145} \end{array}$$

How many 5s in 1? *None*
Write 0 above the 1.

$$\begin{array}{r} 0.029 \\ 5\overline{)0.145} \\ -\,10 \\ \hline 45 \\ -\,45 \\ \hline 0 \end{array}$$

Continue dividing.

Is the answer reasonable?
Estimate: 5 × 0.029 ≈ 0.15
0.15 is close to 0.145.
0.029 is a reasonable answer.

Example H
Horizontal form

26.52 ÷ 68

$$\begin{array}{r} 0.39 \\ 68\overline{)26.52} \\ -\,20\,4 \\ \hline 6\,12 \\ 6\,12 \\ \hline 0 \end{array}$$

Rewrite 26.52 ÷ 68 as shown.
Divide.

Is the answer reasonable?
Estimate: 68 × 0.39 ≈ 28
28 is close to 26.52.
0.39 is a reasonable answer.

Exercises

Set F

1. $5\overline{)33.5}$ 6.7
2. $8\overline{)45.6}$ 5.7
3. $7\overline{)18.2}$ 2.6
4. $2\overline{)1.3174}$ 0.6587
5. $4\overline{)8.64}$ 2.16
6. $9\overline{)50.4}$ 5.6
7. $8\overline{)2.8376}$ 0.3547
8. $6\overline{)75.36}$ 12.56
9. $38\overline{)198.36}$ 5.22
10. $71\overline{)6681.1}$ 94.1
11. $16\overline{)1.824}$ 0.114
12. $27\overline{)99.9}$ 3.7
13. $19\overline{)148.2}$ 7.8
14. $25\overline{)103.25}$ 4.13
15. $18\overline{)16.92}$ 0.94
16. $46\overline{)244.72}$ 5.32
17. $13\overline{)70.72}$ 5.44
18. $42\overline{)2826.6}$ 67.3
19. $508\overline{)812.8}$ 1.6
20. $211\overline{)4937.4}$ 23.4

Set G

1. $3\overline{)0.267}$ 0.089
2. $6\overline{)0.354}$ 0.059
3. $7\overline{)0.0574}$ 0.0082
4. $5\overline{)0.0365}$ 0.0073
5. $9\overline{)0.0432}$ 0.0048
6. $8\overline{)0.03056}$ 0.00382
7. $11\overline{)0.253}$ 0.023
8. $93\overline{)0.558}$ 0.006
9. $51\overline{)1.785}$ 0.035
10. $76\overline{)0.3496}$ 0.0046
11. $12\overline{)0.72}$ 0.06
12. $46\overline{)3.68}$ 0.08
13. $29\overline{)0.0203}$ 0.0007
14. $36\overline{)0.1944}$ 0.0054
15. $28\overline{)0.6384}$ 0.0228
16. $75\overline{)6.525}$ 0.087
17. $96\overline{)1.25184}$ 0.01304
18. $103\overline{)0.0412}$ 0.0004
19. $158\overline{)0.63042}$ 0.00399
20. $271\overline{)1.45798}$ 0.00538

PROBLEM SOLVING
The applications on pages 112–113 may be used anytime after this lesson.

Set H

1. 53.6 ÷ 8
   6.7
2. 0.342 ÷ 6
   0.057
3. 21.56 ÷ 4
   5.39
4. 2.492 ÷ 7
   0.356
5. 0.0126 ÷ 9
   0.0014
6. 3.5298 ÷ 6
   0.5883
7. 12.09 ÷ 3
   4.03
8. 0.3235 ÷ 5
   0.0647
9. 8.84 ÷ 34
   0.26
10. 132.93 ÷ 63
    2.11
11. 0.0265 ÷ 53
    0.0005
12. 0.665 ÷ 19
    0.035
13. 201.02 ÷ 38
    5.29
14. 0.376 ÷ 47
    0.008
15. 49.608 ÷ 72
    0.689
16. 1.0675 ÷ 25
    0.0427
17. 6260.8 ÷ 86
    72.8
18. 0.2414 ÷ 34
    0.0071
19. 393.12 ÷ 126
    3.12
20. 14.067 ÷ 521
    0.027

Mixed Practice

F 1. 92)22.724 — 0.247
F 2. 5)234.5 — 46.9
G 3. 37)0.0296 — 0.0008
F 4. 23)18.86 — 0.82
G 5. 6)0.02886 — 0.00481
G 6. 789)61.542 — 0.078
F 7. 18)82.98 — 4.61

G 15. 81)2.0169 — 0.0249
F 16. 22)29.304 — 1.332
F 17. 3)287.7 — 95.9
F 18. 36)1724.4 — 47.9
G 19. 17)0.1581 — 0.0093
F 20. 7)4.095 — 0.585
F 21. 94)3769.4 — 40.1

H 8. 7.735 ÷ 65 — 0.119
H 9. 0.476 ÷ 7 — 0.068
H 10. 27.36 ÷ 9 — 3.04
H 11. 88.274 ÷ 202 — 0.437
H 12. 3.1997 ÷ 49 — 0.0653
H 13. 48.16 ÷ 8 — 6.02
H 14. 78.54 ÷ 42 — 1.87

H 22. 0.375 ÷ 5 — 0.075
H 23. 1119.72 ÷ 124 — 9.03
H 24. 1.938 ÷ 57 — 0.034
H 25. 3.042 ÷ 9 — 0.338
H 26. 0.03516 ÷ 4 — 0.00879
H 27. 3801.4 ÷ 83 — 45.8
H 28. 4.4170 ÷ 70 — 0.0631

See Skills File, page 420, for more practice.

BREAK TIME

Find the missing digits.

Each symbol represents a different digit. All the 7s are given.

The code is the same for both the addition and the subtraction.

```
  3495
  8655          6637
+ 4375        − 4795
 16525          1842
```

Objective: Multiply or divide a decimal by 10, 100, or 1000.

Multiplying and Dividing a Decimal by 10, 100, or 1000

Example I Without writing zeros in the product

100×0.6897 — 100 has 2 zeros.

$100 \times 0.6897 = 68.97$ — Move the decimal point 2 places to the right.

When you multiply a decimal by 10, 100, or 1000, count the zeros in the multiplier and move the decimal point that many places to the right.

For each exercise type show other examples involving multiplication or division by 10, 100, or 1000.

Example J With writing zeros in the product

1000×15.6 — 1000 has 3 zeros.

$1000 \times 15.600 = 15{,}600$ — Write zeros after the 6 in order to move the decimal point 3 places to the right.

Example K Without writing zeros in the quotient

$116.7 \div 10$ — 10 has 1 zero.

$116.7 \div 10 = 11.67$ — Move the decimal point 1 place to the left.

When you divide a decimal by 10, 100, or 1000, count the zeros in the divisor and move the decimal point that many places to the left.

Example L With writing zeros in the quotient

$5.4 \div 100$ — 100 has 2 zeros.

$05.4 \div 100 = 0.054$ — Write a zero before the 5 so you can move the decimal point 2 places to the left.

Exercises

Set I

1. 10×53.16 531.6
2. 100×1.08 108
3. 1000×0.1685 168.5
4. 10×34.9 349
5. 25.1×10 251
6. 10×1.62 16.2
7. 3.0042×1000 3004.2
8. 1000×0.791 791
9. 10×12.43 124.3
10. 100×0.3895 38.95
11. 10×26.955 269.55
12. 357.1×10 3571
13. 100×64.201 6420.1
14. 1000×0.93642 936.42
15. 1.387×1000 1387
16. 100×2.048 204.8
17. 53.92×100 5392
18. 10×6.072 60.72
19. 704.56×10 7045.6
20. 52.02916×1000 52,029.16

Set J

1. 100×5.6 560
2. 251.8×1000 251,800
3. 100×37.4 3740
4. 1005.4×100 100,540
5. 1000×68.1 68,100
6. 0.3×100 30

PROBLEM SOLVING
The applications on pages 114–117 may be used anytime after this lesson.

7\. 100 × 215.9
21,590

8\. 0.7 × 1000
700

9\. 1000 × 73.51
73,510

10\. 100 × 46.1
4610

11\. 0.08 × 1000
80

12\. 100 × 82.8
8280

13\. 1.9 × 1000
1900

14\. 1000 × 0.56
560

15\. 4.7 × 100
470

16\. 100 × 1256.7
125,670

17\. 1000 × 2.08
2080

18\. 100 × 0.9
90

19\. 930.2 × 1000
930,200

20\. 589.03 × 1000
589,030

Set K

1\. 12.5 ÷ 10
1.25

2\. 376.14 ÷ 100
3.7614

3\. 194.3 ÷ 1000
0.1943

4\. 24.8 ÷ 100
0.248

5\. 801.6 ÷ 100
8.016

6\. 2831.9 ÷ 1000
2.8319

7\. 50.662 ÷ 10
5.0662

8\. 9.33 ÷ 10
0.933

9\. 61,521.5 ÷ 1000
61.5215

10\. 480.45 ÷ 100
4.8045

11\. 63.344 ÷ 10
6.3344

12\. 797.15 ÷ 100
7.9715

13\. 2640.91 ÷ 1000
2.64091

14\. 118.7 ÷ 100
1.187

15\. 56.027 ÷ 10
5.6027

16\. 935.21 ÷ 100
9.3521

17\. 3421.9 ÷ 1000
3.4219

18\. 5602 ÷ 1000
5.602

19\. 4377.81 ÷ 1000
4.37781

20\. 98.3478 ÷ 100
0.983478

Set L

1\. 34.6 ÷ 1000
0.0346

2\. 0.571 ÷ 10
0.0571

3\. 1.7 ÷ 100
0.017

4\. 0.93 ÷ 100
0.0093

5\. 0.6 ÷ 10
0.06

6\. 2.7 ÷ 1000
0.0027

7\. 9.21 ÷ 100
0.0921

8\. 0.05 ÷ 10
0.005

9\. 7.085 ÷ 1000
0.007085

10\. 5.306 ÷ 100
0.05306

11\. 0.2 ÷ 100
0.002

12\. 0.32 ÷ 1000
0.00032

13\. 0.009 ÷ 10
0.0009

14\. 0.456 ÷ 1000
0.000456

15\. 8.4 ÷ 100
0.084

16\. 14.9 ÷ 1000
0.0149

17\. 5.26 ÷ 100
0.0526

18\. 0.0019 ÷ 10
0.00019

19\. 7.43 ÷ 100
0.0743

20\. 21 ÷ 1000
0.021

21\. 39 ÷ 1000
0.039

22\. 8 ÷ 1000
0.008

Mixed Practice

I 1. 9.533 × 10
95.33

K 2. 629.1 ÷ 10
62.91

L 3. 3.4651 ÷ 100
0.034651

J 4. 738.1 × 1000
738,100

L 5. 0.025 ÷ 1000
0.000025

K 6. 901.2 ÷ 100
9.012

J 7. 100 × 506.3
50,630

I 8. 1000 × 12.8956
12,895.6

K 9. 434.4 ÷ 10
43.44

I 10. 100 × 38.6108
3861.08

J 11. 0.78 × 1000
780

L 12. 0.4709 ÷ 10
0.04709

J 13. 100 × 9.8
980

K 14. 6348 ÷ 100
63.48

L 15. 39.1 ÷ 1000
0.0391

I 16. 277.5 × 10
2775

K 17. 30.602 ÷ 100
0.30602

J 18. 20.7 × 100
2070

I 19. 1000 × 0.4651123
465.1123

L 20. 4.0879 ÷ 100
0.040879

I 21. 100 × 68.355
6835.5

J 22. 1000 × 0.09
90

L 23. 4.5 ÷ 1000
0.0045

K 24. 67,801.2 ÷ 100
678.012

L 25. 6 ÷ 1000
0.006

I 26. 8.4127 × 100
841.27

J 27. 1.6 × 1000
1600

K 28. 152 ÷ 10
15.2

Objective: Divide decimals.

Dividing Decimals

Example M Without writing zeros in the dividend

```
      .
0.9)4.3 2
```

Multiply the divisor and the dividend by 10 to make the divisor a whole number.

```
     4.8
0.9)4.3 2
   - 3 6
       7 2
     - 7 2
         0
```

Divide.

Is the answer reasonable?
Estimate: 0.9 × 4.8 ≈ 4.5
4.5 is close to 4.32.
4.8 is a reasonable answer.

The estimation method used in this lesson was taught in Examples D and E.

Example N With writing zeros in the dividend

0.25) 3.5

```
          .
0.25)3.50
```

Multiply the divisor and the dividend by 100 to make the divisor a whole number.

```
       14.
0.25)3.50
    - 2 5
      1 00
    - 1 00
         0
```

Divide.

Is the answer reasonable?
Estimate: 0.25 × 14 ≈ 3
3 is close to 3.5.
14 is a reasonable answer.

Example O Horizontal form

79.8 ÷ 0.019

```
        4 200.
0.019)79.800
     - 76
        3 8
      - 3 8
          000
```

Rewrite 79.8 ÷ 0.019 as shown.
Divide.

Is the answer reasonable?
Estimate: 0.019 × 4200 ≈ 80
80 is close to 79.8.
4200 is a reasonable answer.

Exercises

Set M

1. 0.7)3.22 (4.6)
2. 0.4)167.6 (419)
3. 0.03)0.1647 (5.49)
4. 0.8)0.1888 (0.236)
5. 0.002)0.1786 (89.3)
6. 0.9)5.13 (5.7)
7. 0.06)0.05118 (0.853)
8. 0.08)0.512 (6.4)
9. 0.5)1.535 (3.07)
10. 0.009)0.0369 (4.1)
11. 2.4)0.072 (0.03)
12. 0.61)0.244 (0.4)
13. 9.3)18.972 (2.04)
14. 0.36)3.24 (9)
15. 1.3)7.15 (5.5)
16. 0.74)0.7178 (0.97)
17. 0.57)9.12 (16)
18. 2.8)10.92 (3.9)
19. 0.68)57.12 (84)
20. 1.52)0.5472 (0.36)

Set N

1. 0.05)1.9 (38)
2. 0.8)564 (705)
3. 0.006)2.94 (490)
4. 0.9)7029 (7810)
5. 0.02)8.6 (430)
6. 0.004)3.44 (860)
7. 0.07)3926.3 (56,090)
8. 0.21)12.6 (60)
9. 0.43)344 (800)
10. 0.395)2765 (7000)
11. 8.1)23814 (2940)
12. 2.8)840 (300)
13. 0.017)158.1 (9300)
14. 5.2)2002 (385)
15. 3.7)925 (250)
16. 0.48)112.8 (235)
17. 7.9)44398 (5620)
18. 0.027)232.2 (8600)
19. 0.906)371.46 (410)
20. 0.593)4506.8 (7600)

PROBLEM SOLVING
The applications on pages 118–119 may be used anytime after this lesson.

Set O

1. 0.8 ÷ 0.2
4
2. 0.372 ÷ 0.03
12.4
3. 446 ÷ 0.5
892
4. 0.0588 ÷ 0.006
9.8
5. 0.0021 ÷ 0.7
0.003
6. 4000 ÷ 0.5
8000
7. 63.68 ÷ 0.08
796
8. 355.6 ÷ 0.07
5080
9. 26 ÷ 0.004
6500
10. 39.411 ÷ 0.9
43.79
11. 65.1 ÷ 9.3
7
12. 23.68 ÷ 0.064
370
13. 1.378 ÷ 0.53
2.6
14. 0.1856 ÷ 0.032
5.8
15. 253.58 ÷ 6.2
40.9
16. 615.6 ÷ 0.19
3240
17. 55.44 ÷ 0.088
630
18. 120.195 ÷ 4.5
26.71
19. 8.25 ÷ 0.275
30
20. 0.20475 ÷ 0.315
0.65

Mixed Practice

M 1. $0.4\overline{)0.09416}$ 0.2354
M 2. $0.31\overline{)0.1829}$ 0.59
N 3. $0.05\overline{)30.2}$ 604
M 4. $0.009\overline{)0.423}$ 47
M 5. $4.08\overline{)0.03672}$ 0.009
N 6. $0.15\overline{)8.1}$ 54
M 7. $0.72\overline{)6.192}$ 8.6

O 8. 0.18036 ÷ 0.06
3.006
O 9. 0.0264 ÷ 3.3
0.008
O 10. 7 ÷ 0.002
3500
O 11. 2784 ÷ 4.8
580
O 12. 1.7416 ÷ 6.22
0.28
O 13. 5.27 ÷ 0.085
62
O 14. 0.135 ÷ 2.7
0.05

M 15. $0.09\overline{)0.4734}$ 5.26
M 16. $5.4\overline{)12.96}$ 2.4
N 17. $0.389\overline{)163.38}$ 420
N 18. $0.008\overline{)10.36}$ 1295
M 19. $5.6\overline{)138.32}$ 24.7
M 20. $0.73\overline{)0.00657}$ 0.009
M 21. $1.9\overline{)0.133}$ 0.07

O 22. 1335 ÷ 2.67
500
O 23. 4.611 ÷ 0.53
8.7
O 24. 0.22536 ÷ 0.003
75.12
O 25. 0.048 ÷ 0.8
0.06
O 26. 130.5 ÷ 0.29
450
O 27. 266 ÷ 0.7
380
O 28. 24.648 ÷ 0.78
31.6

See Skills File, page 421, for more practice.

BREAK TIME

A certain basketball league consists of eleven teams.

During a season, each team plays four games with each other team.

How many games are played during a season?
220 games

Objective: Round quotients.

Rounding Quotients

Example P To the nearest tenth

Round the quotient to the nearest tenth.

$$\begin{array}{r} 0.26 \\ 3\overline{)0.79} \\ -6 \\ \hline 19 \\ -18 \\ \hline 1 \end{array} \approx 0.3$$

Divide until the quotient is in hundredths.
Round to the nearest tenth.

Example Q To the nearest hundredth

Round the quotient to the nearest hundredth.

$5.8\overline{)0.198}$

$$\begin{array}{r} 0.034 \\ 5.8\overline{)0.1980} \\ -174 \\ \hline 240 \\ -232 \\ \hline 8 \end{array} \approx 0.03$$

Write one or more zeros in the dividend and divide until the quotient is in thousandths. Round to the nearest hundredth.

Example R To the nearest thousandth

Round the quotient to the nearest thousandth.

$24\overline{)1.7}$

$$\begin{array}{r} 0.0708 \\ 24\overline{)1.7000} \\ -168 \\ \hline 200 \\ -192 \\ \hline 8 \end{array} \approx 0.071$$

Write one or more zeros in the dividend and divide until the quotient is in ten-thousandths. Round to the nearest thousandth.

Exercises

Set P

Round each quotient to the nearest tenth.

1. $0.8\overline{)0.314}$ 0.4
2. $7\overline{)38}$ 5.4
3. $6\overline{)26}$ 4.3
4. $0.9\overline{)0.523}$ 0.6
5. $0.03\overline{)16.12}$ 537.3
6. $0.05\overline{)3.976}$ 79.5
7. $0.04\overline{)2.546}$ 63.7
8. $0.06\overline{)28.34}$ 472.3
9. $3.2\overline{)7.822}$ 2.4
10. $52\overline{)28.7}$ 0.6
11. $0.072\overline{)6.556}$ 91.1
12. $6.4\overline{)9.348}$ 1.5
13. $4.9\overline{)30}$ 6.1
14. $0.093\overline{)2.984}$ 32.1
15. $83\overline{)37.6}$ 0.5
16. $3.8\overline{)20}$ 5.3
17. $71.2\overline{)66.35}$ 0.9
18. $5.93\overline{)4.987}$ 0.8
19. $3.26\overline{)0.8068}$ 0.2
20. $4.17\overline{)0.3719}$ 0.1

Set Q

Round each quotient to the nearest hundredth.

1. $0.2\overline{)0.0735}$ 0.37
2. $0.5\overline{)0.2384}$ 0.48
3. $7\overline{)0.51}$ 0.07
4. $0.03\overline{)0.92029}$ 30.68
5. $8\overline{)0.49}$ 0.06
6. $0.04\overline{)0.81946}$ 20.49
7. $0.9\overline{)5.62}$ 6.24
8. $0.6\overline{)3.26}$ 5.43
9. $5.1\overline{)0.961}$ 0.19
10. $0.62\overline{)0.0863}$ 0.14
11. $47\overline{)3.46}$ 0.07
12. $0.014\overline{)0.05937}$ 4.24
13. $2.8\overline{)3.03}$ 1.08
14. $36\overline{)1.52}$ 0.04
15. $0.024\overline{)0.06746}$ 2.81
16. $3.9\overline{)4.03}$ 1.03
17. $689\overline{)148.235}$ 0.22
18. $507\overline{)75.039}$ 0.15

Set R

Round each quotient to the nearest thousandth.

1. $3\overline{)1.79}$ 0.597
2. $0.7\overline{)0.044336}$ 0.063
3. $0.06\overline{)0.37516}$ 6.253
4. $4\overline{)3.17}$ 0.793
5. $0.8\overline{)0.033865}$ 0.042
6. $0.05\overline{)0.46623}$ 9.325
7. $64\overline{)5.36}$ 0.084
8. $0.28\overline{)0.092}$ 0.329
9. $0.38\overline{)0.168}$ 0.442
10. $73\overline{)4.08}$ 0.056
11. $27\overline{)4.803}$ 0.178
12. $19\overline{)5.013}$ 0.264
13. $4.1\overline{)9.45}$ 2.305
14. $5.2\overline{)7.32}$ 1.408
15. $195\overline{)0.5346}$ 0.003
16. $311\overline{)1.3075}$ 0.004

BREAK TIME

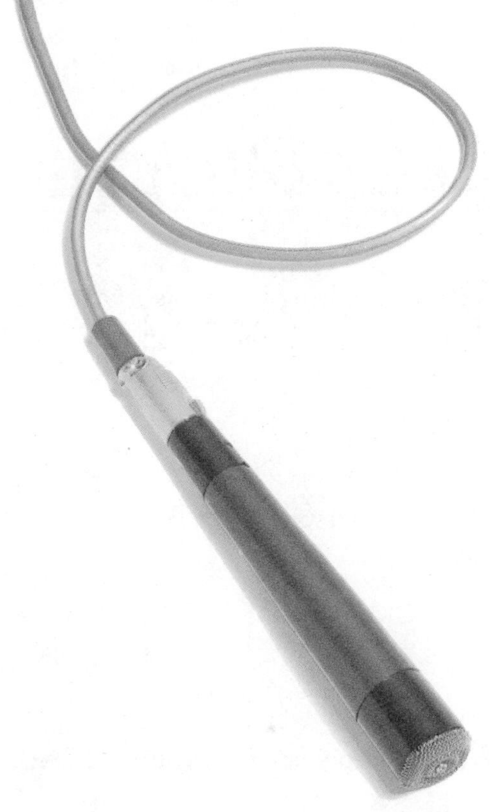

Sally, Jim, and Greg all work at the same television station. One of them is a newscaster, one is a sportscaster, and one reports the weather.

Jim is older than Greg.

Greg does not live in the same town as the newscaster.

The sportscaster, the oldest of the three, often plays tennis with Sally.

What is each person's job?

Sally is the newscaster.
Jim is the sportscaster.
Greg reports the weather.

SKILLS POSTTEST

Number of test items - 18

Number missed	1	2	3	4	5	6	7	8	9
Percent correct	94	89	83	78	72	67	61	56	50

SKILL Multiplying Decimals *pages 96–97*

A 2.49×6.8 16.932 **B** 0.539×0.07 0.03773 **C** 2.8×5.3 14.84

SKILL Estimating Products *pages 98–99*

D Estimate. 0.04×7.9 0.32 **E** Estimate. 3.2×0.8579 2.7

SKILL Dividing a Decimal by a Whole Number *pages 100–101*

F $3\overline{)14.58}$ 4.86 **G** $7\overline{)0.273}$ 0.039 **H** $26.32 \div 47$ 0.56

SKILL Multiplying and Dividing a Decimal by 10, 100, or 1000 *pages 102–103*

I 100×5.962 596.2 **J** 1000×8.6 8600 **K** $395.2 \div 10$ 39.52 **L** $2.3 \div 100$ 0.023

SKILL Dividing Decimals *pages 104–105*

M $0.8\overline{)49.84}$ 62.3 **N** $0.009\overline{)4.05}$ 450 **O** $305.14 \div 0.038$ 8030

SKILL Rounding Quotients *pages 106–107*

P Round the quotient to the nearest tenth.

$4\overline{)2.97}$ 0.7

Q Round the quotient to the nearest hundredth.

$7.2\overline{)0.563}$ 0.08

R Round the quotient to the nearest thousandth.

$6\overline{)0.556}$ 0.093

Problem Solving

CONSUMER APPLICATIONS

See page 14 of *Problem-Solving Masters.*

Objective: Solve problems involving multiplication of decimals.

In this lesson students find the costs of various quantities of meat and fish.

Discuss the importance of wise shopping. The meat and fish purchased by each man has the same nutritional value, even though Mr. Occum's purchases cost more.

Finding the Cost of Groceries

Mr. Occum and Mr. Ruiz shopped at the same market.

Meat	Price per kilogram
Sirloin steak	$7.89
Beef rump roast	$6.19
Ground beef	$3.49
Stew meat	$5.59
Beef liver	$2.68
Beef kidney	$2.08
Pork shoulder	$6.39
Lamb chops	$8.58
Veal roast	$5.98
Sliced ham	$7.19
Perch	$5.09
Fish fillet	$5.29

In each problem, use the prices shown to find the cost of the meat or fish purchased. Round your answer up to the next whole cent.

Answers are rounded up as the actual prices in a grocery store would be.

Mr. Occum

1. 1.3 kg sirloin steak
   $10.26
2. 1.9 kg beef rump roast
   $11.77
3. 2.8 kg lamb chops
   $24.03
4. 1.6 kg veal roast
   $9.57
5. 0.7 kg sliced ham
   $5.04
6. 0.9 kg perch
   $4.59

Mr. Ruiz

7. 1.9 kg ground beef
   $6.64
8. 1.8 kg pork shoulder
   $11.51
9. 1.1 kg beef liver
   $2.95
10. 0.7 kg beef kidney
    $1.46
11. 1.5 kg stew meat
    $8.39
12. 1.4 kg fish fillet
    $7.41

13. What was the total cost of the meat and fish purchased by Mr. Occum?
    $65.26
14. What was the total cost of the meat and fish purchased by Mr. Ruiz?
    $38.36
15. Mr. Occum spent how much more than Mr. Ruiz?
    $26.90

Problem Solving

CONSUMER APPLICATIONS

Objective: Solve problems involving multiplication of decimals.

In this lesson students find the total cost of a nutritious weekly diet for a family of two adults and two children.

Finding the Cost of a Nutritious Diet

These tables list foods in a typical balanced diet. The amounts purchased are for a family of two adults and two children for one week. The average price per unit and the amount purchased are based upon family income level.

Complete each table. Round your answers up to the next whole cent.

Low-Cost Nutritious Diet

	Food	Average price per unit	Amount purchased for one week	Cost	
1.	Meat, fish, poultry	\$4.79 per kilogram	6.3 kilograms	(4.79 × 6.3)	\$30.18
2.	Dry beans, peas, nuts	\$2.03 per kilogram	3.5 kilograms	\$7.11	
3.	Eggs	\$0.95 per dozen	2.5 dozen	\$2.38	
4.	Fresh fruit	\$1.74 per kilogram	1.9 kilograms	\$3.31	
5.	Green vegetables	\$1.08 per kilogram	2.7 kilograms	\$2.92	
6.	Potatoes	\$0.86 per kilogram	3.7 kilograms	\$3.19	
7.	Other vegetables, fruits	\$1.39 per kilogram	6.5 kilograms	\$9.04	
8.	Flour, cereal	\$2.75 per kilogram	3.9 kilograms	\$10.73	
9.	Milk	\$0.43 per liter	16.8 liters	\$7.23	
10.	Fats	\$3.88 per kilogram	0.9 kilogram	\$3.50	
11.			Total cost	\$79.59	

The low-cost diet includes larger quantities of dry beans, peas, nuts, eggs, potatoes, and other vegetables and fruits than the moderate-cost diet.

See page 15 of
Problem-Solving Masters.

Moderate-Cost Nutritious Diet

	Food	Average price per unit	Amount purchased for one week	Cost
12.	Meat, fish, poultry	$5.39 per kilogram	9.5 kilograms	$51.21
13.	Dry beans, peas, nuts	$2.13 per kilogram	0.5 kilogram	$1.07
14.	Eggs	$0.95 per dozen	1.5 dozen	$1.43
15.	Fresh fruit	$1.84 per kilogram	3.9 kilograms	$7.18
16.	Green vegetables	$1.33 per kilogram	3.7 kilograms	$4.93
17.	Potatoes	$0.86 per kilogram	2.8 kilograms	$2.41
18.	Other vegetables, fruits	$1.54 per kilogram	4.6 kilograms	$7.09
19.	Flour, cereal, baked goods	$2.95 per kilogram	4.1 kilograms	$12.10
20.	Milk	$0.43 per liter	17.2 liters	$7.40
21.	Fats	$4.15 per kilogram	0.9 kilogram	$3.74
22.			Total cost	$98.56

23. The total amount spent for the moderate-cost diet is how much more than the total amount spent for the low-cost diet?

$18.97 Point out that if a family saved $18.97 per week on food costs, they could save 52 × $18.97, or $986.44, in one year.
The moderate-cost diet includes larger quantities of meat, fish, poultry, fresh fruit, and green vegetables than the low-cost diet. It allows for more frequent purchases of higher-priced cuts of meat and out-of-season foods. This plan also allows for meals with more variety and less home preparation.

Problem Solving

CONSUMER APPLICATIONS

Borrowing Money to Buy a Car

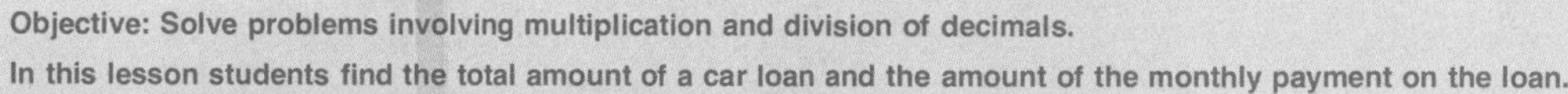

Objective: Solve problems involving multiplication and division of decimals.

In this lesson students find the total amount of a car loan and the amount of the monthly payment on the loan.

Wally Kato is getting a bank loan to buy a new car. The balance due on the car after his down payment is $4759.00. The amount of interest for 1 year is $666.26. He wants to pay back the loan in 3 years (36 months). What will be the total amount of the loan and the amount of his monthly payment?

Interest for 3 years →

$$\begin{array}{r} 666.26 \\ \times \quad 3 \\ \hline 1998.78 \end{array}$$

Multiply the interest for 1 year by 3.

Total amount of loan →

$$\begin{array}{r} 4759.00 \\ +\ 1998.78 \\ \hline 6757.78 \end{array}$$

Add the interest to the balance due on the car.

Monthly payment →

$$36\overline{)6757.780} = 187.716 \approx 187.72$$

Divide the amount of the loan by the number of months. Round up to the next whole cent.

The total amount of the loan will be $6757.78. Wally will pay $187.72 each month for 36 months.

Use the information below to complete each table. Round your answers up to the next whole cent.

Car	Balance due	Interest for 1 year
A	$4806.00	$672.84
B	5358.00	750.12
C	6290.00	880.60
D	5967.35	835.43
E	9282.50	1299.55

After students have completed the tables, have them compare the cost of financing each car for different periods of time. That is, have them compare their answers to Problems 1, 6, and 11; Problems 2, 7, and 12; and so on.

	Car	Interest for 3 years	Total amount of loan	Amount of monthly payment (36 payments)
1.	A	$2018.52	$6824.52	$189.57
2.	B	$2250.36	$7608.36	$211.35
3.	C	$2641.80	$8931.80	$248.11
4.	D	$2506.29	$8473.64	$235.38
5.	E	$3898.65	$13,181.15	$366.15

	Car	Interest for 2.5 years	Total amount of loan	Amount of monthly payment (30 payments)
6.	A	$1682.10	$6488.10	$216.27
7.	B	$1875.30	$7233.30	$241.11
8.	C	$2201.50	$8491.50	$283.05
9.	D	$2088.58	$8055.93	$268.54
10.	E	$3248.88	$12,531.38	$417.72

	Car	Interest for 2 years	Total amount of loan	Amount of monthly payment (24 payments)
11.	A	$1345.68	$6151.68	$256.32
12.	B	$1500.24	$6858.24	$285.76
13.	C	$1761.20	$8051.20	$335.47
14.	D	$1670.86	$7638.21	$318.26
15.	E	$2599.10	$11,881.60	$495.07

Problem Solving

CONSUMER APPLICATIONS

Objective: Solve problems involving multiplication and division of decimals.

In this lesson students compute the cost of using certain electrical appliances for one month.

Finding the Cost of Electricity

The cost of electricity is based upon the number of kilowatt-hours used.

One **kilowatt** is 1000 watts.

One **kilowatt-hour** is the amount of electricity used in one hour by a 1000-watt appliance.

In a certain city, the rate charged for electricity is \$0.06 per kilowatt-hour. Find the cost of using a 950-watt power sander for 2 hours.

First use this formula to find the number of kilowatt-hours used.

Kilowatt-hours = Hours × Watts ÷ 1000

$K = H \times W \div 1000$

$K = 2 \times 950 \div 1000$

$K = 1900 \div 1000$

$K = 1.9$

Then use this formula to find the cost. Round the cost up to the next whole cent.

Cost = Rate × Kilowatt-hours

$C = R \times K$

$C = 0.06 \times 1.9$

$C = 0.114$

$C \approx 0.12$

The cost of using the power sander for 2 hours is about \$0.12.

See page 16 of *Problem-Solving Masters.*

Complete the table to find the cost of using each appliance for a month. Round the cost up to the next whole cent.

	Appliance	Hours used per month (H)	Watts (W)	Kilowatt-hours ($K = H \times W \div 1000$)	Cost ($C = 0.06 \times K$)
	Stereo	35	280	9.8	$0.59
1.	Light bulb	90	60	5.4	$0.33
2.	Dishwasher	8.5	1800	15.3	$0.92
3.	Television	150	275	41.25	$2.48
4.	Coffeemaker	24	600	14.4	$0.87
5.	Power saw	5.5	760	4.18	$0.26
6.	Hair dryer	7.5	810	6.075	$0.37
7.	Vacuum cleaner	10.5	680	7.14	$0.43
8.	Toaster	22	1125	24.75	$1.49
9.	Air conditioner	220	1375	302.5	$18.15
10.	Fan	136	75	10.2	$0.62
11.	Corn popper	3	525	1.575	$0.10
12.	Power drill	3.25	420	1.365	$0.09
13.	Blender	6.75	800	5.4	$0.33
14.	Floodlight	250	500	125	$7.50
15.	Clothes dryer	19	5650	107.35	$6.45

Problem Solving

CAREER APPLICATIONS

Objective: Solve problems involving multiplication and division of decimals.

In this lesson students find the cost of mailing packages of various weights by second- or fourth-class mail.

Postal Clerk

Career Cluster: Business Contact Theresa Sauble is a postal clerk. She often needs to compute the cost of mailing packages.

Second-Class Mail

Zone	Postage rate per pound
1–2	5.2¢
3	5.8¢
4	7.0¢
5	9.0¢
6	11.3¢
7	13.1¢
8	14.9¢

Find the cost of mailing a 37.25-pound package by second-class mail to zone 3.

For second-class mail, the rate varies with the zone. The zone is determined by the distance the package is mailed. The cost is computed by multiplying the weight by the postage rate. If the weight is not a whole number, round it up to the next pound.

Round 37.25 pounds to 38 pounds.
Then multiply. $5.8 \times 38 = 220.4$
Change 220.4¢ to dollars. $220.4 \div 100 = 2.204$
Round to the next whole cent. $2.204 \rightarrow 2.21$

It will cost $2.21 to mail the package.

Complete the table to find the cost of mailing these packages. Round the cost up to the next whole cent.

	Weight (pounds)	Zone	Cost (dollars)
	29	1	$1.51
1.	37	3	$2.15
2.	14.25	5	$1.35
3.	115.5	7	$15.20
4.	45.2	2	$2.40
5.	131.5	8	$19.67
6.	33	4	$2.31
7.	41.8	8	$6.26
8.	125	7	$16.38
9.	147	3	$8.53
10.	56.4	2	$2.97

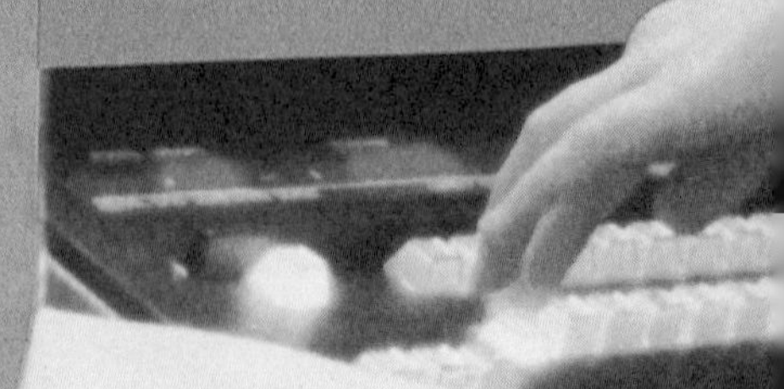

The second-class mail rate used here is for bulk mailings of newspapers and periodicals intended for classroom use.

See page 17 of *Problem-Solving Masters.*

For fourth-class mail, the rate varies according to the weight.

Fourth-Class Mail

Weight	Postage rate
First pound	\$0.59
Each additional pound through 7 pounds	\$0.22
Each additional pound over 7 pounds	\$0.13

Find the cost of mailing an 8.3-pound package by fourth-class mail.

The cost is calculated as follows:

First pound		\$0.59
Pounds two through seven	(6×0.22)	1.32
Pounds eight and nine (Weight was rounded to next pound.)	(2×0.13)	0.26
	Total cost	\$2.17

Find the cost of mailing these items by fourth-class mail.

11. Manuscripts 0.75 pound
\$0.59

12. Film 2 pounds
\$0.81

13. Film catalog 4.5 pounds
\$1.47

14. Periodicals 16 pounds
\$3.08

15. Medical binders 12 pounds
\$2.56

16. Printed music 4 pounds
\$1.25

17. Reference charts 22.5 pounds
\$3.99

18. Play scripts 12.8 pounds
\$2.69

19. Test materials 19 pounds
\$3.47

20. Sound recordings 2.3 pounds
\$1.03

The fourth-class mail rate used here is a special rate for books and records.

Problem Solving

DEVELOPING STRATEGIES

Objective: Solve problems by selecting necessary data from given information.

In this lesson students solve problems involving the number of parking spaces required by town ordinance.

Tactic: Selecting Necessary Data

Sheila Braniff, an architect, must consider town ordinances when designing a building complex.

Building Type	Phase		
	I	II	III
A 28—1 B.R. apartments 10—2 B.R. apartments Building area—21,106 sq. ft.		1 Bldg. 38 units	
B 18—1 B.R. apartments 6—2 B.R. apartments Building area—12,205 sq. ft.	7 Bldg. 168 units	5 Bldg. 120 units	1 Bldg. 24 units
C 8—2 B.R. apartments Building area—5,640 sq. ft.			2 Bldg. 16 units
D 12—3 B.R. apartments Building area—9,247 sq. ft.	5 Bldg. 60 units		3 Bldg. 36 units

Total land area—1,935,983 sq. ft.

TOWN OF WHEATFIELD

BUILDING ORDINANCES

- Minimum distance between buildings—50 feet.
- 1.5 parking spaces per living unit.
- Minimum of 1 parking space per 400 sq. ft. of commercial building.
- All streets to be posted "NO PARKING."
- 1 waste station (64 sq. ft.) per building.
- Minimum distance between street lights—500 feet.
- Maximum building area permitted is 0.25 of total land area.

Problem

According to town ordinances, how many parking spaces must be included in phase III of the building complex?

Solution

The following questions show Sheila's strategy for solving the problem. The tactics she used included selecting necessary data from available information.

a. How many units of each building type are in phase III? Select necessary data.

Type A	Type B	Type C	Type D
0	24	16	36

b. What is the total number of units in phase III? Add. $24 + 16 + 36 = 76$

c. How many parking spaces must be allowed per unit? Read ordinances. 1.5 per unit

d. How many parking spaces are needed? Multiply. $1.5 \times 76 = 114$

Conclusion: The design for phase III of the building complex must include 114 parking spaces.

Related Problems

1. According to the town ordinances, how many parking spaces must be included in phase I of the building complex?
342 parking spaces
2. Find the number of parking spaces necessary for phase II.
237 parking spaces
3. Sheila's original design included a total of 628 parking spaces for the three phases. Had she planned for enough parking spaces according to the town ordinances?
No
4. The complex has 16,800 square feet set aside for commercial use. What is the minimum number of parking spaces required by town ordinance?
42 parking spaces
5. The complex has two swimming pools. Each pool area needs 20 parking spaces. Find the total number of spaces required for the complex.
775 parking spaces

Extensions

6. Parking lot X contains 36 parking spaces as required by ordinance. How many units are in building X?
24 units
7. The design for building Z allows for 2.5 parking spaces per unit. If the parking lot contains 30 spaces, how many units are in building Z?
12 units
8. Buildings E and F share a parking lot. As required by ordinance, the lot contains 57 parking spaces. Building E has two more units than building F. How many units are in building E? How many units are in building F?
20 units; 18 units

CHAPTER 5 TEST

Number of test items - 24

Number missed	1	2	3	4	5	6	7	8	9	10	11	12
Percent correct	96	92	88	83	79	75	71	67	63	58	54	50

A **1.** $\begin{array}{r} 4.37 \\ \times\ 8.5 \\ \hline \end{array}$ 37.145

B **2.** $\begin{array}{r} 0.658 \\ \times\ 0.06 \\ \hline \end{array}$ 0.03948

C **3.** 7.4×5.4 39.96

D **4.** Estimate. 0.03×8.8 0.27

E **5.** Estimate. 9.3×0.3874 3.6

F **6.** $5\overline{)18.75}$ 3.75

G **7.** $3\overline{)0.282}$ 0.094

H **8.** $18.76 \div 28$ 0.67

I **9.** 100×7.326 732.6

J **10.** 1000×5.8 5800

K **11.** $463.9 \div 10$ 46.39

L **12.** $2.9 \div 100$ 0.029

M **13.** $0.7\overline{)65.94}$ 94.2

N **14.** $0.008\overline{)6.08}$ 760

O **15.** $246.96 \div 0.049$ 5040

P **16.** Round the quotient to the nearest tenth.

$6\overline{)5.36}$ 0.9

Q **17.** Round the quotient to the nearest hundredth.

$4.3\overline{)0.318}$ 0.07

R **18.** Round the quotient to the nearest thousandth.

$9\overline{)0.647}$ 0.072

Round to the next whole cent in items 19–23.

19. What is the cost of 1.4 kilograms of chicken priced at \$2.49 per kilogram?
\$3.49

20. What is the cost of 9 kilograms of potatoes priced at \$0.86 per kilogram?
\$7.74

21. Grace Royer is borrowing money to buy a new car. The balance due after her down payment is \$5196.25. Interest on the loan is \$727.48 per year for three years. If Grace pays back the loan in 36 equal payments, what will be the amount of each payment?
\$204.97

22. The rate charged for electricity in a certain city is \$0.073 per kilowatt-hour. What is the cost of using 1025 kilowatt-hours?
\$74.83

23. What is the cost of mailing a 37.5-pound package at a postage rate of 14.9¢ per pound?
\$5.67

24. A city ordinance requires 1.5 parking spaces per apartment. Building A has 48 apartments; building B has 56 apartments; building C has 114 apartments. How many parking spaces are needed for the three buildings?
327 parking spaces

 See pages 11–12 of the *Test Masters* for an alternate form of the Chapter 5 Test.

CHAPTER 6 The Metric System

Materials: Ruler marked in centimeters and millimeters

Number of test items - 16

SKILLS PRETEST

Number missed	1	2	3	4	5	6	7	8
Percent correct	94	88	81	75	69	63	56	50

SKILL Estimating and Measuring Length *page 123*

A Estimate the length of this bar in centimeters. Then measure to the nearest centimeter.

5 centimeters

B Estimate the length of this bar in millimeters. Then measure to the nearest millimeter.

24 millimeters
Accept answers close to this.

SKILL Using Units of Length *pages 124–125*

C Choose the most sensible measure for the length of a pencil.

18 cm

18 mm 18 cm 18 m 18 km

D 3.9 m = ▒ cm

390 cm

SKILL Using Units of Area *page 126*

E Count squares to find the area of this figure in square centimeters.

$4.5\ cm^2$

1 cm

1 cm

F Give the area of the figure in item E in square millimeters.

$450\ mm^2$

SKILL Using Units of Volume *page 127*

G Count cubes to find the volume of this figure in cubic centimeters.

$5\ cm^3$

1 cm

1 cm

1 cm

H Give the volume of the figure in item G in cubic millimeters.

$5000\ mm^3$

Pretest continued on page 122.

Pretest continued from page 121.

SKILL Using Units of Capacity *page 128*

I Choose the more sensible measure for the amount of orange juice a glass holds.
180 mL
180 mL 180 L

J 9.2 L = ▒ mL
9200 mL

SKILL Using Units of Mass *page 129*

K Choose the most sensible measure for the mass of a loaf of bread.
454 g
454 mg 454 g 454 kg

L 3.6 kg = ▒ g
3600 g

SKILL Relating Units of Volume, Capacity, and Mass *page 130*

M Complete this statement.

23 cm^3 of water is ▒ mL of water and has a mass of ▒ g.
23 mL; 23 g

N Complete this statement.

5 dm^3 of water is ▒ L of water and has a mass of ▒ kg.
5 L; 5 kg

SKILL Using Units of Temperature *page 131*

O Tell whether the temperature should be labeled kelvins or degrees Celsius.
degrees Celsius
Warm summer day: 33

P Choose the more sensible temperature for ice skating.
⁻3°C
⁻3°C 20°C

Objective: Estimate and measure the length of a segment to the nearest centimeter or millimeter.

Estimating and Measuring Length

Materials: Ruler marked in centimeters and millimeters

Example A Centimeters

Estimate the length of this bar in centimeters. Then measure to the nearest centimeter.

ESTIMATE: About 5 centimeters

MEASURE: 4 centimeters, to the nearest centimeter

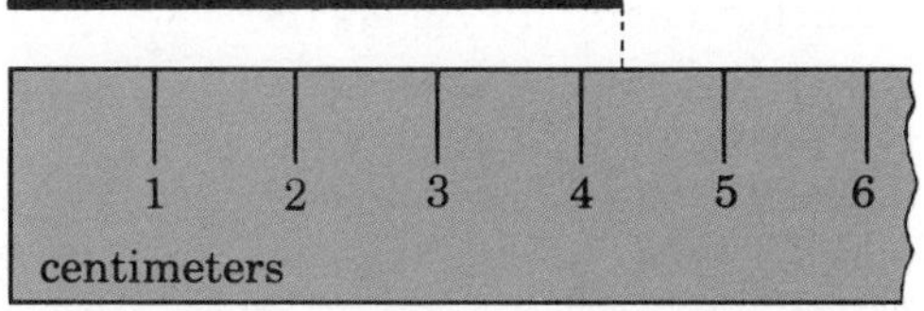

Example B Millimeters

Estimate the length of this bar in millimeters. Then measure to the nearest millimeter.

ESTIMATE: About 55 millimeters

MEASURE: 58 millimeters, to the nearest millimeter

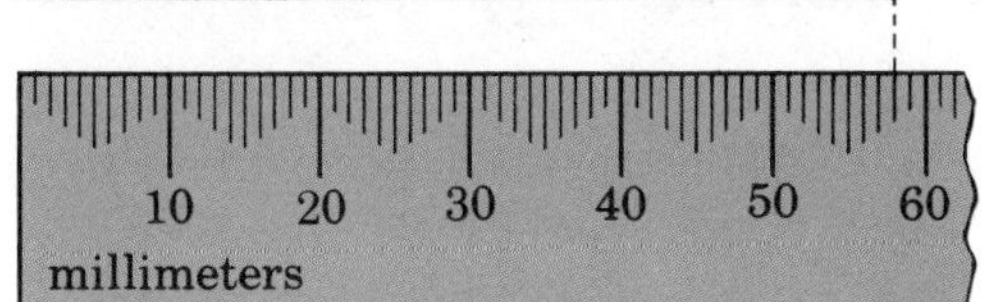

Have students estimate and then measure the lengths of small objects in the room.

Exercises

PROBLEM SOLVING
The applications on pages 138–139 and pages 142–143 may be used anytime after this lesson.

Set A

Estimate the length of each bar in centimeters. Then measure to the nearest centimeter.

1. 4 centimeters
2. 5 centimeters
3. 1 centimeter
4. 2 centimeters
5. 5 centimeters
6. 6 centimeters
7. 2 centimeters
8. 3 centimeters
9. 6 centimeters
10. 4 centimeters

Set B

Estimate the length of each bar in millimeters. Then measure to the nearest millimeter.

Accept answers close to those given.

1. 32 millimeters
2. 48 millimeters
3. 40 millimeters
4. 57 millimeters
5. 22 millimeters
6. 30 millimeters
7. 63 millimeters
8. 9 millimeters
9. 51 millimeters
10. 38 millimeters

Objective: Choose sensible measures and do conversions involving metric units of length.

Using Units of Length

Example C Choosing sensible measures of length

Choose the most sensible measure for the length of a hammer.

35 mm   35 cm   35 m   35 km

A hammer is about 35 cm long.

Remembering these objects will help you choose sensible measures of length.

The thickness of a dime is about 1 **millimeter** (1 mm).

1 millimeter (actual size)

The width of your little finger is about 1 **centimeter** (1 cm).

1 centimeter (actual size)

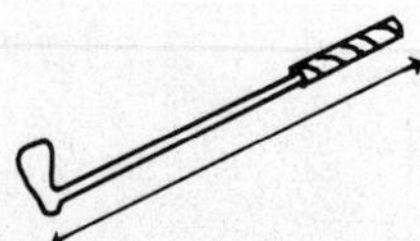

The length of a golf club is about 1 **meter** (1 m).

1 meter (not actual size)

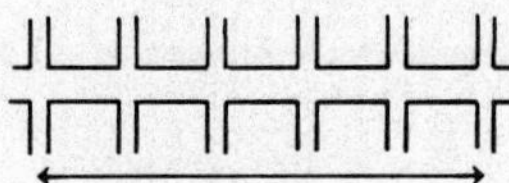

A distance of 5 city blocks is about 1 **kilometer** (1 km).

1 kilometer (not actual size)

Example D Converting units of length

9.82 m = ▒ mm

32.6 cm = ▒ m

Use the table below.

Metric units of length
1 kilometer (km) = 1000 meters (m)
1 hectometer (hm) = 100 meters (m)
1 dekameter (dam) = 10 meters (m)
10 decimeters (dm) = 1 meter (m)
100 centimeters (cm) = 1 meter (m)
1000 millimeters (mm) = 1 meter (m)

Emphasize that each unit of measure is 10 times as large as the next smaller unit.

To convert from a larger metric unit of measure to a smaller one, *multiply* by a number such as 10, 100, or 1000.

9.82 m = ▒ mm   Multiply 9.82 by 1000.

9.82 m = 9820 mm

To convert from a smaller metric unit of measure to a larger one, *divide* by a number such as 10, 100, or 1000.

32.6 cm = ▒ m   Divide 32.6 by 100.

32.6 cm = 0.326 m

Remember, to multiply by 10, 100, or 1000, move the decimal point to the right. To divide by 10, 100, or 1000, move the decimal point to the left.

PROBLEM SOLVING
The applications on pages 136–137 may be used anytime after this lesson.

Exercises

Notice that these exercises stress only the most commonly used units of length: kilometer, meter, centimeter, and millimeter.

Set C

Choose the most sensible measure.

1. Length of a small paper clip
31 mm
31 mm 31 cm 31 m 31 km

2. Length of a tennis racket
68 cm
68 mm 68 cm 68 m 68 km

3. Distance around a track
2 km
2 mm 2 cm 2 m 2 km

4. Length of a canoe
4 m
4 mm 4 cm 4 m 4 km

5. Length of a key
54 mm
54 mm 54 cm 54 m 54 km

6. Height of a woman
160 cm
160 mm 160 cm 160 m 160 km

7. Width of a room
4 m
4 mm 4 cm 4 m 4 km

8. Distance from New York to Boston
348 km
348 mm 348 cm 348 m 348 km

9. Length of a bowling alley
19 m
19 mm 19 cm 19 m 19 km

10. Height of a giant redwood tree
76 m
76 mm 76 cm 76 m 76 km

11. Length of a safety pin
26 mm
26 mm 26 cm 26 m 26 km

12. Width of a desk
75 cm
75 mm 75 cm 75 m 75 km

13. Long-distance run
10,000 m
10,000 cm 10,000 m 10,000 km

Set D

1. 38 km = ▒ m
38,000 m
2. 0.4 m = ▒ cm
40 cm
3. 758 mm = ▒ m
0.758 m
4. 24.3 dm = ▒ m
2.43 m
5. 8.5 m = ▒ mm
8500 mm
6. 7 km = ▒ m
7000 m
7. 155 cm = ▒ m
1.55 m
8. 9.21 m = ▒ dm
92.1 dm
9. 1245 m = ▒ km
1.245 km
10. 247 cm = ▒ m
2.47 m
11. 16.5 m = ▒ cm
1650 cm
12. 1475 mm = ▒ m
1.475 m
13. 65 cm = ▒ m
0.65 m
14. 66.3 m = ▒ dm
663 dm
15. 35.75 m = ▒ km
0.03575 km
16. 93.6 cm = ▒ m
0.936 m
17. 2.58 m = ▒ cm
258 cm
18. 686 mm = ▒ m
0.686 m
19. 4.5 km = ▒ m
4500 m
20. 8 m = ▒ cm
800 cm
21. 39.8 mm = ▒ m
0.0398 m
22. 202 dm = ▒ m
20.2 m
23. 32 m = ▒ mm
32,000 mm
24. 29 km = ▒ m
29,000 m

BREAK TIME

Bonnie has coins totaling more than one dollar, but she cannot make change for a dollar.

What is the greatest amount of money in coins that she could have?
$1.19

Objective: Find areas of figures and do conversions involving metric units of area.

Using Units of Area

Example E Counting square centimeters

Count squares to find the area in square centimeters.

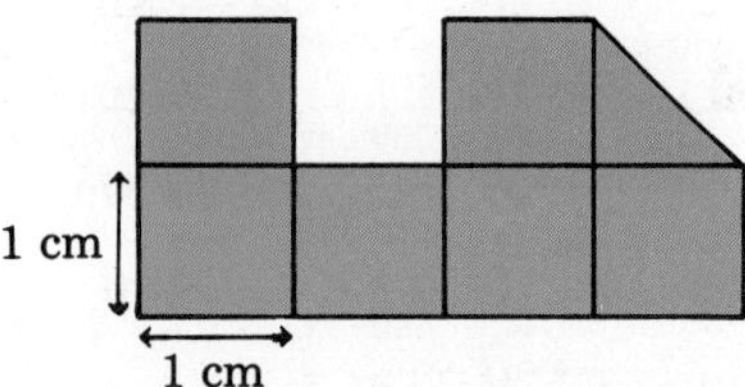

The area of the figure is 6.5 square centimeters (6.5 cm²).

Listed below are some commonly used metric units of area.

Square kilometer (km^2)
Square meter (m^2)
Square centimeter (cm^2)
Square millimeter (mm^2)

Example F Converting units of area

Give the area of the figure in Example E in square millimeters.

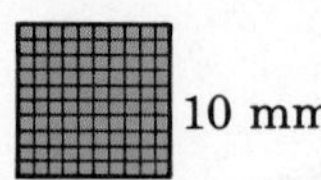

$1\ cm^2 = 100\ mm^2$

The area of the figure in Example E is $6.5\ cm^2$. To convert from square centimeters to square millimeters, multiply by 100.

$6.5\ cm^2 = \square\ mm^2$ Multiply 6.5 by 100.

$6.5\ cm^2 = 650\ mm^2$

The area of the figure in Example E is 650 square millimeters ($650\ mm^2$).

Exercises

Set E

Count to find the area in square centimeters.

1. $8\ cm^2$

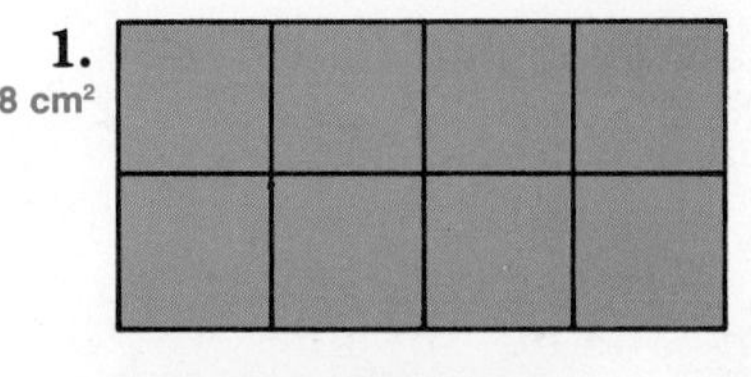

2. $9\ cm^2$

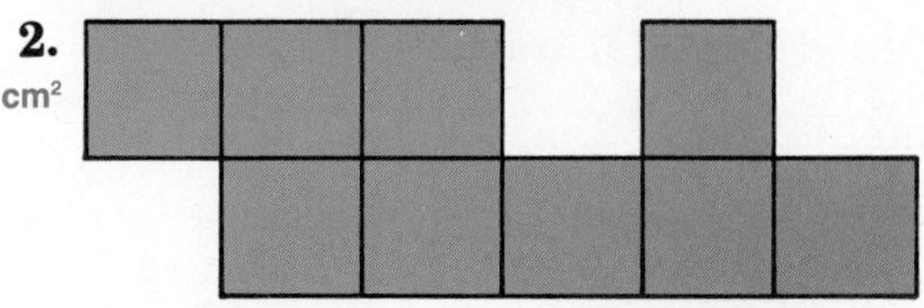

3. $13\ cm^2$

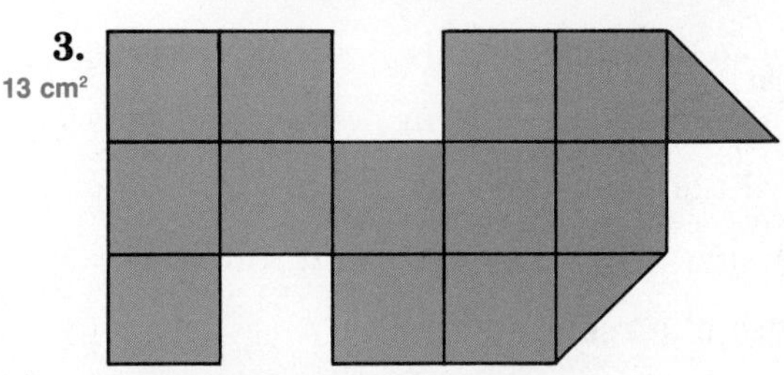

4. $8.5\ cm^2$

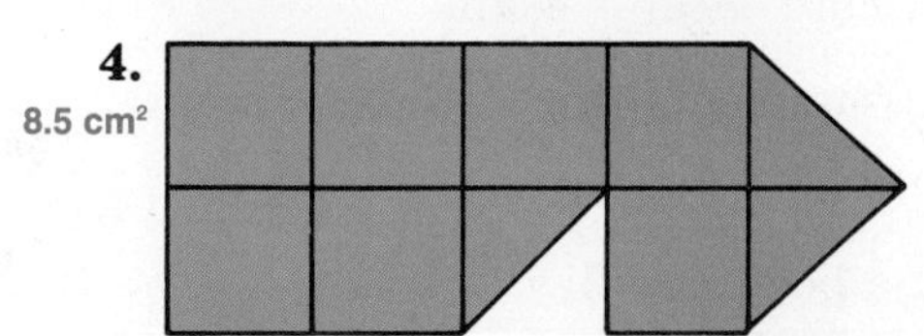

5. $8.5\ cm^2$

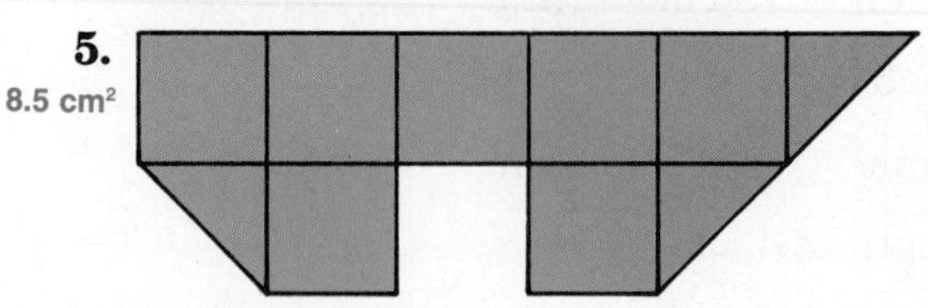

Set F

1–5. Give the area of each figure in Set E in square millimeters.

1. $800\ mm^2$
2. $900\ mm^2$
3. $1300\ mm^2$
4. $850\ mm^2$
5. $850\ mm^2$

Objective: Find volumes of figures and do conversions involving metric units of volume.

Using Units of Volume

Example G Counting cubic centimeters

Count cubes to find the volume in cubic centimeters.

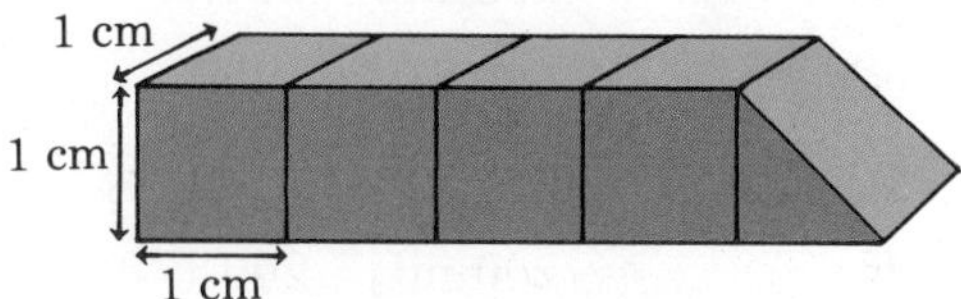

The volume of the figure is 4.5 cubic centimeters (4.5 cm^3).

Listed below are some commonly used metric units of volume.

Cubic meter (m^3)
Cubic decimeter (dm^3)
Cubic centimeter (cm^3)
Cubic millimeter (mm^3)

Example H Converting units of volume

Give the volume of the figure in Example G in cubic millimeters.

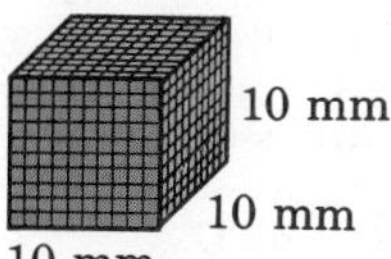

$1\text{ cm}^3 = 1000\text{ mm}^3$

The volume of the figure in Example G is 4.5 cm^3. To convert from cubic centimeters to cubic millimeters, multiply by 1000.

$4.5\text{ cm}^3 = \square\text{ mm}^3$ Multiply 4.5 by 1000.

$4.5\text{ cm}^3 = 4500\text{ mm}^3$

The volume of the figure in Example G is 4500 cubic millimeters (4500 mm^3).

Exercises

Set G

Count to find the volume in cubic centimeters.

1. 10 cm^3

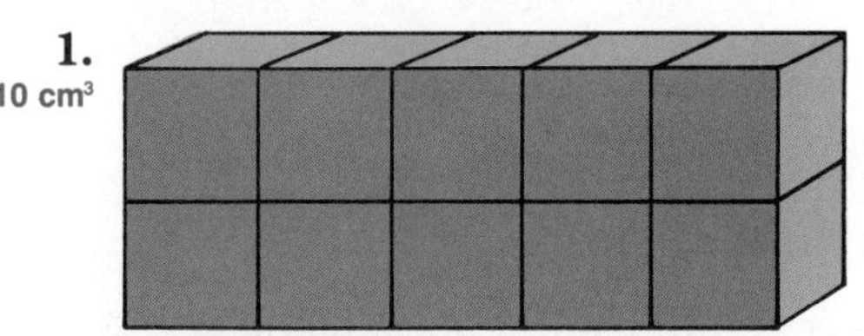

2. 8 cm^3

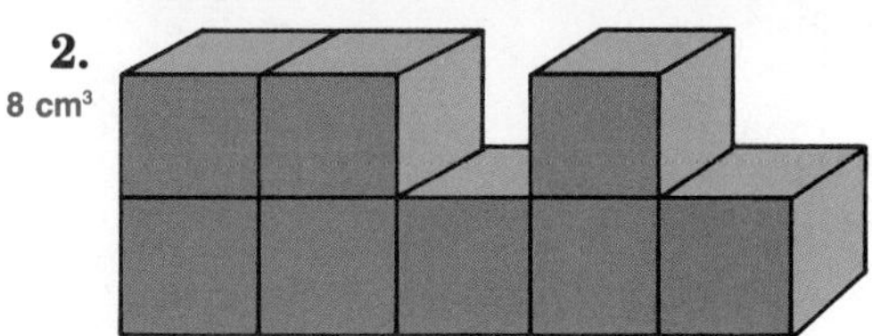

3. 11 cm^3

4. 6 cm^3

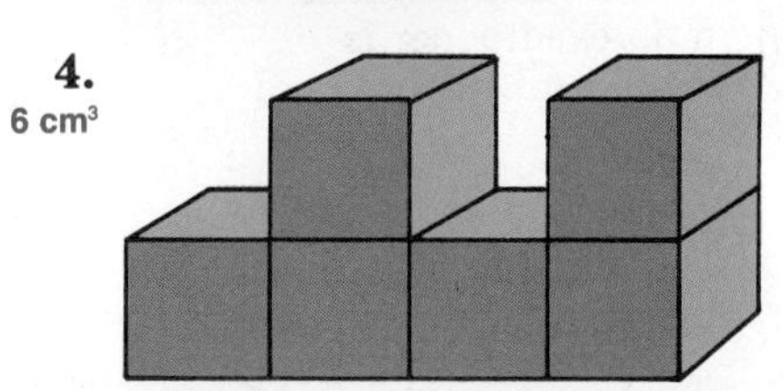

5. 7.5 cm^3

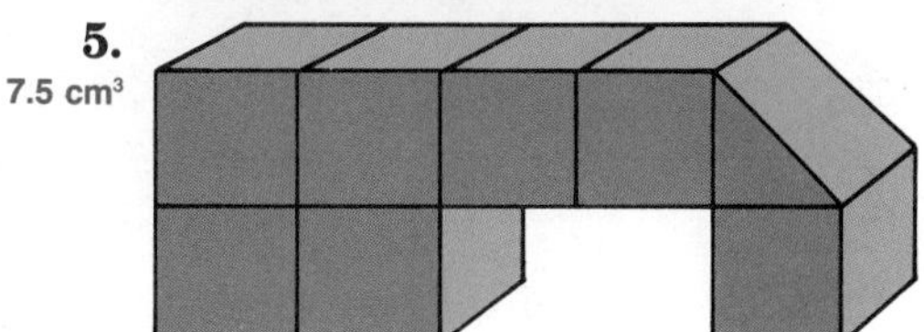

Set H

1–5. Give the volume of each figure in Set G in cubic millimeters.

1. 10,000 mm^3
2. 8000 mm^3
3. 11,000 mm^3
4. 6000 mm^3
5. 7500 mm^3

Objective: Choose sensible measures and do conversions involving metric units of capacity.

Using Units of Capacity

Example I Choosing sensible measures of capacity

Choose the more sensible measure for the amount of milk a glass holds.

250 mL   250 L

The amount of milk that a glass holds is about 250 mL.

Remembering these objects will help you choose sensible measures of capacity.

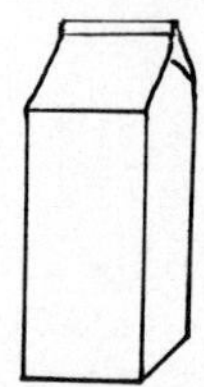

1 liter

The amount of milk in this type of carton is about 1 **liter** (1 L).

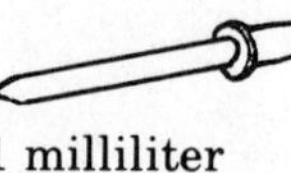

1 milliliter

The amount of liquid in an eyedropper is about 1 **milliliter** (1 mL).

Example J Converting units of capacity

7.4 L = ▒ mL

85 mL = ▒ L

1 L = 1000 mL

To convert from liters to milliliters, multiply by 1000.

7.4 L = 7400 mL   Multiply 7.4 by 1000.

To convert from milliliters to liters, divide by 1000.

85 mL = 0.085 L   Divide 85 by 1000.

Exercises

Set I

Choose the more sensible measure.

1.	Saucepan 2 L	2 mL	2 L
2.	Can of juice 700 mL	700 mL	700 L
3.	Carton of cream 265 mL	265 mL	265 L
4.	Fish tank 20 L	20 mL	20 L
5.	Spoon 3 mL	3 mL	3 L
6.	Bathtub 200 L	200 mL	200 L
7.	Teakettle 700 mL	700 mL	700 L
8.	Test tube 75 mL	75 mL	75 L
9.	Bucket 8 L	8 mL	8 L
10.	Bottle of shampoo 350 mL	350 mL	350 L
11.	Kitchen sink 20 L	20 mL	20 L
12.	Thermos bottle 1 L	1 mL	1 L

Set J

1. 25 L = ▒ mL
   25,000 mL
2. 435 mL = ▒ L
   0.435 L
3. 82.7 mL = ▒ L
   0.0827 L
4. 0.8 L = ▒ mL
   800 mL
5. 375 L = ▒ mL
   375,000 mL
6. 85 mL = ▒ L
   0.085 L
7. 5 L = ▒ mL
   5000 mL
8. 28.2 mL = ▒ L
   0.0282 L
9. 4370 mL = ▒ L
   4.37 L
10. 3.2 L = ▒ mL
    3200 mL
11. 83.4 mL = ▒ L
    0.0834 L
12. 0.25 L = ▒ mL
    250 mL
13. 9164 mL = ▒ L
    9.164 L
14. 9.1 L = ▒ mL
    9100 mL
15. 96 L = ▒ mL
    96,000 mL
16. 98.6 mL = ▒ L
    0.0986 L
17. 4 L = ▒ mL
    4000 mL
18. 752 mL = ▒ L
    0.752 L
19. 3 mL = ▒ L
    0.003 L
20. 0.5 L = ▒ mL
    500 mL
21. 5860 mL = ▒ L
    5.86 L
22. 254 L = ▒ mL
    254,000 mL
23. 600 mL = ▒ L
    0.6 L
24. 0.03 L = ▒ mL
    30 mL
25. 72 mL = ▒ L
    0.072 L
26. 9200 L = ▒ mL
    9,200,000 mL

Objective: Choose sensible measures and do conversions involving metric units of mass.

Using Units of Mass

Example K

Choosing sensible measures of mass

Choose the most sensible measure for the mass of an egg.

54 mg   54 g   54 kg

The mass of an egg is about 54 g.

Remembering these objects will help you choose sensible measures of mass.

1 kilogram

The mass of an adult's pair of shoes is about 1 **kilogram** (1 kg).

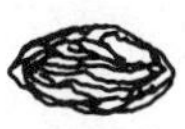

1 gram

The mass of a raisin is about 1 **gram** (1 g).

125 milligrams

The mass of a straight pin is about 125 **milligrams** (125 mg). **1000 mg = 1 g**

See page T33 for information about the terms "weight" and "mass."

Example L

Converting units of mass

9.5 kg = ▒ g

552 g = ▒ kg

1 kg = 1000 g

To convert from kilograms to grams, multiply by 1000.

9.5 kg = 9500 g   Multiply 9.5 by 1000.

To convert from grams to kilograms, divide by 1000.

552 g = 0.552 kg   Divide 552 by 1000.

Exercises

Set K

Choose the most sensible measure.

1.	Dog 8 kg	8 mg	8 g	8 kg
2.	Can of beans 453 g	453 mg	453 g	453 kg
3.	Pencil 5 g	5 mg	5 g	5 kg
4.	Paper clip 515 mg	515 mg	515 g	515 kg
5.	TV set 19 kg	19 mg	19 g	19 kg
6.	Man 90 kg	90 mg	90 g	90 kg
7.	Can of soup 305 g	305 mg	305 g	305 kg
8.	Lion 170 kg	170 mg	170 g	170 kg
9.	Nickel 5 g	5 mg	5 g	5 kg
10.	Basketball 566 g	566 mg	566 g	566 kg
11.	Sewing needle 200 mg	200 mg	200 g	200 kg
12.	Bowling ball 7kg	7 mg	7 g	7 kg

Set L

Notice that these exercises stress only the most commonly used units of mass: kilogram and gram.

1. 38 kg = ▒ g
38,000 g
2. 715 g = ▒ kg
0.715 kg
3. 0.4 kg = ▒ g
400 g
4. 67.2 g = ▒ kg
0.0672 kg
5. 31 g = ▒ kg
0.031 kg
6. 283 kg = ▒ g
283,000 g
7. 7 kg = ▒ g
7000 g
8. 45.8 g = ▒ kg
0.0458 kg
9. 6420 g = ▒ kg
6.42 kg
10. 9.3 kg = ▒ g
9300 g
11. 850 g = ▒ kg
0.85 kg
12. 0.36 kg = ▒ g
360 g
13. 4 g = ▒ kg
0.004 kg
14. 2 kg = ▒ g
2000 g
15. 800 kg = ▒ g
800,000 g
16. 88 g = ▒ kg
0.088 kg
17. 0.9 kg = ▒ g
900 g
18. 415 g = ▒ kg
0.415 kg
19. 7.3 g = ▒ kg
0.0073 kg
20. 53 kg = ▒ g
53,000 g
21. 300 g = ▒ kg
0.3 kg
22. 12.5 kg = ▒ g
12,500 g
23. 0.07 kg = ▒ g
70 g
24. 3000 g = ▒ kg
3 kg
25. 0.6 g = ▒ kg
0.0006 kg
26. 0.004 kg = ▒ g
4 g

Objective: Write measures for given amounts of water using related units of volume, capacity, and mass.

Relating Units of Volume, Capacity, and Mass

Example M Relating cm^3, mL, and g

Complete this statement.

7 cm^3 of water is ▒ mL of water and has a mass of ▒ g.

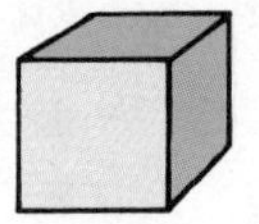

Technically, this relationship holds when the water is at 4°C.

1 cm^3 1 mL	A container with a volume of 1 cubic centimeter holds 1 milliliter of water.
1 g	The mass of the water is 1 gram.

7 cm^3 of water is 7 mL of water and has a mass of 7 g.

Example N Relating dm^3, L, and kg

Complete this statement.

16 dm^3 of water is ▒ L of water and has a mass of ▒ kg.

1 dm^3 1 L	A container with a volume of 1 cubic decimeter holds 1 liter of water.
1 kg	The mass of the water is 1 kilogram.

16 dm^3 of water is 16 L of water and has a mass of 16 kg.

You might demonstrate this relationship by using an approximation of a cubic decimeter in the form of a half-gallon milk carton which has been cut off 1 decimeter above the base. The trimmed carton will hold about 1 liter.

Exercises PROBLEM SOLVING

The applications on pages 140–141 may be used anytime after this lesson.

Set M

Complete each description of an amount of water.

1. 30 cm^3 ▒ mL ▒ g
   30 mL; 30 g
2. 8.2 mL ▒ cm^3 ▒ g
   8.2 cm^3; 8.2 g
3. 950 g ▒ mL ▒ cm^3
   950 mL; 950 cm^3
4. 7 cm^3 ▒ g ▒ mL
   7 g; 7 mL
5. 63 g ▒ mL ▒ cm^3
   63 mL; 63 cm^3
6. 0.4 mL ▒ cm^3 ▒ g
   0.4 cm^3; 0.4 g
7. 16.3 mL ▒ g ▒ cm^3
   16.3 g; 16.3 cm^3
8. 12 cm^3 ▒ mL ▒ g
   12 mL; 12 g
9. 8.9 g ▒ cm^3 ▒ mL
   8.9 cm^3; 8.9 mL
10. 250 cm^3 ▒ mL ▒ g
    250 mL; 250 g
11. 9 mL ▒ cm^3 ▒ g
    9 cm^3; 9 g

Set N

Complete each description of an amount of water.

1. 8 dm^3 ▒ L ▒ kg
   8 L; 8 kg
2. 5.6 L ▒ kg ▒ dm^3
   5.6 kg; 5.6 dm^3
3. 0.3 kg ▒ dm^3 ▒ L
   0.3 dm^3; 0.3 L
4. 2.45 L ▒ dm^3 ▒ kg
   2.45 dm^3; 2.45 kg
5. 12.3 kg ▒ L ▒ dm^3
   12.3 L; 12.3 dm^3
6. 30 dm^3 ▒ kg ▒ L
   30 kg; 30 L
7. 85 L ▒ dm^3 ▒ kg
   85 dm^3; 85 kg
8. 16 dm^3 ▒ L ▒ kg
   16 L; 16 kg
9. 0.7 kg ▒ dm^3 ▒ L
   0.7 dm^3; 0.7 L
10. 280 L ▒ dm^3 ▒ kg
    280 dm^3; 280 kg
11. 5.32 kg ▒ L ▒ dm^3
    5.32 L; 5.32 dm^3

Objective: Choose sensible measures involving metric units of temperature.

Using Units of Temperature

Example O Choosing kelvins or degrees Celsius

Tell whether the temperature should be labeled kelvins or degrees Celsius.

Air in a classroom: 22

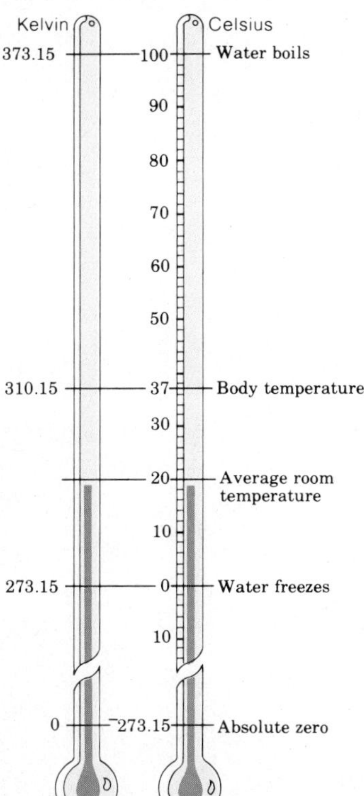

Thermometers in most countries measure temperature in **degrees Celsius** (°C).

Scientists use thermometers that measure temperature in **kelvins** (K).

Notice that the word *kelvins* is not capitalized and that the degree symbol is not used with the symbol K.

The air in a classroom is about 22°C.

Example P Choosing sensible measures in degrees Celsius

Choose the more sensible temperature for the water in a bathtub.

27°C 80°C

Water in a bathtub is about 27°C.

PROBLEM SOLVING
The applications on pages 134–135 may be used anytime after this lesson.

Exercises

Set O

Tell whether the temperature should be labeled kelvins or degrees Celsius.

1. Cold glass of milk: 5
degrees Celsius
2. Summer day: 300
kelvins
3. Hot oven: 220
degrees Celsius
4. Water in river: 11
degrees Celsius
5. Boiling water: 373.15
kelvins
6. Snowball: ⁻2
degrees Celsius
7. Melted butter: 43
degrees Celsius
8. Cold winter day: ⁻15
degrees Celsius
9. Warm bread: 32
degrees Celsius
10. Desert air: 313
kelvins
11. Arctic waters: 1
degrees Celsius
12. Girl with fever: 312
kelvins

Set P

Choose the more sensible temperature.

1.	Hot soup 58°C	25°C	58°C
2.	Spring day 20°C	20°C	65°C
3.	Boiling water 100°C	100°C	50°C
4.	Winter day ⁻7°C	45°C	⁻7°C
5.	Drinking water 10°C	10°C	70°C
6.	Fall day 13°C	13°C	60°C
7.	Warm shower 50°C	110°C	50°C
8.	Refrigerator 4°C	4°C	20°C
9.	Ice cube 0°C	0°C	32°C
10.	Rain water 18°C	60°C	18°C
11.	Warm milk 55°C	15°C	55°C
12.	Frozen food ⁻10°C	⁻10°C	25°C

Materials: Ruler marked in centimeters and millimeters

Number of test items - 16

SKILLS POSTTEST

Number missed	1	2	3	4	5	6	7	8
Percent correct	94	88	81	75	69	63	56	50

SKILL Estimating and Measuring Length *page 123*

A Estimate the length of this bar in centimeters. Then measure to the nearest centimeter.

6 centimeters

B Estimate the length of this bar in millimeters. Then measure to the nearest millimeter.

32 millimeters
Accept answers close to this.

SKILL Using Units of Length *pages 124–125*

C Choose the most sensible measure for the length of a room.
5 m

5 mm   5 cm   5 m   5 km

D 6.5 m = ▒ cm
650 cm

SKILL Using Units of Area *page 126*

E Count squares to find the area of this figure in square centimeters.
3.5 cm²

1 cm

1 cm

F Give the area of the figure in item E in square millimeters.
350 mm²

SKILL Using Units of Volume *page 127*

G Count cubes to find the volume of this figure in cubic centimeters.
3 cm³

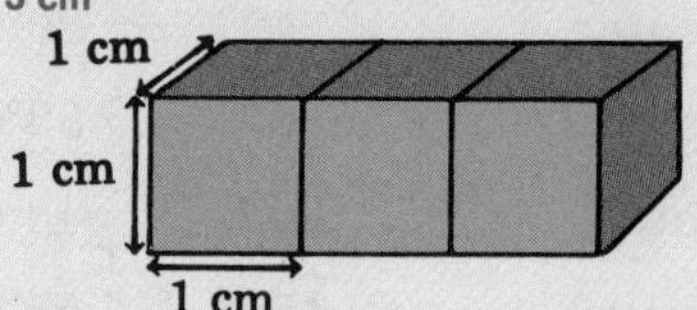

H Give the volume of the figure in item G in cubic millimeters.
3000 mm³

Posttest continued on page 133.

Posttest continued from page 132.

SKILL Using Units of Capacity *page 128*

I Choose the more sensible measure for the capacity of a can of motor oil.
1 L
1 mL 1 L

J 7.3 L = ▒ mL
7300 mL

SKILL Using Units of Mass *page 129*

K Choose the most sensible measure for the mass of a tennis ball.
56 g
56 mg 56 g 56 kg

L 4.6 kg = ▒ g
4600 g

SKILL Relating Units of Volume, Capacity, and Mass *page 130*

M Complete this statement.

91 cm^3 of water is ▒ mL of water and has a mass of ▒ g.
91 mL; 91 g

N Complete this statement.

3 dm^3 of water is ▒ L of water and has a mass of ▒ kg.
3 L; 3 kg

SKILL Using Units of Temperature *page 131*

O Tell whether the temperature should be labeled kelvins or degrees Celsius.
degrees Celsius
Room thermostat setting: 20

P Choose the more sensible temperature for a mild winter day.
9°C
9°C 45°C

Problem Solving

CONSUMER APPLICATIONS

Objective: Solve problems involving metric units of measure.

In this lesson students increase and decrease recipes that use metric measures.

Using Metric Measures in Cooking

GRAHAM MUFFINS

Makes 12 muffins

	1.
165 g graham cracker crumbs	495 g
15 mL baking powder	45 mL
1 egg	3
125 mL milk	375 mL
75 mL corn oil	225 mL
50 mL corn syrup	150 mL
55 g chopped pecans	165 g

Grease 12 muffin cups. Combine cracker crumbs and baking powder. Beat egg. Add milk, oil, and syrup. Add to crumbs. Stir. Add nuts. Bake at 190°C for 20 minutes.

LAZY DAY LASAGNA

Serves 4 people

	3.
170 g lasagna noodles	340 g
1 mL dried, crushed oregano	2 mL
250 mL spaghetti sauce with meat	500 mL
250 mL cream-style cottage cheese	500 mL
180 g sliced mozzarella cheese	360 g

Cook noodles. Add oregano to spaghetti sauce. In baking dish, make layers of noodles, cottage cheese, cheese slices, and sauce. Repeat layers. Bake at 185°C for 30 minutes.

4. 85 g lasagna noodles
0.5 mL dried, crushed oregano
125 mL spaghetti sauce with meat
125 mL cream-style cottage cheese
90 g sliced mozzarella cheese

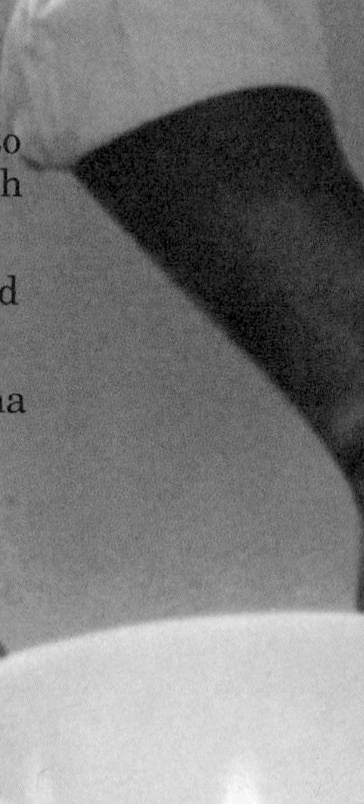

1. Tom wants to triple the recipe for graham muffins. How much of each ingredient should he use?
See recipe above.
2. The Smiths want to serve lasagna to 8 people. They need to multiply each ingredient by ▒. 2
3. How much of each ingredient should they use?
See recipe above.
4. Mr. Williams wants to make lasagna for only his wife and himself. How much of each ingredient should he use?
See recipe above.

Discuss and/or demonstrate ways to measure dry ingredients in grams [spring scale or pan balance] and ways to measure liquid or dry ingredients in milliliters [glass containers, metal containers, or measuring spoons].

Point out the oven temperatures given in degrees Celsius. Here are some other oven temperatures.
Warm: 150°C, Moderate: 180°C, Hot: 210°C, Very hot: 240°C, Broil: 270°C

CEREAL COOKIES

Makes 24 cookies

	6.	8.
100 g shortening	600 g	50 g
140 g sugar	840 g	70 g
2 eggs	12	1
5 mL vanilla extract	30 mL	2.5 mL
6 mL salt	36 mL	3 mL
4 mL baking powder	24 mL	2 mL
150 g flour	900 g	75 g
80 g high-protein cereal	480 g	40 g

Blend shortening, sugar, vanilla. Add eggs and beat. Add dry ingredients and 20 g of cereal. Make into balls. Roll in remaining cereal. Flatten. Bake at 190°C for 11 minutes.

SPECIAL BEEF PATTIES

Serves 6 people

	7.
0.5 kg ground beef	0.25 kg
30 mL finely chopped green pepper	15 mL
60 mL chopped onion	30 mL
80 mL catsup	40 mL
15 mL horseradish	7.5 mL
7 mL dry mustard	3.5 mL
2 mL salt	1 mL

Combine ingredients. Form patties. Bake at 190°C for 30 minutes.

9. 1 kg ground beef
60 mL finely chopped green pepper
120 mL chopped onion
160 mL catsup
30 mL horseradish
14 mL dry mustard
4 mL salt

5. Chris wants to make 144 cereal cookies. Each ingredient should be multiplied by ▒. 6

6. How much of each ingredient should Chris use?
See recipe above.

7. Carolyn Bruder plans to make special beef patties for 3 people. How much of each ingredient should she use?
See recipe above.

Mr. and Mrs. Marchanic plan to make special beef patties and cereal cookies for 12 people.

8. How much of each cookie ingredient should they use to make 12 cookies?
See recipe above.

9. How much of each beef patty ingredient should they use?
See recipe above.

Problem Solving

CONSUMER APPLICATIONS

Objective: Solve problems involving metric units of measure.

In this lesson students compare the cost of sewing a jacket when metric measures are used.

Using Metric Measures in Sewing

Mr. d'Angelo sews clothes for his children. He plans to make a jacket for Melissa.

Here is the information given on the back of the pattern envelope.

Width of material	Length of material in meters			
	Size 8	Size 10	Size 12	Size 14
Jacket				
115 cm	1.60	1.75	1.75	1.85
140 cm	1.40	1.40	1.40	1.40
150 cm	1.40	1.40	1.40	1.40
Interfacing				
90 cm	0.35	0.35	0.35	0.50
Lining				
90 cm	1.50	1.50	1.60	1.60
115 cm	1.15	1.15	1.15	1.15

Interfacing is stiff material used to hold shape.

See pages 18–19 of *Problem-Solving Masters.*

Melissa is size 8. Complete this table to find the cost of her jacket.

	Item	Width	Length needed	Price per meter	Cost rounded up to next whole cent
	Material	115 cm	1.60 meters	$6.50	$10.40
1.	Interfacing	90 cm	0.35 meters	$2.25	$0.79
2.	Lining	90 cm	1.5 meters	$2.60	$3.90
	Zipper				$1.85
3.				Total cost of all items	$16.94

At a second store, similar material in a different width was on sale. Find the costs at that store.

	Item	Width	Length needed	Price per meter	Cost rounded up to next whole cent
4.	Material	150 cm	1.4 meters	$4.95	$6.93
5.	Interfacing	90 cm	0.35 meters	$2.10	$0.74
6.	Lining	115 cm	1.15 meters	$2.90	$3.34
	Zipper				$1.79
7.				Total cost of all items	$12.80

8. The total cost is how much less at the second store?
$4.14

Find the cost of making a size 14 jacket in different material for Melissa's mother.

	Item	Width	Length needed	Price per meter	Cost rounded up to next whole cent
9.	Material	115 cm	1.85 meters	$6.95	$12.86
10.	Interfacing	90 cm	0.5 meters	$2.25	$1.13
11.	Lining	90 cm	1.6 meters	$2.75	$4.40
	Zipper				$2.35
12.				Total cost of all items	$20.74

You might have students bring in patterns which show both metric and U.S. customary measures.

Problem Solving

CAREER APPLICATIONS

Objective: Solve problems involving metric units of measure.

In this lesson students measure parts of metal fasteners to the nearest millimeter and compute diameters of tap drills used with metal fasteners.

Materials: Ruler marked in millimeters

Assembler

Career Cluster: Trades Dorothy Stevens works as an assembler in a factory. She uses metal fasteners to join pieces of metal.

Use a ruler to measure the thread (T), the length (L), and the diameter (D) of each fastener to the nearest millimeter.

Accept answers close to the those given.

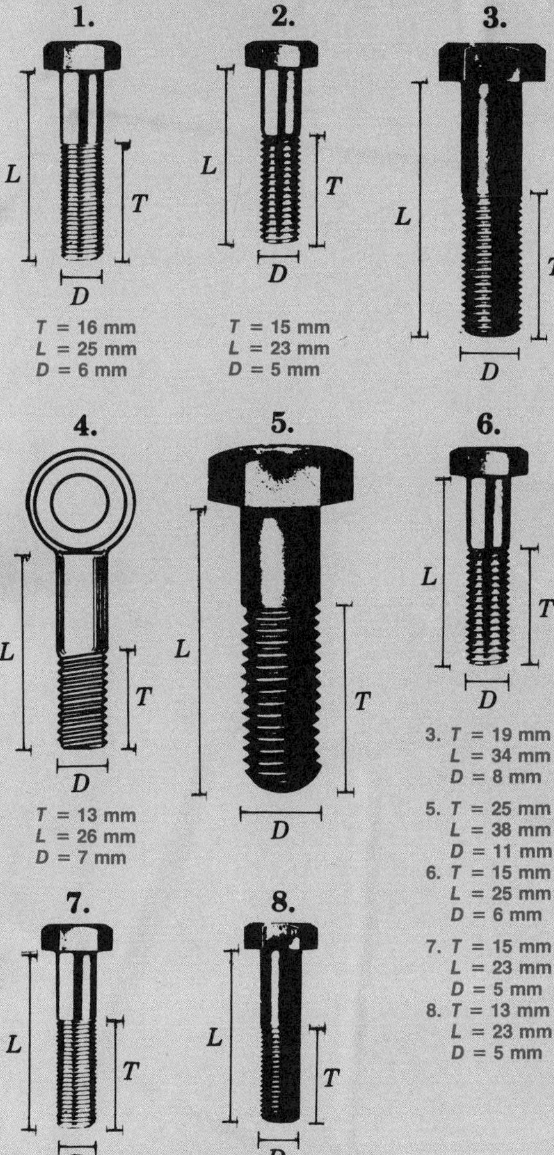

The pitch of a fastener is the distance from the top of one thread to the top of the next thread.

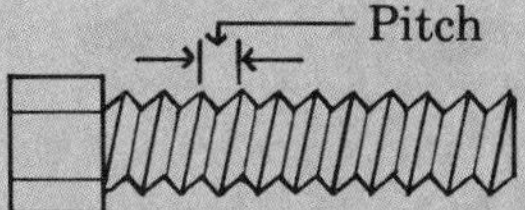

In order to use a fastener, Dorothy must tap drill a hole. She selects a tap drill with a diameter that is slightly smaller than the diameter of the fastener, so that the threads of the fastener will hold in the metal.

The table below lists most of the fastener sizes used in industry.

To select the correct diameter for a tap drill, subtract the pitch of the fastener from the diameter of the fastener.

In the table, size M 3 means a diameter of 3 millimeters. Size M 12 means a diameter of 12 millimeters.

	Diameter of fastener (mm)	Pitch of fastener (mm)	Diameter of tap drill (mm)
	M 3	0.5	2.5
9.	M 4	0.7	3.3
10.	M 5	0.8	4.2
11.	M 6	1.0	5
12.	M 8	1.25	6.75
13.	M 10	1.5	8.5
14.	M 12	1.75	10.25
15.	M 16	2.0	14
16.	M 20	2.5	17.5
17.	M 24	3.0	21
18.	M 30	3.5	26.5

A transparent metric ruler and some bolts can be used to demonstrate which measures are to be taken.

Problem Solving

CAREER APPLICATIONS

Objective: Solve problems involving metric units of measure.

In this lesson students work with dosages of medicines and dispensed units of medicine involving metric measures.

Hospital-Ward Clerk

See the Careers Chart beginning on page 426 for more information about the careers in this cluster.

Career Cluster: Health Yin Lim is a ward clerk in a hospital. He prepares medical records, serves as a receptionist, and handles most of the clerical work involved in management of the third floor.

Yin received the request form shown below. He must compute the supply of each medication that will be needed for that day. Here is an example.

Dosage: 1.5 g Rate: Every 4 hours

Find the total dosage.

First divide 24 hours by the rate to find the number of dosages per day. $24 \div 4 = 6$
Then multiply to find the total daily dosage. $6 \times 1.5 = 9.0$ Total daily dosage: 9.0 g

Complete the request form. The illnesses for which the drugs are prescribed are given below.

	Floor: 3rd	Pharmaceutical Request Form			Date: November 15
	Patient	Medication	Dosage	Rate	Total daily dosage
1.	Vollmer, Mary Heart attack	Digoxin	0.125 mg	Every 6 hours	0.5 mg
2.		Morphine sulfate	10 mg	Every 4 hours	60 mg
3.		Valium	5 mg	Every 6 hours	20 mg
4.	Witts, Ken Stomach spasms	Meprobamate	500 mg	Every 4 hours	3000 mg
5.		Maalox	30 cm³	Every 4 hours	180 cm³
6.		Donnatol elixer	5 cm³	Every 6 hours	20 cm³
7.	Ramirez, Linda High blood pressure with convulsions	Librium	10 mg	Every 4 hours	60 mg
8.		Dilantin	0.1 g	Every 8 hours	0.3 g
9.		Aldomet	250 mg	Every 12 hours	500 mg
10.	Turner, Francis Urinary tract infection	Gantanol	1 g	Every 8 hours	3 g
11.		Darvon plain	65 mg	Every 6 hours	260 mg
12.		Chloral hydrate	500 mg	Every 4 hours	3000 mg
13.	Valdes, Rosalia Appendicitis	Ampicillin	500 mg	Every 24 hours	500 mg
14.		Meperidine	75 mg	Every 6 hours	300 mg

Yin receives medicines from the pharmacy in bulk quantities. He dispenses the medicines to the nurses in smaller quantities called units.

The bulk quantity for staphene is 5 liters. It is dispensed in 250-milliliter units. How many units are dispensed from 5 liters?

First convert 5 liters to milliliters.

Liters		Milliliters per liter		Milliliters
↓		↓		↓
5	×	1000	=	5000

5 L = 5000 mL

Then divide to find the number of units.

Milliliters		Milliliters per unit		Units
↓		↓		↓
5000	÷	250	=	20

5000 mL = 20 units

Find the number of units for each item listed below.

	Item	Bulk amount	Size of dispensed unit	Number of units
15.	Alcohol	5 L	100 mL	50
16.	Penicillin	1 L	20 mL	50
17.	Quinine	1 L	5 mL	200
18.	Iodine	2 kg	2 g	1000
19.	Sodium bicarbonate	5 kg	10 g	500
20.	Saparated creosol	1 L	4 mL	250

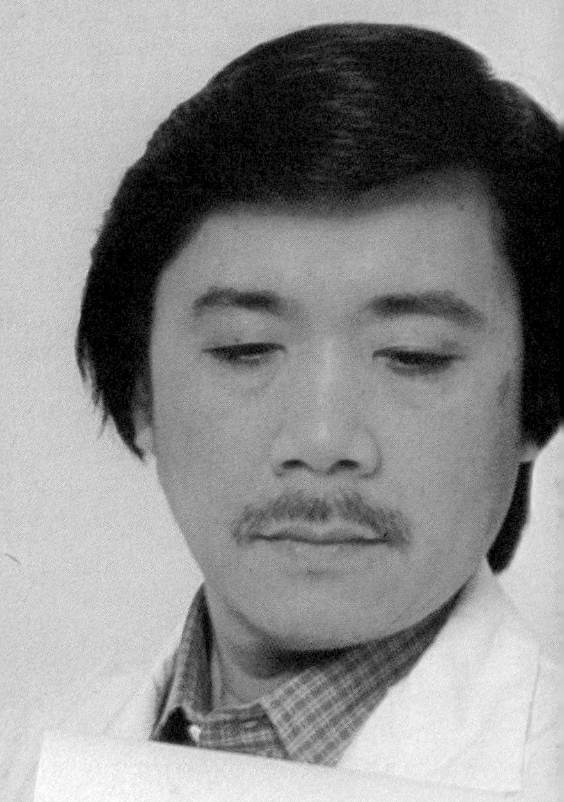

Problem Solving

DEVELOPING STRATEGIES

Objective: Solve problems by measuring.

In this lesson students measure the length of a tooth, choose a file of an appropriate length, and find the adjustment for the file.

Materials: Ruler marked in millimeters

Tactic: Measuring

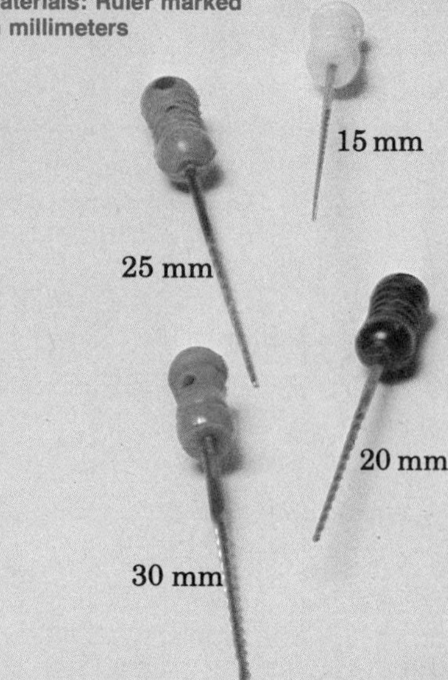

Dr. Larry Whitney, a dentist, often performs a root canal rather than extracting a tooth that is infected. He uses a file to enlarge the canal of the root. In order to choose a file of the correct length, Dr. Whitney uses an X ray of the tooth to measure the distance from the top of the crown to the end of the root. Since the initial opening into the root will be made to a level 3 mm from the end of the root, Dr. Whitney chooses a file that is slightly longer than this distance. Then he makes an adjustment on the file to shorten its length.

Problem

Which file should be used for the tooth shown and what adjustment should be made to shorten the length?

Solution

In his strategy for solving the problem, Dr. Whitney used the tactic of measuring. He asked himself these questions.

a. What is the length of the tooth? Measure. — 22 mm

b. How long should he make the initial opening? Subtract.

$$\begin{array}{r} 22\text{ mm} \\ -\ 3\text{ mm} \\ \hline 19\text{ mm} \end{array}$$

c. Which file should he use? From the files shown, choose the file that is slightly longer than the initial opening. — 20-mm file

d. What adjustment should be made to shorten the length of the file? Subtract.

$$\begin{array}{r} 20\text{ mm} \\ -\ 19\text{ mm} \\ \hline 1\text{ mm} \end{array}$$

Conclusion: Dr. Whitney should use the 20-mm file and make a 1-mm adjustment.

See page 20 of
Problem-Solving Masters.

Related Problems

Measure the tooth in each X ray to the nearest millimeter. After finding the length for the initial opening, tell which file from those shown on page 142 should be used and what adjustment should be made to shorten the length of the file.

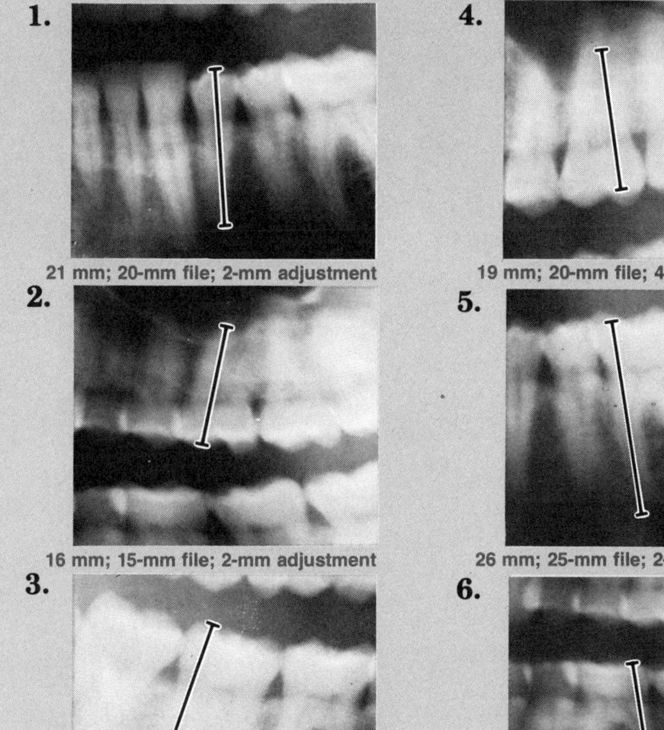

1. 21 mm; 20-mm file; 2-mm adjustment

2. 16 mm; 15-mm file; 2-mm adjustment

3. 24 mm; 25-mm file; 4-mm adjustment

4.

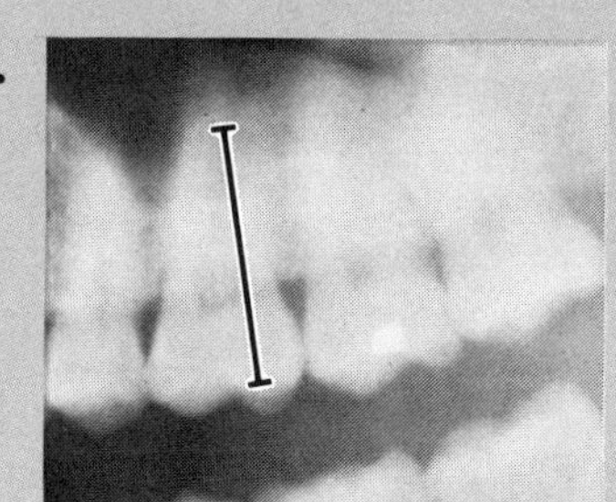

19 mm; 20-mm file; 4-mm adjustment

5.

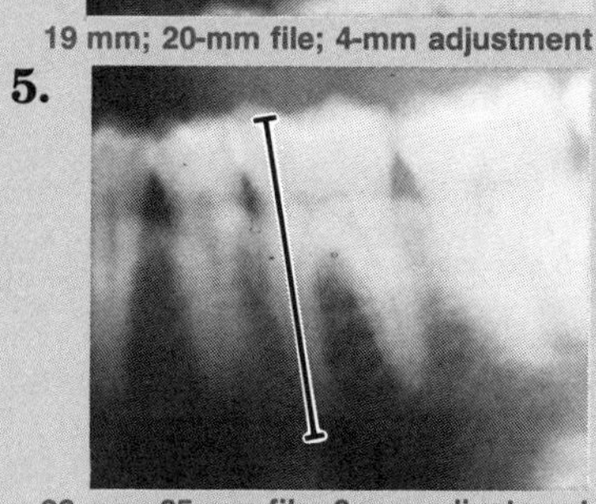

26 mm; 25-mm file; 2-mm adjustment

6.

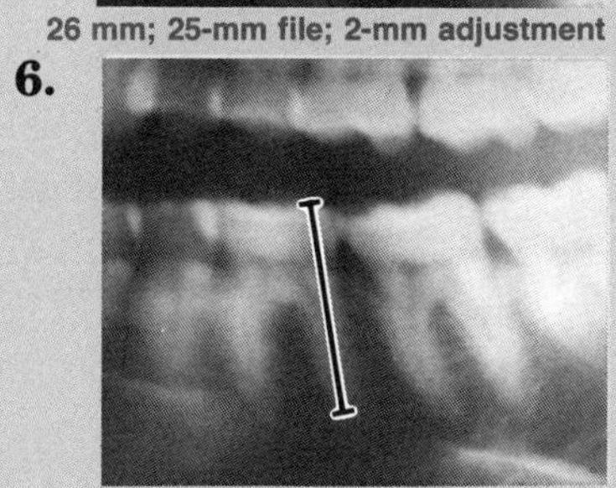

17 mm; 15-mm file; 1-mm adjustment

7.

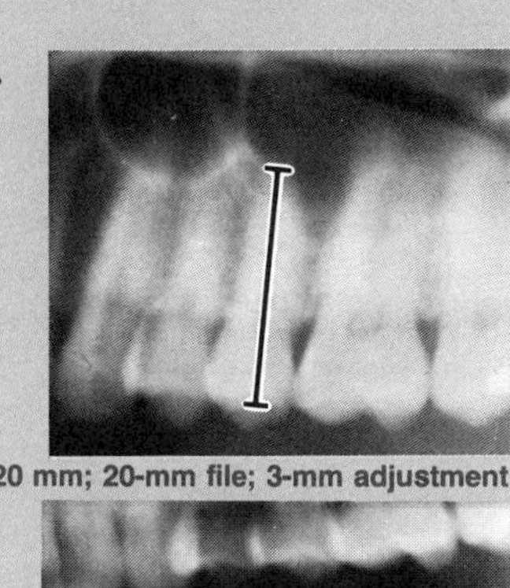

20 mm; 20-mm file; 3-mm adjustment

8.

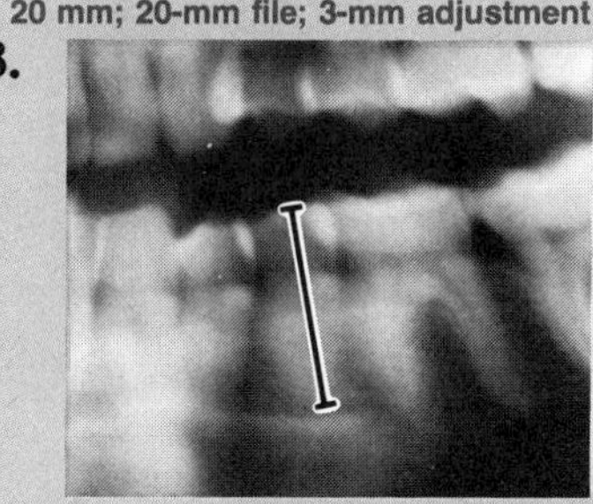

15 mm; 15-mm file; 3-mm adjustment

9.

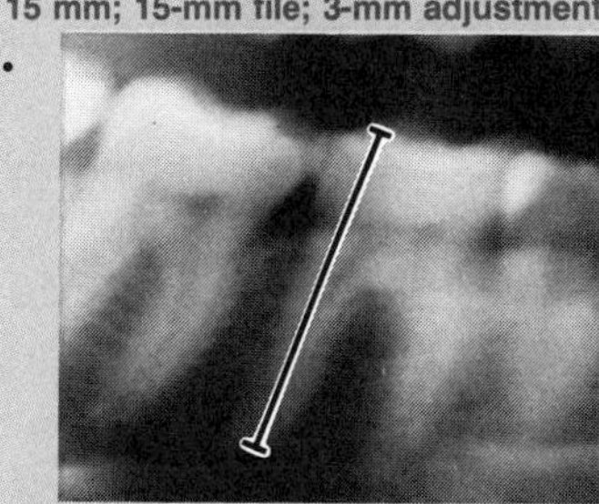

25 mm; 25-mm file; 3-mm adjustment

Extensions

10–18. A reamer is used to remove the diseased nerve tissue from the canal. The reamer is inserted to a point 1 mm from the end of the root. Reamers come in the same sizes as the files shown on page 142. The reamer used must be slightly longer than the distance the reamer is to be inserted. For each tooth shown above, tell what size reamer should be used and what adjustment should be made to shorten the reamer.
See Additional Answers on page T46.

CHAPTER 6 TEST

Number of test items - 21

Number missed	1	2	3	4	5	6	7	8	9	10
Percent correct	95	90	86	81	76	71	67	62	57	52

Materials: Ruler marked in centimeters and millimeters

A **1.** Estimate the length of this bar in centimeters. Then measure to the nearest centimeter.

3 centimeters

B **2.** Estimate the length of this bar in millimeters. Then measure to the nearest millimeter.

Accept answers close to this.

17 millimeters

C **3.** Choose the most sensible measure for the length of a car.

5 m

5 mm   5 cm

5 m   5 km

D **4.** 3.8 m = ▒ mm

3800 mm

E **5.** Count squares to find the area of this figure in square centimeters.

3 cm²

1 cm

1 cm

F **6.** Give the area of the figure in item 5 in square millimeters.

300 mm²

G **7.** Count cubes to find the volume of this figure in cubic centimeters.

2 cm³

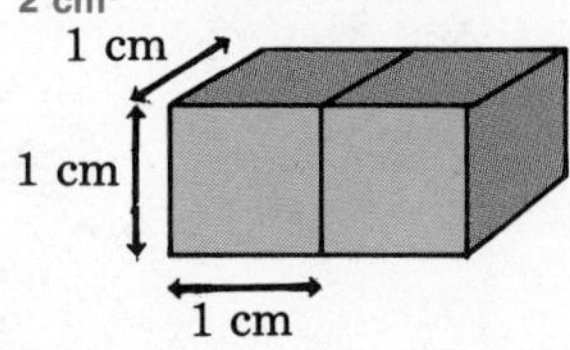

H **8.** Give the volume of the figure in item 7 in cubic millimeters.

2000 mm³

I **9.** Choose the more sensible measure for the amount of water a pail holds.

6 L

6 mL   6 L

J **10.** 8.2 L = ▒ mL

8200 mL

K **11.** Choose the most sensible measure for the mass of a small child.

15 kg

15 mg   15 g   15 kg

L **12.** 4.5 kg = ▒ g

4500 g

M **13.** Complete this statement.

4 cm³ of water is ▒ mL of water and has a mass of ▒ g.

4 mL; 4 g

N **14.** Complete this statement.

9 dm³ of water is ▒ L of water and has a mass of ▒ kg.

9 L; 9 kg

O **15.** Tell whether the temperature should be labeled kelvins or degrees Celsius.

degrees Celsius

Hot toast: 50

P **16.** Choose the more sensible temperature for a cold drink.

6°C

6°C   47°C

17. A recipe calls for 150 mL of milk. How much milk is needed for a triple recipe?

450 mL

18. What is the cost of 1.5 meters of material at $3.50 per meter?

$5.25

19. Measure the thread (T), the length (L), and the diameter (D) of this fastener to the nearest millimeter.

Accept answers close to those given.

T = 14 mm

D = 6 mm

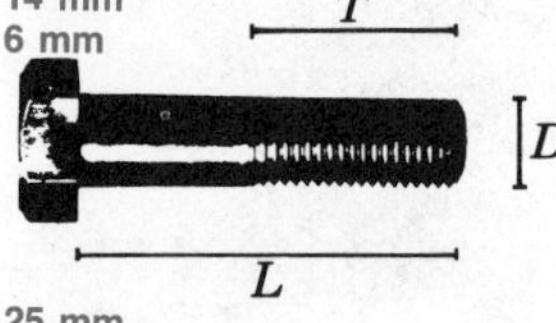

L = 25 mm

20. Dosage: 25 g

Rate: Every 4 hours

Find the total daily dosage.

150 g

21. Find the length of this tooth from the top of the crown to the end of the root.

19 mm

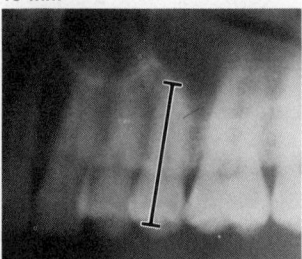

See pages 13–14 of the *Test Masters* for an alternate form of the Chapter 6 Test.
For a test on Unit 2, see pages T58–T59 of this book and pages 15–16 of the *Test Masters*.

SKILLS TUNE-UP

Dividing Whole Numbers, pages 47-58

Give the quotient and remainder.

1. 193 ÷ 4
48 R1
2. 8732 ÷ 6
1455 R2
3. 78 ÷ 29
2 R20
4. 569 ÷ 44
12 R41
5. 527 ÷ 8
65 R7
6. 7610 ÷ 57
133 R29
7. 964 ÷ 3
321 R1
8. 854 ÷ 437
1 R417
9. 3625 ÷ 673
5 R260
10. 451 ÷ 7
64 R3
11. 937 ÷ 37
25 R12
12. 6135 ÷ 18
340 R15
13. 18,566 ÷ 6
3094 R2
14. 800 ÷ 187
4 R52
15. 782 ÷ 6
130 R2
16. 4378 ÷ 24
182 R10
17. 7692 ÷ 183
42 R6
18. 13,545 ÷ 55
246 R15
19. 159,372 ÷ 5
31,874 R2
20. 5582 ÷ 48
115 R62
21. 4885 ÷ 713
6 R607
22. 775,482 ÷ 8
96,935 R2
23. 3781 ÷ 58
65 R11
24. 97,559 ÷ 421
231 R308
25. 87 ÷ 34
2 R19

Adding and Subtracting Decimals, pages 75-84

1. 6.3 + 7.4
13.7
2. 2.4 + 70.7
73.1
3. 0.57 + 0.63
1.2
4. 0.24 + 2.3
2.54
5. 6.7 + 0.791
7.491
6. 0.4 + 0.7 + 0.8
1.9
7. 0.83 + 3.648 + 5.95
10.428
8. 4.293 + 0.4 + 3.49
8.183
9. 0.07 + 3.7 + 0.042
3.812
10. 0.9 + 7.53 + 12.87
21.3
11. 4 + 0.923 + 6.5
11.423
12. 0.94 + 6 + 36.7
43.64
13. 7.9 + 0.063 + 25
32.963
14. 9.3 − 3.7
5.6
15. 0.76 − 0.08
0.68
16. 27.438 − 6.569
20.869
17. 8.104 − 4
4.104
18. 9.37 − 6.289
3.081
19. 18 − 4.263
13.737
20. 0.849 − 0.351
0.498
21. 62.003 − 45.394
16.609
22. 57.48 − 27.117
30.363
23. 76.7 − 71.305
5.395
24. 67.44 − 46
21.44
25. 0.932 − 0.564
0.368
26. 87.14 − 25.343
61.797
27. 48 − 0.013
47.987

Multiplying and Dividing Decimals, pages 95-108

1. 7.6 × 52.9
402.04
2. 0.54 × 0.124
0.06696
3. 0.2 × 3.7
0.74
4. 2.001 × 2.1
4.2021
5. 17.4 × 2.05
35.67
6. 0.031 × 0.7
0.0217
7. 1.7 × 317
538.9
8. 0.37 × 10.64
3.9368
9. 75.36 ÷ 6
12.56
10. 0.444 ÷ 74
0.006
11. 0.0584 ÷ 8
0.0073
12. 10 × 6.215
62.15
13. 0.39 × 1000
390
14. 453.6 ÷ 10
45.36
15. 0.27 ÷ 100
0.0027
16. 7.15 ÷ 1.3
5.5
17. 122.2 ÷ 0.52
235
18. 40.6 ÷ 5.8
7

Round each quotient to the nearest hundredth.

19. 2.171 ÷ 0.4
5.43
20. 0.545 ÷ 2.4
0.23
21. 0.00451 ÷ 0.08
0.06
22. 3.49 ÷ 74
0.05
23. 0.324 ÷ 5.3
0.06
24. 0.07213 ÷ 0.029
2.49
25. 0.345 ÷ 4.9
0.07

CALCULATOR APPLICATIONS

All employees at Seaview Market are hired to work a 40-hour week. If an employee works more than 40 hours a week, the employee is paid an overtime rate of 1.5 times the regular hourly rate for the additional hours.

Ali worked 53.5 hours this week. If her regular hourly rate is $3.80, what was her gross pay this week?

Regular pay

$40 \times \$3.80 = \$152.00$

Number of overtime hours

$53.5 - 40 = 13.5$

Overtime pay

$13.5 \times \$3.80 \times 1.5 = \$76.95$

Regular pay		Overtime pay		Gross pay
$152.00	+	$76.95	=	$228.95

Ali's gross pay this week was $228.95.

Calculator Suggestion: If your calculator has memory keys, try this key sequence.

Press: 40 [×] 3.8 [=] [M+] 53.5 [−] 40 [×] 3.8 [×] 1.5 [=] [M+] [MR]

Display: 228.95

Answer: $228.95

If your display does not show 228.95, consult the instruction book for your calculator to find out how the memory keys work. Be sure to clear the memory before starting each problem.

For each employee, find the gross pay for the week.

1. Robert
   Number of hours worked: 49.5
   Regular hourly rate: $4.20
   $227.85
2. Carole
   Number of hours worked: 51
   Regular hourly rate: $4.50
   $254.25
3. Scott
   Number of hours worked: 43.6
   Regular hourly rate: $3.90
   $177.06
4. Alice
   Number of hours worked: 40.6
   Regular hourly rate: $4.30
   $175.87
5. Beverly
   Number of hours worked: 48.3
   Regular hourly rate: $4.40
   $230.78
6. Dick
   Number of hours worked: 42.2
   Regular hourly rate: $4.10
   $177.53
7. Joyce
   Number of hours worked: 45
   Regular hourly rate: $5.50
   $261.25
8. Yâna
   Number of hours worked: 47.7
   Regular hourly rate: $5.20
   $268.06
9. Nancy
   Number of hours worked: 41.5
   Regular hourly rate: $5.00
   $211.25
10. Theodore
    Number of hours worked: 54.6
    Regular hourly rate: $6.80
    $420.92
11. Chris
    Number of hours worked: 58.2
    Regular hourly rate: $11.50
    $773.95

COMPUTER LITERACY

The LET and INPUT Statements

A computer has thousands of memory locations. Each location can hold exactly one value at a time. When a memory location is used, it is given a name. A name can be either a single letter or a single letter followed by a single digit. A, B3, and Q are examples of names which can be used.

In BASIC, the LET statement is used to put a value in a memory location. In Program A, lines 10 and 20 assign values to memory locations. In line 30, the values for A and B are retrieved from the memory, the computation is performed, and the resulting value is stored in another memory location (C).

Program A

The LET statement is a command to perform calculations, and not a statement of algebraic equality.

Input	Output
10 LET A=3 20 LET B=5 30 LET C=A*B 40 PRINT C 50 END	15

The general form of the LET statement is:
LET (variable) = (expression)

The INPUT statement is another way to put a value in a memory location. The INPUT statement causes the computer to print a question mark and the output is stopped until a value is typed in. This value is stored in a memory location until it is needed in the program. The INPUT statement allows you, the user, to be able to run the program more than once using a different value each time.

1.	2.	3.	4.
? 4 ? 7 R+S= 11 R*S= 28	? 8 ? 8 R+S= 16 R*S= 64	? 12 ? 15 R+S= 27 R*S= 180	? 65 ? 98 R+S= 163 R*S= 6370

In Program B, the user typed 9 for R and 6 for S.

Program B

Input	Output
10 INPUT R 20 INPUT S 30 PRINT "R+S=";R+S 40 PRINT "R*S=";R*S 50 END	? 9 ? 6 R+S= 15 R*S= 54

Give the output for Program B when

See below.

1. R = 4; S = 7.
2. R = 8; S = 8.
3. R = 12; S = 15.
4. R = 65; S = 98.

Give the output for each program.

5.
```
10 LET L=36
20 LET M=12
30 PRINT "SUM =";L+M
40 PRINT "DIFFERENCE =";L-M
50 PRINT "PRODUCT =";L*M
60 PRINT "QUOTIENT =";L/M
70 END
```

SUM = 48
DIFFERENCE = 24
PRODUCT = 432
QUOTIENT = 3

6. Use 7 for A and 8 for B. Then use 12 for A and 9 for B.

```
10 INPUT A
20 INPUT B
30 LET S=(A+B)/2
40 PRINT S
50 END
```

? 7
? 8
7.5

? 12
? 9
10.5

7. Write a program using the INPUT statement that finds the sum and the product of three numbers. Answers may vary.

```
10 INPUT X
20 INPUT Y
30 INPUT Z
40 PRINT X+Y+Z
50 PRINT X*Y*Z
60 END
```

UNIT THREE Fractions, Mixed Numbers, and Probability

CHAPTER 7 Multiplying and Dividing Fractions and Mixed Numbers

SKILLS PRETEST

Number of test items - 19

Number missed	1	2	3	4	5	6	7	8	9
Percent correct	95	89	84	79	74	68	63	58	53

SKILL Writing Fractions and Mixed Numbers *pages 150–151*

A Write a fraction for the shaded part. $\frac{5}{9}$

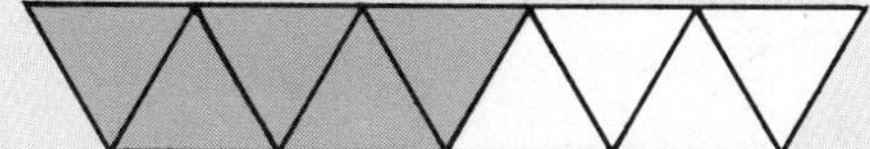

B Write a mixed number for point X. $11\frac{1}{4}$

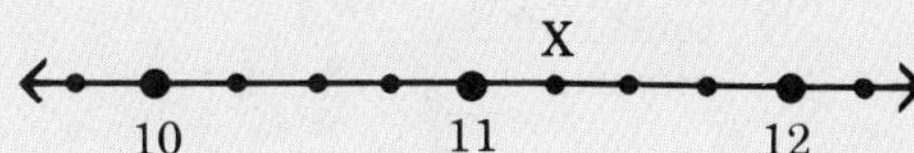

SKILL Renaming Fractions and Mixed Numbers *page 152*

C Reduce $\frac{8}{20}$ to lowest terms. $\frac{2}{5}$

D Write $\frac{17}{2}$ as a mixed number or as a whole number. $8\frac{1}{2}$

E Write $6\frac{3}{4}$ as a fraction. $\frac{27}{4}$

SKILL Writing Fractions as Decimals *page 153*

F Write $\frac{2}{5}$ as a decimal. 0.4

G Write $\frac{7}{15}$ as a decimal. Round your answer to the nearest thousandth. 0.467

SKILL Multiplying Fractions *pages 154–155*

H $\frac{2}{3} \times \frac{5}{7}$ $\frac{10}{21}$

I $\frac{3}{4} \times \frac{8}{9}$ $\frac{2}{3}$

J $\frac{3}{4} \times \frac{2}{5} \times \frac{5}{6}$ $\frac{1}{4}$

K $\frac{5}{8} \times 16$ 10

SKILL Multiplying Mixed Numbers *pages 156–157*

L $4\frac{1}{2} \times \frac{3}{5}$ $2\frac{7}{10}$

M $2\frac{2}{3} \times 10$ $26\frac{2}{3}$

N $1\frac{1}{4} \times 5\frac{2}{3}$ $7\frac{1}{12}$

O $10 \times \frac{3}{5} \times 1\frac{1}{2}$ 9

SKILL Dividing Fractions and Mixed Numbers *pages 158–159*

P Write the reciprocal of $\frac{2}{9}$. $\frac{9}{2}$

Q $\frac{2}{3} \div \frac{5}{8}$ $1\frac{1}{15}$

R $\frac{7}{10} \div 6$ $\frac{7}{60}$

S $3\frac{1}{2} \div 2\frac{3}{4}$ $1\frac{3}{11}$

See page T34 for additional notes on Chapter 7.

Objective: Write fractions and mixed numbers.

Writing Fractions and Mixed Numbers

Example A Writing fractions

Write a fraction for the shaded part.

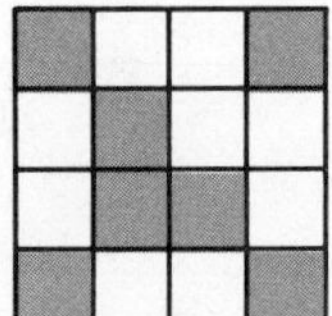

Numerator: number of shaded parts $\longrightarrow$ $\dfrac{7}{16}$ $\longleftarrow$ **Denominator:** total number of parts

$\frac{7}{16}$ is also shown on this number line at point W.

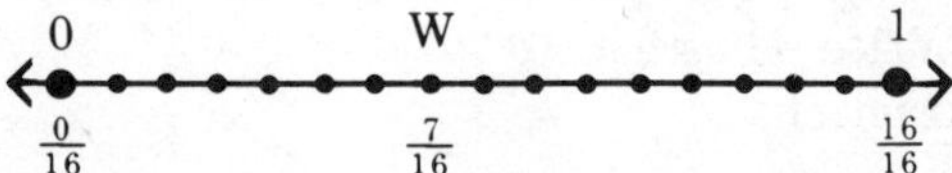

Example B Writing mixed numbers

Write a mixed number for point Y.

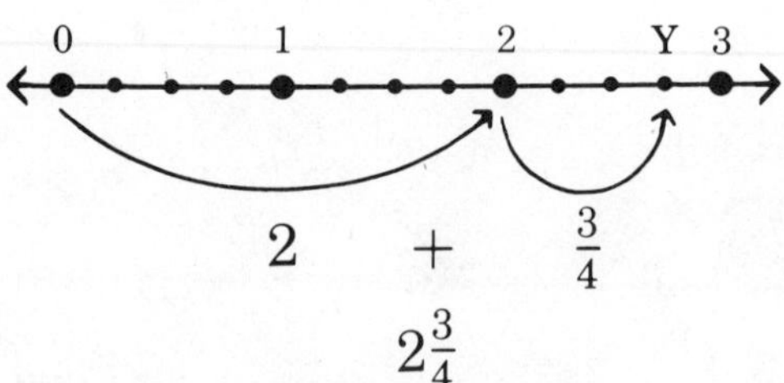

$2\frac{3}{4}$ is also shown as the shaded part in this picture.

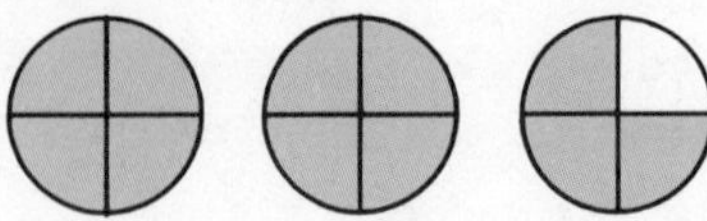

Exercises

Set A

Write a fraction for the shaded part.

1. $\frac{2}{5}$

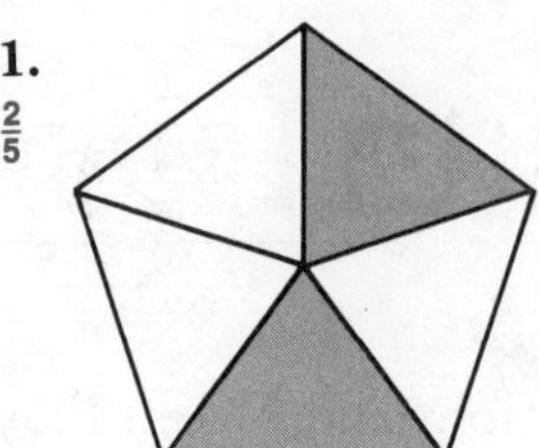

2. $\frac{3}{8}$

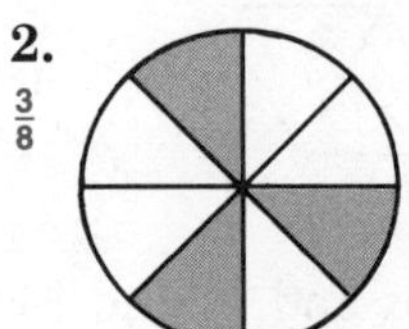

3. $\frac{7}{12}$

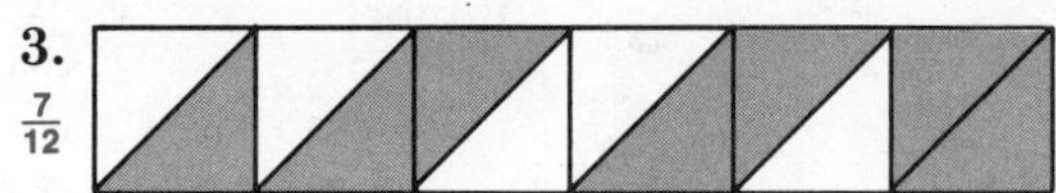

4. $\frac{8}{16}$

5. $\frac{5}{10}$

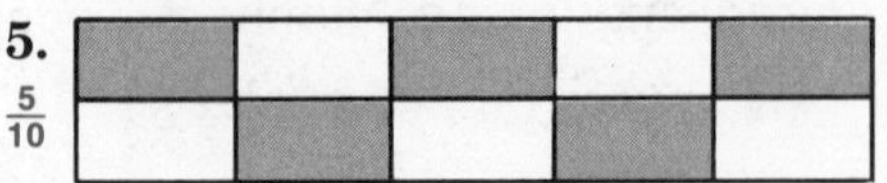

Write a fraction for each point labeled with a letter.

6. 0, W, 1 — $\frac{0}{6}$, $\frac{5}{6}$, $\frac{6}{6}$

7. 0, T, 1 — $\frac{0}{4}$, $\frac{1}{4}$, $\frac{4}{4}$

8. 0, V, 1 — $\frac{0}{3}$, $\frac{2}{3}$, $\frac{3}{3}$

9. 0, L, 1 — $\frac{0}{8}$, $\frac{5}{8}$, $\frac{8}{8}$

10. 0, U, 1 — $\frac{0}{10}$, $\frac{3}{10}$, $\frac{10}{10}$

Set B

Write a mixed number for each point labeled with a letter.

1. 0, 1, X, 2 — $1\frac{1}{2}$

2. 5, D, 6, 7 — $5\frac{2}{3}$

3. 6, Z, 7, 8 — $6\frac{3}{4}$

4. 8, 9, M, 10 — $9\frac{1}{4}$

5. 2, 3, R, 4 — $3\frac{2}{5}$

Write a mixed number for the shaded part.

6. $2\frac{2}{3}$

7. $2\frac{1}{4}$

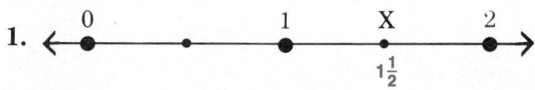

8. $6\frac{2}{5}$

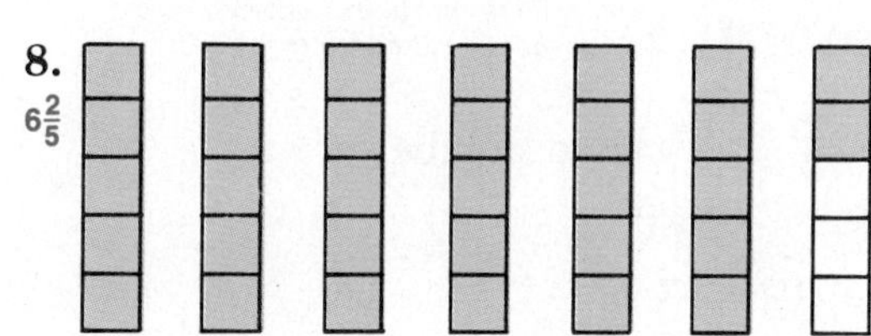

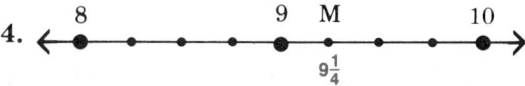

9. $4\frac{1}{2}$

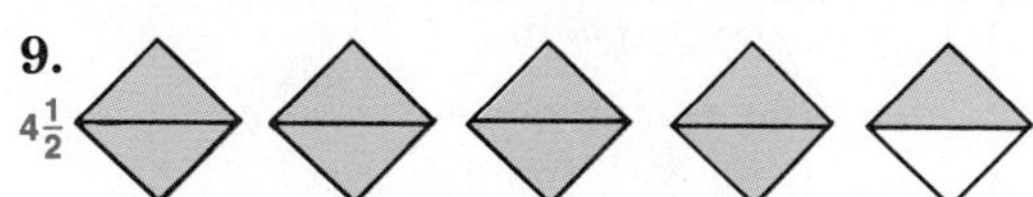

10. $1\frac{5}{6}$

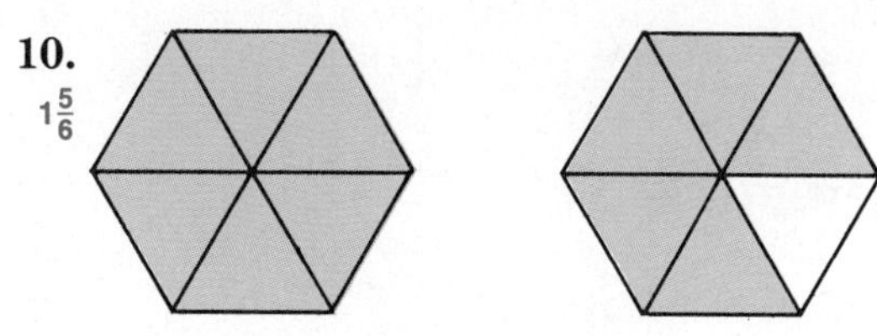

11. $3\frac{5}{8}$

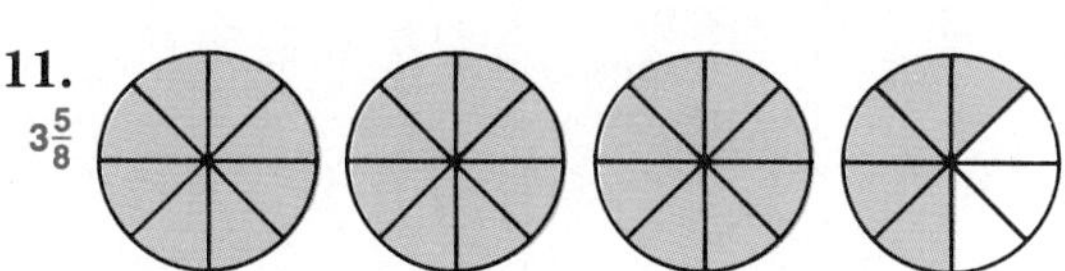

Objective: Rename fractions and mixed numbers.

Renaming Fractions and Mixed Numbers

Example C Reducing fractions

Reduce $\frac{28}{42}$ to lowest terms.

$$\frac{28}{42} \underset{42 \div 7}{\overset{28 \div 7}{=}} \frac{4}{6} \underset{6 \div 2}{\overset{4 \div 2}{=}} \frac{2}{3}$$

To reduce a fraction, divide the numerator and the denominator by a common factor greater than 1.

A fraction is in lowest terms when it cannot be reduced.

$$\frac{28}{42} = \frac{2}{3}$$

Example D Writing improper fractions as mixed numbers or as whole numbers

Write $\frac{63}{5}$ as a mixed number or as a whole number.

$$\frac{63}{5} = 63 \div 5$$

$$\begin{array}{r} 12\frac{3}{5} \\ 5\overline{)63} \\ -5 \\ \hline 13 \\ -10 \\ \hline 3 \end{array}$$

Divide the numerator by the denominator.

If the remainder is not zero, write a fraction with the remainder as the numerator and the divisor as the denominator.

Example E Writing mixed numbers as fractions

Write $7\frac{1}{2}$ as a fraction.

$$7\frac{1}{2} = \frac{15}{2}$$

Multiply 2 and 7 to find how many halves are in 7. Then add 1.
The numerator is 15.
The denominator is 2.

Exercises

Set C

Reduce each fraction to lowest terms.

1. $\frac{8}{12}$ $\frac{2}{3}$
2. $\frac{6}{24}$ $\frac{1}{4}$
3. $\frac{10}{20}$ $\frac{1}{2}$
4. $\frac{9}{27}$ $\frac{1}{3}$
5. $\frac{12}{16}$ $\frac{3}{4}$
6. $\frac{4}{32}$ $\frac{1}{8}$
7. $\frac{33}{55}$ $\frac{3}{5}$
8. $\frac{21}{35}$ $\frac{3}{5}$
9. $\frac{30}{36}$ $\frac{5}{6}$
10. $\frac{24}{40}$ $\frac{3}{5}$
11. $\frac{15}{80}$ $\frac{3}{16}$
12. $\frac{42}{90}$ $\frac{7}{15}$
13. $\frac{24}{72}$ $\frac{1}{3}$
14. $\frac{56}{84}$ $\frac{2}{3}$
15. $\frac{48}{64}$ $\frac{3}{4}$

Set D

Write each fraction as a mixed number or as a whole number.

1. $\frac{23}{4}$ $5\frac{3}{4}$
2. $\frac{73}{9}$ $8\frac{1}{9}$
3. $\frac{35}{7}$ 5
4. $\frac{59}{6}$ $9\frac{5}{6}$
5. $\frac{38}{6}$ $6\frac{1}{3}$
6. $\frac{52}{8}$ $6\frac{1}{2}$
7. $\frac{48}{2}$ 24
8. $\frac{109}{5}$ $21\frac{4}{5}$
9. $\frac{44}{3}$ $14\frac{2}{3}$
10. $\frac{197}{6}$ $32\frac{5}{6}$
11. $\frac{283}{10}$ $28\frac{3}{10}$
12. $\frac{130}{10}$ 13
13. $\frac{188}{12}$ $15\frac{2}{3}$
14. $\frac{300}{15}$ 20
15. $\frac{485}{20}$ $24\frac{1}{4}$

Set E

Write each mixed number as a fraction.

1. $1\frac{2}{5}$ $\frac{7}{5}$
2. $2\frac{3}{4}$ $\frac{11}{4}$
3. $3\frac{7}{8}$ $\frac{31}{8}$
4. $2\frac{5}{9}$ $\frac{23}{9}$
5. $9\frac{5}{6}$ $\frac{59}{6}$
6. $8\frac{4}{5}$ $\frac{44}{5}$
7. $12\frac{1}{2}$ $\frac{25}{2}$
8. $10\frac{5}{8}$ $\frac{85}{8}$
9. $21\frac{2}{3}$ $\frac{65}{3}$
10. $36\frac{1}{2}$ $\frac{73}{2}$
11. $25\frac{9}{10}$ $\frac{259}{10}$
12. $14\frac{1}{3}$ $\frac{43}{3}$
13. $6\frac{1}{16}$ $\frac{97}{16}$
14. $5\frac{5}{16}$ $\frac{85}{16}$
15. $85\frac{3}{4}$ $\frac{343}{4}$

Objective: Write a fraction as a decimal.

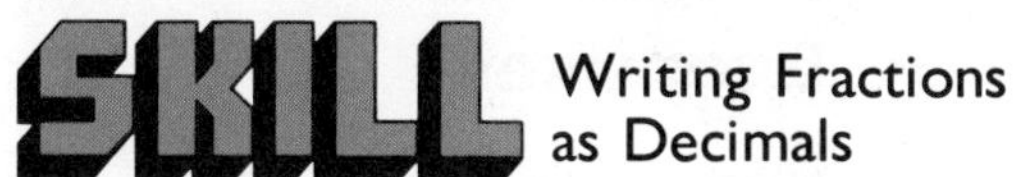

Writing Fractions as Decimals

Example F Terminating decimals

Write $\frac{7}{8}$ as a decimal.

$\frac{7}{8} = 7 \div 8$

$$\begin{array}{r} 0.875 \\ 8\overline{)7.000} \\ -6\,4 \\ \hline 60 \\ -56 \\ \hline 40 \\ -40 \\ \hline 0 \end{array}$$

Divide the numerator by the denominator.

Write zeros in the dividend and continue dividing until the remainder is zero.

Example G Nonterminating decimals

Write $\frac{1}{6}$ as a decimal. Round your answer to the nearest thousandth.

$\frac{1}{6} = 1 \div 6$

$$\begin{array}{r} 0.1666 \approx 0.167 \\ 6\overline{)1.0000} \\ -6 \\ \hline 40 \\ -36 \\ \hline 40 \\ -36 \\ \hline 40 \\ -36 \\ \hline 4 \end{array}$$

Divide the numerator by the denominator.

Write zeros in the dividend and divide until the quotient is in ten-thousandths. Round to the nearest thousandth.

Exercises

Set F

Write each fraction as a decimal. Divide until the remainder is zero.

1. $\frac{1}{2}$ 0.5
2. $\frac{1}{5}$ 0.2
3. $\frac{1}{4}$ 0.25
4. $\frac{4}{5}$ 0.8
5. $\frac{7}{10}$ 0.7
6. $\frac{3}{4}$ 0.75
7. $\frac{3}{5}$ 0.6
8. $\frac{9}{10}$ 0.9
9. $\frac{1}{20}$ 0.05
10. $\frac{5}{8}$ 0.625
11. $\frac{3}{8}$ 0.375
12. $\frac{17}{100}$ 0.17
13. $\frac{3}{20}$ 0.15
14. $\frac{8}{25}$ 0.32
15. $\frac{9}{50}$ 0.18
16. $\frac{11}{20}$ 0.55
17. $\frac{13}{1000}$ 0.013
18. $\frac{19}{40}$ 0.475
19. $\frac{1}{80}$ 0.0125
20. $\frac{7}{16}$ 0.4375
21. $\frac{5}{16}$ 0.3125
22. $\frac{1}{32}$ 0.03125
23. $\frac{3}{16}$ 0.1875
24. $\frac{9}{16}$ 0.5625

Set G

Write each fraction as a decimal. Round each answer to the nearest thousandth.

1. $\frac{1}{3}$ 0.333
2. $\frac{1}{9}$ 0.111
3. $\frac{2}{9}$ 0.222
4. $\frac{2}{3}$ 0.667
5. $\frac{5}{9}$ 0.556
6. $\frac{8}{9}$ 0.889
7. $\frac{5}{6}$ 0.833
8. $\frac{3}{7}$ 0.429
9. $\frac{4}{7}$ 0.571
10. $\frac{9}{11}$ 0.818
11. $\frac{4}{11}$ 0.364
12. $\frac{10}{11}$ 0.909
13. $\frac{5}{12}$ 0.417
14. $\frac{7}{12}$ 0.583
15. $\frac{8}{21}$ 0.381
16. $\frac{1}{12}$ 0.083
17. $\frac{11}{12}$ 0.917
18. $\frac{5}{21}$ 0.238
19. $\frac{13}{19}$ 0.684
20. $\frac{1}{18}$ 0.056
21. $\frac{17}{18}$ 0.944
22. $\frac{3}{17}$ 0.176
23. $\frac{1}{15}$ 0.067
24. $\frac{4}{15}$ 0.267

Objective: Multiply fractions.

Multiplying Fractions

Example H Two fractions, without reducing

$\frac{3}{4}\times\frac{1}{5}=\frac{3}{20}$ Multiply the numerators. Multiply the denominators.

The product of fractions less than 1 is a fraction less than 1. The answer is reasonable.

Example I Two fractions, with reducing

$\frac{5}{8}\times\frac{7}{10}=\frac{35}{80}=\frac{7}{16}$ Multiply. Reduce $\frac{35}{80}$ to lowest terms.

Sometimes you can use a shortcut when you multiply.

$\frac{\overset{1}{\cancel{5}}}{8}\times\frac{7}{\underset{2}{\cancel{10}}}=\frac{7}{16}$ If possible, divide a denominator and a numerator by the same number. Then multiply.

Example J Three fractions

$\frac{1}{6}\times\frac{9}{10}\times\frac{5}{7}$

$\frac{1}{\underset{2}{\cancel{6}}}\times\frac{\overset{3}{\cancel{9}}}{\underset{2}{\cancel{10}}}\times\frac{\overset{1}{\cancel{5}}}{7}=\frac{3}{28}$ Use the shortcut. Divide the denominator, 6, and the numerator, 9, by 3. Divide the denominator, 10, and the numerator, 5, by 5. Multiply.

Example K A fraction and a whole number

$\frac{7}{8}\times 36$

Write 36 as $\frac{36}{1}$.

$\frac{7}{\underset{2}{\cancel{8}}}\times\frac{\overset{9}{\cancel{36}}}{1}=\frac{63}{2}=31\frac{1}{2}$ Use the shortcut. Multiply. Write $\frac{63}{2}$ as a mixed number.

The product of a whole number and a fraction less than 1 is less than the whole number. The answer is reasonable.

Exercises

Set H

1. $\frac{2}{3}\times\frac{4}{5}$ **$\frac{8}{15}$**
2. $\frac{1}{8}\times\frac{3}{4}$ **$\frac{3}{32}$**
3. $\frac{5}{6}\times\frac{1}{3}$ **$\frac{5}{18}$**
4. $\frac{3}{4}\times\frac{5}{8}$ **$\frac{15}{32}$**
5. $\frac{1}{7}\times\frac{2}{5}$ **$\frac{2}{35}$**
6. $\frac{1}{2}\times\frac{3}{8}$ **$\frac{3}{16}$**
7. $\frac{3}{5}\times\frac{7}{8}$ **$\frac{21}{40}$**
8. $\frac{1}{4}\times\frac{11}{12}$ **$\frac{11}{48}$**
9. $\frac{9}{10}\times\frac{3}{7}$ **$\frac{27}{70}$**
10. $\frac{5}{9}\times\frac{7}{8}$ **$\frac{35}{72}$**
11. $\frac{7}{16}\times\frac{1}{3}$ **$\frac{7}{48}$**
12. $\frac{7}{12}\times\frac{5}{8}$ **$\frac{35}{96}$**

Set I

1. $\frac{3}{8}\times\frac{4}{5}$ **$\frac{3}{10}$**
2. $\frac{2}{7}\times\frac{14}{15}$ **$\frac{4}{15}$**
3. $\frac{5}{8}\times\frac{4}{7}$ **$\frac{5}{14}$**
4. $\frac{6}{11}\times\frac{5}{12}$ **$\frac{5}{22}$**
5. $\frac{8}{9}\times\frac{5}{16}$ **$\frac{5}{18}$**
6. $\frac{7}{12}\times\frac{3}{4}$ **$\frac{7}{16}$**
7. $\frac{9}{10}\times\frac{1}{6}$ **$\frac{3}{20}$**
8. $\frac{6}{7}\times\frac{7}{8}$ **$\frac{3}{4}$**
9. $\frac{4}{9}\times\frac{3}{16}$ **$\frac{1}{12}$**
10. $\frac{3}{10}\times\frac{5}{6}$ **$\frac{1}{4}$**
11. $\frac{2}{3}\times\frac{9}{16}$ **$\frac{3}{8}$**
12. $\frac{3}{4}\times\frac{8}{9}$ **$\frac{2}{3}$**
13. $\frac{4}{5}\times\frac{9}{10}$ **$\frac{18}{25}$**
14. $\frac{8}{9}\times\frac{5}{12}$ **$\frac{10}{27}$**
15. $\frac{6}{7}\times\frac{14}{15}$ **$\frac{4}{5}$**
16. $\frac{9}{10}\times\frac{5}{12}$ **$\frac{3}{8}$**
17. $\frac{2}{5}\times\frac{15}{16}$ **$\frac{3}{8}$**
18. $\frac{5}{6}\times\frac{18}{25}$ **$\frac{3}{5}$**
19. $\frac{4}{9}\times\frac{15}{16}$ **$\frac{5}{12}$**
20. $\frac{9}{10}\times\frac{20}{21}$ **$\frac{6}{7}$**
21. $\frac{5}{12}\times\frac{3}{20}$ **$\frac{1}{16}$**
22. $\frac{7}{32}\times\frac{8}{21}$ **$\frac{1}{12}$**
23. $\frac{8}{9}\times\frac{27}{28}$ **$\frac{6}{7}$**
24. $\frac{9}{10}\times\frac{5}{24}$ **$\frac{3}{16}$**
25. $\frac{14}{15}\times\frac{25}{42}$ **$\frac{5}{9}$**
26. $\frac{20}{21}\times\frac{35}{36}$ **$\frac{25}{27}$**
27. $\frac{15}{16}\times\frac{24}{25}$ **$\frac{9}{10}$**
28. $\frac{48}{49}\times\frac{35}{36}$ **$\frac{20}{21}$**

Set J

1. $\frac{2}{3} \times \frac{6}{7} \times \frac{14}{15}$ $\frac{8}{15}$
2. $\frac{10}{21} \times \frac{3}{5} \times \frac{7}{8}$ $\frac{1}{4}$
3. $\frac{8}{9} \times \frac{3}{5} \times \frac{1}{4}$ $\frac{2}{15}$
4. $\frac{3}{4} \times \frac{1}{2} \times \frac{5}{9}$ $\frac{5}{24}$
5. $\frac{9}{16} \times \frac{5}{6} \times \frac{12}{25}$ $\frac{9}{40}$
6. $\frac{3}{8} \times \frac{4}{5} \times \frac{1}{2}$ $\frac{3}{20}$
7. $\frac{16}{25} \times \frac{10}{27} \times \frac{3}{8}$ $\frac{4}{45}$
8. $\frac{5}{6} \times \frac{2}{3} \times \frac{9}{16}$ $\frac{5}{16}$
9. $\frac{2}{3} \times \frac{1}{2} \times \frac{3}{4}$ $\frac{1}{4}$
10. $\frac{5}{8} \times \frac{3}{14} \times \frac{7}{10}$ $\frac{3}{32}$
11. $\frac{8}{15} \times \frac{9}{10} \times \frac{5}{21}$ $\frac{4}{35}$
12. $\frac{3}{8} \times \frac{7}{9} \times \frac{4}{5}$ $\frac{7}{30}$
13. $\frac{3}{10} \times \frac{4}{7} \times \frac{5}{9}$ $\frac{2}{21}$
14. $\frac{10}{27} \times \frac{3}{8} \times \frac{9}{20}$ $\frac{1}{16}$
15. $\frac{4}{9} \times \frac{3}{16} \times \frac{2}{5}$ $\frac{1}{30}$
16. $\frac{2}{9} \times \frac{21}{22} \times \frac{9}{14}$ $\frac{3}{22}$
17. $\frac{6}{7} \times \frac{14}{27} \times \frac{15}{28}$ $\frac{5}{21}$
18. $\frac{24}{25} \times \frac{15}{16} \times \frac{3}{4}$ $\frac{27}{40}$

Set K

1. $\frac{2}{3} \times 18$ 12
2. $\frac{5}{8} \times 16$ 10
3. $\frac{4}{5} \times 30$ 24
4. $\frac{7}{10} \times 50$ 35
5. $9 \times \frac{1}{6}$ $1\frac{1}{2}$
6. $\frac{3}{8} \times 20$ $7\frac{1}{2}$
7. $\frac{2}{3} \times 32$ $21\frac{1}{3}$
8. $\frac{2}{5} \times 21$ $8\frac{2}{5}$
9. $4 \times \frac{5}{6}$ $3\frac{1}{3}$
10. $\frac{1}{6} \times 16$ $2\frac{2}{3}$
11. $60 \times \frac{3}{4}$ 45
12. $10 \times \frac{7}{16}$ $4\frac{3}{8}$
13. $90 \times \frac{1}{4}$ $22\frac{1}{2}$
14. $75 \times \frac{2}{3}$ 50
15. $148 \times \frac{1}{4}$ 37
16. $\frac{1}{5} \times 235$ 47
17. $\frac{2}{3} \times 9000$ 6000
18. $\frac{3}{4} \times 8000$ 6000

Mixed Practice

H 1. $\frac{2}{3} \times \frac{5}{9}$ $\frac{10}{27}$

I 2. $\frac{3}{5} \times \frac{1}{6}$ $\frac{1}{10}$

J 3. $\frac{8}{9} \times \frac{3}{8} \times \frac{6}{7}$ $\frac{2}{7}$

K 4. $\frac{1}{6} \times 348$ 58

I 5. $\frac{7}{8} \times \frac{4}{25}$ $\frac{7}{50}$

I 6. $\frac{3}{8} \times \frac{6}{7}$ $\frac{9}{28}$

I 7. $\frac{9}{10} \times \frac{5}{24}$ $\frac{3}{16}$

I 8. $\frac{8}{9} \times \frac{9}{10}$ $\frac{4}{5}$

K 9. $27 \times \frac{3}{4}$ $20\frac{1}{4}$

I 10. $\frac{7}{10} \times \frac{4}{5}$ $\frac{14}{25}$

J 11. $\frac{3}{8} \times \frac{4}{15} \times \frac{5}{9}$ $\frac{1}{18}$

K 12. $18 \times \frac{4}{5}$ $14\frac{2}{5}$

I 13. $\frac{8}{15} \times \frac{11}{16}$ $\frac{11}{30}$

K 14. $\frac{4}{5} \times 6000$ 4800

I 15. $\frac{8}{9} \times \frac{27}{32}$ $\frac{3}{4}$

K 16. $22 \times \frac{3}{11}$ 6

J 17. $\frac{6}{25} \times \frac{10}{27} \times \frac{9}{16}$ $\frac{1}{20}$

H 18. $\frac{3}{5} \times \frac{7}{8}$ $\frac{21}{40}$

BREAK TIME

A boy has as many sisters as brothers.
Each sister has only half as many sisters as brothers.
How many sisters and brothers are there?
3 sisters, 4 brothers

Objective: Multiply mixed numbers.

Multiplying Mixed Numbers

Example L A mixed number and a fraction

$2\frac{3}{4} \times \frac{1}{6}$

$\frac{11}{4} \times \frac{1}{6} = \frac{11}{24}$

Write $2\frac{3}{4}$ as a fraction.
Multiply.

The product of a mixed number and a fraction less than 1 is less than the mixed number. The answer is reasonable.

Example M A mixed number and a whole number

$3\frac{1}{4} \times 5$

$\frac{13}{4} \times \frac{5}{1} = \frac{65}{4} = 16\frac{1}{4}$

Write $3\frac{1}{4}$ and 5 as fractions.
Multiply.
Write $\frac{65}{4}$ as a mixed number.

The product of a mixed number and a whole number is greater than the product of the two whole numbers. The answer is reasonable.

Example N Two mixed numbers

$2\frac{1}{3} \times 5\frac{1}{6}$

$\frac{7}{3} \times \frac{31}{6} = \frac{217}{18} = 12\frac{1}{18}$

Write $2\frac{1}{3}$ and $5\frac{1}{6}$ as fractions.
Multiply.
Write $\frac{217}{18}$ as a mixed number.

The product of two mixed numbers is greater than the product of the whole numbers. The answer is reasonable.

Example O Three factors

$4\frac{1}{5} \times \frac{5}{7} \times 9$

$\frac{\overset{3}{\cancel{21}}}{\underset{1}{\cancel{5}}} \times \frac{\overset{1}{\cancel{5}}}{\underset{1}{\cancel{7}}} \times \frac{9}{1} = \frac{27}{1} = 27$

Write $4\frac{1}{5}$ and 9 as fractions.
Use the shortcut.
Multiply.
Write $\frac{27}{1}$ as a whole number.

Exercises

Set L

1. $1\frac{2}{5} \times \frac{5}{8}$ **$\frac{7}{8}$**
2. $2\frac{1}{4} \times \frac{1}{3}$ **$\frac{3}{4}$**
3. $\frac{1}{6} \times 3\frac{2}{5}$ **$\frac{17}{30}$**
4. $5\frac{1}{2} \times \frac{1}{3}$ **$1\frac{5}{6}$**
5. $2\frac{2}{3} \times \frac{3}{8}$ **1**
6. $\frac{9}{10} \times 1\frac{1}{9}$ **1**
7. $9\frac{1}{2} \times \frac{4}{7}$ **$5\frac{3}{7}$**
8. $5\frac{1}{3} \times \frac{3}{4}$ **4**
9. $\frac{2}{3} \times 8\frac{2}{5}$ **$5\frac{3}{5}$**
10. $6\frac{3}{10} \times \frac{5}{7}$ **$4\frac{1}{2}$**
11. $\frac{8}{9} \times 1\frac{11}{16}$ **$1\frac{1}{2}$**
12. $3\frac{1}{7} \times \frac{3}{4}$ **$2\frac{5}{14}$**
13. $4\frac{1}{8} \times \frac{5}{9}$ **$2\frac{7}{24}$**
14. $6\frac{2}{5} \times \frac{5}{8}$ **4**
15. $21\frac{1}{3} \times \frac{3}{8}$ **8**
16. $24\frac{1}{2} \times \frac{4}{7}$ **14**

Set M

1. $3\frac{2}{3} \times 9$ **33**
2. $6 \times 4\frac{1}{2}$ **27**
3. $5\frac{1}{3} \times 4$ **$21\frac{1}{3}$**
4. $7 \times 5\frac{1}{2}$ **$38\frac{1}{2}$**
5. $8\frac{1}{4} \times 12$ **99**
6. $7\frac{1}{5} \times 10$ **72**
7. $1\frac{3}{4} \times 13$ **$22\frac{3}{4}$**
8. $3 \times 4\frac{3}{5}$ **$13\frac{4}{5}$**
9. $7\frac{1}{3} \times 6$ **44**
10. $4\frac{3}{4} \times 8$ **38**
11. $9\frac{3}{8} \times 6$ **$56\frac{1}{4}$**
12. $6 \times 3\frac{9}{10}$ **$23\frac{2}{5}$**
13. $2\frac{7}{8} \times 32$ **92**
14. $2\frac{3}{8} \times 40$ **95**
15. $10\frac{3}{7} \times 14$ **146**
16. $30 \times 12\frac{1}{3}$ **370**

Set N

1. $1\frac{1}{2} \times 3\frac{1}{4}$ **$4\frac{7}{8}$**
2. $2\frac{1}{2} \times 2\frac{2}{3}$ **$6\frac{2}{3}$**
3. $5\frac{1}{4} \times 2\frac{2}{7}$ **12**
4. $1\frac{7}{10} \times 3\frac{1}{3}$ **$5\frac{2}{3}$**
5. $3\frac{3}{5} \times 1\frac{1}{6}$ **$4\frac{1}{5}$**
6. $1\frac{4}{5} \times 2\frac{7}{9}$ **5**

7. $6\frac{2}{3} \times 2\frac{1}{4}$ 15

8. $3\frac{3}{4} \times 9\frac{1}{3}$ 35

9. $8\frac{3}{4} \times 2\frac{1}{7}$ $18\frac{3}{4}$

10. $10\frac{2}{3} \times 1\frac{3}{8}$ $14\frac{2}{3}$

11. $3\frac{3}{7} \times 2\frac{5}{8}$ 9

12. $2\frac{4}{5} \times 3\frac{4}{7}$ 10

13. $7\frac{5}{8} \times 3\frac{1}{5}$ $24\frac{2}{5}$

14. $9\frac{1}{3} \times 1\frac{3}{7}$ $13\frac{1}{3}$

15. $15\frac{5}{6} \times 1\frac{1}{2}$ $23\frac{3}{4}$

16. $12\frac{4}{5} \times 4\frac{3}{4}$ $60\frac{4}{5}$

Set O

1. $\frac{2}{3} \times 2\frac{1}{2} \times 5\frac{1}{4}$ $8\frac{3}{4}$

2. $\frac{4}{7} \times 2\frac{1}{3} \times 5$ $6\frac{2}{3}$

3. $1\frac{3}{4} \times 12 \times \frac{2}{3}$ 14

4. $3\frac{1}{3} \times 6 \times \frac{4}{5}$ 16

5. $15 \times 2 \times \frac{5}{6}$ 25

6. $4\frac{1}{2} \times 1\frac{1}{7} \times \frac{7}{9}$ 4

7. $7\frac{2}{5} \times \frac{5}{6} \times \frac{1}{2}$ $3\frac{1}{12}$

8. $6\frac{1}{4} \times 5\frac{1}{2} \times 8$ 275

9. $\frac{1}{3} \times \frac{6}{7} \times 2\frac{1}{8}$ $\frac{17}{28}$

10. $24 \times \frac{1}{8} \times 9\frac{1}{2}$ $28\frac{1}{2}$

11. $36 \times \frac{5}{6} \times \frac{7}{10}$ 21

PROBLEM SOLVING
The applications on pages 164–165 may be used anytime after this lesson.

Mixed Practice

L 1. $\frac{1}{8} \times 2\frac{1}{2}$ $\frac{5}{16}$

M 2. $2\frac{1}{3} \times 21$ 49

N 3. $2\frac{1}{4} \times 3\frac{1}{3}$ $7\frac{1}{2}$

O 4. $\frac{4}{5} \times 3\frac{1}{2} \times 10$ 28

M 5. $10 \times 3\frac{1}{2}$ 35

L 6. $\frac{2}{3} \times 7\frac{1}{5}$ $4\frac{4}{5}$

O 7. $6\frac{1}{4} \times 5\frac{3}{5} \times \frac{1}{2}$ $17\frac{1}{2}$

N 8. $3\frac{1}{7} \times 4\frac{2}{3}$ $14\frac{2}{3}$

L 9. $2\frac{2}{3} \times \frac{5}{8}$ $1\frac{2}{3}$

M 10. $36 \times 3\frac{1}{4}$ 117

N 11. $3\frac{1}{7} \times 5\frac{1}{4}$ $16\frac{1}{2}$

O 12. $\frac{1}{2} \times 3\frac{1}{7} \times 10\frac{1}{2}$ $16\frac{1}{2}$

M 13. $10\frac{3}{5} \times 25$ 265

L 14. $6\frac{1}{4} \times \frac{4}{5}$ 5

O 15. $5\frac{1}{6} \times \frac{15}{16} \times \frac{1}{5}$ $\frac{31}{32}$

N 16. $4\frac{2}{5} \times 1\frac{4}{11}$ 6

L 17. $\frac{7}{8} \times 1\frac{5}{9}$ $1\frac{13}{36}$

N 18. $1\frac{7}{8} \times 3\frac{1}{3}$ $6\frac{1}{4}$

N 19. $9\frac{3}{8} \times 4\frac{4}{5}$ 45

L 20. $6\frac{5}{6} \times \frac{2}{3}$ $4\frac{5}{9}$

N 21. $2\frac{5}{8} \times 2\frac{2}{3}$ 7

See Skills File, page 421, for more practice.

BREAK TIME

If a chicken weighs 2 pounds plus three fourths its own weight, how much does it weigh?
8 pounds

Objective: Divide fractions and mixed numbers.

Dividing Fractions and Mixed Numbers

Example P Writing reciprocals

Give the reciprocals of $\frac{2}{5}$, 7, and $3\frac{1}{4}$.

Two numbers whose product is 1 are **reciprocals.**

The reciprocal of $\frac{2}{5}$ is $\frac{5}{2}$. $\quad \frac{2}{5} \times \frac{5}{2} = 1$

The reciprocal of 7 is $\frac{1}{7}$. $\quad 7 = \frac{7}{1} \longrightarrow \frac{7}{1} \times \frac{1}{7} = 1$

The reciprocal of $3\frac{1}{4}$ is $\frac{4}{13}$. $\quad 3\frac{1}{4} = \frac{13}{4} \longrightarrow \frac{13}{4} \times \frac{4}{13} = 1$

Example Q A fraction divisor

$2\frac{3}{4} \div \frac{2}{5}$

$\frac{11}{4} \times \frac{5}{2} = \frac{55}{8} = 6\frac{7}{8}$

Multiply by the reciprocal of the divisor. The reciprocal of $\frac{2}{5}$ is $\frac{5}{2}$.

When the dividend is greater than the divisor, the quotient is greater than 1.

Example R A whole-number divisor

$\frac{4}{5} \div 8$

$\frac{4}{5} \div \frac{8}{1} = \frac{\cancel{4}^{1}}{5} \times \frac{1}{\cancel{8}_{2}} = \frac{1}{10}$

Multiply by the reciprocal of 8.

When the dividend is less than the divisor, the quotient is less than 1.

Example S A mixed-number divisor

$6\frac{2}{3} \div 2\frac{2}{5}$

$\frac{20}{3} \div \frac{12}{5} = \frac{\cancel{20}^{5}}{3} \times \frac{5}{\cancel{12}_{3}} = \frac{25}{9} = 2\frac{7}{9}$

Multiply by the reciprocal of $2\frac{2}{5}$.

Exercises

Set P

Give the reciprocal of each number.

1. $\frac{3}{4}$ $\quad \frac{4}{3}$
2. $\frac{4}{5}$ $\quad \frac{5}{4}$
3. $\frac{1}{9}$ $\quad \frac{9}{1}$
4. $\frac{9}{10}$ $\quad \frac{10}{9}$
5. $\frac{7}{100}$ $\quad \frac{100}{7}$
6. $\frac{11}{12}$ $\quad \frac{12}{11}$
7. 12 $\quad \frac{1}{12}$
8. 6 $\quad \frac{1}{6}$
9. 52 $\quad \frac{1}{52}$
10. 99 $\quad \frac{1}{99}$
11. $2\frac{1}{2}$ $\quad \frac{2}{5}$
12. $3\frac{5}{8}$ $\quad \frac{8}{29}$
13. $4\frac{2}{3}$ $\quad \frac{3}{14}$
14. $7\frac{1}{4}$ $\quad \frac{4}{29}$
15. $5\frac{3}{5}$ $\quad \frac{5}{28}$
16. $8\frac{5}{9}$ $\quad \frac{9}{77}$
17. $12\frac{5}{6}$ $\quad \frac{6}{77}$
18. $15\frac{3}{4}$ $\quad \frac{4}{63}$

Set Q

1. $\frac{3}{4} \div \frac{1}{2}$ $\quad 1\frac{1}{2}$
2. $\frac{5}{6} \div \frac{2}{3}$ $\quad 1\frac{1}{4}$
3. $\frac{6}{7} \div \frac{3}{8}$ $\quad 2\frac{2}{7}$
4. $\frac{9}{16} \div \frac{1}{2}$ $\quad 1\frac{1}{8}$
5. $\frac{2}{3} \div \frac{4}{9}$ $\quad 1\frac{1}{2}$
6. $\frac{5}{8} \div \frac{5}{12}$ $\quad 1\frac{1}{2}$
7. $\frac{5}{6} \div \frac{9}{16}$ $\quad 1\frac{13}{27}$
8. $\frac{1}{6} \div \frac{7}{9}$ $\quad \frac{3}{14}$
9. $10 \div \frac{7}{10}$ $\quad 14\frac{2}{7}$
10. $8 \div \frac{3}{4}$ $\quad 10\frac{2}{3}$
11. $12 \div \frac{1}{5}$ $\quad 60$
12. $10 \div \frac{1}{100}$ $\quad 1000$
13. $9 \div \frac{3}{4}$ $\quad 12$
14. $10 \div \frac{5}{16}$ $\quad 32$
15. $5\frac{2}{5} \div \frac{3}{10}$ $\quad 18$
16. $4\frac{1}{4} \div \frac{3}{8}$ $\quad 11\frac{1}{3}$
17. $4\frac{1}{3} \div \frac{1}{2}$ $\quad 8\frac{2}{3}$
18. $5\frac{1}{2} \div \frac{3}{4}$ $\quad 7\frac{1}{3}$
19. $2\frac{5}{8} \div \frac{3}{8}$ $\quad 7$
20. $4\frac{1}{6} \div \frac{5}{12}$ $\quad 10$

PROBLEM SOLVING
The applications on pages 161–163, 166–169 may be used anytime after this lesson.

Set R

1. $\frac{3}{8} \div 2$	$\frac{3}{16}$	**11.** $1\frac{3}{4} \div 3$	$\frac{7}{12}$
2. $\frac{2}{3} \div 7$	$\frac{2}{21}$	**12.** $3\frac{1}{5} \div 8$	$\frac{2}{5}$
3. $\frac{1}{4} \div 5$	$\frac{1}{20}$	**13.** $4\frac{1}{6} \div 5$	$\frac{5}{6}$
4. $\frac{1}{5} \div 9$	$\frac{1}{45}$	**14.** $7\frac{1}{2} \div 3$	$2\frac{1}{2}$
5. $\frac{5}{16} \div 15$	$\frac{1}{48}$	**15.** $5\frac{1}{4} \div 7$	$\frac{3}{4}$
6. $\frac{2}{3} \div 20$	$\frac{1}{30}$	**16.** $1\frac{1}{2} \div 12$	$\frac{1}{8}$
7. $\frac{11}{12} \div 22$	$\frac{1}{24}$	**17.** $2\frac{1}{3} \div 14$	$\frac{1}{6}$
8. $\frac{1}{2} \div 50$	$\frac{1}{100}$	**18.** $1\frac{2}{3} \div 35$	$\frac{1}{21}$
9. $\frac{6}{7} \div 10$	$\frac{3}{35}$	**19.** $8\frac{3}{4} \div 21$	$\frac{5}{12}$
10. $\frac{9}{10} \div 6$	$\frac{3}{20}$	**20.** $5\frac{5}{8} \div 36$	$\frac{5}{32}$

Set S

1. $\frac{1}{2} \div 1\frac{1}{3}$	$\frac{3}{8}$	**11.** $10 \div 4\frac{3}{8}$	$2\frac{2}{7}$
2. $\frac{3}{4} \div 6\frac{1}{2}$	$\frac{3}{26}$	**12.** $15 \div 2\frac{1}{7}$	7
3. $\frac{1}{10} \div 1\frac{2}{5}$	$\frac{1}{14}$	**13.** $2\frac{3}{4} \div 2\frac{3}{8}$	$1\frac{3}{19}$
4. $\frac{5}{8} \div 3\frac{1}{2}$	$\frac{5}{28}$	**14.** $13\frac{3}{4} \div 1\frac{2}{3}$	$8\frac{1}{4}$
5. $\frac{3}{5} \div 1\frac{1}{5}$	$\frac{1}{2}$	**15.** $8\frac{1}{4} \div 1\frac{1}{2}$	$5\frac{1}{2}$
6. $\frac{5}{6} \div 2\frac{1}{12}$	$\frac{2}{5}$	**16.** $6\frac{1}{4} \div 2\frac{1}{2}$	$2\frac{1}{2}$
7. $4 \div 1\frac{2}{3}$	$2\frac{2}{5}$	**17.** $1\frac{1}{4} \div 7\frac{1}{2}$	$\frac{1}{6}$
8. $5 \div 3\frac{1}{3}$	$1\frac{1}{2}$	**18.** $6\frac{2}{3} \div 7\frac{1}{2}$	$\frac{8}{9}$
9. $1 \div 8\frac{3}{4}$	$\frac{4}{35}$	**19.** $3\frac{1}{4} \div 1\frac{1}{6}$	$2\frac{11}{14}$
10. $7 \div 4\frac{9}{10}$	$1\frac{3}{7}$	**20.** $4\frac{1}{6} \div 7\frac{1}{2}$	$\frac{5}{9}$

Mixed Practice

Q	**1.** $\frac{7}{8} \div \frac{5}{6}$	$1\frac{1}{20}$
Q	**2.** $8 \div \frac{2}{3}$	12
Q	**3.** $2\frac{3}{5} \div \frac{7}{10}$	$3\frac{5}{7}$
R	**4.** $\frac{5}{7} \div 10$	$\frac{1}{14}$
R	**5.** $5\frac{1}{2} \div 2$	$2\frac{3}{4}$
S	**6.** $\frac{3}{4} \div 2\frac{1}{4}$	$\frac{1}{3}$
Q	**7.** $100 \div \frac{1}{2}$	200
S	**8.** $5\frac{1}{2} \div 3\frac{1}{4}$	$1\frac{9}{13}$
Q	**9.** $7 \div \frac{7}{8}$	8
Q	**10.** $6\frac{1}{3} \div \frac{2}{3}$	$9\frac{1}{2}$
R	**11.** $\frac{1}{4} \div 6$	$\frac{1}{24}$
R	**12.** $4\frac{1}{3} \div 3$	$1\frac{4}{9}$
S	**13.** $\frac{5}{6} \div 2\frac{1}{4}$	$\frac{10}{27}$
Q	**14.** $60 \div \frac{1}{3}$	180
S	**15.** $7\frac{1}{3} \div 2\frac{1}{2}$	$2\frac{14}{15}$
Q	**16.** $\frac{9}{10} \div \frac{3}{5}$	$1\frac{1}{2}$
R	**17.** $2\frac{3}{8} \div 12$	$\frac{19}{96}$
S	**18.** $6\frac{1}{3} \div 3\frac{1}{2}$	$1\frac{17}{21}$
Q	**19.** $\frac{3}{4} \div \frac{6}{7}$	$\frac{7}{8}$
Q	**20.** $3\frac{3}{4} \div \frac{5}{8}$	6
S	**21.** $2\frac{3}{5} \div 1\frac{3}{10}$	2

BREAK TIME

The faces on each cube are identical. Which symbol is

opposite the circle?
Arrow

opposite the triangle?
Star

opposite the square?
Diamond

See Skills File, page 421, for more practice.

SKILLS POSTTEST

Number of test items - 19

Number missed	1	2	3	4	5	6	7	8	9
Percent correct	95	89	84	79	74	68	63	58	53

SKILL Writing Fractions and Mixed Numbers *pages 150–151*

A Write a fraction for the shaded part. $\frac{3}{5}$

B Write a mixed number for point Z. $7\frac{2}{3}$

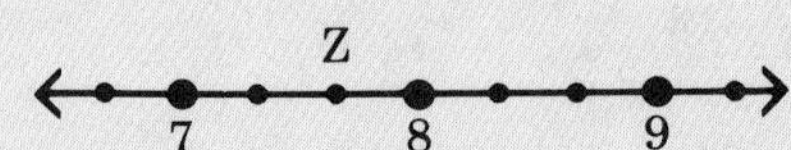

SKILL Renaming Fractions and Mixed Numbers *page 152*

C Reduce $\frac{12}{24}$ to lowest terms. $\frac{1}{2}$

D Write $\frac{35}{8}$ as a mixed number or as a whole number. $4\frac{3}{8}$

E Write $2\frac{3}{5}$ as a fraction. $\frac{13}{5}$

SKILL Writing Fractions as Decimals *page 153*

F Write $\frac{1}{4}$ as a decimal. 0.25

G Write $\frac{1}{7}$ as a decimal. Round your answer to the nearest thousandth. 0.143

SKILL Multiplying Fractions *pages 154–155*

H $\frac{1}{2} \times \frac{3}{5}$ $\frac{3}{10}$

I $\frac{3}{10} \times \frac{5}{9}$ $\frac{1}{6}$

J $\frac{3}{4} \times \frac{1}{6} \times \frac{8}{9}$ $\frac{1}{9}$

K $\frac{2}{3} \times 24$ 16

SKILL Multiplying Mixed Numbers *pages 156–157*

L $2\frac{1}{3} \times \frac{5}{8}$ $1\frac{11}{24}$

M $4\frac{2}{5} \times 4$ $17\frac{3}{5}$

N $2\frac{3}{8} \times 1\frac{2}{3}$ $3\frac{23}{24}$

O $8 \times 5\frac{1}{2} \times \frac{1}{4}$ 11

SKILL Dividing Fractions and Mixed Numbers *pages 158–159*

P Write the reciprocal of $\frac{3}{5}$. $\frac{5}{3}$

Q $\frac{4}{5} \div \frac{1}{3}$ $2\frac{2}{5}$

R $\frac{3}{8} \div 6$ $\frac{1}{16}$

S $5\frac{1}{2} \div 1\frac{3}{4}$ $3\frac{1}{7}$

Problem Solving

CONSUMER APPLICATIONS

See page 21 of *Problem-Solving Masters.*

Objective: Solve problems involving multiplication and division of fractions and mixed numbers.

In this lesson students solve problems involving times and distances for riding a bicycle and jogging.

Finding Exercise Times and Distances

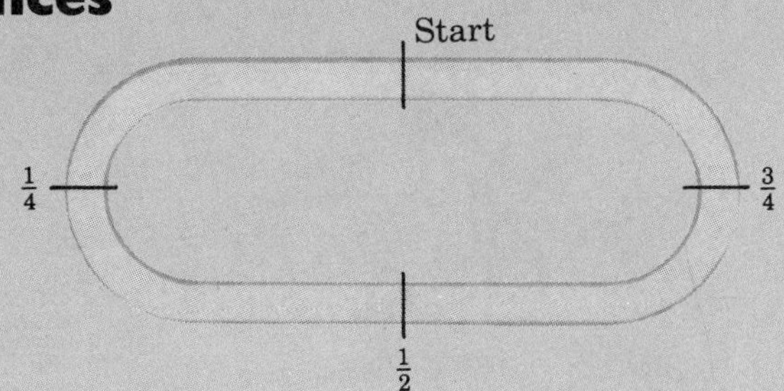

Eva and Luis Ortiz exercise regularly at a nearby track. Luis rides a bicycle and Eva jogs. There are small posts in the ground to mark the fractional parts of one lap of the track.

Luis rides at a speed of one lap every $1\frac{1}{2}$ minutes. How long will it take him to complete

1. 3 laps? $(3 \times 1\frac{1}{2})$ $4\frac{1}{2}$ min.
2. 7 laps? $10\frac{1}{2}$ min.
3. 12 laps? 18 min.
4. $1\frac{1}{2}$ laps? $2\frac{1}{4}$ min.
5. $5\frac{3}{4}$ laps? $8\frac{5}{8}$ min.

How many laps can Luis complete in

6. 3 minutes? $(3 \div 1\frac{1}{2})$ 2 laps
7. 6 minutes? 4 laps
8. $10\frac{1}{2}$ minutes? 7 laps
9. $12\frac{3}{4}$ minutes? $8\frac{1}{2}$ laps
10. 15 minutes? 10 laps

Eva jogs at a speed of one lap every $4\frac{1}{4}$ minutes. How long will it take her to complete

11. 2 laps? $8\frac{1}{2}$ min.
12. 5 laps? $21\frac{1}{4}$ min.
13. $2\frac{1}{2}$ laps? $10\frac{5}{8}$ min.
14. $4\frac{1}{2}$ laps? $19\frac{1}{8}$ min.
15. $\frac{1}{2}$ lap? $2\frac{1}{8}$ min.

How many laps can Eva complete in

16. 17 minutes? 4 laps
17. $21\frac{1}{4}$ minutes? 5 laps
18. $8\frac{1}{2}$ minutes? 2 laps
19. $12\frac{3}{4}$ minutes? 3 laps
20. $38\frac{1}{4}$ minutes? 9 laps

Problem Solving

CONSUMER APPLICATIONS

Objective: Solve problems involving multiplication and division of fractions and mixed numbers.

In this lesson students solve problems involving measuring with a "C" clamp.

Using a "C" Clamp for Measuring

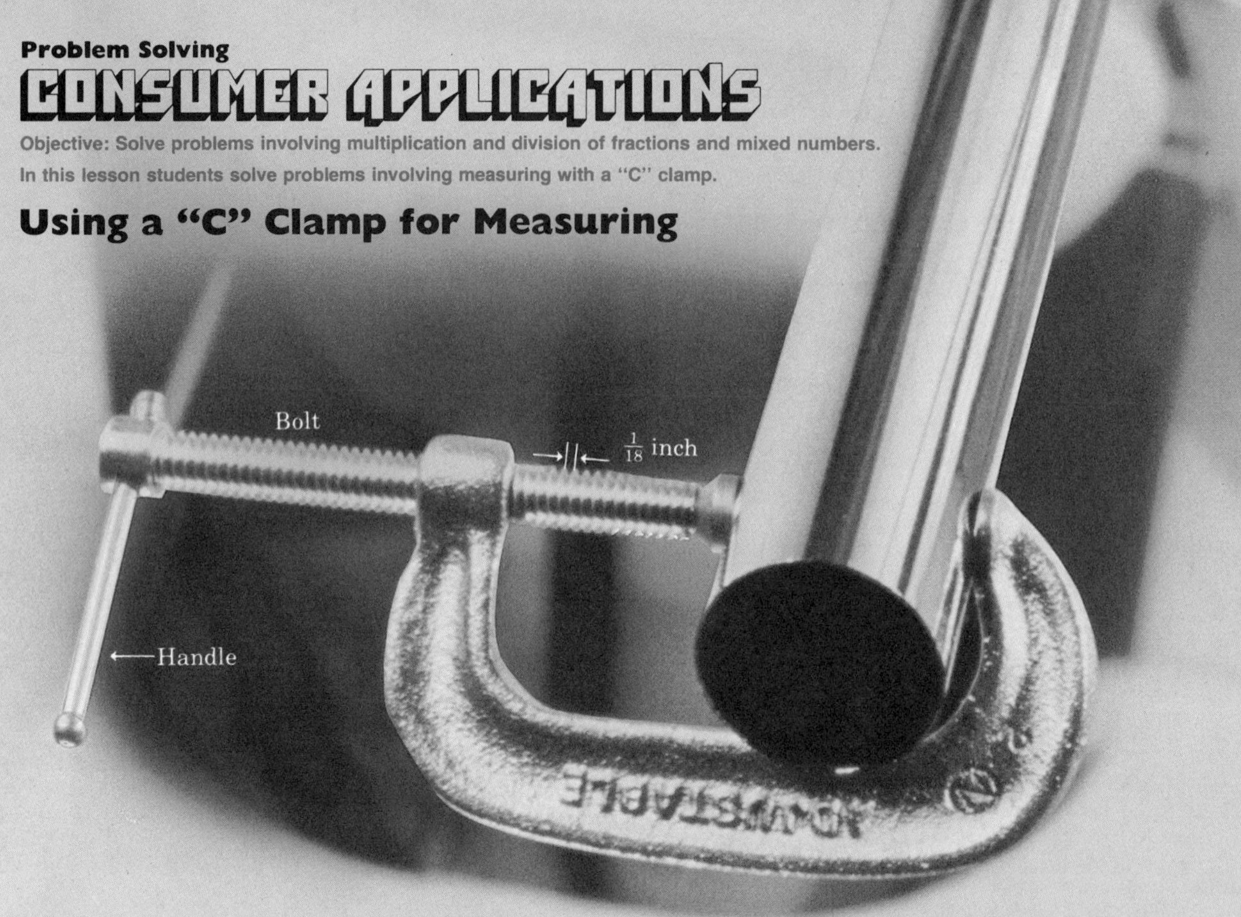

A "C" clamp is used in workshops to hold materials in place. It can also be used to measure the width of an object, such as the pipe shown above.

On the bolt of the "C" clamp, the distance from the top of one thread to the top of the next is $\frac{1}{18}$ inch. If the handle is turned completely around once, the bolt moves $\frac{1}{18}$ inch.

When the pipe is removed from the clamp, it takes $22\frac{1}{2}$ turns of the handle to close the clamp. You can multiply to find the outside diameter of the pipe.

Turns of handle		Amount bolt moves for each turn (inches)		Width of object (inches)		
$22\frac{1}{2}$	$\times$	$\frac{1}{18}$				
$\frac{\overset{5}{\cancel{45}}}{2}$	$\times$	$\frac{1}{\underset{2}{\cancel{18}}}$	$=$	$\frac{5}{4}$	$=$	$1\frac{1}{4}$

The outside diameter of the pipe is about $1\frac{1}{4}$ inches.

Each problem gives the number of turns of the handle needed to close the "C" clamp when an object is removed. Multiply by $\frac{1}{18}$ inch to find the width of each object.

	Object	Turns of handle	
1.	Bolt	9	$\frac{1}{2}$ inch
2.	Pencil	5	$\frac{5}{18}$ inch
3.	Bottle	18	1 inch
4.	Nail	$2\frac{1}{4}$	$\frac{1}{8}$ inch
5.	Chalk	6	$\frac{1}{3}$ inch
6.	Golf ball	30	$1\frac{2}{3}$ inches
7.	Thumb	$10\frac{1}{2}$	$\frac{7}{12}$ inch
8.	Wrist	24	$1\frac{1}{3}$ inches
9.	Spool	14	$\frac{7}{9}$ inch
10.	Magazine	$4\frac{1}{2}$	$\frac{1}{4}$ inch

Each problem gives the width of an object. Divide by $\frac{1}{18}$ inch to find the number of turns needed to close the "C" clamp when the object is removed.

	Object	Width (inches)	
11.	Candle	$1\frac{1}{2}$	27 turns
12.	Drill bit	$\frac{3}{8}$	$6\frac{3}{4}$ turns
13.	Marble	$\frac{3}{4}$	$13\frac{1}{2}$ turns
14.	Crayon	$\frac{5}{8}$	$11\frac{1}{4}$ turns
15.	Grape	$\frac{5}{6}$	15 turns

This design is to be made on a wood lathe. Divide each width by $\frac{1}{18}$ to find how many turns of the "C" clamp are needed to check that width.

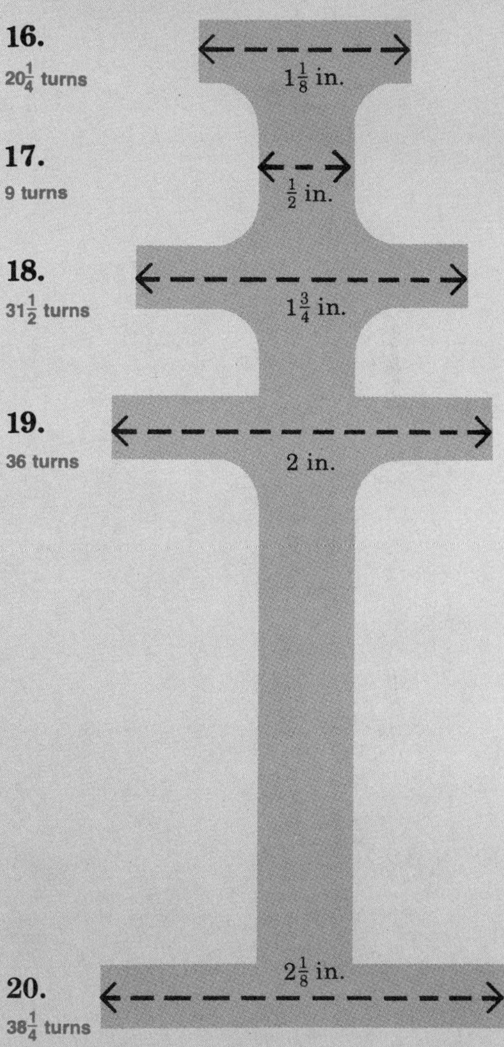

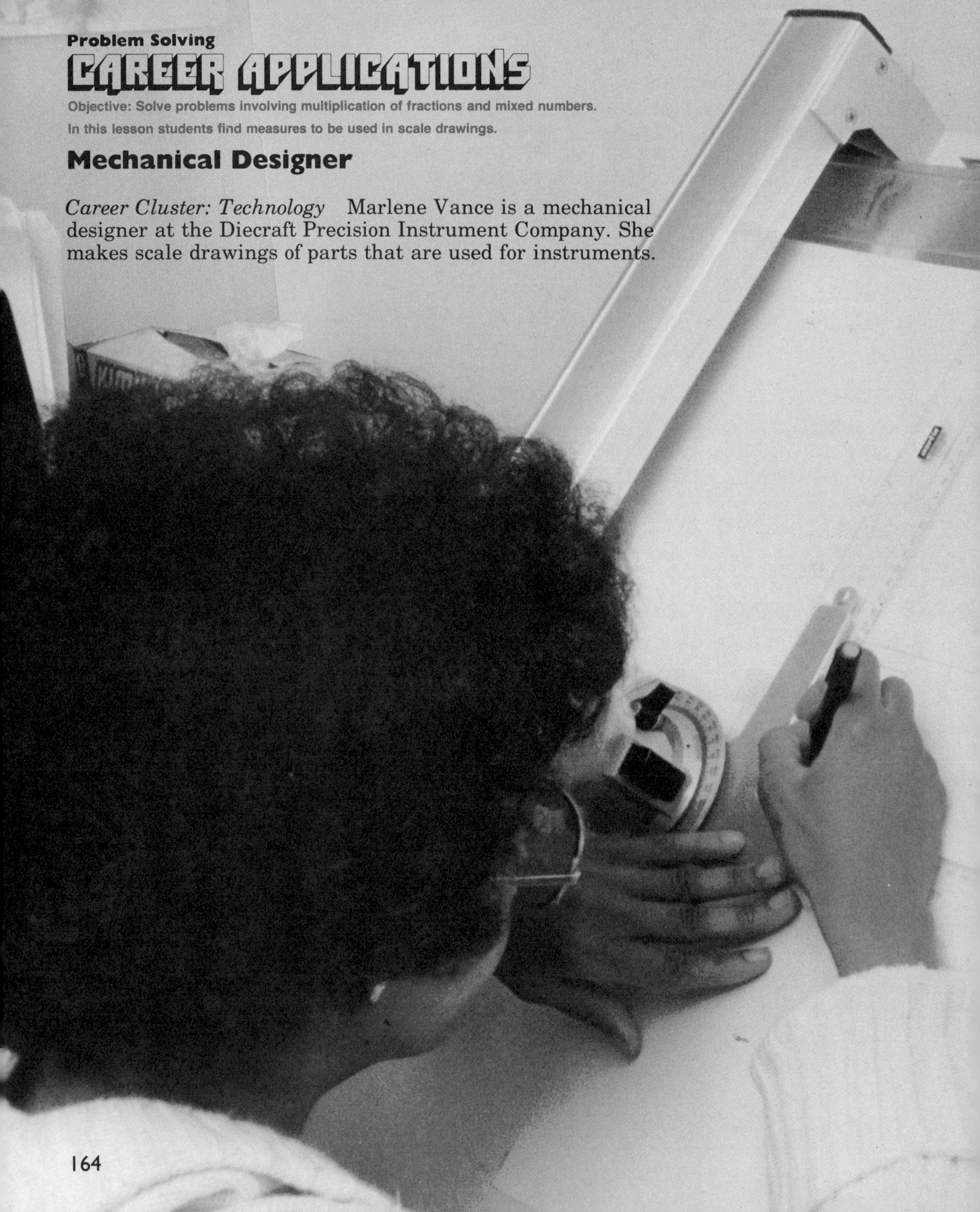

Problem Solving

CAREER APPLICATIONS

Objective: Solve problems involving multiplication of fractions and mixed numbers.

In this lesson students find measures to be used in scale drawings.

Mechanical Designer

Career Cluster: Technology Marlene Vance is a mechanical designer at the Diecraft Precision Instrument Company. She makes scale drawings of parts that are used for instruments.

The pictures show machine parts actual size.
They are not scale drawings.

See page 22 of *Problem-Solving Masters.*

Marlene plans to make a drawing of this part. In her drawing, each length will be $\frac{1}{2}$ as long as the actual length. Multiply to find each measure for the scale drawing.

1. AB $(\frac{1}{2} \times 2\frac{3}{8})$ $1\frac{3}{16}$ in.
2. BC $\frac{1}{8}$ in.
3. CD $\frac{7}{8}$ in.
4. DE $\frac{7}{16}$ in.
5. EF $\frac{11}{16}$ in.
6. FG $\frac{3}{16}$ in.
7. GH $1\frac{3}{8}$ in.
8. HA $\frac{3}{4}$ in.
9. JK $\frac{1}{2}$ in.
10. KL $\frac{5}{16}$ in.

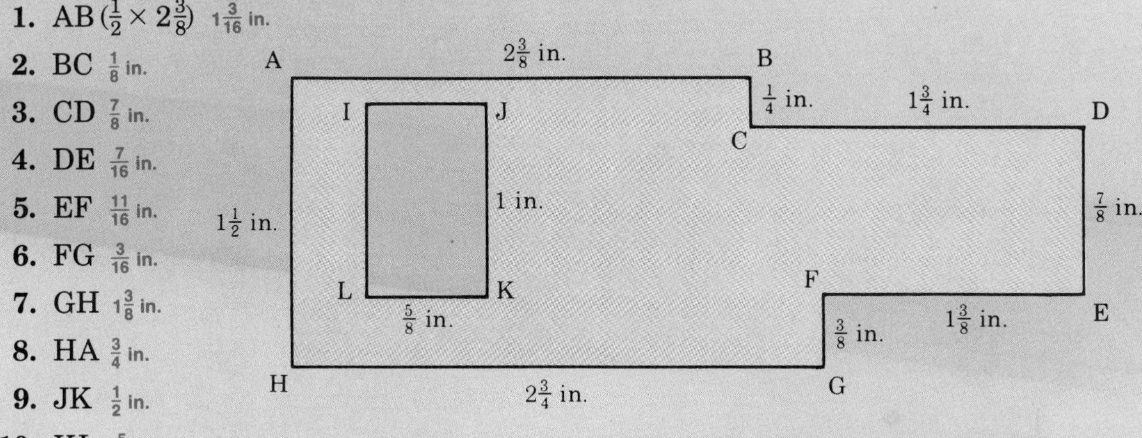

In the scale drawing for this part, each length will be $\frac{3}{4}$ as long as the actual length. Multiply to find each measure for the scale drawing.

11. AB $1\frac{1}{8}$ in.
12. BC $\frac{9}{16}$ in.
13. CD $\frac{3}{4}$ in.
14. DE $\frac{15}{16}$ in.
15. EF $1\frac{7}{8}$ in.
16. FA $\frac{3}{8}$ in.

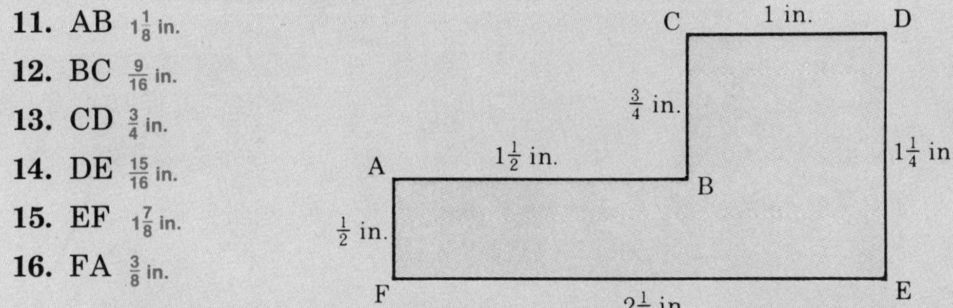

In the scale drawing for this part, each length will be $\frac{5}{8}$ as long as the actual length. In each problem, measure the length of the side to the nearest $\frac{1}{8}$ inch. Then multiply to find each measure for the scale drawing.

	Side	Actual length	Length in scale drawing
17.	AB	$1\frac{1}{2}$ in.	$\frac{15}{16}$ in.
18.	BC	1 in.	$\frac{5}{8}$ in.
19.	GH	$\frac{3}{4}$ in.	$\frac{15}{32}$ in.
20.	HI	$\frac{1}{2}$ in.	$\frac{5}{16}$ in.

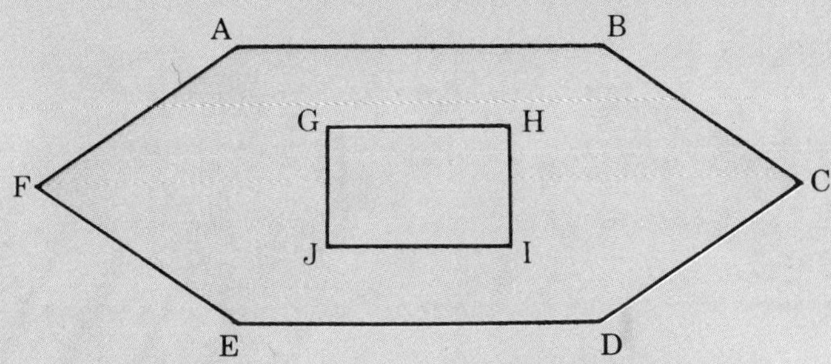

Problem Solving

CAREER APPLICATIONS

Objective: Solve problems involving multiplication and division of fractions and mixed numbers.

In this lesson students find the number of decoys that can be made from a log of a given length.

Wood Carver

See the Careers Chart beginning on page 426 for more information about the careers in this cluster.

Career Cluster: Arts Madison Mitchell is a wood carver who makes duck decoys. Years ago his decoys were used by hunters, but today they are purchased by collectors. Mr. Mitchell uses the wood from discarded utility poles or well-seasoned timbers. He carves the decoys $\frac{3}{4}$ or $\frac{3}{8}$ as long as the actual length of the duck.

If the actual length of a mallard duck is 20 inches, what will be the length of a section of log needed for a $\frac{3}{8}$-scale decoy?

Scale		Actual length (inches)	Length of section for decoy (inches)
$\frac{3}{8}$	$\times$	20	

$$\frac{3}{\cancel{8}_{2}} \times \frac{\cancel{20}^{5}}{1} = \frac{15}{2} = 7\frac{1}{2}$$

The length of the section will be $7\frac{1}{2}$ inches.

How many of these $7\frac{1}{2}$-inch sections can be cut from a 16-foot (192-inch) log?

Length of log (inches)		Length of section for decoy (inches)	Sections per log
192	$\div$	$7\frac{1}{2}$	

$$\frac{192}{1} \div \frac{15}{2} = \frac{\cancel{192}^{64}}{1} \times \frac{2}{\cancel{15}_{5}} = \frac{128}{5} = 25\frac{3}{5}$$

25 sections that are each $7\frac{1}{2}$ inches long can be cut from the log.

Mr. Mitchell can carve 2 decoys from each section. How many decoys can he make from the 16-foot log?

Sections per log		Decoys per section		Decoys per log
25	$\times$	2	=	50

Mr. Mitchell can make 50 mallard duck decoys from a 16-foot log.

Complete the table.

	Type of bird	Scale	Actual length (inches)	Length of section for decoy (inches)	Length of log (inches)	Sections per log	Decoys per section	Decoys per log
	Mallard	$\frac{3}{8}$	20	$7\frac{1}{2}$	192	25	2	50
1.	Black duck	$\frac{3}{8}$	20	$7\frac{1}{2}$	216	28	3	84
2.	Baldpate duck	$\frac{3}{4}$	18	$13\frac{1}{2}$	60	4	2	8
3.	Pintail duck	$\frac{3}{8}$	28	$10\frac{1}{2}$	72	6	2	12
4.	Blue-winged teal	$\frac{3}{4}$	15	$11\frac{1}{4}$	216	19	3	57
5.	Greater snow goose	$\frac{3}{8}$	30	$11\frac{1}{4}$	120	10	1	10
6.	Canada goose	$\frac{3}{8}$	36	$13\frac{1}{2}$	240	17	1	17
7.	Canvasback duck	$\frac{3}{4}$	21	$15\frac{3}{4}$	192	12	2	24
8.	Whistling swan	$\frac{3}{8}$	48	18	192	10	1	10

9. Mr. Mitchell carves a mallard duck decoy in about $1\frac{1}{4}$ hours. How long will it take him to carve 50 decoys? $62\frac{1}{2}$ hours

10. A collector bought a pintail duck decoy from Mr. Mitchell for \$25. The collector sold the decoy in his shop for $2\frac{1}{2}$ times that price. What was the selling price? \$62.50

Problem Solving

DEVELOPING STRATEGIES

Objective: Solve problems by using estimated information.

In this lesson students use an estimate to find the length of time and cost of mowing a lawn.

Tactic: Using Estimated Information

Al Davis charged Mr. Wollen 15 dollars to mow and trim his lawn. He did the job in $2\frac{1}{2}$ hours using a push-type mower. Al has been asked to mow the Sewell lawn. Al estimates that the Sewell lawn is about $1\frac{1}{2}$ times as large as the Wollen lawn.

Problem

How long will it take Al to mow the Sewell lawn, and what should he charge?

Solution

The following questions show Al's strategy for solving the problem. He used the tactic of using estimated information.

a. How does the Sewell job compare to the Wollen job? Use Al's estimation. $1\frac{1}{2}$ times as large

b. Based on Al's estimate, how long will it take Al to do the Sewell job? Multiply. $1\frac{1}{2} \times 2\frac{1}{2} = 3\frac{3}{4}$ hours

c. What was Al's hourly wage for the Wollen job? Divide. $15 \div 2\frac{1}{2} = 6$ dollars

d. What should Al charge for the Sewell job? Multiply. $6 \times 3\frac{3}{4} = 22\frac{1}{2}$ dollars

Conclusion: The Sewell job will take about $3\frac{3}{4}$ hours. Al should charge $22\frac{1}{2}$ dollars, or $22.50.

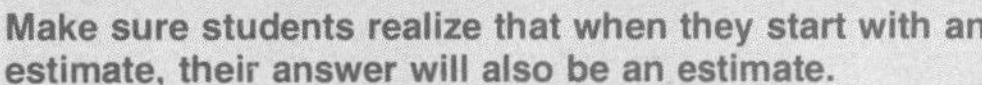
Make sure students realize that when they start with an estimate, their answer will also be an estimate.

Related Problems

Maria Lopez asked Al to mow her lawn. Al estimated that her lawn is $\frac{1}{2}$ as large as the Wollen lawn.

1. How long will it take Al to mow the Lopez lawn? $1\frac{1}{4}$ hours
2. What should Al charge for mowing the Lopez lawn? $7.50

Al estimated that the Jensen lawn is $2\frac{1}{2}$ times as large as the Wollen lawn.

3. How long would it take Al to mow the Jensen lawn? $6\frac{1}{4}$ hours
4. What should Al charge for mowing the Jensen lawn? $37.50

Al estimated that he could cut a lawn in $\frac{3}{4}$ of the time using a power mower.

5. How long would it take Al to mow the Wollen lawn using a power mower? $1\frac{7}{8}$ hours
6. If Al charged the same amount for mowing the Wollen lawn with a power mower as with a push-type mower, what would be his hourly wage? $8
7. Using a power mower, how long would it take Al to mow the Lopez lawn? the Jensen lawn? $\frac{15}{16}$ hour; $4\frac{11}{16}$ hours

Extensions

8. Together the Statz twins can mow a lawn in $\frac{2}{3}$ the time it takes Al using a power mower. They charge $14 an hour. Would Mr. Wollen save money by hiring the Statz twins? No
9. Al estimated that he fills the power mower with gas every $\frac{1}{2}$ hour. How many times would he fill the mower while doing the Wollen lawn? 4 times

CHAPTER 7 TEST

Number of test items - 24

Number missed	1	2	3	4	5	6	7	8	9	10	11	12
Percent correct	96	92	88	83	79	75	71	67	63	58	54	50

A **1.** Write a fraction for the shaded part. $\frac{5}{6}$

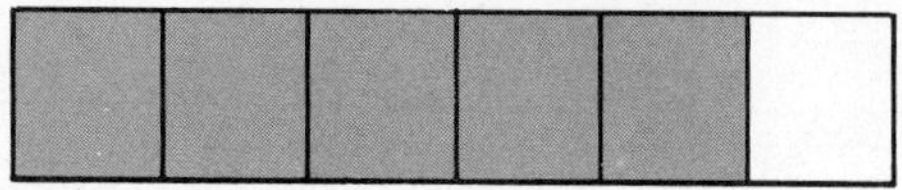

B **2.** Write a mixed number for point R.

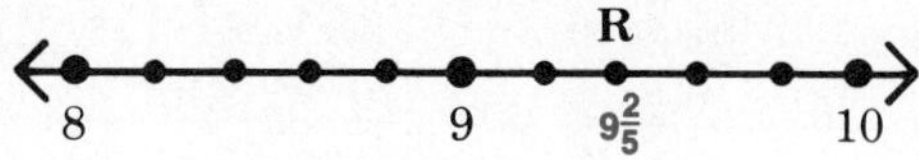

C **3.** Reduce $\frac{16}{28}$ to lowest terms. $\frac{4}{7}$

D **4.** Write $\frac{24}{5}$ as a mixed number or as a whole number. $4\frac{4}{5}$

E **5.** Write $4\frac{3}{8}$ as a fraction. $\frac{35}{8}$

F **6.** Write $\frac{3}{4}$ as a decimal. 0.75

G **7.** Write $\frac{5}{7}$ as a decimal. Round your answer to the nearest thousandth. 0.714

H **8.** $\frac{3}{4} \times \frac{1}{8}$ $\frac{3}{32}$

I **9.** $\frac{2}{3} \times \frac{9}{10}$ $\frac{3}{5}$

J **10.** $\frac{7}{8} \times \frac{4}{5} \times \frac{2}{7}$ $\frac{1}{5}$

K **11.** $\frac{3}{4} \times 20$ 15

L **12.** $3\frac{2}{3} \times \frac{4}{5}$ $2\frac{14}{15}$

M **13.** $1\frac{5}{6} \times 5$ $9\frac{1}{6}$

N **14.** $3\frac{5}{8} \times 1\frac{2}{3}$ $6\frac{1}{24}$

O **15.** $\frac{3}{4} \times 12 \times \frac{5}{6}$ $7\frac{1}{2}$

P **16.** Write the reciprocal of $\frac{4}{9}$. $\frac{9}{4}$

Q **17.** $\frac{7}{10} \div \frac{3}{4}$ $\frac{14}{15}$

R **18.** $\frac{5}{6} \div 10$ $\frac{1}{12}$

S **19.** $1\frac{7}{8} \div 3\frac{1}{2}$ $\frac{15}{28}$

20. Phil jogs around a track at a speed of one lap every $5\frac{1}{2}$ minutes. How many laps can he complete in 22 minutes? 4 laps

21. The bolt of a "C" clamp moves $\frac{1}{20}$ inch in one turn. How far will it move in $7\frac{1}{2}$ turns? $\frac{3}{8}$ inch

22. In the scale drawing for this part, each length will be $\frac{1}{2}$ as long as the actual length. Find the measure of side AB for the scale drawing. $\frac{15}{16}$ inch

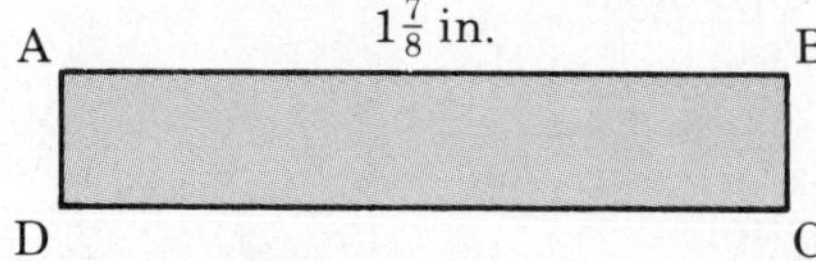

23. How many sections that are each $8\frac{1}{4}$ inches long can be cut from a 192-inch log? 23 sections

24. Betty cut her lawn in $1\frac{1}{4}$ hours. At that rate, how long should she estimate that it would take her to mow a lawn 3 times as large? $3\frac{3}{4}$ hours

 See pages 17–18 of the *Test Masters* for an alternate form of the Chapter 7 Test.

CHAPTER 8 Adding and Subtracting Fractions and Mixed Numbers

SKILLS PRETEST

Number of test items - 21

Number missed	1	2	3	4	5	6	7	8	9	10
Percent correct	95	90	86	81	76	71	67	62	57	52

SKILL Finding Common Denominators *page 172*

A Write $\frac{2}{3}$ and $\frac{3}{5}$ as fractions with a common denominator. $\frac{10}{15}, \frac{9}{15}$

B Write $\frac{2}{3}$, $\frac{5}{6}$, and $\frac{1}{4}$ as fractions with a common denominator. $\frac{8}{12}, \frac{10}{12}, \frac{3}{12}$

SKILL Comparing Fractions and Mixed Numbers *page 173*

C Compare $\frac{7}{8}$ and $\frac{5}{8}$. Replace ● with <, >, or =.

$\frac{7}{8}$ ● $\frac{5}{8}$ >

D Compare $\frac{5}{8}$ and $\frac{3}{4}$. Replace ● with <, >, or =.

$\frac{5}{8}$ ● $\frac{3}{4}$ <

E Compare $2\frac{8}{16}$ and $2\frac{1}{2}$. Replace ● with <, >, or =.

$2\frac{8}{16}$ ● $2\frac{1}{2}$ =

SKILL Adding and Subtracting Fractions *pages 174–175*

F Round $3\frac{1}{3}$ to the nearest whole number. 3

G $\frac{3}{4} + \frac{3}{4}$ $1\frac{1}{2}$

H $\frac{5}{8} - \frac{3}{8}$ $\frac{1}{4}$

I $\frac{7}{12} + \frac{3}{4}$ $1\frac{1}{3}$

J $\frac{7}{16} - \frac{1}{8}$ $\frac{5}{16}$

K $\frac{1}{2} + \frac{2}{3} + \frac{1}{6}$ $1\frac{1}{3}$

SKILL Adding Mixed Numbers *pages 176–177*

L $6\frac{3}{5} + 2\frac{3}{10}$ $8\frac{9}{10}$

M Rename $4\frac{11}{8}$.

$4\frac{11}{8} = 5\frac{■}{8}$ 3

N $2\frac{1}{3} + 6\frac{7}{8}$ $9\frac{5}{24}$

O $7\frac{3}{5} + 4\frac{2}{5}$ 12

SKILL Subtracting Mixed Numbers: Same Denominator *pages 178–179*

P Find the missing number.

$7\frac{5}{8} = 6\frac{■}{8}$ 13

Q $9\frac{5}{8} - 4\frac{7}{8}$ $4\frac{3}{4}$

R $6 - 1\frac{3}{5}$ $4\frac{2}{5}$

SKILL Subtracting Mixed Numbers: Different Denominators *pages 180–181*

S $5\frac{5}{6} - 1\frac{2}{3}$ $4\frac{1}{6}$

T $7\frac{1}{5} - 2\frac{3}{4}$ $4\frac{9}{20}$

U $8\frac{1}{4} - 5\frac{5}{6}$ $2\frac{5}{12}$

See page T35 for additional notes on Chapter 8.

Objective: Find common denominators.

Finding Common Denominators

Example A Two fractions

Write $\frac{2}{3}$ and $\frac{1}{4}$ as fractions with a common denominator.

A **common denominator** of $\frac{2}{3}$ and $\frac{1}{4}$ is a common multiple of 3 and 4.

List the multiples of 4 until you have a common multiple of 3 and 4.

4 8 12

Is 4 a multiple of 3? *No*
Is 8 a multiple of 3? *No*
Is 12 a multiple of 3? *Yes*

12 is a common denominator of $\frac{2}{3}$ and $\frac{1}{4}$.

Now find the fractions equal to $\frac{2}{3}$ and $\frac{1}{4}$ that have a denominator of 12.

$$\frac{2}{3} = \frac{8}{12} \quad (2 \times 4,\ 3 \times 4) \qquad \frac{1}{4} = \frac{3}{12} \quad (1 \times 3,\ 4 \times 3)$$

$$\frac{2}{3} = \frac{8}{12} \qquad \frac{1}{4} = \frac{3}{12}$$

Point out that students could first divide 3 into 12 to get 4, and then multiply 2 and 4 to get 8.

Example B Three fractions

Write $\frac{1}{2}$, $\frac{1}{3}$, and $\frac{5}{8}$ as fractions with a common denominator.

List the multiples of 8 until you have a common multiple of 2, 3, and 8.

8 16 24

24 is a common denominator of $\frac{1}{2}$, $\frac{1}{3}$, and $\frac{5}{8}$.

Now find the fractions equal to $\frac{1}{2}$, $\frac{1}{3}$, and $\frac{5}{8}$ that have a denominator of 24.

$$\frac{1}{2} = \frac{12}{24} \qquad \frac{1}{3} = \frac{8}{24} \qquad \frac{5}{8} = \frac{15}{24}$$

Exercises

Set A

Write these fractions with a common denominator.

1. $\frac{3}{4}$ $\frac{3}{4}$ $\frac{1}{2}$ $\frac{2}{4}$
2. $\frac{1}{3}$ $\frac{2}{6}$ $\frac{5}{6}$ $\frac{5}{6}$
3. $\frac{5}{8}$ $\frac{5}{8}$ $\frac{1}{4}$ $\frac{2}{8}$
4. $\frac{1}{6}$ $\frac{2}{12}$ $\frac{7}{12}$ $\frac{7}{12}$
5. $\frac{1}{2}$ $\frac{3}{6}$ $\frac{1}{3}$ $\frac{2}{6}$
6. $\frac{4}{5}$ $\frac{8}{10}$ $\frac{1}{2}$ $\frac{5}{10}$
7. $\frac{2}{3}$ $\frac{10}{15}$ $\frac{3}{5}$ $\frac{9}{15}$
8. $\frac{2}{3}$ $\frac{16}{24}$ $\frac{1}{8}$ $\frac{3}{24}$
9. $\frac{1}{6}$ $\frac{4}{24}$ $\frac{3}{8}$ $\frac{9}{24}$
10. $\frac{3}{4}$ $\frac{9}{12}$ $\frac{1}{6}$ $\frac{2}{12}$
11. $\frac{3}{8}$ $\frac{9}{24}$ $\frac{7}{12}$ $\frac{14}{24}$
12. $\frac{5}{6}$ $\frac{15}{18}$ $\frac{7}{9}$ $\frac{14}{18}$
13. $\frac{3}{4}$ $\frac{15}{20}$ $\frac{2}{5}$ $\frac{8}{20}$
14. $\frac{7}{8}$ $\frac{21}{24}$ $\frac{1}{3}$ $\frac{8}{24}$
15. $\frac{3}{4}$ $\frac{9}{12}$ $\frac{1}{3}$ $\frac{4}{12}$
16. $\frac{2}{3}$ $\frac{20}{30}$ $\frac{7}{10}$ $\frac{21}{30}$
17. $\frac{5}{8}$ $\frac{10}{16}$ $\frac{3}{16}$ $\frac{3}{16}$
18. $\frac{2}{3}$ $\frac{6}{9}$ $\frac{5}{9}$ $\frac{5}{9}$
19. $\frac{4}{5}$ $\frac{32}{40}$ $\frac{5}{8}$ $\frac{25}{40}$
20. $\frac{7}{9}$ $\frac{35}{45}$ $\frac{3}{5}$ $\frac{27}{45}$
21. $\frac{3}{8}$ $\frac{15}{40}$ $\frac{7}{10}$ $\frac{28}{40}$
22. $\frac{5}{6}$ $\frac{25}{30}$ $\frac{3}{10}$ $\frac{9}{30}$
23. $\frac{5}{12}$ $\frac{25}{60}$ $\frac{7}{10}$ $\frac{42}{60}$
24. $\frac{7}{12}$ $\frac{28}{48}$ $\frac{9}{16}$ $\frac{27}{48}$

Set B

Write these fractions with a common denominator.

1. $\frac{2}{3}$ $\frac{4}{6}$ $\frac{5}{6}$ $\frac{5}{6}$ $\frac{1}{2}$ $\frac{3}{6}$
2. $\frac{7}{8}$ $\frac{7}{8}$ $\frac{1}{2}$ $\frac{4}{8}$ $\frac{3}{4}$ $\frac{6}{8}$
3. $\frac{1}{2}$ $\frac{5}{10}$ $\frac{3}{5}$ $\frac{6}{10}$ $\frac{9}{10}$ $\frac{9}{10}$
4. $\frac{5}{6}$ $\frac{10}{12}$ $\frac{1}{3}$ $\frac{4}{12}$ $\frac{7}{12}$ $\frac{7}{12}$
5. $\frac{3}{5}$ $\frac{6}{10}$ $\frac{1}{2}$ $\frac{5}{10}$ $\frac{9}{10}$ $\frac{9}{10}$
6. $\frac{3}{4}$ $\frac{9}{12}$ $\frac{2}{3}$ $\frac{8}{12}$ $\frac{5}{12}$ $\frac{5}{12}$
7. $\frac{2}{3}$ $\frac{8}{12}$ $\frac{3}{4}$ $\frac{9}{12}$ $\frac{1}{2}$ $\frac{6}{12}$
8. $\frac{5}{8}$ $\frac{15}{24}$ $\frac{1}{4}$ $\frac{6}{24}$ $\frac{2}{3}$ $\frac{16}{24}$
9. $\frac{1}{2}$ $\frac{6}{12}$ $\frac{5}{6}$ $\frac{10}{12}$ $\frac{3}{4}$ $\frac{9}{12}$
10. $\frac{3}{4}$ $\frac{9}{12}$ $\frac{2}{3}$ $\frac{8}{12}$ $\frac{1}{6}$ $\frac{2}{12}$
11. $\frac{4}{5}$ $\frac{24}{30}$ $\frac{2}{3}$ $\frac{20}{30}$ $\frac{7}{10}$ $\frac{21}{30}$
12. $\frac{7}{8}$ $\frac{35}{40}$ $\frac{3}{5}$ $\frac{24}{40}$ $\frac{1}{10}$ $\frac{4}{40}$
13. $\frac{1}{2}$ $\frac{15}{30}$ $\frac{2}{3}$ $\frac{20}{30}$ $\frac{3}{5}$ $\frac{18}{30}$
14. $\frac{1}{3}$ $\frac{20}{60}$ $\frac{3}{5}$ $\frac{36}{60}$ $\frac{3}{4}$ $\frac{45}{60}$
15. $\frac{3}{8}$ $\frac{5}{6}$ $\frac{7}{10}$
16. $\frac{1}{12}$ $\frac{5}{8}$ $\frac{3}{10}$

15. $\frac{45}{120}$ $\frac{100}{120}$ $\frac{84}{120}$
16. $\frac{10}{120}$ $\frac{75}{120}$ $\frac{36}{120}$

Objective: Compare fractions and mixed numbers.

Comparing Fractions and Mixed Numbers

Example C Fractions with common denominators

Compare $\frac{4}{7}$ and $\frac{5}{7}$. Replace ● with $<$, $>$, or $=$.

To compare fractions with a common denominator, compare the numerators.

$\frac{4}{7} < \frac{5}{7}$ $\quad$ $4 < 5$, so $\frac{4}{7} < \frac{5}{7}$.

You may wish to use a number line to illustrate this example.

Example D Fractions with different denominators

Compare $\frac{5}{6}$ and $\frac{2}{3}$. Replace ● with $<$, $>$, or $=$.

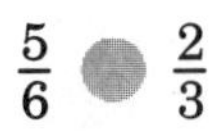

Write $\frac{5}{6}$ and $\frac{2}{3}$ as fractions with a common denominator.

Compare the numerators. $5 > 4$, so $\frac{5}{6} > \frac{4}{6}$.

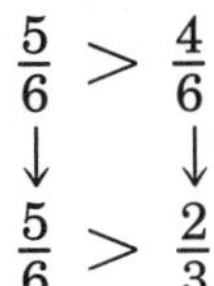

$$\frac{5}{6} > \frac{4}{6}$$
$$\downarrow \quad \downarrow$$
$$\frac{5}{6} > \frac{2}{3}$$

Example E Mixed numbers

Compare $2\frac{1}{2}$ and $2\frac{4}{8}$. Replace ● with $<$, $>$, or $=$.

The whole numbers are the same. Compare the fractions. Write $\frac{1}{2}$ and $\frac{4}{8}$ as fractions with a common denominator.

$2\frac{4}{8}$ ● $2\frac{4}{8}$

Compare the numerators. $4 = 4$, so $\frac{4}{8} = \frac{4}{8}$, and $2\frac{4}{8} = 2\frac{4}{8}$.

$$2\frac{4}{8} = 2\frac{4}{8}$$
$$\downarrow \quad \downarrow$$
$$2\frac{1}{2} = 2\frac{4}{8}$$

Exercises

PROBLEM SOLVING
The applications on pages 190–191 may be used anytime after this lesson.

Set C

Compare these numbers. Replace ● with $<$, $>$, or $=$.

1. $\frac{3}{4}$ ● $\frac{1}{4}$ $>$	4. $\frac{7}{8}$ ● $\frac{6}{8}$ $>$	7. $\frac{7}{12}$ ● $\frac{11}{12}$ $<$
2. $\frac{1}{3}$ ● $\frac{2}{3}$ $<$	5. $\frac{3}{6}$ ● $\frac{5}{6}$ $<$	8. $\frac{3}{10}$ ● $\frac{9}{10}$ $<$
3. $\frac{4}{5}$ ● $\frac{3}{5}$ $>$	6. $\frac{5}{9}$ ● $\frac{4}{9}$ $>$	9. $\frac{5}{16}$ ● $\frac{3}{16}$ $>$

Set D

Compare these numbers. Replace ● with $<$, $>$, or $=$.

1. $\frac{3}{8}$ ● $\frac{1}{4}$ $>$	4. $\frac{1}{2}$ ● $\frac{3}{5}$ $<$	7. $\frac{3}{4}$ ● $\frac{5}{6}$ $<$
2. $\frac{2}{3}$ ● $\frac{5}{12}$ $>$	5. $\frac{1}{3}$ ● $\frac{1}{2}$ $<$	8. $\frac{4}{6}$ ● $\frac{6}{9}$ $=$
3. $\frac{2}{5}$ ● $\frac{7}{10}$ $<$	6. $\frac{3}{5}$ ● $\frac{2}{3}$ $<$	9. $\frac{7}{10}$ ● $\frac{5}{8}$ $>$

Set E

Compare these numbers. Replace ● with $<$, $>$, or $=$.

1. $3\frac{2}{3}$ ● $3\frac{5}{6}$ $<$	4. $5\frac{3}{5}$ ● $5\frac{1}{2}$ $>$	7. $4\frac{3}{8}$ ● $4\frac{5}{6}$ $<$
2. $7\frac{1}{8}$ ● $7\frac{3}{16}$ $<$	5. $9\frac{1}{3}$ ● $9\frac{1}{4}$ $>$	8. $2\frac{5}{8}$ ● $2\frac{7}{10}$ $<$
3. $8\frac{2}{3}$ ● $8\frac{6}{9}$ $=$	6. $5\frac{2}{3}$ ● $6\frac{5}{8}$ $<$	9. $4\frac{5}{12}$ ● $3\frac{9}{10}$ $>$

Mixed Practice

Compare these numbers. Replace ● with $<$, $>$, or $=$.

D 1. $\frac{1}{2}$ ● $\frac{3}{6}$ $=$	D 4. $\frac{5}{6}$ ● $\frac{7}{9}$ $>$	E 7. $1\frac{11}{15}$ ● $1\frac{3}{5}$ $>$
C 2. $\frac{5}{8}$ ● $\frac{3}{8}$ $>$	E 5. $4\frac{1}{3}$ ● $4\frac{2}{9}$ $>$	D 8. $\frac{5}{12}$ ● $\frac{3}{8}$ $>$
E 3. $2\frac{3}{4}$ ● $2\frac{11}{12}$ $<$	C 6. $\frac{9}{10}$ ● $\frac{4}{5}$ $>$	E 9. $5\frac{5}{9}$ ● $5\frac{7}{12}$ $<$

Adding and Subtracting Fractions

Example F Rounding fractions and mixed numbers to the nearest whole number

Round $\frac{1}{4}$, $\frac{2}{3}$, and $3\frac{4}{8}$ to the nearest whole number.

$\frac{1}{4} < \frac{1}{2}$ To round fractions and mixed numbers to the nearest whole number, compare the fractions to $\frac{1}{2}$.

$\frac{2}{3} > \frac{1}{2}$

$\frac{4}{8} = \frac{1}{2}$

$\frac{1}{4}$ rounds to 0. If the fraction is less than $\frac{1}{2}$, round down.

$\frac{2}{3}$ rounds to 1. If the fraction is greater than $\frac{1}{2}$, round up.

$3\frac{4}{8}$ rounds to 4. If the fraction equals $\frac{1}{2}$, round up.

Example G Adding, same denominators

Estimate: $\frac{7}{8} + \frac{5}{8}$
$\downarrow \quad \downarrow$
$1 + 1 = 2$

$$\begin{array}{r} \frac{7}{8} \\ + \frac{5}{8} \\ \hline \end{array}$$

To add fractions that have a common denominator, add the numerators.

$\frac{12}{8} = 1\frac{4}{8} = 1\frac{1}{2}$ Write $\frac{12}{8}$ as a mixed number. Reduce $1\frac{4}{8}$ to lowest terms.

Example H Subtracting, same denominators

Estimate: 1 − 0 = 1

$$\begin{array}{r} \frac{5}{6} \\ - \frac{1}{6} \\ \hline \end{array}$$

To subtract fractions that have a common denominator, subtract the numerators.

$\frac{4}{6} = \frac{2}{3}$ Reduce $\frac{4}{6}$ to lowest terms.

Example I Adding, different denominators

Estimate: 1 + 0 = 1

$$\begin{array}{r} \frac{5}{6} = \frac{5}{6} \\ + \frac{1}{3} = \frac{2}{6} \\ \hline \end{array}$$

Write $\frac{5}{6}$ and $\frac{1}{3}$ as fractions with a common denominator. Then add the numerators.

$\frac{7}{6} = 1\frac{1}{6}$ Write $\frac{7}{6}$ as a mixed number.

Example J Subtracting, different denominators

Estimate: 1 − 0 = 1

$$\begin{array}{r} \frac{7}{8} = \frac{14}{16} \\ - \frac{3}{16} = \frac{3}{16} \\ \hline \frac{11}{16} \end{array}$$

Write $\frac{7}{8}$ and $\frac{3}{16}$ as fractions with a common denominator. Then subtract the numerators.

Example K Horizontal form

$\frac{3}{4} + \frac{1}{3} + \frac{1}{2}$

Estimate: 1 + 0 + 1 = 2

$$\begin{array}{r} \frac{3}{4} = \frac{9}{12} \\ \frac{1}{3} = \frac{4}{12} \\ + \frac{1}{2} = \frac{6}{12} \\ \hline \end{array}$$

Rewrite $\frac{3}{4} + \frac{1}{3} + \frac{1}{2}$ as shown. Write $\frac{3}{4}$, $\frac{1}{3}$, and $\frac{1}{2}$ as fractions with a common denominator. Add the numerators.

$\frac{19}{12} = 1\frac{7}{12}$ Write $\frac{19}{12}$ as a mixed number.

Exercises

Set F

Round to the nearest whole number.

1. $\frac{3}{4}$ 1
2. $\frac{3}{8}$ 0
3. $\frac{6}{12}$ 1
4. $\frac{4}{9}$ 0
5. $2\frac{7}{10}$ 3
6. $5\frac{3}{8}$ 5

Set G

1. $\frac{4}{5} + \frac{3}{5}$ $1\frac{2}{5}$
2. $\frac{3}{8} + \frac{7}{8}$ $1\frac{1}{4}$
3. $\frac{5}{6} + \frac{1}{6}$ 1
4. $\frac{2}{3} + \frac{2}{3}$ $1\frac{1}{3}$
5. $\frac{3}{4} + \frac{3}{4}$ $1\frac{1}{2}$
6. $\frac{7}{10} + \frac{9}{10}$ $1\frac{3}{5}$
7. $\frac{5}{12} + \frac{11}{12}$ $1\frac{1}{3}$
8. $\frac{5}{16} + \frac{13}{16}$ $1\frac{1}{8}$

Set H

1. $\frac{2}{3} - \frac{1}{3}$ $\frac{1}{3}$
2. $\frac{4}{5} - \frac{2}{5}$ $\frac{2}{5}$
3. $\frac{3}{4} - \frac{1}{4}$ $\frac{1}{2}$
4. $\frac{5}{8} - \frac{3}{8}$ $\frac{1}{4}$
5. $\frac{5}{6} - \frac{1}{6}$ $\frac{2}{3}$
6. $\frac{8}{9} - \frac{2}{9}$ $\frac{2}{3}$
7. $\frac{9}{10} - \frac{3}{10}$ $\frac{3}{5}$
8. $\frac{7}{12} - \frac{5}{12}$ $\frac{1}{6}$

Set I

1. $\frac{3}{4} + \frac{5}{8}$ $1\frac{3}{8}$
2. $\frac{2}{3} + \frac{3}{4}$ $1\frac{5}{12}$
3. $\frac{5}{6} + \frac{2}{9}$ $1\frac{1}{18}$
4. $\frac{7}{10} + \frac{3}{5}$ $1\frac{3}{10}$
5. $\frac{5}{6} + \frac{2}{3}$ $1\frac{1}{2}$
6. $\frac{1}{2} + \frac{5}{6}$ $1\frac{1}{3}$
7. $\frac{7}{8} + \frac{5}{16}$ $1\frac{3}{16}$
8. $\frac{2}{3} + \frac{4}{5}$ $1\frac{7}{15}$
9. $\frac{7}{10} + \frac{1}{2}$ $1\frac{1}{5}$
10. $\frac{5}{8} + \frac{7}{12}$ $1\frac{5}{24}$
11. $\frac{3}{4} + \frac{7}{12}$ $1\frac{1}{3}$
12. $\frac{11}{18} + \frac{5}{6}$ $1\frac{4}{9}$

Set J

1. $\frac{5}{6} - \frac{2}{3}$ $\frac{1}{6}$
2. $\frac{7}{8} - \frac{1}{2}$ $\frac{3}{8}$
3. $\frac{3}{4} - \frac{1}{3}$ $\frac{5}{12}$
4. $\frac{2}{3} - \frac{3}{8}$ $\frac{7}{24}$
5. $\frac{3}{5} - \frac{1}{10}$ $\frac{1}{2}$
6. $\frac{3}{4} - \frac{1}{6}$ $\frac{7}{12}$
7. $\frac{4}{5} - \frac{1}{3}$ $\frac{7}{15}$
8. $\frac{2}{3} - \frac{3}{10}$ $\frac{11}{30}$
9. $\frac{9}{10} - \frac{3}{4}$ $\frac{3}{20}$
10. $\frac{11}{12} - \frac{1}{6}$ $\frac{3}{4}$

Set K

1. $\frac{2}{3} + \frac{1}{2}$ $1\frac{1}{6}$
2. $\frac{7}{8} + \frac{1}{2}$ $1\frac{3}{8}$
3. $\frac{2}{3} + \frac{7}{12}$ $1\frac{1}{4}$
4. $\frac{2}{3} - \frac{4}{9}$ $\frac{2}{9}$
5. $\frac{5}{6} - \frac{1}{3}$ $\frac{1}{2}$
6. $\frac{3}{4} - \frac{7}{12}$ $\frac{1}{6}$
7. $\frac{1}{2} + \frac{2}{5} + \frac{1}{3}$ $1\frac{7}{30}$
8. $\frac{1}{3} + \frac{1}{2} + \frac{3}{4}$ $1\frac{7}{12}$
9. $\frac{2}{5} + \frac{1}{2} + \frac{3}{10}$ $1\frac{1}{5}$
10. $\frac{3}{4} + \frac{1}{6} + \frac{1}{3}$ $1\frac{1}{4}$

Mixed Practice

I 1. $\frac{4}{5} + \frac{7}{10}$ $1\frac{1}{2}$

G 2. $\frac{5}{6} + \frac{5}{6}$ $1\frac{2}{3}$

J 3. $\frac{11}{12} - \frac{2}{3}$ $\frac{1}{4}$

I 4. $\frac{3}{4} + \frac{5}{6}$ $1\frac{7}{12}$

K 5. $\frac{5}{6} - \frac{7}{10}$ $\frac{2}{15}$

K 6. $\frac{1}{6} + \frac{5}{8}$ $\frac{19}{24}$

H 7. $\frac{7}{8} - \frac{5}{8}$ $\frac{1}{4}$

G 8. $\frac{3}{8} + \frac{5}{8}$ 1

J 9. $\frac{5}{8} - \frac{1}{3}$ $\frac{7}{24}$

H 10. $\frac{5}{6} - \frac{1}{6}$ $\frac{2}{3}$

K 11. $\frac{4}{5} + \frac{3}{8}$ $1\frac{7}{40}$

K 12. $\frac{11}{12} - \frac{5}{8}$ $\frac{7}{24}$

Objective: Add mixed numbers.

Adding Mixed Numbers

Example L No sums with improper fractions

$$\begin{array}{r} 7\frac{1}{2} = 7\frac{3}{6} \\ +\ 2\frac{1}{6} = 2\frac{1}{6} \\ \hline 9\frac{4}{6} = 9\frac{2}{3} \end{array}$$

Estimate: 8 + 2 = 10
Write $\frac{1}{2}$ and $\frac{1}{6}$ as fractions with a common denominator.
Add the fractions.
Add the whole numbers.

Reduce $9\frac{4}{6}$ to lowest terms.

Example M Renaming mixed numbers having improper fractions

Rename $8\frac{7}{5}$.

$8\frac{7}{5} = 8 + \frac{7}{5}$ Rename $\frac{7}{5}$ as $1\frac{2}{5}$.

$8\frac{7}{5} = 8 + 1\frac{2}{5}$ Add 8 to get $9\frac{2}{5}$.

$8\frac{7}{5} = 9\frac{2}{5}$

Example N Renaming sums having improper fractions

$$\begin{array}{r} 6\frac{5}{6} = 6\frac{10}{12} \\ +\ 1\frac{3}{4} = 1\frac{9}{12} \\ \hline 7\frac{19}{12} = 8\frac{7}{12} \end{array}$$

Estimate: 7 + 2 = 9
Write $\frac{5}{6}$ and $\frac{3}{4}$ as fractions with a common denominator.
Add the fractions.
Add the whole numbers.

Rename $7\frac{19}{12}$.

Example O Horizontal form

$6\frac{7}{8} + 2\frac{7}{8} + 3\frac{7}{8}$

$$\begin{array}{r} 6\frac{7}{8} \\ 2\frac{7}{8} \\ +\ 3\frac{7}{8} \\ \hline 11\frac{21}{8} = 13\frac{5}{8} \end{array}$$

Estimate: 7 + 3 + 4 = 14
Rewrite $6\frac{7}{8} + 2\frac{7}{8} + 3\frac{7}{8}$ as shown.
Add the fractions.
Add the whole numbers.

Rename $11\frac{21}{8}$.

Exercises

Set L

1. $3\frac{1}{5} + 4\frac{2}{5}$ $7\frac{3}{5}$
2. $6\frac{3}{7} + 1\frac{2}{7}$ $7\frac{5}{7}$
3. $5\frac{1}{2} + 6\frac{1}{4}$ $11\frac{3}{4}$
4. $2\frac{3}{8} + 9\frac{1}{4}$ $11\frac{5}{8}$
5. $8\frac{1}{6} + 7\frac{2}{3}$ $15\frac{5}{6}$
6. $7\frac{1}{2} + 1\frac{1}{3}$ $8\frac{5}{6}$
7. $8\frac{1}{4} + 6\frac{2}{3}$ $14\frac{11}{12}$
8. $7\frac{1}{4} + 3\frac{1}{6}$ $10\frac{5}{12}$
9. $4\frac{1}{2} + 3\frac{2}{5}$ $7\frac{9}{10}$
10. $5\frac{3}{8} + 6\frac{1}{3}$ $11\frac{17}{24}$
11. $2\frac{3}{10} + 6\frac{1}{6}$ $8\frac{7}{15}$
12. $4\frac{3}{8} + 5\frac{1}{12}$ $9\frac{11}{24}$

Set M

Rename these mixed numbers.

1. $4\frac{3}{2}$ $5\frac{1}{2}$
2. $5\frac{11}{6}$ $6\frac{5}{6}$
3. $8\frac{7}{5}$ $9\frac{2}{5}$
4. $9\frac{5}{3}$ $10\frac{2}{3}$
5. $3\frac{11}{8}$ $4\frac{3}{8}$
6. $2\frac{5}{5}$ 3
7. $9\frac{5}{4}$ $10\frac{1}{4}$
8. $4\frac{11}{7}$ $5\frac{4}{7}$
9. $7\frac{4}{3}$ $8\frac{1}{3}$
10. $2\frac{7}{4}$ $3\frac{3}{4}$
11. $9\frac{13}{8}$ $10\frac{5}{8}$
12. $3\frac{9}{9}$ 4
13. $5\frac{10}{7}$ $6\frac{3}{7}$
14. $6\frac{11}{10}$ $7\frac{1}{10}$
15. $4\frac{17}{9}$ $5\frac{8}{9}$
16. $6\frac{17}{12}$ $7\frac{5}{12}$
17. $1\frac{6}{4}$ $2\frac{1}{2}$
18. $8\frac{14}{10}$ $9\frac{2}{5}$
19. $9\frac{14}{12}$ $10\frac{1}{6}$
20. $3\frac{10}{8}$ $4\frac{1}{4}$
21. $4\frac{22}{12}$ $5\frac{5}{6}$
22. $7\frac{10}{6}$ $8\frac{2}{3}$
23. $2\frac{18}{10}$ $3\frac{4}{5}$
24. $5\frac{16}{8}$ 7
25. $8\frac{12}{6}$ 10
26. $9\frac{21}{10}$ $11\frac{1}{10}$
27. $10\frac{19}{8}$ $12\frac{3}{8}$

PROBLEM SOLVING
The applications on page 183 may be used anytime after this lesson.

Set N

1. $1\frac{1}{2} + 3\frac{5}{8}$ $5\frac{1}{8}$
2. $7\frac{5}{6} + 2\frac{1}{3}$ $10\frac{1}{6}$
3. $6\frac{7}{10} + 9\frac{3}{5}$ $16\frac{3}{10}$
4. $9\frac{2}{3} + 2\frac{3}{4}$ $12\frac{5}{12}$
5. $8\frac{3}{4} + 6\frac{4}{5}$ $15\frac{11}{20}$
6. $2\frac{1}{3} + 7\frac{4}{5}$ $10\frac{2}{15}$
7. $3\frac{5}{6} + 1\frac{1}{4}$ $5\frac{1}{12}$
8. $7\frac{1}{2} + 6\frac{4}{5}$ $14\frac{3}{10}$
9. $4\frac{3}{5} + 8\frac{5}{6}$ $13\frac{13}{30}$
10. $9\frac{7}{10} + 2\frac{3}{4}$ $12\frac{9}{20}$
11. $7\frac{3}{8} + 6\frac{4}{5}$ $14\frac{7}{40}$
12. $1\frac{7}{10} + 5\frac{2}{3}$ $7\frac{11}{30}$
13. $5\frac{3}{4} + 8\frac{11}{12}$ $14\frac{2}{3}$
14. $8\frac{1}{2} + 1\frac{9}{10}$ $10\frac{2}{5}$
15. $7\frac{5}{6} + 2\frac{1}{2}$ $10\frac{1}{3}$
16. $8\frac{1}{3} + 9\frac{11}{12}$ $18\frac{1}{4}$
17. $2\frac{5}{12} + 4\frac{5}{6}$ $7\frac{1}{4}$
18. $8\frac{7}{10} + 5\frac{5}{6}$ $14\frac{8}{15}$

Set O

1. $6\frac{1}{2} + 3\frac{1}{2}$ 10
2. $2\frac{3}{5} + 1\frac{4}{5}$ $4\frac{2}{5}$
3. $4\frac{3}{5} + 6\frac{3}{10}$ $10\frac{9}{10}$
4. $3\frac{3}{8} + 4\frac{1}{2}$ $7\frac{7}{8}$
5. $3\frac{2}{5} + 2\frac{1}{2}$ $5\frac{9}{10}$
6. $2\frac{1}{8} + 5\frac{2}{3}$ $7\frac{19}{24}$
7. $9\frac{3}{4} + 6\frac{1}{2}$ $16\frac{1}{4}$
8. $2\frac{5}{8} + 6\frac{7}{10}$ $9\frac{13}{40}$
9. $9\frac{3}{8} + 7\frac{11}{12}$ $17\frac{7}{24}$
10. $5\frac{5}{6} + 4\frac{7}{8}$ $10\frac{17}{24}$
11. $2\frac{1}{3} + 7\frac{2}{3} + 4\frac{2}{3}$ $14\frac{2}{3}$
12. $6\frac{3}{8} + 5\frac{5}{8} + 3\frac{7}{8}$ $15\frac{7}{8}$
13. $4\frac{2}{3} + 1\frac{2}{3} + 6\frac{5}{6}$ $13\frac{1}{6}$
14. $7\frac{7}{8} + 5\frac{3}{4} + 8\frac{5}{8}$ $22\frac{1}{4}$
15. $4\frac{3}{5} + 6\frac{9}{10} + 2\frac{1}{2}$ 14
16. $3\frac{5}{6} + 4\frac{1}{2} + 5\frac{11}{12}$ $14\frac{1}{4}$

Mixed Practice

N 1. $8\frac{1}{3} + 6\frac{3}{4}$ $15\frac{1}{12}$
L 2. $5\frac{1}{8} + 7\frac{5}{8}$ $12\frac{3}{4}$
N 3. $1\frac{3}{4} + 4\frac{5}{6}$ $6\frac{7}{12}$
N 4. $3\frac{3}{4} + 1\frac{2}{5}$ $5\frac{3}{20}$
N 5. $9\frac{7}{10} + 5\frac{9}{10}$ $15\frac{3}{5}$
L 6. $3\frac{5}{8} + 4\frac{3}{10}$ $7\frac{37}{40}$
N 7. $2\frac{5}{6} + 8\frac{5}{6}$ $11\frac{2}{3}$
O 8. $3\frac{1}{6} + 4\frac{3}{5}$ $7\frac{23}{30}$
O 9. $5\frac{7}{8} + 2\frac{3}{5}$ $8\frac{19}{40}$
O 10. $6\frac{1}{3} + 8\frac{7}{8}$ $15\frac{5}{24}$
O 11. $9\frac{3}{8} + 7\frac{11}{12}$ $17\frac{7}{24}$
L 12. $9\frac{2}{5} + 5\frac{1}{3}$ $14\frac{11}{15}$
N 13. $3\frac{11}{12} + 9\frac{7}{12}$ $13\frac{1}{2}$
N 14. $9\frac{2}{3} + 5\frac{7}{10}$ $15\frac{11}{30}$
N 15. $7\frac{1}{6} + 3\frac{5}{6}$ 11
L 16. $7\frac{5}{12} + 1\frac{3}{8}$ $8\frac{19}{24}$
L 17. $3\frac{1}{6} + 1\frac{7}{12}$ $4\frac{3}{4}$
N 18. $8\frac{3}{4} + 2\frac{3}{4}$ $11\frac{1}{2}$
O 19. $4\frac{3}{8} + 2\frac{7}{8} + 3\frac{5}{8}$ $10\frac{7}{8}$
O 20. $5\frac{1}{2} + 3\frac{3}{8} + 4\frac{7}{8}$ $13\frac{3}{4}$
O 21. $1\frac{2}{3} + 7\frac{5}{6} + 6\frac{1}{2}$ 16
O 22. $9\frac{4}{5} + 8\frac{9}{10} + 2\frac{1}{2}$ $21\frac{1}{5}$

See Skills File, page 422, for more practice.

BREAK TIME

Gerry gave Mary $\frac{1}{2}$ of his mystery books.
Mary gave Larry $\frac{1}{2}$ of the books she got from Gerry.
Larry gave Harry $\frac{1}{2}$ of the books he got from Mary.
Harry got only 4 books.

How many books did Gerry start with? 32 books

Objective: Subtract mixed numbers with the same denominator.

Subtracting Mixed Numbers: Same Denominator

Example P Renaming a mixed number or a whole number

Rename $9\frac{1}{5}$ to show more fifths.

$$9\frac{1}{5} = 8\frac{\square}{5}$$

$9\frac{1}{5} = 9 + \frac{1}{5}$ Rename 9 as $8\frac{5}{5}$.

$9\frac{1}{5} = 8\frac{5}{5} + \frac{1}{5}$ Add $\frac{1}{5}$ to get $8\frac{6}{5}$.

$9\frac{1}{5} = 8\frac{6}{5}$

Example Q Renaming the minuend

$$\begin{array}{r} 8\frac{5}{8} = 7\frac{13}{8} \\ -\ 5\frac{7}{8} = 5\frac{7}{8} \\ \hline 2\frac{6}{8} = 2\frac{3}{4} \end{array}$$

Estimate: $9 - 6 = 3$

Rename $8\frac{5}{8}$ to show more eighths.
Subtract the fractions.
Subtract the whole numbers.

Reduce $2\frac{6}{8}$ to lowest terms.

Example R Horizontal form

$9 - 2\frac{1}{5}$

$$\begin{array}{r} 9 = 8\frac{5}{5} \\ -\ 2\frac{1}{5} = 2\frac{1}{5} \\ \hline 6\frac{4}{5} \end{array}$$

Estimate: $9 - 2 = 7$

Rewrite $9 - 2\frac{1}{5}$ as shown.
Rename 9 to show fifths.
Subtract the fractions.
Subtract the whole numbers.

Exercises

Set P

Find each missing number.

1. $3\frac{1}{4} = 2\frac{\square}{4}$ 5
2. $4\frac{2}{5} = 3\frac{\square}{5}$ 7
3. $6\frac{1}{3} = 5\frac{\square}{3}$ 4
4. $2\frac{1}{2} = 1\frac{\square}{2}$ 3
5. $3 = 2\frac{\square}{6}$ 6
6. $7 = 6\frac{\square}{8}$ 8
7. $9\frac{1}{6} = 8\frac{\square}{6}$ 7
8. $7\frac{5}{8} = 6\frac{\square}{8}$ 13
9. $2 = 1\frac{\square}{4}$ 4
10. $5 = 4\frac{\square}{2}$ 2
11. $5\frac{2}{9} = 4\frac{\square}{9}$ 11
12. $8\frac{4}{10} = 7\frac{\square}{10}$ 14
13. $1 = \frac{\square}{5}$ 5
14. $8 = 7\frac{\square}{3}$ 3
15. $6 = 5\frac{\square}{10}$ 10
16. $4 = 3\frac{\square}{12}$ 12
17. $3\frac{3}{12} = 2\frac{\square}{12}$ 15
18. $1\frac{8}{24} = \frac{\square}{24}$ 32
19. $10 = 9\frac{\square}{15}$ 15
20. $9 = 8\frac{\square}{16}$ 16

Set Q

1. $6\frac{1}{5} - 3\frac{4}{5}$ $2\frac{2}{5}$
2. $9\frac{1}{3} - 7\frac{2}{3}$ $1\frac{2}{3}$
3. $6\frac{4}{9} - 2\frac{8}{9}$ $3\frac{5}{9}$
4. $8\frac{2}{5} - 3\frac{3}{5}$ $4\frac{4}{5}$
5. $7 - 3\frac{1}{8}$ $3\frac{7}{8}$
6. $8 - 7\frac{2}{3}$ $\frac{1}{3}$
7. $7\frac{1}{8} - 5\frac{5}{8}$ $1\frac{1}{2}$
8. $8\frac{1}{6} - 2\frac{5}{6}$ $5\frac{1}{3}$
9. $9 - 4\frac{7}{8}$ $4\frac{1}{8}$
10. $7 - 3\frac{5}{6}$ $3\frac{1}{6}$
11. $4\frac{1}{4} - 1\frac{3}{4}$ $2\frac{1}{2}$
12. $7\frac{5}{8} - 4\frac{7}{8}$ $2\frac{3}{4}$
13. $8\frac{5}{12} - 6\frac{7}{12}$ $1\frac{5}{6}$
14. $7\frac{3}{16} - 5\frac{11}{16}$ $1\frac{1}{2}$
15. $4 - 2\frac{5}{12}$ $1\frac{7}{12}$

PROBLEM SOLVING
The applications on pages 188–189 may be used anytime after this lesson.

Set R

1. $6 - 4\frac{1}{5}$ $1\frac{4}{5}$
2. $5 - 1\frac{1}{2}$ $3\frac{1}{2}$
3. $9\frac{2}{5} - 2\frac{4}{5}$ $6\frac{3}{5}$
4. $8\frac{3}{8} - 3\frac{7}{8}$ $4\frac{1}{2}$
5. $5\frac{1}{10} - 2\frac{7}{10}$ $2\frac{2}{5}$
6. $6\frac{5}{12} - 5\frac{11}{12}$ $\frac{1}{2}$
7. $2 - 1\frac{3}{4}$ $\frac{1}{4}$
8. $4 - 2\frac{4}{5}$ $1\frac{1}{5}$
9. $9\frac{2}{9} - \frac{5}{9}$ $8\frac{2}{3}$
10. $6\frac{3}{10} - \frac{9}{10}$ $5\frac{2}{5}$

Mixed Practice

Q 1. $7 - 3\frac{3}{8}$ $3\frac{5}{8}$

Q 2. $4\frac{2}{5} - 1\frac{4}{5}$ $2\frac{3}{5}$

Q 3. $9 - 7\frac{1}{6}$ $1\frac{5}{6}$

Q 4. $8 - 4\frac{1}{4}$ $3\frac{3}{4}$

R 5. $3\frac{5}{9} - 2\frac{8}{9}$ $\frac{2}{3}$

R 6. $6\frac{7}{10} - 3\frac{9}{10}$ $2\frac{4}{5}$

R 7. $6 - 2\frac{1}{3}$ $3\frac{2}{3}$

Q 8. $5\frac{1}{12} - 2\frac{7}{12}$ $2\frac{1}{2}$

Q 9. $10 - 3\frac{9}{10}$ $6\frac{1}{10}$

Q 10. $5\frac{1}{5} - 1\frac{3}{5}$ $3\frac{3}{5}$

Q 11. $2\frac{3}{8} - 1\frac{7}{8}$ $\frac{1}{2}$

12. R $7 - 5\frac{7}{12}$ $1\frac{5}{12}$

13. R $4\frac{1}{12} - 2\frac{5}{12}$ $1\frac{2}{3}$

14. R $9 - 5\frac{7}{10}$ $3\frac{3}{10}$

BREAK TIME

Pat had a party for some friends.

10 of the people were on the volleyball team.

10 of the people were on the tennis team.

9 of the people were on the track team.

3 of the track team members were on the volleyball team.

4 of the volleyball team members were on the tennis team.

3 of the tennis team members were on the track team.

No one was on more than two teams.

How many people were at the party?
19 people

Objective: Subtract mixed numbers with different denominators.

Subtracting Mixed Numbers: Different Denominators

Example S No renaming the minuend

$$\begin{array}{r} 7\frac{7}{8} = 7\frac{7}{8} \\ -\ 3\frac{1}{4} = 3\frac{2}{8} \\ \hline 4\frac{5}{8} \end{array}$$

Estimate: 8 − 3 = 5
Write $\frac{7}{8}$ and $\frac{1}{4}$ as fractions with a common denominator.
Subtract the fractions.
Subtract the whole numbers.

Example T Renaming the minuend

$$\begin{array}{r} 6\frac{1}{6} = 6\frac{2}{12} = 5\frac{14}{12} \\ -\ 4\frac{3}{4} = 4\frac{9}{12} = 4\frac{9}{12} \\ \hline 1\frac{5}{12} \end{array}$$

Estimate: 6 − 5 = 1
Write $\frac{1}{6}$ and $\frac{3}{4}$ as fractions with a common denominator.
Rename $6\frac{2}{12}$ to show more twelfths.
Subtract the fractions.
Subtract the whole numbers.

Example U Horizontal form

$8\frac{9}{10} - 2\frac{1}{5}$

$$\begin{array}{r} 8\frac{9}{10} = 8\frac{9}{10} \\ -\ 2\frac{1}{5} = 2\frac{2}{10} \\ \hline 6\frac{7}{10} \end{array}$$

Estimate: 9 − 2 = 7
Rewrite $8\frac{9}{10} - 2\frac{1}{5}$ as shown.
Write $\frac{9}{10}$ and $\frac{1}{5}$ as fractions with a common denominator.
Subtract the fractions.
Subtract the whole numbers.

Exercises

Set S

1. $5\frac{3}{4} - 2\frac{1}{2}$ $3\frac{1}{4}$
2. $4\frac{1}{2} - 1\frac{1}{3}$ $3\frac{1}{6}$
3. $8\frac{2}{3} - 4\frac{1}{6}$ $4\frac{1}{2}$
4. $9\frac{2}{3} - 3\frac{1}{4}$ $6\frac{5}{12}$
5. $7\frac{1}{2} - 2\frac{3}{10}$ $5\frac{1}{5}$
6. $3\frac{5}{6} - 2\frac{3}{4}$ $1\frac{1}{12}$
7. $8\frac{2}{3} - 2\frac{5}{8}$ $6\frac{1}{24}$
8. $6\frac{1}{2} - 2\frac{2}{5}$ $4\frac{1}{10}$
9. $9\frac{4}{5} - 7\frac{3}{4}$ $2\frac{1}{20}$
10. $3\frac{7}{8} - 3\frac{5}{6}$ $\frac{1}{24}$
11. $7\frac{9}{10} - 1\frac{2}{5}$ $6\frac{1}{2}$
12. $2\frac{5}{6} - 1\frac{2}{9}$ $1\frac{11}{18}$

Set T

1. $5\frac{1}{4} - 1\frac{2}{3}$ $3\frac{7}{12}$
2. $9\frac{1}{2} - 7\frac{4}{5}$ $1\frac{7}{10}$
3. $7\frac{1}{2} - 4\frac{2}{3}$ $2\frac{5}{6}$
4. $6\frac{3}{5} - 4\frac{2}{3}$ $1\frac{14}{15}$
5. $8\frac{1}{6} - 5\frac{3}{4}$ $2\frac{5}{12}$
6. $12\frac{1}{3} - 7\frac{5}{8}$ $4\frac{17}{24}$
7. $10\frac{5}{8} - 2\frac{5}{6}$ $7\frac{19}{24}$
8. $6\frac{7}{12} - 2\frac{5}{6}$ $3\frac{3}{4}$
9. $4\frac{1}{6} - 3\frac{4}{9}$ $\frac{13}{18}$
10. $3\frac{1}{3} - 1\frac{5}{6}$ $1\frac{1}{2}$
11. $7\frac{1}{5} - 4\frac{7}{10}$ $2\frac{1}{2}$
12. $14\frac{1}{2} - 3\frac{3}{4}$ $10\frac{3}{4}$
13. $6\frac{3}{10} - 4\frac{1}{2}$ $1\frac{4}{5}$
14. $7\frac{1}{8} - 2\frac{3}{4}$ $4\frac{3}{8}$
15. $15\frac{7}{12} - 9\frac{5}{8}$ $5\frac{23}{24}$
16. $8\frac{1}{4} - 2\frac{5}{6}$ $5\frac{5}{12}$
17. $7\frac{1}{2} - 3\frac{3}{5}$ $3\frac{9}{10}$
18. $9\frac{5}{8} - 5\frac{2}{3}$ $3\frac{23}{24}$
19. $5\frac{3}{8} - 1\frac{7}{12}$ $3\frac{19}{24}$
20. $4\frac{1}{6} - 1\frac{5}{8}$ $2\frac{13}{24}$
21. $9\frac{5}{6} - 3\frac{9}{10}$ $5\frac{14}{15}$

PROBLEM SOLVING
The applications on pages 184–187 may be used anytime after this lesson.

Set U

1. $5\frac{4}{5} - 1\frac{1}{2}$ $4\frac{3}{10}$
2. $8\frac{1}{2} - 3\frac{1}{3}$ $5\frac{1}{6}$
3. $8\frac{1}{4} - 4\frac{1}{8}$ $4\frac{1}{8}$
4. $4\frac{2}{3} - 3\frac{1}{4}$ $1\frac{5}{12}$
5. $7\frac{5}{6} - 2$ $5\frac{5}{6}$
6. $9\frac{7}{12} - 8$ $1\frac{7}{12}$
7. $6\frac{1}{10} - 4\frac{4}{5}$ $1\frac{3}{10}$
8. $5\frac{1}{8} - 2\frac{3}{4}$ $2\frac{3}{8}$
9. $7\frac{1}{3} - 3\frac{4}{9}$ $3\frac{8}{9}$
10. $3\frac{2}{5} - 1\frac{1}{2}$ $1\frac{9}{10}$
11. $8\frac{1}{3} - 6\frac{5}{6}$ $1\frac{1}{2}$
12. $4\frac{1}{5} - 2\frac{7}{10}$ $1\frac{1}{2}$
13. $12\frac{3}{4} - \frac{11}{16}$ $12\frac{1}{16}$
14. $5\frac{5}{6} - \frac{3}{10}$ $5\frac{8}{15}$
15. $4\frac{5}{6} - 1\frac{5}{9}$ $3\frac{5}{18}$
16. $11\frac{3}{8} - 6\frac{7}{12}$ $4\frac{19}{24}$
17. $38\frac{3}{10} - 14\frac{1}{4}$ $24\frac{1}{20}$
18. $47\frac{4}{15} - 35\frac{1}{6}$ $12\frac{1}{10}$
19. $51\frac{3}{8} - 29\frac{13}{16}$ $21\frac{9}{16}$
20. $73\frac{5}{12} - 35\frac{3}{4}$ $37\frac{2}{3}$
21. $39\frac{2}{9} - 25\frac{5}{12}$ $13\frac{29}{36}$

Mixed Practice

S 1. $8\frac{2}{3} - 2\frac{4}{9}$ $6\frac{2}{9}$

T 2. $4\frac{1}{4} - 3\frac{5}{8}$ $\frac{5}{8}$

T 3. $6\frac{5}{8} - 2\frac{2}{3}$ $3\frac{23}{24}$

S 4. $7\frac{5}{6} - 1\frac{3}{4}$ $6\frac{1}{12}$

T 5. $9\frac{3}{10} - 5\frac{3}{4}$ $3\frac{11}{20}$

S 6. $7\frac{2}{3} - 3\frac{1}{6}$ $4\frac{1}{2}$

T 7. $8\frac{1}{6} - 5\frac{5}{9}$ $2\frac{11}{18}$

S 8. $3\frac{2}{3} - 1\frac{2}{9}$ $2\frac{4}{9}$

S 9. $9\frac{3}{10} - 2\frac{1}{5}$ $7\frac{1}{10}$

T 10. $5\frac{1}{6} - 4\frac{2}{3}$ $\frac{1}{2}$

U 11. $3\frac{1}{4} - 1\frac{1}{2}$ $1\frac{3}{4}$

U 12. $9\frac{1}{6} - \frac{7}{8}$ $8\frac{7}{24}$

U 13. $6\frac{3}{4} - 5\frac{7}{10}$ $1\frac{1}{20}$

U 14. $2\frac{3}{8} - \frac{1}{3}$ $2\frac{1}{24}$

T 15. $9\frac{5}{12} - 6\frac{2}{3}$ $2\frac{3}{4}$

T 16. $3\frac{3}{8} - 1\frac{5}{12}$ $1\frac{23}{24}$

S 17. $4\frac{7}{8} - 2\frac{1}{2}$ $2\frac{3}{8}$

T 18. $7\frac{1}{8} - 3\frac{3}{10}$ $3\frac{33}{40}$

S 19. $6\frac{5}{8} - 1\frac{7}{12}$ $5\frac{1}{24}$

T 20. $8\frac{3}{4} - 7\frac{5}{6}$ $\frac{11}{12}$

S 21. $5\frac{3}{10} - 2\frac{1}{6}$ $3\frac{2}{15}$

S 22. $2\frac{5}{6} - 1\frac{3}{10}$ $1\frac{8}{15}$

T 23. $4\frac{1}{8} - 2\frac{1}{2}$ $1\frac{5}{8}$

T 24. $6\frac{5}{8} - 1\frac{9}{10}$ $4\frac{29}{40}$

U 25. $12\frac{2}{3} - 6\frac{4}{5}$ $5\frac{13}{15}$

U 26. $8\frac{5}{6} - 3$ $5\frac{5}{6}$

U 27. $3\frac{1}{2} - 1\frac{4}{9}$ $2\frac{1}{18}$

U 28. $8\frac{5}{6} - 2\frac{3}{4}$ $6\frac{1}{12}$

BREAK TIME

Each face of a large cube was painted. Then the cube was cut into small cubes as shown.

How many small cubes have paint on exactly
1 face? 6
2 faces? 12
3 faces? 8
4 faces? 0

How many small cubes have no paint?
1

See Skills File, page 422, for more practice.

Number of test items - 21

SKILLS POSTTEST

Number missed	1	2	3	4	5	6	7	8	9	10
Percent correct	95	90	86	81	76	71	67	62	57	52

SKILL Finding Common Denominators *page 172*

A Write $\frac{2}{3}$ and $\frac{3}{4}$ as fractions with a common denominator.

$\frac{8}{12}, \frac{9}{12}$

B Write $\frac{1}{2}$, $\frac{1}{3}$, and $\frac{1}{4}$ as fractions with a common denominator.

$\frac{6}{12}, \frac{4}{12}, \frac{3}{12}$

SKILL Comparing Fractions and Mixed Numbers *page 173*

C Compare $\frac{2}{5}$ and $\frac{4}{5}$. Replace ● with $<$, $>$, or $=$.

$\frac{2}{5}$ ● $\frac{4}{5}$ $<$

D Compare $\frac{4}{6}$ and $\frac{2}{3}$. Replace ● with $<$, $>$, or $=$.

$\frac{4}{6}$ ● $\frac{2}{3}$ $=$

E Compare $5\frac{7}{8}$ and $5\frac{3}{4}$. Replace ● with $<$, $>$, or $=$.

$5\frac{7}{8}$ ● $5\frac{3}{4}$ $>$

SKILL Adding and Subtracting Fractions *pages 174–175*

F Round $5\frac{3}{4}$ to the nearest whole number.

6

G $\frac{3}{5} + \frac{4}{5}$

$1\frac{2}{5}$

H $\frac{7}{8} - \frac{3}{8}$

$\frac{1}{2}$

I $\frac{5}{8} + \frac{3}{4}$

$1\frac{3}{8}$

J $\frac{1}{2} - \frac{1}{4}$

$\frac{1}{4}$

K $\frac{5}{8} + \frac{1}{2} + \frac{3}{4}$

$1\frac{7}{8}$

SKILL Adding Mixed Numbers *pages 176–177*

L $7\frac{1}{4} + 2\frac{5}{8}$

$9\frac{7}{8}$

M Rename $6\frac{6}{5}$.

$6\frac{6}{5} = 7\frac{\square}{5}$ 1

N $3\frac{1}{2} + 9\frac{4}{5}$

$13\frac{3}{10}$

O $7\frac{2}{3} + 4\frac{1}{3}$

12

SKILL Subtracting Mixed Numbers: Same Denominator *pages 178–179*

P Find the missing number.

$8\frac{1}{3} = 7\frac{\square}{3}$ 4

Q $7\frac{1}{6} - 3\frac{5}{6}$

$3\frac{1}{3}$

R $3 - 1\frac{2}{3}$

$1\frac{1}{3}$

SKILL Subtracting Mixed Numbers: Different Denominators *pages 180–181*

S $8\frac{3}{4} - 4\frac{1}{2}$ $4\frac{1}{4}$

T $6\frac{1}{3} - 2\frac{3}{4}$ $3\frac{7}{12}$

U $5\frac{1}{6} - 3\frac{2}{3}$

$1\frac{1}{2}$

Problem Solving

CONSUMER APPLICATIONS

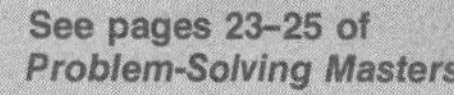
See pages 23–25 of *Problem-Solving Masters.*

Objective: Solve problems involving addition of fractions and mixed numbers.

In this lesson students find the number of hours worked and compute total wages earned for a week.

Computing Weekly Wages

The Torockios' carpenter kept an accurate record of the hours worked each day.

For each week, find the total number of hours the carpenter worked. Then compute the total amount of money earned that week at a rate of $15 per hour.

1.

Day	Number of hours worked
Monday	$7\frac{1}{2}$
Tuesday	$4\frac{1}{4}$
Wednesday	5
Thursday	$3\frac{1}{2}$
Friday	$6\frac{3}{4}$

27 hours, $405

2.

Day	Number of hours worked
Monday	$6\frac{1}{2}$
Tuesday	$7\frac{1}{4}$
Wednesday	$4\frac{1}{4}$
Thursday	$6\frac{1}{2}$
Friday	$5\frac{1}{2}$

30 hours, $450

3.

Day	Number of hours worked
Monday	$8\frac{1}{6}$
Tuesday	$5\frac{1}{2}$
Wednesday	$5\frac{1}{2}$
Thursday	$4\frac{2}{3}$
Friday	6
Saturday	$9\frac{1}{6}$

39 hours, $585

4.

Day	Number of hours worked
Monday	$4\frac{5}{6}$
Tuesday	$7\frac{3}{4}$
Wednesday	$6\frac{3}{4}$
Thursday	$8\frac{1}{2}$
Friday	$8\frac{1}{6}$

36 hours, $540

5.

Day	Number of hours worked
Monday	$3\frac{1}{6}$
Tuesday	$7\frac{5}{6}$
Wednesday	$6\frac{3}{4}$
Thursday	$7\frac{1}{2}$
Friday	$7\frac{3}{4}$

33 hours, $495

6.

Day	Number of hours worked
Monday	$8\frac{2}{3}$
Tuesday	$6\frac{3}{4}$
Wednesday	$5\frac{1}{2}$
Thursday	$7\frac{1}{3}$
Friday	$6\frac{1}{4}$
Saturday	$3\frac{1}{2}$

38 hours, $570

Problem Solving

CONSUMER APPLICATIONS

Objective: Solve problems involving subtraction of fractions and mixed numbers.

In this lesson students read a stock report and compute the difference between the closing price and the highest price for the day, the high and the low for the day, and the high and the low for the year.

Reading a Stock Market Report

Investing money in the stock market is sometimes a way of saving or earning money. Janet Littlebird owns stock in SFN Companies, Inc. Because the price of a stock may change daily, she reads the stock report each day.

She looks first for SFN, the abbreviated name of the company. Then she looks at the columns to the right of SFN.

The *highest price* paid per share that day was $29\frac{3}{4}$ ($29\frac{3}{4}$ dollars). The *lowest price* paid per share that day was 29 (29 dollars). The *closing price* paid per share that day was $29\frac{1}{4}$ ($29\frac{1}{4}$ dollars). The *net change* was $+\frac{1}{2}$. This indicates that the last price paid per share that day was $\frac{1}{2}$ dollar higher than the last price paid on the previous day.

The first two columns give the highest price ($31\frac{7}{8}$ dollars) and the lowest price ($19\frac{3}{8}$ dollars) paid for one share of stock since the first of the year.

Be sure students understand new terms before assigning the problems.

NEW YORK STOCK EXCHANGE
MONDAY

1980 High	1980 Low		High	Low	Close	Net Chg.
High	Low		High	Low	Last	Chg.
19¾	6¾	SCA	16½	16	16¼	+ ⅜
32¼	16⅝	SCM	25⅞	25	25½	+ ¼
31⅞	19⅜	SFN	29¾	29	29¼	+ ½
37½	21⅝	SPSTec	31⅛	30	30⅞	+ 1⅛
73	34	Sabine s	64¼	63¼	63¾	− 7¼
32¼	17	SfgdBus n	30¾	30¼	30½	+ ¼
6¼	3	Safgdin n	5⅝	5	5½	+ ⅞
36¾	27½	Safewy	31	30¾	31	+ ⅛
11¼	6⅞	SagaCp	8¾	8½	8½	− ⅜
75⅛	27⅝	SJoMn	71	70¼	70⅞	+ ⅛
11½	9	StJoLP	10½	9⅞	10¼	.....
108	49¼	StLSaF	107¾	102¾	107½	+ 6½
10½	7⅞	SPaul	8¾	8⅝	8⅝	− ⅛
37	25¼	StRegP	34⅛	33¾	34⅛	+ ½
8⅜	5	Salant	8	7⅝	7⅞	+ ¼
7⅞	3½	Sambos	6⅝	6¼	6⅝	+ ⅜
15¼	11⅛	SDieGs	14⅛	12¼	12½	+ ¼
16½	11½	SJuanB wi	13¾	12⅞	13½	+ ¾
21¼	12	SJuanR	19¼	19	19	+ ⅛
61⅜	24⅛	Sanders	62¼	61¼	62	+ ¾
85¾	47½	SFeInd	88	85¾	86⅞	+ 1¼
64¾	29¾	SFeInt	62⅜	61	62	+ 1½
21½	13½	SgtWel	21¼	21	21¼	+ ¼
10⅝	5⅛	SaulRE	9⅛	9⅛	9⅛	.....
16⅝	7⅝	SavAStp	15⅜	15¼	15¼	+ ⅛
12¼	8¾	SavEIP	9⅜	9¼	9⅜	.....
12⅞	9¾	SavE A	10⅛	10⅛	10⅛	.....
11¼	8½	SavE pf	9⅝	9⅝	9⅝	.....
19	11⅜	Savin	12½	12¼	12¼	.....
23¼	16	Savin pf	16⅞	16¾	16¾	− ¼
9¾	4	Saxon	7¾	7⅜	7½	+ ¼
5⅝	2⅞	Schaefer	4	4	4	.....
45⅝	28¼	SchrPlo	38	36⅝	38	+ 1½

See pages 26–27 of *Problem-Solving Masters.*

What would Janet save per share if she bought each stock at Monday's lowest price instead of Monday's highest price?

1. SFN $(29\frac{3}{4} - 29)$ $\frac{3}{4}$ dollar
2. Sabine 1 dollar
3. StLSaF 5 dollars
4. SJaunB $\frac{7}{8}$ dollar
5. SFeInd $2\frac{1}{4}$ dollars
6. Saxon $\frac{3}{8}$ dollar
7. SchrPlo $1\frac{3}{8}$ dollars

What would Janet save per share if she bought each stock at Monday's closing price instead of Monday's highest price?

8. SFN $(29\frac{3}{4} - 29\frac{1}{4})$ $\frac{1}{2}$ dollar
9. SPSTec $\frac{1}{4}$ dollar
10. SfgdBus $\frac{1}{4}$ dollar
11. SJoMn $\frac{1}{8}$ dollar
12. SDieGs $1\frac{5}{8}$ dollars
13. SavElP 0 dollars
14. Saxon $\frac{1}{4}$ dollar

For each stock, find the difference between the highest and lowest prices paid per share since the first of the year.

15. SFN $(31\frac{7}{8} - 19\frac{3}{8})$ $12\frac{1}{2}$ dollars
16. SfgdBus $15\frac{1}{4}$ dollars
17. Safewy $9\frac{1}{4}$ dollars
18. SPaul $2\frac{5}{8}$ dollars
19. Sanders $37\frac{1}{4}$ dollars
20. SgtWel 8 dollars
21. SchrPlo $17\frac{3}{8}$ dollars

Problem Solving

CAREER APPLICATIONS

Objective: Solve problems involving addition and subtraction of fractions and mixed numbers.

In this lesson students find the cost of producing toys and compute the gross profit.

Toy Manufacturer

Career Cluster: Trades Mr. Richard Metti owns a toy factory. He supervises the purchasing of parts to make the toys and sees that the toys are assembled.

1. Find the total cost of the parts purchased to make each Fly-Rite Plane. $8\frac{1}{4}$¢

Part	Cost in cents
Plastic body	$4\frac{7}{8}$
Wings	$1\frac{5}{8}$
Propeller	$1\frac{1}{4}$
Rubber band	$\frac{1}{2}$

2. Wonderland Toy Company sells the plane for 59 cents. Find the gross profit for each plane. $50\frac{3}{4}$¢
(Selling price − cost)

3. Find the total cost of the parts purchased to make each Playtime Paddle Ball. $13\frac{7}{8}$¢

Part	Cost in cents
Paddle	$10\frac{1}{2}$
Ball	$2\frac{3}{4}$
Rubber band	$\frac{1}{2}$
Staple	$\frac{1}{8}$

4. Wonderland Toy Company sells the paddle ball for 89 cents. Find the gross profit for each paddle ball. $75\frac{1}{8}$¢

5. Find the total cost of all the items in each Mighty Handy Tool Set. $23\frac{5}{8}$¢

Part	Cost in cents
Saw	$4\frac{1}{4}$
Wrench	$3\frac{1}{2}$
Screwdriver	$4\frac{3}{8}$
Pliers	$6\frac{1}{2}$
Hammer	$2\frac{3}{4}$
File	$2\frac{1}{4}$

6. Wonderland Toy Company sells the tool set for 98 cents. Find the gross profit for each tool set. $74\frac{3}{8}$¢

Several suppliers submitted prices to Mr. Metti for the component parts that make up the Mighty Motor Mixer.

Part	Price in cents		
	Toyparts Company	Kids' Stuff, Inc.	Knickknacks, Ltd.
4 wheels with hubcaps	$5\frac{1}{8}$	$4\frac{7}{8}$	$5\frac{1}{4}$
2 metal axles	$6\frac{1}{4}$	5	$5\frac{3}{4}$
Plastic windows and windshield	$2\frac{1}{2}$	$2\frac{3}{4}$	$2\frac{1}{2}$
Metal cab	9	9	$9\frac{1}{8}$
Seats and steering wheel	$2\frac{3}{4}$	$2\frac{1}{2}$	$2\frac{5}{8}$
Metal truck bed	$15\frac{1}{4}$	$14\frac{1}{4}$	$13\frac{3}{4}$
Plastic cement mixer	$5\frac{1}{2}$	$5\frac{1}{4}$	$5\frac{1}{2}$

Find the total price for the component parts submitted by

7. Toyparts Company. $46\frac{3}{8}$¢

8. Kids' Stuff, Inc. $43\frac{5}{8}$¢

9. Knickknacks, Ltd. $44\frac{1}{2}$¢

Which company submitted the

10. lowest price? Kids' Stuff, Inc.

11. highest price? Toyparts Company

12. How much less was the lowest price submitted than the highest price? $2\frac{3}{4}$¢

13. Find the total price of the component parts if Mr. Metti could select each individual part at the lowest price. $42\frac{7}{8}$¢

Mighty Motor Mixer sells for 99 cents. Find the gross profit for each truck if Mr. Metti purchases parts from

14. Toyparts Company. $52\frac{5}{8}$¢

15. Kids' Stuff, Inc. $55\frac{3}{8}$¢

16. Knickknacks, Ltd. $54\frac{1}{2}$¢

Problem Solving

CAREER APPLICATIONS

Objective: Solve problems involving addition and subtraction of fractions and mixed numbers.

In this lesson students find the total time for performing tasks and compute the time saved by making task modifications.

Efficiency Expert

Career Cluster: Trades Don Wong is an efficiency expert. He keeps an accurate record of the time it takes an employee to perform a certain task. He then suggests changes that allow the employee to perform the task more quickly.

1. Find the total time needed to assemble a nut and bolt. 20 seconds

Task	Time in seconds
Obtain bolt from bin.	$4\frac{3}{10}$
Obtain washer from bin.	$5\frac{1}{2}$
Position washer on bolt.	$2\frac{3}{10}$
Obtain nut from bin.	$3\frac{2}{5}$
Place nut on bolt.	$4\frac{1}{2}$

2. Find the total time needed to assemble a nut and bolt after Mr. Wong had the bins moved closer together. $10\frac{7}{10}$ seconds

Task	Time in seconds
Obtain bolt from bin.	$1\frac{1}{5}$
Obtain washer from bin.	$1\frac{1}{5}$
Position washer on bolt.	$2\frac{3}{10}$
Obtain nut from bin.	$1\frac{1}{2}$
Place nut on bolt.	$4\frac{1}{2}$

After Mr. Wong had the bins moved closer together, how many seconds were saved in assembling

3. a nut and bolt? $9\frac{3}{10}$ seconds
4. 10 nuts and bolts? 93 seconds
5. 100 nuts and bolts? 930 seconds

You might ask students to change 930 seconds to minutes. [$15\frac{1}{2}$ minutes]

Mr. Wong recorded how many seconds it took Mr. Woodfield to drill each of the four metal braces.

Task	Time in seconds			
	First brace	Second brace	Third brace	Fourth brace
Pick up piece and place it in drill.	$3\frac{1}{2}$	$3\frac{1}{5}$	$3\frac{4}{5}$	$3\frac{7}{10}$
Tighten set screw.	$1\frac{1}{2}$	$1\frac{3}{4}$	$1\frac{1}{2}$	$1\frac{3}{10}$
Advance drill to work.	$2\frac{1}{5}$	$3\frac{1}{2}$	$3\frac{1}{4}$	$2\frac{4}{5}$
Drill holes.	$5\frac{1}{5}$	$5\frac{1}{2}$	$5\frac{1}{2}$	$5\frac{3}{4}$
Loosen set screw.	$1\frac{1}{5}$	$1\frac{1}{2}$	1	$1\frac{4}{5}$
Remove piece.	$2\frac{1}{10}$	3	$2\frac{1}{10}$	$3\frac{1}{4}$
Blow out chips.	$\frac{1}{2}$	$\frac{1}{2}$	$\frac{3}{4}$	$\frac{3}{4}$

How many seconds were used to drill the

6. first brace? $16\frac{1}{5}$ seconds
7. second brace? $18\frac{19}{20}$ seconds
8. third brace? $17\frac{9}{10}$ seconds
9. fourth brace? $19\frac{7}{20}$ seconds

You may wish to check answers to Problems 6–9 before having students work Problems 10–12.

10. How many seconds were used to drill all four braces? $72\frac{2}{5}$ seconds
11. Divide the total time by 4 to find the average number of seconds used to drill each metal brace. $18\frac{1}{10}$ seconds
12. Mr. Wong made changes that allowed Mr. Woodfield to decrease his average time to $13\frac{1}{2}$ seconds. By how many seconds did his average time decrease? $4\frac{3}{5}$ seconds

Efficiency experts are used throughout all phases of industry. They analyze tasks and then make recommendations that help employees do a task more efficiently and with less fatigue. This results in increased productivity per employee, and the company saves money.

Problem Solving

DEVELOPING STRATEGIES

Objective: Solve problems by drawing a picture.

In this lesson students find the number of tiles needed to install a suspended ceiling.

Tactic: Drawing a Picture

Lou Bowen installs suspended ceilings in large buildings. He must often place partial tiles along the edges of the ceiling to keep the pattern symmetrical. Lou cuts these tiles so that the pieces used at opposite edges of the ceiling are the same size. Each dimension of a partial tile must be greater than half the corresponding dimension of a full-size tile.

Problem

How many tiles must Lou cut for the edges of a ceiling that is $28\frac{2}{3}$ feet by $16\frac{1}{3}$ feet if each tile is 2 feet by 2 feet?

Solution

The following questions show Lou's strategy for solving the problem. He used the tactic of drawing a picture.

a. How many tiles would fit along the length of the ceiling? Divide the length of the ceiling by the length of a tile. The fraction shows that partial tiles are needed.

$28\frac{2}{3} \div 2 = 14\frac{1}{3}$

b. How many full-length tiles will Lou use along the length of the ceiling? 14 would be too many because $\frac{1}{3}$ of a tile is too small to cut the pieces that will be used at opposite edges. Subtract 1 tile from 14. Using 13 full-length tiles leaves $2\frac{2}{3}$ feet to be divided in half and used at each end.

$14 - 1 = 13$

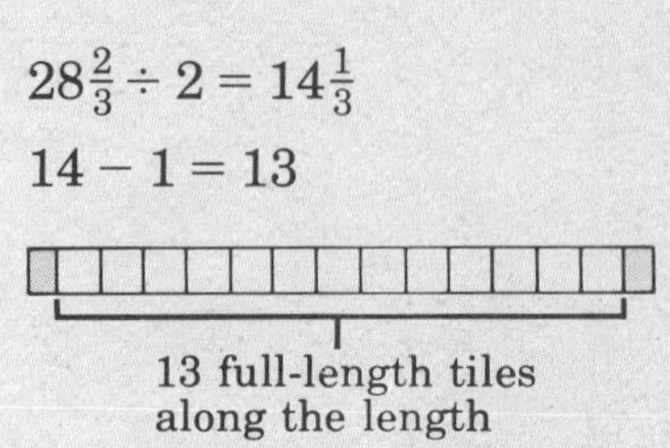
13 full-length tiles along the length

c. How many tiles would fit along the width of the ceiling? Divide the width of the ceiling by the width of a tile.

$16\frac{1}{3} \div 2 = 8\frac{1}{6}$

d. How many full-length tiles will Lou use along the width of the ceiling? Subtract 1 from the number of whole tiles for the width.

$8 - 1 = 7$

e. How many partial tiles are along the edges? Lou drew a picture and counted the shaded tiles along the edges.

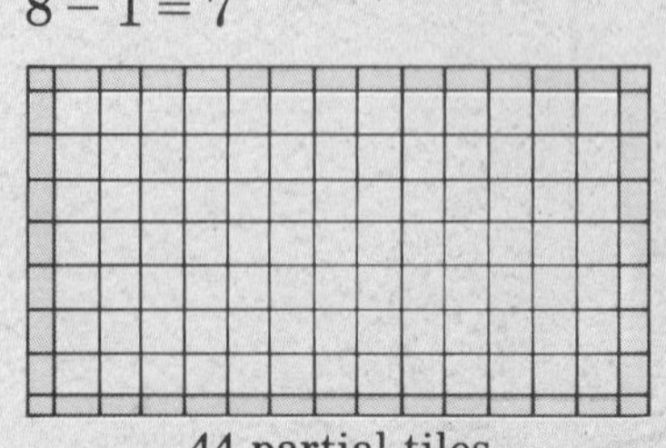
44 partial tiles

Conclusion: Lou must cut 44 tiles for the edges.

Related Problems

1. How many tiles would be used for the entire ceiling in the problem on page 190? (Count the number of tiles in Lou's picture.)
135 tiles

A ceiling is $16\frac{3}{4}$ feet by $24\frac{1}{2}$ feet.
Each tile is 2 feet by 2 feet.

2. How many tiles would be cut for the edges of the ceiling?
40 tiles
3. How many tiles would be used for the entire ceiling?
117 tiles

A ceiling is $18\frac{3}{8}$ feet by $21\frac{3}{4}$ feet.
Each tile is 3 feet by 3 feet.

4. How many tiles would be cut for the edges of the ceiling?
26 tiles
5. How many tiles would be used for the entire ceiling?
56 tiles

A ceiling is $12\frac{3}{4}$ feet by $15\frac{3}{8}$ feet.
Each tile is $1\frac{1}{2}$ feet by $1\frac{1}{2}$ feet.

6. How many tiles would be cut for the edges of the ceiling?
36 tiles
7. How many tiles would be used for the entire ceiling?
99 tiles

A ceiling is 15 feet by 28 feet.
Each tile is $2\frac{1}{2}$ feet by $2\frac{1}{2}$ feet.

8. How many tiles would be cut for the edges of the ceiling?
12 tiles
9. How many tiles would be used for the entire ceiling?
72 tiles

Extensions

10–13. Give the length and width of the corner tiles for each ceiling in Problems 2–9.
See Additional Answers on page T46.

CHAPTER 8 TEST

Number of test items - 26

Number missed	1	2	3	4	5	6	7	8	9	10	11	12	13
Percent correct	96	92	88	85	81	77	73	69	65	62	58	54	50

Write these fractions with a common denominator.

A **1.** $\frac{1}{2}$ $\frac{3}{5}$ $\frac{5}{10}$ $\frac{6}{10}$

B **2.** $\frac{2}{3}$ $\frac{5}{6}$ $\frac{1}{2}$ $\frac{4}{6}$ $\frac{5}{6}$ $\frac{3}{6}$

Compare the numbers. Replace ● with <, >, or =.

C **3.** $\frac{3}{7}$ ● $\frac{4}{7}$ <

D **4.** $\frac{6}{10}$ ● $\frac{3}{5}$ =

E **5.** $6\frac{3}{4}$ ● $6\frac{5}{8}$ >

F **6.** Round $5\frac{2}{3}$ to the nearest whole number. 6

G **7.** $\frac{2}{3} + \frac{2}{3}$ $1\frac{1}{3}$

H **8.** $\frac{3}{4} - \frac{1}{4}$ $\frac{1}{2}$

I **9.** $\frac{5}{6} + \frac{2}{3}$ $1\frac{1}{2}$

J **10.** $\frac{1}{2} - \frac{1}{3}$ $\frac{1}{6}$

K **11.** $\frac{1}{2} + \frac{2}{3} + \frac{1}{4}$ $1\frac{5}{12}$

L **12.** $5\frac{1}{6} + 4\frac{2}{3}$ $9\frac{5}{6}$

M **13.** Rename $4\frac{5}{4}$.

$4\frac{5}{4} = 5\frac{\square}{4}$ 1

N **14.** $3\frac{1}{2} + 9\frac{2}{3}$ $13\frac{1}{6}$

O **15.** $6\frac{3}{4} + 2\frac{1}{4}$ 9

P **16.** Find the missing number.

$8\frac{1}{4} = 7\frac{\square}{4}$ 5

Q **17.** $7\frac{1}{4} - 2\frac{3}{4}$ $4\frac{1}{2}$

R **18.** $9 - 3\frac{3}{4}$ $5\frac{1}{4}$

S **19.** $4\frac{3}{4} - 2\frac{2}{3}$ $2\frac{1}{12}$

T **20.** $8\frac{1}{8} - 6\frac{3}{4}$ $1\frac{3}{8}$

U **21.** $6\frac{1}{2} - 3\frac{5}{6}$ $2\frac{2}{3}$

22. Find the total number of hours Tom worked last week. $16\frac{1}{12}$ hours

Day	Number of hours worked
Monday	$3\frac{2}{3}$
Tuesday	$2\frac{1}{2}$
Wednesday	$4\frac{5}{6}$
Thursday	$1\frac{3}{4}$
Friday	$3\frac{1}{3}$

23. How much money could Sue save if she bought SCM at the day's lowest price per share instead of the day's highest price? $\frac{7}{8}$ dollar

1980 High	Low		High	Low	Close	Net Chg.
High	Low		High	Low	Last	Chg.
19¾	6¾	SCA	16½	16	16¼	+ ⅜
32¼	16⅝	SCM	25⅞	25	25½	+ ¼
31⅞	19⅜	SFN	29¾	29	29¼	+ ½
37½	21⅝	SPSTec	31⅛	30	30⅞	+ 1⅛
73	34	Sabine s	64¼	63¼	63¾	− 7¼

24. Find the total cost of all the items in the toy tool set. $17\frac{3}{4}$¢

Item	Cost in cents
Hammer	$2\frac{3}{4}$
Saw	$4\frac{3}{8}$
Pliers	$6\frac{1}{2}$
Screwdriver	$4\frac{1}{8}$

25. How many seconds did Jenny use to drill all three braces? $52\frac{3}{5}$ seconds

1st brace, $16\frac{1}{5}$ seconds

2nd brace, $18\frac{9}{10}$ seconds

3rd brace, $17\frac{1}{2}$ seconds

26. How many tiles would be cut for the edges of a ceiling that is $12\frac{2}{3}$ feet by $15\frac{3}{4}$ feet if each tile is 2 feet by 2 feet? 26 tiles

 See pages 19–20 of the *Test Masters* for an alternate form of the Chapter 8 Test.

CHAPTER 9 Probability

SKILLS PRETEST

Number of test items - 8

Number missed	1	2	3	4
Percent correct	88	75	63	50

SKILL Finding Probabilities and Predicting Outcomes *pages 194–195*

A Give the probability that the roll of a number cube will show two.
$\frac{1}{6}$

B Give the probability that the roll of a number cube will show three or four.
$\frac{2}{6}$ or $\frac{1}{3}$

C Give the expected number of rolls that will result in two if a number cube were rolled 30 times.
5

SKILL Finding Probabilities by Using Tree Diagrams *pages 196–197*

D Make a tree diagram to find the number of outcomes for tossing three coins.
8 possible outcomes
See below.

E Give the probability of getting three heads if three coins were tossed.
$\frac{1}{8}$

SKILL Finding Probabilities by Using Multiplication *pages 198–199*

F Multiply to find the number of possible outcomes for choosing a five-digit code number if each digit is chosen at random.
100,000

G Give the probability that a five-digit code number chosen at random will be 09644 or 21735.
$\frac{2}{100,000}$ or $\frac{1}{50,000}$

SKILL Finding Probabilities Involving Dependent Events *pages 200–201*

H Give the probability of drawing two cards at random that show *O* if the first card is *not* replaced before the second draw.

$\frac{2}{42}$ or $\frac{1}{21}$

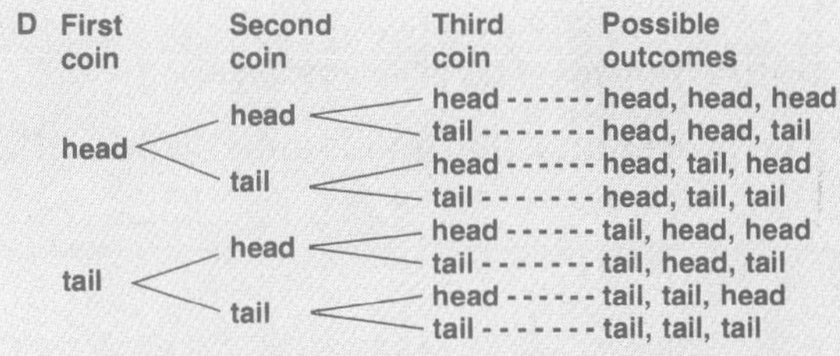

See page T36 for additional notes on Chapter 9.

Objective: Find probabilities and make predictions.

Finding Probabilities and Predicting Outcomes

Example A Finding probability, one favorable outcome

Give the probability that the roll of a number cube will show four.

Use this formula to find the probability of a given outcome when all outcomes are equally likely.

$$\text{Probability} = \frac{\textbf{Number of favorable outcomes}}{\textbf{Number of possible outcomes}}$$

The number cube may land in any of 6 ways. All are equally likely to occur. There are 6 possible outcomes: one, two, three, four, five, six. Four is 1 of the 6 possible outcomes.

$\frac{1}{6}$ ← Number of favorable outcomes / ← Number of possible outcomes

The probability that the number cube will show four is $\frac{1}{6}$.

Example B Finding probability, more than one favorable outcome

Use the formula to give the probability that the roll of a number cube will show four or six.

There are 6 possible outcomes, and all are equally likely to occur. Four is 1 of the possible outcomes. Six is another. Therefore, there are 2 favorable outcomes.

$\frac{2}{6}$ ← Number of favorable outcomes / ← Number of possible outcomes

The probability that the number cube will show four or six is $\frac{2}{6}$, or $\frac{1}{3}$.

Example C Predicting outcomes

Give the expected number of rolls that will result in four if a number cube were rolled 18 times.

First find the probability of rolling a four.

$\frac{1}{6}$ ← Number of favorable outcomes / ← Number of possible outcomes

Then multiply to find the expected number of favorable outcomes.

Probability of rolling a four		Number of rolls		Expected number of favorable outcomes
$\frac{1}{6}$	$\times$	18	$=$	3

You could expect about 3 out of 18 rolls to result in four.

Point out to the students that equally likely means that each possible outcome has an equal chance of occurring.

Exercises

PROBLEM SOLVING
The applications on pages 204–207 may be used anytime after this lesson.

Set A

Give the probability that the roll of a number cube will show

1. two. $\frac{1}{6}$
2. six. $\frac{1}{6}$
3. five. $\frac{1}{6}$
4. one. $\frac{1}{6}$
5. three. $\frac{1}{6}$

Set B

Give the probability that the roll of a number cube will show

1. two or four. $\frac{2}{6}$ or $\frac{1}{3}$
2. one, two, or six. $\frac{3}{6}$ or $\frac{1}{2}$
3. one or five. $\frac{2}{6}$ or $\frac{1}{3}$
4. two, three, or five. $\frac{3}{6}$ or $\frac{1}{2}$
5. five or six. $\frac{2}{6}$ or $\frac{1}{3}$
6. a number less than five. $\frac{4}{6}$ or $\frac{2}{3}$
7. a number greater than one. $\frac{5}{6}$
8. an even number. $\frac{3}{6}$ or $\frac{1}{2}$

Using these cards, give the probability of drawing a card that shows

9. *T*. $\frac{1}{7}$
10. *U*. $\frac{1}{7}$
11. *O*. $\frac{2}{7}$
12. *T* or *U*. $\frac{2}{7}$
13. *T* or *O*. $\frac{3}{7}$
14. *T*, *U*, or *O*. $\frac{4}{7}$

Using these cards, give the probability of drawing a card that shows

15. *P*. $\frac{1}{11}$
16. *R*. $\frac{1}{11}$
17. *B*. $\frac{2}{11}$
18. *I*. $\frac{2}{11}$
19. *P* or *B*. $\frac{3}{11}$
20. *B* or *I*. $\frac{4}{11}$

Set C

Give the expected number of rolls that will result in two if a number cube were rolled

1. 6 times. 1
2. 12 times. 2
3. 24 times. 4
4. 60 times. 10
5. 90 times. 15
6. 120 times. 20

Give the expected number of rolls that will result in five or six if a number cube were rolled

7. 12 times. 4
8. 15 times. 5
9. 21 times. 7
10. 27 times. 9
11. 42 times. 14
12. 90 times. 30

Give the expected number of rolls that will result in a number less than five if a number cube were rolled

13. 9 times. 6
14. 18 times. 12
15. 24 times. 16
16. 30 times. 20
17. 42 times. 28
18. 60 times. 40

Objective: Find probabilities using tree diagrams.

Finding Probabilities by Using Tree Diagrams

Example D Finding possible outcomes

Make a tree diagram to find the number of possible outcomes for choosing one ball from each bowl.

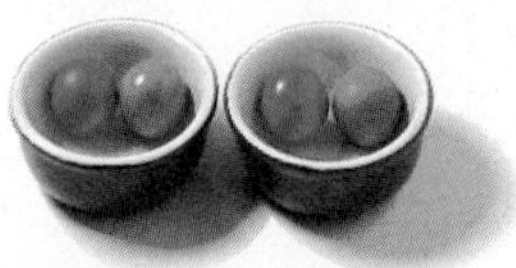

First bowl	Second bowl	Possible outcomes
green	green	green, green
	red	green, red
red	green	red, green
	red	red, red

A tree diagram shows that there are 4 possible outcomes.

Example E Finding probability, independent events

If a ball were chosen from each bowl, give the probability of choosing one green and one red ball.

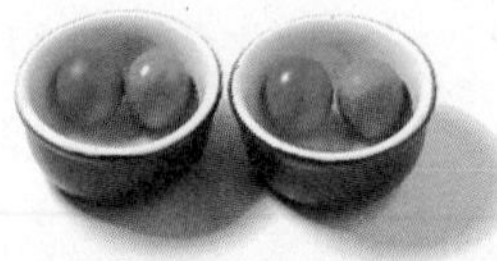

There are 4 possible outcomes.
There are 2 favorable outcomes.
Green, *red* is one; *red*, *green* is the other.

$\frac{2}{4}$ ⟵ Number of favorable outcomes / Number of possible outcomes

The probability of choosing one green and one red ball is $\frac{2}{4}$, or $\frac{1}{2}$.

You may wish to refer students to the tree diagram, which shows the four possible outcomes, in Example D.

Exercises

Set D

Complete each tree diagram to find the number of possible outcomes for

1. choosing a sweater and a skirt from the ones listed.
6 possible outcomes
Sweater—yellow, orange
Skirt—gray, green, brown

Sweater	Skirt	Possible outcomes
yellow	gray	yellow, gray
	green	yellow, green
	brown	yellow, brown
orange	gray	orange, gray
	green	orange, green
	brown	orange, brown

2. choosing a catcher and a pitcher from the athletes listed.
8 possible outcomes
Catcher—Joan, Mona
Pitcher—Donna, Karen, Beth, Paula

Catcher	Pitcher	Possible outcomes
Joan	Donna	Joan, Donna
	Karen	Joan, Karen
	Beth	Joan, Beth
	Paula	Joan, Paula
Mona	Donna	Mona, Donna
	Karen	Mona, Karen
	Beth	Mona, Beth
	Paula	Mona, Paula

3. tossing two coins.
4 possible outcomes

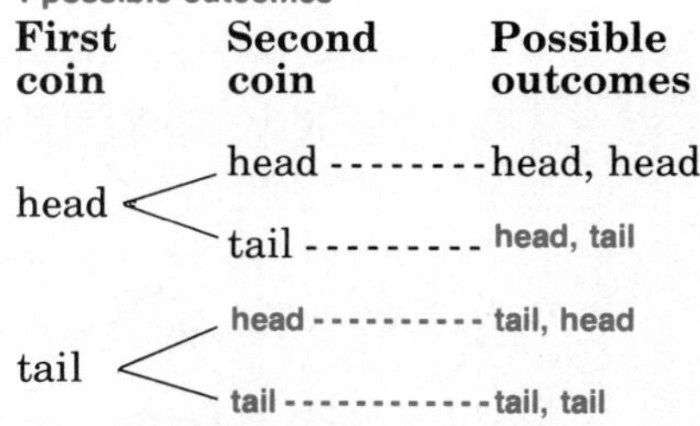

4. tossing three coins.
8 possible outcomes

First coin	Second coin	Third coin	Possible outcomes
head	head	head	head, head, head
		tail	head, head, tail
	tail	head	head, tail, head
		tail	head, tail, tail
tail	head	head	tail, head, head
		tail	tail, head, tail
	tail	head	tail, tail, head
		tail	tail, tail, tail

5. choosing the answers in a true-false test with three questions.
8 possible outcomes

First question	Second question	Third question	Possible outcomes
true	true	true	true, true, true
		false	true, true, false
	false	true	true, false, true
		false	true, false, false
false	true	true	false, true, true
		false	false, true, false
	false	true	false, false, true
		false	false, false, false

Set E

If two coins were tossed, give the probability of getting

1. two heads. $\frac{1}{4}$
2. two tails. $\frac{1}{4}$
3. one head and one tail. $\frac{2}{4}$ or $\frac{1}{2}$
4. one or more heads. $\frac{3}{4}$
5. one or more tails. $\frac{3}{4}$

If three coins were tossed, give the probability of getting

6. three heads. $\frac{1}{8}$
7. two heads and one tail. $\frac{3}{8}$
8. one or more heads. $\frac{7}{8}$
9. three tails. $\frac{1}{8}$
10. one or more tails. $\frac{7}{8}$
11. two or more heads. $\frac{4}{8}$ or $\frac{1}{2}$
12. two or more tails. $\frac{4}{8}$ or $\frac{1}{2}$

If a student guessed the answers to the three questions of a true-false test, give the probability that the student wrote

13. *true* once and *false* twice. $\frac{3}{8}$
14. *true* at least twice. $\frac{4}{8}$ or $\frac{1}{2}$

15. the correct set of answers for the test. $\frac{1}{8}$

Objective: Find probabilities involving independent events using multiplication.

Finding Probabilities by Using Multiplication

Example F Finding possible outcomes

Multiply to find the number of possible outcomes for choosing a three-digit code number if each digit is chosen at random.

There are 10 possible choices for each digit: 0, 1, 2, 3, 4, 5, 6, 7, 8, 9.

Number of choices for first digit		Number of choices for second digit		Number of choices for third digit		Number of possible outcomes
10	×	10	×	10	=	1000

Example G Finding probability, independent events

Give the probability that a three-digit code number chosen at random will be 684 or 092.

There are 1000 possible outcomes.
There are 2 favorable outcomes, 684 and 092.

$\frac{2}{1000}$ ⟵ Number of favorable outcomes / ⟵ Number of possible outcomes

The probability of choosing 684 or 092 at random is $\frac{2}{1000}$, or $\frac{1}{500}$.

Exercises

Set F

Multiply to find the number of possible outcomes for choosing at random a

1. two-digit code number. 100
2. four-digit code number. 10,000
3. five-digit code number. 100,000
4. six-digit code number. 1,000,000

Multiply to find the number of possible outcomes for tossing

5. two coins. ($2 \times 2 = \square$) 4
6. three coins. ($2 \times 2 \times 2 = \square$) 8
7. four coins. 16
8. five coins. 32
9. six coins. 64
10. seven coins. 128
11. two number cubes. ($6 \times 6 = \square$) 36
12. three number cubes. 216
13. two coins and one number cube. ($2 \times 2 \times 6 = \square$) 24
14. two coins and two number cubes. 144
15. three coins and three number cubes. 1728

PROBLEM SOLVING
The applications on page 203 may be used anytime after this lesson.

Set G

See page T36 for more information concerning these answers.

Give the probability that a two-digit code number chosen at random will be

1. 26. $\frac{1}{100}$
2. 30 or 08. $\frac{2}{100}$ or $\frac{1}{50}$
3. 17, 93, or 46. $\frac{3}{100}$
4. a number whose last digit is 5. $\frac{10}{100}$ or $\frac{1}{10}$
5. a number greater than 90. $\frac{9}{100}$
6. a multiple of 10. $\frac{9}{100}$

Give the probability that a three-digit code number chosen at random will be

7. 368 or 792. $\frac{2}{1000}$ or $\frac{1}{500}$
8. 431. $\frac{1}{1000}$
9. a number whose first digit is 7. $\frac{100}{1000}$ or $\frac{1}{10}$
10. a multiple of 100. $\frac{9}{1000}$

Give the probability that a four-digit code number chosen at random will be

11. 7864. $\frac{1}{10,000}$
12. 6392 or 0819. $\frac{2}{10,000}$ or $\frac{1}{5000}$
13. a multiple of 100. $\frac{99}{10,000}$

Give the probability that a five-digit code number chosen at random will be

14. 13,496. $\frac{1}{100,000}$
15. 25,147 or 94,777. See below.
16. a multiple of 1000. $\frac{99}{100,000}$

15. $\frac{2}{100,000}$ or $\frac{1}{50,000}$

BREAK TIME

Marty drew four straight lines to divide the circle into eleven pieces. There was exactly one square in each piece of the circle. Trace the figure and show the four straight lines that Marty could have drawn.

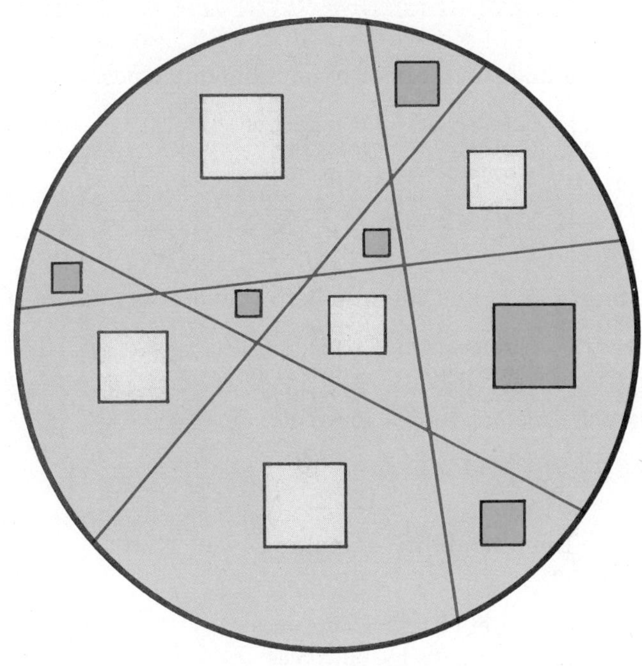

Objective: Find probabilities involving dependent events using multiplication.

Finding Probabilities Involving Dependent Events

Example H Finding probability, dependent events

Give the probability of drawing two cards at random that show *I* if the first card is *not* replaced before the second draw.

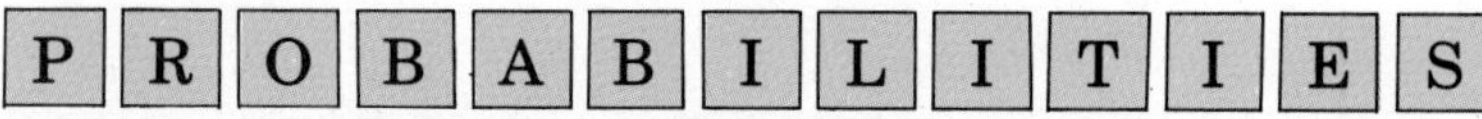

Multiply to find the number of possible outcomes.

Number of choices for first card		Number of choices for second card		Number of possible outcomes
13	×	12	=	156

Next, multiply to find the number of favorable outcomes.

Number of choices of *I* for the first card		Number of choices of *I* for the second card		Number of favorable outcomes
3	×	2	=	6

Then give the probability of making two draws that show *I*.

$\frac{6}{156}$ ← Number of favorable outcomes / Number of possible outcomes

The probability of making two draws that show *I* is $\frac{6}{156}$, or $\frac{1}{26}$.

For Exercises 11–20, the number of possible outcomes is 13 × 12 × 11, or 1716.

Exercises

Set H

Use the cards in Example H for Exercises 1–20. In each exercise, when a card is drawn, it is *not* replaced before the next draw.

Give the probability of making two draws that show

1. *B*. $\frac{2}{156}$ or $\frac{1}{78}$
2. *B*, then *R*. $\frac{2}{156}$ or $\frac{1}{78}$
3. *P*, then *S*. $\frac{1}{156}$
4. *T*, then *I*. $\frac{3}{156}$ or $\frac{1}{52}$
5. *L*, then *B*. $\frac{2}{156}$ or $\frac{1}{78}$
6. *I*, then *E*. $\frac{3}{156}$ or $\frac{1}{52}$
7. *A*, then *T*. $\frac{1}{156}$
8. *B*, then *I*. $\frac{6}{156}$ or $\frac{1}{26}$
9. *R*, then *E*. $\frac{1}{156}$
10. *S*, then *I*. $\frac{3}{156}$ or $\frac{1}{52}$

Give the probability of making three draws in order that show

11. *I*. $\frac{6}{1716}$ or $\frac{1}{286}$
12. *P*, then *B*, then *B*. $\frac{2}{1716}$ or $\frac{1}{858}$
13. *I*, then *A*, then *I*. $\frac{6}{1716}$ or $\frac{1}{286}$
14. *L*, then *B*, then *B*. $\frac{2}{1716}$ or $\frac{1}{858}$
15. *B*, then *I*, then *I*. $\frac{12}{1716}$ or $\frac{1}{143}$
16. *P*, then *R*, then *O*. $\frac{1}{1716}$
17. *B*, then *A*, then *E*. $\frac{2}{1716}$ or $\frac{1}{858}$
18. *S*, then *I*, then *R*. $\frac{3}{1716}$ or $\frac{1}{572}$
19. *B*, then *I*, then *S*. $\frac{6}{1716}$ or $\frac{1}{286}$
20. *L*, then *I*, then *T*. $\frac{3}{1716}$ or $\frac{1}{572}$

PROBLEM SOLVING
The applications on pages 208–209 may be used anytime after this lesson.

Use these cards for Exercises 21–40. Each time a card is drawn, it is *not* replaced before the next draw.

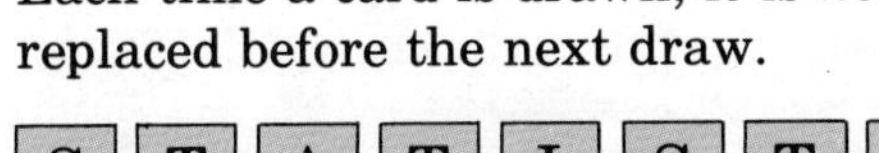

The number of possible outcomes is 10 × 9, or 90.

Give the probability of making two draws that show

21. *S*. $\frac{6}{90}$ or $\frac{1}{15}$
22. *I*. $\frac{2}{90}$ or $\frac{1}{45}$
23. *T*. $\frac{6}{90}$ or $\frac{1}{15}$
24. *A*, then *C*. $\frac{1}{90}$
25. *A*, then *S*. $\frac{3}{90}$ or $\frac{1}{30}$
26. *T*, then *S*. $\frac{9}{90}$ or $\frac{1}{10}$
27. *I*, then *C*. $\frac{2}{90}$ or $\frac{1}{45}$
28. *T*, then *I*. $\frac{6}{90}$ or $\frac{1}{15}$
29. *S*, then *C*. $\frac{3}{90}$ or $\frac{1}{30}$
30. *A*, then *I*. $\frac{2}{90}$ or $\frac{1}{45}$

The number of possible outcomes is 10 × 9 × 8, or 720.

Give the probability of making three draws that show

31. *T*. $\frac{6}{720}$ or $\frac{1}{120}$
32. *S*. $\frac{6}{720}$ or $\frac{1}{120}$
33. *T*, then *C*, then *T*. $\frac{6}{720}$ or $\frac{1}{120}$
34. *S*, then *I*, then *S*. $\frac{12}{720}$ or $\frac{1}{60}$
35. *S*, then *A*, then *S*. $\frac{6}{720}$ or $\frac{1}{120}$
36. *T*, then *S*, then *C*. $\frac{9}{720}$ or $\frac{1}{80}$
37. *S*, then *T*, then *A*. $\frac{9}{720}$ or $\frac{1}{80}$
38. *S*, then *T*, then *I*. $\frac{18}{720}$ or $\frac{1}{40}$
39. *A*, then *C*, then *T*. $\frac{3}{720}$ or $\frac{1}{240}$
40. *I*, then *A*, then *S*. $\frac{6}{720}$ or $\frac{1}{120}$

BREAK TIME

Trace these figures without taking your pencil from the paper and without crossing any lines.
Answers may vary.

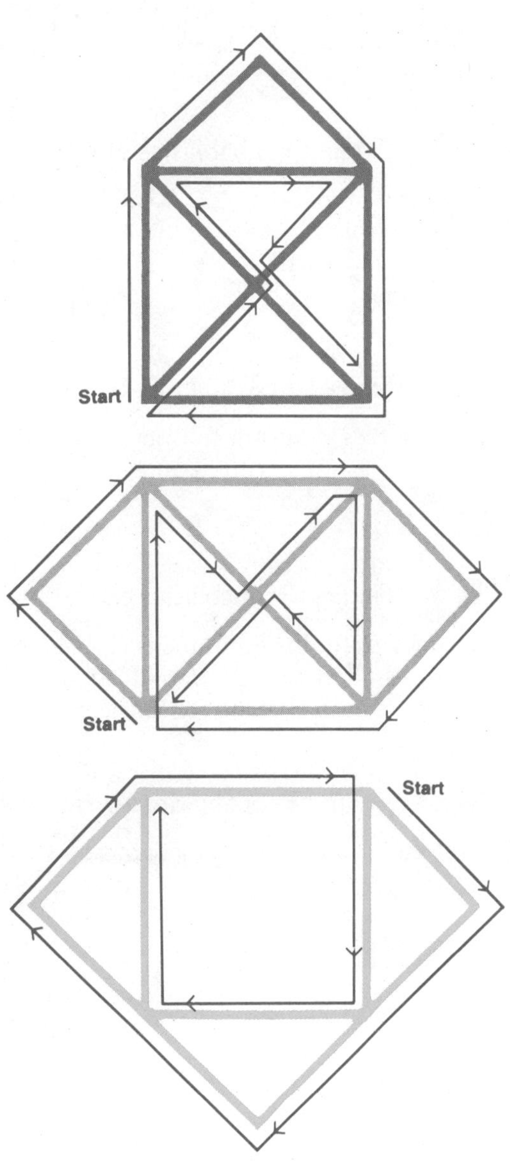

SKILLS POSTTEST

Number of test items - 8

Number missed	1	2	3	4
Percent correct	88	75	63	50

SKILL Finding Probabilities and Predicting Outcomes *pages 194–195*

A Give the probability that the roll of a number cube will show one.
$\frac{1}{6}$

B Give the probability that the roll of a number cube will show one or five.
$\frac{2}{6}$ or $\frac{1}{3}$

C Give the expected number of rolls that will result in one if a number cube were rolled 42 times.
7

SKILL Finding Probabilities by Using Tree Diagrams *pages 196–197*

D Make a tree diagram to find the number of outcomes for tossing two coins.
4 possible outcomes
See below.

E Give the probability of getting two tails if two coins were tossed.
$\frac{1}{4}$

SKILL Finding Probabilities by Using Multiplication *pages 198–199*

F Multiply to find the number of possible outcomes for choosing a two-digit code number if each digit is chosen at random.
100

G Give the probability that a two-digit code number chosen at random will be 34 or 05.
$\frac{2}{100}$ or $\frac{1}{50}$

SKILL Finding Probabilities Involving Dependent Events *pages 200–201*

H Give the probability of drawing two cards at random that show *L* if the first card is *not* replaced before the second draw.

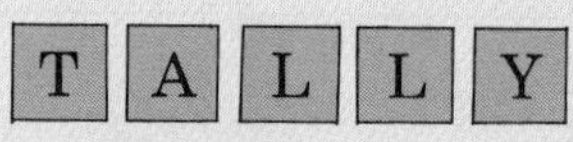

$\frac{2}{20}$ or $\frac{1}{10}$

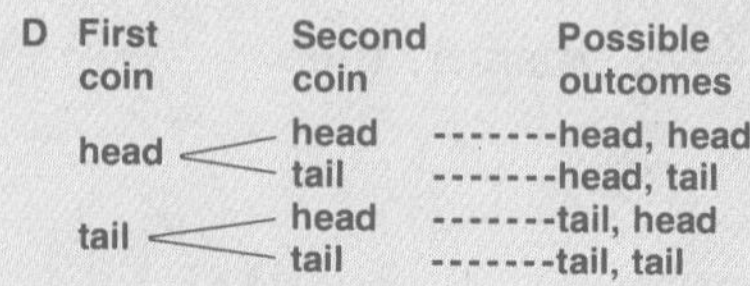

Problem Solving

CONSUMER APPLICATIONS

Objective: Solve problems involving probability.

In this lesson students find the probability of getting a certain license plate.

Finding Probabilities for License Plates

Gus Simpson ordered his license plates. In his area, license plates show two letters followed by four digits, such as **GS 3167.**

1. How many license plates are possible? (Complete Row 1 in the chart below to find the number of possible outcomes.)
6,760,000

What is the probability that Gus will get
See Additional Answers on page T46.

2. GS 3167? (1 favorable outcome)
3. GS 3167 or GS 1978? (2 favorable outcomes)
4. GS followed by any digits? (Complete Row 2 to find favorable outcomes.)
5. any letters followed by 1234 in order? (Complete Row 3.)
6. both letters alike and all digits alike, as in DD 2222? (Complete Row 4.)
7. any letters followed by a number ending in 3? (Complete Row 5.)
8. both letters alike followed by a number greater than 4999? (Complete Row 6.)
9. HI followed by a number greater than 2999?
10. GO followed by all digits alike?

	Number of choices for first letter		Number of choices for second letter		Number of choices for first digit		Number of choices for second digit		Number of choices for third digit		Number of choices for fourth digit		Number of outcomes
Row 1	26	×	26	×	10	×	10	×	10	×	10	=	6,760,000
Row 2	1	×	1	×	10	×	10	×	10	×	10	=	10,000
Row 3	26	×	26	×	1	×	1	×	1	×	1	=	676
Row 4	26	×	1	×	10	×	1	×	1	×	1	=	260
Row 5	26	×	26	×	10	×	10	×	10	×	1	=	676,000
Row 6	26	×	1	×	5	×	10	×	10	×	10	=	130,000

Problem Solving

CAREER APPLICATIONS

Objective: Solve problems involving probability.

In this lesson students use sales records to estimate the probability of selling a certain type of chowder and then use that probability to find expected sales.

Concession Salesperson

Career Cluster: Business Contact
Andrew Scholl sells cups of chowder at a concession near the beach.

1. Andrew kept a record of daily sales at different outdoor temperatures. Find the total for each temperature.

	Number of cups sold at these outdoor temperatures				
Type of chowder	0°C Cold	8°C Cool	16°C Mild	24°C Warm	32°C Hot
Clam	50	35	30	11	6
Oyster	29	22	20	16	9
Shrimp	23	15	14	13	8
Lobster	26	20	16	10	3
Crab meat	28	21	18	9	7
Conch	13	11	9	4	1
Salmon	19	14	10	8	5
Totals	188	138	117	71	39

Actual data can be used to estimate probabilities.

Use Andrew's chart to estimate the probability that a cup of clam chowder will be sold when the outdoor temperature is about 24°C.

$$\frac{\text{Number of favorable outcomes}}{\text{Number of possible outcomes}} = \frac{\text{Number of cups of clam chowder sold when 24°C}}{\text{Total number of cups of chowder sold when 24°C}} = \frac{11}{71}$$

Estimate the probability that a cup of the given type of chowder will be sold at the given outdoor temperature.

2. Oyster, 32°C $\frac{9}{39}$ or $\frac{3}{13}$ **4.** Conch, 24°C $\frac{4}{71}$

3. Clam, 16°C $\frac{30}{117}$ or $\frac{10}{39}$ **5.** Lobster, 0°C $\frac{26}{188}$ or $\frac{13}{94}$

Andrew has permission to sell chowder at an outdoor art fair. The temperature will be about 8°C. Use the data in Andrew's chart to estimate the probability that a cup of the given type of chowder will be sold.

6. Clam $\frac{35}{138}$ **10.** Crab meat $\frac{21}{138}$ or $\frac{7}{46}$

7. Oyster $\frac{22}{138}$ or $\frac{11}{69}$ **11.** Conch $\frac{11}{138}$

8. Shrimp $\frac{15}{138}$ or $\frac{5}{46}$ **12.** Salmon $\frac{14}{138}$ or $\frac{7}{69}$

9. Lobster $\frac{20}{138}$ or $\frac{10}{69}$

Andrew expects to sell 500 cups of chowder at the art fair. How many of these can he expect to be clam chowder? Round the answer up to the next whole number.

Probability of clam chowder		Total number of cups		Expected number of cups of clam chowder		
$\frac{35}{138}$	$\times$	500	$=$	$126\frac{112}{138}$	$\approx$	127

How many of the 500 cups of chowder can he expect to be

13. oyster? 80 cups **16.** crab meat? 77 cups

14. shrimp? 55 cups **17.** conch? 40 cups

15. lobster? 73 cups **18.** salmon? 51 cups

It takes 1 kilogram of seafood to make 20 cups of chowder. How many kilograms of clams will Andrew need for the art fair? Round up to the next whole number.

Expected number of cups of clam chowder		Number of cups of chowder per kilogram of seafood		Number of kilograms of clams needed		
127	$\div$	20	$=$	6.35	$\approx$	7

How many kilograms of each of these types of seafood will Andrew need for the art fair?

19. Oyster 4 kg **22.** Crab meat 4 kg

20. Shrimp 3 kg **23.** Conch 2 kg

21. Lobster 4 kg **24.** Salmon 3 kg

Problem Solving

CAREER APPLICATIONS

Objective: Solve problems involving probability.

In this lesson students use a mortality table to predict the probability of dying at a given age and to predict the probability, in decimal form, that a person of a given age will live to another age.

Insurance Actuary

Career Cluster: Business Detail

Jo Tashi is an actuary and uses mortality tables to determine life insurance rates.

Use the table on page 207 to find the probability of dying at age 10.

$$\frac{\text{Number of deaths at age 10}}{\text{Number living at age 10}} = \frac{12}{9806}$$

Give the probability of dying at

See Additional Answers on page T46.

1. age 2. **4.** age 35. **7.** age 75.

2. age 11. **5.** age 42. **8.** age 80.

3. age 20. **6.** age 65. **9.** age 90.

Probabilities are expressed in the table as deaths per 1000. For example, at age 10:

$\frac{12}{9806} \approx \frac{1.2}{1000}$ or 1.2 deaths per 1000

Use the table to tell at what age or ages

10. the number of deaths per 1000 is highest.
Age 99

11. the number of deaths per 1000 is lowest.
Ages 7–12

12. the number of deaths is highest.
Ages 75 and 76

13. the number of deaths is lowest.
Age 99

What is the probability that a 16-year-old person will live to age 80?

$$\frac{\text{Number living at age 80}}{\text{Number living at age 16}} = \frac{2626}{9729}$$

This fraction can be written as a decimal to the nearest hundredth.

$\frac{2626}{9729} \approx 0.27$ $\qquad 9729\overline{)2626.000}$ gives $0.269 \approx 0.27$

The probability that a 16-year-old will live to age 80 is about 0.27.

Use a fraction and a decimal to the nearest hundredth to give the probability that

See Additional Answers on page T46.

14. a 20-year-old will live to age 30.

15. a 60-year-old will live to age 80.

16. a 4-year-old will live to age 50.

17. a 15-year-old will live to age 30.

18. a 40-year-old will live to age 42.

19. an 80-year-old will live to age 85.

20. a 10-year-old will live to age 75.

See pages 28–29 of
Problem-Solving Masters.

Table of Mortality

Age	Number living	Deaths each year	Deaths per 1000	Age	Number living	Deaths each year	Deaths per 1000	Age	Number living	Deaths each year	Deaths per 1000
0	10,000	71	7.1	34	9396	23	2.4	67	6356	242	38.1
1	9929	17	1.7	35	9373	23	2.5	68	6114	255	41.7
2	9912	15	1.5	36	9350	24	2.6	69	5859	267	45.6
3	9897	15	1.5	37	9326	27	2.9	70	5592	278	49.7
4	9982	14	1.4	38	9299	28	3.0	71	5314	288	54.2
5	9868	13	1.3	39	9271	30	3.2	72	5026	295	58.7
6	9855	13	1.3	40	9241	33	3.6	73	4731	299	63.2
7	9842	12	1.2	41	9208	35	3.8	74	4432	302	68.1
8	9830	12	1.2	42	9173	38	4.1	75	4130	303	73.4
9	9818	12	1.2	43	9135	41	4.5	76	3827	303	79.2
10	9806	12	1.2	44	9094	45	4.9	77	3524	302	85.7
11	9794	12	1.2	45	9049	48	5.3	78	3222	300	93.1
12	9782	12	1.2	46	9001	53	5.9	79	2922	296	101.3
13	9770	13	1.3	47	8948	57	6.4	80	2626	288	109.7
14	9757	14	1.4	48	8891	62	7.0	81	2338	279	119.3
15	9743	14	1.4	49	8829	67	7.6	82	2059	266	129.2
16	9729	15	1.5	50	8762	73	8.3	83	1793	250	139.4
17	9714	16	1.6	51	8689	79	9.1	84	1543	232	150.4
18	9698	16	1.6	52	8610	86	10.0	85	1311	211	158.5
19	9682	17	1.8	53	8524	93	10.9	86	1100	190	172.7
20	9665	17	1.8	54	8431	100	11.9	87	910	169	185.7
21	9648	18	1.9	55	8331	108	13.0	88	741	147	198.4
22	9630	18	1.9	56	8223	117	14.2	89	594	126	212.1
23	9612	18	1.9	57	8106	126	15.5	90	468	107	228.6
24	9594	18	1.9	58	7980	135	16.9	91	361	89	246.5
25	9576	19	2.0	59	7845	146	18.6	92	272	72	264.7
26	9557	19	2.0	60	7699	157	20.4	93	200	58	290.0
27	9538	19	2.0	61	7542	168	22.2	94	142	45	316.9
28	9519	19	2.0	62	7374	179	24.3	95	97	34	350.5
29	9500	20	2.1	63	7195	191	26.5	96	63	25	396.8
30	9480	20	2.1	64	7004	203	29.0	97	38	19	500.0
31	9460	21	2.2	65	6801	216	31.8	98	19	13	684.2
32	9439	21	2.2	66	6585	229	34.8	99	6	6	1000.0
33	9418	22	2.3								

This table is a simplified version of the Table of Mortality, Commissioners 1958 Standard Ordinary which is still in use today.

Problem Solving

DEVELOPING STRATEGIES

Objective: Solve problems by using a simpler case.

In this lesson students find the number of different cards possible for the games of **OK** and **WIN**.

Tactic: Using a Simpler Case

Paula Jeffers works for a company that develops children's games. She is studying the games of **OK** and **WIN.**

In the game of **OK** each player has a card similar to the one shown. A number cannot appear more than once on a card and no two cards are the same. A caller spins a spinner and calls out the number. Any player who has the number covers it with a marker. The first person to have two markers in a row, column, or diagonal calls out "OK" and wins the game.

O	K
5	8
2	10

The game of **WIN** is played the same way, but each card has three rows and three columns.

Problem

How many different cards are possible in the game of **OK** if the numbers 1–5 are used for the **O**-column and 6–10 are used for the **K**-column?

Solution

Remind students that these are dependent events since a number cannot appear more than once on a single card.

The following questions show Paula's strategy for solving the problem. Her tactic was to use a simpler case.

Suppose the numbers 1 and 2 are used in the **O**-column and 3 and 4 are used in the **K**-column.

a. How many different numbers can be placed in the top space of the **O**-column? 2

b. For each number in the top space of the **O**-column, how many different numbers can appear in the bottom space of the **O**-column? 1

c. How many types of **O**-columns are possible? $2 \times 1 = 2$

d. How many types of **K**-columns are possible? $2 \times 1 = 2$

e. How many different cards are possible? $2 \times 2 = 4$

f. If the numbers 1–5 are used for the **O**-column and 6–10 are used for the **K**-column, how many different cards are possible? Use questions **a–d** for this case. $20 \times 20 = 400$

Conclusion: If the numbers 1–5 are used for the **O**-column and 6–10 are used for the **K**-column, 400 different cards are possible.

Related Problems

Suppose the numbers 1–10 are used for the **O**-column and 11–20 are used for the **K**-column.

1. How many types of **O**-columns are possible?
90
2. How many types of **K**-columns are possible?
90
3. How many different cards are possible?
8100 cards

In the **WIN** game each player has a card similar to the one shown. Suppose the numbers 1–5 are used for the **W**-column, 6–10 are used for the **I**-column, and 11–15 are used for the **N**-column.

W	I	N
3	9	15
1	10	12
5	7	14

4. How many different numbers can be placed in the top space of the **W**-column?
5
5. For each number in the top space of the **W**-column, how many different numbers can appear in the middle space of the **W**-column?
4
6. How many different numbers can appear in the bottom space of the **W**-column when the top and middle spaces are filled?
3
7. How many types of **W**-columns are possible?
60
8. How many types of **I**-columns are possible?
60
9. How many types of **N**-columns are possible?
60
10. How many different cards are possible?
216,000 cards

Suppose the numbers 1–10 are used for the **W**-column, 11–20 are used for the **I**-column, and 21–30 are used for the **N**-column.

11. How many types of **W**-columns are possible?
720
12. How many types of **I**-columns are possible?
720
13. How many types of **N**-columns are possible?
720
14. How many different cards are possible?
373,248,000 cards

Extension

15. How many different cards are possible in the game of **WIN** that is described for Problems 11–14 if a "FREE" space appears in the middle of the **I**-column?
46,656,000 cards

CHAPTER 9 TEST

Number of test items - 12						
Number missed	1	2	3	4	5	6
Percent correct	92	83	75	67	58	50

A **1.** Give the probability that the roll of a number cube will show five.
$\frac{1}{6}$

B **2.** Give the probability that the roll of a number cube will show two or six.
$\frac{2}{6}$ or $\frac{1}{3}$

C **3.** Give the expected number of rolls that will result in six if a number cube were rolled 24 times.
4

D **4.** Make a tree diagram to find the number of possible outcomes for tossing a coin and a number cube.
12 possible outcomes See below.

E **5.** If a coin and a number cube are tossed, give the probability that the coin will show heads and the number cube will show five.
$\frac{1}{12}$

F **6.** Multiply to find the number of possible outcomes for choosing a four-digit code number if each digit is chosen at random.
10,000

G **7.** Give the probability that a four-digit code number chosen at random will be 0495 or 7326.
$\frac{2}{10,000}$ or $\frac{1}{5000}$

H **8.** Give the probability of drawing two of these cards at random that show *S* if the first card is *not* replaced before the second draw.

T	O	S	S	E	S

$\frac{6}{30}$ or $\frac{1}{5}$

9. How many license plates are possible that show two letters followed by three digits?
676,000 license plates

10. If the probability that a cup of oyster chowder will be sold is $\frac{29}{188}$ and if a total of 400 cups of chowder will be sold, about how many cups of the total sold will be oyster chowder? Round up to the next whole number.
62 cups

11. If there are 278 deaths at age 70 for every 5592 people living at age 70, give the probability as a fraction that a person will die at age 70.
$\frac{278}{5592}$ or $\frac{139}{2796}$

12. The game **OK** uses cards similar to the one shown. If the numbers 1–7 are used for the **O**-column and 8–14 are used for the **K**-column, how many different cards are possible? (Remember, a number cannot appear more than once on a card.)
1764 cards

O	K
7	12
5	10

4. Coin	Number cube	Possible outcomes
head	1	head, 1
	2	head, 2
	3	head, 3
	4	head, 4
	5	head, 5
	6	head, 6
tail	1	tail, 1
	2	tail, 2
	3	tail, 3
	4	tail, 4
	5	tail, 5
	6	tail, 6

See pages 21–22 of the *Test Masters* for an alternate form of the Chapter 9 Test.
For a test on Unit 3, see pages T60–T61 of this book and pages 23–24 of the *Test Masters*.

SKILLS TUNE-UP

Multiplying Whole Numbers, pages 25-36

1. 19×32 608
2. 30×700 21,000
3. 78×25 1950
4. 48×512 24,576
5. 4×1821 7284
6. 74×46 3404
7. 9×1362 12,258
8. 43×440 18,920
9. 4×7000 28,000
10. 37×4888 180,856
11. 127×326 41,402
12. 17×3545 60,265
13. 40×1000 40,000
14. 33×790 26,070
15. 28×623 17,444
16. 13×3332 43,316
17. 4×752 3008
18. 363×1535 557,205
19. $800 \times 20{,}000$ 16,000,000
20. $83{,}075 \times 23$ 1,910,725
21. 176×2188 385,088
22. 39×6003 234,117
23. 36×17 612
24. 940×45 42,300
25. 634×9276 5,880,984
26. 909×99 89,991
27. 394×654 257,676

Multiplying and Dividing Decimals, pages 95-108

1. 2.9×43.4 125.86
2. 400×0.78 312
3. 3.4×0.023 0.0782
4. 0.0037×0.425 0.0015725
5. 0.07×0.003 0.00021
6. 0.41×0.94 0.3854
7. 4.5×1200 5400
8. 0.0015×6.5255 0.00978825
9. 0.005×0.02 0.0001
10. $0.105 \div 0.07$ 1.5
11. $29.7 \div 9$ 3.3
12. $25.08 \div 57$ 0.44
13. $0.002 \div 0.025$ 0.08
14. $0.423 \div 9$ 0.047
15. $2.365 \div 47.3$ 0.05
16. $984.2 \div 518$ 1.9
17. $229.77 \div 3.7$ 62.1
18. $0.00805 \div 0.575$ 0.014

Round each quotient to the nearest hundredth.

19. $3.128 \div 6.7$ 0.47
20. $0.771 \div 0.53$ 1.45
21. $0.273 \div 0.019$ 14.37
22. $58.31 \div 2.17$ 26.87
23. $3.92 \div 0.057$ 68.77
24. $5.46 \div 0.0027$ 2022.22
25. $75.9 \div 0.014$ 5421.43

Multiplying and Dividing Fractions and Mixed Numbers, pages 149-160

1. $\frac{5}{9} \times \frac{2}{5}$ $\frac{2}{9}$
2. $5 \times 1\frac{1}{3}$ $6\frac{2}{3}$
3. $\frac{5}{8} \times 40$ 25
4. $2\frac{1}{2} \times \frac{1}{10}$ $\frac{1}{4}$
5. $\frac{15}{22} \times \frac{11}{20}$ $\frac{3}{8}$
6. $\frac{5}{9} \times \frac{27}{32}$ $\frac{15}{32}$
7. $3\frac{8}{9} \times 2\frac{1}{10}$ $8\frac{1}{6}$
8. $\frac{7}{12} \times 5$ $2\frac{11}{12}$
9. $1\frac{1}{6} \times 24$ 28
10. $\frac{5}{7} \div \frac{4}{5}$ $\frac{25}{28}$
11. $5\frac{1}{3} \div 8$ $\frac{2}{3}$
12. $\frac{21}{30} \div 1\frac{1}{6}$ $\frac{3}{5}$
13. $28 \div 3\frac{1}{2}$ 8
14. $4\frac{3}{8} \div 6\frac{1}{4}$ $\frac{7}{10}$
15. $1\frac{1}{4} \div 7\frac{1}{2}$ $\frac{1}{6}$
16. $2\frac{3}{4} \div 1\frac{3}{4}$ $1\frac{4}{7}$
17. $2 \div 7\frac{3}{5}$ $\frac{5}{19}$
18. $\frac{1}{40} \div \frac{1}{7}$ $\frac{7}{40}$
19. $7\frac{1}{2} \div \frac{1}{4}$ 30

CALCULATOR APPLICATIONS

At the track meet, Viho jumped 6 feet $8\frac{1}{2}$ inches. Rick jumped 7 feet $2\frac{1}{4}$ inches. How much higher did Rick jump than Viho?

Change each height to inches and write in decimal form.

Since 1 foot = 12 inches, multiply the number of feet by 12.

7 feet $2\frac{1}{4}$ inches
84 inches + $2\frac{1}{4}$ inches

Change the mixed number to a decimal by dividing the numerator by the denominator and adding the whole number. Then add to find the total number of inches.

$2\frac{1}{4} = 2.25$ $\quad$ $84 + 2.25 = 86.25$

7 feet $2\frac{1}{4}$ inches = 86.25 inches

6 feet $8\frac{1}{2}$ inches = 80.5 inches

Subtract to find the difference.

$86.25 - 80.5 = 5.75$

Rick jumped 5.75 inches higher than Viho.

Calculator Suggestion: If your calculator has memory keys, try this key sequence.

Press: 7 [×] 12 [=] [M+] 1 [÷] 4 [+] 2 [=] [M+] 6 [×] 12 [=] [M−] 1 [÷] 2 [+] 8 [=] [M−] [MR]

Display: 5.75

Answer: 5.75 inches

If your display does not show 5.75, consult the instruction book for your calculator to find out how the memory keys work. Be sure to clear the memory before starting each problem.

Find each difference in inches.

1. High jump
   Elena—6 feet $1\frac{1}{4}$ inches
   Stephanie—5 feet $2\frac{3}{4}$ inches
   10.5 inches
2. Shot-put
   Tanya—57 feet $9\frac{1}{2}$ inches
   Sharda—42 feet $10\frac{3}{4}$ inches
   178.75 inches
3. Shot-put
   Ralph—66 feet $8\frac{1}{4}$ inches
   George—59 feet $10\frac{1}{4}$ inches
   82 inches
4. Long jump
   Russ—23 feet 5 inches
   Bruce—19 feet $7\frac{1}{2}$ inches
   45.5 inches
5. Discus throw
   Ruth—176 feet $\frac{3}{4}$ inch
   Helen—131 feet $8\frac{1}{2}$ inches
   532.25 inches
6. Discus throw
   Arnie—198 feet $3\frac{1}{2}$ inches
   Kurt—94 feet 5 inches
   1246.5 inches
7. Javelin throw
   Ellen—149 feet $\frac{1}{4}$ inch
   Barbara—142 feet $8\frac{1}{2}$ inches
   75.75 inches
8. Javelin throw
   Victor—190 feet $7\frac{1}{4}$ inches
   Earl—181 feet $\frac{3}{4}$ inch
   114.5 inches
9. Pole vault
   Elaine—10 feet $7\frac{3}{4}$ inches
   Millie—7 feet 8 inches
   35.75 inches
10. Pole vault
    Frank—12 feet $1\frac{3}{4}$ inches
    Leroy—9 feet $\frac{1}{2}$ inch
    37.25 inches

COMPUTER LITERACY

The GO TO and IF . . . THEN Statements

The BASIC symbols for equality and inequality are as follows:

= (equal)	<> (not equal)
< (less than)	<= (less than or equal)
> (greater than)	>= (greater than or equal)

The GO TO statement tells the computer to skip ahead or to go back to a specified line. In Program A, line 30 sends the computer to line 10 where another value for X is to be entered. The user first typed 4 for X, then 10. The program would continue indefinitely, but the third time the question mark appeared, the program was stopped by the user.

```
1. ? 7
     35
   ? 12
     60
   ? 16
     80
   ? 22
    110
   ? 30
    150
   ? 48
    240
   ? 65
    325
   ?
```

Program A

Input	Output
`10 INPUT X`	`? 4`
`20 PRINT (2*X)+(3*X)`	`20`
`30 GO TO 10`	`? 10`
`40 END`	`50`
	`?`

Consult your manual to learn how to stop this program.

The IF . . . THEN statement transfers the computer to a specified line if a specified condition is true. If the condition is false, the computer goes to the next line of the program. In line 30 of Program B, if A and B are the same value, the program sends the computer to line 90 and the program will end. In line 40, the computer is sent to line 70 if A is greater than B, and the computer will go to line 50 if A is not greater than B. The user first typed 4 for A and 8 for B; then 7 for A and 3 for B; and then 5 for A and 5 for B.

Program B

Input	Output
`10 INPUT A`	`? 4`
`20 INPUT B`	`? 8`
`30 IF A=B THEN 90`	`4 < 8`
`40 IF A>B THEN 70`	`? 7`
`50 PRINT A;"<";B`	`? 3`
`60 GO TO 10`	`7 > 3`
`70 PRINT A;">";B`	`? 5`
`80 GO TO 10`	`? 5`
`90 END`	

```
2. ? 5
   ? 8
    5 < 8
   ? 6
   ? 2
    6 > 2
   ? 15
   ? 12
    15 > 12
   ? 65
   ? 40
    65 > 40
   ? 42
   ? 42
```

1. Give the output for Program A. Use 7, 12, 16, 22, 30, 48, and 65 for X.
   See left.
2. Give the output for Program B when A = 5, B =8; A = 6, B = 2; A = 15, B = 12; A = 65, B = 40; A = 42, B = 42.
   See above.
3. Give the output for this program. Use 3, 12, 26, 45, 63, and 0 for N.

```
10 INPUT N
20 IF N=0 THEN 80
30 IF N>=20 THEN 60
40 PRINT 5*N
50 GO TO 10
60 PRINT N
70 GO TO 10
80 END
```

```
? 3
 15
? 12
 60
? 26
 26
? 45
 45
? 63
 63
? 0
```

4. Rewrite Program A using an IF . . . THEN statement so that the program will not continue indefinitely.
   See Additional Answers on page T47.
5. Write a program similar to Program B which includes PRINT statements containing A;"<";B, A;">";B, and A;"=";B.
   See Additional Answers on page T47.

 Ratio, Percent, and Statistics

CHAPTER 10 Ratio, Proportion, and Similarity

SKILLS PRETEST

Number of test items - 8

Number missed	1	2	3	4
Percent correct	88	75	63	50

SKILL Writing Ratios *pages 216–217*

A Write the ratio of records to dollars.

3 records for $20 **$\frac{3}{20}$**

B Give the next ratio in this list.

$\frac{5}{7} = \frac{10}{14} = \frac{15}{21}$ **$\frac{20}{28}$**

SKILL Solving Proportions *pages 218–219*

C Find cross-products. Then tell whether these ratios are equal. $\frac{8}{15}$ $\frac{12}{21}$

$168 \neq 180$

D Find the missing number in this proportion. $\frac{4}{10} = \frac{22}{n}$

$n = 55$

SKILL Identifying Similar Figures *pages 220–221*

E Give the letter of the figure that is similar to the figure on the left.

a

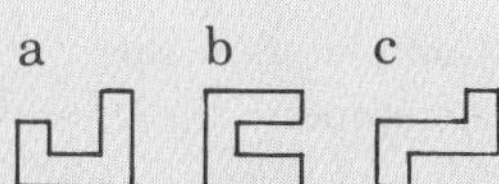

F The triangles are similar. Give 3 pairs of corresponding angles and 3 pairs of corresponding sides.

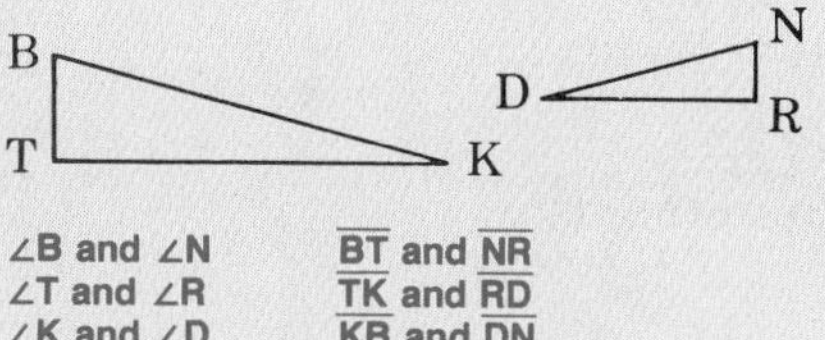

∠B and ∠N
∠T and ∠R
∠K and ∠D

$\overline{BT}$ and $\overline{NR}$
$\overline{TK}$ and $\overline{RD}$
$\overline{KB}$ and $\overline{DN}$

SKILL Finding Missing Sides in Similar Triangles *pages 222–223*

G The triangles are similar. Complete these ratios of the lengths of corresponding sides.

$\frac{16}{▒} = \frac{20}{▒}$

24 **30**

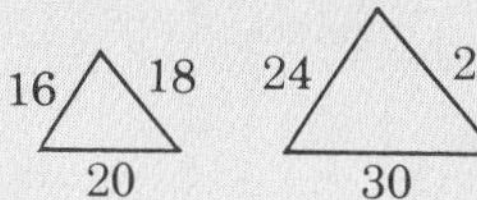

H The triangles are similar. Write a proportion and find n.

Proportions may vary. A sample is given.

60 m 110 m 130 m 48 m n

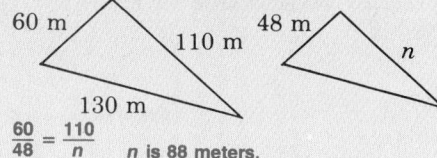

$\frac{60}{48} = \frac{110}{n}$ ***n* is 88 meters.**

Objective: Write ratios and lists of equal ratios.

Writing Ratios

Example A Writing ratios

Write the ratio of pages to hours.

250 pages in 4 hours

$$\frac{250}{4} \begin{array}{l} \longleftarrow \text{Pages} \\ \longleftarrow \text{Hours} \end{array}$$

The **ratio** $\frac{250}{4}$ is read "250 to 4."

Example B Equal ratios

Give the next ratio in this list.

$$\frac{3}{10} = \frac{6}{20} = \frac{9}{30}$$

You can use multiplication to find equal ratios.

$$\frac{3}{10} = \frac{6}{20} = \frac{9}{30} = \frac{12}{40}$$

$$\frac{6}{20} = \frac{2 \times 3}{2 \times 10}, \quad \frac{9}{30} = \frac{3 \times 3}{3 \times 10}, \quad \frac{12}{40} = \frac{4 \times 3}{4 \times 10}$$

$\frac{12}{40}$ is the next ratio in the list.

Point out that students need not always use lists to generate equal ratios. An equal ratio can be found by multiplying or dividing both numbers of a ratio by the same number. For example:

$$\frac{3}{5} = \frac{60}{100} \quad \left(\frac{20 \times 3}{20 \times 5}\right) \qquad \frac{18}{24} = \frac{3}{4} \quad \left(\frac{18 \div 6}{24 \div 6}\right)$$

Exercises

Set A

Write each ratio.

1. 100 kilometers on 12 liters of gasoline

$\frac{100}{12}$ ▒ ⟵ Kilometers / ▒ ⟵ Liters of gasoline

2. 18 girls and 16 boys in the class

$\frac{16}{18}$ ▒ ⟵ Boys / ▒ ⟵ Girls

3. 100 centimeters in 1 meter

$\frac{100}{1}$ ▒ ⟵ Centimeters / ▒ ⟵ Meters

4. 300 milliliters of orange juice and 250 milliliters of grapefruit juice

$\frac{250}{300}$ ▒ ⟵ Milliliters of grapefruit juice / ▒ ⟵ Milliliters of orange juice

5. 60 centimeters high and 21 centimeters wide

$\frac{21}{60}$ ▒ ⟵ Width in centimeters / ▒ ⟵ Height in centimeters

6. 7 completed passes out of 15 attempts

$\frac{7}{15}$ ▒ ⟵ Completed passes / ▒ ⟵ Attempts

7. 7 nickels and 4 dimes

$\frac{4}{7}$ ▒ ⟵ Dimes / ▒ ⟵ Nickels

8. 240 calories in 5 crackers

$\frac{240}{5}$ ▒ ⟵ Calories / ▒ ⟵ Crackers

9. 340 kilometers in 5 hours

$\frac{340}{5}$ $\dfrac{\square}{\square}$ $\begin{matrix}\leftarrow \text{Kilometers}\\ \leftarrow \text{Hours}\end{matrix}$

10. 6 pencils for 29¢

$\frac{6}{29}$ $\dfrac{\square}{\square}$ $\begin{matrix}\leftarrow \text{Pencils}\\ \leftarrow \text{Cents}\end{matrix}$

11. A 35-centimeter post that weighs 15 kilograms

$\frac{35}{15}$ $\dfrac{\square}{\square}$ $\begin{matrix}\leftarrow \text{Length in centimeters}\\ \leftarrow \text{Weight in kilograms}\end{matrix}$

12. 8 heartbeats in 6 seconds

$\frac{8}{6}$ $\dfrac{\square}{\square}$ $\begin{matrix}\leftarrow \text{Heartbeats}\\ \leftarrow \text{Seconds}\end{matrix}$

13. 2 centimeters on a map for an actual distance of 2.5 meters

$\frac{2}{2.5}$ $\dfrac{\square}{\square}$ $\begin{matrix}\leftarrow \text{Centimeters on map}\\ \leftarrow \text{Actual distance in meters}\end{matrix}$

14. 6 batteries for $2.10

$\frac{6}{2.10}$ $\dfrac{\square}{\square}$ $\begin{matrix}\leftarrow \text{Batteries}\\ \leftarrow \text{Dollars}\end{matrix}$

15. 9 turns of a bicycle pedal for 14 turns of the rear wheel

$\frac{9}{14}$ $\dfrac{\square}{\square}$ $\begin{matrix}\leftarrow \text{Pedal turns}\\ \leftarrow \text{Rear-wheel turns}\end{matrix}$

16. 1 centimeter on a model airplane for 32 centimeters on the actual airplane

$\frac{1}{32}$ $\dfrac{\square}{\square}$ $\begin{matrix}\leftarrow \text{Centimeters on model}\\ \leftarrow \text{Centimeters on actual plane}\end{matrix}$

17. 3 drops of red for 4 drops of blue

$\frac{3}{7}$ $\dfrac{\square}{\square}$ $\begin{matrix}\leftarrow \text{Number of red drops}\\ \leftarrow \text{Total number of drops}\end{matrix}$

Set B

Give the next ratio in each list.

1. $\frac{2}{15} = \frac{4}{30} = \frac{6}{45}$ $\frac{8}{60}$

2. $\frac{7}{19} = \frac{14}{38} = \frac{21}{57}$ $\frac{28}{76}$

3. $\frac{8}{5} = \frac{16}{10} = \frac{24}{15}$ $\frac{32}{20}$

4. $\frac{12}{7} = \frac{24}{14} = \frac{36}{21}$ $\frac{48}{28}$

5. $\frac{8}{190} = \frac{16}{380} = \frac{24}{570}$ $\frac{32}{760}$

6. $\frac{6}{140} = \frac{12}{280} = \frac{18}{420}$ $\frac{24}{560}$

7. $\frac{4}{3} = \frac{8}{6} = \frac{12}{9} = \frac{16}{12}$ $\frac{20}{15}$

8. $\frac{4}{9} = \frac{8}{18} = \frac{12}{27} = \frac{16}{36}$ $\frac{20}{45}$

9. $\frac{3}{5} = \frac{6}{10} = \frac{9}{15} = \frac{12}{20}$ $\frac{15}{25}$

10. $\frac{9}{6} = \frac{18}{12} = \frac{27}{18} = \frac{36}{24}$ $\frac{45}{30}$

11. $\frac{15}{13} = \frac{30}{26} = \frac{45}{39} = \frac{60}{52}$ $\frac{75}{65}$

12. $\frac{12}{11} = \frac{24}{22} = \frac{36}{33} = \frac{48}{44}$ $\frac{60}{55}$

13. $\frac{2}{3} = \frac{4}{6} = \frac{6}{9} = \frac{8}{12} = \frac{10}{15}$ $\frac{12}{18}$

14. $\frac{8}{7} = \frac{16}{14} = \frac{24}{21} = \frac{32}{28} = \frac{40}{35}$ $\frac{48}{42}$

Objective: Find a missing number in a proportion by using cross-products.

Solving Proportions

Example C Cross-products

Find cross-products. Then tell whether these ratios are equal.

Point out that these ratios can be found in a list of equal ratios.

$$\frac{2}{5} = \frac{4}{10} = \frac{6}{15} = \frac{8}{20} = \frac{10}{25} = \frac{12}{30} = \frac{14}{35} = \frac{16}{40}$$

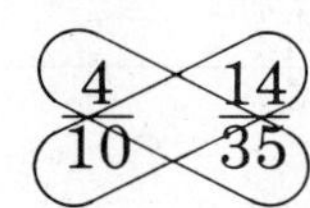

$4 \times 35 \quad 10 \times 14$ — Multiply 4×35 and 10×14 to find **cross-products.**

$140 = 140$ — The cross-products are equal.

$\frac{4}{10} = \frac{14}{35}$ — So the ratios are equal.

If the cross-products were not equal, the ratios would not be equal.

Example D Solving proportions

Find the missing number in this proportion.

$\frac{12}{28} = \frac{k}{42}$ — Equal ratios form a **proportion.**

$12 \times 42 = 28 \times k$ — Multiply to find cross-products.

$504 = 28k$

$\frac{504}{28} = \frac{28k}{28}$ — Divide both sides by 28.

$18 = k$

Exercises

Set C

In each exercise, find cross-products. Then tell whether the ratios are equal.

1. $\frac{3}{6} \quad \frac{2}{5}$ — 15 ≠ 12
2. $\frac{3}{7} \quad \frac{9}{21}$ — 63 = 63
3. $\frac{2}{3} \quad \frac{7}{16}$ — 32 ≠ 21
4. $\frac{3}{8} \quad \frac{10}{27}$ — 81 ≠ 80
5. $\frac{4}{7} \quad \frac{32}{56}$ — 224 = 224
6. $\frac{28}{24} \quad \frac{7}{6}$ — 168 = 168
7. $\frac{6}{11} \quad \frac{40}{77}$ — 462 ≠ 440
8. $\frac{9}{12} \quad \frac{12}{16}$ — 144 = 144
9. $\frac{18}{63} \quad \frac{4}{14}$ — 252 = 252
10. $\frac{30}{9} \quad \frac{40}{12}$ — 360 = 360
11. $\frac{8}{30} \quad \frac{40}{160}$ — 1280 ≠ 1200
12. $\frac{9}{16} \quad \frac{81}{130}$ — 1170 ≠ 1296
13. $\frac{15}{10} \quad \frac{20}{16}$ — 240 ≠ 200
14. $\frac{30}{36} \quad \frac{20}{24}$ — 720 = 720
15. $\frac{24}{42} \quad \frac{36}{60}$ — 1440 ≠ 1512
16. $\frac{14}{22} \quad \frac{21}{33}$ — 462 = 462
17. $\frac{12}{21} \quad \frac{10}{15}$ — 180 ≠ 210
18. $\frac{18}{14} \quad \frac{54}{42}$ — 756 = 756
19. $\frac{0.6}{0.8} \quad \frac{1.5}{2.0}$ — 1.2 = 1.2
20. $\frac{6.5}{1.3} \quad \frac{0.5}{0.1}$ — 0.65 = 0.65
21. $\frac{0.16}{0.36} \quad \frac{0.4}{0.9}$ — 0.144 = 0.144
22. $\frac{0.3}{0.5} \quad \frac{3.0}{4.5}$ — 1.35 ≠ 1.5
23. $\frac{1.1}{0.3} \quad \frac{44}{12}$ — 13.2 = 13.2
24. $\frac{2.4}{0.5} \quad \frac{36}{11}$ — 26.4 ≠ 18
25. $\frac{35.1}{45} \quad \frac{3.9}{5}$ — 175.5 = 175.5
26. $\frac{4.2}{9} \quad \frac{25.2}{50}$ — 210 ≠ 226.8

PROBLEM SOLVING
The applications on pages 225, 228–229, 232–233 may be used anytime after this lesson.

Set D

Find each missing number.

1. $\frac{1}{6} = \frac{t}{78}$ t = 13
2. $\frac{4}{1} = \frac{52}{s}$ s = 13
3. $\frac{1}{17} = \frac{c}{51}$ c = 3
4. $\frac{19}{1} = \frac{76}{x}$ x = 4
5. $\frac{2}{3} = \frac{b}{42}$ b = 28
6. $\frac{5}{7} = \frac{v}{91}$ v = 65
7. $\frac{4}{18} = \frac{10}{n}$ n = 45
8. $\frac{8}{50} = \frac{20}{x}$ x = 125
9. $\frac{6}{21} = \frac{a}{70}$ a = 20
10. $\frac{c}{18} = \frac{10}{4}$ c = 45
11. $\frac{10}{t} = \frac{8}{28}$ t = 35
12. $\frac{15}{g} = \frac{6}{10}$ g = 25
13. $\frac{26}{13} = \frac{8}{r}$ r = 4
14. $\frac{68}{36} = \frac{f}{9}$ f = 17
15. $\frac{4}{g} = \frac{92}{23}$ g = 1
16. $\frac{9}{b} = \frac{57}{19}$ b = 3
17. $\frac{20}{25} = \frac{d}{45}$ d = 36
18. $\frac{k}{40} = \frac{14}{16}$ k = 35
19. $\frac{12}{20} = \frac{n}{25}$ n = 15
20. $\frac{h}{12} = \frac{45}{18}$ h = 30
21. $\frac{75}{100} = \frac{30}{x}$ x = 40
22. $\frac{102}{17} = \frac{36}{d}$ d = 6
23. $\frac{0.7}{0.9} = \frac{k}{36}$ k = 28
24. $\frac{18}{a} = \frac{4.8}{5.6}$ a = 21
25. $\frac{y}{27} = \frac{1.6}{2.4}$ y = 18
26. $\frac{2.4}{2.8} = \frac{18}{a}$ a = 21
27. $\frac{0.4}{0.9} = \frac{4.8}{e}$ e = 10.8
28. $\frac{w}{0.16} = \frac{0.15}{0.40}$ w = 0.06

See Skills File, page 422, for more practice.

BREAK TIME

With a 7-minute timer and an 11-minute timer, find the *quickest* way to time the boiling of an egg for 15 minutes.

Start both timers at the same time the egg is placed in boiling water. When the sand stops in the 7-minute timer, turn it over. When the sand stops in the 11-minute timer, turn over the 7-minute timer again. When the sand stops in the 7-minute timer, 15 minutes will have elapsed.

Objective: Identify similar figures and name corresponding angles and sides.

Identifying Similar Figures

Example E Identifying similar figures

Give the letter of the figure that is similar to the figure on the left.

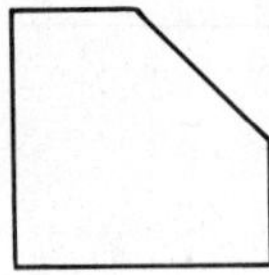

a

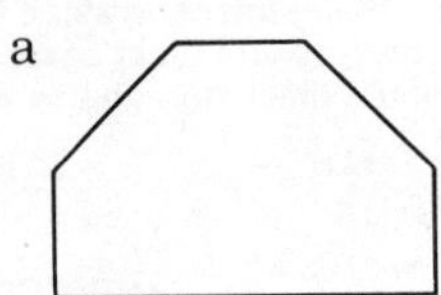

b

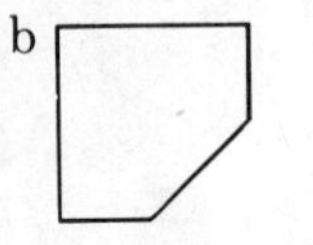

c

Figure b is similar to the figure on the left.

Similar figures have the same shape but not necessarily the same size.

Example F Naming corresponding parts of similar triangles

The triangles are similar. Give 3 pairs of corresponding angles and 3 pairs of corresponding sides.

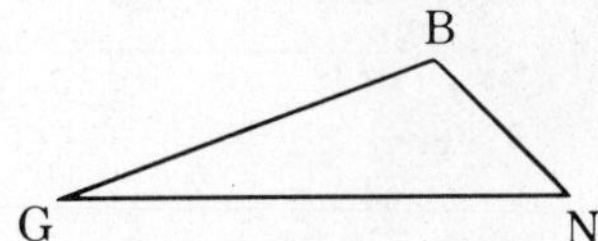

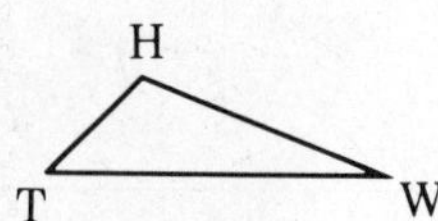

Corresponding angles	Corresponding sides
$\angle G$ and $\angle W$	$\overline{GB}$ and $\overline{WH}$
$\angle B$ and $\angle H$	$\overline{BN}$ and $\overline{HT}$
$\angle N$ and $\angle T$	$\overline{GN}$ and $\overline{WT}$

$\angle G$ means "angle G."

$\overline{GB}$ means "segment GB."

Exercises

Set E

In each exercise, give the letter of the figure that is similar to the figure on the left.

1. b

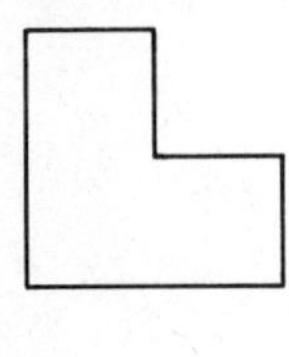

a

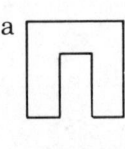

b

c

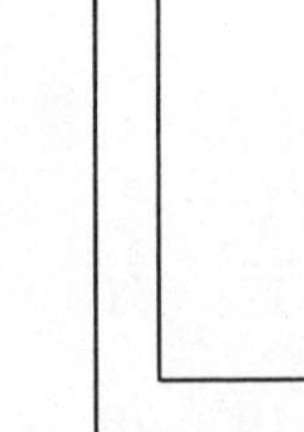

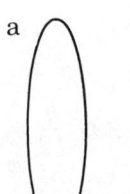

2. c

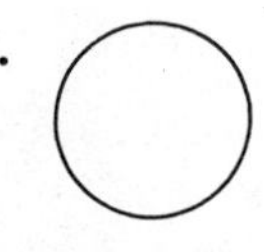

a

b

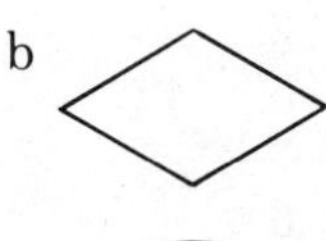

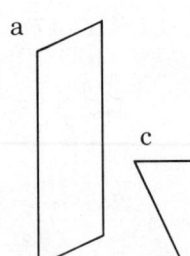

c

3. c

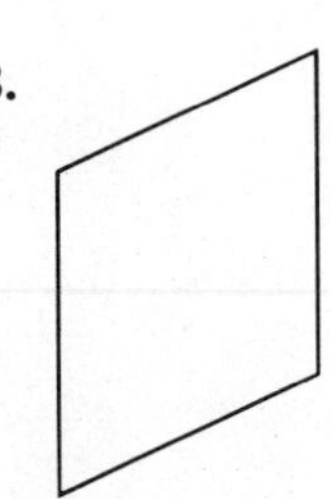

a

b

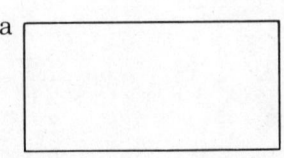

c

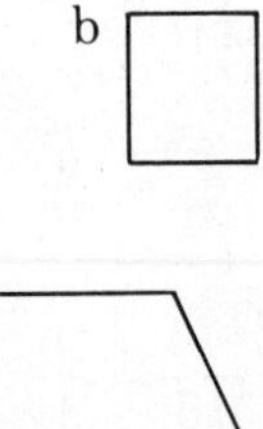

4. a

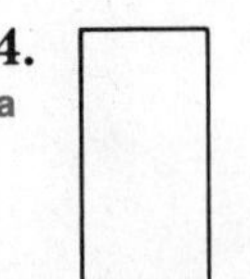

a

b

c

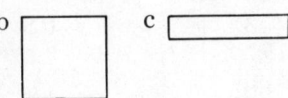

5. b

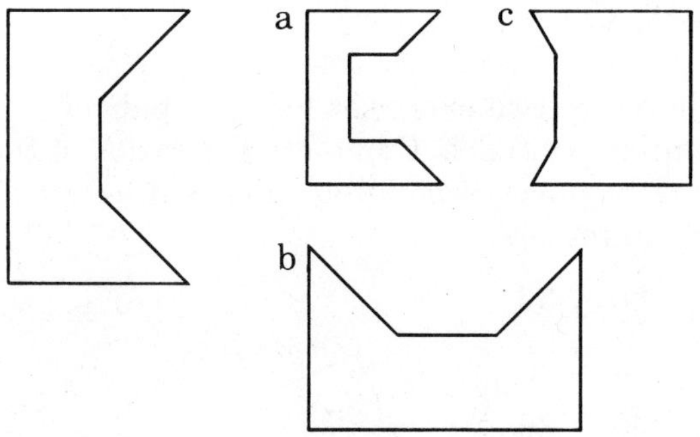

a c

b

6. b

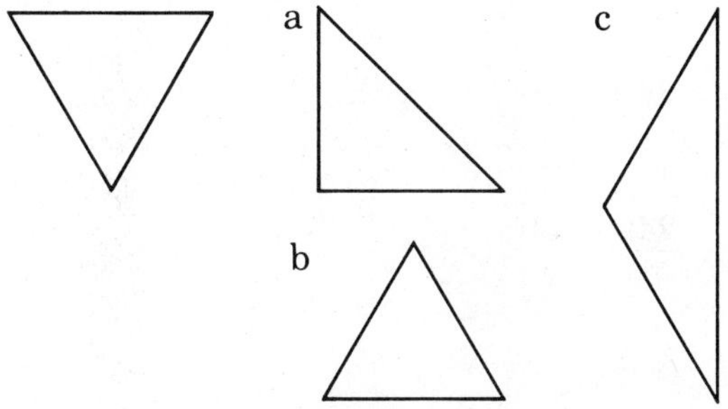

a c

b

7. a

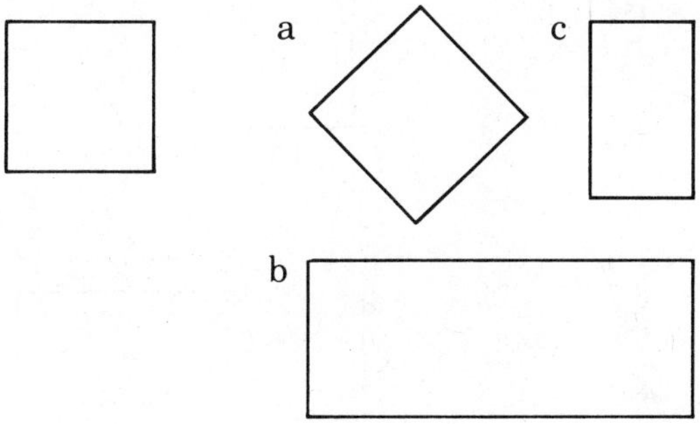

a c

b

8. c

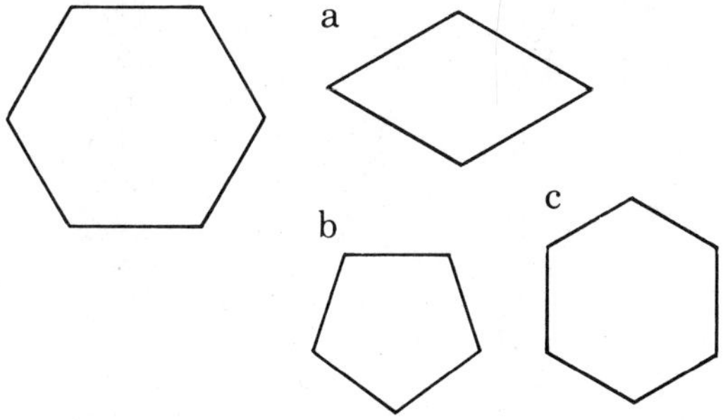

a

b c

Set F

It may help some students to think of corresponding sides as sides opposite corresponding angles.

In each exercise, the triangles are similar. For each exercise, give 3 pairs of corresponding angles and 3 pairs of corresponding sides.

1.

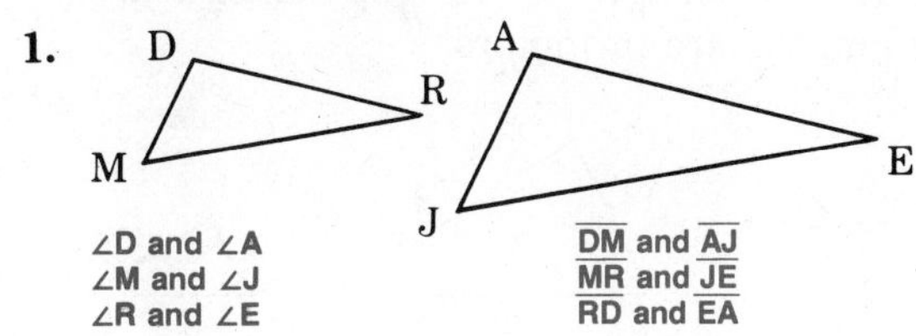

2.

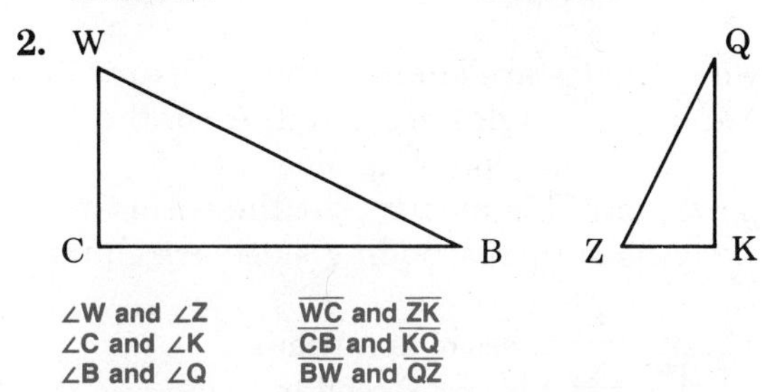

3.

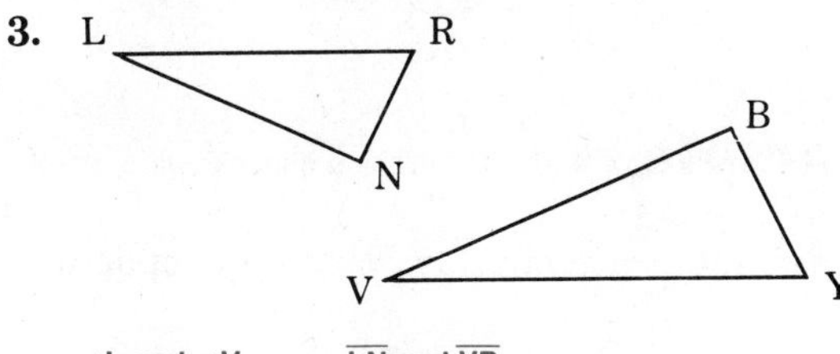

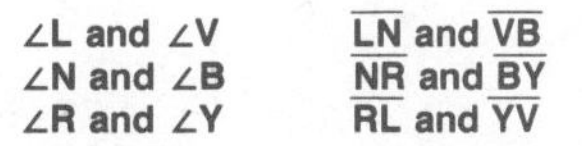

$\overline{LN}$ and $\overline{VB}$
$\overline{NR}$ and $\overline{BY}$
$\overline{RL}$ and $\overline{YV}$

4.

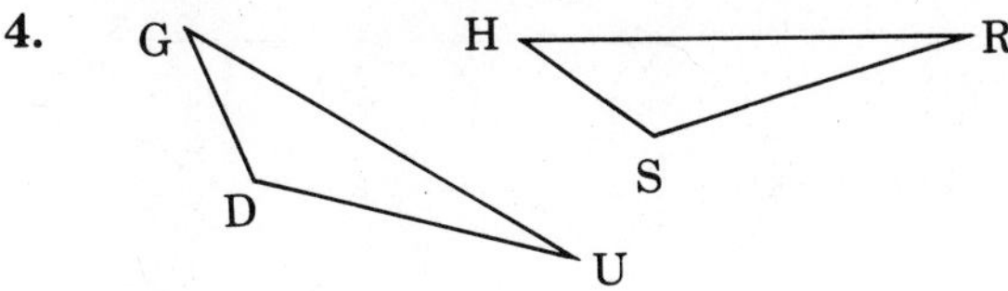

∠G and ∠H
∠D and ∠S
∠U and ∠R

$\overline{GD}$ and $\overline{HS}$
$\overline{DU}$ and $\overline{SR}$
$\overline{UG}$ and $\overline{RH}$

5. T B W

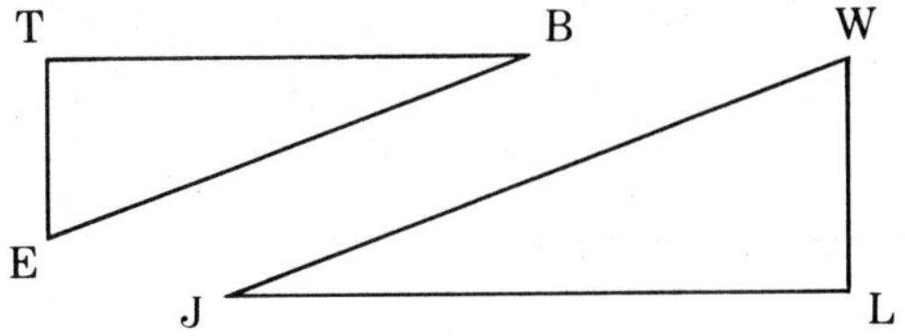

E

J L

∠T and ∠L
∠E and ∠W
∠B and ∠J

$\overline{TE}$ and $\overline{LW}$
$\overline{EB}$ and $\overline{WJ}$
$\overline{BT}$ and $\overline{JL}$

Finding Missing Sides in Similar Triangles

Example G Writing ratios of lengths of corresponding sides

The triangles are similar. Complete these ratios of the lengths of corresponding sides. All lengths are in meters.

$\frac{14}{\square} = \frac{26}{\square}$

14, 24, 26; 7, 12, 13

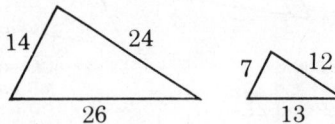

If two triangles are similar, the measures of corresponding angles are equal. Also, the measures of corresponding sides are proportional. This means that the ratios of the lengths of corresponding sides are equal.

$\frac{14}{7} = \frac{26}{13}$ ← Sides of first triangle ← Sides of second triangle

Example H Finding missing dimensions

The triangles are similar. Write a proportion and find n.

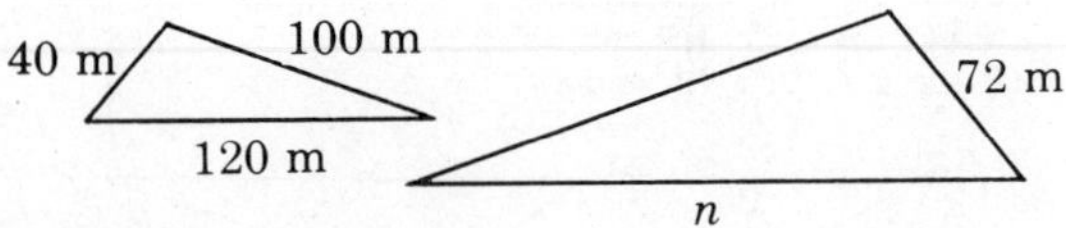

$$\frac{40}{72} = \frac{120}{n}$$

$$40 \times n = 72 \times 120$$

$$40n = 8640$$

$$n = 216$$

n is 216 meters.

Exercises

Set G

There are two exercises for each pair of similar triangles. Complete the ratios of the lengths of corresponding sides. All lengths are in meters.

1. $\frac{60}{\square} = \frac{36}{\square}$ 150 90
2. $\frac{48}{\square} = \frac{36}{\square}$ 120 90

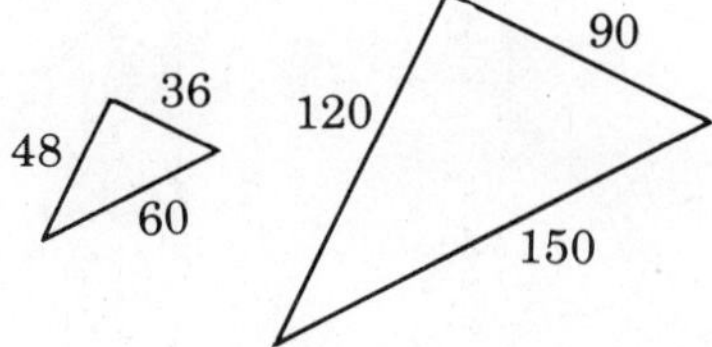

3. $\frac{240}{\square} = \frac{200}{\square}$ 216 180
4. $\frac{240}{\square} = \frac{80}{\square}$ 216 72

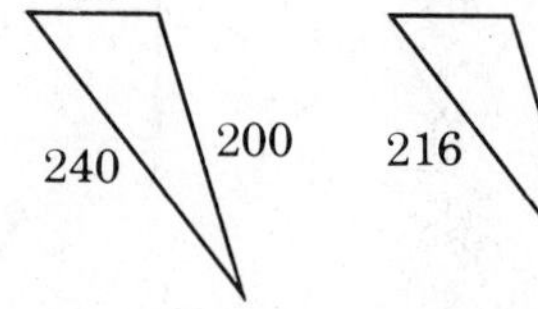

5. $\frac{25}{\square} = \frac{20}{\square}$ 15 12

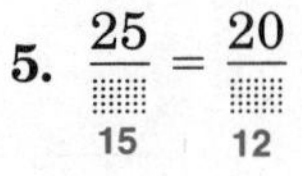

6. $\frac{25}{\square} = \frac{15}{\square}$ 15 9

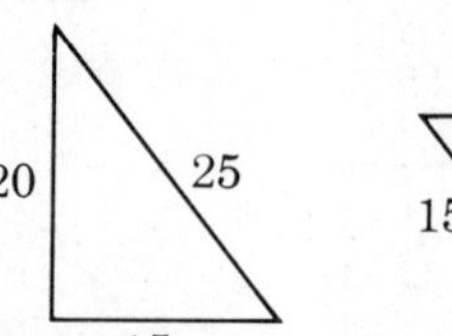

7. $\frac{6.0}{\square} = \frac{3.6}{\square}$ 9.0 5.4

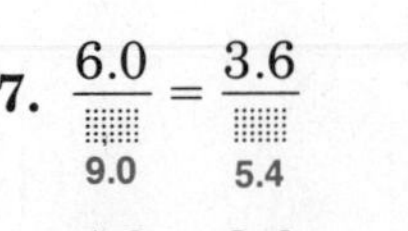

8. $\frac{4.8}{\square} = \frac{3.6}{\square}$ 7.2 5.4

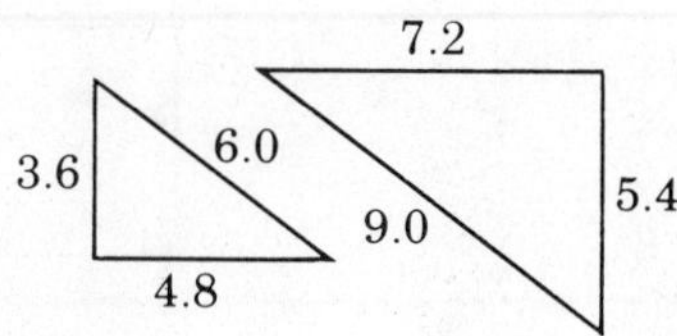

9. $\frac{104}{\square} = \frac{40}{\square}$ 130 50
10. $\frac{104}{\square} = \frac{80}{\square}$ 130 100

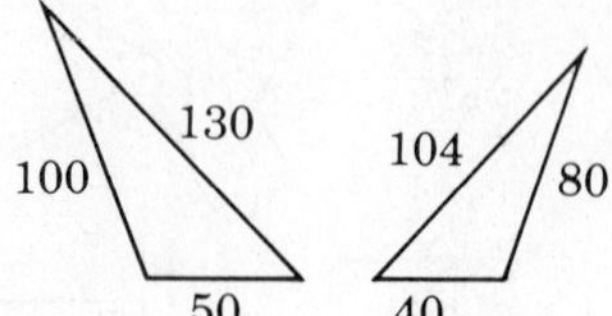

PROBLEM SOLVING
The applications on pages 226–227, 230–231 may be used anytime after this lesson.

Set H

In each exercise, the triangles are similar. Write a proportion and find n. All lengths are in meters.

Proportions may vary. Sample proportions are given.

1.

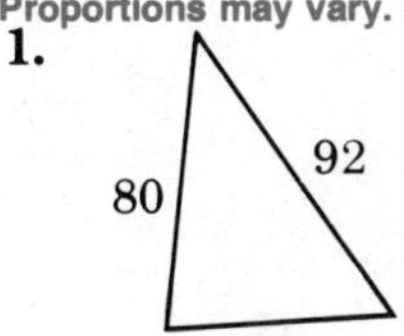

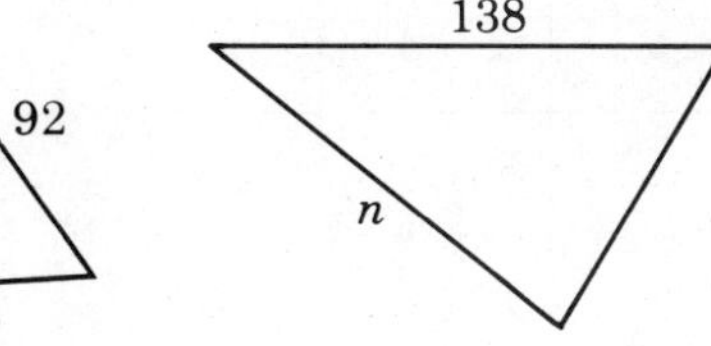

$\frac{92}{138} = \frac{80}{n}$ **n is 120 meters.**

2.

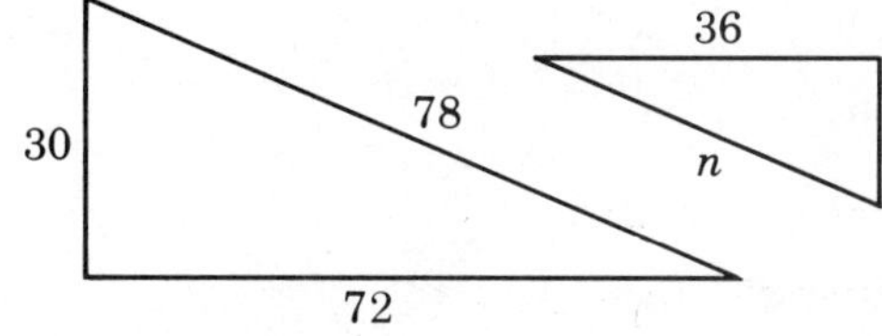

$\frac{72}{36} = \frac{78}{n}$ **n is 39 meters.**

3.

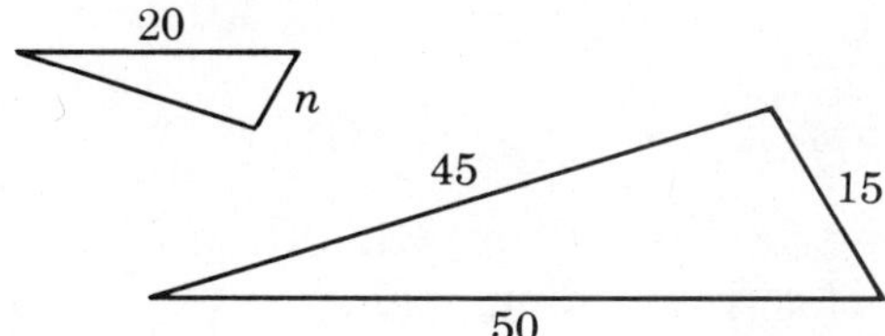

$\frac{20}{50} = \frac{n}{15}$ **n is 6 meters.**

4.

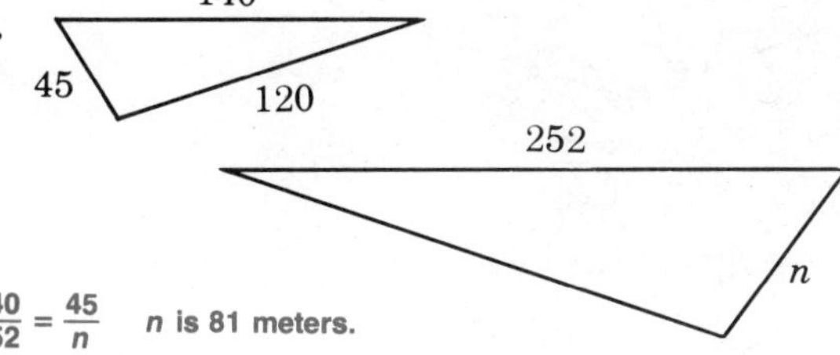

$\frac{140}{252} = \frac{45}{n}$ **n is 81 meters.**

5.

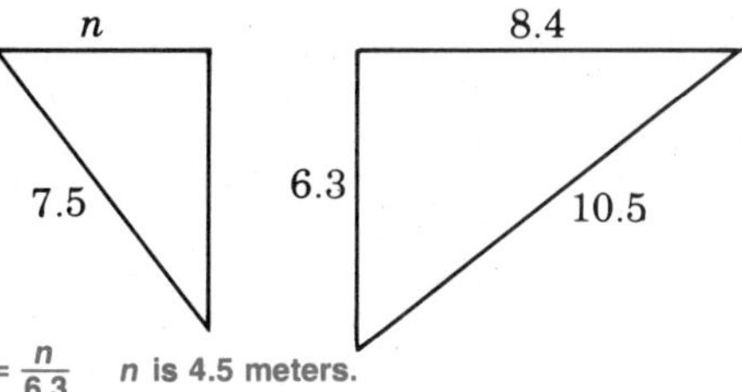

$\frac{7.5}{10.5} = \frac{n}{6.3}$ **n is 4.5 meters.**

6.

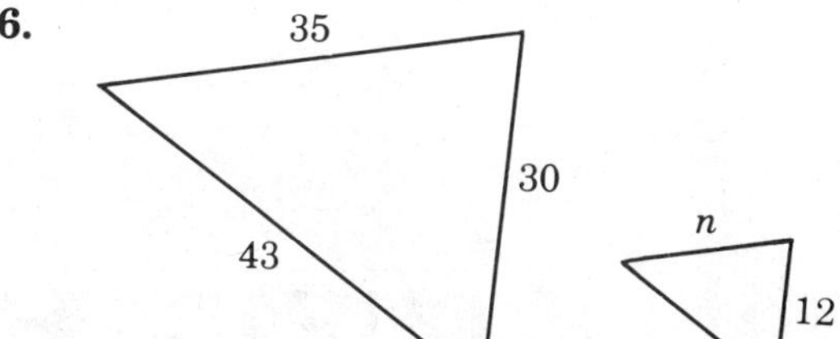

$\frac{30}{12} = \frac{35}{n}$ **n is 14 meters.**

7.

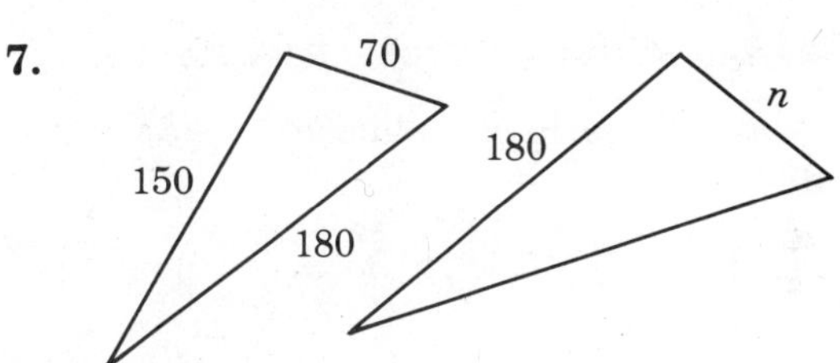

$\frac{150}{180} = \frac{70}{n}$ **n is 84 meters.**

8.

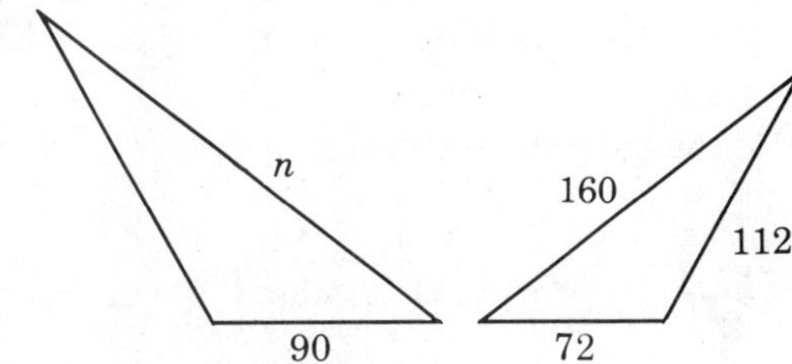

$\frac{90}{72} = \frac{n}{160}$ **n is 200 meters.**

9.

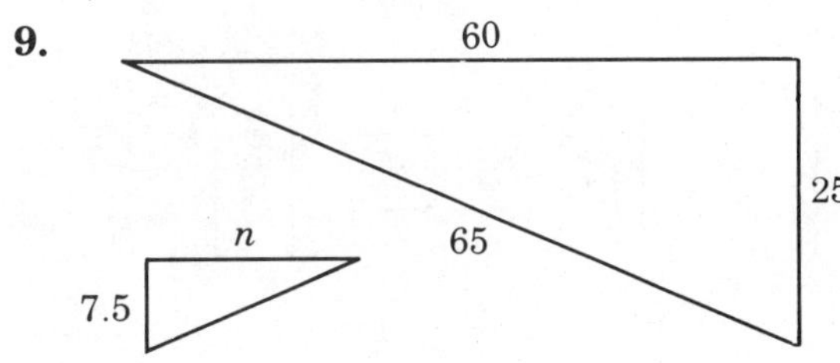

$\frac{7.5}{25} = \frac{n}{60}$ **n is 18 meters.**

10.

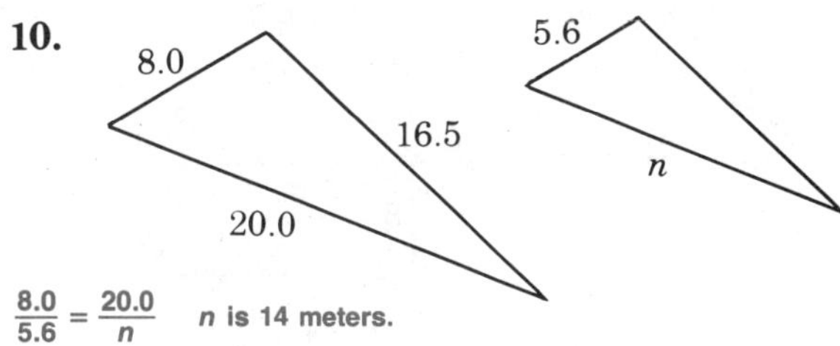

$\frac{8.0}{5.6} = \frac{20.0}{n}$ **n is 14 meters.**

SKILLS POSTTEST

Number of test items - 8

Number missed	1	2	3	4
Percent correct	88	75	63	50

SKILL Writing Ratios *pages 216–217*

A Write the ratio of dollars to days.

$82 earned in 5 days $\frac{82}{5}$

B Give the next ratio in this list.

$\frac{9}{8} = \frac{18}{16} = \frac{27}{24}$ $\frac{36}{32}$

SKILL Solving Proportions *pages 218–219*

C Find cross-products. Then tell whether these ratios are equal. $\frac{6}{16}$ $\frac{15}{40}$

240 = 240

D Find the missing number in this proportion. $\frac{18}{x} = \frac{3}{8}$

x = 48

SKILL Identifying Similar Figures *pages 220–221*

E Give the letter of the figure that is similar to the figure on the left.

b

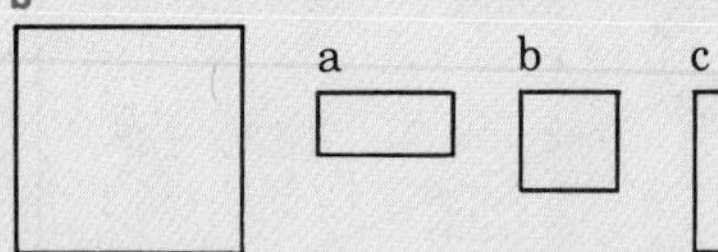

F The triangles are similar. Give 3 pairs of corresponding angles and 3 pairs of corresponding sides.

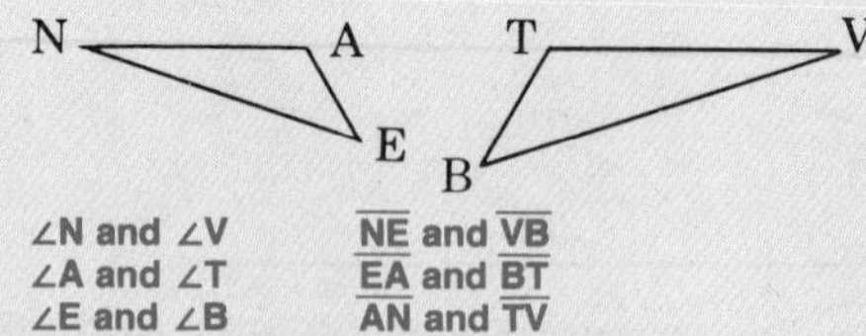

$\angle N$ and $\angle V$ — $\overline{NE}$ and $\overline{VB}$
$\angle A$ and $\angle T$ — $\overline{EA}$ and $\overline{BT}$
$\angle E$ and $\angle B$ — $\overline{AN}$ and $\overline{TV}$

SKILL Finding Missing Sides in Similar Triangles *pages 222–223*

G The triangles are similar. Complete these ratios of the lengths of corresponding sides.

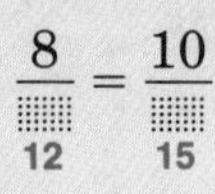

$\frac{8}{12} = \frac{10}{15}$

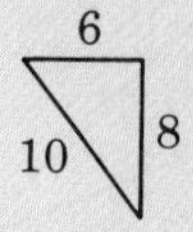

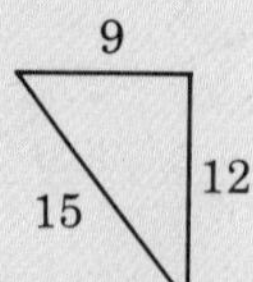

H The triangles are similar. Write a proportion and find n.

Proportions may vary. A sample is given.

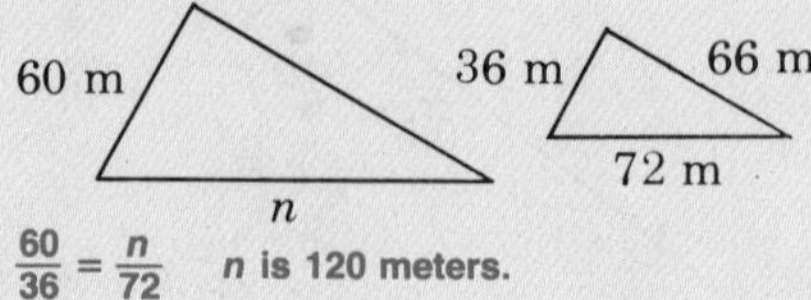

$\frac{60}{36} = \frac{n}{72}$ *n* is 120 meters.

Problem Solving

CONSUMER APPLICATIONS

Objective: Solve problems involving ratio and proportion.

In this lesson students solve problems involving driving rates, gasoline consumption, and expenses for a vacation trip.

Planning a Vacation

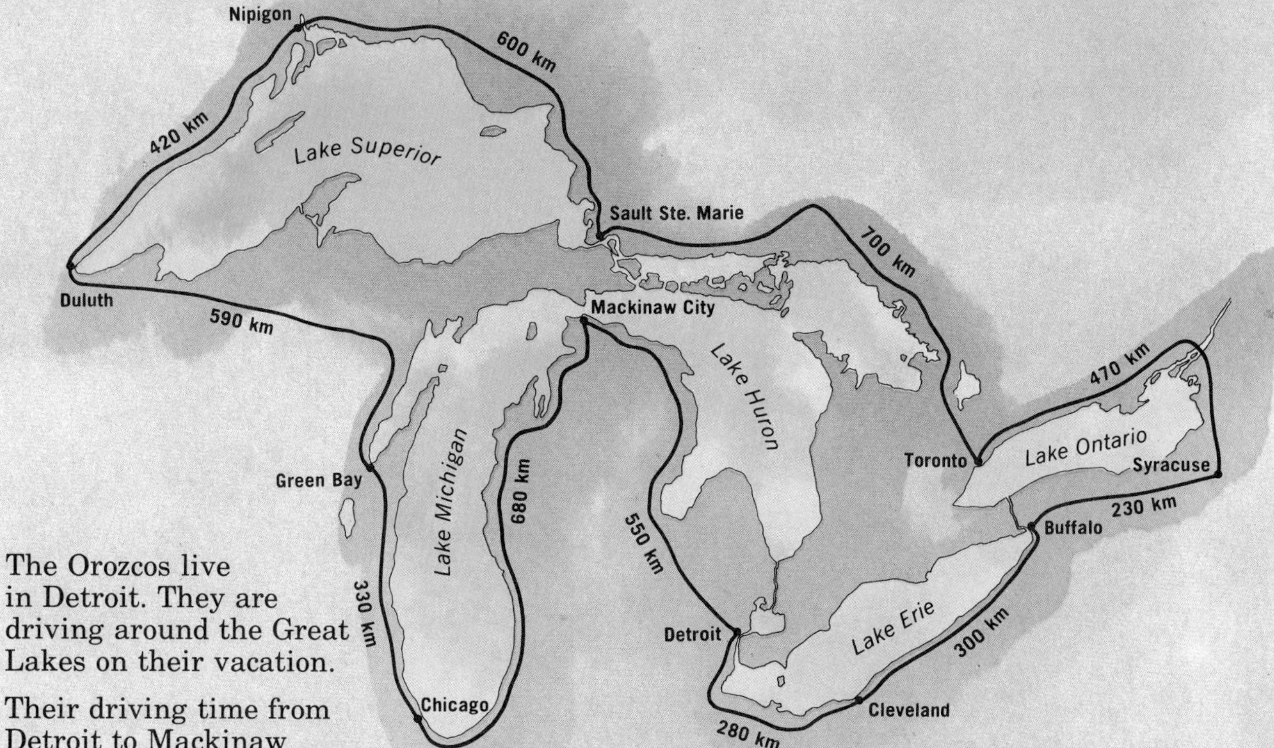

The Orozcos live in Detroit. They are driving around the Great Lakes on their vacation.

Their driving time from Detroit to Mackinaw City was 7 hours. At this rate, what will be their driving time between the following cities? Give each answer to the nearest tenth hour.

1. Mackinaw City to Chicago

   $\frac{550}{7} = \frac{680}{n}$ ← Kilometers, ← Hours

   8.7 hours

2. Chicago to Green Bay

   $\frac{550}{7} = \frac{330}{n}$ ← Kilometers, ← Hours

   4.2 hours

3. Green Bay to Duluth
   7.5 hours
4. Duluth to Nipigon
   5.3 hours
5. Nipigon to Sault Ste. Marie
   7.6 hours
6. Sault Ste. Marie to Toronto
   8.9 hours
7. Toronto to Syracuse
   6.0 hours
8. Syracuse to Buffalo
   2.9 hours
9. Buffalo to Cleveland
   3.8 hours
10. Cleveland to Detroit
    3.6 hours
11. Find the total distance for the trip.
    5150 kilometers
12. If the Orozcos use 4 liters of gasoline every 50 kilometers, how much gasoline will they use for the entire trip?
    412 liters

The Orozcos spent $340 for food and motels the first 4 days. At this rate, how much will they spend for food and motels

13. in 10 days?
    $850
14. in 14 days?
    $1190

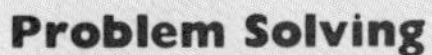

Problem Solving

CONSUMER APPLICATIONS

Objective: Solve problems involving ratio, proportion, and similarity.

In this lesson students find heights and distances through indirect measurement by using similar triangles.

Finding Heights and Distances Using Similarity

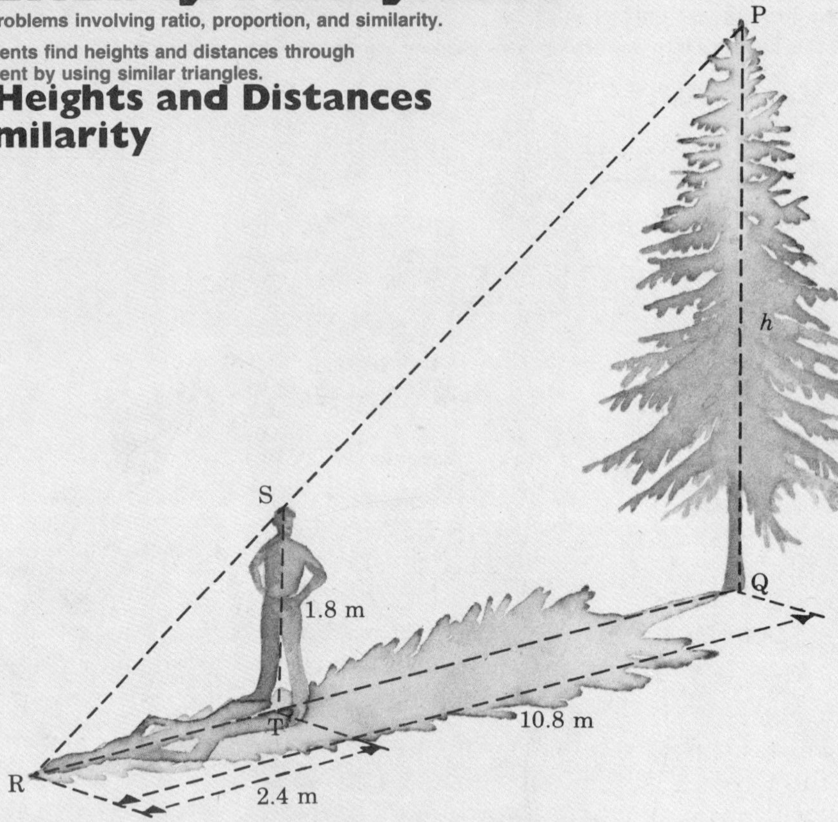

The Conrads visited a state park. Mr. Conrad used the following technique to estimate the height of a pine tree.

He stood so that his shadow extended as far as the shadow of the tree.

He recorded the measure of the tree's shadow, QR, his shadow, TR, and his height, ST.

Triangles PQR and STR are similar. So the measures of corresponding sides are proportional.

$$\frac{PQ}{ST} = \frac{QR}{TR}$$

$$\frac{h}{1.8} = \frac{10.8}{2.4}$$

$$h \times 2.4 = 1.8 \times 10.8$$

$$2.4h = 19.44$$

$$h = 8.1$$

The height of the tree is 8.1 meters.

Find the height of the tree if these were the values for QR, TR, and ST.

	QR (m)	TR (m)	ST (m)	
1.	22.4	2.8	1.6	12.8 m
2.	28.8	7.2	1.6	6.4 m
3.	12.8	0.8	1.7	27.2 m
4.	57.6	6.4	1.8	16.2 m
5.	8.4	1.2	1.5	10.5 m
6.	55.5	3.7	1.5	22.5 m
7.	25.2	1.2	1.8	37.8 m
8.	10.4	1.3	1.7	13.6 m

See page 30 of *Problem-Solving Masters.*

Mrs. Conrad planned to swim across the lake. First she used this technique to estimate the width of the lake.

She stood at B directly across from the tent at A. She turned left, walked 60 paces, and put a stake into the ground. She continued for 40 paces. At D, she turned left and walked until she could line up C and A. This was 50 paces from D.

Triangles ABC and EDC are similar.

$$\frac{AB}{ED} = \frac{BC}{DC}$$

$$\frac{w}{50} = \frac{60}{40}$$

$$w \times 40 = 50 \times 60$$

$$40w = 3000$$

$$w = 75$$

The lake is 75 paces wide.

Each of Mrs. Conrad's paces is about 0.8 meter.

$75 \times 0.8 = 60$

The lake is about 60 meters wide.

Find the width of the lake in paces and in meters if these were the values of BC, DC, and ED. Each pace is about 0.8 meter.

See below.

	BC (paces)	DC (paces)	ED (paces)
9.	16	10	50
10.	15	4	20
11.	42	14	40
12.	36	15	25
13.	40	12	54
14.	25	10	24
15.	60	9	15

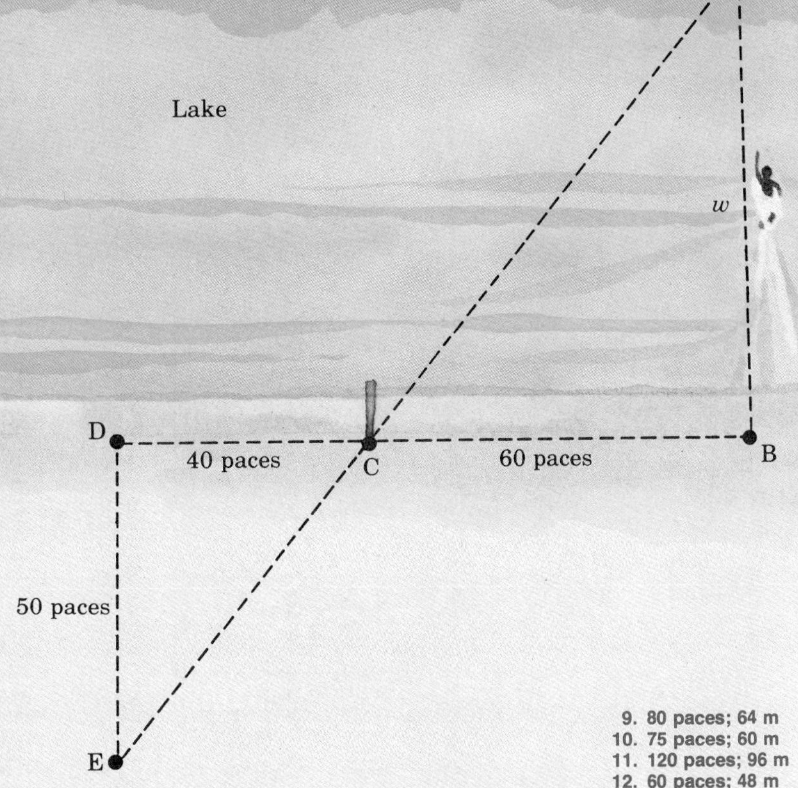

9. 80 paces; 64 m
10. 75 paces; 60 m
11. 120 paces; 96 m
12. 60 paces; 48 m
13. 180 paces; 144 m
14. 60 paces; 48 m
15. 100 paces; 80 m

Problem Solving

CAREER APPLICATIONS

Pharmacist

Objective: Solve problems involving ratio and proportion.

In this lesson students solve problems involving amount of medication and prescription cost.

Career Cluster: Health
Peggy Williams is a pharmacist. She uses proportions when filling prescriptions.

Aminophylline is a medication used to ease breathing for people with asthma. It comes in a solution.

The label says there is 250 mg of medication in 10 cm^3 of solution. The prescription calls for 40 mg of medication. How much solution is needed?

$$\frac{250}{10} = \frac{40}{n} \begin{array}{l} \longleftarrow \text{Medication (mg)} \\ \longleftarrow \text{Solution (cm}^3\text{)} \end{array}$$

$n = 1.6$

1.6 cm^3 of solution is needed.

Complete this table.

	Label on bottle	Amount of medication needed	Amount of solution or number of tablets needed
1.	350 mg in 10 cm^3	105 mg	3 cm^3
2.	0.5 g in 5 cm^3	6 g	60 cm^3
3.	84 mg in 3 tablets	476 mg	17 tablets
4.	1.5 g in 3 mL	0.4 g	0.8 mL
5.	160 mg in 5 cm^3	800 mg	25 cm^3
6.	0.15 mg in 1 tablet	3.6 mg	24 tablets
7.	3.5 mg in 5 tablets	8.4 mg	12 tablets
8.	250 mg in 10 mL	350 mg	14 mL
9.	0.4 g in 5 mL	3.4 g	42.5 mL
10.	2.4 g in 10 cm^3	8.4 g	35 cm^3
11.	0.6 mg in 4 tablets	4.5 mg	30 tablets
12.	1.8 g in 5 mL	9 g	25 mL

Peggy uses proportions to find the cost of prescriptions.

The pharmacy pays $9.10 for 65 tablets of a certain medicine. A prescription calls for 24 tablets. What is the pharmacy's cost for 24 tablets?

$$\frac{9.10}{65} = \frac{n}{24} \begin{array}{l} \leftarrow \text{Dollars} \\ \leftarrow \text{Tablets} \end{array}$$

$$n = 3.36$$

The pharmacy's cost for 24 tablets is $3.36.

Peggy will then add a fee to this cost to determine the price paid by the customer.

Complete this table. Give each answer rounded up to the next whole cent.

	Number of tablets in bottle	Pharmacy's cost for bottle	Number of tablets for prescription	Pharmacy's cost for prescription
13.	65	$10.15	24	$3.75
14.	50	$9.02	36	$6.50
15.	100	$20.50	20	$4.10
16.	56	$13.90	28	$6.95
17.	75	$12.50	35	$5.84
18.	100	$18.00	12	$2.16
19.	50	$7.15	24	$3.44
20.	100	$21.30	30	$6.39
21.	100	$42.50	45	$19.13
22.	50	$7.18	60	$8.62
23.	85	$12.35	100	$14.53
24.	60	$14.70	15	$3.68

Problem Solving

CAREER APPLICATIONS

Photographer

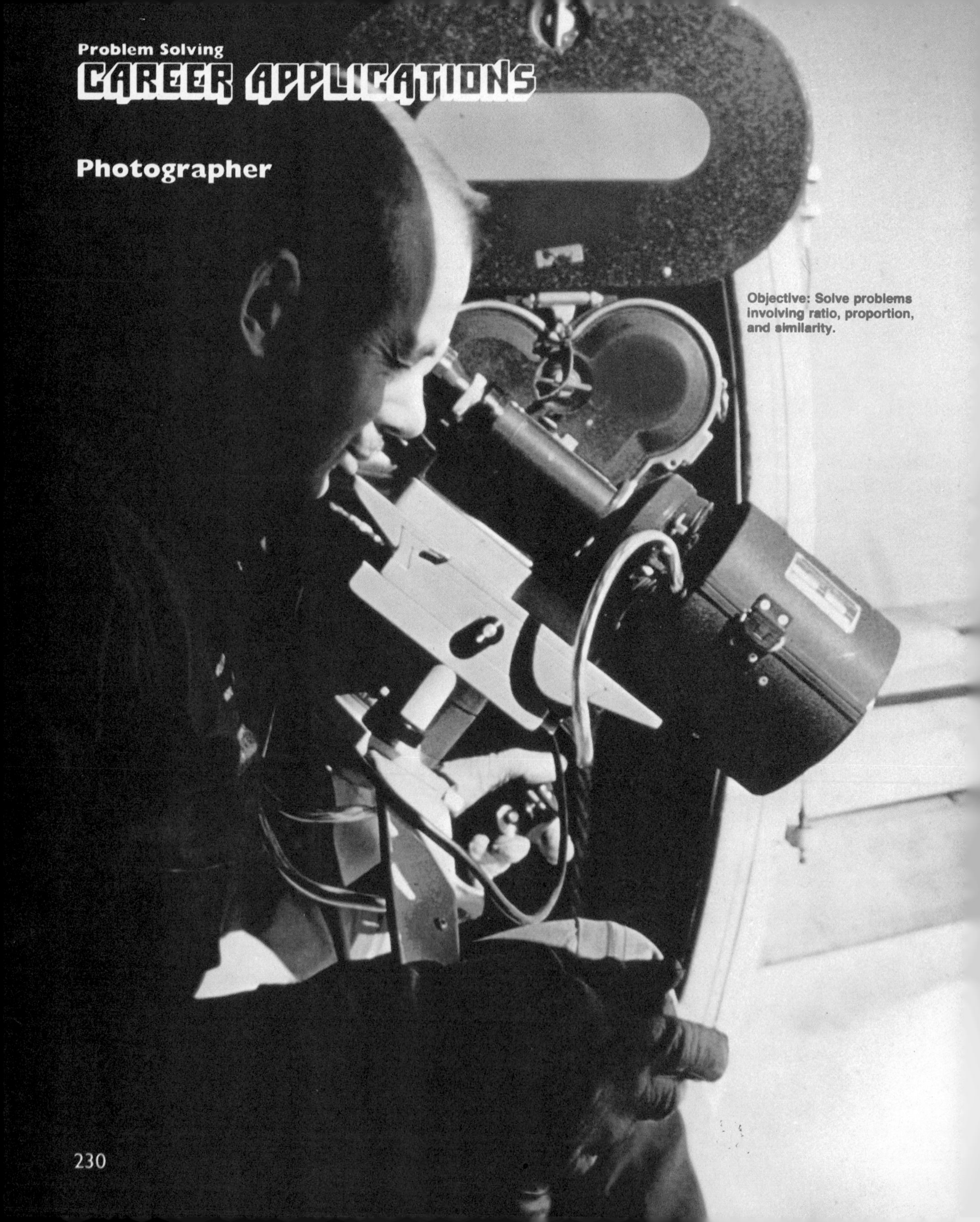

Objective: Solve problems involving ratio, proportion, and similarity.

In this lesson students find the ground distance shown in an aerial photograph, given the focal length of the camera lens, the altitude of the airplane, and the width of the photograph.

See page 31 of *Problem-Solving Masters.*

Career Cluster: Arts David Meyer is an aerial photographer. The photographs he takes from an airplane can be used to find distances on the ground.

In the diagram below, light enters the camera through the lens and strikes the film.

f is the focal length of the lens.

a is the altitude of the airplane.

w is the width of the picture.

d is the ground distance shown in the photograph.

The triangle inside the camera is similar to the triangle outside the camera. Ratios of the lengths of corresponding sides are equal to the ratio of the focal length to the altitude.

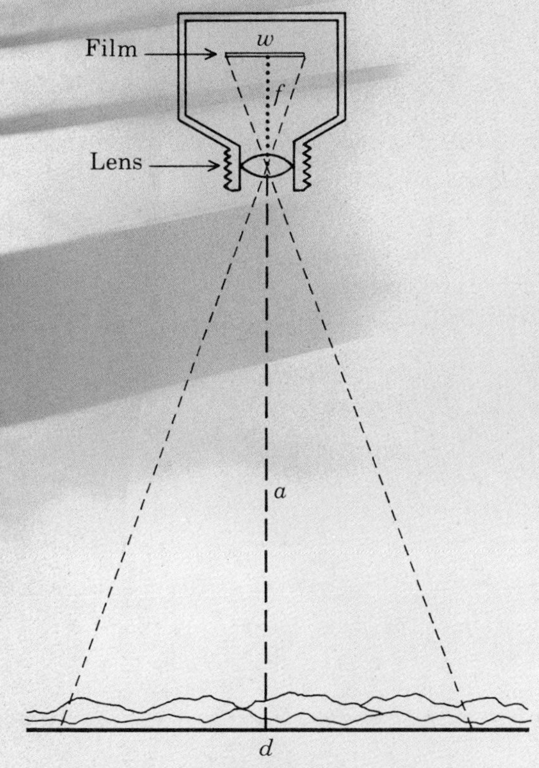

David uses this proportion to find d.

$$\frac{f}{a} = \frac{w}{d}$$

$w \leftarrow$ Centimeters inside camera
$d \leftarrow$ Meters outside camera

If f is 30 cm, a is 10,000 m, and w is 24 cm, David solves this proportion to find d.

$$\frac{30}{10{,}000} = \frac{24}{d}$$

$$d = 8000$$

The ground distance shown in the photograph is 8000 meters.

Find the ground distance (d) in meters for these values of f, a, and w.

	f	a	w	
1.	50 cm	18,000 m	24 cm	8640 m
2.	50 cm	14,000 m	24 cm	6720 m
3.	50 cm	10,000 m	24 cm	4800 m
4.	50 cm	6000 m	24 cm	2880 m
5.	30 cm	18,000 m	24 cm	14,400 m
6.	30 cm	14,000 m	24 cm	11,200 m
7.	30 cm	10,000 m	24 cm	8000 m
8.	30 cm	6000 m	24 cm	4800 m
9.	24 cm	18,000 m	24 cm	18,000 m
10.	24 cm	14,000 m	24 cm	14,000 m
11.	24 cm	10,000 m	24 cm	10,000 m
12.	24 cm	6000 m	24 cm	6000 m

13. For a given focal length, as the altitude decreases, what happens to the ground distance?
It decreases.

14. For a given altitude, as the focal length decreases, what happens to the ground distance?
It increases.

Problem Solving

DEVELOPING STRATEGIES

Objective: Solve problems by using proportions and interpreting remainders.

In this lesson students determine the amount of food needed for a horse and the cost of the food.

Tactics: Using Proportions, Interpreting Remainders

Lauri Stephen works for a stable that boards horses. One of her responsibilities is to buy food for the horses. Each horse eats a combination of hay and sweet feed every day.

Hay: 25-kg bales
$2 per bale

Sweet feed: 25-kg bags
$5.25 per bag

Problem

Buster eats 113 kilograms of hay in 4 weeks. At this rate, how much would it cost to feed Buster hay for one year? (1 year = 52 weeks)

Solution

The following questions show Lauri's strategy for solving the problem. The tactics she used included using proportions and interpreting remainders.

a. How many kilograms of hay will Buster eat in one year? Write a proportion and solve.

$$\frac{113}{4} = \frac{x}{52} \begin{array}{l} \leftarrow \text{Kilograms of hay} \\ \leftarrow \text{Number of weeks} \end{array}$$

$$x = 1469$$

b. How many bales are needed? Divide and interpret remainder.

$$25\overline{)1469} = 58 \text{ R}19 \longrightarrow 59$$

c. How much will the hay cost for one year? Multiply.

$$\begin{array}{r} 59 \\ \times\ 2 \\ \hline 118 \end{array} \begin{array}{l} \leftarrow \text{Number of bales} \\ \leftarrow \text{Dollars per bale} \\ \end{array}$$

Conclusion: If Buster continues to eat hay at a rate of 113 kilograms in 4 weeks, the cost of the hay for one year will be $118.

Related Problems

1. Buster eats 70 kilograms of sweet feed in 4 weeks. At this rate, how much will it cost to feed Buster sweet feed for one year?
$194.25
2. What is the total cost of feeding Buster for one year?
$312.25
3. Lucky Kate eats 90 kilograms of sweet feed in 4 weeks. At this rate, how much will it cost to feed her sweet feed for one year?
$246.75
4. Lucky Kate eats twice as much hay as sweet feed. At this rate, how much will hay for one year cost?
$188
5. What is the total cost of hay and sweet feed for feeding Buster and Lucky Kate for one year?
$747
6. Thunderbolt eats 15 kilograms of hay in 5 days. Bongo eats twice as much hay as Thunderbolt. At this rate, how many bales of hay are needed to feed Bongo for one year? Round your answer to the nearest whole number. (1 year = 365 days)
88 bales
7. How much will hay for Thunderbolt and Bongo cost for one year?
$264

Extensions

8. Lauri needs 100 bales of hay to feed Beulah for one year. To the nearest kilogram, how much hay does Beulah eat in 5 days?
34 kilograms
9. Wild Walker eats 3 bags of sweet feed in 4 weeks. How many kilograms of sweet feed does she eat in one year?
975 kilograms

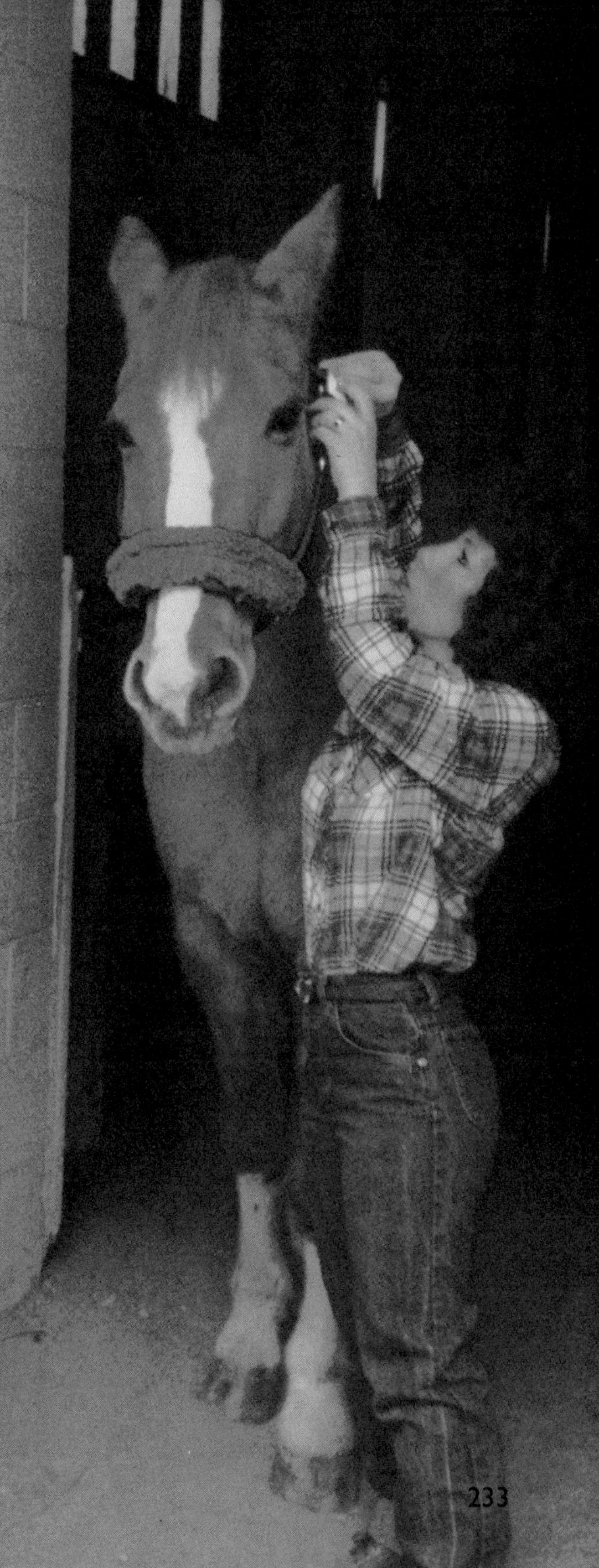

CHAPTER 10 TEST

Number of test items - 13

Number missed	1	2	3	4	5	6
Percent correct	92	85	77	69	62	54

A **1.** Write the ratio of knee bends to seconds.

11 knee bends in 15 seconds $\frac{11}{15}$

B **2.** Give the next ratio in this list.

$\frac{7}{15} = \frac{14}{30} = \frac{21}{45}$ $\frac{28}{60}$

C **3.** Find cross-products. Then tell whether these ratios are equal.

$\frac{6}{34}$ $\frac{12}{75}$

$450 \neq 408$

D **4.** Find the missing number in this proportion.

$\frac{15}{9} = \frac{t}{21}$

$t = 35$

E **5.** Give the letter of the figure that is similar to the figure on the left.

c

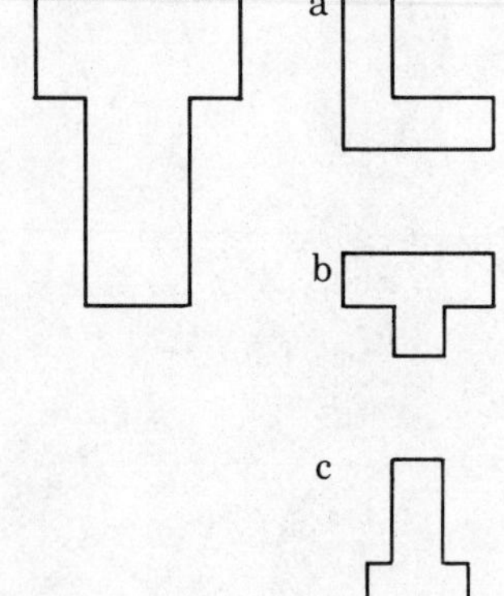

F **6.** The triangles are similar. Give 3 pairs of corresponding angles and 3 pairs of corresponding sides.

∠D and ∠H
∠R and ∠C
∠B and ∠W

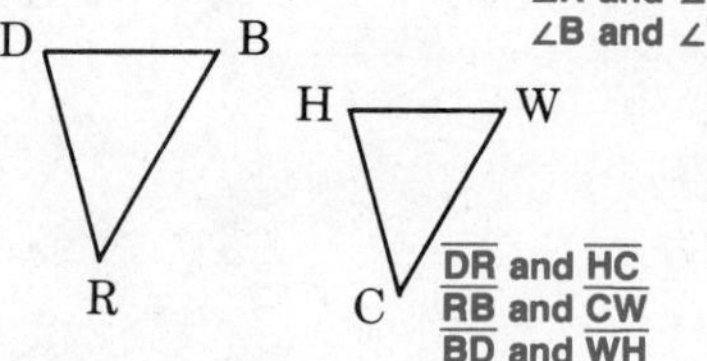

$\overline{DR}$ and $\overline{HC}$
$\overline{RB}$ and $\overline{CW}$
$\overline{BD}$ and $\overline{WH}$

G **7.** The triangles are similar. Complete these ratios of the lengths of corresponding sides. All lengths are in meters.

$\frac{56}{▒} = \frac{98}{▒}$

40 70

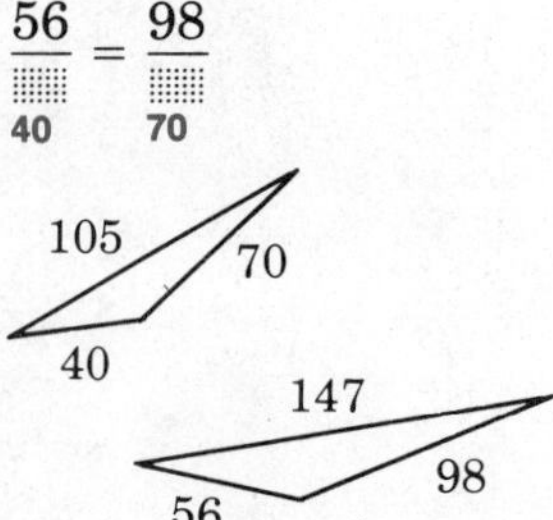

H **8.** The triangles are similar. Write a proportion and find n. All lengths are in meters.

Proportions may vary. A sample is given.

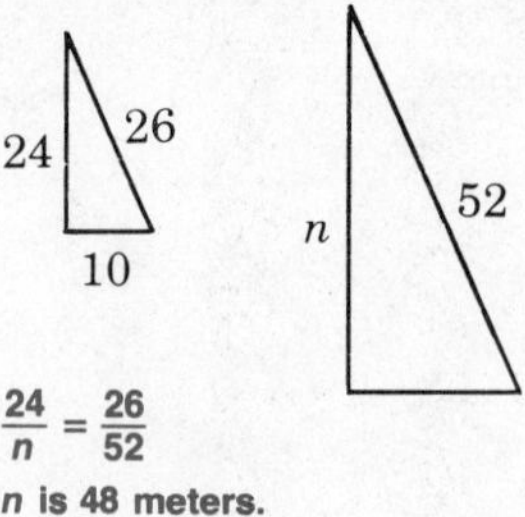

$\frac{24}{n} = \frac{26}{52}$

n is 48 meters.

9. If it takes 4 hours to drive 314 kilometers, how long does it take to drive 785 kilometers?

10 hours

10. Find h in meters.

3.2 meters

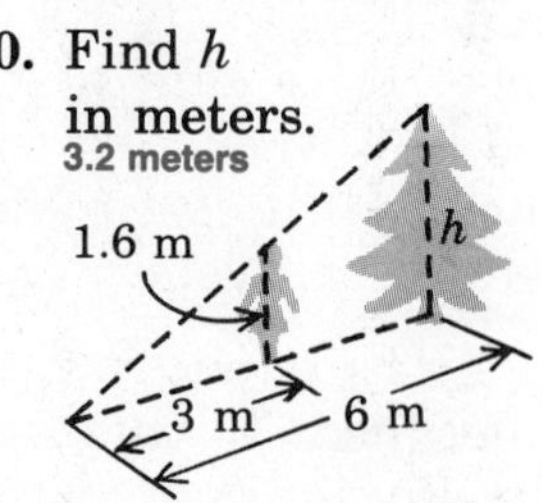

11. There is 250 mg of a medication in 10 cm^3 of solution. How much solution is needed to obtain 600 mg of the medication?

24 cm^3

12. Find d in meters if f is 30 centimeters, a is 14,000 meters, and w is 24 centimeters.

11,200 meters

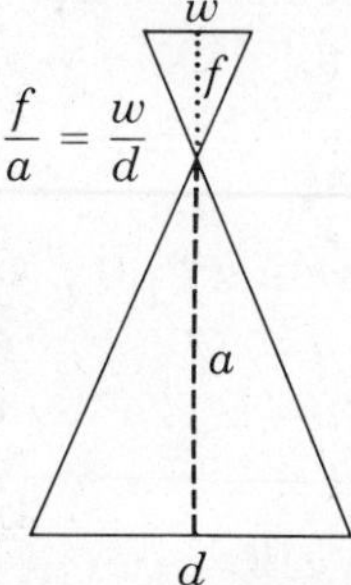

13. A certain horse eats 112 kilograms of hay in 4 weeks. At this rate, how many kilograms of hay does this horse eat in one year? (1 year = 52 weeks)

1456 kilograms

 See pages 25–26 of the *Test Masters* for an alternate form of the Chapter 10 Test.

CHAPTER 11 Percent

SKILLS PRETEST

Number of test items - 11

Number missed	1	2	3	4	5
Percent correct	91	82	73	64	55

SKILL Writing Percents and Decimals *pages 236–237*

A Write 8% as a decimal.
0.08

B Write 0.326 as a percent.
32.6%

SKILL Writing Percents and Fractions *pages 238–239*

C Write 45% as a fraction in lowest terms.
$\frac{9}{20}$

D Write $\frac{4}{5}$ as a percent.
80%

SKILL Finding a Percent of a Number *pages 240–241*

E Find 47% of 93.
43.71

F Find $5\frac{3}{4}$% of 700.
40.25

G Find $66\frac{2}{3}$% of 57.
38

SKILL Finding a Percent *pages 242–243*

H 9 is what percent of 75?
12%

I 21 is what percent of 45?
$46\frac{2}{3}$%

SKILL Finding a Number When a Percent Is Known *pages 244–245*

J 63 is 35% of what number?
180

K 39 is $33\frac{1}{3}$% of what number?
117

See page T38 for additional notes on Chapter 11.

Objective: Write percents as decimals and decimals as percents.

Writing Percents and Decimals

Example A Writing decimals

Write each percent as a decimal.

$49\% = 0.49$

$3\% = 0.03$

$100\% = 1.00$, or 1

$5.7\% = 0.057$

$0.16\% = 0.0016$

$4\frac{1}{2}\% = 4.5\% = 0.045$

Percent means hundredths.

Move the decimal point two places to the left and omit the percent sign.

Encourage students to change a percent like $4\frac{1}{2}\%$ to a decimal without a fraction in order to make computation with the percent easier.

Example B Writing percents

Write each decimal as a percent.

$0.13 = 13\%$

$0.04 = 4\%$

$2.9 = 290\%$

$0.508 = 50.8\%$

$0.001 = 0.1\%$

$0.33\frac{1}{3} = 33\frac{1}{3}\%$

First move the decimal point two places to the right. Then write the numeral with a percent sign.

Point out that a decimal point is not placed between the whole number and the fraction.

Exercises

Students should know the decimal equivalents of $\frac{1}{2}$, $\frac{1}{4}$, and $\frac{3}{4}$.

Set A

Write each percent as a decimal.

1. 9.6% 0.096
2. 53% 0.53
3. 2% 0.02
4. 350% 3.5
5. 0.27% 0.0027
6. 215% 2.15
7. 32% 0.32
8. $6\frac{1}{2}\%$ 0.065
9. 1% 0.01
10. 605% 6.05
11. 95% 0.95
12. 700% 7
13. 8.5% 0.085
14. 9% 0.09
15. 12.7% 0.127
16. 99% 0.99
17. 80.4% 0.804
18. 13% 0.13
19. 800% 8
20. 6.23% 0.0623
21. 41% 0.41
22. 0.15% 0.0015
23. 5.13% 0.0513
24. 0.01% 0.0001
25. 147% 1.47
26. 4% 0.04
27. 100.5% 1.005
28. $3\frac{1}{2}\%$ 0.035
29. 80% 0.8
30. 150% 1.5
31. $1\frac{1}{4}\%$ 0.0125
32. 1.2% 0.012
33. 14% 0.14
34. 64% 0.64
35. $2\frac{1}{2}\%$ 0.025
36. 125% 1.25
37. 0.92% 0.0092
38. $\frac{3}{4}\%$ 0.0075
39. 0.9% 0.009
40. 35% 0.35
41. $7\frac{1}{4}\%$ 0.0725
42. 8% 0.08
43. 300% 3
44. 0.1% 0.001
45. 91.8% 0.918
46. 620% 6.2
47. $9\frac{1}{2}\%$ 0.095
48. 7% 0.07
49. 0.21% 0.0021
50. 4.09% 0.0409
51. $5\frac{3}{4}\%$ 0.0575
52. 0.3% 0.003
53. $6\frac{1}{4}\%$ 0.0625
54. 130% 1.3
55. 82% 0.82
56. $11\frac{1}{2}\%$ 0.115
57. 8.1% 0.081
58. 0.52% 0.0052
59. 5% 0.05
60. 91% 0.91
61. 0.8% 0.008
62. 13.2% 0.132
63. $1\frac{1}{2}\%$ 0.015
64. 79% 0.79
65. $\frac{1}{2}\%$ 0.005
66. 110% 1.1
67. 7.2% 0.072
68. 6% 0.06
69. 0.35% 0.0035
70. 56% 0.56
71. $8\frac{3}{4}\%$ 0.0875
72. 175% 1.75
73. 0.6% 0.006
74. 52.8% 0.528
75. 900% 9

Set B

Write each decimal as a percent.

1. 0.62 62%
2. 0.06 6%
3. 0.8 80%
4. 1.4 140%
5. 0.17 17%
6. 0.201 20.1%
7. 0.005 0.5%
8. 9.5 950%
9. 0.37 37%
10. 0.318 31.8%
11. 5.01 501%
12. $0.16\frac{2}{3}$ $16\frac{2}{3}\%$
13. 0.28 28%
14. 0.047 4.7%
15. 0.79 79%
16. 0.923 92.3%
17. 0.082 8.2%
18. 0.45 45%
19. 0.731 73.1%
20. 0.3 30%
21. $0.37\frac{1}{2}$ $37\frac{1}{2}\%$
22. 0.68 68%
23. 0.009 0.9%
24. 0.44 44%
25. 0.008 0.8%
26. 0.05 5%
27. 0.73 73%
28. $0.04\frac{1}{3}$ $4\frac{1}{3}\%$
29. 0.5 50%
30. 8.25 825%
31. 0.51 51%
32. 0.004 0.4%
33. 0.08 8%
34. 0.411 41.1%
35. 0.84 84%
36. $0.66\frac{2}{3}$ $66\frac{2}{3}\%$
37. 0.03 3%
38. 0.894 89.4%
39. 0.91 91%
40. 0.0061 0.61%
41. 4.92 492%
42. 0.29 29%
43. 0.41 41%
44. $0.62\frac{1}{2}$ $62\frac{1}{2}\%$
45. 0.09 9%
46. 7.2 720%
47. 0.77 77%
48. 0.6 60%
49. $0.55\frac{5}{9}$ $55\frac{5}{9}\%$
50. 0.0035 0.35%
51. 0.551 55.1%
52. 0.4 40%
53. 6.5 650%
54. 0.85 85%
55. 0.907 90.7%
56. 0.131 13.1%
57. 0.07 7%
58. $0.12\frac{1}{2}$ $12\frac{1}{2}\%$
59. 0.88 88%
60. 0.39 39%
61. 0.999 99.9%
62. 0.02 2%
63. 0.007 0.7%
64. $0.23\frac{3}{8}$ $23\frac{3}{8}\%$
65. 0.18 18%
66. 3.7 370%
67. 0.464 46.4%
68. 0.56 56%
69. 0.626 62.6%
70. 0.002 0.2%
71. $0.03\frac{2}{9}$ $3\frac{2}{9}\%$
72. 0.11 11%
73. 0.01 1%
74. 2.36 236%
75. 1.5 150%

BREAK TIME

The people at a party are forming equal teams to play a game. When the people form groups of 2, 3, 4, 5, or 6, there is always exactly one person left.

What is the smallest number of people that could be at the party?

61 people

(The answer is the least common multiple of 2, 3, 4, 5, and 6; plus 1.)

Writing Percents and Fractions

Example C Writing fractions

Write each percent as a fraction in lowest terms.

Percent means hundredths.
Write the numeral as the numerator.
Write 100 as the denominator.
Reduce the fraction to lowest terms.

$61\% = \frac{61}{100}$

$40\% = \frac{40}{100} = \frac{2}{5}$

$135\% = \frac{135}{100} = 1\frac{35}{100} = 1\frac{7}{20}$

$\frac{1}{4}\% = \dfrac{\frac{1}{4}}{100} = \frac{1}{4} \div 100 = \frac{1}{4} \times \frac{1}{100} = \frac{1}{400}$

$16\frac{2}{3}\% = \dfrac{16\frac{2}{3}}{100} = 16\frac{2}{3} \div 100 = \frac{50}{3} \div 100 = \frac{\overset{1}{\cancel{50}}}{3} \times \frac{1}{\underset{2}{\cancel{100}}} = \frac{1}{6}$

Example D Writing percents

Write $\frac{3}{5}$ as a percent.

$$\begin{array}{r} 0.60 = 60\% \\ 5\overline{)3.00} \\ -\,3\,0 \\ \hline 00 \end{array}$$

Divide the numerator by the denominator.
Divide until the quotient is in hundredths.
Write the quotient as a percent.

$\frac{3}{5} = 60\%$

Write $\frac{2}{3}$ as a percent.

$$\begin{array}{r} 0.66\frac{2}{3} = 66\frac{2}{3}\% \\ 3\overline{)2.00} \\ -\,1\,8 \\ \hline 20 \\ -\,18 \\ \hline 2 \end{array}$$

Divide until the quotient is in hundredths.
If the remainder is not zero, write the remainder over the divisor to form a fraction.

$\frac{2}{3} = 66\frac{2}{3}\%$

Percents that contain a fraction such as $\frac{1}{3}$ or $\frac{2}{3}$ are usually written with a fraction rather than with a decimal.

Exercises

Set C

Write each percent as a fraction in lowest terms.

1. 7% $\frac{7}{100}$
2. 53% $\frac{53}{100}$
3. 67% $\frac{67}{100}$
4. 9% $\frac{9}{100}$
5. 25% $\frac{1}{4}$
6. 70% $\frac{7}{10}$
7. 30% $\frac{3}{10}$
8. 75% $\frac{3}{4}$
9. 13% $\frac{13}{100}$
10. 19% $\frac{19}{100}$
11. 80% $\frac{4}{5}$
12. 60% $\frac{3}{5}$
13. 5% $\frac{1}{20}$
14. 27% $\frac{27}{100}$
15. 43% $\frac{43}{100}$
16. 8% $\frac{2}{25}$
17. 107% $1\frac{7}{100}$
18. 150% $1\frac{1}{2}$
19. 110% $1\frac{1}{10}$
20. 103% $1\frac{3}{100}$
21. $\frac{1}{2}$% $\frac{1}{200}$
22. $12\frac{1}{2}$% $\frac{1}{8}$
23. $33\frac{1}{3}$% $\frac{1}{3}$
24. $\frac{3}{4}$% $\frac{3}{400}$
25. $37\frac{1}{2}$% $\frac{3}{8}$
26. $83\frac{1}{3}$% $\frac{5}{6}$
27. 31% $\frac{31}{100}$
28. 50% $\frac{1}{2}$
29. 121% $1\frac{21}{100}$
30. $6\frac{1}{2}$% $\frac{13}{200}$
31. 45% $\frac{9}{20}$
32. 71% $\frac{71}{100}$
33. 2% $\frac{1}{50}$
34. 83% $\frac{83}{100}$
35. $7\frac{1}{2}$% $\frac{3}{40}$
36. $5\frac{3}{4}$% $\frac{23}{400}$
37. 200% 2
38. 35% $\frac{7}{20}$
39. 20% $\frac{1}{5}$
40. 1% $\frac{1}{100}$
41. 90% $\frac{9}{10}$
42. 47% $\frac{47}{100}$
43. $11\frac{1}{9}$% $\frac{1}{9}$
44. 139% $1\frac{39}{100}$
45. 91% $\frac{91}{100}$
46. 10% $\frac{1}{10}$
47. $8\frac{3}{4}$% $\frac{7}{80}$
48. 6% $\frac{3}{50}$
49. 3% $\frac{3}{100}$
50. 300% 3
51. 59% $\frac{59}{100}$
52. $9\frac{1}{11}$% $\frac{1}{11}$

Set D

Write each fraction as a percent.

1. $\frac{17}{100}$ 17%
2. $\frac{13}{100}$ 13%
3. $\frac{9}{10}$ 90%
4. $\frac{7}{10}$ 70%
5. $\frac{1}{2}$ 50%
6. $\frac{29}{50}$ 58%
7. $\frac{1}{4}$ 25%
8. $\frac{1}{5}$ 20%
9. $\frac{38}{50}$ 76%
10. $\frac{3}{4}$ 75%
11. $\frac{1}{6}$ $16\frac{2}{3}$%
12. $\frac{1}{7}$ $14\frac{2}{7}$%
13. $\frac{5}{8}$ $62\frac{1}{2}$%
14. $\frac{5}{6}$ $83\frac{1}{3}$%
15. $\frac{2}{7}$ $28\frac{4}{7}$%
16. $\frac{7}{8}$ $87\frac{1}{2}$%
17. $\frac{3}{10}$ 30%
18. $\frac{4}{9}$ $44\frac{4}{9}$%
19. $\frac{1}{10}$ 10%
20. $\frac{8}{9}$ $88\frac{8}{9}$%
21. $\frac{4}{5}$ 80%
22. $\frac{3}{7}$ $42\frac{6}{7}$%
23. $\frac{61}{100}$ 61%
24. $\frac{18}{25}$ 72%
25. $\frac{9}{40}$ $22\frac{1}{2}$%
26. $\frac{2}{5}$ 40%
27. $\frac{4}{7}$ $57\frac{1}{7}$%
28. $\frac{16}{25}$ 64%
29. $\frac{3}{2}$ 150%
30. $\frac{57}{100}$ 57%
31. $\frac{5}{4}$ 125%
32. $\frac{31}{90}$ $34\frac{4}{9}$%
33. $\frac{11}{15}$ $73\frac{1}{3}$%
34. $\frac{23}{45}$ $51\frac{1}{9}$%
35. $\frac{1}{200}$ $\frac{1}{2}$%
36. $\frac{3}{400}$ $\frac{3}{4}$%
37. $\frac{11}{12}$ $91\frac{2}{3}$%
38. $\frac{3}{11}$ $27\frac{3}{11}$%
39. $\frac{7}{13}$ $53\frac{11}{13}$%
40. $\frac{7}{12}$ $58\frac{1}{3}$%

BREAK TIME

A squirrel has $2\frac{1}{2}$ stacks of walnuts in one field and $3\frac{1}{2}$ stacks of walnuts in another field.

If the squirrel puts all the walnuts together, how many stacks will there be?
1 stack

Objective: Find a percent of a number.

Finding a Percent of a Number

Example E Using a decimal for whole-number and decimal percents

Find 7% of 4.2.

$0.07 \times 4.2 = n$ Write an equation with the percent named as a decimal. $7\% = 0.07$

$$\begin{array}{r} 4.2 \\ \times\, 0.07 \\ \hline 0.294 \end{array}$$

Multiply.

$0.294 = n$

7% of 4.2 is 0.294.

See page T38 for an alternate approach.

Example F Using a decimal for fraction and mixed-number percents

Find $6\frac{1}{2}\%$ of 289.

$0.065 \times 289 = n$ Write an equation with the percent named as a decimal. $6\frac{1}{2}\% = 6.5\% = 0.065$

$$\begin{array}{r} 289 \\ \times\, 0.065 \\ \hline 1\,445 \\ 17\,340 \\ \hline 18.785 \end{array}$$

Multiply.

$18.785 = n$

$6\frac{1}{2}\%$ of 289 is 18.785.

Example G Using a fraction for whole-number and mixed-number percents

Find $66\frac{2}{3}\%$ of 18.

$\frac{2}{3} \times 18 = n$ Write an equation with the percent named as a fraction. $66\frac{2}{3}\% = \frac{2}{3}$

$\frac{2}{\cancel{3}_1} \times \frac{\cancel{18}^{6}}{1} = \frac{12}{1} = 12$ Multiply.

$12 = n$

$66\frac{2}{3}\%$ of 18 is 12.

Exercises

Set E

Find each number.

1. 6% of 29 1.74
2. 5% of 67 3.35
3. 12% of 72 8.64
4. 50% of 19 9.5
5. 78% of 40 31.2
6. 13% of 84 10.92
7. 60% of 29 17.4
8. 54% of 60 32.4
9. 7% of 7.2 0.504
10. 4% of 9.6 0.384
11. 8% of 75.3 6.024
12. 9% of 61.5 5.535
13. 45% of 3.7 1.665
14. 62% of 0.93 0.5766
15. 3.5% of 70 2.45
16. 4.2% of 39 1.638
17. 9.2% of 28 2.576
18. 4.5% of 90 4.05
19. 0.7% of 82 0.574
20. 0.5% of 35 0.175
21. 7.6% of 260 19.76
22. 5.8% of 430 24.94
23. 2.75% of 95 2.6125
24. 6.25% of 75 4.6875
25. 150% of 8 12
26. 125% of 40 50
27. 300% of 6.75 20.25

PROBLEM SOLVING
The applications on pages 247, 250–255 may be used anytime after this lesson.

Set F

Find each number.

1. $2\frac{1}{2}\%$ of 370 9.25
2. $1\frac{1}{2}\%$ of 49 0.735
3. $12\frac{1}{2}\%$ of 2000 250
4. $37\frac{1}{2}\%$ of 1600 600
5. $1\frac{1}{2}\%$ of 27 0.405
6. $2\frac{1}{2}\%$ of 430 10.75
7. $\frac{1}{2}\%$ of 525 2.625
8. $\frac{1}{4}\%$ of 330 0.825
9. $\frac{3}{4}\%$ of 290 2.175
10. $\frac{1}{2}\%$ of 675 3.375
11. $8\frac{1}{4}\%$ of 500 41.25
12. $6\frac{3}{4}\%$ of 700 47.25
13. $5\frac{3}{4}\%$ of 3000 172.5
14. $7\frac{1}{4}\%$ of 1400 101.5
15. $9\frac{1}{2}\%$ of 783 74.385
16. $6\frac{1}{2}\%$ of 945 61.425
17. $37\frac{1}{2}\%$ of 55 20.625
18. $12\frac{1}{2}\%$ of 75 9.375
19. $4\frac{1}{5}\%$ of 400 16.8
20. $3\frac{4}{5}\%$ of 860 32.68
21. $9\frac{3}{5}\%$ of 349 33.504

Set G

Find each number.

1. $66\frac{2}{3}\%$ of 12 8
2. $33\frac{1}{3}\%$ of 27 9
3. $33\frac{1}{3}\%$ of 90 30
4. $66\frac{2}{3}\%$ of 30 20
5. $16\frac{2}{3}\%$ of 18 3
6. $16\frac{2}{3}\%$ of 36 6
7. $83\frac{1}{3}\%$ of 72 60
8. $83\frac{1}{3}\%$ of 96 80
9. $66\frac{2}{3}\%$ of 75 50
10. $33\frac{1}{3}\%$ of 57 19
11. $16\frac{2}{3}\%$ of 240 40
12. $83\frac{1}{3}\%$ of 60 50
13. $33\frac{1}{3}\%$ of 282 94
14. $66\frac{2}{3}\%$ of 123 82
15. 25% of 28 7
16. 75% of 24 18
17. $33\frac{1}{3}\%$ of 48 16
18. $66\frac{2}{3}\%$ of 63 42
19. $22\frac{2}{9}\%$ of 45 10
20. $133\frac{1}{3}\%$ of 21 28
21. $166\frac{2}{3}\%$ of 12 20

Mixed Practice

Find each number.

F 1. $7\frac{1}{2}\%$ of 39.4 2.955
E 2. 13% of 7.7 1.001
E 3. 150% of 400 600
E 4. 7.2% of 5.3 0.3816
G 5. $33\frac{1}{3}\%$ of 81 27
E 6. 4% of 19.87 0.7948
F 7. $12\frac{1}{2}\%$ of 56 7
E 8. 24% of 473 113.52
F 9. $37\frac{1}{2}\%$ of 1700 637.5
E 10. 25% of 47 11.75
E 11. 0.3% of 216 0.648
F 12. $5\frac{1}{2}\%$ of 58.6 3.223
G 13. $66\frac{2}{3}\%$ of 45 30
E 14. 200% of 300 600
E 15. 10% of 1500 150
E 16. 1% of 1200 12
E 17. 4.6% of 2.9 0.1334
G 18. $16\frac{2}{3}\%$ of 84 14
E 19. 2.5% of 290 7.25
F 20. $37\frac{1}{2}\%$ of 48 18
E 21. 15% of 6.3 0.945
F 22. $12\frac{1}{2}\%$ of 2300 287.5
E 23. 32% of 362 115.84
E 24. 0.4% of 613 2.452
E 25. 6% of 24.95 1.497
E 26. 3.5% of 250 8.75
G 27. $83\frac{1}{3}\%$ of 78 65

See Skills File, page 423, for more practice.

Objective: Find what percent one number is of another.

Finding a Percent

Example H Whole-number percents

7 is what percent of 35?

$7 = n \times 35$ Write an equation.

$\frac{7}{35} = \frac{n \times 35}{35}$ Divide both sides by 35.

$\frac{7}{35} = n$

$$\begin{array}{r} 0.20 \\ 35\overline{)7.00} \\ -7\,0 \\ \hline 00 \end{array}$$

Divide until the quotient is in hundredths.

$n = 0.20$, or 20% Write the answer as a percent.

7 is 20% of 35. To check, substitute 20% for *n* in the original equation.

Example I Fraction and mixed-number percents

2 is what percent of 24?

$2 = t \times 24$ Write an equation.

$\frac{2}{24} = \frac{t \times 24}{24}$ Divide both sides by 24.

$\frac{2}{24} = t$

$$\begin{array}{r} 0.08\frac{8}{24} = 0.08\frac{1}{3} \\ 24\overline{)2.00} \\ -1\,92 \\ \hline 8 \end{array}$$

Divide until the quotient is in hundredths.

$t = 0.08\frac{1}{3}$, or $8\frac{1}{3}\%$ Write the answer as a percent.

2 is $8\frac{1}{3}\%$ of 24.

Exercises

Set H

1. 3 is what percent of 10? 30%
2. 9 is what percent of 90? 10%
3. 68 is what percent of 100? 68%
4. 54 is what percent of 200? 27%
5. 13 is what percent of 25? 52%
6. 47 is what percent of 50? 94%
7. 11 is what percent of 20? 55%
8. 28 is what percent of 80? 35%
9. 6 is what percent of 15? 40%
10. 18 is what percent of 24? 75%
11. 4 is what percent of 16? 25%
12. 27 is what percent of 45? 60%
13. 141 is what percent of 470? 30%
14. 364 is what percent of 520? 70%
15. 3.3 is what percent of 55? 6%
16. 18.4 is what percent of 23? 80%
17. 35.1 is what percent of 65? 54%
18. 1.4 is what percent of 35? 4%
19. 13.3 is what percent of 19? 70%
20. 52.7 is what percent of 85? 62%
21. 3.3 is what percent of 7.5? 44%
22. 12.6 is what percent of 22.5? 56%
23. What percent of 25 is 5? 20%
24. What percent of 70 is 7? 10%
25. What percent of 64 is 22.4? 35%
26. What percent of 12 is 5.4? 45%
27. What percent of 9 is 18? 200%
28. What percent of 25 is 30? 120%

Discuss how to write an equation for the problem: "What percent of 35 is 7?" [$n \times 35 = 7$] See Exercises 23–28 in Sets H and I.

PROBLEM SOLVING
The applications on pages 248–249 may be used anytime after this lesson.

Set I

1. 3 is what percent of 24? $12\frac{1}{2}\%$
2. 5 is what percent of 16? $31\frac{1}{4}\%$
3. 28 is what percent of 42? $66\frac{2}{3}\%$
4. 50 is what percent of 90? $55\frac{5}{9}\%$
5. 10 is what percent of 60? $16\frac{2}{3}\%$
6. 6 is what percent of 16? $37\frac{1}{2}\%$
7. 9 is what percent of 63? $14\frac{2}{7}\%$
8. 19 is what percent of 57? $33\frac{1}{3}\%$
9. 7 is what percent of 84? $8\frac{1}{3}\%$
10. 4 is what percent of 56? $7\frac{1}{7}\%$
11. 6 is what percent of 13? $46\frac{2}{13}\%$
12. 7 is what percent of 22? $31\frac{9}{11}\%$
13. 30 is what percent of 35? $85\frac{5}{7}\%$
14. 20 is what percent of 28? $71\frac{3}{7}\%$
15. 49 is what percent of 42? $116\frac{2}{3}\%$
16. 72 is what percent of 54? $133\frac{1}{3}\%$
17. 56 is what percent of 128? $43\frac{3}{4}\%$
18. 88 is what percent of 165? $53\frac{1}{3}\%$
19. 1.1 is what percent of 40? $2\frac{3}{4}\%$
20. 3.3 is what percent of 60? $5\frac{1}{2}\%$
21. 2.1 is what percent of 3.6? $58\frac{1}{3}\%$
22. 3.9 is what percent of 4.5? $86\frac{2}{3}\%$
23. What percent of 300 is 200? $66\frac{2}{3}\%$
24. What percent of 700 is 300? $42\frac{6}{7}\%$
25. What percent of 80 is 23? $28\frac{3}{4}\%$
26. What percent of 40 is 31? $77\frac{1}{2}\%$
27. What percent of 9 is 2? $22\frac{2}{9}\%$
28. What percent of 7 is 4? $57\frac{1}{7}\%$

Mixed Practice

H 1. 14 is what percent of 25? 56%
I 2. 20 is what percent of 48? $41\frac{2}{3}\%$
I 3. 48 is what percent of 54? $88\frac{8}{9}\%$
H 4. 0.43 is what percent of 43? 1%
I 5. 54 is what percent of 48? $112\frac{1}{2}\%$
H 6. 129 is what percent of 300? 43%
H 7. 2.8 is what percent of 35? 8%
I 8. 24 is what percent of 64? $37\frac{1}{2}\%$
H 9. 31 is what percent of 62? 50%
H 10. 56 is what percent of 28? 200%
I 11. 2 is what percent of 4.4? $45\frac{5}{11}\%$
I 12. 15 is what percent of 18? $83\frac{1}{3}\%$
I 13. 4.5 is what percent of 72? $6\frac{1}{4}\%$
H 14. What percent of 75 is 36? 48%
H 15. What percent of 200 is 78? 39%
I 16. 8 is what percent of 13? $61\frac{7}{13}\%$
H 17. 7 is what percent of 28? 25%
I 18. What percent of 112 is 70? $62\frac{1}{2}\%$
I 19. 18 is what percent of 54? $33\frac{1}{3}\%$
H 20. What percent of 32.5 is 1.3? 4%
I 21. 12 is what percent of 45? $26\frac{2}{3}\%$
I 22. 0.3 is what percent of 20? $1\frac{1}{2}\%$
I 23. What percent of 105 is 51? $48\frac{4}{7}\%$
H 24. 76 is what percent of 95? 80%
H 25. What percent of 6.3 is 6.3? 100%
H 26. 33 is what percent of 44? 75%
H 27. 54 is what percent of 18? 300%
I 28. What percent of 42 is 70? $166\frac{2}{3}\%$

See Skills File, page 423, for more practice.

Objective: Find a number when a percent of it is known.

Finding a Number When a Percent Is Known

Example J Using a decimal

22 is 40% of what number?

$22 = 0.4 \times n$ Write an equation with the percent named as a decimal.

$\frac{22}{0.4} = \frac{0.4 \times n}{0.4}$ Divide both sides by 0.4.

$\frac{22}{0.4} = n$

$$\begin{array}{r} 55. \\ 0.4\overline{)22.0} \\ -20 \\ \hline 2\,0 \\ -2\,0 \\ \hline 0 \end{array}$$

Divide.

$55 = n$

22 is 40% of 55.

Discuss how to write an equation for the same problem stated this way: "40% of what number is 22?" [$0.4 \times n = 22$]

See Exercises 23–28 in Set J, and Exercises 19–22 in Set K.

Example K Using a fraction

17 is $33\frac{1}{3}$% of what number?

$17 = \frac{1}{3} \times w$ Write an equation with the percent named as a fraction.

$\frac{3}{1} \times 17 = \frac{3}{1} \times \frac{1}{3} \times w$ Divide both sides by $\frac{1}{3}$. To divide, multiply both sides by the reciprocal of the fraction. The reciprocal of $\frac{1}{3}$ is $\frac{3}{1}$.

$\frac{3}{1} \times \frac{17}{1} = w$

$51 = w$

17 is $33\frac{1}{3}$% of 51.

Exercises

Set J

1. 9 is 20% of what number? 45
2. 14 is 70% of what number? 20
3. 27 is 90% of what number? 30
4. 57 is 60% of what number? 95
5. 6 is 8% of what number? 75
6. 9 is 6% of what number? 150
7. 63 is 75% of what number? 84
8. 39 is 25% of what number? 156
9. 58 is 200% of what number? 29
10. 72 is 300% of what number? 24
11. 48 is 150% of what number? 32
12. 45 is 250% of what number? 18
13. 56 is 35% of what number? 160
14. 11 is 44% of what number? 25
15. 20.4 is 51% of what number? 40
16. 73.8 is 82% of what number? 90
17. 3 is 0.4% of what number? 750
18. 17 is 0.2% of what number? 8500
19. 7.25 is 0.25% of what number? 2900
20. 9.75 is 0.75% of what number? 1300
21. 12 is $1\frac{1}{2}$% of what number? 800
22. 3 is $7\frac{1}{2}$% of what number? 40
23. 10% of what number is 73? 730
24. 4% of what number is 13? 325
25. 2.4% of what number is 144? 6000
26. 30% of what number is 99? 330
27. 5% of what number is 24? 480
28. 3.6% of what number is 108? 3000

Set K

1. 6 is $33\frac{1}{3}\%$ of what number? 18
2. 15 is $33\frac{1}{3}\%$ of what number? 45
3. 10 is $66\frac{2}{3}\%$ of what number? 15
4. 24 is $66\frac{2}{3}\%$ of what number? 36
5. 4 is $16\frac{2}{3}\%$ of what number? 24
6. 29 is $16\frac{2}{3}\%$ of what number? 174
7. 25 is $12\frac{1}{2}\%$ of what number? 200
8. 7 is $12\frac{1}{2}\%$ of what number? 56
9. 24 is $37\frac{1}{2}\%$ of what number? 64
10. 9 is $37\frac{1}{2}\%$ of what number? 24
11. 2 is 25% of what number? 8
12. 30 is 25% of what number? 120
13. 20 is $11\frac{1}{9}\%$ of what number? 180
14. 11 is $11\frac{1}{9}\%$ of what number? 99
15. 56 is 50% of what number? 112
16. 12 is 50% of what number? 24
17. 16 is $133\frac{1}{3}\%$ of what number? 12
18. 52 is $133\frac{1}{3}\%$ of what number? 39
19. $33\frac{1}{3}\%$ of what number is 37? 111
20. $66\frac{2}{3}\%$ of what number is 58? 87
21. $66\frac{2}{3}\%$ of what number is 86? 129
22. $33\frac{1}{3}\%$ of what number is 72? 216

Mixed Practice

J 1. 86 is 40% of what number? 215
K 2. 53 is $33\frac{1}{3}\%$ of what number? 159
J 3. 91 is 65% of what number? 140
J 4. 36 is 0.8% of what number? 4500
K 5. 28 is 25% of what number? 112
K 6. 24 is $16\frac{2}{3}\%$ of what number? 144
J 7. 9 is $1\frac{1}{2}\%$ of what number? 600
J 8. 15 is 2.5% of what number? 600
K 9. 38 is $66\frac{2}{3}\%$ of what number? 57
K 10. 65 is $11\frac{1}{9}\%$ of what number? 585
J 11. 124.8 is 160% of what number? 78
K 12. 19 is $12\frac{1}{2}\%$ of what number? 152
J 13. 66 is 75% of what number? 88
K 14. 45 is $37\frac{1}{2}\%$ of what number? 120
J 15. 72 is 0.9% of what number? 8000
J 16. 120% of what number is 67.2? 56
J 17. 90 is 4.5% of what number? 2000
J 18. 50% of what number is 207? 414
K 19. 63 is $37\frac{1}{2}\%$ of what number? 168
J 20. $5\frac{1}{2}\%$ of what number is 66? 1200
K 21. 27 is $33\frac{1}{3}\%$ of what number? 81
K 22. $66\frac{2}{3}\%$ of what number is 64? 96
K 23. $16\frac{2}{3}\%$ of what number is 14? 84
J 24. 45% of what number is 108? 240
K 25. 39 is $11\frac{1}{9}\%$ of what number? 351
J 26. 25% of what number is 29? 116
K 27. 46 is $12\frac{1}{2}\%$ of what number? 368
J 28. 451 is 50% of what number? 902

See Skills File, page 423, for more practice.

SKILLS POSTTEST

Number of test items - 11

Number missed	1	2	3	4	5
Percent correct	91	82	73	64	55

SKILL Writing Percents and Decimals *pages 236–237*

A Write 6% as a decimal.
0.06

B Write 0.418 as a percent.
41.8%

SKILL Writing Percents and Fractions *pages 238–239*

C Write 15% as a fraction in lowest terms.
$\frac{3}{20}$

D Write $\frac{2}{5}$ as a percent.
40%

SKILL Finding a Percent of a Number *pages 240–241*

E Find 39% of 64.
24.96

F Find $7\frac{1}{4}$% of 900.
65.25

G Find $66\frac{2}{3}$% of 48.
32

SKILL Finding a Percent *pages 242–243*

H 7 is what percent of 25?
28%

I 15 is what percent of 36?
$41\frac{2}{3}$%

SKILL Finding a Number When a Percent Is Known *pages 244–245*

J 91 is 65% of what number?
140

K 57 is $33\frac{1}{3}$% of what number?
171

Problem Solving

CONSUMER APPLICATIONS

Finding Amount of Discount and Sale Price

Objective: Solve problems involving percent.

In this lesson students compute the amount of discount and the sale price of certain sports equipment.

See page 32 of *Problem-Solving Masters*.

Phil Whitewing bought a toboggan on sale at a 25% discount. The regular price of the toboggan was $89.98. How much did he save by purchasing the toboggan on sale?

$89.98	Regular price
× 0.25	Percent of discount (25% = 0.25)
4 4990	
17 9960	
$22.4950 ≈ $22.50	Amount Phil saved

What was the sale price of the toboggan?

$89.98	Regular price
− 22.50	Amount saved
$67.48	Sale price

The amounts of the discounts are rounded to the nearest cent, rather than *always* being rounded *up* to the next whole cent. Stores commonly do not round amounts of money in favor of the customer.

For each item, find the amount saved. Round your answer to the nearest whole cent. Then find the sale price.

The sale price is shown in parentheses.

	Item	Regular price	Discount
1.	Figure skates $9.90 ($39.60)	$49.50	20%
2.	Hockey skates $12.40 ($49.60)	$62.00	20%
3.	Hockey stick $2.10 ($11.89)	$13.99	15%
4.	Skis $23.50 ($211.50)	$235.00	10%
5.	Ski jacket $15.30 ($61.19)	$76.49	20%
6.	Ski gloves $7.50 ($17.49)	$24.99	30%
7.	Ski goggles $5.49 ($12.80)	$18.29	30%
8.	Sled $2.65 ($23.85)	$26.50	10%
9.	Insulated boots $16.24 ($48.71)	$64.95	25%
10.	Snowmobile suit $28.25 ($84.73)	$112.98	25%

Problem Solving

CONSUMER APPLICATIONS

Objective: Solve problems involving percent.

In this lesson students compute amounts of simple interest, total cost, and monthly interest rates for certain loans.

Finding Simple Interest

Mr. Stumfel wanted to buy a $475 stereo system. He borrowed the money for 2 months at an interest rate of 2.5% per month. How much interest did he pay?

Use the **simple-interest** formula:

$$I = P \times R \times T$$

- I — Interest
- P — Principal (Amount borrowed)
- R — Rate (Percent)
- T — Time

$I = P \times R \times T$

$I = 475 \times 2.5\% \times 2$ — Write the percent as a decimal.

$I = 475 \times 0.025 \times 2$ — Multiply.

$I = 23.75$

Mr. Stumfel paid $23.75 interest.

If he paid back the loan in one payment, how much did Mr. Stumfel pay at the end of 2 months?

$475.00	Principal
+ 23.75	Interest
$498.75	Total amount paid

Mr. Stumfel paid a total amount of $498.75.

Monthly interest rates are given. Find the amount of interest charged on a loan to buy each item. Then find the total amount to be paid for each item.

The total amount to be paid is shown in parentheses.

1. Draperies: $98 at 1.5% for 6 months
   $8.82 ($106.82)
2. Dresser: $279 at 3% for 9 months
   $75.33 ($354.33)
3. Chair: $165 at $2\frac{1}{2}$% for 4 months
   $16.50 ($181.50)
4. China: $225 at $1\frac{1}{4}$% for 12 months
   $33.75 ($258.75)
5. Dinette set: $329 at 2% for 3 months
   $19.74 ($348.74)
6. Desk: $236 at $1\frac{1}{2}$% for 7 months
   $24.78 ($260.78)
7. Brass lamp: $245 at $1\frac{3}{4}$% for 8 months
   $34.30 ($279.30)
8. End table: $129 at 2% for 12 months
   $30.96 ($159.96)
9. Bed: $319 at 1.8% for 5 months
   $28.71 ($347.71)
10. Television: $489 at 2.5% for 18 months
    $220.05 ($709.05)

See page 33 of *Problem-Solving Masters.*

Mr. Stumfel borrowed money to buy a sofa priced at \$420. The interest for 3 months was \$31.50. What was the rate of interest?

Use this formula:

$$R = \frac{I}{P \times T} \begin{matrix} \leftarrow \text{Interest} \\ \leftarrow \text{Principal} \times \text{Time} \end{matrix}$$

$\uparrow$ Rate

$$R = \frac{I}{P \times T}$$

$$R = \frac{31.50}{420 \times 3}$$ Multiply 420 and 3.

$$R = \frac{31.50}{1260}$$ Divide 31.50 by 1260.

$$\begin{array}{r} 0.025 \\ 1260\overline{)31.500} \\ -\ 25\ 20 \\ \hline 6\ 300 \\ -\ 6\ 300 \\ \hline 0 \end{array}$$ Divide until the remainder is zero.

$R = 0.025$, or 2.5% Write the rate as a percent.

The rate of interest was 2.5% per month.

Find the monthly interest rate charged by each company on a loan of \$1800.

11. Company A: \$81 interest for 3 months
1.5%

12. Company B: \$216 interest for 6 months
2%

13. Company C: \$90 interest for 4 months
1.25%

14. Company D: \$225 interest for 5 months
2.5%

15. Company E: \$40.50 interest for 1 month
2.25%

16. Company F: \$441 interest for 7 months
3.5%

17. Company G: \$63 interest for 2 months
1.75%

18. Company H: \$243 interest for 9 months
1.5%

19. Company I: \$99 interest for 2 months
2.75%

20. Company J: \$648 interest for 12 months
3%

Problem Solving

CONSUMER APPLICATIONS

Objective: Solve problems involving percent.

In this lesson students find the monthly finance charge for a lawn tractor purchased on credit.

Buying on Credit

Mr. and Mrs. Rogers used a credit plan to buy a $1900 lawn tractor. They paid for the tractor in monthly payments of $180 each. They also paid a monthly finance charge of 2% per month on the unpaid balance.

What was the balance on Mr. and Mrs. Rogers' account after the first monthly payment in April?

Beginning balance	$1900
Subtract April payment.	− 180
New amount	$1720
Find 2% of new amount.	× 0.02
Finance charge	$34.40
Add finance charge and new amount.	+ 1720.00
Balance	$1754.40

After the April payment the balance was $1754.40.

Stores have various plans for buying on installment and with revolving charge accounts. You may wish to have students gather information and discuss the advantages and disadvantages of this type of buying.

See pages 34–35 of *Problem-Solving Masters.*

Complete this table to find the balance on the Rogers' account after each monthly payment. In computing the finance charge, always round your answer up to the next whole cent.

	Month	Balance	Payment	New amount	2% finance charge	Balance
	April	$1900	$180	$1720	$34.40	$1754.40
1.	May	$1754.40	$180	$1574.40 (1754.40 − 180)	$31.49	$1605.89
2.	June	$1605.89	$180	$1425.89	$28.52	$1454.41
3.	July	$1454.41	$180	$1274.41	$25.49	$1299.90
4.	August	$1299.90	$180	$1119.90	$22.40	$1142.30
5.	September	$1142.30	$180	$962.30	$19.25	$981.55
6.	October	$981.55	$180	$801.55	$16.04	$817.59
7.	November	$817.59	$180	$637.59	$12.76	$650.35
8.	December	$650.35	$180	$470.35	$9.41	$479.76
9.	January	$479.76	$180	$299.76	$6.00	$305.76
10.	February	$305.76	$180	$125.76	$2.52	$128.28
11.	March	$128.28	$128.28	0	0	0

12. What was the total amount that Mr. and Mrs. Rogers paid in finance charges? $208.28
13. What was the total amount paid by Mr. and Mrs. Rogers? $2108.28

Problem Solving

CAREER APPLICATIONS

Objective: Solve problems involving percent.

In this lesson students find ohmic value and acceptable tolerance range for resistors.

Television Inspector

Career Cluster: Trades Nancy Parkens inspects television sets. Part of her job is to check the ohmic value of the resistors. Nancy also finds if the resistance is within the acceptable tolerance range.

Resistors resist the flow of electricity. The higher the ohmic value of a resistor, the harder it is for the electrical current to flow through the resistor. Most resistors have colored bands that show their ohmic value. The code for the colored bands is in these tables.

Digit bands	
Black (BK)	0
Brown (BR)	1
Red (R)	2
Orange (O)	3
Yellow (Y)	4
Green (G)	5
Blue (B)	6
Violet (V)	7
Gray (GY)	8
White (W)	9

Factor band	
Gray (GY)	÷ 100
Gold (GD)	÷ 10
Black (BK)	÷ 1
Brown (BR)	× 10
Red (R)	× 100
Orange (O)	× 1000
Yellow (Y)	× 10,000
Green (G)	× 100,000
Blue (B)	× 1,000,000

Tolerance band	
No band	± 20%
Silver (S)	± 10%
Gold (GD)	± 5%
Red (R)	± 2%

Some resistors have a fifth band that gives the reliability rating. For the purpose of this lesson, the fifth band can be ignored.

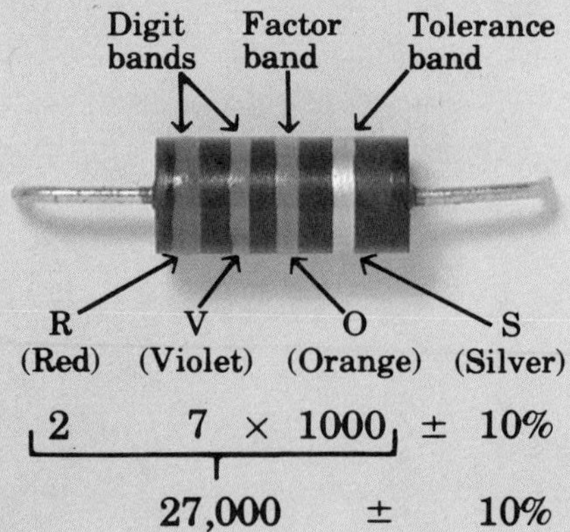

The first two bands form a two-digit number.

The factor band tells you to multiply or to divide by a certain multiple of 10.

The tolerance band gives the possible percent of variation in the ohmic value.

To find the acceptable tolerance range for this resistor, first find 10% of 27,000. Add 10% to 27,000 to find the highest acceptable value. Subtract 10% from 27,000 to find the lowest acceptable value.

The ohmic value of this resistor is 27,000 ± 10%.

10% of 27,000 is 2700.

$$\begin{array}{r} 27000 \\ +\ 2700 \\ \hline 29700 \end{array} \qquad \begin{array}{r} 27000 \\ -\ 2700 \\ \hline 24300 \end{array}$$

The acceptable tolerance range for this resistor is 24,300 ohms to 29,700 ohms.

Find the ohmic value and the acceptable tolerance range for each resistor.

1. 
39,000 ± 10%; 35,100 ohms to 42,900 ohms

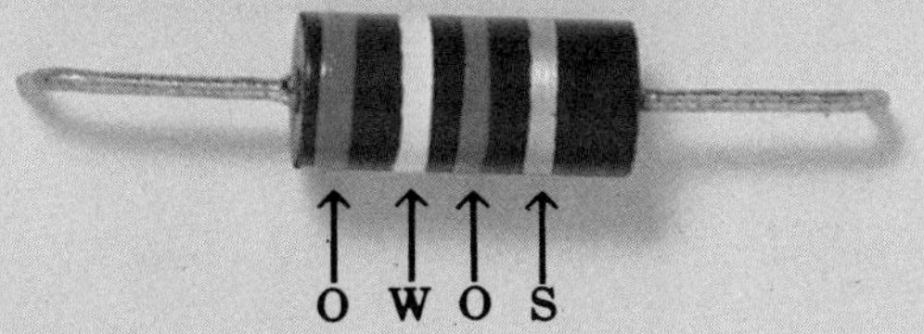

2. 220,000 ± 10%; 198,000 ohms to 242,000 ohms

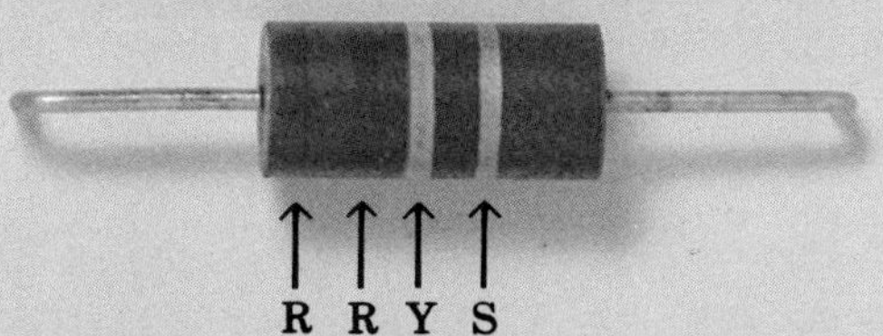

3. 68,000 ± 10%; 61,200 ohms to 74,800 ohms

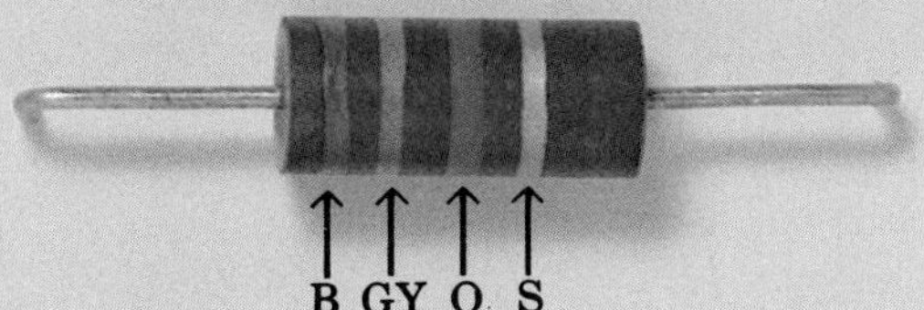

4. 330,000 ± 10%; 297,000 ohms to 363,000 ohms

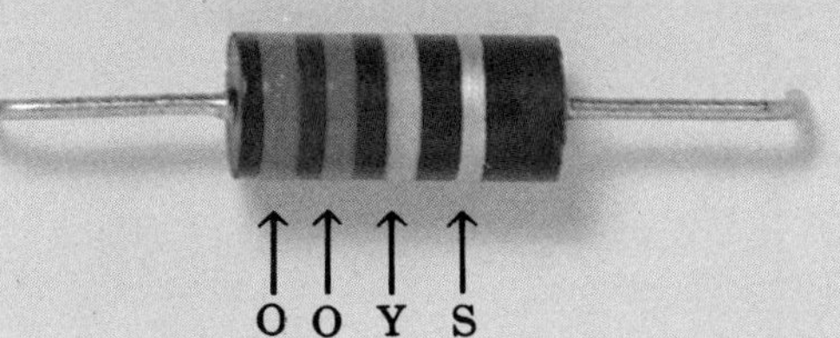

5. 2,700,000 ± 10%; 2,430,000 ohms to 2,970,000 ohms

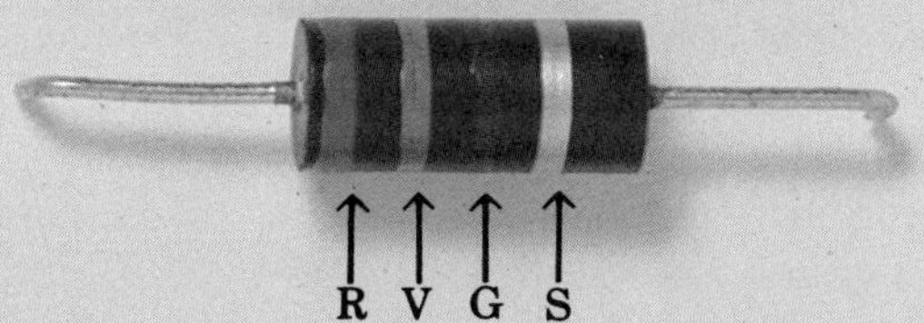

6. 82,000 ± 10%; 73,800 ohms to 90,200 ohms

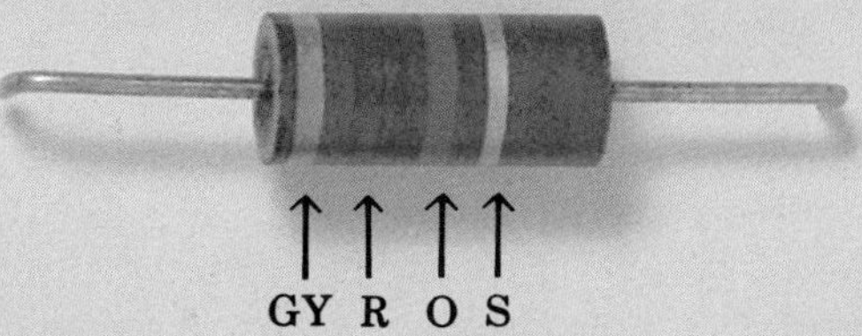

7. 22,000 ± 10%; 19,800 ohms to 24,200 ohms

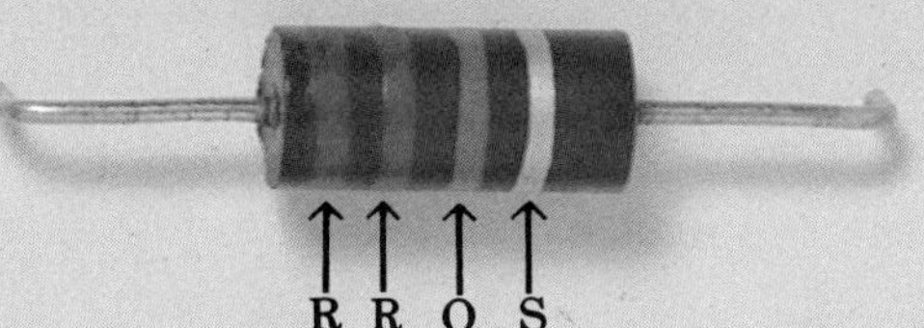

8. 10,000,000 ± 10%; 9,000,000 ohms to 11,000,000 ohms

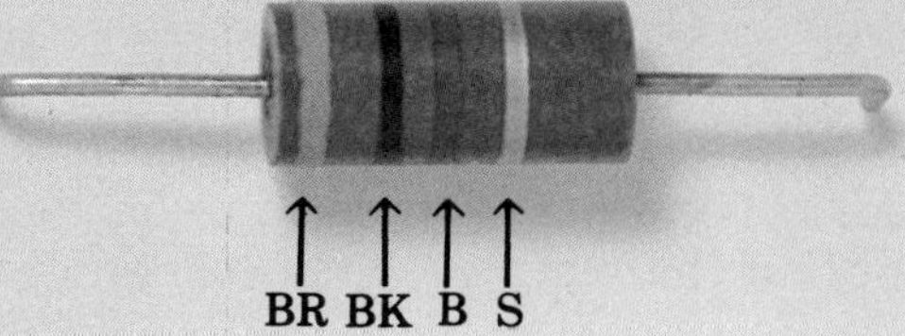

Problem Solving

DEVELOPING STRATEGIES

Objective: Solve problems by reading a table, reading a scale, and working backward.

In this lesson students find the amount of cleaner to be added to a solution.

Tactics: Reading a Table, Reading a Scale, Working Backward

Darlene Parry works for an industrial cleaner company. In her job, she uses a refractometer to check the concentration of cleaner in cleaning solutions. If the solution does not contain the recommended concentration of cleaner, she works backward to find the amount of cleaner needed to raise the concentration close to the recommended level.

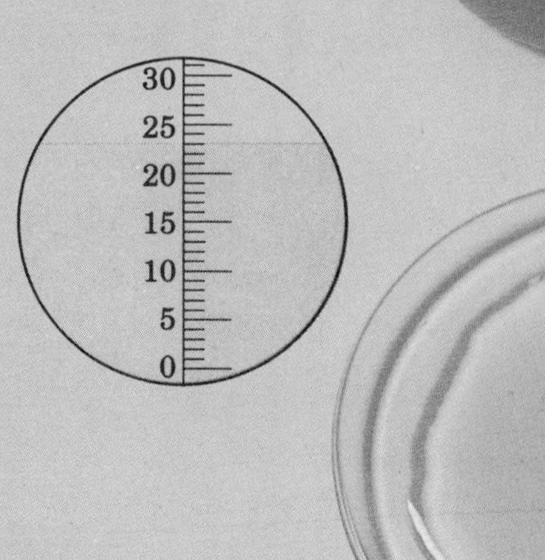

Problem

A Scour solution is used in a machine shop to clean gears. How much Scour should be added to 400 liters of solution to raise the concentration close to the recommended level? Use the refractometer reading in the picture and the table on page 255.

Solution

Darlene's strategy for solving the problem includes the tactics of reading a table, reading a scale, and working backward from the recommended concentration.

a. What is the recommended concentration for Scour? Read the table on page 255. — 12%

b. What is the refractometer reading? Read the scale. — 23

c. What is the conversion factor? Read the table on page 255. — 0.37

d. What is the percent of Scour in the solution? Multiply the refractometer reading by the conversion factor. — $0.37 \times 23 = 8.51$

e. The concentration of Scour in the solution is how much less than the recommended concentration of Scour? Subtract. — $12\% - 8.51\% = 3.49\%$

f. How many liters of Scour will be added? Change 3.49% to a decimal and multiply. — $400 \times 0.0349 = 13.96$

The additional Scour will make the concentration close, but not exactly equal, to 12% because the total amount of solution is now more than 400 liters.

Conclusion: The addition of 13.96 liters of Scour to the solution would raise the concentration close to the recommended level of 12%.

The 0 to 30 scale in the refractometer is plotted in arbitrary units. The conversion factor for each concentrate is determined by taking refractometer readings of 3 to 5 accurately measured, known percents of concentrate in solution.

See page 36 of *Problem-Solving Masters.*

Name of cleaner	Scour	Boast	Ezy	Gone	Lift	Oft	Raze
Recommended concentration	12%	8.7%	6.6%	7.3%	9%	9.2%	10.3%
Conversion factor	0.37	0.27	0.22	0.18	0.41	0.62	0.43

Related Problems

Find the amount of cleaner that must be added to each solution to raise the concentration close to the recommended level.

1. 700 liters of Boast

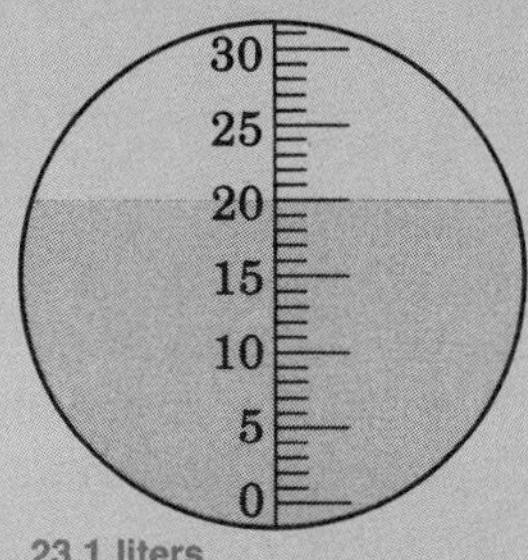

23.1 liters

2. 900 liters of Lift

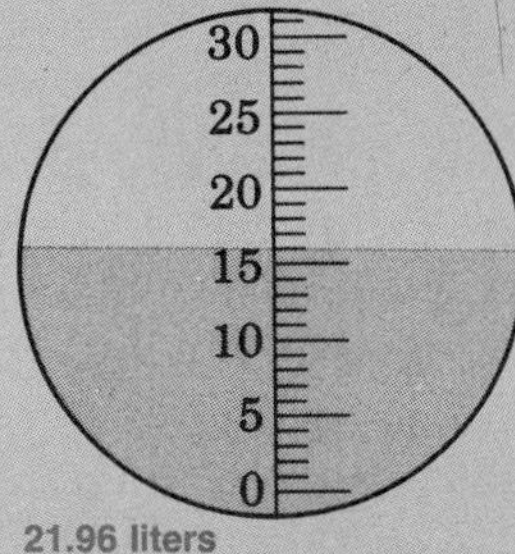

21.96 liters

3. 500 liters of Oft

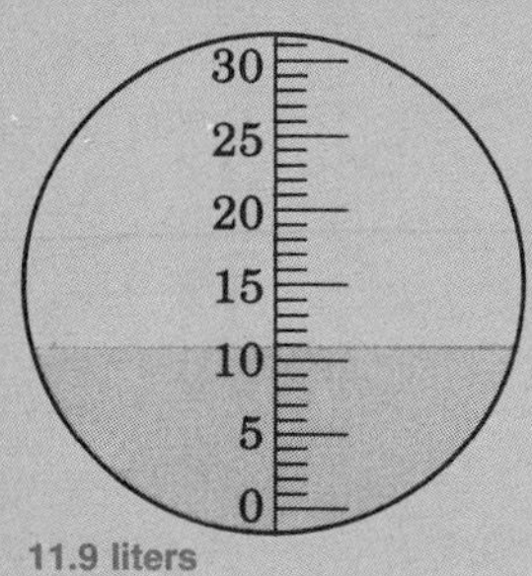

11.9 liters

4. 1000 liters of Ezy

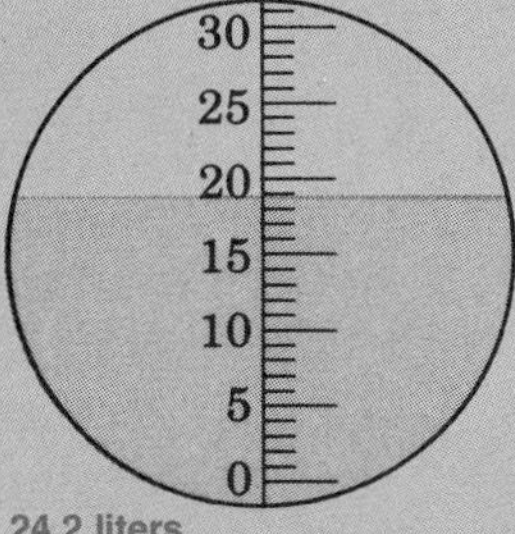

24.2 liters

5. 840 liters of Raze

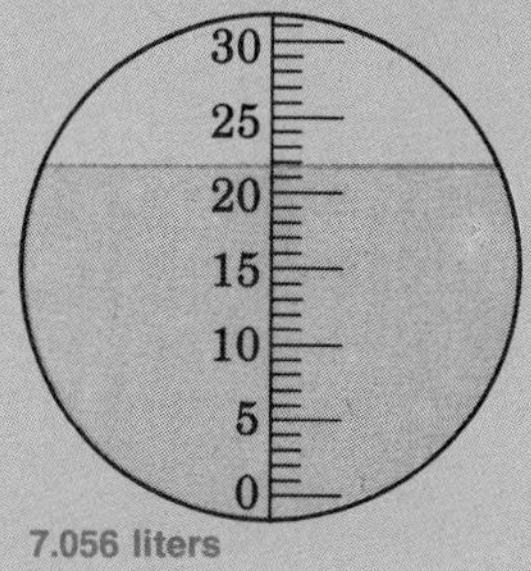

7.056 liters

6. 975 liters of Gone

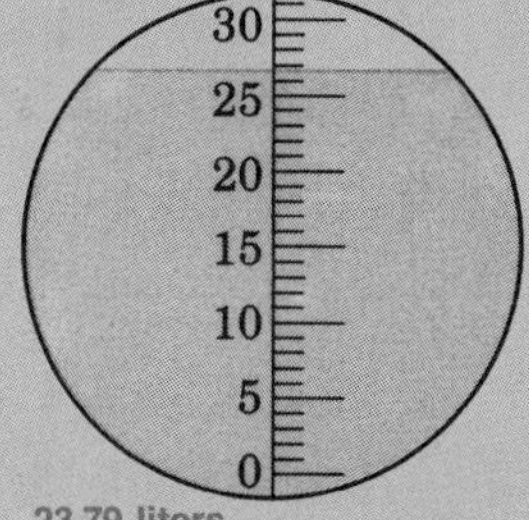

23.79 liters

Extensions

7. Grease is cleaned from machine parts by soaking the parts in a bath containing 700 liters of Ezy solution. The solution being used has a refractometer reading of 16. If Ezy cleaner costs $21 per liter, find the cost of the cleaner needed to raise the concentration close to the recommended level.
$452.76

8. An Oft solution is used to clean the ink rollers on printing presses. In 440 liters of the solution, the refractometer reading was 8. If Oft cleaner costs $24 per liter, find the cost of the cleaner needed to raise the concentration close to the recommended level. Round the answer to the next whole cent.
$447.75

CHAPTER 11 TEST

Number of test items - 17

Number missed	1	2	3	4	5	6	7	8
Percent correct	94	88	82	76	71	65	59	53

A **1.** Write 7% as a decimal. 0.07

B **2.** Write 0.594 as a percent. 59.4%

C **3.** Write 35% as a fraction in lowest terms. $\frac{7}{20}$

D **4.** Write $\frac{3}{4}$ as a percent. 75%

E **5.** Find 58% of 72. 41.76

F **6.** Find $4\frac{3}{4}\%$ of 900. 42.75

G **7.** Find $66\frac{2}{3}\%$ of 51. 34

H **8.** 13 is what percent of 20? 65%

I **9.** 22 is what percent of 24? $91\frac{2}{3}\%$

J **10.** 72 is 45% of what number? 160

K **11.** 45 is $33\frac{1}{3}\%$ of what number? 135

Use this information for item 12.

SALE SKI POLES SALE
Regular Price $21.50
25% Discount

12. How much did Erica save if she bought the ski poles on sale? Round your answer to the nearest whole cent.
$5.38

13. Linda Lauer wanted to buy tires priced at $275. She borrowed the money for 6 months at an interest rate of 1.5% per month. How much interest did she pay? Use this formula: $I = P \times R \times T$
$24.75

14. Mr. Doughty borrowed $1400 to buy a dining room set. The interest for 12 months was $420. What was the monthly interest rate?

Use this formula: $R = \dfrac{I}{P \times T}$
2.5%

15. The balance on Mr. Stillman's charge account was $192. He made a $25 monthly payment. Then he was charged 2% for a finance charge. What was the new balance on his account?
$170.34

16. The ohm value for a resistor is 16.3 ohms $\pm$ 10%. Find the acceptable tolerance range for the resistor.
14.67 ohms to 17.93 ohms

17. The recommended concentration for a solution of Scour cleaner is 12%. A tank containing 500 liters of solution has a 7.5% concentration of Scour. How many liters of Scour need to be added to the solution to raise the concentration close to the recommended level?
22.5 liters

 See pages 27–28 of the *Test Masters* for an alternate form of the Chapter 11 Test.

CHAPTER 12 Statistics

SKILLS PRETEST

Materials: Graph paper, protractor

Number of test items - 10

Number missed	1	2	3	4	5
Percent correct	90	80	70	60	50

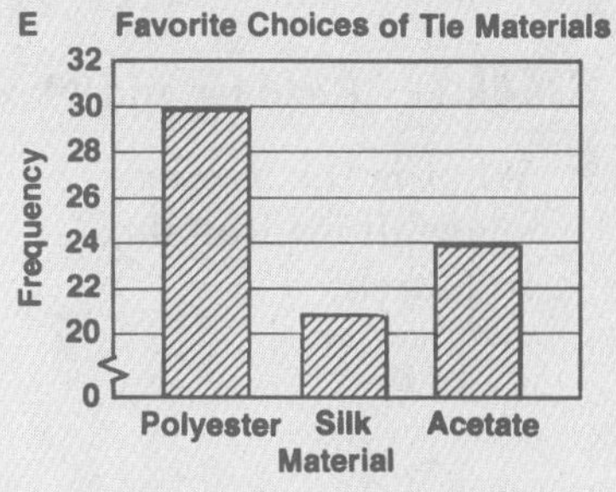

SKILL Finding the Mean *page 259*

A Find the mean for the set of data below. Round your answer to the nearest tenth.
171.3

178 168 163 180
172 178 160

SKILL Finding the Median and the Mode *pages 260–261*

B Find the median for the set of data in item A.
172

C Find the mode for the set of data in item A.
178

SKILL Reading and Making a Bar Graph *pages 262–263*

D On which days were more than 24 ties sold?
Monday, Wednesday

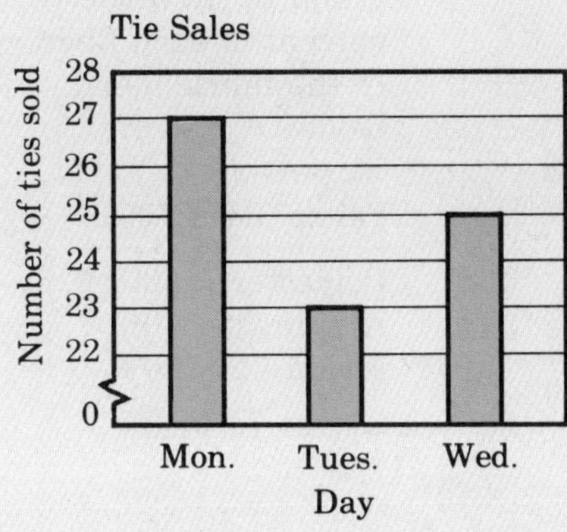

E Make a bar graph for this frequency table.
See above.

Favorite Choices of Tie Materials

Material	Frequency (Number of times chosen)
Polyester	30
Silk	21
Acetate	24

Throughout this Chapter, graphs may vary depending upon choice of scale.

Pretest continued on page 258.

See page T39 for additional notes on Chapter 12.

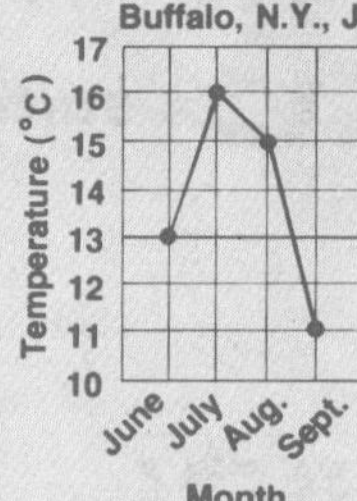

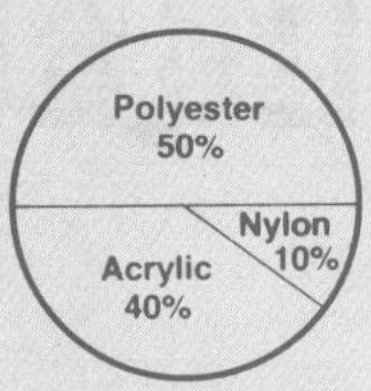

Pretest continued from page 257.

SKILL Reading and Making a Line Graph *pages 264–265*

F What is the average snowfall for Buffalo in March?

30 centimeters

Average Snowfall for Buffalo, N.Y., December–March

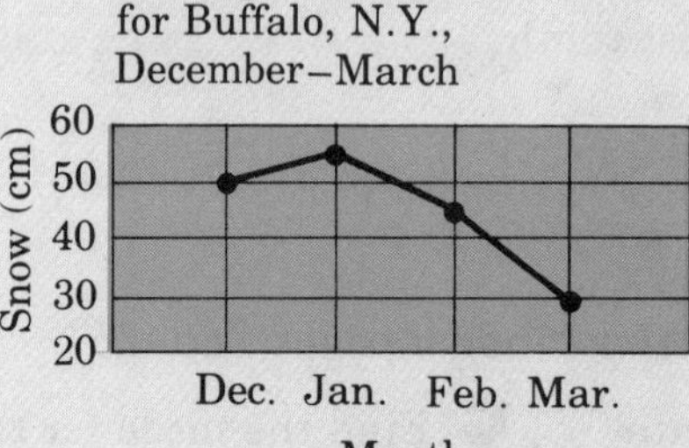

G Make a line graph to show the average monthly temperature for Buffalo from June through September.

See above.

Month	Temperature
June	13°C
July	16°C
August	15°C
September	11°C

SKILL Reading and Making a Circle Graph *pages 266–267*

H Which ingredient makes up the greatest part of dry concrete mix?

Gravel

Dry Concrete Mix

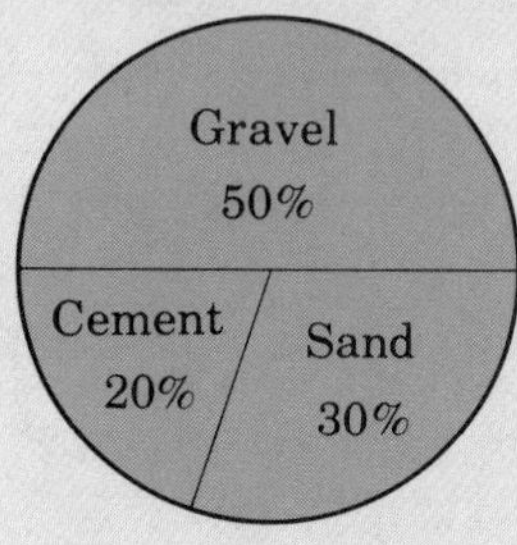

I Use the circle graph in item H to find how much gravel is needed to make 120 kilograms of dry concrete mix.

60 kilograms

J Make a circle graph to show the percent of each fiber in the fabric blend below.

See above.

Fabric Blend Fibers		Central angle
Polyester	50%	180°
Acrylic	40%	144°
Nylon	10%	36°

Objective: Find the mean for a set of data.

Finding the Mean

Example A Finding the mean

The numbers below are the weights in kilograms of a group of students. Find the mean of the weights to the nearest tenth of a kilogram.

47   52   60   75   58   63

The **mean** of a set of data is the same as the average.

To find the mean, first add the items.

$$\begin{array}{r} 47 \\ 52 \\ 60 \\ 75 \\ 58 \\ +\ 63 \\ \hline 355 \end{array} \longleftarrow \text{Sum of items}$$

Then divide the sum of the items by the number of items. Round to the nearest tenth.

$$\text{Number of items} \longrightarrow 6\overline{)355.00} \longleftarrow \text{Sum of items}; \quad \mathbf{59.16} \approx \mathbf{59.2} \longleftarrow \text{Mean}$$

The mean is 59.2 kilograms.

Exercises

PROBLEM SOLVING
The applications on pages 276–277 may be used anytime after this lesson.

Set A

Find the mean for each set of data.
Round each answer to the nearest tenth.

1. 10   3   12   7
8

2. 24   28   16   17
21.3

3. 284   267   225   213
247.3

4. 387   963   435   171
489

5. 9   16   12   8   4
9.8

6. 15   23   25   16   19
19.6

7. 24   86   71   82   91   71
70.8

8. 16   38   92   75   43   67
55.2

9. 7   8   21   32   18
17.2

10. 46   45   32   37   39
39.8

11. 87   81   75   76   92   88   80
82.7

12. 95   43   67   88   76   79   59
72.4

13. 135   97   98   101   156   123
118.3

14. 109   132   145   168   173   198
154.2

15. 256   259   213   298   251   207
247.3

16. 916   102   168   521   798   812
552.8

17. 17   16   19   28   12   11   15   19
17.1

18. 28   25   23   17   34   27   26   25
25.6

19. 102   119   98   135   141   123   134
121.7

20. 359   254   287   301   321   290   288
300

21. 105   196   173   98   117   95
128   189
137.6

22. 207   123   58   396   148   275
312   251
221.3

23. 446   384   567   339   448   502
496   532
464.3

24. 4453   5602   4872   5406   4992   5001
5054.3

25. 1331   2009   2114   1890   1904   2358
1934.3

Additional exercises may be given by assigning several exercises as one.

Finding the Median and the Mode

Example B Finding the median

The numbers below are the lengths in millimeters of pieces of chalk. Find the median of the lengths.

25 40 68 75 32 59
85 79 88 28 46

Arrange the data in order. The **median** is the middle number. It has as many numbers above it as below it.

88
85
79
75
68
59 ← 59 is the median.
46
40
32
28
25

The median is 59 millimeters.

In this set of data, there are two middle numbers, 83 and 78. The median is the average of 83 and 78.

90
90 $83 + 78 = 161$
85 $161 \div 2 = 80.5$
83 ← 80.5 is the median.
78
74
74
70

You may need to review finding averages.

Example C Finding the mode

Find the mode of the test scores below.

76 39 45 76 98 27 19
98 76 18 93 52 76 21

Arrange the data in order. The **mode** is the number that appears most often.

98
98
93
76
76
76 ← 76 is the mode.
76
52
45
39
27
21
19
18

The mode is 76.

The first set of data in Example B has no mode. The second set has two modes, 90 and 74.

Exercises

You might have students find the mean for each set of data. Have them round their answers to the nearest tenth when appropriate. The means are given in the Additional Answers on page T47.

Set B

Find the median for each set of data.

1. 8 7 6 1 2 3 7
   6 (7)
2. 9 2 7 2 2 5 8
   5 (2)
3. 7 8 4 3 2 9 5 6
   5.5 (none)
4. 8 9 5 6 8 5 4 5
   5.5 (5)
5. 16 19 18 14 12 10 16
   12 16 12 11 19 12 18
   15 (12)
6. 75 93 91 16 89 92 72
   89 (none)
7. 178 177 175 178
   178 174 171 175
   176 (178)
8. 769 768 793 772 768 793 782
   772 (768, 793)
9. 12 23 49 12 29 46 12 39
   26 (12)
10. 39 38 35 35 32 38 35 39
    36.5 (35)
11. 359 357 350 352 363 356 362
    357 (none)
12. 986 981 986 984
    988 984 987 984
    985 (984)
13. 15 12 6 9 7 9 9 13 15 14
    10.5 (9)
14. 16 28 15 18 19 23 27 12 14
    18 (none)
15. 76 77 98 59 76 78 76 79
    76.5 (76)
16. 210 200 208 216
    201 209 202 201
    205 (201)
17. 3168 3109 3213 3217 3213
    3189 3192 3068 3105
    3189 (3213)
18. 8764 8772 8760 8762
    8761 8769 8762 8769
    8763 (8762, 8769)
19. 12 16 16 19 30 16 25
    16 (16)
20. 58 75 63 72 54 75 67
    74 63 72 79 75 75 78
    73 (75)
21. 19 17 16 21 28 19 25 19
    16 23 21 18 16 20 21
    19 (16, 19, 21)
22. 12 36 92 95 47 58 76 58
    76 20 76 62 91 87 58
    62 (58, 76)
23. 36 29 38 32 25 23 39 45 31
    37 29 20 31 36 29 38 40 43
    34 (29)
24. 368 374 379 362 375 371 376
    375 368 371 369 375 375 368
    365 371 379
    371 (375)
25. 8719 8907 8019 8791 8279 8709
    8018 8792 8297 8719 8710 8017
    8791 8931 8129 8791 8718
    8718 (8791)

Set C

1–25. Find the mode for each set of data in Set B.

The mode for each set is shown in parentheses.

BREAK TIME

Fill in the missing digits.

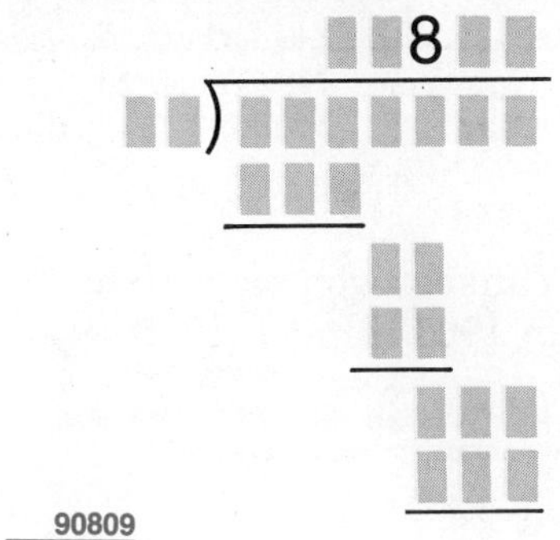


```
     90809
12)1089708
   108
     97
     96
      108
      108
```

Objective: Read and make a bar graph.

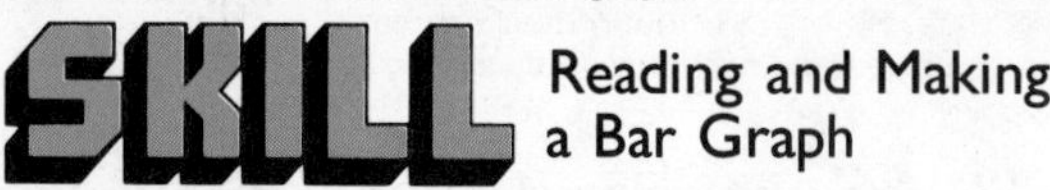

Reading and Making a Bar Graph

Example D Reading a bar graph

Which baseball teams named in the **bar graph** below won more than 20 pennants from 1903 through 1978?

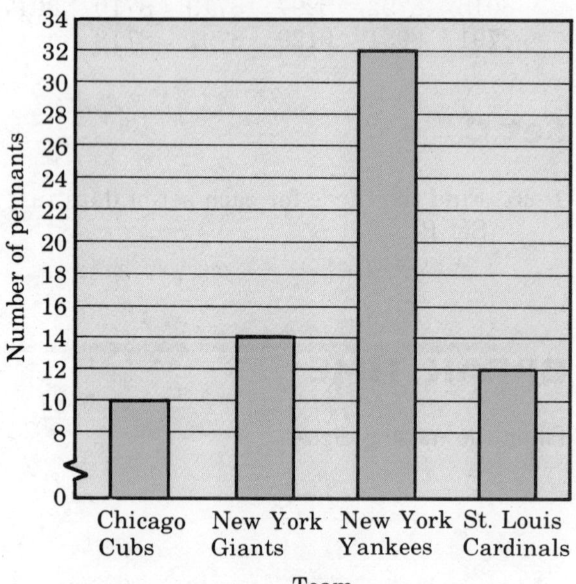

The New York Yankees won more than 20 pennants from 1903 through 1978.

Discuss with students how the choice of scale can make the differences in the data more or less dramatic.

Example E Making a bar graph

Make a bar graph for this frequency table. The table lists some of the National Football League Conference Champions from 1934 through 1979.

NFL Conference Champions, 1934–1979

Team	Frequency (Number of times champion)
Chicago Bears	9
Cleveland Browns	11
Dallas Cowboys	7
Green Bay Packers	10
New York Giants	13

First draw and label a vertical scale to show the number of times a team was the champion. The break in the vertical scale shows that the numbers between 0 and 6 have been omitted. Next draw and label a horizontal scale to show teams.

Finally, draw bars to show the number of times each team was the conference champion, and write a title for the graph.

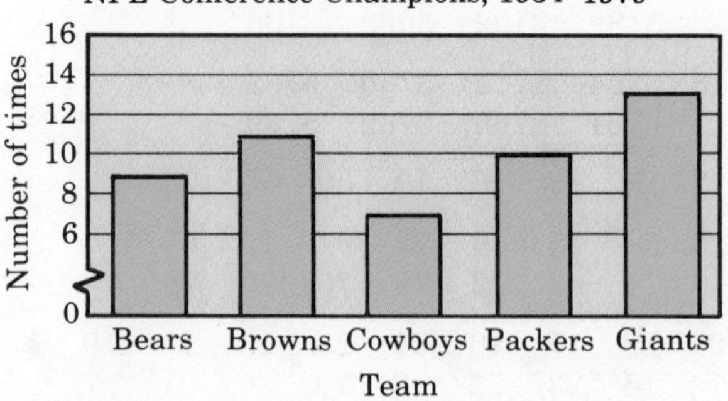

Exercises

Set D

Use the bar graph below for Exercises 1–12.

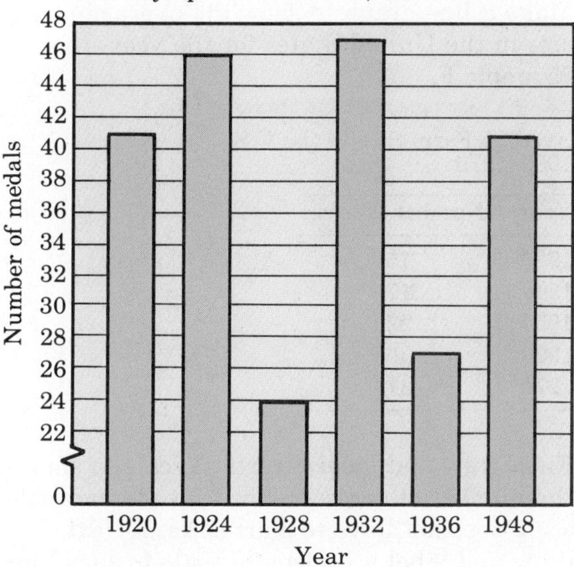

How many gold medals did the U.S. win in

1. 1920? 41 gold medals
2. 1924? 46 gold medals
3. 1928? 24 gold medals
4. 1932? 47 gold medals
5. 1936? 27 gold medals
6. 1948? 41 gold medals

In which years did the U.S. win

7. more than 30 gold medals? 1920, 1924, 1932, 1948
8. 40 or more gold medals? 1920, 1924, 1932, 1948
9. fewer than 28 gold medals? 1928, 1936
10. the same number of gold medals? 1920, 1948

Did the U.S. win more gold medals in

11. 1928 or 1936? 1936
12. 1924 or 1932? 1932

You may wish to include questions that require computation, such as: "How many more gold medals were won in 1932 than in 1936?" [20 more gold medals]

Set E

Make a bar graph for each frequency table.
See Additional Answers on page T47.

1. U.S. Olympic Gold Medals, 1956–1976

Year	Frequency (Number of gold medals)
1956	34
1960	37
1964	37
1968	46
1972	36
1976	37

2. U.S.S.R. Olympic Gold Medals, 1956–1976

Year	Frequency (Number of gold medals)
1956	43
1960	49
1964	41
1968	33
1972	58
1976	60

3. Winter Olympic Medals, 1980

Country	Frequency (Number of medals)
East Germany	23
Finland	9
Norway	10
U.S.	12
U.S.S.R.	22

Objective: Read and make a line graph.

SKILL Reading and Making a Line Graph

See pages 63–64 of *Problem-Solving Masters.*

Materials: Graph paper

Example F Reading a line graph

Use the **line graph** below to tell how many million farms there were in the United States in 1960.

Data has been rounded to the nearest 500,000 farms.

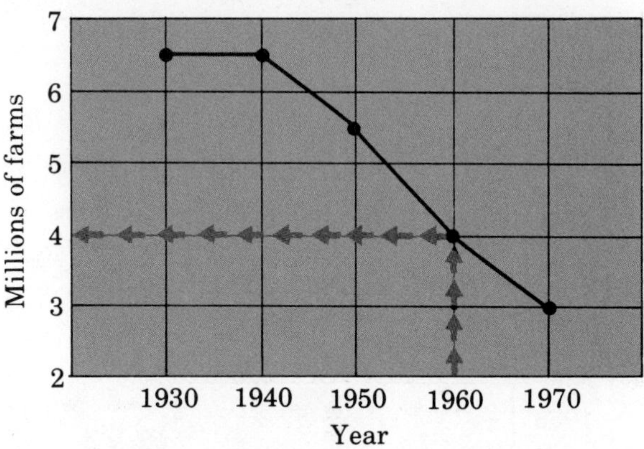

Locate 1960 on the horizontal scale. Follow the arrows up to the point on the graph. Then follow the arrows left to the number on the vertical scale.

The vertical scale shows that there were 4 million farms in the United States in 1960.

A line graph such as this is often called a "broken-line graph." It is not a linear function.
Note that here, too, the choice of scale can make the differences in the data appear more or less extreme.

Example G Making a line graph

Make a line graph to show the average farm size in the United States for the years in Example F.

Data has been rounded to the nearest 25 acres.

Average Farm Size in the U.S., 1930–1970

Year	Number of acres
1930	150
1940	175
1950	225
1960	300
1970	375

First draw and label a vertical scale to show the number of acres. Notice that the vertical scale does not have to start at zero. Next draw and label a horizontal scale to show the years.

Find the lines for 150 acres and the year 1930. Locate the point where the lines meet. Then locate the points for the other farm sizes and years. Connect the points with a line.

Write a title for the graph.

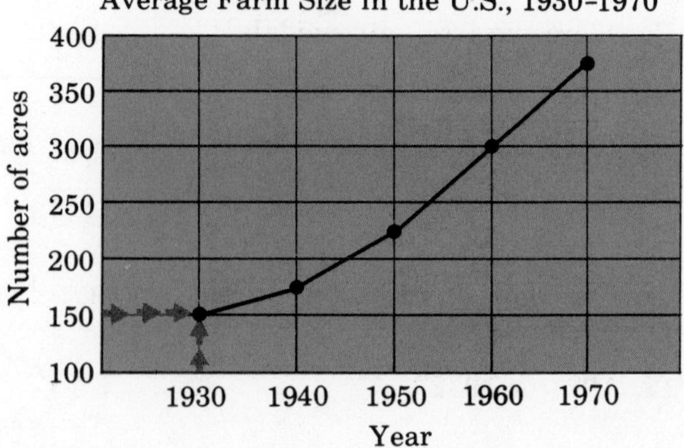

PROBLEM SOLVING
The applications on pages 270–275
may be used anytime after this lesson.

Exercises

Set F

Use the line graph below for Exercises 1–13.

Data has been rounded to the nearest 25 minutes.

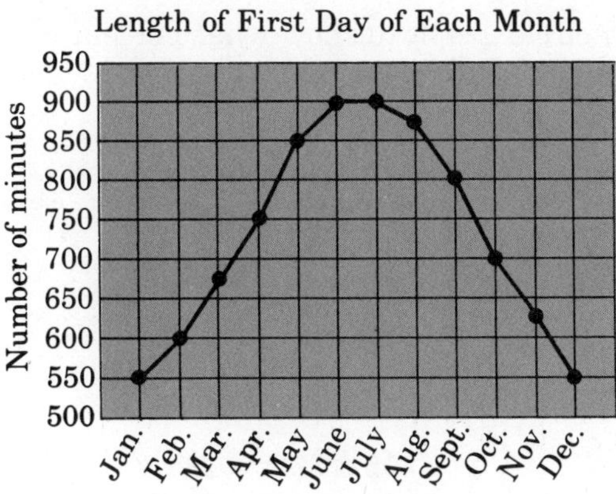

For which months is the first day

1. longer than 750 minutes?
   May, June, July, Aug., Sept.
2. shorter than 700 minutes?
   Jan., Feb., Mar., Nov., Dec.
3. 800 minutes or longer?
   May, June, July, Aug., Sept.
4. 750 minutes or shorter?
   Jan., Feb., Mar., Apr., Oct., Nov., Dec.
5. shorter than 600 minutes?
   Jan., Dec.
6. longer than 850 minutes?
   June, July, Aug.
7. 700 minutes or longer?
   Apr., May, June, July, Aug., Sept., Oct.

Was the first day longer in

8. March or October?
   October
9. May or September?
   May
10. April or October?
    April
11. June or August?
    June
12. February or November?
    November
13. How long was the first day of each month?
    J–550 F–600 M–675 A–750 M–850 J–900
    J–900 A–875 S–800 O–700 N–625 D–550

The answers to Exercise 13 have been given in minutes. You might also have students give the answers in hours.

Set G

Make a line graph for each set of data.

Data has been rounded to the nearest 1000 graduates.

1. U.S. Law Graduates

Year	Number
1955	8000
1960	9000
1965	12,000
1970	15,000
1975	29,000

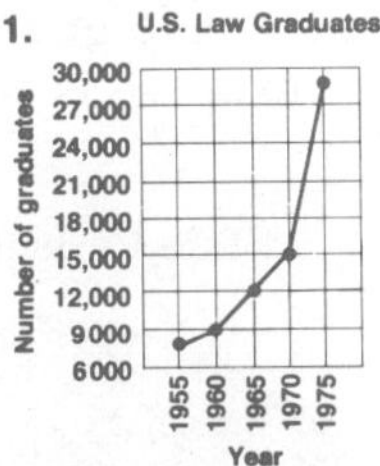

Data has been rounded to the nearest 5000 graduates.

2. U.S. Engineering Graduates

Year	Number
1950	60,000
1955	30,000
1960	45,000
1965	50,000
1970	65,000
1975	65,000

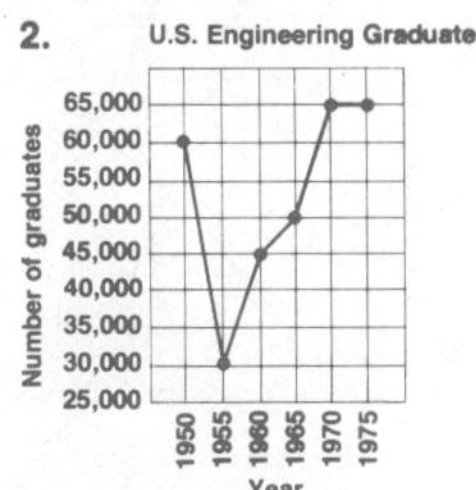

Data has been rounded to the nearest 5000 graduates.

3. U.S. Nursing Graduates

Year	Number
1973	15,000
1974	20,000
1975	25,000
1976	25,000
1977	30,000

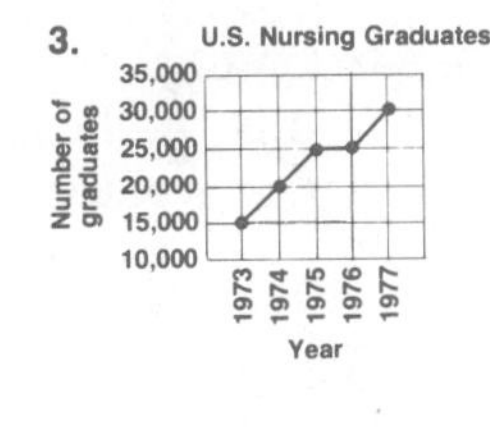

Data has been rounded to the nearest 10,000 graduates.

4. U.S. Elementary Education Graduates

Year	Number
1973	90,000
1974	80,000
1975	70,000
1976	60,000
1977	50,000

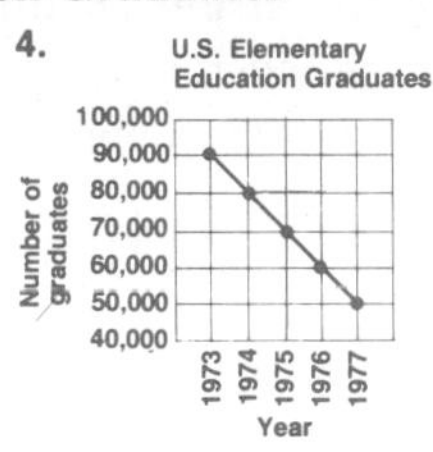

Objective: Read and make a circle graph.

Reading and Making a Circle Graph

Materials: Protractor

Example H Reading a circle graph and comparing the data

Use the **circle graph** below to tell which college expense is the greatest.

State College Expenses

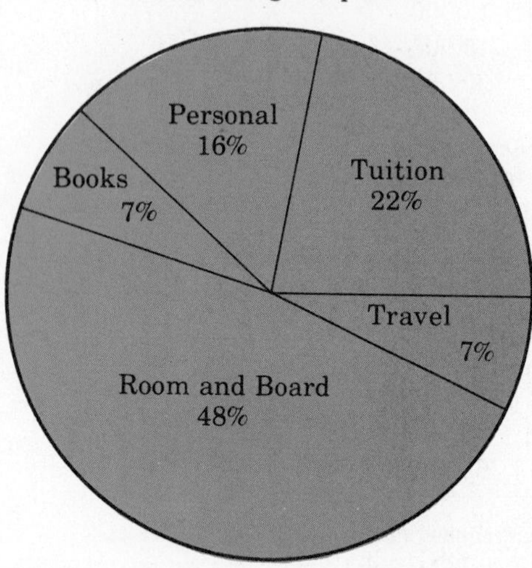

The section of the circle graph showing room and board is the largest; therefore, room and board is the greatest expense at a state college.

Example I Using data in a circle graph to find a percent of a given total

Use the circle graph in Example H to find how much money is spent on tuition if the total college expenses are $3400 per year.

Find 22% of $3400.

$0.22 \times 3400 = 748$ Write 22% as a decimal and multiply.

Tuition at a state college is $748 per year.

Example J Making a circle graph for a set of data

Make a circle graph to show what percent of a student's budget is designated for each expense at a private college.

Travel	5%	Room and board	26%
Books	4%	Tuition	55%
Personal	10%		

Remind students that there are 360° in a circle.

Write each percent as a decimal and multiply by 360° to find the size of each **central angle.** Round the answers to the nearest degree.

Travel	$0.05 \times 360° = 18°$
Books	$0.04 \times 360° = 14.4° \approx 14°$
Personal	$0.10 \times 360° = 36°$
Room and board	$0.26 \times 360° = 93.6° \approx 94°$
Tuition	$0.55 \times 360° = 198°$

Review circle and central-angle construction.

Draw a circle with a central angle for each measure listed above. Label each section. Then write a title for the graph.

Private College Expenses

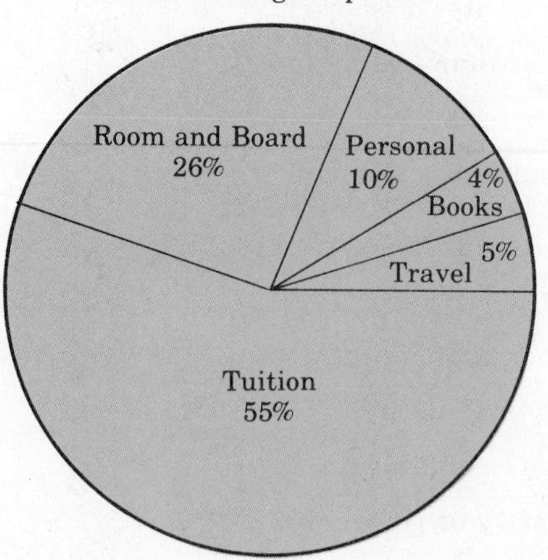

You may wish to discuss reasons for differences in expenses for various types of colleges.

Exercises

The measure of each central angle is given to the nearest degree. For graphs, see Additional Answers on page T48.

Set H

Use this circle graph to answer the questions.

Materials That Make Up the Human Body

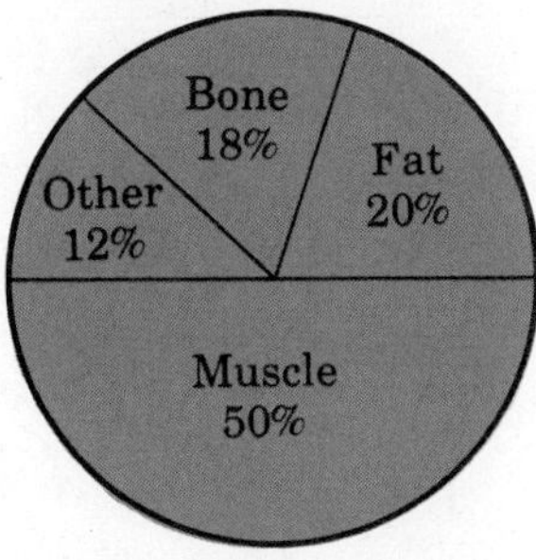

Which material makes up

1. the greatest part of the human body?
Muscle
2. 50% of the human body?
Muscle
3. 18% of the human body?
Bone
4. 20% of the human body?
Fat

Which materials make up

5. 15% or more of the human body?
Muscle, Fat, Bone
6. less than 50% of the human body?
Fat, Bone, Other
7. 20% or less of the human body?
Fat, Bone, Other

Which of these materials make up the greater part of the human body?

8. Muscle or fat
Muscle
9. Fat or bone
Fat
10. Bone or muscle
Muscle

Set I

Use the circle graphs on page 266 to answer the questions.

At a state college, about how much is spent on each item if total expenses are

1. $3400 per year?
   a. Room and board
   $1632
   b. Travel
   $238
   c. Personal
   $544
   d. Books
   $238
2. $4000 per year?
   a. Tuition
   $880
   b. Room and board
   $1920
   c. Books
   $280

At a private college, about how much is spent on each item if total expenses are

3. $6000 per year?
   a. Tuition
   $3300
   b. Room and board
   $1560
   c. Books
   $240
   d. Travel
   $300
4. $7200 per year?
   a. Tuition
   $3960
   b. Room and board
   $1872
   c. Personal
   $720

Set J

Make a circle graph to show each set of data.

1. Elements of Earth's Crust

Oxygen	47%	169°
Silicon	28%	101°
Aluminum	8%	29°
Other	17%	61°

2. Sources of Water Pollution

Industry	60%	216°
Urban sewage	25%	90°
Agriculture	15%	54°

3. Sources of Air Pollution

Transportation	42%	151°
Fuel combustion	21%	76°
Industry	14%	50°
Solid waste	6%	22°
Other	17%	61°

4. Earth's Water

Atlantic Ocean	23%	83°
Pacific Ocean	46%	166°
Indian Ocean	20%	72°
Arctic Ocean	4%	14°
Other	7%	25°

5. Earth's Land

Africa	20%	72°
Asia	30%	108°
Australia	5%	18°
North America	16%	58°
South America	12%	43°
Europe	7%	25°
Antarctica	9%	32°
Other	1%	4°

Have students construct smaller angles first; discuss *reflex* angles.

SKILLS POSTTEST

Materials: Graph paper, protractor

Number of test items - 10

Number missed	1	2	3	4	5
Percent correct	90	80	70	60	50

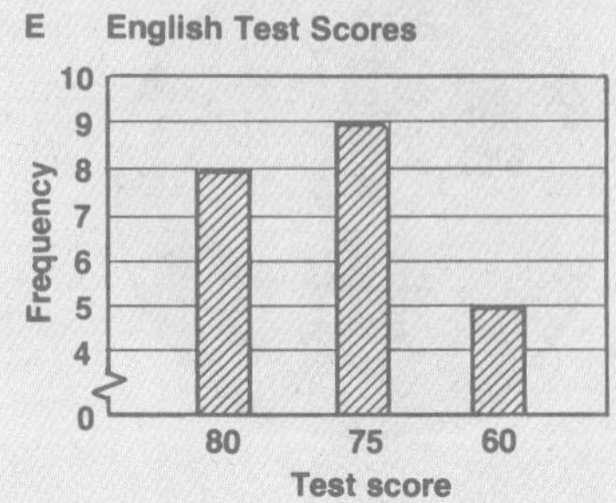

SKILL Finding the Mean *page 259*

A Find the mean for the set of data below. Round your answer to the nearest tenth.
86.1

77 90 87 87
98 96 68

SKILL Finding the Median and the Mode *pages 260–261*

B Find the median for the set of data in item A.
87

C Find the mode for the set of data in item A.
87

SKILL Reading and Making a Bar Graph *pages 262–263*

D Which of these clubs have 18 or fewer members?
Latin Club, French Club

Club Membership

Number of members: 21, 20, 19, 18, 17, 16, 15, 0

Spanish Latin French

Club

E Make a bar graph for this frequency table.
See above.

English Test Scores

Test score	Frequency (Number of times scored)
80	8
75	9
60	5

Posttest continued on page 269.

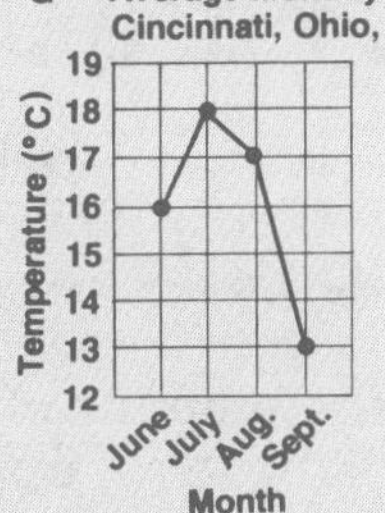

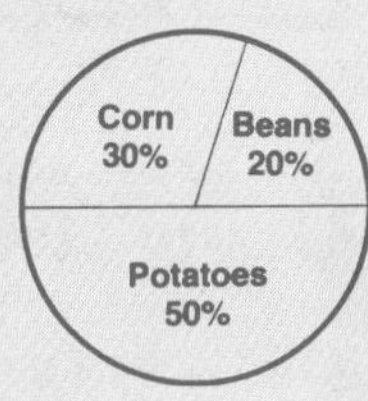

Posttest continued from page 268.

SKILL Reading and Making a Line Graph *pages 264–265*

F What is the average snowfall for Cincinnati in December?
10 centimeters

Average Snowfall for Cincinnati, Ohio, December–March

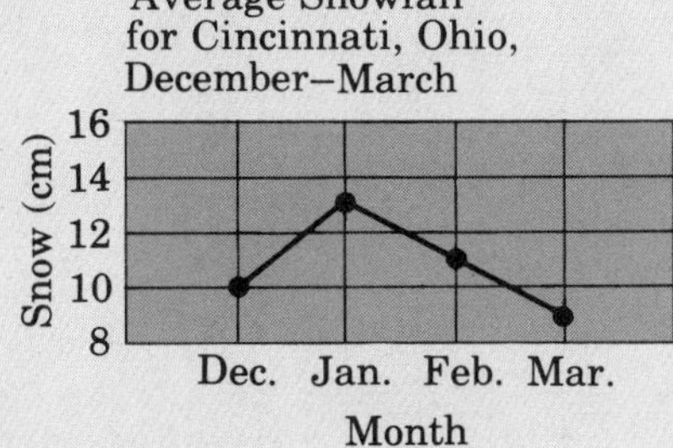

G Make a line graph to show the average monthly temperature for Cincinnati from June through September.
See above.

Month	Temperature
June	16°C
July	18°C
August	17°C
September	13°C

SKILL Reading and Making a Circle Graph *pages 266–267*

H Which type of book is favored by the greatest number of students?
Novels

Favorite Books of 2500 Students

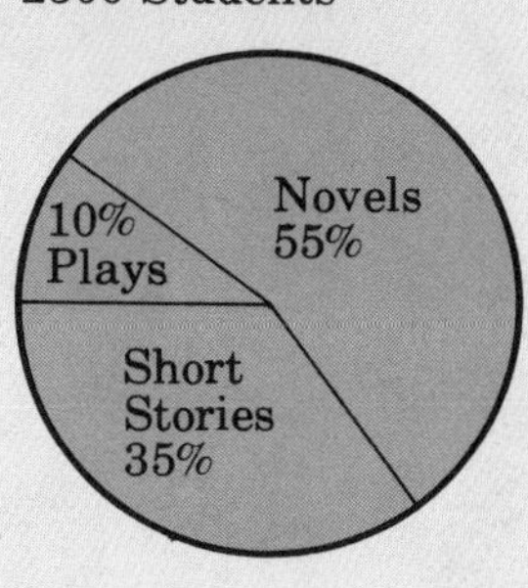

I Use the circle graph in Item H to find how many of the 2500 students favored short stories.
875 students

J Make a circle graph to show the percent of land planted in each crop.
See above.

Crops Planted		Central angle
Corn	30%	108°
Beans	20%	72°
Potatoes	50%	180°

Problem Solving

CONSUMER APPLICATIONS

Objective: Solve problems involving statistics.

In this lesson students read line graphs to compare electric expenses for 1978, 1979, and 1980. They also determine the appropriate amount for equal monthly payments.

Using Graphs: Electric Bills

Maureen DeCourcey graphed the amount of money she paid each month for electricity in 1978, 1979, and 1980.

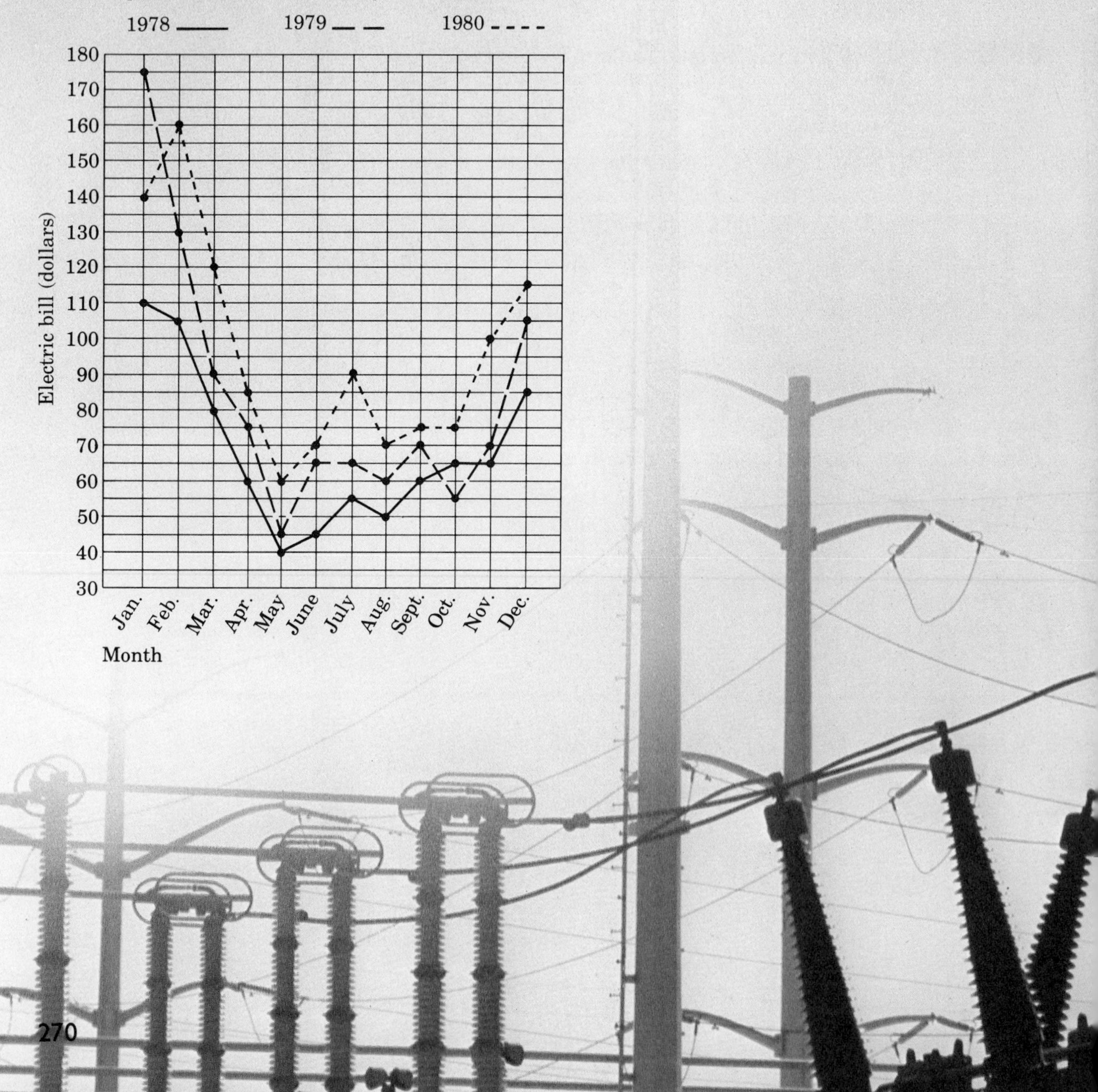

See pages 37–38 of *Problem-Solving Masters.*

During which months in 1978 was the electric bill

1. less than $60?
May through Aug.

2. $80 or less?
Mar. through Nov.

3. $65 or more?
Jan., Feb., Mar., Oct., Nov., Dec.

4. more than $40?
Jan. through Apr., June through Dec.

During which months in 1979 was the electric bill

5. more than $100?
Jan., Feb., Dec.

6. less than $80?
Apr. through Nov.

7. $65 or less?
May through Aug., Oct.

8. $70 or more?
Jan. through Apr., Sept., Nov., Dec.

During which months in 1980 was the electric bill

9. less than $75?
May, June, Aug.

10. $90 or more?
Jan., Feb., Mar., July, Nov., Dec.

11. $75 or less?
May, June, Aug., Sept., Oct.

12. more than $100?
Jan., Feb., Mar., Dec.

Give the amount of the electric bill for each month in
See Additional Answers on page T48.

13. 1978. **14.** 1979. **15.** 1980.

To avoid exceptionally large payments, many consumers make equal monthly payments. Each payment is the average of the previous year's bills. What equal monthly payments could Maureen have made in each of these three years? Round your answers to the nearest dollar.

16. 1979 (To find the average of the electric bills for 1978, add the monthly bills and divide by 12.)
$68

17. 1980
$84 (The 1979 average)

18. 1981
$97 (The 1980 average)

Equal monthly payments are generally adjusted each year to accommodate changes in the cost of electricity.

For each of these months, give the year and the amount of the highest bill and the lowest bill. Then, for each month, find the difference between the highest and the lowest bills.
See Additional Answers on page T48.

19. January **21.** April **23.** October

20. February **22.** July **24.** December

Problem Solving

CAREER APPLICATIONS

Objective: Solve problems involving statistics.

Materials: Graph paper

In this lesson students find mean temperature and precipitation for certain cities, and make line graphs to show normal monthly temperature and precipitation for these cities.

Meteorologist

Career Cluster: Science Dail Currier is a meteorologist. She uses this table to compare temperatures of various cities.

See the Careers Chart beginning on page 426 for more information about the careers in this cluster.

Normal Monthly Temperature (degrees Celsius)

	Jan.	Feb.	Mar.	Apr.	May	June	July	Aug.	Sept.	Oct.	Nov.	Dec.
Asheville	3	4	8	13	18	22	23	23	19	17	11	7
Birmingham	7	8	12	17	22	25	27	26	23	17	11	7
Dodge City	0	2	5	12	17	23	26	26	20	14	6	1
New York City	0	1	5	11	17	22	25	24	20	14	8	2
Miami	19	20	22	24	26	27	28	28	28	26	22	20
Honolulu	22	22	23	24	25	26	27	27	27	26	25	23

1. Find the annual mean temperature for each city. Round your answers to the nearest degree.
   Asheville, 14°C; Birmingham, 17°C; Dodge City, 13°C; New York City, 12°C; Miami, 24°C; Honolulu, 25°C
2. For each city, make a line graph that shows the normal monthly temperature.
   See Additional Answers on pages T49–T50.

For Problems 2 and 4, you might have students draw two graphs per grid, pairing Asheville and Birmingham, Dodge City and New York City, and Miami and Honolulu. The temperatures for each pair of cities are similar, but the amounts of precipitation vary widely.

See pages 39, and 63–64 of *Problem-Solving Masters.*

Dail uses this table to compare amounts of precipitation for various cities.

Normal Monthly Precipitation (centimeters)

	Jan.	Feb.	Mar.	Apr.	May	June	July	Aug.	Sept.	Oct.	Nov.	Dec.
Asheville	8.6	9.1	11.9	8.9	8.4	10.2	12.4	11.4	9.1	8.4	7.4	9.1
Birmingham	12.2	13.5	15.7	11.7	9.1	10.2	13.2	10.9	9.1	6.6	9.4	13.2
Dodge City	1.3	1.5	2.8	4.3	7.9	8.4	7.9	6.6	4.3	4.3	1.5	1.3
New York City	7.4	7.9	10.2	9.1	8.6	7.4	9.9	11.4	8.1	7.6	9.7	9.1
Miami	5.6	5.1	5.3	9.1	15.5	22.9	17.5	17.0	22.1	20.8	6.9	4.1
Honolulu	11.1	6.4	8.1	3.6	2.5	0.8	1.5	2.0	1.8	3.8	7.6	9.4

3. Find the annual mean precipitation for each city. Round your answers to the nearest tenth of a centimeter.
Asheville, 9.6 cm; Birmingham, 11.2 cm; Dodge City, 4.3 cm; New York City, 8.9 cm; Miami, 12.7 cm; Honolulu, 4.9 cm

4. For each city, make a line graph that shows the normal monthly precipitation.
See Additional Answers on pages T49–T50.

In Problem 4, you might have students label each unit on the vertical scale in intervals of 0.5 degrees. The graphs in the Teacher's Edition are shown in intervals of 1 degree because of limited space.

Problem Solving

CAREER APPLICATIONS

Objective: Solve problems involving statistics.

Materials: Graph paper

In this lesson students make line graphs and analyze data on hydrocarbons, carbon monoxide, and ozone.

Ecologist

Career Cluster: Science Mike Goldstein is an ecologist. He studies air pollution and its effect on animal and plant life.

For each type of pollutant in the table below, the average for the day is determined from hourly readings. The high and the low are the day's highest and lowest hourly readings.

October 5-11 Pollutants		Sunday	Monday	Tuesday	Wednesday	Thursday	Friday	Saturday
Hydrocarbons (Parts per billion)	Low	1800	1900	1700	1800	1800	1700	1800
	Average	2300	3300	3700	2600	3500	2300	5300
	High	3200	8000	8200	5400	6600	3800	9400
Carbon monoxide (Parts per billion)	Low	500	1000	500	1000	1500	1000	500
	Average	2900	7400	9900	4800	9500	3000	3600
	High	6000	23,000	31,500	20,000	21,000	10,000	14,000
Ozone (Parts per billion)	Low	5	5	5	10	5	5	10
	Average	26	17	11	28	11	22	29
	High	45	45	25	45	30	35	40

Danger zones: Hydrocarbons—any reading greater than 6500
Carbon monoxide—any reading greater than 36,000
Ozone—any reading greater than 30

Before assigning the problems on page 275, make sure that the students can read the table and the graph by asking questions about the information presented on hydrocarbons. Discuss how the graph was constructed.

Mike used the data in the table to make the graph below. The shaded portion of the graph shows the danger zone.

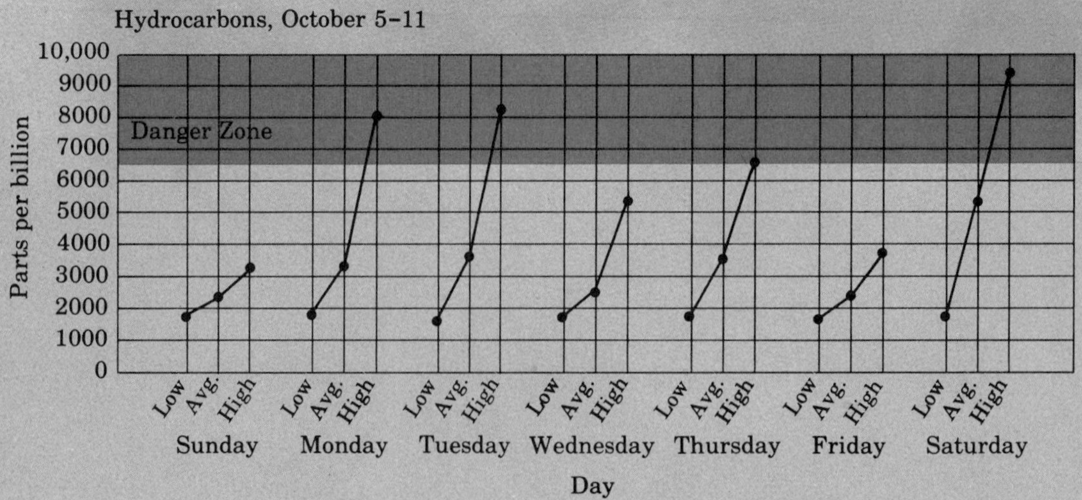

See pages 63–64 of *Problem-Solving Masters*.

Use the table on page 274 to make a graph for each pollutant. Use the same horizontal scale that was used for hydrocarbons. Shade and label the danger zone.

1. Carbon monoxide
See right.
2. Ozone
See right.

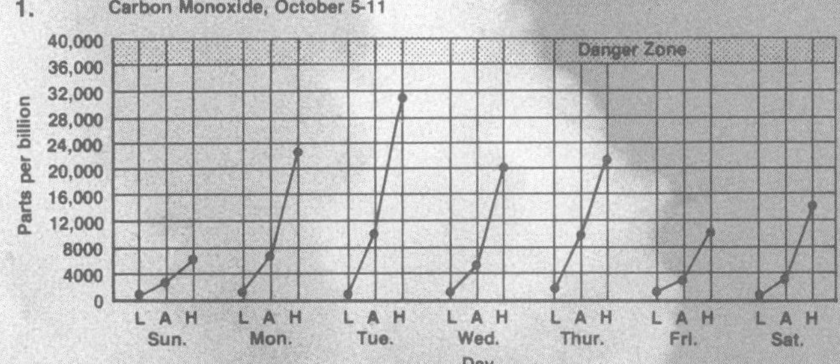

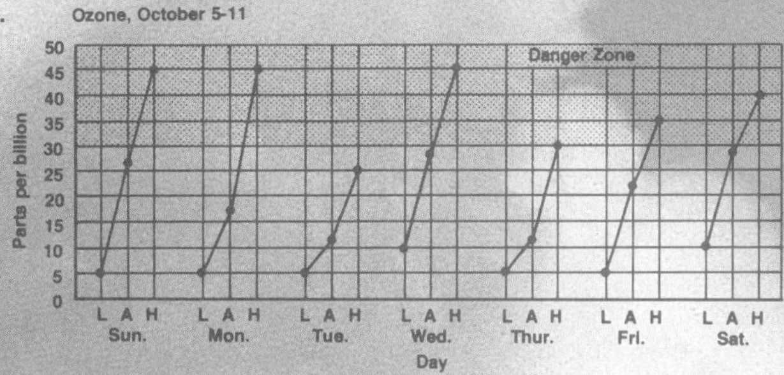

Mike uses this code to report special conditions.

A Danger zone

B Any high reading that is preceded by two consecutive increases in the high readings In evaluating B, remind students to consider three consecutive readings.

C Any significant increase in the high reading from the day before:

Hydrocarbons, an increase of 5000 or more
Carbon monoxide, an increase of 7000 or more
Ozone, an increase of 20 or more

Use the table and the graph on page 274 for Problems 3–5.

3. On which days were the readings for hydrocarbons in the danger zone?
Monday, Tuesday, Thursday, Saturday
4. On which days was the high reading for hydrocarbons preceded by two consecutive increases in the high readings?
Tuesday
5. On which days did the high reading for hydrocarbons increase by 5000 or more from the day before?
Saturday

The answers to Problems 3–5 were used to indicate the special conditions for hydrocarbons in the table below. Complete the table by indicating the special conditions that Mike must report for carbon monoxide and ozone.

	October 5-11 Special Conditions	Sunday	Monday	Tuesday	Wednesday	Thursday	Friday	Saturday
	Hydrocarbons		**A**	**A,B**		**A**		**A,C**
6.	Carbon monoxide		C	B,C				
7.	Ozone	A	A		A,C		A	A,B

Point out that because statistics for the previous week are not presented, Sunday and Monday cannot be evaluated for condition B, and Sunday cannot be evaluated for condition C.

Problem Solving

DEVELOPING STRATEGIES

Objective: Solve problems by making a table and interpreting data.

In this lesson students learn to make a table with tally marks and to interpret a manufacturer's code numbers.

Tactics: Making a Table, Interpreting Data

Hiroko Kawai is the manager of The Bootery. Each month she must write reports on the shoe sales for that month. The sales slips for September showed the following Style 80 Loafer code numbers. The first two digits indicate shoe style, the third digit stands for color, and the last digit is the size.

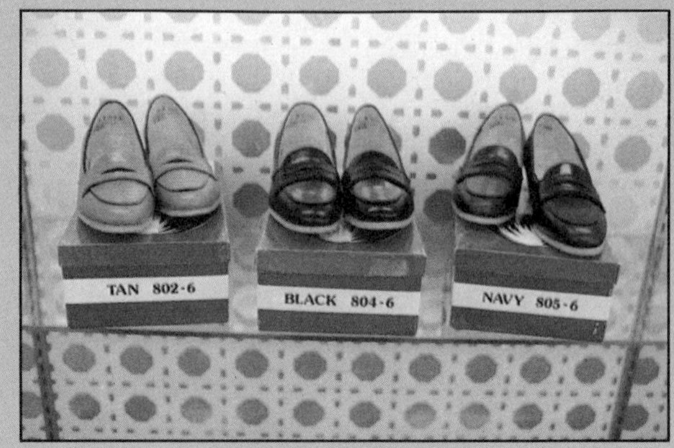

802-7	804-8	805-9	804-7	802-8	804-7
804-8	802-9	805-8	805-8	802-8	805-8
802-8	805-7	804-7	802-8	805-6	802-7
805-8	804-7	802-8	805-7	802-9	804-7
805-9	802-8	802-5	804-6	805-7	802-8

Problem

For each color, how many pairs of each size of Style 80 Loafer were sold by The Bootery in September?

Solution

Hiroko's strategy for solving the problem included the tactics of making a table and interpreting data.

a. How can the list of code numbers be organized? Make a table with a section for each number.

b. How can the sales be recorded? Make a tally mark for each code number.

c. How many pairs of shoes with each code number were sold? Count the tally marks and record the number.

d. What do the code numbers mean? Interpret the code numbers like this:

802 - 5: Tan, Size 5   804 - 8: Black, Size 8   805 - 7: Navy, Size 7

Shoe Sales - Style 80, September

802-5 / ①	804-5 ⓪	805-5 ⓪
802-6 ⓪	804-6 / ①	805-6 / ①
802-7 // ②	804-7 ~~////~~ ⑤	805-7 /// ③
802-8 ~~////~~ // ⑦	804-8 // ②	805-8 //// ④
802-9 // ②	804-9 ⓪	805-9 // ②

Conclusion: In September, sales of Style 80 Loafer were as listed at the right.

Tan		Black		Navy	
	Size 5: 1 pair		Size 6: 1 pair		Size 6: 1 pair
	Size 7: 2 pairs		Size 7: 5 pairs		Size 7: 3 pairs
	Size 8: 7 pairs		Size 8: 2 pairs		Size 8: 4 pairs
	Size 9: 2 pairs				Size 9: 2 pairs

Related Problems

Use the table for Style 80 shoes on page 276 for Problems 1–9.

Find the total number of pairs of Style 80 shoes sold by The Bootery in September that were

1. size 5. 1 pair
2. size 6. 2 pairs
3. size 7. 10 pairs
4. size 8. 13 pairs
5. size 9. 4 pairs
6. tan. 12 pairs
7. black. 8 pairs
8. navy. 10 pairs
9. What was the total number of pairs of Style 80 shoes sold by The Bootery in September? 30 pairs

10. Make a table for July sales of Style 98 shoes. The sales slips listed these code numbers. Remember, the first two digits indicate the style and the last digits are the size. The third digit stands for color: 6—gray; 7—green; 3—blue. See Additional Answers on page T51.

986-11	986-12	983-11	986-10	987-12
986-10	987-11	986-11	987-8	986-10
986-11	983-10	986-10	983-8	987-10
983-10	986-12	987-10	986-11	983-10
987-10	986-11	983-10	986-11	983-11
983-8	987-10	987-11	986-9	986-10
986-10	983-9	986-10	987-12	986-9
983-9	986-10	987-8	983-10	983-10

Use your table for Style 98 shoes for Problems 11–14.

11. For each color, how many pairs of each size of Style 98 shoes were sold by The Bootery in July? See Additional Answers on page T51.

Find the total number of pairs of Style 98 shoes sold by The Bootery in July for

12. each size. See Additional Answers on page T51.
13. each color. Blue: 12 pairs Gray: 18 pairs Green: 10 pairs
14. What was the total number of pairs of Style 98 shoes sold by The Bootery in July? 40 pairs

Extensions

15. What percent of the Style 80 shoes sold in September were tan? 40%
16. What percent of the Style 80 shoes sold in September were size 7? $33\frac{1}{3}\%$
17. What percent of the navy Style 80 shoes sold in September were size 9? 20%
18. Based on September sales, Hiroko wishes to order 90 pairs of Style 80 shoes for another month. For each color, how many pairs of each size should she order? See Additional Answers on page T51.

CHAPTER 12 TEST

Materials: Graph paper, protractor

Number of test items - 14

Number missed	1	2	3	4	5	6	7
Percent correct	93	86	79	71	64	57	50

A **1.** Find the mean for the set of data below. Round to the nearest tenth.
11.3

15 17 9 8
10 9 11

B **2.** Find the median for the set of data in item 1.
10

C **3.** Find the mode for the set of data in item 1.
9

D **4.** In which year was the volume of mail more than 90 billion?
1974

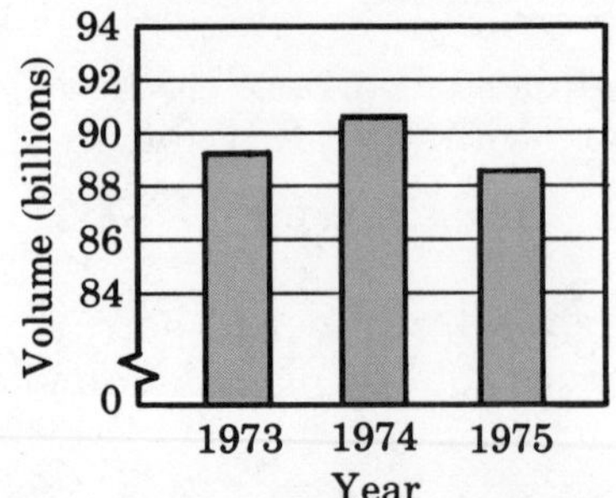

E **5.** Make a bar graph for this frequency table.
See Additional Answers on page T51.

Summer Birthdays

Month	Frequency (Number of birthdays)
June	12
July	8
August	9

F **6.** How many bushels of soybeans were produced per acre in the United States in 1976?
26 bushels per acre

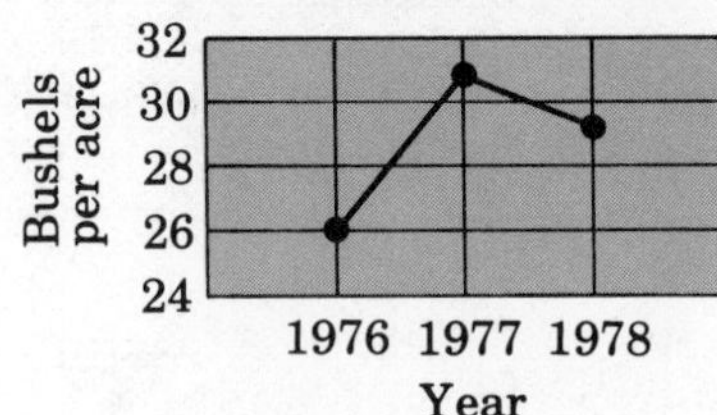

G **7.** Make a line graph to show this set of data.
See Additional Answers on page T51.

Egg Use per Person

Year	Number of eggs
1960	340
1965	310
1970	310
1975	280

H **8.** Which expense makes up the greatest part of this budget?
Room and board

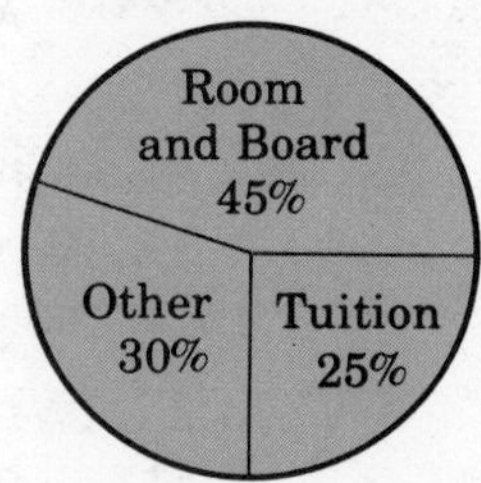

I **9.** Use item 8 to find how much is budgeted for tuition if the student's total budget is $4800.
$1200

J **10.** Make a circle graph to show this set of data.
See Additional Answers on page T51.

Fabric Blend Fibers		Central angle
Acetate	55%	198°
Acrylic	40%	144°
Cotton	5%	18°

11. Find the average of these 1980 bills to get the equal monthly payments for 1981.
$92

$152 $95 $59 $65
$160 $71 $63 $86
$127 $60 $68 $98

12. The normal monthly precipitation for Oklahoma City is given in centimeters. Find the annual mean precipitation to the nearest tenth.
6.6 centimeters

2.8 8.8 6.8 6.5
3.4 13.2 6.5 3.6
5.2 10.7 9.0 3.2

13. High ozone readings for two consecutive days were 27 and 43. Find the increase.
16

14. *Shoe Sales – Style 73*

731-8	733-8	734-8
IIII	~~IIII~~ I	~~IIII~~

How many pairs of Style 73 shoes in size 8 were sold? (Last digit is size.)
15 pairs

See pages 29–30 of the *Test Masters* for an alternate form of the Chapter 12 Test.
For a test on Unit 4, see pages T62–T63 of this book and pages 31–32 of the *Test Masters*.

SKILLS TUNE-UP

Adding and Subtracting Whole Numbers, pages 3-14

1. 45 + 52 — 97
2. 37 + 13 — 50
3. 175 + 209 — 384
4. 3847 + 1953 — 5800
5. 64,042 + 34,178 — 98,220
6. 88 + 57 + 48 — 193
7. 107 + 39 + 14 — 160
8. 38 + 279 + 304 — 621
9. 102 + 44 + 95 — 241
10. 5963 + 36 + 969 — 6968
11. 104 + 9 + 27 + 16 — 156
12. 7 + 928 + 5 + 36 — 976
13. 84 − 62 — 22
14. 73 − 56 — 17
15. 618 − 509 — 109
16. 768 − 241 — 527
17. 703 − 615 — 88
18. 2725 − 206 — 2519
19. 9335 − 474 — 8861
20. 4102 − 237 — 3865
21. 2666 − 418 — 2248
22. 3915 − 287 — 3628
23. 7000 − 2162 — 4838
24. 82,587 − 78,252 — 4335
25. 93,109 − 47,721 — 45,388
26. 17,433 − 16,786 — 647

Adding and Subtracting Decimals, pages 75-84

1. 5.3 + 7.6 — 12.9
2. 11.7 + 18.7 — 30.4
3. 0.87 + 0.22 — 1.09
4. 0.29 + 4.3 — 4.59
5. 8.5 + 0.461 — 8.961
6. 0.6 + 0.3 + 0.8 — 1.7
7. 0.9 + 0.261 + 0.43 — 1.591
8. 1.394 + 0.75 + 2.7 — 4.844
9. 2.72 + 2.162 + 0.81 — 5.692
10. 0.009 + 2.7 + 4.58 — 7.289
11. 4 + 0.013 + 6.2 — 10.213
12. 0.084 + 0.005 + 2.042 — 2.131
13. 6 + 0.37 + 17.8 — 24.17
14. 9.8 − 4.6 — 5.2
15. 0.66 − 0.07 — 0.59
16. 8.035 − 5 — 3.035
17. 6.84 − 4.659 — 2.181
18. 9 − 1.172 — 7.828
19. 0.959 − 0.483 — 0.476
20. 15.007 − 12.138 — 2.869
21. 76.41 − 48 — 28.41
22. 12.9 − 7.154 — 5.746
23. 17.61 − 9.349 — 8.261
24. 0.416 − 0.027 — 0.389
25. 15.1 − 9.701 — 5.399
26. 16 − 14.25 — 1.75
27. 13.5 − 12.843 — 0.657

Adding and Subtracting Fractions and Mixed Numbers, pages 171-182

1. $\frac{2}{5} + \frac{7}{10}$ — $1\frac{1}{10}$
2. $6\frac{5}{6} + 3\frac{1}{12}$ — $9\frac{11}{12}$
3. $\frac{13}{16} + \frac{11}{16}$ — $1\frac{1}{2}$
4. $\frac{2}{5} + \frac{2}{3} + \frac{3}{5}$ — $1\frac{2}{3}$
5. $2\frac{2}{3} + 7\frac{11}{12}$ — $10\frac{7}{12}$
6. $\frac{1}{4} + \frac{7}{8}$ — $1\frac{1}{8}$
7. $3\frac{4}{5} + 3\frac{8}{15}$ — $7\frac{1}{3}$
8. $5\frac{11}{12} + 7\frac{1}{8}$ — $13\frac{1}{24}$
9. $1\frac{1}{3} + 3\frac{1}{4} + 1\frac{1}{3}$ — $5\frac{11}{12}$
10. $\frac{7}{10} + \frac{3}{5}$ — $1\frac{3}{10}$
11. $9\frac{13}{16} - 5\frac{5}{16}$ — $4\frac{1}{2}$
12. $\frac{23}{24} - \frac{7}{24}$ — $\frac{2}{3}$
13. $8\frac{1}{4} - 4\frac{2}{3}$ — $3\frac{7}{12}$
14. $\frac{3}{4} - \frac{2}{3}$ — $\frac{1}{12}$
15. $6\frac{3}{8} - 2\frac{2}{3}$ — $3\frac{17}{24}$
16. $\frac{7}{12} - \frac{3}{8}$ — $\frac{5}{24}$
17. $5\frac{4}{7} - 3\frac{6}{7}$ — $1\frac{5}{7}$
18. $7\frac{3}{5} - 4\frac{2}{3}$ — $2\frac{14}{15}$
19. $3 - 1\frac{3}{5}$ — $1\frac{2}{5}$
20. $7 - 6\frac{2}{3}$ — $\frac{1}{3}$

CALCULATOR APPLICATIONS

In 1980 the population of the world was about 4.4 billion. The annual rate of increase in the population was about 2%. If that rate continues, what will the population be in 1983? Round your answer to the nearest hundredth of a billion.

Since the annual rate of increase is 2%, the population in each year is 102% of the population the previous year. Multiply by 1.02 and round to the nearest hundredth.

All population figures are in billions.

$1.02 \times 4.4 \approx 4.49$	Population in 1981
$1.02 \times 4.49 \approx 4.58$	Population in 1982
$1.02 \times 4.58 \approx 4.67$	Population in 1983

The population in 1983 will be about 4.67 billion.

Calculator Suggestion: If your calculator has the automatic constant feature for multiplication, try this key sequence.

Press: 1.02 [×] 4.4 [=] [=] [=]

Display: 4.6693152

Answer: 4.67 billion

On some calculators the key sequence would be 4.4 [×] 1.02 [=] [=] [=].

Notice that the number of times you press the [=] key is determined by the number of years. In this case, it is three (1981, 1982, 1983).

Be sure students know whether their calculator uses the first number or the second number for the automatic constant.

Find each answer.

1. If the annual rate of increase continues at 2%, what will be the world population to the nearest hundredth of a billion in 1990?
5.36 billion

In 1980 the population of Japan was about 114 million. The annual rate of increase was about 1%.

2. To the nearest tenth of a million, what will be the population in 1992?
128.5 million
3. In what year will the population be about 135 million?
1997

In 1980 the population of China was about 873 million. The annual rate of increase was about 1.5%.

4. To the nearest million, what will be the population in 1988?
983 million
5. In what year will the population reach one billion?
1990

In 1980 the population of the United States was about 233 million. The annual rate of increase was about 1.4%.

6. To the nearest hundredth of a million, what will be the population in the year 2000?
307.69 million
7. How many years from 1980 will it take the United States to double the 1980 population?
50 years
8. If the annual rate of increase had also been about 1.4% before 1980, what was the population in 1975? Round your answer to the nearest million. Hint: Check your calculator to see if it has the automatic constant feature for division.
217 million

COMPUTER LITERACY

The FOR and NEXT Statements

The FOR and NEXT statements work together to form a loop. The FOR statement is always the first statement in the loop and the NEXT statement is always the last. The steps that are repeated are placed between the FOR and NEXT statements.

In Program A, line 10 tells the computer to go through the loop using 1 as the first value for X. Line 30 sends the computer back to line 10 and the computer goes through the loop using 2 as the value for X. Each time the loop is executed, the value for X increases by 1. The loop is completed after the last value of X (4) which is indicated in the FOR statement, and the computer goes to the line following the NEXT statement.

Program A

Input	Output
`10 FOR X=1 TO 4`	1
`20 PRINT X`	2
`30 NEXT X`	3
`40 END`	4

In Program B, STEP 2 tells the computer to increase the value of Y by 2 each time the loop is executed. If no step is given, the value increases by 1.

Program B

Input	Output
`10 FOR Y=4 TO 10 STEP 2`	4
`20 PRINT Y`	6
`30 NEXT Y`	8
`40 END`	10

Program C adds the whole numbers from 1 to 5, printing each sum as it goes. Notice that in line 30, a different value is assigned to S each time the loop is executed.

Program C

Input	Output
`10 LET S=0`	1
`20 FOR N=1 TO 5`	3
`30 LET S=S+N`	6
`40 PRINT S`	10
`50 NEXT N`	15
`60 END`	

LET S=S+N can be a difficult concept for students. Work through Program C with your students before assigning exercise 3.

Give the output for each program.

1.
```
10 FOR N=5 TO 12
20 PRINT N
30 NEXT N
40 END
```

1. 5 6 7 8 9 10 11 12

2.
```
10 FOR A=1 TO 16 STEP 3
20 PRINT A
30 NEXT A
40 END
```

2. 1 4 7 10 13 16

3.
```
10 LET S=0
20 FOR N=2 TO 10 STEP 2
30 LET S=S+N
40 PRINT S
50 NEXT N
60 END
```

3. 2 6 12 20 30

4. Write a program that will print the cost of buying 1 to 10 items selling for $1.29 each.

Answers may vary.

```
10 FOR N=1 TO 10
20 PRINT N;"COST: $";N*1.29
30 NEXT N
40 END
```

UNIT FIVE Algebra

CHAPTER 13 Positive and Negative Numbers

SKILLS PRETEST

Number of test items - 21

Number missed	1	2	3	4	5	6	7	8	9	10
Percent correct	95	90	86	81	76	71	67	62	57	52

SKILL Writing and Ordering Positive and Negative Numbers *pages 284–285*

A Write a number for point N on the number line.

N

$^{-}4$ $^{-}3$ ■ $^{-}1$ 0 1 2

$^{-}2$

B Compare these numbers. Replace ● with < or >.

2 ● $^{-}1$

>

C Arrange these numbers in order from the least to the greatest.

3 6 $^{-}1$ 0

$^{-}1$ 0 3 6

SKILL Adding Positive and Negative Numbers *pages 286–287*

D $5 + 2$
7

E $^{-}3 + {}^{-}2$
$^{-}5$

F $2 + {}^{-}6$
$^{-}4$

G $^{-}6 + 2 + {}^{-}5 + 1$
$^{-}8$

SKILL Subtracting Positive and Negative Numbers *pages 288–289*

H Name the opposite of $^{-}7$.
7

I $4 - 6$
$^{-}2$

J $^{-}3 - {}^{-}4$
1

K $^{-}4 - 3$
$^{-}7$

L $5 - {}^{-}1$
6

M $1 - (6 - {}^{-}3)$
$^{-}8$

SKILL Multiplying Positive and Negative Numbers *pages 290–291*

N 9×3
27

O $^{-}2 \times {}^{-}6$
12

P $4 \times {}^{-}5$
$^{-}20$

Q $5(3) - 6(^{-}2)$
27

SKILL Dividing Positive and Negative Numbers *pages 292–293*

R $18 \div 2$
9

S $^{-}21 \div {}^{-}3$
7

T $^{-}15 \div 3$
$^{-}5$

U $\frac{7 - 12}{^{-}5}$
1

See page T40 for additional notes on Chapter 13.

Objective: Write, compare, and order positive and negative numbers.

Writing and Ordering Positive and Negative Numbers

Example A Writing integers

Write a positive or a negative number for each point labeled by a letter.

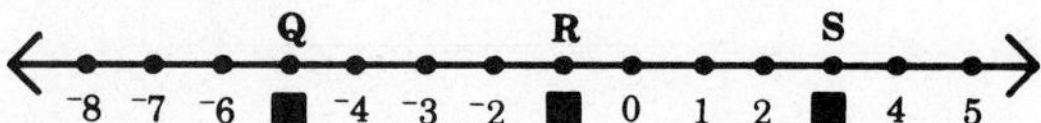

The numbers on this number line are called **integers.** The integers to the left of zero are negative. The integers to the right of zero are positive. Zero is neither positive nor negative.

Point Q	$^{-}5$	negative 5
Point R	$^{-}1$	negative 1
Point S	3	positive 3

Example B Comparing integers

Compare each pair of numbers below.
Replace ● with $<$ or $>$.

Think of the numbers as they would appear on a number line.

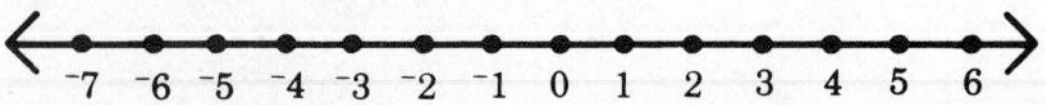

6 ● 4	$6 > 4$	The number farther to the right on the number line is greater.
3 ● $^{-}3$	$3 > {}^{-}3$	
$^{-}2$ ● $^{-}7$	$^{-}2 > {}^{-}7$	
0 ● $^{-}1$	$0 > {}^{-}1$	

$^{-}2$ ● 6	$^{-}2 < 6$	The number farther to the left on the number line is less.
$^{-}5$ ● $^{-}1$	$^{-}5 < {}^{-}1$	
$^{-}3$ ● 0	$^{-}3 < 0$	
0 ● 2	$0 < 2$	

Example C Ordering integers

Arrange these numbers in order from the least to the greatest.

1 $\quad ^{-}5 \quad$ 0 $\quad ^{-}3$

Write the numbers in the same order that they would appear on a number line.

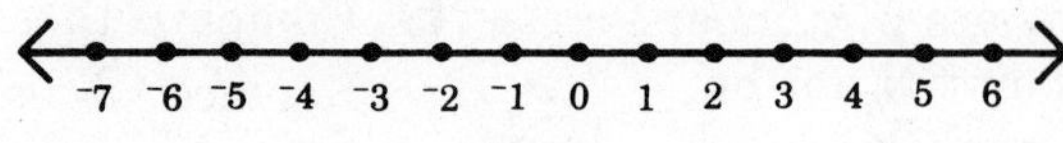

$^{-}5 \quad ^{-}3 \quad$ 0 $\quad$ 1

Exercises

Set A

Write a positive or negative number for each point labeled by a letter.

1. 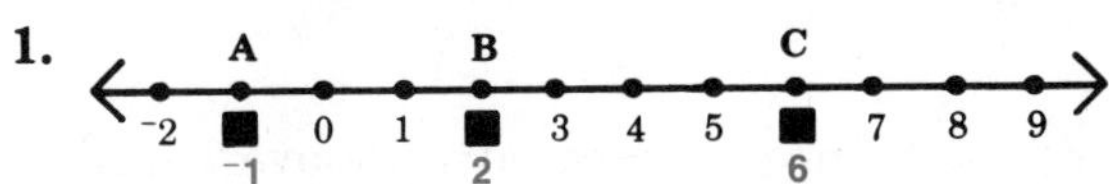

2. 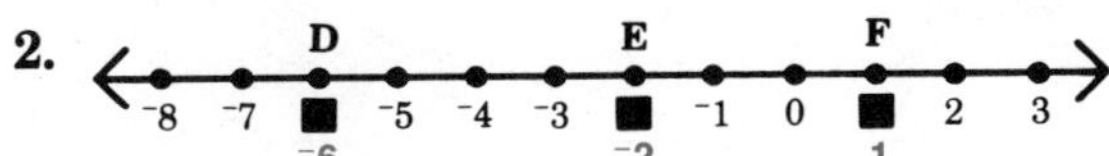

3. 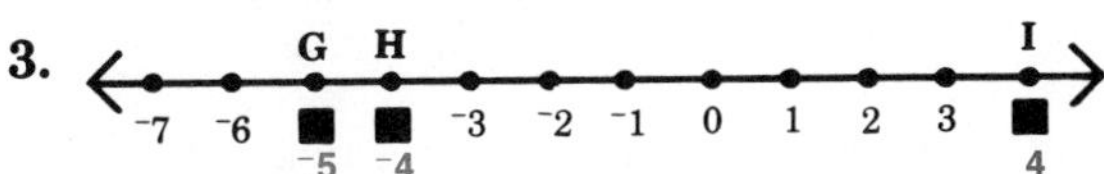

4. 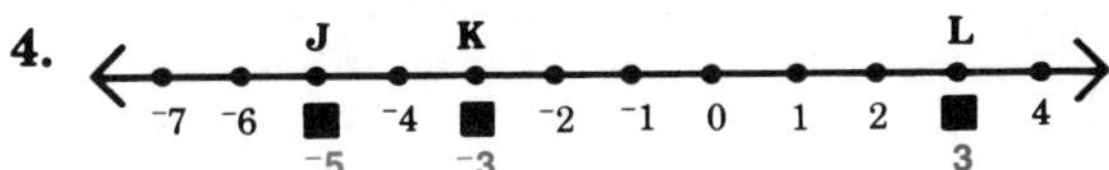

5. 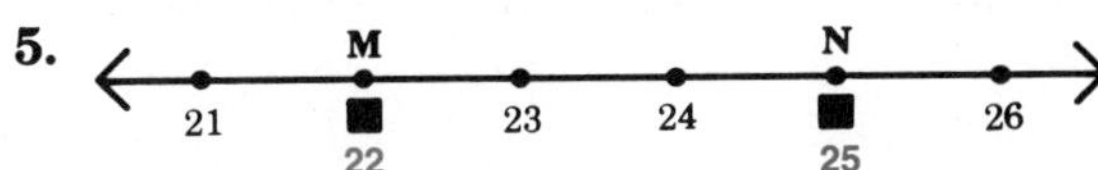

6. 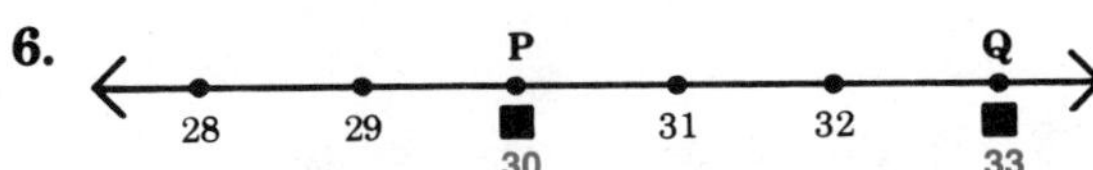

7. 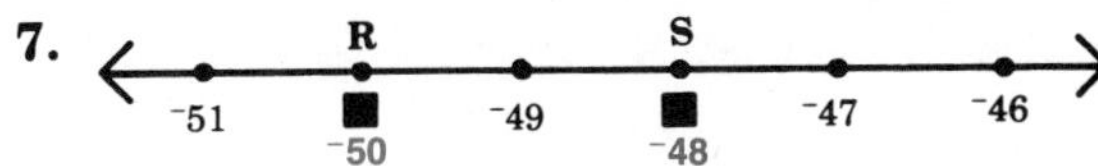

8. 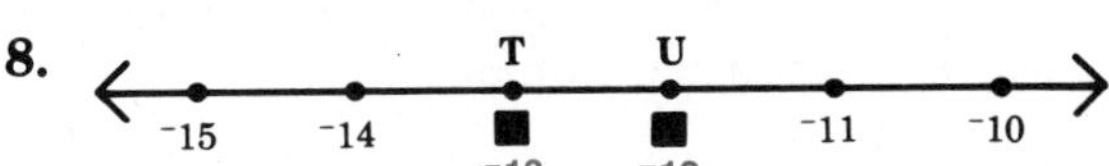

Set B

Compare each pair of numbers.
Replace ● with $<$ or $>$.

1. $^-8$ ● 0 — $<$
2. 4 ● 2 — $>$
3. 6 ● 10 — $<$
4. $^-7$ ● 7 — $<$
5. $^-4$ ● $^-6$ — $>$
6. 1 ● $^-9$ — $>$
7. $^-8$ ● $^-3$ — $<$
8. 0 ● 8 — $<$
9. $^-13$ ● $^-17$ — $>$
10. $^-16$ ● 3 — $<$
11. $^-19$ ● $^-13$ — $<$
12. 78 ● 74 — $>$
13. $^-38$ ● $^-62$ — $>$
14. $^-14$ ● 10 — $<$
15. $^-72$ ● $^-64$ — $<$
16. $^-35$ ● $^-51$ — $>$
17. 12 ● 3 — $>$
18. $^-49$ ● 15 — $<$
19. $^-31$ ● $^-42$ — $>$
20. 37 ● $^-98$ — $>$

Set C

For each exercise, arrange the numbers in order from least to greatest.

1. 6 $^-4$ 3 $^-1$ — $^-4$ $^-1$ 3 6
2. 1 $^-1$ 2 $^-2$ — $^-2$ $^-1$ 1 2
3. 7 $^-3$ $^-5$ 9 — $^-5$ $^-3$ 7 9
4. $^-13$ $^-15$ $^-19$ 14 — $^-19$ $^-15$ $^-13$ 14
5. 25 $^-10$ $^-30$ 40 — $^-30$ $^-10$ 25 40
6. 5 $^-7$ 8 3 $^-4$ — $^-7$ $^-4$ 3 5 8
7. $^-7$ 8 0 $^-8$ $^-9$ — $^-9$ $^-8$ $^-7$ 0 8
8. $^-6$ 7 $^-8$ 9 $^-10$ — $^-10$ $^-8$ $^-6$ 7 9
9. 8 0 $^-9$ 9 7 — $^-9$ 0 7 8 9
10. 5 $^-4$ 0 6 $^-2$ — $^-4$ $^-2$ 0 5 6
11. $^-16$ 13 $^-14$ 0 8 — $^-16$ $^-14$ 0 8 13
12. 35 25 $^-18$ 10 $^-10$ — $^-18$ $^-10$ 10 25 35
13. 1 5 7 $^-1$ $^-5$ $^-7$ — $^-7$ $^-5$ $^-1$ 1 5 7
14. 8 $^-1$ 16 $^-12$ $^-8$ — $^-12$ $^-8$ $^-1$ 8 16
15. $^-2$ 10 $^-7$ $^-10$ 6 — $^-10$ $^-7$ $^-2$ 6 10
16. $^-15$ 15 $^-16$ 16 $^-17$ 17 — $^-17$ $^-16$ $^-15$ 15 16 17
17. $^-21$ $^-28$ 14 16 $^-9$ $^-5$ — $^-28$ $^-21$ $^-9$ $^-5$ 14 16
18. $^-6$ 3 $^-8$ 6 $^-7$ $^-9$ 10 — $^-9$ $^-8$ $^-7$ $^-6$ 3 6 10
19. $^-4$ $^-2$ $^-9$ 4 9 6 $^-5$ — $^-9$ $^-5$ $^-4$ $^-2$ 4 6 9
20. 78 $^-39$ $^-92$ 46 52 $^-14$ — $^-92$ $^-39$ $^-14$ 46 52 78
21. 27 $^-46$ 33 $^-24$ $^-30$ 39 — $^-46$ $^-30$ $^-24$ 27 33 39

Objective: Add positive and negative numbers.

Adding Positive and Negative Numbers

Example D Two positive numbers

$1 + 4$

Start at 1. Since 4 is positive, move 4 units to the right.

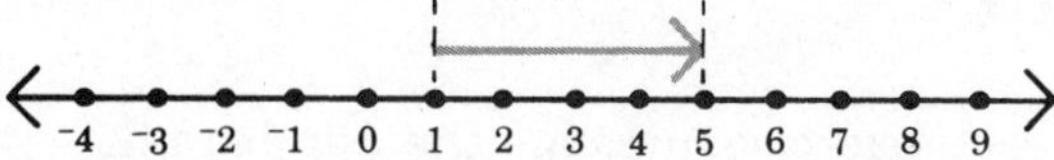

To add two positive numbers, find the sum of the two numbers. The answer is positive.

$1 + 4 = 5$

Example E Two negative numbers

${}^-2 + {}^-4$

Start at ${}^-2$. Since ${}^-4$ is negative, move 4 units to the left.

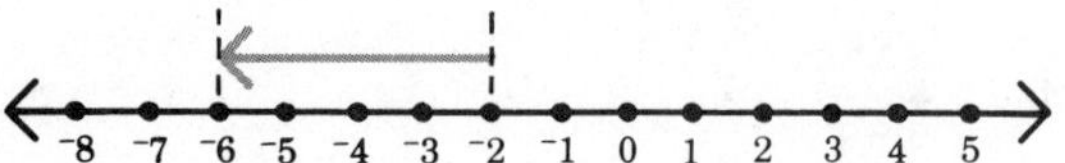

To add two negative numbers, find the sum without regard to the signs. The answer is negative.

${}^-2 + {}^-4 = {}^-6$

Example F One positive and one negative number

$3 + {}^-7$

Start at 3. Since ${}^-7$ is negative, move 7 units to the left.

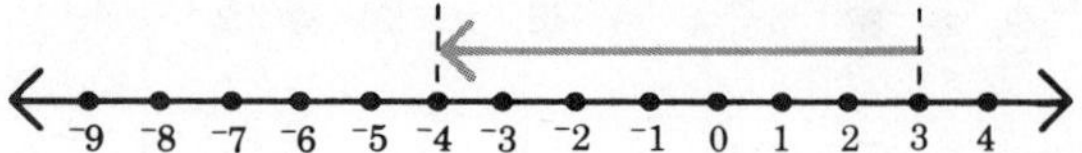

To add a positive number and a negative number, subtract without regard to the signs. The answer is positive if the number farther from zero is positive. The answer is negative if the number farther from zero is negative.

$3 + {}^-7 = {}^-4$

Example G Three or more addends

$8 + 2 + {}^-3 + 1 + {}^-9$

Here is any easy way to add more than two positive and negative numbers.

$8 + 2 + {}^-3 + 1 + {}^-9$ — Add the positive numbers.

$11 + {}^-3 + {}^-9$ — Add the negative numbers.

$11 + {}^-12$ — Find the sum of the two answers.

${}^-1$

$8 + 2 + {}^-3 + 1 + {}^-9 = {}^-1$

Exercises

PROBLEM SOLVING
The applications on pages 295–297 may be used anytime after this lesson.

Set D

1. $3 + 6$
   9
2. $92 + 48$
   140
3. $18 + 26$
   44
4. $813 + 295$
   1108
5. $156 + 975$
   1131
6. $295 + 167$
   462
7. $36 + 45$
   81
8. $15 + 37$
   52
9. $75 + 16$
   91
10. $748 + 976$
    1724
11. $12.9 + 7.6$
    20.5
12. $9.3 + 0.8$
    10.1
13. $8.37 + 4.96$
    13.33

Set E

1. ${}^-5 + {}^-6$
   $^-11$
2. ${}^-12 + {}^-8$
   $^-20$
3. ${}^-94 + {}^-29$
   $^-123$
4. ${}^-876 + {}^-135$
   $^-1011$
5. ${}^-35 + {}^-47$
   $^-82$
6. ${}^-28 + {}^-165$
   $^-193$
7. ${}^-64 + {}^-18$
   $^-82$
8. ${}^-108 + {}^-792$
   $^-900$
9. ${}^-49 + {}^-62$
   $^-111$
10. ${}^-84 + {}^-67$
    $^-151$
11. ${}^-1.14 + {}^-1.27$
    $^-2.41$
12. ${}^-3.9 + {}^-5.6$
    $^-9.5$
13. ${}^-8.17 + {}^-9.54$
    $^-17.71$

Set F

1. $4 + {}^-8$
   $^-4$
2. $9 + {}^-7$
   2
3. ${}^-16 + 4$
   $^-12$
4. ${}^-12 + 10$
   $^-2$
5. ${}^-8 + 23$
   15
6. $25 + {}^-76$
   $^-51$
7. $19 + {}^-24$
   $^-5$
8. ${}^-92 + 69$
   $^-23$
9. $501 + {}^-372$
   129
10. ${}^-43 + 58$
    15
11. ${}^-27.3 + 68.2$
    40.9
12. ${}^-0.97 + 0.35$
    $^-0.62$
13. $7.36 + {}^-5.24$
    2.12

Set G

1. ${}^-6 + 4 + {}^-9$
   $^-11$
2. ${}^-7 + {}^-6 + 5$
   $^-8$
3. $8 + 3 + {}^-4$
   7
4. $10 + {}^-12 + 3$
   1
5. ${}^-25 + {}^-16 + {}^-14$
   $^-55$
6. $45 + {}^-29 + {}^-30$
   $^-14$
7. ${}^-2 + {}^-4 + {}^-5 + {}^-6$
   $^-17$
8. $7 + {}^-13 + 2 + {}^-1$
   $^-5$
9. ${}^-375 + 215 + 30$
   $^-130$
10. ${}^-204 + 913 + {}^-408$
    301
11. $18 + {}^-6 + 12 + {}^-2$
    22
12. ${}^-85 + {}^-4 + 12 + {}^-3$
    $^-80$
13. $2.7 + {}^-1.9 + 0.7$
    1.5

Mixed Practice

F 1. $34 + {}^-50$
   $^-16$
F 2. $15 + {}^-37$
   $^-22$
D 3. $473 + 859$
   1332
G 4. ${}^-6 + {}^-14 + 35$
   15
G 5. ${}^-12 + 5 + 6 + {}^-8$
   $^-9$
E 6. ${}^-562 + {}^-183$
   $^-745$
G 7. ${}^-16 + {}^-24 + 8$
   $^-32$
G 8. ${}^-6 + {}^-3 + 28$
   19
F 9. $67 + {}^-21$
   46
F 10. ${}^-46 + 31$
   $^-15$
G 11. $4 + {}^-6 + {}^-9 + 10$
   $^-1$
F 12. $132 + {}^-46$
   86
F 13. ${}^-201 + 167$
   $^-34$
E 14. ${}^-86 + {}^-37$
   $^-123$
G 15. ${}^-13 + 6 + {}^-5 + {}^-2$
   $^-14$
F 16. $98 + {}^-45$
   53
E 17. ${}^-472 + {}^-378$
   $^-850$
F 18. $79 + {}^-101$
   $^-22$
F 19. ${}^-76 + 38$
   $^-38$
G 20. $2 + {}^-4 + 5 + {}^-6$
   $^-3$
F 21. ${}^-175 + 89$
   $^-86$
F 22. $118 + {}^-374$
   $^-256$
G 23. $68 + 5 + {}^-72$
   1
D 24. $426 + 217$
   643
E 25. ${}^-512 + {}^-682$
   $^-1194$
G 26. $408 + {}^-965 + 126$
   $^-431$
G 27. $34 + {}^-62 + 48 + {}^-17$
   3
G 28. ${}^-37 + 25 + 88 + {}^-91$
   $^-15$
G 29. $605 + {}^-109 + {}^-576$
   $^-80$

See Skills File, page 424, for more practice.

Objective: Subtract positive and negative numbers.

Subtracting Positive and Negative Numbers

Example H Writing the opposite of a given number

Name the opposite of ${}^{-}3$.

On a number line, a number and its **opposite** are the same distance from zero. Zero is its own opposite.

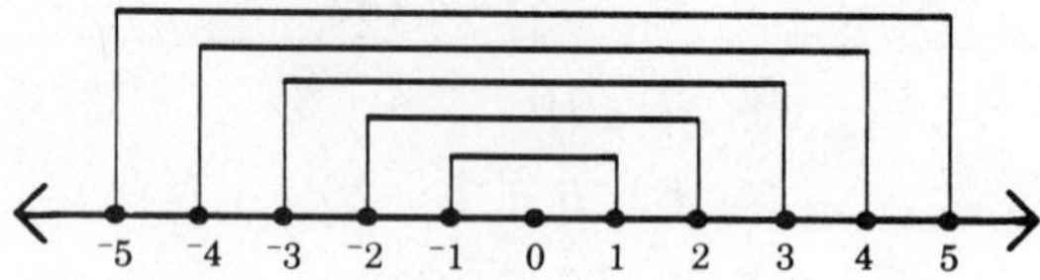

The opposite of ${}^{-}3$ is 3.

Example I Two positive numbers

$3 - 4$

Study the pattern.

$3 - 1 = 2$ $\quad 3 + {}^{-}1 = 2$

$3 - 2 = 1$ $\quad 3 + {}^{-}2 = 1$

$3 - 3 = 0$ $\quad 3 + {}^{-}3 = 0$

$3 - 4 = {}^{-}1$ $\quad 3 + {}^{-}4 = {}^{-}1$

$3 - 5 = {}^{-}2$ $\quad 3 + {}^{-}5 = {}^{-}2$

$3 - 6 = {}^{-}3$ $\quad 3 + {}^{-}6 = {}^{-}3$

To subtract a positive or a negative number, add its opposite.

$3 - 4 = \square$

$3 + {}^{-}4 = {}^{-}1$ Add the opposite of 4.

$3 - 4 = {}^{-}1$

Example J Two negative numbers

${}^{-}6 - {}^{-}8$

${}^{-}6 + 8 = 2$ Add the opposite of ${}^{-}8$.

${}^{-}6 - {}^{-}8 = 2$

Example K A negative minuend and a positive subtrahend

${}^{-}5 - 2$

${}^{-}5 + {}^{-}2 = {}^{-}7$ Add the opposite of 2.

${}^{-}5 - 2 = {}^{-}7$

Example L A positive minuend and a negative subtrahend

$7 - {}^{-}4$

$7 + 4 = 11$ Add the opposite of ${}^{-}4$.

$7 - {}^{-}4 = 11$

Example M Order of operations involving addition and subtraction

$15 - ({}^{-}8 + 2)$ First do operations inside parentheses. Then subtract.

$15 - {}^{-}6$

21

PROBLEM SOLVING
The applications on pages 298–301 may be used anytime after this lesson.

Exercises

Set H

Name the opposite of each number.

1. 7 — $^{-}7$
2. $^{-}6$ — 6
3. 1 — $^{-}1$
4. $^{-}35$ — 35
5. 48 — $^{-}48$
6. $^{-}965$ — 965

Set I

1. $8-9$ — $^{-}1$
2. $7-3$ — 4
3. $25-38$ — $^{-}13$
4. $17-16$ — 1
5. $48-62$ — $^{-}14$
6. $125-338$ — $^{-}213$
7. $824-931$ — $^{-}107$
8. $3.8-4.6$ — $^{-}0.8$
9. $7.9-12.5$ — $^{-}4.6$
10. $3.15-4.24$ — $^{-}1.09$

Set J

1. $^{-}4-{}^{-}9$ — 5
2. $^{-}5-{}^{-}8$ — 3
3. $^{-}21-{}^{-}18$ — $^{-}3$
4. $^{-}32-{}^{-}29$ — $^{-}3$
5. $^{-}35-{}^{-}91$ — 56
6. $^{-}389-{}^{-}462$ — 73
7. $^{-}913-{}^{-}628$ — $^{-}285$
8. $^{-}4.9-{}^{-}5.6$ — 0.7
9. $^{-}14.8-{}^{-}6.3$ — $^{-}8.5$
10. $^{-}4.86-{}^{-}3.17$ — $^{-}1.69$

Set K

1. $^{-}3-6$ — $^{-}9$
2. $^{-}9-3$ — $^{-}12$
3. $^{-}41-17$ — $^{-}58$
4. $^{-}65-48$ — $^{-}113$
5. $^{-}19-25$ — $^{-}44$
6. $^{-}137-462$ — $^{-}599$
7. $^{-}792-218$ — $^{-}1010$
8. $^{-}6.3-11.8$ — $^{-}18.1$
9. $^{-}1.16-0.78$ — $^{-}1.94$
10. $^{-}0.42-3.16$ — $^{-}3.58$

Set L

1. $9-{}^{-}6$ — 15
2. $5-{}^{-}3$ — 8
3. $13-{}^{-}12$ — 25
4. $23-{}^{-}49$ — 72
5. $16-{}^{-}12$ — 28
6. $482-{}^{-}186$ — 668
7. $381-{}^{-}469$ — 850
8. $6.8-{}^{-}3.4$ — 10.2
9. $6.3-{}^{-}12.1$ — 18.4
10. $1.28-{}^{-}0.39$ — 1.67

Set M

1. $16-({}^{-}9+{}^{-}4)$ — 29
2. $(15-{}^{-}8)-{}^{-}3$ — 26
3. $({}^{-}19+{}^{-}3)-16$ — $^{-}38$
4. $(20-{}^{-}6)-(6-7)$ — 27
5. $({}^{-}3+{}^{-}8)-{}^{-}9$ — $^{-}2$
6. $26-(39-{}^{-}19)$ — $^{-}32$
7. $({}^{-}5-4)-(1-{}^{-}2)$ — $^{-}12$
8. $(67+48)-16$ — 99
9. $^{-}78-(19-{}^{-}59)$ — $^{-}156$
10. $^{-}52-({}^{-}98+65)$ — $^{-}19$
11. $({}^{-}8-{}^{-}3)-({}^{-}4-5)$ — 4
12. $119-({}^{-}34+102)$ — 51
13. $^{-}48-(14+{}^{-}16)$ — $^{-}46$
14. $^{-}84-({}^{-}123-49)$ — 88
15. $(6+{}^{-}9)-(5-{}^{-}6)$ — $^{-}14$

Mixed Practice

I 1. $95-103$ — $^{-}8$
K 2. $^{-}18-56$ — $^{-}74$
L 3. $29-{}^{-}48$ — 77
M 4. $^{-}10-(12+{}^{-}38)$ — 16
M 5. $(19+{}^{-}9)-{}^{-}16$ — 26
I 6. $63-79$ — $^{-}16$
J 7. $^{-}89-{}^{-}45$ — $^{-}44$
L 8. $89-{}^{-}67$ — 156
K 9. $^{-}81-42$ — $^{-}123$
J 10. $^{-}65-{}^{-}81$ — 16
M 11. $(28-7)-{}^{-}19$ — 40
I 12. $14-83$ — $^{-}69$
M 13. $({}^{-}94+{}^{-}6)-100$ — $^{-}200$
K 14. $^{-}32-61$ — $^{-}93$
J 15. $^{-}145-{}^{-}302$ — 157
M 16. $936-(21-{}^{-}9)$ — 906
L 17. $42-{}^{-}256$ — 298

See Skills File, page 424, for more practice.

Objective: Multiply positive and negative numbers.

Multiplying Positive and Negative Numbers

Example N Two positive numbers

8×6

Before developing the rules for multiplying positive and negative numbers, you may wish to have students study patterns like those below.

The product of two positive numbers is positive.

$8 \times 6 = 48$

$5 \times 2 = 10$	$^-5 \times 2 = {}^-10$
$5 \times 1 = 5$	$^-5 \times 1 = {}^-5$
$5 \times 0 = 0$	$^-5 \times 0 = 0$
$5 \times {}^-1 = {}^-5$	$^-5 \times {}^-1 = 5$
$5 \times {}^-2 = {}^-10$	$^-5 \times {}^-2 = 10$

Example O Two negative numbers

$^-3 \times {}^-4$

The product of two negative numbers is positive.

$^-3 \times {}^-4 = 12$

Example P One positive and one negative number

$7 \times {}^-5$ $\quad$ $^-8 \times 6$

The product of a positive number and a negative number is negative.

$7 \times {}^-5 = {}^-35$ $\quad$ $^-8 \times 6 = {}^-48$

Example Q Order of operations involving addition, subtraction, and multiplication

$6({}^-5) - 7({}^-8 + 2)$ First do operations inside parentheses.

$6({}^-5) - 7({}^-6)$ Then multiply.

$^-30 - {}^-42$ Then subtract.

12

Exercises

Set N

1. 9×6 54
2. 5×4 20
3. 7×8 56
4. 6×3 18
5. 2×9 18
6. 36×4 144
7. 3×25 75
8. 16×2 32
9. 18×3 54
10. 4×32 128
11. 9×45 405
12. 10×34 340
13. 11×62 682
14. 40×16 640
15. 24×18 432
16. 12×95 1140
17. 37×46 1702
18. 18×36 648
19. 25×48 1200
20. 76×13 988
21. 105×37 3885
22. 7.6×10 76
23. 0.7×0.9 0.63
24. 0.89×0.72 0.6408

Set O

1. $^-8 \times {}^-4$ 32
2. $^-7 \times {}^-5$ 35
3. $^-9 \times {}^-7$ 63
4. $^-6 \times {}^-4$ 24
5. $^-3 \times {}^-9$ 27
6. $^-2 \times {}^-14$ 28
7. $^-6 \times {}^-29$ 174
8. $^-7 \times {}^-35$ 245
9. $^-14 \times {}^-11$ 154
10. $^-16 \times {}^-98$ 1568
11. $^-10 \times {}^-72$ 720
12. $^-8 \times {}^-45$ 360
13. $^-18 \times {}^-100$ 1800
14. $^-32 \times {}^-125$ 4000
15. $^-202 \times {}^-68$ 13,736
16. $^-167 \times {}^-103$ 17,201
17. $^-71 \times {}^-98$ 6958
18. $^-65 \times {}^-79$ 5135
19. $^-13 \times {}^-86$ 1118
20. $^-45 \times {}^-62$ 2790
21. $^-12 \times {}^-42$ 504
22. $^-13 \times {}^-2.7$ 35.1
23. $^-1.6 \times {}^-2.5$ 4
24. $^-0.82 \times {}^-3.1$ 2.542

Exercises

Set P

1. $^{-}4 \times 7$
   $^{-}28$
2. $8 \times {}^{-}3$
   $^{-}24$
3. $^{-}9 \times 7$
   $^{-}63$
4. $^{-}6 \times 5$
   $^{-}30$
5. $7 \times {}^{-}8$
   $^{-}56$
6. $2 \times {}^{-}16$
   $^{-}32$
7. $5 \times {}^{-}78$
   $^{-}390$
8. $^{-}7 \times 12$
   $^{-}84$
9. $98 \times {}^{-}45$
   $^{-}4410$
10. $^{-}35 \times 21$
    $^{-}735$
11. $71 \times {}^{-}83$
    $^{-}5893$
12. $^{-}92 \times 76$
    $^{-}6992$
13. $19 \times {}^{-}25$
    $^{-}475$
14. $^{-}42 \times 36$
    $^{-}1512$
15. $^{-}25 \times 48$
    $^{-}1200$
16. $3 \times {}^{-}124$
    $^{-}372$
17. $^{-}68 \times 954$
    $^{-}64{,}872$
18. $^{-}2 \times 0.4$
    $^{-}0.8$
19. $3 \times {}^{-}0.16$
    $^{-}0.48$
20. $100 \times {}^{-}0.95$
    $^{-}95$

Set Q

1. $^{-}4(^{-}5 + 1)$
   16
2. $(1 + {}^{-}8)2$
   $^{-}14$
3. $6(9) - {}^{-}2(7)$
   68
4. $4(^{-}29) + {}^{-}3(8)$
   $^{-}140$
5. $^{-}15 + 6(7) - {}^{-}1$
   28
6. $^{-}7(^{-}3 + 2 + {}^{-}6)$
   49
7. $12 - {}^{-}8(2)(^{-}1)$
   $^{-}4$
8. $9(^{-}2)(^{-}3) - {}^{-}22$
   76
9. $^{-}70 - 5(^{-}13 + 9)$
   $^{-}50$
10. $8(^{-}18 + 9) - 42$
    $^{-}114$
11. $^{-}5(^{-}3 - {}^{-}1)$
    10
12. $9 - 2(^{-}4 + {}^{-}2)$
    21
13. $2(8 - {}^{-}3)$
    22
14. $23 - {}^{-}7(2)$
    37
15. $^{-}2(8 - {}^{-}3)$
    $^{-}22$
16. $^{-}10(^{-}3 - {}^{-}6 + 2)$
    $^{-}50$
17. $^{-}8(^{-}9 - 2 - {}^{-}5)$
    48
18. $12(7 - 8)$
    $^{-}12$
19. $9(^{-}2) + 4(3 - {}^{-}2)$
    2
20. $^{-}4(^{-}3) - 6(4 + {}^{-}1)$
    $^{-}6$

Mixed Practice

Q 1. $39 - {}^{-}6(^{-}6)$
   3
P 2. $9 \times {}^{-}9$
   $^{-}81$
P 3. $52 \times {}^{-}14$
   $^{-}728$
N 4. 12×14
   168
O 5. $^{-}62 \times {}^{-}12$
   744
P 6. $78 \times {}^{-}96$
   $^{-}7488$
Q 7. $(^{-}9 - {}^{-}10) + 3(^{-}1)$
   $^{-}2$
Q 8. $8(^{-}7) + {}^{-}3(2)$
   $^{-}62$
P 9. $^{-}24 \times 39$
   $^{-}936$
O 10. $^{-}57 \times {}^{-}2$
   114
Q 11. $(7 + {}^{-}6) - 4(^{-}8)$
   33
P 12. $10 \times {}^{-}621$
   $^{-}6210$
N 13. 15×45
   675
Q 14. $^{-}6(3) + (4 - {}^{-}9)$
   $^{-}5$
P 15. $^{-}45 \times 251$
   $^{-}11{,}295$
O 16. $^{-}43 \times {}^{-}87$
   3741
Q 17. $^{-}9(25 + {}^{-}38)$
   117
N 18. 100×32
   3200
Q 19. $12(19 + {}^{-}21) - {}^{-}3$
   $^{-}21$
P 20. $^{-}21 \times 38$
   $^{-}798$

See Skills File, page 424, for more practice.

BREAK TIME

Find the total number of triangles.
27

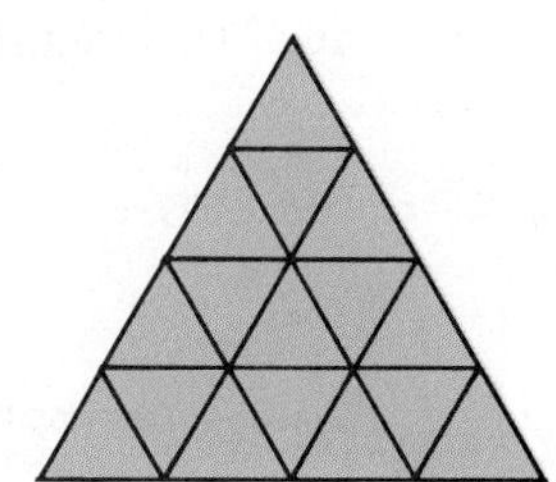

Find the total number of squares.
13

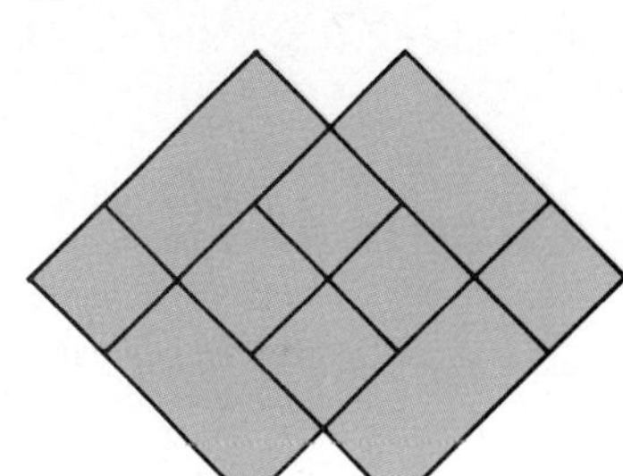

Objective: Divide positive and negative numbers.

Dividing Positive and Negative Numbers

Example R Two positive numbers

$24 \div 6$

Before developing the rules for dividing positive and negative numbers, you might have students study patterns relating division and multiplication as shown below.

The quotient of two positive numbers is positive.

$24 \div 6 = 4$

$5 \times 3 = 15$	$^-5 \times 3 = {}^-15$
$15 \div 3 = 5$	$^-15 \div 3 = {}^-5$
$5 \times {}^-3 = {}^-15$	$^-5 \times {}^-3 = 15$
$^-15 \div {}^-3 = 5$	$15 \div {}^-3 = {}^-5$

Example S Two negative numbers

$^-14 \div {}^-2$

The quotient of two negative numbers is positive.

$^-14 \div {}^-2 = 7$

Example T One positive and one negative number

$^-56 \div 8$ $\quad$ $54 \div {}^-9$

The quotient of a positive number and a negative number is negative.

$^-56 \div 8 = {}^-7$ $\quad$ $54 \div {}^-9 = {}^-6$

Example U Order of operations involving addition, subtraction, and division

$\frac{8 - 17}{3}$ First do all operations above and below the division bar.

$\frac{^-9}{3}$ Then divide.

$^-3$

Exercises

Set R

1. $18 \div 3$ 6
2. $48 \div 6$ 8
3. $72 \div 8$ 9
4. $24 \div 4$ 6
5. $36 \div 6$ 6
6. $40 \div 5$ 8
7. $49 \div 7$ 7
8. $72 \div 9$ 8
9. $25 \div 5$ 5
10. $54 \div 9$ 6
11. $99 \div 11$ 9
12. $75 \div 15$ 5
13. $84 \div 21$ 4
14. $96 \div 32$ 3
15. $108 \div 12$ 9
16. $504 \div 14$ 36
17. $756 \div 28$ 27
18. $672 \div 32$ 21
19. $540 \div 18$ 30
20. $930 \div 62$ 15
21. $962 \div 37$ 26
22. $0.9 \div 3$ 0.3
23. $0.4 \div 0.2$ 2
24. $6.4 \div 1.6$ 4

Set S

1. $^-15 \div {}^-3$ 5
2. $^-63 \div {}^-9$ 7
3. $^-21 \div {}^-7$ 3
4. $^-59 \div {}^-1$ 59
5. $^-35 \div {}^-5$ 7
6. $^-56 \div {}^-8$ 7
7. $^-81 \div {}^-9$ 9
8. $^-25 \div {}^-5$ 5
9. $^-64 \div {}^-8$ 8
10. $^-84 \div {}^-12$ 7
11. $^-75 \div {}^-5$ 15
12. $^-124 \div {}^-4$ 31
13. $^-72 \div {}^-12$ 6
14. $^-414 \div {}^-9$ 46
15. $^-901 \div {}^-17$ 53
16. $^-594 \div {}^-18$ 33
17. $^-986 \div {}^-29$ 34
18. $^-162 \div {}^-18$ 9
19. $^-196 \div {}^-14$ 14
20. $^-203 \div {}^-29$ 7
21. $^-152 \div {}^-38$ 4
22. $^-70.8 \div {}^-12$ 5.9
23. $^-2.52 \div {}^-1.8$ 1.4
24. $^-0.253 \div {}^-0.11$ 2.3

Set T

1. $^-12 \div 6$
   $^-2$
2. $18 \div {^-3}$
   $^-6$
3. $21 \div {^-7}$
   $^-3$
4. $^-35 \div 5$
   $^-7$
5. $^-36 \div 6$
   $^-6$
6. $48 \div {^-8}$
   $^-6$
7. $^-18 \div 2$
   $^-9$
8. $^-24 \div 3$
   $^-8$
9. $^-96 \div 6$
   $^-16$
10. $140 \div {^-7}$
    $^-20$
11. $^-112 \div 8$
    $^-14$
12. $300 \div {^-25}$
    $^-12$
13. $144 \div {^-12}$
    $^-12$
14. $^-676 \div 26$
    $^-26$
15. $345 \div {^-15}$
    $^-23$
16. $^-182 \div 14$
    $^-13$
17. $^-902 \div 82$
    $^-11$
18. $0.48 \div {^-4}$
    $^-0.12$
19. $^-5.4 \div 0.6$
    $^-9$
20. $^-0.72 \div 1.2$
    $^-0.6$

Set U

1. $\dfrac{4 - 16}{3}$
   $^-4$
2. $\dfrac{^-28 - 14}{7}$
   $^-6$
3. $\dfrac{13 - {^-7}}{10}$
   2
4. $\dfrac{25 + {^-21}}{^-4}$
   $^-1$
5. $\dfrac{^-6 + {^-18}}{^-4}$
   6
6. $\dfrac{^-35 + 13}{11}$
   $^-2$
7. $\dfrac{^-42 - 18}{13 + {^-7}}$
   $^-10$
8. $\dfrac{^-8 - {^-9}}{^-1}$
   $^-1$
9. $\dfrac{102 - {^-42}}{^-56 + 8}$
   $^-3$
10. $\dfrac{800 + {^-464}}{^-100 + 58}$
    $^-8$

Mixed Practice

R 1. $42 \div 3$
   14

U 2. $\dfrac{49 - 7}{^-7}$
   $^-6$

T 3. $48 \div {^-16}$
   $^-3$

U 4. $\dfrac{^-27 + {^-9}}{^-11 + 2}$
   4

T 5. $^-49 \div 7$
   $^-7$

T 6. $156 \div {^-13}$
   $^-12$

U 7. $\dfrac{^-2842}{^-100 + 51}$
   58

S 8. $^-78 \div {^-6}$
   13

U 9. $\dfrac{4 + 10}{^-1 + 3}$
   7

R 10. $176 \div 11$
   16

S 11. $^-28 \div {^-7}$
   4

T 12. $^-455 \div 13$
   $^-35$

S 13. $^-841 \div {^-29}$
   29

See Skills File, page 424, for more practice.

BREAK TIME

The number of eggs in a basket doubled every minute.

The basket was full of eggs at 3:25 P.M.

When was the basket half full?

3:24 P.M.

SKILLS POSTTEST

Number of test items - 21

Number missed	1	2	3	4	5	6	7	8	9	10
Percent correct	95	90	86	81	76	71	67	62	57	52

SKILL Writing and Ordering Positive and Negative Numbers *pages 284–285*

A Write a number for point R on the number line.

R ■ $^{-}2$ $^{-}1$ 0 1 2

$^{-}3$

B Compare these numbers. Replace ● with $<$ or $>$.

$^{-}2$ ● 2

$<$

C Arrange these numbers in order from the least to the greatest.

$^{-}8$ 0 4 $^{-}3$

$^{-}8$ $^{-}3$ 0 4

SKILL Adding Positive and Negative Numbers *pages 286–287*

D $7 + 3$
10

E $^{-}4 + {}^{-}5$
$^{-}9$

F $^{-}6 + 8$
2

G $^{-}9 + 5 + {}^{-}1 + 3$
$^{-}2$

SKILL Subtracting Positive and Negative Numbers *pages 288–289*

H Name the opposite of $^{-}9$.
9

I $3 - 8$
$^{-}5$

J $^{-}2 - {}^{-}3$
1

K $^{-}6 - 7$
$^{-}13$

L $4 - {}^{-}5$
9

M $20 - (2 - {}^{-}5)$
13

SKILL Multiplying Positive and Negative Numbers *pages 290–291*

N 7×8
56

O $^{-}9 \times {}^{-}2$
18

P $^{-}6 \times 3$
$^{-}18$

Q $9(7) - 5({}^{-}2)$
73

SKILL Dividing Positive and Negative Numbers *pages 292–293*

R $63 \div 9$
7

S $^{-}48 \div {}^{-}6$
8

T $12 \div {}^{-}2$
$^{-}6$

U $\frac{8 - {}^{-}6}{^{-}2}$
$^{-}7$

Problem Solving

CONSUMER APPLICATIONS

Objective: Solve problems involving positive and negative numbers.

In this lesson students compute total yardage.

Charting Football Plays

Coach Buchheister charted the plays for the first half of Milford's football game with Barrington High. Each time the team gained at least 10 yards in four plays or less, they received a first down. If they did not gain 10 yards in three plays, they usually punted. You may wish to discuss that it is not mandatory to punt on the fourth play.

Complete the chart below before doing Problems 5–8. For each play, positive numbers represent yards gained; negative numbers represent yards lost.

First-Half Plays

	Play	Type of play: Run	Pass	Penalty	Total yardage in three plays
	1	4			
	2		0		
	3			⁻5	4+0+⁻5=⁻1
	1	7			
	2	2			
	3		9		7+2+9=18
	1	-4			
	2		13		
1.	3	8			⁻4 + 13 + 8 = 17
	1			5	
	2		⁻3		
2.	3	7			5 + ⁻3 + 7 = 9
	1	-7			
	2		0		
3.	3			10	⁻7 + 0 + 10 = 3
	1	4			
	2		5		
4.	3	7			4 + 5 + 7 = 16

5. Give a positive number for total yards gained.
81 yards
6. Give a negative number for total yards lost.
⁻19 yards
7. Find the total offense. (Yards gained + yards lost)
62 yards
8. How many first downs did Milford receive in the first half?
3 first downs

In Problems 2 and 3, yards were gained as a result of penalties on the opposing team.

Problem Solving

CONSUMER APPLICATIONS

Objective: Solve problems involving positive and negative numbers.

In this lesson students find the times and heights of morning and evening high tides.

Finding the Times and Heights of High Tides

Harry Alvarez enjoys fishing during high tide, when the fish leave deep water to feed in creeks and shallow waters. He uses charts to determine when the tide will be high in a given area. He also uses charts to help him find the height of the tide at that time.

His charts contain complete tide tables for Boston with correction tables for other areas of the United States. Parts of these tables are shown below.

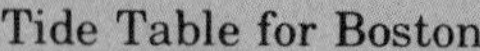

Tide Table for Boston

Day	Time of high tide		Tide height in meters	
	Morning	Evening	Morning	Evening
June 1	5:00	5:45	2.70	2.62
2	6:00	6:30	2.62	2.65
3	6:45	7:25	2.56	2.68
4	7:45	8:15	2.53	2.74
5	8:30	9:00	2.56	2.65
July 1	5:15	5:45	2.62	2.71
2	6:00	6:30	2.53	2.71
3	7:00	7:30	2.50	2.77
4	8:00	8:15	2.47	2.83
5	8:45	9:00	2.50	2.96
Aug. 16	7:30	8:00	2.62	3.02
17	8:30	9:00	2.59	2.99
18	9:30	9:45	2.62	3.02

Be sure students understand that the negative sign used with a time difference refers to the entire quantity (both hours and minutes).

Tide-Correction Table

Location	Time difference	Height difference
MAINE		
Bar Harbor	-0 hr. 34 min.	0.27 m
Portland	-0 hr. 12 min.	-0.18 m
Eastport	-0 hr. 28 min.	2.56 m
Machias	-0 hr. 28 min.	0.85 m
NEW YORK		
Coney Island	-3 hr. 33 min.	-1.49 m
Oyster Bay	0 hr. 04 min.	-0.55 m
NEW JERSEY		
Atlantic City	-3 hr. 56 min.	-1.68 m
Cape May	-3 hr. 28 min.	-1.62 m
MARYLAND		
Havre de Grace	11 hr. 21 min.	-2.35 m
Annapolis	4 hr. 25 min.	-2.29 m
CALIFORNIA		
Los Angeles	-1 hr. 33 min.	-1.43 m
San Francisco	-0 hr. 45 min.	-1.34 m
ALASKA		
Anchorage	-4 hr. 58 min.	5.33 m
Juneau	3 hr. 08 min.	1.86 m
Kodiak	1 hr. 53 min.	-0.52 m

Harry plans to go fishing near Atlantic City, New Jersey, on June 2. He wants to know the time and the height of the morning high tide.

First he finds the time of the morning high tide in Boston on June 2. It is 6:00 A.M. Then he finds Atlantic City in the tide-correction table. The correction (time difference) is $^{-}3$ hours 56 minutes.

He adds to find the time of the morning high tide in Atlantic City.

$$\begin{array}{rcr} 6 \text{ hours} \quad 0 \text{ minutes} & = & 5 \text{ hours } 60 \text{ minutes} \\ + \, ^{-}3 \text{ hours } 56 \text{ minutes} & = & \underline{^{-}3 \text{ hours } 56 \text{ minutes}} \\ & & 2 \text{ hours} \quad 4 \text{ minutes, or 2:04 A.M.} \end{array}$$

Then he computes the height of the morning high tide for June 2. First he finds the height of the morning high tide for Boston on June 2. It is 2.62 meters. Then he finds the correction (height difference) for Atlantic City in the tide-correction table. It is $^{-}1.68$ meters.

He adds to find the height of the morning high tide in Atlantic City.

2.62 meters + $^{-}1.68$ meters = 0.94 meters

Find the time and the height of the morning high tide for each city on the given date.

1. Portland, Maine, June 1
   4:48 A.M.; 2.52 m
2. Portland, Maine, July 1
   5:03 A.M.; 2.44 m
3. Eastport, Maine, August 17
   8:02 A.M.; 5.15 m
4. Eastport, Maine, June 4
   7:17 A.M.; 5.09 m
5. Coney Island, New York, June 5
   4:57 A.M.; 1.07 m
6. Coney Island, New York, July 5
   5:12 A.M.; 1.01 m
7. Cape May, New Jersey, July 2
   2:32 A.M.; 0.91 m
8. Cape May, New Jersey, July 3
   3:32 A.M.; 0.88 m
9. Annapolis, Maryland, June 2
   10:25 A.M.; 0.33 m
10. Annapolis, Maryland, July 3
   11:25 A.M.; 0.21 m
11. Los Angeles, California, June 3
   5:12 A.M.; 1.13 m
12. San Francisco, California, June 3
   6:00 A.M.; 1.22 m
13. Anchorage, Alaska, July 2
   1:02 A.M.; 7.86 m
14. Anchorage, Alaska, August 18
   4:32 A.M.; 7.95 m
15. Kodiak, Alaska, July 2
   7:53 A.M.; 2.01 m

16–30. Find the time and the height of the evening high tide for each city in Problems 1–15.

16. 5:33 P.M.; 2.44 m
17. 5:33 P.M.; 2.53 m
18. 8:32 P.M.; 5.55 m
19. 7:47 P.M.; 5.3 m
20. 5:27 P.M.; 1.16 m
21. 5:27 P.M.; 1.47 m
22. 3:02 P.M.; 1.09 m
23. 4:02 P.M.; 1.15 m
24. 10:55 P.M.; 0.36 m
25. 11:55 P.M.; 0.48 m
26. 5:52 P.M.; 1.25 m
27. 6:40 P.M.; 1.34 m
28. 1:32 P.M.; 8.04 m
29. 4:47 P.M.; 8.35 m
30. 8:23 P.M.; 2.19 m

Problem Solving

CAREER APPLICATIONS

Objective: Solve problems involving positive and negative numbers.

In this lesson students read a wind-chill table.

Radio Announcer

Career Cluster: Arts Doris Jackson is an announcer at Radio Station WMIL. She gives the wind-chill index in addition to the Weather Bureau forecast. The wind-chill index is an estimate of how cold the air feels. A temperature of $^-20$°C combined with a wind speed of 25 kilometers per hour is equivalent to a temperature of $^-40$°C without the wind. The wind-chill index is $^-40$°C.

After reading the thermometer and the anemometer (an instrument that measures wind speed), Doris uses this table to determine the wind-chill index.

Wind–Chill Index

Wind speed (kilometers per hour)	Thermometer reading (°C) 0	$^-5$	$^-10$	$^-15$	$^-20$	$^-25$	$^-30$	$^-35$	$^-40$
	Equivalent temperature (°C)								
Calm	0	$^-5$	$^-10$	$^-15$	$^-20$	$^-25$	$^-30$	$^-35$	$^-40$
10	$^-4$	$^-10$	$^-15$	$^-21$	$^-27$	$^-32$	$^-38$	$^-43$	$^-49$
15	$^-8$	$^-14$	$^-20$	$^-26$	$^-32$	$^-38$	$^-45$	$^-51$	$^-57$
20	$^-10$	$^-17$	$^-23$	$^-30$	$^-37$	$^-43$	$^-50$	$^-56$	$^-63$
25	$^-12$	$^-19$	$^-26$	$^-33$	$^-40$	$^-47$	$^-54$	$^-61$	$^-68$
30	$^-14$	$^-21$	$^-28$	$^-36$	$^-43$	$^-50$	$^-57$	$^-64$	$^-71$
35	$^-16$	$^-23$	$^-30$	$^-38$	$^-45$	$^-52$	$^-60$	$^-67$	$^-74$
40	$^-17$	$^-24$	$^-32$	$^-39$	$^-47$	$^-54$	$^-62$	$^-69$	$^-77$
45	$^-18$	$^-25$	$^-33$	$^-41$	$^-48$	$^-56$	$^-64$	$^-71$	$^-79$
50	$^-19$	$^-26$	$^-34$	$^-42$	$^-50$	$^-57$	$^-65$	$^-73$	$^-81$
55	$^-19$	$^-27$	$^-35$	$^-43$	$^-51$	$^-59$	$^-67$	$^-74$	$^-82$
60	$^-20$	$^-28$	$^-36$	$^-44$	$^-52$	$^-60$	$^-68$	$^-76$	$^-83$

Little danger — Increasing danger — Great danger

You may wish to discuss that even when people are properly clothed for cold weather, there is a danger of freezing exposed flesh.

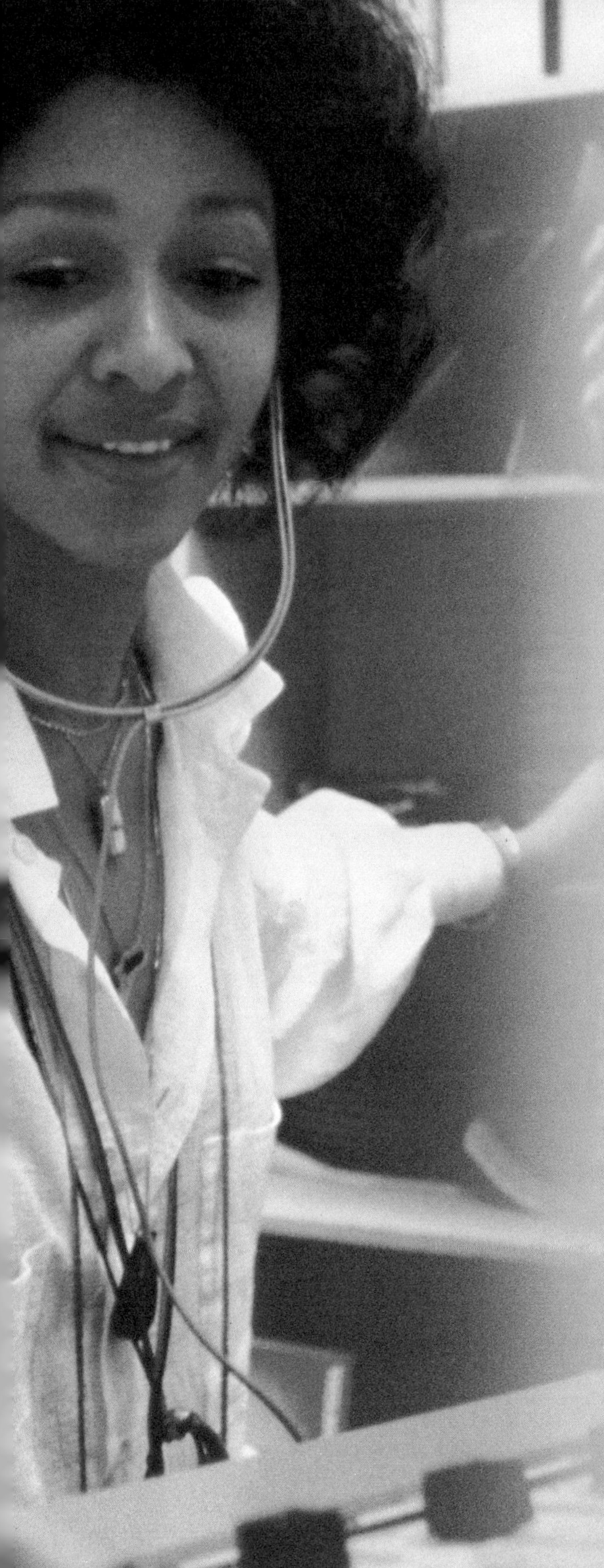

See page 40 of *Problem-Solving Masters.*

Doris keeps a record of the instrument readings for her morning broadcasts. Use the table on page 298 to complete Doris's tables for Monday and Tuesday.

Be sure students know how to read the wind-chill table.

Monday

	Time (A.M.)	Thermometer reading (°C)	Wind speed (km/h)	Wind-chill index (°C)
	5:00	⁻20	10	⁻27
	6:00	⁻15	10	⁻21
1.	7:00	⁻15	15	⁻26
2.	8:00	⁻10	20	⁻23
3.	9:00	⁻5	25	⁻19
4.	10:00	0	30	⁻14

5. What was the difference in the thermometer readings at 5:00 and 10:00 on Monday? (0 – ⁻20)
20°C

6. What was the difference in the wind-chill indexes at 5:00 and 10:00 on Monday?
13°C

Tuesday

	Time (A.M.)	Thermometer reading (°C)	Wind speed (km/h)	Wind-chill index (°C)
7.	5:00	⁻25	15	⁻38
8.	6:00	⁻25	25	⁻47
9.	7:00	⁻20	30	⁻43
10.	8:00	⁻15	30	⁻36
11.	9:00	⁻10	35	⁻30
12.	10:00	0	40	⁻17

13. What was the difference in the thermometer readings at 5:00 and 10:00 on Tuesday?
25°C

14. What was the difference in the wind-chill indexes at 5:00 and 10:00 on Tuesday?
21°C

Problem Solving

DEVELOPING STRATEGIES

Objective: Balance a check register by using positive and negative numbers.

In this lesson students learn to use positive and negative numbers to complete a check register.

Tactic: Using Positive and Negative Numbers

Susan Smith has a checking account with a **line-of-credit** provision. With this feature, if Susan writes a check for more money than she has in her account, the bank will pay the amount but will charge a loan fee. Without this feature, the bank would not pay the amount, and Susan's check would "bounce."

While on vacation, Susan had to write a check for unexpected engine repairs for her car. She also paid her motel bill by check. Since her checking account did not contain enough money to cover the bills, the account was "overdrawn." At the end of the month, Susan made a deposit into her account. Part of her check register is shown below.

NUMBER	DATE	DESCRIPTION OF TRANSACTION	PAYMENT/DEBIT (−)		√ T	FEE (IF ANY) (−)	DEPOSIT/CREDIT (+)		BALANCE	
									$ 78	80
1061	10/31	Moran's Auto Repair Engine Repair	$128	80		$	$			
1062	11/12	Milton Motor Inn	75	50						
	11/30	Deposit					225	00		

Problem

How much money was in Susan's checking account after her November 30 deposit?

Solution

Susan's strategy for solving the problem involved the tactic of using positive and negative numbers.

a. What was the balance in the account before the two checks were written? Read the check register. 78.80

b. What was the balance in the account after Susan wrote the check to Moran's Auto Repair? Subtract. $78.80 - 128.80 = {}^{-}50.00$

c. What was the balance in the account after Susan wrote the check to Milton Motor Inn? Subtract. ${}^{-}50.00 - 75.50 = {}^{-}125.50$

d. What was the balance in the account after Susan made the November 30 deposit? Add. ${}^{-}125.50 + 225.00 = 99.50$

BALANCE	
$ 78	80
128	80
⁻50	00
75	50
⁻125	50
225	00
99	50

Conclusion: After her November 30 deposit, Susan had $99.50 in her checking account.

See pages 41–42 of *Problem-Solving Masters.*

Related Problems

Find the balance in Susan's checking account after each payment or deposit listed in the check register below.

	NUMBER	DATE	DESCRIPTION OF TRANSACTION	PAYMENT/DEBIT (−)	√ T	FEE (IF ANY) (−)	DEPOSIT/CREDIT (+)	BALANCE
								$ 127 50
	1085	12/14	City Charge	$ 50 00		$	$	50 00
1.			Payment					77 50
	1086	12/15	Getty Oil Company	83 75				83 75
2.			Gasoline					−6 25
	1087	12/17	Mirror Magic	15 00				15 00
3.			Haircut					−21 25
		12/17	Deposit				150 00	150 00
4.								128 75
	1088	12/18	Rolling Green Apartments	245 00				245 00
5.			Rent					−116 25
		12/20	Deposit				250 00	250 00
6.								133 75

Extensions

The bank charges a loan fee of 0.05% per day on the overdrawn amount.

7. What is the loan fee if Susan's account is overdrawn by $140 for 5 days?
$0.35

8. What is the loan fee if Susan's account is overdrawn by $90 for 20 days?
$0.90

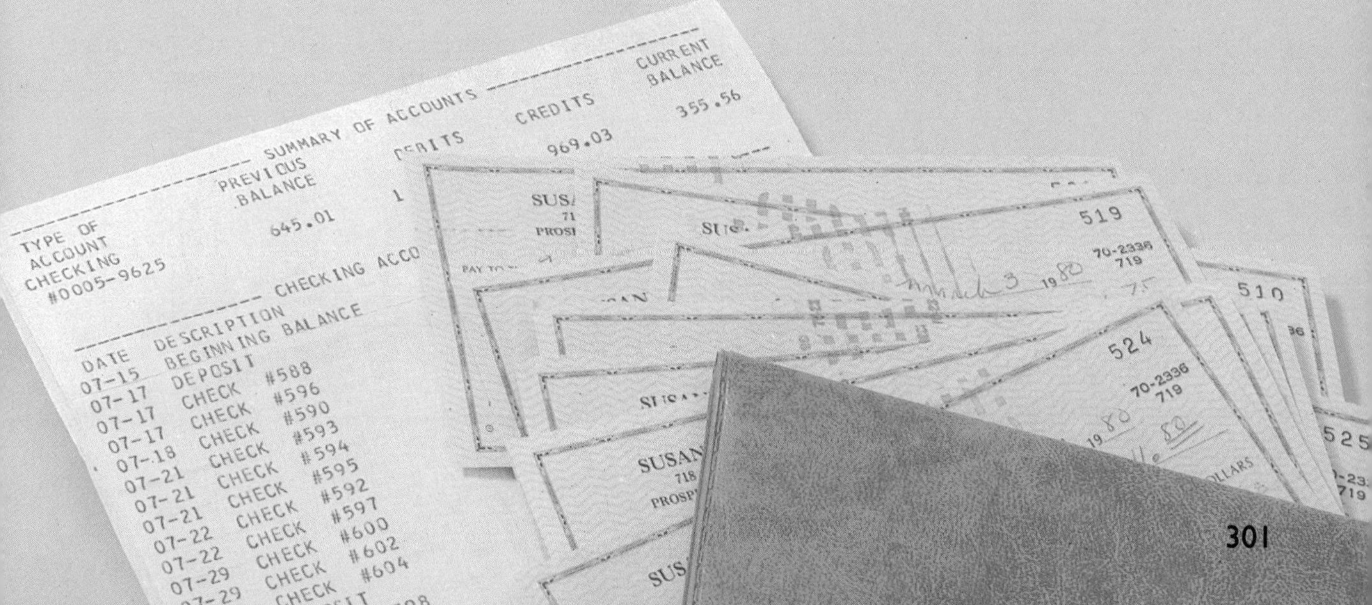

CHAPTER 13 TEST

Number of test items - 25

Number missed	1	2	3	4	5	6	7	8	9	10	11	12
Percent correct	96	92	88	84	80	76	72	68	64	60	56	52

A **1.** Write a number for point T on the number line.

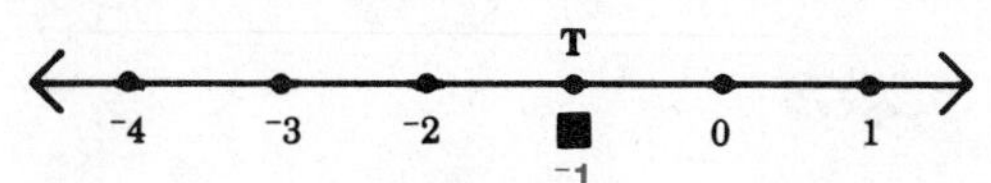

B **2.** Compare these numbers. Replace ● with < or >.

4 ● ⁻9
>

C **3.** Arrange these numbers in order from the least to the greatest.

6 ⁻7 ⁻8 9
⁻8 ⁻7 6 9

D **4.** $8 + 9$
17

E **5.** $^-6 + {}^-4$
⁻10

F **6.** $7 + {}^-8$
⁻1

G **7.** $5 + {}^-7 + 6 + {}^-2$
2

H **8.** Name the opposite of ⁻1.
1

I **9.** $2 - 3$
⁻1

J **10.** $^-5 - {}^-1$
⁻4

K **11.** $^-1 - 8$
⁻9

L **12.** $2 - {}^-9$
11

M **13.** $16 - ({}^-8 - {}^-3)$
21

N **14.** 6×4
24

O **15.** $^-5 \times {}^-2$
10

P **16.** $7 \times {}^-4$
⁻28

Q **17.** $8(2) - 3({}^-4)$
28

R **18.** $42 \div 6$
7

S **19.** $^-36 \div {}^-9$
4

T **20.** $^-28 \div 4$
⁻7

U **21.** $\frac{6 - {}^-4}{^-2}$
⁻5

22. Use the football-play chart below to find total yardage in three plays.

Play	Type of play: Run	Pass	Penalty	Total yards in three plays
1	8			
2	⁻5			
3		12		8 + ⁻5 + 12 = 15

23. Find the height of the evening high tide for Juneau, Alaska, on July 1. Use the table on page 296.
4.57 m

24. Find the wind-chill index if the thermometer reading is ⁻25°C and the wind speed is 15 kilometers per hour. Use the table on page 298.
⁻38°C

25. Find the balance in the checking account after the deposit listed in the check register.

PAYMENT/DEBIT (−)		√ T	FEE (IF ANY) (−)	DEPOSIT/CREDIT (+)		BALANCE	
						$ 45	50
$ 85	30		$	$		85	30
						⁻39	80
				50	00	50	00
						10	20

 See pages 33–34 of the *Test Masters* for an alternate form of the Chapter 13 Test.

Expressions and Equations

SKILLS PRETEST

Number of test items - 14

Number missed	1	2	3	4	5	6	7
Percent correct	93	86	79	71	64	57	50

SKILL Evaluating Expressions *pages 304–305*

A Evaluate $a + 1.7 + b$ when $a = 2.3$ and $b = 0.6$.
4.6

B Evaluate $3.7 - x - z$ when $x = 0.9$ and $z = 2$.
0.8

C Evaluate ^-4sw when $s = 5$ and $w = {^-2}$.
40

D Evaluate $\frac{72}{d}$ when $d = {^-6}$.
$^-12$

SKILL Evaluating Expressions Involving Order of Operations *pages 306–307*

E Evaluate $\frac{25}{x} + 3y$ when $x = 5$ and $y = 7$.
26

F Evaluate $\frac{2n}{5} + 6(d - 0.3)$ when $n = 10$ and $d = 1.4$.
10.6

SKILL Solving Addition and Subtraction Equations *pages 308–309*

G Find r. $r + 0.83 = 5.7$
$r = 4.87$

H Find a. $a - 0.16 = 0.35$
$a = 0.51$

SKILL Solving Multiplication and Division Equations *pages 310–311*

I Find c. $6c = 420$
$c = 70$

J Find x. $\frac{x}{4} = {^-32}$
$x = {^-128}$

SKILL Solving Two-Step Equations *pages 312–313*

K Find y. $3y + 8 = 53$
$y = 15$

L Find m. $\frac{m}{7} - 1 = 8$
$m = 63$

SKILL Combining Like Terms to Solve Equations *pages 314–315*

M Find n. $4n + 3n = 63$
$n = 9$

N Find c. $12c + 3c - 7 = 68$
$c = 5$

See page T41 for additional notes on Chapter 14.

Objective: Evaluate expressions.

Evaluating Expressions

Example A Involving addition

Evaluate $g + 0.23 + h$ when $g = 1.7$ and $h = 0.2$.

$g + 0.23 + h$

$1.7 + 0.23 + 0.2$

2.13

Substitute the given values for g and h in the expression. Then add.

Example B Involving subtraction

Evaluate $n - p - 4.6$ when $n = 17.08$ and $p = 0.6$.

$n - p - 4.6$

$17.08 - 0.6 - 4.6$

11.88

Substitute the given values for n and p in the expression. Then subtract.

Example C Involving multiplication

Evaluate ^-3ab when $a = {}^-4$ and $b = 6$.

^-3ab

$^-3(^-4)(6)$

72

Substitute the given values for a and b in the expression. Then multiply.

Example D Involving division

Evaluate $\frac{51}{s}$ when $s = {}^-3$.

$\frac{51}{s}$ Substitute the given value for s in the expression.

$\frac{51}{^-3}$ Then divide.

$^-17$

Exercises

Set A

Evaluate each expression when $a = 0.19$, $b = 4.2$, $x = {}^-6$, and $y = 57$.

1. $17 + x + 8$ 19
2. $^-60 + y$ $^-3$
3. $^-15 + x + y$ 36
4. $x + y$ 51
5. $48 + b$ 52.2
6. $a + 5.4$ 5.59
7. $9.4 + a + b$ 13.79
8. $2.1 + b$ 6.3
9. $a + 3.89 + y$ 61.08
10. $b + 0.08$ 4.28
11. $0.71 + 0.053 + a$ 0.953
12. $105 + y$ 162
13. $22 + b + 0.7$ 26.9
14. $y + 21 + x$ 72
15. $b + 0.4 + a$ 4.79
16. $x + {}^-25$ $^-31$
17. $a + {}^-0.19 + b$ 4.2
18. $^-98 + x$ $^-104$
19. $a + b + 0.99$ 5.38
20. $x + 62 + y$ 113
21. $a + 5.078$ 5.268
22. $y + 30 + b$ 91.2
23. $72.9 + b + y$ 134.1
24. $b + {}^-6.13 + a$ $^-1.74$
25. $x + x + 17$ 5
26. $a + a + b$ 4.58

Set B

Evaluate each expression when $g = 45$, $h = {}^{-}21$, $t = 3.7$, and $u = 0.9$.

1. $100 - h$
   121
2. ${}^{-}45 - g$
   ${}^{-}90$
3. $h - g$
   ${}^{-}66$
4. ${}^{-}36 - h$
   ${}^{-}15$
5. $g - 16 - t$
   25.3
6. $t - u$
   2.8
7. $t - 2.5$
   1.2
8. $t - 1.9$
   1.8
9. $2.1 - u$
   1.2
10. $g - 32 - h$
    34
11. $2.6 - t$
    ${}^{-}1.1$
12. $u - t$
    ${}^{-}2.8$
13. $t - 1.5 - u$
    1.3
14. $u - {}^{-}0.3$
    1.2
15. $41.8 - 3.7 - t$
    34.4
16. $1.1 - u$
    0.2
17. $58.4 - t - g$
    9.7
18. $100.2 - u$
    99.3
19. $56 - h - g$
    32
20. $u - 0.005$
    0.895
21. $9.051 - t$
    5.351
22. $t - 0.6 - u$
    2.2
23. $g - h$
    66
24. ${}^{-}4.51 - t$
    ${}^{-}8.21$
25. $9.1 - u - t$
    4.5
26. $2000 - g - u$
    1954.1

Set C

Evaluate each expression when $c = 14$, $d = {}^{-}90$, $k = 0.07$, and $n = 8.5$.

1. $26c$
   364
2. $4cd$
   ${}^{-}5040$
3. ${}^{-}8c$
   ${}^{-}112$
4. $2d$
   ${}^{-}180$
5. cn
   119
6. $16k$
   1.12
7. $25d$
   ${}^{-}2250$
8. ${}^{-}7n$
   ${}^{-}59.5$
9. ${}^{-}3d$
   270
10. $12n$
    102
11. $31k$
    2.17
12. $52c$
    728
13. ${}^{-}45k$
    ${}^{-}3.15$
14. ${}^{-}10c$
    ${}^{-}140$
15. ${}^{-}4d$
    360
16. kn
    0.595
17. ${}^{-}5cd$
    6300
18. $100n$
    850
19. $2kn$
    1.19
20. $9ck$
    8.82

Set D

Evaluate each expression when $m = 0.24$, $p = 0.6$, $w = {}^{-}5$, and $z = 50$.

1. $\frac{{}^{-}100}{z}$
   ${}^{-}2$
2. $\frac{35}{w}$
   ${}^{-}7$
3. $\frac{m}{4}$
   0.06
4. $\frac{m}{p}$
   0.4
5. $\frac{p}{3}$
   0.2
6. $\frac{m}{0.12}$
   2
7. $\frac{w}{5}$
   ${}^{-}1$
8. $\frac{z}{w}$
   ${}^{-}10$
9. $\frac{z}{25}$
   2
10. $\frac{m}{0.8}$
    0.3
11. $\frac{43.8}{p}$
    73
12. $\frac{{}^{-}3000}{z}$
    ${}^{-}60$

Mixed Practice

Evaluate each expression when $e = 0.35$, $f = {}^{-}12$, $r = 4$, and $s = 2.7$.

B 1. $s - 1.3$
   1.4

C 2. $5e$
   1.75

A 3. ${}^{-}12 + r$
   ${}^{-}8$

B 4. ${}^{-}23 - f$
   ${}^{-}11$

D 5. $\frac{e}{5}$
   0.07

C 6. $3es$
   2.835

B 7. $f - r$
   ${}^{-}16$

D 8. $\frac{f}{r}$
   ${}^{-}3$

B 9. $1.2 - e$
   0.85

C 10. $8f$
   ${}^{-}96$

A 11. $35 + s$
   37.7

B 12. $48 - r - s$
   41.3

D 13. $\frac{s}{3}$
   0.9

C 14. ${}^{-}2s$
   ${}^{-}5.4$

A 15. $f + 18 + r$
   10

A 16. $e + s$
   3.05

D 17. $\frac{{}^{-}48}{f}$
   4

A 18. $e + 8.2$
   8.55

Objective: Evaluate expressions involving order of operations.

Evaluating Expressions Involving Order of Operations

You may wish to review order of operations on page 54 before explaining this lesson.

Example E Without grouping symbols

Evaluate $\frac{45}{a} + 7k$ when $a = 15$ and $k = 4$.

$\frac{45}{a} + 7k$ Substitute the given values for a and k in the expression.

$\frac{45}{15} + 7(4)$ Do division and multiplication.

$3 + 28$ Do remaining addition.

31

Example F With grouping symbols

Evaluate $\frac{x+7}{9-6} - 2(y+1)$ when $x = 26$ and $y = {}^{-}5$.

$\frac{x+7}{9-6} - 2(y+1)$ Substitute the given values for x and y in the expression.

$\frac{26+7}{9-6} - 2({}^{-}5+1)$ Do operations above and below the division bar and inside parentheses.

$\frac{33}{3} - 2({}^{-}4)$ Do remaining division and multiplication.

$11 - {}^{-}8$ Do remaining subtraction.

19

Exercises

Set E

Evaluate each expression when $c = 0.3, s = 5,$ $v = {}^{-}4$, and $y = 20$.

1. $5v + 2y$ 20
2. $2vy - 1$ ${}^{-}161$
3. $\frac{y}{2} - \frac{16}{v}$ 14
4. $9v + 13 + {}^{-}2y$ ${}^{-}63$
5. $\frac{c}{3} + 3y$ 60.1
6. $8s + 3.9$ 43.9
7. $10s - 8c$ 47.6
8. $3y + 11v$ 16
9. $7c + \frac{20}{s}$ 6.1
10. $61 + 2v + 5y$ 153
11. $84 - 2vy$ 244
12. $\frac{180}{y} + 17c$ 14.1
13. $5s - 25c$ 17.5
14. $\frac{72}{v} + \frac{v}{4}$ ${}^{-}19$
15. $905c + 6.2$ 277.7
16. $10y - 30s$ 50
17. $\frac{{}^{-}2.7}{c} + {}^{-}5$ ${}^{-}14$

PROBLEM SOLVING
The applications on pages 318–321, 324–325 may be used anytime after this lesson.

Set F

Evaluate each expression when $b = 60, t = {}^{-}8$, $w = 3$, and $n = 15$.

1. $\frac{b+4}{16} + 3t$
   $^{-}20$
2. $7w(2 + n) - 1$
   356
3. $\frac{b}{4} + \frac{36}{t+10}$
   33
4. $\frac{n(b+20)}{2} + w$
   603
5. $3(w + n) + 2wn$
   144
6. $\frac{488+t}{2b} - \frac{t+13}{5}$
   3
7. $w(23 + 6) - \frac{95}{5}$
   68
8. $\frac{2.2n-3}{w+4.5}$
   4
9. $b(16 - 13) + 4t$
   148
10. $12(n + w) + \frac{130}{6.5}$
    236
11. $4(b + w) - 6$
    246
12. $0.8n(1.1 + w + 0.7)$
    57.6
13. $\frac{6bt}{5} + \frac{b-12}{8}$
    $^{-}570$
14. $\frac{3t}{12} + {}^{-}4b$
    $^{-}242$
15. $2.6n + 14(w + 1)$
    95

Mixed Practice

Evaluate each expression when $a = 36, g = 50$, $h = 9$, and $k = {}^{-}4$.

E 1. $\frac{a}{k} + \frac{a}{12}$
   $^{-}6$

E 2. $47 + \frac{100}{g}$
   49

F 3. $3hk(g - 28)$
   $^{-}2376$

E 4. $g - 3h$
   23

F 5. $\frac{21+h}{5} - \frac{100}{2g}$
   5

E 6. $\frac{h}{3} + 0.21$
   3.21

F 7. $\frac{5(k+1)}{1.5} + \frac{a}{6}$
   $^{-}4$

F 8. $gk(14 - 7)$
   $^{-}1400$

E 9. $a + g + 4k$
   70

F 10. $h(g - 45) + \frac{a}{2}$
    63

E 11. ${}^{-}7g + a$
    $^{-}314$

E 12. $gh - ak$
    594

F 13. $\frac{{}^{-}3g}{10} - 8$
    $^{-}23$

F 14. $\frac{2h}{{}^{-}6} + \frac{h+26}{7}$
    2

F 15. $\frac{a+h}{1.5} + 0.5g$
    55

E 16. $5h + 3k$
    33

F 17. $ah(g - a)$
    4536

E 18. $\frac{45}{h} + k$
    1

F 19. $3(a + 4) + \frac{g}{10}$
    125

E 20. $\frac{a}{h} - k$
    8

E 21. $2.5g - 3a$
    17

E 22. ${}^{-}5k + g - a$
    34

F 23. $\frac{2g}{25} + \frac{a}{hk}$
    3

BREAK TIME

These answers were given on a matching quiz. No two answers can be the same.

Item	Jo	Lin	Sue	Jim
1	a	d	a	b
2	c	a	b	c
3	d	c	d	a
4	b	b	c	d

Three students each have exactly two answers correct. One student has them all wrong. What were the correct answers?
(1) d; (2) c; (3) a; (4) b

Objective: Solve addition and subtraction equations involving integers and decimals.

Solving Addition and Subtraction Equations

Example G Missing addend

Find n.

$$n + 5.6 = 9.2$$
$$n + 5.6 - 5.6 = 9.2 - 5.6$$
$$n = 3.6$$

5.6 is added to n.
To undo the addition, subtract 5.6 from both sides of the equation.

Check: $n + 5.6 = 9.2$
$3.6 + 5.6 \stackrel{?}{=} 9.2$
$9.2 = 9.2$

Check by substituting 3.6 for n in the original equation.
Since the two sides of the equation are equal, n does equal 3.6.

Example H Missing minuend

Find c.

$$c - 4 = {}^-17$$
$$c - 4 + 4 = {}^-17 + 4$$
$$c = {}^-13$$

4 is subtracted from c.
To undo the subtraction, add 4 to both sides of the equation.

Check: $c - 4 = {}^-17$
${}^-13 - 4 \stackrel{?}{=} {}^-17$
${}^-17 = {}^-17$

Check by substituting ${}^-13$ for c in the original equation.

Exercises

Set G

Find each missing number.

1. $x + 54 = 31$ $x = {}^-23$
2. $b + {}^-7 = 18$ $b = 25$
3. $27 + a = 35$ $a = 8$
4. ${}^-9 + c = 32$ $c = 41$
5. $n + 22 = {}^-8$ $n = {}^-30$
6. $1.92 + y = 2.3$ $y = 0.38$
7. $51 = w + 33$ $w = 18$
8. $6.1 = d + 2.8$ $d = 3.3$
9. $z + 4.6 = 7.12$ $z = 2.52$
10. ${}^-6 + f = 15$ $f = 21$
11. $62 = t + 9$ $t = 53$
12. $9.04 + x = 31.5$ $x = 22.46$
13. $g + {}^-12 = {}^-12$ $g = 0$
14. $108 = u + 92$ $u = 16$
15. $1.15 + h = 3.06$ $h = 1.91$
16. $v + 8.4 = 9.1$ $v = 0.7$
17. $4 = {}^-13 + k$ $k = 17$
18. $41 + w = 54.9$ $w = 13.9$
19. $n + {}^-2 = 81$ $n = 83$
20. $3.8 + a = 7.4$ $a = 3.6$
21. $0.07 + p = 0.38$ $p = 0.31$
22. ${}^-49 = d + 25$ $d = {}^-74$
23. $r + 8.9 = 64.2$ $r = 55.3$
24. ${}^-23 + f = 73$ $f = 96$
25. $11.8 + s = 30$ $s = 18.2$
26. $3.72 + n = 10.7$ $n = 6.98$

Set H

Find each missing number.

1. $a - 4 = 26$ $a = 30$
2. $n - 25 = 15$ $n = 40$
3. $z - 7 = {}^{-}9$ $z = {}^{-}2$
4. $10 = b - 13$ $b = 23$
5. ${}^{-}8 = d - 17$ $d = 9$
6. $s - 7.08 = 1.32$ $s = 8.4$
7. $r - 0.8 = 0.9$ $r = 1.7$
8. $t - {}^{-}2 = 46$ $t = 44$
9. $c - 3.8 = 1.9$ $c = 5.7$
10. $f - 0.72 = 0.8$ $f = 1.52$
11. $x - 2.38 = 6.7$ $x = 9.08$
12. ${}^{-}35 = y - 14$ $y = {}^{-}21$
13. $21 = w - 98$ $w = 119$
14. $n - 3.3 = 6.06$ $n = 9.36$
15. $g - 0.081 = 0.95$ $g = 1.031$
16. $71 = k - 82$ $k = 153$
17. $3 = x - 18$ $x = 21$
18. $a - 45.92 = 6.02$ $a = 51.94$
19. $h - 8.3 = 4.77$ $h = 13.07$
20. ${}^{-}9 = m - 103$ $m = 94$
21. $2.8 = z - 5.35$ $z = 8.15$
22. $k - 8 = {}^{-}29$ $k = {}^{-}21$
23. $b - 6.2 = 0.49$ $b = 6.69$
24. $m - 0.76 = 0.8$ $m = 1.56$
25. $3.09 = w - 62.2$ $w = 65.29$
26. $c - 40 = {}^{-}37$ $c = 3$
27. $d - {}^{-}28 = {}^{-}74$ $d = {}^{-}102$

Mixed Practice

Find each missing number.

G 1. $h + 3.6 = 7.92$ $h = 4.32$
G 2. $0.48 = 0.3 + t$ $t = 0.18$
H 3. $f - 98.6 = 32.7$ $f = 131.3$
G 4. $n + {}^{-}21 = {}^{-}6$ $n = 15$
H 5. $p - 15 = {}^{-}64$ $p = {}^{-}49$
H 6. $z - 7 = 19$ $z = 26$
G 7. $0.231 + k = 1.08$ $k = 0.849$
H 8. ${}^{-}19 = h - 53$ $h = 34$
G 9. $v + 107 = 4$ $v = {}^{-}103$
G 10. $3 = 11 + p$ $p = {}^{-}8$
H 11. $q - 4.04 = 30.17$ $q = 34.21$
G 12. $62 + a = 35$ $a = {}^{-}27$
H 13. $74 = g - {}^{-}12$ $g = 62$
H 14. $5.4 = f - 9.6$ $f = 15$
G 15. ${}^{-}41 = {}^{-}9 + y$ $y = {}^{-}32$
H 16. $17 = r - 4.5$ $r = 21.5$
G 17. $49 = d + 88$ $d = {}^{-}39$
H 18. $t - 4.11 = 1.3$ $t = 5.41$
G 19. $5.5 + p = 19.4$ $p = 13.9$
G 20. ${}^{-}60 + z = 31$ $z = {}^{-}29$
H 21. $m - 43.15 = 2.11$ $m = 45.26$
G 22. $a + 5.3 = 40$ $a = 34.7$
H 23. ${}^{-}8 = t - 48$ $t = 40$
H 24. $n - 9 = {}^{-}10$ $n = {}^{-}1$
H 25. $v - 100 = {}^{-}4$ $v = 96$
G 26. $3 = c + {}^{-}12$ $c = 15$
H 27. $w - 33.7 = 4.9$ $w = 38.6$
G 28. $a + 4.7 = 6.8$ $a = 2.1$
H 29. $h - 73 = {}^{-}15$ $h = 58$
H 30. $w - 5.28 = 7.95$ $w = 13.23$
G 31. $n + {}^{-}6 = 24$ $n = 30$
G 32. ${}^{-}51 + s = 33$ $s = 84$
H 33. $19 = b - {}^{-}3$ $b = 16$
G 34. $0.276 + d = {}^{-}6.2$ $d = {}^{-}6.476$
H 35. $y - 22.5 = 8.7$ $y = 31.2$
G 36. $72 = 45 + c$ $c = 27$
G 37. $f + {}^{-}9 = {}^{-}21$ $f = {}^{-}12$
H 38. $k - 1.7 = 3.9$ $k = 5.6$

BREAK TIME

Sam put $75 in the bank and later made a series of withdrawals. His records showed a discrepancy of $1.

Deposit—$75

Withdrawals	Balance
$35	$40
20	20
10	10
4	6
6	0
$75	$76

What happened to the missing dollar?
The sum of the balances is not related to the sum of the withdrawals.

Objective: Solve multiplication and division equations involving integers and decimals.

Solving Multiplication and Division Equations

Example I Missing factor

Find b.

$$^{-}30b = 240$$

b is multiplied by $^{-}30$.
To undo the multiplication, divide both sides of the equation by $^{-}30$.

$$\frac{^{-}30b}{^{-}30} = \frac{240}{^{-}30}$$

$$b = {}^{-}8$$

Check:
$$^{-}30b = 240$$
$$^{-}30(^{-}8) \stackrel{?}{=} 240$$
$$240 = 240$$

Example J Missing dividend

Find w.

$$\frac{w}{1.8} = 5.2$$

w is divided by 1.8.
To undo the division, multiply both sides of the equation by 1.8.

$$(1.8)\frac{w}{1.8} = (1.8)5.2$$

$$w = 9.36$$

Check:
$$\frac{w}{1.8} = 5.2$$
$$\frac{9.36}{1.8} \stackrel{?}{=} 5.2$$
$$5.2 = 5.2$$

Exercises

Set I

Find each missing number.

1. $^{-}3w = 159$ $w = {}^{-}53$
2. $12a = 84$ $a = 7$
3. $^{-}63 = 7m$ $m = {}^{-}9$
4. $^{-}8t = {}^{-}744$ $t = 93$
5. $4d = {}^{-}196$ $d = {}^{-}49$
6. $0.9x = 0.72$ $x = 0.8$
7. $3.1y = 3.1$ $y = 1$
8. $1.85 = 0.05h$ $h = 37$
9. $0.62c = 4.774$ $c = 7.7$
10. $34.4 = 4.3w$ $w = 8$
11. $172.8 = 7.2g$ $g = 24$
12. $0.186 = 0.02u$ $u = 9.3$
13. $54 = {}^{-}18y$ $y = {}^{-}3$
14. $95g = 570$ $g = 6$
15. $26k = {}^{-}130$ $k = {}^{-}5$
16. $^{-}9v = {}^{-}756$ $v = 84$
17. $^{-}561 = {}^{-}33d$ $d = 17$
18. $4.05 = 4.5y$ $y = 0.9$
19. $1.62 = 0.27q$ $q = 6$
20. $3.8c = 7.98$ $c = 2.1$
21. $^{-}3n = 120$ $n = {}^{-}40$
22. $390 = 6b$ $b = 65$
23. $70z = {}^{-}5670$ $z = {}^{-}81$
24. $21.5 = 0.5r$ $r = 43$
25. $10.44 = 3.6t$ $t = 2.9$
26. $9.2p = 6.44$ $p = 0.7$

PROBLEM SOLVING
The applications on pages 317, 322–323 may be used anytime after this lesson.

Set J

Find each missing number.

1. $\frac{g}{^{-}9} = {^{-}8}$ $g = 72$
2. $\frac{n}{^{-}3} = 52$ $n = {^{-}156}$
3. $\frac{r}{31} = 28$ $r = 868$
4. $^{-}6 = \frac{h}{17}$ $h = {^{-}102}$
5. $\frac{c}{35} = 0.08$ $c = 2.8$
6. $9.1 = \frac{k}{0.9}$ $k = 8.19$
7. $\frac{b}{3.4} = 1.8$ $b = 6.12$
8. $\frac{d}{^{-}5} = 75$ $d = {^{-}375}$
9. $0.46 = \frac{a}{0.7}$ $a = 0.322$
10. $\frac{c}{4.7} = 0.25$ $c = 1.175$
11. $^{-}1 = \frac{g}{44}$ $g = {^{-}44}$
12. $16 = \frac{b}{^{-}7}$ $b = {^{-}112}$
13. $0.04 = \frac{s}{92}$ $s = 3.68$
14. $\frac{m}{0.07} = 5.3$ $m = 0.371$
15. $\frac{y}{0.16} = 0.29$ $y = 0.0464$
16. $26 = \frac{w}{^{-}6}$ $w = {^{-}156}$
17. $\frac{y}{0.73} = 1.29$ $y = 0.9417$
18. $\frac{r}{^{-}3} = 70$ $r = {^{-}210}$
19. $\frac{y}{^{-}5} = {^{-}400}$ $y = 2000$
20. $\frac{d}{1.26} = {^{-}3.05}$ $d = {^{-}3.843}$

Mixed Practice

Find each missing number.

I 1. $0.583 = 0.53f$ $f = 1.1$
I 2. $^{-}17s = {^{-}340}$ $s = 20$
J 3. $\frac{h}{1.9} = 2.4$ $h = 4.56$
I 4. $^{-}80x = 1040$ $x = {^{-}13}$
J 5. $38 = \frac{a}{20.9}$ $a = 794.2$
J 6. $\frac{z}{^{-}9} = {^{-}52}$ $z = 468$
I 7. $^{-}2.5w = 20$ $w = {^{-}8}$
I 8. $0.54 = 0.09n$ $n = 6$
J 9. $\frac{t}{39} = {^{-}3}$ $t = {^{-}117}$
J 10. $9.2 = \frac{u}{0.6}$ $u = 5.52$
I 11. $0.423 = 4.7k$ $k = 0.09$
J 12. $\frac{y}{^{-}18} = 34$ $y = {^{-}612}$
I 13. $83b = {^{-}83}$ $b = {^{-}1}$
I 14. $^{-}11u = 0$ $u = 0$
J 15. $^{-}14 = \frac{n}{^{-}14}$ $n = 196$
J 16. $\frac{p}{5.09} = 10.2$ $p = 51.918$
I 17. $0.008z = 0.01096$ $z = 1.37$
I 18. $8d = 432$ $d = 54$
J 19. $\frac{t}{^{-}85} = 4$ $t = {^{-}340}$
J 20. $3.9 = \frac{x}{52.5}$ $x = 204.75$
I 21. $^{-}0.0588 = 0.98c$ $c = {^{-}0.06}$
I 22. $^{-}14h = 1778$ $h = {^{-}127}$
J 23. $1.25 = \frac{u}{0.38}$ $u = 0.475$
J 24. $26 = \frac{a}{^{-}17}$ $a = {^{-}442}$

Objective: Solve two-step equations.

Solving Two-Step Equations

Example K Missing factor

Find n.

$$4n + 12 = 32$$

First find $4n$.

To undo the addition, subtract 12 from both sides of the equation.

$$4n + 12 - 12 = 32 - 12$$

$$4n = 20$$

Then find n.

To undo the multiplication, divide both sides of the equation by 4.

$$\frac{4n}{4} = \frac{20}{4}$$

$$n = 5$$

Check: $4n + 12 = 32$

$4(5) + 12 \stackrel{?}{=} 32$

$20 + 12 \stackrel{?}{=} 32$

$32 = 32$

Example L Missing dividend

Find t.

$$\frac{t}{^-6} + 15 = 10$$

First find $\frac{t}{^-6}$.

To undo the addition, subtract 15 from both sides of the equation.

$$\frac{t}{^-6} + 15 - 15 = 10 - 15$$

$$\frac{t}{^-6} = {}^-5$$

Then find t.

To undo the division, multiply both sides of the equation by $^-6$.

$$(^-6)\frac{t}{^-6} = (^-6)(^-5)$$

$$t = 30$$

Check: $\frac{t}{^-6} + 15 = 10$

$\frac{30}{^-6} + 15 \stackrel{?}{=} 10$

$^-5 + 15 \stackrel{?}{=} 10$

$10 = 10$

Exercises

Set K

Find each missing number.

1. $3x + 1 = 13$ x = 4
2. $7n + 2 = 51$ n = 7
3. $4t + 4 = 40$ t = 9
4. $5a + 8 = 3$ a = $^-1$
5. $^-2s + 6 = 0$ s = 3
6. $^-9b + 2 = 56$ b = $^-6$
7. $10y + 3 = 83$ y = 8
8. $12c - 4 = 20$ c = 2
9. $6m + 2 = 80$ m = 13
10. $^-8r + 10 = {}^-30$ r = 5
11. $^-5d + 100 = 50$ d = 10
12. $1.4k + 0.2 = 3$ k = 2
13. $^-3n + 14 = 17$ n = $^-1$
14. $20g - 25 = {}^-25$ g = 0
15. $11w - 7 = 37$ w = 4
16. $^-4z + 12 = 32$ z = $^-5$
17. $2h + 8 = 11$ h = 1.5
18. $7s + 2 = 65$ s = 9
19. $30p + 10 = 340$ p = 11
20. $9n - 15 = 93$ n = 12
21. $0.5x + 0.7 = 2.1$ x = 2.8
22. $2t - 13 = {}^-1$ t = 6
23. $8a - 12 = 124$ a = 17
24. $0.7g + 0.5 = 3.3$ g = 4
25. $^-10k + {}^-5 = {}^-35$ k = 3
26. $5c - 6 = 39$ c = 9
27. $0.03b + 0.08 = 0.14$ b = 2

Set L

Find each missing number.

1. $\frac{m}{3} + 2 = 5$ m = 9
2. $\frac{a}{^-5} + 8 = 6$ a = 10
3. $\frac{x}{2} + 7 = 11$ x = 8
4. $\frac{n}{6} + 13 = 15$ n = 12
5. $\frac{t}{0.7} + 9 = 10$ t = 0.7
6. $\frac{s}{^-9} + 7 = 9$ s = ⁻18
7. $\frac{y}{8} - 3 = 2$ y = 40
8. $\frac{w}{10} - 1 = 2$ w = 30
9. $\frac{z}{12} - 8 = {}^-4$ z = 48
10. $\frac{n}{3} + 19 = 14$ n = ⁻15
11. $\frac{b}{2} - 7 = 12$ b = 38
12. $\frac{d}{4} - 6 = {}^-1$ d = 20
13. $\frac{c}{5} + 12 = 25$ c = 65
14. $\frac{a}{20} + 26 = 31$ a = 100
15. $\frac{h}{16} - 2 = 0$ h = 32
16. $\frac{s}{^-1} + 18 = 35$ s = ⁻17
17. $\frac{n}{^-8} + {}^-2 = {}^-10$ n = 64
18. $\frac{a}{9} - 6 = 2$ a = 72
19. $\frac{c}{3} - 3 = 4$ c = 21
20. $\frac{t}{6} - 9 = {}^-6$ t = 18
21. $\frac{k}{30} + 62 = 65$ k = 90
22. $\frac{g}{10} - 5 = 3$ g = 80
23. $\frac{d}{^-11} + 17 = 13$ d = 44
24. $\frac{h}{0.4} + 2 = 11$ h = 3.6
25. $\frac{x}{0.3} + 0.5 = 1.4$ x = 0.27
26. $\frac{r}{9} - 1 = 4$ r = 45
27. $\frac{b}{1.2} + 4.6 = 11.6$ b = 8.4
28. $\frac{s}{7} - 4 = 4$ s = 56

Mixed Practice

Find each missing number.

K 1. $4z - 27 = 13$ z = 10

K 2. $18m + 14 = 104$ m = 5

L 3. $\frac{y}{9} + 31 = 40$ y = 81

L 4. $\frac{h}{0.8} + 16 = 25$ h = 7.2

K 5. $21h + 3 = 150$ h = 7

K 6. $3r + {}^-3 = {}^-30$ r = ⁻9

L 7. $\frac{u}{9} + 6.2 = 16.2$ u = 90

K 8. $5s - 8 = {}^-23$ s = ⁻3

K 9. $8q - {}^-2 = {}^-38$ q = ⁻5

L 10. $\frac{z}{13} + {}^-2 = 0$ z = 26

L 11. $\frac{c}{40} - 8 = {}^-5$ c = 120

L 12. $\frac{g}{2} - 11 = 3$ g = 28

K 13. $15d + 63 = 363$ d = 20

K 14. $2x + 20 = 4$ x = ⁻8

L 15. $\frac{v}{0.9} + 0.7 = 1.3$ v = 0.54

L 16. $\frac{d}{5} + 29 = 35$ d = 30

Combining Like Terms to Solve Equations

Example M Missing factor, one-step equation

Find y.

$$7y + 6y = 65$$
$$13y = 65$$
$$\frac{13y}{13} = \frac{65}{13}$$
$$y = 5$$

First combine like terms. Remind students that $n = 1n$.
$7y$ and $6y$ are like terms because both 7 and 6 are multiplied by y. $7y + 6y = (7 + 6)y = 13y$

Then divide both sides of the equation by 13 to find y.

Check:
$$7y + 6y = 65$$
$$7(5) + 6(5) \stackrel{?}{=} 65$$
$$35 + 30 \stackrel{?}{=} 65$$
$$65 = 65$$

Example N Missing factor, two-step equation

Find x.

$$8x + 18 + {}^{-}3x - 4 = 64$$
$$5x + 14 = 64$$
$$5x + 14 - 14 = 64 - 14$$
$$5x = 50$$
$$\frac{5x}{5} = \frac{50}{5}$$
$$x = 10$$

Combine like terms.
$8x + {}^{-}3x = 5x$
$18 - 4 = 14$

Subtract 14 from both sides of the equation to find $5x$.

Then divide both sides of the equation by 5 to find x.

Check:
$$8x + 18 + {}^{-}3x - 4 = 64$$
$$8(10) + 18 + {}^{-}3(10) - 4 \stackrel{?}{=} 64$$
$$80 + 18 + {}^{-}30 - 4 \stackrel{?}{=} 64$$
$$64 = 64$$

Exercises

Set M

Find each missing number.

1. $3n + 7n = 80$ $n = 8$
2. ${}^{-}4x + 2x = 18$ $x = {}^{-}9$
3. $9z + 8z = 34$ $z = 2$
4. $a + 5a = 72$ $a = 12$
5. $2t + {}^{-}3t + 4t = 27$ $t = 9$
6. $14m + m = 75$ $m = 5$
7. $3b + 8b = 99$ $b = 9$
8. $10c - 2c = 56$ $c = 7$
9. $12p - 6p = 36$ $p = 6$
10. $r + r = 46$ $r = 23$
11. $7s + 9s = 48$ $s = 3$
12. $4v + {}^{-}11v = 49$ $v = {}^{-}7$
13. ${}^{-}2z + 10z = 16$ $z = 2$
14. $5d + 5d + 5d = 30$ $d = 2$
15. ${}^{-}3w + {}^{-}4w = 140$ $w = {}^{-}20$
16. $2y + {}^{-}7y = 70$ $y = {}^{-}14$
17. $3.1u + 0.2u = 6.6$ $u = 2$
18. $6x + 0.5x = 32.5$ $x = 5$
19. ${}^{-}9f + 5f = 40$ $f = {}^{-}10$
20. $1.8n + 0.7n = 10$ $n = 4$
21. ${}^{-}6z + 21z = 45$ $z = 3$
22. $40a - 20a = 180$ $a = 9$
23. $q + 3q + q = 135$ $q = 27$
24. $2b + 17b + b = 20$ $b = 1$
25. ${}^{-}4x + x - 8x = 0$ $x = 0$
26. $6n - n - 3n = 14$ $n = 7$
27. $d + 3d + {}^{-}7d = {}^{-}27$ $d = 9$

Set N

Find each missing number.

1. $2c + 3 + 5c = 52$ $c = 7$
2. $n + 8n + 9 = 27$ $n = 2$
3. $4x + {}^-9 + 3x = {}^-16$ $x = {}^-1$
4. $9w - 2w + 10 = 31$ $w = 3$
5. $6d - 4d - 3 = 7$ $d = 5$
6. $7m + 25 + m = {}^-7$ $m = {}^-4$
7. $2p - p + 1 = 10$ $p = 9$
8. $30a + 1.6 + 1.4 + 2a = 22.2$ $a = 0.6$
9. $5x + 2x - 17 = {}^-52$ $x = {}^-5$
10. $6 + n + 3n + 9 = 47$ $n = 8$
11. $4b + {}^-6 + 7b + b = 114$ $b = 10$
12. $7q + 4 + {}^-3q - 7 = 13$ $q = 4$
13. $19k + 8 - 6 - 12 = 560$ $k = 30$
14. $27 + c + 11c - 15 = 96$ $c = 7$
15. $3g + 4.6 + 0.7 + 13g = 11.7$ $g = 0.4$
16. $t + 15 + 6t - 9 = 41$ $t = 5$
17. $2h + 9.5 + 0.7 + 3 = 17$ $h = 1.9$
18. $47 + k + 8k + {}^-6 = 68$ $k = 3$
19. $17v + {}^-8 + {}^-11v - 2 = 20$ $v = 5$
20. $12z - 6z + 4z - 21 = 39$ $z = 6$
21. $8u + 70 - 4u = 30$ $u = {}^-10$
22. $3y + 8 - y = 9$ $y = 0.5$
23. $4b + b + 19 + {}^-2b - 5 = 41$ $b = 9$
24. ${}^-17x + 2 + {}^-3x + 23 = 145$ $x = {}^-6$
25. $4d + 1.7 + 0.2d + 7 = 21.3$ $d = 3$
26. $3a + 9a + a + {}^-6 = 137$ $a = 11$
27. $19 + s + 10s + {}^-2s + 8 = 27$ $s = 0$
28. $1.5g + 2.5 + 0.8g = 2.96$ $g = 0.2$

Mixed Practice

Find each missing number.

N 1. $63 + 7c - 3c - 1 = 90$ $c = 7$
M 2. $6p + {}^-8p = 10$ $p = {}^-5$
N 3. $1.5w + 0.8w + 8 = 8.46$ $w = 0.2$
N 4. ${}^-5x + 37 - 10 + 9x = 7$ $x = {}^-5$
M 5. $5z + 2z + 8z = {}^-105$ $z = {}^-7$
N 6. $8.3a + 1.8a + 3.2 + 5.3 = 38.8$ $a = 3$
M 7. $d + 4d = 12$ $d = 2.4$
M 8. $3.42r + 0.18r + 4.9r = 12.75$ $r = 1.5$
N 9. $21k + {}^-7 - 16k + 2 = 0$ $k = 1$
N 10. $9t + 11t + 52 - 44 = {}^-12$ $t = {}^-1$
M 11. $4c - 2c + 3c = 250$ $c = 50$
M 12. $3m + {}^-7m + 9m = {}^-35$ $m = {}^-7$
N 13. $5g + 15 + 2g + 7g = 155$ $g = 10$
M 14. $s + s + s + s = 44$ $s = 11$
N 15. $5n + 75 - 4n - 62 = 17$ $n = 4$
M 16. ${}^-9z + 16z = 56$ $z = 8$

BREAK TIME

9 8 7 6 5 4 3 2 1

Place 3 addition signs and 1 subtraction sign between the digits so that the answer is 100. Do not change the order of the digits.

$98 - 76 + 54 + 3 + 21 = 100$

Here is an example that is wrong because the answer is 109.

$98 - 76 + 54 + 32 + 1 = 109$

SKILLS POSTTEST

Number of test items - 14

Number missed	1	2	3	4	5	6	7
Percent correct	93	86	79	71	64	57	50

SKILL Evaluating Expressions *pages 304–305*

A Evaluate $n + 0.4 + a$ when $n = 0.7$ and $a = 3.1$.
4.2

B Evaluate $b - 3.7 - d$ when $b = 14.2$ and $d = 5$.
5.5

C Evaluate $3xy$ when $x = {}^{-}7$ and $y = 2$.
$^{-}42$

D Evaluate $\frac{64}{m}$ when $m = 8$.
8

SKILL Evaluating Expressions Involving Order of Operations *pages 306–307*

E Evaluate $\frac{20}{c} + 6d$ when $c = 4$ and $d = {}^{-}5$.
$^{-}25$

F Evaluate $3(t + 0.5) + \frac{9v}{2}$ when $t = 1.5$ and $v = 4$.
24

SKILL Solving Addition and Subtraction Equations *pages 308–309*

G Find k. $k + 8.6 = 13.5$
$k = 4.9$

H Find g. $g - 4.3 = 17.8$
$g = 22.1$

SKILL Solving Multiplication and Division Equations *pages 310–311*

I Find w. $5w = 350$
$w = 70$

J Find v. $\frac{v}{9} = {}^{-}21$
$v = {}^{-}189$

SKILL Solving Two-Step Equations *pages 312–313*

K Find d. $2d + 6 = 44$
$d = 19$

L Find h. $\frac{h}{3} + 6 = 10$
$h = 12$

SKILL Combining Like Terms to Solve Equations *pages 314–315*

M Find x. $6x + 2x = 72$
$x = 9$

N Find u. $14u + 8 + 2u = 40$
$u = 2$

Problem Solving See page 43 of *Problem-Solving Masters.*

CONSUMER APPLICATIONS

Objective: Solve problems involving equations.

In this lesson students solve problems using the formulas $E = IR$ and $W = EI$.

Checking the Safety of Electrical Circuits

Electricity flows through circuits under a constant pressure (volts), at a certain rate (amperes), and encounters resistance (ohms). The number of volts is equal to the number of amperes times the number of ohms.

$E = IR$ — E: Volts; I: Amperes; R: Ohms

These units are given on many electrical appliances.

The amount of electrical power required to operate appliances is measured in watts. The number of watts is equal to the number of volts times the number of amperes.

$W = EI$ — W: Watts; E: Volts; I: Amperes

The resistance of a radio is 60 ohms when the radio is using 120 volts. How many amperes of current is the radio drawing?

$$E = IR$$

$$120 = I \times 60$$

$$\frac{120}{60} = \frac{I \times 60}{60}$$

$$2 = I$$

The radio is drawing 2 amperes of current.

How many watts is the radio using?

$$W = EI$$

$$W = 120(2)$$

$$W = 240$$

The radio is using 240 watts.

An overloaded circuit could cause a fire. To check the safety of each circuit given below, first use the information to find the amperes (I) and the watts (W) for each appliance on the circuit. Round your answers to the nearest tenth.

	Circuit A				
	Appliance	Ohms (R)	Volts (E)	Amps (I)	Watts (W)
1.	Toaster	22	110	5	550
2.	Percolator	20	110	5.5	605
3.	Frying pan	11	110	10	1100
4.	Clock	270	110	0.4	44
5.	Doorbell	220	110	0.5	55

	Circuit B				
	Appliance	Ohms (R)	Volts (E)	Amps (I)	Watts (W)
6.	Dishwasher	70	220	3.1	682
7.	Heater	55	220	4	880
8.	Dryer	25	220	8.8	1936

9. What is the total wattage of circuit A? 2354 watts
10. Circuit A can safely handle up to 1800 watts. Is circuit A safe? No
11. What is the total wattage of circuit B? 3498 watts
12. Circuit B can safely handle up to 3600 watts. Is circuit B safe? Yes

Problem Solving

CONSUMER APPLICATIONS

Objective: Solve problems involving equations.

In this lesson students solve problems relating to a coinsurance policy by using the formula $P = \frac{IL}{0.8V}$.

Interpreting a Coinsurance Clause

Some homeowner's insurance policies have an 80% coinsurance clause. This means that if the property is insured for less than 80% of its value, the insurance company will pay only part of any loss. The insurance company uses this formula to determine the amount it will pay.

$$P = \frac{IL}{0.8V}$$

P is the amount paid by the company.
I is the amount of insurance carried.
L is the amount of the loss.
V is the value of the property.

Point out that if the property is insured for 80% of its value or more, the entire loss would be covered by insurance, and the formula would not be used.

Francisca's home, valued at $80,000, was damaged by fire. Francisca has a $40,000 insurance policy with an 80% coinsurance clause. The loss due to fire damage was $10,000. How much money would the insurance company pay Francisca?

$$P = \frac{IL}{0.8V}$$

$$P = \frac{40{,}000(10{,}000)}{0.8(80{,}000)}$$

Encourage students to simplify before multiplying.

$$P = 6250$$

The insurance company would pay $6250 for the damages.

How much more money would Francisca have to pay to completely repair the damages?

$$\begin{array}{r} \$10000 \\ -\quad 6250 \\ \hline \$\ \ 3750 \end{array}$$

Francisca would have to pay $3750.

See page 44 of *Problem-Solving Masters.*

Each of these properties is insured by a policy with an 80% coinsurance clause. Find each amount paid by the insurance company. Round this amount to the nearest dollar. Then subtract to find the amount paid by each owner.

	Value of property (*V*)	Insurance carried (*I*)	Loss (*L*)	Paid by insurance company (*P*)	Paid by owner
1.	$25,000	$18,000	$8000	$7200	$800
2.	$80,000	$40,000	$5000	$3125	$1875
3.	$10,400	$6500	$3000	$2344	$656
4.	$165,000	$130,000	$2950	$2905	$45
5.	$125,000	$85,000	$90,000	$76,500	$13,500
6.	$50,000	$30,000	$15,000	$11,250	$3750
7.	$34,500	$25,000	$25,000	$22,645	$2355
8.	$54,000	$36,000	$11,500	$9583	$1917
9.	$95,000	$47,000	$12,800	$7916	$4884
10.	$100,000	$75,000	$60,000	$56,250	$3750
11.	$72,000	$54,000	$8950	$8391	$559
12.	$86,800	$62,000	$9300	$8304	$996
13.	$97,000	$65,000	$58,400	$48,918	$9482
14.	$146,000	$90,000	$6000	$4623	$1377
15.	$180,500	$120,000	$6800	$5651	$1149

Problem Solving

CAREER APPLICATIONS

Objective: Solve problems involving equations.

In this lesson students use the formula $P = \frac{2wh}{s + 1}$ to determine the safe load for a pile that has been driven into the ground.

Heavy-Equipment Operator

Career Cluster: Trades Paul Becker is working on the construction of homes built on pile foundations. Paul operates the equipment used to drive the piles into the ground.

The pile driver drops a heavy "hammer" on the pile to push it into the ground. Paul uses this formula to determine the safe load. The safe load is the weight that could be supported by a pile when it has been driven into the ground.

$$P = \frac{2wh}{s + 1}$$

P is the safe load in pounds.
w is the weight of the hammer in pounds.
h is the distance in feet the hammer falls.
s is the distance in inches the pile moves under the blow.

Suppose the weight of the hammer is 3000 pounds, and when the hammer falls 10 feet, it moves the pile 2 inches into the ground. What is the safe load of the pile?

$$P = \frac{2wh}{s + 1}$$

$$P = \frac{2(3000)(10)}{2 + 1}$$

$$P = \frac{60{,}000}{3}$$

$$P = 20{,}000$$

The safe load of the pile is 20,000 pounds.

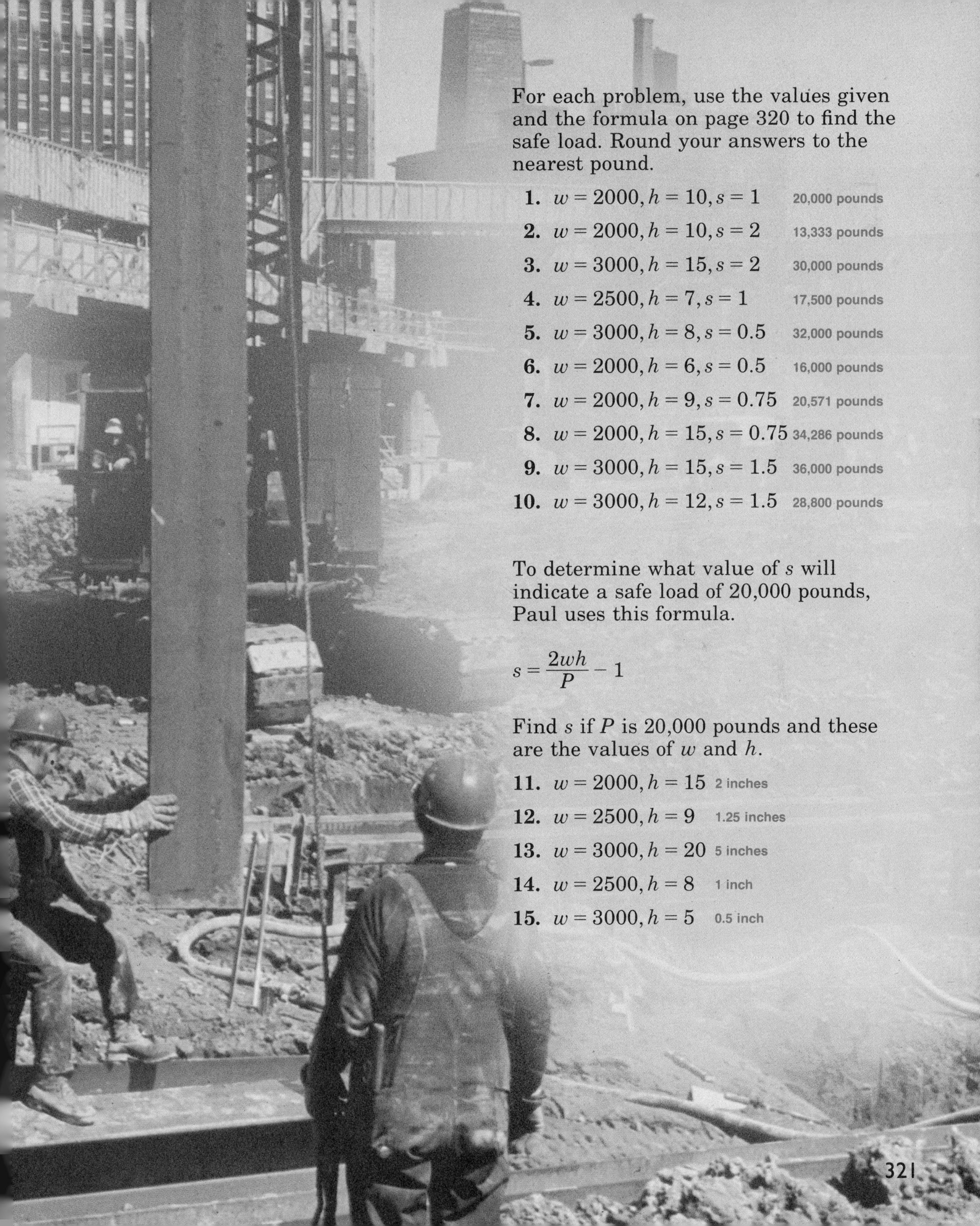

For each problem, use the values given and the formula on page 320 to find the safe load. Round your answers to the nearest pound.

1. $w = 2000, h = 10, s = 1$ 20,000 pounds
2. $w = 2000, h = 10, s = 2$ 13,333 pounds
3. $w = 3000, h = 15, s = 2$ 30,000 pounds
4. $w = 2500, h = 7, s = 1$ 17,500 pounds
5. $w = 3000, h = 8, s = 0.5$ 32,000 pounds
6. $w = 2000, h = 6, s = 0.5$ 16,000 pounds
7. $w = 2000, h = 9, s = 0.75$ 20,571 pounds
8. $w = 2000, h = 15, s = 0.75$ 34,286 pounds
9. $w = 3000, h = 15, s = 1.5$ 36,000 pounds
10. $w = 3000, h = 12, s = 1.5$ 28,800 pounds

To determine what value of s will indicate a safe load of 20,000 pounds, Paul uses this formula.

$$s = \frac{2wh}{P} - 1$$

Find s if P is 20,000 pounds and these are the values of w and h.

11. $w = 2000, h = 15$ 2 inches
12. $w = 2500, h = 9$ 1.25 inches
13. $w = 3000, h = 20$ 5 inches
14. $w = 2500, h = 8$ 1 inch
15. $w = 3000, h = 5$ 0.5 inch

Problem Solving

CAREER APPLICATIONS

Objective: Solve problems involving equations.

In this lesson students find rates of vehicles in meters per second and in kilometers per hour.

Police Officer

See the Careers Chart beginning on page 426 for more information about the careers in this cluster.

Career Cluster: Social Service Tracy Collier is a police officer. She uses electronic equipment to time a vehicle when it passes certain checkpoints. The equipment also measures the distance between these checkpoints. The speed of the vehicle is then computed by the equipment. If it is necessary for Tracy to appear in court, she must be prepared to explain the mathematics involved in finding the speed.

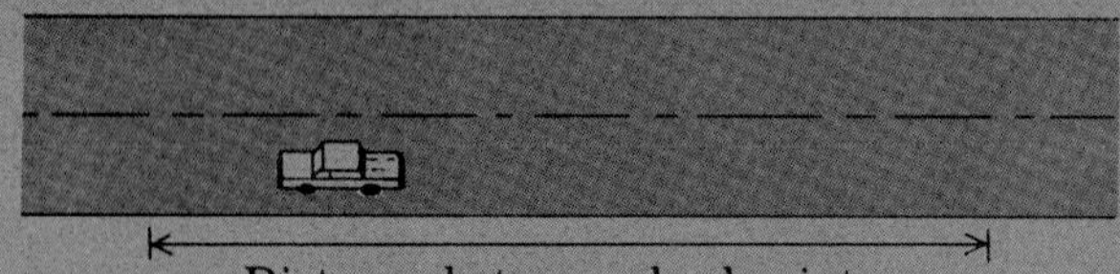

Distance between checkpoints: 140 meters
Time: 8 seconds

This formula is used to find speed (rate).

$$D = RT$$

D: Distance; R: Rate; T: Time

What is the speed of the automobile in the diagram?

$$D = RT$$
$$140 = R \times 8$$
$$\frac{140}{8} = \frac{R \times 8}{8}$$
$$17.5 = R$$

Distances are often measured between landmarks, such as overpasses, trees, culverts, and utility poles.

The speed is 17.5 meters per second (17.5 m/s).

Use the formula to find each missing distance, rate, or time. Round your answers to the nearest tenth.

	Distance (meters)	Rate (m/s)	Time (seconds)
1.	250	25	10
2.	340	26.2	13
3.	185	26.4	7
4.	216	18	12
5.	73.2	12	6.1
6.	455	13	35
7.	150	15	10
8.	244	20	12.2
9.	360	14	25.7
10.	240	22.9	10.5

90

Officer Collier is checking speeds in an 80-kilometer-per-hour (80 km/h) zone. She finds that the rate of a certain vehicle is 25 m/s. Is this a violation?

To convert meters per second to kilometers per hour, multiply by 3.6. $3.6 \times 25 = 90$

The speed of the vehicle is 90 km/h. This is a violation because it is greater than the speed limit of 80 km/h.

Complete this table. First find the rate in meters per second. Round your answer to the nearest tenth. Then find the rate in kilometers per hour and decide if the speed is a violation of the speed limit given.

	Distance (meters)	Time (seconds)	Rate (m/s)	Rate (km/h)	Speed limit (km/h)	Violation (*yes* or *no*)
11.	200	13	15.4	55.44	60	No
12.	325	14	23.2	83.52	90	No
13.	250	10	25	90	80	Yes
14.	235	8	29.4	105.84	90	Yes
15.	450	25	18	64.8	80	No
16.	432	24	18	64.8	60	Yes
17.	360	18	20	72	65	Yes
18.	500	20	25	90	90	No
19.	1000	35	28.6	102.96	85	Yes
20.	275	15	18.3	65.88	60	Yes

Problem Solving

DEVELOPING STRATEGIES

Objective: Solve problems by using a formula and making a graph.

In this lesson students use the distance formula $R = \frac{3600D}{T}$ to make a graph showing the speed of boats at different RPM readings.

Materials: Graph paper

Tactics: Using a Formula, Making a Graph

Ray Fischer's boat does not have a speedometer. It does have a tachometer which measures engine speed in revolutions per minute (RPM). Ray timed his boat on a special 0.5-nautical-mile course. (One nautical mile equals 1.15 land miles.) Then he made the table at the right.

RPM	Time (seconds)
1000	300
1500	225
2000	120
2500	81
3000	75

Problem

How can Ray tell the speed of his boat at different RPM readings?

Solution

Ray's strategy for solving the problem included the tactics of using a formula and making a graph.

a. What was the distance traveled? Information given. — 0.5 nautical mile

b. How long did it take Ray's boat to travel the course at 1000 RPM? Information from table. — 300 seconds

c. To the nearest knot, what was the speed of Ray's boat at 1000 RPM? (One knot equals one nautical mile per hour.)

Use this formula: $R = \frac{3600D}{T}$

R is the rate (speed) in knots.
D is the distance in nautical miles.
T is the time in seconds. (3600 seconds = 1 hour)

$$R = \frac{3600D}{T}$$

$$R = \frac{3600(0.5)}{300}$$

$$R = 6$$

d. Ray started to make a graph to use as a speed chart. The horizontal scale represented the RPM readings and the vertical scale represented the speed. On the line for 1000 RPM he located the point for 6 knots.

e. Ray repeated steps **a–c** for the other RPM readings. He completed the graph by locating the points and connecting them.

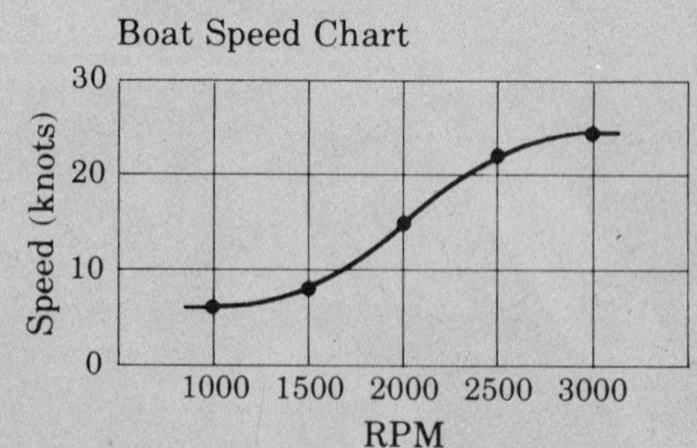

Conclusion: Ray can read his graph to find the speed of his boat at different RPM readings.

See pages 45, 63–64 of *Problem-Solving Masters.*

Related Problems

The following boats were timed at different RPM readings on a special 0.5-nautical-mile course. Make a graph to use as a speed chart for each boat.
For graphs, see Additional Answers on page T51.

1. *Morning Star*

RPM	Time (seconds)	Speed (nearest knot)
1000	257	7
1500	180	10
2000	138	13
2500	90	20
3000	69	26

2. *Friendship*

RPM	Time (seconds)	Speed (nearest knot)
1000	225	8
1500	180	10
2000	95	19
2500	67	27
3000	62	29

3. *Felicidad*

RPM	Time (seconds)	Speed (nearest knot)
1000	225	8
1500	138	13
2000	86	21
2500	72	25
3000	67	27

Extensions

Cruisers and small boats are said to plane when they reach a speed where they "climb" to the surface and move across the top of the water. The greatest increase in speed between RPM readings is where the boat planes.

4. Between which RPM readings does the *Morning Star* plane?
2000 RPM and 2500 RPM

5. Between which RPM readings does the *Friendship* plane?
1500 RPM and 2000 RPM

6. Between which RPM readings does the *Felicidad* plane?
1500 RPM and 2000 RPM

CHAPTER 14 TEST

Materials: Graph paper

Number of test items - 19

Number missed	1	2	3	4	5	6	7	8	9
Percent correct	95	89	84	79	74	68	63	58	53

Evaluate each expression when $a = 5$, $b = {}^{-}3$, $x = 1.8$, and $y = 90$.

A **1.** $14 + a + y$
109

B **2.** $37.2 - x - a$
30.4

C **3.** $2ab$
$^{-}30$

D **4.** $\frac{15}{b}$
$^{-}5$

E **5.** $2y - 3a$
165

F **6.** $7(x + 0.2) + \frac{54a}{30}$
23

Find each missing number.

G **7.** $2.5 + a = 17.1$
$a = 14.6$

H **8.** $n - 15 = {}^{-}60$
$n = {}^{-}45$

I **9.** $13y = {}^{-}299$
$y = {}^{-}23$

J **10.** $\frac{w}{15} = 4$
$w = 60$

K **11.** $7c - 16 = 68$
$c = 12$

L **12.** $\frac{v}{6} + 25 = 31$
$v = 36$

M **13.** $2x + 17x = 57$
$x = 3$

N **14.** $10d + 9 - 3d = 37$
$d = 4$

15. The resistance of an iron is 20 ohms when the iron is using 120 volts. How many amperes of current is the iron drawing?
6 amperes

16. The value of a home was $80,000. The home was insured for $40,000 by a policy with an 80% coinsurance clause. If $5000 damage was done to the home, how much money would the insurance company pay the owner?
$3125

17. The weight of a hammer on a pile driver is 2000 pounds. When the hammer fell 8 feet, it moved the pile 1 inch into the ground. What weight could be supported by the pile?
16,000 pounds

18. A truck traveled 220 meters in 11 seconds. What was the speed of the truck in meters per second?
20 meters per second

19. Jack's boat was timed on a special 0.5-nautical-mile course. Make a graph to use as a speed chart.

RPM	Time (seconds)	Speed (nearest knot)
1000	240	8
1500	138	13
2000	100	18
2500	90	20
3000	86	21

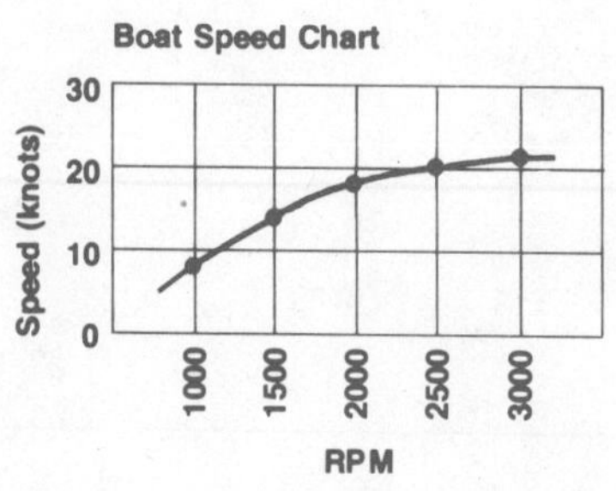

You may wish to have students refer to the applications lessons on pages 317–325 to find the formulas needed for items 15–19.

 See pages 35–36 of the *Test Masters* for an alternate form of the Chapter 14 Test.

CHAPTER 15 Graphing

Materials: Graph paper

Number of test items - 8

Number missed	1	2	3	4
Percent correct	88	75	63	50

SKILLS PRETEST

SKILL Locating Points on a Grid *page 329*

A Give the ordered pair for point Q.
(3, 5)

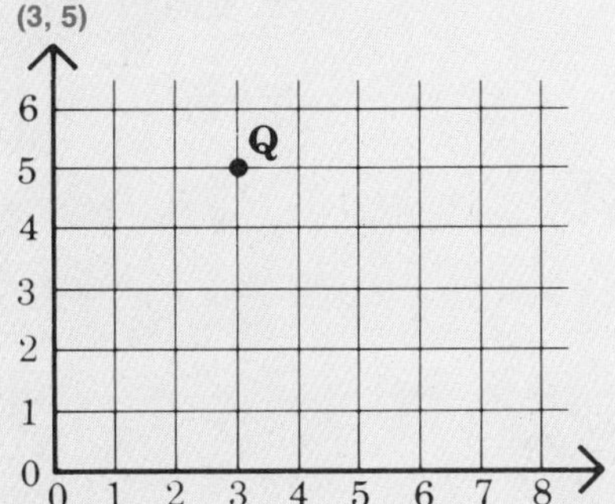

B Plot and label point R(6, 2) on a grid like the one below.

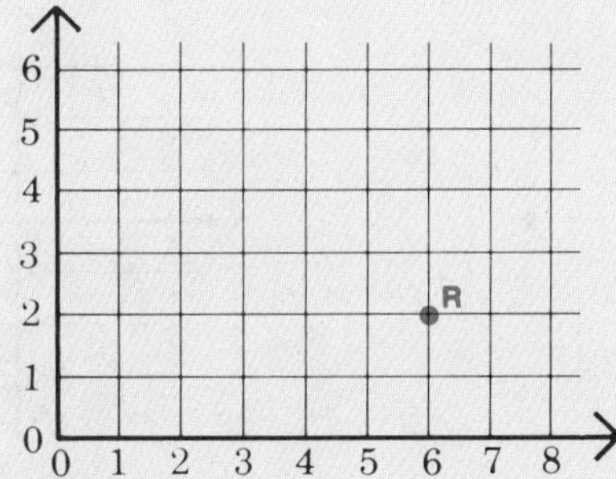

SKILL Reading and Making Graphs on a Grid *pages 330–331*

C Read the graph on the grid below to find the missing numbers in the table at the right.

x	y	
3	▒	1
▒	2	5
7	▒	3

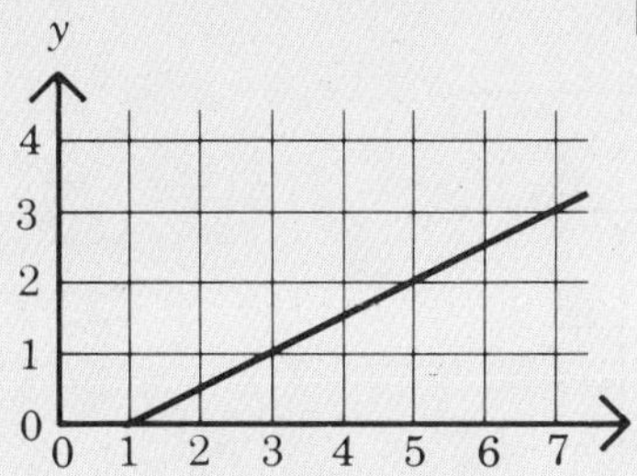

D Draw the graph of the equation $y = 2x + 2$ on a grid like the one below.

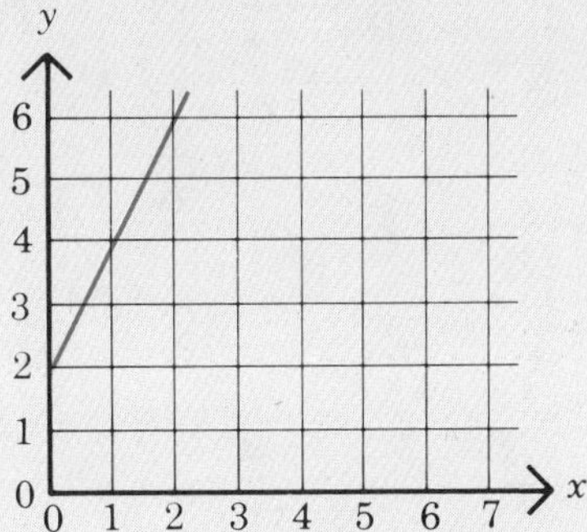

Pretest continued on page 328.

Pretest continued from page 327.

SKILL Locating Points in Four Quadrants *pages 332–333*

E Give the ordered pair for point N.
(⁻2, 1)

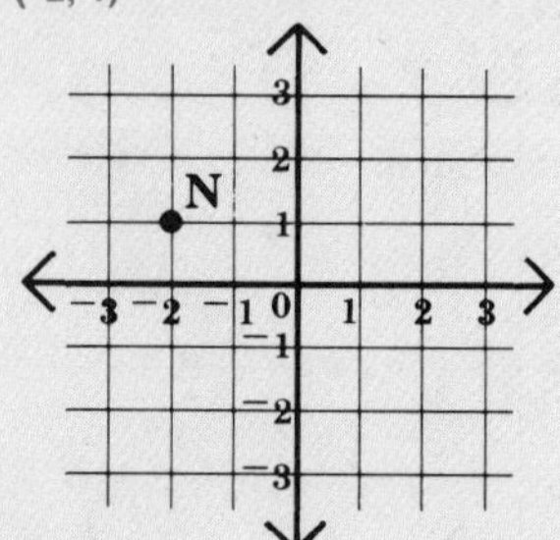

F Plot and label point T(⁻2, ⁻1) on a grid like the one below.

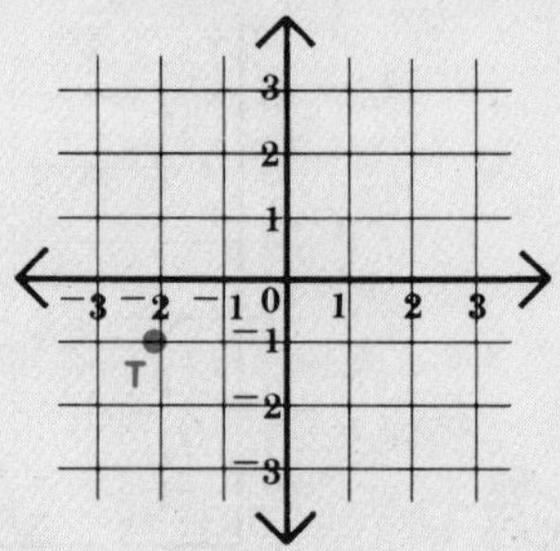

SKILL Reading and Making Graphs in Four Quadrants *pages 334–335*

G Read the graph below to find the missing numbers in the table at the right.

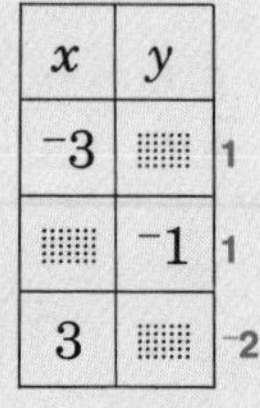

x	y	
⁻3	▒	1
▒	⁻1	1
3	▒	⁻2

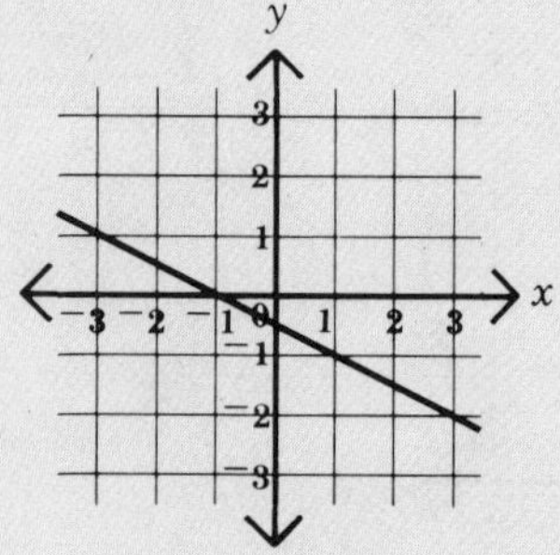

H Draw the graph of the equation $y = x + 2$ on a grid like the one below.

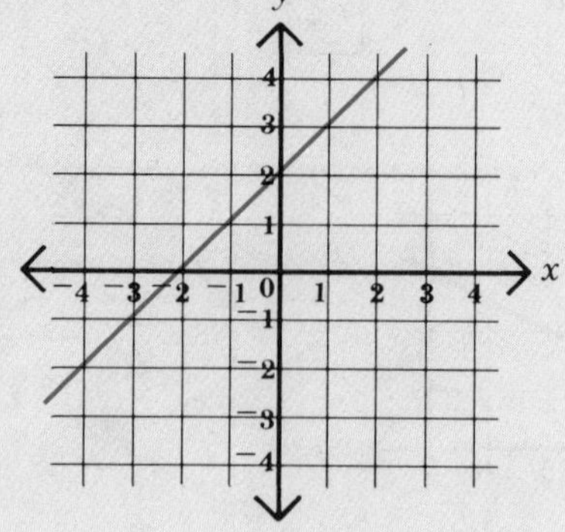

Objective: Give ordered pairs for points, and locate points for ordered pairs.

Locating Points on a Grid

Materials: Graph paper

Example A Giving ordered pairs

Give the **ordered pair** for point A.

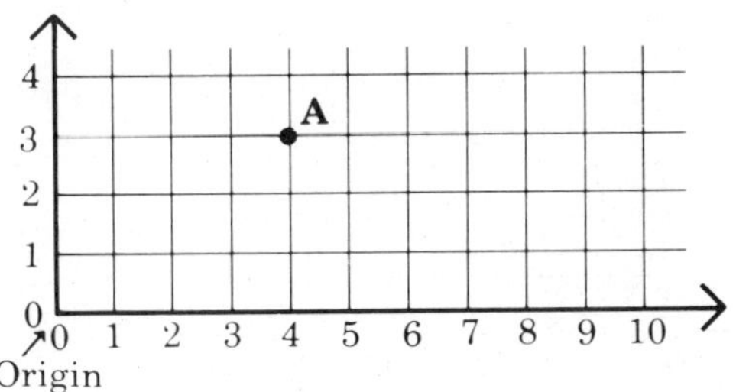

Start at the **origin,** the point where the horizontal axis and the vertical axis meet. Point A is 4 units to the right and 3 units up.

The first number tells how many units to the right.

The second number tells how many units up.

A(4, 3)

The ordered pair for point A is (4, 3).

Stress that the first number of an ordered pair indicates horizontal distance, and the second number indicates vertical distance.

Example B Plotting points

Plot and label point B(7, 2) on a grid like the one below.

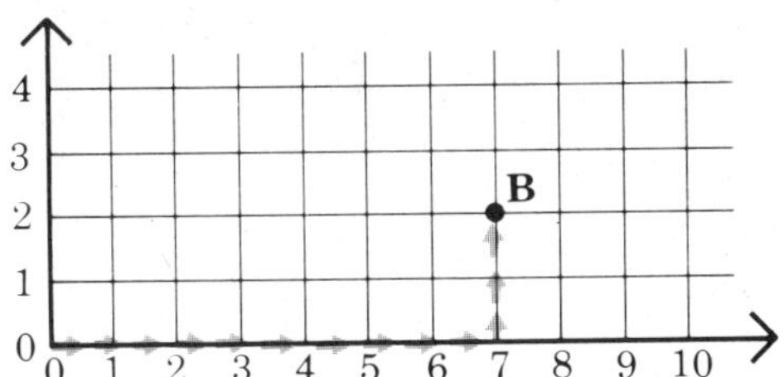

Start at the origin (0, 0). Move 7 units to the right and 2 units up. Label the point B.

Exercises

See pages 63–64 of *Problem-Solving Masters.*

Set A

Give the ordered pair for each point shown on the grid below.

1. Point C (6, 4)
2. Point D (3, 4)
3. Point E (4, 2)
4. Point F (0, 3)
5. Point G (1, 5)
6. Point H (1, 0)
7. Point I (8, 4)
8. Point J (10, 5)
9. Point K (8, 2)
10. Point L (5, 0)

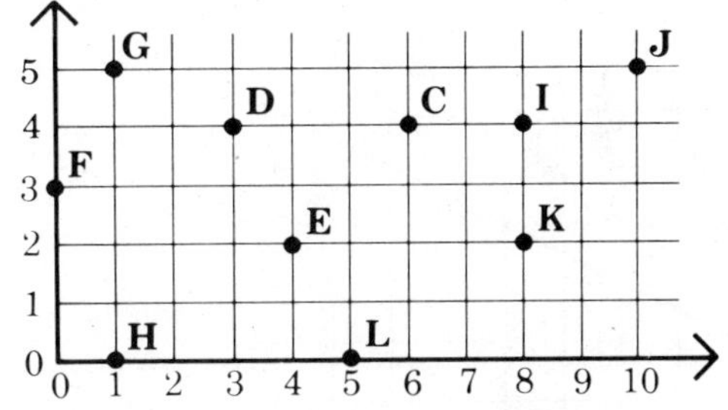

Set B

Note, to avoid confusion with zero, O has not been used to label points.

Plot and label these points on a grid like the one below.

1. M(2, 5)
2. N(5, 2)
3. P(3, 3)
4. Q(0, 4)
5. R(8, 4)
6. S(9, 1)
7. T(7, 0)
8. U(2, 1)
9. V(1, 3)
10. W(5, 5)

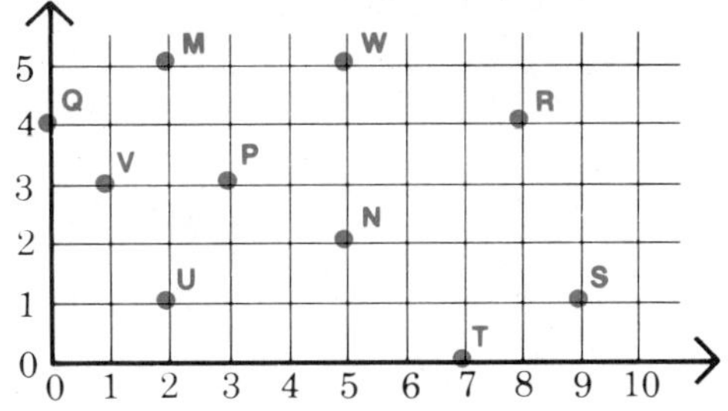

For more practice, students can draw simple pictures on a grid, using straight line segments. They can write ordered pairs for points in the pictures and give the pairs to other students to recreate the pictures.

Objective: Read a graph on a grid, and draw the graph of an equation.

Reading and Making Graphs on a Grid

See pages 63-64 of *Problem-Solving Masters.*

Materials: Graph paper

Example C Reading a graph

Read the graph on the grid below to find the missing numbers in the table at the right.

x	y
4	
	4
8	
	6

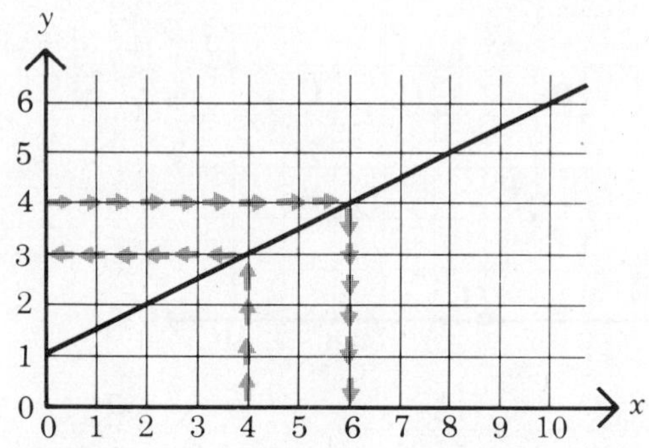

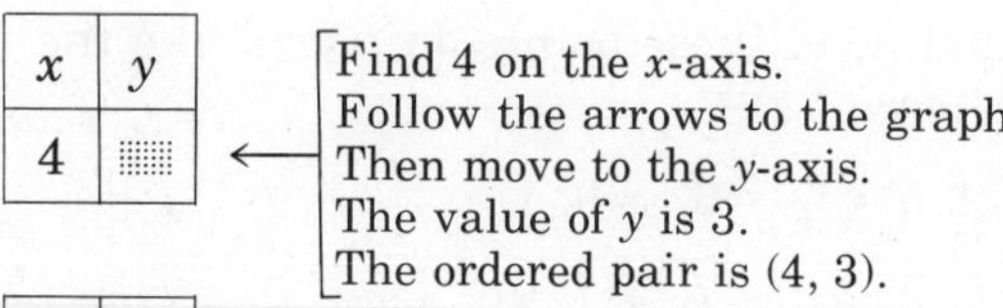

x	y
4	

Find 4 on the x-axis.
Follow the arrows to the graph.
Then move to the y-axis.
The value of y is 3.
The ordered pair is (4, 3).

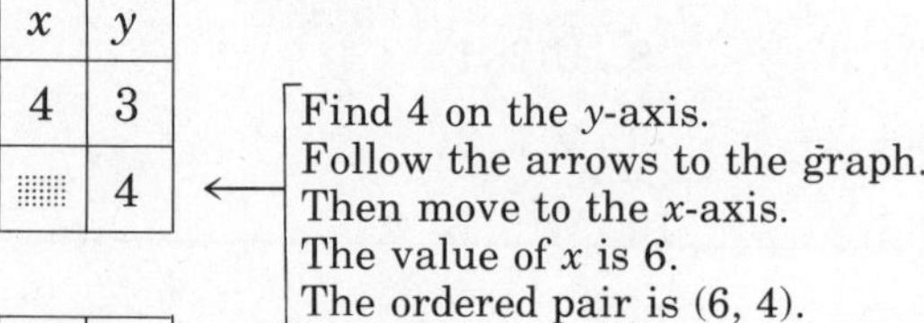

x	y
4	3
	4

Find 4 on the y-axis.
Follow the arrows to the graph.
Then move to the x-axis.
The value of x is 6.
The ordered pair is (6, 4).

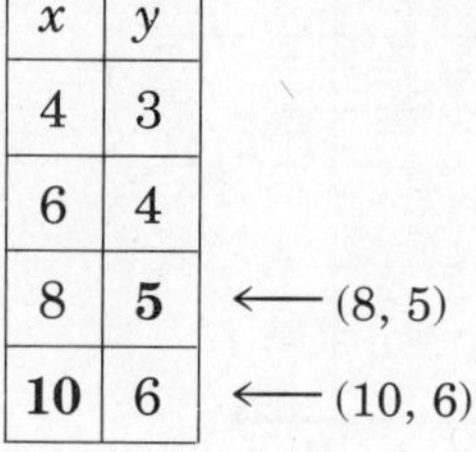

x	y	
4	3	
6	4	
8	**5**	⟵ (8, 5)
10	6	⟵ (10, 6)

Example D Drawing a graph

Draw the graph of the equation $y = 2x + 1$ on a grid like the one below.

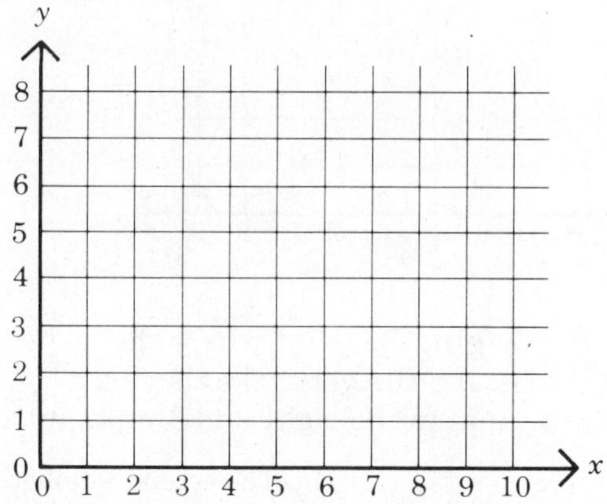

x	y	$y = 2x + 1$
0	1	$y = 2(0) + 1$
1	3	$y = 2(1) + 1$
2	5	$y = 2(2) + 1$
3	7	$y = 2(3) + 1$

Make a table.
Pick some values for x.
Substitute the values for x in the equation to compute values for y.

Plot the points and connect them.

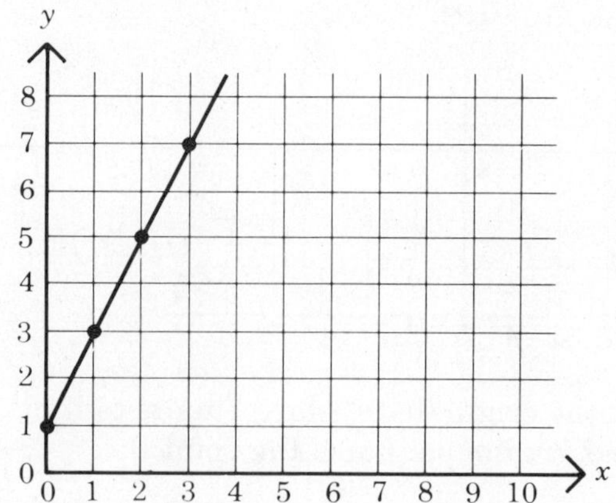

PROBLEM SOLVING
The applications on pages 342–345 may be used anytime after this lesson.

Exercises

Set C

Read the graphs to find the missing numbers in the tables.

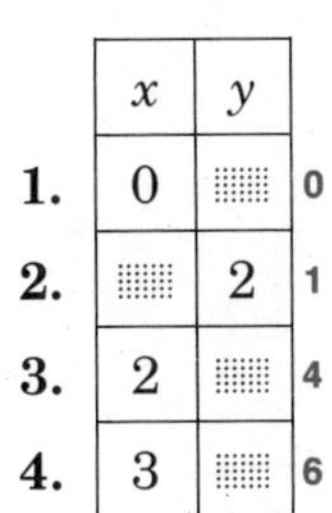

	x	y	
1.	0		0
2.		2	1
3.	2		4
4.	3		6

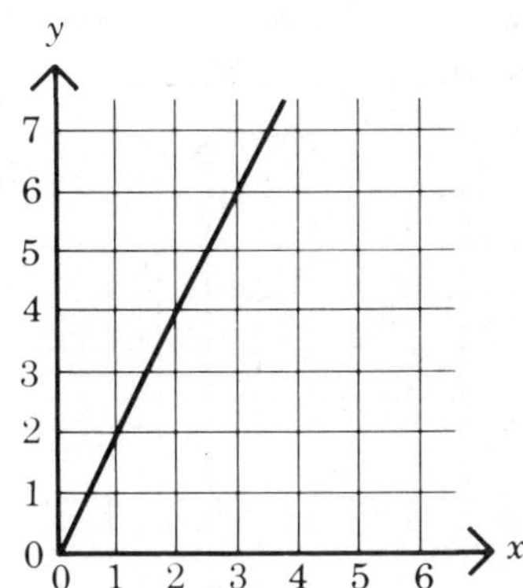

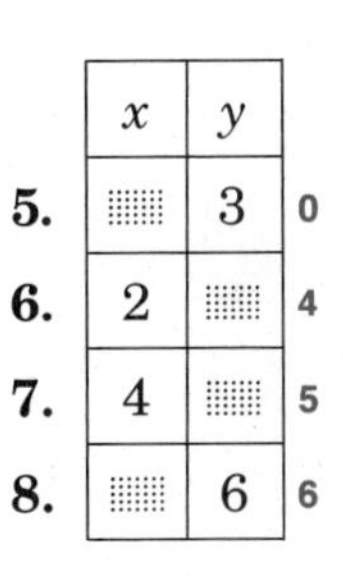

	x	y	
5.		3	0
6.	2		4
7.	4		5
8.		6	6

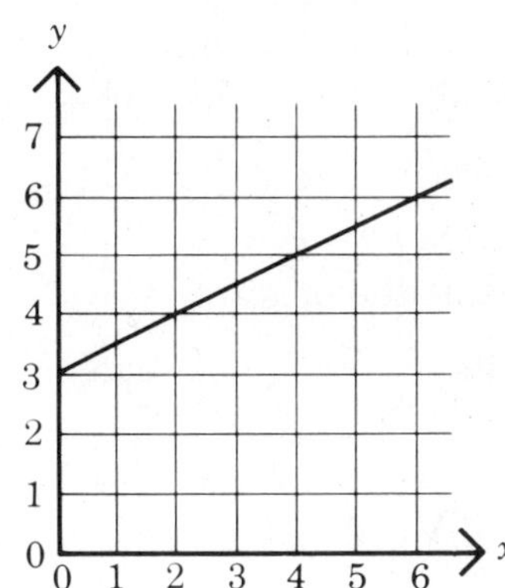

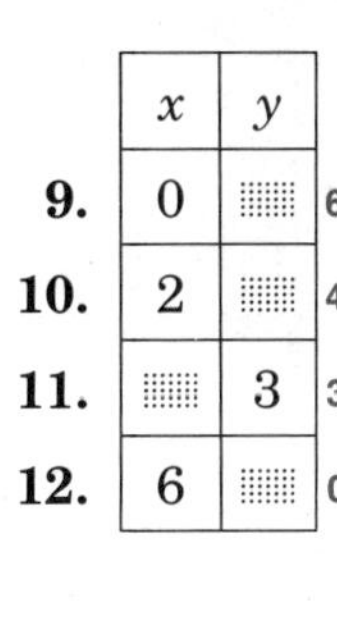

	x	y	
9.	0		6
10.	2		4
11.		3	3
12.	6		0

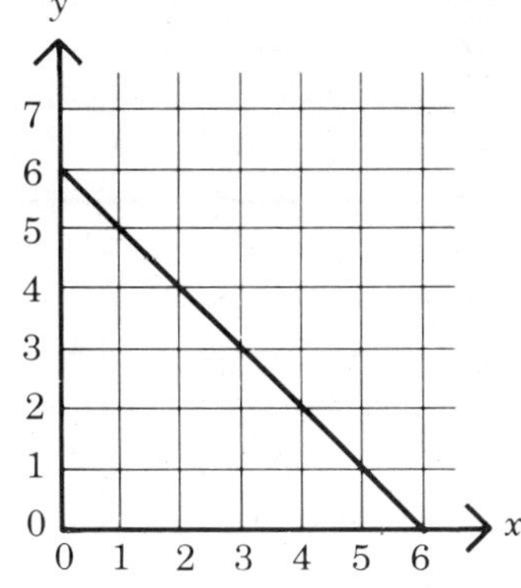

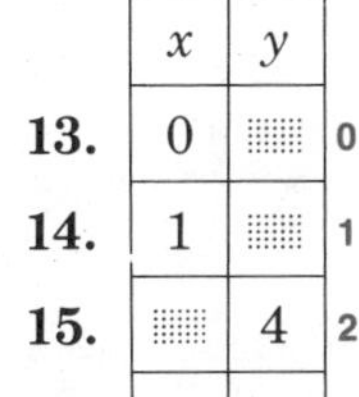

	x	y	
13.	0		0
14.	1		1
15.		4	2
16.		9	3

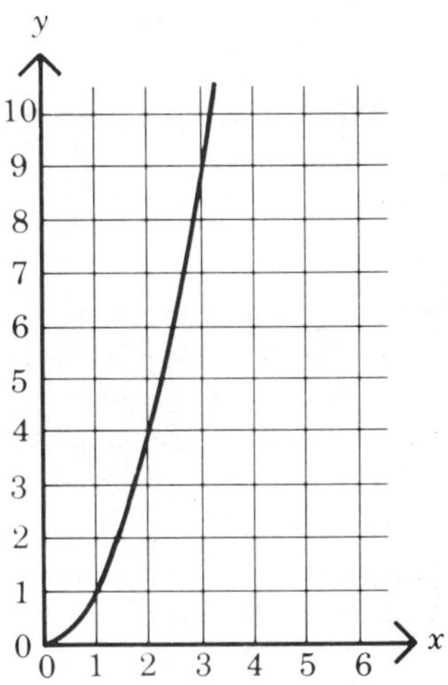

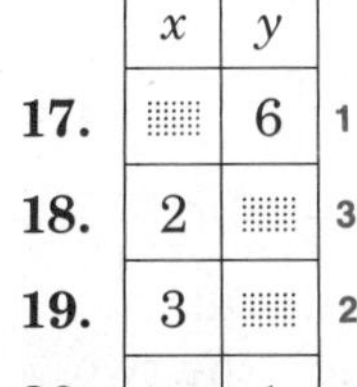

	x	y	
17.		6	1
18.	2		3
19.	3		2
20.		1	6

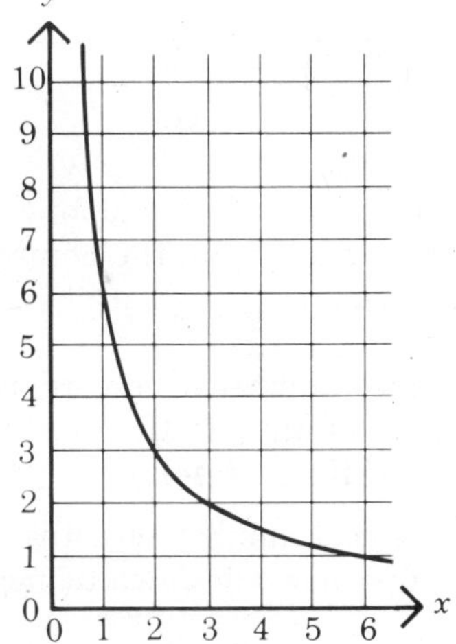

Set D

Lead students to choose appropriate values for x to avoid negative values for y.

Draw graphs of these equations on grids like the one in Example D.

See Additional Answers on page T52.

1. $y = x$

2. $y = x + 3$

3. $y = 2x$

4. $y = 2x - 1$

5. $y = 3x - 5$

6. $y = x - 4$

7. $y = 4 - x$

8. $y = 8 - 2x$

Locating Points in Four Quadrants

See pages 63–64 of *Problem-Solving Masters.*

Materials: Graph paper

Example E Giving ordered pairs

Give the ordered pair for point R.

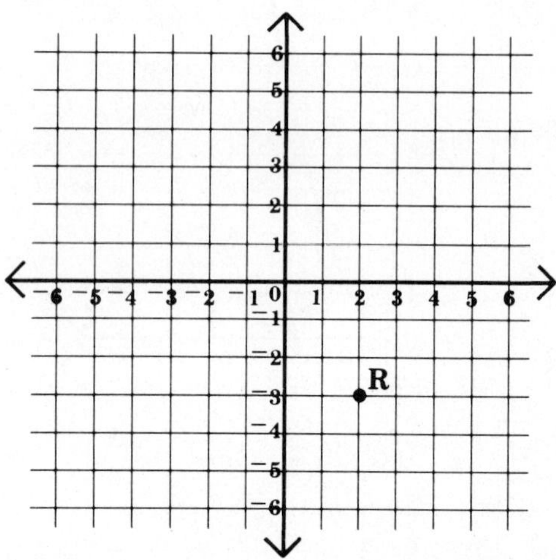

The grid is divided into four **quadrants.** Start at the origin, the point where the two axes meet.

The first number of the ordered pair tells the number of units to the right (if positive) or to the left (if negative).

The second number tells the number of units up (if positive) or down (if negative).

Point R is 2 units to the right (positive) and 3 units down (negative).

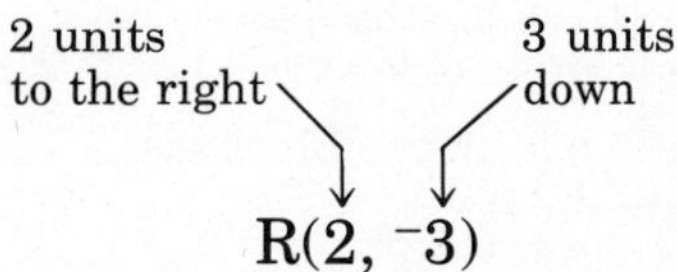

The ordered pair for point R is (2, $^-3$).

Stress again that the first number of an ordered pair indicates horizontal distance, and the second number indicates vertical distance.

Example F Plotting points

Plot and label point V($^-4$, $^-2$) on a grid like the one below.

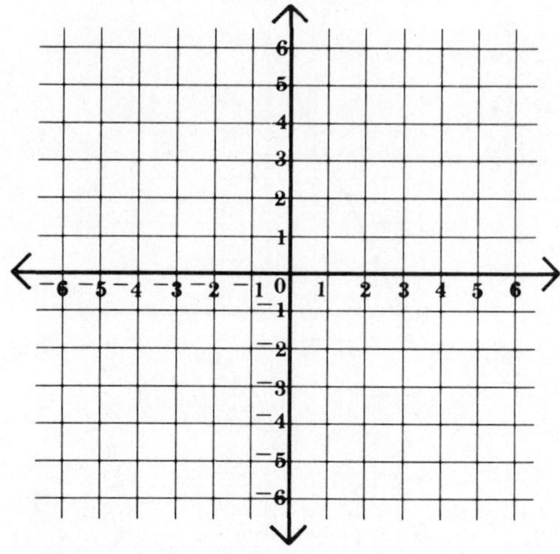

Start at the origin.

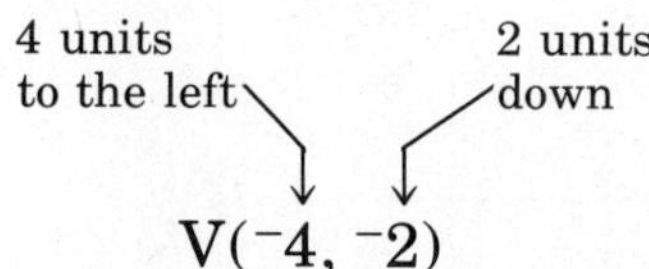

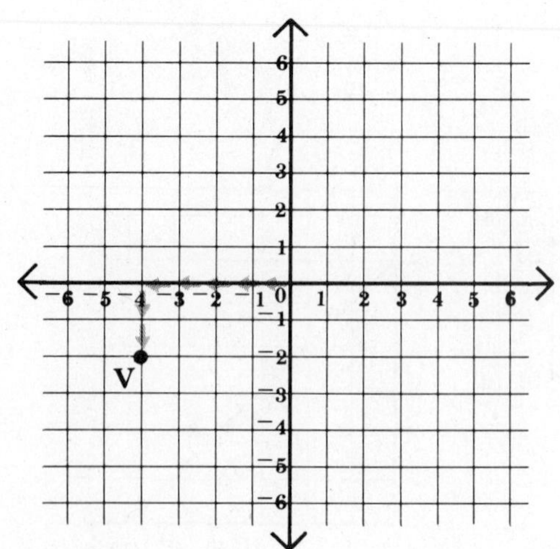

PROBLEM SOLVING
The applications on pages 340–341 may be used anytime after this lesson.

Exercises

Set E

Give the ordered pair for each point.

1. Point A (⁻3, 2)
2. Point B (⁻5, 5)
3. Point C (3, 2)
4. Point D (6, 7)
5. Point E (⁻4, ⁻4)
6. Point F (5, ⁻3)
7. Point G (⁻8, 7)
8. Point H (⁻7, ⁻9)
9. Point I (⁻3, ⁻7)
10. Point J (7, 1)
11. Point K (8, 5)
12. Point L (7, ⁻9)
13. Point M (2, ⁻6)
14. Point N (0, ⁻5)
15. Point P (4, 0)
16. Point Q (3, 8)
17. Point R (⁻8, ⁻3)
18. Point S (0, 6)
19. Point T (4, ⁻8)
20. Point U (⁻8, 0)
21. Point V (⁻6, ⁻6)
22. Point W (⁻2, 8)
23. Point X (⁻6, 3)
24. Point Y (2, ⁻2)

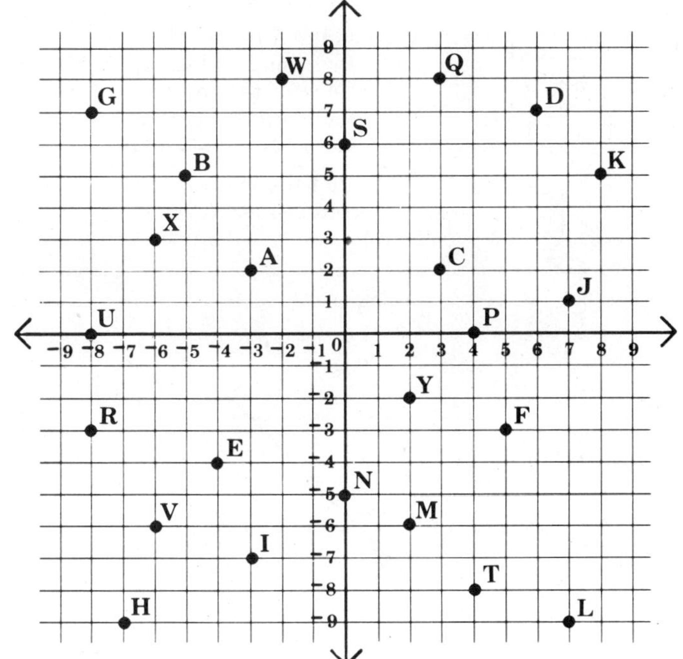

Set F

Plot and label these points on a grid like the one in Example F.
See Additional Answers on page T52.

1. A(3, ⁻6)
2. B(0, 3)
3. C(⁻4, ⁻3)
4. D(4, 3)
5. E(3, ⁻3)
6. F(5, ⁻4)
7. G(1, 6)
8. H(⁻3, ⁻4)
9. I(⁻4, 3)
10. J(5, 0)
11. K(6, 5)
12. L(⁻5, 5)
13. M(⁻4, 0)
14. N(⁻5, ⁻2)
15. P(⁻5, 2)
16. Q(0, ⁻5)
17. R(⁻6, ⁻6)
18. S(⁻3, ⁻6)
19. T(2, ⁻2)
20. U(3, 2)

BREAK TIME

Copy this picture of nine dots in a square. Draw two more squares to divide the large square into nine sections with exactly one dot in each section.

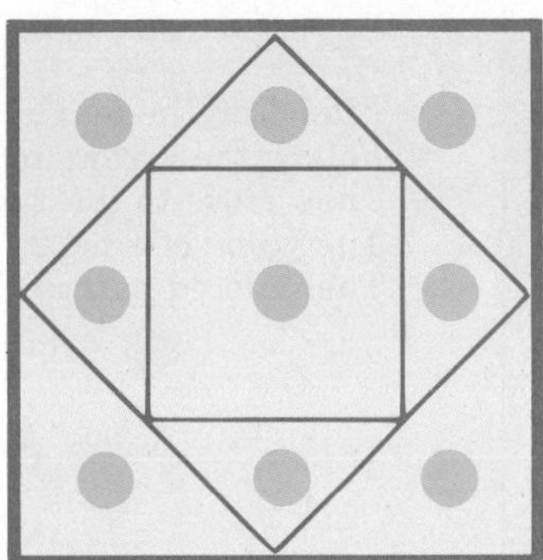

Objective: Read a graph on a four-quadrant grid, and draw the graph of an equation on a four-quadrant grid.

Reading and Making Graphs in Four Quadrants

See pages 63–64 of *Problem-Solving Masters.*

Materials: Graph paper

Example G Reading a graph

Read the graph below to find the missing numbers in the table at the right.

x	y
$^-4$	
	1
2	
	$^-4$

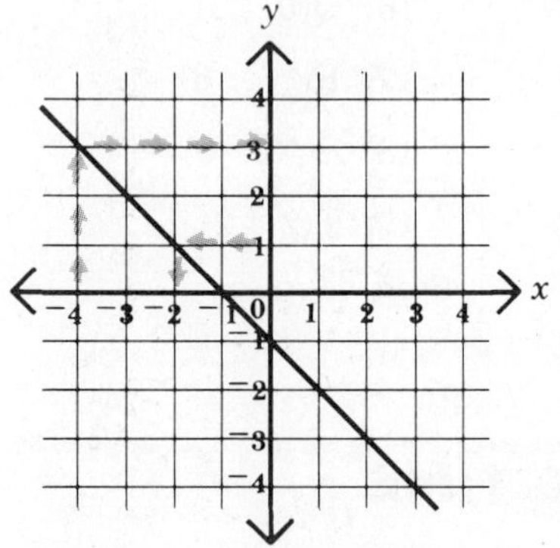

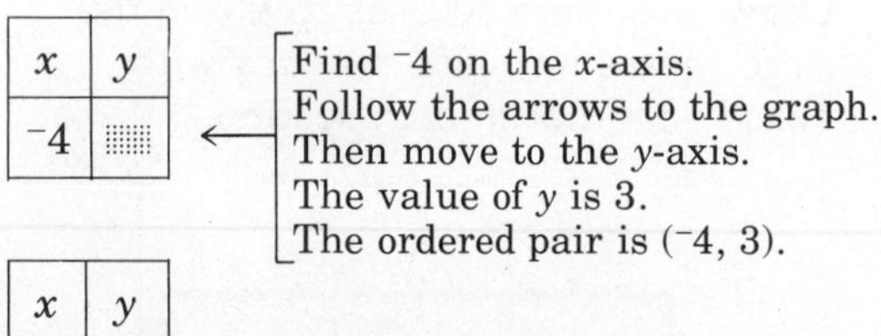

x	y
$^-4$	

Find $^-4$ on the x-axis.
Follow the arrows to the graph.
Then move to the y-axis.
The value of y is 3.
The ordered pair is ($^-4$, 3).

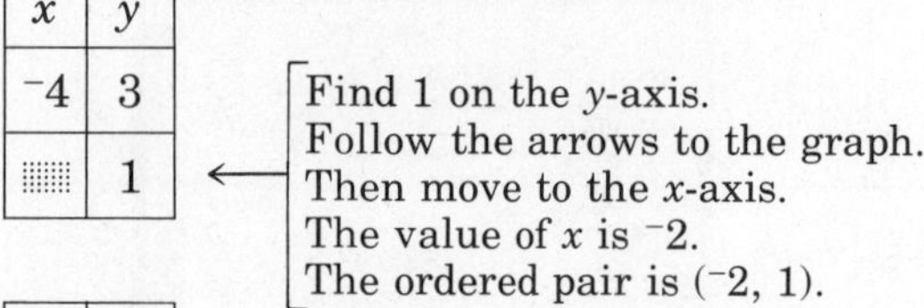

x	y
$^-4$	3
	1

Find 1 on the y-axis.
Follow the arrows to the graph.
Then move to the x-axis.
The value of x is $^-2$.
The ordered pair is ($^-2$, 1).

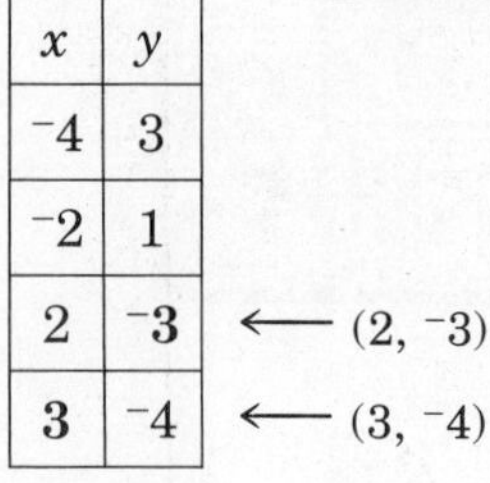

x	y	
$^-4$	3	
$^-2$	1	
2	$^-3$	← (2, $^-3$)
3	$^-4$	← (3, $^-4$)

Example H Drawing a graph

Draw the graph of the equation $y = x - 2$ on a grid like the one below.

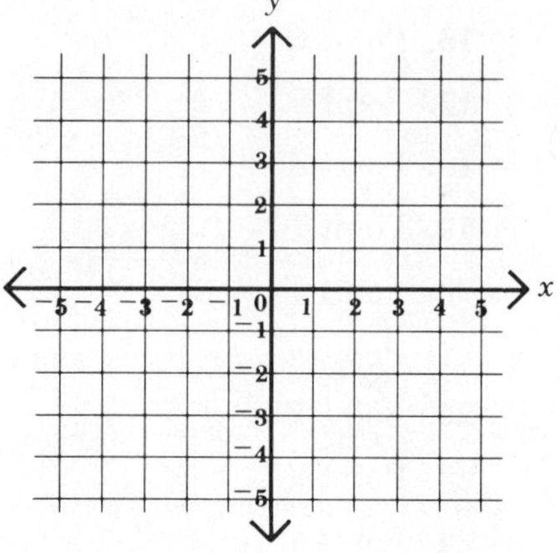

x	y	$y = x - 2$
$^-3$	$^-5$	$y = {^-3} - 2$
$^-1$	$^-3$	$y = {^-1} - 2$
1	$^-1$	$y = 1 - 2$
3	1	$y = 3 - 2$

Make a table.
Pick some values for x.
Substitute the values for x in the equation to compute values for y.

Plot the points and connect them.

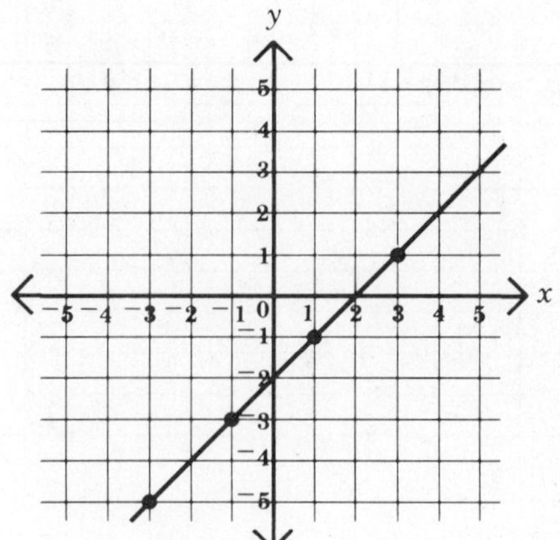

PROBLEM SOLVING
The applications on pages 338–339 may be used anytime after this lesson.

Exercises

Set G

Read the graphs to find the missing numbers in the tables.

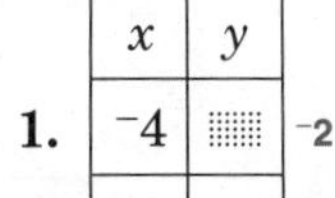

	x	y	
1.	$^-4$	▒	$^-2$
2.	▒	$^-1$	$^-2$
3.	2	▒	1
4.	▒	2	4

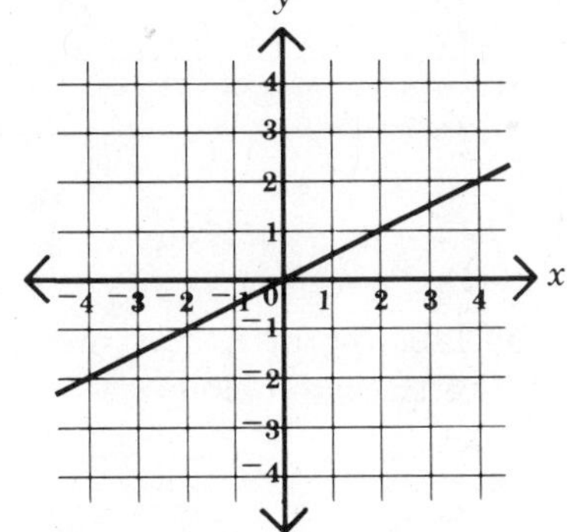

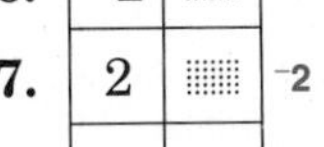
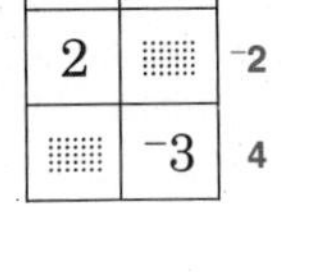

	x	y	
5.	▒	1	$^-4$
6.	$^-2$	▒	0
7.	2	▒	$^-2$
8.	▒	$^-3$	4

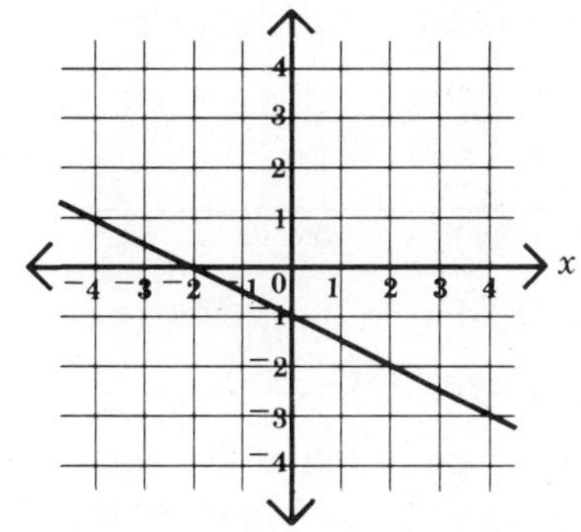

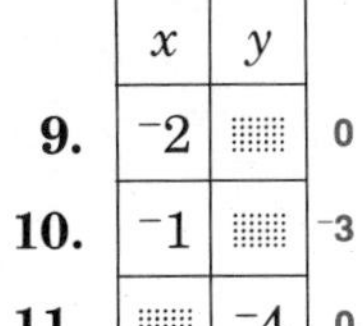
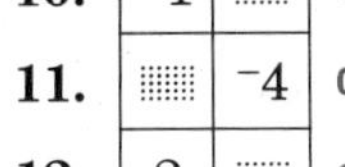
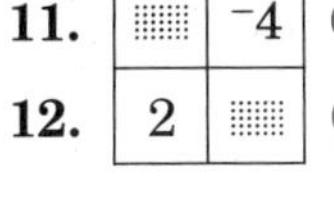

	x	y	
9.	$^-2$	▒	0
10.	$^-1$	▒	$^-3$
11.	▒	$^-4$	0
12.	2	▒	0

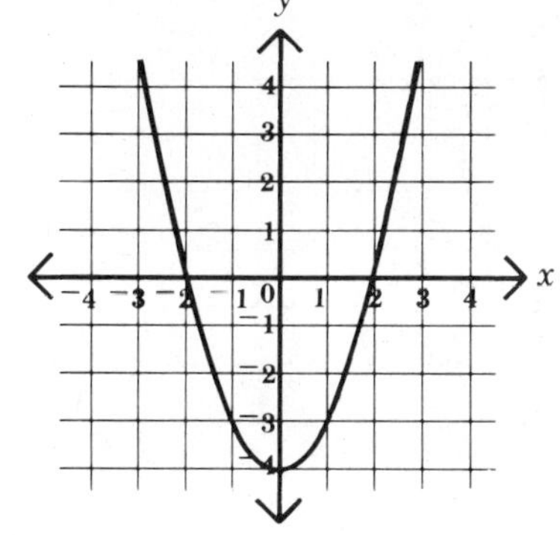

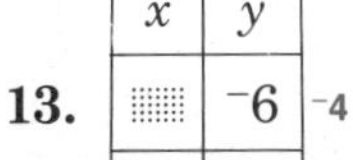

	x	y	
13.	▒	$^-6$	$^-4$
14.	$^-2$	▒	$^-3$
15.	0	▒	0
16.	▒	6	4

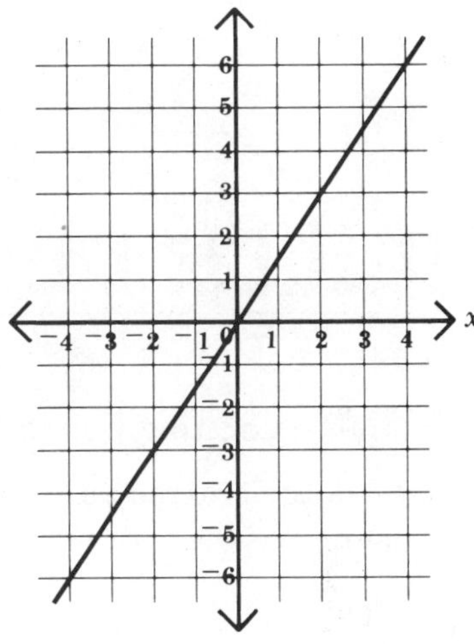

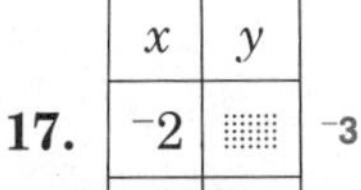

	x	y	
17.	$^-2$	▒	$^-3$
18.	$^-1$	▒	2
19.	▒	6	1
20.	▒	$^-3$	$^-2$ or 4

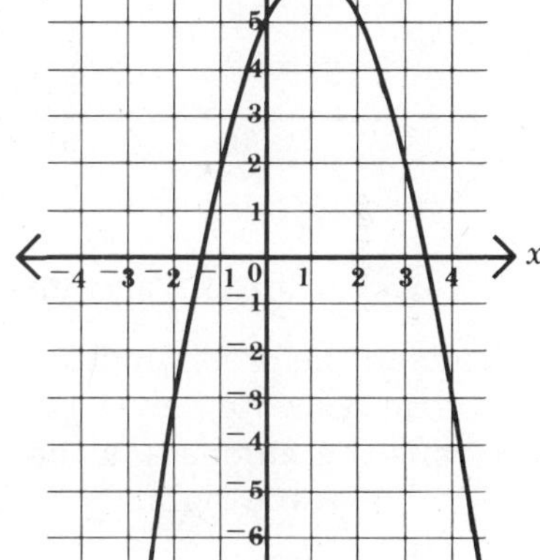

Set H

Draw graphs of these equations on grids like the one in Example H.

See Additional Answers on page T52.

1. $y = x + 1$
2. $y = {}^-2x$
3. $y = x - 3$
4. $y = x$
5. $y = 2x - 1$
6. $y = {}^-2 - x$
7. $y = 3 - x$
8. $y = x + 3$

SKILLS POSTTEST

Materials: Graph paper

Number of test items - 8

Number missed	1	2	3	4
Percent correct	88	75	63	50

SKILL Locating Points on a Grid *page 329*

A Give the ordered pair for point W.
(6, 4)

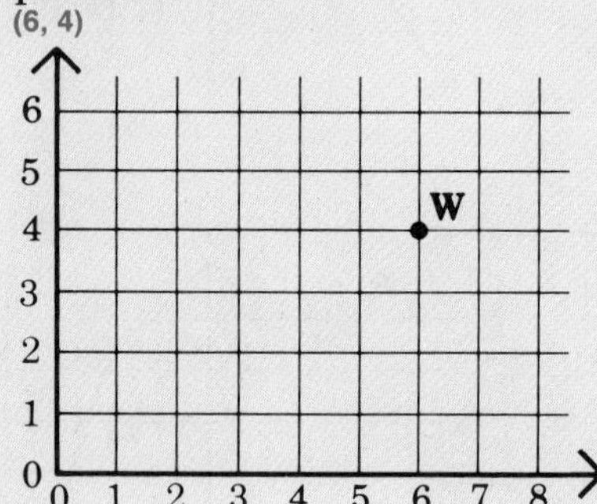

B Plot and label point K(5, 3) on a grid like the one below.

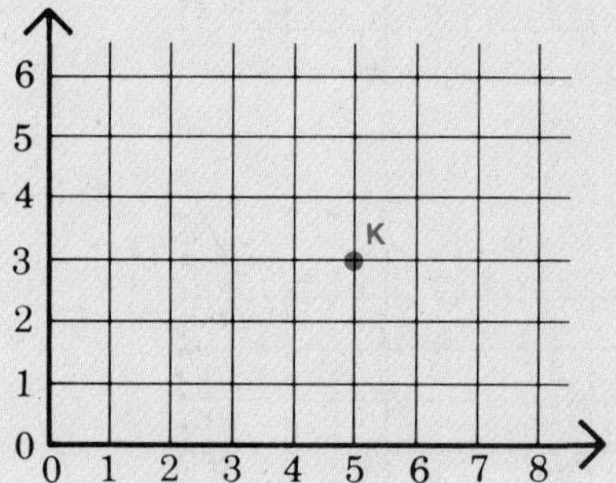

SKILL Reading and Making Graphs on a Grid *pages 330–331*

C Read the graph on the grid below to find the missing numbers in the table at the right.

x	y	
▒	2	3
5	▒	3
▒	4	7

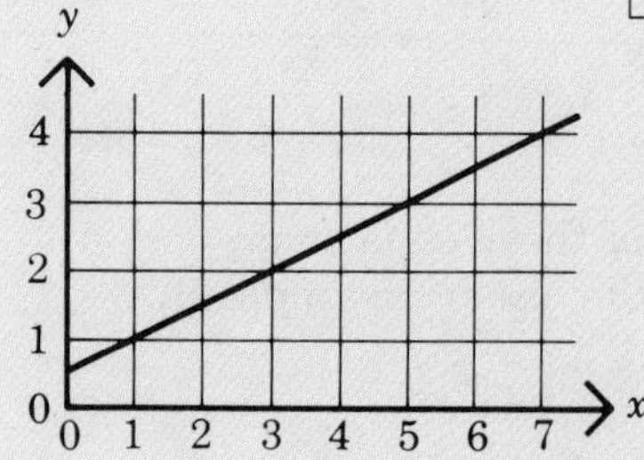

D Draw the graph of the equation $y = 3x$ on a grid like the one below.

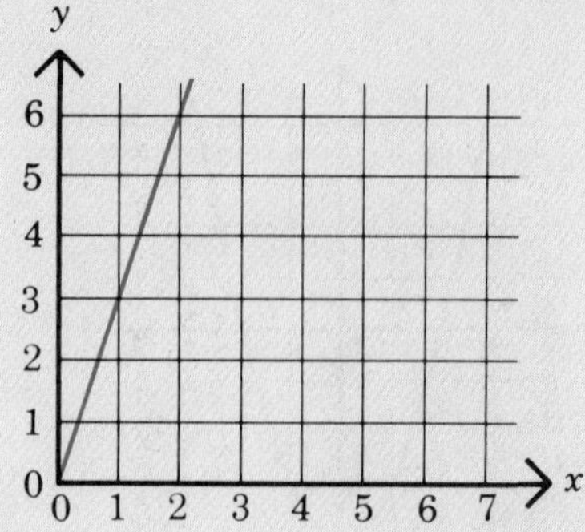

Posttest continued on page 337.

Posttest continued from page 336.

SKILL Locating Points in Four Quadrants *pages 332–333*

E Give the ordered pair for point K.
(2, $^-3$)

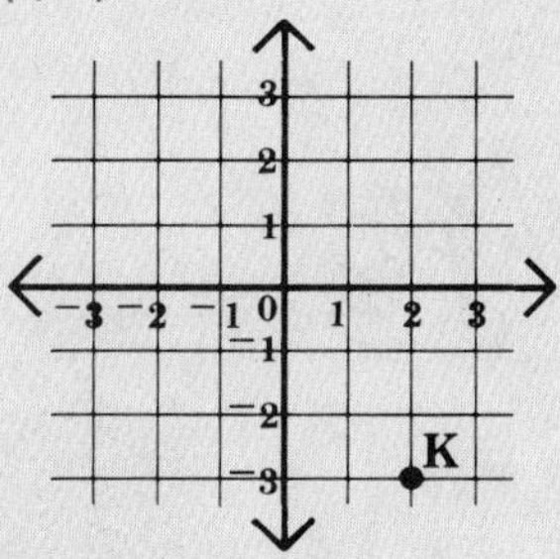

F Plot and label point M($^-3$, 1) on a grid like the one below.

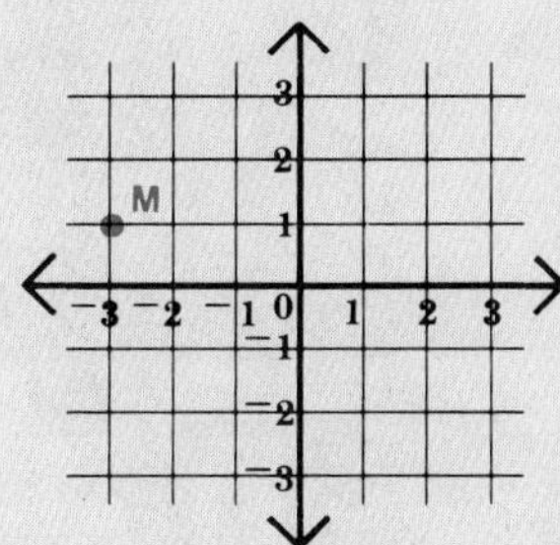

SKILL Reading and Making Graphs in Four Quadrants *pages 334–335*

G Read the graph below to find the missing numbers in the table at the right.

x	y	
$^-1$		$^-2$
1		$^-1$
	0	3

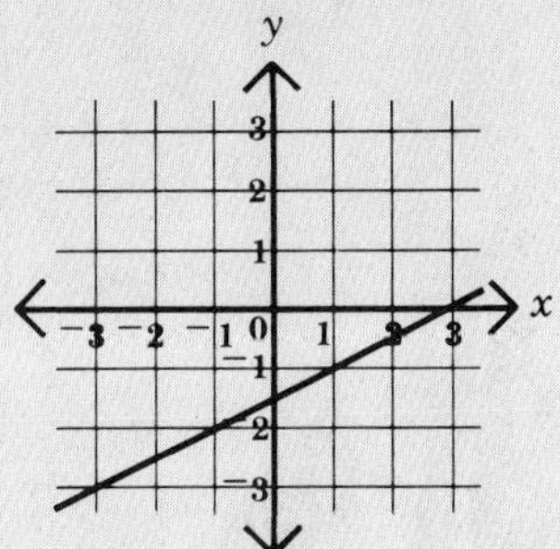

H Draw the graph of the equation $y = x - 3$ on a grid like the one below.

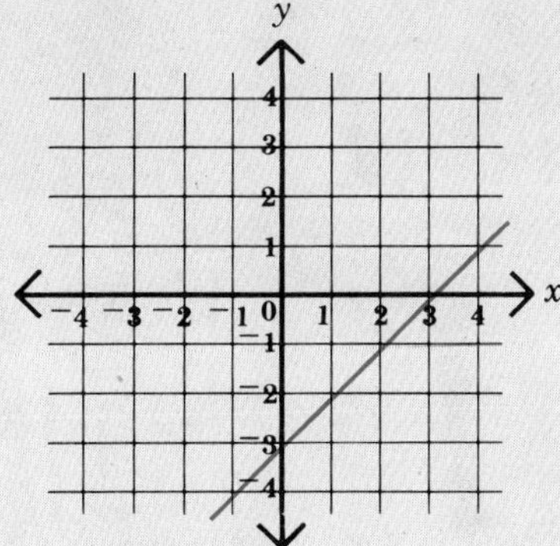

Problem Solving

CONSUMER APPLICATIONS

Objective: Solve problems involving coordinate graphing.

In this lesson students draw graphs that show the freezing points for various concentrations of three types of antifreeze.

Buying Antifreeze

Materials: Graph paper

Patty Redwing needed permanent antifreeze to protect the engine of her car. Antifreeze is added to the water in the cooling system of a car to prevent the engine parts from cracking.

Patty read an article about three major types of antifreeze: ethylene glycol, methanol, and ethanol.

Type of antifreeze	Concentration (percent antifreeze)	Freezing point	Ordered pairs
Ethylene glycol	0%	0°C	(0, 0)
	15%	$^{-}$6°C	(15, $^{-}$6)
	32%	$^{-}$18°C	(32, $^{-}$18)
	45%	$^{-}$34°C	(45, $^{-}$34)
	50%	$^{-}$40°C	(50, $^{-}$40)
	58%	$^{-}$51°C	(58, $^{-}$51)
Methanol	0%	0°C	(0, 0)
	10%	$^{-}$6°C	(10, $^{-}$6)
	20%	$^{-}$12°C	(20, $^{-}$12)
	32%	$^{-}$23°C	(32, $^{-}$23)
	42%	$^{-}$34°C	(42, $^{-}$34)
	55%	$^{-}$51°C	(55, $^{-}$51)
Ethanol	0%	0°C	(0, 0)
	18%	$^{-}$6°C	(18, $^{-}$6)
	28%	$^{-}$12°C	(28, $^{-}$12)
	43%	$^{-}$23°C	(43, $^{-}$23)
	55%	$^{-}$34°C	(55, $^{-}$34)
	81%	$^{-}$51°C	(81, $^{-}$51)

See pages 63–64 of *Problem-Solving Masters.*
Suggest that students draw each graph in a different color.

1. Use the data in the table to draw a graph for ethylene glycol. Plot points and connect them. Use a grid like the one below.
See grid.

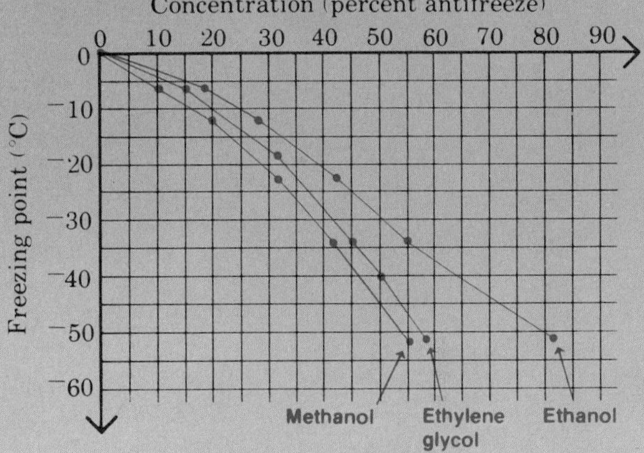

2. Draw a graph for methanol on the same grid.
See grid.
3. Draw a graph for ethanol on the same grid.
See grid.
4. Which antifreeze has the lowest freezing point for a 30% concentration?
Methanol
5. Which antifreezes will prevent freezing at $^{-}$35°C with a 50% concentration?
Ethylene glycol, methanol
6. Which antifreeze provides the most protection (has the lowest freezing point) for any concentration?
Methanol
7. Which antifreeze provides the least protection for any concentration?
Ethanol

Ethylene glycol is a year-round permanent antifreeze with a boiling point of 104°C. Methanol and ethanol are non-permanent, alcohol-based antifreezes that can boil off in the summer. Their boiling points are 85°C and 84°C, respectively.

Methanol and ethanol are no longer commonly used antifreezes.

Problem Solving

CAREER APPLICATIONS

Objective: Solve problems involving coordinate graphing.

Materials: Graph paper

Drill-Press Operator

In this lesson students use a grid to show the location of holes that are to be drilled by a computer-controlled drill press.

See pages 63–64 of *Problem-Solving Masters.*

Career Cluster: Trades Fred Willis operates a computer-controlled drill press that is used in mass production.

He prepares a program for the computer. The computer directs the drill to the spot where the hole is to be drilled.

The drill moves left (L) or right (R) and up (U) or down (D) *from the previous hole* to get to the next hole. The drill starts at the center of a grid.

Hole	Drill movements	Location of hole
A	R3 U2	(3, 2)
B	L5 D6	($^-2$, $^-4$)
C	R3 U0	(1, $^-4$)

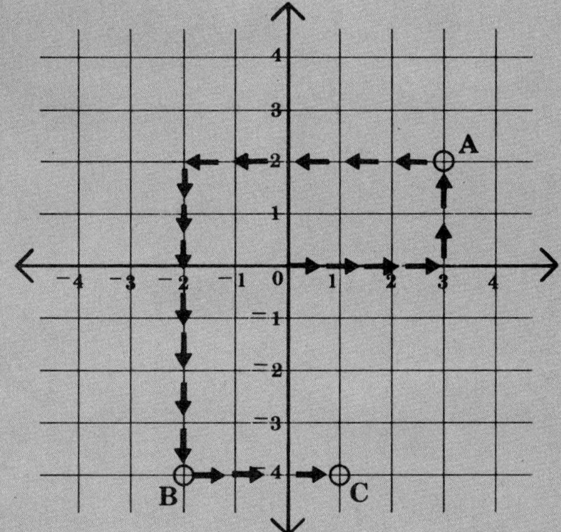

For each table, plot and label the holes on a grid. Use an ordered pair to give the location of each hole.
Have students use a different grid for each table.

	Hole	Drill movements	Location of hole
	A	R5 D5	(5, $^-5$)
	B	L2 U0	(3, $^-5$)
1.	C	L6 U0	($^-3$, $^-5$)
2.	D	R0 U3	($^-3$, $^-2$)
3.	E	R1 U4	($^-2$, 2)
4.	F	R7 D1	(5, 1)

For grid, see Additional Answers on page T52.

	Hole	Drill movements	Location of hole
5.	A	L2 U1	($^-2$, 1)
6.	B	R1 U3	($^-1$, 4)
7.	C	R5 U0	(4, 4)
8.	D	L1 D3	(3, 1)
9.	E	L2 D2	(1, $^-1$)
10.	F	L4 U0	($^-3$, $^-1$)

For grid, see Additional Answers on page T52.

	Hole	Drill movements	Location of hole
11.	A	L2 U3	($^-2$, 3)
12.	B	R6 D2	(4, 1)
13.	C	R1 D4	(5, $^-3$)
14.	D	L7 U0	($^-2$, $^-3$)
15.	E	L3 D1	($^-5$, $^-4$)
16.	F	R0 U2	($^-5$, $^-2$)
17.	G	R1 U3	($^-4$, 1)
18.	H	L1 U3	($^-5$, 4)

For grid, see Additional Answers on page T52.

Problem Solving

CAREER APPLICATIONS

Objective: Solve problems involving coordinate graphing.

In this lesson students determine the thickness of various layers of rock by using graphs of data obtained from a geophone.

Geologist

Materials: Graph paper

Career Cluster: Science The Campbell Stone Company bought three sections of land. Steve Haverl, a geologist, was asked to prepare a report on the various layers of rock in each section of land.

Steve set off a small charge of dynamite. He used a geophone to record how long it took the compression waves from the dynamite to travel various distances through the ground. He used his data to make graphs like these.

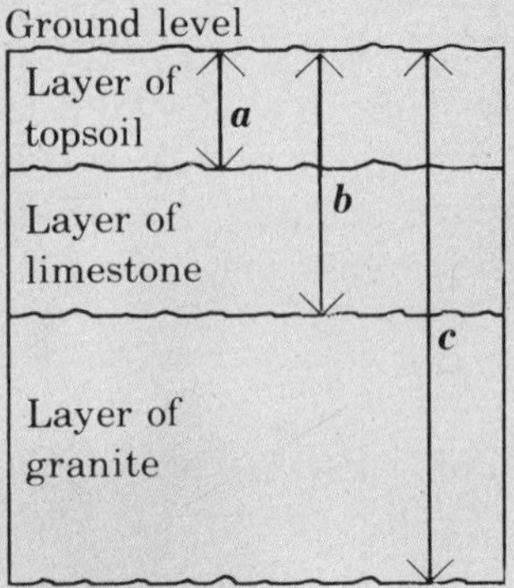

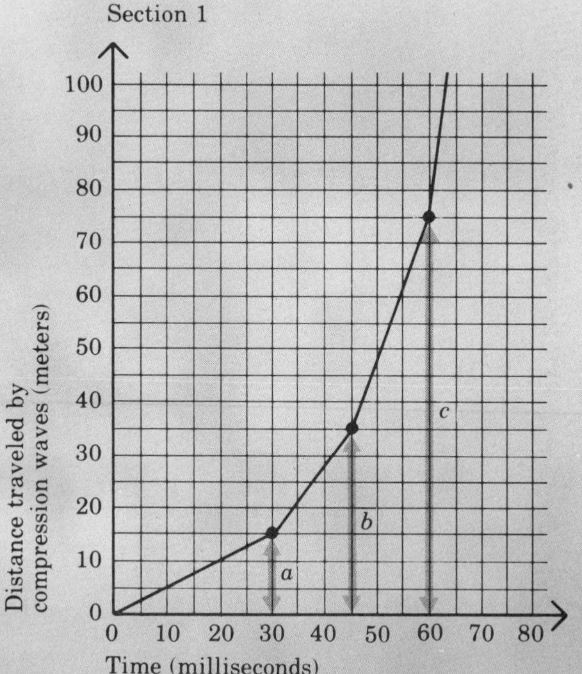

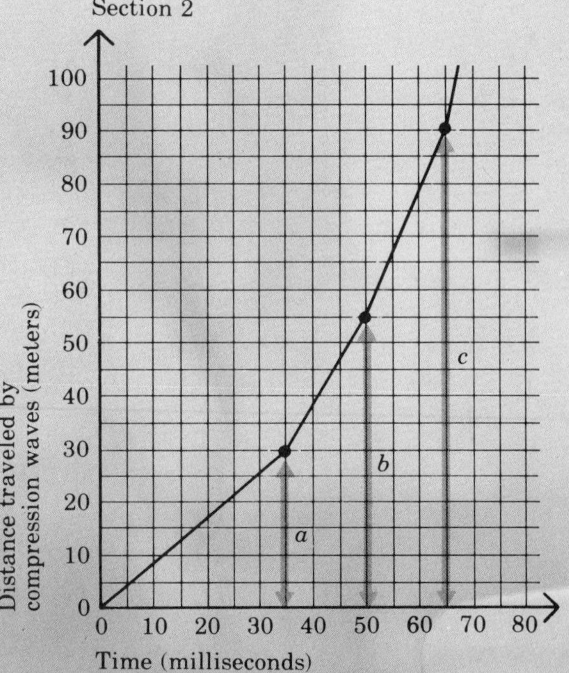

The changes in steepness on each graph indicate changes in the speed of the compression waves. These changes occur where the layers end. For example, the graph for Section 1 shows that the topsoil ends at 15 meters.

See pages 63–64 of *Problem-Solving Masters.*

1. Use this data to draw a graph for Section 3. (time in milliseconds, distance in meters)
See Additional Answers on page T53.
(0, 0) (15, 5) (30, 10) (45, 15) (55, 25)
(65, 35) (75, 45) (85, 65) (95, 85) (100, 125)

2. At what three points on your graph does the steepness of the graph change?
(45, 15) (75, 45) (95, 85)

3. Label the distances a, b, and c on your graph.
See Additional Answers on page T53.

In addition to finding the levels at which various layers end, Steve must determine the thickness of each layer of rock.

Use the graphs for the three sections of land to complete the table below.

		Level at which topsoil ends a	Level at which limestone ends b	Thickness of limestone layer $b - a$	Level at which granite ends c	Thickness of granite layer $c - b$
4.	Section 1	15 m	35 m	20 m	75 m	40 m
5.	Section 2	30 m	55 m	25 m	90 m	35 m
6.	Section 3	15 m	45 m	30 m	85 m	40 m

Problem Solving

DEVELOPING STRATEGIES

Objective: Solve problems by reading and interpreting graphs.

In this lesson students read graphs depicting weekly sales in 1980 and 1981, and use the information to determine total and average increases.

Tactic: Reading and Interpreting Graphs

Jo Rheinbolt is a sales analyst for a chain of small grocery stores. Sales graphs for each store help her to find sales increases from one year to the next, total sales for a given period, and lowest and highest sales periods. Jo used this graph when she analyzed the sales of Manchester Super Thrift in 1980 and 1981.

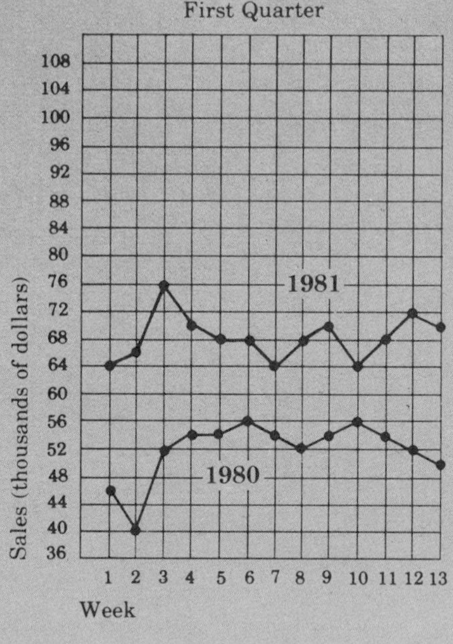

Problem

What was the total increase in first-quarter sales from 1980 to 1981 for the Manchester Super Thrift?

Solution

In her strategy for solving the problem, Jo used the tactic of reading and interpreting graphs.

a. What were the sales for each week in the first quarters of 1980 and 1981? Read the graphs.

b. What were the total first-quarter sales for each year? Add.

Discuss with students the business practice of dividing the year into periods of 13 weeks, or quarters.

The fiscal year here is the calendar year.

1980	**1981**
$46,000	$64,000
40,000	66,000
52,000	76,000
54,000	70,000
54,000	68,000
56,000	68,000
54,000	64,000
52,000	68,000
54,000	70,000
56,000	64,000
54,000	68,000
52,000	72,000
+ 50,000	+ 70,000
$674,000	$888,000

c. What was the total increase in first-quarter sales? Subtract.

$888,000 − $674,000 = $214,000

Conclusion: The total increase in first-quarter sales from 1980 to 1981 for the Manchester Super Thrift was $214,000.

See pages 46–47 of *Problem-Solving Masters*.

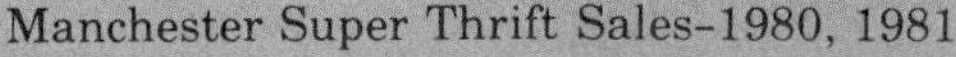

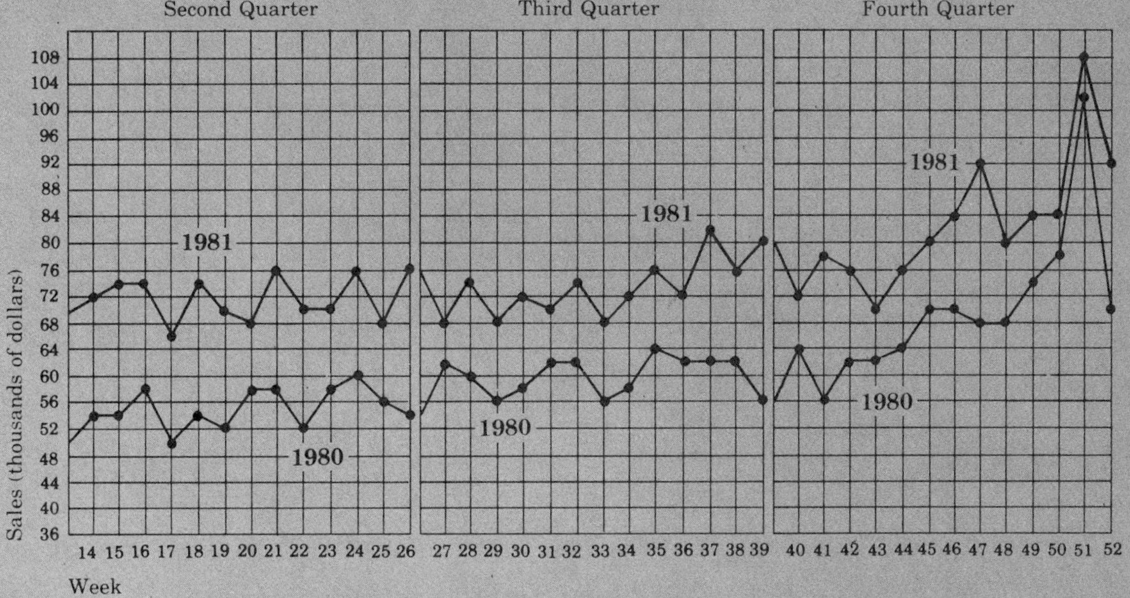

Related Problems

Use the graphs above for Problems 1–3.

What was the total increase in sales from 1980 to 1981 for the

1. second quarter?
   $216,000
2. third quarter?
   $172,000
3. fourth quarter?
   $168,000

Use the graphs for all four quarters for Problems 4–8.

4. Which week in 1980 had the lowest sales?
   Week 2
5. Which week in 1981 had the highest sales?
   Week 51
6. Find the total sales for 1980.
   $3,080,000
7. Find the total sales for 1981.
   $3,850,000
8. Find the total increase in sales from 1980 to 1981.
   $770,000
9. Find the average weekly increase to the nearest thousand dollars for the first quarter. (Since a quarter has 13 weeks, divide the total increase in first-quarter sales by 13.)
   $16,000

Use your answers to Problems 1–3 to find the average weekly increase to the nearest thousand dollars for the

10. second quarter.
    $17,000
11. third quarter.
    $13,000
12. fourth quarter.
    $13,000

Extensions

Point out that the percent of increase is based on the lower figure.

13. The total increase in sales from 1980 to 1981 is what percent of total sales in 1980?
    25%
14. Assuming that sales will increase by the same percent, predict total sales for 1982.
    $4,812,500

CHAPTER 15 TEST

Number of test items - 12						
Number missed	1	2	3	4	5	6
Percent correct	92	83	75	67	58	50

Materials: Graph paper

A **1.** Give the ordered pair for point J.
(3, 2)

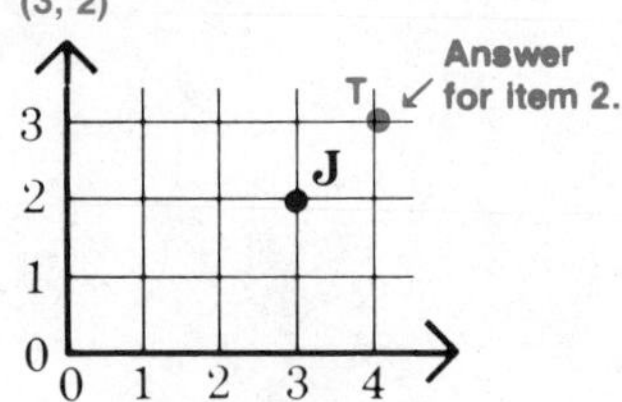

B **2.** Plot and label point T(4, 3) on a grid like the one in item 1.
See grid in item 1.

C **3.** Read the graph below to find the missing numbers in the table.

x	y	
0	▒	2
▒	3	2
4	▒	4

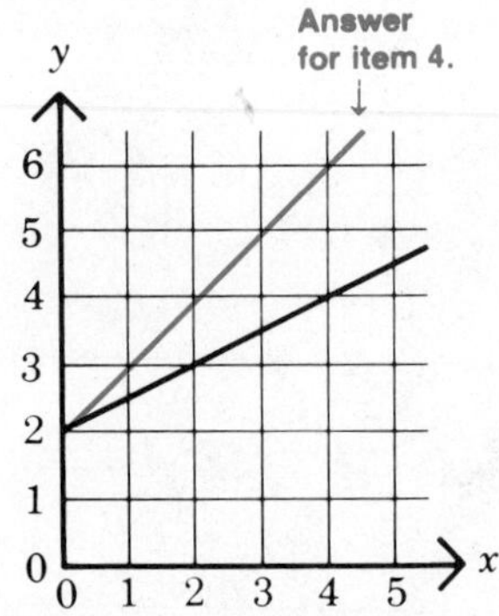

D **4.** Draw the graph of the equation $y = x + 2$ on a grid like the one in item 3.
See grid in item 3.

E **5.** Give the ordered pair for point R.
($^-3$, 2)

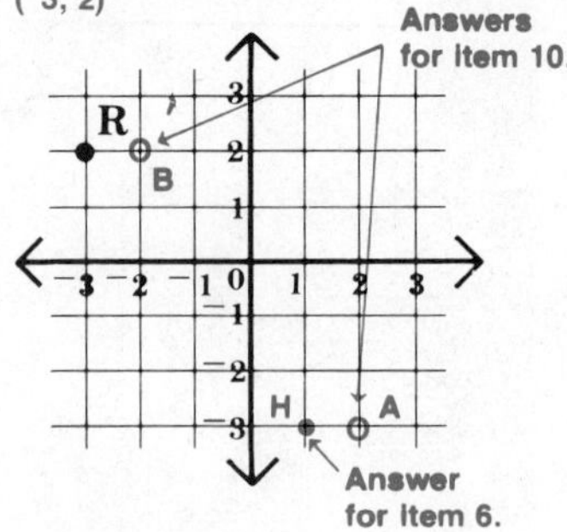

F **6.** Plot and label point H(1, $^-3$) on a grid like the one in item 5.
See grid in item 5.

G **7.** Read the graph below to find the missing numbers in the table.

x	y	
$^-2$	▒	$^-3$
▒	1	0
1	▒	3

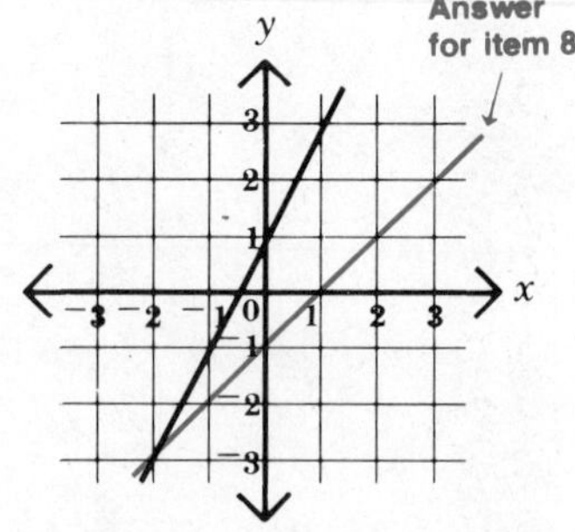

H **8.** Draw the graph of the equation $y = x - 1$ on a grid like the one in item 7.
See grid in item 7.

9. What is the freezing point for solution that is 20% antifreeze?
$^-15$°C

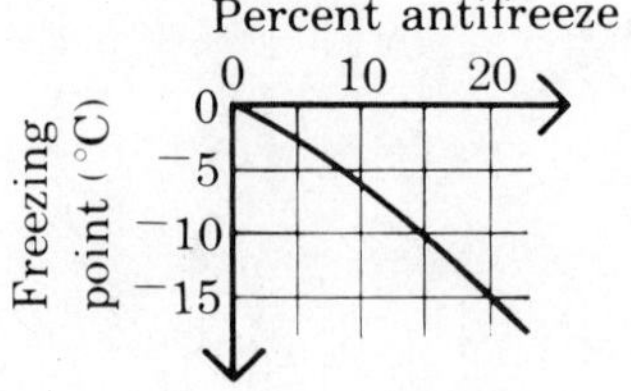

10. Plot and label holes A and B on a grid like the one in item 5. Start at (0, 0).
See grid in item 5.

Hole	Drill movements	
A	R2 D3	(2, $^-3$)
B	L4 U5	($^-2$, 2)

11. What is the depth of the topsoil (a)?
15 m

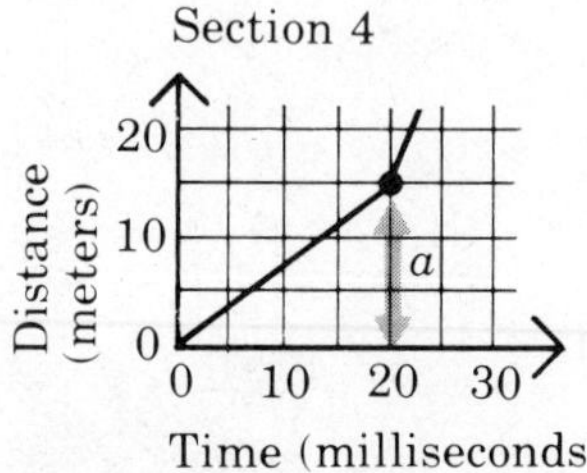

12. What were total sales for the first six weeks for the Super Thrift?
$302,000

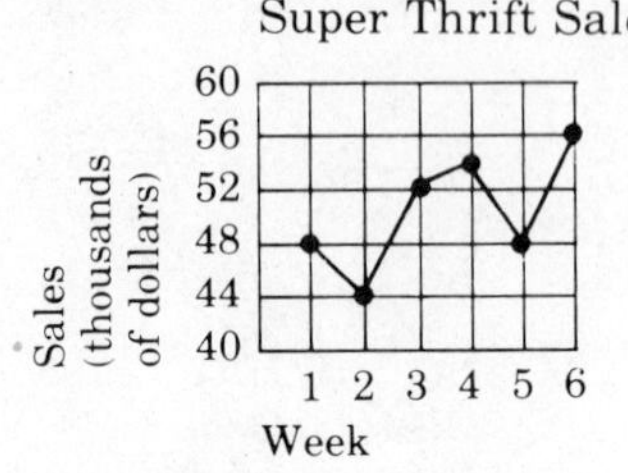

See pages 37–38 of the *Test Masters* for an alternate form of the Chapter 15 Test.
For a test on Unit 5, see pages T64–T65 of this book and pages 39–40 of the *Test Masters*.

SKILLS TUNE-UP

Multiplying and Dividing Fractions and Mixed Numbers, pages 149–160

1. $\frac{3}{5} \times \frac{7}{8}$ $\frac{21}{40}$
2. $\frac{4}{9} \times \frac{3}{16}$ $\frac{1}{12}$
3. $\frac{7}{8} \times \frac{1}{2}$ $\frac{7}{16}$
4. $\frac{3}{5} \times \frac{1}{2} \times \frac{5}{6}$ $\frac{1}{4}$
5. $6 \times \frac{6}{7}$ $5\frac{1}{7}$
6. $\frac{7}{8} \times 24$ 21
7. $\frac{5}{7} \times 1\frac{5}{9}$ $1\frac{1}{9}$
8. $1\frac{14}{25} \times 15$ $23\frac{2}{5}$
9. $1\frac{5}{9} \times 3\frac{3}{14}$ 5
10. $1\frac{1}{4} \times 5\frac{1}{2}$ $6\frac{7}{8}$
11. $\frac{20}{21} \times \frac{3}{8} \times 1\frac{7}{10}$ $\frac{17}{28}$
12. $5\frac{2}{7} \times \frac{2}{3} \times \frac{7}{8}$ $3\frac{1}{12}$
13. $\frac{27}{56} \times \frac{35}{36}$ $\frac{15}{32}$
14. $7 \div \frac{2}{3}$ $10\frac{1}{2}$
15. $\frac{3}{8} \div 2$ $\frac{3}{16}$
16. $17\frac{1}{2} \div 7$ $2\frac{1}{2}$
17. $1\frac{1}{4} \div 7\frac{1}{2}$ $\frac{1}{6}$
18. $9\frac{3}{4} \div 3\frac{1}{2}$ $2\frac{11}{14}$
19. $7 \div 1\frac{2}{5}$ 5

Percent, pages 235–246

Write each percent as a decimal.

1. 9% 0.09
2. 35% 0.35
3. 92.1% 0.921
4. 0.35% 0.0035
5. 6.24% 0.0624
6. 0.1% 0.001
7. 27% 0.27
8. $5\frac{1}{4}$% 0.0525

Write each decimal as a percent.

9. 0.04 4%
10. 0.923 92.3%
11. $0.37\frac{1}{2}$ $37\frac{1}{2}$%
12. 2.36 236%
13. 0.79 79%
14. 0.243 24.3%
15. 0.8 80%
16. 0.03 3%

Write each percent as a fraction in lowest terms.

17. 6% $\frac{3}{50}$
18. 25% $\frac{1}{4}$
19. $\frac{1}{2}$% $\frac{1}{200}$
20. 124% $1\frac{6}{25}$
21. 8% $\frac{2}{25}$
22. $66\frac{2}{3}$% $\frac{2}{3}$
23. 13% $\frac{13}{100}$
24. 75% $\frac{3}{4}$

Write each fraction as a percent.

25. $\frac{3}{5}$ 60%
26. $\frac{5}{8}$ $62\frac{1}{2}$%
27. $\frac{5}{4}$ 125%
28. $\frac{1}{200}$ $\frac{1}{2}$%
29. $\frac{5}{6}$ $83\frac{1}{3}$%
30. $\frac{4}{7}$ $57\frac{1}{7}$%
31. $\frac{9}{16}$ $56\frac{1}{4}$%
32. $\frac{3}{2}$ 150%
33. $\frac{1}{6}$ $16\frac{2}{3}$%
34. $\frac{3}{8}$ $37\frac{1}{2}$%

Percent, pages 235–246

1. Find 5% of 52. 2.6
2. Find 81% of 40. 32.4
3. Find 8% of 85. 6.8
4. Find 25% of 84. 21
5. Find $33\frac{1}{3}$% of 24. 8
6. Find 125% of 40. 50
7. 24 is what percent of 40? 60%
8. 27 is what percent of 135? 20%
9. 9 is what percent of 45? 20%
10. 86 is what percent of 200? 43%
11. 5 is what percent of 12? $41\frac{2}{3}$%
12. 6 is what percent of 72? $8\frac{1}{3}$%
13. 3 is 6% of what number? 50
14. 76 is 80% of what number? 95
15. 66 is 20% of what number? 330
16. 3 is $12\frac{1}{2}$% of what number? 24
17. 42 is $16\frac{2}{3}$% of what number? 252
18. 54 is 25% of what number? 216

CALCULATOR APPLICATIONS

Laba's Sport Store is having a sale.

All bicycles are on sale at a 20% discount. If there is a 5% sales tax, what is the total cost of a bicycle that regularly sells for $168.99?

Round the amount saved and the sales tax to the nearest cent.

$0.20 \times 168.99 \approx 33.80$	Amount saved
$168.99 - 33.80 = 135.19$	Sale price
$0.05 \times 135.19 \approx 6.76$	Sales tax
$135.19 + 6.76 = 141.95$	Total cost

The total cost of the bicycle is $141.95.

> **Calculator Suggestion:** If your calculator has a [%] key, try this key sequence.
>
> Press: 168.99 [−] 20 [%] [=] [+] 5 [%] [=]
>
> Display: 141.9516
>
> Answer: $141.95
>
> If your display does not show 141.9516, consult the instruction book for your calculator to find out how the percent key works. Notice that when this key sequence is used, all you need to round is the number in the display.

Find the total cost of each item. There is a 5% sales tax on all goods.

1. 10-speed bicycle
   Regular price: $295.75
   Discount: 20%
   $248.43
2. Bicycle tire
   Regular price: $49.95
   Discount: 15%
   $44.58
3. 1 pair of skis
   Regular price: $195.95
   Discount: 25%
   $154.31
4. Tent
   Regular price: $275.99
   Discount: 10%
   $260.81
5. Back pack
   Regular price: $53.99
   Discount: 20%
   $45.35
6. Camp stove
   Regular price: $12.49
   Discount: 15%
   $11.15
7. Running shoes
   Regular price: $28.50
   Discount: 10%
   $26.93
8. Warm-up suit
   Regular price: $65.95
   Discount: 30%
   $48.47
9. Tennis racket
   Regular price: $45.95
   Discount: 15%
   $41.01

Find each answer. There is a 5% sales tax on all goods.

10. A bicycle team bought 7 competition racing bicycles at a 25% discount. The regular price for each bicycle was $695.98. How much did the team pay for all these bicycles?
    $3836.59
11. A community group bought camping equipment that regularly sells for $1365.75 and ten bicycles that regularly sell for $175 each. They were given a 15% discount on the camping equipment and a 25% discount on the bicycles. What was the total amount that the group spent?
    $2597.06

COMPUTER LITERACY

The INT Function

INT(X) is the greatest integer function. The greatest integer in a number, X, is that greatest integer which is less than or equal to X. Some examples are:

INT(6) = 6	INT(0.009) = 0
INT(2.34) = 2	INT(8/3) = 2
INT(3.689) = 3	

Examine these sentences and the reason each is true or false.

INT(6.09) = 6	True by definition
INT(9.89) = 10	False because 10 is an integer greater than 9.89
INT(10/5) = 10/5	True because 10/5 = 2 and INT(2) = 2
INT(7/6) = 7/6	False because INT(7/6) = INT(1.1666) = 1 and $1 \neq 1.1666$

In line 20 of Program A, the values for X are tested using the INT function to determine which numbers from 1 to 28 are multiples of 4.

Program A

Input	Output
`10 FOR X=1 TO 28`	4
`20 IF INT(X/4)=X/4 THEN 50`	8
`30 NEXT X`	12
`40 GO TO 70`	16
`50 PRINT X`	20
`60 GO TO 30`	24
`70 END`	28

4.
```
10 INPUT N
20 IF N=0 THEN 80
30 IF INT(N/5)=N/5 THEN 60
40 PRINT N;"IS NOT A MULTIPLE OF 5."
50 GO TO 10
60 PRINT N;"IS A MULTIPLE OF 5."
70 GO TO 10
80 END
```

Give the output for each program.

1. Use 3, 6, 10, 15, 24, 25, and 0 for X.
See Additional Answers on page T53.
```
10 INPUT X
20 IF X=0 THEN 80
30 IF INT(X/2)=X/2 THEN 60
40 PRINT X;"IS AN ODD NUMBER."
50 GO TO 10
60 PRINT X;"IS AN EVEN NUMBER."
70 GO TO 10
80 END
```

2. Use 24, 36, 41, 64, 120, and 0 for N.
See Additional Answers on page T53.
```
10 INPUT N
20 IF N=0 THEN 90
30 PRINT "DIVISORS OF";N;"ARE:"
40 FOR D=1 TO N
50 IF INT(N/D)<>N/D THEN 70
60 PRINT D
70 NEXT D
80 GO TO 10
90 END
```

3. Use A = 12, B = 3; A = 15, B = 6; A = 51, B = 3; A = 63, B = 12; A = 0.
See Additional Answers on page T54.
```
10 INPUT A
20 IF A=0 THEN 90
30 INPUT B
40 IF INT(A/B)=A/B THEN 70
50 PRINT A;"IS NOT A MULTIPLE OF";B
60 GO TO 10
70 PRINT A;"IS A MULTIPLE OF";B
80 GO TO 10
90 END
```

4. Write a program that will test if a number is a multiple of 5.
Answers may vary. A sample program is given at left.
5. Write a program that will test if a number is divisible by 2 and 3.
See Additional Answers on page T54.

UNIT SIX Geometry and Right-Triangle Relations

CHAPTER 16 Perimeter and Area

SKILLS PRETEST

Number of test items - 11

Number missed	1	2	3	4	5
Percent correct	91	82	73	64	55

SKILL Finding Perimeter of a Geometric Figure *pages 352–353*

A Find the perimeter of this polygon.
35 m

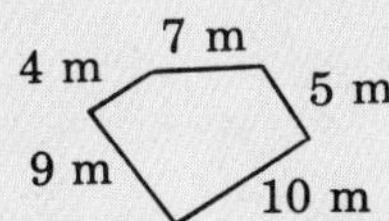

B Find the perimeter of this rectangle.
50 cm

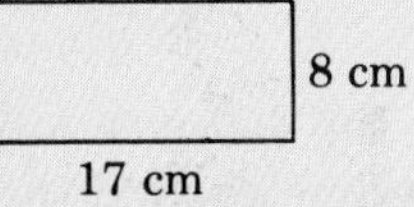

SKILL Finding Circumference of a Circle *pages 354–355*

C Find the circumference of this circle.
53.38 m

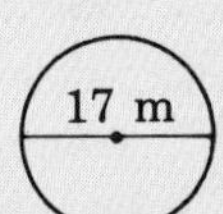

D Find the circumference of this circle.
56.52 m

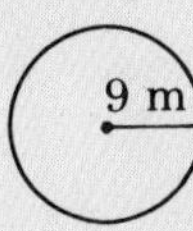

SKILL Finding Area of a Rectangle, a Square, and a Parallelogram *pages 356–357*

E Find the area of this rectangle.
35.84 cm²

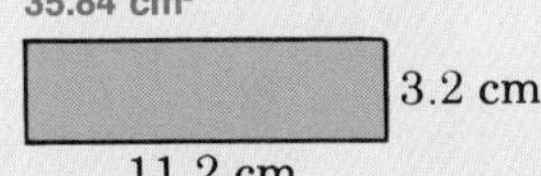

F Find the area of this square.
23.04 mm²

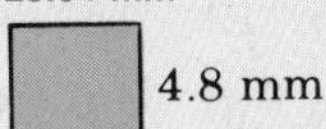

G Find the area of this parallelogram.
200 m²

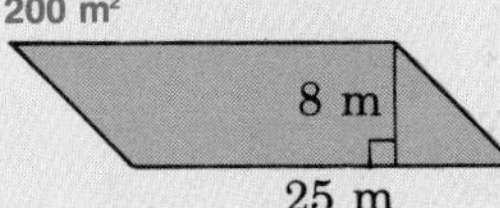

SKILL Finding Area of a Triangle and a Trapezoid *pages 358–359*

H Find the area of this triangle.
600 cm²

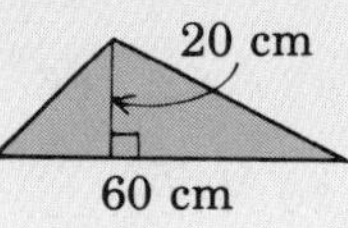

I Find the area of this trapezoid.
29.4 cm²

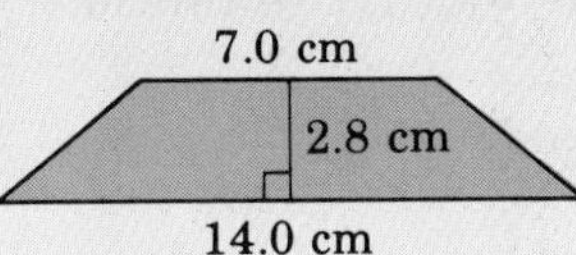

SKILL Finding Area of a Circle *pages 360–361*

J Find the area of this circle.
113.04 m²

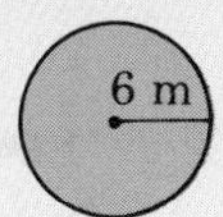

K Find the area of this circle.
452.16 cm²

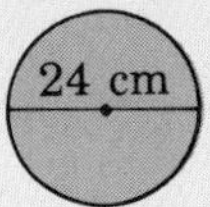

See page T43 for additional notes on Chapter 16.

Objective: Find the perimeter of a geometric figure.

Finding Perimeter of a Geometric Figure

Example A

Polygon, when given the measures of all sides

Find the perimeter of this polygon.

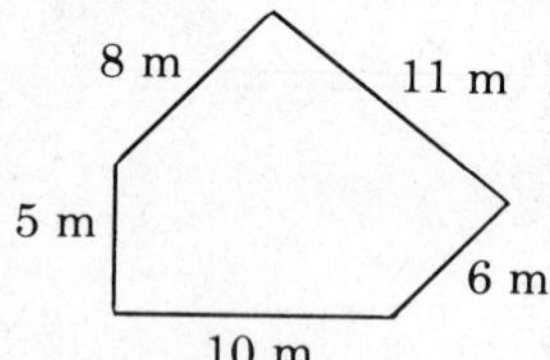

Perimeter is the distance around a **polygon.** To find the perimeter, add the lengths of the sides.

$P = 11 + 6 + 10 + 5 + 8$

$P = 40$

The perimeter is 40 m.

Example B

Rectangle, when given the length and the width

Find the perimeter of this rectangle.

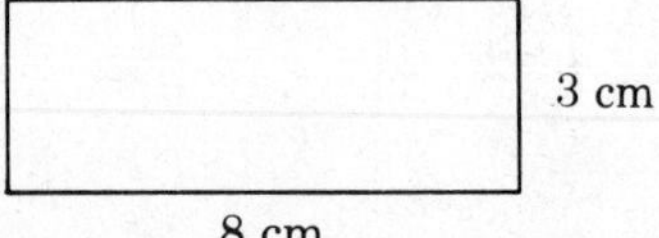

The perimeter of a rectangle is twice the length plus twice the width. Use this formula.

$P = 2l + 2w$

$P = 2(8) + 2(3)$

$P = 16 + 6$

$P = 22$

The perimeter is 22 cm.

Exercises

Set A

Find the perimeter of each polygon. All measures are given in centimeters.

1.
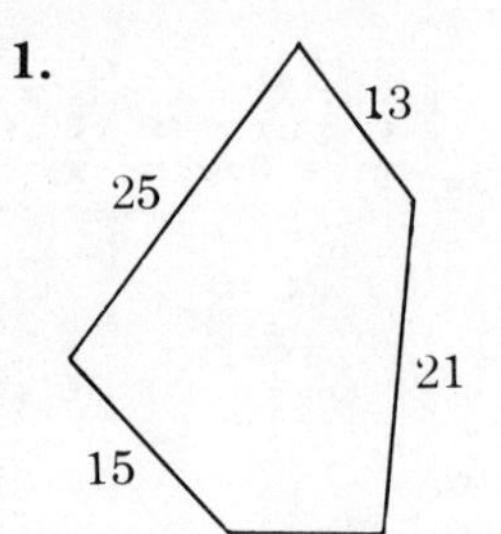

84 cm

3.
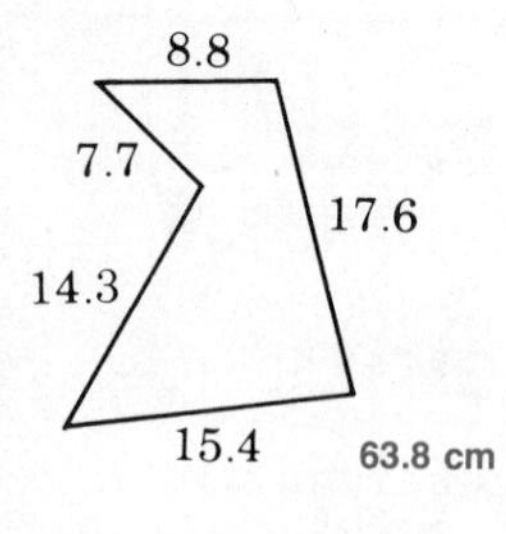

63.8 cm

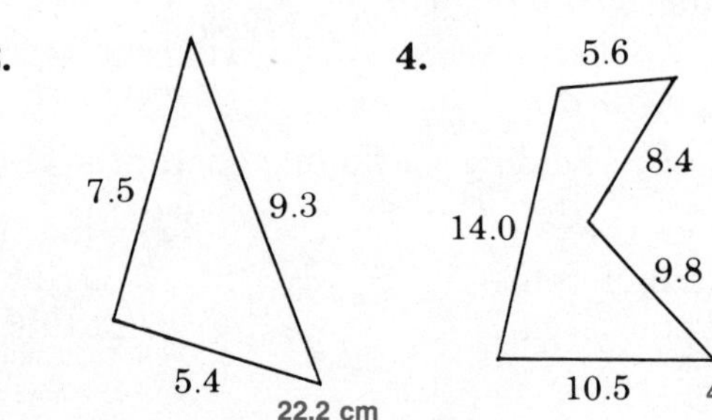

2. 22.2 cm

4. 48.3 cm

Find the perimeter of each polygon. Use these dimensions for the sides. All measures are given in meters.

5. 12 15 44 28 — 99 m
6. 30 17 39 41 — 127 m
7. 5.6 12.0 8.8 — 26.4 m
8. 39 27 62 18 — 146 m
9. 76 42 68 35 47 — 268 m
10. 63 58 49 52 86 — 308 m
11. 0.91 0.84 0.35 — 2.1 m
12. 5.4 9.0 4.5 7.2 9.9 — 36 m
13. 146 234 197 168 203 — 948 m
14. 27.5 15.2 12.8 20.9 24.6 — 101 m
15. 2.17 1.93 1.85 1.94 1.79 2.06 — 11.74 m

Set B

Find the perimeter of each rectangle. All measures are given in centimeters.

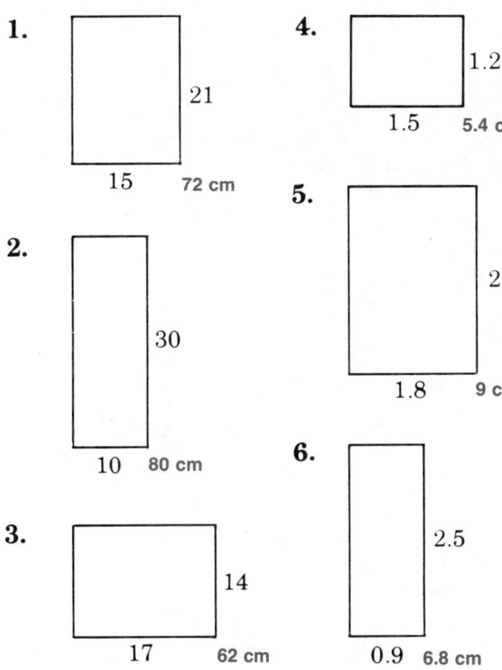

Find the perimeter of each rectangle. Use these dimensions.

	Length	Width	
7.	23 mm	15 mm	76 mm
8.	28 cm	22 cm	100 cm
9.	47 mm	34 mm	162 mm
10.	15.4 m	4.8 m	40.4 m
11.	30.3 m	27.8 m	116.2 m
12.	186 mm	97 mm	566 mm
13.	223 cm	166 cm	778 cm
14.	7.37 m	6.96 m	28.66 m
15.	16.39 m	11.04 m	54.86 m

BREAK TIME

At a track meet, Janice, Machiko, and Virginia ran a 50-meter dash.

Virginia did not come in second, and Machiko did not come in third.

Virginia's time was two seconds faster than that of the oldest girl in the race.

In what order did the girls finish the race?
First: Virginia
Second: Machiko
Third: Janice

Objective: Find the circumference of a circle.

Finding Circumference of a Circle

Example C Given the diameter

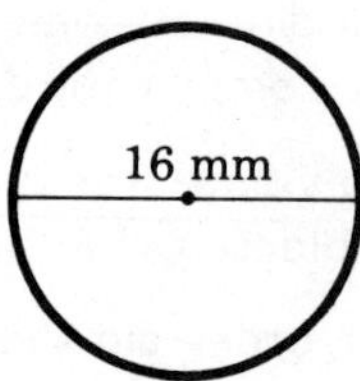

Find the circumference of this circle. The diameter is 16 mm.

The **circumference** is the distance around a circle.

The circumference is π (pi) times the **diameter.** π is approximately equal to 3.14. Use this formula.

$C = \pi d$

$C \approx 3.14 \times 16$

$C \approx 50.24$

The circumference is 50.24 mm.

Example D Given the radius

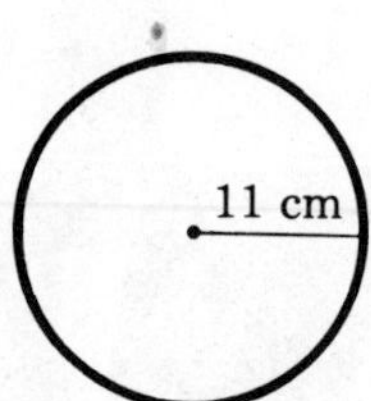

Find the circumference of this circle. The radius is 11 cm.

Since the diameter is twice the **radius,** you can use this formula.

$C = 2\pi r$

$C \approx 2 \times 3.14 \times 11$

$C \approx 69.08$

The circumference is 69.08 cm.

Exercises

Set C

Find the circumference of each circle.

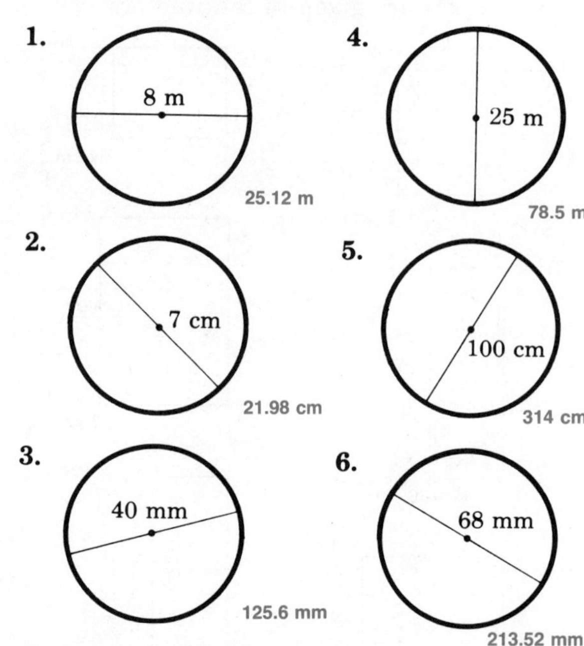

Find the circumference of each circle. Use the given dimension for the diameter.

7. 10 cm 31.4 cm
8. 50 mm 157 mm
9. 90 m 282.6 m
10. 200 mm 628 mm
11. 400 m 1256 m
12. 700 cm 2198 cm
13. 99 mm 310.86 mm
14. 15 mm 47.1 mm
15. 37 cm 116.18 cm
16. 19 km 59.66 km
17. 42 m 131.88 m
18. 61 cm 191.54 cm
19. 75 cm 235.5 cm
20. 22 km 69.08 km
21. 160 km 502.4 km
22. 280 m 879.2 m
23. 350 cm 1099 cm
24. 110 mm 345.4 mm
25. 960 mm 3014.4 mm
26. 570 cm 1789.8 cm
27. 680 m 2135.2 m
28. 890 km 2794.6 km

PROBLEM SOLVING
The applications on pages 366–367 may be used anytime after this lesson.

Set D

Find the circumference of each circle.

1.

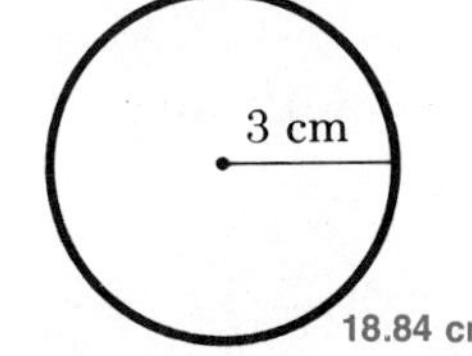

18.84 cm

2.

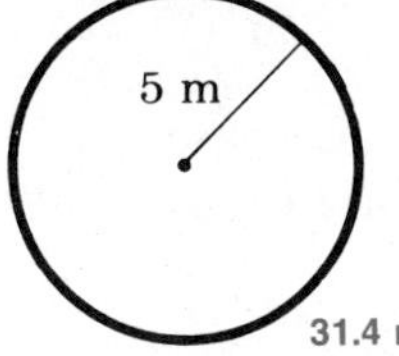

31.4 m

3.

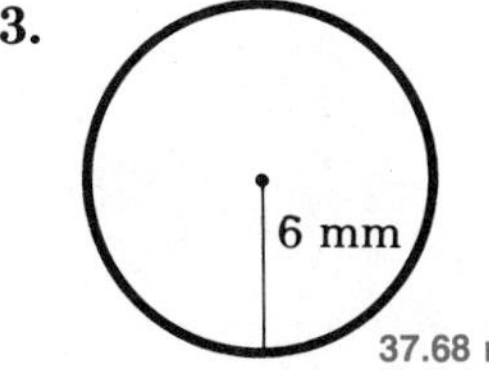

37.68 mm

4.

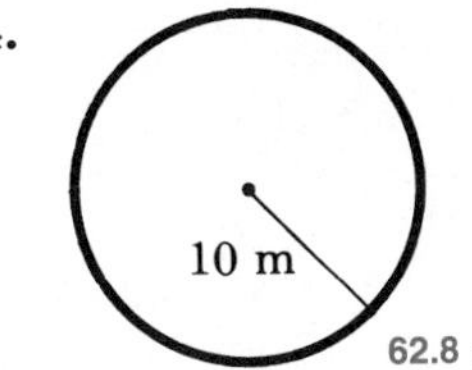

62.8 m

5.

75.36 cm

6.

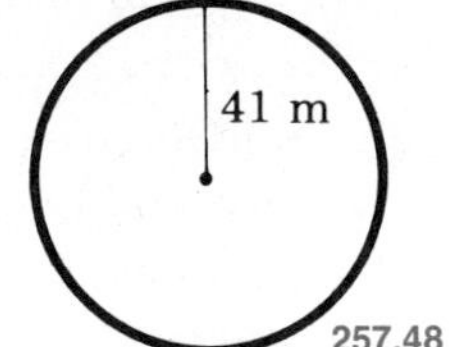

257.48 m

7.

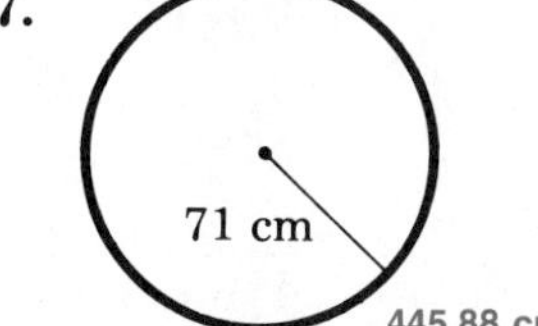

445.88 cm

8.

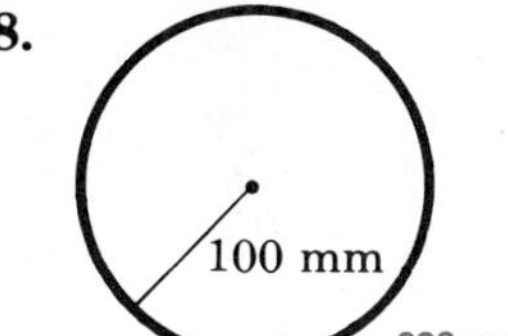

628 mm

Find the circumference of each circle.
Use the given dimension for the radius.

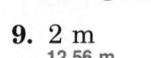

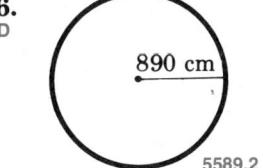

9. 2 m
12.56 m

10. 4 cm
25.12 cm

11. 7 km
43.96 km

12. 20 cm
125.6 cm

13. 50 m
314 m

14. 80 mm
502.4 mm

15. 90 cm
565.2 cm

16. 300 mm
1884 mm

17. 600 mm
3768 mm

18. 900 mm
5652 mm

19. 15 km
94.2 km

20. 38 cm
238.64 cm

21. 92 cm
577.76 cm

22. 120 mm
753.6 mm

23. 740 cm
4647.2 cm

24. 560 mm
3516.8 mm

Mixed Practice

Find the circumference of each circle.

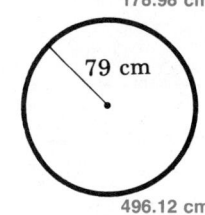

1. C

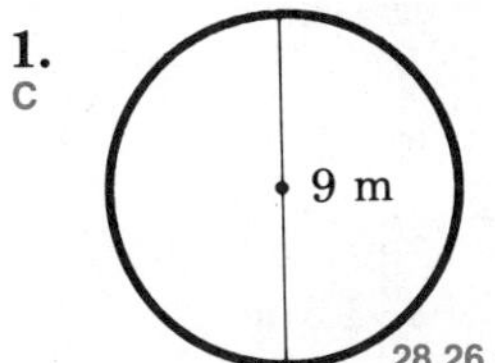

28.26 m

2. D

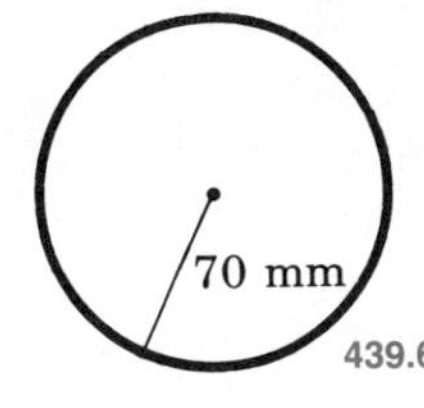

439.6 mm

3. C

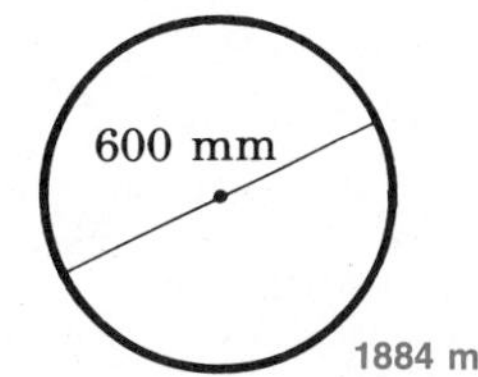

1884 mm

4. D

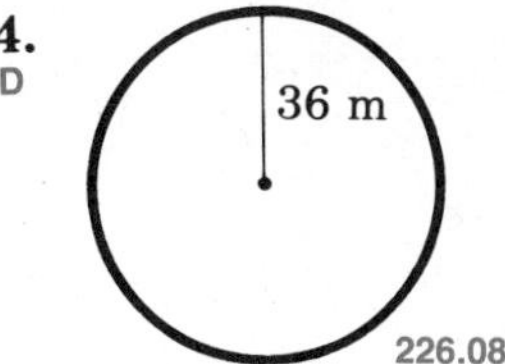

226.08 m

5. C

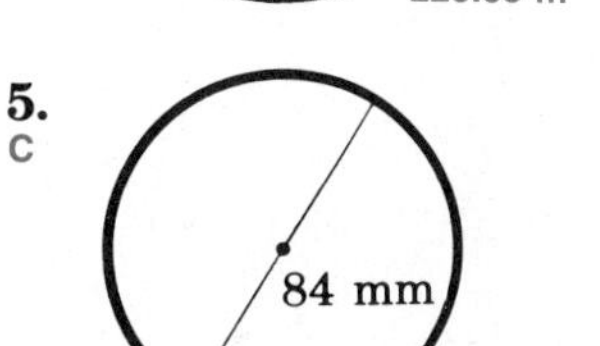

263.76 mm

6. D

890 cm

5589.2 cm

7. D

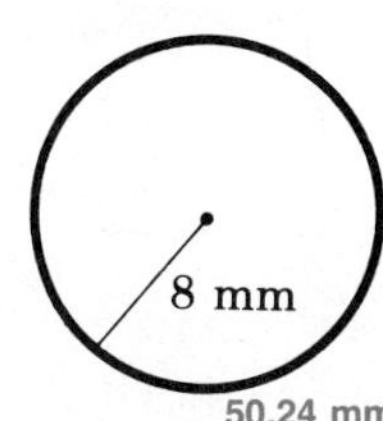

50.24 mm

8. C

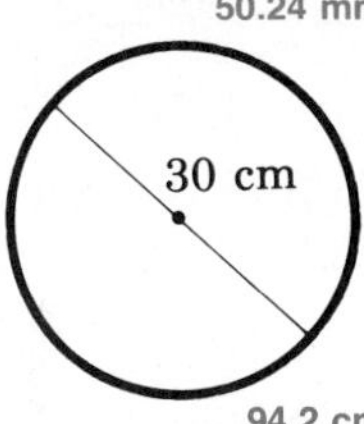

94.2 cm

9. D

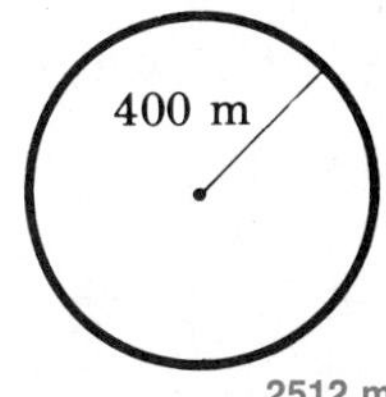

2512 m

10. C

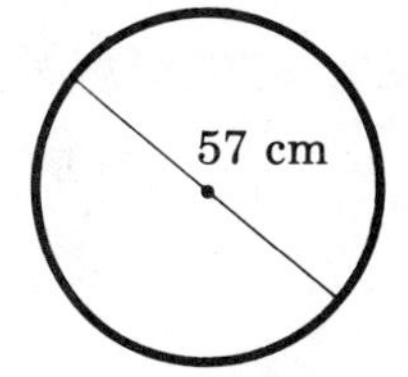

178.98 cm

11. D

79 cm

496.12 cm

12. C

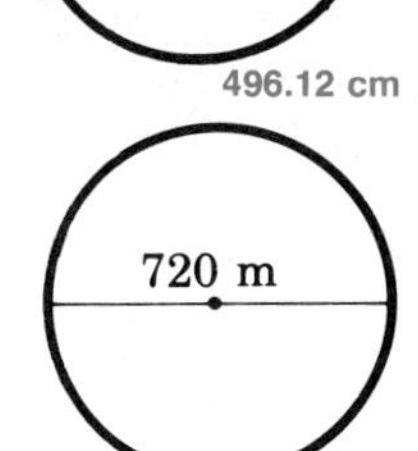

2260.8 m

Objective: Find the area of a rectangle, a square, and a parallelogram.

SKILL Finding Area of a Rectangle, a Square, and a Parallelogram

Example E Rectangle, when given the length and the width

Find the area of this rectangle.

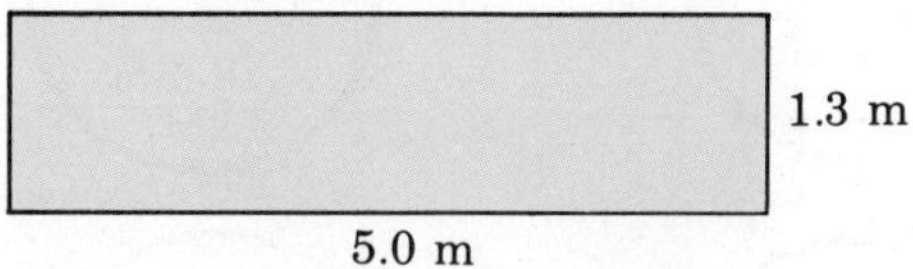

To find the **area** of a rectangle, multiply the length times the width. Use this formula.

$A = lw$

$A = 5.0 \times 1.3$

$A = 6.5$

The area is 6.5 square meters (6.5 m^2).

Example F Square, when given the measure of a side

Find the area of this square.

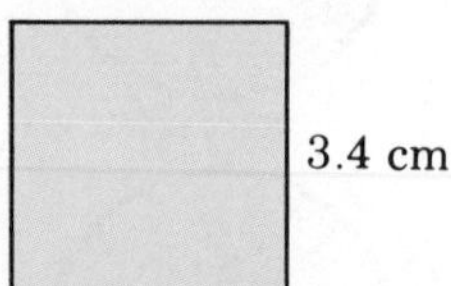

To find the area of a square, multiply the length of one side by itself. Use this formula.

$A = s^2$ s^2 is read "s squared" and means $s \times s$.

$A = (3.4)^2$

$A = 3.4 \times 3.4$

$A = 11.56$

The area is 11.56 cm^2.

Example G Parallelogram, when given the height and the base

Find the area of this **parallelogram.**

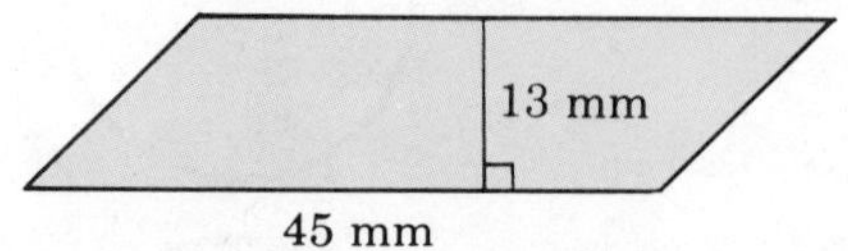

To find the area of a parallelogram, multiply the base times the height. Use this formula.

$A = bh$

$A = 45 \times 13$

$A = 585$

The area is 585 mm^2.

PROBLEM SOLVING
The applications on pages 363–365 may be used anytime after this lesson.

Exercises

Set E

Find the area of each rectangle.

1. 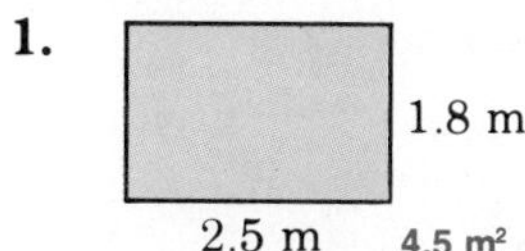

2. 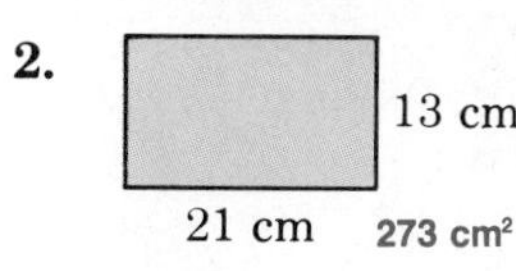

3. 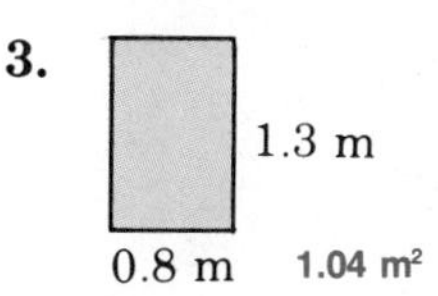

Find the area of each rectangle. Use these dimensions.

	Length	Width	
4.	12 mm	10 mm	120 mm²
5.	10.0 cm	8.4 cm	84 cm²
6.	1.5 m	0.7 m	1.05 m²
7.	2.6 cm	0.9 cm	2.34 cm²
8.	4.5 cm	3.6 cm	16.2 cm²
9.	0.52 m	0.06 m	0.0312 m²
10.	0.38 m	0.14 m	0.0532 m²
11.	1.07 m	0.96 m	1.0272 m²
12.	2.9 cm	0.7 cm	2.03 cm²
13.	4.09 cm	2.70 cm	11.043 cm²
14.	7.16 m	3.80 m	27.208 m²
15.	24.8 mm	16.2 mm	401.76 mm²
16.	57.6 m	34.5 m	1987.2 m²

Set F

Find the area of each square.

1. 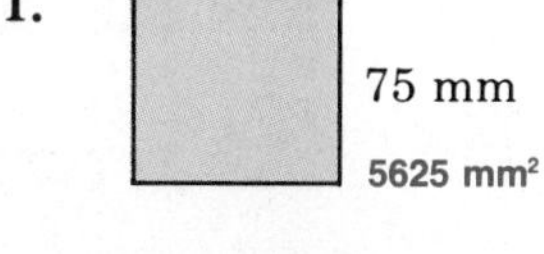

2. 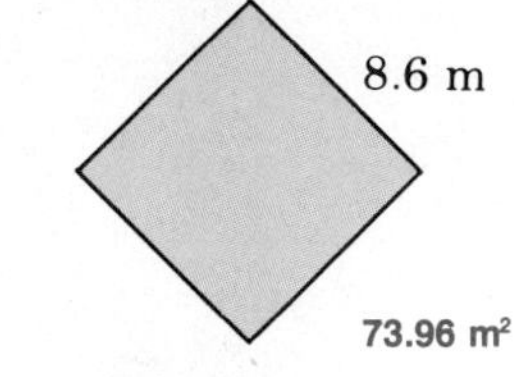

3. 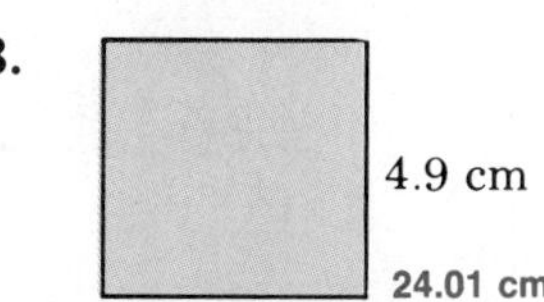

Find the area of each square. Use these dimensions.

	Side	
4.	10 mm	100 mm²
5.	15 mm	225 mm²
6.	1.8 cm	3.24 cm²
7.	2.5 m	6.25 m²
8.	3.8 cm	14.44 cm²
9.	12.1 cm	146.41 cm²
10.	0.48 m	0.2304 m²
11.	0.92 m	0.8464 m²
12.	7.6 cm	57.76 cm²
13.	4.12 m	16.9744 m²
14.	1.7 cm	2.89 cm²
15.	9.46 mm	89.4916 mm²

Set G

Find the area of each parallelogram.

1. 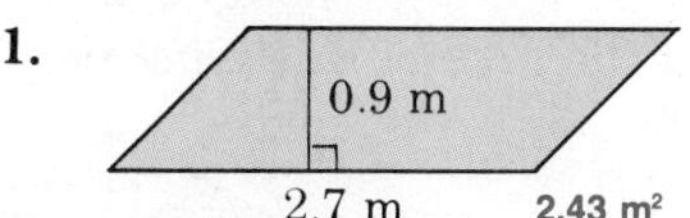

2. 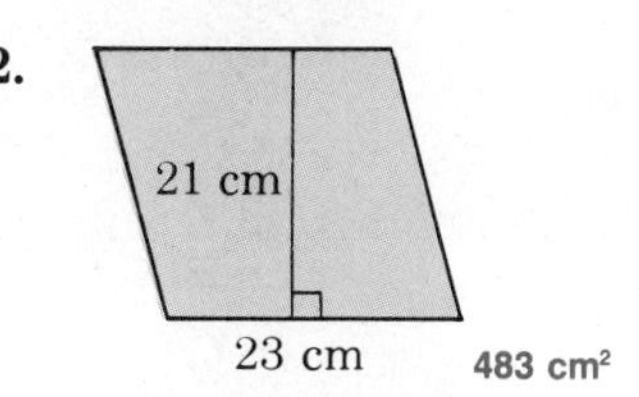

3. 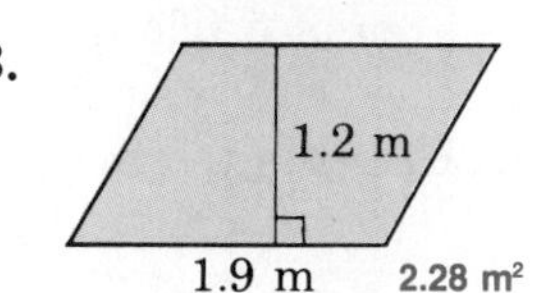

Find the area of each parallelogram. Use these dimensions.

	Base	Height	
4.	18 mm	10 mm	180 mm²
5.	25 mm	30 mm	750 mm²
6.	2.3 cm	0.9 cm	2.07 cm²
7.	1.7 m	0.6 m	1.02 m²
8.	0.5 m	0.8 m	0.4 m²
9.	5.8 cm	2.4 cm	13.92 cm²
10.	0.75 m	0.38 m	0.285 m²
11.	2.38 m	0.74 m	1.7612 m²
12.	1.6 m	0.8 m	1.28 m²
13.	5.49 m	2.16 m	11.8584 m²
14.	26.1 cm	18.3 cm	477.63 cm²
15.	79.8 cm	45.2 cm	3606.96 cm²

Objective: Find the area of a triangle and a trapezoid.

Finding Area of a Triangle and a Trapezoid

Example H Triangle, when given the height and the base

Find the area of this triangle.

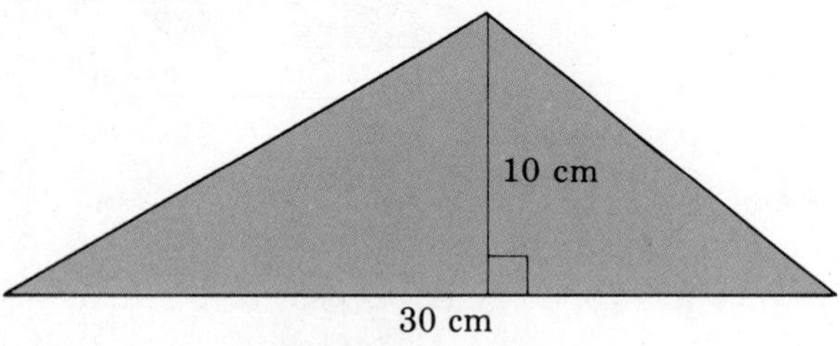

To find the area of a triangle, multiply $\frac{1}{2}$ times the base times the height. Use this formula.

$A = \frac{1}{2}bh$

$A = \frac{1}{2} \times 30 \times 10$

$A = 150$

The area is 150 cm^2.

Example I Trapezoid, when given the height and the measures of the top and bottom bases

Find the area of this trapezoid.

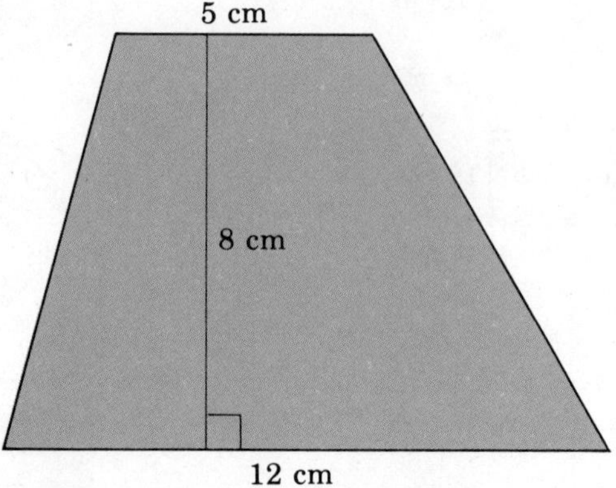

To find the area of a **trapezoid,** multiply $\frac{1}{2}$ times the height times the sum of the bases. Use this formula.

$A = \frac{1}{2}h(a + b)$

$A = \frac{1}{2} \times 8 \times (5 + 12)$

$A = \frac{1}{2} \times 8 \times 17$

$A = 4 \times 17$

$A = 68$

The area is 68 cm^2.

Exercises

Set H

Find the area of each triangle.

1.

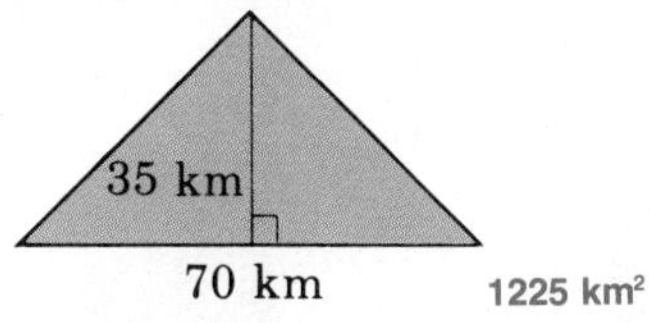

1225 km²

2.

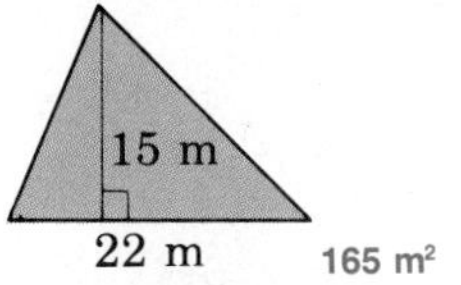

165 m²

3.

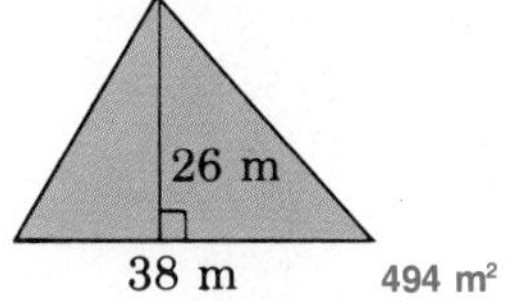

494 m²

Find the area of each triangle. Use these dimensions.

	Base	Height	
4.	7 km	4 km	14 km²
5.	27 mm	16 mm	216 mm²
6.	1.5 cm	1.0 cm	0.75 cm²
7.	25 mm	11 mm	137.5 mm²
8.	3.1 m	2.5 m	3.875 m²
9.	0.36 m	0.12 m	0.0216 m²
10.	1.5 cm	2.4 cm	1.8 cm²
11.	4.4 cm	3.8 cm	8.36 cm²
12.	10.5 cm	31.5 cm	165.375 cm²
13.	34.5 m	11.5 m	198.375 m²
14.	11.2 m	6.5 m	36.4 m²

Set I

Find the area of each trapezoid.

1.

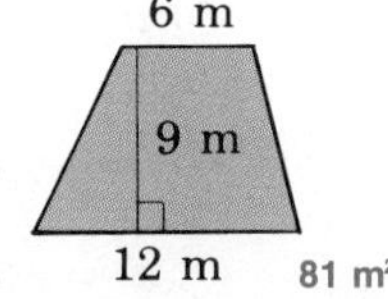

81 m²

2.

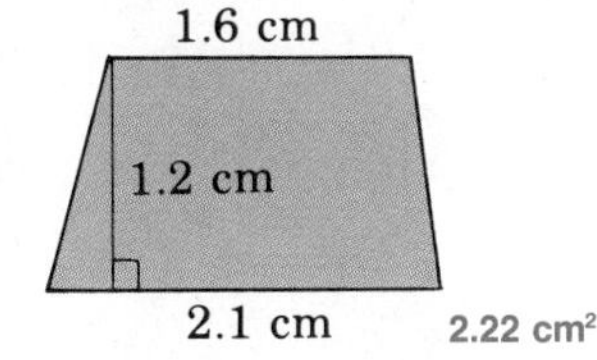

2.22 cm²

3.

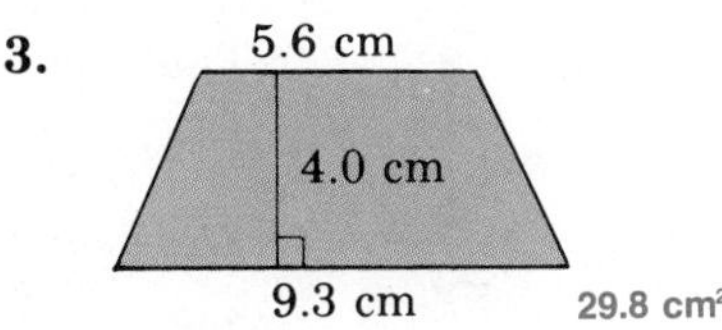

29.8 cm²

Find the area of each trapezoid. Use these dimensions. All measures are given in centimeters.

	Height	Base (a)	Base (b)	
4.	8	13	21	136 cm²
5.	2.0	1.5	2.5	4 cm²
6.	9.0	5.6	14.0	88.2 cm²
7.	6	8	19	81 cm²
8.	50	30	20	1250 cm²
9.	0.6	1.5	2.4	1.17 cm²
10.	2.0	2.0	3.5	5.5 cm²
11.	4.2	3.0	7.1	21.21 cm²
12.	2.5	2.0	4.0	7.5 cm²

BREAK TIME

Fill in the missing digits.

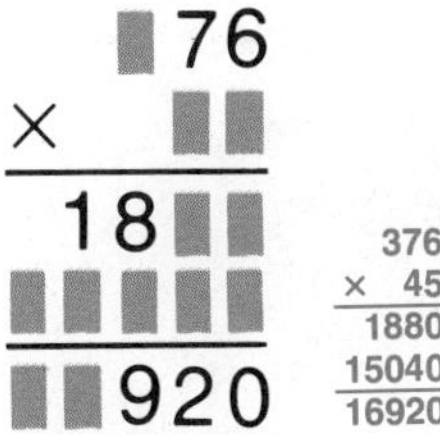

376
× 45
1880
15040
16920

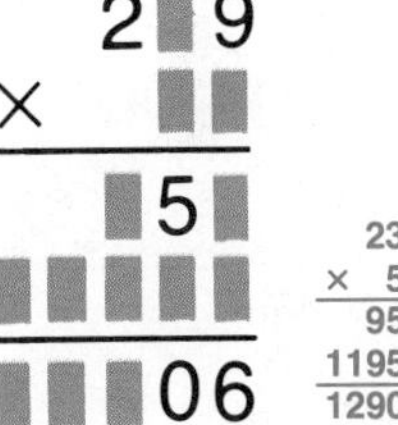

239
× 54
956
11950
12906

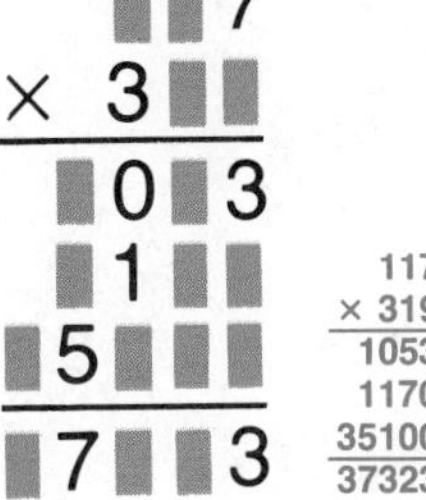

117
× 319
1053
1170
35100
37323

Objective: Find the area of a circle.

SKILL Finding Area of a Circle

Example J Given the radius

Find the area of this circle.

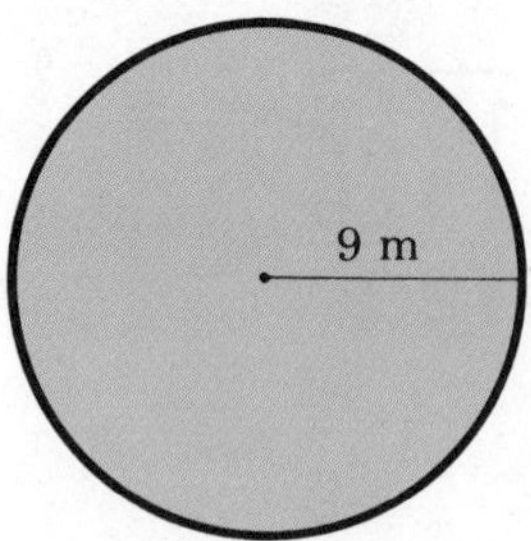

To find the area of a circle, multiply π times the radius squared. Use this formula.

$A = \pi r^2$

$A \approx 3.14 \times 9^2$

$A \approx 3.14 \times 9 \times 9$

$A \approx 3.14 \times 81$

$A \approx 254.34$

The area is 254.34 m^2.

Example K Given the diameter

Find the area of this circle.

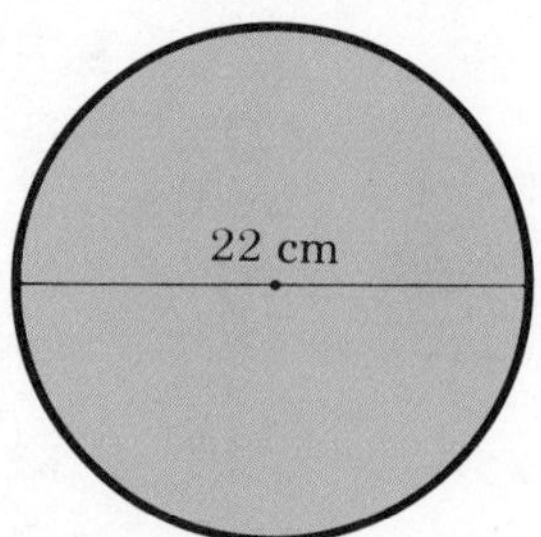

First, find the radius. It is half the diameter, or 11 centimeters. Then use the formula.

$A = \pi r^2$

$A \approx 3.14 \times 11^2$

$A \approx 3.14 \times 11 \times 11$

$A \approx 3.14 \times 121$

$A \approx 379.94$

The area is 379.94 cm^2.

PROBLEM SOLVING
The applications on pages 368–369 may be used anytime after this lesson.

Exercises

Set J

Find the area of each circle.

1. 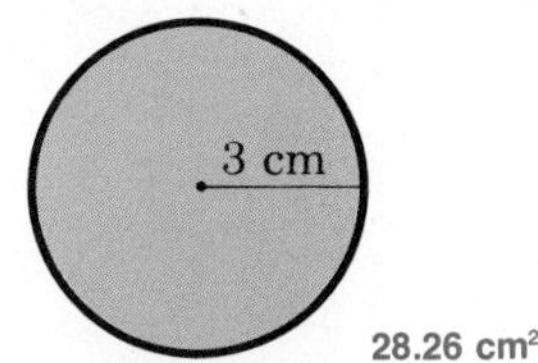

28.26 cm^2

2. 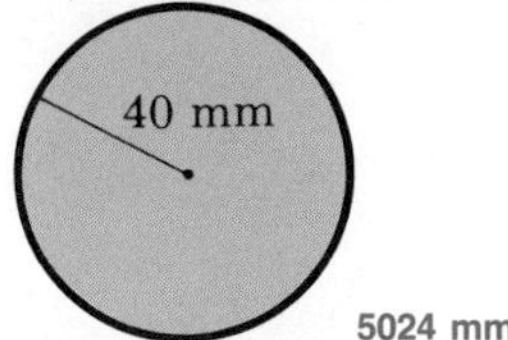

5024 mm^2

3. 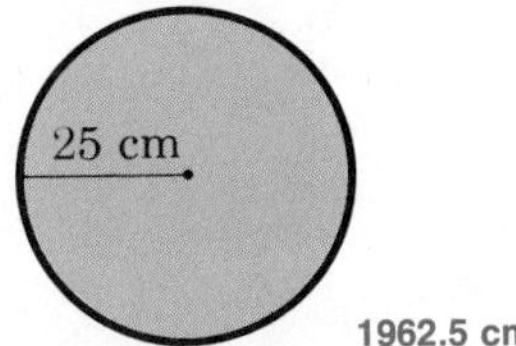

1962.5 cm^2

Find the area of each circle. Use the given dimension for the radius.

4. 6 mm
113.04 mm^2
5. 5 mm
78.5 mm^2
6. 2 km
12.56 km^2
7. 1 km
3.14 km^2
8. 7 m
153.86 m^2
9. 9 cm
254.34 cm^2
10. 10 mm
314 mm^2
11. 100 mm
31,400 mm^2
12. 80 mm
20,096 mm^2
13. 90 cm
25,434 cm^2
14. 40 cm
5024 cm^2
15. 30 m
2826 m^2
16. 60 cm
11,304 cm^2
17. 25 m
1962.5 m^2
18. 75 mm
17,662.5 mm^2
19. 21 mm
1384.74 mm^2
20. 54 mm
9156.24 mm^2
21. 39 cm
4775.94 cm^2
22. 78 cm
19,103.76 cm^2
23. 17 m
907.46 m^2
24. 32 cm
3215.36 cm^2
25. 64 mm
12,861.44 mm^2

Set K

Find the area of each circle.

1. 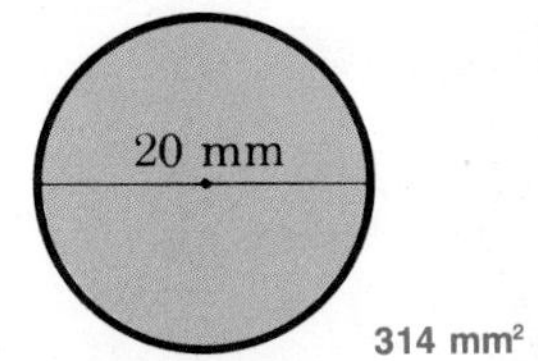

314 mm^2

2. 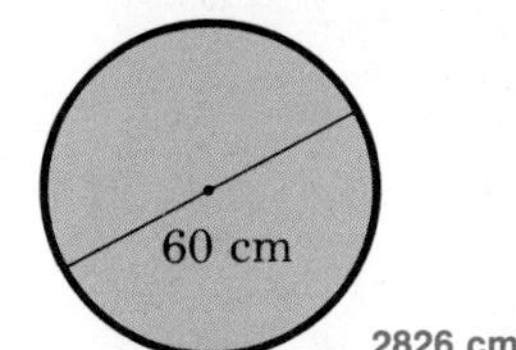

2826 cm^2

3. 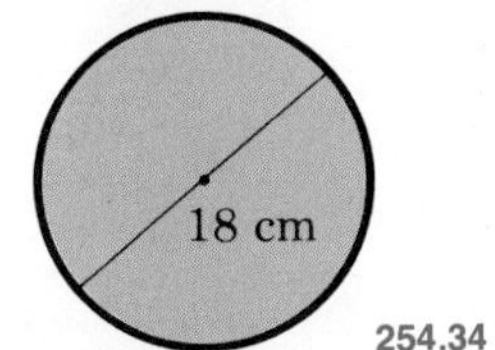

254.34 cm^2

4. 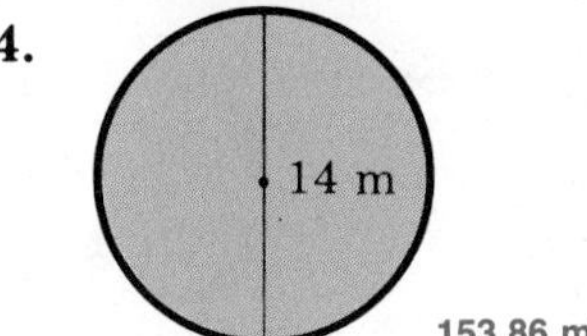

153.86 m^2

Find the area of each circle. Use the given dimension for the diameter.

5. 10 m
78.5 m^2
6. 4 m
12.56 m^2
7. 12 cm
113.04 cm^2
8. 8 mm
50.24 mm^2
9. 160 mm
20,096 mm^2
10. 100 mm
7850 mm^2
11. 200 mm
31,400 mm^2
12. 24 m
452.16 m^2
13. 46 mm
1661.06 mm^2
14. 32 cm
803.84 cm^2
15. 50 cm
1962.5 cm^2
16. 70 cm
3846.5 cm^2
17. 28 cm
615.44 cm^2
18. 36 mm
1017.36 mm^2

Mixed Practice

Find the area of each circle.

J 1. 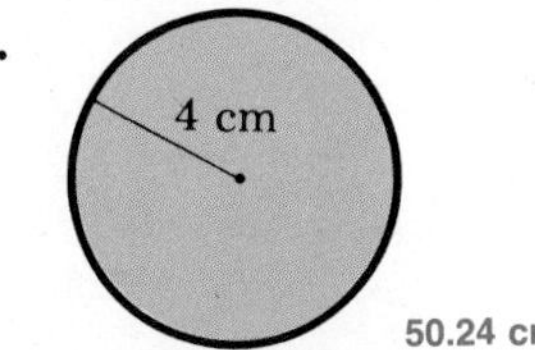

50.24 cm^2

K 2. 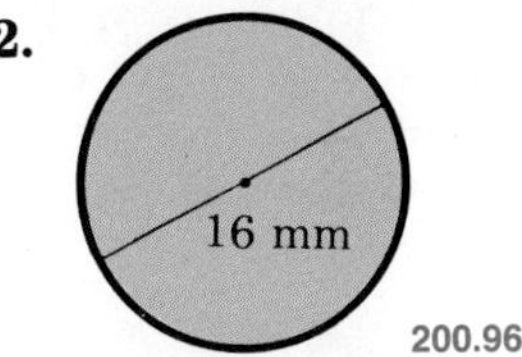

200.96 mm^2

J 3. 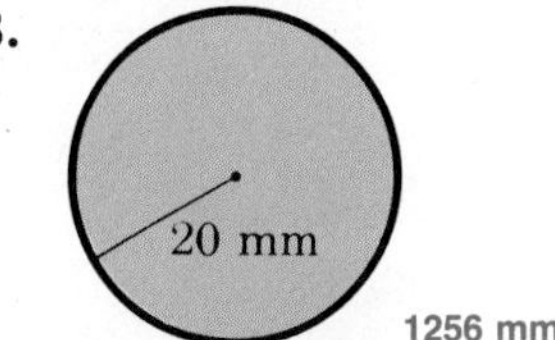

1256 mm^2

K 4. 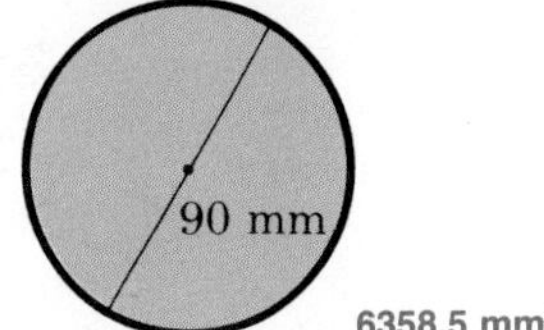

6358.5 mm^2

J 5. 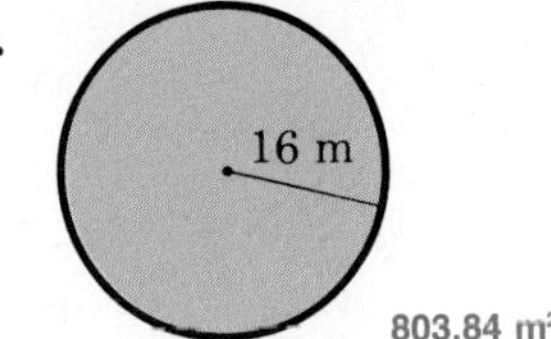

803.84 m^2

K 6. 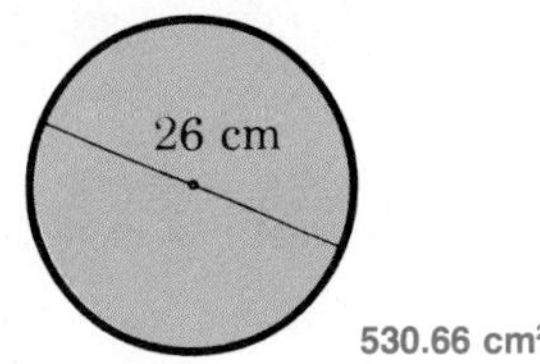

530.66 cm^2

SKILLS POSTTEST

Number of test items - 11

Number missed	1	2	3	4	5
Percent correct	91	82	73	64	55

SKILL Finding Perimeter of a Geometric Figure *pages 352–353*

A Find the perimeter of this polygon.
22 m

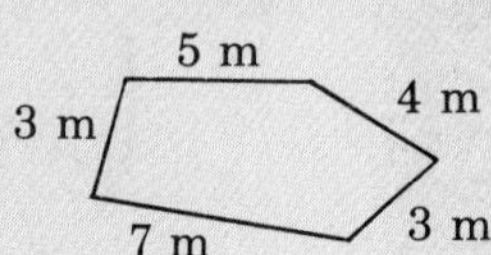

B Find the perimeter of this rectangle.
46 cm

8 cm
15 cm

SKILL Finding Circumference of a Circle *pages 354–355*

C Find the circumference of this circle.
40.82 m

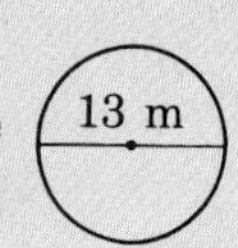

D Find the circumference of this circle.
43.96 m

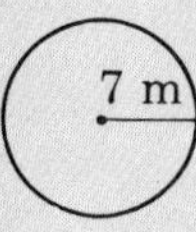

SKILL Finding Area of a Rectangle, a Square, and a Parallelogram *pages 356–357*

E Find the area of this rectangle.
46.08 cm^2

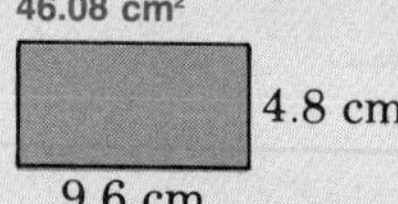

F Find the area of this square.
51.84 mm^2

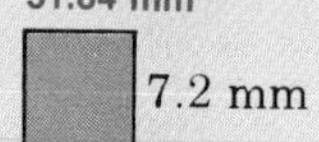

G Find the area of this parallelogram.
800 cm^2

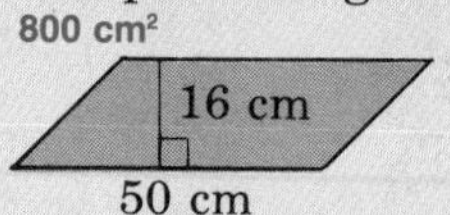

SKILL Finding Area of a Triangle and a Trapezoid *pages 358–359*

H Find the area of this triangle.
216 mm^2

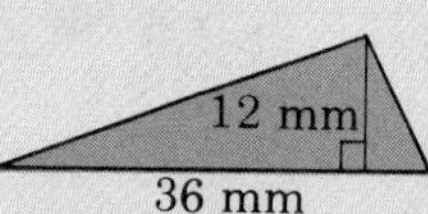

I Find the area of this trapezoid.
152 m^2

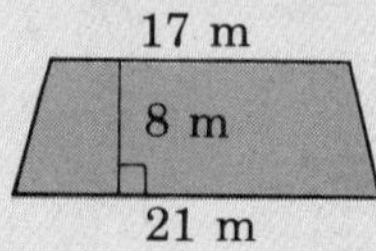

SKILL Finding Area of a Circle *pages 360–361*

J Find the area of this circle.
78.5 m^2

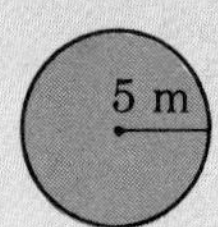

K Find the area of this circle.
615.44 cm^2

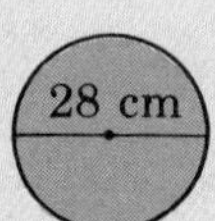

Problem Solving

CONSUMER APPLICATIONS

See pages 48–49 of *Problem-Solving Masters.*

Objective: Solve problems involving area.

In this lesson students find the actual length and width of a room by using a blueprint, then find the area of a room in square meters, and compute the cost of buying carpet for a room.

Buying Carpet

Susan and Dave Sanner are going to put textured carpeting in their dining room. They measured to find the length and width of each room. They wrote these measures on the blueprint.

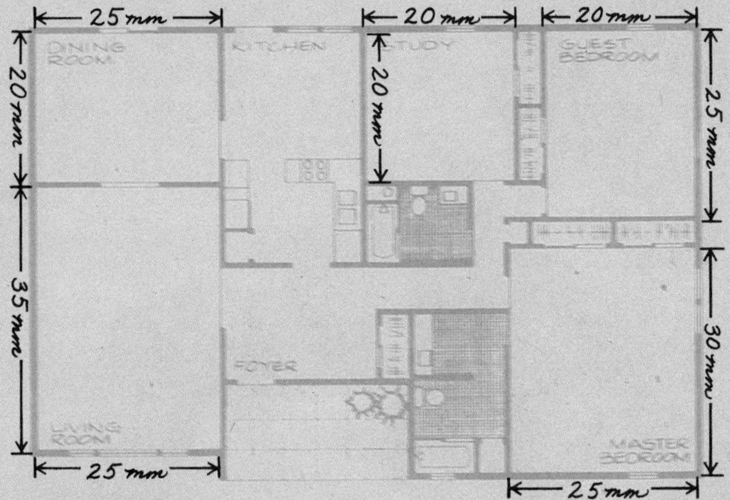

On this blueprint of their home, the length of the dining room is 25 millimeters and the width is 20 millimeters. 1 millimeter represents 0.2 meters. The Sanners multiplied by 0.2 to find the actual dimensions.

Actual length: 0.2×25, or 5 m

Actual width: 0.2×20, or 4 m

Then they multiplied the length and width to find the area, or the number of square meters.

Area: 5×4, or 20 m^2

Next, they multiplied to find the cost of carpeting the dining room at $11.63 per square meter.

Number of square meters		Price per square meter		Cost
20	×	$11.63	=	$232.60

The cost of putting textured carpeting in the dining room is $232.60.

Find the actual length and width of each room. Then find the area of each.

1. Living room
   5 m by 7 m; 35 m^2
2. Master bedroom
   5 m by 6 m; 30 m^2
3. Guest bedroom
   4 m by 5 m; 20 m^2
4. Study
   4 m by 4 m; 16 m^2

Find the cost of buying carpeting for each room in Problems 1–4 if the Sanners choose

5. plush carpeting at $12.79 per square meter.
   See below.
6. textured carpeting at $11.63 per square meter.
   See below.

	Living room	Master bedroom	Guest bedroom	Study
5.	$447.65	$383.70	$255.80	$204.64
6.	$407.05	$348.90	$232.60	$186.08

Problem Solving

CONSUMER APPLICATIONS

Objective: Solve problems involving area.

In this lesson students find the area of the entire property, area of the house, and area of the lawn in order to compute how much fertilizer to buy for a lawn.

Caring for a Lawn

Jean Stephens works hard to make her lawn attractive.

See page 50 of *Problem-Solving Masters.*

Jean uses this scale drawing of her property to help her find how much fertilizer she should buy for the lawn.

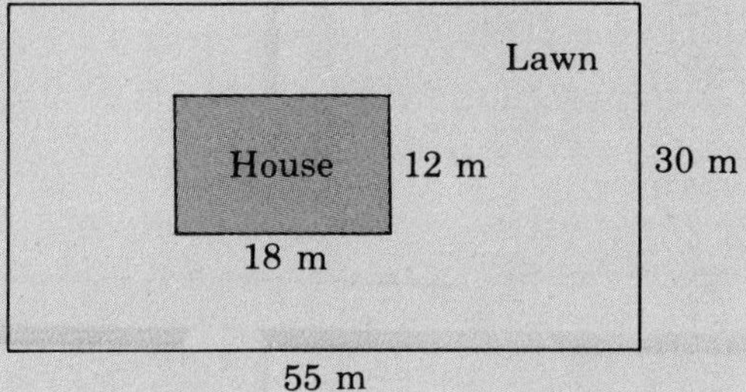

First, she must find the total area of the property and the area of the ground floor of her house.

Total area: 55×30, or 1650 m^2

Area of house: 18×12, or 216 m^2

Then she must subtract to find the area of the lawn.

Area of lawn: $1650 \text{ m}^2 - 216 \text{ m}^2 = 1434 \text{ m}^2$

Jean needs 30 kilograms of fertilizer for each 1500 square meters of lawn. She uses this proportion to find the amount of fertilizer she should buy.

$$\frac{30}{1500} = \frac{n}{1434} \begin{array}{l} \longleftarrow \text{Kilograms} \\ \longleftarrow \text{Square meters} \end{array}$$

$$30 \times 1434 = 1500 \times n$$

$$43{,}020 = 1500n$$

$$28.68 = n$$

Jean rounds her answer up to the next whole number. She should buy 29 kilograms of fertilizer.
The answer must always be rounded up or there will not be enough fertilizer.

Find the area of each lawn if these are the dimensions of the property and the house. All measures are given in meters.

	Property Length	Property Width	Area	House Length	House Width	Amount of fertilizer
1.	50	30	1320 m²	18	10	27 kg
2.	50	25	1090 m²	16	10	22 kg
3.	70	50	3330 m²	17	10	67 kg
4.	65	40	2360 m²	20	12	48 kg
5.	90	60	5100 m²	20	15	102 kg
6.	70	55	3584 m²	19	14	72 kg
7.	75	50	3563 m²	17	11	72 kg
8.	55	40	1996 m²	17	12	40 kg
9.	60	45	2508 m²	16	12	51 kg
10.	80	40	3002 m²	18	11	61 kg
11.	45	30	1206 m²	16	9	25 kg
12.	70	45	2814 m²	21	16	57 kg
13.	85	60	4533 m²	27	21	91 kg
14.	80	55	3963 m²	23	19	80 kg
15.	60	40	2166 m²	18	13	44 kg
16.	50	35	1465 m²	19	15	30 kg
17.	75	60	4126 m²	22	17	83 kg
18.	55	35	1621 m²	19	16	33 kg
19.	65	50	2914 m²	21	16	59 kg

20. For each of Problems 1–19, find how much fertilizer should be bought. Use 30 kilograms of fertilizer for each 1500 square meters of lawn. When necessary, round your answer up to the next whole number.
See above.

Problem Solving

CAREER APPLICATIONS

Objective: Solve problems involving circumference.

In this lesson students find the total length of pipes used in plumbing.

Plumber

Career Cluster: Trades Oliver Graham is a plumber. He installs and repairs water pipes and fixtures in buildings. He needs to know the total length of this pipe.

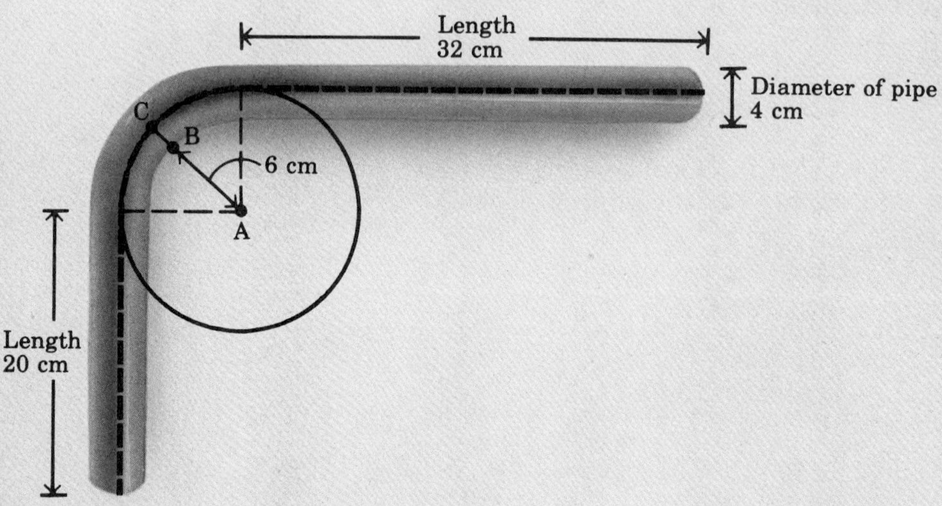

Oliver followed these steps to find the length of the curved section of pipe.

Step 1: Find $\frac{1}{2}$ of the diameter of the pipe to get CB. $\frac{1}{2} \times 4\text{ cm} = 2\text{ cm}$

Step 2: Add this to AB to find radius AC. $6\text{ cm} + 2\text{ cm} = 8\text{ cm}$

Step 3: Find the circumference of the circle shown. Use radius AC. $2 \times 3.14 \times 8\text{ cm} = 50.24\text{ cm}$

Step 4: Find $\frac{1}{4}$ of the circumference because the bend is 90° ($\frac{1}{4}$ of a circle). Round answer to the nearest centimeter. $\frac{1}{4} \times 50.24\text{ cm} = 12.56\text{ cm} \approx 13\text{ cm}$

The length of the curved section is about 13 centimeters.

Then Oliver found the total length of the pipe by adding the lengths of the three sections.

$32\text{ cm} + 13\text{ cm} + 20\text{ cm} = 65\text{ cm}$

The total length of the pipe is about 65 centimeters.

Find the total length of each pipe. Remember to round the length of each curved section to the nearest centimeter.

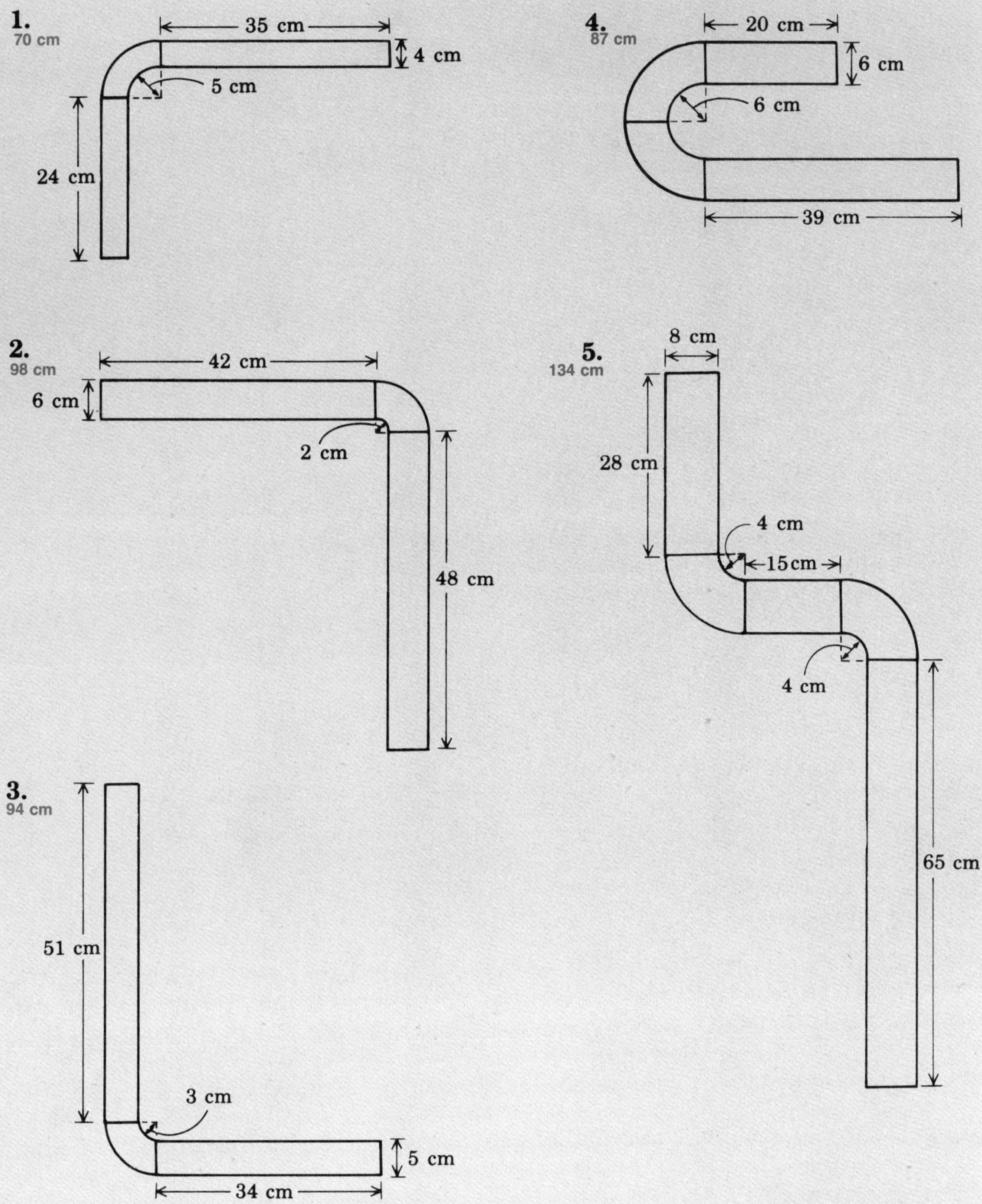

Problem Solving

DEVELOPING STRATEGIES

Objective: Solve problems by obtaining information from a picture, using a formula, and selecting necessary data. In this lesson students find the number of lifeguard stands needed and the number of people allowed in a swimming pool at one time.

Tactics: Obtaining Information from a Picture, Using a Formula, Selecting Necessary Data

Ed Jackson is an inspector for the State Health Board. As part of his job, Ed checks plans for new swimming pools to ensure that builders are meeting the health and safety standards set forth by law.

Specifications for Swimming Pool Construction
1. 1 lifeguard stand per 2000 sq. ft. of water surface. 2. Diving end: 24 sq. ft. per person. Shallow end: 12 sq. ft. per person. 3. Land enclosed around pool: 20 sq. ft. per person.

Problem

Ed was checking plans for the new Ridge Pool. To meet the specifications, how many lifeguard stands must there be and how many people will be allowed in the pool at one time?

Solution

Ed's strategy for solving the problem included the tactics of obtaining information from a picture, using a formula, and selecting necessary data.

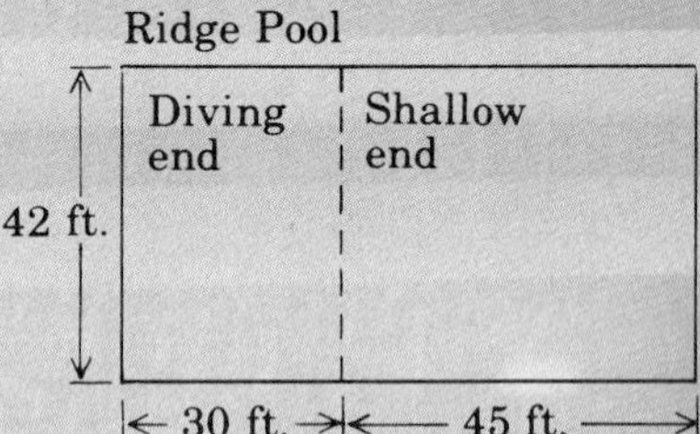

a. What is the area of the water surface in each end of the pool? Obtain the dimensions from the picture and use the formula for the area of a rectangle.

Diving End	Shallow End
$A = lw$	$A = lw$
$A = 42 \times 30$	$A = 45 \times 42$
$A = 1260$ sq. ft.	$A = 1890$ sq. ft.

b. What is the total area of the water surface? Add.

$1260 + 1890 = 3150$ sq. ft.

c. How many lifeguard stands should be provided? Select the necessary data and divide. Round your answer to the next whole number.

1 lifeguard stand required per 2000 sq. ft. of water surface.
$3150 \div 2000 = 1.575$
$1.575 \approx 2$

d. How many people will be allowed in each end of the pool? Select the necessary data and divide.

Diving End	Shallow End
$1260 \div 24 = 52\,R12$	$1890 \div 12 = 157\,R6$

e. How many people will be allowed in the pool? Add. Do not use the remainders.

$52 + 157 = 209$

Conclusion: The Ridge Pool will need 2 lifeguard stands and 209 people will be allowed in the pool at one time.

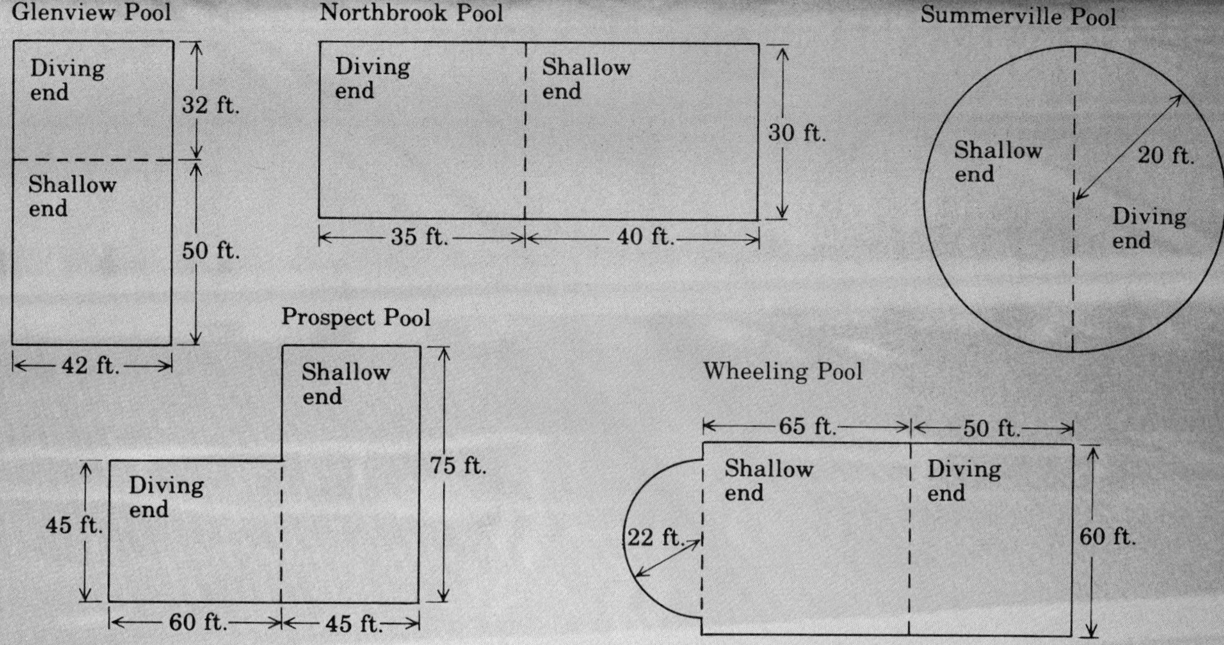

Related Problems

At one time, how many people will be allowed in the

1. Glenview Pool?
   231 people
2. Northbrook Pool?
   143 people
3. Prospect Pool?
   393 people

For each pool, how many lifeguard stands must be built? Round your answer up.

4. Glenview Pool
   2 stands
5. Northbrook Pool
   2 stands
6. Prospect Pool
   4 stands

Use the specifications and your answers for Problems 1, 2, and 3 to help you find the amount of land that should be enclosed around the

7. Glenview Pool.
   4620 sq. ft.
8. Northbrook Pool.
   2860 sq. ft.
9. Prospect Pool.
   7860 sq. ft.

Extensions

For the Summerville Pool, use the specifications to find

10. the number of people who will be allowed in the pool at one time.
    78 people
11. the number of lifeguard stands that must be built.
    1 stand
12. the amount of land that should be enclosed around the pool.
    1560 sq. ft.

For the Wheeling Pool, use the specifications to find

13. the number of people who will be allowed in the pool at one time.
    513 people
14. the number of lifeguard stands that must be built.
    4 stands
15. the amount of land that should be enclosed around the pool.
    10,260 sq. ft.

Discuss with students the need for safety standards when building swimming pools for public use.

CHAPTER 16 TEST

Number of test items - 15

Number missed	1	2	3	4	5	6	7
Percent correct	93	87	80	73	67	60	53

Find the perimeter of each polygon.

A **1.**

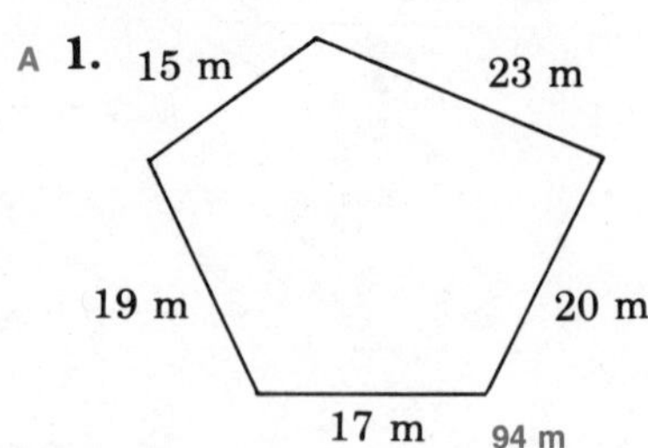

94 m

B **2.**

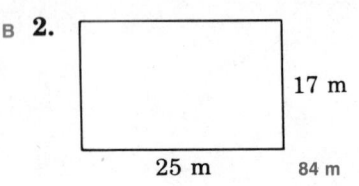

17 m

25 m

84 m

Find the circumference of each circle.

C **3.**

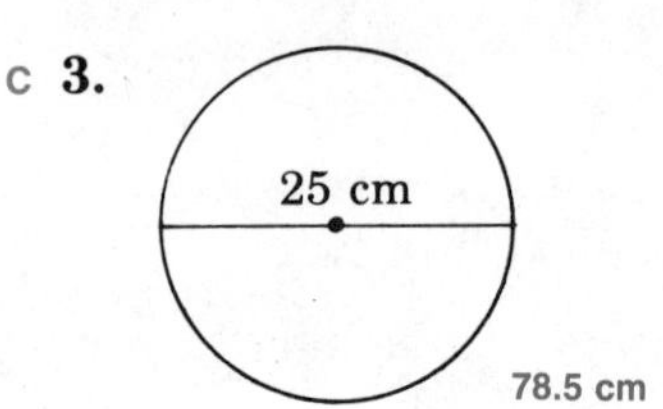

78.5 cm

D **4.**

15 mm

94.2 mm

Find the area of this rectangle.

E **5.**

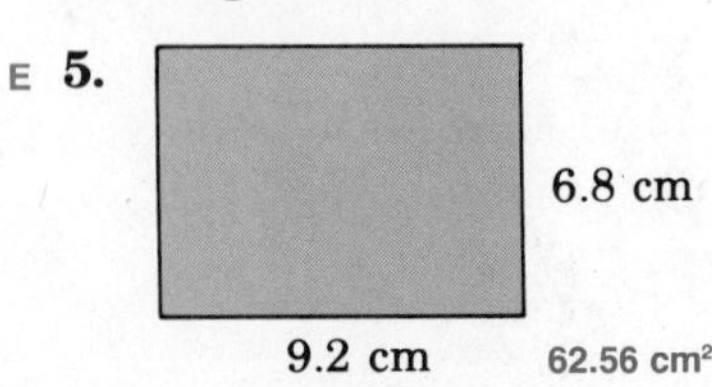

62.56 cm²

Find the area of each figure.

F **6.**

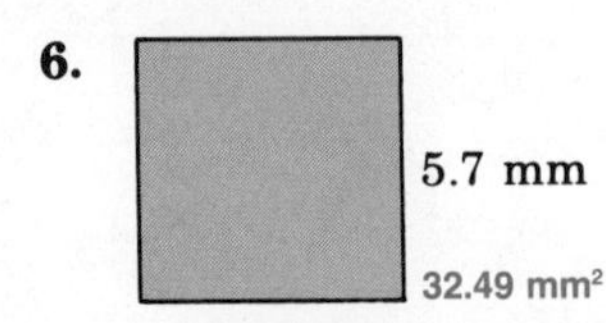

32.49 mm²

G **7.**

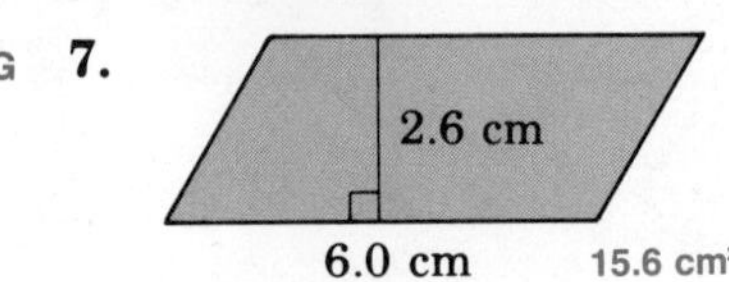

15.6 cm²

H **8.**

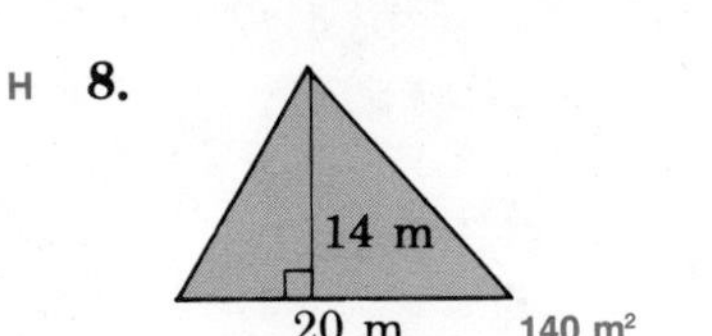

140 m²

I **9.**

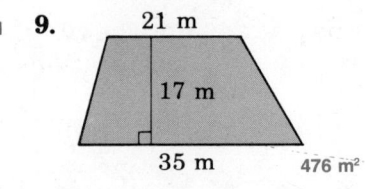

21 m

17 m

35 m

476 m²

Find the area of each circle.

J **10.**

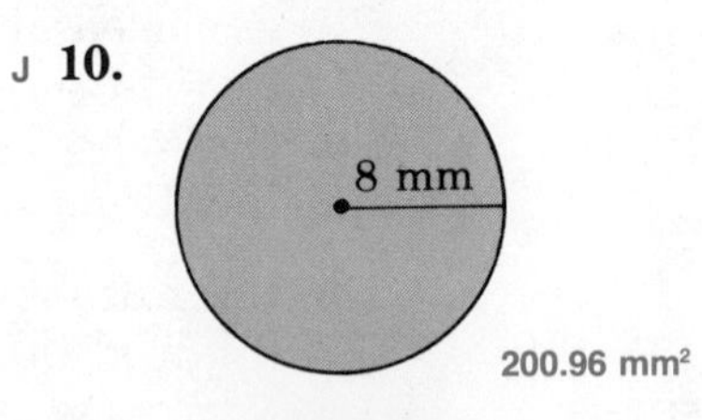

200.96 mm²

K **11.**

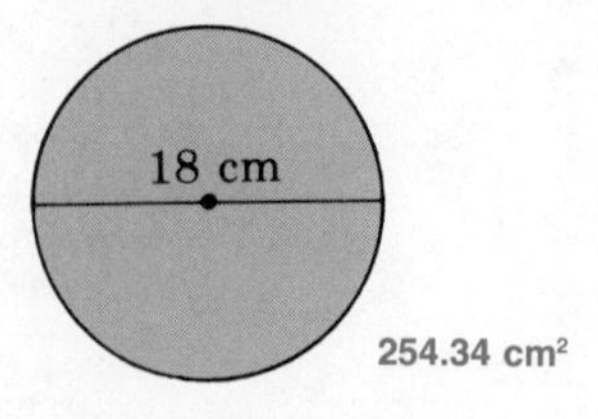

254.34 cm²

12. Carpeting costs $12 per square meter. Find the cost of carpeting a living room with these dimensions.
$288
Length: 6 m Width: 4 m

13. The area of John's lawn is 2600 square meters. He uses 30 kilograms of fertilizer on each 1500 square meters of lawn. How many kilograms of fertilizer should he buy?
52 kilograms

14. Find the total length of this pipe.
65.42 cm

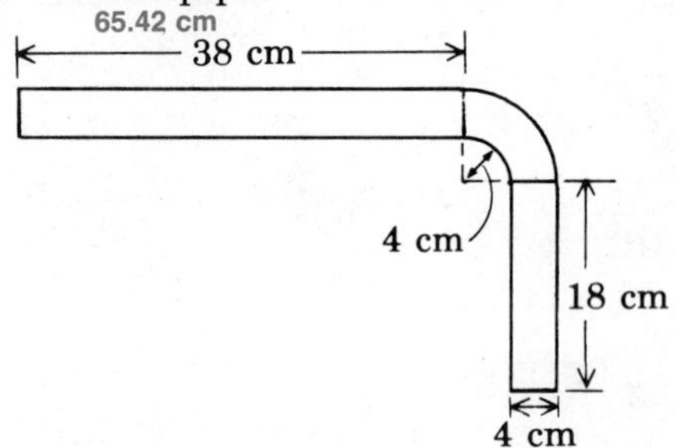

15. Pool specifications state that there must be one lifeguard stand per 2000 square feet of water surface. How many lifeguard stands must there be for the Freeport Pool?
3 stands

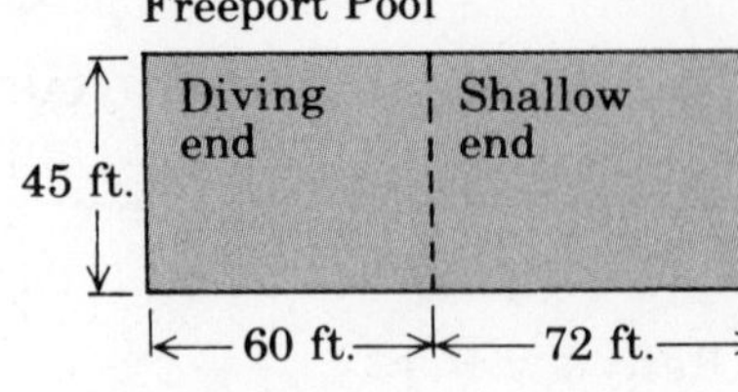

 See pages 41–42 of the *Test Masters* for an alternate form of the Chapter 16 Test.

CHAPTER 17 Surface Area and Volume

SKILLS PRETEST

Number of test items - 11

Number missed	1	2	3	4	5
Percent correct	91	82	73	64	55

SKILL Finding Surface Area of a Rectangular Prism *page 373*

A Find the surface area of this rectangular prism.
550 cm²

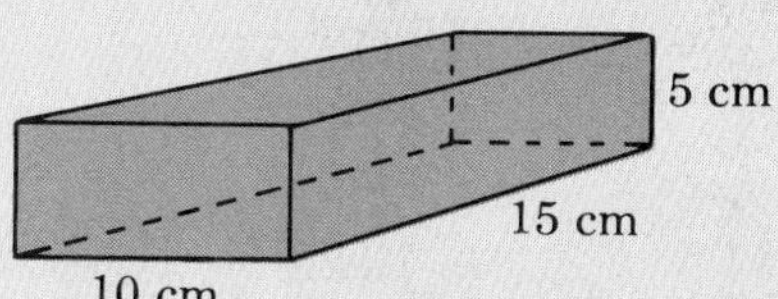

SKILL Finding Surface Area of a Cube *page 374*

B Find the surface area of this cube.
4704 mm²

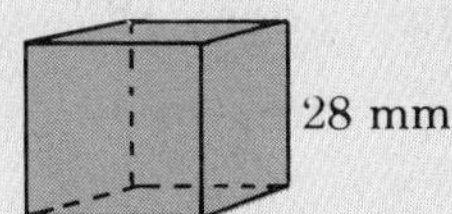

SKILL Finding Surface Area of a Cylinder *page 375*

C Find the surface area of this cylinder.
2009.6 m²

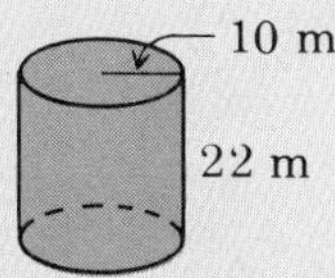

SKILL Finding Volume of a Rectangular Prism and a Cube *pages 376–377*

D Find the volume of this rectangular prism.
4320 m³

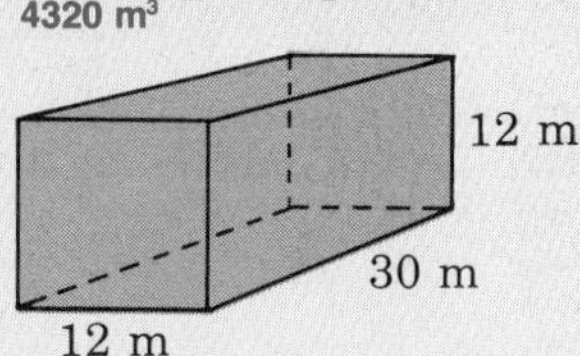

E Find the volume of this cube.
753,571 cm³

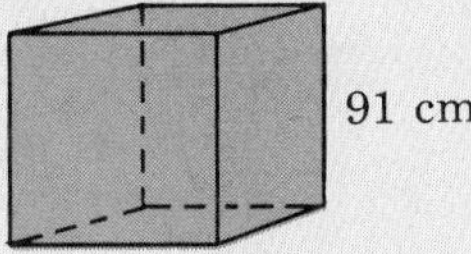

Pretest continued on page 372.

Pretest continued from page 371.

SKILL Finding Volume of a Cylinder *pages 378–379*

F Find the volume of this cylinder.
226.08 cm^3

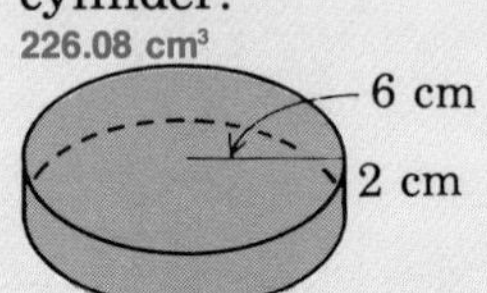

G Find the volume of this cylinder.
763.02 cm^3

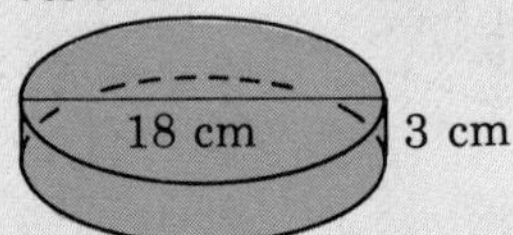

SKILL Finding Volume of a Pyramid and a Cone *pages 380–381*

H Find the volume of this pyramid. The base is a rectangle.
192 m^3

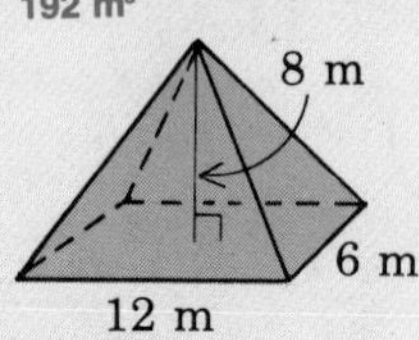

I Find the volume of this cone.
1186.92 cm^3

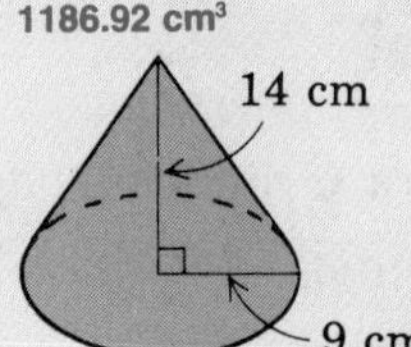

SKILL Finding Volume of a Sphere *page 382*

J Find the volume of this sphere.
14,130 m^3

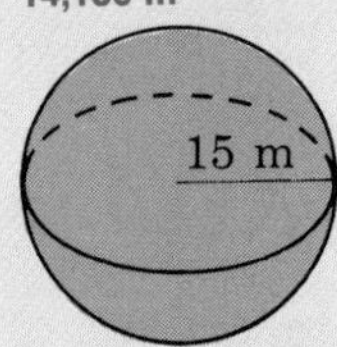

K Find the volume of this sphere.
7234.56 cm^3

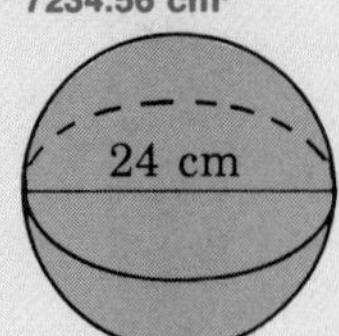

Objective: Find the surface area of a rectangular prism.

Finding Surface Area of a Rectangular Prism

Example A Given the length, width, and height

Find the surface area of this rectangular prism.

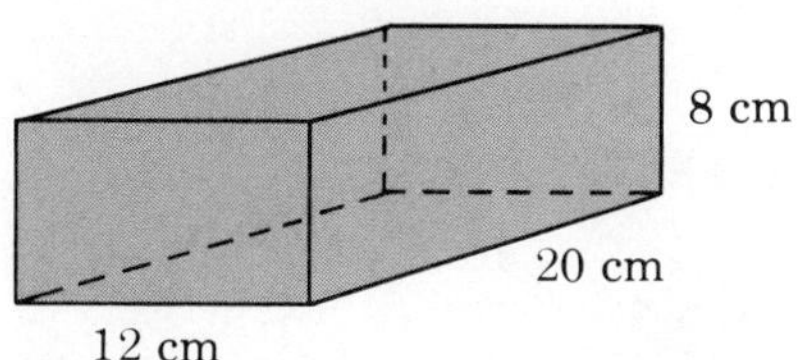

To find the **surface area** of a **rectangular prism,** add the areas of the six rectangular faces. Use this formula.

A	$=$	$2lw$	$+$	$2lh$	$+$	$2wh$
↑		↑		↑		↑
Surface area		Area of top and bottom		Area of two sides		Area of front and back

$A = 2lw + 2lh + 2wh$

$A = 2(20)(12) + 2(20)(8) + 2(12)(8)$

$A = 480 + 320 + 192$

$A = 992$

The surface area is 992 cm^2.

The formula could also be written
$A = 2(lw + lh + wh)$.

Have students identify the length, width, and height in the example and in each of the first three exercises.

Exercises

PROBLEM SOLVING
The applications on pages 390–391 may be used anytime after this lesson.

Set A

Find the surface area of each rectangular prism.

1.

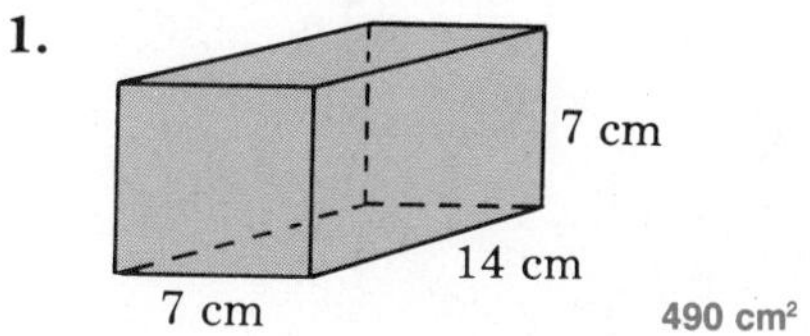

490 cm^2

2.

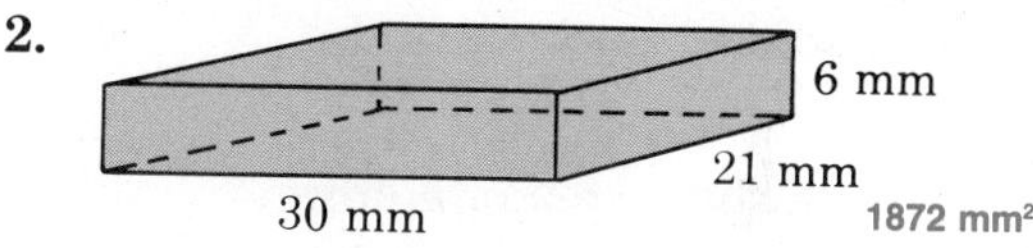

1872 mm^2

3.

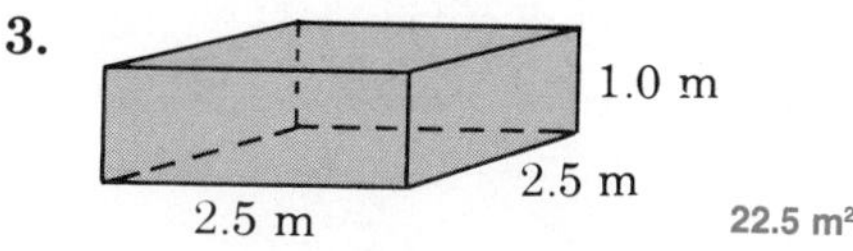

22.5 m^2

Find the surface area of each rectangular prism. Use these dimensions.

	Length (l)	Width (w)	Height (h)	
4.	43 cm	2 cm	4 cm	532 cm^2
5.	21 mm	6 mm	9 mm	738 mm^2
6.	54 cm	40 cm	19 cm	7892 cm^2
7.	36 m	20 m	18 m	3456 m^2
8.	101 mm	92 mm	24 mm	27,848 mm^2
9.	204 mm	87 mm	39 mm	58,194 mm^2
10.	0.8 m	0.4 m	0.5 m	1.84 m^2
11.	7.0 cm	4.5 cm	3.5 cm	143.5 cm^2
12.	8.1 m	6.4 m	1.2 m	138.48 m^2
13.	7.5 m	4.6 m	2.3 m	124.66 m^2
14.	5.2 cm	1.5 cm	5.2 cm	85.28 cm^2

Objective: Find the surface area of a cube.

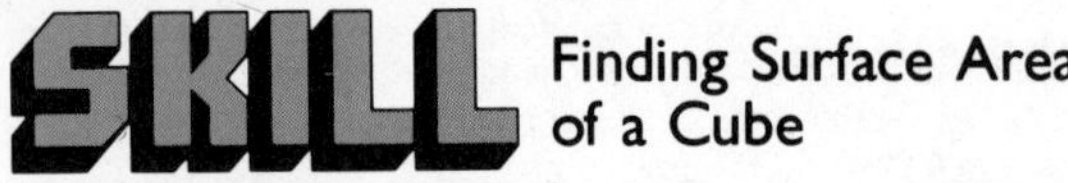

Finding Surface Area of a Cube

Example B Given the measure of one side

Find the surface area of this cube.

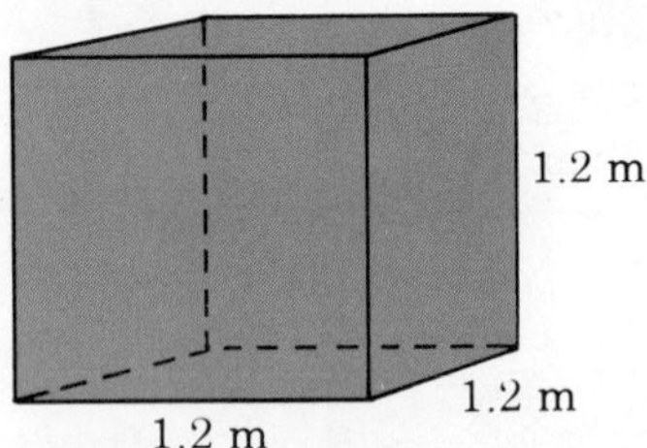

To find the surface area of a **cube,** find the area of one square face and multiply by 6. Use this formula.

Number of faces

$$A = 6s^2$$

Surface area (A); Area of each square face (s^2)

$A = 6s^2$

$A = 6(1.2)^2$ Emphasize that 1.2 must be squared before it is multiplied by 6.

$A = 6(1.44)$

$A = 8.64$

The surface area is 8.64 m^2.

Exercises

Set B

Find the surface area of each cube.

1.

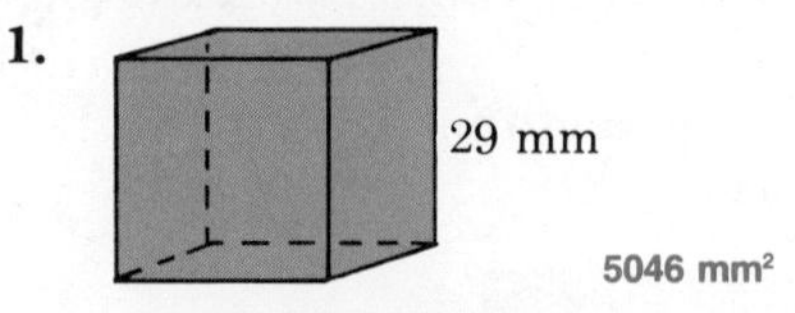

5046 mm^2

2.

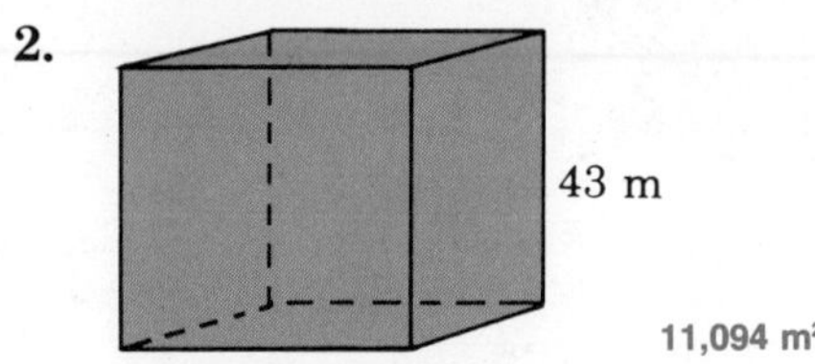

11,094 m^2

3.

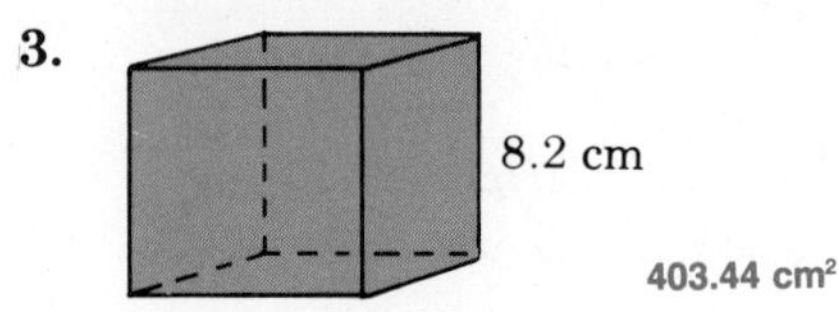

403.44 cm^2

Find the surface area of each cube. The length of a side (s) is given.

4. 12 mm 864 mm^2
5. 65 cm 25,350 cm^2
6. 58 mm 20,184 mm^2
7. 26 mm 4056 mm^2
8. 48 mm 13,824 mm^2
9. 31 m 5766 m^2
10. 40 cm 9600 cm^2
11. 23 m 3174 m^2
12. 42 mm 10,584 mm^2
13. 50 cm 15,000 cm^2
14. 37 cm 8214 cm^2
15. 291 cm 508,086 cm^2
16. 110 cm 72,600 cm^2
17. 0.7 m 2.94 m^2
18. 0.3 m 0.54 m^2
19. 0.9 cm 4.86 cm^2
20. 0.5 m 1.5 m^2
21. 1.4 m 11.76 m^2
22. 6.1 cm 223.26 cm^2
23. 9.2 cm 507.84 cm^2
24. 3.5 m 73.5 m^2
25. 5.3 m 168.54 m^2
26. 6.5 m 253.5 m^2
27. 7.8 cm 365.04 cm^2
28. 9.9 cm 588.06 cm^2
29. 8.6 m 443.76 m^2

Objective: Find the surface area of a cylinder.

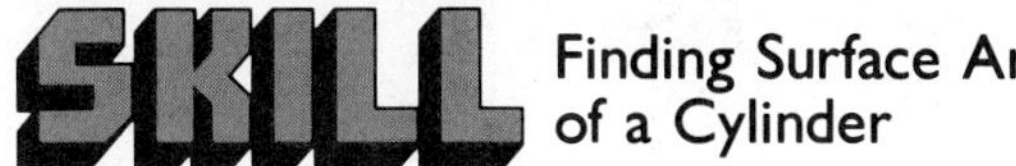

Finding Surface Area of a Cylinder

Example C Given the radius and height

Find the surface area of this cylinder.

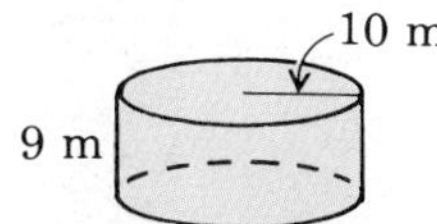

The flat diagram below shows the surface of the **cylinder.** The length of the rectangle is the circumference of the circle ($2\pi r$). The width of the rectangle is the height of the cylinder.

Review finding the circumference and area of a circle.

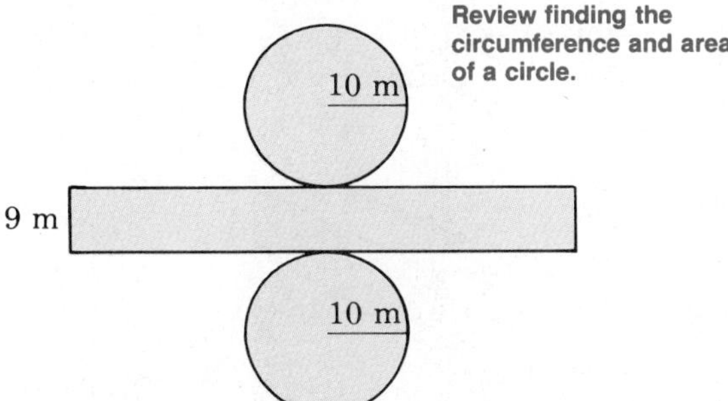

To find the surface area, add the area of the rectangle and the areas of the two circles. Use this formula.

A	$=$	$2\pi rh$	$+$	$2\pi r^2$
↑		↑		↑
Surface area		Area of rectangle		Area of two circles

$A = 2\pi rh + 2\pi r^2$

$A \approx 2(3.14)(10)(9) + 2(3.14)(10)^2$

$A \approx 2(3.14)(10)(9) + 2(3.14)(100)$

$A \approx 565.2 + 628$

$A \approx 1193.2$

The surface area is about 1193.2 m^2.

Exercises

Set C

Find the surface area of each cylinder.

1. 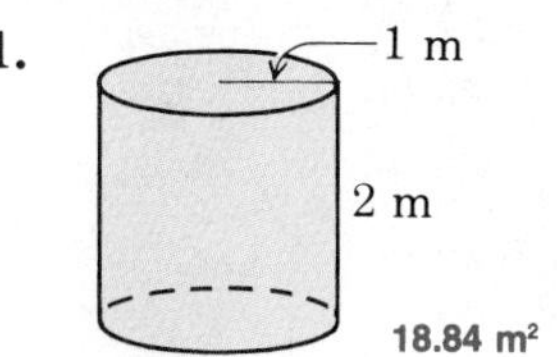

18.84 m^2

2. 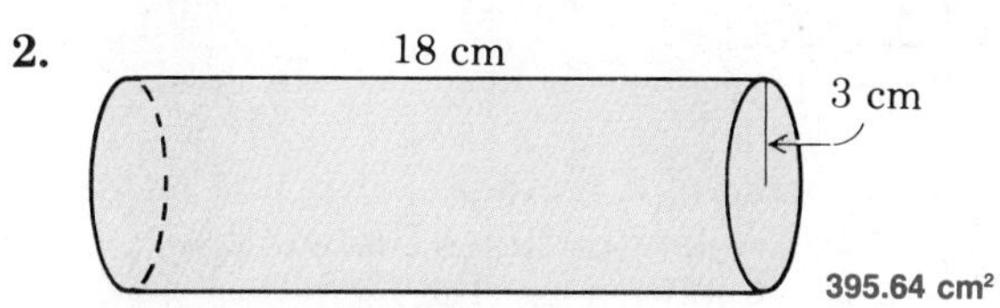

395.64 cm^2

3. 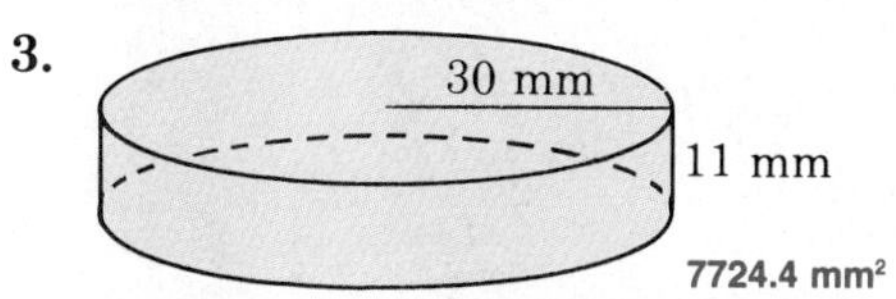

7724.4 mm^2

Find the surface area of each cylinder. Use these dimensions.

	Radius (r)	Height (h)	
4.	1 cm	9 cm	62.8 cm^2
5.	2 m	5 m	87.92 m^2
6.	4 m	3 m	175.84 m^2
7.	7 cm	8 cm	659.4 cm^2
8.	5 m	14 m	596.6 m^2
9.	6 cm	17 cm	866.64 cm^2
10.	10 cm	18 cm	1758.4 cm^2
11.	20 mm	24 mm	5526.4 mm^2
12.	50 mm	30 mm	25,120 mm^2
13.	30 mm	25 mm	10,362 mm^2
14.	12 m	15 m	2034.72 m^2
15.	13 cm	29 cm	3428.88 cm^2

Objective: Find the volume of a rectangular prism and a cube.

Finding Volume of a Rectangular Prism and a Cube

Example D

Rectangular prism, when given the length, width, and height

Find the volume of this rectangular prism.

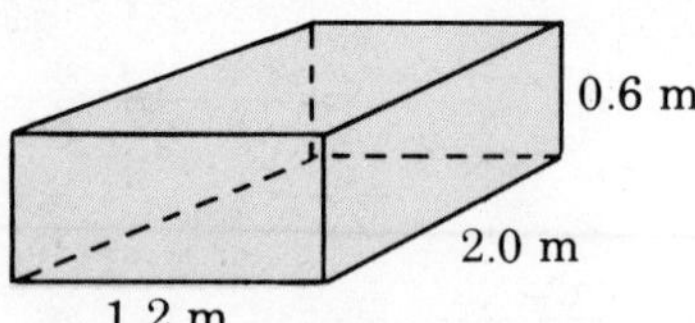

The **volume** of a rectangular prism is equal to the length times the width times the height. Use this formula.

$V = lwh$

$V = 2.0 \times 1.2 \times 0.6$

$V = 1.44$

You might point out that the three dimensions can be multiplied in any order.

The volume is 1.44 cubic meters (1.44 m^3).

Example E

Cube, when given the measure of one side

Find the volume of this cube.

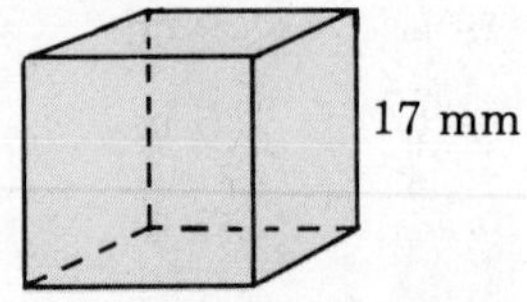

The volume of a cube is equal to the length of a side times the same length times the same length. Use this formula.

$V = s^3$ — s^3 is read "s cubed" and means $s \times s \times s$.

$V = 17^3$

$V = 17 \times 17 \times 17$

$V = 4913$

The volume is 4913 mm^3.

Exercises

Set D

Find the volume of each rectangular prism.

1. 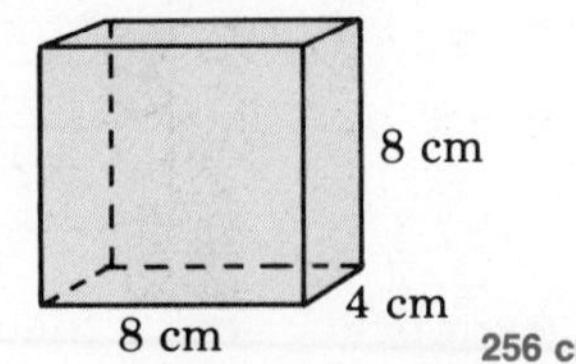

256 cm^3

2. 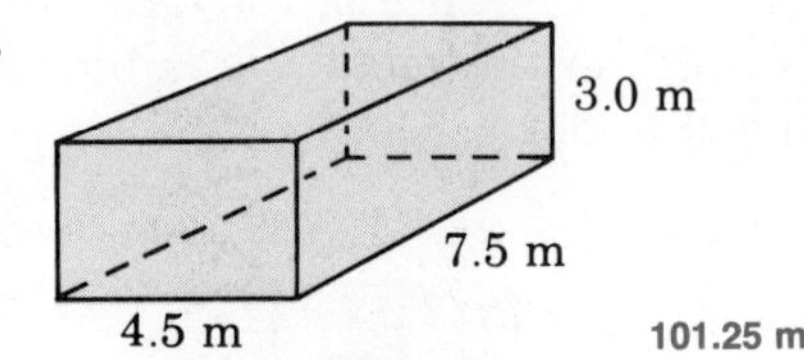

101.25 m^3

3. 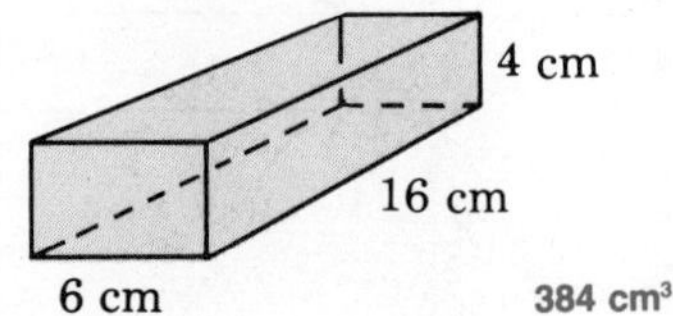

384 cm^3

Find the volume of each rectangular prism. Use these dimensions.

	Length (l)	Width (w)	Height (h)
4.	19 mm 3344 mm^3	8 mm	22 mm
5.	25 cm 1625 cm^3	13 cm	5 cm
6.	94 cm 253,800 cm^3	60 cm	45 cm
7.	21 cm 10,710 cm^3	15 cm	34 cm
8.	58 mm 194,996 mm^3	41 mm	82 mm
9.	70 mm 165,550 mm^3	55 mm	43 mm
10.	3.1 m 3.41 m^3	2.2 m	0.5 m
11.	4.7 m 5.264 m^3	0.8 m	1.4 m
12.	2.9 m 6.96 m^3	0.6 m	4.0 m
13.	7.0 cm 23.94 cm^3	3.8 cm	0.9 cm

PROBLEM SOLVING
The applications on pages 386–387 may be used anytime after this lesson.

Set E

Find the volume of each cube.

1\.
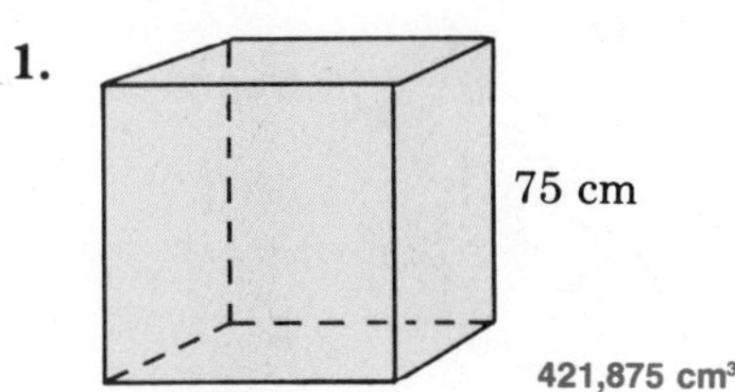

421,875 cm^3

2\.
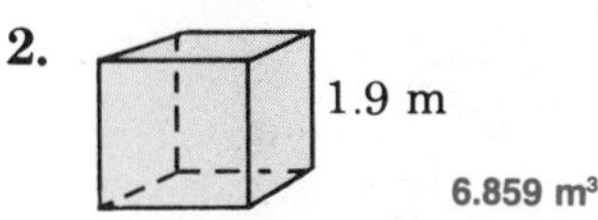

6.859 m^3

3\.
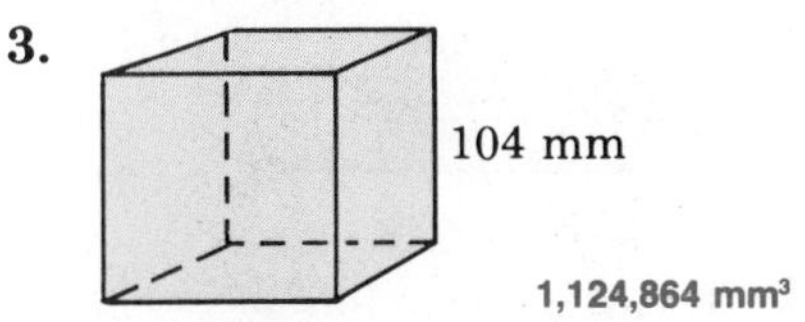

1,124,864 mm^3

Find the volume of each cube.
The length of a side (s) is given.

4. 7 m — 343 m^3
5. 6 m — 216 m^3
6. 10 m — 1000 m^3
7. 20 m — 8000 m^3
8. 50 cm — 125,000 cm^3
9. 23 m — 12,167 m^3
10. 42 mm — 74,088 mm^3
11. 94 cm — 830,584 cm^3
12. 32 cm — 32,768 cm^3
13. 48 cm — 110,592 cm^3
14. 81 mm — 531,441 mm^3
15. 56 mm — 175,616 mm^3
16. 63 cm — 250,047 cm^3
17. 87 mm — 658,503 mm^3
18. 100 cm — 1,000,000 cm^3
19. 300 m — 27,000,000 m^3
20. 0.4 m — 0.064 m^3
21. 0.8 m — 0.512 m^3
22. 9.2 m — 778.688 m^3
23. 1.5 m — 3.375 m^3
24. 2.9 m — 24.389 m^3
25. 5.8 cm — 195.112 cm^3
26. 12.1 cm — 1771.561 cm^3
27. 25.2 cm — 16,003.008 cm^3

BREAK TIME

How many complete turns will be made by gear C when gear A makes one complete turn?
3 turns

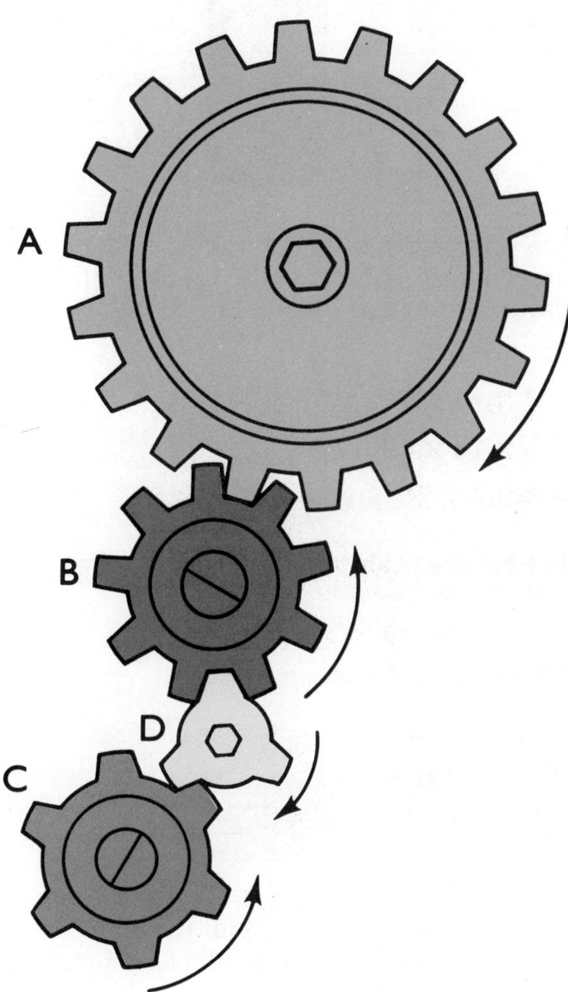

Objective: Find the volume of a cylinder.

Finding Volume of a Cylinder

Example F Given the radius

Find the volume of this cylinder.

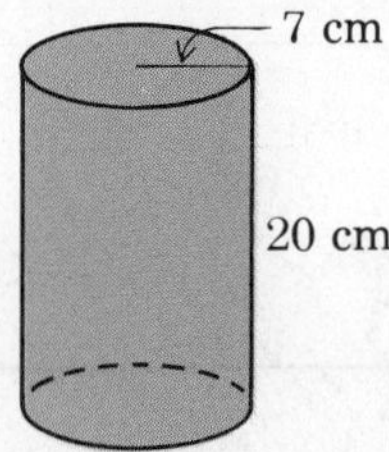

The volume of a cylinder is equal to the area of the circular base (πr^2) times the height of the cylinder. Use this formula.

$V = \pi r^2 h$

$V \approx 3.14 \times 7^2 \times 20$

$V \approx 3.14 \times 49 \times 20$

$V \approx 3077.2$

The volume is about 3077.2 cm^3.

Example G Given the diameter

Find the volume of this cylinder.

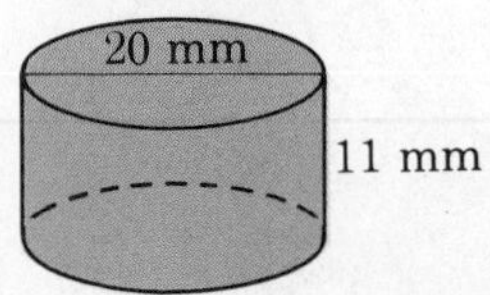

First find the radius. It is half the diameter, or 10 millimeters. Then use the formula.

$V = \pi r^2 h$

$V \approx 3.14 \times 10^2 \times 11$

$V \approx 3.14 \times 100 \times 11$

$V \approx 3454$

The volume is about 3454 mm^3.

Exercises

Set F

Find the volume of each cylinder.

1.
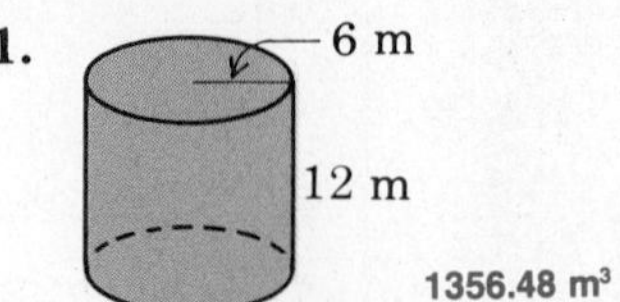

1356.48 m^3

2.
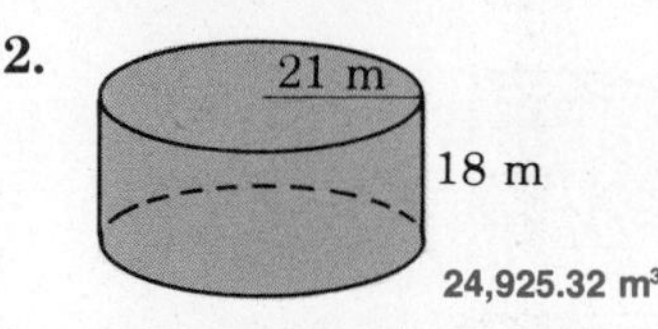

24,925.32 m^3

3.
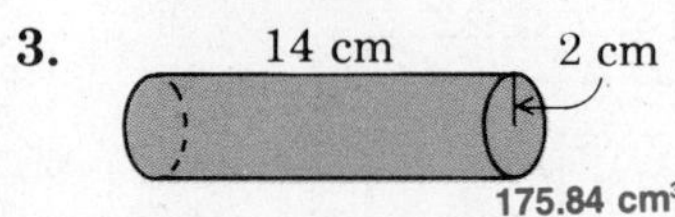

175.84 cm^3

Find the volume of each cylinder. Use these dimensions.

	Radius (r)	Height (h)
4.	7 m 461.58 m^3	3 m
5.	9 m 2034.72 m^3	8 m
6.	1 m 59.66 m^3	19 m
7.	3 cm 791.28 cm^3	28 cm
8.	8 mm 5024 mm^3	25 mm
9.	12 cm 3165.12 cm^3	7 cm
10.	23 cm 6644.24 cm^3	4 cm
11.	10 cm 4082 cm^3	13 cm
12.	40 cm 80,384 cm^3	16 cm
13.	26 mm 125,235.76 mm^3	59 mm
14.	38 cm 408,074.4 cm^3	90 cm
15.	10 mm 31,400 mm^3	100 mm

PROBLEM SOLVING
The applications on pages 388–389 may be used anytime after this lesson.

Set G

Find the volume of each cylinder.

1. 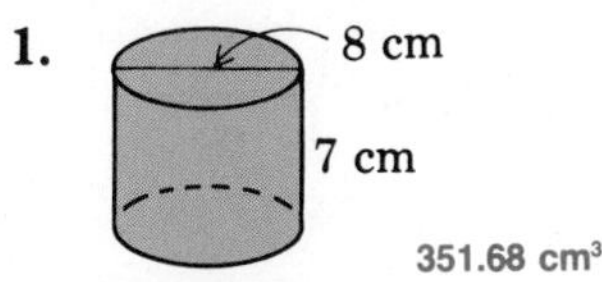

351.68 cm³

2. 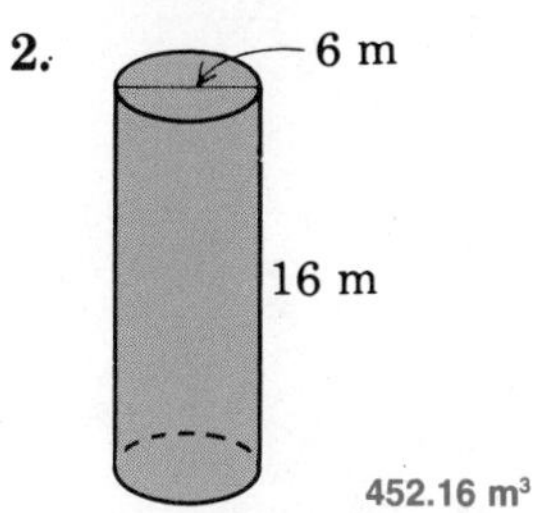

452.16 m³

3. 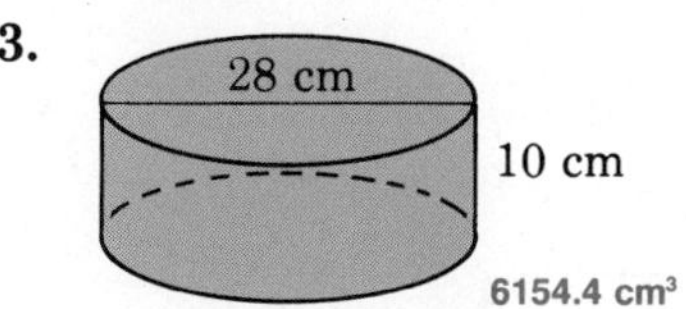

6154.4 cm³

Find the volume of each cylinder. Use these dimensions.

	Diameter	Height	
4.	6 m	9 m	254.34 m³
5.	4 m	7 m	87.92 m³
6.	2 cm	21 cm	65.94 cm³
7.	4 cm	19 cm	238.64 cm³
8.	10 m	8 m	628 m³
9.	50 cm	6 cm	11,775 cm³
10.	70 mm	40 mm	153,860 mm³
11.	30 cm	20 cm	14,130 cm³
12.	14 cm	95 cm	14,616.7 cm³
13.	18 mm	83 mm	21,110.22 mm³

BREAK TIME

This is the top view of four grain elevators. When the elevators were filled, the grain overflowed to fill the space in the middle.

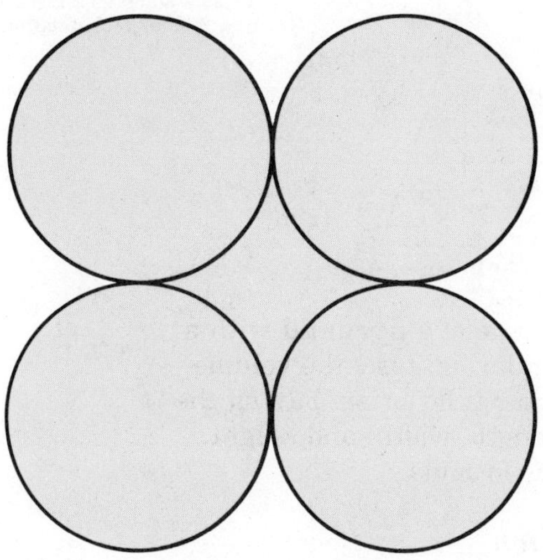

The radius of each elevator is 2 meters, and the height is 10 meters. Find the total volume of the four elevators and the space in the middle.

536.8 m³

Objective: Find the volume of a pyramid and a cone.

Finding Volume of a Pyramid and a Cone

Example H
Pyramid, when given the length, width, and height

Find the volume of this pyramid. The base is a rectangle.

Be sure students understand how the height is determined.

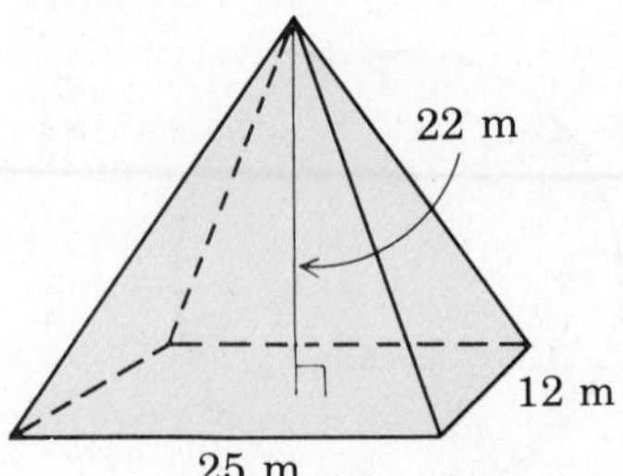

The volume of a **pyramid** with a rectangular base is $\frac{1}{3}$ the volume of a rectangular prism having the same length, width, and height. Use this formula.

$$V = \frac{1}{3}lwh$$

$$V = \frac{1}{3} \times 25 \times 12 \times 22$$

$$V = \frac{1}{\cancel{3}_1} \times \frac{25}{1} \times \frac{\cancel{12}^4}{1} \times \frac{22}{1}$$

$$V = 2200$$

The volume is 2200 m³.

Example I
Cone, when given the radius and height

Find the volume of this cone.

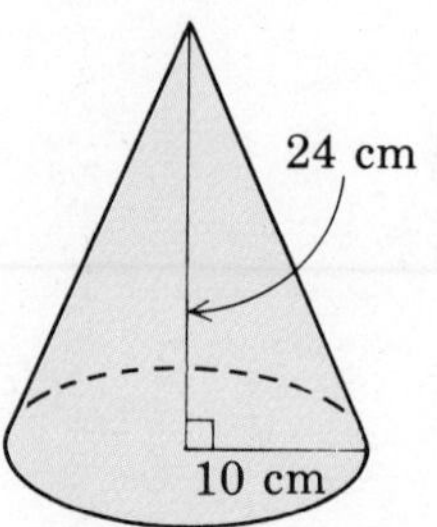

The volume of a **cone** is $\frac{1}{3}$ the volume of a cylinder having the same radius and height. Use this formula.

$$V = \frac{1}{3}\pi r^2 h$$

$$V \approx \frac{1}{3} \times 3.14 \times 10^2 \times 24$$

$$V \approx \frac{1}{3} \times 3.14 \times 100 \times 24$$

$$V \approx \frac{1}{\cancel{3}_1} \times \frac{3.14}{1} \times \frac{100}{1} \times \frac{\cancel{24}^8}{1}$$

$$V \approx 2512$$

The volume is about 2512 cm³.

Exercises

Set H

Find the volume of each pyramid.

1. 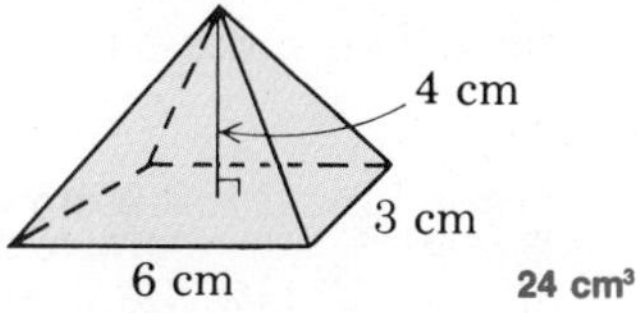

24 cm³

2. 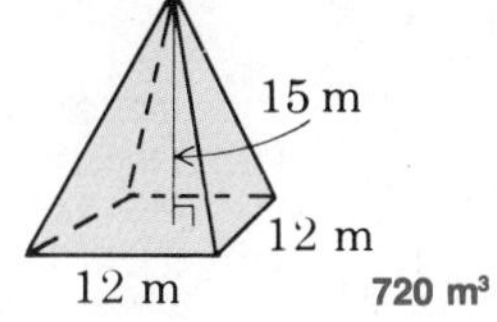

720 m³

3. 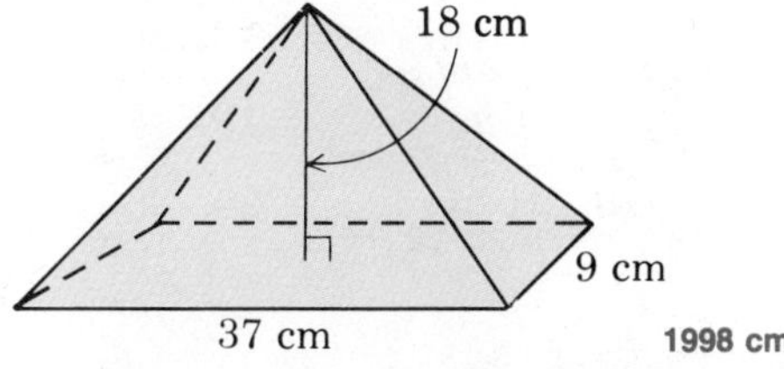

1998 cm³

Find the volume of each pyramid. Use these dimensions.

	Length (l)	Width (w)	Height (h)	
4.	14 cm	8 cm	9 cm	336 cm³
5.	19 m	6 m	5 m	190 m³
6.	20 cm	20 cm	36 cm	4800 cm³
7.	50 mm	50 mm	42 mm	35,000 mm³
8.	45 mm	22 mm	15 mm	4950 mm³
9.	17 cm	13 cm	60 cm	4420 cm³
10.	93 mm	87 mm	52 mm	140,244 mm³
11.	61 mm	59 mm	78 mm	93,574 mm³
12.	3.2 m	3.0 m	8.5 m	27.2 m³
13.	6.0 m	2.3 m	9.2 m	42.32 m³
14.	7.2 cm	5.5 cm	1.3 cm	17.16 cm³

Set I

Find the volume of each cone.

1. 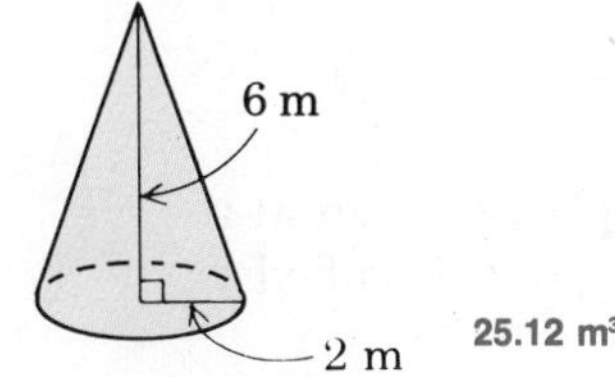

25.12 m³

2. 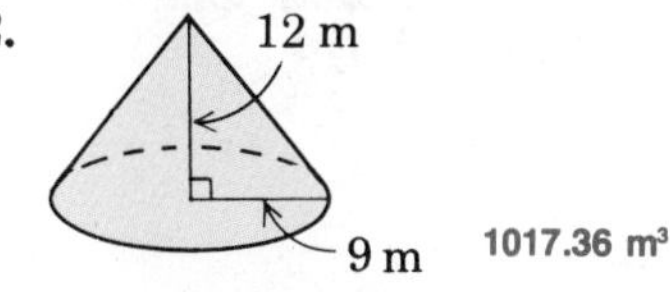

1017.36 m³

3. 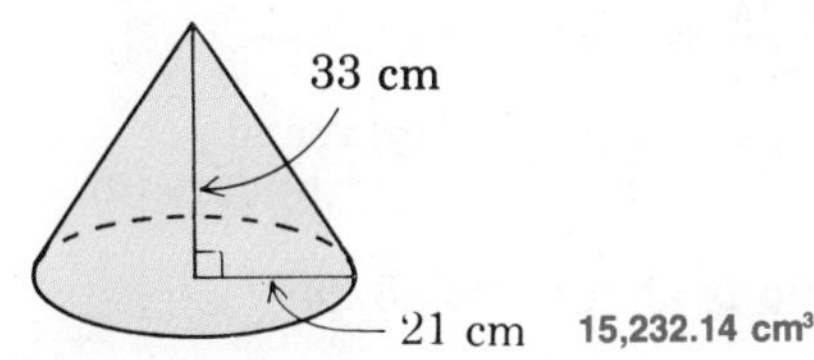

15,232.14 cm³

Find the volume of each cone. Use these dimensions.

	Radius (r)	Height (h)	
4.	5 m	3 m	78.5 m³
5.	8 cm	9 cm	602.88 cm³
6.	6 m	6 m	226.08 m³
7.	4 cm	12 cm	200.96 cm³
8.	3 cm	16 cm	150.72 cm³
9.	15 m	5 m	1177.5 m³
10.	12 m	7 m	1055.04 m³
11.	11 cm	3 cm	379.94 cm³
12.	10 cm	51 cm	5338 cm³
13.	30 mm	43 mm	40,506 mm³
14.	20 mm	36 mm	15,072 mm³
15.	25 cm	24 cm	15,700 cm³

Objective: Find the volume of a sphere.

Finding Volume of a Sphere

Example J Given the radius

Find the volume of this sphere.

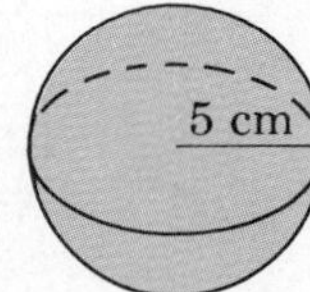

The volume of a **sphere** is equal to $\frac{4}{3}$ times π times the radius cubed. Use this formula.

$V = \frac{4}{3}\pi r^3$

Some students may write 5^3 as $5 \times 5 \times 5$ before multiplying.

$V \approx \frac{4}{3} \times 3.14 \times 5^3$

$V \approx \frac{4}{3} \times 3.14 \times 125$

$V \approx \frac{4}{3} \times \frac{3.14}{1} \times \frac{125}{1}$

$V \approx 523.33$ If necessary, round to the nearest hundredth.

The volume is about 523.33 cm³.

Example K Given the diameter

Find the volume of this sphere.

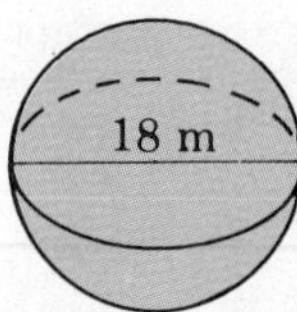

First find the radius. It is half the diameter, or 9 meters. Then use the formula.

$V = \frac{4}{3}\pi r^3$

$V \approx \frac{4}{3} \times 3.14 \times 9^3$

$V \approx \frac{4}{3} \times 3.14 \times 729$

$V \approx \frac{4}{\cancel{3}_1} \times \frac{3.14}{1} \times \frac{\overset{243}{\cancel{729}}}{1}$

$V \approx 3052.08$

The volume is about 3052.08 m³.

Exercises

PROBLEM SOLVING The applications on page 385 may be used anytime after this lesson.

Set J

Find the volume of each sphere to the nearest hundredth. The radius (r) is given.

1. 8 m — 2143.57 m³
2. 2 m — 33.49 m³
3. 4 cm — 267.95 cm³
4. 1 m — 4.19 m³
5. 7 m — 1436.03 m³
6. 6 m — 904.32 m³
7. 30 mm — 113,040 mm³
8. 10 cm — 4186.67 cm³
9. 16 mm — 17,148.59 mm³
10. 21 cm — 38,772.72 cm³
11. 40 cm — 267,946.67 cm³
12. 36 mm — 195,333.12 mm³
13. 12 cm — 7234.56 cm³
14. 29 cm — 102,108.61 cm³
15. 18 mm — 24,416.64 mm³
16. 27 cm — 82,406.16 cm³
17. 33 cm — 150,456.24 cm³
18. 20 mm — 33,493.33 mm³
19. 17 mm — 20,569.09 mm³
20. 35 cm — 179,503.33 cm³

Set K

Find the volume of each sphere to the nearest hundredth. The diameter is given.

1. 6 cm — 113.04 cm³
2. 30 mm — 14,130 mm³
3. 44 mm — 44,579.63 mm³
4. 70 cm — 179,503.33 cm³
5. 52 mm — 73,584.85 mm³
6. 28 cm — 11,488.21 cm³
7. 50 mm — 65,416.67 mm³
8. 22 cm — 5572.45 cm³
9. 76 mm — 229,730.77 mm³
10. 64 mm — 137,188.69 mm³
11. 38 cm — 28,716.35 cm³
12. 78 mm — 248,348.88 mm³
13. 62 mm — 124,724.99 mm³
14. 46 cm — 50,939.17 cm³
15. 68 mm — 164,552.75 mm³
16. 74 mm — 212,067.23 mm³
17. 56 cm — 91,905.71 cm³
18. 26 cm — 9198.11 cm³
19. 48 mm — 57,876.48 mm³
20. 32 mm — 17,148.59 mm³

SKILLS POSTTEST

Number of test items - 11

Number missed	1	2	3	4	5
Percent correct	91	82	73	64	55

SKILL Finding Surface Area of a Rectangular Prism *page 373*

A Find the surface area of this rectangular prism.
1062 m²

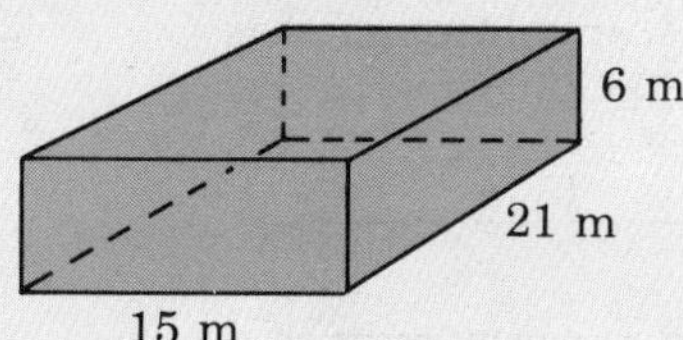

SKILL Finding Surface Area of a Cube *page 374*

B Find the surface area of this cube.
7776 mm²

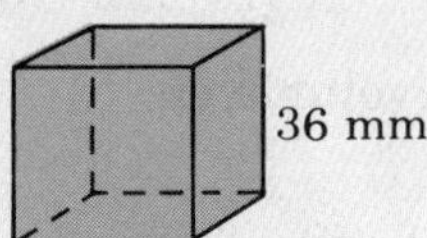

SKILL Finding Surface Area of a Cylinder *page 375*

C Find the surface area of this cylinder.
565.2 m²

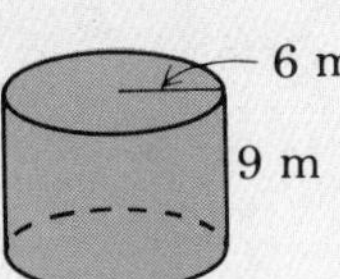

SKILL Finding Volume of a Rectangular Prism and a Cube *pages 376–377*

D Find the volume of this rectangular prism.
10,290 mm³

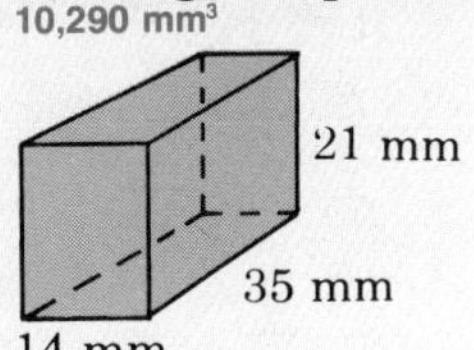

E Find the volume of this cube.
438,976 mm³

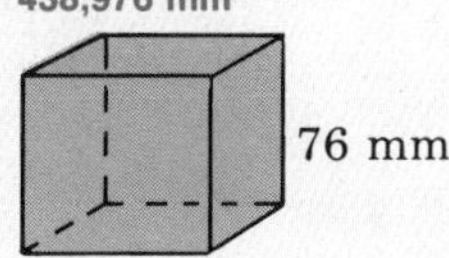

Posttest continued on page 384.

Posttest continued from page 383.

SKILL Finding Volume of a Cylinder *pages 378–379*

F Find the volume of this cylinder.
314 m^3

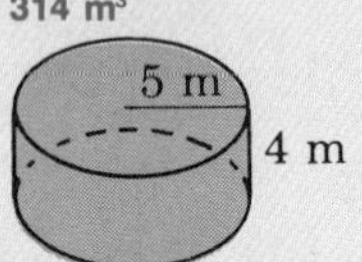

G Find the volume of this cylinder.
226.08 m^3

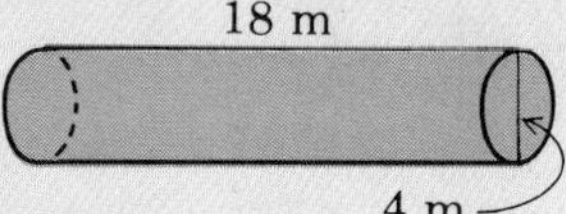

SKILL Finding Volume of a Pyramid and a Cone *pages 380–381*

H Find the volume of this pyramid. The base is a rectangle.
360 m^3

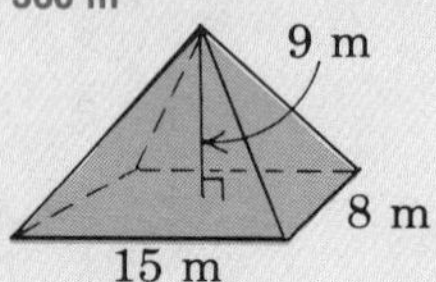

I Find the volume of this cone.
414.48 cm^3

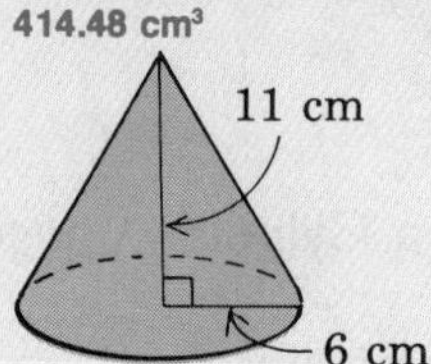

SKILL Finding Volume of a Sphere *page 382*

J Find the volume of this sphere.
7234.56 m^3

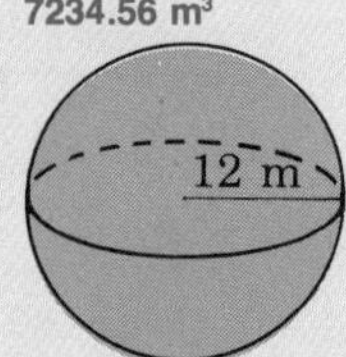

K Find the volume of this sphere.
904.32 cm^3

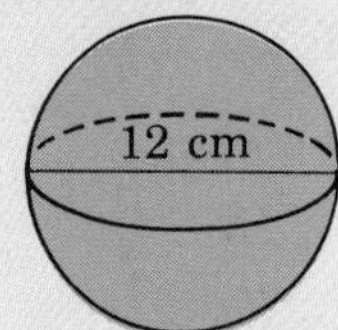

Problem Solving

CONSUMER APPLICATIONS

Objective: Solve problems involving volume.

In this lesson students compute the amount of wax needed to make candles.

Buying Wax to Make Candles

As a hobby, Mr. and Mrs. Gonzalez make candles in shapes like these. They make several candles at a time and use them for gifts.

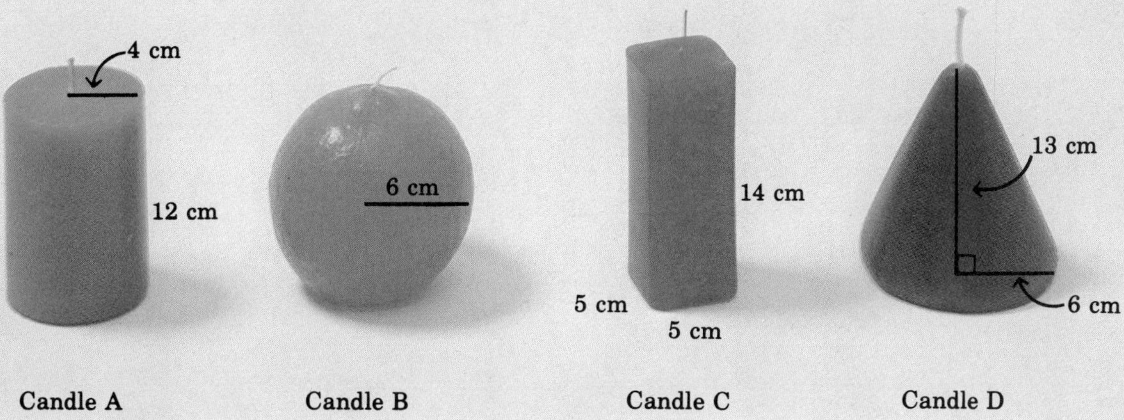

Candle A Candle B Candle C Candle D

How many cubic centimeters of wax are needed to make

1. candle A? 602.88 cm^3
2. candle B? 904.32 cm^3
3. candle C? 350 cm^3
4. candle D? 489.84 cm^3

A cubic centimeter of wax has a mass of about 0.9 gram. To the nearest gram, how many grams of wax are needed to make

5. candle A? 543 grams
6. candle B? 814 grams
7. candle C? 315 grams
8. candle D? 441 grams

How many grams of wax are needed to make

9. 5 candles like candle A? 2715 grams
10. 6 candles like candle B? 4884 grams
11. 7 candles like candle C? 2205 grams
12. 4 candles like candle D? 1764 grams
13. How many grams of wax are needed to make all of the candles listed in Problems 9–12? 11,568 grams
14. How many 500-gram slabs of wax will be needed to make all of the candles listed in Problems 9–12? 24 slabs
15. A slab of wax costs $1.50. How much will it cost to buy the wax to make all of the candles listed in Problems 9–12? $36

Problem Solving

CONSUMER APPLICATIONS

Objective: Solve problems involving surface area and volume.

In this lesson students estimate the cost of building a garage.

Buying Building Materials

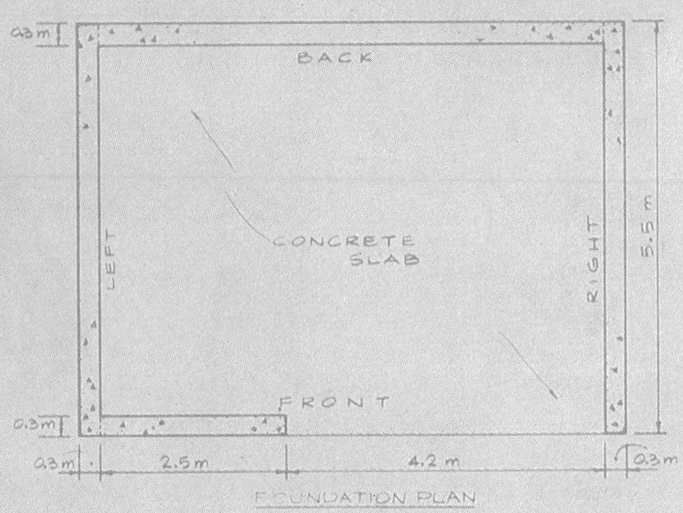

Jeff Scott is buying materials to build a garage. First he buys concrete for the footings. Footings are trenches filled with concrete. They run the length of each side and support the weight of the garage. The first picture is a top view of the footings.

The footings will be 0.9 meter deep. Other dimensions are given in the picture. Complete the table to find the amount of concrete needed for each footing.

	Footing	Dimensions (meters)	Volume (cubic meters)
1.	Front	2.5 × 0.3 × 0.9	0.675
2.	Back	6.7 × 0.3 × 0.9	1.809
3.	Right	5.5 × 0.3 × 0.9	1.485
4.	Left	5.5 × 0.3 × 0.9	1.485

5. Find the total number of cubic meters of concrete needed for the footings. Round your answer up to the next whole number.
6 m³
6. If concrete costs $65 per cubic meter, how much will the concrete for the footings cost?
$390
7. About 4 cubic meters of concrete are needed for the floor of the garage. At $65 per cubic meter, how much will the concrete for the floor cost?
$260

See pages 51–52 of *Problem-Solving Masters.*

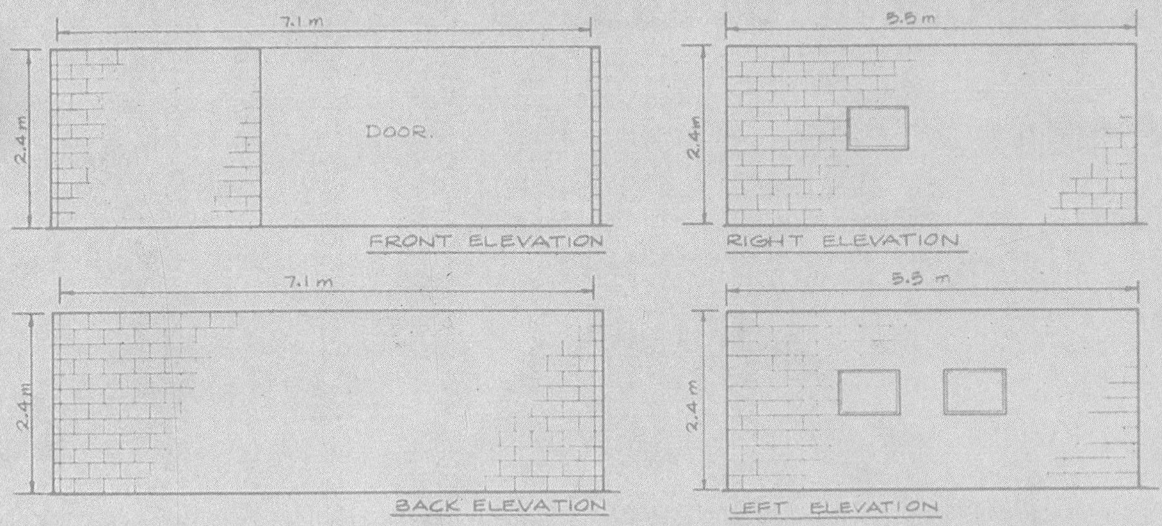

The walls of the garage will be concrete block. Use the dimensions in the four pictures of the walls to complete this table.

	Wall	Dimensions (meters)	Total area (square meters)	Area subtracted for windows or door (square meters)	Area covered with concrete blocks (square meters)
8.	Front	7.1 × 2.4	17.04	10.08 (Door)	6.96 (17.04 − 10.08)
9.	Back	7.1 × 2.4	17.04	———	17.04
10.	Right	5.5 × 2.4	13.2	0.5 (Window)	12.7
11.	Left	5.5 × 2.4	13.2	1.0 (Two windows)	12.2
12.				Total area covered	48.9

13. Give the total area to be covered in square millimeters. ($1\ m^2 = 1{,}000{,}000\ mm^2$)
48,900,000 mm²

14. Jeff bought concrete blocks like this one. Find the area of the front face.
80,000 mm²

15. To find the number of concrete blocks needed, divide the total area to be covered by the area of the front face of the block. Round up to the next whole number.
612 blocks

16. If concrete blocks cost $1.40 per block, how much will the blocks for the walls cost?
$856.80

17. To finish the garage, Jeff estimates he will spend $350 for the roof, $400 for the door, and a total of $95 for the windows. Add these amounts to the cost of the footings, the cost of the floor, and the cost of the concrete blocks to estimate the total cost of the garage.
$2351.80

Problem Solving

CAREER APPLICATIONS

Objective: Solve problems involving volume.

In this lesson students compute piston displacement and engine displacement.

Automobile Mechanic

Career Cluster: Trades Don Loloma is an automobile mechanic. In order to repair and maintain automobiles, he must know how an automobile engine runs.

See page 53 of *Problem-Solving Masters.*

A gasoline engine works by burning a mixture of gasoline and air inside a cylinder. This causes the piston to move up and down (stroke). The piston is attached to the crankshaft; and the crankshaft is connected, through a series of gears, to the rear wheels of the automobile. In some cars the crankshaft is connected to the front wheels (front-wheel drive) or all four wheels (four-wheel drive).

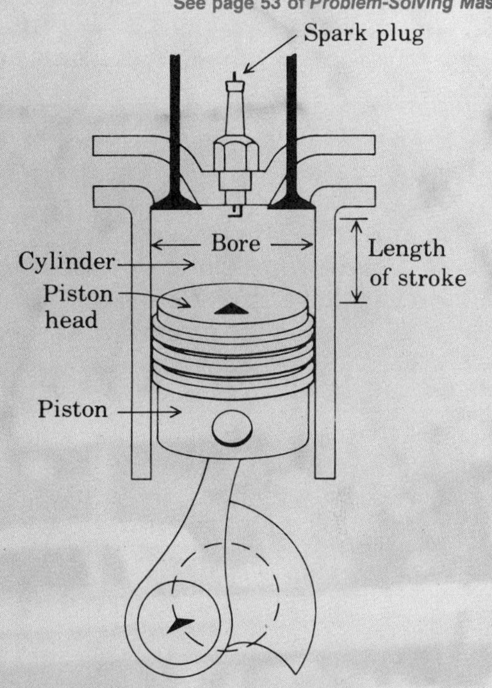

The **piston displacement** is the volume found by multiplying the area of the piston head by the length of the stroke. The greater the piston displacement, the greater the power that is obtained from the engine.

Engine displacement is found by multiplying the piston displacement by the number of cylinders in the engine. Most automobiles have an engine with 4, 6, or 8 cylinders.

Complete this table to find the displacement for various engines.
You may wish to have students round their final answers to the nearest whole number.

	Bore (B)	Radius of piston head ($r = \frac{1}{2}B$)	Area of piston head ($A = \pi r^2$)	Length of stroke (S)	Piston displacement ($P = A \times S$)	Number of cylinders (N)	Engine displacement ($E = P \times N$)
	8 cm	4 cm	50.24 cm^2	7 cm	351.68 cm^3	6	2110.08 cm^3
1.	10 cm	5 cm	78.5 cm^2 (3.14 × 5^2)	5 cm	392.5 cm^3	4	1570 cm^3
2.	6 cm	3 cm	28.26 cm^2	10 cm	282.6 cm^3	6	1695.6 cm^3
3.	7 cm	3.5 cm	38.465 cm^2	8 cm	307.72 cm^3	8	2461.76 cm^3
4.	6 cm	3 cm	28.26 cm^2	8.2 cm	231.732 cm^3	8	1853.856 cm^3
5.	5 cm	2.5 cm	19.625 cm^2	8 cm	157 cm^3	8	1256 cm^3
6.	4 cm	2 cm	12.56 cm^2	4 cm	50.24 cm^3	4	200.96 cm^3
7.	9 cm	4.5 cm	63.585 cm^2	7 cm	445.095 cm^3	6	2670.57 cm^3
8.	4 cm	2 cm	12.56 cm^2	5 cm	62.8 cm^3	6	376.8 cm^3
9.	3.8 cm	1.9 cm	11.3354 cm^2	6 cm	68.0124 cm^3	4	272.0496 cm^3
10.	7.2 cm	3.6 cm	40.6944 cm^2	8 cm	325.5552 cm^3	8	2604.4416 cm^3

Problem Solving

DEVELOPING STRATEGIES

Objective: Solve problems by obtaining information from a picture, using a formula, and reading a table.

In this lesson students compute the costs of materials to pave certain surfaces.

Tactics: Obtaining Information from a Picture, Using a Formula, Reading a Table

Jamie Lauren's job is to quote prices for materials to pave roads and driveways. The tables shown here and the specifications for each job provide her with the data to determine the amount of materials needed and their cost.

Pavement cross section

← Surface course

← Base course

← Crusher run

Table A

Blacktop Surface course $26/metric ton Base course $24/metric ton	
Depth (cm)	Area covered per metric ton (m^2)
2.5	14
3.5	10
5	8
7.5	6
10	4

Table B

Crusher run $21/metric ton $\frac{\text{Square meters}}{\text{Depth factor}} \times 1.9 = \text{Number of metric tons}$	
Depth (cm)	Depth factor
5	18
7.5	12
10	9
12.5	7.2
15	6

Point out to the students that depth is used here to mean thickness.

Problem

Find the cost of the blacktop for the surface-course layer of this driveway.

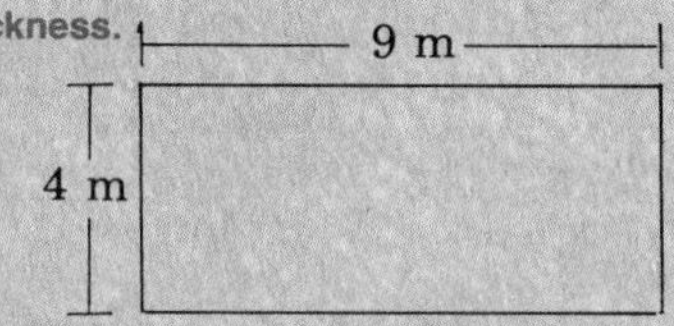

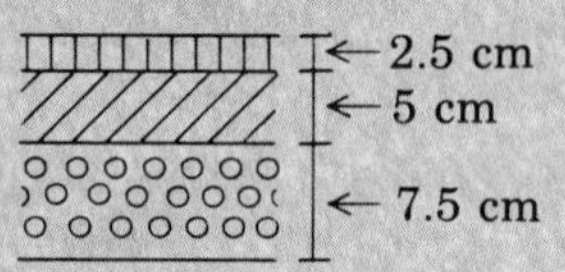

Solution

In her strategy for solving this problem, Jamie used the tactics of obtaining information from a picture, using a formula, and reading a table.

a. What is the area of this driveway? Obtain the necessary information from the picture and use the area formula for a rectangle.

$A = lw$
$A = 9 \times 4$
$A = 36\ m^2$

b. How many metric tons of blacktop are needed for the surface course? First read Table A. Then divide. If necessary, round to the nearest hundredth.

Area of driveway

$36 \div 14 \approx 2.57$ metric tons

Area covered per metric ton

c. What is the cost of the blacktop for the surface course? Read Table A, then multiply.

$2.57 \times 26 = 66.82$

Conclusion: The cost of the blacktop for the surface-course layer is $66.82.

See page 54 of *Problem-Solving Masters.*

Related Problems

Use the driveway described on page 390 for Problems 1–3.

1. Find the cost of the blacktop for the base-course layer.
$108
2. Find the cost of the crusher run. To find the number of metric tons needed, use the formula given in Table B.
$119.70
3. Find the total cost of materials for the three layers of this driveway.
$294.52

Use this diagram for Problems 4–6.

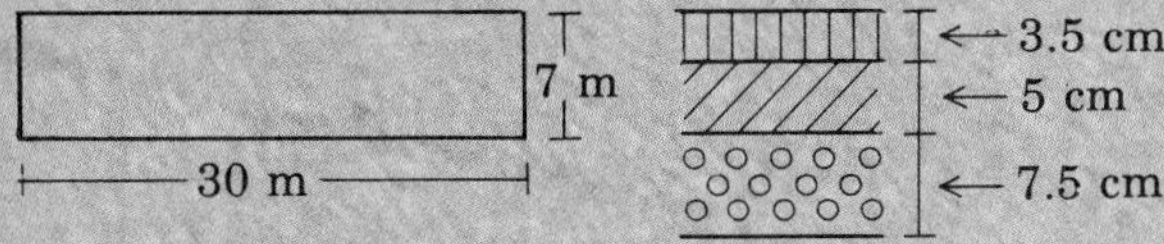

4. Find the cost of the blacktop for the surface course and the base course.
$1176
5. Find the cost of the crusher run.
$698.25
6. Find the total cost of materials to pave the driveway.
$1874.25

Find the total cost of materials to pave these areas. If necessary, round the number of metric tons to the nearest hundredth.

7. Two-lane road $4815

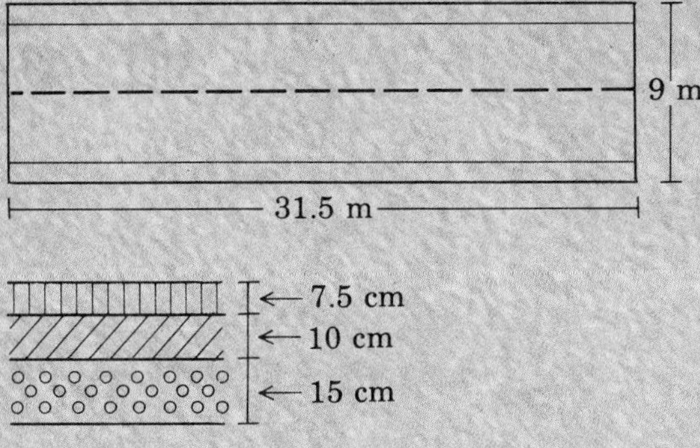

8. Tennis court $6925.57

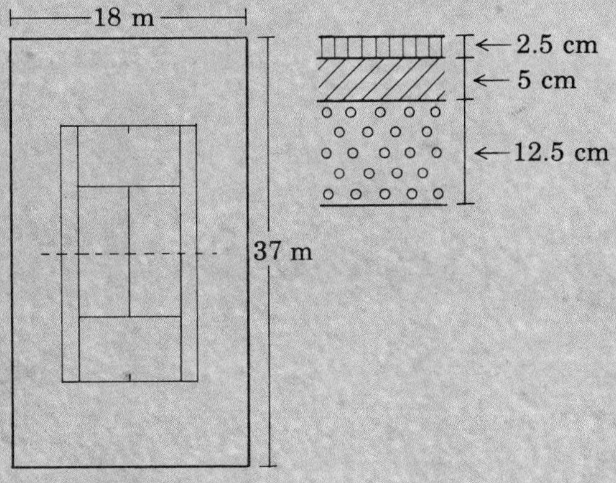

Extension

9. Find the total cost of materials to pave this parking lot. If necessary, round the number of metric tons to the nearest hundredth. $8634.61

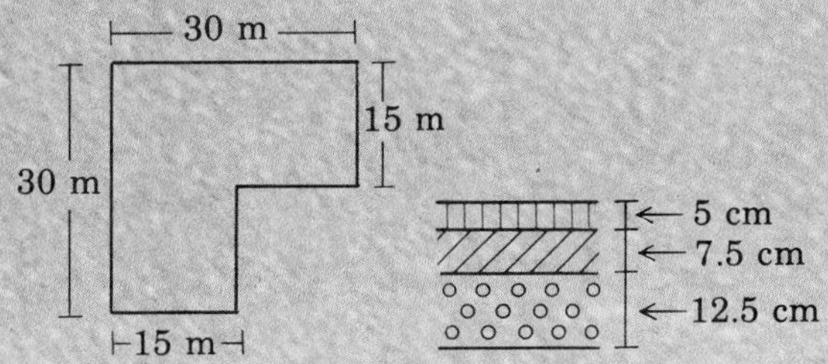

CHAPTER 17 TEST

Number of test items - 15

Number missed	1	2	3	4	5	6	7
Percent correct	93	87	80	73	67	60	53

Find the surface area of each figure.

A **1.** Rectangular prism 990 m^2

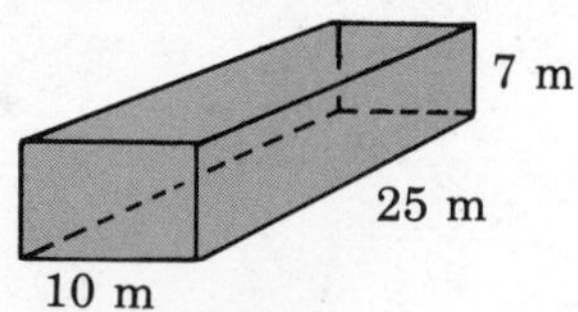

B **2.** Cube 3456 mm^2

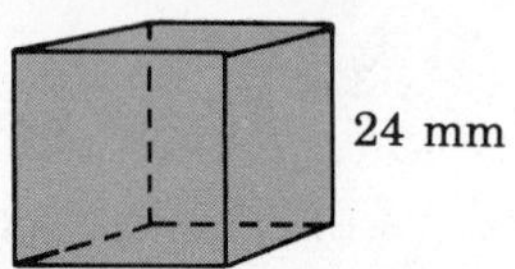

C **3.** Cylinder 1230.88 m^2

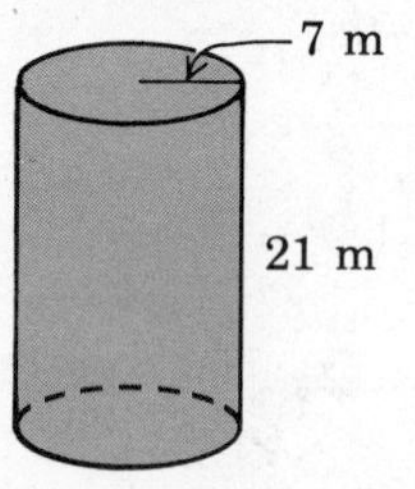

Find the volume of each figure.

D **4.** Rectangular prism 600 m^3

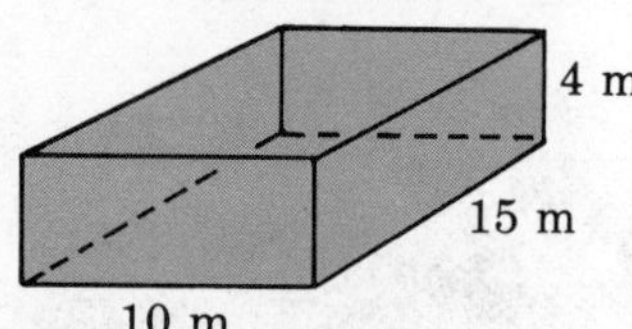

E **5.** Cube 15,625 cm^3

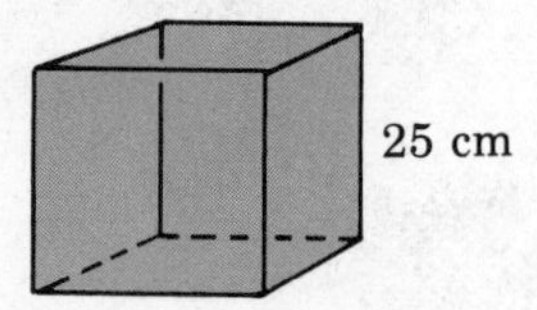

F **6.** Cylinder 1384.74 m^3

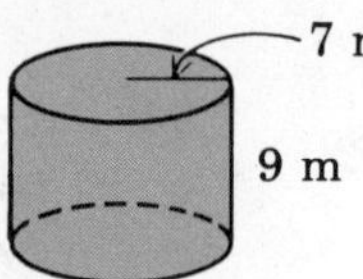

G **7.** Cylinder 942 m^3

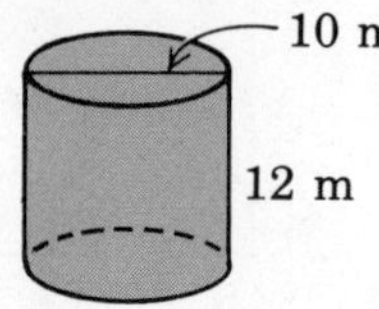

H **8.** Pyramid 324 m^3

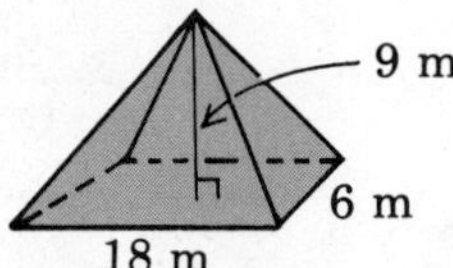

I **9.** Cone 923.16 cm^3

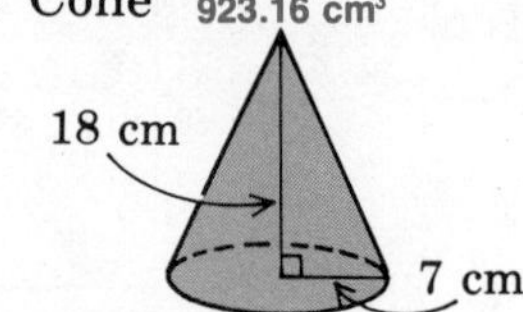

J **10.** Sphere 38,772.72 m^3

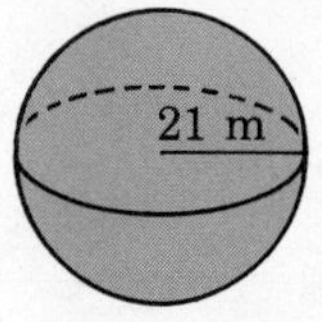

K **11.** Sphere 5572.45 cm^3

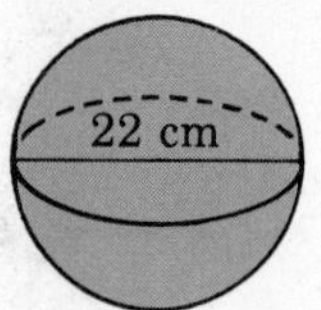

12. How many cubic centimeters of wax are needed to make this candle?
1205.76 cm^3

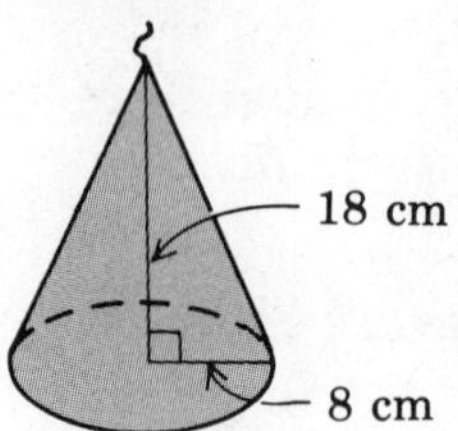

13. How many cubic meters of concrete are needed for a footing that is 7.5 m by 0.3 m by 0.9 m?
2.025 m^3

14. In a cylinder of an engine, the bore (B) is 10 centimeters. What is the area of the piston head?
($r = \frac{1}{2}B$ and $A = \pi r^2$)
78.5 cm^2

15.

Blacktop	
Depth (cm)	Area covered per metric ton (m^2)
2.5	14
3.75	11

How many metric tons of blacktop are needed for the surface course of this driveway? The depth of the surface course is 2.5 cm.
16 metric tons

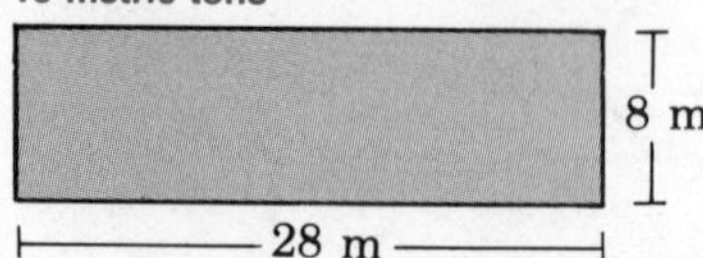

 See pages 43–44 of the *Test Masters* for an alternate form of the Chapter 17 Test.

CHAPTER 18 The Pythagorean Rule and Trigonometry

SKILLS PRETEST

Number of test items-16

Number missed	1	2	3	4	5	6	7	8
Percent correct	94	88	81	75	69	63	56	50

SKILL Using Exponents and Square Roots *page 395*

A Compute 5^4.
625

B Find $\sqrt{64}$.
8

SKILL Reading a Table of Squares and Square Roots *pages 396–397*

C Find 35^2. Use the table on page 397.
1225

D Find $\sqrt{46}$ to the nearest tenth. Use the table on page 397.
6.8

E Find $\sqrt{7921}$. Use the table on page 397.
89

SKILL Using the Pythagorean Rule *pages 398–399*

F Use the Pythagorean Rule to find the length of the hypotenuse to the nearest tenth. Use the table on page 397.
7.8 cm

6 cm

5 cm

G Use the Pythagorean Rule to find the missing length to the nearest tenth. Use the table on page 397.
7.2 cm

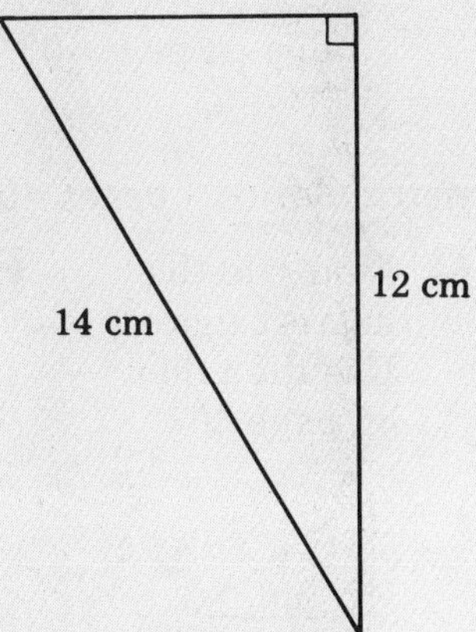

Pretest continued on page 394.

Pretest continued from page 393.

SKILL Writing Trigonometric Ratios *pages 400–401*

H Give the tangent of ∠R as a ratio and as a decimal to the nearest thousandth.

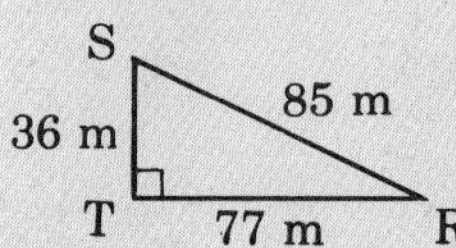

I Give the sine of ∠R in item H as a ratio and as a decimal to the nearest thousandth.

J Give the cosine of ∠R in item H as a ratio and as a decimal to the nearest thousandth.

tan ∠R = $\frac{36}{77} \approx 0.468$

sin ∠R = $\frac{36}{85} \approx 0.424$

cos ∠R = $\frac{77}{85} \approx 0.906$

SKILL Reading a Table of Trigonometric Ratios *pages 402–403*

K Give the tangent of 18° as a decimal to the nearest thousandth. Use the table on page 403.
0.325

L Give the sine of 43° as a decimal to the nearest thousandth. Use the table on page 403.
0.682

M Give the cosine of 52° as a decimal to the nearest thousandth. Use the table on page 403.
0.616

SKILL Using Trigonometric Ratios *pages 404–405*

N Find n to the nearest tenth. Use the table on page 403.
19.2 cm

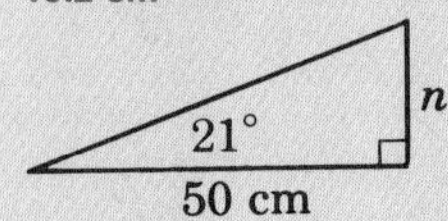

O Find k to the nearest tenth. Use the table on page 403.
51.7 cm

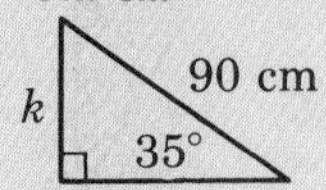

P Find w to the nearest tenth. Use the table on page 403.
37.5 m

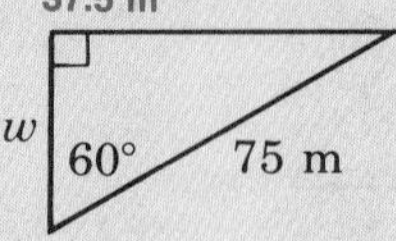

Objective: Find powers of numbers by using positive exponents, and find square roots of numbers by trial and error.

Using Exponents and Square Roots

Example A Exponents

Compute 3^4.

In 3^4 the 4 is called an **exponent.** It tells how many times to use 3 as a factor.

$3^1 = 3$
3^1 is read "three to the first power."

$3^2 = 3 \times 3 = 9$
3^2 is read "three squared" or "three to the second power."

$3^3 = 3 \times 3 \times 3 = 27$
3^3 is read "three cubed" or "three to the third power."

$3^4 = 3 \times 3 \times 3 \times 3 = 81$
3^4 is read "three to the fourth power."

Example B Finding square roots

Find $\sqrt{25}$.

$\sqrt{25}$ is read "**square root** of 25."
The square root of 25 is a number that when squared equals 25.

$25 = \square^2$	Try different numbers until you find a number that when squared equals 25.
$25 = 5^2$	25 is 5 squared.
$\sqrt{25} = 5$	So 5 is a square root of 25.

The meaning of square root is emphasized in this lesson. A square root table is used in the next lesson.

Exercises

Set A

Compute each number.

1. 6^3 216
2. 2^4 16
3. 7^1 7
4. 1^7 1
5. 2^3 8
6. 3^5 243
7. 7^2 49
8. 2^5 32
9. 5^2 25
10. 4^4 256
11. 1^3 1
12. 5^4 625
13. 4^2 16
14. 5^3 125
15. 10^1 10
16. 10^2 100
17. 10^3 1000
18. 10^4 10,000
19. 10^5 100,000
20. 10^7 10,000,000
21. 10^9 1,000,000,000
22. 13^2 169
23. 78^1 78
24. 18^2 324
25. 20^3 8000
26. 25^2 625
27. $(5.1)^2$ 26.01
28. $(0.7)^2$ 0.49
29. $(0.2)^4$ 0.0016
30. $(1.2)^3$ 1.728

Set B

Find each square root. Try different numbers until you find the correct answer.

1. $\sqrt{9}$ 3
2. $\sqrt{4}$ 2
3. $\sqrt{1}$ 1
4. $\sqrt{16}$ 4
5. $\sqrt{49}$ 7
6. $\sqrt{100}$ 10
7. $\sqrt{144}$ 12
8. $\sqrt{121}$ 11
9. $\sqrt{225}$ 15
10. $\sqrt{900}$ 30
11. $\sqrt{400}$ 20
12. $\sqrt{196}$ 14
13. $\sqrt{625}$ 25
14. $\sqrt{169}$ 13
15. $\sqrt{576}$ 24
16. $\sqrt{4900}$ 70
17. $\sqrt{2500}$ 50
18. $\sqrt{1600}$ 40
19. $\sqrt{3600}$ 60
20. $\sqrt{10,000}$ 100

Objective: Find squares and square roots of numbers by reading a table.

Reading a Table of Squares and Square Roots

Example C Finding squares

Find 84^2. Use the table on page 397.

Find 84 in the column labeled "n." Read the number to the right in the column labeled "n^2."

n	n^2	$\sqrt{n}$
84	7056	9.165

$84^2 = 7056$

Example D Finding square roots

Find $\sqrt{42}$ to the nearest tenth. Use the table on page 397.

Find 42 in the column labeled "n." Read the number in the column labeled "$\sqrt{n}$."

n	n^2	$\sqrt{n}$
42	1764	6.481

The table gives an approximation correct to thousandths. Round to the nearest tenth.

$\sqrt{42} \approx 6.5$

Example E Finding the square root of a perfect square

Find $\sqrt{6241}$. Use the table on page 397.

$6241 = \square^2$ — 6241 is not shown in the column labeled "n." Look in the column labeled "n^2."

$6241 = 79^2$ — 6241 is 79 squared.

$\sqrt{6241} = 79$ — So 79 is a square root of 6241.

Exercises

Set C

Find each number. Use the table on page 397.

1. 61^2 3721
2. 19^2 361
3. 87^2 7569
4. 54^2 2916
5. 38^2 1444
6. 57^2 3249
7. 30^2 900
8. 17^2 289
9. 83^2 6889
10. 21^2 441
11. 177^2 31,329
12. 196^2 38,416
13. 110^2 12,100
14. 145^2 21,025
15. 189^2 35,721

Set D

Find each square root to the nearest tenth. Use the table on page 397.

1. $\sqrt{15}$ 3.9
2. $\sqrt{88}$ 9.4
3. $\sqrt{40}$ 6.3
4. $\sqrt{56}$ 7.5
5. $\sqrt{2}$ 1.4
6. $\sqrt{23}$ 4.8
7. $\sqrt{59}$ 7.7
8. $\sqrt{3}$ 1.7
9. $\sqrt{64}$ 8.0
10. $\sqrt{8}$ 2.8
11. $\sqrt{180}$ 13.4
12. $\sqrt{174}$ 13.2
13. $\sqrt{101}$ 10.1
14. $\sqrt{143}$ 12.0
15. $\sqrt{197}$ 14.0

Set E

Find each square root. Use the table on page 397.

1. $\sqrt{676}$ 26
2. $\sqrt{225}$ 15
3. $\sqrt{484}$ 22
4. $\sqrt{841}$ 29
5. $\sqrt{324}$ 18
6. $\sqrt{7744}$ 88
7. $\sqrt{4356}$ 66
8. $\sqrt{3481}$ 59
9. $\sqrt{2401}$ 49
10. $\sqrt{1156}$ 34
11. $\sqrt{14,884}$ 122
12. $\sqrt{36,100}$ 190
13. $\sqrt{39,601}$ 199
14. $\sqrt{15,376}$ 124
15. $\sqrt{27,889}$ 167

Squares and Square Roots

n	n^2	$\sqrt{n}$	n	n^2	$\sqrt{n}$	n	n^2	$\sqrt{n}$	n	n^2	$\sqrt{n}$
1	1	1.000	**51**	2601	7.141	**101**	10,201	10.050	**151**	22,801	12.288
2	4	1.414	**52**	2704	7.211	**102**	10,404	10.100	**152**	23,104	12.329
3	9	1.732	**53**	2809	7.280	**103**	10,609	10.149	**153**	23,409	12.369
4	16	2.000	**54**	2916	7.348	**104**	10,816	10.198	**154**	23,716	12.410
5	25	2.236	**55**	3025	7.416	**105**	11,025	10.247	**155**	24,025	12.450
6	36	2.449	**56**	3136	7.483	**106**	11,236	10.296	**156**	24,336	12.490
7	49	2.646	**57**	3249	7.550	**107**	11,449	10.344	**157**	24,649	12.530
8	64	2.828	**58**	3364	7.616	**108**	11,664	10.392	**158**	24,964	12.570
9	81	3.000	**59**	3481	7.681	**109**	11,881	10.440	**159**	25,281	12.610
10	100	3.162	**60**	3600	7.746	**110**	12,100	10.488	**160**	25,600	12.649
11	121	3.317	**61**	3721	7.810	**111**	12,321	10.536	**161**	25,921	12.689
12	144	3.464	**62**	3844	7.874	**112**	12,544	10.583	**162**	26,244	12.728
13	169	3.606	**63**	3969	7.937	**113**	12,769	10.630	**163**	26,569	12.767
14	196	3.742	**64**	4096	8.000	**114**	12,996	10.677	**164**	26,896	12.806
15	225	3.873	**65**	4225	8.062	**115**	13,225	10.724	**165**	27,225	12.845
16	256	4.000	**66**	4356	8.124	**116**	13,456	10.770	**166**	27,556	12.884
17	289	4.123	**67**	4489	8.185	**117**	13,689	10.817	**167**	27,889	12.923
18	324	4.243	**68**	4624	8.246	**118**	13,924	10.863	**168**	28,224	12.961
19	361	4.359	**69**	4761	8.307	**119**	14,161	10.909	**169**	28,561	13.000
20	400	4.472	**70**	4900	8.367	**120**	14,400	10.954	**170**	28,900	13.038
21	441	4.583	**71**	5041	8.426	**121**	14,641	11.000	**171**	29,241	13.077
22	484	4.690	**72**	5184	8.485	**122**	14,884	11.045	**172**	29,584	13.115
23	529	4.796	**73**	5329	8.544	**123**	15,129	11.091	**173**	29,929	13.153
24	576	4.899	**74**	5476	8.602	**124**	15,376	11.136	**174**	30,276	13.191
25	625	5.000	**75**	5625	8.660	**125**	15,625	11.180	**175**	30,625	13.229
26	676	5.099	**76**	5776	8.718	**126**	15,876	11.225	**176**	30,976	13.266
27	729	5.196	**77**	5929	8.775	**127**	16,129	11.269	**177**	31,329	13.304
28	784	5.292	**78**	6084	8.832	**128**	16,384	11.314	**178**	31,684	13.342
29	841	5.385	**79**	6241	8.888	**129**	16,641	11.358	**179**	32,041	13.379
30	900	5.477	**80**	6400	8.944	**130**	16,900	11.402	**180**	32,400	13.416
31	961	5.568	**81**	6561	9.000	**131**	17,161	11.446	**181**	32,761	13.454
32	1024	5.657	**82**	6724	9.055	**132**	17,424	11.489	**182**	33,124	13.491
33	1089	5.745	**83**	6889	9.110	**133**	17,689	11.533	**183**	33,489	13.528
34	1156	5.831	**84**	7056	9.165	**134**	17,956	11.576	**184**	33,856	13.565
35	1225	5.916	**85**	7225	9.220	**135**	18,225	11.619	**185**	34,225	13.601
36	1296	6.000	**86**	7396	9.274	**136**	18,496	11.662	**186**	34,596	13.638
37	1369	6.083	**87**	7569	9.327	**137**	18,769	11.705	**187**	34,969	13.675
38	1444	6.164	**88**	7744	9.381	**138**	19,044	11.747	**188**	35,344	13.711
39	1521	6.245	**89**	7921	9.434	**139**	19,321	11.790	**189**	35,721	13.748
40	1600	6.325	**90**	8100	9.487	**140**	19,600	11.832	**190**	36,100	13.784
41	1681	6.403	**91**	8281	9.539	**141**	19,881	11.874	**191**	36,481	13.820
42	1764	6.481	**92**	8464	9.592	**142**	20,164	11.916	**192**	36,864	13.856
43	1849	6.557	**93**	8649	9.644	**143**	20,449	11.958	**193**	37.249	13.892
44	1936	6.633	**94**	8836	9.695	**144**	20,736	12.000	**194**	37,636	13.928
45	2025	6.708	**95**	9025	9.747	**145**	21,025	12.042	**195**	38,025	13.964
46	2116	6.782	**96**	9216	9.798	**146**	21,316	12.083	**196**	38,416	14.000
47	2209	6.856	**97**	9409	9.849	**147**	21,609	12.124	**197**	38,809	14.036
48	2304	6.928	**98**	9604	9.899	**148**	21,904	12.166	**198**	39,204	14.071
49	2401	7.000	**99**	9801	9.950	**149**	22,201	12.207	**199**	39,601	14.107
50	2500	7.071	**100**	10,000	10.000	**150**	22,500	12.247	**200**	40,000	14.142

Objective: Find the length of a side of a right triangle by using the Pythagorean Rule.

Using the Pythagorean Rule

See page T45 for an activity that develops the Pythagorean Rule.

Example F Finding the hypotenuse

Use the Pythagorean Rule to find the length of the hypotenuse to the nearest tenth. Use the table on page 397.

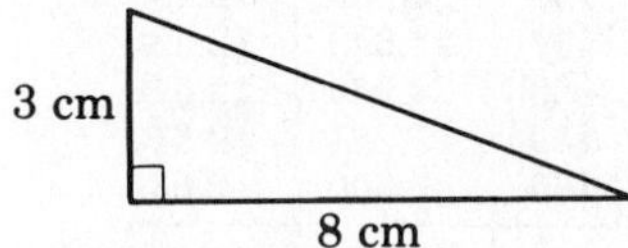

A **right triangle** has a right angle (90°). The longest side of a right triangle is called the **hypotenuse.** The hypotenuse is always opposite the right angle. The other two sides are called **legs.**

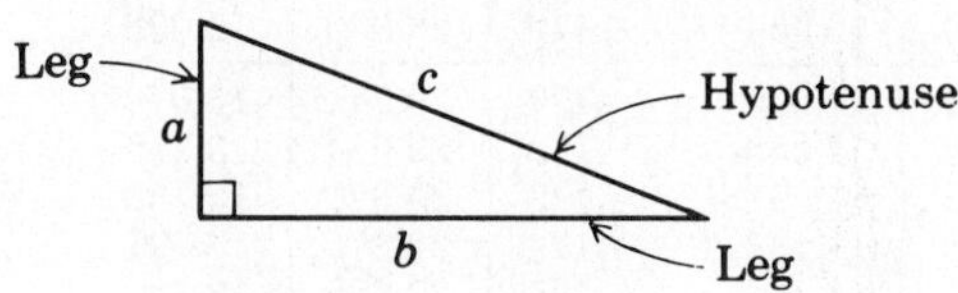

The **Pythagorean Rule** states that for any right triangle with hypotenuse of length c and legs of lengths a and b, $a^2 + b^2 = c^2$.

$a^2 + b^2 = c^2$	Substitute 3 for a and 8 for b.
$3^2 + 8^2 = c^2$	Find 3^2 and 8^2.
$9 + 64 = c^2$	
$73 = c^2$	Since 73 is c squared, c is a square root of 73.
$\sqrt{73} = c$	The table on page 397 shows that $\sqrt{73}$ is 8.544. Round 8.544 to the nearest tenth.
$8.5 \approx c$	

The hypotenuse is about 8.5 centimeters long.

Example G Finding a missing leg

Use the Pythagorean Rule to find the missing length. Use the table on page 397.

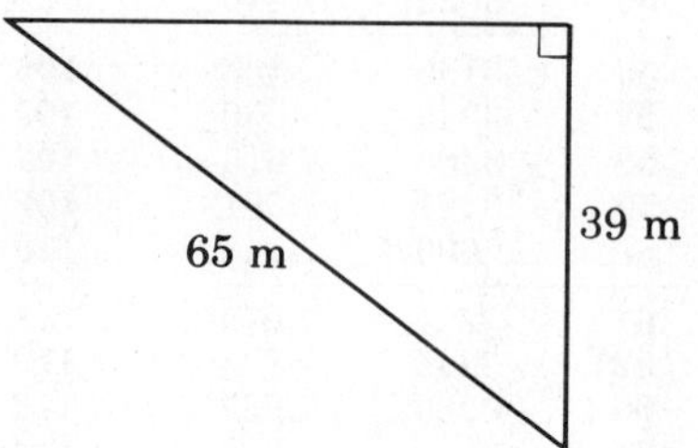

$a^2 + b^2 = c^2$	Substitute 39 for a and 65 for c.
$39^2 + b^2 = 65^2$	Find 39^2 and 65^2 by multiplying or by using the table on page 397.
$1521 + b^2 = 4225$	Subtract 1521 from both sides of the equation.
$b^2 = 2704$	Since 2704 is b^2, b is a square root of 2704.
$b = \sqrt{2704}$	The table on page 397 shows that 52^2 is 2704. So 52 is a square root of 2704.
$b = 52$	

The missing length is 52 meters.

Exercises

PROBLEM SOLVING
The applications on pages 408–411 may be used anytime after this lesson.

Set F

Use the Pythagorean Rule to find the length of each hypotenuse to the nearest tenth. Use the table on page 397.

1.

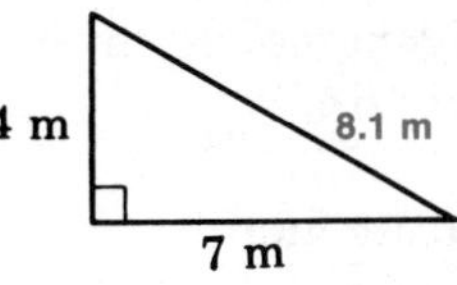

2.

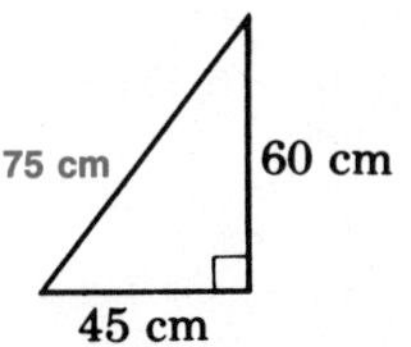

3.

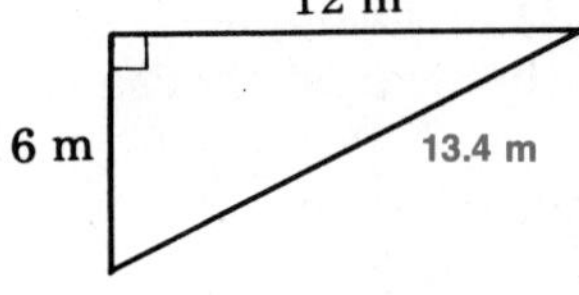

4.

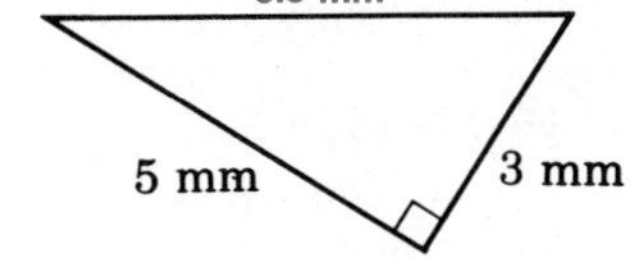

5.

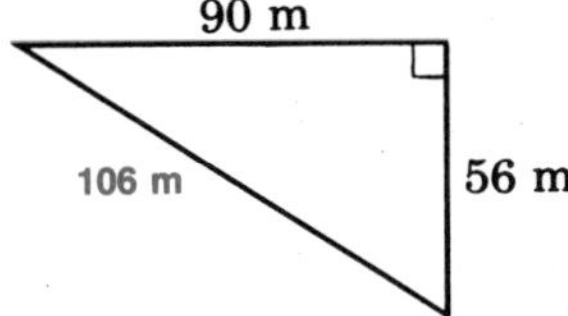

	Length in meters		
	Leg	Leg	Hypotenuse
6.	8	10	▦ 12.8
7.	40	9	▦ 41
8.	7	7	▦ 9.9
9.	11	3	▦ 11.4
10.	5	12	▦ 13
11.	6	4	▦ 7.2
12.	8	11	▦ 13.6
13.	20	21	▦ 29
14.	7	24	▦ 25
15.	10	9	▦ 13.5
16.	12	7	▦ 13.9
17.	8	15	▦ 17
18.	6	3	▦ 6.7

Set G

Use the Pythagorean Rule to find each missing length to the nearest tenth. Use the table on page 397.

1.

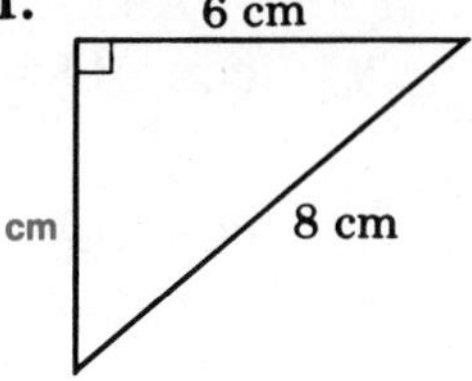

2.

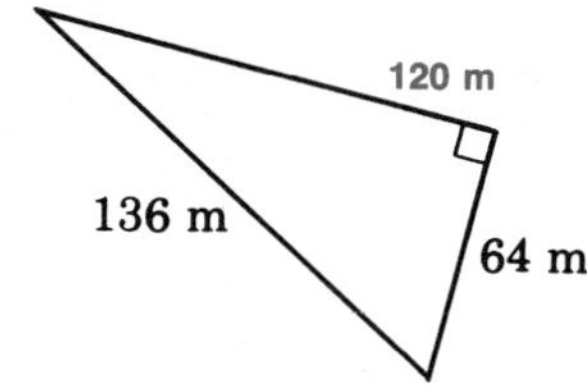

3.

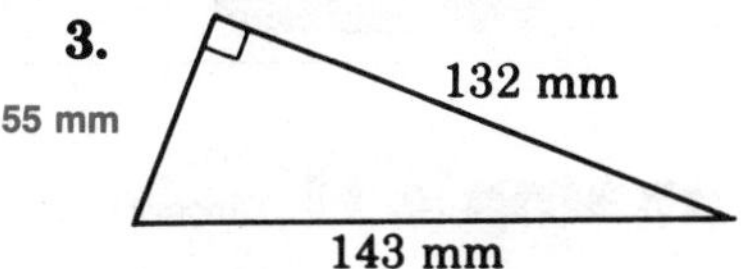

4.

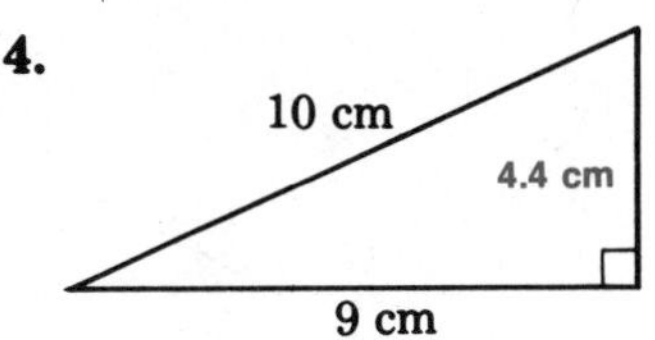

5.

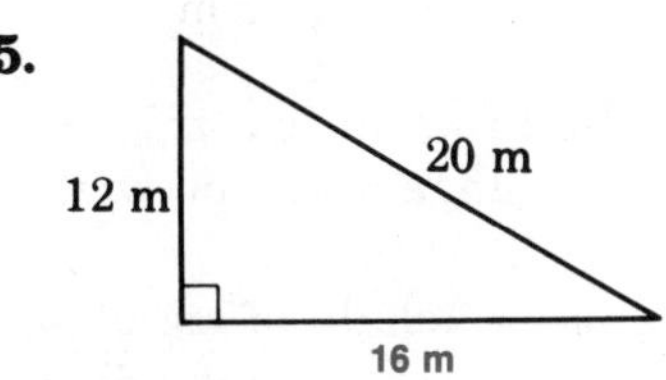

	Length in meters		
	Leg	Leg	Hypotenuse
6.	11	▦ 6.9	13
7.	▦ 40	30	50
8.	▦ 42	40	58
9.	10	▦ 13.7	17
10.	▦ 10.7	9	14
11.	84	▦ 135	159
12.	1	▦ 1.7	2
13.	▦ 72	21	75
14.	▦ 9.8	5	11
15.	18	▦ 8.7	20
16.	▦ 90	120	150
17.	41	▦ 9.1	42
18.	▦ 120	27	123

Objective: Write the tangent, the sine, and the cosine of a given angle as a ratio and as a decimal.

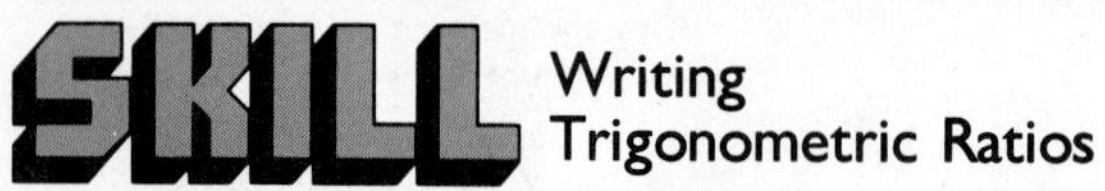

Writing Trigonometric Ratios

Example H Tangent

Give the tangent of ∠Q as a ratio and as a decimal to the nearest thousandth.

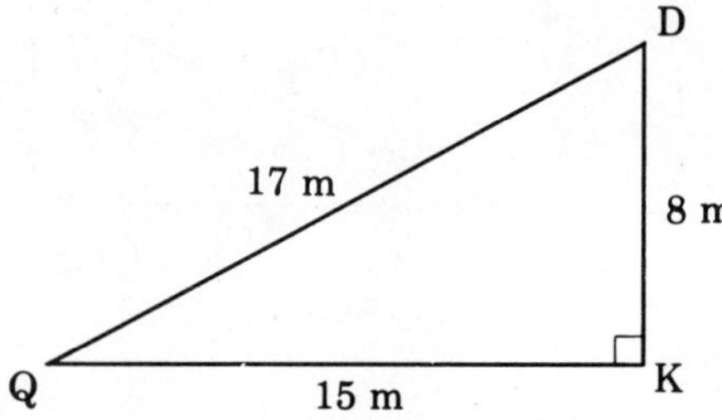

The **tangent** is a **trigonometric ratio.** The tangent can be written "tan."

$$\text{tan} = \frac{\textbf{length of leg opposite angle}}{\textbf{length of leg adjacent to angle}}$$

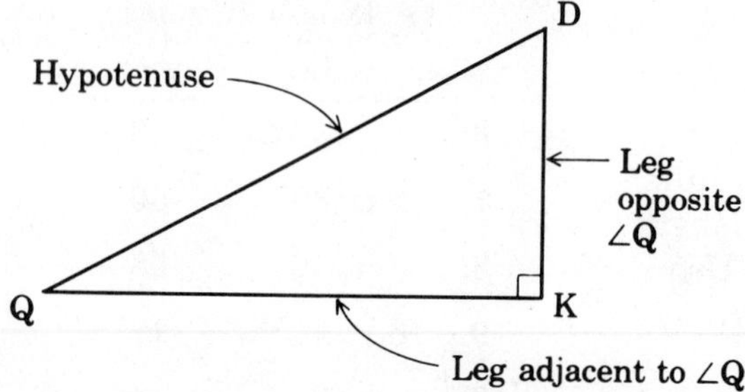

$\tan \angle Q = \frac{8}{15}$

$\tan \angle Q \approx 0.533$

Divide 8 by 15. Give the quotient to the nearest thousandth.

$15\overline{)8.0000}$ = 0.5333 ≈ 0.533

Example I Sine

Give the sine of ∠Q in Example H as a ratio and as a decimal to the nearest thousandth.

The **sine** is another trigonometric ratio. The sine can be written "sin."

$$\text{sin} = \frac{\textbf{length of leg opposite angle}}{\textbf{length of hypotenuse}}$$

$\sin \angle Q = \frac{8}{17}$

$\sin \angle Q \approx 0.471$

Divide 8 by 17.

$17\overline{)8.0000}$ = 0.4705 ≈ 0.471

Example J Cosine

Give the cosine of ∠Q in Example H as a ratio and as a decimal to the nearest thousandth.

The **cosine** is another trigonometric ratio. The cosine can be written "cos."

$$\text{cos} = \frac{\textbf{length of leg adjacent to angle}}{\textbf{length of hypotenuse}}$$

$\cos \angle Q = \frac{15}{17}$

$\cos \angle Q \approx 0.882$

Divide 15 by 17.

$17\overline{)15.0000}$ = 0.8823 ≈ 0.882

Exercises

Set H

For each angle listed, give the tangent as a ratio and as a decimal to the nearest thousandth. All lengths are given in meters.

1. $\angle J$ $\tan \angle J = \frac{20}{21} \approx 0.952$

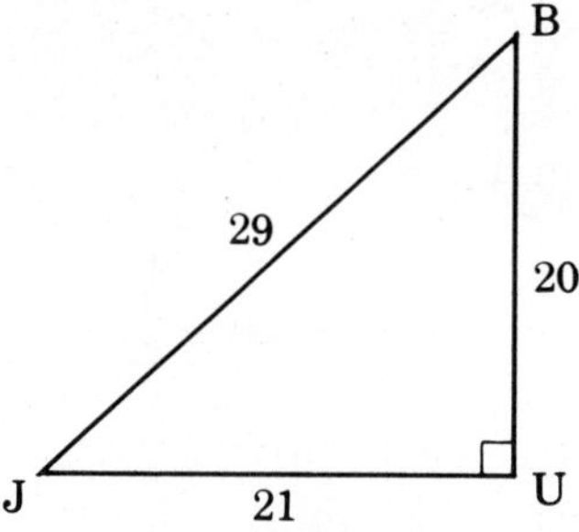

2. $\angle V$ $\tan \angle V = \frac{8}{6} \approx 1.333$

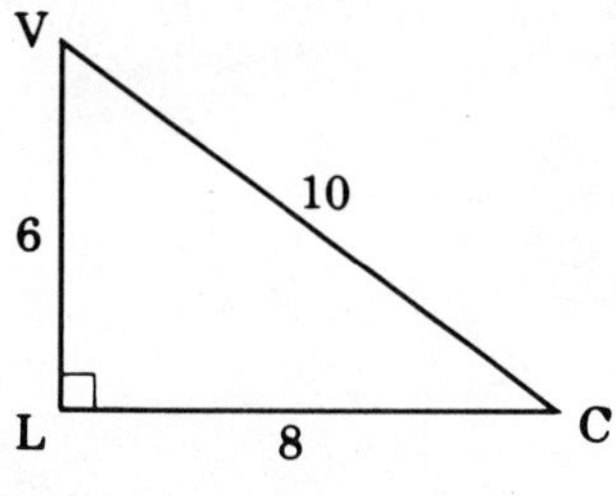

3. $\angle M$ $\tan \angle M = \frac{5}{12} \approx 0.417$

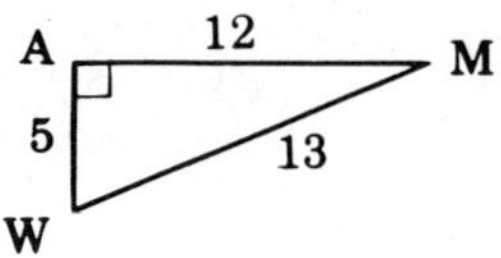

4. $\angle Y$ $\tan \angle Y = \frac{7}{24} \approx 0.292$
5. $\angle K$ $\tan \angle K = \frac{24}{7} \approx 3.429$

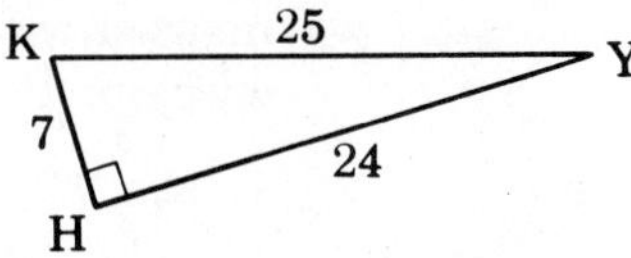

6. $\angle T$ $\tan \angle T = \frac{35}{12} \approx 2.917$
7. $\angle X$ $\tan \angle X = \frac{12}{35} \approx 0.343$

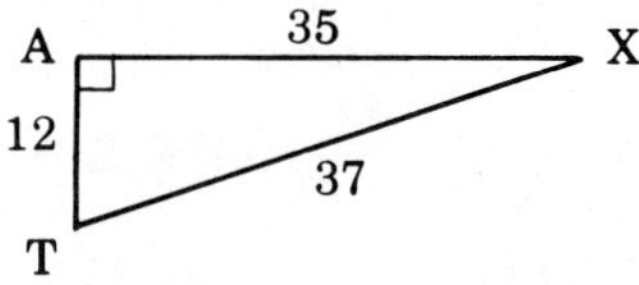

8. $\angle S$ $\tan \angle S = \frac{28}{45} \approx 0.622$
9. $\angle D$ $\tan \angle D = \frac{45}{28} \approx 1.607$

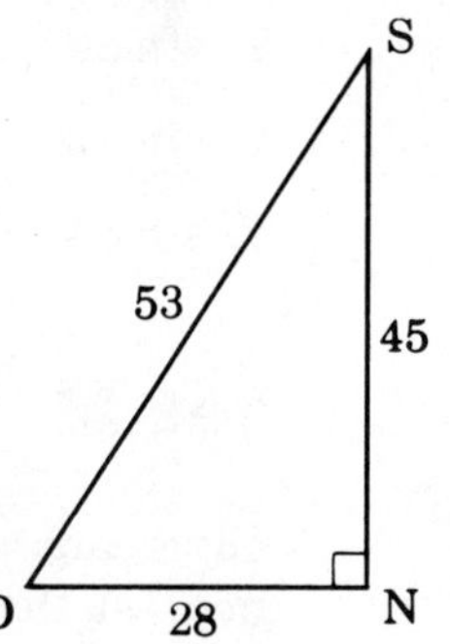

10. $\angle B$ $\tan \angle B = \frac{9}{40} \approx 0.225$
11. $\angle P$ $\tan \angle P = \frac{40}{9} \approx 4.444$

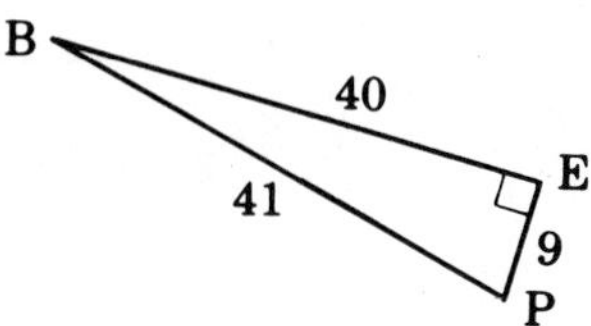

12. $\angle R$ $\tan \angle R = \frac{154}{72} \approx 2.139$
13. $\angle G$ $\tan \angle G = \frac{72}{154} \approx 0.468$

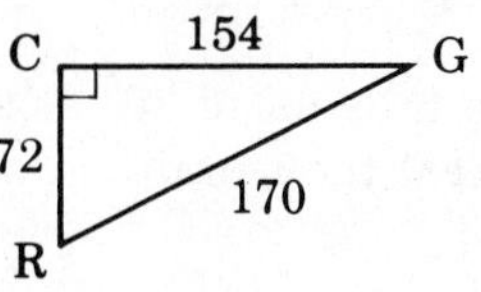

14. $\angle Z$ $\tan \angle Z = \frac{63}{16} \approx 3.938$
15. $\angle F$ $\tan \angle F = \frac{16}{63} \approx 0.254$

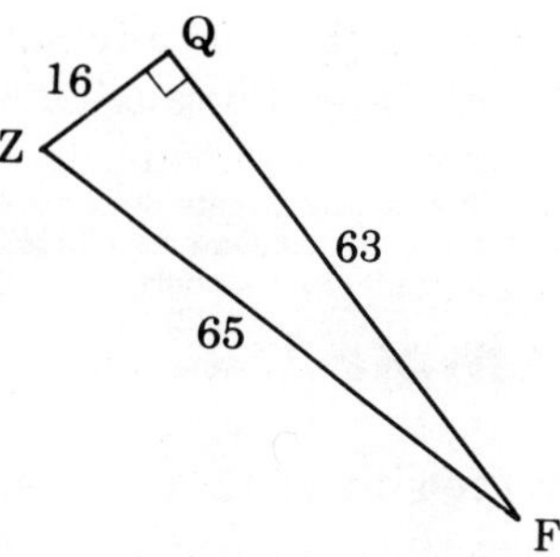

Set I

1–15. For each exercise in Set H, give the sine of the angle as a ratio and as a decimal to the nearest thousandth.
See Additional Answers on page T54.

Set J

1–15. For each exercise in Set H, give the cosine of the angle as a ratio and as a decimal to the nearest thousandth.
See Additional Answers on page T54.

Objective: Give the tangent, the sine, and the cosine of a given angle by reading a table.

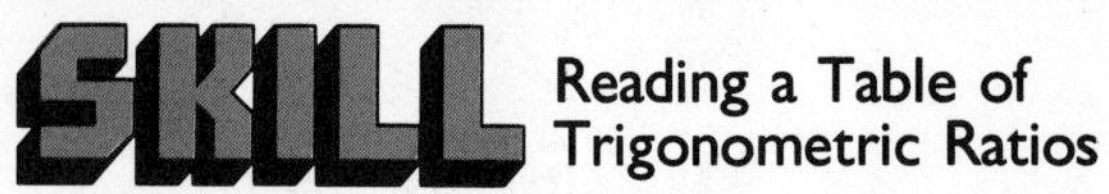

Reading a Table of Trigonometric Ratios

Example K Tangent

Give the tangent of 36° as a decimal to the nearest thousandth. Use the table on page 403.

Locate 36° in the table. Read the number to the right in the column labeled "tan."

$\tan 36° \approx 0.727$

This means that for any 36° angle in any right triangle, the tangent will be 0.727 to the nearest thousandth.
To show this, have students draw several right triangles with 36° angles, measure sides opposite and adjacent, and then write the tangents as decimals.

Example L Sine

Give the sine of 15° as a decimal to the nearest thousandth. Use the table on page 403.

Locate 15° in the table. Read the number to the right in the column labeled "sin."

$\sin 15° \approx 0.259$

Example M Cosine

Give the cosine of 72° as a decimal to the nearest thousandth. Use the table on page 403.

Locate 72° in the table. Read the number to the right in the column labeled "cos."

$\cos 72° \approx 0.309$

Exercises

Set K

Give each tangent as a decimal to the nearest thousandth. Use the table on page 403.

1. tan 9° 0.158
2. tan 28° 0.532
3. tan 75° 3.732
4. tan 13° 0.231
5. tan 56° 1.483
6. tan 42° 0.900
7. tan 86° 14.301
8. tan 23° 0.424
9. tan 88° 28.636
10. tan 4° 0.070

Set L

Give each sine as a decimal to the nearest thousandth. Use the table on page 403.

1. sin 71° 0.946
2. sin 54° 0.809
3. sin 30° 0.500
4. sin 12° 0.208
5. sin 84° 0.995
6. sin 37° 0.602
7. sin 49° 0.755
8. sin 63° 0.891
9. sin 16° 0.276
10. sin 68° 0.927

Set M

Give each cosine as a decimal to the nearest thousandth. Use the table on page 403.

1. cos 19° 0.946
2. cos 4° 0.998
3. cos 50° 0.643
4. cos 82° 0.139
5. cos 31° 0.857
6. cos 67° 0.391
7. cos 58° 0.530
8. cos 24° 0.914
9. cos 45° 0.707
10. cos 62° 0.469

Trigonometric Ratios

Measure of angle	tan	sin	cos
1°	0.017	0.017	1.000
2°	0.035	0.035	0.999
3°	0.052	0.052	0.999
4°	0.070	0.070	0.998
5°	0.087	0.087	0.996
6°	0.105	0.105	0.995
7°	0.123	0.122	0.993
8°	0.141	0.139	0.990
9°	0.158	0.156	0.988
10°	0.176	0.174	0.985
11°	0.194	0.191	0.982
12°	0.213	0.208	0.978
13°	0.231	0.225	0.974
14°	0.249	0.242	0.970
15°	0.268	0.259	0.966
16°	0.287	0.276	0.961
17°	0.306	0.292	0.956
18°	0.325	0.309	0.951
19°	0.344	0.326	0.946
20°	0.364	0.342	0.940
21°	0.384	0.358	0.934
22°	0.404	0.375	0.927
23°	0.424	0.391	0.921
24°	0.445	0.407	0.914
25°	0.466	0.423	0.906
26°	0.488	0.438	0.899
27°	0.510	0.454	0.891
28°	0.532	0.469	0.883
29°	0.554	0.485	0.875
30°	0.577	0.500	0.866
31°	0.601	0.515	0.857
32°	0.625	0.530	0.848
33°	0.649	0.545	0.839
34°	0.675	0.559	0.829
35°	0.700	0.574	0.819
36°	0.727	0.588	0.809
37°	0.754	0.602	0.799
38°	0.781	0.616	0.788
39°	0.810	0.629	0.777
40°	0.839	0.643	0.766
41°	0.869	0.656	0.755
42°	0.900	0.669	0.743
43°	0.933	0.682	0.731
44°	0.966	0.695	0.719
45°	1.000	0.707	0.707

Measure of angle	tan	sin	cos
46°	1.036	0.719	0.695
47°	1.072	0.731	0.682
48°	1.111	0.743	0.669
49°	1.150	0.755	0.656
50°	1.192	0.766	0.643
51°	1.235	0.777	0.629
52°	1.280	0.788	0.616
53°	1.327	0.799	0.602
54°	1.376	0.809	0.588
55°	1.428	0.819	0.574
56°	1.483	0.829	0.559
57°	1.540	0.839	0.545
58°	1.600	0.848	0.530
59°	1.664	0.857	0.515
60°	1.732	0.866	0.500
61°	1.804	0.875	0.485
62°	1.881	0.883	0.469
63°	1.963	0.891	0.454
64°	2.050	0.899	0.438
65°	2.145	0.906	0.423
66°	2.246	0.914	0.407
67°	2.356	0.921	0.391
68°	2.475	0.927	0.375
69°	2.605	0.934	0.358
70°	2.748	0.940	0.342
71°	2.904	0.946	0.326
72°	3.078	0.951	0.309
73°	3.271	0.956	0.292
74°	3.487	0.961	0.276
75°	3.732	0.966	0.259
76°	4.011	0.970	0.242
77°	4.332	0.974	0.225
78°	4.705	0.978	0.208
79°	5.145	0.982	0.191
80°	5.671	0.985	0.174
81°	6.314	0.988	0.156
82°	7.115	0.990	0.139
83°	8.144	0.993	0.122
84°	9.514	0.995	0.105
85°	11.430	0.996	0.087
86°	14.301	0.998	0.070
87°	19.081	0.999	0.052
88°	28.636	0.999	0.035
89°	57.290	1.000	0.017

BREAK TIME

Each side of the square is 5 meters long. Find the circumference of each circle to the nearest tenth of a meter.

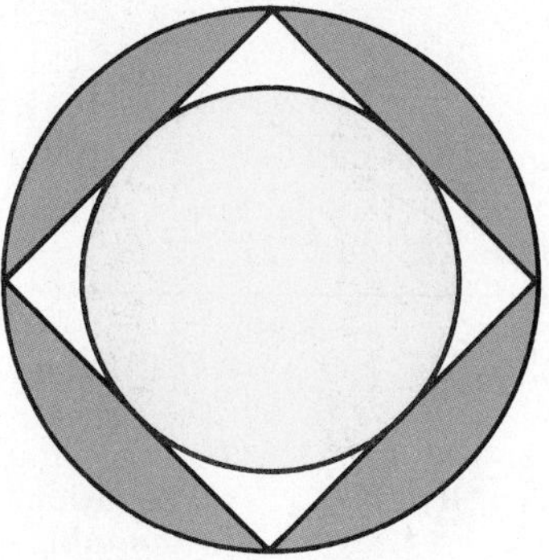

Smaller circle: 15.7 m

Larger circle: 22.2 m

The radius of the circle is 9 meters. Find the perimeter of each square to the nearest tenth of a meter.

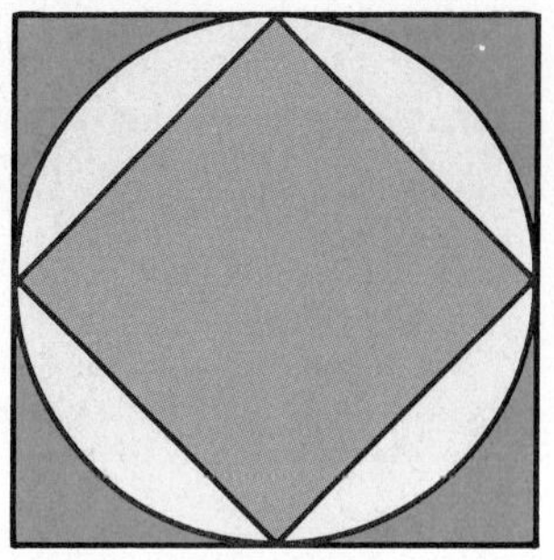

Smaller square: 50.9 m

Larger square: 72.0 m

Objective: Find the length of a side of a right triangle by using a trigonometric ratio.

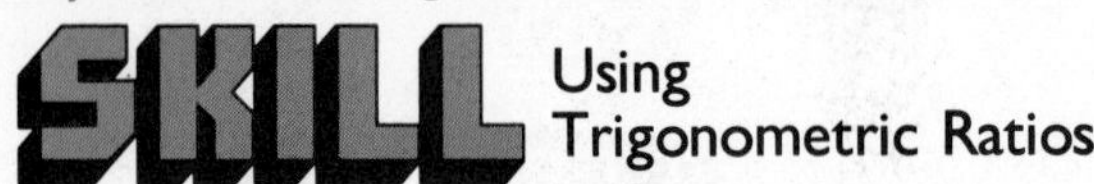

Using Trigonometric Ratios

Example N Tangent

Find n to the nearest tenth. Use the table on page 403.

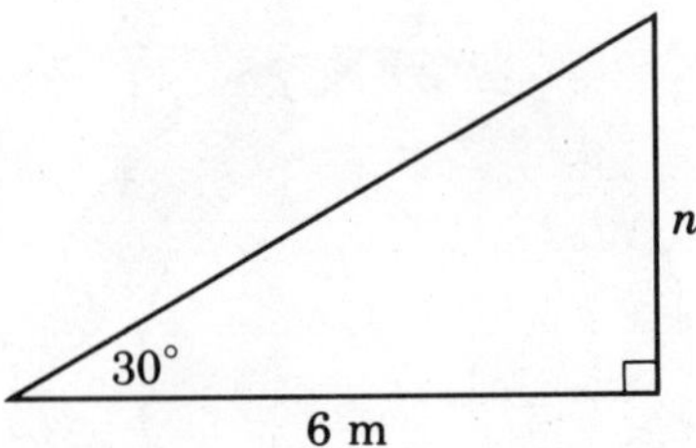

$\tan 30° = \frac{n}{6}$ — Use the tangent ratio to write an equation. Find tan 30° in the table on page 403. $\tan 30° \approx 0.577$

$0.577 \approx \frac{n}{6}$ — Multiply both sides of the equation by 6.

$3.462 \approx n$ — Round to the nearest tenth.

$3.5 \approx n$

n is about 3.5 meters.

Example O Sine

Find k to the nearest tenth.

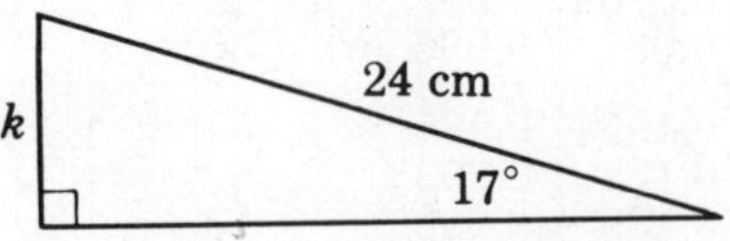

$\sin 17° = \frac{k}{24}$ — Use the sine ratio to write an equation. Use the table on page 403. $\sin 17° \approx 0.292$

$0.292 \approx \frac{k}{24}$ — Multiply both sides by 24.

$7.008 \approx k$ — Round to the nearest tenth.

$7.0 \approx k$

k is about 7.0 centimeters.

Example P Cosine

Find w to the nearest tenth.

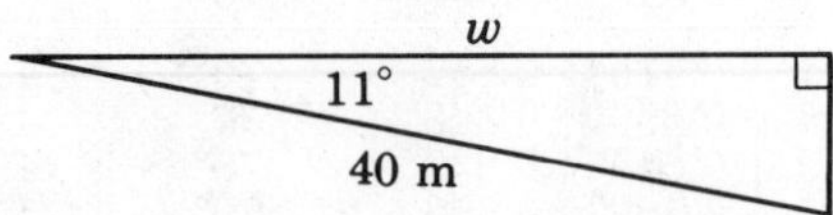

$\cos 11° = \frac{w}{40}$ — Use the cosine ratio to write an equation. Use the table on page 403. $\cos 11° \approx 0.982$

$0.982 \approx \frac{w}{40}$ — Multiply both sides by 40.

$39.280 \approx w$ — Round to the nearest tenth.

$39.3 \approx w$

w is about 39.3 meters.

PROBLEM SOLVING
The applications on pages 412–413 may be used anytime after this lesson.

Exercises

Set N

Find n to the nearest tenth. Use the table on page 403.

1.

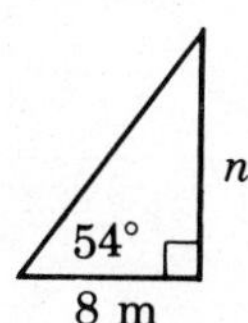

11.0 m

2.

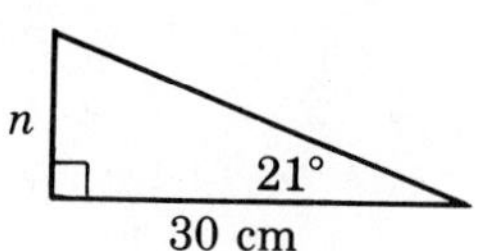

11.5 cm

3.

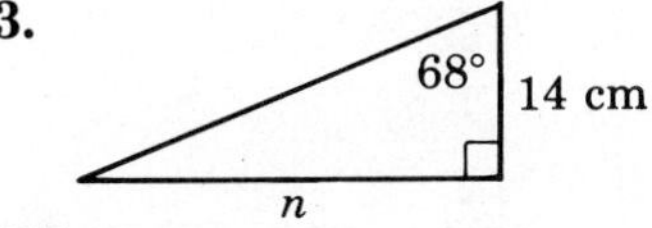

34.7 cm

4.

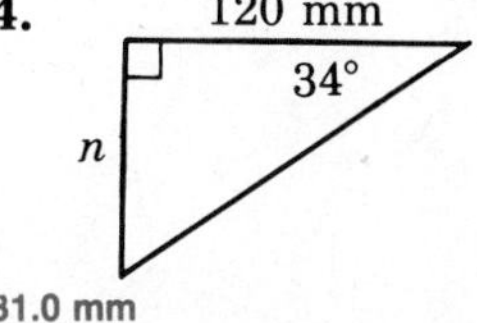

81.0 mm

5.

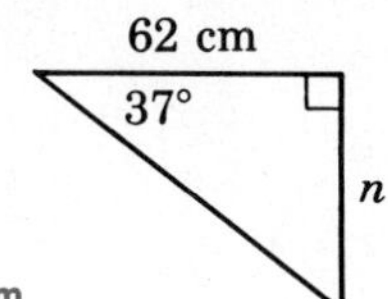

46.7 cm

6.

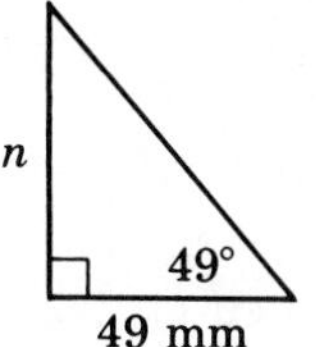

56.4 mm

Set O

Find k to the nearest tenth. Use the table on page 403.

1.

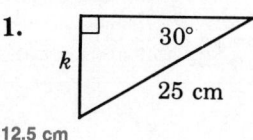

30°
k
25 cm

12.5 cm

2.

k
7 m
45°

4.9 m

3.

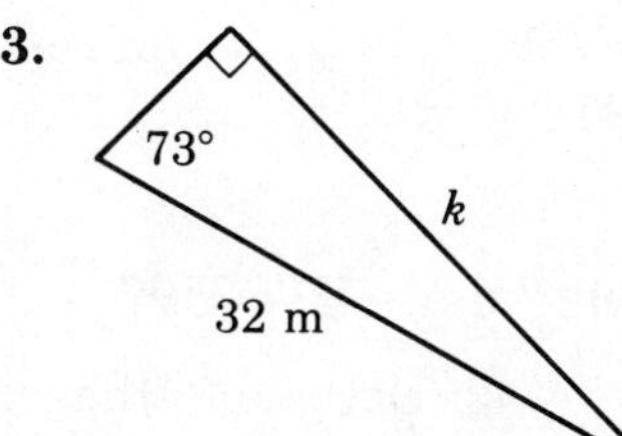

30.6 m

4.

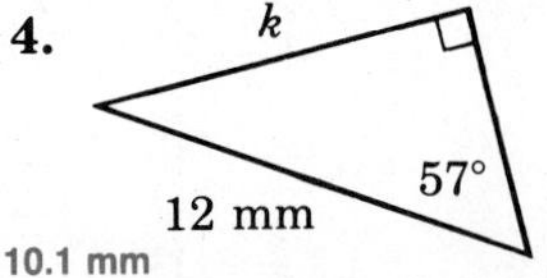

10.1 mm

5.

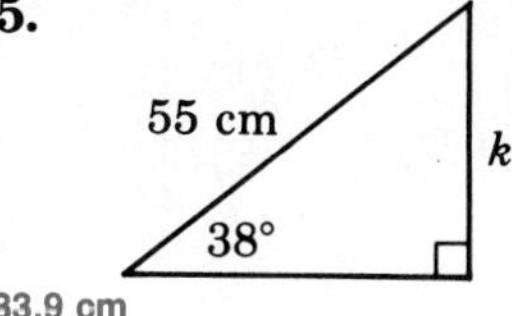

33.9 cm

6.

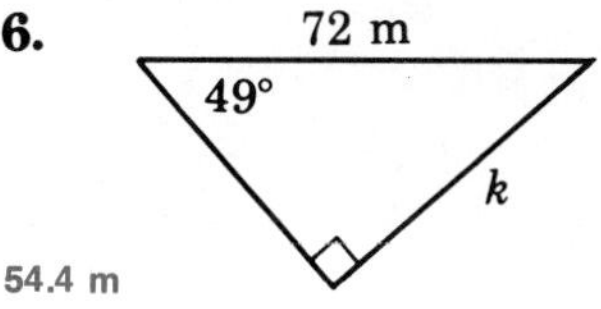

54.4 m

Set P

Find w to the nearest tenth. Use the table on page 403.

1.

15 m
26°
w

13.5 m

2.

w
56°
7 cm

3.9 cm

3.

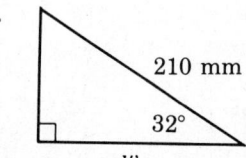

210 mm
32°
w

178.1 mm

4.

w
58°
85 m

45.1 m

5.

150 mm
47°
w

102.3 mm

6.

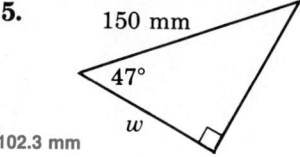

76 cm
62°
w

35.6 cm

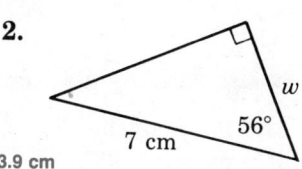

SKILLS POSTTEST

Number of test items - 16

Number missed	1	2	3	4	5	6	7	8
Percent correct	94	88	81	75	69	63	56	50

SKILL Using Exponents and Square Roots *page 395*

A Compute 4^3.
64

B Find $\sqrt{36}$.
6

SKILL Reading a Table of Squares and Square Roots *pages 396–397*

C Find 17^2. Use the table on page 397.
289

D Find $\sqrt{29}$ to the nearest tenth. Use the table on page 397.
5.4

E Find $\sqrt{8464}$. Use the table on page 397.
92

SKILL Using the Pythagorean Rule *pages 398–399*

F Use the Pythagorean Rule to find the length of the hypotenuse to the nearest tenth. Use the table on page 397.
9.2 m

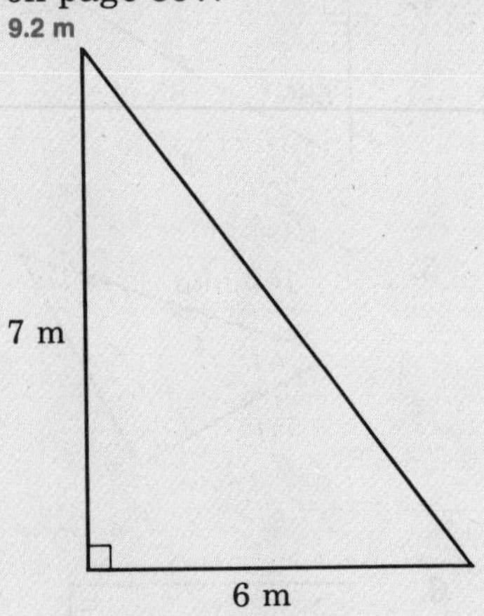

G Use the Pythagorean Rule to find the missing length to the nearest tenth. Use the table on page 397.
14 m

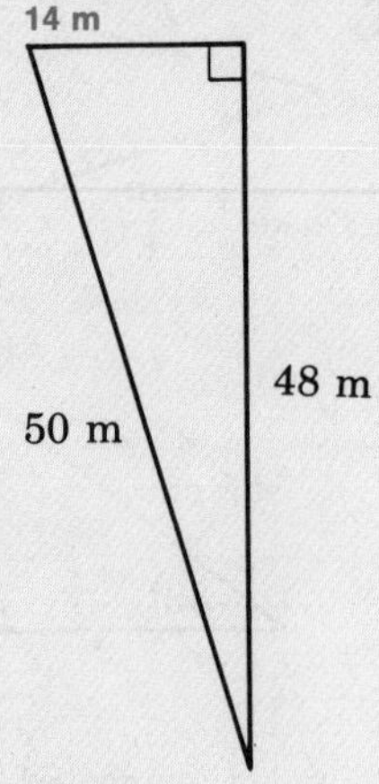

Posttest continued on page 407.

Posttest continued from page 406.

SKILL Writing Trigonometric Ratios *pages 400–401*

H Give the tangent of $\angle X$ as a ratio and as a decimal to the nearest thousandth.

Y
26 m
10 m
X 24 m Z

I Give the sine of $\angle X$ in item H as a ratio and as a decimal to the nearest thousandth.

$\tan \angle X = \frac{10}{24} \approx 0.417$

$\sin \angle X = \frac{10}{26} \approx 0.385$

$\cos \angle X = \frac{24}{26} \approx 0.923$

J Give the cosine of $\angle X$ in item H as a ratio and as a decimal to the nearest thousandth.

SKILL Reading a Table of Trigonometric Ratios *pages 402–403*

K Give the tangent of 24° as a decimal to the nearest thousandth. Use the table on page 403.
0.445

L Give the sine of 74° as a decimal to the nearest thousandth. Use the table on page 403.
0.961

M Give the cosine of 39° as a decimal to the nearest thousandth. Use the table on page 403.
0.777

SKILL Using Trigonometric Ratios *pages 404–405*

N Find n to the nearest tenth. Use the table on page 403.
9.9 m

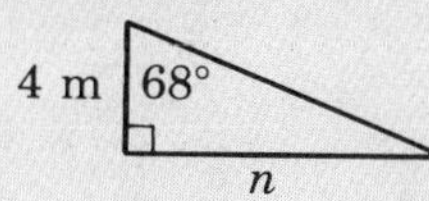

O Find k to the nearest tenth. Use the table on page 403.
12.3 cm

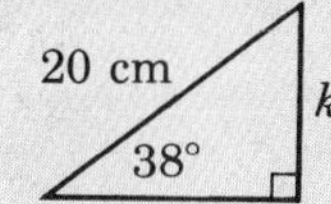

P Find w to the nearest tenth. Use the table on page 403.
6.5 cm

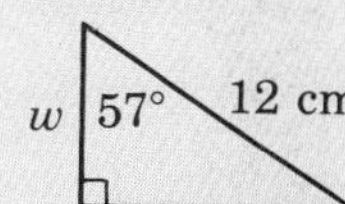

Problem Solving

CONSUMER APPLICATIONS

Objective: Solve problems involving the Pythagorean Rule and trigonometry.

In this lesson students tell whether a given set of lengths on a baseball field will form a right triangle at home plate, by using the Pythagorean Rule.

Laying Out a Baseball Diamond

Yvonne and her friends plan to lay out a baseball diamond in a vacant field.

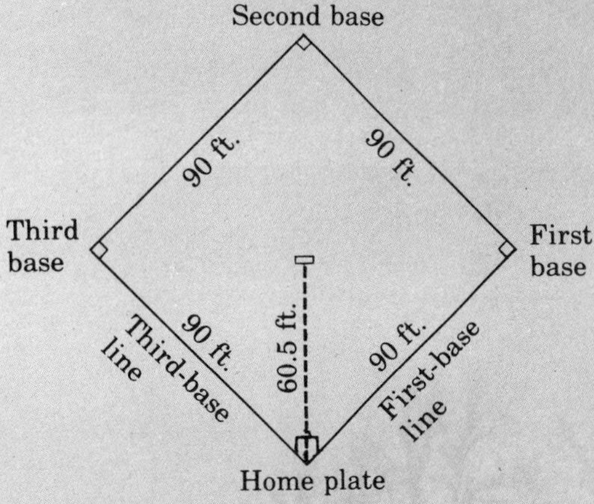

They have a tape measure to measure the base lines, but they need to be sure the angle at home plate is a right angle.

Yvonne knows that if the lengths of the sides of a triangle fit the Pythagorean Rule, then the triangle is a right triangle. She knows that sides of 3, 4, and 5 will fit the Pythagorean Rule.

$$a^2 + b^2 = c^2$$

$$3^2 + 4^2 = 5^2$$

$$9 + 16 = 25$$

$$25 = 25$$

See pages 55–56 of *Problem-Solving Masters.*

Yvonne said:

"Measure 4 feet from home plate down the first-base line and put a stake into the ground.

"Measure 3 feet down the third-base line and put a stake into the ground.

"Measure the distance between the stakes. If it is 5 feet, then the angle at home plate is a right angle."

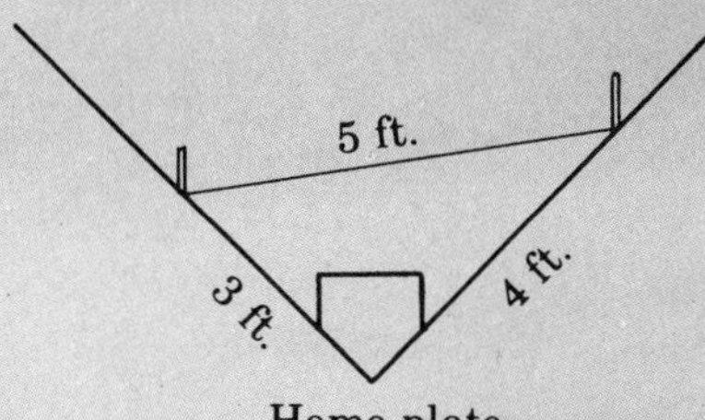

For each problem, tell whether or not the distances would form a right angle. Use the Pythagorean Rule and the table on page 397.

	Distance to stake on first-base line (a)	Distance to stake on third-base line (b)	Distance between stakes (c)	
1.	5 feet	12 feet	14 feet	No
2.	15 feet	8 feet	17 feet	Yes
3.	12 feet	36 feet	37 feet	No
4.	20 feet	28 feet	42 feet	No
5.	7 feet	11 feet	13 feet	No
6.	80 feet	18 feet	82 feet	Yes
7.	9 feet	9 feet	12 feet	No
8.	12 feet	35 feet	37 feet	Yes
9.	60 feet	63 feet	87 feet	Yes
10.	7 feet	24 feet	25 feet	Yes

Problem Solving

CAREER APPLICATIONS

Objective: Solve problems involving the Pythagorean Rule and trigonometry.

In this lesson students use the Pythagorean Rule to find the hypotenuse of a 45°-45°-90° right triangle determined by an angled pipeline, given the length of one leg, and to find the legs of a 30°-60°-90° right triangle, given the hypotenuse.

Pipeline Engineer

Career Cluster: Technology Karen Ilfeld is an engineer who designs pipelines.

Sometimes a pipeline has to be installed at an angle to avoid an obstacle. To do this, the crew connects a piece of pipe on a diagonal by using fittings called elbows.

Karen uses the Pythagorean Rule to find various distances. The offset, the run, and the diagonal shown below form a right triangle.

$(\text{offset})^2 + (\text{run})^2 = (\text{diagonal})^2$

$o^2 + r^2 = d^2$

When 45° elbows are used, the offset is equal to the run. When 60° elbows are used, the run is half as long as the diagonal.

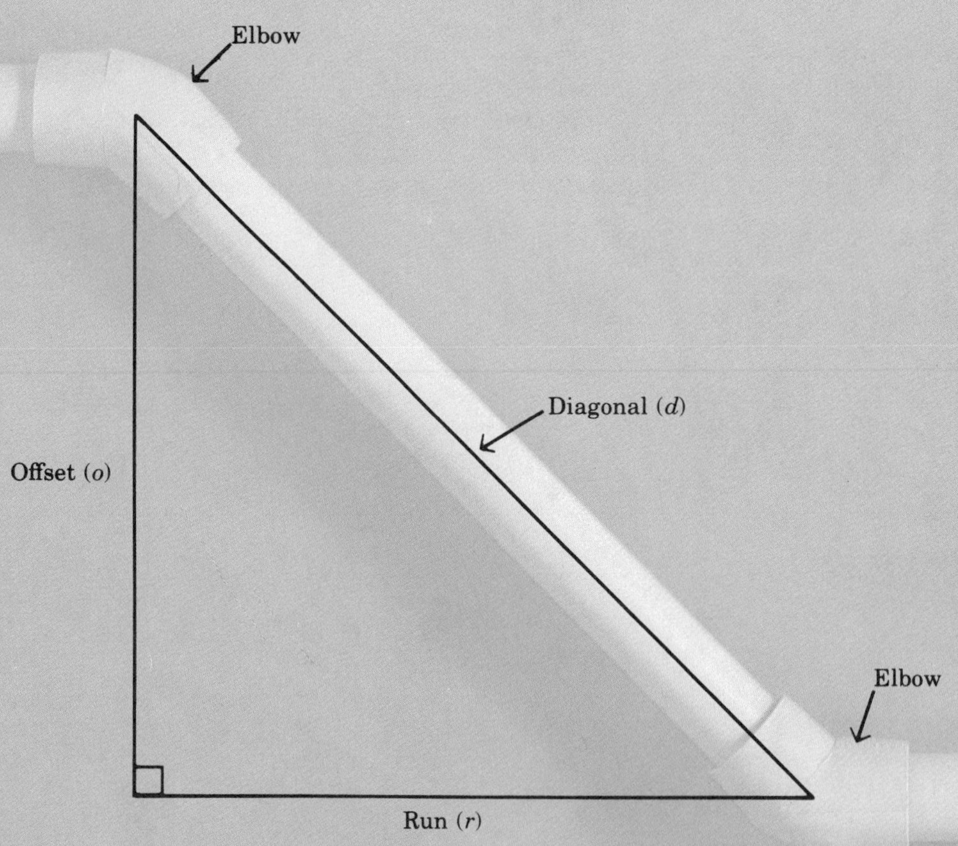

Karen planned 45° elbows for one job. She needed to find the run and the diagonal for an offset of 8 decimeters.

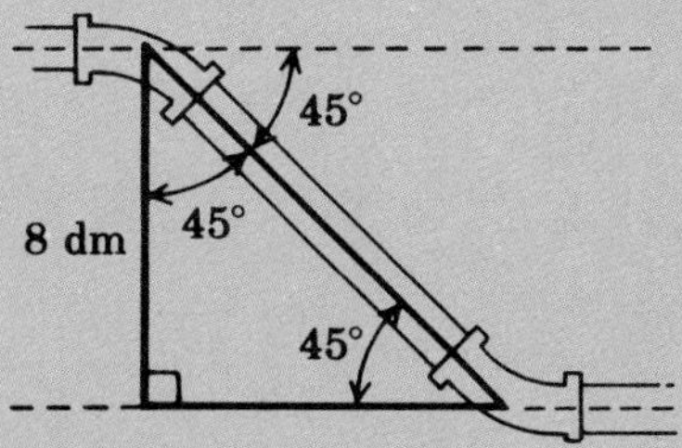

Since 45° elbows are used, the offset is equal to the run. In this case, both are 8 decimeters.

$$o^2 + r^2 = d^2$$

$$8^2 + 8^2 = d^2$$

$$64 + 64 = d^2$$

$$128 = d^2$$

$$\sqrt{128} = d$$

$$11.3 \approx d$$

The run is 8 decimeters. The diagonal is 11.3 decimeters to the nearest tenth.

On another job, Karen planned for 60° elbows. She needed to find the run and the offset for a diagonal of 14 decimeters.

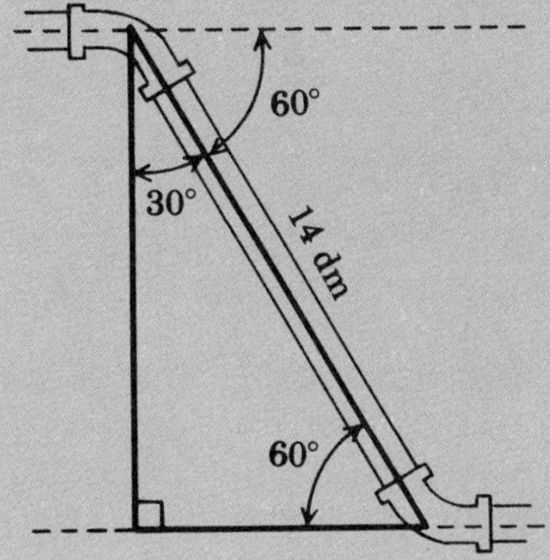

Since 60° elbows are used, the run is half as long as the diagonal. The diagonal is 14 decimeters. The run is 7 decimeters.

$$o^2 + r^2 = d^2$$

$$o^2 + 7^2 = 14^2$$

$$o^2 + 49 = 196$$

$$o^2 = 147$$

$$o = \sqrt{147}$$

$$o \approx 12.1$$

The run is 7 decimeters. The offset is 12.1 decimeters to the nearest tenth.

Find the missing numbers if 45° elbows are used. Use the table on page 397. All lengths are given in decimeters. Round answers to the nearest tenth.

	Offset (o)	Run (r)	Diagonal (d)
1.	7	7	9.9
2.	4	4	5.7
3.	5	5	7.1
4.	3	3	4.2
5.	9	9	12.7
6.	10	10	14.1
7.	2	2	2.8
8.	1	1	1.4

Find the missing numbers if 60° elbows are used. Use the table on page 397. All lengths are given in decimeters. Round answers to the nearest tenth.

	Offset (o)	Run (r)	Diagonal (d)
9.	13.9	8	16
10.	10.4	6	12
11.	6.9	4	8
12.	8.7	5	10
13.	3.5	2	4
14.	5.2	3	6
15.	1.7	1	2

Problem Solving

DEVELOPING STRATEGIES

Objective: Solve problems by drawing a picture and using trigonometric ratios.

In this lesson students find the dimensions of the minimum rectangular space requirement for a standard antenna tower and its guy wires.

Tactics: Drawing a Picture, Using Trigonometric Ratios

Chuck Fester works for a company that installs antenna towers for two-way radio systems. It is important to know the minimum rectangular space requirement (guying space) for a tower and its guy wires. Each size tower has a different guying space.

The diagram at the right shows a plan for a standard tower. The guy radius is the distance from the base of the tower to the point at which the guy wire is anchored at ground level (guy point). A standard tower has three guy points and the guy radius is the same for each. The angles indicated are the same for all standard towers.

Overview of a Standard Tower

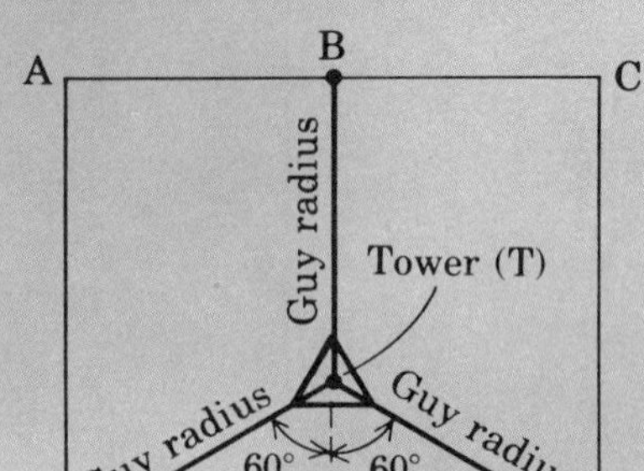

Problem

What are the dimensions of the guying space for a tower with a guy radius of 24 meters?

Solution

Chuck's tactics for solving the problem included drawing a picture and using trigonometric ratios.

a. What are the specifications? Draw a picture and label the given information.

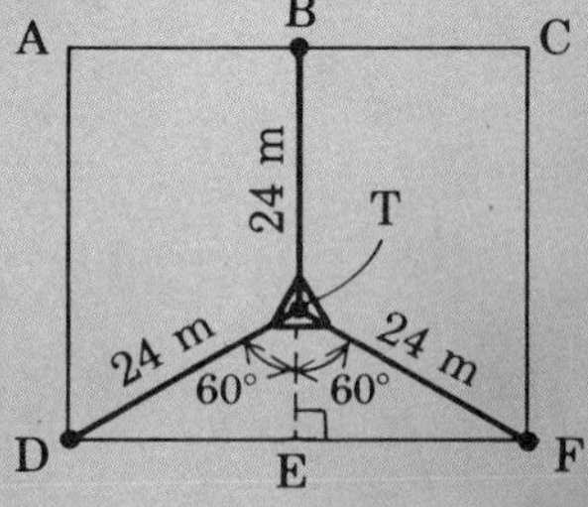

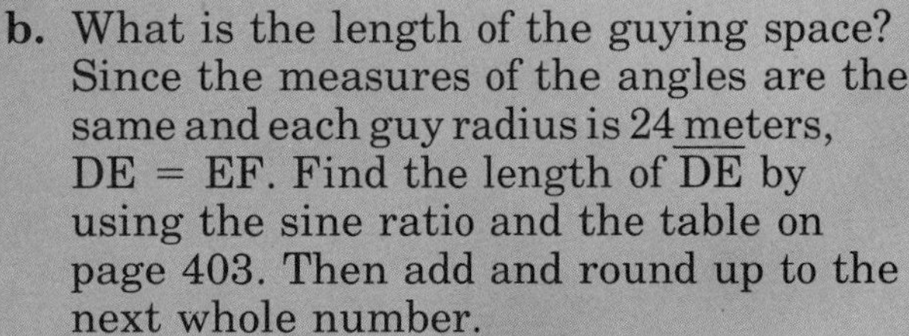

b. What is the length of the guying space? Since the measures of the angles are the same and each guy radius is 24 meters, DE = EF. Find the length of $\overline{DE}$ by using the sine ratio and the table on page 403. Then add and round up to the next whole number.

$$\sin 60° = \frac{DE}{24}$$

$$0.866 \approx \frac{DE}{24}$$

$$20.784 \approx DE$$

$$\begin{array}{rl} 20.784 & \leftarrow \text{length of } \overline{DE} \\ +\ 20.784 & \leftarrow \text{length of } \overline{EF} \\ \hline 41.568 & \approx 42 \end{array}$$

c. What is the width of the guying space? Find the length of $\overline{TE}$ by using the cosine ratio and the table on page 403. Then add the lengths of $\overline{BT}$ and TE.

$$\cos 60° = \frac{TE}{24}$$

$$0.500 = \frac{TE}{24}$$

$$12 = TE$$

$$\begin{array}{rl} 24 & \leftarrow \text{length of } \overline{BT} \\ +\ 12 & \leftarrow \text{length of } \overline{TE} \\ \hline 36 & \end{array}$$

Conclusion: The dimensions of the guying space are 42 meters by 36 meters.

Related Problems

1. What are the dimensions of the guying space for a tower with a guy radius of 16 meters? Remember, round the length up to the next whole meter.
28 meters by 24 meters
2. What are the dimensions of the guying space for a tower with a guy radius of 38 meters?
66 meters by 57 meters
3. What are the dimensions of the guying space for a tower with a guy radius of 40 meters?
70 meters by 60 meters
4. What are the dimensions of the guying space for a tower with a guy radius of 60 meters?
104 meters by 90 meters
5. What is the perimeter (distance around) of the guying space for the tower in Problem 4?
388 meters
6. What is the perimeter of the guying space for a tower with a guy radius of 52 meters?
338 meters

Extensions

7. The guy radius for a standard tower is 80% of the tower height. To the nearest meter, what is the perimeter of the guying space for an 80-meter tower?
414 meters
8. This diagram shows the arrangement of the wires at one of the three guy points. Each guy point has the same arrangement of wires. Find the total amount of wire needed to support this 12-meter tower. Round your answer up to the next meter. (Hint: Use the Pythagorean Rule and the table on page 397.)
78 meters
Note that this guy radius is not 80% of the tower height. This length may vary depending on job specifications.

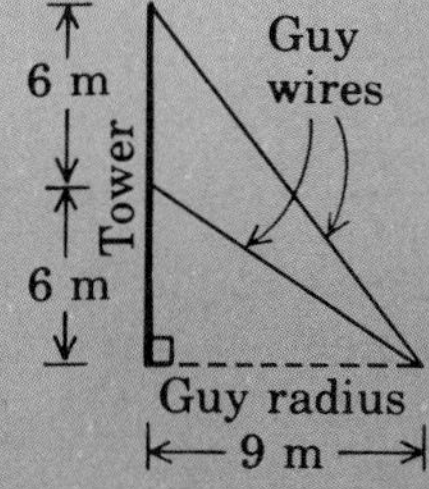

CHAPTER 18 TEST

Number of test items - 19

Number missed	1	2	3	4	5	6	7	8	9
Percent correct	95	89	84	79	74	68	63	58	53

A **1.** Compute 2^4.
16

B **2.** Find $\sqrt{81}$.
9

Find items 3–7, use the table on page 397.

C **3.** Find 53^2.
2809

D **4.** Find $\sqrt{96}$ to the nearest tenth.
9.8

E **5.** Find $\sqrt{7396}$.
86

F **6.** Use the Pythagorean Rule to find the length of the hypotenuse to the nearest tenth.
7.6 m

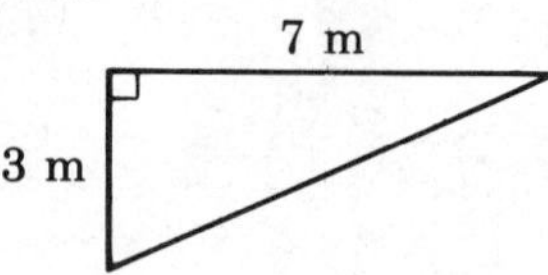

G **7.** Use the Pythagorean Rule to find the missing length.
63 m

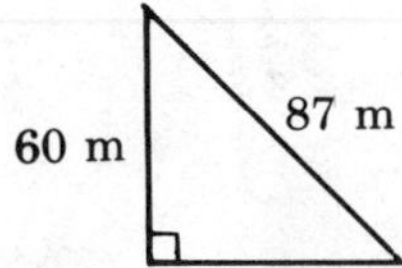

H **8.** Give the tangent of $\angle W$ as a ratio and as a decimal to the nearest thousandth.

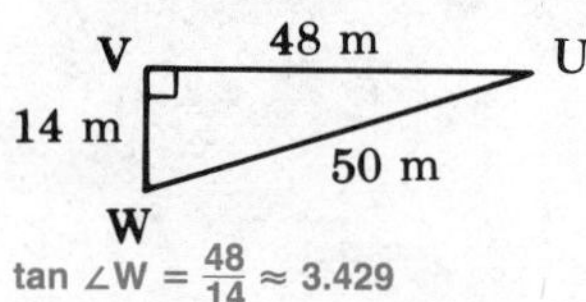

$\tan \angle W = \frac{48}{14} \approx 3.429$

I **9.** Give the sine of $\angle W$ in item 8 as a ratio and as a decimal to the nearest thousandth.
$\sin \angle W = \frac{48}{50} \approx 0.960$

J **10.** Give the cosine of $\angle W$ in item 8 as a ratio and as a decimal to the nearest thousandth.
$\cos \angle W = \frac{14}{50} \approx 0.280$

For items 11–16, use the table on page 403.

K **11.** Give the tangent of 28° as a decimal to the nearest thousandth.
0.532

L **12.** Give the sine of 41° as a decimal to the nearest thousandth.
0.656

M **13.** Give the cosine of 67° as a decimal to the nearest thousandth.
0.391

N **14.** Find n to the nearest tenth.
5.6 cm

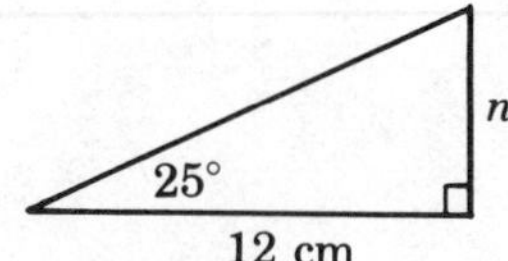

O **15.** Find k to the nearest tenth.
20.6 cm

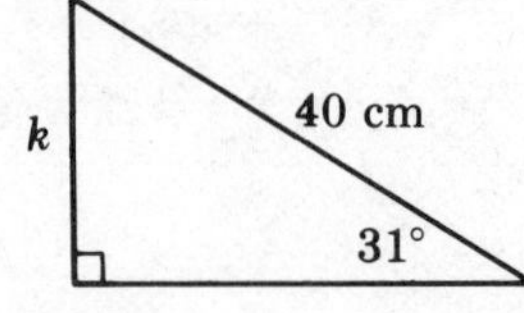

P **16.** Find w to the nearest tenth.
5.2 m

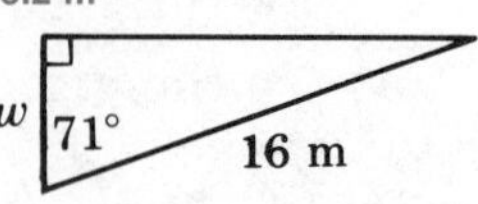

17. Would these lengths form a right triangle?
No

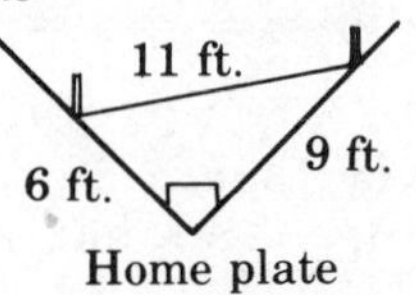

18. Find the length of the diagonal to the nearest tenth of a decimeter. Use the table on page 397.
8.5 dm

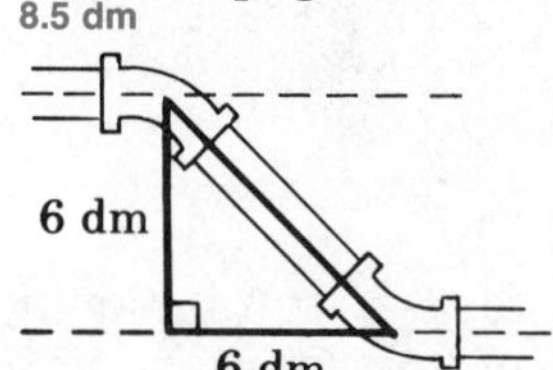

19. To the nearest meter, what is the length (AC) of the guying space for a tower with a guy radius of 68 meters? Use the table on page 403.
118 m

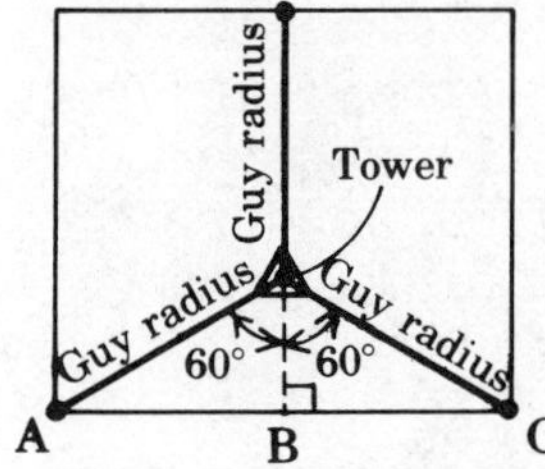

See pages 45–46 of the *Test Masters* for an alternate form of the Chapter 18 Test.
For a test on Unit 6, see pages T66–T67 of this book and pages 47–48 of the *Test Masters*.
For an end-of-book test, see pages T68–T71 of this book and pages 49–52 of the *Test Masters*.

SKILLS TUNE-UP

Ratio, Proportion, and Similarity, pages 215-224

Find each missing number.

1. $\frac{8}{26} = \frac{28}{n}$ $n = 91$
2. $\frac{18}{t} = \frac{30}{25}$ $t = 15$
3. $\frac{27}{45} = \frac{h}{35}$ $h = 21$
4. $\frac{112}{k} = \frac{84}{30}$ $k = 40$
5. $\frac{d}{9.1} = \frac{0.4}{0.7}$ $d = 5.2$
6. $\frac{5}{6} = \frac{45}{m}$ $m = 54$
7. $\frac{w}{9} = \frac{19}{57}$ $w = 3$
8. $\frac{3.2}{48} = \frac{a}{27}$ $a = 1.8$
9. $\frac{27}{15} = \frac{45}{c}$ $c = 25$
10. $\frac{f}{45} = \frac{12}{18}$ $f = 30$
11. $\frac{84}{j} = \frac{25.2}{3.6}$ $j = 12$
12. $\frac{18}{45} = \frac{m}{15}$ $m = 6$

Percent, pages 235-246

1. Find 6% of 40. 2.4
2. Find 63% of 64. 40.32
3. Find $12\frac{1}{2}$% of 200. 25
4. Find 10% of 93. 9.3
5. Find $33\frac{1}{3}$% of 27. 9
6. Find 250% of 36. 90
7. 21 is what percent of 70? 30%
8. 47 is what percent of 188? 25%
9. 38 is what percent of 95? 40%
10. 117 is what percent of 260? 45%
11. 49 is what percent of 147? $33\frac{1}{3}$%
12. 7 is what percent of 84? $8\frac{1}{3}$%
13. 3 is 6% of what number? 50
14. 30 is 75% of what number? 40
15. 25 is $12\frac{1}{2}$% of what number? 200
16. 44 is $66\frac{2}{3}$% of what number? 66
17. 22 is 50% of what number? 44
18. 180 is 18% of what number? 1000

Positive and Negative Numbers, pages 283-294

1. $^-4 + 6$ 2
2. $9 + {}^-7$ 2
3. $^-14 + {}^-24$ $^-38$
4. $^-13 + 5$ $^-8$
5. $7.2 + {}^-2.7$ 4.5
6. $^-3.7 + {}^-5.2$ $^-8.9$
7. $^-3 - 8$ $^-11$
8. $4 - {}^-15$ 19
9. $^-82 - {}^-34$ $^-48$
10. $5 - 17$ $^-12$
11. $^-18.4 - 7.2$ $^-25.6$
12. $^-9.3 - {}^-8.6$ $^-0.7$
13. $6 \times {}^-9$ $^-54$
14. $6 \times {}^-16$ $^-96$
15. $^-25 \times 3$ $^-75$
16. $^-7 \times {}^-24$ 168
17. $5.6 \times {}^-3$ $^-16.8$
18. $^-3.1 \times 9.5$ $^-29.45$
19. $56 \div {}^-7$ $^-8$
20. $^-105 \div 5$ $^-21$
21. $^-144 \div {}^-12$ 12
22. $^-22.5 \div 9$ $^-2.5$
23. $280 \div {}^-70$ $^-4$
24. $^-27.6 \div 6$ $^-4.6$
25. $^-291 \div {}^-30$ 9.7

CALCULATOR APPLICATIONS

Butch's Meat Market is having its grand opening sale.

Three kilograms of ham sells for $12.75, and 5 kilograms of beef roast sells for $23.25. What is the total cost of 2 kilograms of ham and 3 kilograms of beef roast?

$$\frac{3}{12.75} = \frac{2}{x}$$ Write a proportion to find the cost of the ham.

$$3x = 25.5$$

$$x = 8.5$$

$$\frac{5}{23.25} = \frac{3}{x}$$ Write a proportion to find the cost of the beef roast.

$$5x = 69.75$$

$$x = 13.95$$

Cost of ham		Cost of beef roast		Total cost
$8.50	+	$13.95	=	$22.45

The total cost is $22.45.

Calculator Suggestion: If your calculator has memory keys, try this key sequence.

Press: 12.75 [×] 2 [÷] 3 [=] [M+]
23.25 [×] 3 [÷] 5 [=] [M+] [MR]

Display: 22.45

Answer: $22.45

If your display does not show 22.45, consult the instruction book for your calculator to find out how the memory keys work. Be sure to clear the memory before starting each problem.

Find each answer. Some students may find writing proportions helpful.

1. T-bone steak: 2 kg for $12.30
Porterhouse steak: 2 kg for $12.80
Find the total cost of 5 kilograms of T-bone steak and 5 kilograms of porterhouse steak.
$62.75
2. Leg of lamb: 5 kg for $22.50
Lamb chops: 3 kg for $9.18
Find the total cost of 4 kilograms of leg of lamb and 4 kilograms of lamb chops.
$30.24
3. Pork chops: 3 kg for $8.70
Beef liver: 4 kg for $10.48
Find the total cost of 7 kilograms of pork chops and 3 kilograms of beef liver.
$28.16
4. Short ribs: 6 kg for $27.60
Veal chops: $10.98 per kg
Find the total cost of 4 kilograms of short ribs and 2 kilograms of veal chops.
$40.36
5. Italian sausage: 4 kg for $15
Polish sausage: 4 kg for $15
Find the total cost of 7 kilograms of Italian sausage and 6 kilograms of Polish sausage.
$48.75
6. Game hens: 9 kg for $25.65
Chicken: 5 kg for $8.70
How much more does 3 kilograms of game hens cost than 3 kilograms of chicken?
$3.33
7. Ground beef: 8 kg for $24.48
Ground chuck: 8 kg for $17.44
How much more does 3 kilograms of ground beef cost than 3 kilograms of ground chuck?
$2.64

COMPUTER LITERACY

The READ and DATA Statements

The LET and INPUT statements were used to put values into a program. Another way to tell the computer the values of A and B is to use the READ and DATA statements. The READ statement tells the computer that the values of A and B are to be found in the program. When the computer finds a READ statement, it looks for a line beginning with the word DATA. The word DATA is followed by the values, each value separated from the next by a comma.

In Program A, the first time the computer reads A and B it uses A = 2, B = 3. The second time it uses A = 5, B = 6. The computer keeps track of where it is in the data line. On the fourth pass through Program A, the computer will type a message that it is out of data and stop.

Program A

Input

```
10 READ A,B
20 PRINT "A+B=";A+B
30 GO TO 10
40 DATA 2,3,5,6,9,4
50 END
```

Output

```
A+B= 5
A+B= 11
A+B= 13
OUT OF DATA AT LINE 10
```

2. PERIMETER: 26
PERIMETER: 31
PERIMETER: 28
OUT OF DATA AT LINE 10

Give the output for each program.

1.
```
10 PRINT "AREA"
20 READ L,W
30 PRINT L*W
40 GO TO 20
50 DATA 2,5,6,10,12,15
60 END
```
AREA
10
60
180
OUT OF DATA AT LINE 20

2.
```
10 READ L,W
20 LET P=2*L+2*W
30 PRINT "PERIMETER:";P
40 GO TO 10
50 DATA 5,8,9.2,6.3,4.3,9.7
60 END
```
See below.

3.
```
10 READ X
20 LET Y=INT(X)
30 PRINT Y
40 GO TO 10
50 DATA 3.6,2.7,4,5.3
60 END
```
3
2
4
5
OUT OF DATA AT LINE 10

4.
```
10 PRINT "BOWLING AVERAGE"
20 READ A,B,C
30 LET M=(A+B+C)/3
40 PRINT M
50 GO TO 20
60 DATA 140,135,127,136,132,113
70 END
```
See Additional Answers on page T54.

5.
```
10 READ A,B,C
20 IF A>B THEN 90
30 IF B>C THEN 70
40 LET Q=C
50 PRINT Q
60 GO TO 10
70 LET Q=B
80 GO TO 50
90 IF A>C THEN 110
100 GO TO 40
110 LET Q=A
120 GO TO 50
130 DATA 3,1,4,9,2,6,7,6,5
140 END
```
See Additional Answers on page T54.

6. Write a program using the READ and DATA statements that will find areas of triangles. $(A = \frac{1}{2}bh)$

See Additional Answers on page T54.

Some computers will print an error message to indicate when the computer is out of data. Check your computer before assigning these exercises so that you can tell your students what to expect when the computer runs out of data.

SKILLS FILE

Use after page 7.

1.	63 + 24	87
2.	718 + 50	768
3.	560 + 319	879
4.	2416 + 383	2799
5.	2356 + 1431	3787
6.	7561 + 234	7795
7.	27 + 46	73
8.	38 + 76	114
9.	596 + 35	631
10.	68 + 477	545
11.	324 + 696	1020
12.	748 + 363	1111
13.	3196 + 845	4041
14.	8456 + 778	9234
15.	7817 + 4726	12,543
16.	5273 + 7128	12,401
17.	69768 + 3649	73,417
18.	57974 + 3228	61,202
19.	433, 796, + 562	1791
20.	379, 52, + 2513	2944
21.	91, 73, 66, + 74	304
22.	2753, 34, 582, + 4610	7979
23.	22, 933, 71, 9, + 9401	10,436
24.	42, 967, 56, 8, + 2564	3637

Use after page 9.

1.	574 − 152	422
2.	438 − 17	421
3.	8456 − 7321	1135
4.	9643 − 6322	3321
5.	7459 − 307	7152
6.	5587 − 264	5323
7.	49868 − 27342	22,526
8.	35487 − 2176	33,311
9.	53 − 26	27
10.	31 − 17	14
11.	532 − 465	67
12.	307 − 149	158
13.	836 − 59	777
14.	923 − 68	855
15.	2060 − 1378	682
16.	4000 − 2496	1504
17.	1564 − 586	978
18.	1241 − 837	404
19.	6043 − 715	5328
20.	5904 − 247	5657
21.	4010 − 667	3343
22.	2600 − 524	2076
23.	3267 − 89	3178
24.	6205 − 39	6166
25.	75832 − 4756	71,076
26.	40206 − 5787	34,419
27.	87951 − 36452	51,499
28.	49137 − 25699	23,438

Use after page 33.

1.	1000 × 800	800,000
2.	100 × 40	4000
3.	6000 × 80	480,000
4.	4000 × 900	3,600,000
5.	52 × 3	156
6.	63 × 2	126
7.	24 × 8	192
8.	39 × 5	195
9.	387 × 6	2322
10.	548 × 7	3836
11.	3855 × 8	30,840
12.	3295 × 7	23,065
13.	37 × 40	1480
14.	65 × 90	5850
15.	53 × 82	4346
16.	92 × 64	5888
17.	566 × 87	49,242
18.	727 × 94	68,338
19.	4228 × 39	164,892
20.	2364 × 49	115,836
21.	723 × 700	506,100
22.	849 × 600	509,400
23.	762 × 507	386,334
24.	994 × 803	798,182
25.	341 × 982	334,862
26.	386 × 742	286,412
27.	4986 × 384	1,914,624
28.	7791 × 856	6,669,096

SKILLS FILE

Use after page 51.

1. 5)97 (19 R2)
2. 3)83 (27 R2)
3. 6)879 (146 R3)
4. 8)345 (43 R1)
5. 4)8932 (2233)
6. 7)2144 (306 R2)
7. 5)32693 (6538 R3)
8. 8)15718 (1964 R6)
9. 24)98 (4 R2)
10. 31)79 (2 R17)
11. 63)427 (6 R49)
12. 42)963 (22 R39)
13. 86)265 (3 R7)
14. 67)944 (14 R6)
15. 18)752 (41 R14)
16. 25)5787 (231 R12)
17. 74)4392 (59 R26)
18. 93)36427 (391 R64)
19. 37)22645 (612 R1)
20. 76)876254 (11,529 R50)
21. 53)157183 (2965 R38)

Use after page 52.

1. 6)185 (30 R5)
2. 4)362 (90 R2)
3. 8)3442 (430 R2)
4. 2)6015 (3007 R1)
5. 9)4776 (530 R6)
6. 7)2802 (400 R2)
7. 6)18157 (3026 R1)
8. 5)37604 (7520 R4)
9. 8)48643 (6080 R3)
10. 7)21004 (3000 R4)
11. 24)501 (20 R21)
12. 67)724 (10 R54)
13. 24)6738 (280 R18)
14. 37)7696 (208)
15. 33)66258 (2007 R27)
16. 82)49239 (600 R39)
17. 28)84179 (3006 R11)
18. 66)41635 (630 R55)
19. 63)36552 (580 R12)
20. 75)378293 (5043 R68)
21. 92)646783 (7030 R23)

Use after page 79.

1. 17.4 + 6.7 (24.1)
2. 48.5 + 72.8 (121.3)
3. 3.76 + 5.92 (9.68)
4. 4.68 + 12.25 (16.93)
5. 0.096 + 0.243 (0.339)
6. 7.427 + 8.395 (15.822)
7. 0.659 + 0.826 (1.485)
8. 0.764 + 0.453 (1.217)
9. 36.49 + 7.95 (44.44)
10. 42.57 + 8.42 (50.99)
11. 6.826 + 4.637 (11.463)
12. 8.251 + 6.567 (14.818)
13. 2.367 + 15.289 (17.656)
14. 32.168 + 7.438 (39.606)
15. 20.98 0.53 + 18.46 (39.97)
16. 15.67 2.35 + 7.23 (25.25)
17. 8.956 3.409 + 6.738 (19.103)
18. 5.215 0.779 + 2.241 (8.235)
19. 0.036 0.42 + 0.98 (1.436)
20. 0.7 0.438 + 0.29 (1.428)
21. 0.492 0.06 + 0.5 (1.052)
22. 8.246 0.3 + 4.72 (13.266)
23. 5.362 8.6 3.401 + 0.24 (17.603)
24. 30.024 7.88 0.053 + 43.7 (81.657)

SKILLS FILE

Use after page 81.

1.	$6.8 - 2.9$	3.9
2.	$7.2 - 5.8$	1.4
3.	$0.84 - 0.18$	0.66
4.	$7.32 - 1.95$	5.37
5.	$6.73 - 3.48$	3.25
6.	$13.04 - 6.28$	6.76
7.	$21.26 - 7.53$	13.73
8.	$0.724 - 0.482$	0.242
9.	$0.821 - 0.376$	0.445
10.	$0.653 - 0.081$	0.572
11.	$9.508 - 2.726$	6.782
12.	$6.385 - 2.048$	4.337
13.	$5.003 - 1.426$	3.577
14.	$7.025 - 3.679$	3.346
15.	$9.7 - 1.42$	8.28
16.	$5.8 - 3.26$	2.54
17.	$7.4 - 2.55$	4.85
18.	$3.17 - 1.9$	1.27
19.	$3.2 - 2.45$	0.75
20.	$8.4 - 5.67$	2.73
21.	$7.7 - 2.73$	4.97
22.	$0.85 - 0.468$	0.382
23.	$0.52 - 0.159$	0.361
24.	$0.812 - 0.36$	0.452
25.	$9.16 - 1.857$	7.303
26.	$7.278 - 2.32$	4.958
27.	$8.2 - 3.591$	4.609
28.	$5.4 - 2.833$	2.567

Use after page 97.

1.	52.8×0.5	26.4
2.	17.4×7	121.8
3.	2379×0.04	95.16
4.	2.07×8	16.56
5.	2.6×1.8	4.68
6.	0.43×5.6	2.408
7.	2.26×4.3	9.718
8.	8.54×2.7	23.058
9.	6000×2.8	16,800
10.	400×0.37	148
11.	68.3×0.8	54.64
12.	30.7×2.9	89.03
13.	8.65×2.6	22.49
14.	47.6×4.1	195.16
15.	3.22×0.003	0.00966
16.	3.6×0.007	0.0252
17.	3.18×0.002	0.00636
18.	0.0079×0.08	0.000632
19.	0.42×0.006	0.00252
20.	0.083×0.03	0.00249
21.	0.0047×0.04	0.000188
22.	0.24×0.058	0.01392
23.	0.504×0.068	0.034272
24.	0.7234×0.035	0.025319
25.	0.02706×0.636	0.01721016
26.	4.1064×0.0073	0.02997672
27.	0.0834×0.145	0.012093
28.	0.0403×0.524	0.0211172

Use after page 101.

1.	6)34.8	5.8
2.	5)16.5	3.3
3.	3)4.86	1.62
4.	7)1.05	0.15
5.	53)23.32	0.44
6.	12)40.8	3.4
7.	72)424.8	5.9
8.	17)105.57	6.21
9.	89)5090.8	57.2
10.	8)0.296	0.037
11.	5)0.0165	0.0033
12.	7)0.0259	0.0037
13.	3)0.1068	0.0356
14.	48)3.36	0.07
15.	12)0.1392	0.0116
16.	64)1.856	0.029
17.	27)2.916	0.108
18.	55)0.1045	0.0019
19.	86)5.074	0.059
20.	388)7.372	0.019
21.	628)16.328	0.026

SKILLS FILE

Use after page 105.

1. $0.8\overline{)4.56}$ 5.7
2. $0.3\overline{)92.4}$ 308
3. $0.02\overline{)0.0876}$ 4.38
4. $0.06\overline{)0.324}$ 5.4
5. $0.008\overline{)0.0416}$ 5.2
6. $3.6\overline{)0.144}$ 0.04
7. $0.72\overline{)0.432}$ 0.6
8. $0.47\overline{)1.88}$ 4
9. $2.4\overline{)15.84}$ 6.6
10. $0.68\overline{)18.36}$ 27
11. $1.7\overline{)4.76}$ 2.8
12. $0.06\overline{)3.3}$ 55
13. $0.5\overline{)29}$ 58
14. $0.08\overline{)44}$ 550
15. $2.4\overline{)84}$ 35
16. $0.38\overline{)9.5}$ 25
17. $3.2\overline{)208}$ 65
18. $0.74\overline{)25.9}$ 35
19. $0.35\overline{)7256.9}$ 20,734
20. $5.05\overline{)20.2}$ 4
21. $8.46\overline{)42.3}$ 5

Use after page 157.

1. $\frac{1}{3} \times \frac{2}{3}$ $\frac{2}{9}$
2. $\frac{1}{2} \times \frac{3}{4}$ $\frac{3}{8}$
3. $\frac{3}{8} \times \frac{1}{3}$ $\frac{1}{8}$
4. $\frac{3}{4} \times \frac{2}{3}$ $\frac{1}{2}$
5. $\frac{7}{8} \times \frac{4}{5}$ $\frac{7}{10}$
6. $\frac{3}{4} \times \frac{5}{6}$ $\frac{5}{8}$
7. $\frac{3}{4} \times 8$ 6
8. $\frac{1}{4} \times 1\frac{5}{6}$ $\frac{11}{24}$
9. $2\frac{2}{3} \times \frac{7}{8}$ $2\frac{1}{3}$
10. $\frac{5}{8} \times 3\frac{1}{5}$ 2
11. $3\frac{1}{2} \times 4$ 14
12. $4\frac{2}{3} \times 5$ $23\frac{1}{3}$
13. $5\frac{3}{8} \times 6$ $32\frac{1}{4}$
14. $2\frac{2}{5} \times 1\frac{7}{8}$ $4\frac{1}{2}$
15. $1\frac{4}{5} \times 5\frac{5}{6}$ $10\frac{1}{2}$
16. $1\frac{3}{5} \times 2\frac{3}{4}$ $4\frac{2}{5}$
17. $4\frac{1}{5} \times 1\frac{3}{7}$ 6
18. $1\frac{7}{8} \times \frac{3}{5} \times \frac{2}{9}$ $\frac{1}{4}$
19. $2\frac{2}{5} \times 2\frac{1}{2} \times 1\frac{3}{4}$ $10\frac{1}{2}$
20. $1\frac{3}{5} \times 2\frac{1}{4} \times 3\frac{1}{3}$ 12
21. $3\frac{1}{2} \times 2\frac{3}{4} \times \frac{4}{5}$ $7\frac{7}{10}$

Use after page 159.

1. $\frac{2}{3} \div \frac{3}{8}$ $1\frac{7}{9}$
2. $\frac{3}{4} \div \frac{4}{5}$ $\frac{15}{16}$
3. $\frac{1}{2} \div \frac{3}{4}$ $\frac{2}{3}$
4. $\frac{7}{9} \div \frac{2}{3}$ $1\frac{1}{6}$
5. $\frac{3}{8} \div \frac{3}{4}$ $\frac{1}{2}$
6. $\frac{3}{5} \div \frac{9}{10}$ $\frac{2}{3}$
7. $1\frac{3}{5} \div \frac{2}{3}$ $2\frac{2}{5}$
8. $1\frac{1}{4} \div \frac{5}{8}$ 2
9. $1\frac{5}{6} \div \frac{1}{3}$ $5\frac{1}{2}$
10. $2\frac{3}{4} \div \frac{2}{3}$ $4\frac{1}{8}$
11. $1\frac{3}{4} \div 2$ $\frac{7}{8}$
12. $2\frac{4}{5} \div 6$ $\frac{7}{15}$
13. $1\frac{1}{8} \div 3$ $\frac{3}{8}$
14. $1\frac{7}{8} \div 5$ $\frac{3}{8}$
15. $2\frac{5}{8} \div 1\frac{3}{4}$ $1\frac{1}{2}$
16. $2\frac{1}{4} \div 1\frac{1}{4}$ $1\frac{4}{5}$
17. $2\frac{1}{2} \div 3\frac{3}{4}$ $\frac{2}{3}$
18. $4\frac{1}{2} \div 1\frac{1}{2}$ 3
19. $3\frac{1}{5} \div 1\frac{1}{5}$ $2\frac{2}{3}$
20. $4\frac{1}{8} \div 2\frac{3}{4}$ $1\frac{1}{2}$
21. $8 \div 2\frac{2}{5}$ $3\frac{1}{3}$

SKILLS FILE

Use after page 177.

1. $\frac{5}{8} + \frac{7}{8}$ $1\frac{1}{2}$
2. $\frac{2}{5} + \frac{4}{5}$ $1\frac{1}{5}$
3. $\frac{3}{4} + \frac{7}{8}$ $1\frac{5}{8}$
4. $\frac{1}{3} + \frac{3}{4}$ $1\frac{1}{12}$
5. $\frac{5}{6} + \frac{1}{3}$ $1\frac{1}{6}$
6. $\frac{1}{2} + \frac{3}{5}$ $1\frac{1}{10}$
7. $\frac{1}{2} + \frac{3}{4}$ $1\frac{1}{4}$
8. $\frac{8}{9} + \frac{2}{3}$ $1\frac{5}{9}$
9. $\frac{3}{5} + \frac{2}{3}$ $1\frac{4}{15}$
10. $\frac{4}{9} + \frac{1}{2}$ $\frac{17}{18}$
11. $\frac{3}{4} + \frac{5}{6}$ $1\frac{7}{12}$
12. $\frac{9}{10} + \frac{1}{4}$ $1\frac{3}{20}$
13. $2\frac{3}{4} + 4\frac{1}{8}$ $6\frac{7}{8}$
14. $8\frac{3}{5} + 3\frac{1}{3}$ $11\frac{14}{15}$
15. $5\frac{1}{2} + 7\frac{1}{6}$ $12\frac{2}{3}$
16. $9\frac{1}{6} + 1\frac{3}{8}$ $10\frac{13}{24}$
17. $4\frac{1}{2} + 7\frac{7}{8}$ $12\frac{3}{8}$
18. $2\frac{9}{10} + 5\frac{3}{5}$ $8\frac{1}{2}$
19. $7\frac{3}{4} + 2\frac{5}{6}$ $10\frac{7}{12}$
20. $3\frac{7}{10} + 6\frac{4}{5}$ $10\frac{1}{2}$
21. $4\frac{9}{10} + 3\frac{3}{4}$ $8\frac{13}{20}$
22. $9\frac{2}{3} + 4\frac{2}{5}$ $14\frac{1}{15}$
23. $4\frac{9}{10} + 8\frac{1}{3}$ $13\frac{7}{30}$
24. $2\frac{3}{4} + 6\frac{7}{12}$ $9\frac{1}{3}$

Use after page 181.

1. $\frac{4}{5} - \frac{1}{5}$ $\frac{3}{5}$
2. $\frac{7}{8} - \frac{3}{8}$ $\frac{1}{2}$
3. $\frac{3}{4} - \frac{1}{2}$ $\frac{1}{4}$
4. $\frac{3}{4} - \frac{5}{8}$ $\frac{1}{8}$
5. $\frac{4}{5} - \frac{1}{2}$ $\frac{3}{10}$
6. $\frac{5}{6} - \frac{2}{3}$ $\frac{1}{6}$
7. $\frac{3}{4} - \frac{2}{5}$ $\frac{7}{20}$
8. $\frac{3}{5} - \frac{1}{2}$ $\frac{1}{10}$
9. $\frac{3}{4} - \frac{2}{3}$ $\frac{1}{12}$
10. $\frac{7}{10} - \frac{1}{2}$ $\frac{1}{5}$
11. $\frac{4}{5} - \frac{3}{10}$ $\frac{1}{2}$
12. $\frac{11}{12} - \frac{3}{4}$ $\frac{1}{6}$
13. $9\frac{5}{8} - 2\frac{1}{2}$ $7\frac{1}{8}$
14. $7\frac{5}{6} - 4\frac{1}{3}$ $3\frac{1}{2}$
15. $8\frac{1}{4} - 2\frac{1}{6}$ $6\frac{1}{12}$
16. $3\frac{3}{4} - 1\frac{2}{5}$ $2\frac{7}{20}$
17. $6\frac{2}{5} - 3\frac{7}{10}$ $2\frac{7}{10}$
18. $5\frac{3}{8} - 2\frac{2}{3}$ $2\frac{17}{24}$
19. $4\frac{5}{6} - 1\frac{7}{8}$ $2\frac{23}{24}$
20. $9\frac{1}{3} - 6\frac{5}{9}$ $2\frac{7}{9}$
21. $2\frac{1}{4} - 1\frac{2}{3}$ $\frac{7}{12}$
22. $15\frac{1}{2} - 9\frac{4}{5}$ $5\frac{7}{10}$
23. $12\frac{2}{9} - 7\frac{5}{6}$ $4\frac{7}{18}$
24. $10\frac{5}{12} - 1\frac{7}{8}$ $8\frac{13}{24}$

Use after page 219.

Find each missing number.

1. $\frac{1}{5} = \frac{t}{60}$ $t = 12$
2. $\frac{3}{1} = \frac{42}{a}$ $a = 14$
3. $\frac{3}{4} = \frac{x}{98}$ $x = 73.5$
4. $\frac{4}{9} = \frac{w}{63}$ $w = 28$
5. $\frac{12}{27} = \frac{20}{n}$ $n = 45$
6. $\frac{15}{35} = \frac{r}{56}$ $r = 24$
7. $\frac{c}{27} = \frac{14}{6}$ $c = 63$
8. $\frac{65}{35} = \frac{f}{7}$ $f = 13$
9. $\frac{15}{18} = \frac{d}{48}$ $d = 40$
10. $\frac{16}{24} = \frac{a}{39}$ $a = 26$
11. $\frac{18}{48} = \frac{h}{56}$ $h = 21$
12. $\frac{30}{n} = \frac{45}{63}$ $n = 42$
13. $\frac{28}{36} = \frac{56}{d}$ $d = 72$
14. $\frac{36}{e} = \frac{48}{52}$ $e = 39$
15. $\frac{35}{42} = \frac{b}{78}$ $b = 65$
16. $\frac{20}{x} = \frac{35}{77}$ $x = 44$
17. $\frac{39}{45} = \frac{65}{m}$ $m = 75$
18. $\frac{42}{51} = \frac{c}{85}$ $c = 70$
19. $\frac{39}{57} = \frac{52}{w}$ $w = 76$
20. $\frac{0.4}{0.7} = \frac{k}{42}$ $k = 24$
21. $\frac{2.1}{2.7} = \frac{14}{e}$ $e = 18$
22. $\frac{0.5}{0.7} = \frac{6.5}{h}$ $h = 9.1$
23. $\frac{v}{1.12} = \frac{0.28}{0.32}$ $v = 0.98$
24. $\frac{0.2}{0.5} = \frac{1.6}{p}$ $p = 4$
25. $\frac{1.5}{t} = \frac{3.5}{5.6}$ $t = 2.4$
26. $\frac{0.6}{1.4} = \frac{2.1}{r}$ $r = 4.9$

SKILLS FILE

Use after page 241.

Find each number.

1. 7% of 31 2.17
2. 4% of 56 2.24
3. 15% of 65 9.75
4. 40% of 28 11.2
5. 6% of 5.4 0.324
6. 32% of 62.7 20.064
7. 4.6% of 80 3.68
8. 8.2% of 160 13.12
9. 175% of 30 52.5
10. $4\frac{1}{2}\%$ of 290 13.05
11. $10\frac{1}{2}\%$ of 3000 315
12. $1\frac{1}{2}\%$ of 35 0.525
13. $\frac{1}{2}\%$ of 650 3.25
14. $\frac{1}{4}\%$ of 240 0.6
15. $6\frac{1}{4}\%$ of 400 25
16. $8\frac{3}{4}\%$ of 2000 175
17. $37\frac{1}{2}\%$ of 85 31.875
18. $6\frac{2}{5}\%$ of 920 58.88
19. $66\frac{2}{3}\%$ of 18 12
20. $33\frac{1}{3}\%$ of 24 8
21. $16\frac{2}{3}\%$ of 42 7
22. $83\frac{1}{3}\%$ of 66 55
23. $33\frac{1}{3}\%$ of 51 17
24. $66\frac{2}{3}\%$ of 144 96
25. $33\frac{1}{3}\%$ of 108 36
26. 25% of 24 6

Use after page 243.

1. 4 is what percent of 20? 20%
2. 7 is what percent of 70? 10%
3. 84 is what percent of 200? 42%
4. 17 is what percent of 25? 68%
5. 43 is what percent of 50? 86%
6. 13 is what percent of 20? 65%
7. 24 is what percent of 32? 75%
8. 87 is what percent of 290? 30%
9. 16.2 is what percent of 45? 36%
10. 29.6 is what percent of 37? 80%
11. 40.8 is what percent of 85? 48%
12. 2.7 is what percent of 7.5? 36%
13. What percent of 45 is 18? 40%
14. What percent of 36 is 16.2? 45%
15. 6 is what percent of 32? $18\frac{3}{4}\%$
16. 24 is what percent of 36? $66\frac{2}{3}\%$
17. 40 is what percent of 90? $44\frac{4}{9}\%$
18. 18 is what percent of 63? $28\frac{4}{7}\%$
19. 10 is what percent of 16? $62\frac{1}{2}\%$
20. 17 is what percent of 51? $33\frac{1}{3}\%$
21. 12 is what percent of 56? $21\frac{3}{7}\%$
22. 9 is what percent of 26? $34\frac{8}{13}\%$
23. 20 is what percent of 35? $57\frac{1}{7}\%$
24. 64 is what percent of 48? $133\frac{1}{3}\%$
25. 2.2 is what percent of 80? $2\frac{3}{4}\%$
26. 1.5 is what percent of 3.6? $41\frac{2}{3}\%$
27. What percent of 800 is 500? $62\frac{1}{2}\%$

Use after page 245.

1. 26 is 40% of what number? 65
2. 36 is 90% of what number? 40
3. 3 is 4% of what number? 75
4. 51 is 75% of what number? 68
5. 46 is 200% of what number? 23
6. 96 is 150% of what number? 64
7. 63 is 45% of what number? 140
8. 21.5 is 43% of what number? 50
9. 31 is 0.5% of what number? 6200
10. 4.25 is 0.25% of what number? 1700
11. 5 is $2\frac{1}{2}\%$ of what number? 200
12. 43 is 5% of what number? 860
13. 3.6% of what number is 288? 8000
14. 8% of what number is 32? 400
15. 12 is $33\frac{1}{3}\%$ of what number? 36
16. 20 is $66\frac{2}{3}\%$ of what number? 30
17. 15 is $16\frac{2}{3}\%$ of what number? 90
18. 32 is $12\frac{1}{2}\%$ of what number? 256
19. 18 is $37\frac{1}{2}\%$ of what number? 48
20. 16 is 25% of what number? 64
21. 24 is $11\frac{1}{9}\%$ of what number? 216
22. 37 is 50% of what number? 74
23. 20 is $133\frac{1}{3}\%$ of what number? 15
24. $33\frac{1}{3}\%$ of what number is 42? 126
25. $66\frac{2}{3}\%$ of what number is 76? 114
26. 8 is $16\frac{2}{3}\%$ of what number? 48
27. 9 is $12\frac{1}{2}\%$ of what number? 72

SKILLS FILE

Use after page 287.

1. $2 + 5$ — 7
2. $^-4 + {}^-5$ — $^-9$
3. $3 + {}^-7$ — $^-4$
4. $8 + {}^-6$ — 2
5. $^-16 + {}^-6$ — $^-22$
6. $^-15 + 6$ — $^-9$
7. $^-86 + {}^-35$ — $^-121$
8. $84 + 36$ — 120
9. $^-45 + {}^-56$ — $^-101$
10. $^-14 + 11$ — $^-3$
11. $^-38 + {}^-74$ — $^-112$
12. $16 + 23$ — 39
13. $27 + {}^-64$ — $^-37$
14. $24 + 37$ — 61
15. $^-34 + {}^-248$ — $^-282$
16. $23 + {}^-36$ — $^-13$
17. $742 + 567$ — 1309
18. $^-694 + {}^-223$ — $^-917$
19. $329 + {}^-284$ — 45
20. $129 + 892$ — 1021
21. $^-4.8 + {}^-5.3$ — $^-10.1$
22. $^-0.86 + 0.27$ — $^-0.59$
23. $^-7.92 + {}^-6.89$ — $^-14.81$
24. $1.2 + 2.6$ — 3.8
25. $8.42 + {}^-6.33$ — 2.09
26. $6.23 + 8.78$ — 15.01

Use after page 289.

1. $6 - 7$ — $^-1$
2. $^-6 - {}^-8$ — 2
3. $^-4 - 8$ — $^-12$
4. $7 - {}^-2$ — 9
5. $^-7 - 2$ — $^-9$
6. $9 - 4$ — 5
7. $3 - {}^-5$ — 8
8. $^-39 - 23$ — $^-62$
9. $^-23 - {}^-14$ — $^-9$
10. $27 - 39$ — $^-12$
11. $^-36 - {}^-88$ — 52
12. $^-16 - 35$ — $^-51$
13. $27 - {}^-36$ — 63
14. $18 - 14$ — 4
15. $18 - {}^-11$ — 29
16. $^-153 - 582$ — $^-735$
17. $^-265 - {}^-573$ — 308
18. $156 - 385$ — $^-229$
19. $492 - {}^-585$ — 1077
20. $^-7.1 - 10.3$ — $^-17.4$
21. $^-3.8 - {}^-5.2$ — 1.4
22. $5.6 - 7.2$ — $^-1.6$
23. $^-6.92 - {}^-4.19$ — $^-2.73$
24. $^-1.22 - 0.64$ — $^-1.86$
25. $5.6 - {}^-2.7$ — 8.3
26. $3.1 - {}^-10.8$ — 13.9

Use after page 291.

1. 8×5 — 40
2. $^-7 \times {}^-6$ — 42
3. $^-3 \times 8$ — $^-24$
4. $^-5 \times {}^-8$ — 40
5. 7×4 — 28
6. $^-8 \times 6$ — $^-48$
7. $5 \times {}^-6$ — $^-30$
8. $^-7 \times {}^-26$ — 182
9. 4×35 — 140
10. $4 \times {}^-64$ — $^-256$
11. 3×43 — 129
12. $^-15 \times {}^-76$ — 1140
13. $79 \times {}^-35$ — $^-2765$
14. 12×68 — 816
15. $^-14 \times {}^-74$ — 1036
16. $17 \times {}^-27$ — $^-459$
17. $^-15 \times {}^-36$ — 540
18. 14×85 — 1190
19. $83 \times {}^-92$ — $^-7636$
20. 27×46 — 1242
21. $^-29 \times 36$ — $^-1044$
22. $^-16 \times {}^-100$ — 1600
23. $^-143 \times {}^-108$ — $15{,}444$
24. 0.5×0.8 — 0.4
25. $^-2.4 \times {}^-3.2$ — 7.68
26. $^-4 \times 0.6$ — $^-2.4$

Use after page 293.

1. $20 \div 4$ — 5
2. $^-16 \div {}^-4$ — 4
3. $^-15 \div 5$ — $^-3$
4. $^-25 \div {}^-5$ — 5
5. $32 \div 8$ — 4
6. $^-64 \div {}^-8$ — 8
7. $32 \div {}^-4$ — $^-8$
8. $45 \div 9$ — 5
9. $^-40 \div 5$ — $^-8$
10. $56 \div 7$ — 8
11. $^-27 \div 3$ — $^-9$
12. $^-60 \div 4$ — $^-15$
13. $108 \div {}^-9$ — $^-12$
14. $69 \div 23$ — 3
15. $^-52 \div {}^-13$ — 4
16. $^-66 \div {}^-11$ — 6
17. $225 \div {}^-15$ — $^-15$
18. $^-560 \div {}^-16$ — 35
19. $448 \div 28$ — 16
20. $^-169 \div {}^-13$ — 13
21. $312 \div {}^-12$ — $^-26$
22. $^-230 \div {}^-46$ — 5
23. $512 \div 32$ — 16
24. $^-832 \div 64$ — $^-13$
25. $^-1.92 \div {}^-1.6$ — 1.2
26. $0.8 \div 2$ — 0.4

TABLES

Metric System

Length

10 millimeters (mm) = 1 centimeter (cm)
10 centimeters, 100 millimeters = 1 decimeter (dm)
10 decimeters, 100 centimeters = 1 meter (m)
1000 meters = 1 kilometer (km)

Area

100 square millimeters (mm^2) = 1 square centimeter (cm^2)
10,000 square centimeters = 1 square meter (m^2)
100 square meters = 1 are (a)
10,000 square meters = 1 hectare (ha)

Volume

1000 cubic millimeters (mm^3) = 1 cubic centimeter (cm^3)
1000 cubic centimeters = 1 cubic decimeter (dm^3)
1,000,000 cubic centimeters = 1 cubic meter (m^3)

Mass

1000 milligrams (mg) = 1 gram (g)
1000 grams = 1 kilogram (kg)
1000 kilograms = 1 metric ton (t)

Capacity

1000 milliliters (mL) = 1 liter (L)
1000 liters = 1 kiloliter (kL)

United States Customary System

Length

12 inches (in.) = 1 foot (ft.)
3 feet, 36 inches = 1 yard (yd.)
1760 yards, 5280 feet = 1 mile (mi.)
6076 feet = 1 nautical mile

Area

144 square inches (sq. in.) = 1 square foot (sq. ft.)
9 square feet = 1 square yard (sq. yd.)
4840 square yards = 1 acre (A.)

Volume

1728 cubic inches (cu. in.) = 1 cubic foot (cu. ft.)
27 cubic feet = 1 cubic yard (cu. yd.)

Weight

16 ounces (oz.) = 1 pound (lb.)
2000 pounds = 1 ton (T.)

Capacity

8 fluid ounces (fl. oz.) = 1 cup (c.)
2 cups = 1 pint (pt.)
2 pints = 1 quart (qt.)
4 quarts = 1 gallon (gal.)

Symbols

$\approx$	approximately equal to
$\overline{AB}$	segment AB
$\angle G$	angle G
45°	45 degrees
∟	right angle
$\sqrt{25}$	square root of 25

Geometric Formulas

Perimeter
rectangle $P = 2l + 2w$

Circumference
circle $C = \pi d$ or $C = 2\pi r$

Area
rectangle $A = lw$
square $A = s^2$
parallelogram $A = bh$
triangle $A = \frac{1}{2}bh$
trapezoid $A = \frac{1}{2}h(a + b)$
circle $A = \pi r^2$

Surface area
rectangular prism $A = 2lw + 2lh + 2wh$
cube $A = 6s^2$
cylinder $A = 2\pi rh + 2\pi r^2$

Volume
rectangular prism $V = lwh$
cube $V = s^3$
cylinder $V = \pi r^2 h$
rectangular pyramid $V = \frac{1}{3}lwh$
cone $V = \frac{1}{3}\pi r^2 h$
sphere $V = \frac{4}{3}\pi r^3$

CAREERS CHART

This four-page chart gives information about selected careers in eight career clusters: Trades, Technology, Science, Health, Arts, Social Service, Business Contact, and Business Detail.* Information given includes training qualifications of most workers, estimated employment in 1978, and projected average annual openings to 1990 due to growth and replacement needs.

The following code is used under the heading "Qualifications."

C 4 years or more of college required
S Special training required (technical or vocational school, junior college, or apprenticeship)
— No college or special training required

Trades	Qualifications	Estimated employment in 1978	Average annual openings to 1990
Air-conditioning, refrigeration, or heating mechanic	S	210,000	8200
Aircraft mechanic	S	132,000	3500
Appliance repairer	—	145,000	6900
Assembler	—	1,164,000	77,000
Automobile mechanic	—	860,000	37,000
Bricklayer	S	205,000	6200
Carpenter	S	1,253,000	58,000
Electrician (construction)	S	290,000	12,900
Industrial machinery repairer	S	655,000	58,000
Inspector (manufacturing)	—	771,000	35,000
Instrument maker (mechanical)	S	6000	300
Machine tool operator	—	542,000	19,600
Machinist	S	484,000	22,500
Maintenance electrician	S	300,000	15,500
Meatcutter	S	204,000	5200
Millwright	S	95,000	4700
Painter or paperhanger	—	504,000	27,000
Plumber or pipefitter	S	428,000	20,000
Power truck operator	—	363,000	14,000
Supervisor	S	1,671,000	69,000
Television or radio service technician	S	131,000	6100
Tool and die maker	S	170,000	8600
Truck and bus mechanic	—	165,000	6800
Welder	—	679,000	35,000

*Cluster titles are based on interest areas measured by the Vocational Interest Profile used in The American College Testing Career Planning Program. Reprinted by permission. Information about qualifications and employment is from *Occupational Projections and Training Data, 1980 Edition.*

The eight career clusters are first mentioned in career lessons on pages 20–21, 40–41, 42–43, 64–65, 140–141, 166–167, 272–273, 322–323. When a cluster is first mentioned, you might have the students turn to this chart and read the data for the careers in that cluster. Remind students that employment prospects depend on many factors, such as the number of people seeking employment in a particular career.

Technology

Technology	Qualifications	Estimated employment in 1978	Average annual openings to 1990
Aerospace engineer	C	60,000	1900
Air traffic controller	C	21,000	700
Chemical engineer	C	53,000	1800
Civil engineer	C	155,000	7800
Drafter	S	296,000	11,000
Electrical engineer	C	300,000	10,500
Engineering and science technician	S	600,000	23,000
Forester	C	31,200	1400
Mechanical engineer	C	195,000	7500
Pilot or copilot	S	76,000	3800
Surveyor or surveying technician	S	62,000	2300

Science

Science	Qualifications	Estimated employment in 1978	Average annual openings to 1990
Chemist	C	143,000	6100
Economist	C	130,000	7800
Geologist	C	31,000	1700
Life scientist	C	215,000	11,200
Mathematician	C	33,500	1000
Meteorologist	C	7300	300
Physicist	C	44,000	1000

Health

Health	Qualifications	Estimated employment in 1978	Average annual openings to 1990
Dental assistant	—	150,000	11,000
Dental hygienist	S	35,000	6000
Dentist	C	120,000	5500
Dietitian	C	35,000	3300
Hospital attendant or nursing aide	—	1,037,000	94,000
Licensed practical nurse	S	518,000	60,000
Medical laboratory worker	S,C	210,000	14,800
Pharmacist	C	135,000	7800
Physician	C	405,000	19,000
Radiologic technologist	S	100,000	9000
Registered nurse	S,C	1,060,000	85,000
Surgical technician	S	35,000	2600
Veterinarian	C	33,500	1700

CAREERS CHART

Arts	Qualifications	Estimated employment in 1978	Average annual openings to 1990
Actor or actress	S	13,400	850
Architect	C	54,000	4000
Dancer	S	8000	550
Display worker	—	44,000	3300
Interior designer	S	79,000	3600
Musician or music teacher	S,C	127,000	8900
Newspaper reporter	C	45,000	2400
Photographer	—	93,000	3800
Radio or television announcer	—	27,000	850
Singer or singing teacher	S,C	22,000	1600

Social Service			
Barber	S	121,000	9700
Building custodian	—	2,251,000	176,000
College or university teacher	C	673,000	11,000
Cook or chef	—	1,186,000	86,000
Cosmetologist	S	542,000	29,000
Firefighter	—	220,000	7500
Flight attendant	S	48,000	4800
Gasoline service station attendant	—	340,000	5200
Guard	—	550,000	70,000
Kindergarten or elementary school teacher	C	1,322,000	86,000
Lawyer	C	487,000	37,000
Librarian	C	142,000	8000
Mail carrier	—	245,000	7000
Mortician	S	45,000	2200
Personnel or labor relations worker	C	405,000	17,000
Police officer (municipal)	—	450,000	16,500
Private household worker	—	1,162,000	45,000
School counselor	C	45,000	1700
Secondary school teacher	C	1,087,000	7200
Social service aide	—	134,000	7500
Social worker	C	385,000	22,000
State police officer	—	47,000	1800
Teacher aide	—	342,000	26,000
Telephone operator	—	311,000	9900
Waiter or waitress	—	1,383,000	70,000

Business Contact	Qualifications	Estimated employment in 1978	Average annual openings to 1990
Airline passenger agent	—	56,000	2200
Automobile parts clerk	—	97,000	4200
Automobile sales agent	—	158,000	10,400
Bank officer or manager	C	330,000	28,000
Bank teller	—	410,000	17,000
Conductor (railroad)	—	37,000	1700
Hotel manager or assistant	C	168,000	8900
Local truckdriver	—	1,720,000	64,000
Long-distance truckdriver	—	584,000	21,500
Manufacturers' sales representative	C	402,000	21,700
Postal clerk	—	260,000	2000
Public relations worker	C	185,000	7500
Purchasing agent	C	185,000	13,400
Real estate sales agent or broker	S	555,000	50,000
Retail sales worker	—	2,851,000	226,000
Securities sales worker	S	109,000	5500
Taxi driver	—	94,000	4300
Wholesale trade salesworker	—	840,000	40,000

Business Detail	Qualifications	Estimated employment in 1978	Average annual openings to 1990
Accountant	C	985,000	61,000
Bank clerk	—	505,000	45,000
Bookkeeping worker	—	1,830,000	96,000
Cashier	—	1,400,000	119,000
Computer operator	—	666,000	12,500
File clerk	—	273,000	16,500
Front office clerk (hotel)	—	79,000	5400
Insurance actuary	C	9000	500
Office machine operator	—	160,000	9700
Programmer	S,C	247,000	9200
Receptionist	—	588,000	41,000
Shipping and receiving clerk	—	461,000	22,000
Stenographer or secretary	—	3,684,000	305,000
Stock clerk	—	507,000	23,000
Systems analyst	C	182,000	7900
Typist	—	1,044,000	59,000

GLOSSARY

Brief descriptions of terms are listed in this glossary. These descriptions need not be considered definitions.

acute angle
Any angle whose measure is less than 90 degrees.

addend
One of the numbers used in addition. In 25 + 37 = 62, 25 and 37 are addends.

adjacent side
Side AB is next to, or adjacent to, angle A.

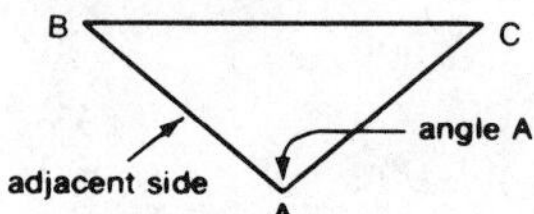

angle
Two rays with the same endpoint. The measure of an angle is given in degrees.

annual
For one year or 12 months.

area
The measure, given in square units, of an amount of surface inside a closed, plane figure.

average
A number obtained by dividing the sum of two or more addends by the number of addends.

axis
A horizontal or vertical line used for reference on a grid.

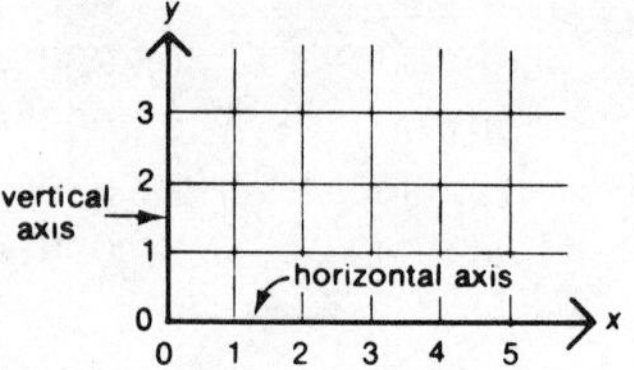

calorie
Unit of energy supplied by food.

capacity
The greatest number of units a container can hold.

central angle
An angle whose vertex is the center of a circle.

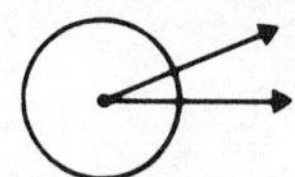

checking account
An account into which money is paid (deposited). The money is taken out (withdrawn) by using forms called checks.

circle
A closed curve in a plane. Each point on the circle is the same distance from the center.

circumference
The measure of the distance around a circle.

common denominator
A common multiple of two or more denominators. A common denominator for $\frac{3}{4}$ and $\frac{5}{6}$ is 12.

common factor
A number that is a factor of two or more numbers. 2 is a common factor of 6 and 14.

common multiple
A number that is a multiple of two or more numbers. 18 is a common multiple of 3, 6, and 9.

computer program
A set of instructions that tells a computer what to do.

cone
A space figure shaped like the one shown below.

corresponding angles or sides
The matching angles or sides in similar figures.

cosine
For a given acute angle in a right triangle, the ratio:
$\frac{\text{length of adjacent side}}{\text{length of hypotenuse}}$

cross-products
The cross-products for the ratios below are 3×8 and 4×6. Two ratios are equal if their cross-products are equal.
$\frac{3}{4} = \frac{6}{8}$ because $3 \times 8 = 4 \times 6$.

cube
A prism with all square faces (sides).

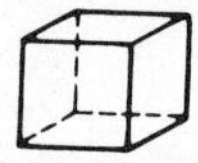

cylinder
A space figure shaped like the one shown below.

data
Information such as scores, measurements, and values.

decimal
A decimal point and place value are used to write decimals, such as 3.8, 0.015, and 8.00.

denominator
In the fraction $\frac{7}{8}$, 8 is the denominator.

diameter
In a circle, a segment that passes through the center and has its endpoints on the circle.

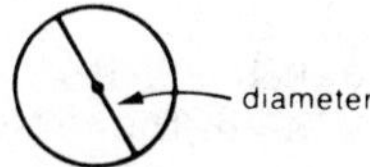

difference
The answer when numbers are subtracted. In $88 - 23 = 65$, 65 is the difference.

digits
One of the symbols used to show numbers. In base ten, the digits are 0, 1, 2, 3, 4, 5, 6, 7, 8, and 9.

discount
Amount deducted from list price to obtain sale price; a percent of the list price.

dividend
In $450 \div 25 = 18$, 450 is the dividend.

divisor
In $450 \div 25 = 18$, 25 is the divisor.

equal fractions
Fractions that name the same number. $\frac{2}{3}$ and $\frac{6}{9}$ are equal fractions.

equal ratios
Ratios that indicate the same rate or comparison. The cross-products of equal ratios are equal.

equation
A mathematical sentence that uses the equals sign (=), such as $5 + 6 = 11$ and $14n = 98$.

exponent
In 4^3, 3 is the exponent. It tells that 4 is to be used as a factor three times.
$4^3 = 4 \times 4 \times 4 = 64$

face
A plane region of a space figure.

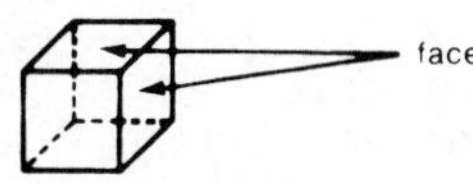

factor
One of the numbers used in multiplication. In $14 \times 8 = 112$, 14 and 8 are factors.

finance charge
A fee paid for buying an item on credit or on an installment plan.

fraction
Any number of the form $\frac{2}{3}$, $\frac{8}{8}$, $\frac{9}{5}$, or $\frac{4}{7}$.

frequency
The number of times an outcome or event occurs.

frequency table
A listing of data and how many times each item of the data occurred.

graph
A picture used to show data. The picture could be a bar, line, or circle graph, or a pictograph. It might also be points on a grid matched with given ordered pairs.

greater than (>)
An inequality relation between two numbers, such as $51 > 15$, $9 > 1.4$, and $\frac{1}{3} > \frac{1}{5}$.

gross income
Income before any deductions are made.

gross profit
The amount left after the cost of parts is deducted from the selling price.

hypotenuse
The side opposite the right angle of a right triangle.

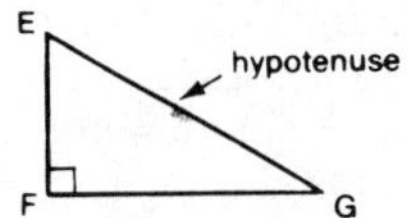

inequality
A mathematical sentence that uses >, <, or ≠, such as $9 > 4$, $5 < 7$, and $3(5) \neq 9$.

input
Coded information fed into a computer.

integers
The whole numbers and their opposites. $^-83$, $^-52$, 0, 106, and 14,679 are integers.

interest
An amount paid for the use of money, usually a percent of the amount invested, loaned, or borrowed.

inventory
A detailed list of articles, usually with their estimated values.

lease
The right to use property for a given length of time. Money (rent) is usually paid for the use of the property.

less than (<)
An inequality relation between two numbers, such as $15 < 51$, $1.4 < 9$, and $\frac{1}{5} < \frac{1}{3}$.

list price
Original or regular price before subtracting the discount.

loan
An amount of money borrowed for a certain period of time. Interest is usually paid for the use of the money.

lowest terms
A fraction is in lowest terms if 1 is the only common factor of the numerator and denominator. $\frac{1}{5}$, $\frac{8}{3}$, and $\frac{4}{7}$ are in lowest terms.

mass
The measure of quantity of matter an object contains.

mean
Another name for average. The mean of 1, 5, and 6 is $12 \div 3$, or 4.

median
The middle number in a series of numbers when the numbers are in order. The median of 2, 2, 3, 4, 5 is 3.

mixed number
Any number of the form $15\frac{3}{7}$, $7\frac{9}{10}$, or $34\frac{1}{2}$.

mode
The number occurring most often in a series of numbers. The mode of 1, 1, and 3 is 1.

multiple
The product of a given number and a whole number. Multiples of 5 are 5, 10, 15, 20, 25, and so on.

multiplier
A number by which another number is to be multiplied.

negative number
A number less than zero, such as $^-8$, $^-15$, and $^-96$.

net gain
Actual profit after expenses have been deducted from gross income; expenses are less than income.

net income
Income remaining after deductions are made.

net loss
Actual losses after expenses have been deducted from gross income; expenses are greater than income.

numerator
In the fraction $\frac{7}{8}$, 7 is the numerator.

operation
Addition, subtraction, multiplication, and division are examples of operations.

opposites
Two numbers whose sum is zero. 9 and $^-9$ are opposites because $9 + {}^-9 = 0$.

ordered pair
Two numbers used in a certain order, such as (4, 0).

origin
On a grid, the point (0, 0). The two number lines, or axes, meet at this point.

output
Data resulting from execution of a computer program.

parallel lines
Lines that are in the same plane and do not meet.

parallelogram
A four-sided polygon whose opposite sides are parallel.

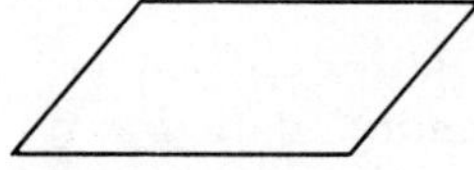

percent
A word that indicates "hundredths" or "out of 100." 4 percent (4%) means 0.04 or $\frac{4}{100}$.

perimeter
The measure of the distance around a closed figure.

pi (π)
The ratio of the circumference to the diameter of a circle. Approximately equal to 3.14.

place value
The value a digit has because of its position. In 78, the 7 has a value of 7(10), or 70, and the 8 has a value of 8(1).

polygon
A closed figure made up of segments.

positive number
A number greater than zero, such as 9, 146, and 32,508.

principal
Amount of money upon which interest is computed.

prism
A space figure with two parallel faces (bases) that have the same measure.

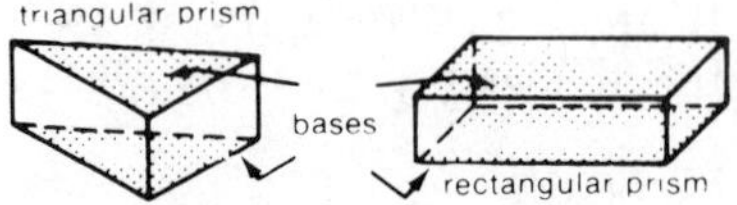

probability
A number that tells how likely it is that a certain event will happen. Expressed as:
$$\frac{\text{number of favorable outcomes}}{\text{number of possible outcomes}}$$

product
The answer when numbers are multiplied. In $35 \times 26 = 910$, 910 is the product.

proportion
A statement that two ratios are equal.
$$\frac{4}{6} = \frac{10}{15}$$

pyramid
A space figure with one base. All sides are triangles.

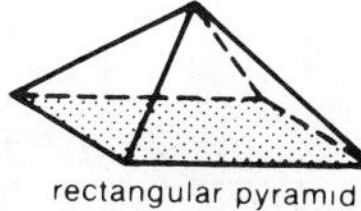

quadrant
The axes separate a grid into four sections. Each section is a quadrant.

quotient
In $450 \div 9 = 50$, 50 is the quotient.

radius
In a circle, a segment with endpoints that are the center of the circle and a point on the circle.

ratio
A pair of numbers that expresses a rate or a comparison.

ray
Part of a line that has one endpoint and extends in one direction.

reciprocals
Two numbers whose product is 1. $\frac{3}{4}$ and $\frac{4}{3}$ are reciprocals because $\frac{3}{4} \times \frac{4}{3} = 1$.

rectangle
A parallelogram with four right angles.

rectangular prism
See prism.

remainder
When 15 is divided by 6, the remainder is 3.

$$6\overline{)15}\ \ 2\text{ R3}$$

right angle
An angle whose measure is 90 degrees.

right triangle
A triangle with one right angle.

salary
Money paid to a person for work completed. It is usually paid weekly, twice a month, or monthly.

sale price
The price after the discount is subtracted from the list price; also called net price.

segment
Part of a line, which includes two endpoints.

share of stock
One unit of ownership in a company or corporation. Shares are traded (bought or sold) through a business called a stock exchange.

similar figures
Figures having the same shape but not necessarily the same size.

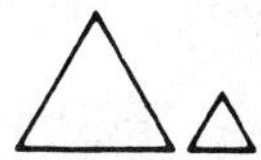

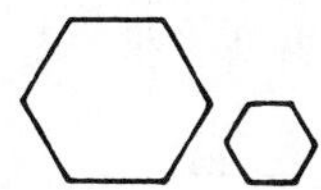

sine
For a given acute angle in a right triangle, the ratio:

$$\frac{\text{length of opposite side}}{\text{length of hypotenuse}}$$

sphere
A round space figure shaped like a basketball. All points on a sphere are the same distance from the center.

square
A rectangle with four sides having the same measure.

square root
One of two equal factors of a number. 5 is the square root of 25 because $5 \times 5 = 25$.

sum
The answer when numbers are added. In $76 + 48 = 124$, 124 is the sum.

surface area
The total area of all the faces of a space figure.

tangent
For a given acute angle in a right triangle, the ratio:

$$\frac{\text{length of opposite side}}{\text{length of adjacent side}}$$

trapezoid
A four-sided polygon with one pair of parallel sides.

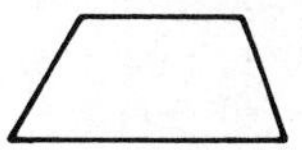

triangle
A polygon with three sides.

trigonometric ratios
See cosine, sine, tangent.

volume
The measure, given in cubic units, of an amount of space inside a space figure.

whole number
Any number in the set 0, 1, 2, 3, 4, 5, and so on.

SELECTED ANSWERS

Page 4

Set A **1.** 60 **3.** 90 **5.** 90 **7.** 50 **9.** 260 **11.** 140 **13.** 290 **15.** 1000 **17.** 4330 **19.** 10 **21.** 4400

Set B **1.** 600 **3.** 800 **5.** 100 **7.** 300 **9.** 5400 **11.** 3200 **13.** 2300 **15.** 11,800 **17.** 1000 **19.** 100 **21.** 8000

Set C **1.** 7000 **3.** 2000 **5.** 5000 **7.** 4000 **9.** 8000 **11.** 9000 **13.** 36,000 **15.** 73,000 **17.** 17,000 **19.** 1000 **21.** 30,000

Page 5

Set D **1.** 70 **3.** 600 **5.** 500 **7.** 1300 **9.** 4000 **11.** 10,000

Set E **1.** 60 **3.** 600 **5.** 300 **7.** 7000 **9.** 2000 **11.** 50,000

Set F **1.** 3700 **3.** 2000 **5.** 17,000 **7.** 5600 **9.** 33,000

Pages 6–7

Set G **1.** 89 **3.** 399 **5.** 925 **7.** 8895 **9.** 5986 **11.** 17,377

Set H **1.** 66 **3.** 905 **5.** 500 **7.** 1002 **9.** 2020 **11.** 11,728 **13.** 92,300

Set I **1.** 162 **3.** 234 **5.** 2835 **7.** 83,581 **9.** 9317

Set J **1.** 7268 **3.** 41,627 **5.** 5993 **7.** 256 **9.** 3783 **11.** 390

Mixed Practice **1.** 456 **3.** 87 **5.** 273 **7.** 3429 **9.** 276 **11.** 63,618 **13.** 2630 **15.** 47,061 **17.** 1023 **19.** 989 **21.** 114 **23.** 34,456 **25.** 8888 **27.** 9102 **29.** 14,582

Pages 8–9

Set K **1.** 11 **3.** 612 **5.** 137 **7.** 1123 **9.** 2121 **11.** 41,102

Set L **1.** 56 **3.** 419 **5.** 88 **7.** 886 **9.** 1720 **11.** 5765 **13.** 7285 **15.** 2184 **17.** 3867 **19.** 2532 **21.** 19,379 **23.** 18,168

Set M **1.** 14 **3.** 261 **5.** 92 **7.** 589 **9.** 14 **11.** 4138 **13.** 7752 **15.** 7321 **17.** 30,867

Mixed Practice **1.** 226 **3.** 4263 **5.** 74,808 **7.** 2465 **9.** 8629 **11.** 27 **13.** 5239 **15.** 2756 **17.** 377 **19.** 4658 **21.** 354 **23.** 39,182 **25.** 317 **27.** 295 **29.** 2386 **31.** 31,373 **33.** 26,346 **35.** 18,276 **37.** 75,629

Pages 10–11

Set N **1.** 7 **3.** 25 **5.** 40 **7.** 32 **9.** 24 **11.** 40 **13.** 85 **15.** 17 **17.** 52 **19.** 9 **21.** 11 **23.** 315 **25.** 170 **27.** 35

Set O **1.** 12 **3.** 7 **5.** 53 **7.** 122 **9.** 24 **11.** 167 **13.** 28 **15.** 0 **17.** 111 **19.** 21 **21.** 162 **23.** 12 **25.** 508 **27.** 25

Mixed Practice **1.** 13 **3.** 36 **5.** 130 **7.** 0 **9.** 10 **11.** 36 **13.** 64 **15.** 22 **17.** 0 **19.** 2 **21.** 2 **23.** 52 **25.** 22 **27.** 42

Pages 12-13

Set P **1.** $x = 35$ **3.** $a = 25$ **5.** $t = 12$ **7.** $d = 25$ **9.** $z = 57$ **11.** $g = 64$

Set Q **1.** $k = 33$ **3.** $a = 23$ **5.** $n = 139$ **7.** $g = 129$ **9.** $y = 90$ **11.** $x = 885$

Mixed Practice **1.** $c = 21$ **3.** $d = 86$ **5.** $h = 27$ **7.** $h = 123$ **9.** $j = 157$ **11.** $v = 13$ **13.** $b = 52$ **15.** $k = 35$ **17.** $a = 18$ **19.** $w = 13$ **21.** $n = 114$ **23.** $a = 320$ **25.** $w = 345$ **27.** $c = 43$

Page 15 **1.** Monday's Totals: 2490; 110 Tuesday's Totals: 1585; 242 **3.** 142 grams

Pages 16-17 **1.** $768 **3.** $451 **5.** Train **7.** $317 **9.** $599 **11.** $944 **13.** $682 **15.** $539 **17.** $1392 **19.** $823 **21.** $370

Pages 18-19 **1.** $6393; $5927; $5334 **3.** $8018; $7419; $6677 **5.** $9608; $8876; $7988 **7.** $11,151; $10,286; $9257 **9.** $12,648; $11,650; $10,485 **11.** $14,087; $12,956; $11,660 **13.** $15,487; $14,223; $12,801

Pages 20-21 **1.** 5 degree-days **3.** 2 degree-days **5.** 14 degree-days **7.** 18 degree-days **9.** 428 degree-days **11.** 207 degree-days **13.** 812 **15.** 703 **17.** 1352 **19.** 972 **21.** 983 **23.** 709 **25.** 6044

Pages 22-23 **1.** 29748 **3.** 30602 **5.** 31653 **7.** 24 kilowatt-hours **9.** 35 kilowatt-hours **11.** 192 kilowatt-hours

Page 26

Set A **1.** 8000 **3.** 100 **5.** 5000 **7.** 200,000 **9.** 4600 **11.** 5,000,000 **13.** 10,000,000 **15.** 8,000,000

Set B **1.** 1200 **3.** 3600 **5.** 180,000 **7.** 10,000 **9.** 30,000 **11.** 5,400,000 **13.** 2,000,000 **15.** 56,000,000

Mixed Practice **1.** 18,000 **3.** 40,000 **5.** 42,000,000 **7.** 68,000 **9.** 1,000,000 **11.** 3,000,000 **13.** 600,000 **15.** 32,000,000

Page 27

Set C **1.** 160 **3.** 400 **5.** 4200 **7.** 4800 **9.** 1800 **11.** 36,000 **13.** 72,000

Set D **1.** 800 **3.** 42,000 **5.** 490,000 **7.** 27,000 **9.** 300,000 **11.** 320,000 **13.** 4,500,000

Mixed Practice **1.** 1500 **3.** 5600 **5.** 72,000 **7.** 160,000 **9.** 2,000,000 **11.** 180,000 **13.** 24,000

Pages 28–29

Set E **1.** 48 **3.** 324 **5.** 128 **7.** 144 **9.** 166

Set F **1.** 175 **3.** 330 **5.** 329 **7.** 396 **9.** 576 **11.** 152 **13.** 145 **15.** 456

Set G **1.** 3344 **3.** 1610 **5.** 2031 **7.** 51,426 **9.** 40,280 **11.** 67,921 **13.** 588,192 **15.** 274,842

Set H **1.** 357 **3.** 288 **5.** 5556 **7.** 1767 **9.** 23,456 **11.** 15,875 **13.** 57,042 **15.** 207,432 **17.** 320,632 **19.** 429,478

Mixed Practice **1.** 203 **3.** 10,390 **5.** 295,624 **7.** 4809 **9.** 184 **11.** 186 **13.** 480 **15.** 486 **17.** 567 **19.** 207,720 **21.** 129 **23.** 297,888 **25.** 2691 **27.** 41,706 **29.** 1832 **31.** 28,863 **33.** 38,312 **35.** 339,715 **37.** 3556

Pages 30–31

Set I **1.** 1920 **3.** 2820 **5.** 2850 **7.** 4080 **9.** 6840

Set J **1.** 828 **3.** 3392 **5.** 2988 **7.** 1105 **9.** 2436 **11.** 2106 **13.** 2200 **15.** 7448

Set K **1.** 46,332 **3.** 53,801 **5.** 388,523 **7.** 221,238 **9.** 370,760 **11.** 3,207,225 **13.** 8,876,276 **15.** 1,471,176

Set L **1.** 4770 **3.** 2814 **5.** 5046 **7.** 19,499 **9.** 68,328 **11.** 706,496 **13.** 461,040 **15.** 3,215,932 **17.** 3,431,664 **19.** 897,876

Mixed Practice **1.** 60,371 **3.** 334,184 **5.** 28,380 **7.** 284,130 **9.** 38,175 **11.** 441,504 **13.** 412,908 **15.** 26,598 **17.** 4,536,252 **19.** 2,117,580 **21.** 4,376,580 **23.** 756 **25.** 3,760,896 **27.** 2340 **29.** 3920 **31.** 15,998 **33.** 3002 **35.** 2,024,948 **37.** 48,100

Pages 32–33

Set M **1.** 173,400 **3.** 495,600 **5.** 635,400 **7.** 450,100 **9.** 159,200

Set N **1.** 66,674 **3.** 103,477 **5.** 370,670 **7.** 587,476 **9.** 368,192 **11.** 498,590 **13.** 110,430 **15.** 485,616

Set O **1.** 95,128 **3.** 247,043 **5.** 1,353,408 **7.** 20,399,632 **9.** 6,227,199 **11.** 42,391,888

Mixed Practice **1.** 366,561 **3.** 99,840 **5.** 8,471,034 **7.** 493,240 **9.** 562,800 **11.** 547,398 **13.** 3,709,472

Pages 34–35

Set P **1.** 23 **3.** 8 **5.** 43 **7.** 19 **9.** 62 **11.** 18 **13.** 36 **15.** 33 **17.** 50 **19.** 8 **21.** 26 **23.** 94 **25.** 62 **27.** 45

Set Q **1.** 30 **3.** 42 **5.** 16 **7.** 33 **9.** 47 **11.** 44 **13.** 210 **15.** 105 **17.** 46 **19.** 27 **21.** 52 **23.** 15 **25.** 54 **27.** 44

Mixed Practice **1.** 16 **3.** 50 **5.** 6 **7.** 96 **9.** 33 **11.** 25 **13.** 80 **15.** 58 **17.** 380 **19.** 60 **21.** 68 **23.** 27 **25.** 76 **27.** 48

Page 37 **1.** \$1590 **3.** \$204 **5.** \$3861 **7.** \$2715 **9.** \$4131

Pages 38–39 **1.** \$686 **3.** \$1257 **5.** \$554 **7.** \$1334 **9.** \$1300 **11.** \$5610 **13.** \$506 **15.** \$793 **17.** \$10,229 **19.** Mr. Diaz

Pages 40–41 **1.** a. 3720 L b. 1320 L c. 5760 L d. 6960 L e. 1560 L f. 3000 L g. 1440 L h. 3960 L i. 3240 L j. 11,400 L k. 4200 L l. 11,520 L m. 6720 L n. 2520 L
3. a. 279 metric tons b. 99 metric tons c. 432 metric tons d. 522 metric tons e. 117 metric tons f. 225 metric tons g. 108 metric tons h. 297 metric tons i. 243 metric tons j. 855 metric tons k. 315 metric tons l. 864 metric tons m. 504 metric tons n. 189 metric tons
5. 5426 kilograms **7.** 8098 kilograms **9.** 7666 kilograms **11.** 141,372 cases **13.** $1,130,976

Pages 42–43 **1.** 576; 768 **3.** 180; 360; 540; 720 **5.** 360; 720; 1080; 1440 **7.** 360; 720; 1080; 1440 **9.** 2100; 2200; 1900 **11.** 4200; 4400; 3800 **13.** 8400; 8800; 8300 **15.** 2800; 2880; 2770

Pages 44–45 **1.** 188 pounds **3.** 162 pounds **5.** 312 pounds **7.** 79 pounds

Pages 48–49
Set A **1.** 19 **3.** 28 **5.** 21 R3 **7.** 46 R1 **9.** 17 R3
Set B **1.** 83 **3.** 29 R2 **5.** 72 R4 **7.** 57 R2 **9.** 285 **11.** 182 R1 **13.** 271 R1 **15.** 189 R2
Set C **1.** 575 **3.** 1329 **5.** 294 R6 **7.** 1255 R5 **9.** 7663 **11.** 3791 R6 **13.** 15,237 **15.** 57,543 R1 **17.** 115,516 R7
Set D **1.** 23 R1 **3.** 78 **5.** 325 **7.** 195 R1 **9.** 1156 **11.** 1368 R3 **13.** 23,778 R2 **15.** 97,488 **17.** 428,377
Mixed Practice **1.** 562 R4 **3.** 87,239 R2 **5.** 167 R3 **7.** 239 **9.** 89 **11.** 95 R1 **13.** 7562 R1 **15.** 116 R5 **17.** 13 R1

Pages 50–51
Set E **1.** 2 **3.** 1 R7 **5.** 2 R10 **7.** 2 R23 **9.** 3 R1 **11.** 1 R15
Set F **1.** 4 R80 **3.** 5 R36 **5.** 34 R3 **7.** 12 R53 **9.** 12 R49 **11.** 15 R19 **13.** 14 R59 **15.** 18 R8 **17.** 27 R10 **19.** 68 R1
Set G **1.** 4 R14 **3.** 5 R19 **5.** 8 R2 **7.** 32 R10 **9.** 51 R12 **11.** 61 R12 **13.** 19 R2 **15.** 28 R14 **17.** 26 R4 **19.** 59 R13
Set H **1.** 75 R7 **3.** 158 R26 **5.** 3592 R5 **7.** 1594 R5 **9.** 5819 R64
Mixed Practice **1.** 24 R6 **3.** 131 R36 **5.** 4 R2 **7.** 25 R2 **9.** 28,782 R15 **11.** 4525 R6 **13.** 19 R32 **15.** 1 R22

Page 52
Set I **1.** 60 R5 **3.** 250 **5.** 705 R2 **7.** 7010 R3 **9.** 4003 R3 **11.** 3602 R4
Set J **1.** 30 R17 **3.** 206 R2 **5.** 107 R8 **7.** 260 R37 **9.** 1060 R18 **11.** 3006 R12
Mixed Practice **1.** 30 R4 **3.** 602 R22 **5.** 10 R25 **7.** 5602 R7 **9.** 4020 R12 **11.** 7006 R5

Page 53
Set K **1.** 8 R19 **3.** 2 R264 **5.** 2 R297 **7.** 5 R20 **9.** 3 R54 **11.** 2 R220
Set L **1.** 5 R490 **3.** 29 R47 **5.** 83 R389 **7.** 29 R307 **9.** 50 R376 **11.** 870 R844
Mixed Practice **1.** 670 R743 **3.** 185 R192 **5.** 2 R191 **7.** 3 R4 **9.** 390 **11.** 7 R20

Pages 54–55
Set M **1.** 4 **3.** 3 **5.** 31 **7.** 2 **9.** 27 **11.** 0 **13.** 17
Set N **1.** 3 **3.** 4 **5.** 3 **7.** 13 **9.** 9 **11.** 0 **13.** 1
Mixed Practice **1.** 7 **3.** 13 **5.** 9 **7.** 5 **9.** 11 **11.** 19 **13.** 73

Pages 56–57
Set O **1.** $c = 26$ **3.** $q = 42$ **5.** $z = 25$ **7.** $t = 18$ **9.** $y = 14$ **11.** $n = 4$ **13.** $r = 27$ **15.** $v = 16$ **17.** $d = 9$ **19.** $c = 6$ **21.** $u = 3$ **23.** $d = 8$ **25.** $h = 7$
Set P **1.** $e = 52$ **3.** $s = 475$ **5.** $a = 427$ **7.** $s = 80$ **9.** $k = 108$ **11.** $n = 135$ **13.** $x = 315$ **15.** $t = 112$ **17.** $w = 169$ **19.** $s = 1488$ **21.** $x = 294$ **23.** $n = 800$ **25.** $m = 1280$ **27.** $t = 4500$
Mixed Practice **1.** $g = 6000$ **3.** $t = 841$ **5.** $a = 234$ **7.** $c = 255$ **9.** $y = 627$ **11.** $b = 254$ **13.** $d = 1575$ **15.** $x = 5400$

Page 59 **1.** \$1326; \$306 **3.** \$1170; \$270 **5.** \$793; \$183 **7.** \$1638; \$378 **9.** \$1222; \$282 **11.** \$1651; \$381 **13.** \$1625; \$375 **15.** \$1495; \$345

Pages 60–61 **1.** 42¢ **3.** 20¢ **5.** 44¢ **7.** 37¢ **9.** 46¢ **11.** 33¢ **13.** 45¢ **15.** 50¢ **17.** Brand X **19.** Brand X **21.** Brand X **23.** Brand X **25.** Brand Y **27.** Brand X **29.** Brand Y

Pages 62–63 **1.** 10; 8; 18 **3.** 9; 7; 16 **5.** 26; 22; 48 **7.** 2; 2; 4 **9.** 8; 6; 14

Pages 64–65 **1.** 12 **3.** 6720; 5760 **5.** 39 cases **7.** 1560 cases **9.** 134,400 cases **11.** 1,497,600 cases **13.** 30 minutes **15.** 50 minutes **17.** 90 minutes **19.** 3600 cases **21.** 2000 cases **23.** 73,000 cases

Pages 66–67 **1. a.** Happ's: \$19,955; Greco's: \$16,653; Lee's: \$17,212 **b.** Happ's: \$3991; Greco's: \$2379; Lee's: \$4303 **c.** Happ's: 5; Greco's: 7; Lee's: 4 **3.** Greco's

Pages 68–69 **1.** 261 cartons **3.** 142 flats **5.** 286 flats **7.** 429 flats **9.** 14 pallets

Page 71
Adding and Subtracting Whole Numbers **1.** 89 **3.** 760 **5.** 101 **7.** 120 **9.** 6052 **11.** 4150 **13.** 255 **15.** 62 **17.** 619 **19.** 6545 **21.** 2048 **23.** 3769 **25.** 20,157
Multiplying Whole Numbers **1.** 87 **3.** 15,500 **5.** 12,033 **7.** 81,500 **9.** 1972 **11.** 30,000 **13.** 33,522 **15.** 13,818 **17.** 1,200,000 **19.** 10,950 **21.** 106,398 **23.** 515,570 **25.** 4,119,276 **27.** 536,536
Dividing Whole Numbers **1.** 181 **3.** 1812 R2 **5.** 34 R35 **7.** 600 **9.** 20,076 **11.** 8 **13.** 35 **15.** 49 R10 **17.** 90 **19.** 600 **21.** 809 **23.** 35 R313 **25.** 189 **27.** 261 R22

Page 72 **1.** \$840 **3.** \$673 **5.** \$2045 **7.** \$1102 **9.** \$1496 **11.** \$2

Page 73 **1.** KATHY LIKES TO WRITE PROGRAMS.

3.
```
9+4= 13
8-5= 3
4*7= 28
3/2= 1.5
```

5.
```
10 PRINT 6+3
20 PRINT 6-3
30 PRINT 6*3
40 PRINT 6/3
50 END
```

Pages 76–77

Set A **1.** hundredths **3.** ten-thousandths **5.** thousandths **7.** hundred-thousandths **9.** hundreds **11.** hundredths **13.** tenths **15.** millionths **17.** hundred-thousandths **19.** thousands **21.** hundreds

Set B **1.** 0.60, 0.600 **3.** 0.38, 0.380 **5.** 0.10, 0.100 **7.** 0.91, 0.910 **9.** 0.63, 0.630 **11.** 0.90, 0.900 **13.** 1.60, 1.600 **15.** 0.37, 0.370 **17.** 0.50, 0.500 **19.** 3.25, 3.250

Set C **1.** < **3.** < **5.** > **7.** > **9.** > **11.** = **13.** < **15.** < **17.** < **19.** < **21.** > **23.** = **25.** < **27.** < **29.** = **31.** < **33.** < **35.** = **37.** < **39.** < **41.** > **43.** < **45.** > **47.** > **49.** <

Pages 78–79

Set D **1.** 18.7 **3.** 15.18 **5.** 0.207 **7.** 8.642 **9.** 278.3 **11.** 19.857

Set E **1.** 0.864 **3.** 1.955 **5.** 12.531 **7.** 22.253 **9.** 81.761

Set F **1.** 7.9 **3.** 1.38 **5.** 5.71 **7.** 4.723 **9.** 1.2 **11.** 1.928 **13.** 26.5

Set G **1.** 3.69 **3.** 3.027 **5.** 10.602 **7.** 2.122 **9.** 11.415 **11.** 12.141 **13.** 10.442

Mixed Practice **1.** 15.71 **3.** 26.914 **5.** 8.3 **7.** 28.26 **9.** 14.563 **11.** 8.896 **13.** 3.42 **15.** 9.883 **17.** 100.18 **19.** 72.454 **21.** 18.3 **23.** 2.398

Pages 80–81

Set H **1.** 2.4 **3.** 0.39 **5.** 1.85 **7.** 0.521 **9.** 0.684 **11.** 3.288

Set I **1.** 4.04 **3.** 3.65 **5.** 1.62 **7.** 0.218 **9.** 0.191 **11.** 4.881

Set J **1.** 1.4 **3.** 2.56 **5.** 3.871 **7.** 5.89 **9.** 0.889 **11.** 4.889 **13.** 0.7315

Set K **1.** 6.15 **3.** 2.15 **5.** 2.085 **7.** 4.274 **9.** 2.279 **11.** 5.175 **13.** 12.64

Mixed Practice **1.** 1.45 **3.** 276.572 **5.** 1.4 **7.** 5.87 **9.** 0.114 **11.** 2.3 **13.** 3.104 **15.** 2.87 **17.** 12.305 **19.** 3.168 **21.** 3.619 **23.** 11.389 **25.** 3.877

Page 82

Set L **1.** 8 **3.** 16 **5.** 58 **7.** 95 **9.** 104 **11.** 201 **13.** 599 **15.** 0

Set M **1.** 2.3 **3.** 0.1 **5.** 0.4 **7.** 101.3 **9.** 72.4 **11.** 27.2 **13.** 0.9 **15.** 12.0 **17.** 0.62 **19.** 6.12 **21.** 0.39 **23.** 3.17 **25.** 0.01 **27.** 1.44 **29.** 7.50 **31.** 0.004 **33.** 0.285 **35.** 0.428 **37.** 0.205 **39.** 8.338 **41.** 0.626 **43.** 71.114 **45.** 0.380

Page 83

Set N **1.** 130 **3.** 10 **5.** 980

Set O **1.** 5 **3.** 9 **5.** 6

Set P **1.** 1.2 **3.** 0.1 **5.** 0.1

Mixed Practice **1.** 3; 3.47 **3.** 10; 10.25 **5.** 160; 155.95 **7.** 0.9; 0.85 **9.** 0.5; 0.548 **11.** 400; 399.52

Page 85 **1.** $8.20 **3.** $14.08 **5.** $36.11 **7.** $80.08

Pages 86–87 **1.** $85.98; $85.98 **3.** $778.79; $778.79 **5.** $597.07; $499.07 **7.** $664.73; $589.73 **9.** $12,661.88; $12,661.88

Pages 88–89 **1.** May 8, 1981 **3.** $35.75 **5.** Dental work **7.** $293.99 **9.** $359.04 **11.** $442.15 **13.** $194.68 **15.** $178.76 **17.** $493.05 **19.** $134.39 **21.** $282.04

Pages 90–91 **1.** $220.27 **3.** $71.62; $228.08 **5.** $1173.09; $289.41; $883.68 **7.** $69.50; $164.40 **9.** $55.58; $139.66 **11.** $1245.34; $350.77; $894.57 **13.** $93.94; $236.39 **15.** $80.54; $211.46

Pages 92–93 **1.** 23.24 cm **3.** 6.426 cm **5.** 3.25 cm **7.** 3.342 cm

Pages 96–97

Set A **1.** 26.22 **3.** 428.96 **5.** 36.54 **7.** 3.978 **9.** 3600 **11.** 82.08 **13.** 181.44 **15.** 11.256 **17.** 1293.1 **19.** 7262.7

Set B **1.** 0.00462 **3.** 0.06405 **5.** 0.02212 **7.** 0.0019 **9.** 0.055872 **11.** 0.0052683 **13.** 0.0504 **15.** 0.0010778 **17.** 0.06758 **19.** 0.0019136 **21.** 0.0165474

Set C **1.** 17.85 **3.** 1.088 **5.** 0.0384 **7.** 30.87 **9.** 0.06306 **11.** 168.4 **13.** 0.01886 **15.** 14.5 **17.** 0.09195 **19.** 15.498 **21.** 1.01973

Mixed Practice **1.** 0.046215 **3.** 5.5836 **5.** 0.7802 **7.** 251.04 **9.** 0.003084 **11.** 2.835 **13.** 1.38 **15.** 0.0259 **17.** 960 **19.** 298.2 **21.** 0.01825148 **23.** 0.02821 **25.** 0.0002616 **27.** 0.0017073 **29.** 0.04256 **31.** 114.72 **33.** 52.5 **35.** 249.682 **37.** 51.84

Pages 98–99

Set D **1.** 2.5 **3.** 0.12 **5.** 14 **7.** 240 **9.** 0.54 **11.** 0.045

Set E **1.** 1.5 **3.** 24 **5.** 0.16 **7.** 48 **9.** 4.5 **11.** 0.56

Mixed Practice **1.** 0.35; 0.35256 **3.** 25; 25.4518 **5.** 0.24; 0.2352 **7.** 0.015; 0.0147 **9.** 0.32; 0.3246885 **11.** 4.5; 4.534 **13.** 0.48; 0.476 **15.** 0.2; 0.2016 **17.** 640; 644.96 **19.** 0.49; 0.49112 **21.** 5.4; 5.364 **23.** 2.4; 2.43 **25.** 0.012; 0.012444 **27.** 0.56; 0.55944

Pages 100–101

Set F **1.** 6.7 **3.** 2.6 **5.** 2.16 **7.** 0.3547 **9.** 5.22 **11.** 0.114 **13.** 7.8 **15.** 0.94 **17.** 5.44 **19.** 1.6

Set G **1.** 0.089 **3.** 0.0082 **5.** 0.0048 **7.** 0.023 **9.** 0.035 **11.** 0.06 **13.** 0.0007 **15.** 0.0228 **17.** 0.01304 **19.** 0.00399

Set H **1.** 6.7 **3.** 5.39 **5.** 0.0014 **7.** 4.03 **9.** 0.26 **11.** 0.0005 **13.** 5.29 **15.** 0.689 **17.** 72.8 **19.** 3.12

Mixed Practice **1.** 0.247 **3.** 0.0008 **5.** 0.00481 **7.** 4.61 **9.** 0.068 **11.** 0.437 **13.** 6.02 **15.** 0.0249 **17.** 95.9 **19.** 0.0093 **21.** 40.1 **23.** 0.075 **25.** 0.338 **27.** 45.8

Pages 102–103
Set I **1.** 531.6 **3.** 168.5 **5.** 251 **7.** 3004.2 **9.** 124.3 **11.** 269.55 **13.** 6420.1 **15.** 1387 **17.** 5392 **19.** 7045.6
Set J **1.** 560 **3.** 3740 **5.** 68,100 **7.** 21,590 **9.** 73,510 **11.** 80 **13.** 1900 **15.** 470 **17.** 2080 **19.** 930,200
Set K **1.** 1.25 **3.** 0.1943 **5.** 8.016 **7.** 5.0662 **9.** 61.5215 **11.** 6.3344 **13.** 2.64091 **15.** 5.6027 **17.** 3.4219 **19.** 4.37781
Set L **1.** 0.0346 **3.** 0.017 **5.** 0.06 **7.** 0.0921 **9.** 0.007085 **11.** 0.002 **13.** 0.0009 **15.** 0.084 **17.** 0.0526 **19.** 0.0743 **21.** 0.039
Mixed Practice **1.** 95.33 **3.** 0.034651 **5.** 0.000025 **7.** 50,630 **9.** 43.44 **11.** 780 **13.** 980 **15.** 0.0391 **17.** 0.30602 **19.** 465.1123 **21.** 6835.5 **23.** 0.0045 **25.** 0.006 **27.** 1600

Pages 104–105
Set M **1.** 4.6 **3.** 5.49 **5.** 89.3 **7.** 0.853 **9.** 3.07 **11.** 0.03 **13.** 2.04 **15.** 5.5 **17.** 16 **19.** 84
Set N **1.** 38 **3.** 490 **5.** 430 **7.** 56,090 **9.** 800 **11.** 2940 **13.** 9300 **15.** 250 **17.** 5620 **19.** 410
Set O **1.** 4 **3.** 892 **5.** 0.003 **7.** 796 **9.** 6500 **11.** 7 **13.** 2.6 **15.** 40.9 **17.** 630 **19.** 30
Mixed Practice **1.** 0.2354 **3.** 604 **5.** 0.009 **7.** 8.6 **9.** 0.008 **11.** 580 **13.** 62 **15.** 5.26 **17.** 420 **19.** 24.7 **21.** 0.07 **23.** 8.7 **25.** 0.06 **27.** 380

Pages 106–107
Set P **1.** 0.4 **3.** 4.3 **5.** 537.3 **7.** 63.7 **9.** 2.4 **11.** 91.1 **13.** 6.1 **15.** 0.5 **17.** 0.9 **19.** 0.2
Set Q **1.** 0.37 **3.** 0.07 **5.** 0.06 **7.** 6.24 **9.** 0.19 **11.** 0.07 **13.** 1.08 **15.** 2.81 **17.** 0.22
Set R **1.** 0.597 **3.** 6.253 **5.** 0.042 **7.** 0.084 **9.** 0.442 **11.** 0.178 **13.** 2.305 **15.** 0.003

Page 109 **1.** $10.26 **3.** $24.03 **5.** $5.04 **7.** $6.64 **9.** $2.95 **11.** $8.39 **13.** $65.26 **15.** $26.90

Pages 110–111 **1.** $30.18 **3.** $2.38 **5.** $2.92 **7.** $9.04 **9.** $7.23 **11.** $79.59 **13.** $1.07 **15.** $7.18 **17.** $2.41 **19.** $12.10 **21.** $3.74 **23.** $18.97

Pages 112–113 **1.** $2018.52; $6824.52; $189.57 **3.** $2641.80; $8931.80; $248.11 **5.** $3898.65; $13,181.15; $366.15 **7.** $1875.30; $7233.30; $241.11 **9.** $2088.58; $8055.93; $268.54 **11.** $1345.68; $6151.68; $256.32 **13.** $1761.20; $8051.20; $335.47 **15.** $2599.10; $11,881.60; $495.07

Pages 114–115 **1.** 5.4; $0.33 **3.** 41.25; $2.48 **5.** 4.18; $0.26 **7.** 7.14; $0.43 **9.** 302.5; $18.15 **11.** 1.575; $0.10 **13.** 5.4; $0.33 **15.** 107.35; $6.45

Pages 116–117 **1.** $2.15 **3.** $15.20 **5.** $19.67 **7.** $6.26 **9.** $8.53 **11.** $0.59 **13.** $1.47 **15.** $2.56 **17.** $3.99 **19.** $3.47

Pages 118–119 **1.** 342 parking spaces **3.** No **5.** 775 parking spaces **7.** 12 units

Page 123

Set A **1.** 4 cm **3.** 1 cm **5.** 5 cm **7.** 2 cm **9.** 6 cm

Set B **1.** 32 mm **3.** 40 mm **5.** 22 mm **7.** 63 mm **9.** 51 mm

Pages 124–125

Set C **1.** 31 mm **3.** 2 km **5.** 54 mm **7.** 4 m **9.** 19 m **11.** 26 mm **13.** 10,000 m

Set D **1.** 38,000 m **3.** 0.758 m **5.** 8500 mm **7.** 1.55 m **9.** 1.245 km **11.** 1650 cm **13.** 0.65 m **15.** 0.03575 km **17.** 258 cm **19.** 4500 m **21.** 0.0398 m **23.** 32,000 mm

Page 126

Set E **1.** 8 cm^2 **3.** 13 cm^2 **5.** 8.5 cm^2

Set F **1.** 800 mm^2 **3.** 1300 mm^2 **5.** 850 mm^2

Page 127

Set G **1.** 10 cm^3 **3.** 11 cm^3 **5.** 7.5 cm^3

Set H **1.** 10,000 mm^3 **3.** 11,000 mm^3 **5.** 7500 mm^3

Page 128

Set I **1.** 2 L **3.** 265 mL **5.** 3 mL **7.** 700 mL **9.** 8 L **11.** 20 L

Set J **1.** 25,000 mL **3.** 0.0827 L **5.** 375,000 mL **7.** 5000 mL **9.** 4.37 L **11.** 0.0834 L **13.** 9.164 L **15.** 96,000 mL **17.** 4000 mL **19.** 0.003 L **21.** 5.86 L **23.** 0.6 L **25.** 0.072 L

Page 129

Set K **1.** 8 kg **3.** 5 g **5.** 19 kg **7.** 305 g **9.** 5 g **11.** 200 mg

Set L **1.** 38,000 g **3.** 400 g **5.** 0.031 kg **7.** 7000 g **9.** 6.42 kg **11.** 0.85 kg **13.** 0.004 kg **15.** 800,000 g **17.** 900 g **19.** 0.0073 kg **21.** 0.3 kg **23.** 70 g **25.** 0.0006 kg

Page 130

Set M **1.** 30 mL; 30 g **3.** 950 mL; 950 cm^3 **5.** 63 mL; 63 cm^3 **7.** 16.3 g; 16.3 cm^3 **9.** 8.9 cm^3; 8.9 mL **11.** 9 cm^3; 9 g

Set N **1.** 8 L; 8 kg **3.** 0.3 dm^3; 0.3 L **5.** 12.3 L; 12.3 dm^3 **7.** 85 dm^3; 85 kg **9.** 0.7 dm^3; 0.7 L **11.** 5.32 L; 5.32 dm^3

Page 131

Set O **1.** degrees Celsius **3.** degrees Celsius **5.** kelvins **7.** degrees Celsius **9.** degrees Celsius **11.** degrees Celsius

Set P **1.** 58°C **3.** 100°C **5.** 10°C **7.** 50°C **9.** 0°C **11.** 55°C

Pages 134–135 **1.** 495 g graham cracker crumbs; 45 mL baking powder; 3 eggs; 375 mL milk; 225 mL corn oil; 150 mL corn syrup; 165 g chopped pecans **3.** 340 g lasagna noodles; 2 mL dried, crushed oregano; 500 mL spaghetti sauce with meat; 500 mL cream-style cottage cheese; 360 g sliced mozzarella cheese **5.** 6 **7.** 0.25 kg ground beef; 15 mL finely chopped green pepper; 30 mL chopped onion; 40 mL catsup; 7.5 mL horseradish; 3.5 mL dry mustard; 1 mL salt **9.** 1 kg ground beef; 60 mL finely chopped green pepper; 120 mL chopped onion; 160 mL catsup; 30 mL horseradish; 14 mL dry mustard; 4 mL salt

Pages 136–137 **1.** 0.35 m; $0.79 **3.** $16.94 **5.** 0.35 m; $0.74 **7.** $12.80 **9.** 1.85 m; $12.86 **11.** 1.6 m; $4.40

Pages 138–139 **1.** T = 16 mm; L = 25 mm; D = 6 mm **3.** T = 19 mm; L = 34 mm; D = 8 mm **5.** T = 25 mm; L = 38 mm; D = 11 mm **7.** T = 15 mm; L = 23 mm; D = 5 mm **9.** 3.3 mm **11.** 5 mm **13.** 8.5 mm **15.** 14 mm **17.** 21 mm

Pages 140–141 **1.** 0.5 mg **3.** 20 mg **5.** 180 cm^3 **7.** 60 mg **9.** 500 mg **11.** 260 mg **13.** 500 mg **15.** 50 **17.** 200 **19.** 500

Pages 142–143 **1.** 21 mm; 20-mm file; 2-mm adjustment **3.** 24 mm; 25-mm file; 4-mm adjustment **5.** 26 mm; 25-mm file; 2-mm adjustment **7.** 20 mm; 20-mm file; 3-mm adjustment **9.** 25 mm; 25-mm file; 3-mm adjustment **11.** 20-mm reamer; 5-mm adjustment **13.** 20-mm reamer; 2-mm adjustment **15.** 20-mm reamer; 4-mm adjustment **17.** 15-mm reamer; 1-mm adjustment

Page 145

Dividing Whole Numbers **1.** 48 R1 **3.** 2 R20 **5.** 65 R7 **7.** 321 R1 **9.** 5 R260 **11.** 25 R12 **13.** 3094 R2 **15.** 130 R2 **17.** 42 R6 **19.** 31,874 R2 **21.** 6 R607 **23.** 65 R11 **25.** 2 R19

Adding and Subtracting Decimals **1.** 13.7 **3.** 1.2 **5.** 7.491 **7.** 10.428 **9.** 3.812 **11.** 11.423 **13.** 32.963 **15.** 0.68 **17.** 4.104 **19.** 13.737 **21.** 16.609 **23.** 5.395 **25.** 0.368 **27.** 47.987

Multiplying and Dividing Decimals **1.** 402.04 **3.** 0.74 **5.** 35.67 **7.** 538.9 **9.** 12.56 **11.** 0.0073 **13.** 390 **15.** 0.0027 **17.** 235 **19.** 5.43 **21.** 0.06 **23.** 0.06 **25.** 0.07

Page 146 **1.** $227.85 **3.** $177.06 **5.** $230.78 **7.** $261.25 **9.** $211.25 **11.** $773.95

Page 147

1.
```
? 4
? 7
  R+S= 11
  R*S= 28
```

3.
```
? 12
? 15
  R+S= 27
  R*S= 180
```

5.
```
SUM = 48
DIFFERENCE = 24
PRODUCT = 432
QUOTIENT = 3
```

7. Answers may vary.
```
10 INPUT X
20 INPUT Y
30 INPUT Z
40 PRINT X+Y+Z
50 PRINT X*Y*Z
60 END
```

Pages 150–151

Set A **1.** $\frac{2}{5}$ **3.** $\frac{7}{12}$ **5.** $\frac{5}{10}$ **7.** $\frac{1}{4}$ **9.** $\frac{5}{8}$

Set B **1.** $1\frac{1}{2}$ **3.** $6\frac{3}{4}$ **5.** $3\frac{2}{5}$ **7.** $2\frac{1}{4}$ **9.** $4\frac{1}{2}$ **11.** $3\frac{5}{8}$

Page 152

Set C **1.** $\frac{2}{3}$ **3.** $\frac{1}{2}$ **5.** $\frac{3}{4}$ **7.** $\frac{3}{5}$ **9.** $\frac{5}{6}$ **11.** $\frac{3}{16}$ **13.** $\frac{1}{3}$ **15.** $\frac{3}{4}$

Set D **1.** $5\frac{3}{4}$ **3.** 5 **5.** $6\frac{1}{3}$ **7.** 24 **9.** $14\frac{2}{3}$ **11.** $28\frac{3}{10}$ **13.** $15\frac{2}{3}$ **15.** $24\frac{1}{4}$

Set E **1.** $\frac{7}{5}$ **3.** $\frac{31}{8}$ **5.** $\frac{59}{6}$ **7.** $\frac{25}{2}$ **9.** $\frac{65}{3}$ **11.** $\frac{259}{10}$ **13.** $\frac{97}{16}$ **15.** $\frac{343}{4}$

Page 153

Set F **1.** 0.5 **3.** 0.25 **5.** 0.7 **7.** 0.6 **9.** 0.05 **11.** 0.375 **13.** 0.15 **15.** 0.18 **17.** 0.013 **19.** 0.0125 **21.** 0.3125 **23.** 0.1875

Set G **1.** 0.333 **3.** 0.222 **5.** 0.556 **7.** 0.833 **9.** 0.571 **11.** 0.364 **13.** 0.417 **15.** 0.381 **17.** 0.917 **19.** 0.684 **21.** 0.944 **23.** 0.067

Pages 154–155

Set H **1.** $\frac{8}{15}$ **3.** $\frac{5}{18}$ **5.** $\frac{2}{35}$ **7.** $\frac{21}{40}$ **9.** $\frac{27}{70}$ **11.** $\frac{7}{48}$

Set I **1.** $\frac{3}{10}$ **3.** $\frac{5}{14}$ **5.** $\frac{5}{18}$ **7.** $\frac{3}{20}$ **9.** $\frac{1}{12}$ **11.** $\frac{3}{8}$ **13.** $\frac{18}{25}$ **15.** $\frac{4}{5}$ **17.** $\frac{3}{8}$ **19.** $\frac{5}{12}$ **21.** $\frac{1}{16}$ **23.** $\frac{6}{7}$ **25.** $\frac{5}{9}$ **27.** $\frac{9}{10}$

Set J **1.** $\frac{8}{15}$ **3.** $\frac{2}{15}$ **5.** $\frac{9}{40}$ **7.** $\frac{4}{45}$ **9.** $\frac{1}{4}$ **11.** $\frac{4}{35}$ **13.** $\frac{2}{21}$ **15.** $\frac{1}{30}$ **17.** $\frac{5}{21}$

Set K **1.** 12 **3.** 24 **5.** $1\frac{1}{2}$ **7.** $21\frac{1}{3}$ **9.** $3\frac{1}{3}$ **11.** 45 **13.** $22\frac{1}{2}$ **15.** 37 **17.** 6000

Mixed Practice **1.** $\frac{10}{27}$ **3.** $\frac{2}{7}$ **5.** $\frac{7}{50}$ **7.** $\frac{3}{16}$ **9.** $20\frac{1}{4}$ **11.** $\frac{1}{18}$ **13.** $\frac{11}{30}$ **15.** $\frac{3}{4}$ **17.** $\frac{1}{20}$

Pages 156–157

Set L **1.** $\frac{7}{8}$ **3.** $\frac{17}{30}$ **5.** 1 **7.** $5\frac{3}{7}$ **9.** $5\frac{3}{5}$ **11.** $1\frac{1}{2}$ **13.** $2\frac{7}{24}$ **15.** 8

Set M **1.** 33 **3.** $21\frac{1}{3}$ **5.** 99 **7.** $22\frac{3}{4}$ **9.** 44 **11.** $56\frac{1}{4}$ **13.** 92 **15.** 146

Set N **1.** $4\frac{7}{8}$ **3.** 12 **5.** $4\frac{1}{5}$ **7.** 15 **9.** $18\frac{3}{4}$ **11.** 9 **13.** $24\frac{2}{5}$ **15.** $23\frac{3}{4}$

Set O **1.** $8\frac{3}{4}$ **3.** 14 **5.** 25 **7.** $3\frac{1}{12}$ **9.** $\frac{17}{28}$ **11.** 21

Mixed Practice **1.** $\frac{5}{16}$ **3.** $7\frac{1}{2}$ **5.** 35 **7.** $17\frac{1}{2}$ **9.** $1\frac{2}{3}$ **11.** $16\frac{1}{2}$ **13.** 265 **15.** $\frac{31}{32}$ **17.** $1\frac{13}{36}$ **19.** 45 **21.** 7

Pages 158–159

Set P **1.** $\frac{4}{3}$ **3.** $\frac{9}{1}$ **5.** $\frac{100}{7}$ **7.** $\frac{1}{12}$ **9.** $\frac{1}{52}$ **11.** $\frac{2}{5}$ **13.** $\frac{3}{14}$ **15.** $\frac{5}{28}$ **17.** $\frac{6}{77}$

Set Q **1.** $1\frac{1}{2}$ **3.** $2\frac{2}{7}$ **5.** $1\frac{1}{2}$ **7.** $1\frac{13}{27}$ **9.** $14\frac{2}{7}$ **11.** 60 **13.** 12 **15.** 18 **17.** $8\frac{2}{3}$ **19.** 7

Set R **1.** $\frac{3}{16}$ **3.** $\frac{1}{20}$ **5.** $\frac{1}{48}$ **7.** $\frac{1}{24}$ **9.** $\frac{3}{35}$ **11.** $\frac{7}{12}$ **13.** $\frac{5}{6}$ **15.** $\frac{3}{4}$ **17.** $\frac{1}{6}$ **19.** $\frac{5}{12}$

Set S **1.** $\frac{3}{8}$ **3.** $\frac{1}{14}$ **5.** $\frac{1}{2}$ **7.** $2\frac{2}{5}$ **9.** $\frac{4}{35}$ **11.** $2\frac{2}{7}$ **13.** $1\frac{3}{19}$ **15.** $5\frac{1}{2}$ **17.** $\frac{1}{6}$ **19.** $2\frac{11}{14}$

Mixed Practice **1.** $1\frac{1}{20}$ **3.** $3\frac{5}{7}$ **5.** $2\frac{3}{4}$ **7.** 200 **9.** 8 **11.** $\frac{1}{24}$ **13.** $\frac{10}{27}$ **15.** $2\frac{14}{15}$ **17.** $\frac{19}{96}$ **19.** $\frac{7}{8}$ **21.** 2

Page 161 **1.** $4\frac{1}{2}$ min. **3.** 18 min. **5.** $8\frac{5}{8}$ min. **7.** 4 laps **9.** $8\frac{1}{2}$ laps **11.** $8\frac{1}{2}$ min. **13.** $10\frac{5}{8}$ min. **15.** $2\frac{1}{8}$ min. **17.** 5 laps **19.** 3 laps

Pages 162–163 **1.** $\frac{1}{2}$ in. **3.** 1 in. **5.** $\frac{1}{3}$ in. **7.** $\frac{7}{12}$ in. **9.** $\frac{7}{9}$ in. **11.** 27 turns **13.** $13\frac{1}{2}$ turns **15.** 15 turns **17.** 9 turns **19.** 36 turns

Pages 164–165 **1.** $1\frac{3}{16}$ in. **3.** $\frac{7}{8}$ in. **5.** $\frac{11}{16}$ in. **7.** $1\frac{3}{8}$ in. **9.** $\frac{1}{2}$ in. **11.** $1\frac{1}{8}$ in. **13.** $\frac{3}{4}$ in. **15.** $1\frac{7}{8}$ in. **17.** $1\frac{1}{2}$ in.; $\frac{15}{16}$ in. **19.** $\frac{3}{4}$ in.; $\frac{15}{32}$ in.

Pages 166–167 **1.** $7\frac{1}{2}$; 28; 84 **3.** $10\frac{1}{2}$; 6; 12 **5.** $11\frac{1}{4}$; 10; 10 **7.** $15\frac{3}{4}$; 12; 24 **9.** $62\frac{1}{2}$ hours

Pages 168–169 **1.** $1\frac{1}{4}$ hours **3.** $6\frac{1}{4}$ hours **5.** $1\frac{7}{8}$ hours **7.** $\frac{15}{16}$ hour; $4\frac{11}{16}$ hours **9.** 4 times

Page 172

Set A **1.** $\frac{3}{4}$, $\frac{2}{4}$ **3.** $\frac{5}{8}$, $\frac{2}{8}$ **5.** $\frac{3}{6}$, $\frac{2}{6}$ **7.** $\frac{10}{15}$, $\frac{9}{15}$ **9.** $\frac{4}{24}$, $\frac{9}{24}$ **11.** $\frac{9}{24}$, $\frac{14}{24}$ **13.** $\frac{15}{20}$, $\frac{8}{20}$ **15.** $\frac{9}{12}$, $\frac{4}{12}$ **17.** $\frac{10}{16}$, $\frac{3}{16}$ **19.** $\frac{32}{40}$, $\frac{25}{40}$ **21.** $\frac{15}{40}$, $\frac{28}{40}$ **23.** $\frac{25}{60}$, $\frac{42}{60}$

Set B **1.** $\frac{4}{6}$, $\frac{5}{6}$, $\frac{3}{6}$ **3.** $\frac{5}{10}$, $\frac{6}{10}$, $\frac{9}{10}$ **5.** $\frac{6}{10}$, $\frac{5}{10}$, $\frac{9}{10}$ **7.** $\frac{8}{12}$, $\frac{9}{12}$, $\frac{6}{12}$ **9.** $\frac{6}{12}$, $\frac{10}{12}$, $\frac{9}{12}$ **11.** $\frac{24}{30}$, $\frac{20}{30}$, $\frac{21}{30}$ **13.** $\frac{15}{30}$, $\frac{20}{30}$, $\frac{18}{30}$ **15.** $\frac{45}{120}$, $\frac{100}{120}$, $\frac{84}{120}$

Page 173

Set C **1.** $>$ **3.** $>$ **5.** $<$ **7.** $<$ **9.** $>$

Set D **1.** $>$ **3.** $<$ **5.** $<$ **7.** $<$ **9.** $>$

Set E **1.** $<$ **3.** $=$ **5.** $>$ **7.** $<$ **9.** $>$

Mixed Practice **1.** $=$ **3.** $<$ **5.** $>$ **7.** $>$ **9.** $<$

Pages 174–175

Set F **1.** 1 **3.** 1 **5.** 3

Set G **1.** $1\frac{2}{5}$ **3.** 1 **5.** $1\frac{1}{2}$ **7.** $1\frac{1}{3}$

Set H **1.** $\frac{1}{3}$ **3.** $\frac{1}{2}$ **5.** $\frac{2}{3}$ **7.** $\frac{3}{5}$

Set I **1.** $1\frac{3}{8}$ **3.** $1\frac{1}{18}$ **5.** $1\frac{1}{2}$ **7.** $1\frac{3}{16}$ **9.** $1\frac{1}{5}$ **11.** $1\frac{1}{3}$

Set J **1.** $\frac{1}{6}$ **3.** $\frac{5}{12}$ **5.** $\frac{1}{2}$ **7.** $\frac{7}{15}$ **9.** $\frac{3}{20}$

Set K **1.** $1\frac{1}{6}$ **3.** $1\frac{1}{4}$ **5.** $\frac{1}{2}$ **7.** $1\frac{7}{30}$ **9.** $1\frac{1}{5}$

Mixed Practice **1.** $1\frac{1}{2}$ **3.** $\frac{1}{4}$ **5.** $\frac{2}{15}$ **7.** $\frac{1}{4}$ **9.** $\frac{7}{24}$ **11.** $1\frac{7}{40}$

Pages 176–177

Set L **1.** $7\frac{3}{5}$ **3.** $11\frac{3}{4}$ **5.** $15\frac{5}{6}$ **7.** $14\frac{11}{12}$ **9.** $7\frac{9}{10}$ **11.** $8\frac{7}{15}$

Set M **1.** $5\frac{1}{2}$ **3.** $9\frac{2}{5}$ **5.** $4\frac{3}{8}$ **7.** $10\frac{1}{4}$ **9.** $8\frac{1}{3}$ **11.** $10\frac{5}{8}$ **13.** $6\frac{3}{7}$ **15.** $5\frac{8}{9}$ **17.** $2\frac{1}{2}$ **19.** $10\frac{1}{6}$ **21.** $5\frac{5}{6}$ **23.** $3\frac{4}{5}$ **25.** 10 **27.** $12\frac{3}{8}$

Set N **1.** $5\frac{1}{8}$ **3.** $16\frac{3}{10}$ **5.** $15\frac{11}{20}$ **7.** $5\frac{1}{12}$ **9.** $13\frac{13}{30}$ **11.** $14\frac{7}{40}$ **13.** $14\frac{2}{3}$ **15.** $10\frac{1}{3}$ **17.** $7\frac{1}{4}$

Set O **1.** 10 **3.** $10\frac{9}{10}$ **5.** $5\frac{9}{10}$ **7.** $16\frac{1}{4}$ **9.** $17\frac{7}{24}$ **11.** $14\frac{2}{3}$ **13.** $13\frac{1}{6}$ **15.** 14

Mixed Practice **1.** $15\frac{1}{12}$ **3.** $6\frac{7}{12}$ **5.** $15\frac{3}{5}$ **7.** $11\frac{2}{3}$ **9.** $8\frac{19}{40}$ **11.** $17\frac{7}{24}$ **13.** $13\frac{1}{2}$ **15.** 11 **17.** $4\frac{3}{4}$ **19.** $10\frac{7}{8}$ **21.** 16

Pages 178–179

Set P **1.** 5 **3.** 4 **5.** 6 **7.** 7 **9.** 4 **11.** 11 **13.** 5 **15.** 10 **17.** 15 **19.** 15

Set Q **1.** $2\frac{2}{5}$ **3.** $3\frac{5}{9}$ **5.** $3\frac{7}{8}$ **7.** $1\frac{1}{2}$ **9.** $4\frac{1}{8}$ **11.** $2\frac{1}{2}$ **13.** $1\frac{5}{6}$ **15.** $1\frac{7}{12}$

Set R **1.** $1\frac{4}{5}$ **3.** $6\frac{3}{5}$ **5.** $2\frac{2}{5}$ **7.** $\frac{1}{4}$ **9.** $8\frac{2}{3}$

Mixed Practice **1.** $3\frac{5}{8}$ **3.** $1\frac{5}{6}$ **5.** $\frac{2}{3}$ **7.** $3\frac{2}{3}$ **9.** $6\frac{1}{10}$ **11.** $\frac{1}{2}$ **13.** $1\frac{2}{3}$

Pages 180–181

Set S **1.** $3\frac{1}{4}$ **3.** $4\frac{1}{2}$ **5.** $5\frac{1}{5}$ **7.** $6\frac{1}{24}$ **9.** $2\frac{1}{20}$ **11.** $6\frac{1}{2}$

Set T **1.** $3\frac{7}{12}$ **3.** $2\frac{5}{6}$ **5.** $2\frac{5}{12}$ **7.** $7\frac{19}{24}$ **9.** $\frac{13}{18}$ **11.** $2\frac{1}{2}$ **13.** $1\frac{4}{5}$ **15.** $5\frac{23}{24}$ **17.** $3\frac{9}{10}$ **19.** $3\frac{19}{24}$ **21.** $5\frac{14}{15}$

Set U **1.** $4\frac{3}{10}$ **3.** $4\frac{1}{8}$ **5.** $5\frac{5}{6}$ **7.** $1\frac{3}{10}$ **9.** $3\frac{8}{9}$ **11.** $1\frac{1}{2}$ **13.** $12\frac{1}{16}$ **15.** $3\frac{5}{18}$ **17.** $24\frac{1}{20}$ **19.** $21\frac{9}{16}$ **21.** $13\frac{29}{36}$

Mixed Practice **1.** $6\frac{2}{9}$ **3.** $3\frac{23}{24}$ **5.** $3\frac{11}{20}$ **7.** $2\frac{11}{18}$ **9.** $7\frac{1}{10}$ **11.** $1\frac{3}{4}$ **13.** $1\frac{1}{20}$ **15.** $2\frac{3}{4}$ **17.** $2\frac{3}{8}$ **19.** $5\frac{1}{24}$ **21.** $3\frac{2}{15}$ **23.** $1\frac{5}{8}$ **25.** $5\frac{13}{15}$ **27.** $2\frac{1}{18}$

Page 183 **1.** 27 hours; \$405 **3.** 39 hours; \$585 **5.** 33 hours; \$495

Pages 184–185 **1.** $\frac{3}{4}$ dollar **3.** 5 dollars **5.** $2\frac{1}{4}$ dollars **7.** $1\frac{3}{8}$ dollars **9.** $\frac{1}{4}$ dollar **11.** $\frac{1}{8}$ dollar **13.** 0 dollars **15.** $12\frac{1}{2}$ dollars **17.** $9\frac{1}{4}$ dollars **19.** $37\frac{1}{4}$ dollars **21.** $17\frac{3}{8}$ dollars

Pages 186–187 **1.** $8\frac{1}{4}$¢ **3.** $13\frac{7}{8}$¢ **5.** $23\frac{5}{8}$¢ **7.** $46\frac{3}{8}$¢ **9.** $44\frac{1}{2}$¢ **11.** Toyparts Company **13.** $42\frac{7}{8}$¢ **15.** $55\frac{3}{8}$¢

Pages 188–189 **1.** 20 seconds **3.** $9\frac{3}{10}$ seconds **5.** 930 seconds **7.** $18\frac{19}{20}$ seconds **9.** $19\frac{7}{20}$ seconds **11.** $18\frac{1}{10}$ seconds

Pages 190–191 **1.** 135 tiles **3.** 117 tiles **5.** 56 tiles **7.** 99 tiles **9.** 72 tiles **11.** $1\frac{11}{16}$ feet by $1\frac{7}{8}$ feet **13.** $2\frac{1}{2}$ feet by $1\frac{1}{2}$ feet

Pages 194–195

Set A **1.** $\frac{1}{6}$ **3.** $\frac{1}{6}$ **5.** $\frac{1}{6}$

Set B **1.** $\frac{2}{6}$ or $\frac{1}{3}$ **3.** $\frac{2}{6}$ or $\frac{1}{3}$ **5.** $\frac{2}{6}$ or $\frac{1}{3}$ **7.** $\frac{5}{6}$ **9.** $\frac{1}{7}$ **11.** $\frac{2}{7}$ **13.** $\frac{3}{7}$ **15.** $\frac{1}{11}$ **17.** $\frac{2}{11}$ **19.** $\frac{3}{11}$

Set C **1.** 1 **3.** 4 **5.** 15 **7.** 4 **9.** 7 **11.** 14 **13.** 6 **15.** 16 **17.** 28

Pages 196–197

Set D Tree diagrams will vary. **1.** The 6 possible outcomes are 1) yellow, gray; 2) yellow, green; 3) yellow, brown; 4) orange, gray; 5) orange, green; 6) orange, brown. **3.** The 4 possible outcomes are 1) head, head; 2) head, tail; 3) tail, head; 4) tail, tail. **5.** The 8 possible outcomes are 1) true, true, true; 2) true, true, false; 3) true, false, true; 4) true, false, false; 5) false, true, true; 6) false, true, false; 7) false, false, true; 8) false, false, false.

Set E **1.** $\frac{1}{4}$ **3.** $\frac{2}{4}$ or $\frac{1}{2}$ **5.** $\frac{3}{4}$ **7.** $\frac{3}{8}$ **9.** $\frac{1}{8}$ **11.** $\frac{4}{8}$ or $\frac{1}{2}$ **13.** $\frac{3}{8}$ **15.** $\frac{1}{8}$

Pages 198–199

Set F **1.** 100 **3.** 100,000 **5.** 4 **7.** 16 **9.** 64 **11.** 36 **13.** 24 **15.** 1728

Set G **1.** $\frac{1}{100}$ **3.** $\frac{3}{100}$ **5.** $\frac{9}{100}$ **7.** $\frac{2}{1000}$ or $\frac{1}{500}$ **9.** $\frac{100}{1000}$ or $\frac{1}{10}$ **11.** $\frac{1}{10,000}$ **13.** $\frac{99}{10,000}$ **15.** $\frac{2}{100,000}$ or $\frac{1}{50,000}$

Pages 200–201

Set H **1.** $\frac{2}{156}$ or $\frac{1}{78}$ **3.** $\frac{1}{156}$ **5.** $\frac{2}{156}$ or $\frac{1}{78}$ **7.** $\frac{1}{156}$ **9.** $\frac{1}{156}$ **11.** $\frac{6}{1716}$ or $\frac{1}{286}$ **13.** $\frac{6}{1716}$ or $\frac{1}{286}$ **15.** $\frac{12}{1716}$ or $\frac{1}{143}$ **17.** $\frac{2}{1716}$ or $\frac{1}{858}$ **19.** $\frac{6}{1716}$ or $\frac{1}{286}$ **21.** $\frac{6}{90}$ or $\frac{1}{15}$ **23.** $\frac{6}{90}$ or $\frac{1}{15}$ **25.** $\frac{3}{90}$ or $\frac{1}{30}$ **27.** $\frac{2}{90}$ or $\frac{1}{45}$ **29.** $\frac{3}{90}$ or $\frac{1}{30}$ **31.** $\frac{6}{720}$ or $\frac{1}{120}$ **33.** $\frac{6}{720}$ or $\frac{1}{120}$ **35.** $\frac{6}{720}$ or $\frac{1}{120}$ **37.** $\frac{9}{720}$ or $\frac{1}{80}$ **39.** $\frac{3}{720}$ or $\frac{1}{240}$

Page 203 **1.** 6,760,000 **3.** $\frac{2}{6,760,000}$ or $\frac{1}{3,380,000}$ **5.** $\frac{676}{6,760,000}$ or $\frac{1}{10,000}$ **7.** $\frac{676,000}{6,760,000}$ or $\frac{1}{10}$ **9.** $\frac{7000}{6,760,000}$ or $\frac{7}{6760}$

Pages 204–205 **1.** 188; 138; 117; 71; 39 **3.** $\frac{30}{117}$ or $\frac{10}{39}$ **5.** $\frac{26}{188}$ or $\frac{13}{94}$ **7.** $\frac{22}{138}$ or $\frac{11}{69}$ **9.** $\frac{20}{138}$ or $\frac{10}{69}$ **11.** $\frac{11}{138}$ **13.** 80 cups **15.** 73 cups **17.** 40 cups **19.** 4 kg **21.** 4 kg **23.** 2 kg

Pages 206–207 **1.** $\frac{15}{9912}$ or $\frac{5}{3304}$ **3.** $\frac{17}{9665}$ **5.** $\frac{38}{9173}$ **7.** $\frac{303}{4130}$ **9.** $\frac{107}{468}$ **11.** Ages 7-12 **13.** Age 99 **15.** $\frac{2626}{7699} \approx 0.34$ **17.** $\frac{9480}{9743} \approx 0.97$ **19.** $\frac{1311}{2626} \approx 0.50$

Pages 208–209 **1.** 90 **3.** 8100 cards **5.** 4 **7.** 60 **9.** 60 **11.** 720 **13.** 720 **15.** 46,656,000 cards

Page 211

Multiplying Whole Numbers **1.** 608 **3.** 1950 **5.** 7284 **7.** 12,258 **9.** 28,000 **11.** 41,402 **13.** 40,000 **15.** 17,444 **17.** 3008 **19.** 16,000,000 **21.** 385,088 **23.** 612 **25.** 5,880,984 **27.** 257,676

Multiplying and Dividing Decimals **1.** 125.86 **3.** 0.0782 **5.** 0.00021 **7.** 5400 **9.** 0.0001 **11.** 3.3 **13.** 0.08 **15.** 0.05 **17.** 62.1 **19.** 0.47 **21.** 14.37 **23.** 68.77 **25.** 5421.43

Multiplying and Dividing Fractions and Mixed Numbers **1.** $\frac{2}{9}$ **3.** 25 **5.** $\frac{3}{8}$ **7.** $8\frac{1}{6}$ **9.** 28 **11.** $\frac{2}{3}$ **13.** 8 **15.** $\frac{1}{6}$ **17.** $\frac{5}{19}$ **19.** 30

Page 212 **1.** 10.5 inches **3.** 82 inches **5.** 532.25 inches **7.** 75.75 inches **9.** 35.75 inches

Page 213 **1.**

```
? 7
 35
? 12
 60
? 16
 80
? 22
 110
? 30
 150
? 48
 240
? 65
 325
?
```

3.

```
? 3
 15
? 12
 60
? 26
 26
? 45
 45
? 63
 63
? 0
```

5. Answers may vary.

```
10 INPUT A
20 INPUT B
30 IF A=0 THEN 120
40 IF A=B THEN 100
50 IF A>B THEN 80
60 PRINT A;"<";B
70 GO TO 10
80 PRINT A;">";B
90 GO TO 10
100 PRINT A;"=";B
110 GO TO 10
120 END
```

Pages 216–217

Set A **1.** $\frac{100}{12}$ **3.** $\frac{100}{1}$ **5.** $\frac{21}{60}$ **7.** $\frac{4}{7}$ **9.** $\frac{340}{5}$ **11.** $\frac{35}{15}$ **13.** $\frac{2}{2.5}$ **15.** $\frac{9}{14}$ **17.** $\frac{3}{7}$

Set B **1.** $\frac{8}{60}$ **3.** $\frac{32}{20}$ **5.** $\frac{32}{760}$ **7.** $\frac{20}{15}$ **9.** $\frac{15}{25}$ **11.** $\frac{75}{65}$ **13.** $\frac{12}{18}$

Pages 218–219

Set C **1.** $15 \neq 12$ **3.** $32 \neq 21$ **5.** $224 = 224$ **7.** $462 \neq 440$ **9.** $252 = 252$ **11.** $1280 \neq 1200$ **13.** $240 \neq 200$ **15.** $1440 \neq 1512$ **17.** $180 \neq 210$ **19.** $1.2 = 1.2$ **21.** $0.144 = 0.144$ **23.** $13.2 = 13.2$ **25.** $175.5 = 175.5$

Set D **1.** $t = 13$ **3.** $c = 3$ **5.** $b = 28$ **7.** $n = 45$ **9.** $a = 20$ **11.** $t = 35$ **13.** $r = 4$ **15.** $g = 1$ **17.** $d = 36$ **19.** $n = 15$ **21.** $x = 40$ **23.** $k = 28$ **25.** $y = 18$ **27.** $e = 10.8$

Pages 220–221

Set E **1.** b **3.** c **5.** b **7.** a

Set F **1.** $\angle D$ and $\angle A$, $\angle M$ and $\angle J$, $\angle R$ and $\angle E$; $\overline{DM}$ and $\overline{AJ}$, $\overline{MR}$ and $\overline{JE}$, $\overline{RD}$ and $\overline{EA}$ **3.** $\angle L$ and $\angle V$, $\angle N$ and $\angle B$, $\angle R$ and $\angle Y$; $\overline{LN}$ and $\overline{VB}$, $\overline{NR}$ and $\overline{BY}$, $\overline{RL}$ and $\overline{YV}$ **5.** $\angle T$ and $\angle L$, $\angle E$ and $\angle W$, $\angle B$ and $\angle J$; $\overline{TE}$ and $\overline{LW}$, $\overline{EB}$ and $\overline{WJ}$, $\overline{BT}$ and $\overline{JL}$

Pages 222–223

Set G **1.** 150; 90 **3.** 216; 180 **5.** 15; 12 **7.** 9.0; 5.4 **9.** 130; 50

Set H **1.** $\frac{92}{138} = \frac{80}{n}$; n is 120 m. **3.** $\frac{20}{50} = \frac{n}{15}$; n is 6 m. **5.** $\frac{7.5}{10.5} = \frac{n}{6.3}$; n is 4.5 m. **7.** $\frac{150}{180} = \frac{70}{n}$; n is 84 m. **9.** $\frac{7.5}{25} = \frac{n}{60}$; n is 18 m.

Page 225 **1.** 8.7 hours **3.** 7.5 hours **5.** 7.6 hours **7.** 6.0 hours **9.** 3.8 hours **11.** 5150 kilometers **13.** $850

Pages 226–227 **1.** 12.8 m **3.** 27.2 m **5.** 10.5 m **7.** 37.8 m **9.** 80 paces; 64 m **11.** 120 paces; 96 m **13.** 180 paces; 144 m **15.** 100 paces; 80 m

Pages 228–229 **1.** 3 cm^3 **3.** 17 tablets **5.** 25 cm^3 **7.** 12 tablets **9.** 42.5 mL **11.** 30 tablets **13.** $3.75 **15.** $4.10 **17.** $5.84 **19.** $3.44 **21.** $19.13 **23.** $14.53

Pages 230–231 **1.** 8640 m **3.** 4800 m **5.** 14,400 m **7.** 8000 m **9.** 18,000 m **11.** 10,000 m **13.** It decreases.

Pages 232–233 **1.** $194.25 **3.** $246.75 **5.** $747 **7.** $264 **9.** 975 kilograms

Pages 236–237

Set A **1.** 0.096 **3.** 0.02 **5.** 0.0027 **7.** 0.32 **9.** 0.01 **11.** 0.95 **13.** 0.085 **15.** 0.127 **17.** 0.804 **19.** 8 **21.** 0.41 **23.** 0.0513 **25.** 1.47 **27.** 1.005 **29.** 0.8 **31.** 0.0125 **33.** 0.14 **35.** 0.025 **37.** 0.0092 **39.** 0.009 **41.** 0.0725 **43.** 3 **45.** 0.918 **47.** 0.095 **49.** 0.0021 **51.** 0.0575 **53.** 0.0625 **55.** 0.82 **57.** 0.081 **59.** 0.05 **61.** 0.008 **63.** 0.015 **65.** 0.005 **67.** 0.072 **69.** 0.0035 **71.** 0.0875 **73.** 0.006 **75.** 9

Set B **1.** 62% **3.** 80% **5.** 17% **7.** 0.5% **9.** 37% **11.** 501% **13.** 28% **15.** 79% **17.** 8.2% **19.** 73.1% **21.** $37\frac{1}{2}$% **23.** 0.9% **25.** 0.8% **27.** 73% **29.** 50% **31.** 51% **33.** 8% **35.** 84% **37.** 3% **39.** 91% **41.** 492% **43.** 41% **45.** 9% **47.** 77% **49.** $55\frac{5}{9}$% **51.** 55.1% **53.** 650% **55.** 90.7% **57.** 7% **59.** 88% **61.** 99.9% **63.** 0.7% **65.** 18% **67.** 46.4% **69.** 62.6% **71.** $3\frac{2}{9}$% **73.** 1% **75.** 150%

Pages 238–239

Set C **1.** $\frac{7}{100}$ **3.** $\frac{67}{100}$ **5.** $\frac{1}{4}$ **7.** $\frac{3}{10}$ **9.** $\frac{13}{100}$ **11.** $\frac{4}{5}$ **13.** $\frac{1}{20}$ **15.** $\frac{43}{100}$ **17.** $1\frac{7}{100}$ **19.** $1\frac{1}{10}$ **21.** $\frac{1}{200}$ **23.** $\frac{1}{3}$ **25.** $\frac{3}{8}$ **27.** $\frac{31}{100}$ **29.** $1\frac{21}{100}$ **31.** $\frac{9}{20}$ **33.** $\frac{1}{50}$ **35.** $\frac{3}{40}$ **37.** 2 **39.** $\frac{1}{5}$ **41.** $\frac{9}{10}$ **43.** $\frac{1}{9}$ **45.** $\frac{91}{100}$ **47.** $\frac{7}{80}$ **49.** $\frac{3}{100}$ **51.** $\frac{59}{100}$

Set D **1.** 17% **3.** 90% **5.** 50% **7.** 25% **9.** 76% **11.** $16\frac{2}{3}$% **13.** $62\frac{1}{2}$% **15.** $28\frac{4}{7}$% **17.** 30% **19.** 10% **21.** 80% **23.** 61% **25.** $22\frac{1}{2}$% **27.** $57\frac{1}{7}$% **29.** 150% **31.** 125% **33.** $73\frac{1}{3}$% **35.** $\frac{1}{2}$% **37.** $91\frac{2}{3}$% **39.** $53\frac{11}{13}$%

Pages 240–241

Set E **1.** 1.74 **3.** 8.64 **5.** 31.2 **7.** 17.4 **9.** 0.504 **11.** 6.024 **13.** 1.665 **15.** 2.45 **17.** 2.576 **19.** 0.574 **21.** 19.76 **23.** 2.6125 **25.** 12 **27.** 20.25

Set F **1.** 9.25 **3.** 250 **5.** 0.405 **7.** 2.625 **9.** 2.175 **11.** 41.25 **13.** 172.5 **15.** 74.385 **17.** 20.625 **19.** 16.8 **21.** 33.504

Set G **1.** 8 **3.** 30 **5.** 3 **7.** 60 **9.** 50 **11.** 40 **13.** 94 **15.** 7 **17.** 16 **19.** 10 **21.** 20

Mixed Practice **1.** 2.955 **3.** 600 **5.** 27 **7.** 7 **9.** 637.5 **11.** 0.648 **13.** 30 **15.** 150 **17.** 0.1334 **19.** 7.25 **21.** 0.945 **23.** 115.84 **25.** 1.497 **27.** 65

Pages 242–243

Set H **1.** 30% **3.** 68% **5.** 52% **7.** 55% **9.** 40% **11.** 25% **13.** 30% **15.** 6% **17.** 54% **19.** 70% **21.** 44% **23.** 20% **25.** 35% **27.** 200%

Set I **1.** $12\frac{1}{2}\%$ **3.** $66\frac{2}{3}\%$ **5.** $16\frac{2}{3}\%$ **7.** $14\frac{2}{7}\%$ **9.** $8\frac{1}{3}\%$ **11.** $46\frac{2}{13}\%$ **13.** $85\frac{5}{7}\%$ **15.** $116\frac{2}{3}\%$ **17.** $43\frac{3}{4}\%$ **19.** $2\frac{3}{4}\%$ **21.** $58\frac{1}{3}\%$ **23.** $66\frac{2}{3}\%$ **25.** $28\frac{3}{4}\%$ **27.** $22\frac{2}{9}\%$

Mixed Practice **1.** 56% **3.** $88\frac{8}{9}\%$ **5.** $112\frac{1}{2}\%$ **7.** 8% **9.** 50% **11.** $45\frac{5}{11}\%$ **13.** $6\frac{1}{4}\%$ **15.** 39% **17.** 25% **19.** $33\frac{1}{3}\%$ **21.** $26\frac{2}{3}\%$ **23.** $48\frac{4}{7}\%$ **25.** 100% **27.** 300%

Pages 244–245

Set J **1.** 45 **3.** 30 **5.** 75 **7.** 84 **9.** 29 **11.** 32 **13.** 160 **15.** 40 **17.** 750 **19.** 2900 **21.** 800 **23.** 730 **25.** 6000 **27.** 480

Set K **1.** 18 **3.** 15 **5.** 24 **7.** 200 **9.** 64 **11.** 8 **13.** 180 **15.** 112 **17.** 12 **19.** 111 **21.** 129

Mixed Practice **1.** 215 **3.** 140 **5.** 112 **7.** 600 **9.** 57 **11.** 78 **13.** 88 **15.** 8000 **17.** 2000 **19.** 168 **21.** 81 **23.** 84 **25.** 351 **27.** 368

Page 247 **1.** \$9.90; \$39.60 **3.** \$2.10; \$11.89 **5.** \$15.30; \$61.19 **7.** \$5.49; \$12.80 **9.** \$16.24; \$48.71

Pages 248–249 **1.** \$8.82; \$106.82 **3.** \$16.50; \$181.50 **5.** \$19.74; \$348.74 **7.** \$34.30; \$279.30 **9.** \$28.71; \$347.71 **11.** 1.5% **13.** 1.25% **15.** 2.25% **17.** 1.75% **19.** 2.75%

Pages 250–251 **1.** \$1574.40; \$31.49; \$1605.89 **3.** \$1454.41; \$1274.41; \$25.49; \$1299.90 **5.** \$1142.30; \$962.30; \$19.25; \$981.55 **7.** \$817.59; \$637.59; \$12.76; \$650.35 **9.** \$479.76; \$299.76; \$6.00; \$305.76 **11.** \$128.28; 0; 0; 0 **13.** \$2108.28

Pages 252–253 **1.** 39,000±10%; 35,100 ohms to 42,900 ohms **3.** 68,000±10%; 61,200 ohms to 74,800 ohms **5.** 2,700,000±10%; 2,430,000 ohms to 2,970,000 ohms **7.** 22,000±10%; 19,800 ohms to 24,200 ohms

Pages 254–255 **1.** 23.1 liters **3.** 11.9 liters **5.** 7.056 liters **7.** \$452.76

Page 259

Set A **1.** 8 **3.** 247.3 **5.** 9.8 **7.** 70.8 **9.** 17.2 **11.** 82.7 **13.** 118.3 **15.** 247.3 **17.** 17.1 **19.** 121.7 **21.** 137.6 **23.** 464.3 **25.** 1934.3

Pages 260–261

Set B **1.** 6 **3.** 5.5 **5.** 15 **7.** 176 **9.** 26 **11.** 357 **13.** 10.5 **15.** 76.5 **17.** 3189 **19.** 16 **21.** 19 **23.** 34 **25.** 8718

Set C **1.** 7 **3.** none **5.** 12 **7.** 178 **9.** 12 **11.** none **13.** 9 **15.** 76 **17.** 3213 **19.** 16 **21.** 16, 19, 21 **23.** 29 **25.** 8791

Pages 262–263

Set D **1.** 41 gold medals **3.** 24 gold medals **5.** 27 gold medals **7.** 1920, 1924, 1932, 1948 **9.** 1928, 1936 **11.** 1936

Set E **1.**

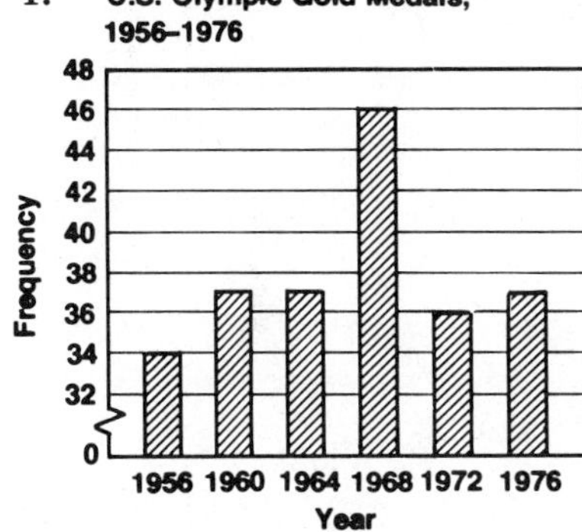

3.

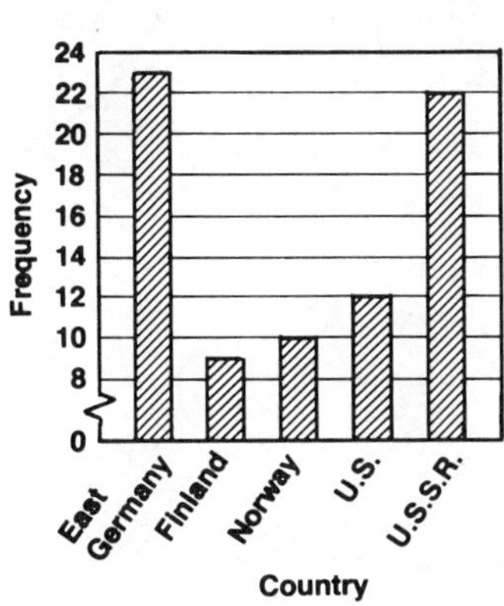

Pages 264–265

Set F **1.** May, June, July, August, September **3.** May, June, July, August, September **5.** January, December **7.** April, May, June, July, August, September, October **9.** May **11.** June **13.** January 550 min.; February 600 min.; March 675 min.; April 750 min.; May 850 min.; June 900 min.; July 900 min.; August 875 min.; September 800 min.; October 700 min.; November 625 min.; December 550 min.

Set G **1.**

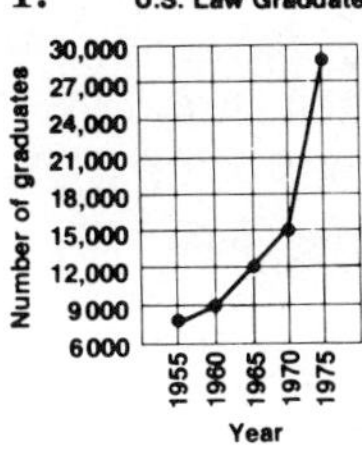

3.

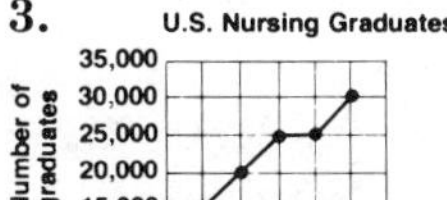

Pages 266–267

Set H **1.** Muscle **3.** Bone **5.** Muscle, Fat, Bone **7.** Fat, Bone, Other **9.** Fat

Set I **1. a.** $1632 **b.** $238 **c.** $544 **d.** $238 **3. a.** $3300 **b.** $1560 **c.** $240 **d.** $300

Set J **1.** Elements of Earth's Crust **3.** Sources of Air Pollution

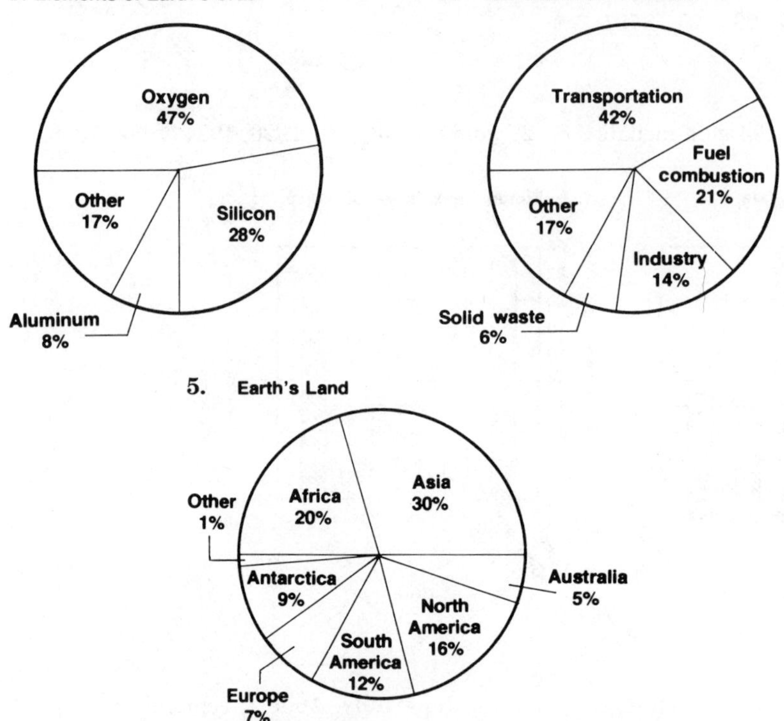

Pages 270–271 **1.** May through August **3.** January, February, March, October, November, December **5.** January, February, December **7.** May through August, October **9.** May, June, August **11.** May, June, August, September, October **13.** January $110; February $105; March $80; April $60; May $40; June $45; July $55; August $50; September $60; October $65; November $65; December $85 **15.** January $140; February $160; March $120; April $85; May $60; June $70; July $90; August $70; September $75; October $75; November $100; December $115 **17.** $84 **19.** High 1979 $175; Low 1978 $110; Difference $65 **21.** High 1980 $85; Low 1978 $60; Difference $25 **23.** High 1980 $75; Low 1979 $55; Difference $20

Pages 272–273 **1.** Asheville 14°C; Birmingham 17°C; Dodge City 13°C; New York City 12°C; Miami 24°C; Honolulu 25°C **3.** Asheville 9.6 cm; Birmingham 11.2 cm; Dodge City 4.3 cm; New York City 8.9 cm; Miami 12.7 cm; Honolulu 4.9 cm

Pages 274–275 **1.**

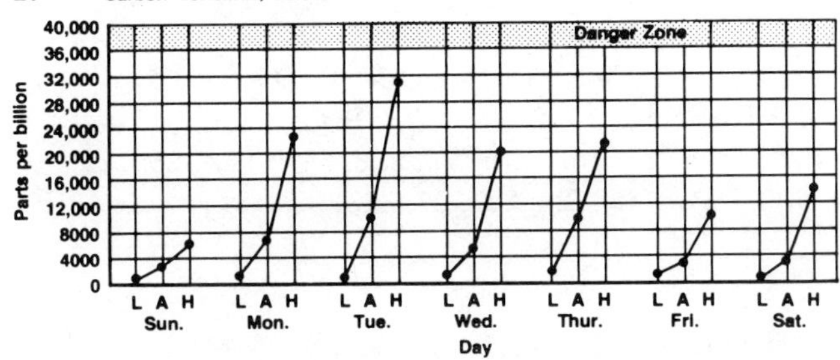

3. Monday, Tuesday, Thursday, Saturday **5.** Saturday **7.** Sunday: A; Monday: A; Wednesday: A, C; Friday: A; Saturday: A, B

Pages 276–277 **1.** 1 pair **3.** 10 pairs **5.** 4 pairs **7.** 8 pairs **9.** 30 pairs

11.

Gray	**Blue**	**Green**
Size 9: 2 pairs	Size 8: 2 pairs	Size 8: 2 pairs
Size 10: 8 pairs	Size 9: 2 pairs	Size 10: 4 pairs
Size 11: 6 pairs	Size 10: 6 pairs	Size 11: 2 pairs
Size 12: 2 pairs	Size 11: 2 pairs	Size 12: 2 pairs

13. Blue: 12 pairs; Gray: 18 pairs; Green: 10 pairs **15.** 40% **17.** 20%

Page 279

Adding and Subtracting Whole Numbers **1.** 97 **3.** 384 **5.** 98,220 **7.** 160 **9.** 241 **11.** 156 **13.** 22 **15.** 109 **17.** 88 **19.** 8861 **21.** 2248 **23.** 4838 **25.** 45,388

Adding and Subtracting Decimals **1.** 12.9 **3.** 1.09 **5.** 8.961 **7.** 1.591 **9.** 5.692 **11.** 10.213 **13.** 24.17 **15.** 0.59 **17.** 2.181 **19.** 0.476 **21.** 28.41 **23.** 8.261 **25.** 5.399 **27.** 0.657

Adding and Subtracting Fractions and Mixed Numbers **1.** $1\frac{1}{10}$ **3.** $1\frac{1}{2}$ **5.** $10\frac{7}{12}$ **7.** $7\frac{1}{3}$ **9.** $5\frac{11}{12}$ **11.** $4\frac{1}{2}$ **13.** $3\frac{7}{12}$ **15.** $3\frac{17}{24}$ **17.** $1\frac{5}{7}$ **19.** $1\frac{2}{5}$

Page 280 **1.** 5.36 billion **3.** 1997 **5.** 1990 **7.** 50 years

Page 281 **1.** 5
6
7
8
9
10
11
12 **3.** 2
6
12
20
30

Pages 284–285

Set A **1.** $^{-}1$, 2, 6 **3.** $^{-}5$, $^{-}4$, 4 **5.** 22, 25 **7.** $^{-}50$, $^{-}48$

Set B **1.** $<$ **3.** $<$ **5.** $>$ **7.** $<$ **9.** $>$ **11.** $<$ **13.** $>$ **15.** $<$ **17.** $>$ **19.** $>$

Set C **1.** $^{-}4$, $^{-}1$, 3, 6 **3.** $^{-}5$, $^{-}3$, 7, 9 **5.** $^{-}30$, $^{-}10$, 25, 40 **7.** $^{-}9$, $^{-}8$, $^{-}7$, 0, 8 **9.** $^{-}9$, 0, 7, 8, 9 **11.** $^{-}16$, $^{-}14$, 0, 8, 13 **13.** $^{-}7$, $^{-}5$, $^{-}1$, 1, 5, 7 **15.** $^{-}10$, $^{-}7$, $^{-}2$, 6, 10 **17.** $^{-}28$, $^{-}21$, $^{-}9$, $^{-}5$, 14, 16 **19.** $^{-}9$, $^{-}5$, $^{-}4$, $^{-}2$, 4, 6, 9 **21.** $^{-}46$, $^{-}30$, $^{-}24$, 27, 33, 39

Pages 286–287

Set D **1.** 9 **3.** 44 **5.** 1131 **7.** 81 **9.** 91 **11.** 20.5 **13.** 13.33

Set E **1.** $^{-}11$ **3.** $^{-}123$ **5.** $^{-}82$ **7.** $^{-}82$ **9.** $^{-}111$ **11.** $^{-}2.41$ **13.** $^{-}17.71$

Set F **1.** $^{-}4$ **3.** $^{-}12$ **5.** 15 **7.** $^{-}5$ **9.** 129 **11.** 40.9 **13.** 2.12

Set G **1.** $^{-}11$ **3.** 7 **5.** $^{-}55$ **7.** $^{-}17$ **9.** $^{-}130$ **11.** 22 **13.** 1.5

Mixed Practice **1.** $^{-}16$ **3.** 1332 **5.** $^{-}9$ **7.** $^{-}32$ **9.** 46 **11.** $^{-}1$ **13.** $^{-}34$ **15.** $^{-}14$ **17.** $^{-}850$ **19.** $^{-}38$ **21.** $^{-}86$ **23.** 1 **25.** $^{-}1194$ **27.** 3 **29.** $^{-}80$

Pages 288–289

Set H **1.** $^{-}7$ **3.** $^{-}1$ **5.** $^{-}48$

Set I **1.** $^{-}1$ **3.** $^{-}13$ **5.** $^{-}14$ **7.** $^{-}107$ **9.** $^{-}4.6$

Set J **1.** 5 **3.** $^{-}3$ **5.** 56 **7.** $^{-}285$ **9.** $^{-}8.5$

Set K **1.** $^{-}9$ **3.** $^{-}58$ **5.** $^{-}44$ **7.** $^{-}1010$ **9.** $^{-}1.94$

Set L **1.** 15 **3.** 25 **5.** 28 **7.** 850 **9.** 18.4

Set M **1.** 29 **3.** $^{-}38$ **5.** $^{-}2$ **7.** $^{-}12$ **9.** $^{-}156$ **11.** 4 **13.** $^{-}46$ **15.** $^{-}14$

Mixed Practice **1.** $^{-}8$ **3.** 77 **5.** 26 **7.** $^{-}44$ **9.** $^{-}123$ **11.** 40 **13.** $^{-}200$ **15.** 157 **17.** 298

Pages 290–291

Set N **1.** 54 **3.** 56 **5.** 18 **7.** 75 **9.** 54 **11.** 405 **13.** 682 **15.** 432 **17.** 1702 **19.** 1200 **21.** 3885 **23.** 0.63

Set O **1.** 32 **3.** 63 **5.** 27 **7.** 174 **9.** 154 **11.** 720 **13.** 1800 **15.** 13,736 **17.** 6958 **19.** 1118 **21.** 504 **23.** 4

Set P **1.** $^{-}28$ **3.** $^{-}63$ **5.** $^{-}56$ **7.** $^{-}390$ **9.** $^{-}4410$ **11.** $^{-}5893$ **13.** $^{-}475$ **15.** $^{-}1200$ **17.** $^{-}64{,}872$ **19.** $^{-}0.48$

Set Q **1.** 16 **3.** 68 **5.** 28 **7.** $^{-}4$ **9.** $^{-}50$ **11.** 10 **13.** 22 **15.** $^{-}22$ **17.** 48 **19.** 2

Mixed Practice **1.** 3 **3.** $^{-}728$ **5.** 744 **7.** $^{-}2$ **9.** $^{-}936$ **11.** 33 **13.** 675 **15.** $^{-}11{,}295$ **17.** 117 **19.** $^{-}21$

Pages 292–293

Set R **1.** 6 **3.** 9 **5.** 6 **7.** 7 **9.** 5 **11.** 9 **13.** 4 **15.** 9 **17.** 27 **19.** 30 **21.** 26 **23.** 2

Set S **1.** 5 **3.** 3 **5.** 7 **7.** 9 **9.** 8 **11.** 15 **13.** 6 **15.** 53 **17.** 34 **19.** 14 **21.** 4 **23.** 1.4

Set T **1.** $^{-}2$ **3.** $^{-}3$ **5.** $^{-}6$ **7.** $^{-}9$ **9.** $^{-}16$ **11.** $^{-}14$ **13.** $^{-}12$ **15.** $^{-}23$ **17.** $^{-}11$ **19.** $^{-}9$

Set U **1.** $^{-}4$ **3.** 2 **5.** 6 **7.** $^{-}10$ **9.** $^{-}3$

Mixed Practice **1.** 14 **3.** $^{-}3$ **5.** $^{-}7$ **7.** 58 **9.** 7 **11.** 4 **13.** 29

Page 295 **1.** $^{-}4 + 13 + 8 = 17$ **3.** $^{-}7 + 0 + 10 = 3$ **5.** 81 yards **7.** 62 yards

Pages 296–297 **1.** 4:48 A.M., 2.52 m **3.** 8:02 A.M., 5.15 m **5.** 4:57 A.M., 1.07 m **7.** 2:32 A.M., 0.91 m **9.** 10:25 A.M., 0.33 m **11.** 5:12 A.M., 1.13 m **13.** 1:02 A.M., 7.86 m **15.** 7:53 A.M., 2.01 m **17.** Portland, July 1–5:33 P.M., 2.53 m **19.** Eastport, June 4–7:47 P.M., 5.3 m **21.** Coney Island, July 5–5:27 P.M., 1.47 m **23.** Cape May, July 3–4:02 P.M., 1.15 m **25.** Annapolis, July 3–11:55 P.M., 0.48 m **27.** San Franscisco, June 3–6:40 P.M.,1.34 m **29.** Anchorage, August 18–4:47 P.M., 8.35 m

Pages 298–299 **1.** $^{-}26$ **3.** $^{-}19$ **5.** 20°C **7.** $^{-}38$ **9.** $^{-}43$ **11.** $^{-}30$ **13.** 25°C

Pages 300–301 **1.** 77.50 **3.** $^{-}21.25$ **5.** $^{-}116.25$ **7.** \$0.35

Pages 304–305

Set A **1.** 19 **3.** 36 **5.** 52.2 **7.** 13.79 **9.** 61.08 **11.** 0.953 **13.** 26.9 **15.** 4.79 **17.** 4.2 **19.** 5.38 **21.** 5.268 **23.** 134.1 **25.** 5

Set B **1.** 121 **3.** $^{-}66$ **5.** 25.3 **7.** 1.2 **9.** 1.2 **11.** $^{-}1.1$ **13.** 1.3 **15.** 34.4 **17.** 9.7 **19.** 32 **21.** 5.351 **23.** 66 **25.** 4.5

Set C **1.** 364 **3.** $^{-}112$ **5.** 119 **7.** $^{-}2250$ **9.** 270 **11.** 2.17 **13.** $^{-}3.15$ **15.** 360 **17.** 6300 **19.** 1.19

Set D **1.** $^{-}2$ **3.** 0.06 **5.** 0.2 **7.** $^{-}1$ **9.** 2 **11.** 73

Mixed Practice **1.** 1.4 **3.** $^{-}8$ **5.** 0.07 **7.** $^{-}16$ **9.** 0.85 **11.** 37.7 **13.** 0.9 **15.** 10 **17.** 4

Pages 306–307

Set E **1.** 20 **3.** 14 **5.** 60.1 **7.** 47.6 **9.** 6.1 **11.** 244 **13.** 17.5 **15.** 277.7 **17.** $^{-}14$

Set F **1.** $^{-}20$ **3.** 33 **5.** 144 **7.** 68 **9.** 148 **11.** 246 **13.** $^{-}570$ **15.** 95

Mixed Practice **1.** $^{-}6$ **3.** $^{-}2376$ **5.** 5 **7.** $^{-}4$ **9.** 70 **11.** $^{-}314$ **13.** $^{-}23$ **15.** 55 **17.** 4536 **19.** 125 **21.** 17 **23.** 3

Pages 308–309

Set G **1.** $x = {}^{-}23$ **3.** $a = 8$ **5.** $n = {}^{-}30$ **7.** $w = 18$ **9.** $z = 2.52$ **11.** $t = 53$ **13.** $g = 0$ **15.** $h = 1.91$ **17.** $k = 17$ **19.** $n = 83$ **21.** $p = 0.31$ **23.** $r = 55.3$ **25.** $s = 18.2$

Set H **1.** $a = 30$ **3.** $z = {}^{-}2$ **5.** $d = 9$ **7.** $r = 1.7$ **9.** $c = 5.7$ **11.** $x = 9.08$ **13.** $w = 119$ **15.** $g = 1.031$ **17.** $x = 21$ **19.** $h = 13.07$ **21.** $z = 8.15$ **23.** $b = 6.69$ **25.** $w = 65.29$ **27.** $d = {}^{-}102$

Mixed Practice **1.** $h = 4.32$ **3.** $f = 131.3$ **5.** $p = {}^{-}49$ **7.** $k = 0.849$ **9.** $v = {}^{-}103$ **11.** $q = 34.21$ **13.** $g = 62$ **15.** $y = {}^{-}32$ **17.** $d = {}^{-}39$ **19.** $p = 13.9$ **21.** $m = 45.26$ **23.** $t = 40$ **25.** $v = 96$ **27.** $w = 38.6$ **29.** $h = 58$ **31.** $n = 30$ **33.** $b = 16$ **35.** $y = 31.2$ **37.** $f = {}^{-}12$

Pages 310–311

Set I **1.** $w = {}^{-}53$ **3.** $m = {}^{-}9$ **5.** $d = {}^{-}49$ **7.** $y = 1$ **9.** $c = 7.7$ **11.** $g = 24$ **13.** $y = {}^{-}3$ **15.** $k = {}^{-}5$ **17.** $d = 17$ **19.** $q = 6$ **21.** $n = {}^{-}40$ **23.** $z = {}^{-}81$ **25.** $t = 2.9$

Set J **1.** $g = 72$ **3.** $r = 868$ **5.** $c = 2.8$ **7.** $b = 6.12$ **9.** $a = 0.322$ **11.** $g = {}^{-}44$ **13.** $s = 3.68$ **15.** $y = 0.0464$ **17.** $y = 0.9417$ **19.** $y = 2000$

Mixed Practice **1.** $f = 1.1$ **3.** $h = 4.56$ **5.** $a = 794.2$ **7.** $w = {}^{-}8$ **9.** $t = {}^{-}117$ **11.** $k = 0.09$ **13.** $b = {}^{-}1$ **15.** $n = 196$ **17.** $z = 1.37$ **19.** $t = {}^{-}340$ **21.** $c = {}^{-}0.06$ **23.** $u = 0.475$

Pages 312-313
Set K **1.** $x = 4$ **3.** $t = 9$ **5.** $s = 3$ **7.** $y = 8$ **9.** $m = 13$ **11.** $d = 10$ **13.** $n = {}^{-}1$ **15.** $w = 4$ **17.** $h = 1.5$ **19.** $p = 11$ **21.** $x = 2.8$ **23.** $a = 17$ **25.** $k = 3$ **27.** $b = 2$
Set L **1.** $m = 9$ **3.** $x = 8$ **5.** $t = 0.7$ **7.** $y = 40$ **9.** $z = 48$ **11.** $b = 38$ **13.** $c = 65$ **15.** $h = 32$ **17.** $n = 64$ **19.** $c = 21$ **21.** $k = 90$ **23.** $d = 44$ **25.** $x = 0.27$ **27.** $b = 8.4$
Mixed Practice **1.** $z = 10$ **3.** $y = 81$ **5.** $h = 7$ **7.** $u = 90$ **9.** $q = {}^{-}5$ **11.** $c = 120$ **13.** $d = 20$ **15.** $v = 0.54$

Pages 314-315
Set M **1.** $n = 8$ **3.** $z = 2$ **5.** $t = 9$ **7.** $b = 9$ **9.** $p = 6$ **11.** $s = 3$ **13.** $z = 2$ **15.** $w = {}^{-}20$ **17.** $u = 2$ **19.** $f = {}^{-}10$ **21.** $z = 3$ **23.** $q = 27$ **25.** $x = 0$ **27.** $d = 9$
Set N **1.** $c = 7$ **3.** $x = {}^{-}1$ **5.** $d = 5$ **7.** $p = 9$ **9.** $x = {}^{-}5$ **11.** $b = 10$ **13.** $k = 30$ **15.** $g = 0.4$ **17.** $h = 1.9$ **19.** $v = 5$ **21.** $u = {}^{-}10$ **23.** $b = 9$ **25.** $d = 3$ **27.** $s = 0$
Mixed Practice **1.** $c = 7$ **3.** $w = 0.2$ **5.** $z = {}^{-}7$ **7.** $d = 2.4$ **9.** $k = 1$ **11.** $c = 50$ **13.** $g = 10$ **15.** $n = 4$

Page 317 **1.** 5; 550 **3.** 10; 1100 **5.** 0.5; 55 **7.** 4; 880 **9.** 2354 watts **11.** 3498 watts

Pages 318-319 **1.** \$7200; \$800 **3.** \$2344; \$656 **5.** \$76,500; \$13,500 **7.** \$22,645; \$2355 **9.** \$7916; \$4884 **11.** \$8391; \$559 **13.** \$48,918; \$9482 **15.** \$5651; \$1149

Pages 320-321 **1.** 20,000 pounds **3.** 30,000 pounds **5.** 32,000 pounds **7.** 20,571 pounds **9.** 36,000 pounds **11.** 2 inches **13.** 5 inches **15.** 0.5 inch

Pages 322-323 **1.** 25 m/s **3.** 26.4 m/s **5.** 73.2 m **7.** 10 seconds **9.** 25.7 seconds **11.** 15.4 m/s; 55.44 km/h; No **13.** 25 m/s; 90 km/h; Yes **15.** 18 m/s; 64.8 km/h; No **17.** 20 m/s; 72 km/h; Yes **19.** 28.6 m/s; 102.96 km/h; Yes

Pages 324-325 **1.**

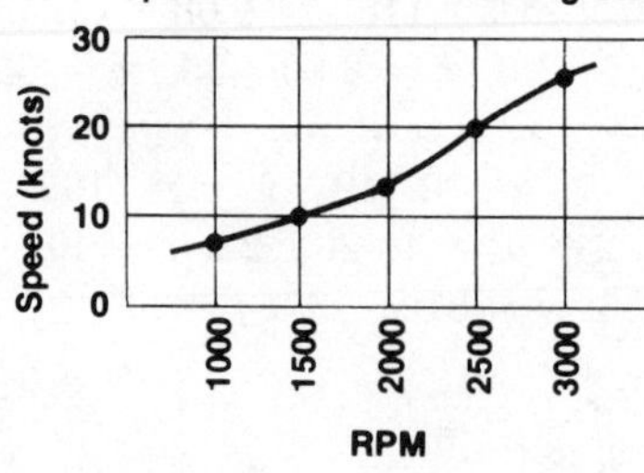

3.

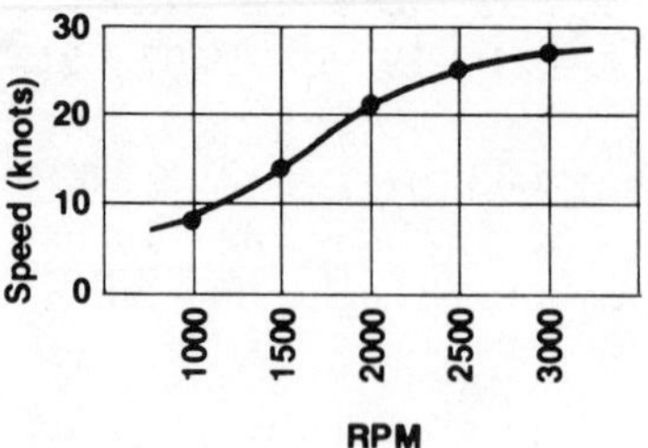

5. 1500 RPM and 2000 RPM

Page 329

Set A **1.** (6, 4) **3.** (4, 2) **5.** (1, 5) **7.** (8, 4) **9.** (8, 2)

Set B

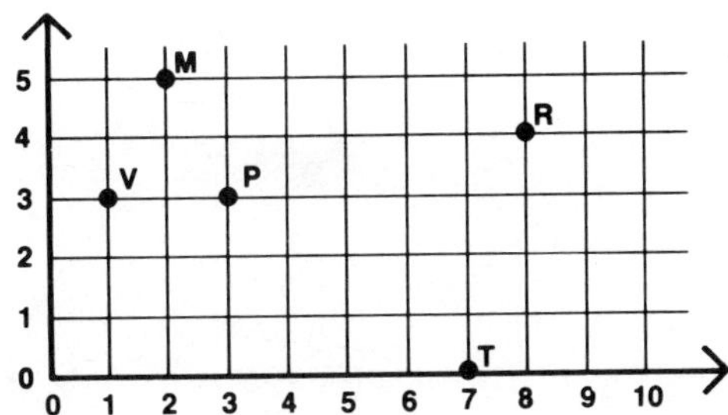

Pages 330–331

Set C **1.** 0 **3.** 4 **5.** 0 **7.** 5 **9.** 6 **11.** 3 **13.** 0 **15.** 2 **17.** 1 **19.** 2

Set D **1.** $y = x$

3. $y = 2x$

5. $y = 3x - 5$

7. $y = 4 - x$

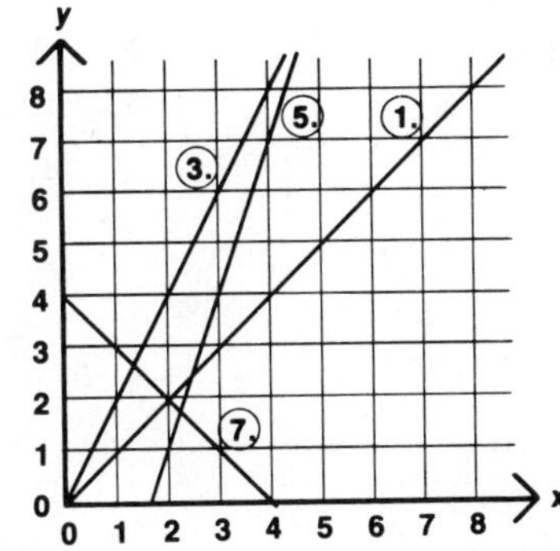

Pages 332–333

Set E **1.** (⁻3, 2) **3.** (3, 2) **5.** (⁻4, ⁻4) **7.** (⁻8, 7) **9.** (⁻3, ⁻7) **11.** (8, 5) **13.** (2, ⁻6) **15.** (4, 0) **17.** (⁻8, ⁻3) **19.** (4, ⁻8) **21.** (⁻6, ⁻6) **23.** (⁻6, 3)

Set F

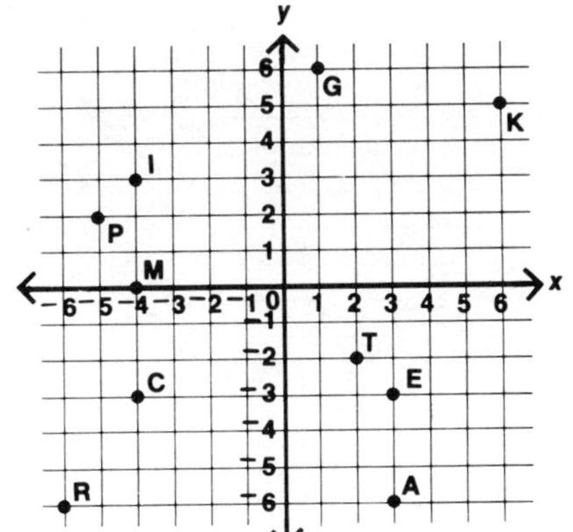

Pages 334-335

Set G **1.** $^-2$ **3.** 1 **5.** $^-4$ **7.** $^-2$ **9.** 0 **11.** 0 **13.** $^-4$ **15.** 0 **17.** $^-3$ **19.** 1

Set H **1.** $y = x + 1$

3. $y = x - 3$

5. $y = 2x - 1$

7. $y = 3 - x$

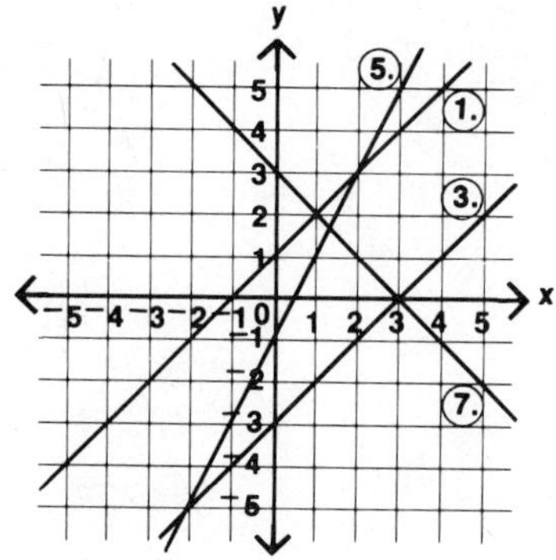

Pages 338-339 1 and 3.

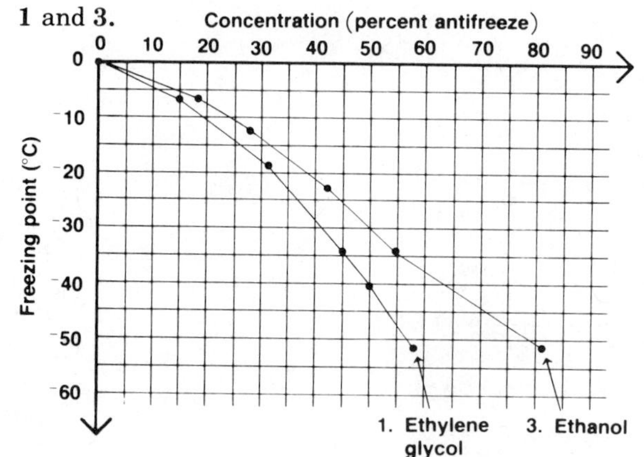

5. Ethylene glycol, methanol

7. Ethanol

Pages 340-341

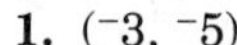

1. $(^-3, ^-5)$

3. $(^-2, 2)$

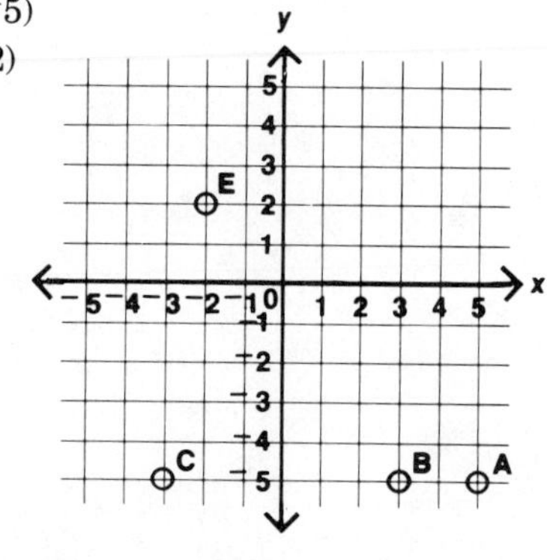

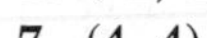

5. $(^-2, 1)$

7. $(4, 4)$

9. $(1, ^-1)$

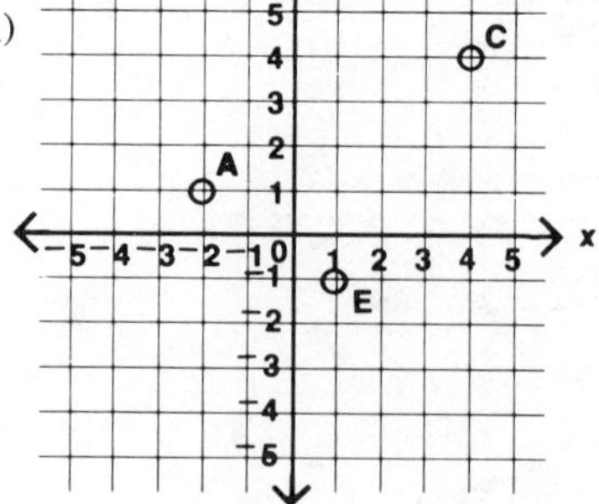

11. $(^-2, 3)$
13. $(5, ^-3)$
15. $(^-5, ^-4)$
17. $(^-4, 1)$

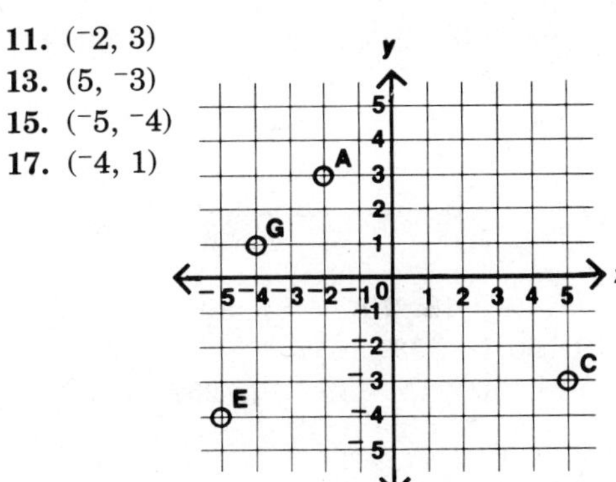

Pages 342–343 **1** and **3.**

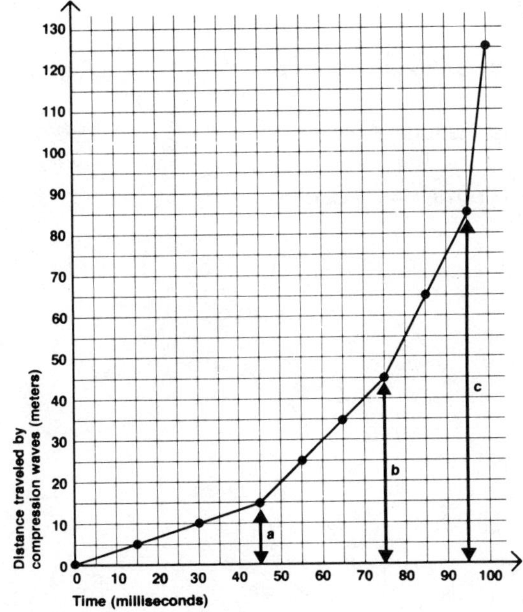

5. 30 m; 55 m; 25 m; 90 m; 35 m

Pages 344–345 **1.** $216,000 **3.** $168,000 **5.** Week 51 **7.** $3,850,000 **9.** $16,000 **11.** $13,000 **13.** 25%

Page 347

Multiplying and Dividing Fractions and Mixed Numbers **1.** $\frac{21}{40}$ **3.** $\frac{7}{16}$ **5.** $5\frac{1}{7}$ **7.** $1\frac{1}{9}$ **9.** 5 **11.** $\frac{17}{28}$ **13.** $\frac{15}{32}$ **15.** $\frac{3}{16}$ **17.** $\frac{1}{6}$ **19.** 5

Percent **1.** 0.09 **3.** 0.921 **5.** 0.0624 **7.** 0.27 **9.** 4% **11.** $37\frac{1}{2}\%$ **13.** 79% **15.** 80% **17.** $\frac{3}{50}$ **19.** $\frac{1}{200}$ **21.** $\frac{2}{25}$ **23.** $\frac{13}{100}$ **25.** 60% **27.** 125% **29.** $83\frac{1}{3}\%$ **31.** $56\frac{1}{4}\%$ **33.** $16\frac{2}{3}\%$

Percent **1.** 2.6 **3.** 6.8 **5.** 8 **7.** 60% **9.** 20% **11.** $41\frac{2}{3}\%$ **13.** 50 **15.** 330 **17.** 252

Page 348 **1.** $248.43 **3.** $154.31 **5.** $45.35 **7.** $26.93 **9.** $41.01 **11.** $2597.06

Page 349 **1.**

```
? 3
 3 IS AN ODD NUMBER.
? 6
 6 IS AN EVEN NUMBER.
? 10
 10 IS AN EVEN NUMBER.
? 15
 15 IS AN ODD NUMBER.
? 24
 24 IS AN EVEN NUMBER.
? 25
 25 IS AN ODD NUMBER.
? 0
```

3.

```
? 12
? 3
 12 IS A MULTIPLE OF 3
? 15
? 6
 15 IS NOT A MULTIPLE OF 6
? 51
? 3
 51 IS A MULTIPLE OF 3
? 63
? 12
 63 IS NOT A MULTIPLE OF 12
? 0
```

5. Answers may vary.

```
10 INPUT N
20 IF N=0 THEN 100
30 IF INT(N/2)=N/2 THEN 60
40 PRINT N;"IS NOT DIVISIBLE BY 2 AND 3."
50 GO TO 10
60 IF INT(N/3)=N/3 THEN 80
70 GO TO 40
80 PRINT N;"IS DIVISIBLE BY 2 AND 3."
90 GO TO 10
100 END
```

Pages 352–353

Set A **1.** 84 cm **3.** 63.8 cm **5.** 99 m **7.** 26.4 m **9.** 268 m **11.** 2.1 m **13.** 948 m **15.** 11.74 m

Set B **1.** 72 cm **3.** 62 cm **5.** 9 cm **7.** 76 mm **9.** 162 mm **11.** 116.2 m **13.** 778 cm **15.** 54.86 m

Pages 354–355

Set C **1.** 25.12 m **3.** 125.6 mm **5.** 314 cm **7.** 31.4 cm **9.** 282.6 m **11.** 1256 m **13.** 310.86 mm **15.** 116.18 cm **17.** 131.88 m **19.** 235.5 cm **21.** 502.4 km **23.** 1099 cm **25.** 3014.4 mm **27.** 2135.2 m

Set D **1.** 18.84 cm **3.** 37.68 mm **5.** 75.36 cm **7.** 445.88 cm **9.** 12.56 m **11.** 43.96 km **13.** 314 m **15.** 565.2 cm **17.** 3768 mm **19.** 94.2 km **21.** 577.76 cm **23.** 4647.2 cm

Mixed Practice **1.** 28.26 m **3.** 1884 mm **5.** 263.76 mm **7.** 50.24 mm **9.** 2512 m **11.** 496.12 cm

Pages 356–357

Set E **1.** 4.5 m^2 **3.** 1.04 m^2 **5.** 84 cm^2 **7.** 2.34 cm^2 **9.** 0.0312 m^2 **11.** 1.0272 m^2 **13.** 11.043 cm^2 **15.** 401.76 mm^2

Set F **1.** 5625 mm^2 **3.** 24.01 cm^2 **5.** 225 mm^2 **7.** 6.25 m^2 **9.** 146.41 cm^2 **11.** 0.8464 m^2 **13.** 16.9744 m^2 **15.** 89.4916 mm^2

Set G **1.** 2.43 m^2 **3.** 2.28 m^2 **5.** 750 mm^2 **7.** 1.02 m^2 **9.** 13.92 cm^2 **11.** 1.7612 m^2 **13.** 11.8584 m^2 **15.** 3606.96 cm^2

Pages 358–359

Set H **1.** 1225 km^2 **3.** 494 m^2 **5.** 216 mm^2 **7.** 137.5 mm^2 **9.** 0.0216 m^2 **11.** 8.36 cm^2 **13.** 198.375 m^2

Set I **1.** 81 m^2 **3.** 29.8 cm^2 **5.** 4 cm^2 **7.** 81 cm^2 **9.** 1.17 cm^2 **11.** 21.21 cm^2

Pages 360–361

Set J **1.** 28.26 cm^2 **3.** 1962.5 cm^2 **5.** 78.5 mm^2 **7.** 3.14 km^2 **9.** 254.34 cm^2 **11.** 31,400 mm^2 **13.** 25,434 cm^2 **15.** 2826 m^2 **17.** 1962.5 m^2 **19.** 1384.74 mm^2 **21.** 4775.94 cm^2 **23.** 907.46 m^2 **25.** 12,861.44 mm^2

Set K **1.** 314 mm^2 **3.** 254.34 cm^2 **5.** 78.5 m^2 **7.** 113.04 cm^2 **9.** 20,096 mm^2 **11.** 31,400 mm^2 **13.** 1661.06 mm^2 **15.** 1962.5 cm^2 **17.** 615.44 cm^2

Mixed Practice **1.** 50.24 cm^2 **3.** 1256 mm^2 **5.** 803.84 m^2

Page 363 **1.** 5 m by 7 m; 35 m^2 **3.** 4 m by 5 m; 20 m^2 **5.** Living room \$447.65; Master bedroom \$383.70; Guest bedroom \$255.80; Study \$204.64

Pages 364–365 The first answer given is the area of the lawn; the second answer is the amount of fertilizer that should be bought for Problem 20. **1.** 1320 m^2; 27 kg **3.** 3330 m^2; 67 kg **5.** 5100 m^2; 102 kg **7.** 3563 m^2; 72 kg **9.** 2508 m^2; 51 kg **11.** 1206 m^2; 25 kg **13.** 4533 m^2; 91 kg **15.** 2166 m^2; 44 kg **17.** 4126 m^2; 83 kg **19.** 2914 m^2; 59 kg

Pages 366–367 **1.** 70 cm **3.** 94 cm **5.** 134 cm

Pages 368–369 **1.** 231 people **3.** 393 people **5.** 2 stands **7.** 4620 sq. ft. **9.** 7860 sq. ft. **11.** 1 stand **13.** 513 people **15.** 10,260 sq. ft.

Page 373
Set A **1.** 490 cm^2 **3.** 22.5 m^2 **5.** 738 mm^2 **7.** 3456 m^2 **9.** 58,194 mm^2 **11.** 143.5 cm^2 **13.** 124.66 m^2

Page 374
Set B **1.** 5046 mm^2 **3.** 403.44 cm^2 **5.** 25,350 cm^2 **7.** 4056 mm^2 **9.** 5766 m^2 **11.** 3174 m^2 **13.** 15,000 cm^2 **15.** 508,086 cm^2 **17.** 2.94 m^2 **19.** 4.86 cm^2 **21.** 11.76 m^2 **23.** 507.84 cm^2 **25.** 168.54 m^2 **27.** 365.04 cm^2 **29.** 443.76 m^2

Page 375
Set C **1.** 18.84 m^2 **3.** 7724.4 mm^2 **5.** 87.92 m^2 **7.** 659.4 cm^2 **9.** 866.64 cm^2 **11.** 5526.4 mm^2 **13.** 10,362 mm^2 **15.** 3428.88 cm^2

Pages 376–377
Set D **1.** 256 cm^3 **3.** 384 cm^3 **5.** 1625 cm^3 **7.** 10,710 cm^3 **9.** 165,550 mm^3 **11.** 5.264 m^3 **13.** 23.94 cm^3
Set E **1.** 421,875 cm^3 **3.** 1,124,864 mm^3 **5.** 216 m^3 **7.** 8000 m^3 **9.** 12,167 m^3 **11.** 830,584 cm^3 **13.** 110,592 cm^3 **15.** 175,616 mm^3 **17.** 658,503 mm^3 **19.** 27,000,000 m^3 **21.** 0.512 m^3 **23.** 3.375 m^3 **25.** 195.112 cm^3 **27.** 16,003.008 cm^3

Pages 378–379
Set F **1.** 1356.48 m^3 **3.** 175.84 cm^3 **5.** 2034.72 m^3 **7.** 791.28 cm^3 **9.** 3165.12 cm^3 **11.** 4082 cm^3 **13.** 125,235.76 mm^3 **15.** 31,400 mm^3
Set G **1.** 351.68 cm^3 **3.** 6154.4 cm^3 **5.** 87.92 m^3 **7.** 238.64 cm^3 **9.** 11,775 cm^3 **11.** 14,130 cm^3 **13.** 21,110.22 mm^3

Pages 380–381
Set H **1.** 24 cm^3 **3.** 1998 cm^3 **5.** 190 m^3 **7.** 35,000 mm^3 **9.** 4420 cm^3 **11.** 93,574 mm^3 **13.** 42.32 m^3
Set I **1.** 25.12 m^3 **3.** 15,232.14 cm^3 **5.** 602.88 cm^3 **7.** 200.96 cm^3 **9.** 1177.5 m^3 **11.** 379.94 cm^3 **13.** 40,506 mm^3 **15.** 15,700 cm^3

Page 382

Set J **1.** 2143.57 m^3 **3.** 267.95 cm^3 **5.** 1436.03 m^3 **7.** 113,040 mm^3 **9.** 17,148.59 mm^3 **11.** 267,946.67 cm^3 **13.** 7234.56 cm^3 **15.** 24,416.64 mm^3 **17.** 150,456.24 cm^3 **19.** 20,569.09 mm^3

Set K **1.** 113.04 cm^3 **3.** 44,579.63 mm^3 **5.** 73,584.85 mm^3 **7.** 65,416.67 mm^3 **9.** 229,730.77 mm^3 **11.** 28,716.35 cm^3 **13.** 124,724.99 mm^3 **15.** 164,552.75 mm^3 **17.** 91,905.71 cm^3 **19.** 57,876.48 mm^3

Page 385 **1.** 602.88 cm^3 **3.** 350 cm^3 **5.** 543 grams **7.** 315 grams **9.** 2715 grams **11.** 2205 grams **13.** 11,568 grams **15.** $36

Pages 386–387 **1.** 0.675 m^3 **3.** 5.5 × 0.3 × 0.9; 1.485 m^3 **5.** 6 m^3 **7.** $260 **9.** 7.1 × 2.4; 17.04; 17.04 m^2 **11.** 5.5 × 2.4; 13.2; 12.2 m^2 **13.** 48,900,000 mm^2 **15.** 612 blocks **17.** $2351.80

Pages 388–389 **1.** 78.5 cm^2; 392.5 cm^3; 1570 cm^3 **3.** 3.5 cm; 38.465 cm^2; 307.72 cm^3; 2461.76 cm^3 **5.** 2.5 cm; 19.625 cm^2; 157 cm^3; 1256 cm^3 **7.** 4.5 cm; 63.585 cm^2; 445.095 cm^3; 2670.57 cm^3 **9.** 1.9 cm; 11.3354 cm^2; 68.0124 cm^3; 272.0496 cm^3

Pages 390–391 **1.** $108 **3.** $294.52 **5.** $698.25 **7.** $4815 **9.** $8634.61

Page 395

Set A **1.** 216 **3.** 7 **5.** 8 **7.** 49 **9.** 25 **11.** 1 **13.** 16 **15.** 10 **17.** 1000 **19.** 100,000 **21.** 1,000,000,000 **23.** 78 **25.** 8000 **27.** 26.01 **29.** 0.0016

Set B **1.** 3 **3.** 1 **5.** 7 **7.** 12 **9.** 15 **11.** 20 **13.** 25 **15.** 24 **17.** 50 **19.** 60

Pages 396–397

Set C **1.** 3721 **3.** 7569 **5.** 1444 **7.** 900 **9.** 6889 **11.** 31,329 **13.** 12,100 **15.** 35,721

Set D **1.** 3.9 **3.** 6.3 **5.** 1.4 **7.** 7.7 **9.** 8.0 **11.** 13.4 **13.** 10.1 **15.** 14.0

Set E **1.** 26 **3.** 22 **5.** 18 **7.** 66 **9.** 49 **11.** 122 **13.** 199 **15.** 167

Pages 398–399

Set F **1.** 8.1 m **3.** 13.4 m **5.** 106 m **7.** 41 m **9.** 11.4 m **11.** 7.2 m **13.** 29 m **15.** 13.5 m **17.** 17 m

Set G **1.** 5.3 cm **3.** 55 mm **5.** 16 m **7.** 40 m **9.** 13.7 m **11.** 135 m **13.** 72 m **15.** 8.7 m **17.** 9.1 m

Pages 400–401

Set H **1.** $\tan \angle J = \frac{20}{21} \approx 0.952$ **3.** $\tan \angle M = \frac{5}{12} \approx 0.417$ **5.** $\tan \angle K = \frac{24}{7} \approx 3.429$

7. $\tan \angle X = \frac{12}{35} \approx 0.343$ **9.** $\tan \angle D = \frac{45}{28} \approx 1.607$ **11.** $\tan \angle P = \frac{40}{9} \approx 4.444$

13. $\tan \angle G = \frac{72}{154} \approx 0.468$ **15.** $\tan \angle F = \frac{16}{63} \approx 0.254$

Set I **1.** $\sin \angle J = \frac{20}{29} \approx 0.690$ **3.** $\sin \angle M = \frac{5}{13} \approx 0.385$ **5.** $\sin \angle K = \frac{24}{25} \approx 0.960$

7. $\sin \angle X = \frac{12}{37} \approx 0.324$ **9.** $\sin \angle D = \frac{45}{53} \approx 0.849$ **11.** $\sin \angle P = \frac{40}{41} \approx 0.976$

13. $\sin \angle G = \frac{72}{170} \approx 0.424$ **15.** $\sin \angle F = \frac{16}{65} \approx 0.246$

Set J **1.** $\cos \angle J = \frac{21}{29} \approx 0.724$ **3.** $\cos \angle M = \frac{12}{13} \approx 0.923$ **5.** $\cos \angle K = \frac{7}{25} \approx 0.280$

7. $\cos \angle X = \frac{35}{37} \approx 0.946$ **9.** $\cos \angle D = \frac{28}{53} \approx 0.528$ **11.** $\cos \angle P = \frac{9}{41} \approx 0.220$

13. $\cos \angle G = \frac{154}{170} \approx 0.906$ **15.** $\cos \angle F = \frac{63}{65} \approx 0.969$

Pages 402–403

Set K **1.** 0.158 **3.** 3.732 **5.** 1.483 **7.** 14.301 **9.** 28.636

Set L **1.** 0.946 **3.** 0.500 **5.** 0.995 **7.** 0.755 **9.** 0.276

Set M **1.** 0.946 **3.** 0.643 **5.** 0.857 **7.** 0.530 **9.** 0.707

Pages 404–405

Set N **1.** 11.0 m **3.** 34.7 cm **5.** 46.7 cm

Set O **1.** 12.5 cm **3.** 30.6 m **5.** 33.9 cm

Set P **1.** 13.5 m **3.** 178.1 mm **5.** 102.3 mm

Pages 408–409 **1.** No **3.** No **5.** No **7.** No **9.** Yes

Pages 410–411 **1.** 9.9 dm **3.** 7.1 dm **5.** 9 dm; 12.7 dm **7.** 2 dm; 2.8 dm **9.** 13.9 dm **11.** 6.9 dm **13.** 3.5 dm; 2 dm **15.** 1.7 dm; 1 dm

Pages 412–413 **1.** 28 m by 24 m **3.** 70 m by 60 m **5.** 388 m **7.** 414 m

Page 415

Ratio, Proportion, and Similarity **1.** $n = 91$ **3.** $h = 21$ **5.** $d = 5.2$ **7.** $w = 3$ **9.** $c = 25$ **11.** $j = 12$

Percent **1.** 2.4 **3.** 25 **5.** 9 **7.** 30% **9.** 40% **11.** $33\frac{1}{3}\%$ **13.** 50 **15.** 200 **17.** 44

Positive and Negative Numbers **1.** 2 **3.** $^-38$ **5.** 4.5 **7.** $^-11$ **9.** $^-48$ **11.** $^-25.6$ **13.** $^-54$ **15.** $^-75$ **17.** $^-16.8$ **19.** $^-8$ **21.** 12 **23.** $^-4$ **25.** 9.7

Page 416 **1.** $62.75 **3.** $28.16 **5.** $48.75 **7.** $2.64

Page 417

1.
```
AREA
10
60
180
OUT OF DATA AT LINE 20
```

3.
```
3
2
4
5
OUT OF DATA AT LINE 10
```

5.
```
4
9
7
OUT OF DATA AT LINE 10
```

Page 418

Use after page 7. **1.** 87 **3.** 879 **5.** 3787 **7.** 73 **9.** 631 **11.** 1020 **13.** 4041 **15.** 12,543 **17.** 73,417 **19.** 1791 **21.** 304 **23.** 10,436

Use after page 9. **1.** 422 **3.** 1135 **5.** 7152 **7.** 22,526 **9.** 27 **11.** 67 **13.** 777 **15.** 682 **17.** 978 **19.** 5328 **21.** 3343 **23.** 3178 **25.** 71,076 **27.** 51,499

Use after page 33. **1.** 800,000 **3.** 480,000 **5.** 156 **7.** 192 **9.** 2322 **11.** 30,840 **13.** 1480 **15.** 4346 **17.** 49,242 **19.** 164,892 **21.** 506,100 **23.** 386,334 **25.** 334,862 **27.** 1,914,624

Page 419

Use after page 51. **1.** 19 R2 **3.** 146 R3 **5.** 2233 **7.** 6538 R3 **9.** 4 R2 **11.** 6 R49 **13.** 3 R7 **15.** 41 R14 **17.** 59 R26 **19.** 612 R1 **21.** 2965 R38

Use after page 52. **1.** 30 R5 **3.** 430 R2 **5.** 530 R6 **7.** 3026 R1 **9.** 6080 R3 **11.** 20 R21 **13.** 280 R18 **15.** 2007 R27 **17.** 3006 R11 **19.** 580 R12 **21.** 7030 R23

Use after page 79. **1.** 24.1 **3.** 9.68 **5.** 0.339 **7.** 1.485 **9.** 44.44 **11.** 11.463 **13.** 17.656 **15.** 39.97 **17.** 19.103 **19.** 1.436 **21.** 1.052 **23.** 14.202

Page 420

Use after page 81. **1.** 3.9 **3.** 0.66 **5.** 3.25 **7.** 13.73 **9.** 0.445 **11.** 6.782 **13.** 3.577 **15.** 8.28 **17.** 4.85 **19.** 0.75 **21.** 4.97 **23.** 0.361 **25.** 7.303 **27.** 4.609

Use after page 97. **1.** 26.4 **3.** 95.16 **5.** 4.68 **7.** 9.718 **9.** 16,800 **11.** 54.64 **13.** 22.49 **15.** 0.00966 **17.** 0.00636 **19.** 0.00252 **21.** 0.000188 **23.** 0.034272 **25.** 0.01721016 **27.** 0.012093

Use after page 101. **1.** 5.8 **3.** 1.62 **5.** 0.44 **7.** 5.9 **9.** 57.2 **11.** 0.0033 **13.** 0.0356 **15.** 0.0116 **17.** 0.108 **19.** 0.059 **21.** 0.026

Page 421

Use after page 105. **1.** 5.7 **3.** 4.38 **5.** 5.2 **7.** 0.6 **9.** 6.6 **11.** 2.8 **13.** 58 **15.** 35 **17.** 65 **19.** 20,734 **21.** 5

Use after page 157. **1.** $\frac{2}{9}$ **3.** $\frac{1}{8}$ **5.** $\frac{7}{10}$ **7.** 6 **9.** $2\frac{1}{3}$ **11.** 14 **13.** $32\frac{1}{4}$ **15.** $10\frac{1}{2}$ **17.** 6 **19.** $10\frac{1}{2}$ **21.** $7\frac{7}{10}$

Use after page 159. **1.** $1\frac{7}{9}$ **3.** $\frac{2}{3}$ **5.** $\frac{1}{2}$ **7.** $2\frac{2}{5}$ **9.** $5\frac{1}{2}$ **11.** $\frac{7}{8}$ **13.** $\frac{3}{8}$ **15.** $1\frac{1}{2}$ **17.** $\frac{2}{3}$ **19.** $2\frac{2}{3}$ **21.** $3\frac{1}{3}$

Page 422

Use after page 177. **1.** $1\frac{1}{2}$ **3.** $1\frac{5}{8}$ **5.** $1\frac{1}{6}$ **7.** $1\frac{1}{4}$ **9.** $1\frac{4}{15}$ **11.** $1\frac{7}{12}$ **13.** $6\frac{7}{8}$ **15.** $12\frac{2}{3}$ **17.** $12\frac{3}{8}$ **19.** $10\frac{7}{12}$ **21.** $8\frac{13}{20}$ **23.** $13\frac{7}{30}$

Use after page 181. **1.** $\frac{3}{5}$ **3.** $\frac{1}{4}$ **5.** $\frac{3}{10}$ **7.** $\frac{7}{20}$ **9.** $\frac{1}{12}$ **11.** $\frac{1}{2}$ **13.** $7\frac{1}{8}$ **15.** $6\frac{1}{12}$ **17.** $2\frac{7}{10}$ **19.** $2\frac{23}{24}$ **21.** $\frac{7}{12}$ **23.** $4\frac{7}{18}$

Use after page 219. **1.** $t = 12$ **3.** $x = 73.5$ **5.** $n = 45$ **7.** $c = 63$ **9.** $d = 40$ **11.** $h = 21$ **13.** $d = 72$ **15.** $b = 65$ **17.** $m = 75$ **19.** $w = 76$ **21.** $e = 18$ **23.** $v = 0.98$ **25.** $t = 2.4$

Page 423

Use after page 241. **1.** 2.17 **3.** 9.75 **5.** 0.324 **7.** 3.68 **9.** 52.5 **11.** 315 **13.** 3.25 **15.** 25 **17.** 31.875 **19.** 12 **21.** 7 **23.** 17 **25.** 36

Use after page 243. **1.** 20% **3.** 42% **5.** 86% **7.** 75% **9.** 36% **11.** 48% **13.** 40% **15.** $18\frac{3}{4}\%$ **17.** $44\frac{4}{9}\%$ **19.** $62\frac{1}{2}\%$ **21.** $21\frac{3}{7}\%$ **23.** $57\frac{1}{7}\%$ **25.** $2\frac{3}{4}\%$ **27.** $62\frac{1}{2}\%$

Use after page 245. **1.** 65 **3.** 75 **5.** 23 **7.** 140 **9.** 6200 **11.** 200 **13.** 8000 **15.** 36 **17.** 90 **19.** 48 **21.** 216 **23.** 15 **25.** 114 **27.** 72

Page 424

Use after page 287. **1.** 7 **3.** $^-4$ **5.** $^-22$ **7.** $^-121$ **9.** $^-101$ **11.** $^-112$ **13.** $^-37$ **15.** $^-282$ **17.** 1309 **19.** 45 **21.** $^-10.1$ **23.** $^-14.81$ **25.** 2.09

Use after page 289. **1.** $^-1$ **3.** $^-12$ **5.** $^-9$ **7.** 8 **9.** $^-9$ **11.** 52 **13.** 63 **15.** 29 **17.** 308 **19.** 1077 **21.** 1.4 **23.** $^-2.73$ **25.** 8.3

Use after page 291. **1.** 40 **3.** $^-24$ **5.** 28 **7.** $^-30$ **9.** 140 **11.** 129 **13.** $^-2765$ **15.** 1036 **17.** 540 **19.** $^-7636$ **21.** $^-1044$ **23.** 15,444 **25.** 7.68

Use after page 293. **1.** 5 **3.** $^-3$ **5.** 4 **7.** $^-8$ **9.** $^-8$ **11.** $^-9$ **13.** $^-12$ **15.** 4 **17.** $^-15$ **19.** 16 **21.** $^-26$ **23.** 16 **25.** 1.2

INDEX